LUCIUS ANNAEUS SENECA

STOICISM COLLECTION

Moral Letters to Lucilius,
On Benefits, On Anger, On the Shortness of Life,
On a Happy Life, On Leisure, On Peace of Mind,
On Providence, On Clemency, and On Consolation

by

LUCIUS ANNAEUS SENECA

Translated by
Richard Mott Gummere
Aubrey Stewart

CLASSY
PUBLISHING

LUCIUS ANNAEUS SENECA STOICISM COLLECTION
by Lucius Annaeus Seneca
Published by Classy Publishing, 2023

www.classypublishing.com
info@classypublishing.com

ISBN: 978-93-5522-656-3

No part of this publication may be reproduced, stored in a retrieval system, or transmitted, in any form or by any means, electronic, mechanical, photocopying, recording or otherwise, without the prior permission of the publisher.

Cover Design by Classy Publishing

CONTENTS

Letter 1. On saving time — 1
Letter 2. On discursiveness in reading — 2
Letter 3. On true and false friendship — 3
Letter 4. On the terrors of death — 4
Letter 5. On the philosopher's mean — 5
Letter 6. On sharing knowledge — 7
Letter 7. On crowds — 8
Letter 8. On the philosopher's seclusion — 10
Letter 9. On philosophy and friendship — 12
Letter 10. On living to oneself — 15
Letter 11. On the blush of modesty — 16
Letter 12. On old age — 17
Letter 13. On groundless fears — 19
Letter 14. On the reasons for withdrawing from the world — 22
Letter 15. On brawn and brains — 25
Letter 16. On philosophy, the guide of life — 27
Letter 17. On philosophy and riches — 29
Letter 18. On festivals and fasting — 30
Letter 19. On worldliness and retirement — 33
Letter 20. On practising what you preach — 35
Letter 21. On the renown which my writings will bring you — 37
Letter 22. On the futility of half-way measures — 39
Letter 23. On the true joy which comes from philosophy — 42
Letter 24. On despising death — 43
Letter 25. On reformation — 48
Letter 26. On old age and death — 49
Letter 27. On the good which abides — 50
Letter 28. On travel as a cure for discontent — 52
Letter 29. On the critical condition of Marcellinus — 53
Letter 30. On conquering the conqueror — 55
Letter 31. On siren songs — 58
Letter 32. On progress — 60
Letter 33. On the futility of learning maxims — 61
Letter 34. On a promising pupil — 63

Letter 35. On the friendship of kindred minds	64
Letter 36. On the value of retirement	64
Letter 37. On allegiance to virtue	66
Letter 38. On quiet conversation	67
Letter 39. On noble aspirations	68
Letter 40. On the proper style for a philosopher's discourse	69
Letter 41. On the god within us	71
Letter 42. On values	73
Letter 43. On the relativity of fame	74
Letter 44. On philosophy and pedigrees	75
Letter 45. On sophistical argumentation	76
Letter 46. On a new book by Lucilius	78
Letter 47. On master and slave	79
Letter 48. On quibbling as unworthy of the philosopher	82
Letter 49. On the shortness of life	84
Letter 50. On our blindness and its cure	86
Letter 51. On Baiae and morals	88
Letter 52. On choosing our teachers	90
Letter 53. On the faults of the spirit	92
Letter 54. On asthma and death	94
Letter 55. On Vatia's villa	95
Letter 56. On quiet and study	97
Letter 57. On the trials of travel	100
Letter 58. On being	101
Letter 59. On pleasure and joy	107
Letter 60. On harmful prayers	110
Letter 61. On meeting death cheerfully	111
Letter 62. On good company	112
Letter 63. On grief for lost friends	112
Letter 64. On the philosopher's task	114
Letter 65. On the first cause	116
Letter 66. On various aspects of virtue	120
Letter 67. On ill-health and endurance of suffering	128
Letter 68. On wisdom and retirement	131
Letter 69. On rest and restlessness	133
Letter 70. On the proper time to slip the cable	134
Letter 71. On the supreme good	138
Letter 72. On business as the enemy of philosophy	144
Letter 73. On philosophers and kings	146

Letter 74. On virtue as a refuge from worldly distractions	148
Letter 75. On the diseases of the soul	154
Letter 76. On learning wisdom in old age	157
Letter 77. On taking one's own life	162
Letter 78. On the healing power of the mind	166
Letter 79. On the rewards of scientific discovery	171
Letter 80. On worldly deceptions	174
Letter 81. On benefits	176
Letter 82. On the natural fear of death	181
Letter 83. On drunkenness	186
Letter 84. On gathering ideas	190
Letter 85. On some vain syllogisms	193
Letter 86. On Scipio's villa	199
Letter 87. Some arguments in favour of the simple life	203
Letter 88. On liberal and vocational studies	209
Letter 89. On the parts of philosophy	217
Letter 90. On the part played by philosophy in the progress of man	221
Letter 91. On the lesson to be drawn from the burning of Lyons	230
Letter 92. On the happy life	234
Letter 93. On the quality, as contrasted with the length, of life	240
Letter 94. On the value of advice	243
Letter 95. On the usefulness of basic principles	255
Letter 96. On facing hardships	267
Letter 97. On the degeneracy of the age	268
Letter 98. On the fickleness of fortune	270
Letter 99. On consolation to the bereaved	273
Letter 100. On the writings of Fabianus	278
Letter 101. On the futility of planning ahead	281
Letter 102. On the intimations of our immortality	283
Letter 103. On the dangers of association with our fellow-men	288
Letter 104. On care of health and peace of mind	289
Letter 105. On facing the world with confidence	295
Letter 106. On the corporeality of virtue	296
Letter 107. On obedience to the universal will	297
Letter 108. On the approaches to philosophy	299
Letter 109. On the fellowship of wise men	306
Letter 110. On true and false riches	309
Letter 111. On the vanity of mental gymnastics	312
Letter 112. On reforming hardened sinners	313

Letter 113. On the vitality of the soul and its attributes	313
Letter 114. On style as a mirror of character	318
Letter 115. On the superficial blessings	323
Letter 116. On self-control	326
Letter 117. On real ethics as superior to syllogistic subtleties	328
Letter 118. On the vanity of place-seeking	334
Letter 119. On nature as our best provider	336
Letter 120. More about virtue	339
Letter 121. On instinct in animals	343
Letter 122. On darkness as a veil for wickedness	347
Letter 123. On the conflict between pleasure and virtue	350
Letter 124. On the true good as attained by reason	353
On Benefits	358
Book 1	358
Book 2	371
Book 3	393
Book 4	415
Book 5	440
Book 6	461
Book 7	488
On Anger	509
Book 1	509
Book 2	527
Book 3	553
On the Shortness of Life	584
On a Happy Life	604
On Leisure	627
On Peace of Mind	634
On Providence	657
On Clemency	670
Book 1	670
Book 2	693
To Marcia, On Consolation	699
To Helvia, On Consolation	726
To Polybius, On Consolation	746

MORAL LETTERS TO LUCILIUS

I. ON SAVING TIME

Greetings from Seneca to his friend Lucilius.
   1. Continue to act thus, my dear Lucilius – set yourself free for your own sake; gather and save your time, which till lately has been forced from you, or filched away, or has merely slipped from your hands. Make yourself believe the truth of my words, – that certain moments are torn from us, that some are gently removed, and that others glide beyond our reach. The most disgraceful kind of loss, however, is that due to carelessness. Furthermore, if you will pay close heed to the problem, you will find that the largest portion of our life passes while we are doing ill, a goodly share while we are doing nothing, and the whole while we are doing that which is not to the purpose. **2.** What man can you show me who places any value on his time, who reckons the worth of each day, who understands that he is dying daily? For we are mistaken when we look forward to death; the major portion of death has already passed. Whatever years be behind us are in death's hands.
   Therefore, Lucilius, do as you write me that you are doing: hold every hour in your grasp. Lay hold of to-day's task, and you will not need to depend so much upon to-morrow's. While we are postponing, life speeds by. **3.** Nothing, Lucilius, is ours, except time. We were entrusted by nature with the ownership of this single thing, so fleeting and slippery that anyone who will can oust us from possession. What fools these mortals be! They allow the cheapest and most useless things, which can easily be replaced, to be charged in the reckoning, after they have acquired them; but they never regard themselves as in debt when they have received some of that precious commodity, – time! And yet time is the one loan which even a grateful recipient cannot repay.
   4. You may desire to know how I, who preach to you so freely, am practising. I confess frankly: my expense account balances, as you would expect from one who is free-handed but careful. I cannot boast that I waste nothing, but I can at least tell you what I am wasting, and the cause and manner of the loss; I can give you the

reasons why I am a poor man. My situation, however, is the same as that of many who are reduced to slender means through no fault of their own: every one forgives them, but no one comes to their rescue.

5. What is the state of things, then? It is this: I do not regard a man as poor, if the little which remains is enough for him. I advise you, however, to keep what is really yours; and you cannot begin too early. For, as our ancestors believed, it is too late to spare when you reach the dregs of the cask. Of that which remains at the bottom, the amount is slight, and the quality is vile. Farewell.

II. ON DISCURSIVENESS IN READING

1. Judging by what you write me, and by what I hear, I am forming a good opinion regarding your future. You do not run hither and thither and distract yourself by changing your abode; for such restlessness is the sign of a disordered spirit. The primary indication, to my thinking, of a well-ordered mind is a man's ability to remain in one place and linger in his own company. **2.** Be careful, however, lest this reading of many authors and books of every sort may tend to make you discursive and unsteady. You must linger among a limited number of master thinkers, and digest their works, if you would derive ideas which shall win firm hold in your mind. Everywhere means nowhere. When a person spends all his time in foreign travel, he ends by having many acquaintances, but no friends. And the same thing must hold true of men who seek intimate acquaintance with no single author, but visit them all in a hasty and hurried manner. **3.** Food does no good and is not assimilated into the body if it leaves the stomach as soon as it is eaten; nothing hinders a cure so much as frequent change of medicine; no wound will heal when one salve is tried after another; a plant which is often moved can never grow strong. There is nothing so efficacious that it can be helpful while it is being shifted about. And in reading of many books is distraction.

Accordingly, since you cannot read all the books which you may possess, it is enough to possess only as many books as you can read. **4.** "But," you reply, "I wish to dip first into one book and then into another." I tell you that it is the sign of an overnice appetite to toy with many dishes; for when they are manifold and varied, they cloy but do not nourish. So you should always read standard authors; and when you crave a change, fall back upon those whom you read before. Each day acquire something that will fortify you against poverty, against death, indeed against other misfortunes as well; and after you have run over many thoughts, select one to be thoroughly digested that day. **5.** This is my own custom; from the many things which I have read, I claim some one part for myself.

The thought for today is one which I discovered in Epicurus; for I am wont to cross over even into the enemy's camp, – not as a deserter, but as a scout. **6.** He says: "Contented poverty is an honourable estate." Indeed, if it be contented, it is not poverty at all. It is not the man who has too little, but the man who craves more, that is poor. What does it matter how much a man has laid up in his safe, or in his warehouse, how large are his flocks and how fat his dividends, if he covets his neighbour's property, and reckons, not his past gains, but his hopes of gains to come? Do you ask what is the proper limit to wealth? It is, first, to have what is necessary, and, second, to have what is enough. Farewell.

III. ON TRUE AND FALSE FRIENDSHIP

1. You have sent a letter to me through the hand of a "friend" of yours, as you call him. And in your very next sentence you warn me not to discuss with him all the matters that concern you, saying that even you yourself are not accustomed to do this; in other words, you have in the same letter affirmed and denied that he is your friend. **2.** Now if you used this word of ours in the popular sense, and called him "friend" in the same way in which we speak of all candidates for election as "honourable gentlemen," and as we greet all men whom we meet casually, if their names slip us for the moment, with the salutation "my dear sir," – so be it. But if you consider any man a friend whom you do not trust as you trust yourself, you are mightily mistaken and you do not sufficiently understand what true friendship means. Indeed, I would have you discuss everything with a friend; but first of all discuss the man himself. When friendship is settled, you must trust; before friendship is formed, you must pass judgment. Those persons indeed put last first and confound their duties, who, violating the rules of Theophrastus, judge a man after they have made him their friend, instead of making him their friend after they have judged him. Ponder for a long time whether you shall admit a given person to your friendship; but when you have decided to admit him, welcome him with all your heart and soul. Speak as boldly with him as with yourself. **3.** As to yourself, although you should live in such a way that you trust your own self with nothing which you could not entrust even to your enemy, yet, since certain matters occur which convention keeps secret, you should share with a friend at least all your worries and reflections. Regard him as loyal, and you will make him loyal. Some, for example, fearing to be deceived, have taught men to deceive; by their suspicions they have given their friend the right to do wrong. Why need I keep back any words in the presence of my friend? Why should I not regard myself as alone when in his company?

4. There is a class of men who communicate, to anyone whom they meet, matters which should be revealed to friends alone, and unload upon the chance listener whatever irks them. Others, again, fear to confide in their closest intimates; and if it were possible, they would not trust even themselves, burying their secrets deep in their hearts. But we should do neither. It is equally faulty to trust everyone and to trust no one. Yet the former fault is, I should say, the more ingenuous, the latter the more safe. **5.** In like manner you should rebuke these two kinds of men, – both those who always lack repose, and those who are always in repose. For love of bustle is not industry, – it is only the restlessness of a hunted mind. And true repose does not consist in condemning all motion as merely vexation; that kind of repose is slackness and inertia. **6.** Therefore, you should note the following saying, taken from my reading in Pomponius: "Some men shrink into dark corners, to such a degree that they see darkly by day." No, men should combine these tendencies, and he who reposes should act and he who acts should take repose. Discuss the problem with Nature; she will tell you that she has created both day and night. Farewell.

IV. ON THE TERRORS OF DEATH

1. Keep on as you have begun, and make all possible haste, so that you may have longer enjoyment of an improved mind, one that is at peace with itself. Doubtless you will derive enjoyment during the time when you are improving your mind and setting it at peace with itself; but quite different is the pleasure which comes from contemplation when one's mind is so cleansed from every stain that it shines. **2.** You remember, of course, what joy you felt when you laid aside the garments of boyhood and donned the man's toga, and were escorted to the forum; nevertheless, you may look for a still greater joy when you have laid aside the mind of boyhood and when wisdom has enrolled you among men. For it is not boyhood that still stays with us, but something worse, – boyishness. And this condition is all the more serious because we possess the authority of old age, together with the follies of boyhood, yea, even the follies of infancy. Boys fear trifles, children fear shadows, we fear both.

3. All you need to do is to advance; you will thus understand that some things are less to be dreaded, precisely because they inspire us with great fear. No evil is great which is the last evil of all. Death arrives; it would be a thing to dread, if it could remain with you. But death must either not come at all, or else must come and pass away.

4. "It is difficult, however," you say, "to bring the mind to a point where it can scorn life." But do you not see what trifling reasons impel men to scorn life? One hangs himself before the door of his mistress; another hurls himself from the housetop that he may no longer be compelled to bear the taunts of a bad-tempered master; a third, to be saved from arrest after running away, drives a sword into his vitals. Do you not suppose that virtue will be as efficacious as excessive fear? No man can have a peaceful life who thinks too much about lengthening it, or believes that living through many consulships is a great blessing. **5.** Rehearse this thought every day, that you may be able to depart from life contentedly; for many men clutch and cling to life, even as those who are carried down a rushing stream clutch and cling to briars and sharp rocks.

Most men ebb and flow in wretchedness between the fear of death and the hardships of life; they are unwilling to live, and yet they do not know how to die. **6.** For this reason, make life as a whole agreeable to yourself by banishing all worry about it. No good thing renders its possessor happy, unless his mind is reconciled to the possibility of loss; nothing, however, is lost with less discomfort than that which, when lost, cannot be missed. Therefore, encourage and toughen your spirit against the mishaps that afflict even the most powerful. **7.** For example, the fate of Pompey was settled by a boy and a eunuch, that of Crassus by a cruel and insolent Parthian. Gaius Caesar ordered Lepidus to bare his neck for the axe of the tribune Dexter; and he himself offered his own throat to Chaerea. No man has ever been so far advanced by Fortune that she did not threaten him as greatly as she had previously indulged him. Do not trust her seeming calm; in a moment the sea is moved to its depths. The very day the ships have made a brave show in the games, they are engulfed. **8.** Reflect that a highwayman or an enemy may cut your throat; and, though he is not your master, every slave wields the power of life and death over you. Therefore I declare to you: he is lord of your life that scorns his own. Think of those who have perished through plots in their own home, slain either openly or by guile; you will that just as many have been killed by angry slaves as by angry kings. What matter, therefore, how powerful he be whom you fear, when every one possesses the power which inspires your fear? **9.** "But," you will say, "if you should chance to fall into the hands of the enemy, the conqueror will command that you be led away," – yes, whither you are already being led. Why do you voluntarily deceive yourself and require to be told now for the first time what fate it is that you have long been labouring under? Take my word for it: since the day you were born you are being led thither. We must ponder this thought, and thoughts of the like nature, if we desire to be calm as we await that last hour, the fear of which makes all previous hours uneasy.

10. But I must end my letter. Let me share with you the saying which pleased me to-day. It, too, is culled from another man's Garden: "Poverty brought into conformity with the law of nature, is great wealth." Do you know what limits that law of nature ordains for us? Merely to avert hunger, thirst, and cold. In order to banish hunger and thirst, it is not necessary for you to pay court at the doors of the purse-proud, or to submit to the stern frown, or to the kindness that humiliates; nor is it necessary for you to scour the seas, or go campaigning; nature's needs are easily provided and ready to hand. **11.** It is the superfluous things for which men sweat, – the superfluous things that wear our togas threadbare, that force us to grow old in camp, that dash us upon foreign shores. That which is enough is ready to our hands. He who has made a fair compact with poverty is rich. Farewell.

V. ON THE PHILOSOPHER'S MEAN

1. I commend you and rejoice in the fact that you are persistent in your studies, and that, putting all else aside, you make it each day your endeavour to become a better man. I do not merely exhort you to keep at it; I actually beg you to do so. I warn you, however, not to act after the fashion of those who desire to be conspicuous rather than to improve, by doing things which will rouse comment as regards your dress or general way of living. **2.** Repellent attire, unkempt hair, slovenly beard, open scorn of silver dishes, a couch on the bare earth, and any other perverted forms of self-display, are to be avoided. The mere name of philosophy, however quietly pursued, is an object of sufficient scorn; and what would happen if we should begin to separate ourselves from the customs of our fellow-men? Inwardly, we ought to be different in all respects, but our exterior should conform to society. **3.** Do not wear too fine, nor yet too frowzy, a toga. One needs no silver plate, encrusted and embossed in solid gold; but we should not believe the lack of silver and gold to be proof of the simple life. Let us try to maintain a higher standard of life than that of the multitude, but not a contrary standard; otherwise, we shall frighten away and repel the very persons whom we are trying to improve. We also bring it about that they are unwilling to imitate us in anything, because they are afraid lest they might be compelled to imitate us in everything.

4. The first thing which philosophy undertakes to give is fellow-feeling with all men; in other words, sympathy and sociability. We part company with our promise if we are unlike other men. We must see to it that the means by which we wish to draw admiration be not absurd and odious. Our motto, as you know, is "Live according to Nature"; but it is quite contrary to nature to torture the body, to hate unlaboured elegance, to be dirty on purpose, to eat food that is not only plain, but disgusting and forbidding. **5.** Just as it is a sign of luxury to seek out dainties, so it is madness to avoid that which is customary and can be purchased at no great price. Philosophy calls for plain living, but not for penance; and we may perfectly well be plain and neat at the same time. This is the mean of which I approve; our life should observe a happy medium between the ways of a sage and the ways of the world at large; all men should admire it, but they should understand it also.

6. "Well then, shall we act like other men? Shall there be no distinction between ourselves and the world?" Yes, a very great one; let men find that we are unlike the common herd, if they look closely. If they visit us at home, they should admire us, rather than our household appointments. He is a great man who uses earthenware dishes as if they were silver; but he is equally great who uses silver as if it were earthenware. It is the sign of an unstable mind not to be able to endure riches.

7. But I wish to share with you to-day's profit also. I find in the writings of our Hecato that the limiting of desires helps also to cure fears: "Cease to hope," he says, "and you will cease to fear." "But how," you will reply, "can things so different go side by side?" In this way, my dear Lucilius: though they do seem at variance, yet they are really united. Just as the same chain fastens the prisoner and the soldier who guards him, so hope and fear, dissimilar as they are, keep step together; fear follows hope. **8.** I am not surprised that they proceed in this way; each alike belongs to a mind that is in suspense, a mind that is fretted by looking forward to the future. But the chief cause of both these ills is that we do not adapt ourselves to the present, but send our thoughts a long way ahead. And so foresight, the noblest blessing of the human race, becomes perverted. **9.** Beasts avoid the dangers which they see, and when they have escaped them are free from care; but we men torment ourselves over that which is to come as well as over that which is past. Many of our blessings bring bane to us; for memory recalls the tortures of fear, while foresight anticipates them. The present alone can make no man wretched. Farewell.

VI. ON SHARING KNOWLEDGE

1. I feel, my dear Lucilius, that I am being not only reformed, but transformed. I do not yet, however, assure myself, or indulge the hope, that there are no elements left in me which need to be changed. Of course there are many that should be made more compact, or made thinner, or be brought into greater prominence. And indeed this very fact is proof that my spirit is altered into something better, – that it can see its own faults, of which it was previously ignorant. In certain cases sick men are congratulated because they themselves have perceived that they are sick.

2. I therefore wish to impart to you this sudden change in myself; I should then begin to place a surer trust in our friendship, – the true friendship which hope and fear and self-interest cannot sever, the friendship in which and for the sake of which men meet death.

3. I can show you many who have lacked, not a friend, but a friendship; this, however, cannot possibly happen when souls are drawn together by identical inclinations into an alliance of honourable desires. And why can it not happen? Because in such cases men know that they have all things in common, especially their troubles.

You cannot conceive what distinct progress I notice that each day brings to me. **4.** And when you say: "Give me also a share in these gifts which you have found so helpful," I reply that I am anxious to heap all these privileges upon you, and that I am glad to learn in order that I may teach. Nothing will ever please me, no matter how excellent or beneficial, if I must retain the knowledge of it to myself. And if wisdom were given me under the express condition that it must be kept hidden and not uttered, I should refuse it. No good thing is pleasant to possess, without friends to share it.

5. I shall therefore send to you the actual books; and in order that you may not waste time in searching here and there for profitable topics, I shall mark certain passages, so that you can turn at once to those which I approve and admire. Of course, however, the living voice and the intimacy of a common life will help you more than the written word. You must go to the scene of action, first, because men put more faith in their eyes than in their ears, and second, because the way is long if one follows precepts, but short and helpful, if one follows patterns.

6. Cleanthes could not have been the express image of Zeno, if he had merely heard his lectures; he shared in his life, saw into his hidden purposes, and watched him to see whether he lived according to his own rules. Plato, Aristotle, and the whole throng of sages who were destined to go each his different way, derived more benefit from the character than from the words of Socrates. It was not the classroom of Epicurus, but living together under the same roof, that made great men of Metrodorus, Hermarchus, and Polyaenus. Therefore I summon you, not merely that you may derive benefit, but that you may confer benefit; for we can assist each other greatly.

7. Meanwhile, I owe you my little daily contribution; you shall be told what pleased me to-day in the writings of Hecato; it is these words: "What progress, you ask, have I made? I have begun to be a friend to myself." That was indeed a great benefit; such a person can never be alone. You may be sure that such a man is a friend to all mankind. Farewell.

VII. ON CROWDS

1. Do you ask me what you should regard as especially to be avoided? I say, crowds; for as yet you cannot trust yourself to them with safety. I shall admit my own weakness, at any rate; for I never bring back home the same character that I took abroad with me. Something of that which I have forced to be calm within me is disturbed; some of the foes that I have routed return again. Just as the sick man, who has been weak for a long time, is in such a condition that he cannot be taken out of the house without suffering a relapse, so we ourselves are affected when our souls are recovering from a lingering disease. **2.** To consort with the crowd is harmful; there is no person who does not make some vice attractive to us, or stamp it upon us, or taint us unconsciously therewith. Certainly, the greater the mob with which we mingle, the greater the danger.

But nothing is so damaging to good character as the habit of lounging at the games; for then it is that vice steals subtly upon one through the avenue of pleasure. **3.** What do you think I mean? I mean that I come home more greedy, more ambitious, more voluptuous, and even more cruel and inhuman, because I have been among human beings. By chance I attended a mid-day exhibition, expecting some fun, wit, and relaxation, – an exhibition at which men's eyes have respite from the slaughter of their fellow-men. But it was quite the reverse. The previous combats were the essence of compassion; but now all the trifling is put aside and it is pure murder. The men have no defensive armour. They are exposed to blows at all points, and no one ever strikes in vain. **4.** Many persons prefer this programme to the usual pairs and to the bouts "by request." Of course they do; there is no helmet or shield to deflect the weapon. What is the need of defensive armour, or of skill? All these mean delaying death. In the morning they throw men to the lions and the bears; at noon, they throw them to the spectators. The spectators demand that the slayer shall face the man who is to slay him in his turn; and they always reserve the latest conqueror for another butchering. The outcome of every fight is death, and the means are fire and sword. This sort of thing goes on while the arena is empty. **5.** You may retort: "But he was a highway robber; he killed a man!" And what of it? Granted that, as a murderer, he deserved this punishment, what crime have you committed, poor fellow, that you should deserve to sit and see this show? In the morning they cried "Kill him! Lash him! Burn him! Why does he meet the sword in so cowardly a way? Why does he strike so feebly? Why doesn't he die game? Whip him to meet his wounds! Let them receive blow for blow, with chests bare and exposed to the stroke!" And when the games stop for the intermission, they announce: "A little throatcutting in the meantime, so that there may still be something going on!"

Come now; do you not understand even this truth, that a bad example reacts on the agent? Thank the immortal gods that you are teaching cruelty to a person who cannot learn to be cruel. **6.** The young character, which cannot hold fast to righteousness, must be rescued from the mob; it is too easy to side with the majority. Even Socrates, Cato, and Laelius might have been shaken in their moral strength by a crowd that was unlike them; so true it is that none of us, no matter how much he cultivates his abilities, can withstand the shock of faults that approach, as it were, with so great a retinue. **7.** Much harm is done by a single case of indulgence or greed; the familiar friend, if he be luxurious, weakens and softens us imperceptibly; the neighbour, if he be rich, rouses our covetousness; the companion, if he be slanderous, rubs off some of his rust upon us, even though we be spotless and sincere. What then do you think the effect will be on character, when the world at large assaults it! You must either imitate or loathe the world.

8. But both courses are to be avoided; you should not copy the bad simply because they are many, nor should you hate the many because they are unlike you. Withdraw into yourself, as far as you can. Associate with those who will make a better man of you. Welcome those whom you yourself can improve. The process is mutual; for men learn while they teach. **9.** There is no reason why pride in advertising your abilities should lure you into publicity, so that you should desire to recite or harangue before the general public. Of course I should be willing for you to do so if you had a stock-in-trade that suited such a mob; as it is, there is not a man of them who can understand you. One or two individuals will perhaps come in your way, but even these will have to be moulded and trained by you so that they will understand you. You may say: "For what purpose did I learn all these things?" But you need not fear that you have wasted your efforts; it was for yourself that you learned them.

10. In order, however, that I may not to-day have learned exclusively for myself, I shall share with you three excellent sayings, of the same general purport, which have come to my attention. This letter will give you one of them as payment of my debt; the other two you may accept as a contribution in advance. Democritus says: "One man means as much to me as a multitude, and a multitude only as much as one man." **11.** The following also was nobly spoken by someone or other, for it is doubtful who the author was; they asked him what was the object of all this study applied to an art that would reach but very few. He replied: "I am content with few, content with one, content with none at all." The third saying – and a noteworthy one, too – is by Epicurus, written to one of the partners of his studies: "I write this not for the many, but for you; each of us is enough of an audience for the other." **12.** Lay these words to heart, Lucilius, that you may scorn the pleasure which comes from the applause of the majority. Many men praise you; but have you any reason for being pleased with yourself, if you are a person whom the many can understand? Your good qualities should face inwards. Farewell.

VIII. ON THE PHILOSOPHER'S SECLUSION

1. "Do you bid me," you say, "shun the throng, and withdraw from men, and be content with my own conscience? Where are the counsels of your school, which order a man to die in the midst of active work?" As to the course which I seem to you to be urging on you now and then, my object in shutting myself up and locking the door is to be able to help a greater number. I never spend a day in idleness; I appropriate even a part of the night for study. I do not allow time for sleep but yield to it when I must, and when my eyes are wearied with waking and ready to fall shut, I keep them at their task. **2.** I have withdrawn not only from men, but from affairs, especially from my own affairs; I am working for later generations, writing down some ideas that may be of assistance to them. There are certain wholesome counsels, which may be compared to prescriptions of useful drugs; these I am putting into writing; for I have found them helpful in ministering to my own sores, which, if not wholly cured, have at any rate ceased to spread.

3. I point other men to the right path, which I have found late in life, when wearied with wandering. I cry out to them: "Avoid whatever pleases the throng: avoid the gifts of Chance! Halt before every good which Chance brings to you, in a spirit of doubt and fear; for it is the dumb animals and fish that are deceived by tempting hopes. Do you call these things the 'gifts' of Fortune? They are snares. And any man among you who wishes to live a life of safety will avoid, to the utmost of his power, these limed twigs of her favour, by which we mortals, most wretched in this respect also, are deceived; for we think that we hold them in our grasp, but they hold us in theirs. **4.** Such a career leads us into precipitous ways, and life on such heights ends in a fall. Moreover, we cannot even stand up against prosperity when she begins to drive us to leeward; nor can we go down, either, 'with the ship at least on her course,' or once for all; Fortune does not capsize us, – she plunges our bows under and dashes us on the rocks.

5. "Hold fast, then, to this sound and wholesome rule of life – that you indulge the body only so far as is needful for good health. The body should be treated more rigorously, that it may not be disobedient to the mind. Eat merely to relieve your hunger; drink merely to quench your thirst; dress merely to keep out the cold; house yourself merely as a protection against personal discomfort. It matters little whether the house be built of turf, or of variously coloured imported marble; understand that a man is sheltered just as well by a thatch as by a roof of gold. Despise everything that useless toil creates as an ornament and an object of beauty. And reflect that nothing except the soul is worthy of wonder; for to the soul, if it be great, naught is great." **6.** When I commune in such terms with myself and with future generations, do you not think that I am doing more good than when I appear as counsel in court, or stamp my seal upon a will, or lend my assistance in the senate, by word or action, to a candidate? Believe me, those who seem to be busied with nothing are busied with the greater tasks; they are dealing at the same time with things mortal and things immortal.

7. But I must stop, and pay my customary contribution, to balance this letter. The payment shall not be made from my own property; for I am still conning Epicurus. I read to-day, in his works, the following sentence: "If you would enjoy real freedom, you must be the slave of Philosophy." The man who submits and surrenders himself to her is not kept waiting; he is emancipated on the spot. For the very service of Philosophy is freedom.

8. It is likely that you will ask me why I quote so many of Epicurus's noble words instead of words taken from our own school. But is there any reason why you should regard them as sayings of Epicurus and not common property? How many poets give forth ideas that have been uttered, or may be uttered, by philosophers! I need not touch upon the tragedians and our writers of national drama; for these last are also somewhat serious, and stand half-way between comedy and tragedy. What a quantity of sagacious verses lie buried in the mime! How many of Publilius's lines are worthy of being spoken by buskin-clad actors, as well as by wearers of the slipper! **9.** I shall quote one verse of his, which concerns philosophy, and particularly that phase of it which we were discussing a moment ago, wherein he says that the gifts of Chance are not to be regarded as part of our possessions:

> Still alien is whatever you have gained
> By coveting.

10. I recall that you yourself expressed this idea much more happily and concisely:

> What Chance has made yours is not really yours.

And a third, spoken by you still more happily, shall not be omitted:

> The good that could be given, can be removed.

I shall not charge this up to the expense account, because I have given it to you from your own stock. Farewell.

IX. ON PHILOSOPHY AND FRIENDSHIP

1. You desire to know whether Epicurus is right when, in one of his letters, he rebukes those who hold that the wise man is self-sufficient and for that reason does not stand in need of friendships. This is the objection raised by Epicurus against Stilbo and those who believe that the Supreme Good is a soul which is insensible to feeling.

2. We are bound to meet with a double meaning if we try to express the Greek term "lack of feeling" summarily, in a single word, rendering it by the Latin word *impatientia*. For it may be understood in the meaning the opposite to that which we wish it to have. What we mean to express is, a soul which rejects any sensation of evil; but people will interpret the idea as that of a soul which can endure no evil. Consider, therefore, whether it is not better to say "a soul that cannot be harmed," or "a soul entirely beyond the realm of suffering." **3.** There is this difference between ourselves and the other school: our ideal wise man feels his troubles, but overcomes them; their wise man does not even feel them. But we and they alike hold this idea, – that the wise man is self-sufficient. Nevertheless, he desires friends, neighbours, and associates, no matter how much he is sufficient unto himself. **4.** And mark how self-sufficient he is; for on occasion he can be content with a part of himself. If he lose a hand through disease or war, or if some accident puts out one or both of his eyes, he will be satisfied with what is left, taking as much pleasure in his impaired and maimed body as he took when it was sound. But while he does not pine for these parts if they are missing, he prefers not to lose them. **5.** In this sense the wise man is self-sufficient, that he can do without friends, not that he desires to do without them. When I say "can," I mean this: he endures the loss of a friend with equanimity.

But he need never lack friends, for it lies in his own control how soon he shall make good a loss. Just as Phidias, if he lose a statue, can straightway carve another, even so our master in the art of making friendships can fill the place of a friend he has lost. **6.** If you ask how one can make oneself a friend quickly, I will tell you, provided we are agreed that I may pay my debt at once and square the account, so far as this letter is concerned. Hecato, says: "I can show you a philtre, compounded without drugs, herbs, or any witch's incantation: 'If you would be loved, love.'" Now there is great pleasure, not only in maintaining old and established friendships, but also in beginning and acquiring new ones. **7.** There is the same difference between winning a new friend and having already won him, as there is between the farmer who sows and the farmer who reaps. The philosopher Attalus used to say: "It is more pleasant to make than to keep a friend, as it is more pleasant to the artist to paint than to have finished painting." When one is busy and absorbed in one's work, the very absorption affords great delight; but when one has withdrawn one's hand from the completed masterpiece, the pleasure is not so keen. Henceforth it is the fruits of his art that he enjoys; it was the art itself that he enjoyed while he was painting. In the case of our children, their young manhood yields the more abundant fruits, but their infancy was sweeter.

8. Let us now return to the question. The wise man, I say, self-sufficient though he be, nevertheless desires friends if only for the purpose of practising friendship, in order that his noble qualities may not lie dormant. Not, however, for the purpose mentioned by Epicurus in the letter quoted above: "That there may be someone to sit by him when he is ill, to help him when he is in prison or in want;" but that he may have someone by whose sick-bed he himself may sit, someone a prisoner in hostile hands whom he himself may set free. He who regards himself only, and enters upon friendships for this reason, reckons wrongly. The end will be like the beginning: he has made friends with one who might assist him out of bondage; at the first rattle of the chain such a friend will desert him. **9.** These are the so-called "fair-weather" friendships; one who is chosen for the sake of utility will be satisfactory only so long as he is useful. Hence prosperous men are blockaded by troops of friends; but those who have failed stand amid vast loneliness their friends fleeing from the very crisis which is to test their worth. Hence, also, we notice those many shameful cases of persons who, through fear, desert or betray. The beginning and the end cannot but harmonize. He who begins to be your friend because it pays will also cease because it pays. A man will be attracted by some reward offered in exchange for his friendship, if he be attracted by aught in friendship other than friendship itself.

10. For what purpose, then, do I make a man my friend? In order to have someone for whom I may die, whom I may follow into exile, against whose death I may stake my own life, and pay the pledge, too. The friendship which you portray is a bargain and not a friendship; it regards convenience only, and looks to the results. **11.** Beyond question the feeling of a lover has in it something akin to friendship; one might call it friendship run mad. But, though this is true, does anyone love for the sake of gain, or promotion, or renown? Pure love, careless of all other things, kindles the soul with desire for the beautiful object, not without the hope of a return of the affection. What then? Can a cause which is more honourable produce a passion that is base? **12.** You may retort: "We are now discussing the question whether friendship is to be cultivated for its own sake." On the contrary, nothing more urgently requires demonstration; for if friendship is to be sought for its own sake, he may seek it who is self-sufficient. "How, then," you ask, "does he seek it?" Precisely as he seeks an object of great beauty, not attracted to it by desire for gain, nor yet frightened by the instability of Fortune. One who seeks friendship for favourable occasions, strips it of all its nobility.

13. "The wise man is self-sufficient." This phrase, my dear Lucilius, is incorrectly explained by many; for they withdraw the wise man from the world, and force him to dwell within his own skin. But we must mark with care what this sentence signifies and how far it applies; the wise man is sufficient unto himself for a happy existence, but not for mere existence. For he needs many helps towards mere existence; but for a happy existence he needs only a sound and upright soul, one that despises Fortune.

14. I should like also to state to you one of the distinctions of Chrysippus, who declares that the wise man is in want of nothing, and yet needs many things. "On the other hand," he says, "nothing is needed by the fool, for he does not understand how to use anything, but he is in want of everything." The wise man needs hands, eyes, and many things that are necessary for his daily use; but he is in want of nothing. For want implies a necessity, and nothing is necessary to the wise man. **15.** Therefore, although he is self-sufficient, yet he has need of friends. He craves as many friends as possible, not, however, that he may live happily; for he will live happily even without friends. The Supreme Good calls for no practical aids from outside; it is developed at home, and arises entirely within itself. If the good seeks any portion of itself from without, it begins to be subject to the play of Fortune.

16. People may say: "But what sort of existence will the wise man have, if he be left friendless when thrown into prison, or when stranded in some foreign nation, or when delayed on a long voyage, or when out upon a lonely shore?" His life will be like that of Jupiter, who, amid the dissolution of the world, when the gods are confounded together and Nature rests for a space from her work, can retire into himself and give himself over to his own thoughts. In some such way as this the sage will act; he will retreat into himself, and live with himself. **17.** As long as he is allowed to order his affairs according to his judgment, he is self-sufficient – and marries a wife; he is self-sufficient – and brings up children; he is self-sufficient – and yet could not live if he had to live without the society of man. Natural promptings, and not his own selfish needs, draw him into Friendships. For just as other things have for us an inherent attractiveness, so has friendship. As we hate solitude and crave society, as nature draws men to each other, so in this matter also there is an attraction which makes us desirous of friendship. **18.** Nevertheless, though the sage may love his friends dearly, often comparing them with himself, and putting them ahead of himself, yet all the good will be limited to his own being, and he will speak the words which were spoken by the very Stilbo whom Epicurus criticizes in his letter. For Stilbo, after his country was captured and his children and his wife lost, as he emerged from the general desolation alone and yet happy, spoke as follows to Demetrius, called Sacker of Cities because of the destruction he brought upon them, in answer to the question whether he had lost anything: "I have all my goods with me!" **19.** There is a brave and stouthearted man for you! The enemy conquered, but Stilbo conquered his conqueror. "I have lost nothing!" Aye, he forced Demetrius to wonder whether he himself had conquered after all. "My goods are all with me!" In other words, he deemed nothing that might be taken from him to be a good.

We marvel at certain animals because they can pass through fire and suffer no bodily harm; but how much more marvellous is a man who has marched forth unhurt and unscathed through fire and sword and devastation! Do you understand now how much easier it is to conquer a whole tribe than to conquer one *man*? This saying of Stilbo makes common ground with Stoicism; the Stoic also can carry his goods unimpaired through cities that have been burned to ashes; for he is self-sufficient. Such are the bounds which he sets to his own happiness.

20. But you must not think that our school alone can utter noble words; Epicurus himself, the reviler of Stilbo, spoke similar language; put it down to my credit, though I have already wiped out my debt for the present day. He says: "Whoever does not regard what he has as most ample wealth, is unhappy, though he be master of the whole world." Or, if the following seems to you a more suitable phrase, – for we must try to render the meaning and not the mere words: "A man may rule the world and still be unhappy, if he does not feel that he is supremely happy." **21.** In order, however, that you may know that these sentiments are universal, suggested, of course, by Nature, you will find in one of the comic poets this verse;

Unblest is he who thinks himself unblest.

or what does your condition matter, if it is bad in your own eyes? **22.** You may say; "What then? If yonder man, rich by base means, and yonder man, lord of many but slave of more, shall call themselves happy, will their own opinion make them happy?" It matters not what one says, but what one feels; also, not how one feels on one particular day, but how one feels at all times. There is no reason, however, why you should fear that this great privilege will fall into unworthy hands; only the wise man is pleased with his own. Folly is ever troubled with weariness of itself. Farewell.

X. ON LIVING TO ONESELF

1. Yes, I do not change my opinion: avoid the many, avoid the few, avoid even the individual. I know of no one with whom I should be willing to have you shared. And see what an opinion of you I have; for I dare to trust you with your own self. Crates, they say, the disciple of the very Stilbo whom I mentioned in a former letter, noticed a young man walking by himself, and asked him what he was doing all alone. "I am communing with myself," replied the youth. "Pray be careful, then," said Crates, "and take good heed; you are communing with a bad man!"

2. When persons are in mourning, or fearful about something, we are accustomed to watch them that we may prevent them from making a wrong use of their loneliness. No thoughtless person ought to be left alone; in such cases he only plans folly, and heaps up future dangers for himself or for others; he brings into play his base desires; the mind displays what fear or shame used to repress; it whets his boldness, stirs his passions, and goads his anger. And finally, the only benefit that solitude confers, – the habit of trusting no man, and of fearing no witnesses, – is lost to the fool; for he betrays himself.

Mark therefore what my hopes are for you, – nay, rather, what I am promising myself, inasmuch as hope is merely the title of an uncertain blessing: I do not know any person with whom I should prefer you to associate rather than yourself. **3.** I remember in what a great-souled way you hurled forth certain phrases, and how full of strength they were! I immediately congratulated myself and said: "These words did not come from the edge of the lips; these utterances have a solid foundation. This man is not one of the many; he has regard for his real welfare." **4.** Speak, and live, in this way; see to it that nothing keeps you down. As for your former prayers, you may dispense the gods from answering them; offer new prayers; pray for a sound mind and for good health, first of soul and then of body. And of course you should offer those prayers frequently. Call boldly upon God; you will not be asking him for that which belongs to another.

5. But I must, as is my custom, send a little gift along with this letter. It is a true saying which I have found in Athenodorus: "Know that thou art freed from all desires when thou hast reached such a point that thou prayest to God for nothing except what thou canst pray for openly." But how foolish men are now! They whisper the basest of prayers to heaven; but if anyone listens, they are silent at once. That which they are unwilling for men to know, they communicate to God. Do you not think, then, that some such wholesome advice as this could be given you: "Live among men as if God beheld you; speak with God as if men were listening"? Farewell.

XI. ON THE BLUSH OF MODESTY

1. Your friend and I have had a conversation. He is a man of ability; his very first words showed what spirit and understanding he possesses, and what progress he has already made. He gave me a foretaste, and he will not fail to answer thereto. For he spoke not from forethought, but was suddenly caught off his guard. When he tried to collect himself, he could scarcely banish that hue of modesty, which is a good sign in a young man; the blush that spread over his face seemed so to rise from the depths. And I feel sure that his habit of blushing will stay with him after he has strengthened his character, stripped off all his faults, and become wise. For by no wisdom can natural weaknesses of the body be removed. That which is implanted and inborn can be toned down by training, but not overcome. **2.** The steadiest speaker, when before the public, often breaks into a perspiration, as if he had wearied or over-heated himself; some tremble in the knees when they rise to speak; I know of some whose teeth chatter, whose tongues falter, whose lips quiver. Training and experience can never shake off this habit; nature exerts her own power and through such a weakness makes her presence known even to the strongest. **3.** I know that the blush, too, is a habit of this sort, spreading suddenly over the faces of the most dignified men. It is, indeed more prevalent in youth, because of the warmer blood and the sensitive countenance; nevertheless, both seasoned men and aged men are affected by it. Some are most dangerous when they redden, as if they were letting all their sense of shame escape. **4.** Sulla, when the blood mantled his cheeks, was in his fiercest mood. Pompey had the most sensitive cast of countenance; he always blushed in the presence of a gathering, and especially at a public assembly. Fabianus also, I remember, reddened when he appeared as a witness before the senate; and his embarrassment became him to a remarkable degree. **5.** Such a habit is not due to mental weakness, but to the novelty of a situation; an inexperienced person is not necessarily confused, but is usually affected, because he slips into this habit by natural tendency of the body. Just as certain men are full-blooded, so others are of a quick and mobile blood, that rushes to the face at once.

6. As I remarked, Wisdom can never remove this habit; for if she could rub out all our faults, she would be mistress of the universe. Whatever is assigned to us by the terms of our birth and the blend in our constitutions, will stick with us, no matter how hard or how long the soul may have tried to master itself. And we cannot forbid these feelings any more than we can summon them. **7.** Actors in the theatre, who imitate the emotions, who portray fear and nervousness, who depict sorrow, imitate bashfulness by hanging their heads, lowering their voices, and keeping their eyes fixed and rooted upon the ground. They cannot, however, muster a blush; for the blush cannot be prevented or acquired. Wisdom will not assure us of a remedy, or give us help against it; it comes or goes unbidden, and is a law unto itself.

8. But my letter calls for its closing sentence. Hear and take to heart this useful and wholesome motto: "Cherish some man of high character, and keep him ever before your eyes, living as if he were watching you, and ordering all your actions as if he beheld them." **9.** Such, my dear Lucilius, is the counsel of Epicurus; he has quite properly given us a guardian and an attendant. We can get rid of most sins, if we have a witness who stands near us when we are likely to go wrong. The soul should have someone whom it can respect, – one by whose authority it may make even its inner shrine more hallowed. Happy is the man who can make others better, not merely when he is in their company, but even when he is in their thoughts! And happy also is he who can so revere a man as to calm and regulate himself by calling him to mind! One who can so revere another, will soon be himself worthy of reverence. **10.** Choose therefore a Cato; or, if Cato seems too severe a model, choose some Laelius, a gentler spirit. Choose a master whose life, conversation, and soul-expressing face have satisfied you; picture him always to yourself as your protector or your pattern. For we must indeed have someone according to whom we may regulate our characters; you can never straighten that which is crooked unless you use a ruler. Farewell.

XII. ON OLD AGE

1. Wherever I turn, I see evidences of my advancing years. I visited lately my country-place, and protested against the money which was spent on the tumble-down building. My bailiff maintained that the flaws were not due to his own carelessness; "he was doing everything possible, but the house was old." And this was the house which grew under my own hands! What has the future in store for me, if stones of my own age are already crumbling? **2.** I was angry, and I embraced the first opportunity to vent my spleen in the bailiff's presence. "It is clear," I cried, "that these plane-trees are neglected; they have no leaves. Their branches are so gnarled and shrivelled; the boles are so rough and unkempt! This would not happen, if someone loosened the earth at their feet, and watered them." The bailiff swore by my protecting deity that "he was doing everything possible, and never relaxed his efforts, but those trees were old." Between you and me, I had planted those trees myself, I had seen them in their first leaf. **3.** Then I turned to the door and asked: "Who is that broken-down dotard? You have done well to place him at the entrance; for he is outward bound. Where did you get him? What pleasure did it give you to take up for burial some other man's dead?" But the slave said: "Don't you know me, sir? I am Felicio; you used to bring me little images. My father was Philositus the steward, and I am your pet slave." "The man is clean crazy," I remarked. "Has my pet slave become a little boy again? But it is quite possible; his teeth are just dropping out."

4. I owe it to my country-place that my old age became apparent whithersoever I turned. Let us cherish and love old age; for it is full of pleasure if one knows how to use it. Fruits are most welcome when almost over; youth is most charming at its close; the last drink delights the toper, the glass which souses him and puts the finishing touch on his drunkenness. **5.** Each pleasure reserves to the end the greatest delights which it contains. Life is most delightful when it is on the downward slope, but has not yet reached the abrupt decline. And I myself believe that the period which stands, so to speak, on the edge of the roof, possesses pleasures of its own. Or else the very fact of our not wanting pleasures has taken the place of the pleasures themselves. How comforting it is to have tired out one's appetites, and to have done with them! **6.** "But," you say, "it is a nuisance to be looking death in the face!" Death, however, should be looked in the face by young and old alike. We are not summoned according to our rating on the censor's list. Moreover, no one is so old that it would be improper for him to hope for another day of existence. And one day, mind you, is a stage on life's journey.

Our span of life is divided into parts; it consists of large circles enclosing smaller. One circle embraces and bounds the rest; it reaches from birth to the last day of existence. The next circle limits the period of our young manhood. The third confines all of childhood in its circumference. Again, there is, in a class by itself, the year; it contains within itself all the divisions of time by the multiplication of which we get the total of life. The month is bounded by a narrower ring. The smallest circle of all is the day; but even a day has its beginning and its ending, its sunrise and its sunset. **7.** Hence Heraclitus, whose obscure style gave him his surname, remarked: "One day is equal to every day." Different persons have interpreted the saying in different ways. Some hold that days are equal in number of hours, and this is true; for if by "day" we mean twenty-four hours' time, all days must be equal, inasmuch as the night acquires what the day loses. But others maintain that one day is equal to all days through resemblance, because the very longest space of time possesses no element which cannot be found in a single day, – namely, light and darkness, – and even to eternity day makes these alternations more numerous, not different when it is shorter and different again when it is longer. **8.** Hence, every day ought to be regulated as if it closed the series, as if it rounded out and completed our existence.

Pacuvius, who by long occupancy made Syria his own, used to hold a regular burial sacrifice in his own honour, with wine and the usual funeral feasting, and then would have himself carried from the dining-room to his chamber, while eunuchs applauded and sang in Greek to a musical accompaniment: "He has lived his life, he has lived his life!" **9.** Thus Pacuvius had himself carried out to burial every day. Let us, however, do from a good motive what he used to do from a debased motive; let us go to our sleep with joy and gladness; let us say:

> I have lived; the course which Fortune set for me
> Is finished.

And if God is pleased to add another day, we should welcome it with glad hearts. That man is happiest, and is secure in his own possession of himself, who can await the morrow without apprehension. When a man has said: "I have lived!", every morning he arises he receives a bonus.

10. But now I ought to close my letter. "What?" you say; "shall it come to me without any little offering? "Be not afraid; it brings something, – nay, more than something, a great deal. For what is more noble than the following saying of which I make this letter the bearer: "It is wrong to live under constraint; but no man is constrained to live under constraint." Of course not. On all sides lie many short and simple paths to freedom; and let us thank God that no man can be kept in life. We may spurn the very constraints that hold us. **11.** "Epicurus," you reply, "uttered these words; what are you doing with another's property?" Any truth, I maintain, is my own property. And I shall continue to heap quotations from Epicurus upon you, so that all persons who swear by the words of another, and put a value upon the speaker and not upon the thing spoken, may understand that the best ideas are common property. Farewell.

XIII. ON GROUNDLESS FEARS

1. I know that you have plenty of spirit; for even before you began to equip yourself with maxims which were wholesome and potent to overcome obstacles, you were taking pride in your contest with Fortune; and this is all the more true, now that you have grappled with Fortune and tested your powers. For our powers can never inspire in us implicit faith in ourselves except when many difficulties have confronted us on this side and on that, and have occasionally even come to close quarters with us. It is only in this way that the true spirit can be tested, – the spirit that will never consent to come under the jurisdiction of things external to ourselves. **2.** This is the touchstone of such a spirit; no prizefighter can go with high spirits into the strife if he has never been beaten black and blue; the only contestant who can confidently enter the lists is the man who has seen his own blood, who has felt his teeth rattle beneath his opponent's fist, who has been tripped and felt the full force of his adversary's charge, who has been downed in body but not in spirit, one who, as often as he falls, rises again with greater defiance than ever. **3.** So then, to keep up my figure, Fortune has often in the past got the upper hand of you, and yet you have not surrendered, but have leaped up and stood your ground still more eagerly. For manliness gains much strength by being challenged; nevertheless, if you approve, allow me to offer some additional safeguards by which you may fortify yourself.

4. There are more things, Lucilius, likely to frighten us than there are to crush us; we suffer more often in imagination than in reality. I am not speaking with you in the Stoic strain but in my milder style. For it is our Stoic fashion to speak of all those things, which provoke cries and groans, as unimportant and beneath notice; but you and I must drop such great-sounding words, although, heaven knows, they are true enough. What I advise you to do is, not to be unhappy before the crisis comes; since it may be that the dangers before which you paled as if they were threatening you, will never come upon you; they certainly have not yet come. **5.** Accordingly, some things torment us more than they ought; some torment us before they ought; and some torment us when they ought not to torment us at all. We are in the habit of exaggerating, or imagining, or anticipating, sorrow.

The first of these three faults may be postponed for the present, because the subject is under discussion and the case is still in court, so to speak. That which I should call trifling, you will maintain to be most serious; for of course I know that some men laugh while being flogged, and that others wince at a box on the ear. We shall consider later whether these evils derive their power from their own strength, or from our own weakness.

6. Do me the favour, when men surround you and try to talk you into believing that you are unhappy, to consider not what you hear but what you yourself feel, and to take counsel with your feelings and question yourself independently, because you know your own affairs better than anyone else does. Ask: "Is there any reason why these persons should condole with me? Why should they be worried or even fear some infection from me, as if troubles could be transmitted? Is there any evil involved, or is it a matter merely of ill report, rather than an evil?" Put the question voluntarily to yourself: "Am I tormented without sufficient reason, am I morose, and do I convert what is not an evil into what is an evil?" **7.** You may retort with the question: "How am I to know whether my sufferings are real or imaginary?" Here is the rule for such matters: we are tormented either by things present, or by things to come, or by both. As to things present, the decision is easy. Suppose that your person enjoys freedom and health, and that you do not suffer from any external injury. As to what may happen to it in the future, we shall see later on. To-day there is nothing wrong with it. **8.** "But," you say, "something will happen to it." First of all, consider whether your proofs of future trouble are sure. For it is more often the case that we are troubled by our apprehensions, and that we are mocked by that mocker, rumour, which is wont to settle wars, but much more often settles individuals. Yes, my dear Lucilius; we agree too quickly with what people say. We do not put to the test those things which cause our fear; we do not examine into them; we blench and retreat just like soldiers who are forced to abandon their camp because of a dust-cloud raised by stampeding cattle, or are thrown into a panic by the spreading of some unauthenticated rumour. **9.** And somehow or other it is the idle report that disturbs us most. For truth has its own definite boundaries, but that which arises from uncertainty is delivered over to guesswork and the irresponsible license of a frightened mind. That is why no fear is so ruinous and so uncontrollable as panic fear. For other fears are groundless, but this fear is witless.

10. Let us, then, look carefully into the matter. It is likely that some troubles will befall us; but it is not a present fact. How often has the unexpected happened! How often has the expected never come to pass! And even though it is ordained to be, what does it avail to run out to meet your suffering? You will suffer soon enough, when it arrives; so look forward meanwhile to better things. **11.** What shall you gain by doing this? Time. There will be many happenings meanwhile which will serve to postpone, or end, or pass on to another person, the trials which are near or even in your very presence. A fire has opened the way to flight. Men have been let down softly by a catastrophe. Sometimes the sword has been checked even at the victim's throat. Men have survived their own executioners. Even bad fortune is fickle. Perhaps it will come, perhaps not; in the meantime it is not. So look forward to better things.

12. The mind at times fashions for itself false shapes of evil when there are no signs that point to any evil; it twists into the worst construction some word of doubtful meaning; or it fancies some personal grudge to be more serious than it really is, considering not how angry the enemy is, but to what lengths he may go if he is angry. But life is not worth living, and there is no limit to our sorrows, if we indulge our fears to the greatest possible extent; in this matter, let prudence help you, and contemn with a resolute spirit even when it is in plain sight. If you cannot do this, counter one weakness with another, and temper your fear with hope. There is nothing so certain among these objects of fear that it is not more certain still that things we dread sink into nothing and that things we hope for mock us.

13. Accordingly, weigh carefully your hopes as well as your fears, and whenever all the elements are in doubt, decide in your own favour; believe what you prefer. And if fear wins a majority of the votes, incline in the other direction anyhow, and cease to harass your soul, reflecting continually that most mortals, even when no troubles are actually at hand or are certainly to be expected in the future, become excited and disquieted. No one calls a halt on himself, when he begins to be urged ahead; nor does he regulate his alarm according to the truth. No one says; "The author of the story is a fool, and he who has believed it is a fool, as well as he who fabricated it." We let ourselves drift with every breeze; we are frightened at uncertainties, just as if they were certain. We observe no moderation. The slightest thing turns the scales and throws us forthwith into a panic.

14. But I am ashamed either to admonish you sternly or to try to beguile you with such mild remedies. Let another say. "Perhaps the worst will not happen." You yourself must say. "Well, what if it does happen? Let us see who wins! Perhaps it happens for my best interests; it may be that such a death will shed credit upon my life." Socrates was ennobled by the hemlock draught. Wrench from Cato's hand his sword, the vindicator of liberty, and you deprive him of the greatest share of his glory. **15.** I am exhorting you far too long, since you need reminding rather than exhortation. The path on which I am leading you is not different from that on which your nature leads you; you were born to such conduct as I describe. Hence there is all the more reason why you should increase and beautify the good that is in you.

16. But now, to close my letter, I have only to stamp the usual seal upon it, in other words, to commit thereto some noble message to be delivered to you: "The fool, with all his other faults, has this also, he is always getting ready to live." Reflect, my esteemed Lucilius, what this saying means, and you will see how revolting is the fickleness of men who lay down every day new foundations of life, and begin to build up fresh hopes even at the brink of the grave. **17.** Look within your own mind for individual instances; you will think of old men who are preparing themselves at that very hour for a political career, or for travel, or for business. And what is baser than getting ready to live when you are already old? I should not name the author of this motto, except that it is somewhat unknown to fame and is not one of those popular sayings of Epicurus which I have allowed myself to praise and to appropriate. Farewell.

XIV. ON THE REASONS FOR WITHDRAWING FROM THE WORLD

1. I confess that we all have an inborn affection for our body; I confess that we are entrusted with its guardianship. I do not maintain that the body is not to be indulged at all; but I maintain that we must not be slaves to it. He will have many masters who makes his body his master, who is over-fearful in its behalf, who judges everything according to the body. **2.** We should conduct ourselves not as if we ought to live for the body, but as if we could not live without it. Our too great love for it makes us restless with fears, burdens us with cares, and exposes us to insults. Virtue is held too cheap by the man who counts his body too dear. We should cherish the body with the greatest care; but we should also be prepared, when reason, self-respect, and duty demand the sacrifice, to deliver it even to the flames.

3. Let us, however, in so far as we can, avoid discomforts as well as dangers, and withdraw to safe ground, by thinking continually how we may repel all objects of fear. If I am not mistaken, there are three main classes of these: we fear want, we fear sickness, and we fear the troubles which result from the violence of the stronger. **4.** And of all these, that which shakes us most is the dread which hangs over us from our neighbour's ascendancy; for it is accompanied by great outcry and uproar. But the natural evils which I have mentioned, – want and sickness, steal upon us silently with no shock of terror to the eye or to the ear. The other kind of evil comes, so to speak, in the form of a huge parade. Surrounding it is a retinue of swords and fire and chains and a mob of beasts to be let loose upon the disembowelled entrails of men. **5.** Picture to yourself under this head the prison, the cross, the rack, the hook, and the stake which they drive straight through a man until it protrudes from his throat. Think of human limbs torn apart by chariots driven in opposite directions, of the terrible shirt smeared and interwoven with inflammable materials, and of all the other contrivances devised by cruelty, in addition to those which I have mentioned! **6.** It is not surprising, then, if our greatest terror is of such a fate; for it comes in many shapes and its paraphernalia are terrifying. For just as the torturer accomplishes more in proportion to the number of instruments which he displays, – indeed, the spectacle overcomes those who would have patiently withstood the suffering, – similarly, of all the agencies which coerce and master our minds, the most effective are those which can make a display. Those other troubles are of course not less serious; I mean hunger, thirst, ulcers of the stomach, and fever that parches our very bowels. They are, however, secret; they have no bluster and no heralding; but these, like huge arrays of war, prevail by virtue of their display and their equipment.

7. Let us, therefore, see to it that we abstain from giving offence. It is sometimes the people that we ought to fear; or sometimes a body of influential oligarchs in the Senate, if the method of governing the State is such that most of the business is done by that body; and sometimes individuals equipped with power by the people and against the people. It is burdensome to keep the friendship of all such persons; it is enough not to make enemies of them. So the wise man will never provoke the anger of those in power; nay, he will even turn his course, precisely as he would turn from a storm if he were steering a ship. **8.** When you travelled to Sicily, you crossed the Straits. The reckless pilot scorned the blustering South Wind, – the wind which roughens the Sicilian Sea and forces it into choppy currents; he sought not the shore on the left, but the strand hard by the place where Charybdis throws the seas into confusion. Your more careful pilot, however, questions those who know the locality as to the tides and the meaning of the clouds; he holds his course far from that region notorious for its swirling waters. Our wise man does the same he shuns a strong man who may be injurious to him, making a point of not seeming to avoid him, because an important part of one's safety lies in not seeking safety openly; for what one avoids, one condemns,

9. We should therefore look about us, and see how we may protect ourselves from the mob. And first of all, we should have no cravings like theirs; for rivalry results in strife. Again, let us possess nothing that can be snatched from us to the great profit of a plotting foe. Let there be as little booty as possible on your person. No one sets out to shed the blood of his fellow-men for the sake of bloodshed, – at any rate very few. More murderers speculate on their profits than give vent to hatred. If you are empty-handed, the highwayman passes you by: even along an infested road, the poor may travel in peace. **10.** Next, we must follow the old adage and avoid three things with special care: hatred, jealousy, and scorn. And wisdom alone can show you how this may be done. It is hard to observe a mean; we must be chary of letting the fear of jealousy lead us into becoming objects of scorn, lest, when we choose not to stamp others down, we let them think that they can stamp us down. The power to inspire fear has caused many men to be in fear. Let us withdraw ourselves in every way; for it is as harmful to be scorned as to be admired.

11. One must therefore take refuge in philosophy; this pursuit, not only in the eyes of good men, but also in the eyes of those who are even moderately bad, is a sort of protecting emblem. For speechmaking at the bar, or any other pursuit that claims the people's attention, wins enemies for a man; but philosophy is peaceful and minds her own business. Men cannot scorn her; she is honoured by every profession, even the vilest among them. Evil can never grow so strong, and nobility of character can never be so plotted against, that the name of philosophy shall cease to be worshipful and sacred.

Philosophy itself, however should be practised with calmness and moderation. **12.** "Very well, then," you retort, "do you regard the philosophy of Marcus Cato as moderate? Cato's voice strove to check a civil war. Cato parted the swords of maddened chieftains. When some fell foul of Pompey and others fell foul of Caesar, Cato defied both parties at once!" **13.** Nevertheless, one may well question whether, in those days, a wise man ought to have taken any part in public affairs, and ask: "What do you mean, Marcus Cato? It is not now a question of freedom; long since has freedom gone to rack and ruin. The question is, whether it is Caesar or Pompey who controls the State. Why, Cato, should you take sides in that dispute? It is no business of yours; a tyrant is being selected. What does it concern you who conquers? The better man may win; but the winner is bound to be the worse man." I have referred to Cato's final rôle. But even in previous years the wise man was not permitted to intervene in such plundering of the state; for what could Cato do but raise his voice and utter unavailing words? At one time he was "bustled" by the mob and spat upon and forcibly removed from the forum and marked for exile; at another, he was taken straight to prison from the senate-chamber.

14. However, we shall consider later whether the wise man ought to give his attention to politics; meanwhile, I beg you to consider those Stoics who, shut out from public life, have withdrawn into privacy for the purpose of improving men's existence and framing laws for the human race without incurring the displeasure of those in power. The wise man will not upset the customs of the people, nor will he invite the attention of the populace by any novel ways of living.

15. "What then? Can one who follows out this Plan be safe in any case?" I cannot guarantee you this any more than I can guarantee good health in the case of a man who observes moderation; although, as a matter of fact, good health results from such moderation. Sometimes a vessel perishes in harbour; but what do you think happens on the open sea? And how much more beset with danger that man would be, who even in his leisure is not secure, if he were busily working at many things! Innocent persons sometimes perish; who would deny that? But the guilty perish more frequently. A soldier's skill is not at fault if he receives the death-blow through his armour. **16.** And finally, the wise man regards the reason for all his actions, but not the results. The beginning is in our own power; fortune decides the issue, but I do not allow her to pass sentence upon myself. You may say: "But she can inflict a measure of suffering and of trouble." The highwayman does not pass sentence when he slays.

17. Now you are stretching forth your hand for the daily gift. Golden indeed will be the gift with which I shall load you; and, inasmuch as we have mentioned gold, let me tell you how its use and enjoyment may bring you greater pleasure. "He who needs riches least, enjoys riches most." "Author's name, please!" you say. Now, to show you how generous I am, it is my intent to praise the dicta of other schools. The phrase belongs to Epicurus, or Metrodorus, or some one of that particular thinking-shop. **18.** But what difference does it make who spoke the words? They were uttered for the world. He who craves riches feels fear on their account. No man, however, enjoys a blessing that brings anxiety; he is always trying to add a little more. While he puzzles over increasing his wealth, he forgets how to use it. He collects his accounts, he wears out the pavement in the forum, he turns over his ledger, – in short, he ceases to be master and becomes a steward. Farewell.

XV. ON BRAWN AND BRAINS

1. The old Romans had a custom which survived even into my lifetime. They would add to the opening words of a letter: "If you are well, it is well; I also am well." Persons like ourselves would do well to say. "If you are studying philosophy, it is well." For this is just what "being well" means. Without philosophy the mind is sickly, and the body, too, though it may be very powerful, is strong only as that of a madman or a lunatic is strong. **2.** This, then, is the sort of health you should primarily cultivate; the other kind of health comes second, and will involve little effort, if you wish to be well physically. It is indeed foolish, my dear Lucilius, and very unsuitable for a cultivated man, to work hard over developing the muscles and broadening the shoulders and strengthening the lungs. For although your heavy feeding produce good results and your sinews grow solid, you can never be a match, either in strength or in weight, for a first-class bull. Besides, by overloading the body with food you strangle the soul and render it less active. Accordingly, limit the flesh as much as possible, and allow free play to the spirit. **3.** Many inconveniences beset those who devote themselves to such pursuits. In the first place, they have their exercises, at which they must work and waste their life-force and render it less fit to bear a strain or the severer studies.

Second, their keen edge is dulled by heavy eating. Besides, they must take orders from slaves of the vilest stamp, – men who alternate between the oil-flask and the flagon, whose day passes satisfactorily if they have got up a good perspiration and quaffed, to make good what they have lost in sweat, huge draughts of liquor which will sink deeper because of their fasting. Drinking and sweating, – it's the life of a dyspeptic!

4. Now there are short and simple exercises which tire the body rapidly, and so save our time; and time is something of which we ought to keep strict account. These exercises are running, brandishing weights, and jumping, – high-jumping or broad-jumping, or the kind which I may call, "the Priest's dance," or, in slighting terms, "the clothes-cleaner's jump." Select for practice any one of these, and you will find it plain and easy. **5.** But whatever you do, come back soon from body to mind. The mind must be exercised both day and night, for it is nourished by moderate labour. and this form of exercise need not be hampered by cold or hot weather, or even by old age. Cultivate that good which improves with the years. **6.** Of course I do not command you to be always bending over your books and your writing materials; the mind must have a change, – but a change of such a kind that it is not unnerved, but merely unbent. Riding in a litter shakes up the body, and does not interfere with study: one may read, dictate, converse, or listen to another; nor does walking prevent any of these things.

7. You need not scorn voice-culture; but I forbid you to practise raising and lowering your voice by scales and specific intonations. What if you should next propose to take lessons in walking! If you consult the sort of person whom starvation has taught new tricks, you will have someone to regulate your steps, watch every mouthful as you eat, and go to such lengths as you yourself, by enduring him and believing in him, have encouraged his effrontery to go. "What, then?" you will ask; "is my voice to begin at the outset with shouting and straining the lungs to the utmost?" No; the natural thing is that it be aroused to such a pitch by easy stages, just as persons who are wrangling begin with ordinary conversational tones and then pass to shouting at the top of their lungs. No speaker cries "Help me, citizens!" at the outset of his speech. **8.** Therefore, whenever your spirit's impulse prompts you, raise a hubbub, now in louder now in milder tones, according as your voice, as well as your spirit, shall suggest to you, when you are moved to such a performance. Then let your voice, when you rein it in and call it back to earth, come down gently, not collapse; it should trail off in tones half way between high and low, and should not abruptly drop from its raving in the uncouth manner of countrymen. For our purpose is, not to give the voice exercise, but to make it give us exercise.

9. You see, I have relieved you of no slight bother; and I shall throw in a little complementary present, – it is Greek, too. Here is the proverb; it is an excellent one: "The fool's life is empty of gratitude and full of fears; its course lies wholly toward the future." "Who uttered these words?" you say. The same writer whom I mentioned before. And what sort of life do you think is meant by the fool's life? That of Baba and Isio? No; he means our own, for we are plunged by our blind desires into ventures which will harm us, but certainly will never satisfy us; for if we could be satisfied with anything, we should have been satisfied long ago; nor do we reflect how pleasant it is to demand nothing, how noble it is to be contented and not to be dependent upon Fortune. **10.** Therefore continually remind yourself, Lucilius, how many ambitions you have attained. When you see many ahead of you, think how many are behind! If you would thank the gods, and be grateful for your past life, you should contemplate how many men you have outstripped. But what have you to do with the others? You have outstripped yourself.

11. Fix a limit which you will not even desire to pass, should you have the power. At last, then, away with all these treacherous goods! They look better to those who hope for them than to those who have attained them. If there were anything substantial in them, they would sooner or later satisfy you; as it is, they merely rouse the drinkers' thirst. Away with fripperies which only serve for show! As to what the future's uncertain lot has in store, why should I demand of Fortune that she give rather than demand of myself that I should not crave? And why should l crave? Shall I heap up my winnings, and forget that man's lot is unsubstantial? For what end should I toil? Lo, to-day is the last; if not, it is near the last. Farewell.

XVI. ON PHILOSOPHY, THE GUIDE OF LIFE

1. It is clear to you, I am sure, Lucilius, that no man can live a happy life, or even a supportable life, without the study of wisdom; you know also that a happy life is reached when our wisdom is brought to completion, but that life is at least endurable even when our wisdom is only begun. This idea, however, clear though it is, must be strengthened and implanted more deeply by daily reflection; it is more important for you to keep the resolutions you have already made than to go on and make noble ones. You must persevere, must develop new strength by continuous study, until that which is only a good inclination becomes a good settled purpose. **2.** Hence you no longer need to come to me with much talk and protestations; I know that you have made great progress. I understand the feelings which prompt your words; they are not feigned or specious words. Nevertheless I shall tell you what I think, – that at present I have hopes for you, but not yet perfect trust. And I wish that you would adopt the same attitude towards yourself; there is no reason why you should put confidence in yourself too quickly and readily. Examine yourself; scrutinize and observe yourself in divers ways; but mark, before all else, whether it is in philosophy or merely in life itself that you have made progress. **3.** Philosophy is no trick to catch the public; it is not devised for show. It is a matter, not of words, but of facts. It is not pursued in order that the day may yield some amusement before it is spent, or that our leisure may be relieved of a tedium that irks us. It moulds and constructs the soul; it orders our life, guides our conduct, shows us what we should do and what we should leave undone; it sits at the helm and directs our course as we waver amid uncertainties. Without it, no one can live fearlessly or in peace of mind. Countless things that happen every hour call for advice; and such advice is to be sought in philosophy.

4. Perhaps someone will say: "How can philosophy help me, if Fate exists? Of what avail is philosophy, if God rules the universe? Of what avail is it, if Chance governs everything? For not only is it impossible to change things that are determined, but it is also impossible to plan beforehand against what is undetermined; either God has forestalled my plans, and decided what I am to do, or else Fortune gives no free play to my plans." **5.** Whether the truth, Lucilius, lies in one or in all of these views, we must be philosophers; whether Fate binds us down by an inexorable law, or whether God as arbiter of the universe has arranged everything, or whether Chance drives and tosses human affairs without method, philosophy ought to be our defence. She will encourage us to obey God cheerfully, but Fortune defiantly; she will teach us to follow God and endure Chance. **6.** But it is not my purpose now to be led into a discussion as to what is within our own control, – if foreknowledge is supreme, or if a chain of fated events drags us along in its clutches, or if the sudden and the unexpected play the tyrant over us; I return now to my warning and my exhortation, that you should not allow the impulse of your spirit to weaken and grow cold. Hold fast to it and establish it firmly, in order that what is now impulse may become a habit of the mind.

7. If I know you well, you have already been trying to find out, from the very beginning of my letter, what little contribution it brings to you. Sift the letter, and you will find it. You need not wonder at any genius of mine; for as yet I am lavish only with other men's property. – But why did I say "other men"? Whatever is well said by anyone is mine. This also is a saying of Epicurus: "If you live according to nature, you will never be poor; if you live according to opinion, you will never be rich." **8.** Nature's wants are slight; the demands of opinion are boundless. Suppose that the property of many millionaires is heaped up in your possession. Assume that fortune carries you far beyond the limits of a private income, decks you with gold, clothes you in purple, and brings you to such a degree of luxury and wealth that you can bury the earth under your marble floors; that you may not only possess, but tread upon, riches. Add statues, paintings, and whatever any art has devised for the luxury; you will only learn from such things to crave still greater.

9. Natural desires are limited; but those which spring from false opinion can have no stopping-point. The false has no limits. When you are travelling on a road, there must be an end; but when astray, your wanderings are limitless. Recall your steps, therefore, from idle things, and when you would know whether that which you seek is based upon a natural or upon a misleading desire, consider whether it can stop at any definite point. If you find, after having travelled far, that there is a more distant goal always in view, you may be sure that this condition is contrary to nature. Farewell.

XVII. ON PHILOSOPHY AND RICHES

1. Cast away everything of that sort, if you are wise; nay, rather that you may be wise; strive toward a sound mind at top speed and with your whole strength. If any bond holds you back, untie it, or sever it. "But," you say, "my estate delays me; I wish to make such disposition of it that it may suffice for me when I have nothing to do, lest either poverty be a burden to me, or I myself a burden to others." **2.** You do not seem, when you say this, to know the strength and power of that good which you are considering. You do indeed grasp the all important thing, the great benefit which philosophy confers, but you do not yet discern accurately its various functions, nor do you yet know how great is the help we receive from philosophy in everything, everywhere, – how, (to use Cicero's language,) it not only succours us in the greatest matters but also descends to the smallest. Take my advice; call wisdom into consultation; she will advise you not to sit for ever at your ledger. **3.** Doubtless, your object, what you wish to attain by such postponement of your studies, is that poverty may not have to be feared by you. But what if it is something to be desired? Riches have shut off many a man from the attainment of wisdom; poverty is unburdened and free from care. When the trumpet sounds, the poor man knows that he is not being attacked; when there is a cry of "Fire," he only seeks a way of escape, and does not ask what he can save; if the poor man must go to sea, the harbour does not resound, nor do the wharves bustle with the retinue of one individual. No throng of slaves surrounds the poor man, – slaves for whose mouths the master must covet the fertile crops of regions beyond the sea. **4.** It is easy to fill a few stomachs, when they are well trained and crave nothing else but to be filled. Hunger costs but little; squeamishness costs much. Poverty is contented with fulfilling pressing needs.

Why, then, should you reject Philosophy as a comrade? **5.** Even the rich man copies her ways when he is in his senses. If you wish to have leisure for your mind, either be a poor man, or resemble a poor man. Study cannot be helpful unless you take pains to live simply; and living simply is voluntary poverty. Away, then, with all excuses like: "I have not yet enough; when I have gained the desired amount, then I shall devote myself wholly to philosophy." And yet this ideal, which you are putting off and placing second to other interests, should be secured first of all; you should begin with it. You retort: "I wish to acquire something to live on." Yes, but learn while you are acquiring it; for if anything forbids you to live nobly, nothing forbids you to die nobly. **6.** There is no reason why poverty should call us away from philosophy, – no, nor even actual want. For when hastening after wisdom, we must endure even hunger. Men have endured hunger when their towns were besieged, and what other reward for their endurance did they obtain than that they did not fall under the conqueror's power? How much greater is the promise of the prize of everlasting liberty, and the assurance that we need fear neither God nor man! Even though we starve, we must reach that goal. **7.** Armies have endured all manner of want, have lived on roots, and have resisted hunger by means of food too revolting to mention. All this they have suffered to gain a kingdom, and, – what is more marvellous, – to gain a kingdom that will be another's. Will any man hesitate to endure poverty, in order that he may free his mind from madness?

Therefore one should not seek to lay up riches first; one may attain to philosophy, however, even without money for the journey. **8.** It is indeed so. After you have come to possess all other things, shall you then wish to possess wisdom also? Is philosophy to be the last requisite in life, – a sort of supplement? Nay, your plan should be this: be a philosopher now, whether you have anything or not, – for if you have anything, how do you know that you have not too much already? – but if you have nothing, seek understanding first, before anything else. **9.** "But," you say, "I shall lack the necessities of life." In the first place, you cannot lack them; because nature demands but little, and the wise man suits his needs to nature. But if the utmost pinch of need arrives, he will quickly take leave of life and cease being a trouble to himself. If, however, his means of existence are meagre and scanty, he will make the best of them, without being anxious or worried about anything more than the bare necessities; he will do justice to his belly and his shoulders; with free and happy spirit he will laugh at the bustling of rich men, and the flurried ways of those who are hastening after wealth, **10.** and say: "Why of your own accord postpone your real life to the distant future? Shall you wait for some interest to fall due, or for some income on your merchandise, or for a place in the will of some wealthy old man, when you can be rich here and now. Wisdom offers wealth in ready money, and pays it over to those in whose eyes she has made wealth superfluous." These remarks refer to other men; you are nearer the rich class. Change the age in which you live, and you have too much. But in every age, what is enough remains the same.

11. I might close my letter at this point, if I had not got you into bad habits. One cannot greet Parthian royalty without bringing a gift; and in your case I cannot say farewell without paying a price. But what of it? I shall borrow from Epicurus: "The acquisition of riches has been for many men, not an end, but a change, of troubles." **12.** I do not wonder. For the fault is not in the wealth, but in the mind itself. That which had made poverty a burden to us, has made riches also a burden. Just as it matters little whether you lay a sick man on a wooden or on a golden bed, for whithersoever he be moved he will carry his malady with him; so one need not care whether the diseased mind is bestowed upon riches or upon poverty. His malady goes with the man. Farewell,

XVIII. ON FESTIVALS AND FASTING

1. It is the month of December, and yet the city is at this very moment in a sweat. License is given to the general merrymaking. Everything resounds with mighty preparations, – as if the Saturnalia differed at all from the usual business day! So true it is that the difference is nil, that I regard as correct the remark of the man who said: "Once December was a month; now it is a year."

2. If I had you with me, I should be glad to consult you and find out what you think should be done, – whether we ought to make no change in our daily routine, or whether, in order not to be out of sympathy with the ways of the public, we should dine in gayer fashion and doff the toga. As it is now, we Romans have changed our dress for the sake of pleasure and holiday-making, though in former times that was only customary when the State was disturbed and had fallen on evil days. **3.** I am sure that, if I know you aright, playing the part of an umpire you would have wished that we should be neither like the liberty-capped throng in all ways, nor in all ways unlike them; unless, perhaps, this is just the season when we ought to lay down the law to the soul, and bid it be alone in refraining from pleasures just when the whole mob has let itself go in pleasures; for this is the surest proof which a man can get of his own constancy, if he neither seeks the things which are seductive and allure him to luxury, nor is led into them. **4.** It shows much more courage to remain dry and sober when the mob is drunk and vomiting; but it shows greater self-control to refuse to withdraw oneself and to do what the crowd does, but in a different way, – thus neither making oneself conspicuous nor becoming one of the crowd. For one may keep holiday without extravagance.

5. I am so firmly determined, however, to test the constancy of your mind that, drawing from the teachings of great men, I shall give you also a lesson: Set aside a certain number of days, during which you shall be content with the scantiest and cheapest fare, with coarse and rough dress, saying to yourself the while: "Is this the condition that I feared?" **6.** It is precisely in times of immunity from care that the soul should toughen itself beforehand for occasions of greater stress, and it is while Fortune is kind that it should fortify itself against her violence. In days of peace the soldier performs manoeuvres, throws up earthworks with no enemy in sight, and wearies himself by gratuitous toil, in order that he may be equal to unavoidable toil. If you would not have a man flinch when the crisis comes, train him before it comes. Such is the course which those men have followed who, in their imitation of poverty, have every month come almost to want, that they might never recoil from what they had so often rehearsed.

7. You need not suppose that I mean meals like Timon's, or "paupers' huts," or any other device which luxurious millionaires use to beguile the tedium of their lives. Let the pallet be a real one, and the coarse cloak; let the bread be hard and grimy. Endure all this for three or four days at a time, sometimes for more, so that it may be a test of yourself instead of a mere hobby. Then, I assure you, my dear Lucilius, you will leap for joy when filled with a pennyworth of food, and you will understand that a man's peace of mind does not depend upon Fortune; for, even when angry she grants enough for our needs.

8. There is no reason, however, why you should think that you are doing anything great; for you will merely be doing what many thousands of slaves and many thousands of poor men are doing every day. But you may credit yourself with this item, – that you will not be doing it under compulsion, and that it will be as easy for you to endure it permanently as to make the experiment from time to time. Let us practise our strokes on the "dummy"; let us become intimate with poverty, so that Fortune may not catch us off our guard. We shall be rich with all the more comfort, if we once learn how far poverty is from being a burden.

9. Even Epicurus, the teacher of pleasure, used to observe stated intervals, during which he satisfied his hunger in niggardly fashion; he wished to see whether he thereby fell short of full and complete happiness, and, if so, by what amount he fell short, and whether this amount was worth purchasing at the price of great effort. At any rate, he makes such a statement in the well known letter written to Polyaenus in the archonship of Charinus. Indeed, he boasts that he himself lived on less than a penny, but that Metrodorus, whose progress was not yet so great, needed a whole penny. **10.** Do you think that there can be fullness on such fare? Yes, and there is pleasure also, – not that shifty and fleeting Pleasure which needs a fillip now and then, but a pleasure that is steadfast and sure. For though water, barley-meal, and crusts of barley-bread, are not a cheerful diet, yet it is the highest kind of Pleasure to be able to derive pleasure from this sort of food, and to have reduced one's needs to that modicum which no unfairness of Fortune can snatch away. **11.** Even prison fare is more generous; and those who have been set apart for capital punishment are not so meanly fed by the man who is to execute them. Therefore, what a noble soul must one have, to descend of one's own free will to a diet which even those who have been sentenced to death have not to fear! This is indeed forestalling the spearthrusts of Fortune.

12. So begin, my dear Lucilius, to follow the custom of these men, and set apart certain days on which you shall withdraw from your business and make yourself at home with the scantiest fare. Establish business relations with poverty.

> Dare, O my friend, to scorn the sight of wealth,
> And mould thyself to kinship with thy God.

13. For he alone is in kinship with God who has scorned wealth. Of course I do not forbid you to possess it, but I would have you reach the point at which you possess it dauntlessly; this can be accomplished only by persuading yourself that you can live happily without it as well as with it, and by regarding riches always as likely to elude you.

14. But now I must begin to fold up my letter. "Settle your debts first," you cry. Here is a draft on Epicurus; he will pay down the sum: "Ungoverned anger begets madness." You cannot help knowing the truth of these words, since you have had not only slaves, but also enemies. **15.** But indeed this emotion blazes out against all sorts of persons; it springs from love as much as from hate, and shows itself not less in serious matters than in jest and sport. And it makes no difference how important the provocation may be, but into what kind of soul it penetrates. Similarly with fire;

it does not matter how great is the flame, but what it falls upon. For solid timbers have repelled a very great fire; conversely, dry and easily inflammable stuff nourishes the slightest spark into a conflagration. So it is with anger, my dear Lucilius; the outcome of a mighty anger is madness, and hence anger should be avoided, not merely that we may escape excess, but that we may have a healthy mind. Farewell.

XIX. ON WORLDLINESS AND RETIREMENT

1. I leap for joy whenever I receive letters from you. For they fill me with hope; they are now not mere assurances concerning you, but guarantees. And I beg and pray you to proceed in this course; for what better request could I make of a friend than one which is to be made for his own sake? If possible, withdraw yourself from all the business of which you speak; and if you cannot do this, tear yourself away. We have dissipated enough of our time already – let us in old age begin to pack up our baggage. **2.** Surely there is nothing in this that men can begrudge us. We have spent our lives on the high seas; let us die in harbour. Not that I would advise you to try to win fame by your retirement; one's retirement should neither be paraded nor concealed. Not concealed, I say, for I shall not go so far in urging you as to expect you to condemn all men as mad and then seek out for yourself a hiding-place and oblivion; rather make this your business, that your retirement be not conspicuous, though it should be obvious. **3.** In the second place, while those whose choice is unhampered from the start will deliberate on that other question, whether they wish to pass their lives in obscurity, in your case there is not a free choice. Your ability and energy have thrust you into the work of the world; so have the charm of your writings and the friendships you have made with famous and notable men. Renown has already taken you by storm. You may sink yourself into the depths of obscurity and utterly hide yourself; yet your earlier acts will reveal you. **4.** You cannot keep lurking in the dark; much of the old gleam will follow you wherever you fly.

Peace you can claim for yourself without being disliked by anyone, without any sense of loss, and without any pangs of spirit. For what will you leave behind you that you can imagine yourself reluctant to leave? Your clients? But none of these men courts you for yourself; they merely court something from you. People used to hunt friends, but now they hunt pelf; if a lonely old man changes his will, the morning-caller transfers himself to another door. Great things cannot be bought for small sums; so reckon up whether it is preferable to leave your own true self, or merely some of your belongings. **5.** Would that you had had the privilege of growing old amid the limited circumstances of your origin, and that fortune had not raised you to such heights! You were removed far from the sight of wholesome living by your swift rise to prosperity, by your province, by your position as procurator, and by all that such things promise; you will next acquire more important duties and after them still more. And what will be the result? **6.** Why wait until there is nothing left for you to crave? That time will never come. We hold that there is a succession of causes, from which fate is woven; similarly, you may be sure, there is a succession in our desires; for one begins where its predecessor ends. You have been thrust into an existence which will never of itself put an end to your wretchedness and your slavery. Withdraw your chafed neck from the yoke; it is better that it should be cut off once for all, than galled for ever. **7.** If you retreat to privacy, everything will be on a smaller scale, but you will be satisfied abundantly; in your present condition, however, there is no satisfaction in the plenty which is heaped upon you on all sides. Would you rather be poor and sated, or rich and hungry? Prosperity is not only greedy, but it also lies exposed to the greed of others. And as long as nothing satisfies you, you yourself cannot satisfy others.

8. "But," you say, "how can I take my leave?" Any way you please. Reflect how many hazards you have ventured for the sake of money, and how much toil you have undertaken for a title! You must dare something to gain leisure, also, – or else grow old amid the worries of procuratorships abroad and subsequently of civil duties at home, living in turmoil and in ever fresh floods of responsibilities, which no man has ever succeeded in avoiding by unobtrusiveness or by seclusion of life. For what bearing on the case has your personal desire for a secluded life? Your position in the world desires the opposite! What if, even now, you allow that position to grow greater? But all that is added to your successes will be added to your fears. **9.** At this point I should like to quote a saying of Maecenas, who spoke the truth when he stood on the very summit: "There's thunder even on the loftiest peaks." If you ask me in what book these words are found, they occur in the volume entitled *Prometheus*. He simply meant to say that these lofty peaks have their tops surrounded with thunder-storms. But is any power worth so high a price that a man like you would ever, in order to obtain it, adopt a style so debauched as that? Maecenas was indeed a man of parts, who would have left a great pattern for Roman oratory to follow, had his good fortune not made him effeminate, – nay, had it not emasculated him! An end like his awaits you also, unless you forthwith shorten sail and, – as Maecenas was not willing to do until it was too late, – hug the shore!

10. This saying of Maecenas's might have squared my account with you; but I feel sure, knowing you, that you will get out an injunction against me, and that you will be unwilling to accept payment of my debt in such crude and debased currency. However that may be, I shall draw on the account of Epicurus. He says: "You must reflect carefully beforehand with whom you are to eat and drink, rather than what you are to eat and drink. For a dinner of meats without the company of a friend is like the life of a lion or a wolf." **11.** This privilege will not be yours unless you withdraw from the world; otherwise, you will have as guests only those whom your slave-secretary sorts out from the throng of callers. It is, however, a mistake to select your friend in the reception-hall or to test him at the dinner-table. The most serious misfortune for a busy man who is overwhelmed by his possessions is, that he believes men to be his friends when he himself is not a friend to them, and that he deems his favours to be effective in winning friends, although, in the case of certain men, the more they owe, the more they hate. A trifling debt makes a man your debtor; a large one makes him an enemy. **12.** "What," you say, "do not kindnesses establish friendships?" They do, if one has had the privilege of choosing those who are to receive them, and if they are placed judiciously, instead of being scattered broadcast.

Therefore, while you are beginning to call your mind your own, meantime apply this maxim of the wise: consider that it is more important who receives a thing, than what it is he receives. Farewell.

XX. ON PRACTISING WHAT YOU PREACH

1. If you are in good health and if you think yourself worthy of becoming at last your own master, I am glad. For the credit will be mine, if I can drag you from the floods in which you are being buffeted without hope of emerging. This, however, my dear Lucilius, I ask and beg of you, on your part, that you let wisdom sink into your soul, and test your progress, not by mere speech or writings, but by stoutness of heart and decrease of desire. Prove your words by your deeds.

2. Far different is the purpose of those who are speech-making and trying to win the approbation of a throng of hearers, far different that of those who allure the ears of young men and idlers by many-sided or fluent argumentation; philosophy teaches us to act, not to speak; it exacts of every man that he should live according to his own standards, that his life should not be out of harmony with his words, and that, further, his inner life should be of one hue and not out of harmony with all his activities. This, I say, is the highest duty and the highest proof of wisdom, – that deed and word should be in accord, that a man should be equal to himself under all conditions, and always the same.

"But," you reply, "who can maintain this standard?" Very few, to be sure; but there are some. It is indeed a hard undertaking, and I do not say that the philosopher can always keep the same pace. But he can always travel the same path. **3.** Observe yourself, then, and see whether your dress and your house are inconsistent, whether you treat yourself lavishly and your family meanly, whether you eat frugal dinners and yet build luxurious houses. You should lay hold, once for all, upon a single norm to live by, and should regulate your whole life according to this norm. Some men restrict themselves at home, but strut with swelling port before the public; such discordance is a fault, and it indicates a wavering mind which cannot yet keep its balance. **4.** And I can tell you, further, whence arise this unsteadiness and disagreement of action and purpose; it is because no man resolves upon what he wishes, and, even if he has done so, he does not persist in it, but jumps the track; not only does he change, but he returns and slips back to the conduct which he has abandoned and abjured. **5.** Therefore, to omit the ancient definitions of wisdom and to include the whole manner of human life, I can be satisfied with the following: "What is wisdom? Always desiring the same things, and always refusing the same things." You may be excused from adding the little proviso, – that what you wish, should be right; since no man can always be satisfied with the same thing, unless it is right.

6. For this reason men do not know what they wish, except at the actual moment of wishing; no man ever decided once and for all to desire or to refuse. Judgment varies from day to day, and changes to the opposite, making many a man pass his life in a kind of game. Press on, therefore, as you have begun; perhaps you will be led to perfection, or to a point which you alone understand is still short of perfection.

7. "But what," you say, "will become of my crowded household without a household income?" If you stop supporting that crowd, it will support itself; or perhaps you will learn by the bounty of poverty what you cannot learn by your own bounty. Poverty will keep for you your true and tried friends; you will be rid of the men who were not seeking you for yourself, but for something which you have. Is it not true, however, that you should love poverty, if only for this single reason, – that it will show you those by whom you are loved? O when will that time come, when no one shall tell lies to compliment you! **8.** Accordingly, let your thoughts, your efforts, your desires, help to make you content with your own self and with the goods that spring from yourself; and commit all your other prayers to God's keeping! What happiness could come closer home to you? Bring yourself down to humble conditions, from which you cannot be ejected and in order that you may do so with greater alacrity, the contribution contained in this letter shall refer to that subject; I shall bestow it upon you forthwith.

9. Although you may look askance, Epicurus will once again be glad to settle my indebtedness: "Believe me, your words will be more imposing if you sleep on a cot and wear rags. For in that case you will not be merely saying them; you will be demonstrating their truth." I, at any rate, listen in a different spirit to the utterances of our friend Demetrius, after I have seen him reclining without even a cloak to cover him, and, more than this, without rugs to lie upon. He is not only a teacher of the truth, but a witness to the truth. **10.** "May not a man, however, despise wealth when it lies in his very pocket?" Of course; he also is great-souled, who sees riches heaped up round him and, after wondering long and deeply because they have come into his possession, smiles, and hears rather than feels that they are his. It means much not to be spoiled by intimacy with riches; and he is truly great who is poor amidst riches. **11.** "Yes, but I do not know," you say, "how the man you speak of will endure poverty, if he falls into it suddenly." Nor do I, Epicurus, know whether the poor man you speak of will despise riches, should he suddenly fall into them; accordingly, in the case of both, it is the mind that must be appraised, and we must investigate whether your man is pleased with his poverty, and whether my man is displeased with his riches. Otherwise, the cot-bed and the rags are slight proof of his good intentions, if it has not been made clear that the person concerned endures these trials not from necessity but from preference.

12. It is the mark, however, of a noble spirit not to precipitate oneself into such things on the ground that they are better, but to practise for them on the ground that they are thus easy to endure. And they are easy to endure, Lucilius; when, however, you come to them after long rehearsal, they are even pleasant; for they contain a sense of freedom from care, – and without this nothing is pleasant. **13.** I hold it essential, therefore, to do as I have told you in a letter that great men have often done: to reserve a few days in which we may prepare ourselves for real poverty by means of fancied poverty. There is all the more reason for doing this, because we have been steeped in luxury and regard all duties as hard and onerous. Rather let the soul be roused from its sleep and be prodded, and let it be reminded that nature has prescribed very little for us. No man is born rich. Every man, when he first sees light, is commanded to be content with milk and rags. Such is our beginning, and yet kingdoms are all too small for us! Farewell.

XXI. ON THE RENOWN WHICH MY WRITINGS WILL BRING YOU

1. Do you conclude that you are having difficulties with those men about whom you wrote to me? Your greatest difficulty is with yourself; for you are your own stumbling-block. You do not know what you want. You are better at approving the right course than at following it out. You see where the true happiness lies, but you have not the courage to attain it. Let me tell you what it is that hinders you, inasmuch as you do not of yourself discern it.

2. You think that this condition, which you are to abandon, is one of importance, and after resolving upon that ideal state of calm into which you hope to pass, you are held back by the lustre of your present life, from which it is your intention to depart, just as if you were about to fall into a state of filth and darkness. This is a mistake, Lucilius; to go from your present life into the other is a promotion. There is the same difference between these two lives as there is between mere brightness and real light; the latter has a definite source within itself, the other borrows its radiance; the one is called forth by an illumination coming from the outside, and anyone who stands between the source and the object immediately turns the latter into a dense shadow; but the other has a glow that comes from within.

It is your own studies that will make you shine and will render you eminent, Allow me to mention the case of Epicurus. **3.** He was writing to Idomeneus and trying to recall him from a showy existence to sure and steadfast renown. Idomeneus was at that time a minister of state who exercised a rigorous authority and had important affairs in hand. "If," said Epicurus, "you are attracted by fame, my letters will make you more renowned than all the things which you cherish and which make you cherished." **4.** Did Epicurus speak falsely? Who would have known of Idomeneus, had not the philosopher thus engraved his name in those letters of his? All the grandees and satraps, even the king himself, who was petitioned for the title which Idomeneus sought, are sunk in deep oblivion. Cicero's letters keep the name of Atticus from perishing. It would have profited Atticus nothing to have an Agrippa for a son-in-law, a Tiberius for the husband of his grand-daughter, and a Drusus Caesar for a great-grandson; amid these mighty names his name would never be spoken, had not Cicero bound him to himself. **5.** The deep flood of time will roll over us; some few great men will raise their heads above it, and, though destined at the last to depart into the same realms of silence, will battle against oblivion and maintain their ground for long.

That which Epicurus could promise his friend, this I promise you, Lucilius. I shall find favour among later generations; I can take with me names that will endure as long as mine. Our poet Vergil promised an eternal name to two heroes, and is keeping his promise:

> Blest heroes twain! If power my song possess,
> The record of your names shall never be
> Erased from out the book of Time, while yet
> Aeneas' tribe shall keep the Capitol,
> That rock immovable, and Roman sire
> Shall empire hold.

6. Whenever men have been thrust forward by fortune, whenever they have become part and parcel of another's influence, they have found abundant favour, their houses have been thronged, only so long as they themselves have kept their position; when they themselves have left it, they have slipped at once from the memory of men. But in the case of innate ability, the respect in which it is held increases, and not only does honour accrue to the man himself, but whatever has attached itself to his memory is passed on from one to another.

7. In order that Idomeneus may not be introduced free of charge into my letter, he shall make up the indebtedness from his own account. It was to him that Epicurus addressed the well-known saying urging him to make Pythocles rich, but not rich in the vulgar and equivocal way. "If you wish," said he, "to make Pythocles rich, do not add to his store of money, but subtract from his desires." **8.** This idea is too clear to need explanation, and too clever to need reinforcement. There is, however, one point on which I would warn you, – not to consider that this statement applies only to riches; its value will be the same, no matter how you apply it. "If you wish to make Pythocles honourable, do not add to his honours, but subtract from his desires"; "if you wish Pythocles to have pleasure for ever, do not add to his pleasures, but subtract from his desires"; "if you wish to make Pythocles an old man, filling his life to the full, do not add to his years, but subtract from his desires." **9.** There is no reason why you should hold that these words belong to Epicurus alone; they are public property. I think we ought to do in philosophy as they are wont to do in the Senate: when someone has made a motion, of which I approve to a certain extent, I ask him to make his motion in two parts, and I vote for the part which I approve. So I am all the more glad to repeat the distinguished words of Epicurus, in order that I may prove to those who have recourse to him through a bad motive, thinking that they will have in him a screen for their own vices, that they must live honourably, no matter what school they follow.

10. Go to his Garden and read the motto carved there:

"Stranger, here you will do well to tarry; here our highest good is pleasure."

The care-taker of that abode, a kindly host, will be ready for you; he will welcome you with barley-meal and serve you water also in abundance, with these words: "Have you not been well entertained?" "This garden," he says, "does not whet your appetite; it quenches it. Nor does it make you more thirsty with every drink; it slakes the thirst by a natural cure, a cure that demands no fee. This is the 'pleasure' in which I have grown old."

11. In speaking with you, however, I refer to those desires which refuse alleviation, which must be bribed to cease. For in regard to the exceptional desires, which may be postponed, which may be chastened and checked, I have this one thought to share with you: a pleasure of that sort is according to our nature, but it is not according to our needs; one owes nothing to it; whatever is expended upon it is a free gift. The belly will not listen to advice; it makes demands, it importunes. And yet it is not a troublesome creditor; you can send it away at small cost, provided only that you give it what you owe, not merely all you are able to give. Farewell.

XXII. ON THE FUTILITY OF HALF-WAY MEASURES

1. You understand by this time that you must withdraw yourself from those showy and depraved pursuits; but you still wish to know how this may be accomplished. There are certain things which can be pointed out only by someone who is present. The physician cannot prescribe by letter the proper time for eating or bathing; he must feel the pulse. There is an old adage about gladiators, – that they plan their fight in the ring; as they intently watch, something in the adversary's glance, some movement of his hand, even some slight bending of his body, gives a warning. **2.** We can formulate general rules and commit them to writing, as to what is usually done, or ought to be done; such advice may be given, not only to our absent friends, but also to succeeding generations. In regard, however, to that second question, – when or how your plan is to be carried out, – no one will advise at long range; we must take counsel in the presence of the actual situation. **3.** You must be not only present in the body, but watchful in mind, if you would avail yourself of the fleeting opportunity. Accordingly, look about you for the opportunity; if you see it, grasp it, and with all your energy and with all your strength devote yourself to this task – to rid yourself of those business duties.

Now listen carefully to the opinion which I shall offer; it is my opinion that you should withdraw either from that kind of existence, or else from existence altogether. But I likewise maintain that you should take a gentle path, that you may loosen rather than cut the knot which you have bungled so badly in tying, – provided that if there shall be no other way of loosening it, you may actually cut it. No man is so faint-hearted that he would rather hang in suspense for ever than drop once for all. **4.** Meanwhile, – and this is of first importance, – do not hamper yourself; be content with the business into which you have lowered yourself, or, as you prefer to have people think, have tumbled. There is no reason why you should be struggling on to something further; if you do, you will lose all grounds of excuse, and men will see that it was not a tumble. The usual explanation which men offer is wrong: "I was compelled to do it. Suppose it was against my will; I had to do it." But no one is compelled to pursue prosperity at top speed; it means something to call a halt, – even if one does not offer resistance, – instead of pressing eagerly after favouring fortune. **5.** Shall you then be put out with me, if I not only come to advise you, but also call in others to advise you, – wiser heads than my own, men before whom I am wont to lay any problem upon which I am pondering? Read the letter of Epicurus which appears on this matter; it is addressed to Idomeneus. The writer asks him to hasten as fast as he can, and beat a retreat before some stronger influence comes between and takes from him the liberty to withdraw. **6.** But he also adds that one should attempt nothing except at the time when it can be attempted suitably and seasonably. Then, when the long-sought occasion comes, let him be up and doing. Epicurus forbids us to doze when we are meditating escape; he bids us hope for a safe release from even the hardest trials, provided that we are not in too great a hurry before the time, nor too dilatory when the time arrives.

7. Now, I suppose, you are looking for a Stoic motto also. There is really no reason why anyone should slander that school to you on the ground of its rashness; as a matter of fact, its caution is greater than its courage. You are perhaps expecting the sect to utter such words as these: "It is base to flinch under a burden. Wrestle with the duties which you have once undertaken. No man is brave and earnest if he avoids danger, if his spirit does not grow with the very difficulty of his task." **8.** Words like these will indeed be spoken to you, if only your perseverance shall have an object that is worth while, if only you will not have to do or to suffer anything unworthy of a good man; besides, a good man will not waste himself upon mean and discreditable work or be busy merely for the sake of being busy. Neither will he, as you imagine, become so involved in ambitious schemes that he will have continually to endure their ebb and flow. Nay, when he sees the dangers, uncertainties, and hazards in which he was formerly tossed about, he will withdraw, – not turning his back to the foe, but falling back little by little to a safe position. **9.** From business, however, my dear Lucilius, it is easy to escape, if only you will despise the rewards of business. We are held back and kept from escaping by thoughts like these: "What then? Shall I leave behind me these great prospects? Shall I depart at the very time of harvest? Shall I have no slaves at my side? no retinue for my litter? no crowd in my reception room?"

Hence men leave such advantages as these with reluctance; they love the reward of their hardships, but curse the hardships themselves. **10.** Men complain about their ambitions as they complain about their mistresses; in other words, if you penetrate their real feelings, you will find, not hatred, but bickering. Search the minds of those who cry down what they have desired, who talk about escaping from things which they are unable to do without; you will comprehend that they are lingering of their own free will in a situation which they declare they find it hard and wretched to endure. **11.** It is so, my dear Lucilius; there are a few men whom slavery holds fast, but there are many more who hold fast to slavery.

If, however, you intend to be rid of this slavery; if freedom is genuinely pleasing in your eyes; and if you seek counsel for this one purpose, – that you may have the good fortune to accomplish this purpose without perpetual annoyance, – how can the whole company of Stoic thinkers fail to approve your course? Zeno, Chrysippus, and all their kind will give you advice that is temperate, honourable, and suitable. **12.** But if you keep turning round and looking about, in order to see how much you may carry away with you, and how much money you may keep to equip yourself for the life of leisure, you will never find a way out. No man can swim ashore and take his baggage with him. Rise to a higher life, with the favour of the gods; but let it not be favour of such a kind as the gods give to men when with kind and genial faces they bestow magnificent ills, justified in so doing by the one fact that the things which irritate and torture have been bestowed in answer to prayer.

13. I was just putting the seal upon this letter; but it must be broken again, in order that it may go to you with its customary contribution, bearing with it some noble word. And lo, here is one that occurs to my mind; I do not know whether its truth or its nobility of utterance is the greater. "Spoken by whom?" you ask. By Epicurus; for I am still appropriating other men's belongings. **14.** The words are: "Everyone goes out of life just as if he had but lately entered it." Take anyone off his guard, young, old, or middle-aged; you will find that all are equally afraid of death, and equally ignorant of life. No one has anything finished, because we have kept putting off into the future all our undertakings. No thought in the quotation given above pleases me more than that it taunts old men with being infants. **15.** "No one," he says, "leaves this world in a different manner from one who has just been born." That is not true; for we are worse when we die than when we were born; but it is our fault, and not that of Nature. Nature should scold us, saying: "What does this mean? I brought you into the world without desires or fears, free from superstition, treachery and the other curses. Go forth as you were when you entered!"

16. A man has caught the message of wisdom, if he can die as free from care as he was at birth; but as it is we are all a-flutter at the approach of the dreaded end. Our courage fails us, our cheeks blanch; our tears fall, though they are unavailing. But what is baser than to fret at the very threshold of peace? **17.** The reason, however is, that we are stripped of all our goods, we have jettisoned our cargo of life and are in distress; for no part of it has been packed in the hold; it has all been heaved overboard and has drifted away. Men do not care how nobly they live, but only how long, although it is within the reach of every man to live nobly, but within no man's power to live long. Farewell.

XXIII. ON THE TRUE JOY WHICH COMES FROM PHILOSOPHY

1. Do you suppose that I shall write you how kindly the winter season has dealt with us, – a short season and a mild one, – or what a nasty spring we are having, – cold weather out of season, – and all the other trivialities which people write when they are at a loss for topics of conversation? No; I shall communicate something which may help both you and myself. And what shall this "something" be, if not an exhortation to soundness of mind? Do you ask what is the foundation of a sound mind? It is, not to find joy in useless things. I said that it was the foundation; it is really the pinnacle. **2.** We have reached the heights if we know what it is that we find joy in and if we have not placed our happiness in the control of externals. The man who is goaded ahead by hope of anything, though it be within reach, though it be easy of access, and though his ambitions have never played him false, is troubled and unsure of himself. **3.** Above all, my dear Lucilius, make this your business: learn how to feel joy.

Do you think that I am now robbing you of many pleasures when I try to do away with the gifts of chance, when I counsel the avoidance of hope, the sweetest thing that gladdens our hearts? Quite the contrary; I do not wish you ever to be deprived of gladness. I would have it born in your house; and it is born there, if only it be inside of you. Other objects of cheer do not fill a man's bosom; they merely smooth his brow and are inconstant, – unless perhaps you believe that he who laughs has joy. The very soul must be happy and confident, lifted above every circumstance.

4. Real joy, believe me, is a stern matter. Can one, do you think, despise death with a care-free countenance, or with a "blithe and gay" expression, as our young dandies are accustomed to say? Or can one thus open his door to poverty, or hold the curb on his pleasures, or contemplate the endurance of pain? He who ponders these things in his heart is indeed full of joy; but it is not a cheerful joy. It is just this joy, however, of which I would have you become the owner; for it will never fail you when once you have found its source. **5.** The yield of poor mines is on the surface; those are really rich whose veins lurk deep, and they will make more bountiful returns to him who delves unceasingly. So too those baubles which delight the common crowd afford but a thin pleasure, laid on as a coating, and even joy that is only plated lacks a real basis. But the joy of which I speak, that to which I am endeavouring to lead you, is something solid, disclosing itself the more fully as you penetrate into it. **6.** Therefore I pray you, my dearest Lucilius, do the one thing that can render you really happy: cast aside and trample under foot all the things that glitter outwardly and are held out to you by another or as obtainable from another; look toward the true good, and rejoice only in that which comes from your own store. And what do I mean by "from your own store"? I mean from your very self, that which is the best part of you. The frail body, also, even though we can accomplish nothing without it, is to be regarded as necessary rather than as important; it involves us in vain pleasures, short-lived, and soon to be regretted, which, unless they are reined in by extreme self-control, will be transformed into the opposite. This is what I mean: pleasure, unless it has been kept within bounds, tends to rush headlong into the abyss of sorrow.

But it is hard to keep within bounds in that which you believe to be good. The real good may be coveted with safety. **7.** Do you ask me what this real good is, and whence it derives? I will tell you: it comes from a good conscience, from honourable purposes, from right actions, from contempt of the gifts of chance, from an even and calm way of living which treads but one path. For men who leap from one purpose to another, or do not even leap but are carried over by a sort of hazard, – how can such wavering and unstable persons possess any good that is fixed and lasting? **8.** There are only a few who control themselves and their affairs by a guiding purpose; the rest do not proceed; they are merely swept along, like objects afloat in a river. And of these objects, some are held back by sluggish waters and are transported gently; others are torn along by a more violent current; some, which are nearest the bank, are left there as the current slackens; and others are carried out to sea by the onrush of the stream. Therefore, we should decide what we wish, and abide by the decision.

9. Now is the time for me to pay my debt. I can give you a saying of your friend Epicurus and thus clear this letter of its obligation. "It is bothersome always to be beginning life." Or another, which will perhaps express the meaning better: "They live ill who are always beginning to live." **10.** You are right in asking why; the saying certainly stands in need of a commentary. It is because the life of such persons is always incomplete. But a man cannot stand prepared for the approach of death if he has just begun to live. We must make it our aim already to have lived long enough. No one deems that he has done so, if he is just on the point of planning his life. **11.** You need not think that there are few of this kind; practically everyone is of such a stamp. Some men, indeed, only begin to live when it is time for them to leave off living. And if this seems surprising to you, I shall add that which will surprise you still more: Some men have left off living before they have begun. Farewell.

XXIV. ON DESPISING DEATH

1. You write me that you are anxious about the result of a lawsuit, with which an angry opponent is threatening you; and you expect me to advise you to picture to yourself a happier issue, and to rest in the allurements of hope. Why, indeed, is it necessary to summon trouble, – which must be endured soon enough when it has once arrived, or to anticipate trouble and ruin the present through fear of the future? It is indeed foolish to be unhappy now because you may be unhappy at some future time. **2.** But I shall conduct you to peace of mind by another route: if you would put off all worry, assume that what you fear may happen will certainly happen in any event; whatever the trouble may be, measure it in your own mind, and estimate the amount of your fear. You will thus understand that what you fear is either insignificant or short-lived. **3.** And you need not spend a long time in gathering illustrations which will strengthen you; every epoch has produced them. Let your thoughts travel into any era of Roman or foreign history, and there will throng before you notable examples of high achievement or of high endeavour.

If you lose this case, can anything more severe happen to you than being sent into exile or led to prison? Is there a worse fate that any man may fear than being burned or being killed? Name such penalties one by one, and mention the men who have scorned them; one does not need to hunt for them, – it is simply a matter of selection. **4.** Sentence of conviction was borne by Rutilius as if the injustice of the decision were the only thing which annoyed him. Exile was endured by Metellus with courage, by Rutilius even with gladness; for the former consented to come back only because his country called him; the latter refused to return when Sulla summoned him, – and nobody in those days said "No" to Sulla! Socrates in prison discoursed, and declined to flee when certain persons gave him the opportunity; he remained there, in order to free mankind from the fear of two most grievous things, death and imprisonment. **5.** Mucius put his hand into the fire. It is painful to be burned; but how much more painful to inflict such suffering upon oneself! Here was a man of no learning, not primed to face death and pain by any words of wisdom, and equipped only with the courage of a soldier, who punished himself for his fruitless daring; he stood and watched his own right hand falling away piecemeal on the enemy's brazier, nor did he withdraw the dissolving limb, with its uncovered bones, until his foe removed the fire. He might have accomplished something more successful in that camp, but never anything more brave. See how much keener a brave man is to lay hold of danger than a cruel man is to inflict it: Porsenna was more ready to pardon Mucius for wishing to slay him than Mucius to pardon himself for failing to slay Porsenna!

6. "Oh," say you, "those stories have been droned to death in all the schools; pretty soon, when you reach the topic 'On Despising Death,' you will be telling me about Cato." But why should I not tell you about Cato, how he read Plato's book on that last glorious night, with a sword laid at his pillow? He had provided these two requisites for his last moments, – the first, that he might have the will to die, and the second, that he might have the means. So he put his affairs in order, – as well as one could put in order that which was ruined and near its end, – and thought that he ought to see to it that no one should have the power to slay or the good fortune to save Cato. **7.** Drawing the sword, – which he had kept unstained from all bloodshed against the final day, he cried: "Fortune, you have accomplished nothing by resisting all my endeavours. I have fought, till now, for my country's freedom, and not for my own, I did not strive so doggedly to be free, but only to live among the free. Now, since the affairs of mankind are beyond hope, let Cato be withdrawn to safety." **8.** So saying, he inflicted a mortal wound upon his body. After the physicians had bound it up, Cato had less blood and less strength, but no less courage; angered now not only at Caesar but also at himself, he rallied his unarmed hands against his wound, and expelled, rather than dismissed, that noble soul which had been so defiant of all worldly power.

9. I am not now heaping up these illustrations for the purpose of exercising my wit, but for the purpose of encouraging you to face that which is thought to be most terrible. And I shall encourage you all the more easily by showing that not only resolute men have despised that moment when the soul breathes its last, but that certain persons, who were craven in other respects, have equalled in this regard the courage of the bravest. Take, for example, Scipio, the father-in-law of Gnaeus Pompeius: he was driven back upon the African coast by a head-wind and saw his ship in the power of the enemy. He therefore pierced his body with a sword; and when they asked where the commander was, he replied: "All is well with the commander." **10.** These words brought him up to the level of his ancestors and suffered not the glory which fate gave to the Scipios in Africa to lose its continuity. It was a great deed to conquer Carthage, but a greater deed to conquer death. "All is well with the commander!" Ought a general to die otherwise, especially one of Cato's generals? **11.** I shall not refer you to history, or collect examples of those men who throughout the ages have despised death; for they are very many. Consider these times of ours, whose enervation and over-refinement call forth our complaints; they nevertheless will include men of every rank, of every lot in life, and of every age, who have cut short their misfortunes by death.

Believe me, Lucilius; death is so little to be feared that through its good offices nothing is to be feared. **12.** Therefore, when your enemy threatens, listen unconcernedly. Although your conscience makes you confident, yet, since many things have weight which are outside your case, both hope for that which is utterly just, and prepare yourself against that which is utterly unjust. Remember, however, before all else, to strip things of all that disturbs and confuses, and to see what each is at bottom; you will then comprehend that they contain nothing fearful except the actual fear. **13.** That you see happening to boys happens also to ourselves, who are only slightly bigger boys: when those whom they love, with whom they daily associate, with whom they play, appear with masks on, the boys are frightened out of their wits. We should strip the mask, not only from men, but from things, and restore to each object its own aspect.

14. "Why dost thou hold up before my eyes swords, fires, and a throng of executioners raging about thee? Take away all that vain show, behind which thou lurkest and scarest fools! Ah! thou art naught but Death, whom only yesterday a manservant of mine and a maid-servant did despise! Why dost thou again unfold and spread before me, with all that great display, the whip and the rack? Why are those engines of torture made ready, one for each several member of the body, and all the other innumerable machines for tearing a man apart piecemeal? Away with all such stuff, which makes us numb with terror! And thou, silence the groans the cries, and the bitter shrieks ground out of the victim as he is torn on the rack! Forsooth thou are naught but Pain, scorned by yonder gout-ridden wretch, endured by yonder dyspeptic in the midst of his dainties, borne bravely by the girl in travail. Slight thou art, if I can bear thee; short thou art if I cannot bear thee!"

15. Ponder these words which you have often heard and often uttered. Moreover, prove by the result whether that which you have heard and uttered is true. For there is a very disgraceful charge often brought against our school, – that we deal with the words, and not with the deeds, of philosophy.

What, have you only at this moment learned that death is hanging over your head, at this moment exile, at this moment grief? You were born to these perils. Let us think of everything that can happen as something which will happen. **16.** I know that you have really done what I advise you to do; I now warn you not to drown your soul in these petty anxieties of yours; if you do, the soul will be dulled and will have too little vigour left when the time comes for it to arise. Remove the mind from this case of yours to the case of men in general. Say to yourself that our petty bodies are mortal and frail; pain can reach them from other sources than from wrong or the might of the stronger. Our pleasures themselves become torments; banquets bring indigestion, carousals paralysis of the muscles and palsy, sensual habits affect the feet, the hands, and every joint of the body.

17. I may become a poor man; I shall then be one among many. I may be exiled; I shall then regard myself as born in the place to which I shall be sent. They may put me in chains. What then? Am I free from bonds now? Behold this clogging burden of a body, to which nature has fettered me! "I shall die," you say; you mean to say "I shall cease to run the risk of sickness; I shall cease to run the risk of imprisonment; I shall cease to run the risk of death." **18.** I am not so foolish as to go through at this juncture the arguments which Epicurus harps upon, and say that the terrors of the world below are idle, – that Ixion does not whirl round on his wheel, that Sisyphus does not shoulder his stone uphill, that a man's entrails cannot be restored and devoured every day; no one is so childish as to fear Cerberus, or the shadows, or the spectral garb of those who are held together by naught but their unfleshed bones. Death either annihilates us or strips us bare. If we are then released, there remains the better part, after the burden has been withdrawn; if we are annihilated, nothing remains; good and bad are alike removed.

19. Allow me at this point to quote a verse of yours, first suggesting that, when you wrote it, you meant it for yourself no less than for others. It is ignoble to say one thing and mean another; and how much more ignoble to write one thing and mean another! I remember one day you were handling the well-known commonplace, – that we do not suddenly fall on death, but advance towards it by slight degrees; we die every day. **20.** For every day a little of our life is taken from us; even when we are growing, our life is on the wane. We lose our childhood, then our boyhood, and then our youth. Counting even yesterday, all past time is lost time; the very day which we are now spending is shared between ourselves and death. It is not the last drop that empties the water-clock, but all that which previously has flowed out; similarly, the final hour when we cease to exist does not of itself bring death; it merely of itself completes the death-process. We reach death at that moment, but we have been a long time on the way. **21.** In describing this situation, you said in your customary, style (for you are always impressive, but never more pungent than when you are putting the truth in appropriate words):

> Not single is the death which comes; the death
> Which takes us off is but the last of all.

I prefer that you should read your own words rather than my letter; for then it will be clear to you that this death, of which we are afraid, is the last but not the only death. **22.** I see what you are looking for; you are asking what I have packed into my letter, what inspiriting saying from some master-mind, what useful precept. So I shall send you something dealing with this very subject which has been under discussion. Epicurus upbraids those who crave, as much as those who shrink from, death: "It is absurd," he says, "to run towards death because you are tired of life, when it is your manner of life that has made you run towards death." **23.** And in another passage: "What is so absurd as to seek death, when it is through fear of death that you have robbed your life of peace?" And you may add a third statement, of the same stamp: "Men are so thoughtless, nay, so mad, that some, through fear of death, force themselves to die."

24. Whichever of these ideas you ponder, you will strengthen your mind for the endurance alike of death and of life. For we need to be warned and strengthened in both directions, – not to love or to hate life overmuch; even when reason advises us to make an end of it, the impulse is not to be adopted without reflection or at headlong speed. **25.** The grave and wise man should not beat a hasty retreat from life; he should make a becoming exit. And above all, he should avoid the weakness which has taken possession of so many, – the lust for death. For just as there is an unreflecting tendency of the mind towards other things, so, my dear Lucilius, there is an unreflecting tendency towards death; this often seizes upon the noblest and most spirited men, as well as upon the craven and the abject. The former despise life; the latter find it irksome.

26. Others also are moved by a satiety of doing and seeing the same things, and not so much by a hatred of life as because they are cloyed with it. We slip into this condition, while philosophy itself pushes us on, and we say; "How long must I endure the same things? Shall I continue to wake and sleep, be hungry and be cloyed, shiver and perspire? There is an end to nothing; all things are connected in a sort of circle; they flee and they are pursued. Night is close at the heels of day, day at the heels of night; summer ends in autumn, winter rushes after autumn, and winter softens into spring; all nature in this way passes, only to return. I do nothing new; I see nothing new; sooner or later one sickens of this, also." There are many who think that living is not painful, but superfluous. Farewell.

XXV. ON REFORMATION

1. With regard to these two friends of ours, we must proceed along different lines; the faults of the one are to be corrected, the other's are to be crushed out. I shall take every liberty; for I do not love this one if I am unwilling to hurt his feelings. "What," you say, "do you expect to keep a forty-year-old ward under your tutelage? Consider his age, how hardened it now is, and past handling! **2.** Such a man cannot be re-shaped; only young minds are moulded." I do not know whether I shall make progress; but I should prefer to lack success rather than to lack faith. You need not despair of curing sick men even when the disease is chronic, if only you hold out against excess and force them to do and submit to many things against their will. As regards our other friend I am not sufficiently confident, either, except for the fact that he still has sense of shame enough to blush for his sins. This modesty should be fostered; so long as it endures in his soul, there is some room for hope. But as for this veteran of yours, I think we should deal more carefully with him, that he may not become desperate about himself. **3.** There is no better time to approach him than now, when he has an interval of rest and seems like one who has corrected his faults. Others have been cheated by this interval of virtue on his part, but he does not cheat me. I feel sure that these faults will return, as it were, with compound interest, for just now, I am certain, they are in abeyance but not absent. I shall devote some time to the matter, and try to see whether or not something can be done.

4. But do you yourself, as indeed you are doing, show me that you are stout-hearted; lighten your baggage for the march. None of our possessions is essential. Let us return to the law of nature; for then riches are laid up for us. The things which we actually need are free for all, or else cheap; nature craves only bread and water. No one is poor according to this standard; when a man has limited his desires within these bounds, he can challenge the happiness of Jove himself, as Epicurus says. I must insert in this letter one or two more of his sayings: **5.** "Do everything as if Epicurus were watching you." There is no real doubt that it is good for one to have appointed a guardian over oneself, and to have someone whom you may look up to, someone whom you may regard as a witness of your thoughts. It is, indeed, nobler by far to live as you would live under the eyes of some good man, always at your side; but nevertheless I am content if you only act, in whatever you do, as you would act if anyone at all were looking on; because solitude prompts us to all kinds of evil. **6.** And when you have progressed so far that you have also respect for yourself, you may send away your attendant; but until then, set as a guard over yourself the authority of some man, whether your choice be the great Cato or Scipio, or Laelius,

– or any man in whose presence even abandoned wretches would check their bad impulses. Meantime, you are engaged in making of yourself the sort of person in whose company you would not dare to sin. When this aim has been accomplished and you begin to hold yourself in some esteem, I shall gradually allow you to do what Epicurus, in another passage, suggests: "The time when you should most of all withdraw into yourself is when you are forced to be in a crowd."

7. You ought to make yourself of a different stamp from the multitude. Therefore, while it is not yet safe to withdraw into solitude, seek out certain individuals; for everyone is better off in the company of somebody or other, – no matter who, – than in his own company alone. "The time when you should most of all withdraw into yourself is when you are forced to be in a crowd." Yes, provided that you are a good, tranquil, and self-restrained man; otherwise, you had better withdraw into a crowd in order to get away from your self. Alone, you are too close to a rascal. Farewell.

XXVI. ON OLD AGE AND DEATH

1. I was just lately telling you that I was within sight of old age. I am now afraid that I have left old age behind me. For some other word would now apply to my years, or at any rate to my body; since old age means a time of life that is weary rather than crushed. You may rate me in the worn-out class, – of those who are nearing the end.

2. Nevertheless, I offer thanks to myself, with you as witness; for I feel that age has done no damage to my mind, though I feel its effects on my constitution. Only my vices, and the outward aids to these vices, have reached senility; my mind is strong and rejoices that it has but slight connexion with the body. It has laid aside the greater part of its load. It is alert; it takes issue with me on the subject of old age; it declares that old age is its time of bloom. **3.** Let me take it at its word, and let it make the most of the advantages it possesses. The mind bids me do some thinking and consider how much of this peace of spirit and moderation of character I owe to wisdom and how much to my time of life; it bids me distinguish carefully what I cannot do and what I do not want to do. . . . For why should one complain or regard it as a disadvantage, if powers which ought to come to an end have failed? **4.** "But," you say, "it is the greatest possible disadvantage to be worn out and to die off, or rather, if I may speak literally, to melt away! For we are not suddenly smitten and laid low; we are worn away, and every day reduces our powers to a certain extent."

But is there any better end to it all than to glide off to one's proper haven, when nature slips the cable? Not that there is anything painful in a shock and a sudden departure from existence; it is merely because this other way of departure is easy, – a gradual withdrawal. I, at any rate, as if the test were at hand and the day were come which is to pronounce its decision concerning all the years of my life, watch over myself and commune thus with myself: **5.** "The showing which we have made up to the present time, in word or deed, counts for nothing. All this is but a trifling and deceitful pledge of our spirit, and is wrapped in much charlatanism. I shall leave it to Death to determine what progress I have made. Therefore with no faint heart I am making ready for the day when, putting aside all stage artifice and actor's rouge, I am to pass judgment upon myself, – whether I am merely declaiming brave sentiments, or whether I really feel them; whether all the bold threats I have uttered against fortune are a pretence and a farce. **6.** Put aside the opinion of the world; it is always wavering and always takes both sides. Put aside the studies which you have pursued throughout your life; Death will deliver the final judgment in your case. This is what I mean: your debates and learned talks, your maxims gathered from the teachings of the wise, your cultured conversation, – all these afford no proof of the real strength of your soul. Even the most timid man can deliver a bold speech. What you have done in the past will be manifest only at the time when you draw your last breath. I accept the terms; I do not shrink from the decision." **7.** This is what I say to myself, but I would have you think that I have said it to you also. You are younger; but what does that matter? There is no fixed count of our years. You do not know where death awaits you; so be ready for it everywhere.

8. I was just intending to stop, and my hand was making ready for the closing sentence; but the rites are still to be performed and the travelling money for the letter disbursed. And just assume that I am not telling where I intend to borrow the necessary sum; you know upon whose coffers I depend. Wait for me but a moment, and I will pay you from my own account; meanwhile, Epicurus will oblige me with these words: "Think on death," or rather, if you prefer the phrase, on "migration to heaven." **9.** The meaning is clear, – that it is a wonderful thing to learn thoroughly how to die. You may deem it superfluous to learn a text that can be used only once; but that is just the reason why we ought to think on a thing. When we can never prove whether we really know a thing, we must always be learning it. **10.** "Think on death." In saying this, he bids us think on freedom. He who has learned to die has unlearned slavery; he is above any external power, or, at any rate, he is beyond it. What terrors have prisons and bonds and bars for him? His way out is clear. There is only one chain which binds us to life, and that is the love of life. The chain may not be cast off, but it may be rubbed away, so that, when necessity shall demand, nothing may retard or hinder us from being ready to do at once that which at some time we are bound to do. Farewell.

XXVII. ON THE GOOD WHICH ABIDES

1. "What," say you, "are you giving me advice? Indeed, have you already advised yourself, already corrected your own faults? Is this the reason why you have leisure to reform other men?" No, I am not so shameless as to undertake to cure my fellow-men when I am ill myself. I am, however, discussing with you troubles which concern us both, and sharing the remedy with you, just as if we were lying ill in the same hospital. Listen to me, therefore, as you would if I were talking to myself. I am admitting you to my inmost thoughts, and am having it out with myself, merely making use of you as my pretext. **2.** I keep crying out to myself: "Count your years, and you will be ashamed to desire and pursue the same things you desired in your boyhood days. Of this one thing make sure against your dying day, – let your faults die before you die. Away with those disordered pleasures, which must be dearly paid for; it is not only those which are to come that harm me, but also those which have come and gone. Just as crimes, even if they have not been detected when they were committed, do not allow anxiety to end with them; so with guilty pleasures, regret remains even after the pleasures are over. They are not substantial, they are not trustworthy; even if they do not harm us, they are fleeting. **3.** Cast about rather for some good which will abide. But there can be no such good except as the soul discovers it for itself within itself. Virtue alone affords everlasting and peace-giving joy; even if some obstacle arise, it is but like an intervening cloud, which floats beneath the sun but never prevails against it."

4. When will it be your lot to attain this joy? Thus far, you have indeed not been sluggish, but you must quicken your pace. Much toil remains; to confront it, you must yourself lavish all your waking hours, and all your efforts, if you wish the result to be accomplished. This matter cannot be delegated to someone else. **5.** The other kind of literary activity admits of outside assistance. Within our own time there was a certain rich man named Calvisius Sabinus; he had the bank-account and the brains of a freedman. I never saw a man whose good fortune was a greater offence against propriety. His memory was so faulty that he would sometimes forget the name of Ulysses, or Achilles, or Priam, – names which we know as well as we know those of our own attendants. No major-domo in his dotage, who cannot give men their right names, but is compelled to invent names for them, – no such man, I say, calls off the names of his master's tribesmen so atrociously as Sabinus used to call off the Trojan and Achaean heroes. But none the less did he desire to appear learned. **6.** So he devised this short cut to learning: he paid fabulous prices for slaves, – one to know Homer by heart and another to know Hesiod; he also delegated a special slave to each of the nine lyric poets. You need not wonder that he paid high prices for these slaves; if he did not find them ready to hand he had them made to order. After collecting this retinue, he began to make life miserable for his guests; he would keep these fellows at the foot of his couch, and ask them from time to time for verses which he might repeat, and then frequently break down in the middle of a word. **7.** Satellius Quadratus, a feeder, and consequently a fawner, upon addle-pated millionaires, and also (for this quality goes with the other two) a flouter of them, suggested to Sabinus that he should have philologists to gather up the bits. Sabinus remarked that each slave cost him one hundred thousand sesterces; Satellius replied: "You might have bought as many book-cases for a smaller sum." But Sabinus held to the opinion that what any member of his household knew, he himself knew also. **8.** This same Satellius began to advise Sabinus to take wrestling lessons, – sickly, pale, and thin as he was, Sabinus answered: "How can I? I can scarcely stay alive now." "Don't say that, I implore you," replied the other, "consider how many perfectly healthy slaves you have!" No man is able to borrow or buy a sound mind; in fact, as it seems to me, even though sound minds were for sale, they would not find buyers. Depraved minds, however, are bought and sold every day.

9. But let me pay off my debt and say farewell: "Real wealth is poverty adjusted to the law of Nature." Epicurus has this saying in various ways and contexts; but it can never be repeated too often, since it can never be learned too well. For some persons the remedy should be merely prescribed; in the case of others, it should be forced down their throats. Farewell.

XXVIII. ON TRAVEL AS A CURE FOR DISCONTENT

1. Do you suppose that you alone have had this experience? Are you surprised, as if it were a novelty, that after such long travel and so many changes of scene you have not been able to shake off the gloom and heaviness of your mind? You need a change of soul rather than a change of climate. Though you may cross vast spaces of sea, and though, as our Vergil remarks,

> Lands and cities are left astern,

your faults will follow you whithersoever you travel. **2.** Socrates made the same remark to one who complained; he said: "Why do you wonder that globe-trotting does not help you, seeing that you always take yourself with you? The reason which set you wandering is ever at your heels." What pleasure is there in seeing new lands? Or in surveying cities and spots of interest? All your bustle is useless. Do you ask why such flight does not help you? It is because you flee along with yourself. You must lay aside the burdens of the mind; until you do this, no place will satisfy you. **3.** Reflect that your present behaviour is like that of the prophetess whom Vergil describes: she is excited and goaded into fury, and contains within herself much inspiration that is not her own:

> The priestess raves, if haply she may shake
> The great god from her heart.

You wander hither and yon, to rid yourself of the burden that rests upon you, though it becomes more troublesome by reason of your very restlessness, just as in a ship the cargo when stationary makes no trouble, but when it shifts to this side or that, it causes the vessel to heel more quickly in the direction where it has settled. Anything you do tells against you, and you hurt yourself by your very unrest; for you are shaking up a sick man.

4. That trouble once removed, all change of scene will become pleasant; though you may be driven to the uttermost ends of the earth, in whatever corner of a savage land you may find yourself, that place, however forbidding, will be to you a hospitable abode. The person you are matters more than the place to which you go; for that reason we should not make the mind a bondsman to any one place. Live in this belief: "I am not born for any one corner of the universe; this whole world is my country." **5.** If you saw this fact clearly, you would not be surprised at getting no benefit from the fresh scenes to which you roam each time through weariness of the old scenes. For the first would have pleased you in each case, had you believed it wholly yours. As it is, however, you are not journeying; you are drifting and being driven, only exchanging one place for another, although that which you seek, – to live well, – is found everywhere. **6.** Can there be any spot so full of confusion as the Forum? Yet you can live quietly even there, if necessary. Of course, if one were allowed to make one's own arrangements, I should flee far from the very sight and neighbourhood of the Forum. For just as pestilential places assail even the strongest constitution, so there are some places which are also unwholesome for a healthy mind which is not yet quite sound, though recovering from its ailment. **7.** I disagree with those who strike out into the midst of the billows and, welcoming a stormy existence, wrestle daily in hardihood of soul with life's problems. The wise man will endure all that, but will not choose it; he will prefer to be at peace rather than at war. It helps little to have cast out your own faults if you must quarrel with those of others. **8.** Says one: "There were thirty tyrants surrounding Socrates, and yet they could not break his spirit"; but what does it matter how many masters a man has? "Slavery" has no plural; and he who has scorned it is free, – no matter amid how large a mob of over-lords he stands.

9. It is time to stop, but not before I have paid duty. "The knowledge of sin is the beginning of salvation." This saying of Epicurus seems to me to be a noble one. For he who does not know that he has sinned does not desire correction; you must discover yourself in the wrong before you can reform yourself. **10.** Some boast of their faults. Do you think that the man has any thought of mending his ways who counts over his vices as if they were virtues? Therefore, as far as possible, prove yourself guilty, hunt up charges against yourself; play the part, first of accuser, then of judge, last of intercessor. At times be harsh with yourself. Farewell.

XXIX. ON THE CRITICAL CONDITION OF MARCELLINUS

1. You have been inquiring about our friend Marcellinus and you desire to know how he is getting along. He seldom comes to see me, for no other reason than that he is afraid to hear the truth, and at present he is removed from my danger of hearing it; for one must not talk to a man unless he is willing to listen. That is why it is often doubted whether Diogenes and the other Cynics, who employed an undiscriminating freedom of speech and offered advice to any who came in their way, ought to have pursued such a plan. **2.** For what if one should chide the deaf or those who are speechless from birth or by illness? But you answer: "Why should I spare words? They cost nothing. I cannot know whether I shall help the man to whom I give advice; but I know well that I shall help someone if I advise many. I must scatter this advice by the handful. It is impossible that one who tries often should not sometime succeed."

3. This very thing, my dear Lucilius, is, I believe, exactly what a great-souled man ought not to do; his influence is weakened; it has too little effect upon those whom it might have set right if it had not grown so stale. The archer ought not to hit the mark only sometimes; he ought to miss it only sometimes. That which takes effect by chance is not an art. Now wisdom is an art; it should have a definite aim, choosing only those who will make progress, but withdrawing from those whom it has come to regard as hopeless, – yet not abandoning them too soon, and just when the case is becoming hopeless trying drastic remedies.

4. As to our friend Marcellinus, I have not yet lost hope. He can still be saved, but the helping hand must be offered soon. There is indeed danger that he may pull his helper down; for there is in him a native character of great vigour, though it is already inclining to wickedness. Nevertheless I shall brave this danger and be bold enough to show him his faults. **5.** He will act in his usual way; he will have recourse to his wit, – the wit that can call forth smiles even from mourners. He will turn the jest, first against himself, and then against me. He will forestall every word which I am about to utter. He will quiz our philosophic systems; he will accuse philosophers of accepting doles, keeping mistresses, and indulging their appetites. He will point out to me one philosopher who has been caught in adultery, another who haunts the cafes, and another who appears at court. **6.** He will bring to my notice Aristo, the philosopher of Marcus Lepidus, who used to hold discussions in his carriage; for that was the time which he had taken for editing his researches, so that Scaurus said of him when asked to what school he belonged: "At any rate, he isn't one of the Walking Philosophers." Julius Graecinus, too, a man of distinction, when asked for an opinion on the same point, replied: "I cannot tell you; for I don't know what he does when dismounted," as if the query referred to a chariot-gladiator. **7.** It is mountebanks of that sort, for whom it would be more creditable to have left philosophy alone than to traffic in her, whom Marcellinus will throw in my teeth. But I have decided to put up with taunts; he may stir my laughter, but I perchance shall stir him to tears; or, if he persist in his jokes, I shall rejoice, so to speak, in the midst of sorrow, because he is blessed with such a merry sort of lunacy. But that kind of merriment does not last long. Observe such men, and you will note that within a short space of time they laugh to excess and rage to excess. **8.** It is my plan to approach him and to show him how much greater was his worth when many thought it less. Even though I shall not root out his faults, I shall put a check upon them; they will not cease, but they will stop for a time; and perhaps they will even cease, if they get the habit of stopping. This is a thing not to be despised, since to men who are seriously stricken the blessing of relief is a substitute for health. **9.** So while I prepare myself to deal with Marcellinus, do you in the meantime, who are able, and who understand whence and whither you have made your way, and who for that reason have an inkling of the distance yet to go, regulate your character, rouse your courage, and stand firm in the face of things which have terrified you. Do not count the number of those who inspire fear in you. Would you not regard as foolish one who was afraid of a multitude in a place where only one at a time could pass? Just so, there are not many who have access to you to slay you, though there are many who threaten you with death. Nature has so ordered it that, as only one has given you life, so only one will take it away.

10. If you had any shame, you would have let me off from paying the last instalment. Still, I shall not be niggardly either, but shall discharge my debts to the last penny and force upon you what I still owe: "I have never wished to cater to the crowd; for what I know, they do not approve, and what they approve, I do not know." **11.** "Who said this?" you ask, as if you were ignorant whom I am pressing into service; it is Epicurus. But this same watchword rings in your ears from every sect, – Peripatetic, Academic, Stoic, Cynic. For who that is pleased by virtue can please the crowd? It takes trickery to win popular approval; and you must needs make yourself like unto them; they will withhold their approval if they do not recognise you as one of themselves. However, what you think of yourself is much more to the point than what others think of you. The favour of ignoble men can be won only by ignoble means. **12.** What benefit, then, will that vaunted philosophy confer, whose praises we sing, and which, we are told, is to be preferred to every art and every possession? Assuredly, it will make you prefer to please yourself rather than the populace, it will make you weigh, and not merely count, men's judgments, it will make you live without fear of gods or men, it will make you either overcome evils or end them. Otherwise, if I see you applauded by popular acclamation, if your entrance upon the scene is greeted by a roar of cheering and clapping, marks of distinction meet only for actors, – if the whole state, even the women and children, sing your praises, how can I help pitying you? For I know what pathway leads to such popularity. Farewell.

XXX. ON CONQUERING THE CONQUEROR

1. I have beheld Aufidius Bassus, that noble man, shattered in health and wrestling with his years. But they already bear upon him so heavily that he cannot be raised up; old age has settled down upon him with great, – yes, with its entire, weight. You know that his body was always delicate and sapless. For a long time he has kept it in hand, or, to speak more correctly, has kept it together; of a sudden it has collapsed. **2.** Just as in a ship that springs a leak, you can always stop the first or the second fissure, but when many holes begin to open and let in water, the gaping hull cannot be saved; similarly, in an old man's body, there is a certain limit up to which you can sustain and prop its weakness. But when it comes to resemble a decrepit building, when every joint begins to spread and while one is being repaired another falls apart, – then it is time for a man to look about him and consider how he may get out.

3. But the mind of our friend Bassus is active. Philosophy bestows this boon upon us; it makes us joyful in the very sight of death, strong and brave no matter in what state the body may be, cheerful and never failing though the body fail us. A great pilot can sail even when his canvas is rent; if his ship be dismantled, he can yet put in trim what remains of her hull and hold her to her course. This is what our friend Bassus is doing; and he contemplates his own end with the courage and countenance which you would regard as undue indifference in a man who so contemplated another's.

4. This is a great accomplishment, Lucilius, and one which needs long practice to learn, – to depart calmly when the inevitable hour arrives. Other kinds of death contain an ingredient of hope: a disease comes to an end; a fire is quenched; falling houses have set down in safety those whom they seemed certain to crush; the sea has cast ashore unharmed those whom it had engulfed, by the same force through which it drew them down; the soldier has drawn back his sword from the very neck of his doomed foe. But those whom old age is leading away to death have nothing to hope for; old age alone grants no reprieve. No ending, to be sure, is more painless; but there is none more lingering.

5. Our friend Bassus seemed to me to be attending his own funeral, and laying out his own body for burial, and living almost as if he had survived his own death, and bearing with wise resignation his grief at his own departure. For he talks freely about death, trying hard to persuade us that if this process contains any element of discomfort or of fear, it is the fault of the dying person, and not of death itself; also, that there is no more inconvenience at the actual moment than there is after it is over. **6.** "And it is just as insane," he adds, "for a man to fear what will not happen to him, as to fear what he will not feel if it does happen." Or does anyone imagine it to be possible that the agency by which feeling is removed can be itself felt? "Therefore," says Bassus, "death stands so far beyond all evil that it is beyond all fear of evils."

7. I know that all this has often been said and should be often repeated; but neither when I read them were such precepts so effective with me, nor when I heard them from the lips of those who were at a safe distance from the fear of the things which they declared were not to be feared. But this old man had the greatest weight with me when he discussed death and death was near. **8.** For I must tell you what I myself think: I hold that one is braver at the very moment of death than when one is approaching death. For death, when it stands near us, gives even to inexperienced men the courage not to seek to avoid the inevitable. So the gladiator, who throughout the fight has been no matter how faint-hearted, offers his throat to his opponent and directs the wavering blade to the vital spot. But an end that is near at hand, and is bound to come, calls for tenacious courage of soul; this is a rarer thing, and none but the wise man can manifest it.

9. Accordingly, I listened to Bassus with the deepest pleasure; he was casting his vote concerning death and pointing out what sort of a thing it is when it is observed, so to speak, nearer at hand. I suppose that a man would have your confidence in a larger degree, and would have more weight with you, if he had come back to life and should declare from experience that there is no evil in death; and so, regarding the approach of death, those will tell you best what disquiet it brings who have stood in its path, who have seen it coming and have welcomed it. **10.** Bassus may be included among these men; and he had no wish to deceive us. He says that it is as foolish to fear death as to fear old age; for death follows old age precisely as old age follows youth. He who does not wish to die cannot have wished to live. For life is granted to us with the reservation that we shall die; to this end our path leads. Therefore, how foolish it is to fear it, since men simply await that which is sure, but fear only that which is uncertain! **11.** Death has its fixed rule, – equitable and unavoidable. Who can complain when he is governed by terms which include everyone? The chief part of equity, however, is equality.

But it is superfluous at the present time to plead Nature's cause; for she wishes our laws to be identical with her own; she but resolves that which she has compounded, and compounds again that which she has resolved. **12.** Moreover, if it falls to the lot of any man to be set gently adrift by old age, – not suddenly torn from life, but withdrawn bit by bit, oh, verily he should thank the gods, one and all, because, after he has had his fill, he is removed to a rest which is ordained for mankind, a rest that is welcome to the weary. You may observe certain men who crave death even more earnestly than others are wont to beg for life. And I do not know which men give us greater courage, – those who call for death, or those who meet it cheerfully and tranquilly, – for the first attitude is sometimes inspired by madness and sudden anger, the second is the calm which results from fixed judgment. Before now men have gone to meet death in a fit of rage; but when death comes to meet him, no one welcomes it cheerfully, except the man who has long since composed himself for death.

13. I admit, therefore, that I have visited this dear friend of mine more frequently on many pretexts, but with the purpose of learning whether I should find him always the same, and whether his mental strength was perhaps waning in company with his bodily powers. But it was on the increase, just as the joy of the charioteer is wont to show itself more clearly when he is on the seventh round of the course, and nears the prize. **14.** Indeed, he often said, in accord with the counsels of Epicurus: "I hope, first of all, that there is no pain at the moment when a man breathes his last; but if there is, one will find an element of comfort in its very shortness. For no great pain lasts long. And at all events, a man will find relief at the very time when soul and body are being torn asunder, even though the process be accompanied by excruciating pain, in the thought that after this pain is over he can feel no more pain. I am sure, however, that an old man's soul is on his very lips, and that only a little force is necessary to disengage it from the body. A fire which has seized upon a substance that sustains it needs water to quench it, or, sometimes, the destruction of the building itself; but the fire which lacks sustaining fuel dies away of its own accord."

15. I am glad to hear such words, my dear Lucilius, not as new to me, but as leading me into the presence of an actual fact. And what then? Have I not seen many men break the thread of life? I have indeed seen such men; but those have more weight with me who approach death without any loathing for life, letting death in, so to speak, and not pulling it towards them. **16.** Bassus kept saying: "It is due to our own fault that we feel this torture, because we shrink from dying only when we believe that our end is near at hand." But who is not near death? It is ready for us in all places and at all times. "Let us consider," he went on to say, "when some agency of death seems imminent, how much nearer are other varieties of dying which are not feared by us." **17.** A man is threatened with death by an enemy, but this form of death is anticipated by an attack of indigestion. And if we are willing to examine critically the various causes of our fear, we shall find that some exist, and others only seem to be. We do not fear death; we fear the thought of death. For death itself is always the same distance from us; wherefore, if it is to be feared at all, it is to be feared always. For what season of our life is exempt from death?

18. But what I really ought to fear is that you will hate this long letter worse than death itself; so I shall stop. Do you, however, always think on death in order that you may never fear it. Farewell.

XXXI. ON SIREN SONGS

1. Now I recognize my Lucilius! He is beginning to reveal the character of which he gave promise. Follow up the impulse which prompted you to make for all that is best, treading under your feet that which is approved by the crowd. I would not have you greater or better than you planned; for in your case the mere foundations have covered a large extent of ground; only finish all that you have laid out, and take in hand the plans which you have had in mind. **2.** In short, you will be a wise man, if you stop up your ears; nor is it enough to close them with wax; you need a denser stopple than that which they say Ulysses used for his comrades. The song which he feared was alluring, but came not from every side; the song, however, which you have to fear, echoes round you not from a single headland, but from every quarter of the world. Sail, therefore, not past one region which you mistrust because of its treacherous delights, but past every city. Be deaf to those who love you most of all; they pray for bad things with good intentions. And, if you would be happy, entreat the gods that none of their fond desires for you may be brought to pass. **3.** What they wish to have heaped upon you are not really good things; there is only one good, the cause and the support of a happy life, – trust in oneself. But this cannot be attained, unless one has learned to despise toil and to reckon it among the things which are neither good nor bad. For it is not possible that a single thing should be bad at one time and good at another, at times light and to be endured, and at times a cause of dread. **4.** Work is not a good. Then what is a good? I say, the scorning of work. That is why I should rebuke men who toil to no purpose. But when, on the other hand, a man is struggling towards honourable things, in proportion as he applies himself more and more, and allows himself less and less to be beaten or to halt, I shall recommend his conduct and shout my encouragement, saying: "By so much you are better! Rise, draw a fresh breath, and surmount that hill, if possible, at a single spurt!"

5. Work is the sustenance of noble minds. There is, then, no reason why, in accordance with that old vow of your parents, you should pick and choose what fortune you wish should fall to your lot, or what you should pray for; besides, it is base for a man who has already travelled the whole round of highest honours to be still importuning the gods. What need is there of vows? Make yourself happy through your own efforts; you can do this, if once you comprehend that whatever is blended with virtue is good, and that whatever is joined to vice is bad. Just as nothing gleams if it has no light blended with it, and nothing is black unless it contains darkness or draws to itself something of dimness, and as nothing is hot without the aid of fire, and nothing cold without air; so it is the association of virtue and vice that makes things honourable or base.

6. What then is good? The knowledge of things. What is evil? The lack of knowledge of things. Your wise man, who is also a craftsman, will reject or choose in each case as it suits the occasion; but he does not fear that which he rejects, nor does he admire that which he chooses, if only he has a stout and unconquerable soul. I forbid you to be cast down or depressed. It is not enough if you do not shrink from work; ask for it. **7.** "But," you say, "is not trifling and superfluous work, and work that has been inspired by ignoble causes, a bad sort of work?" No; no more than that which is expended upon noble endeavours, since the very quality that endures toil and rouses itself to hard and uphill effort, is of the spirit, which says: "Why do you grow slack? It is not the part of a man to fear sweat." **8.** And besides this, in order that virtue may be perfect, there should be an even temperament and a scheme of life that is consistent with itself throughout; and this result cannot be attained without knowledge of things, and without the art which enables us to understand things human and things divine. That is the greatest good. If you seize this good, you begin to be the associate of the gods, and not their suppliant.

9. "But how," you ask, "does one attain that goal?" You do not need to cross the Pennine or Graian hills, or traverse the Candavian waste, or face the Syrtes, or Scylla, or Charybdis, although you have travelled through all these places for the bribe of a petty governorship; the journey for which nature has equipped you is safe and pleasant. She has given you such gifts that you may, if you do not prove false to them, rise level with God. **10.** Your money, however, will not place you on a level with God; for God has no property. Your bordered robe will not do this; for God is not clad in raiment; nor will your reputation, nor a display of self, nor a knowledge of your name wide-spread throughout the world; for no one has knowledge of God; many even hold him in low esteem, and do not suffer for so doing. The throng of slaves which carries your litter along the city streets and in foreign places will not help you; for this God of whom I speak, though the highest and most powerful of beings, carries all things on his own shoulders. Neither can beauty or strength make you blessed, for none of these qualities can withstand old age.

11. What we have to seek for, then, is that which does not each day pass more and more under the control of some power which cannot be withstood. And what is this? It is the soul, – but the soul that is upright, good, and great. What else could you call such a soul than a god dwelling as a guest in a human body? A soul like this may descend into a Roman knight just as well as into a freedman's son or a slave. For what is a Roman knight, or a freedmen's son, or a slave? They are mere titles, born of ambition or of wrong. One may leap to heaven from the very slums. Only rise

And mould thyself to kinship with thy God.

This moulding will not be done in gold or silver; an image that is to be in the likeness of God cannot be fashioned of such materials; remember that the gods, when they were kind unto men, were moulded in clay. Farewell.

XXXII. ON PROGRESS

1. I have been asking about you, and inquiring of everyone who comes from your part of the country, what you are doing, and where you are spending your time, and with whom. You cannot deceive me; for I am with you. Live just as if I were sure to get news of your doings, nay, as if I were sure to behold them. And if you wonder what particularly pleases me that I hear concerning you, it is that I hear nothing, that most of those whom I ask do not know what you are doing.

2. This is sound practice – to refrain from associating with men of different stamp and different aims. And I am indeed confident that you cannot be warped, that you will stick to your purpose, even though the crowd may surround and seek to distract you. What, then, is on my mind? I am not afraid lest they work a change in you; but I am afraid lest they may hinder your progress. And much harm is done even by one who holds you back, especially since life is so short; and we make it still shorter by our unsteadiness, by making ever fresh beginnings at life, now one and immediately another. We break up life into little bits, and fritter it away. **3.** Hasten ahead, then, dearest Lucilius, and reflect how greatly you would quicken your speed if an enemy were at your back, or if you suspected the cavalry were approaching and pressing hard upon your steps as you fled. It is true; the enemy is indeed pressing upon you; you should therefore increase your speed and escape away and reach a safe position, remembering continually what a noble thing it is to round out your life before death comes, and then await in peace the remaining portion of your time, claiming nothing for yourself, since you are in possession of the happy life; for such a life is not made happier for being longer. **4.** O when shall you see the time when you shall know that time means nothing to you, when you shall be peaceful and calm, careless of the morrow, because you are enjoying your life to the full?

Would you know what makes men greedy for the future? It is because no one has yet found himself. Your parents, to be sure, asked other blessings for you; but I myself pray rather that you may despise all those things which your parents wished for you in abundance. Their prayers plunder many another person, simply that you may be enriched. Whatever they make over to you must be removed from someone else. **5.** I pray that you may get such control over yourself that your mind, now shaken by wandering thoughts, may at last come to rest and be steadfast, that it may be content with itself and, having attained an understanding of what things are truly good, – and they are in our possession as soon as we have this knowledge, – that it may have no need of added years. He has at length passed beyond all necessities – he has won his honourable discharge and is free, – who still lives after his life has been completed. Farewell.

XXXIII. ON THE FUTILITY OF LEARNING MAXIMS

1. You wish me to close these letters also, as I closed my former letters, with certain utterances taken from the chiefs of our school. But they did not interest themselves in choice extracts; the whole texture of their work is full of strength. There is unevenness, you know, when some objects rise conspicuous above others. A single tree is not remarkable if the whole forest rises to the same height. **2.** Poetry is crammed with utterances of this sort, and so is history. For this reason I would not have you think that these utterances belong to Epicurus. they are common property and are emphatically our own. They are, however, more noteworthy in Epicurus, because they appear at infrequent intervals and when you do not expect them, and because it is surprising that brave words should be spoken at any time by a man who made a practice of being effeminate. For that is what most persons maintain. In my own opinion, however, Epicurus is really a brave man, even though he did wear long sleeves. Fortitude, energy, and readiness for battle are to be found among the Persians, just as much as among men who have girded themselves up high.

3. Therefore, you need not call upon me for extracts and quotations; such thoughts as one may extract here and there in the works of other philosophers run through the whole body of our writings. Hence we have no "show-window goods," nor do we deceive the purchaser in such a way that, if he enters our shop, he will find nothing except that which is displayed in the window. We allow the purchasers themselves to get their samples from anywhere they please. **4.** Suppose we should desire to sort out each separate motto from the general stock; to whom shall we credit them? To Zeno, Cleanthes, Chrysippus, Panaetius, or Posidonius? We Stoics are not subjects of a despot: each of us lays claim to his own freedom. With them, on the other hand, whatever Hermarchus says or Metrodorus, is ascribed to one source. In that brotherhood, everything that any man utters is spoken under the leadership and commanding authority of one alone. We cannot, I maintain, no matter how we try, pick out anything from so great a multitude of things equally good.

Only the poor man counts his flock.

Wherever you direct your gaze, you will meet with something that might stand out from the rest, if the context in which you read it were not equally notable.

5. For this reason, give over hoping that you can skim, by means of epitomes, the wisdom of distinguished men. Look into their wisdom as a whole; study it as a whole. They are working out a plan and weaving together, line upon line, a masterpiece, from which nothing can be taken away without injury to the whole. Examine the separate parts, if you like, provided you examine them as parts of the man himself. She is not a beautiful woman whose ankle or arm is praised, but she whose general appearance makes you forget to admire her single attributes.

6. If you insist, however, I shall not be niggardly with you, but lavish; for there is a huge multitude of these passages; they are scattered about in profusion, – they do not need to be gathered together, but merely to be picked up. They do not drip forth occasionally; they flow continuously. They are unbroken and are closely connected. Doubtless they would be of much benefit to those who are still novices and worshipping outside the shrine; for single maxims sink in more easily when they are marked off and bounded like a line of verse. **7.** That is why we give to children a proverb, or that which the Greeks call *Chria*, to be learned by heart; that sort of thing can be comprehended by the young mind, which cannot as yet hold more. For a man, however, whose progress is definite, to chase after choice extracts and to prop his weakness by the best known and the briefest sayings and to depend upon his memory, is disgraceful; it is time for him to lean on himself. He should make such maxims and not memorize them. For it is disgraceful even for an old man, or one who has sighted old age, to have a note-book knowledge. "This is what Zeno said." But what have you yourself said? "This is the opinion of Cleanthes." But what is your own opinion? How long shall you march under another man's orders? Take command, and utter some word which posterity will remember. Put forth something from your own stock. **8.** For this reason I hold that there is nothing of eminence in all such men as these, who never create anything themselves, but always lurk in the shadow of others, playing the rôle of interpreters, never daring to put once into practice what they have been so long in learning. They have exercised their memories on other men's material. But it is one thing to remember, another to know. Remembering is merely safeguarding something entrusted to the memory; knowing, however, means making everything your own; it means not depending upon the copy and not all the time glancing back at the master. **9.** "Thus said Zeno, thus said Cleanthes, indeed!" Let there be a difference between yourself and your book! How long shall you be a learner? From now on be a teacher as well! "But why," one asks, "should I have to continue hearing lectures on what I can read?" "The living voice," one replies, "is a great help." Perhaps, but not the voice which merely makes itself the mouthpiece of another's words, and only performs the duty of a reporter.

10. Consider this fact also. Those who have never attained their mental independence begin, in the first place, by following the leader in cases where everyone has deserted the leader; then, in the second place, they follow him in matters where the truth is still being investigated. However, the truth will never be discovered if we rest contented with discoveries already made. Besides, he who follows another not only discovers nothing but is not even investigating. **11.** What then? Shall I not follow in the footsteps of my predecessors? I shall indeed use the old road, but if I find one that makes a shorter cut and is smoother to travel, I shall open the new road. Men who have made these discoveries before us are not our masters, but our guides. Truth lies open for all; it has not yet been monopolized. And there is plenty of it left even for posterity to discover. Farewell.

XXXIV. ON A PROMISING PUPIL

1. I grow in spirit and leap for joy and shake off my years and my blood runs warm again, whenever I understand, from your actions and your letters, how far you have outdone yourself; for as to the ordinary man, you left him in the rear long ago. If the farmer is pleased when his tree develops so that it bears fruit, if the shepherd takes pleasure in the increase of his flocks, if every man regards his pupil as though he discerned in him his own early manhood, – what, then, do you think are the feelings of those who have trained a mind and moulded a young idea, when they see it suddenly grown to maturity?

2. I claim you for myself; you are my handiwork. When I saw your abilities, I laid my hand upon you, I exhorted you, I applied the goad and did not permit you to march lazily, but roused you continually. And now I do the same; but by this time I am cheering on one who is in the race and so in turn cheers me on.

3. "What else do you want of me, then?" you ask; "the will is still mine." Well, the will in this case is almost everything, and not merely the half, as in the proverb "A task once begun is half done." It is more than half, for the matter of which we speak is determined by the soul. Hence it is that the larger part of goodness is the will to become good. You know what I mean by a good man? One who is complete, finished, – whom no constraint or need can render bad. **4.** I see such a person in you, if only you go steadily on and bend to your task, and see to it that all your actions and words harmonize and correspond with each other and are stamped in the same mould. If a man's acts are out of harmony, his soul is crooked. Farewell.

XXXV. ON THE FRIENDSHIP OF KINDRED MINDS

1. When I urge you so strongly to your studies, it is my own interest which I am consulting; I want your friendship, and it cannot fall to my lot unless you proceed, as you have begun, with the task of developing yourself. For now, although you love me, you are not yet my friend. "But," you reply, "are these words of different meaning?" Nay, more, they are totally unlike in meaning. A friend loves you, of course; but one who loves you is not in every case your friend. Friendship, accordingly, is always helpful, but love sometimes even does harm. Try to perfect yourself, if for no other reason, in order that you may learn how to love.

2. Hasten, therefore, in order that, while thus perfecting yourself for my benefit, you may not have learned perfection for the benefit of another. To be sure, I am already deriving some profit by imagining that we two shall be of one mind, and that whatever portion of my strength has yielded to age will return to me from your strength, although there is not so very much difference in our ages. **3.** But yet I wish to rejoice in the accomplished fact. We feel a joy over those whom we love, even when separated from them, but such a joy is light and fleeting; the sight of a man, and his presence, and communion with him, afford something of living pleasure; this is true, at any rate, if one not only sees the man one desires, but the sort of man one desires. Give yourself to me, therefore, as a gift of great price, and, that you may strive the more, reflect that you yourself are mortal, and that I am old. **4.** Hasten to find me, but hasten to find yourself first. Make progress, and, before all else, endeavour to be consistent with yourself. And when you would find out whether you have accomplished anything, consider whether you desire the same things today that you desired yesterday. A shifting of the will indicates that the mind is at sea, heading in various directions, according to the course of the wind. But that which is settled and solid does not wander from its place. This is the blessed lot of the completely wise man, and also, to a certain extent, of him who is progressing and has made some headway. Now what is the difference between these two classes of men? The one is in motion, to be sure, but does not change its position; it merely tosses up and down where it is; the other is not in motion at all. Farewell.

XXXVI. ON THE VALUE OF RETIREMENT

1. Encourage your friend to despise stout-heartedly those who upbraid him because he has sought the shade of retirement and has abdicated his career of honours, and, though he might have attained more, has preferred tranquillity to them all. Let him prove daily to these detractors how wisely he has looked out for his own interests. Those whom men envy will continue to march past him; some will be pushed out of the ranks, and others will fall. Prosperity is a turbulent thing; it torments itself. It stirs the brain in more ways than one, goading men on to various aims, – some to power, and others to high living. Some it puffs up; others it slackens and wholly enervates.

2. "But," the retort comes, "so-and-so carries his prosperity well." Yes; just as he carries his liquor. So you need not let this class of men persuade you that one who is besieged by the crowd is happy; they run to him as crowds rush for a pool of water, rendering it muddy while they drain it. But you say: "Men call our friend a trifler and a sluggard." There are men, you know, whose speech is awry, who use the contrary terms. They called him happy; what of it? Was he happy? **3.** Even the fact that to certain persons he seems a man of a very rough and gloomy cast of mind, does not trouble me. Aristo used to say that he preferred a youth of stern disposition to one who was a jolly fellow and agreeable to the crowd. "For," he added, "wine which, when new, seemed harsh and sour, becomes good wine; but that which tasted well at the vintage cannot stand age." So let them call him stern and a foe to his own advancement, it is just this sternness that will go well when it is aged, provided only that he continues to cherish virtue and to absorb thoroughly the studies which make for culture, – not those with which it is sufficient for a man to sprinkle himself, but those in which the mind should be steeped. **4.** Now is the time to learn. "What? Is there any time when a man should not learn?" By no means; but just as it is creditable for every age to study, so it is not creditable for every age to be instructed. An old man learning his A B C is a disgraceful and absurd object; the young man must store up, the old man must use. You will therefore be doing a thing most helpful to yourself if you make this friend of yours as good a man as possible; those kindnesses, they tell us, are to be both sought for and bestowed, which benefit the giver no less than the receiver; and they are unquestionably the best kind.

5. Finally, he has no longer any freedom in the matter; he has pledged his word. And it is less disgraceful to compound with a creditor than to compound with a promising future. To pay his debt of money, the business man must have a prosperous voyage, the farmer must have fruitful fields and kindly weather; but the debt which your friend owes can be completely paid by mere goodwill. **6.** Fortune has no jurisdiction over character. Let him so regulate his character that in perfect peace he may bring to perfection that spirit within him which feels neither loss nor gain, but remains in the same attitude, no matter how things fall out. A spirit like this, if it is heaped with worldly goods, rises superior to its wealth; if, on the other hand, chance has stripped him of a part of his wealth, or even all, it is not impaired.

7. If your friend had been born in Parthia, he would have begun, when a child, to bend the bow; if in Germany, he would forthwith have been brandishing his slender spear; if he had been born in the days of our forefathers, he would have learned to ride a horse and smite his enemy hand to hand. These are the occupations which the system of each race recommends to the individual, – yes, prescribes for him. **8.** To what, then, shall this friend of yours devote his attention? I say, let him learn that which is helpful against all weapons, against every kind of foe, – contempt of death; because no one doubts that death has in it something that inspires terror, so that it shocks even our souls, which nature has so moulded that they love their own existence; for otherwise there would be no need to prepare ourselves, and to whet our courage, to face that towards which we should move with a sort of voluntary instinct, precisely as all men tend to preserve their existence. **9.** No man learns a thing in order that, if necessity arises, he may lie down with composure upon a bed of roses; but he steels his courage to this end, that he may not surrender his plighted faith to torture, and that, if need be, he may some day stay out his watch in the trenches, even though wounded, without even leaning on his spear; because sleep is likely to creep over men who support themselves by any prop whatsoever.

In death there is nothing harmful; for there must exist something to which it is harmful. **10.** And yet, if you are possessed by so great a craving for a longer life, reflect that none of the objects which vanish from our gaze and are re-absorbed into the world of things, from which they have come forth and are soon to come forth again, is annihilated; they merely end their course and do not perish. And death, which we fear and shrink from, merely interrupts life, but does not steal it away; the time will return when we shall be restored to the light of day; and many men would object to this, were they not brought back in forgetfulness of the past.

11. But I mean to show you later, with more care, that everything which seems to perish merely changes. Since you are destined to return, you ought to depart with a tranquil mind. Mark how the round of the universe repeats its course; you will see that no star in our firmament is extinguished, but that they all set and rise in alternation. Summer has gone, but another year will bring it again; winter lies low, but will be restored by its own proper months; night has overwhelmed the sun, but day will soon rout the night again. The wandering stars retrace their former courses; a part of the sky is rising unceasingly, and a part is sinking. **12.** One word more, and then I shall stop; infants, and boys, and those who have gone mad, have no fear of death, and it is most shameful if reason cannot afford us that peace of mind to which they have been brought by their folly. Farewell.

XXXVII. ON ALLEGIANCE TO VIRTUE

1. You have promised to be a good man; you have enlisted under oath; that is the strongest chain which will hold you to a sound understanding. Any man will be but mocking you, if he declares that this is an effeminate and easy kind of soldiering. I will not have you deceived. The word of this most honourable compact are the same as the words of that most disgraceful one, to wit: "Through burning, imprisonment, or death by the sword." **2.** From the men who hire out their strength for the arena, who eat and drink what they must pay for with their blood, security is taken that they will endure such trials even though they be unwilling; from you, that you will endure them willingly and with alacrity. The gladiator may lower his weapon and test the pity of the people; but you will neither lower your weapon nor beg for life.

You must die erect and unyielding. Moreover, what profit is it to gain a few days or a few years? There is no discharge for us from the moment we are born.

3. "Then how can I free myself?" you ask. You cannot escape necessities, but you can overcome them

> By force a way is made.

And this way will be afforded you by philosophy. Betake yourself therefore to philosophy if you would be safe, untroubled, happy, in fine, if you wish to be, – and that is most important, – free. There is no other way to attain this end. **4.** Folly is low, abject, mean, slavish, and exposed to many of the cruellest passions. These passions, which are heavy taskmasters, sometimes ruling by turns, and sometimes together, can be banished from you by wisdom, which is the only real freedom. There is but one path leading thither, and it is a straight path; you will not go astray. Proceed with steady step, and if you would have all things under your control, put yourself under the control of reason; if reason becomes your ruler, you will become ruler over many. You will learn from her what you should undertake, and how it should be done; you will not blunder into things. **5.** You can show me no man who knows how he began to crave that which he craves. He has not been led to that pass by forethought; he has been driven to it by impulse. Fortune attacks us as often as we attack Fortune. It is disgraceful, instead of proceeding ahead, to be carried along, and then suddenly, amid the whirlpool of events, to ask in a dazed way: "How did I get into this condition?" Farewell.

XXXVIII. ON QUIET CONVERSATION

1. You are right when you urge that we increase our mutual traffic in letters. But the greatest benefit is to be derived from conversation, because it creeps by degrees into the soul. Lectures prepared beforehand and spouted in the presence of a throng have in them more noise but less intimacy. Philosophy is good advice; and no one can give advice at the top of his lungs. Of course we must sometimes also make use of these harangues, if I may so call them, when a doubting member needs to be spurred on; but when the aim is to make a man learn and not merely to make him wish to learn, we must have recourse to the low-toned words of conversation. They enter more easily, and stick in the memory; for we do not need many words, but, rather, effective words.

2. Words should be scattered like seed; no matter how small the seed may be, if it has once found favourable ground, it unfolds its strength and from an insignificant thing spreads to its greatest growth. Reason grows in the same way; it is not large to the outward view, but increases as it does its work. Few words are spoken; but if the mind has truly caught them, they come into their strength and spring up. Yes, precepts and seeds have the same quality; they produce much, and yet they are slight things. Only, as I said, let a favourable mind receive and assimilate them. Then of itself the mind also will produce bounteously in its turn, giving back more than it has received. Farewell.

XXXIX. ON NOBLE ASPIRATIONS

1. I shall indeed arrange for you, in careful order and narrow compass, the notes which you request. But consider whether you may not get more help from the customary method than from that which is now commonly called a "breviary," though in the good old days, when real Latin was spoken, it was called a "summary." The former is more necessary to one who is learning a subject, the latter to one who knows it. For the one teaches, the other stirs the memory. But I shall give you abundant opportunity for both. A man like you should not ask me for this authority or that; he who furnishes a voucher for his statements argues himself unknown. **2.** I shall therefore write exactly what you wish, but I shall do it in my own way; until then, you have many authors whose works will presumably keep your ideas sufficiently in order. Pick up the list of the philosophers; that very act will compel you to wake up, when you see how many men have been working for your benefit. You will desire eagerly to be one of them yourself, for this is the most excellent quality that the noble soul has within itself, that it can be roused to honourable things.

No man of exalted gifts is pleased with that which is low and mean; the vision of great achievement summons him and uplifts him. **3.** Just as the flame springs straight into the air and cannot be cabined or kept down any more than it can repose in quiet, so our soul is always in motion, and the more ardent it is, the greater its motion and activity. But happy is the man who has given it this impulse toward better things! He will place himself beyond the jurisdiction of chance; he will wisely control prosperity; he will lessen adversity, and will despise what others hold in admiration. **4.** It is the quality of a great soul to scorn great things and to prefer that which is ordinary rather than that which is too great. For the one condition is useful and life-giving; but the other does harm just because it is excessive. Similarly, too rich a soil makes the grain fall flat, branches break down under too heavy a load, excessive productiveness does not bring fruit to ripeness. This is the case with the soul also; for it is ruined by uncontrolled prosperity, which is used not only to the detriment of others, but also to the detriment of itself. **5.** What enemy was ever so insolent to any opponent as are their pleasures to certain men? The only excuse that we can allow for the incontinence and mad lust of these men is the fact that they suffer the evils which they have inflicted upon others. And they are rightly harassed by this madness, because desire must have unbounded space for its excursions, if it transgresses nature's mean. For this has its bounds, but waywardness and the acts that spring from wilful lust are without boundaries. **6.** Utility measures our needs; but by what standard can you check the superfluous? It is for this reason that men sink themselves in pleasures, and they cannot do without them when once they have become accustomed to them, and for this reason they are most wretched, because they have reached such a pass that what was once superfluous to them has become indispensable. And so they are the slaves of their pleasures instead of enjoying them; they even love their own ills, – and that is the worst ill of all! Then it is that the height of unhappiness is reached, when men are not only attracted, but even pleased, by shameful things, and when there is no longer any room for a cure, now that those things which once were vices have become habits. Farewell.

XL. ON THE PROPER STYLE FOR A PHILOSOPHER'S DISCOURSE

1. I thank you for writing to me so often; for you are revealing your real self to me in the only way you can. I never receive a letter from you without being in your company forthwith. If the pictures of our absent friends are pleasing to us, though they only refresh the memory and lighten our longing by a solace that is unreal and unsubstantial, how much more pleasant is a letter, which brings us real traces, real evidences, of an absent friend! For that which is sweetest when we meet face to face is afforded by the impress of a friend's hand upon his letter, – recognition.

2. You write me that you heard a lecture by the philosopher Serapio, when he landed at your present place of residence. "He is wont," you say, "to wrench up his words with a mighty rush, and he does not let them flow forth one by one, but makes them crowd and dash upon each other. For the words come in such quantity that a single voice is inadequate to utter them." I do not approve of this in a philosopher; his speech, like his life, should be composed; and nothing that rushes headlong and is hurried is well ordered. That is why, in Homer, the rapid style, which sweeps down without a break like a snow-squall, is assigned to the younger speaker; from the old man eloquence flows gently, sweeter than honey.

3. Therefore, mark my words; that forceful manner of speech, rapid and copious, is more suited to a mountebank than to a man who is discussing and teaching an important and serious subject. But I object just as strongly that he should drip out his words as that he should go at top speed; he should neither keep the ear on the stretch, nor deafen it. For that poverty-stricken and thin-spun style also makes the audience less attentive because they are weary of its stammering slowness; nevertheless, the word which has been long awaited sinks in more easily than the word which flits past us on the wing. Finally, people speak of "handing down" precepts to their pupils; but one is not "handing down" that which eludes the grasp. **4.** Besides, speech that deals with the truth should be unadorned and plain. This popular style has nothing to do with the truth; its aim is to impress the common herd, to ravish heedless ears by its speed; it does not offer itself for discussion, but snatches itself away from discussion. But how can that speech govern others which cannot itself be governed? May I not also remark that all speech which is employed for the purpose of healing our minds, ought to sink into us? Remedies do not avail unless they remain in the system.

5. Besides, this sort of speech contains a great deal of sheer emptiness; it has more sound than power. My terrors should be quieted, my irritations soothed, my illusions shaken off, my indulgences checked, my greed rebuked. And which of these cures can be brought about in a hurry? What physician can heal his patient on a flying visit? May I add that such a jargon of confused and ill-chosen words cannot afford pleasure, either? **6.** No; but just as you are well satisfied, in the majority of cases, to have seen through tricks which you did not think could possibly be done, so in the case of these word-gymnasts to have heard them once is amply sufficient. For what can a man desire to learn or to imitate in them? What is he to think of their souls, when their speech is sent into the charge in utter disorder, and cannot be kept in hand? **7.** Just as, when you run down hill, you cannot stop at the point where you had decided to stop, but your steps are carried along by the momentum of your body and are borne beyond the place where you wished to halt; so this speed of speech has no control over itself, nor is it seemly for philosophy; since philosophy should carefully place her words, not fling them out, and should proceed step by step.

8. "What then?" you say; "should not philosophy sometimes take a loftier tone?" Of course she should; but dignity of character should be preserved, and this is stripped away by such violent and excessive force. Let philosophy possess great forces, but kept well under control; let her stream flow unceasingly, but never become a torrent. And I should hardly allow even to an orator a rapidity of speech like this, which cannot be called back, which goes lawlessly ahead; for how could it be followed by jurors, who are often inexperienced and untrained? Even when the orator is carried away by his desire to show off his powers, or by uncontrollable emotion, even then he should not quicken his pace and heap up words to an extent greater than the ear can endure.

9. You will be acting rightly, therefore, if you do not regard those men who seek how much they may say, rather than how they shall say it, and if for yourself you choose, provided a choice must be made, to speak as Publius Vinicius the stammerer does. When Asellius was asked how Vinicius spoke, he replied: "Gradually"! (It was a remark of Geminus Varius, by the way: "I don't see how you can call that man 'eloquent'; why, he can't get out three words together.") Why, then, should you not choose to speak as Vinicius does? **10.** Though of course some wag may cross your path, like the person who said, when Vinicius was dragging out his words one by one, as if he were dictating and not speaking. "Say, haven't you anything to say?" And yet that were the better choice, for the rapidity of Quintus Haterius, the most famous orator of his age, is, in my opinion, to be avoided by a man of sense. Haterius never hesitated, never paused; he made only one start, and only one stop.

11. However, I suppose that certain styles of speech are more or less suitable to nations also; in a Greek you can put up with the unrestrained style, but we Romans, even when writing, have become accustomed to separate our words. And our compatriot Cicero, with whom Roman oratory sprang into prominence, was also a slow pacer. The Roman language is more inclined to take stock of itself, to weigh, and to offer something worth weighing. **12.** Fabianius, a man noteworthy because of his life, his knowledge, and, less important than either of these, his eloquence also, used to discuss a subject with dispatch rather than with haste; hence you might call it ease rather than speed. I approve this quality in the wise man; but I do not demand it; only let his speech proceed unhampered, though I prefer that it should be deliberately uttered rather than spouted.

13. However, I have this further reason for frightening you away from the latter malady, namely, that you could only be successful in practising this style by losing your sense of modesty; you would have to rub all shame from your countenance, and refuse to hear yourself speak. For that heedless flow will carry with it many expressions which you would wish to criticize. **14.** And, I repeat, you could not attain it and at the same time preserve your sense of shame. Moreover, you would need to practise every day, and transfer your attention from subject matter to words. But words, even if they came to you readily and flowed without any exertion on your part, yet would have to be kept under control. For just as a less ostentatious gait becomes a philosopher, so does a restrained style of speech, far removed from boldness. Therefore, the ultimate kernel of my remarks is this: I bid you be slow of speech. Farewell

XLI. ON THE GOD WITHIN US

1. You are doing an excellent thing, one which will be wholesome for you, if, as you write me, you are persisting in your effort to attain sound understanding; it is foolish to pray for this when you can acquire it from yourself. We do not need to uplift our hands towards heaven, or to beg the keeper of a temple to let us approach his idol's ear, as if in this way our prayers were more likely to be heard. God is near you, he is with you, he is within you. **2.** This is what I mean, Lucilius: a holy spirit indwells within us, one who marks our good and bad deeds, and is our guardian. As we treat this spirit, so are we treated by it. Indeed, no man can be good without the help of God. Can one rise superior to fortune unless God helps him to rise? He it is that gives noble and upright counsel. In each good man

> A god doth dwell, but what god know we not.

3. If ever you have come upon a grove that is full of ancient trees which have grown to an unusual height, shutting out a view of the sky by a veil of pleached and intertwining branches, then the loftiness of the forest, the seclusion of the spot, and your marvel at the thick unbroken shade in the midst of the open spaces, will prove to you the presence of deity. Or if a cave, made by the deep crumbling of the rocks, holds up a mountain on its arch, a place not built with hands but hollowed out into such spaciousness by natural causes, your soul will be deeply moved by a certain intimation of the existence of God. We worship the sources of mighty rivers; we erect altars at places where great streams burst suddenly from hidden sources; we adore springs of hot water as divine, and consecrate certain pools because of their dark waters or their immeasurable depth. **4.** If you see a man who is unterrified in the midst of dangers, untouched by desires, happy in adversity, peaceful amid the storm, who looks down upon men from a higher plane, and views the gods on a footing of equality, will not a feeling of reverence for him steal over you, will you not say: "This quality is too great and too lofty to be regarded as resembling this petty body in which it dwells? A divine power has descended upon that man." **5.** When a soul rises superior to other souls, when it is under control, when it passes through every experience as if it were of small account, when it smiles at our fears and at our prayers, it is stirred by a force from heaven. A thing like this cannot stand upright unless it be propped by the divine. Therefore, a greater part of it abides in that place from whence it came down to earth. Just as the rays of the sun do indeed touch the earth, but still abide at the source from which they are sent; even so the great and hallowed soul, which has come down in order that we may have a nearer knowledge of divinity, does indeed associate with us, but still cleaves to its origin; on that source it depends, thither it turns its gaze and strives to go, and it concerns itself with our doings only as a being superior to ourselves.

6. What, then, is such a soul? One which is resplendent with no external good, but only with its own. For what is more foolish than to praise in a man the qualities which come from without? And what is more insane than to marvel at characteristics which may at the next instant be passed on to someone else? A golden bit does not make a better horse. The lion with gilded mane, in process of being trained and forced by weariness to endure the decoration, is sent into the arena in quite a different way from the wild lion whose spirit is unbroken; the latter, indeed, bold in his attack, as nature wished him to be, impressive because of his wild appearance, – and it is his glory that none can look upon him without fear, – is favoured in preference to the other lion, that languid and gilded brute.

7. No man ought to glory except in that which is his own. We praise a vine if it makes the shoots teem with increase, if by its weight it bends to the ground the very poles which hold its fruit; would any man prefer to this vine one from which golden grapes and golden leaves hang down? In a vine the virtue peculiarly its own is fertility; in man also we should praise that which is his own. Suppose that he has a retinue of comely slaves and a beautiful house, that his farm is large and large his income; none of these things is in the man himself; they are all on the outside. **8.** Praise the quality in him which cannot be given or snatched away, that which is the peculiar property of the man. Do you ask what this is? It is soul, and reason brought to perfection in the soul. For man is a reasoning animal. Therefore, man's highest good is attained, if he has fulfilled the good for which nature designed him at birth. **9.** And what is it which this reason demands of him? The easiest thing in the world,

– to live in accordance with his own nature. But this is turned into a hard task by the general madness of mankind; we push one another into vice. And how can a man be recalled to salvation, when he has none to restrain him, and all mankind to urge him on? Farewell.

XLII. ON VALUES

1. Has that friend of yours already made you believe that he is a good man? And yet it is impossible in so short a time for one either to become good or be known as such. Do you know what kind of man I now mean when I speak of "a good man"? I mean one of the second grade, like your friend. For one of the first class perhaps springs into existence, like the phoenix, only once in five hundred years. And it is not surprising, either, that greatness develops only at long intervals; Fortune often brings into being commonplace powers, which are born to please the mob; but she holds up for our approval that which is extraordinary by the very fact that she makes it rare.

2. This man, however, of whom you spoke, is still far from the state which he professes to have reached. And if he knew what it meant to be "a good man," he would not yet believe himself such; perhaps he would even despair of his ability to become good. "But," you say, "he thinks ill of evil men." Well, so do evil men themselves; and there is no worse penalty for vice than the fact that it is dissatisfied with itself and all its fellows. **3.** "But he hates those who make an ungoverned use of great power suddenly acquired." I retort that he will do the same thing as soon as he acquires the same powers. In the case of many men, their vices, being powerless, escape notice; although, as soon as the persons in question have become satisfied with their own strength, the vices will be no less daring than those which prosperity has already disclosed. **4.** These men simply lack the means whereby they may unfold their wickedness. Similarly, one can handle even a poisonous snake while it is stiff with cold; the poison is not lacking; it is merely numbed into inaction. In the case of many men, their cruelty, ambition, and indulgence only lack the favour of Fortune to make them dare crimes that would match the worst. That their wishes are the same you will in a moment discover, in this way: give them the power equal to their wishes.

5. Do you remember how, when you declared that a certain person was under your influence, I pronounced him fickle and a bird of passage, and said that you held him not by the foot but merely by a wing? Was I mistaken? You grasped him only by a feather; he left it in your hands and escaped. You know what an exhibition he afterwards made of himself before you, how many of the things he attempted were to recoil upon his own head. He did not see that in endangering others he was tottering to his own downfall. He did not reflect how burdensome were the objects which he was bent upon attaining, even if they were not superfluous.

6. Therefore, with regard to the objects which we pursue, and for which we strive with great effort, we should note this truth; either there is nothing desirable in them, or the undesirable is preponderant. Some objects are superfluous; others are not worth the price we pay for them. But we do not see this clearly, and we regard things as free gifts when they really cost us very dear. **7.** Our stupidity may be clearly proved by the fact that we hold that "buying" refers only to the objects for which we pay cash, and we regard as free gifts the things for which we spend our very selves. These we should refuse to buy, if we were compelled to give in payment for them our houses or some attractive and profitable estate; but we are eager to attain them at the cost of anxiety, of danger, and of lost honour, personal freedom, and time; so true it is that each man regards nothing as cheaper than himself.

8. Let us therefore act, in all our plans and conduct, just as we are accustomed to act whenever we approach a huckster who has certain wares for sale; let us see how much we must pay for that which we crave. Very often the things that cost nothing cost us the most heavily; I can show you many objects the quest and acquisition of which have wrested freedom from our hands. We should belong to ourselves, if only these things did not belong to us.

9. I would therefore have you reflect thus, not only when it is a question of gain, but also when it is a question of loss. "This object is bound to perish." Yes, it was a mere extra; you will live without it just as easily as you have lived before. If you have possessed it for a long time, you lose it after you have had your fill of it; if you have not possessed it long, then you lose it before you have become wedded to it. "You will have less money." Yes, and less trouble. **10.** "Less influence." Yes, and less envy. Look about you and note the things that drive us mad, which we lose with a flood of tears; you will perceive that it is not the loss that troubles us with reference to these things, but a notion of loss. No one feels that they have been lost, but his mind tells him that it has been so. He that owns himself has lost nothing. But how few men are blessed with ownership of self! Farewell.

XLIII. ON THE RELATIVITY OF FAME

1. Do you ask how the news reached me, and who informed me, that you were entertaining this idea, of which you had said nothing to a single soul? It was that most knowing of persons, – gossip. "What," you say, "am I such a great personage that I can stir up gossip?" Now there is no reason why you should measure yourself according to this part of the world; have regard only to the place where you are dwelling. **2.** Any point which rises above adjacent points is great, at the spot where it rises. For greatness is not absolute; comparison increases it or lessens it. A ship which looms large in the river seems tiny when on the ocean. A rudder which is large for one vessel, is small for another.

3. So you in your province are really of importance, though you scorn yourself. Men are asking what you do, how you dine, and how you sleep, and they find out, too; hence there is all the more reason for your living circumspectly. Do not, however, deem yourself truly happy until you find that you can live before men's eyes, until your walls protect but do not hide you; although we are apt to believe that these walls surround us, not to enable us to live more safely, but that we may sin more secretly. 4. I shall mention a fact by which you may weigh the worth of a man's character: you will scarcely find anyone who can live with his door wide open. It is our conscience, not our pride, that has put doorkeepers at our doors; we live in such a fashion that being suddenly disclosed to view is equivalent to being caught in the act. What profits it, however, to hide ourselves away, and to avoid the eyes and ears of men? 5. A good conscience welcomes the crowd, but a bad conscience, even in solitude, is disturbed and troubled. If your deeds are honourable, let everybody know them; if base, what matters it that no one knows them, as long as you yourself know them? How wretched you are if you despise such a witness! Farewell.

XLIV. ON PHILOSOPHY AND PEDIGREES

1. You are again insisting to me that you are a nobody, and saying that nature in the first place, and fortune in the second, have treated you too scurvily, and this in spite of the fact that you have it in your power to separate yourself from the crowd and rise to the highest human happiness! If there is any good in philosophy, it is this, – that it never looks into pedigrees. All men, if traced back to their original source, spring from the gods. 2. You are a Roman knight, and your persistent work promoted you to this class; yet surely there are many to whom the fourteen rows are barred; the senate-chamber is not open to all; the army, too, is scrupulous in choosing those whom it admits to toil and danger. But a noble mind is free to all men; according to this test, we may all gain distinction. Philosophy neither rejects nor selects anyone; its light shines for all. 3. Socrates was no aristocrat. Cleanthes worked at a well and served as a hired man watering a garden. Philosophy did not find Plato already a nobleman; it made him one. Why then should you despair of becoming able to rank with men like these? They are all your ancestors, if you conduct yourself in a manner worthy of them; and you will do so if you convince yourself at the outset that no man outdoes you in real nobility. 4. We have all had the same number of forefathers; there is no man whose first beginning does not transcend memory. Plato says: "Every king springs from a race of slaves, and every slave has had kings among his ancestors." The flight of time, with its vicissitudes, has jumbled all such things together, and Fortune has turned them upside down. 5. Then who is well-born? He who is by nature well fitted for virtue. That is the one point to be considered; otherwise, if you hark back to antiquity, every one traces back to a date before which there is nothing. From the earliest beginnings of the universe to the present time, we have been led forward out of origins that were alternately illustrious and ignoble. A hall full of smoke-begrimed busts does not make the nobleman. No past life has been lived to lend us glory, and that which has existed before us is not ours; the soul alone renders us noble, and it may rise superior to Fortune out of any earlier condition, no matter what that condition has been.

6. Suppose, then, that you were not that Roman knight, but a freedman, you might nevertheless by your own efforts come to be the only free man amid a throng of gentlemen. "How?" you ask. Simply by distinguishing between good and bad things without patterning your opinion from the populace. You should look, not to the source from which these things come, but to the goal towards which they tend. If there is anything that can make life happy, it is good on its own merits; for it cannot degenerate into evil. 7. Where, then, lies the mistake, since all men crave the happy life? It is that they regard the means for producing happiness as happiness itself, and, while seeking happiness, they are really fleeing from it. For although the sum and substance of the happy life is unalloyed freedom from care, and though the secret of such freedom is unshaken confidence, yet men gather together that which causes worry, and, while travelling life's treacherous road, not only have burdens to bear, but even draw burdens to themselves; hence they recede farther and farther from the achievement of that which they seek, and the more effort they expend, the more they hinder themselves and are set back. This is what happens when you hurry through a maze; the faster you go, the worse you are entangled. Farewell.

XLV. ON SOPHISTICAL ARGUMENTATION

1. You complain that in your part of the world there is a scant supply of books. But it is quality, rather than quantity, that matters; a limited list of reading benefits; a varied assortment serves only for delight. He who would arrive at the appointed end must follow a single road and not wander through many ways. What you suggest is not travelling; it is mere tramping.

2. "But," you say, "I should rather have you give me advice than books." Still, I am ready to send you all the books I have, to ransack the whole storehouse. If it were possible, I should join you there myself; and were it not for the hope that you will soon complete your term of office, I should have imposed upon myself this old man's journey; no Scylla or Charybdis or their storied straits could have frightened me away. I should not only have crossed over, but should have been willing to swim over those waters, provided that I could greet you and judge in your presence how much you had grown in spirit.

3. Your desire, however, that I should dispatch to you my own writings does not make me think myself learned, any more than a request for my picture would flatter my beauty. I know that it is due to your charity rather than to your judgment. And even if it is the result of judgment, it was charity that forced the judgment upon you. 4. But whatever the quality of my works may be, read them as if I were still seeking, and were not aware of, the truth, and were seeking it obstinately, too. For I have sold myself to no man; I bear the name of no master. I give much credit to the judgment of great men; but I claim something also for my own. For these men, too, have left to us, not positive discoveries, but problems whose solution is still to be sought. They might perhaps have discovered the essentials, had they not sought the

superfluous also. **5.** They lost much time in quibbling about words and in sophistical argumentation; all that sort of thing exercises the wit to no purpose. We tie knots and bind up words in double meanings, and then try to untie them.

Have we leisure enough for this? Do we already know how to live, or die? We should rather proceed with our whole souls towards the point where it is our duty to take heed lest things, as well as words, deceive us. **6.** Why, pray, do you discriminate between similar words, when nobody is ever deceived by them except during the discussion? It is things that lead us astray: it is between things that you must discriminate. We embrace evil instead of good; we pray for something opposite to that which we have prayed for in the past. Our prayers clash with our prayers, our plans with our plans. **7.** How closely flattery resembles friendship! It not only apes friendship, but outdoes it, passing it in the race; with wide-open and indulgent ears it is welcomed and sinks to the depths of the heart, and it is pleasing precisely wherein it does harm. Show me how I may be able to see through this resemblance! An enemy comes to me full of compliments, in the guise of a friend. Vices creep into our hearts under the name of virtues, rashness lurks beneath the appellation of bravery, moderation is called sluggishness, and the coward is regarded as prudent; there is great danger if we go astray in these matters. So stamp them with special labels.

8. Then, too, the man who is asked whether he has horns on his head is not such a fool as to feel for them on his forehead, nor again so silly or dense that you can persuade him by means of argumentation, no matter how subtle, that he does not know the facts. Such quibbles are just as harmlessly deceptive as the juggler's cup and dice, in which it is the very trickery that pleases me. But show me how the trick is done, and I have lost my interest therein. And I hold the same opinion about these tricky word-plays; for by what other name can one call such sophistries? Not to know them does no harm, and mastering them does no good. **9.** At any rate, if you wish to sift doubtful meanings of this kind, teach us that the happy man is not he whom the crowd deems happy, namely, he into whose coffers mighty sums have flowed, but he whose possessions are all in his soul, who is upright and exalted, who spurns inconstancy, who sees no man with whom he wishes to change places, who rates men only at their value as men, who takes Nature for his teacher, conforming to her laws and living as she commands, whom no violence can deprive of his possessions, who turns evil into good, is unerring in judgment, unshaken, unafraid, who may be moved by force but never moved to distraction, whom Fortune when she hurls at him with all her might the deadliest missile in her armoury, may graze, though rarely, but never wound. For Fortune's other missiles, with which she vanquishes mankind in general, rebound from such a one, like hail which rattles on the roof with no harm to the dweller therein, and then melts away.

10. Why do you bore me with that which you yourself call the "liar fallacy," about which so many books have been written? Come now, suppose that my whole life is a lie; prove that to be wrong and, if you are sharp enough, bring that back to the truth.

At present it holds things to be essential of which the greater part is superfluous. And even that which is not superfluous is of no significance in respect to its power of making one fortunate and blest. For if a thing be necessary, it does not follow that it is a good. Else we degrade the meaning of "good," if we apply that name to bread and barley-porridge and other commodities without which we cannot live. **11.** The good must in every case be necessary; but that which is necessary is not in every case a good, since certain very paltry things are indeed necessary. No one is to such an extent ignorant of the noble meaning of the word "good," as to debase it to the level of these humdrum utilities.

12. What, then? Shall you not rather transfer your efforts to making it clear to all men that the search for the superfluous means a great outlay of time, and that many have gone through life merely accumulating the instruments of life? Consider individuals, survey men in general; there is none whose life does not look forward to the morrow. **13.** "What harm is there in this," you ask? Infinite harm; for such persons do not live, but are preparing to live. They postpone everything. Even if we paid strict attention, life would soon get ahead of us; but as we are now, life finds us lingering and passes us by as if it belonged to another, and though it ends on the final day, it perishes every day.

But I must not exceed the bounds of a letter, which ought not to fill the reader's left hand. So I shall postpone to another day our case against the hair-splitters, those over-subtle fellows who make argumentation supreme instead of subordinate. Farewell.

XLVI. ON A NEW BOOK BY LUCILIUS

1. I received the book of yours which you promised me. I opened it hastily with the idea of glancing over it at leisure; for I meant only to taste the volume. But by its own charm the book coaxed me into traversing it more at length. You may understand from this fact how eloquent it was; for it seemed to be written in the smooth style, and yet did not resemble your handiwork or mine, but at first sight might have been ascribed to Titus Livius or to Epicurus. Moreover, I was so impressed and carried along by its charm that I finished it without any postponement. The sunlight called to me, hunger warned, and clouds were lowering; but I absorbed the book from beginning to end.

2. I was not merely pleased; I rejoiced. So full of wit and spirit it was! I should have added "force," had the book contained moments of repose, or had it risen to energy only at intervals. But I found that there was no burst of force, but an even flow, a style that was vigorous and chaste. Nevertheless I noticed from time to time your sweetness, and here and there that mildness of yours. Your style is lofty and noble; I want you to keep to this manner and this direction. Your subject also contributed something; for this reason you should choose productive topics, which will lay hold of the mind and arouse it.

3. I shall discuss the book more fully after a second perusal; meantime, my judgment is somewhat unsettled, just as if I had heard it read aloud, and had not read it myself. You must allow me to examine it also. You need not be afraid; you shall hear the truth. Lucky fellow, to offer a man no opportunity to tell you lies at such long range! Unless perhaps, even now, when excuses for lying are taken away, custom serves as an excuse for our telling each other lies! Farewell.

XLVII. ON MASTER AND SLAVE

1. I am glad to learn, through those who come from you, that you live on friendly terms with your slaves. This befits a sensible and well-educated man like yourself. "They are slaves," people declare. Nay, rather they are men. "Slaves!" No, comrades. "Slaves!" No, they are unpretentious friends. "Slaves!" No, they are our fellow-slaves, if one reflects that Fortune has equal rights over slaves and free men alike.

2. That is why I smile at those who think it degrading for a man to dine with his slave. But why should they think it degrading? It is only because purse-proud etiquette surrounds a householder at his dinner with a mob of standing slaves. The master eats more than he can hold, and with monstrous greed loads his belly until it is stretched and at length ceases to do the work of a belly; so that he is at greater pains to discharge all the food than he was to stuff it down. **3.** All this time the poor slaves may not move their lips, even to speak. The slightest murmur is repressed by the rod; even a chance sound, – a cough, a sneeze, or a hiccup, – is visited with the lash. There is a grievous penalty for the slightest breach of silence. All night long they must stand about, hungry and dumb.

4. The result of it all is that these slaves, who may not talk in their master's presence, talk about their master. But the slaves of former days, who were permitted to converse not only in their master's presence, but actually with him, whose mouths were not stitched up tight, were ready to bare their necks for their master, to bring upon their own heads any danger that threatened him; they spoke at the feast, but kept silence during torture. **5.** Finally, the saying, in allusion to this same high-handed treatment, becomes current: "As many enemies as you have slaves." They are not enemies when we acquire them; we make them enemies.

I shall pass over other cruel and inhuman conduct towards them; for we maltreat them, not as if they were men, but as if they were beasts of burden. When we recline at a banquet, one slave mops up the disgorged food, another crouches beneath the table and gathers up the left-overs of the tipsy guests. **6.** Another carves the priceless game birds; with unerring strokes and skilled hand he cuts choice morsels along the breast or the rump. Hapless fellow, to live only for the purpose of cutting fat capons correctly – unless, indeed, the other man is still more unhappy than he, who teaches this art for pleasure's sake, rather than he who learns it because he must. **7.** Another, who serves the wine, must dress like a woman and wrestle with his advancing years; he cannot get away from his boyhood; he is dragged back to it; and though he has already acquired a soldier's figure, he is kept beardless by having his hair smoothed away or plucked out by the roots, and he must remain awake throughout the night, dividing his time between his master's drunkenness and his lust; in the chamber he must be a man, at the feast a boy. **8.** Another, whose duty it is to put a valuation on the guests, must stick to his task, poor fellow, and watch to see whose flattery and whose immodesty, whether of appetite or of language, is to get them an invitation for to-morrow. Think also of the poor purveyors of food, who note their masters' tastes with delicate skill, who know what special flavours will sharpen their appetite, what will please their eyes, what new combinations will rouse their cloyed stomachs, what food will excite their loathing through sheer satiety, and what will stir them to hunger on that particular day. With slaves like these the master cannot bear to dine; he would think it beneath his dignity to associate with his slave at the same table! Heaven forfend!

But how many masters is he creating in these very men! **9.** I have seen standing in the line, before the door of Callistus, the former master, of Callistus; I have seen the master himself shut out while others were welcomed, – the master who once fastened the "For Sale" ticket on Callistus and put him in the market along with the good-for-nothing slaves. But he has been paid off by that slave who was shuffled into the first lot of those on whom the crier practises his lungs; the slave, too, in his turn has cut his name from the list and in his turn has adjudged him unfit to enter his house. The master sold Callistus, but how much has Callistus made his master pay for!

10. Kindly remember that he whom you call your slave sprang from the same stock, is smiled upon by the same skies, and on equal terms with yourself breathes, lives, and dies. It is just as possible for you to see in him a free-born man as for him to see in you a slave. As a result of the massacres in Marius's day, many a man of distinguished birth, who was taking the first steps toward senatorial rank by service in the army, was humbled by fortune, one becoming a shepherd, another a caretaker of a country cottage. Despise, then, if you dare, those to whose estate you may at any time descend, even when you are despising them.

11. I do not wish to involve myself in too large a question, and to discuss the treatment of slaves, towards whom we Romans are excessively haughty, cruel, and insulting. But this is the kernel of my advice: Treat your inferiors as you would be treated by your betters. And as often as you reflect how much power you have over a slave, remember that your master has just as much power over you. **12.** "But I have no master," you say. You are still young; perhaps you will have one. Do you not know at what age Hecuba entered captivity, or Croesus, or the mother of Darius, or Plato, or Diogenes?

13. Associate with your slave on kindly, even on affable, terms; let him talk with you, plan with you, live with you. I know that at this point all the exquisites will cry out against me in a body; they will say: "There is nothing more debasing, more disgraceful, than this." But these are the very persons whom I sometimes surprise kissing the hands of other men's slaves. **14.** Do you not see even this, how our ancestors removed from masters everything invidious, and from slaves everything insulting? They called the master "father of the household," and the slaves "members of the household," a custom which still holds in the mime. They established a holiday on which masters and slaves should eat together, – not as the only day for this custom, but as obligatory on that day in any case. They allowed the slaves to attain honours in the household and to pronounce judgment; they held that a household was a miniature commonwealth.

15. "Do you mean to say," comes the retort, "that I must seat all my slaves at my own table?" No, not any more than that you should invite all free men to it. You are mistaken if you think that I would bar from my table certain slaves whose duties are more humble, as, for example, yonder muleteer or yonder herdsman; I propose to value them according to their character, and not according to their duties. Each man acquires his character for himself, but accident assigns his duties. Invite some to your table because they deserve the honor, and others that they may come to deserve it. For if there is any slavish quality in them as the result of their low associations, it will be shaken off by intercourse with men of gentler breeding. **16.** You need not, my dear Lucilius, hunt for friends only in the forum or in the Senate-house; if you are careful and attentive, you will find them at home also. Good material often stands idle for want of an artist; make the experiment, and you will find it so. As he is a fool who, when purchasing a horse, does not consider the animal's points, but merely his saddle and bridle; so he is doubly a fool who values a man from his clothes or from his rank, which indeed is only a robe that clothes us.

17. "He is a slave." His soul, however, may be that of a freeman. "He is a slave." But shall that stand in his way? Show me a man who is not a slave; one is a slave to lust, another to greed, another to ambition, and all men are slaves to fear. I will name you an ex-consul who is slave to an old hag, a millionaire who is slave to a serving-maid; I will show you youths of the noblest birth in serfdom to pantomime players! No servitude is more disgraceful than that which is self-imposed.

You should therefore not be deterred by these finicky persons from showing yourself to your slaves as an affable person and not proudly superior to them; they ought to respect you rather than fear you. **18.** Some may maintain that I am now offering the liberty-cap to slaves in general and toppling down lords from their high estate, because I bid slaves respect their masters instead of fearing them. They say: "This is what he plainly means: slaves are to pay respect as if they were clients or early-morning callers!" Anyone who holds this opinion forgets that what is enough for a god cannot be too little for a master. Respect means love, and love and fear cannot be mingled. **19.** So I hold that you are entirely right in not wishing to be feared by your slaves, and in lashing them merely with the tongue; only dumb animals need the thong.

That which annoys us does not necessarily injure us; but we are driven into wild rage by our luxurious lives, so that whatever does not answer our whims arouses our anger. **20.** We don the temper of kings. For they, too, forgetful alike of their own strength and of other men's weakness, grow white-hot with rage, as if they had received an injury, when they are entirely protected from danger of such injury by their exalted station. They are not unaware that this is true, but by finding fault they seize upon opportunities to do harm; they insist that they have received injuries, in order that they may inflict them.

21. I do not wish to delay you longer; for you need no exhortation. This, among other things, is a mark of good character: it forms its own judgments and abides by them; but badness is fickle and frequently changing, not for the better, but for something different. Farewell.

XLVIII. ON QUIBBLING AS UNWORTHY OF THE PHILOSOPHER

1. In answer to the letter which you wrote me while travelling, – a letter as long as the journey itself, – I shall reply later. I ought to go into retirement, and consider what sort of advice I should give you. For you yourself, who consult me, also reflected for a long time whether to do so; how much more, then, should I myself reflect, since more deliberation is necessary in settling than in propounding a problem! And this is particularly true when one thing is advantageous to you and another to me. Am I speaking again in the guise of an Epicurean? **2.** But the fact is, the same thing is advantageous to me which is advantageous to you; for I am not your friend unless whatever is at issue concerning you is my concern also. Friendship produces between us a partnership in all our interests. There is no such thing as good or bad fortune for the individual; we live in common. And no one can live happily who has regard to himself alone and transforms everything into a question of his own utility; you must live for your neighbour, if you would live for yourself. **3.** This fellowship, maintained with scrupulous care, which makes us mingle as men with our fellow-men and holds that the human race have certain rights in common, is also of great help in cherishing the more intimate fellowship which is based on friendship, concerning which I began to speak above. For he that has much in common with a fellow-man will have all things in common with a friend.

4. And on this point, my excellent Lucilius, I should like to have those subtle dialecticians of yours advise me how I ought to help a friend, or how a fellow man, rather than tell me in how many ways the word "friend" is used, and how many meanings the word "man" possesses. Lo, Wisdom and Folly are taking opposite sides. Which shall I join? Which party would you have me follow? On that side, "man" is the equivalent of "friend"; on the other side, "friend" is not the equivalent of "man." The one wants a friend for his own advantage; the other wants to make himself an advantage to his friend. What *you* have to offer me is nothing but distortion of words and splitting of syllables. **5.** It is clear that unless I can devise some very tricky premises and by false deductions tack on to them a fallacy which springs from the truth, I shall not be able to distinguish between what is desirable and what is to be avoided! I am ashamed! Old men as we are, dealing with a problem so serious, we make play of it!

6. "'Mouse' is a syllable. Now a mouse eats its cheese; therefore, a syllable eats cheese." Suppose now that I cannot solve this problem; see what peril hangs over my head as a result of such ignorance! What a scrape I shall be in! Without doubt I must beware, or some day I shall be catching syllables in a mousetrap, or, if I grow careless, a book may devour my cheese! Unless, perhaps, the following syllogism is shrewder still: "'Mouse' is a syllable. Now a syllable does not eat cheese. Therefore a mouse does not eat cheese." **7.** What childish nonsense! Do we knit our brows over this sort of problem? Do we let our beards grow long for this reason? Is this the matter which we teach with sour and pale faces?

Would you really know what philosophy offers to humanity? Philosophy offers counsel. Death calls away one man, and poverty chafes another; a third is worried either by his neighbour's wealth or by his own. So-and-so is afraid of bad luck; another desires to get away from his own good fortune. Some are ill-treated by men, others by the gods. **8.** Why, then, do you frame for me such games as these? It is no occasion for jest; you are retained as counsel for unhappy mankind. You have promised to help those in peril by sea, those in captivity, the sick and the needy, and those whose heads are under the poised axe. Whither are you straying? What are you doing?

This friend, in whose company you are jesting, is in fear. Help him, and take the noose from about his neck. Men are stretching out imploring hands to you on all sides; lives ruined and in danger of ruin are begging for some assistance; men's hopes, men's resources, depend upon you. They ask that you deliver them from all their restlessness, that you reveal to them, scattered and wandering as they are, the clear light of truth. **9.** Tell them what nature has made necessary, and what superfluous; tell them how simple are the laws that she has laid down, how pleasant and unimpeded life is for those who follow these laws, but how bitter and perplexed it is for those who have put their trust in opinion rather than in nature.

I should deem your games of logic to be of some avail in relieving men's burdens, if you could first show me what part of these burdens they will relieve. What among these games of yours banishes lust? Or controls it? Would that I could say that they were merely of no profit! They are positively harmful. I can make it perfectly clear to you whenever you wish, that a noble spirit when involved in such subtleties is impaired and weakened. **10.** I am ashamed to say what weapons they supply to men who are destined to go to war with fortune, and how poorly they equip them! Is this the path to the greatest good? Is philosophy to proceed by such claptrap and by quibbles which would be a disgrace and a reproach even for expounders of the law? For what else is it that you men are doing, when you deliberately ensnare the person to whom you are putting questions, than making it appear that the man has lost his case on a technical error? But just as the judge can reinstate those who have lost a suit in this way, so philosophy has reinstated these victims of quibbling to their former condition. **11.** Why do you men abandon your mighty promises, and, after having assured me in high-sounding language that you will permit the glitter of gold to dazzle my eyesight no more than the gleam of the sword, and that I shall, with mighty steadfastness, spurn both that which all men crave and that which all men fear, why do you descend to the ABC's of scholastic pedants? What is your answer?

Is this the path to heaven?

For that is exactly what philosophy promises to me, that I shall be made equal to God. For this I have been summoned, for this purpose have I come. Philosophy, keep your promise!

12. Therefore, my dear Lucilius, withdraw yourself as far as possible from these exceptions and objections of so-called philosophers. Frankness, and simplicity beseem true goodness. Even if there were many years left to you, you would have had to spend them frugally in order to have enough for the necessary things; but as it is, when your time is so scant, what madness it is to learn superfluous things! Farewell.

XLIX. ON THE SHORTNESS OF LIFE

1. A man is indeed lazy and careless, my dear Lucilius, if he is reminded of a friend only by seeing some landscape which stirs the memory; and yet there are times when the old familiar haunts stir up a sense of loss that has been stored away in the soul, not bringing back dead memories, but rousing them from their dormant state, just as the sight of a lost friend's favourite slave, or his cloak, or his house, renews the mourner's grief, even though it has been softened by time.

Now, lo and behold, Campania, and especially Naples and your beloved Pompeii, struck me, when I viewed them, with a wonderfully fresh sense of longing for you. You stand in full view before my eyes. I am on the point of parting from you. I see you choking down your tears and resisting without success the emotions that well up at the very moment when you try to check them. I seem to have lost you but a moment ago. For what is not "but a moment ago" when one begins to use the memory? **2.** It was but a moment ago that I sat, as a lad, in the school of the philosopher Sotion, but a moment ago that I began to plead in the courts, but a moment ago that I lost the desire to plead, but a moment ago that I lost the ability. Infinitely swift is the flight of time, as those see more clearly who are looking backwards. For when we are intent on the present, we do not notice it, so gentle is the passage of time's headlong flight. **3.** Do you ask the reason for this? All past time is in the same place; it all presents the same aspect to us, it lies together. Everything slips into the same abyss. Besides, an event which in its entirety is of brief compass cannot contain long intervals. The time which we spend in living is but a point, nay, even less than a point. But this point of time, infinitesimal as it is, nature has mocked by making it seem outwardly of longer duration; she has taken one portion thereof and made it infancy, another childhood, another youth, another the gradual slope, so to speak, from youth to old age, and old age itself is still another. How many steps for how short a climb! **4.** It was but a moment ago that I saw you off on your journey; and yet this "moment ago" makes up a goodly share of our existence, which is so brief, we should reflect, that it will soon come to an end altogether. In other years time did not seem to me to go so swiftly; now, it seems fast beyond belief, perhaps, because I feel that the finish-line is moving closer to me, or it may be that I have begun to take heed and reckon up my losses.

5. For this reason I am all the more angry that some men claim the major portion of this time for superfluous things, – time which, no matter how carefully it is guarded, cannot suffice even for necessary things. Cicero declared that if the number of his days were doubled, he should not have time to read the lyric poets. And you may rate the dialecticians in the same class; but they are foolish in a more melancholy way. The lyric poets are avowedly frivolous; but the dialecticians believe that they are themselves engaged upon serious business. **6.** I do not deny that one must cast a glance at dialectic; but it ought to be a mere glance, a sort of greeting from the threshold, merely that one may not be deceived, or judge these pursuits to contain any hidden matters of great worth.

Why do you torment yourself and lose weight over some problem which it is more clever to have scorned than to solve? When a soldier is undisturbed and travelling at his ease, he can hunt for trifles along his way; but when the enemy is closing in on the rear, and a command is given to quicken the pace, necessity makes him throw away everything which he picked up in moments of peace and leisure. **7.** I have no time to investigate disputed inflections of words, or to try my cunning upon them.

> Behold the gathering clans, the fast-shut gates,
> And weapons whetted ready for the war.

I need a stout heart to hear without flinching this din of battle which sounds round about. **8.** And all would rightly think me mad if, when graybeards and women were heaping up rocks for the fortifications, when the armour-clad youths inside the gates were awaiting, or even demanding, the order for a sally, when the spears of the foemen were quivering in our gates and the very ground was rocking with mines and subterranean passages, – I say, they would rightly think me mad if I were to sit idle, putting such petty posers as this: "What you have not lost, you have. But you have not lost any horns. Therefore, you have horns," or other tricks constructed after the model of this piece of sheer silliness. **9.** And yet I may well seem in your eyes no less mad, if I spend my energies on that sort of thing; for even now I am in a state of siege. And yet, in the former case it would be merely a peril from the outside that threatened me, and a wall that sundered me from the foe;

as it is now, death-dealing perils are in my very presence. I have no time for such nonsense; a mighty undertaking is on my hands. What am I to do? Death is on my trail, and life is fleeting away; **10.** teach me something with which to face these troubles. Bring it to pass that I shall cease trying to escape from death, and that life may cease to escape from me. Give me courage to meet hardships; make me calm in the face of the unavoidable. Relax the straitened limits of the time which is allotted me. Show me that the good in life does not depend upon life's length, but upon the use we make of it; also, that it is possible, or rather usual, for a man who has lived long to have lived too little. Say to me when I lie down to sleep: "You may not wake again!" And when I have waked: "You may not go to sleep again!" Say to me when I go forth from my house: "You may not return!" And when I return: "You may never go forth again!" **11.** You are mistaken if you think that only on an ocean voyage there is a very slight space between life and death. No, the distance between is just as narrow everywhere. It is not everywhere that death shows himself so near at hand; yet everywhere he is as near at hand.

Rid me of these shadowy terrors; then you will more easily deliver to me the instruction for which I have prepared myself. At our birth nature made us teachable, and gave us reason, not perfect, but capable of being perfected. **12.** Discuss for me justice, duty, thrift, and that twofold purity, both the purity which abstains from another's person, and that which takes care of one's own self. If you will only refuse to lead me along by-paths, I shall more easily reach the goal at which I am aiming. For, as the tragic poet says:

> The language of truth is simple.

We should not, therefore, make that language intricate; since there is nothing less fitting for a soul of great endeavour than such crafty cleverness. Farewell.

L. ON OUR BLINDNESS AND ITS CURE

1. I received your letter many months after you had posted it; accordingly, I thought it useless to ask the carrier what you were busied with. He must have a particularly good memory if he can remember that! But I hope by this time you are living in such a way that I can be sure what it is you are busied with, no matter where you may be. For what else are you busied with except improving yourself every day, laying aside some error, and coming to understand that the faults which you attribute to circumstances are in yourself? We are indeed apt to ascribe certain faults to the place or to the time; but those faults will follow us, no matter how we change our place.

2. You know Harpaste, my wife's female clown; she has remained in my house, a burden incurred from a legacy. I particularly disapprove of these freaks; whenever I wish to enjoy the quips of a clown, I am not compelled to hunt far; I can laugh at myself. Now this clown suddenly became blind. The story sounds incredible, but I assure you that it is true: she does not know that she is blind. She keeps asking her attendant to change her quarters; she says that her apartments are too dark.

3. You can see clearly that that which makes us smile in the case of Harpaste happens to all the rest of us; nobody understands that he is himself greedy, or that he is covetous. Yet the blind ask for a guide, while we wander without one, saying: "I am not self-seeking; but one cannot live at Rome in any other way. I am not extravagant, but mere living in the city demands a great outlay. It is not my fault that I have a choleric disposition, or that I have not settled down to any definite scheme of life; it is due to my youth." **4.** Why do we deceive ourselves? The evil that afflicts us is not external, it is within us, situated in our very vitals; for that reason we attain soundness with all the more difficulty, because we do not know that we are diseased.

Suppose that we have begun the cure; when shall we throw off all these diseases, with all their virulence? At present, we do not even consult the physician, whose work would be easier if he were called in when the complaint was in its early stages. The tender and the inexperienced minds would follow his advice if he pointed out the right way. **5.** No man finds it difficult to return to nature, except the man who has deserted nature. We blush to receive instruction in sound sense; but, by Heaven, if we think it base to seek a teacher of this art, we should also abandon any hope that so great a good could be instilled into us by mere chance.

No, we must work. To tell the truth, even the work is not great, if only, as I said, we begin to mould and reconstruct our souls before they are hardened by sin. But I do not despair even of a hardened sinner. **6.** There is nothing that will not surrender to persistent treatment, to concentrated and careful attention; however much the timber may be bent, you can make it straight again. Heat unbends curved beams, and wood that grew naturally in another shape is fashioned artificially according to our needs. How much more easily does the soul permit itself to be shaped, pliable as it is and more yielding than any liquid! For what else is the soul than air in a certain state? And you see that air is more adaptable than any other matter, in proportion as it is rarer than any other.

7. There is nothing, Lucilius, to hinder you from entertaining good hopes about us, just because we are even now in the grip of evil, or because we have long been possessed thereby. There is no man to whom a good mind comes before an evil one. It is the evil mind that gets first hold on all of us. Learning virtue means unlearning vice. **8.** We should therefore proceed to the task of freeing ourselves from faults with all the more courage because, when once committed to us, the good is an everlasting possession; virtue is not unlearned. For opposites find difficulty in clinging where they do not belong, therefore they can be driven out and hustled away; but qualities that come to a place which is rightfully theirs abide faithfully. Virtue is according to nature; vice is opposed to it and hostile. **9.** But although virtues, when admitted, cannot depart and are easy to guard, yet the first steps in the approach to them are toilsome, because it is characteristic of a weak and diseased mind to fear that which is unfamiliar. The mind must, therefore, be forced to make a beginning; from then on, the medicine is not bitter; for just as soon as it is curing us it begins to give pleasure. One enjoys other cures only after health is restored, but a draught of philosophy is at the same moment wholesome and pleasant. Farewell.

LI. ON BAIAE AND MORALS

1. Every man does the best he can, my dear Lucilius! You over there have Etna, that lofty and most celebrated mountain of Sicily; (although I cannot make out why Messala, – or was it Valgius? for I have been reading in both, – has called it "unique," inasmuch as many regions belch forth fire, not merely the lofty ones where the phenomenon is more frequent, – presumably because fire rises to the greatest possible height, – but low-lying places also.) As for myself, I do the best I can; I have had to be satisfied with Baiae; and I left it the day after I reached it; for Baiae is a place to be avoided, because, though it has certain natural advantages, luxury has claimed it for her own exclusive resort. **2.** "What then," you say, "should any place be singled out as an object of aversion?" Not at all. But just as, to the wise and upright man, one style of clothing is more suitable than another, without his having an aversion for any particular colour, but because he thinks that some colours do not befit one who has adopted the simple life; so there are places also, which the wise man or he who is on the way toward wisdom will avoid as foreign to good morals. **3.** Therefore, if he is contemplating withdrawal from the world, he will not select Canopus (although Canopus does not keep any man from living simply), nor Baiae either; for both places have begun to be resorts of vice. At Canopus luxury pampers itself to the utmost degree; at Baiae it is even more lax, as if the place itself demanded a certain amount of licence.

4. We ought to select abodes which are wholesome not only for the body but also for the character. Just as I do not care to live in a place of torture, neither do I care to live in a cafe. To witness persons wandering drunk along the beach, the riotous revelling of sailing parties, the lakes a-din with choral song, and all the other ways in which luxury, when it is, so to speak, released from the restraints of law not merely sins, but blazons its sins abroad, – why must I witness all this? **5.** We ought to see to it that we flee to the greatest possible distance from provocations to vice. We should toughen our minds, and remove them far from the allurements of pleasure. A single winter relaxed Hannibal's fibre; his pampering in Campania took the vigour out of that hero who had triumphed over Alpine snows. He conquered with his weapons, but was conquered by his vices. **6.** We too have a war to wage, a type of warfare in which there is allowed no rest or furlough. To be conquered, in the first place, are pleasures, which, as you see, have carried off even the sternest characters. If a man has once understood how great is the task which he has entered upon, he will see that there must be no dainty or effeminate conduct. What have I to do with those hot baths or with the sweating-room where they shut in the dry steam which is to drain your strength? Perspiration should flow only after toil.

7. Suppose we do what Hannibal did, – check the course of events, give up the war, and give over our bodies to be coddled. Every one would rightly blame us for our untimely sloth, a thing fraught with peril even for the victor, to say nothing of one who is only on the way to victory. And we have even less right to do this than those followers of the Carthaginian flag; for our danger is greater than theirs if we slacken, and our toil is greater than theirs even if we press ahead. **8.** Fortune is fighting against me, and I shall not carry out her commands. I refuse to submit to the yoke; nay rather, I shake off the yoke that is upon me, – an act which demands even greater courage. The soul is not to be pampered; surrendering to pleasure means also surrendering to pain, surrendering to toil, surrendering to poverty. Both ambition and anger will wish to have the same rights over me as pleasure, and I shall be torn asunder, or rather pulled to pieces, amid all these conflicting passions. **9.** I have set freedom before my eyes; and I am striving for that reward. And what is freedom, you ask? It means not being a slave to any circumstance, to any constraint, to any chance; it means compelling Fortune to enter the lists on equal terms. And on the day when I know that I have the upper hand, her power will be naught. When I have death in my own control, shall I take orders from her?

10. Therefore, a man occupied with such reflections should choose an austere and pure dwelling-place. The spirit is weakened by surroundings that are too pleasant, and without a doubt one's place of residence can contribute towards impairing its vigour. Animals whose hoofs are hardened on rough ground can travel any road; but when they are fattened on soft marshy meadows their hoofs are soon worn out. The bravest soldier comes from rock-ribbed regions; but the town-bred and the home-bred are sluggish in action. The hand which turns from the plough to the sword never objects to toil; but your sleek and well-dressed dandy quails at the first cloud of dust. **11.** Being trained in a rugged country strengthens the character and fits it for great undertakings. It was more honourable in Scipio to spend his exile at Liternum, than at Baiae; his downfall did not need a setting so effeminate. Those also into whose hands the rising fortunes of Rome first transferred the wealth of the state, Gaius Marius, Gnaeus Pompey, and Caesar, did indeed build villas near Baiae; but they set them on the very tops of the mountains. This seemed more soldier-like, to look down from a lofty height upon lands spread far and wide below. Note the situation, position, and type of building which they chose; you will see that they were not country-places, – they were camps. **12.** Do you suppose that Cato would ever have dwelt in a pleasure-palace, that he might count the lewd women as they sailed past, the many kinds of barges painted in all sorts of colours, the roses which were wafted about the lake, or that he might listen to the nocturnal brawls of serenaders? Would he not have preferred to remain in the shelter of a trench thrown up by his own hands to serve for a single night? Would not anyone who is a man have his slumbers broken by a war-trumpet rather than by a chorus of serenaders?

13. But I have been haranguing against Baiae long enough; although I never could harangue often enough against vice. Vice, Lucilius, is what I wish you to proceed against, without limit and without end. For it has neither limit nor end. If any vice rend your heart, cast it away from you; and if you cannot be rid of it in any other way, pluck out your heart also. Above all, drive pleasures from your sight. Hate them beyond all other things, for they are like the bandits whom the Egyptians call "lovers," who embrace us only to garrotte us. Farewell.

LII. ON CHOOSING OUR TEACHERS

1. What is this force, Lucilius, that drags us in one direction when we are aiming in another, urging us on to the exact place from which we long to withdraw? What is it that wrestles with our spirit, and does not allow us to desire anything once for all? We veer from plan to plan. None of our wishes is free, none is unqualified, none is lasting. **2.** "But it is the fool," you say, "who is inconsistent; nothing suits him for long." But how or when can we tear ourselves away from this folly? No man by himself has sufficient strength to rise above it; he needs a helping hand, and some one to extricate him.

3. Epicurus remarks that certain men have worked their way to the truth without any one's assistance, carving out their own passage. And he gives special praise to these, for their impulse has come from within, and they have forged to the front by themselves. Again, he says, there are others who need outside help, who will not proceed unless someone leads the way, but who will follow faithfully. Of these, he says, Metrodorus was one; this type of man is also excellent, but belongs to the second grade. We ourselves are not of that first class, either; we shall be well treated if we are admitted into the second. Nor need you despise a man who can gain salvation only with the assistance of another; the will to be saved means a great deal, too.

4. You will find still another class of man, – and a class not to be despised, – who can be forced and driven into righteousness, who do not need a guide as much as they require someone to encourage and, as it were, to force them along. This is the third variety. If you ask me for a man of this pattern also, Epicurus tells us that Hermarchus was such. And of the two last-named classes, he is more ready to congratulate the one, but he feels more respect for the other; for although both reached the same goal, it is a greater credit to have brought about the same result with the more difficult material upon which to work.

5. Suppose that two buildings have been erected, unlike as to their foundations, but equal in height and in grandeur. One is built on faultless ground, and the process of erection goes right ahead. In the other case, the foundations have exhausted the building materials, for they have been sunk into soft and shifting ground and much labour has been wasted in reaching the solid rock. As one looks at both of them, one sees clearly what progress the former has made but the larger and more difficult part of the latter is hidden. **6.** So with men's dispositions; some are pliable and easy to manage, but others have to be laboriously wrought out by hand, so to speak, and are wholly employed in the making of their own foundations. I should accordingly deem more fortunate the man who has never had any trouble with himself; but the other, I feel, has deserved better of himself, who has won a victory over the meanness of his own nature, and has not gently led himself, but has wrestled his way, to wisdom.

7. You may be sure that this refractory nature, which demands much toil, has been implanted in us. There are obstacles in our path; so let us fight, and call to our assistance some helpers. "Whom," you say, "shall I call upon? Shall it be this man or that?" There is another choice also open to you; you may go to the ancients; for they have the time to help you. We can get assistance not only from the living, but from those of the past. 8. Let us choose, however, from among the living, not men who pour forth their words with the greatest glibness, turning out commonplaces and holding. as it were, their own little private exhibitions, – not these, I say, but men who teach us by their lives, men who tell us what we ought to do and then prove it by practice, who show us what we should avoid, and then are never caught doing that which they have ordered us to avoid.

Choose as a guide one whom you will admire more when you see him act than when you hear him speak. 9. Of course I would not prevent you from listening also to those philosophers who are wont to hold public meetings and discussions, provided they appear before the people for the express purpose of improving themselves and others, and do not practise their profession for the sake of self-seeking. For what is baser than philosophy courting applause? Does the sick man praise the surgeon while he is operating? 10. In silence and with reverent awe submit to the cure. Even though you cry applause, I shall listen to your cries as if you were groaning when your sores were touched. Do you wish to bear witness that you are attentive, that you are stirred by the grandeur of the subject? You may do this at the proper time; I shall of course allow you to pass judgment and cast a vote as to the better course. Pythagoras made his pupils keep silence for five years; do you think that they had the right on that account to break out immediately into applause?

11. How mad is he who leaves the lecture-room in a happy frame of mind simply because of applause from the ignorant! Why do you take pleasure in being praised by men whom you yourself cannot praise? Fabianus used to give popular talks, but his audience listened with self-control. Occasionally a loud shout of praise would burst forth, but it was prompted by the greatness of his subject, and not by the sound of oratory that slipped forth pleasantly and softly. 12. There should be a difference between the applause of the theatre and the applause of the school; and there is a certain decency even in bestowing praise. If you mark them carefully, all acts are always significant, and you can gauge character by even the most trifling signs. The lecherous man is revealed by his gait, by a movement of the hand, sometimes by a single answer, by his touching his head with a finger, by the shifting of his eye. The scamp is shown up by his laugh; the madman by his face and general appearance. These qualities become known by certain marks; but

you can tell the character of every man when you see how he gives and receives praise. **13.** The philosopher's audience, from this corner and that, stretch forth admiring hands, and sometimes the adoring crowd almost hang over the lecturer's head. But, if you really understand, that is not praise; it is merely applause. These outcries should be left for the arts which aim to please the crowd; let philosophy be worshipped in silence. **14.** Young men, indeed, must sometimes have free play to follow their impulses, but it should only be at times when they act from impulse, and when they cannot force themselves to be silent. Such praise as that gives a certain kind of encouragement to the hearers themselves, and acts as a spur to the youthful mind. But let them be roused to the matter, and not to the style; otherwise, eloquence does them harm, making them enamoured of itself, and not of the subject.

15. I shall postpone this topic for the present; it demands a long and special investigation, to show how the public should be addressed, what indulgences should be allowed to a speaker on a public occasion, and what should be allowed to the crowd itself in the presence of the speaker. There can be no doubt that philosophy has suffered a loss, now that she has exposed her charms for sale. But she can still be viewed in her sanctuary, if her exhibitor is a priest and not a pedlar. Farewell.

LIII. ON THE FAULTS OF THE SPIRIT

1. You can persuade me into almost anything now, for I was recently persuaded to travel by water. We cast off when the sea was lazily smooth; the sky, to be sure, was heavy with nasty clouds, such as usually break into rain or squalls. Still, I thought that the few miles between Puteoli and your dear Parthenope might be run off in quick time, despite the uncertain and lowering sky. So, in order to get away more quickly, I made straight out to sea for Nesis, with the purpose of cutting across all the inlets. **2.** But when we were so far out that it made little difference to me whether I returned or kept on, the calm weather, which had enticed me, came to naught. The storm had not yet begun, but the ground-swell was on, and the waves kept steadily coming faster. I began to ask the pilot to put me ashore somewhere; he replied that the coast was rough and a bad place to land, and that in a storm he feared a lee shore more than anything else. **3.** But I was suffering too grievously to think of the danger, since a sluggish seasickness which brought no relief was racking me, the sort that upsets the liver without clearing it. Therefore I laid down the law to my pilot, forcing him to make for the shore, willy-nilly. When we drew near, I did not wait for things to be done in accordance with Vergil's orders, until

> Prow faced seawards

or

> Anchor plunged from bow;

I remembered my profession as a veteran devotee of cold water, and, clad as I was in my cloak, let myself down into the sea, just as a cold-water bather should. 4. What do you think my feelings were, scrambling over the rocks, searching out the path, or making one for myself? I understood that sailors have good reason to fear the land. It is hard to believe what I endured when I could not endure myself; you may be sure that the reason why Ulysses was shipwrecked on every possible occasion was not so much because the sea-god was angry with him from his birth; he was simply subject to seasickness. And in the future I also, if I must go anywhere by sea, shall only reach my destination in the twentieth year.

5. When I finally calmed my stomach (for you know that one does not escape seasickness by escaping from the sea) and refreshed my body with a rubdown, I began to reflect how completely we forget or ignore our failings, even those that affect the body, which are continually reminding us of their existence, – not to mention those which are more serious in proportion as they are more hidden. 6. A slight ague deceives us; but when it has increased and a genuine fever has begun to burn, it forces even a hardy man, who can endure much suffering, to admit that he is ill. There is pain in the foot, and a tingling sensation in the joints; but we still hide the complaint and announce that we have sprained a joint, or else are tired from over-exercise. Then the ailment, uncertain at first, must be given a name; and when it begins to swell the ankles also, and has made both our feet "right" feet, we are bound to confess that we have the gout. 7. The opposite holds true of diseases of the soul; the worse one is, the less one perceives it. You need not be surprised, my beloved Lucilius. For he whose sleep is light pursues visions during slumber, and sometimes, though asleep, is conscious that he is asleep; but sound slumber annihilates our very dreams and sinks the spirit down so deep that it has no perception of self. 8. Why will no man confess his faults? Because he is still in their grasp; only he who is awake can recount his dream, and similarly a confession of sin is a proof of sound mind.

Let us, therefore, rouse ourselves, that we may be able to correct our mistakes. Philosophy, however, is the only power that can stir us, the only power that can shake off our deep slumber. Devote yourself wholly to philosophy. You are worthy of her; she is worthy of you; greet one another with a loving embrace. Say farewell to all other interests with courage and frankness. Do not study philosophy merely during your spare time.

9. If you were ill, you would stop caring for your personal concerns, and forget your business duties; you would not think highly enough of any client to take active charge of his case during a slight abatement of your sufferings. You would try your hardest to be rid of the illness as soon as possible. What, then? Shall you not do the same thing now? Throw aside all hindrances and give up your time to getting a sound mind; for no man can attain it if he is engrossed in other matters. Philosophy wields her own authority; she appoints her own time and does not allow it to be appointed for her. She is not a thing to be followed at odd times, but a subject for daily practice; she is mistress, and she commands our attendance. 10. Alexander,

when a certain state promised him a part of its territory and half its entire property, replied: "I invaded Asia with the intention, not of accepting what you might give, but of allowing you to keep what I might leave." Philosophy likewise keeps saying to all occupations: "I do not intend to accept the time which you have left over, but I shall allow you to keep what I myself shall leave."

11. Turn to her, therefore, with all your soul, sit at her feet, cherish her; a great distance will then begin to separate you from other men. You will be far ahead of all mortals, and even the gods will not be far ahead of you. Do you ask what will be the difference between yourself and the gods? They will live longer. But, by my faith, it is the sign of a great artist to have confined a full likeness to the limits of a miniature. The wise man's life spreads out to him over as large a surface as does all eternity to a god. There is one point in which the sage has an advantage over the god; for a god is freed from terrors by the bounty of nature, the wise man by his own bounty. **12.** What a wonderful privilege, to have the weaknesses of a man and the serenity of a god! The power of philosophy to blunt the blows of chance is beyond belief. No missile can settle in her body; she is well-protected and impenetrable. She spoils the force of some missiles and wards them off with the loose folds of her gown, as if they had no power to harm; others she dashes aside, and hurls them back with such force that they recoil upon the sender. Farewell.

LIV. ON ASTHMA AND DEATH

1. My ill-health had allowed me a long furlough, when suddenly it resumed the attack. "What kind of ill-health?" you say. And you surely have a right to ask; for it is true that no kind is unknown to me. But I have been consigned, so to speak, to one special ailment. I do not know why I should call it by its Greek name; for it is well enough described as "shortness of breath." Its attack is of very brief duration, like that of a squall at sea; it usually ends within an hour. Who indeed could breathe his last for long? **2.** I have passed through all the ills and dangers of the flesh; but nothing seems to me more troublesome than this. And naturally so; for anything else may be called illness; but this is a sort of continued "last gasp." Hence physicians call it "practising how to die." For some day the breath will succeed in doing what it has so often essayed. **3.** Do you think I am writing this letter in a merry spirit, just because I have escaped? It would be absurd to take delight in such supposed restoration to health, as it would be for a defendant to imagine that he had won his case when he had succeeded in postponing his trial. Yet in the midst of my difficult breathing I never ceased to rest secure in cheerful and brave thoughts.

4. "What?" I say to myself; "does death so often test me? Let it do so; I myself have for a long time tested death." "When?" you ask. Before I was born. Death is non-existence, and I know already what that means. What was before me will happen again after me. If there is any suffering in this state, there must have been such suffering also in the past, before we entered the light of day. As a matter of fact, however, we felt no discomfort then. **5.** And I ask you, would you not say that one was the greatest of fools who believed that a lamp was worse off when it was extinguished than before it was lighted? We mortals also are lighted and extinguished; the period of suffering comes in between, but on either side there is a deep peace. For, unless I am very much mistaken, my dear Lucilius, we go astray in thinking that death only follows, when in reality it has both preceded us and will in turn follow us. Whatever condition existed before our birth, is death. For what does it matter whether you do not begin at all, or whether you leave off, inasmuch as the result of both these states is non-existence?

6. I have never ceased to encourage myself with cheering counsels of this kind, silently, of course, since I had not the power to speak; then little by little this shortness of breath, already reduced to a sort of panting, came on at greater intervals, and then slowed down and finally stopped. Even by this time, although the gasping has ceased, the breath does not come and go normally; I still feel a sort of hesitation and delay in breathing. Let it be as it pleases, provided there be no sigh from the soul. **7.** Accept this assurance from me – I shall never be frightened when the last hour comes; I am already prepared and do not plan a whole day ahead. But do you praise and imitate the man whom it does not irk to die, though he takes pleasure in living. For what virtue is there in going away when you are thrust out? And yet there is virtue even in this: I am indeed thrust out, but it is as if I were going away willingly. For that reason the wise man can never be thrust out, because that would mean removal from a place which he was unwilling to leave; and the wise man does nothing unwillingly. He escapes necessity, because he wills to do what necessity is about to force upon him. Farewell.

LV. ON VATIA'S VILLA

1. I have just returned from a ride in my litter; and I am as weary as if I had walked the distance, instead of being seated. Even to be carried for any length of time is hard work, perhaps all the more so because it is an unnatural exercise; for Nature gave us legs with which to do our own walking, and eyes with which to do our own seeing. Our luxuries have condemned us to weakness; we have ceased to be able to do that which we have long declined to do. **2.** Nevertheless, I found it necessary to give my body a shaking up, in order that the bile which had gathered in my throat, if that was my trouble, might be shaken out, or, if the very breath within me had become, for some reason, too thick, that the jolting, which I have felt was a good thing for me, might make it thinner. So I insisted on being carried longer than usual, along an attractive beach, which bends between Cumae and Servilius Vatia's country-house, shut in by the sea on one side and the lake on the other, just like a narrow path. It was packed firm under foot, because of a recent storm; since, as you know, the waves, when they beat upon the beach hard and fast, level it out; but a continuous period of fair weather loosens it, when the sand, which is kept firm by the water, loses its moisture.

3. As my habit is, I began to look about for something there that might be of service to me, when my eyes fell upon the villa which had once belonged to Vatia. So this was the place where that famous praetorian millionaire passed his old age! He was famed for nothing else than his life of leisure, and he was regarded as lucky only for that reason. For whenever men were ruined by their friendship with Asinius Gallus whenever others were ruined by their hatred of Sejanus, and later by their intimacy with him, – for it was no more dangerous to have offended him than to have loved him, – people used to cry out: "O Vatia, you alone know how to live!" **4.** But what he knew was how to hide, not how to live; and it makes a great deal of difference whether your life be one of leisure or one of idleness. So I never drove past his country-place during Vatia's lifetime without saying to myself: "Here lies Vatia!"

But, my dear Lucilius, philosophy is a thing of holiness, something to be worshipped, so much so that the very counterfeit pleases. For the mass of mankind consider that a person is at leisure who has withdrawn from society, is free from care, self-sufficient, and lives for himself; but these privileges can be the reward only of the wise man. Does he who is a victim of anxiety know how to live for himself? What? Does he even know (and that is of first importance) how to live at all? **5.** For the man who has fled from affairs and from men, who has been banished to seclusion by the unhappiness which his own desires have brought upon him, who cannot see his neighbour more happy than himself, who through fear has taken to concealment, like a frightened and sluggish animal. – this person is not living for himself he is living for his belly, his sleep, and his lust, – and that is the most shameful thing in the world. He who lives for no one does not necessarily live for himself. Nevertheless, there is so much in steadfastness and adherence to one's purpose that even sluggishness, if stubbornly maintained, assumes an air of authority with us.

6. I could not describe the villa accurately; for I am familiar only with the front of the house, and with the parts which are in public view and can be seen by the mere passer-by. There are two grottoes, which cost a great deal of labour, as big as the most spacious hall, made by hand. One of these does not admit the rays of the sun, while the other keeps them until the sun sets. There is also a stream running through a grove of plane-trees, which draws for its supply both on the sea and on Lake Acheron; it intersects the grove just like a race-way and is large enough to support fish, although its waters are continually being drawn off. When the sea is calm, however, they do not use the stream, only touching the well-stocked waters when the storms give the fishermen a forced holiday. **7.** But the most convenient thing about the villa is the fact that Baiae is next door, it is free from all the inconveniences of that resort, and yet enjoys its pleasures. I myself understand these attractions, and I believe that it is a villa suited to every season of the year. It fronts the west wind, which it intercepts in such a way that Baiae is denied it. So it seems that Vatia was no fool when he selected this place as the best in which to spend his leisure when it was already unfruitful and decrepit.

8. The place where one lives, however, can contribute little towards tranquillity; it is the mind which must make everything agreeable to itself. I have seen men despondent in a gay and lovely villa, and I have seen them to all appearance full of business in the midst of a solitude. For this reason you should not refuse to believe that your life is well-placed merely because you are not now in Campania. But why are you not there? Just let your thoughts travel, even to this place. **9.** You may hold converse with your friends when they are absent, and indeed as often as you wish and for as long as you wish. For we enjoy this, the greatest of pleasures, all the more when we are absent from one another. For the presence of friends makes us fastidious; and because we can at any time talk or sit together, when once we have parted we give not a thought to those whom we have just beheld. **10.** And we ought to bear the absence of friends cheerfully, just because everyone is bound to be often absent from his friends even when they are present. Include among such cases, in the first place, the nights spent apart, then the different engagements which each of two friends has, then the private studies of each and their excursions into the country, and you will see that foreign travel does not rob us of much. **11.** A friend should be retained in the spirit; such a friend can never be absent. He can see every day whomsoever he desires to see.

I would therefore have you share your studies with me, your meals, and your walks. We should be living within too narrow limits if anything were barred to our thoughts. I see you, my dear Lucilius, and at this very moment I hear you; I am with you to such an extent that I hesitate whether I should not begin to write you notes instead of letters. Farewell.

LVI. ON QUIET AND STUDY

1. Beshrew me if I think anything more requisite than silence for a man who secludes himself in order to study! Imagine what a variety of noises reverberates about my ears! I have lodgings right over a bathing establishment. So picture to yourself the assortment of sounds, which are strong enough to make me hate my very powers of hearing! When your strenuous gentleman, for example, is exercising himself by flourishing leaden weights; when he is working hard, or else pretends to be working hard, I can hear him grunt; and whenever he releases his imprisoned breath, I can hear him panting in wheezy and high-pitched tones. Or perhaps I notice some lazy fellow, content with a cheap rubdown, and hear the crack of the pummelling hand on his shoulder, varying in sound according as the hand is laid on flat or hollow. Then, perhaps, a professional comes along, shouting out the score; that is the finishing touch. **2.** Add to this the arresting of an occasional roisterer or pickpocket, the racket of the man who always likes to hear his own voice in the bathroom, or the enthusiast who plunges into the swimming-tank with unconscionable noise and splashing. Besides all those whose voices, if nothing else, are good, imagine the hair-plucker with his penetrating, shrill voice, – for purposes of advertisement, – continually giving it vent and never holding his tongue except when he is plucking the armpits and making his victim yell instead. Then the cakeseller with his varied cries, the sausageman, the confectioner, and all the vendors of food hawking their wares, each with his own distinctive intonation.

3. So you say: "What iron nerves or deadened ears, you must have, if your mind can hold out amid so many noises, so various and so discordant, when our friend Chrysippus is brought to his death by the continual good-morrows that greet him!" But I assure you that this racket means no more to me than the sound of waves or falling water; although you will remind me that a certain tribe once moved their city merely because they could not endure the din of a Nile cataract. 4. Words seem to distract me more than noises; for words demand attention, but noises merely fill the ears and beat upon them. Among the sounds that din round me without distracting, I include passing carriages, a machinist in the same block, a saw-sharpener near by, or some fellow who is demonstrating with little pipes and flutes at the Trickling Fountain, shouting rather than singing.

5. Furthermore, an intermittent noise upsets me more than a steady one. But by this time I have toughened my nerves against all that sort of thing, so that I can endure even a boatswain marking the time in high-pitched tones for his crew. For I force my mind to concentrate, and keep it from straying to things outside itself; all outdoors may be bedlam, provided that there is no disturbance within, provided that fear is not wrangling with desire in my breast, provided that meanness and lavishness are not at odds, one harassing the other. For of what benefit is a quiet neighbourhood, if our emotions are in an uproar?

6. 'Twas night, and all the world was lulled to rest.

This is not true; for no real rest can be found when reason has not done the lulling. Night brings our troubles to the light, rather than banishes them; it merely changes the form of our worries. For even when we seek slumber, our sleepless moments are as harassing as the daytime. Real tranquillity is the state reached by an unperverted mind when it is relaxed. 7. Think of the unfortunate man who courts sleep by surrendering his spacious mansion to silence, who, that his ear may be disturbed by no sound, bids the whole retinue of his slaves be quiet and that whoever approaches him shall walk on tiptoe; he tosses from this side to that and seeks a fitful slumber amid his frettings! 8. He complains that he has heard sounds, when he has not heard them at all. The reason, you ask? His soul's in an uproar; it must be soothed, and its rebellious murmuring checked. You need not suppose that the soul is at peace when the body is still. Sometimes quiet means disquiet.

We must therefore rouse ourselves to action and busy ourselves with interests that are good, as often as we are in the grasp of an uncontrollable sluggishness. 9. Great generals, when they see that their men are mutinous, check them by some sort of labour or keep them busy with small forays. The much occupied man has no time for wantonness, and it is an obvious commonplace that the evils of leisure can be shaken off by hard work. Although people may often have thought that I sought seclusion because I was disgusted with politics and regretted my hapless and thankless position, yet, in the retreat to which apprehension and weariness have driven me, my ambition sometimes develops afresh. For it is not because my ambition was rooted out that it has abated, but because it was wearied or perhaps even put out of temper by the failure of its plans. **10.** And so with luxury, also, which sometimes seems to have departed, and then when we have made a profession of frugality, begins to fret us and, amid our economies, seeks the pleasures which we have merely left but not condemned. Indeed, the more stealthily it comes, the greater is its force. For all unconcealed vices are less serious; a disease also is farther on the road to being cured when it breaks forth from concealment and manifests its power. So with greed, ambition, and the other evils of the mind, – you may be sure that they do most harm when they are hidden behind a pretence of soundness.

11. Men think that we are in retirement, and yet we are not. For if we have sincerely retired, and have sounded the signal for retreat, and have scorned outward attractions, then, as I remarked above, no outward thing will distract us; no music of men or of birds can interrupt good thoughts, when they have once become steadfast and sure. **12.** The mind which starts at words or at chance sounds is unstable and has not yet withdrawn into itself; it contains within itself an element of anxiety and rooted fear, and this makes one a prey to care, as our Vergil says:

> I, whom of yore no dart could cause to flee,
> Nor Greeks, with crowded lines of infantry.
> Now shake at every sound, and fear the air,
> Both for my child and for the load I bear.

13. This man in his first state is wise; he blenches neither at the brandished spear, nor at the clashing armour of the serried foe, nor at the din of the stricken city. This man in his second state lacks knowledge fearing for his own concerns, he pales at every sound; any cry is taken for the battle-shout and overthrows him; the slightest disturbance renders him breathless with fear. It is the load that makes him afraid. **14.** Select anyone you please from among your favourites of Fortune, trailing their many responsibilities, carrying their many burdens, and you will behold a picture of Vergil's hero, "fearing both for his child and for the load he bears."

You may therefore be sure that you are at peace with yourself, when no noise readies you, when no word shakes you out of yourself, whether it be of flattery or of threat, or merely an empty sound buzzing about you with unmeaning din. **15.** "What then?" you say, "is it not sometimes a simpler matter just to avoid the uproar?" I admit this. Accordingly, I shall change from my present quarters. I merely wished to test myself and to give myself practice. Why need I be tormented any longer, when Ulysses found so simple a cure for his comrades even against the songs of the Sirens? Farewell.

LVII. ON THE TRIALS OF TRAVEL

1. When it was time for me to return to Naples from Baiae, I easily persuaded myself that a storm was raging, that I might avoid another trip by sea; and yet the road was so deep in mud, all the way, that I may be thought none the less to have made a voyage. On that day I had to endure the full fate of an athlete; the anointing with which we began was followed by the sand-sprinkle in the Naples tunnel. **2.** No place could be longer than that prison; nothing could be dimmer than those torches, which enabled us, not to see amid the darkness, but to see the darkness. But, even supposing that there was light in the place, the dust, which is an oppressive and disagreeable thing even in the open air, would destroy the light; how much worse the dust is there, where it rolls back upon itself, and, being shut in without ventilation, blows back in the faces of those who set it going! So we endured two inconveniences at the same time, and they were diametrically different: we struggled both with mud and with dust on the same road and on the same day.

3. The gloom, however, furnished me with some food for thought; I felt a certain mental thrill, and a transformation unaccompanied by fear, due to the novelty and the unpleasantness of an unusual occurrence. Of course I am not speaking to you of myself at this point, because I am far from being a perfect person, or even a man of middling qualities; I refer to one over whom fortune has lost her control. Even such a man's mind will be smitten with a thrill and he will change colour. **4.** For there are certain emotions, my dear Lucilius, which no courage can avoid; nature reminds courage how perishable a thing it is. And so he will contract his brow when the prospect is forbidding, will shudder at sudden apparitions, and will become dizzy when he stands at the edge of a high precipice and looks down. This is not fear; it is a natural feeling which reason cannot rout. **5.** That is why certain brave men, most willing to shed their own blood, cannot bear to see the blood of others. Some persons collapse and faint at the sight of a freshly inflicted wound; others are affected similarly on handling or viewing an old wound which is festering. And others meet the sword-stroke more readily than they see it dealt.

6. Accordingly, as I said, I experienced a certain transformation, though it could not be called confusion. Then at the first glimpse of restored daylight my good spirits returned without forethought or command. And I began to muse and think how foolish we are to fear certain objects to a greater or less degree, since all of them end in the same way. For what difference does it make whether a watchtower or a mountain crashes down upon us? No difference at all, you will find. Nevertheless, there will be some men who fear the latter mishap to a greater degree, though both accidents are equally deadly; so true it is that fear looks not to the effect, but to the cause of the effect. **7.** Do you suppose that I am now referring to the Stoics, who hold that the soul of a man crushed by a great weight cannot abide, and is scattered forthwith, because it has not had a free opportunity to depart? That is not what I am doing; those who think thus are, in my opinion, wrong. **8.** Just as fire cannot be crushed out, since it will escape round the edges of the body which overwhelms it; just as the air cannot be damaged by lashes and blows, or even cut into, but flows back about the object to which it gives place; similarly the soul, which consists of the subtlest particles, cannot be arrested or destroyed inside the body, but, by virtue of its delicate substance, it will rather escape through the very object by which it is being crushed. Just as lightning, no matter how widely it strikes and flashes, makes its return through a narrow opening, so the soul, which is still subtler than fire, has a way of escape through any part of the body. **9.** We therefore come to this question, – whether the soul can be immortal. But be sure of this: if the soul survives the body after the body is crushed, the soul can in no wise be crushed out, precisely because it does not perish; for the rule of immortality never admits of exceptions, and nothing can harm that which is everlasting. Farewell.

LVIII. ON BEING

1. How scant of words our language is, nay, how poverty-stricken, I have not fully understood until to-day. We happened to be speaking of Plato, and a thousand subjects came up for discussion, which needed names and yet possessed none; and there were certain others which once possessed, but have since lost, their words because we were too nice about their use. But who can endure to be nice in the midst of poverty? **2.** There is an insect, called by the Greeks *oestrus*, which drives cattle wild and scatters them all over their pasturing grounds; it used to be called *asilus* in our language, as you may believe on the authority of Vergil:-

> Near Silarus groves, and eke Alburnus' shades
> Of green-clad oak-trees flits an insect, named
> *Asilus* by the Romans; in the Greek
> The word is rendered *oestrus*. With a rough
> And strident sound it buzzes and drives wild
> The terror-stricken herds throughout the woods.

3. By which I infer that the word has gone out of use. And, not to keep you waiting too long, there were certain uncompounded words current, like *cernere ferro inter se*, as will be proved again by Vergil:-

> Great heroes, born in various lands, had come
> To *settle matters* mutually with the sword.

This "settling matters" we now express by *decernere*. The plain word has become obsolete. **4.** The ancients used to say *iusso*, instead of *iussero*, in conditional clauses. You need not take my word, but you may turn again to Vergil:-

> The other soldiers shall conduct the fight
> With me, where I *shall bid*.

5. It is not in my purpose to show, by this array of examples, how much time I have wasted on the study of language; I merely wish you to understand how many words, that were current in the works of Ennius and Accius, have become mouldy with age; while even in the case of Vergil, whose works are explored daily, some of his words have been filched away from us.

6. You will say, I suppose: "What is the purpose and meaning of this preamble?" I shall not keep you in the dark; I desire, if possible, to say the word *essentia* to you and obtain a favourable hearing. If I cannot do this, I shall risk it even though it put you out of humour. I have Cicero, as authority for the use of this word, and I regard him as a powerful authority. If you desire testimony of a later date, I shall cite Fabianus, careful of speech, cultivated, and so polished in style that he will suit even our nice tastes. For what can we do, my dear Lucilius? How otherwise can we find a word for that which the Greeks call οὐσία, something that is indispensable, something that is the natural substratum of everything? I beg you accordingly to allow me to use this word *essentia*. I shall nevertheless take pains to exercise the privilege, which you have granted me, with as sparing a hand as possible; perhaps I shall be content with the mere right. **7.** Yet what good will your indulgence do me, if, lo and behold, I can in no wise express in Latin the meaning of the word which gave me the opportunity to rail at the poverty of our language? And you will condemn our narrow Roman limits even more, when you find out that there is a word of one syllable which I cannot translate. "What is this?" you ask. It is the word ὄν. You think me lacking in facility; you believe that the word is ready to hand, that it might be translated by *quod est*. I notice, however, a great difference; you are forcing me to render a noun by a verb. **8.** But if I must do so, I shall render it by *quod est*. There are six ways in which Plato expresses this idea, according to a friend of ours, a man of great learning, who mentioned the fact to-day. And I shall explain all of them to you, if I may first point out that there is something called *genus* and something called *species*.

For the present, however, we are seeking the primary idea of *genus*, on which the others, the different *species*, depend, which is the source of all classification, the term under which universal ideas are embraced. And the idea of *genus* will be reached if we begin to reckon back from particulars; for in this way we shall be conducted back to the primary notion. **9.** Now "man" is a *species*, as Aristotle says; so is "horse," or "dog." We must therefore discover some common bond for all these terms, one which embraces them and holds them subordinate to itself. And what is this? It is "animal." And so there begins to be a *genus* "animal," including all these terms, "man," "horse," and "dog." **10.** But there are certain things which have life (*anima*) and yet are not "animals." For it is agreed that plants and trees possess life, and that is why we speak of them as living and dying. Therefore the term "living things" will occupy a still higher place, because both animals and plants are included in this category. Certain objects, however, lack life, – such as rocks. There will therefore be another term to take precedence over "living things," and that is "substance." I shall classify "substance" by saying that all substances are either animate or inanimate. **11.** But there is still something superior to "substance"; for we speak of certain things as possessing substance, and certain things as lacking substance. What, then, will be the term from which these things are derived? It is that to which we lately gave an inappropriate name, "that which exists." For by using this term they will be divided into *species*, so that we can say: that which exists either possesses, or lacks, substance.

12. This, therefore, is what *genus* is, – the primary, original, and (to play upon the word) "general." Of course there are the other *genera*: but they are "special" *genera*: "man" being, for example, a *genus*. For "man" comprises species: by nations, – Greek, Roman, Parthian; by colours, – white, black, yellow. The term comprises individuals also: Cato, Cicero, Lucretius. So "man" falls into the category *genus*, in so far as it includes many kinds; but in so far as it is subordinate to another term, it falls into the category *species*. But the *genus* "that which exists" is general, and has no term superior to it. It is the first term in the classification of things, and all things are included under it.

13. The Stoics would set ahead of this still another *genus*, even more primary; concerning which I shall immediately speak, after proving that the *genus* which has been discussed above, has rightly been placed first, being, as it is, capable of including everything. **14.** I therefore distribute "that which exists" into these two species, – things with, and things without, substance. There is no third class. And how do I distribute "substance"? By saying that it is either animate or inanimate. And how do I distribute the "animate"? By saying: "Certain things have mind, while others have only life." Or the idea may be expressed as follows: "Certain things have the power of movement, of progress, of change of position, while others are rooted in the ground; they are fed and they grow only through their roots." Again, into what species do I divide "animals"? They are either perishable or imperishable. **15.** Certain of the Stoics regard the primary *genus* as the "something." I shall add the reasons they give for their belief; they say: "in the order of nature some things exist, and other things do not exist. And even the things that do not exist are really part of the order of nature. What these are will readily occur to the mind, for example centaurs, giants, and all other figments of unsound reasoning, which have begun to have a definite shape, although they have no bodily consistency."

16. But I now return to the subject which I promised to discuss for you, namely, how it is that Plato divides all existing things in six different ways. The first class of "that which exists" cannot be grasped by the sight or by the touch, or by any of the senses; but it can be grasped by the thought. Any generic conception, such as the generic idea "man," does not come within the range of the eyes; but "man" in particular does; as, for example, Cicero, Cato. The term "animal" is not seen; it is grasped by thought alone. A particular animal, however, is seen, for example, a horse, a dog.

17. The second class of "things which exist," according to Plato, is that which is prominent and stands out above everything else; this, he says, exists in a pre-eminent degree. The word "poet" is used indiscriminately, for this term is applied to all writers of verse; but among the Greeks it has come to be the distinguishing mark of a single individual. You know that Homer is meant when you hear men say "the poet." What, then, is this pre-eminent Being? God, surely, one who is greater and more powerful than anyone else.

18. The third class is made up of those things which exist in the proper sense of the term; they are countless in number, but are situated beyond our sight. "What are these?" you ask. They are Plato's own furniture, so to speak; he calls them "ideas," and from them all visible things are created, and according to their pattern all things are fashioned. They are immortal, unchangeable, inviolable. **19.** And this "idea," or rather, Plato's conception of it, is as follows: "The 'idea' is the everlasting pattern of those things which are created by nature." I shall explain this definition, in order to set the subject before you in a clearer light: Suppose that I wish to make a likeness of you; I possess in your own person the pattern of this picture, wherefrom my mind receives a certain outline, which it is to embody in its own handiwork. That outward appearance, then, which gives me instruction and guidance, this pattern for me to imitate, is the "idea." Such patterns, therefore, nature possesses in infinite number, – of men, fish, trees, according to whose model everything that nature has to create is worked out.

20. In the fourth place we shall put "form." And if you would know what "form" means, you must pay close attention, calling Plato, and not me, to account for the difficulty of the subject. However, we cannot make fine distinctions without encountering difficulties. A moment ago I made use of the artist as an illustration. When the artist desired to reproduce Vergil in colours he would gaze upon Vergil himself. The "idea" was Vergil's outward appearance, and this was the pattern of the intended work. That which the artist draws from this "idea" and has embodied in his own work, is the "form." **21.** Do you ask me where the difference lies? The former is the pattern; while the latter is the shape taken from the pattern and embodied in the work. Our artist follows the one, but the other he creates. A statue has a certain external appearance; this external appearance of the statue is the "form." And the pattern itself has a certain external appearance, by gazing upon which the sculptor has fashioned his statue; this is the "idea." If you desire a further distinction, I will say that the "form" is in the artist's work, the "idea" outside his work, and not only outside it, but prior to it.

22. The fifth class is made up of the things which exist in the usual sense of the term. These things are the first that have to do with us; here we have all such things as men, cattle, and things. In the sixth class goes all that which has a fictitious existence, like void, or time.

Whatever is concrete to the sight or touch, Plato does not include among the things which he believes to be existent in the strict sense of the term. These things are the first that have to do with us: here we have all such things as men, cattle, and things. For they are in a state of flux, constantly diminishing or increasing. None of us is the same man in old age that he was in youth; nor the same on the morrow as on the day preceding. Our bodies are burned along like flowing waters; every visible object accompanies time in its flight; of the things which we see, nothing is fixed. Even I myself as I comment on this change, am changed myself. **23.** This is just what Heraclitus says: "We go down twice into the same river, and yet into a different river." For the stream still keeps the same name, but the water has already flowed past. Of course this is much more evident in rivers than in human beings. Still, we mortals are also carried past in no less speedy a course; and this prompts me to marvel at our madness in cleaving with great affection to such a fleeting thing as the body, and in fearing lest some day we may die, when every instant means the death of our previous condition. Will you not stop fearing lest that may happen once which really happens every day? **24.** So much for man, – a substance that flows away and falls, exposed to every influence; but the universe, too, immortal and enduring as it is, changes and never remains the same. For though it has within itself all that it has had, it has it in a different way from that in which it has had it; it keeps changing its arrangement.

25. "Very well," say you, "what good shall I get from all this fine reasoning?" None, if you wish me to answer your question. Nevertheless, just as an engraver rests his eyes when they have long been under a strain and are weary, and calls them from their work, and "feasts" them, as the saying is; so we at times should slacken our minds and refresh them with some sort of entertainment. But let even your entertainment be work; and even from these various forms of entertainment you will select, if you have been watchful, something that may prove wholesome. **26.** That is my habit, Lucilius: I try to extract and render useful some element from every field of thought, no matter how far removed it may be from philosophy. Now what could be less likely to reform character than the subjects which we have been discussing? And how can I be made a better man by the "ideas" of Plato? What can I draw from them that will put a check on my appetites? Perhaps the very thought, that all these things which minister to our senses, which arouse and excite us, are by Plato denied a place among the things that really exist. **27.** Such things are therefore imaginary, and though they for the moment present a certain external appearance, yet they are in no case permanent or substantial; none the less, we crave them as if they were always to exist, or as if we were always to possess them.

We are weak, watery beings standing in the midst of unrealities; therefore let us turn our minds to the things that are everlasting. Let us look up to the ideal outlines of all things, that flit about on high, and to the God who moves among them and plans how he may defend from death that which he could not make imperishable because its substance forbade, and so by reason may overcome the defects of the body. **28.** For all things abide, not because they are everlasting, but because they are protected by the care of him who governs all things; but that which was imperishable would need no guardian. The Master Builder keeps them safe, overcoming the weakness of their fabric by his own power. Let us despise everything that is so little an object of value that it makes us doubt whether it exists at all. **29.** Let us at the same time reflect, seeing that Providence rescues from its perils the world itself, which is no less mortal than we ourselves, that to some extent our petty bodies can be made to tarry longer upon earth by our own providence, if only we acquire the ability to control and check those pleasures whereby the greater portion of mankind perishes. **30.** Plato himself, by taking pains, advanced to old age. To be sure, he was the fortunate possessor of a strong and sound body (his very name was given him because of his broad chest); but his strength was much impaired by sea voyages and desperate adventures. Nevertheless, by frugal living, by setting a limit upon all that rouses the appetites, and by painstaking attention to himself, he reached that advanced age in spite of many hindrances. **31.** You know, I am sure, that Plato had the good fortune, thanks to his careful living, to die on his birthday, after exactly completing his eighty-first year. For this reason wise men of the East, who happened to be in Athens at that time, sacrificed to him after his death, believing that his length of days was too full for a mortal man, since he had rounded out the perfect number of nine times nine. I do not doubt that he would have been quite willing to forgo a few days from this total, as well as the sacrifice.

32. Frugal living can bring one to old age; and to my mind old age is not to be refused any more than is to be craved. There is a pleasure in being in one's own company as long as possible, when a man has made himself worth enjoying. The question, therefore, on which we have to record our judgment is, whether one should shrink from extreme old age and should hasten the end artificially, instead of waiting for it to come. A man who sluggishly awaits his fate is almost a coward, just as he is immoderately given to wine who drains the jar dry and sucks up even the dregs. **33.** But we shall ask this question also: "Is the extremity of life the dregs, or is it the clearest and purest part of all, provided only that the mind is unimpaired, and the senses, still sound, give their support to the spirit, and the body is not worn out and dead before its time?" For it makes a great deal of difference whether a man is lengthening his life or his death. **34.** But if the body is useless for service, why should one not free the struggling soul? Perhaps one ought to do this a little before the debt is due, lest, when it falls due, he may be unable to perform the act. And since the danger of living in wretchedness is greater than the danger of dying soon, he is a fool who refuses to stake a little time and win a hazard of great gain.

Few have lasted through extreme old age to death without impairment, and many have lain inert, making no use of themselves. How much more cruel, then, do you suppose it really is to have lost a portion of your life, than to have lost your right to end that life? **35.** Do not hear me with reluctance, as if my statement applied directly to you, but weigh what I have to say. It is this, that I shall not abandon old age, if old age preserves me intact for myself, and intact as regards the better part of myself; but if old age begins to shatter my mind, and to pull its various faculties to pieces, if it leaves me, not life, but only the breath of life, I shall rush out of a house that is crumbling and tottering. **36.** I shall not avoid illness by seeking death, as long as the illness is curable and does not impede my soul. I shall not lay violent hands upon myself just because I am in pain; for death under such circumstances is defeat. But if I find out that the pain must always be endured, I shall depart, not because of the pain but because it will be a hindrance to me as regards all my reasons for living. He who dies just because he is in pain is a weakling, a coward; but he who lives merely to brave out this pain, is a fool.

37. But I am running on too long; and, besides, there is matter here to fill a day. And how can a man end his life, if he cannot end a letter? So farewell. This last word you will read with greater pleasure than all my deadly talk about death. Farewell.

LIX. ON PLEASURE AND JOY

1. I received great pleasure from your letter; kindly allow me to use these words in their everyday meaning, without insisting upon their Stoic import. For we Stoics hold that pleasure is a vice. Very likely it is a vice; but we are accustomed to use the word when we wish to indicate a happy state of mind. **2.** I am aware that if we test words by our formula, even pleasure is a thing of ill repute, and joy can be attained only by the wise. For "joy" is an elation of spirit, of a spirit which trusts in the goodness and truth of its own possessions. The common usage, however, is that we derive great "joy" from a friend's position as consul, or from his marriage, or from the birth of his child; but these events, so far from being matters of joy, are more often the beginnings of sorrow to come. No, it is a characteristic of real joy that it never ceases, and never changes into its opposite.

3. Accordingly, when our Vergil speaks of

> The evil joys of the mind,

his words are eloquent, but not strictly appropriate. For no "joy" can be evil. He has given the name "joy" to pleasures, and has thus expressed his meaning. For he has conveyed the idea that men take delight in their own evil. **4.** Nevertheless, I was not wrong in saying that I received great "pleasure" from your letter; for although an ignorant man may derive "joy" if the cause be an honourable one, yet, since his emotion is wayward, and is likely soon to take another direction, I call it "pleasure"; for it is inspired by an opinion concerning a spurious good; it exceeds control and is carried to excess.

But, to return to the subject, let me tell you what delighted me in your letter. You have your words under control. You are not carried away by your language, or borne beyond the limits which you have determined upon. **5.** Many writers are tempted by the charm of some alluring phrase to some topic other than that which they had set themselves to discuss. But this has not been so in your case; all your words are compact, and suited to the subject, You say all that you wish, and you mean still more than you say. This is a proof of the importance of your subject matter, showing that your mind, as well as your words, contains nothing superfluous or bombastic.

6. I do, however, find some metaphors, not, indeed, daring ones, but the kind which have stood the test of use. I find similes also; of course, if anyone forbids us to use them, maintaining that poets alone have that privilege, he has not, apparently, read any of our ancient prose writers, who had not yet learned to affect a style that should win applause. For those writers, whose eloquence was simple and directed only towards proving their case, are full of comparisons; and I think that these are necessary, not for the same reason which makes them necessary for the poets, but in order that they may serve as props to our feebleness, to bring both speaker and listener face to face with the subject under discussion. **7.** For example, I am at this very moment reading Sextius; he is a keen man, and a philosopher who, though he writes in Greek, has the Roman standard of ethics. One of his similes appealed especially to me, that of an army marching in hollow square, in a place where the enemy might be expected to appear from any quarter, ready for battle. "This," said he, "is just what the wise man ought to do; he should have all his fighting qualities deployed on every side, so that wherever the attack threatens, there his supports may be ready to hand and may obey the captain's command without confusion." This is what we notice in armies which serve under great leaders; we see how all the troops simultaneously understand their general's orders, since they are so arranged that a signal given by one man passes down the ranks of cavalry and infantry at the same moment. **8.** This, he declares, is still more necessary for men like ourselves; for soldiers have often feared an enemy without reason, and the march which they thought most dangerous has in fact been most secure; but folly brings no repose, fear haunts it both in the van and in the rear of the column, and both flanks are in a panic. Folly is pursued, and confronted, by peril. It blenches at everything; it is unprepared; it is frightened even by auxiliary troops. But the wise man is fortified against all inroads; he is alert; he will not retreat before the attack of poverty, or of sorrow, or of disgrace, or of pain. He will walk undaunted both against them and among them.

9. We human beings are fettered and weakened by many vices; we have wallowed in them for a long time and it is hard for us to be cleansed. We are not merely defiled; we are dyed by them. But, to refrain from passing from one figure to another, I will raise this question, which I often consider in my own heart: why is it that folly holds us with such an insistent grasp? It is, primarily, because we do not combat it strongly enough, because we do not struggle towards salvation with all our might; secondly, because we do not put sufficient trust in the discoveries of the wise, and do not drink in their words with open hearts; we approach this great problem in too trifling a spirit. **10.** But how can a man learn, in the struggle against his vices, an amount that is enough, if the time which he gives to learning is only the amount left over from his vices? None of us goes deep below the surface. We skim the top only, and we regard the smattering of time spent in the search for wisdom as enough and to spare for a busy man. **11.** What hinders us most of all is that we are too readily satisfied with ourselves; if we meet with someone who calls us good men, or sensible men, or holy men, we see ourselves in his description, not content with praise in moderation, we accept everything that shameless flattery heaps upon us, as if it were our due. We agree with those who declare us to be the best and wisest of men, although we know that they are given to much lying. And we are so self-complacent that we desire praise for certain actions when we are especially addicted to the very opposite. Yonder person hears himself called "most gentle" when he is inflicting tortures, or "most generous" when he is engaged in looting, or "most temperate" when he is in the midst of drunkenness and lust. Thus it follows that we are unwilling to be reformed, just because we believe ourselves to be the best of men.

12. Alexander was roaming as far as India, ravaging tribes that were but little known, even to their neighbours. During the blockade of a certain city, while he was reconnoitring the walls and hunting for the weakest spot in the fortifications, he was wounded by an arrow. Nevertheless, he long continued the siege, intent on finishing what he had begun. The pain of his wound, however, as the surface became dry and as the flow of blood was checked, increased; his leg gradually became numb as he sat his horse; and finally, when he was forced to withdraw, he exclaimed: "All men swear that I am the son of Jupiter, but this wound cries out that I am mortal." **13.** Let us also act in the same way. Each man, according to his lot in life, is stultified by flattery. We should say to him who flatters us: "You call me a man of sense, but I understand how many of the things which I crave are useless, and how many of the things which I desire will do me harm. I have not even the knowledge, which satiety teaches to animals, of what should be the measure of my food or my drink. I do not yet know how much I can hold."

14. I shall now show you how you may know that you are not wise. The wise man is joyful, happy and calm, unshaken, he lives on a plane with the gods. Now go, question yourself; if you are never downcast, if your mind is not harassed by my apprehension, through anticipation of what is to come, if day and night your soul keeps on its even and unswerving course, upright and content with itself, then you have attained to the greatest good that mortals can possess. If, however, you seek pleasures of all kinds in all directions, you must know that you are as far short of wisdom as you are short of joy. Joy is the goal which you desire to reach, but you are wandering from the path, if you expect to reach your goal while you are in the midst of riches and official titles, – in other words, if you seek joy in the midst of cares, these objects for which you strive so eagerly, as if they would give you happiness and pleasure, are merely causes of grief.

15. All men of this stamp, I maintain, are pressing on in pursuit of joy, but they do not know where they may obtain a joy that is both great and enduring. One person seeks it in feasting and self-indulgence; another, in canvassing for honours and in being surrounded by a throng of clients; another, in his mistress; another, in idle display of culture and in literature that has no power to heal; all these men are led astray by delights which are deceptive and short-lived – like drunkenness for example, which pays for a single hour of hilarious madness by a sickness of many days, or like applause and the popularity of enthusiastic approval which are gained, and atoned for, at the cost of great mental disquietude.

16. Reflect, therefore, on this, that the effect of wisdom is a joy that is unbroken and continuous. The mind of the wise man is like the ultra-lunar firmament; eternal calm pervades that region. You have, then, a reason for wishing to be wise, if the wise man is never deprived of joy. This joy springs only from the knowledge that you possess the virtues. None but the brave, the just, the self-restrained, can rejoice. **17.** And when you query: "What do you mean? Do not the foolish and the wicked also rejoice?" I reply, no more than lions who have caught their prey. When men have wearied themselves with wine and lust, when night fails them before their debauch is done, when the pleasures which they have heaped upon a body that is too small to hold them begin to fester, at such times they utter in their wretchedness those lines of Vergil:

> Thou knowest how, amid false-glittering joys,
> We spent that last of nights.

18. Pleasure-lovers spend every night amid false-glittering joys, and just as if it were their last. But the joy which comes to the gods, and to those who imitate the gods, is not broken off, nor does it cease; but it would surely cease were it borrowed from without. Just because it is not in the power of another to bestow, neither is it subject to another's whims. That which Fortune has not given, she cannot take away. Farewell.

LX. ON HARMFUL PRAYERS

1. I file a complaint, I enter a suit, I am angry. Do you still desire what your nurse, your guardian, or your mother, have prayed for in your behalf? Do you not yet understand what evil they prayed for? Alas, how hostile to us are the wishes of our own folk! And they are all the more hostile in proportion as they are more completely fulfilled. It is no surprise to me, at my age, that nothing but evil attends us from our early youth; for we have grown up amid the curses invoked by our parents. And may the gods give ear to our cry also, uttered in our own behalf, – one which asks no favours!

2. How long shall we go on making demands upon the gods, as if we were still unable to support ourselves? How long shall we continue to fill with grain the market-places of our great cities? How long must the people gather it in for us? How long shall many ships convey the requisites for a single meal, bringing them from no single sea? The bull is filled when he feeds over a few acres; and one forest is large enough for a herd of elephants. Man, however, draws sustenance both from the earth and from the sea. **3.** What, then? Did nature give us bellies so insatiable, when she gave us these puny bodies, that we should outdo the hugest and most voracious animals in greed? Not at all. How small is the amount which will satisfy nature? A very little will send her away contented. It is not the natural hunger of our bellies that costs us dear, but our solicitous cravings. **4.** Therefore those who, as Sallust puts it, "hearken to their bellies," should be numbered among the animals, and not among men; and certain men, indeed, should be numbered, not even among the animals, but among the dead. He really lives who is made use of by many; he really lives who makes use of himself. Those men, however, who creep into a hole and grow torpid are no better off in their homes than if they were in their tombs. Right there on the marble lintel of the house of such a man you may inscribe his name, for he has died before he is dead. Farewell.

LXI. ON MEETING DEATH CHEERFULLY

1. Let us cease to desire that which we have been desiring. I, at least, am doing this: in my old age I have ceased to desire what I desired when a boy. To this single end my days and my nights are passed; this is my task, this the object of my thoughts, – to put an end to my chronic ills. I am endeavouring to live every day as if it were a complete life. I do not indeed snatch it up as if it were my last; I do regard it, however, as if it might even be my last. **2.** The present letter is written to you with this in mind as if death were about to call me away in the very act of writing. I am ready to depart, and I shall enjoy life just because I am not over-anxious as to the future date of my departure.

Before I became old I tried to live well; now that I am old, I shall try to die well; but dying well means dying gladly. See to it that you never do anything unwillingly. **3.** That which is bound to be a necessity if you rebel, is not a necessity if you desire it. This is what I mean: he who takes his orders gladly, escapes the bitterest part of slavery, – doing what one does not want to do. The man who does something under orders is not unhappy; he is unhappy who does something against his will. Let us therefore so set our minds in order that we may desire whatever is demanded of us by circumstances, and above all that we may reflect upon our end without sadness. **4.** We must make ready for death before we make ready for life. Life is well enough furnished, but we are too greedy with regard to its furnishings; something always seems to us lacking, and will always seem lacking. To have lived long enough depends neither upon our years nor upon our days, but upon our minds. I have lived, my dear friend Lucilius, long enough. I have had my fill; I await death. Farewell.

LXII. ON GOOD COMPANY

1. We are deceived by those who would have us believe that a multitude of affairs blocks their pursuit of liberal studies; they make a pretence of their engagements, and multiply them, when their engagements are merely with themselves. As for me, Lucilius, my time is free; it is indeed free, and wherever I am, I am master of myself. For I do not surrender myself to my affairs, but loan myself to grief, and I do not hunt out excuses for wasting my time. And wherever I am situated, I carry on my own meditations and ponder in my mind some wholesome thought. **2.** When I give myself to my friends, I do not withdraw from my own company, nor do I linger with those who are associated with me through some special occasion or some case which arises from my official position. But I spend my time in the company of all the best; no matter in what lands they may have lived, or in what age, I let my thoughts fly to them. **3.** Demetrius, for instance, the best of men, I take about with me, and, leaving the wearers of purple and fine linen, I talk with him, half-naked as he is, and hold him in high esteem. Why should I not hold him in high esteem? I have found that he lacks nothing. It is in the power of any man to despise all things, but of no man to possess all things. The shortest cut to riches is to despise riches. Our friend Demetrius, however, lives not merely as if he has learned to despise all things, but as if he has handed them over for others to possess. Farewell.

LXIII. ON GRIEF FOR LOST FRIENDS

1. I am grieved to hear that your friend Flaccus is dead, but I would not have you sorrow more than is fitting. That you should not mourn at all I shall hardly dare to insist; and yet I know that it is the better way. But what man will ever be so blessed with that ideal steadfastness of soul, unless he has already risen far above the reach of Fortune? Even such a man will be stung by an event like this, but it will be only a sting. We, however, may be forgiven for bursting into tears, if only our tears have not flowed to excess, and if we have checked them by our own efforts. Let not the eyes be dry when we have lost a friend, nor let them overflow. We may weep, but we must not wail.

2. Do you think that the law which I lay down for you is harsh, when the greatest of Greek poets has extended the privilege of weeping to one day only, in the lines where he tells us that even Niobe took thought of food? Do you wish to know the reason for lamentations and excessive weeping? It is because we seek the proofs of our bereavement in our tears, and do not give way to sorrow, but merely parade it. No man goes into mourning for his own sake. Shame on our ill-timed folly! There is an element of self-seeking even in our sorrow.

3. "What," you say, "am I to forget my friend?" It is surely a short-lived memory that you vouchsafe to him, if it is to endure only as long as your grief; presently that brow of yours will be smoothed out in laughter by some circumstance, however casual. It is to a time no more distant than this that I put off the soothing of every regret, the quieting of even the bitterest grief. As soon as you cease to observe yourself, the picture of sorrow which you have contemplated will fade away; at present you are keeping watch over your own suffering. But even while you keep watch it slips away from you, and the sharper it is, the more speedily it comes to an end.

4. Let us see to it that the recollection of those whom we have lost becomes a pleasant memory to us. No man reverts with pleasure to any subject which he will not be able to reflect upon without pain. So too it cannot but be that the names of those whom we have loved and lost come back to us with a sort of sting; but there is a pleasure even in this sting. **5.** For, as my friend Attalus used to say: "The remembrance of lost friends is pleasant in the same way that certain fruits have an agreeably acid taste, or as in extremely old wines it is their very bitterness that pleases us. Indeed, after a certain lapse of time, every thought that gave pain is quenched, and the pleasure comes to us unalloyed." **6.** If we take the word of Attalus for it, "to think of friends who are alive and well is like enjoying a meal of cakes and honey; the recollection of friends who have passed away gives a pleasure that is not without a touch of bitterness. Yet who will deny that even these things, which are bitter and contain an element of sourness, do serve to arouse the stomach?" **7.** For my part, I do not agree with him. To me, the thought of my dead friends is sweet and appealing. For I have had them as if I should one day lose them; I have lost them as if I have them still.

Therefore, Lucilius, act as befits your own serenity of mind, and cease to put a wrong interpretation on the gifts of Fortune. Fortune has taken away, but Fortune has given. **8.** Let us greedily enjoy our friends, because we do not know how long this privilege will be ours. Let us think how often we shall leave them when we go upon distant journeys, and how often we shall fail to see them when we tarry together in the same place; we shall thus understand that we have lost too much of their time while they were alive. **9.** But will you tolerate men who are most careless of their friends, and then mourn them most abjectly, and do not love anyone unless they have lost him? The reason why they lament too unrestrainedly at such times is that they are afraid lest men doubt whether they really have loved; all too late they seek for proofs of their emotions. **10.** If we have other friends, we surely deserve ill at their hands and think ill of them, if they are of so little account that they fail to console us for the loss of one. If, on the other hand, we have no other friends, we have injured ourselves more than Fortune has injured us; since Fortune has robbed us of one friend, but we have robbed ourselves of every friend whom we have failed to make. **11.** Again, he who has been unable to love more than one, has had none too much love even for that one. If a man who has lost his one and only tunic through robbery chooses to bewail his plight rather than look about him for some way to escape the cold, or for something with which to cover his shoulders, would you not think him an utter fool?

You have buried one whom you loved; look about for someone to love. It is better to replace your friend than to weep for him. **12.** What I am about to add is, I know, a very hackneyed remark, but I shall not omit it simply because it is a common phrase: a man ends his grief by the mere passing of time, even if he has not ended it of his own accord. But the most shameful cure for sorrow, in the case of a sensible man, is to grow weary of sorrowing. I should prefer you to abandon grief, rather than have grief abandon you; and you should stop grieving as soon as possible, since, even if you wish to do so, it is impossible to keep it up for a long time. **13.** Our forefathers have enacted that, in the case of women, a year should be the limit for mourning; not that they needed to mourn for so long, but that they should mourn no longer. In the case of men, no rules are laid down, because to mourn at all is not regarded as honourable. For all that, what woman can you show me, of all the pathetic females that could scarcely be dragged away from the funeral-pile or torn from the corpse, whose tears have lasted a whole month? Nothing becomes offensive so quickly as grief; when fresh, it finds someone to console it and attracts one or another to itself; but after becoming chronic, it is ridiculed, and rightly. For it is either assumed or foolish.

14. He who writes these words to you is no other than I, who wept so excessively for my dear friend Annaeus Serenus that, in spite of my wishes, I must be included among the examples of men who have been overcome by grief. To-day, however, I condemn this act of mine, and I understand that the reason why I lamented so greatly was chiefly that I had never imagined it possible for his death to precede mine. The only thought which occurred to my mind was that he was the younger, and much younger, too, – as if the Fates kept to the order of our ages!

15. Therefore let us continually think as much about our own mortality as about that of all those we love. In former days I ought to have said: "My friend Serenus is younger than I; but what does that matter? He would naturally die after me, but he may precede me." It was just because I did not do this that I was unprepared when Fortune dealt me the sudden blow. Now is the time for you to reflect, not only that all things are mortal, but also that their mortality is subject to no fixed law. Whatever can happen at any time can happen to-day. **16.** Let us therefore reflect, my beloved Lucilius, that we shall soon come to the goal which this friend, to our own sorrow, has reached. And perhaps, if only the tale told by wise men is true and there is a bourne to welcome us, then he whom we think we have lost has only been sent on ahead. Farewell.

LXIV. ON THE PHILOSOPHER'S TASK

1. Yesterday you were with us. You might complain if I said "yesterday" merely. This is why I have added "with us." For, so far as I am concerned, you are always with me. Certain friends had happened in, on whose account a somewhat brighter fire was laid, – not the kind that generally bursts from the kitchen chimneys of the rich and scares the watch, but the moderate blaze which means that guests have come. **2.** Our talk ran on various themes, as is natural at a dinner; it pursued no chain of thought to the end, but jumped from one topic to another. We then had read to us a book by Quintus Sextius the Elder. He is a great man, if you have any confidence in my opinion, and a real Stoic, though he himself denies it. **3.** Ye Gods, what strength and spirit one finds in him! This is not the case with all philosophers; there are some men of illustrious name whose writings are sapless. They lay down rules, they argue, and they quibble; they do not infuse spirit simply because they have no spirit. But when you come to read Sextius you will say: "He is alive; he is strong; he is free; he is more than a man; he fills me with a mighty confidence before I close his book." **4.** I shall acknowledge to you the state of mind I am in when I read his works: I want to challenge every hazard; I want to cry: "Why keep me waiting, Fortune? Enter the lists! Behold, I am ready for you!" I assume the spirit of a man who seeks where he may make trial of himself where he may show his worth:

> And fretting 'mid the unwarlike flocks he prays
> Some foam-flecked boar may cross his path, or else
> A tawny lion stalking down the hills.

5. I want something to overcome, something on which I may test my endurance. For this is another remarkable quality that Sextius possesses: he will show you the grandeur of the happy life and yet will not make you despair of attaining it; you will understand that it is on high, but that it is accessible to him who has the will to seek it.

6. And virtue herself will have the same effect upon you, of making you admire her and yet hope to attain her. In my own case, at any rate the very contemplation of wisdom takes much of my time; I gaze upon her with bewilderment, just as I sometimes gaze upon the firmament itself, which I often behold as if I saw it for the first time. **7.** Hence I worship the discoveries of wisdom and their discoverers; to enter, as it were, into the inheritance of many predecessors is a delight. It was for me that they laid up this treasure; it was for me that they toiled. But we should play the part of a careful householder; we should increase what we have inherited. This inheritance shall pass from me to my descendants larger than before. Much still remains to do, and much will always remain, and he who shall be born a thousand ages hence will not be barred from his opportunity of adding something further. **8.** But even if the old masters have discovered everything, one thing will be always new, – the application and the scientific study and classification of the discoveries made by others. Assume that prescriptions have been handed down to us for the healing of the eyes; there is no need of my searching for others in addition; but for all that, these prescriptions must be adapted to the particular disease and to the particular stage of the disease. Use this prescription to relieve granulation of the eyelids, that to reduce the swelling of the lids, this to prevent sudden pain or a rush of tears, that to sharpen the vision. Then compound these several prescriptions, watch for the right time of their application, and supply the proper treatment in each case.

The cures for the spirit also have been discovered by the ancients; but it is our task to learn the method and the time of treatment. **9.** Our predecessors have worked much improvement, but have not worked out the problem. They deserve respect, however, and should be worshipped with a divine ritual. Why should I not keep statues of great men to kindle my enthusiasm, and celebrate their birthdays? Why should I not continually greet them with respect and honour? The reverence which I owe to my own teachers I owe in like measure to those teachers of the human race, the source from which the beginnings of such great blessings have flowed. **10.** If I meet a consul or a praetor, I shall pay him all the honour which his post of honour is wont to receive: I shall dismount, uncover, and yield the road. What, then? Shall I admit into my soul with less than the highest marks of respect Marcus Cato, the Elder and the Younger, Laelius the Wise, Socrates and Plato, Zeno and Cleanthes? I worship them in very truth, and always rise to do honour to such noble names. Farewell.

LXV. ON THE FIRST CAUSE

1. I shared my time yesterday with ill health; it claimed for itself all the period before noon; in the afternoon, however, it yielded to me. And so I first tested my spirit by reading; then, when reading was found to be possible, I dared to make more demands upon the spirit, or perhaps I should say, to make more concessions to it. I wrote a little, and indeed with more concentration than usual, for I am struggling with a difficult subject and do not wish to be downed. In the midst of this, some friends visited me, with the purpose of employing force and of restraining me, as if I were a sick man indulging in some excess. **2.** So conversation was substituted for writing; and from this conversation I shall communicate to you the topic which is still the subject of debate; for we have appointed you referee. You have more of a task on your hands than you suppose, for the argument is threefold.

Our Stoic philosophers, as you know, declare that there are two things in the universe which are the source of everything, – namely, cause and matter. Matter lies sluggish, a substance ready for any use, but sure to remain unemployed if no one sets it in motion. Cause, however, by which we mean reason, moulds matter and turns it in whatever direction it will, producing thereby various concrete results. Accordingly, there must be, in the case of each thing, that from which it is made, and, next, an agent by which it is made. The former is its material, the latter its cause.

3. All art is but imitation of nature; therefore, let me apply these statements of general principles to the things which have to be made by man. A statue, for example, has afforded matter which was to undergo treatment at the hands of the artist, and has had an artist who was to give form to the matter. Hence, in the case of the statue, the material was bronze, the cause was the workman. And so it goes with all things, – they consist of that which is made and of the maker. **4.** The Stoics believe in one cause only – the maker; but Aristotle thinks that the word "cause" can be used in three ways: "The first cause," he says, "is the actual matter, without which nothing can be created. The second is the workman. The third is the form, which is impressed upon every work, – a statue, for example." This last is what Aristotle calls the *idos*. "There is, too," says he, "a fourth, – the purpose of the work as a whole." **5.** Now I shall show you what this last means. Bronze is the "first cause" of the statue, for it could never have been made unless there had been something from which it could be cast and moulded. The "second cause" is the artist; for without the skilled hands of a workman that bronze could not have been shaped to the outlines of the statue. The "third cause" is the form, inasmuch as our statue could never be called The Lance-Bearer or The Boy Binding his Hair had not this special shape been stamped upon it. The "fourth cause" is the purpose of the work. For if this purpose had not existed, the statue would not have been made. **6.** Now what is this purpose? It is that which attracted the artist which he followed when he made the statue. It may have been money, if he has made it for sale; or renown, if he has worked for reputation; or religion, if he has wrought it as a gift for a temple. Therefore this also is a cause contributing towards the making of the statue; or do you think that we should avoid including, among the causes of a thing which has been made, that element without which the thing in question would not have been made?

7. To these four Plato adds a fifth cause, – the pattern which he himself calls the "idea"; for it is this that the artist gazed upon when he created the work which he had decided to carry out. Now it makes no difference whether he has this pattern outside himself, that he may direct his glance to it, or within himself, conceived and placed there by himself. God has within himself these patterns of all things, and his mind comprehends the harmonies and the measures of the whole totality of things which are to be carried out; he is filled with these shapes which Plato calls the "ideas," – imperishable, unchangeable, not subject to decay. And therefore, though men die, humanity itself, or the idea of man, according to which man is moulded, lasts on, and though men toil and perish, it suffers no change. **8.** Accordingly, there are five causes, as Plato says: the material, the agent, the make-up, the model, and the end in view. Last comes the result of all these. Just as in the case of the statue, – to go back to the figure with which we began, – the material is the bronze, the agent is the artist, the make-up is the form which is adapted to the material, the model is the pattern imitated by the agent, the end in view is the purpose in the maker's mind, and, finally, the result of all these is the statue itself. **9.** The universe also, in Plato's opinion, possesses all these elements. The agent is God; the source, matter; the form, the shape and the arrangement of the visible world. The pattern is doubtless the model according to which God has made this great and most beautiful creation. **10.** The purpose is his object in so doing. Do you ask what God's purpose is? It is goodness. Plato, at any rate, says: "What was God's reason for creating the world? God is good, and no good person is grudging of anything that is good. Therefore, God made it the best world possible." Hand down your opinion, then, O judge; state who seems to you to say what is truest, and not who says what is absolutely true. For to do that is as far beyond our ken as truth itself.

11. This throng of causes, defined by Aristotle and by Plato, embraces either too much or too little. For if they regard as "causes" of an object that is to be made everything without which the object cannot be made, they have named too few. Time must be included among the causes; for nothing can be made without time. They must also include place; for if there be no place where a thing can be made, it will not be made. And motion too; nothing is either made or destroyed without motion. There is no art without motion, no change of any kind. **12.** Now, however, I am searching for the first, the general cause; this must be simple, inasmuch as matter, too, is simple. Do we ask what cause is? It is surely Creative Reason, – in other words, God. For those elements to which you referred are not a great series of independent causes; they all hinge on one alone, and that will be the creative cause. **13.** Do you maintain that form is a cause? This is only what the artist stamps upon his work; it is part of a cause, but not the cause. Neither is the pattern a cause, but an indispensable tool of the cause. His pattern is as indispensable to the artist as the chisel or the file; without these, art can make no progress. But for all that, these things are neither parts of the art, nor causes of it. **14.** "Then," perhaps you will say, "the purpose of the artist, that which leads him to undertake to create something, is the cause." It may be a cause; it is not, however, the efficient cause, but only an accessory cause. But there are countless accessory causes; what we are discussing is the general cause. Now the statement of Plato and Aristotle is not in accord with their usual penetration, when they maintain that the whole universe, the perfectly wrought work, is a cause. For there is a great difference between a work and the cause of a work.

15. Either give your opinion, or, as is easier in cases of this kind, declare that the matter is not clear and call for another hearing. But you will reply: "What pleasure do you get from wasting your time on these problems, which relieve you of none of your emotions, rout none of your desires?" So far as I am concerned, I treat and discuss them as matters which contribute greatly toward calming the spirit, and I search myself first, and then the world about me. **16.** And not even now am I, as you think, wasting my time. For all these questions, provided that they be not chopped up and torn apart into such unprofitable refinements, elevate and lighten the soul, which is weighted down by a heavy burden and desires to be freed and to return to the elements of which it was once a part. For this body of ours is a weight upon the soul and its penance; as the load presses down the soul is crushed and is in bondage, unless philosophy has come to its assistance and has bid it take fresh courage by contemplating the universe, and has turned it from things earthly to things divine. There it has its liberty, there it can roam abroad; meantime it escapes the custody in which it is bound, and renews its life in heaven. **17.** Just as skilled workmen, who have been engaged upon some delicate piece of work which wearies their eyes with straining, if the light which they have is niggardly or uncertain, go forth into the open air and in some park devoted to the people's recreation delight their eyes in the generous light of day; so the soul, imprisoned as it has been in this gloomy and darkened house, seeks the open sky whenever it can, and in the contemplation of the universe finds rest.

18. The wise man, the seeker after wisdom, is bound closely, indeed, to his body, but he is an absentee so far as his better self is concerned, and he concentrates his thoughts upon lofty things. Bound, so to speak, to his oath of allegiance, he regards the period of life as his term of service. He is so trained that he neither loves nor hates life; he endures a mortal lot, although he knows that an ampler lot is in store for him. 19. Do you forbid me to contemplate the universe? Do you compel me to withdraw from the whole and restrict me to a part? May I not ask what are the beginnings of all things, who moulded the universe, who took the confused and conglomerate mass of sluggish matter, and separated it into its parts? May I not inquire who is the Master-Builder of this universe, how the mighty bulk was brought under the control of law and order, who gathered together the scattered atoms, who separated the disordered elements and assigned an outward form to elements that lay in one vast shapelessness? Or whence came all the expanse of light? And whether is it fire, or even brighter than fire? 20. Am I not to ask these questions? Must I be ignorant of the heights whence I have descended? Whether I am to see this world but once, or to be born many times? What is my destination afterwards? What abode awaits my soul on its release from the laws of slavery among men? Do you forbid me to have a share in heaven? In other words, do you bid me live with my head bowed down? 21. No, I am above such an existence; I was born to a greater destiny than to be a mere chattel of my body, and I regard this body as nothing but a chain which manacles my freedom. Therefore, I offer it as a sort of buffer to fortune, and shall allow no wound to penetrate through to my soul. For my body is the only part of me which can suffer injury. In this dwelling, which is exposed to peril, my soul lives free. 22. Never shall this flesh drive me to feel fear or to assume any pretence that is unworthy of a good man. Never shall I lie in order to honour this petty body. When it seems proper, I shall sever my connexion with it. And at present, while we are bound together, our alliance shall nevertheless not be one of equality; the soul shall bring all quarrels before its own tribunal. To despise our bodies is sure freedom.

23. To return to our subject; this freedom will be greatly helped by the contemplation of which we were just speaking. All things are made up of matter and of God; God controls matter, which encompasses him and follows him as its guide and leader. And that which creates, in other words, God, is more powerful and precious than matter, which is acted upon by God. 24. God's place in the universe corresponds to the soul's relation to man. World-matter corresponds to our mortal body; therefore let the lower serve the higher. Let us be brave in the face of hazards. Let us not fear wrongs, or wounds, or bonds, or poverty. And what is death? It is either the end, or a process of change. I have no fear of ceasing to exist; it is the same

as not having begun. Nor do I shrink from changing into another state, because I shall, under no conditions, be as cramped as I am now. Farewell.

LXVI. ON VARIOUS ASPECTS OF VIRTUE

1. I have just seen my former school-mate Claranus for the first time in many years. You need not wait for me to add that he is an old man; but I assure you that I found him hale in spirit and sturdy, although he is wrestling with a frail and feeble body. For Nature acted unfairly when she gave him a poor domicile for so rare a soul; or perhaps it was because she wished to prove to us that an absolutely strong and happy mind can lie hidden under any exterior. Be that as it may, Claranus overcomes all these hindrances, and by despising his own body has arrived at a stage where he can despise other things also. **2.** The poet who sang

> Worth shows more pleasing in a form that's fair,

is, in my opinion, mistaken. For virtue needs nothing to set it off; it is its own great glory, and it hallows the body in which it dwells. At any rate, I have begun to regard Claranus in a different light; he seems to me handsome, and as well-setup in body as in mind. **3.** A great man can spring from a hovel; so can a beautiful and great soul from an ugly and insignificant body. For this reason Nature seems to me to breed certain men of this stamp with the idea of proving that virtue springs into birth in any place whatever. Had it been possible for her to produce souls by themselves and naked, she would have done so; as it is, Nature does a still greater thing, for she produces certain men who, though hampered in their bodies, none the less break through the obstruction. **4.** I think Claranus has been produced as a pattern, that we might be enabled to understand that the soul is not disfigured by the ugliness of the body, but rather the opposite, that the body is beautified by the comeliness of the soul.

Now, though Claranus and I have spent very few days together, we have nevertheless had many conversations, which I will at once pour forth and pass on to you. **5.** The first day we investigated this problem: how can goods be equal if they are of three kinds? For certain of them, according to our philosophical tenets, are primary, such as joy, peace, and the welfare of one's country. Others are of the second order, moulded in an unhappy material, such as the endurance of suffering, and self-control during severe illness. We shall pray outright for the goods of the first class; for the second class we shall pray only if the need shall arise. There is still a third variety, as, for example, a modest gait, a calm and honest countenance, and a bearing that suits the man of wisdom. **6.** Now how can these things be equal when we compare them, if you grant that we ought to pray for the one and avoid the other? If we would make distinctions among them, we had better return to the First Good, and consider what its nature is: the soul that gazes upon truth, that is skilled in what should be sought and what should be avoided, establishing standards of value not according to opinion, but according to nature, – the soul that penetrates the whole world and directs its contemplating gaze upon all its Phenomena, paying strict attention to thoughts and actions, equally great and forceful, superior alike to hardships and blandishments, yielding itself to neither extreme of fortune, rising above all blessings and tribulations, absolutely beautiful, perfectly equipped with grace as well as with strength, healthy and sinewy, unruffled, undismayed, one which no violence can shatter, one which acts of chance can neither exalt nor depress, – a soul like this is virtue itself. **7.** There you have its outward appearance, if it should ever come under a single view and show itself once in all its completeness. But there are many aspects of it. They unfold themselves according as life varies and as actions differ; but virtue itself does not become less or greater. For the Supreme Good cannot diminish, nor may virtue retrograde; rather is it transformed, now into one quality and now into another, shaping itself according to the part which it is to play. **8.** Whatever it has touched it brings into likeness with itself, and dyes with its own colour. It adorns our actions, our friendships, and sometimes entire households which it has entered and set in order. Whatever it has handled it forthwith makes lovable, notable, admirable.

Therefore the power and the greatness of virtue cannot rise to greater heights, because increase is denied to that which is superlatively great. You will find nothing straighter than the straight, nothing truer than the truth, and nothing more temperate than that which is temperate. **9.** Every virtue is limitless; for limits depend upon definite measurements. Constancy cannot advance further, any more than fidelity, or truthfulness, or loyalty. What can be added to that which is perfect? Nothing otherwise that was not perfect to which something has been added. Nor can anything be added to virtue, either, for if anything can be added thereto, it must have contained a defect. Honour, also, permits of no addition; for it is honourable because of the very qualities which I have mentioned. What then? Do you think that propriety, justice, lawfulness, do not also belong to the same type, and that they are kept within fixed limits? The ability to increase is proof that a thing is still imperfect.

10. The good, in every instance, is subject to these same laws. The advantage of the state and that of the individual are yoked together; indeed it is as impossible to separate them as to separate the commendable from the desirable. Therefore, virtues are mutually equal; and so are the works of virtue, and all men who are so fortunate as to possess these virtues. **11.** But, since the virtues of plants and of animals are perishable, they are also frail and fleeting and uncertain. They spring up, and they sink down again, and for this reason they are not rated at the same value; but to human virtues only one rule applies. For right reason is single and of but one kind. Nothing is more divine than the divine, or more heavenly than the heavenly. **12.** Mortal things decay, fall, are worn out, grow up, are exhausted, and replenished. Hence, in their case, in view of the uncertainty of their lot, there is inequality; but of things divine the nature is one. Reason, however, is nothing else than a portion of the divine spirit set in a human body. If reason is divine, and the good in no case lacks reason, then the good in every case is divine. And furthermore, there is no distinction between things divine; hence there is none between goods, either. Therefore it follows that joy and a brave unyielding endurance of torture are equal goods; for in both there is the same greatness of soul relaxed and cheerful in the one case, in the other combative and braced for action. **13.** What? Do you not think that the virtue of him who bravely storms the enemy's stronghold is equal to that of him who endures a siege with the utmost patience? Great is Scipio when he invests Numantia, and constrains and compels the hands of an enemy, whom he could not conquer, to resort to their own destruction. Great also are the souls of the defenders – men who know that, as long as the path to death lies open, the blockade is not complete, men who breathe their last in the arms of liberty. In like manner, the other virtues are also equal as compared with one another: tranquillity, simplicity, generosity, constancy, equanimity, endurance. For underlying them all is a single virtue – that which renders the soul straight and unswerving.

14. "What then," you say; "is there no difference between joy and unyielding endurance of pain?" None at all, as regards the virtues themselves; very great, however, in the circumstances in which either of these two virtues is displayed. In the one case, there is a natural relaxation and loosening of the soul; in the other there is an unnatural pain. Hence these circumstances, between which a great distinction can be drawn, belong to the category of indifferent things, but the virtue shown in each case is equal. **15.** Virtue is not changed by the matter with which it deals; if the matter is hard and stubborn, it does not make the virtue worse; if pleasant and joyous, it does not make it better. Therefore, virtue necessarily remains equal. For, in each case, what is done is done with equal uprightness, with equal wisdom, and with equal honour. Hence the states of goodness involved are equal, and it is impossible for a man to transcend these states of goodness by conducting himself better, either the one man in his joy, or the other amid his suffering. And two goods, neither of which can possibly be better, are equal. **16.** For if things which are extrinsic to virtue can either diminish or increase virtue, then that which is honourable ceases to be the only good. If you grant this, honour has wholly perished. And why? Let me tell you: it is because no act is honourable that is done by an unwilling agent, that is compulsory. Every honourable act is voluntary. Alloy it with reluctance, complaints, cowardice, or fear, and it loses its best characteristic – self-approval. That which is not free cannot be honourable; for fear means slavery. **17.** The honourable is wholly free from anxiety and is calm; if it ever objects, laments, or regards anything as an evil, it becomes subject to disturbance and begins to flounder about amid great confusion. For on one side the semblance of right calls to it, on the other the suspicion of evil drags it back, therefore, when a man is about to do something honourable, he should not regard any obstacles as evils, even though he regard them as inconvenient, but he should will to do the deed, and do it willingly. For every honourable act is done without commands or compulsion; it is unalloyed and contains no admixture of evil.

18. I know what you may reply to me at this point: "Are you trying to make us believe that it does not matter whether a man feels joy, or whether he lies upon the rack and tires out his torturer?" I might say in answer: "Epicurus also maintains that the wise man, though he is being burned in the bull of Phalaris, will cry out: 'Tis pleasant, and concerns me not at all.'" Why need you wonder, if I maintain that he who reclines at a banquet and the victim who stoutly withstands torture possess equal goods, when Epicurus maintains a thing that is harder to believe, namely, that it is pleasant to be roasted in this way? **19.** But the reply which I do make, is that there is great difference between joy and pain; if I am asked to choose, I shall seek the former and avoid the latter. The former is according to nature, the latter contrary to it. So long as they are rated by this standard, there is a great gulf between; but when it comes to a question of the virtue involved, the virtue in each case is the same, whether it comes through joy or through sorrow. **20.** Vexation and pain and other inconveniences are of no consequence, for they are overcome by virtue. Just as the brightness of the sun dims all lesser lights, so virtue, by its own greatness, shatters and overwhelms all pains, annoyances, and wrongs; and wherever its radiance reaches, all lights which shine without the help of virtue are extinguished; and inconveniences, when they come in contact with virtue, play no more important a part than does a storm-cloud at sea.

21. This can be proved to you by the fact that the good man will hasten unhesitatingly to any noble deed; even though he be confronted by the hangman, the torturer, and the stake, he will persist, regarding not what he must suffer, but what he must do; and he will entrust himself as readily to an honourable deed as he would to a good man; he will consider it advantageous to himself, safe, propitious. And he will hold the same view concerning an honourable deed, even though it be fraught with sorrow and hardship, as concerning a good man who is poor or wasting away in exile. **22.** Come now, contrast a good man who is rolling in wealth with a man who has nothing, except that in himself he has all things; they will be equally good, though they experience unequal fortune. This same standard, as I have remarked, is to be applied to things as well as to men; virtue is just as praiseworthy if it dwells in a sound and free body, as in one which is sickly or in bondage. **23.** Therefore, as regards your own virtue also, you will not praise it any more, if fortune has favoured it by granting you a sound body, than if fortune has endowed you with a body that is crippled in some member, since that would mean rating a master low because he is dressed like a slave. For all those things over which Chance holds sway are chattels, money, person, position; they are weak, shifting, prone to perish, and of uncertain tenure. On the other hand, the works of virtue are free and unsubdued, neither more worthy to be sought when fortune treats them kindly, nor less worthy when any adversity weighs upon them.

24. Now friendship in the case of men corresponds to desirability in the case of things. You would not, I fancy, love a good man if he were rich any more than if he were poor, nor would you love a strong and muscular person more than one who was slender and of delicate constitution. Accordingly, neither will you seek or love a good thing that is mirthful and tranquil more than one that is full of perplexity and toil. **25.** Or, if you do this, you will, in the case of two equally good men, care more for him who is neat and well-groomed than for him who is dirty and unkempt. You would next go so far as to care more for a good man who is sound in all his limbs and without blemish, than for one who is weak or purblind; and gradually your fastidiousness would reach such a point that, of two equally just and prudent men, you would choose him who has long curling hair! Whenever the virtue in each one is equal, the inequality in their other attributes is not apparent. For all other things are not parts, but merely accessories. **26.** Would any man judge his children so unfairly as to care more for a healthy son than for one who was sickly, or for a tall child of unusual stature more than for one who was short or of middling height? Wild beasts show no favouritism among their offspring; they lie down in order to suckle all alike; birds make fair distribution of their food. Ulysses hastens back to the rocks of his Ithaca as eagerly as Agamemnon speeds to the kingly walls of Mycenae. For no man loves his native land because it is great; he loves it because it is his own.

27. And what is the purpose of all this? That you may know that virtue regards all her works in the same light, as if they were her children, showing equal kindness to all, and still deeper kindness to those which encounter hardships; for even parents lean with more affection towards those of their offspring for whom they feel pity. Virtue, too, does not necessarily love more deeply those of her works which she beholds in trouble and under heavy burdens, but, like good parents, she gives them more of her fostering care.

28. Why is no good greater than any other good? It is because nothing can be more fitting than that which is fitting, and nothing more level than that which is level. You cannot say that one thing is more equal to a given object than another thing; hence also nothing is more honourable than that which is honourable. **29.** Accordingly, if all the virtues are by nature equal, the three varieties of goods are equal. This is what I mean: there is an equality between feeling joy with self-control and suffering pain with self-control. The joy in the one case does not surpass in the other the steadfastness of soul that gulps down the groan when the victim is in the clutches of the torturer; goods of the first kind are desirable, while those of the second are worthy of admiration; and in each case they are none the less equal, because whatever inconvenience attaches to the latter is compensated by the qualities of the good, which is so much greater. **30.** Any man who believes them to be unequal is turning away from the virtues themselves and is surveying mere externals; true goods have the same weight and the same width. The spurious sort contain much emptiness; hence, when they are weighed in the balance, they are found wanting, although they look imposing and grand to the gaze.

31. Yes, my dear Lucilius, the good which true reason approves is solid and everlasting; it strengthens the spirit and exalts it, so that it will always be on the heights; but those things which are thoughtlessly praised, and are goods in the opinion of the mob merely puff us up with empty joy. And again, those things which are feared as if they were evils merely inspire trepidation in men's minds, for the mind is disturbed by the semblance of danger, just as animals are disturbed. 32. Hence it is without reason that both these things distract and sting the spirit; the one is not worthy of joy, nor the other of fear. It is reason alone that is unchangeable, that holds fast to its decisions. For reason is not a slave to the senses, but a ruler over them. Reason is equal to reason, as one straight line to another; therefore virtue also is equal to virtue. Virtue is nothing else than right reason. All virtues are reasons. Reasons are reasons, if they are right reasons. If they are right, they are also equal. 33. As reason is, so also are actions; therefore all actions are equal. For since they resemble reason, they also resemble each other. Moreover, I hold that actions are equal to each other in so far as they are honourable and right actions. There will be, of course, great differences according as the material varies, as it becomes now broader and now narrower, now glorious and now base, now manifold in scope and now limited. However, that which is best in all these cases is equal; they are all honourable. 34. In the same way, all good men, in so far as they are good, are equal. There are, indeed, differences of age, one is older, another younger; of body, – one is comely, another is ugly; of fortune, – this man is rich, that man poor, this one is influential, powerful, and well-known to cities and peoples, that man is unknown to most, and is obscure. But all, in respect of that wherein they are good, are equal. 35. The senses do not decide upon things good and evil; they do not know what is useful and what is not useful. They cannot record their opinion unless they are brought face to face with a fact; they can neither see into the future nor recollect the past; and they do not know what results from what. But it is from such knowledge that a sequence and succession of actions is woven, and a unity of life is created, – a unity which will proceed in a straight course. Reason, therefore, is the judge of good and evil; that which is foreign and external she regards as dross, and that which is neither good nor evil she judges as merely accessory, insignificant and trivial. For all her good resides in the soul.

36. But there are certain goods which reason regards as primary, to which she addresses herself purposely; these are, for example, victory, good children, and the welfare of one's country. Certain others she regards as secondary; these become manifest only in adversity, – for example, equanimity in enduring severe illness or exile. Certain goods are indifferent; these are no more according to nature than contrary to nature, as, for example, a discreet gait and a sedate posture in a chair. For sitting is an act that is not less according to nature than standing or walking. 37. The two kinds of goods which are of a higher order are different; the primary are according to nature, – such as deriving joy from the dutiful behaviour of one's children and from the well-being of one's country. The secondary are contrary to nature, – such as fortitude in resisting torture or in enduring thirst when illness makes the vitals feverish. 38. "What then," you say; "can anything that is contrary

to nature be a good?" Of course not; but that in which this good takes its rise is sometimes contrary to nature. For being wounded, wasting away over a fire, being afflicted with bad health, – such things are contrary to nature; but it is in accordance with nature for a man to preserve an indomitable soul amid such distresses. **39.** To explain my thought briefly, the material with which a good is concerned is sometimes contrary to nature, but a good itself never is contrary, since no good is without reason, and reason is in accordance with nature.

"What, then," you ask, "is reason?" It is copying nature. "And what," you say, "is the greatest good that man can possess?" It is to conduct oneself according to what nature wills. **40.** "There is no doubt," says the objector, "that peace affords more happiness when it has not been assailed than when it has been recovered at the cost of great slaughter." "There is no doubt also," he continues, "that health which has not been impaired affords more happiness than health which has been restored to soundness by means of force, as it were, and by endurance of suffering, after serious illnesses that threaten life itself. And similarly there will be no doubt that joy is a greater good than a soul's struggle to endure to the bitter end the torments of wounds or burning at the stake." **41.** By no means. For things that result from hazard admit of wide distinctions, since they are rated according to their usefulness in the eyes of those who experience them, but with regard to goods, the only point to be considered is that they are in agreement with nature; and this is equal in the case of all goods. When at a meeting of the Senate we vote in favour of someone's motion, it cannot be said, "A. is more in accord with the motion than B." All alike vote for the same motion. I make the same statement with regard to virtues, – they are all in accord with nature; and I make it with regard to goods also, – they are all in accord with nature. **42.** One man dies young, another in old age, and still another in infancy, having enjoyed nothing more than a mere glimpse out into life. They have all been equally subject to death, even though death has permitted the one to proceed farther along the pathway of life, has cut off the life of the second in his flower, and has broken off the life of the third at its very beginning. **43.** Some get their release at the dinner-table. Others extend their sleep into the sleep of death. Some are blotted out during dissipation. Now contrast with these persons individuals who have been pierced by the sword, or bitten to death by snakes, or crushed in ruins, or tortured piecemeal out of existence by the prolonged twisting of their sinews. Some of these departures may be regarded as better, some as worse; but the act of dying is equal in all. The methods of ending life are different; but the end is one and the same. Death has no degrees of greater or less; for it has the same limit in all instances, – the finishing of life.

44. The same thing holds true, I assure you, concerning goods; you will find one amid circumstances of pure pleasure, another amid sorrow and bitterness. The one controls the favours of fortune; the other overcomes her onslaughts. Each is equally a good, although the one travels a level and easy road, and the other a rough road. And the end of them all is the same – they are goods, they are worthy of praise, they accompany virtue and reason. Virtue makes all the things that it acknowledges equal to one another. **45.** You need not wonder that this is one of our principles; we find mentioned in the works of Epicurus two goods, of which his Supreme Good, or blessedness, is composed, namely, a body free from pain and a soul free from disturbance. These goods, if they are complete, do not increase; for how can that which is complete increase? The body is, let us suppose, free from pain; what increase can there be to this absence of pain? The soul is composed and calm; what increase can there be to this tranquillity? **46.** Just as fair weather, purified into the purest brilliancy, does not admit of a still greater degree of clearness; so, when a man takes care of his body and of his soul, weaving the texture of his good from both, his condition is perfect, and he has found the consummation of his prayers, if there is no commotion in his soul or pain in his body. Whatever delights fall to his lot over and above these two things do not increase his Supreme Good; they merely season it, so to speak, and add spice to it. For the absolute good of man's nature is satisfied with peace in the body and peace in the soul. **47.** I can show you at this moment in the writings of Epicurus a graded list of goods just like that of our own school. For there are some things, he declares, which he prefers should fall to his lot, such as bodily rest free from all inconvenience, and relaxation of the soul as it takes delight in the contemplation of its own goods. And there are other things which, though he would prefer that they did not happen, he nevertheless praises and approves, for example, the kind of resignation, in times of ill-health and serious suffering, to which I alluded a moment ago, and which Epicurus displayed on that last and most blessed day of his life. For he tells us that he had to endure excruciating agony from a diseased bladder and from an ulcerated stomach, so acute that it permitted no increase of pain; "and yet," he says, "that day was none the less happy." And no man can spend such a day in happiness unless he possesses the Supreme Good.

48. We therefore find mentioned, even by Epicurus, those goods which one would prefer not to experience; which, however, because circumstances have decided thus, must be welcomed and approved and placed on a level with the highest goods. We cannot say that the good which has rounded out a happy life, the good for which Epicurus rendered thanks in the last words he uttered, is not equal to the greatest. **49.** Allow me, excellent Lucilius, to utter a still bolder word: if any goods could be greater than others, I should prefer those which seem harsh to those which are mild and alluring, and should pronounce them greater. For it is more of an accomplishment to break one's way through difficulties than to keep joy within bounds. **50.** It requires the same use of reason, I am fully aware, for a man to endure prosperity well and also to endure misfortune bravely. What man may be just as brave who sleeps in front of the ramparts without fear of danger when no enemy attacks the camp, as the man who, when the tendons of his legs have been severed, holds himself up on his knees and does not let fall his weapons; but it is to the blood-stained soldier returning from the front that men cry: "Well done, thou hero!" And therefore I should bestow greater praise upon those goods that have stood trial and show courage, and have fought it out with fortune. 51. Should I hesitate whether to give greater praise to the maimed and shrivelled hand of Mucius than to the uninjured hand of the bravest man in the world? There stood Mucius, despising the enemy and despising the fire, and watched his hand as it dripped blood over the fire on his enemy's altar, until Porsenna, envying the fame of the hero whose punishment he was advocating, ordered the fire to be removed against the will of the victim.

52. Why should I not reckon this good among the primary goods, and deem it in so far greater than those other goods which are unattended by danger and have made no trial of fortune, as it is a rarer thing to have overcome a foe with a hand lost than with a hand armed? "What then?" you say; "shall you desire this good for yourself?" Of course I shall. For this is a thing that a man cannot achieve unless he can also desire it. 53. Should I desire, instead, to be allowed to stretch out my limbs for my slaves to massage, or to have a woman, or a man changed into the likeness of a woman, pull my finger-joints? I cannot help believing that Mucius was all the more lucky because he manipulated the flames as calmly as if he were holding out his hand to the manipulator. He had wiped out all his previous mistakes; he finished the war unarmed and maimed; and with that stump of a hand he conquered two kings. Farewell.

LXVII. ON ILL-HEALTH AND ENDURANCE OF SUFFERING

1. If I may begin with a commonplace remark, spring is gradually disclosing itself; but though it is rounding into summer, when you would expect hot weather, it has kept rather cool, and one cannot yet be sure of it. For it often slides back into winter weather. Do you wish to know how uncertain it still is? I do not yet trust myself to a bath which is absolutely cold; even at this time I break its chill. You may say that this is no way to show the endurance either of heat or of cold; very true, dear Lucilius, but at my time of life one is at length contented with the natural chill of the body. I can scarcely thaw out in the middle of summer. Accordingly, I spend most of the time bundled up; 2. and I thank old age for keeping me fastened to my bed. Why should I not thank old age on this account? That which I ought not to wish to do, I lack the ability to do. Most of my converse is with books. Whenever your letters arrive, I imagine that I am with you, and I have the feeling that I am about to speak my answer, instead of writing it. Therefore let us together investigate the nature of this problem of yours, just as if we were conversing with one another.

3. You ask me whether every good is desirable. You say: "If it is a good to be brave under torture, to go to the stake with a stout heart, to endure illness with resignation, it follows that these things are desirable. But I do not see that any of them is worth praying for. At any rate I have as yet known of no man who has paid

a vow by reason of having been cut to pieces by the rod, or twisted out of shape by the gout, or made taller by the rack." **4.** My dear Lucilius, you must distinguish between these cases; you will then comprehend that there is something in them that is to be desired. I should prefer to be free from torture; but if the time comes when it must be endured, I shall desire that I may conduct myself therein with bravery, honour, and courage. Of course I prefer that war should not occur; but if war does occur, I shall desire that I may nobly endure the wounds, the starvation, and all that the exigency of war brings. Nor am I so mad as to crave illness; but if I must suffer illness, I shall desire that I may do nothing which shows lack of restraint, and nothing that is unmanly. The conclusion is, not that hardships are desirable, but that virtue is desirable, which enables us patiently to endure hardships.

5. Certain of our school, think that, of all such qualities, a stout endurance is not desirable, – though not to be deprecated either – because we ought to seek by prayer only the good which is unalloyed, peaceful, and beyond the reach of trouble. Personally, I do not agree with them. And why? First, because it is impossible for anything to be good without being also desirable. Because, again, if virtue is desirable, and if nothing that is good lacks virtue, then everything good is desirable. And, lastly, because a brave endurance even under torture is desirable. **6.** At this point I ask you: is not bravery desirable? And yet bravery despises and challenges danger. The most beautiful and most admirable part of bravery is that it does not shrink from the stake, advances to meet wounds, and sometimes does not even avoid the spear, but meets it with opposing breast. If bravery is desirable, so is patient endurance of torture; for this is a part of bravery. Only sift these things, as I have suggested; then there will be nothing which can lead you astray. For it is not mere endurance of torture, but brave endurance, that is desirable. I therefore desire that "brave" endurance; and this is virtue.

7. "But," you say, "who ever desired such a thing for himself?" Some prayers are open and outspoken, when the requests are offered specifically; other prayers are indirectly expressed, when they include many requests under one title. For example, I desire a life of honour. Now a life of honour includes various kinds of conduct; it may include the chest in which Regulus was confined, or the wound of Cato which was torn open by Cato's own hand, or the exile of Rutilius, or the cup of poison which removed Socrates from gaol to heaven. Accordingly, in praying for a life of honour, I have prayed also for those things without which, on some occasions, life cannot be honourable

> **8.** O thrice and four times blest were they
> Who underneath the lofty walls of Troy
> Met happy death before their parents' eyes!

What does it matter whether you offer this prayer for some individual, or admit that it was desirable in the past? **9.** Decius sacrificed himself for the State; he set spurs to his horse and rushed into the midst of the foe, seeking death. The second

Decius, rivalling his father's valour, reproducing the words which had become sacred and already household words, dashed into the thickest of the fight, anxious only that his sacrifice might bring omen of success, and regarding a noble death as a thing to be desired. Do you doubt, then, whether it is best to die glorious and performing some deed of valour? 10. When one endures torture bravely, one is using all the virtues. Endurance may perhaps be the only virtue that is on view and most manifest; but bravery is there too, and endurance and resignation and long-suffering are its branches. There, too, is foresight; for without foresight no plan can be undertaken; it is foresight that advises one to bear as bravely as possible the things one cannot avoid. There also is steadfastness, which cannot be dislodged from its position, which the wrench of no force can cause to abandon its purpose. There is the whole inseparable company of virtues; every honourable act is the work of one single virtue, but it is in accordance with the judgment of the whole council. And that which is approved by all the virtues, even though it seems to be the work of one alone, is desirable.

11. What? Do you think that those things only are desirable which come to us amid pleasure and ease, and which we bedeck our doors to welcome? There are certain goods whose features are forbidding. There are certain prayers which are offered by a throng, not of men who rejoice, but of men who bow down reverently and worship. 12. Was it not in this fashion, think you, that Regulus prayed that he might reach Carthage? Clothe yourself with a hero's courage, and withdraw for a little space from the opinions of the common man. Form a proper conception of the image of virtue, a thing of exceeding beauty and grandeur; this image is not to be worshipped by us with incense or garlands, but with sweat and blood. 13. Behold Marcus Cato, laying upon that hallowed breast his unspotted hands, and tearing apart the wounds which had not gone deep enough to kill him! Which, pray, shall you say to him: "I hope all will be as you wish," and "I am grieved," or shall it be "Good fortune in your undertaking!"?

14. In this connexion I think of our friend Demetrius, who calls an easy existence, untroubled by the attacks of Fortune, a "Dead Sea." If you have nothing to stir you up and rouse you to action, nothing which will test your resolution by its threats and hostilities; if you recline in unshaken comfort, it is not tranquillity; it is merely a flat calm. 15. The Stoic Attalus was wont to say: "I should prefer that Fortune keep me in her camp rather than in the lap of luxury. If I am tortured, but bear it bravely, all is well; if I die, but die bravely, it is also well." Listen to Epicurus; he will tell you that it is actually pleasant. I myself shall never apply an effeminate word to an act so honourable and austere. If I go to the stake, I shall go unbeaten. 16. Why should I not regard this as desirable – not because the fire, burns me, but because it does not overcome me? Nothing is more excellent or more beautiful than virtue; whatever we do in obedience to her orders is both good and desirable. Farewell.

LXVIII. ON WISDOM AND RETIREMENT

1. I fall in with your plan; retire and conceal yourself in repose. But at the same time conceal your retirement also. In doing this, you may be sure that you will be following the example of the Stoics, if not their precept. But you will be acting according to their precept also; you will thus satisfy both yourself and any Stoic you please. **2.** We Stoics do not urge men to take up public life in every case, or at all times, or without any qualification. Besides, when we have assigned to our wise man that field of public life which is worthy of him, – in other words, the universe, – he is then not apart from public life, even if he withdraws; nay, perhaps he has abandoned only one little corner thereof and has passed over into greater and wider regions; and when he has been set in the heavens, he understands how lowly was the place in which he sat when he mounted the curule chair or the judgment-seat. Lay this to heart, that the wise man is never more active in affairs than when things divine as well as things human have come within his ken.

3. I now return to the advice which I set out to give you, – that you keep your retirement in the background. There is no need to fasten a placard upon yourself with the words: "Philosopher and Quietist." Give your purpose some other name; call it ill-health and bodily weakness, or mere laziness. To boast of our retirement is but idle self-seeking. **4.** Certain animals hide themselves from discovery by confusing the marks of their foot-prints in the neighbourhood of their lairs. You should do the same. Otherwise, there will always be someone dogging your footsteps. Many men pass by that which is visible, and peer after things hidden and concealed; a locked room invites the thief. Things which lie in the open appear cheap; the house-breaker passes by that which is exposed to view. This is the way of the world, and the way of all ignorant men: they crave to burst in upon hidden things. It is therefore best not to vaunt one's retirement. **5.** It is, however, a sort of vaunting to make too much of one's concealment and of one's withdrawal from the sight of men. So-and-so has gone into his retreat at Tarentum; that other man has shut himself up at Naples; this third person for many years has not crossed the threshold of his own house. To advertise one's retirement is to collect a crowd. **6.** When you withdraw from the world your business is to talk with yourself, not to have men talk about you. But what shall you talk about? Do just what people are fond of doing when they talk about their neighbours, – speak ill of yourself when by yourself; then you will become accustomed both to speak and to hear the truth. Above all, however, ponder that which you come to feel is your greatest weakness. **7.** Each man knows best the defects of his own body. And so one relieves his stomach by vomiting, another props it up by frequent eating, another drains and purges his body by periodic fasting. Those whose feet are visited by pain abstain either from wine or from the bath. In general, men who are careless in other respects go out of their way to relieve the disease which frequently afflicts them. So it is with our souls; there are in them certain parts which are, so to speak, on the sick-list, and to these parts the cure must be applied.

8. What, then, am I myself doing with my leisure? I am trying to cure my own sores. If I were to show you a swollen foot, or an inflamed hand, or some shrivelled sinews in a withered leg, you would permit me to lie quiet in one place and to apply lotions to the diseased member. But my trouble is greater than any of these, and I cannot show it to you. The abscess, or ulcer, is deep within my breast. Pray, pray, do not commend me, do not say: "What a great man! He has learned to despise all things; condemning the madnesses of man's life, he has made his escape!" I have condemned nothing except myself. **9.** There is no reason why you should desire to come to me for the sake of making progress. You are mistaken if you think that you will get any assistance from this quarter; it is not a physician that dwells here, but a sick man. I would rather have you say, on leaving my presence: "I used to think him a happy man and a learned one, and I had pricked up my ears to hear him; but I have been defrauded. I have seen nothing, heard nothing which I craved and which I came back to hear." If you feel thus, and speak thus, some progress has been made. I prefer you to pardon rather than envy my retirement.

10. Then you say: "Is it retirement, Seneca, that you are recommending to me? You will soon be falling back upon the maxims of Epicurus!" I do recommend retirement to you, but only that you may use it for greater and more beautiful activities than those which you have resigned; to knock at the haughty doors of the influential, to make alphabetical lists of childless old men, to wield the highest authority in public life, – this kind of power exposes you to hatred, is short-lived, and, if you rate it at its true value, is tawdry. **11.** One man shall be far ahead of me as regards his influence in public life, another in salary as an army officer and in the position which results from this, another in the throng of his clients; but it is worth while to be outdone by all these men, provided that I myself can outdo Fortune. And I am no match for her in the throng; she has the greater backing.

12. Would that in earlier days you had been minded to follow this purpose! Would that we were not discussing the happy life in plain view of death! But even now let us have no delay. For now we can take the word of experience, which tells us that there are many superfluous and hostile things; for this we should long since have taken the word of reason. **13.** Let us do what men are wont to do when they are late in setting forth, and wish to make up for lost time by increasing their speed – let us ply the spur. Our time of life is the best possible for these pursuits; for the period of boiling and foaming is now past. The faults that were uncontrolled in the first fierce heat of youth are now weakened, and but little further effort is needed to extinguish them.

14. "And when," you ask, "will that profit you which you do not learn until your departure, and how will it profit you?" Precisely in this way, that I shall depart a better man. You need not think, however, that any time of life is more fitted to the attainment of a sound mind than that which has gained the victory over itself by many trials and by long and oft-repeated regret for past mistakes, and, its passions assuaged, has reached a state of health. This is indeed the time to have acquired this good; he who has attained wisdom in his old age, has attained it by his years. Farewell.

LXIX. ON REST AND RESTLESSNESS

1. I do not like you to change your headquarters and scurry about from one place to another. My reasons are, – first, that such frequent flitting means an unsteady spirit. And the spirit cannot through retirement grow into unity unless it has ceased from its inquisitiveness and its wanderings. To be able to hold your spirit in check, you must first stop the runaway flight of the body. **2.** My second reason is, that the remedies which are most helpful are those which are not interrupted. You should not allow your quiet, or the oblivion to which you have consigned your former life, to be broken into. Give your eyes time to unlearn what they have seen, and your ears to grow accustomed to more wholesome words. Whenever you stir abroad you will meet, even as you pass from one place to another, things that will bring back your old cravings. **3.** Just as he who tries to be rid of an old love must avoid every reminder of the person once held dear (for nothing grows again so easily as love), similarly, he who would lay aside his desire for all the things which he used to crave so passionately, must turn away both eyes and ears from the objects which he has abandoned. The emotions soon return to the attack; **4.** at every turn they will notice before their eyes an object worth their attention. There is no evil that does not offer inducements. Avarice promises money; luxury, a varied assortment of pleasures; ambition, a purple robe and applause, and the influence which results from applause, and all that influence can do. **5.** Vices tempt you by the rewards which they offer; but in the life of which I speak, you must live without being paid. Scarcely will a whole life-time suffice to bring our vices into subjection and to make them accept the yoke, swollen as they are by long-continued indulgence; and still less, if we cut into our brief span by any interruptions. Even constant care and attention can scarcely bring any one undertaking to full completion. **6.** If you will give ear to my advice, ponder and practise this, – how to welcome death, or even, if circumstances commend that course, to invite it. There is no difference whether death comes to us, or whether we go to death. Make yourself believe that all ignorant men are wrong when they say: "It is a beautiful thing to die one's own death." But there is no man who does not die his own death. What is more, you may reflect on this thought: No one dies except on his own day. You are throwing away none of your own time; for what you leave behind does not belong to you. Farewell.

LXX. ON THE PROPER TIME TO SLIP THE CABLE

1. After a long space of time I have seen your beloved Pompeii. I was thus brought again face to face with the days of my youth. And it seemed to me that I could still do, nay, had only done a short time ago, all the things which I did there when a young man. 2. We have sailed past life, Lucilius, as if we were on a voyage, and just as when at sea, to quote from our poet Vergil,

> Lands and towns are left astern,

even so, on this journey where time flies with the greatest speed, we put below the horizon first our boyhood and then our youth, and then the space which lies between young manhood and middle age and borders on both, and next, the best years of old age itself. Last of all, we begin to sight the general bourne of the race of man. 3. Fools that we are, we believe this bourne to be a dangerous reef; but it is the harbour, where we must some day put in, which we may never refuse to enter; and if a man has reached this harbour in his early years, he has no more right to complain than a sailor who has made a quick voyage. For some sailors, as you know, are tricked and held back by sluggish winds, and grow weary and sick of the slow-moving calm; while others are carried quickly home by steady gales.

4. You may consider that the same thing happens to us: life has carried some men with the greatest rapidity to the harbour, the harbour they were bound to reach even if they tarried on the way, while others it has fretted and harassed. To such a life, as you are aware, one should not always cling. For mere living is not a good, but living well. Accordingly, the wise man will live as long as he ought, not as long as he can. 5. He will mark in what place, with whom, and how he is to conduct his existence, and what he is about to do. He always reflects concerning the quality, and not the quantity, of his life. As soon as there are many events in his life that give him trouble and disturb his peace of mind, he sets himself free. And this privilege is his, not only when the crisis is upon him, but as soon as Fortune seems to be playing him false; then he looks about carefully and sees whether he ought, or ought not, to end his life on that account. He holds that it makes no difference to him whether his taking-off be natural or self-inflicted, whether it comes later or earlier. He does not regard it with fear, as if it were a great loss; for no man can lose very much when but a driblet remains. 6. It is not a question of dying earlier or later, but of dying well or ill. And dying well means escape from the danger of living ill.

That is why I regard the words of the well-known Rhodian as most unmanly. This person was thrown into a cage by his tyrant, and fed there like some wild animal. And when a certain man advised him to end his life by fasting, he replied: "A man may hope for anything while he has life." 7. This may be true; but life is not to be purchased at any price. No matter how great or how well-assured certain rewards may be I shall not strive to attain them at the price of a shameful confession of weakness. Shall I reflect that Fortune has all power over one who lives, rather than reflect that she has no power over one who knows how to die? **8.** There are times, nevertheless, when a man, even though certain death impends and he knows that torture is in store for him, will refrain from lending a hand to his own punishment, to himself, however, he would lend a hand. It is folly to die through fear of dying. The executioner is upon you; wait for him. Why anticipate him? Why assume the management of a cruel task that belongs to another? Do you grudge your executioner his privilege, or do you merely relieve him of his task? **9.** Socrates might have ended his life by fasting; he might have died by starvation rather than by poison. But instead of this he spent thirty days in prison awaiting death, not with the idea "everything may happen," or "so long an interval has room for many a hope" but in order that he might show himself submissive to the laws and make the last moments of Socrates an edification to his friends. What would have been more foolish than to scorn death, and yet fear poison?

10. Scribonia, a woman of the stern old type, was an aunt of Drusus Libo. This young man was as stupid as he was well born, with higher ambitions than anyone could have been expected to entertain in that epoch, or a man like himself in any epoch at all. When Libo had been carried away ill from the senate-house in his litter, though certainly with a very scanty train of followers, – for all his kinsfolk undutifully deserted him, when he was no longer a criminal but a corpse, – he began to consider whether he should commit suicide, or await death. Scribonia said to him: "What pleasure do you find in doing another man's work?" But he did not follow her advice; he laid violent hands upon himself. And he was right, after all; for when a man is doomed to die in two or three days at his enemy's pleasure, he is really "doing another man's work" if he continues to live.

11. No general statement can be made, therefore, with regard to the question whether, when a power beyond our control threatens us with death, we should anticipate death, or await it. For there are many arguments to pull us in either direction. If one death is accompanied by torture, and the other is simple and easy, why not snatch the latter? Just as I shall select my ship when I am about to go on a voyage or my house when I propose to take a residence, so I shall choose my death when I am about to depart from life. **12.** Moreover, just as a long-drawn out life does not necessarily mean a better one, so a long-drawn-out death necessarily means a worse one. There is no occasion when the soul should be humoured more than at the moment of death. Let the soul depart as it feels itself impelled to go; whether it seeks the sword, or the halter, or some drought that attacks the veins, let it proceed and burst the bonds of its slavery. Every man ought to make his life acceptable to others besides himself, but his death to himself alone. The best form of death is the one we like. **13.** Men are foolish who reflect thus: "One person will say that my conduct was not brave enough; another, that I was too headstrong; a third, that a particular kind of death would have betokened more spirit." What you should really reflect is: "I have under consideration a purpose with which the talk of men has no concern!" Your sole aim should be to escape from Fortune as speedily as possible; otherwise, there will be no lack of persons who will think ill of what you have done.

14. You can find men who have gone so far as to profess wisdom and yet maintain that one should not offer violence to one's own life, and hold it accursed for a man to be the means of his own destruction; we should wait, say they, for the end decreed by nature. But one who says this does not see that he is shutting off the path to freedom. The best thing which eternal law ever ordained was that it allowed to us one entrance into life, but many exits. **15.** Must I await the cruelty either of disease or of man, when I can depart through the midst of torture, and shake off my troubles? This is the one reason why we cannot complain of life; it keeps no one against his will. Humanity is well situated, because no man is unhappy except by his own fault. Live, if you so desire; if not, you may return to the place whence you came. **16.** You have often been cupped in order to relieve headaches. You have had veins cut for the purpose of reducing your weight. If you would pierce your heart, a gaping wound is not necessary – a lancet will open the way to that great freedom, and tranquillity can be purchased at the cost of a pin-prick.

What, then, is it which makes us lazy and sluggish? None of us reflects that some day he must depart from this house of life; just so old tenants are kept from moving by fondness for a particular place and by custom, even in spite of ill-treatment. **17.** Would you be free from the restraint of your body? Live in it as if you were about to leave it. Keep thinking of the fact that some day you will be deprived of this tenure; then you will be more brave against the necessity of departing. But how will a man take thought of his own end, if he craves all things without end? **18.** And yet there is nothing so essential for us to consider. For our training in other things is perhaps superfluous. Our souls have been made ready to meet poverty; but our riches have held out. We have armed ourselves to scorn pain; but we have had the good fortune to possess sound and healthy bodies, and so have never been forced to put this virtue to the test. We have taught ourselves to endure bravely the loss of those we love; but Fortune has preserved to us all whom we loved. **19.** It is in this one matter only that the day will come which will require us to test our training.

You need not think that none but great men have had the strength to burst the bonds of human servitude; you need not believe that this cannot be done except by a Cato, – Cato, who with his hand dragged forth the spirit which he had not succeeded in freeing by the sword. Nay, men of the meanest lot in life have by a mighty impulse escaped to safety, and when they were not allowed to die at their own convenience, or to suit themselves in their choice of the instruments of death, they have snatched up whatever was lying ready to hand, and by sheer strength have turned objects which were by nature harmless into weapons of their own. **20.** For example, there was lately in a training-school for wild-beast gladiators a German, who was making ready for the morning exhibition; he withdrew in order to relieve himself, – the only thing which he was allowed to do in secret and without the presence of a guard. While so engaged, he seized the stick of wood, tipped with a sponge, which was devoted to the vilest uses, and stuffed it, just as it was, down his throat; thus he blocked up his windpipe, and choked the breath from his body. That was truly to insult death! **21.** Yes, indeed; it was not a very elegant or becoming way to die; but what is more foolish than to be over-nice about dying? What a brave fellow! He surely deserved to be allowed to choose his fate! How bravely he would have wielded a sword! With what courage he would have hurled himself into the depths of the sea, or down a precipice! Cut off from resources on every hand, he yet found a way to furnish himself with death, and with a weapon for death. Hence you can understand that nothing but the will need postpone death. Let each man judge the deed of this most zealous fellow as he likes, provided we agree on this point, – that the foulest death is preferable to the fairest slavery.

22. Inasmuch as I began with an illustration taken from humble life I shall keep on with that sort. For men will make greater demands upon themselves, if they see that death can be despised even by the most despised class of men. The Catos, the Scipios, and the others whose names we are wont to hear with admiration, we regard as beyond the sphere of imitation; but I shall now prove to you that the virtue of which I speak is found as frequently in the gladiators' training-school as among the leaders in a civil war. **23.** Lately a gladiator, who had been sent forth to the morning exhibition, was being conveyed in a cart along with the other prisoners; nodding as if he were heavy with sleep, he let his head fall over so far that it was caught in the spokes; then he kept his body in position long enough to break his neck by the revolution of the wheel. So he made his escape by means of the very wagon which was carrying him to his punishment.

24. When a man desires to burst forth and take his departure, nothing stands in his way. It is an open space in which Nature guards us. When our plight is such as to permit it, we may look about us for an easy exit. If you have many opportunities ready to hand, by means of which you may liberate yourself, you may make a selection and think over the best way of gaining freedom; but if a chance is hard to find, instead of the best, snatch the next best, even though it be something unheard of, something new. If you do not lack the courage, you will not lack the cleverness, to die. **25.** See how even the lowest class of slave, when suffering goads him on, is aroused and discovers a way to deceive even the most watchful guards! He is truly great who not only has given himself the order to die, but has also found the means.

I have promised you, however, some more illustrations drawn from the same games. **26.** During the second event in a sham sea-fight one of the barbarians sank deep into his own throat a spear which had been given him for use against his foe. "Why, oh why," he said, "have I not long ago escaped from all this torture and all this mockery? Why should I be armed and yet wait for death to come?" This exhibition was all the more striking because of the lesson men learn from it that dying is more honourable than killing.

27. What then? If such a spirit is possessed by abandoned and dangerous men, shall it not be possessed also by those who have trained themselves to meet such contingencies by long meditation, and by reason, the mistress of all things? It is reason which teaches us that fate has various ways of approach, but the same end, and that it makes no difference at what point the inevitable event begins. **28.** Reason, too, advises us to die, if we may, according to our taste; if this cannot be, she advises us to die according to our ability, and to seize upon whatever means shall offer itself for doing violence to ourselves. It is criminal to "live by robbery"; but, on the other hand, it is most noble to "die by robbery." Farewell.

LXXI. ON THE SUPREME GOOD

1. You are continually referring special questions to me, forgetting that a vast stretch of sea sunders us. Since, however, the value of advice depends mostly on the time when it is given, it must necessarily result that by the time my opinion on certain matters reaches you, the opposite opinion is the better. For advice conforms to circumstances; and our circumstances are carried along, or rather whirled along. Accordingly, advice should be produced at short notice; and even this is too late; it should "grow while we work," as the saying is. And I propose to show you how you may discover the method.

2. As often as you wish to know what is to be avoided or what is to be sought, consider its relation to the Supreme Good, to the purpose of your whole life. For whatever we do ought to be in harmony with this; no man can set in order the details unless he has already set before himself the chief purpose of his life. The artist may have his colours all prepared, but he cannot produce a likeness unless he has already made up his mind what he wishes to paint. The reason we make mistakes is because we all consider the parts of life, but never life as a whole. **3.** The archer must know what he is seeking to hit; then he must aim and control the weapon by his skill. Our plans miscarry because they have no aim. When a man does not know what harbour he is making for, no wind is the right wind. Chance must necessarily have great influence over our lives, because we live by chance. **4.** It is the case with certain men, however, that they do not know that they know certain things. Just as we often go searching for those who stand beside us, so we are apt to forget that the goal of the Supreme Good lies near us.

To infer the nature of this Supreme Good, one does not need many words or any round-about discussion; it should be pointed out with the forefinger, so to speak, and not be dissipated into many parts. For what good is there in breaking it up into tiny bits, when you can say: the Supreme Good is that which is honourable? Besides (and you may be still more surprised at this), that which is honourable is the only good; all other goods are alloyed and debased. **5.** If you once convince yourself of this, and if you come to love virtue devotedly (for mere loving is not enough), anything that has been touched by virtue will be fraught with blessing and prosperity for you, no matter how it shall be regarded by others. Torture, if only, as you lie suffering, you are more calm in mind than your very torturer; illness, if only you curse not Fortune and yield not to the disease – in short, all those things which others regard as ills will become manageable and will end in good, if you succeed in rising above them.

Let this once be clear, that there is nothing good except that which is honourable, and all hardships will have a just title to the name of "goods," when once virtue has made them honourable. 6. Many think that we Stoics are holding out expectations greater than our human lot admits of; and they have a right to think so. For they have regard to the body only. But let them turn back to the soul, and they will soon measure man by the standard of God. Rouse yourself, most excellent Lucilius, and leave off all this word-play of the philosophers, who reduce a most glorious subject to a matter of syllables, and lower and wear out the soul by teaching fragments; then you will become like the men who discovered these precepts, instead of those who by their teaching do their best to make philosophy seem difficult rather than great.

7. Socrates, who recalled the whole of philosophy to rules of conduct, and asserted that the highest wisdom consisted in distinguishing between good and evil, said: "Follow these rules, if my words carry weight with you, in order that you may be happy; and let some men think you even a fool. Allow any man who so desires to insult you and work you wrong; but if only virtue dwells with you, you will suffer nothing. If you wish to be happy, if you would be in good faith a good man let one person or another despise you." No man can accomplish this unless he has come to regard all goods as equal, for the reason that no good exists without that which is honourable, and that which is honourable is in every case equal. 8. You may say: "What then? Is there no difference between Cato's being elected praetor and his failure at the polls? Or whether Cato is conquered or conqueror in the battle-line of Pharsalia? And when Cato could not be defeated, though his party met defeat, was not this goodness of his equal to that which would have been his if he had returned victorious to his native land and arranged a peace?" Of course it was; for it is by the same virtue that evil fortune is overcome and good fortune is controlled. Virtue however, cannot be increased or decreased; its stature is uniform. 9. "But," you will object, "Gnaeus Pompey will lose his army; the patricians, those noblest patterns of the State's creation, and the front-rank men of Pompey's party, a senate under arms, will be routed in a single engagement; the ruins of that great oligarchy will be scattered all over the world; one division will fall in Egypt, another in Africa, and another in Spain! And the poor State will not be allowed even the privilege of being ruined once for all!" 10. Yes, all this may happen; Juba's familiarity with every position in his own kingdom may be of no avail to him, of no avail the resolute bravery of his people when fighting for their king; even the men of Utica, crushed by their troubles, may waver in their allegiance; and the good fortune which ever attended men of the name of Scipio may desert Scipio in Africa. But long ago destiny "saw to it that Cato should come to no harm."

11. "He was conquered in spite of it all!" Well, you may include this among Cato's "failures"; Cato will bear with an equally stout heart anything that thwarts

him of his victory, as he bore that which thwarted him of his praetorship. The day whereon he failed of election, he spent in play; the night wherein he intended to die, he spent in reading. He regarded in the same light both the loss of his praetorship and the loss of his life; he had convinced himself that he ought to endure anything which might happen. 12. Why should he not suffer, bravely and calmly, a change in the government? For what is free from the risk of change? Neither earth, nor sky, nor the whole fabric of our universe, though it be controlled by the hand of God. It will not always preserve its present order; it will be thrown from its course in days to come. 13. All things move in accord with their appointed times; they are destined to be born, to grow, and to be destroyed. The stars which you see moving above us, and this seemingly immovable earth to which we cling and on which we are set, will be consumed and will cease to exist. There is nothing that does not have its old age; the intervals are merely unequal at which Nature sends forth all these things towards the same goal. Whatever is will cease to be, and yet it will not perish, but will be resolved into its elements. 14. To our minds, this process means perishing, for we behold only that which is nearest; our sluggish mind, under allegiance to the body, does not penetrate to bournes beyond. Were it not so, the mind would endure with greater courage its own ending and that of its possessions, if only it could hope that life and death, like the whole universe about us, go by turns, that whatever has been put together is broken up again, that whatever has been broken up is put together again, and that the eternal craftsmanship of God, who controls all things is working at this task.

15. Therefore the wise man will say just what a Marcus Cato would say, after reviewing his past life: "The whole race of man, both that which is and that which is to be, is condemned to die. Of all the cities that at any time have held sway over the world, and of all that have been the splendid ornaments of empires not their own, men shall some day ask where they were, and they shall be swept away by destructions of various kinds; some shall be ruined by wars, others shall be wasted away by inactivity and by the kind of peace which ends in sloth, or by that vice which is fraught with destruction even for mighty dynasties, – luxury. All these fertile plains shall be buried out of sight by a sudden overflowing of the sea, or a slipping of the soil, as it settles to lower levels, shall draw them suddenly into a yawning chasm. Why then should I be angry or feel sorrow, if I precede the general destruction by a tiny interval of time?" 16. Let great souls comply with God's wishes, and suffer unhesitatingly whatever fate the law of the universe ordains; for the soul at death is either sent forth into a better life, destined to dwell with deity amid greater radiance and calm, or else, at least, without suffering any harm to itself, it will be mingled with nature again, and will return to the universe.

Therefore Cato's honourable death was no less a good than his honourable life, since virtue admits of no stretching. Socrates used to say that verity and virtue were the same. Just as truth does not grow, so neither does virtue grow; for it has its due proportions and is complete. 17. You need not, therefore, wonder that goods are equal, both those which are to be deliberately chosen, and those which circumstances have imposed. For if you once adopt the view that they are unequal, deeming, for instance, a brave endurance of torture as among the lesser goods, you will be including it among the evils also; you will pronounce Socrates unhappy in his prison, Cato unhappy when he reopens his wounds with more courage than he allowed in inflicting them, and Regulus the most ill-starred of all when he pays the penalty for keeping his word even with his enemies. And yet no man, even the most effeminate person in the world, has ever dared to maintain such an opinion. For though such persons deny that a man like Regulus is happy, yet for all that they also deny that he is wretched. **18.** The earlier Academics do indeed admit that a man is happy even amid such tortures, but do not admit that he is completely or fully happy. With this view we cannot in any wise agree; for unless a man is happy, he has not attained the Supreme Good; and the good which is supreme admits of no higher degree, if only virtue exists within this man, and if adversity does not impair his virtue, and if, though the body be injured, the virtue abides unharmed. And it does abide. For I understand virtue to be high-spirited and exalted, so that it is aroused by anything that molests it. **19.** This spirit, which young men of noble breeding often assume, when they are so deeply stirred by the beauty of some honourable object that they despise all the gifts of chance, is assuredly infused in us and communicated to us by wisdom. Wisdom will bring the conviction that there is but one good – that which is honourable; that this can neither be shortened nor extended, any more than a carpenter's rule, with which straight lines are tested, can be bent. Any change in the rule means spoiling the straight line. **20.** Applying, therefore, this same figure to virtue, we shall say: virtue also is straight, and admits of no bending. What can be made more tense than a thing which is already rigid? Such is virtue, which passes judgment on everything, but nothing passes judgment on virtue. And if this rule, virtue, cannot itself be made more straight, neither can the things created by virtue be in one case straighter and in another less straight. For they must necessarily correspond to virtue; hence they are equal.

21. "What," you say, "do you call reclining at a banquet and submitting to torture equally good?" Does this seem surprising to you? You may be still more surprised at the following, – that reclining at a banquet is an evil, while reclining on the rack is a good, if the former act is done in a shameful, and the latter in an honourable manner. It is not the material that makes these actions good or bad; it is the virtue. All acts in which virtue has disclosed itself are of the same measure and value. **22.** At this moment the man who measures the souls of all men by his own is shaking his fist in my face because I hold that there is a parity between the goods involved in the case of one who passes sentence honourably, and of one who suffers sentence honourably; or because I hold that there is a parity between the goods of one who celebrates a triumph, and of one who, unconquered in spirit, is carried before the victor's chariot. For such critics think that whatever they themselves cannot do, is not done; they pass judgment on virtue in the light of their own weaknesses.

23. Why do you marvel if it helps a man, and on occasion even pleases him, to be burned, wounded, slain, or bound in prison? To a luxurious man, a simple life is a penalty; to a lazy man, work is punishment; the dandy pities the diligent man; to the slothful, studies are torture. Similarly, we regard those things with respect to which we are all infirm of disposition, as hard and beyond endurance, forgetting what a torment it is to many men to abstain from wine or to be routed from their beds at break of day. These actions are not essentially difficult; it is we ourselves that are soft and flabby. 24. We must pass judgment concerning great matters with greatness of soul; otherwise, that which is really our fault will seem to be their fault. So it is that certain objects which are perfectly straight, when sunk in water appear to the onlooker as bent or broken off. It matters not only what you see, but with what eyes you see it; our souls are too dull of vision to perceive the truth. 25. But give me an unspoiled and sturdy-minded young man; he will pronounce more fortunate one who sustains on unbending shoulders the whole weight of adversity, who stands out superior to Fortune. It is not a cause for wonder that one is not tossed about when the weather is calm; reserve your wonderment for cases where a man is lifted up when all others sink, and keeps his footing when all others are prostrate.

26. What element of evil is there in torture and in the other things which we call hardships? It seems to me that there is this evil, – that the mind sags, and bends, and collapses. But none of these things can happen to the sage; he stands erect under any load. Nothing can subdue him; nothing that must be endured annoys him. For he does not complain that he has been struck by that which can strike any man. He knows his own strength; he knows that he was born to carry burdens. 27. I do not withdraw the wise man from the category of man, nor do I deny to him the sense of pain as though he were a rock that has no feelings at all. I remember that he is made up of two parts: the one part is irrational, – it is this that may be bitten, burned, or hurt; the other part is rational, – it is this which holds resolutely to opinions, is courageous, and unconquerable. In the latter is situated man's Supreme Good. Before this is completely attained, the mind wavers in uncertainty; only when it is fully achieved is the mind fixed and steady. 28. And so when one has just begun, or is on one's way to the heights and is cultivating virtue, or even if one is drawing near the perfect good but has not yet put the finishing touch upon it, one will retrograde at times and there will be a certain slackening of mental effort. For such a man has not yet traversed the doubtful ground; he is still standing in slippery places. But the happy man, whose virtue is complete, loves himself most of all when his bravery has been submitted to the severest test, and when he not only, endures but welcomes that which all other men regard with fear, if it is the price which he must pay for the performance of a duty which honour imposes, and he greatly prefers to have men say of him: "how much more noble!" rather than "how much more lucky!"

29. And now I have reached the point to which your patient waiting summons me. You must not think that our human virtue transcends nature; the wise man will tremble, will feel pain, will turn pale, For all these are sensations of the body. Where,

then, is the abode of utter distress, of that which is truly an evil? In the other part of us, no doubt, if it is the mind that these trials drag down, force to a confession of its servitude, and cause to regret its existence. **30.** The wise man, indeed, overcomes Fortune by his virtue, but many who profess wisdom are sometimes frightened by the most unsubstantial threats. And at this stage it is a mistake on our part to make the same demands upon the wise man and upon the learner. I still exhort myself to do that which I recommend; but my exhortations are not yet followed. And even if this were the case, I should not have these principles so ready for practice, or so well trained, that they would rush to my assistance in every crisis. **31.** Just as wool takes up certain colours at once, while there are others which it will not absorb unless it is soaked and steeped in them many times; so other systems of doctrine can be immediately applied by men's minds after once being accepted, but this system of which I speak, unless it has gone deep and has sunk in for a long time, and has not merely coloured but thoroughly permeated the soul, does not fulfil any of its promises. **32.** The matter can be imparted quickly and in very few words: "Virtue is the only good; at any rate there is no good without virtue; and virtue itself is situated in our nobler part, that is, the rational part." And what will this virtue be? A true and never-swerving judgment. For therefrom will spring all mental impulses, and by its agency every external appearance that stirs our impulses will be clarified. **33.** It will be in keeping with this judgment to judge all things that have been coloured by virtue as goods, and as equal goods.

Bodily goods are, to be sure, good for the body; but they are not absolutely good. There will indeed be some value in them; but they will possess no genuine merit, for they will differ greatly; some will be less, others greater. **34.** And we are constrained to acknowledge that there are great differences among the very followers of wisdom. One man has already made so much progress that he dares to raise his eyes and look Fortune in the face, but not persistently, for his eyes soon drop, dazzled by her overwhelming splendour; another has made so much progress that he is able to match glances with her, – that is, unless he has already reached the summit and is full of confidence. **35.** That which is short of perfection must necessarily be unsteady, at one time progressing, at another slipping or growing faint; and it will surely slip back unless it keeps struggling ahead; for if a man slackens at all in zeal and faithful application, he must retrograde. No one can resume his progress at the point where he left off. **36.** Therefore let us press on and persevere. There remains much more of the road than we have put behind us; but the greater part of progress is the desire to progress.

I fully understand what this task is. It is a thing which I desire, and I desire it with all my heart. I see that you also have been aroused and are hastening with great zeal towards infinite beauty. Let us, then, hasten; only on these terms will life be a boon to us; otherwise, there is delay, and indeed disgraceful delay, while we busy ourselves with revolting things. Let us see to it that all time belongs to us. This, however, cannot be unless first of all our own selves begin to belong to us.

37. And when will it be our privilege to despise both kinds of fortune? When will it be our privilege, after all the passions have been subdued and brought under our own control, to utter the words "I have conquered!"? Do you ask me whom I have conquered? Neither the Persians, nor the far-off Medes, nor any warlike race that lies beyond the Dahae; not these, but greed, ambition, and the fear of death that has conquered the conquerors of the world. Farewell.

LXXII. ON BUSINESS AS THE ENEMY OF PHILOSOPHY

1. The subject concerning which you question me was once clear to my mind, and required no thought, so thoroughly had I mastered it. But I have not tested my memory of it for some time, and therefore it does not readily come back to me. I feel that I have suffered the fate of a book whose rolls have stuck together by disuse; my mind needs to be unrolled, and whatever has been stored away there ought to be examined from time to time, so that it may be ready for use when occasion demands. Let us therefore put this subject off for the present; for it demands much labour and much care. As soon as I can hope to stay for any length of time in the same place, I shall then take your question in hand. 2. For there are certain subjects about which you can write even while travelling in a gig, and there are also subjects which need a study-chair, and quiet, and seclusion. Nevertheless I ought to accomplish something even on days like these, – days which are fully employed, and indeed from morning till night. For there is never a moment when fresh employments will not come along; we sow them, and for this reason several spring up from one. Then, too, we keep adjourning our own cases by saying: "As soon as I am done with this, I shall settle down to hard work," or: "If I ever set this troublesome matter in order, I shall devote myself to study."

3. But the study of philosophy is not to be postponed until you have leisure; everything else is to be neglected in order that we may attend to philosophy, for no amount of time is long enough for it, even though our lives be prolonged from boyhood to the uttermost bounds of time allotted to man. It makes little difference whether you leave philosophy out altogether or study it intermittently; for it does not stay as it was when you dropped it, but, because its continuity has been broken, it goes back to the position in which it was at the beginning, like things which fly apart when they are stretched taut. We must resist the affairs which occupy our time; they must not be untangled, but rather put out of the way. Indeed, there is no time that is unsuitable for helpful studies; and yet many a man fails to study amid the very circumstances which make study necessary. 4. He says: "Something will happen to hinder me." No, not in the case of the man whose spirit, no matter what his business may be, is happy and alert. It is those who are still short of perfection whose happiness can be broken off; the joy of a wise man, on the other hand, is a woven fabric, rent by no chance happening and by no change of fortune; at all times and in all places he is at peace. For his joy depends on nothing external and looks for

no boon from man or fortune. His happiness is something within himself; it would depart from his soul if it entered in from the outside; it is born there. **5.** Sometimes an external happening reminds him of his mortality, but it is a light blow, and merely grazes the surface of his skin. Some trouble, I repeat, may touch him like a breath of wind, but that Supreme Good of his is unshaken. This is what I mean: there are external disadvantages, like pimples and boils that break out upon a body which is normally strong and sound; but there is no deep-seated malady. **6.** The difference, I say, between a man of perfect wisdom and another who is progressing in wisdom is the same as the difference between a healthy man and one who is convalescing from a severe and lingering illness, for whom "health" means only a lighter attack of his disease. If the latter does not take heed, there is an immediate relapse and a return to the same old trouble; but the wise man cannot slip back, or slip into any more illness at all. For health of body is a temporary matter which the physician cannot guarantee, even though he has restored it; nay, he is often roused from his bed to visit the same patient who summoned him before. The mind, however, once healed, is healed for good and all.

7. I shall tell you what I mean by health: if the mind is content with its own self; if it has confidence in itself; if it understands that all those things for which men pray, all the benefits which are bestowed and sought for, are of no importance in relation to a life of happiness; under such conditions it is sound. For anything that can be added to is imperfect; anything that can suffer loss is not lasting; but let the man whose happiness is to be lasting, rejoice in what is truly his own. Now all that which the crowd gapes after, ebbs and flows. Fortune gives us nothing which we can really own. But even these gifts of Fortune please us when reason has tempered and blended them to our taste; for it is reason which makes acceptable to us even external goods that are disagreeable to use if we absorb them too greedily. **8.** Attalus used to employ the following simile: "Did you ever see a dog snapping with wide-open jaws at bits of bread or meat which his master tosses to him? Whatever he catches, he straightway swallows whole, and always opens his jaws in the hope of something more. So it is with ourselves; we stand expectant, and whatever Fortune has thrown to us we forthwith bolt, without any real pleasure, and then stand alert and frantic for something else to snatch." But it is not so with the wise man; he is satisfied. Even if something falls to him, he merely accepts it carelessly and lays it aside. **9.** The happiness that he enjoys is supremely great, is lasting, is his own. Assume that a man has good intentions, and has made progress, but is still far from the heights; the result is a series of ups and downs; he is now raised to heaven, now brought down to earth. For those who lack experience and training, there is no limit to the downhill course; such a one falls into the Chaos of Epicurus, – empty and boundless. **10.** There is still a third class of men, – those who toy with wisdom, – they have not indeed touched it, but yet are in sight of it, and have it, so to speak, within striking distance. They are not dashed about, nor do they drift back either; they are not on dry land, but are already in port.

11. Therefore, considering the great difference between those on the heights and those in the depths, and seeing that even those in the middle are pursued by an ebb and flow peculiar to their state and pursued also by an enormous risk of returning to their degenerate ways, we should not give ourselves up to matters which occupy our time. They should be shut out; if they once gain an entrance, they will bring in still others to take their places. Let us resist them in their early stages. It is better that they shall never begin than that they shall be made to cease. Farewell.

LXXIII. ON PHILOSOPHERS AND KINGS

1. It seems to me erroneous to believe that those who have loyally dedicated themselves to philosophy are stubborn and rebellious, scorners of magistrates or kings or of those who control the administration of public affairs. For, on the contrary, no class of man is so popular with the philosopher as the ruler is; and rightly so, because rulers bestow upon no men a greater privilege than upon those who are allowed to enjoy peace and leisure. **2.** Hence, those who are greatly profited, as regards their purpose of right living, by the security of the State, must needs cherish as a father the author of this good; much more so, at any rate, than those restless persons who are always in the public eye, who owe much to the ruler, but also expect much from him, and are never so generously loaded with favours that their cravings, which grow by being supplied, are thoroughly satisfied. And yet he whose thoughts are of benefits to come has forgotten the benefits received; and there is no greater evil in covetousness than its ingratitude. **3.** Besides, no man in public life thinks of the many whom he has outstripped; he thinks rather of those by whom he is outstripped. And these men find it less pleasing to see many behind them than annoying to see anyone ahead of them. That is the trouble with every sort of ambition; it does not look back. Nor is it ambition alone that is fickle, but also every sort of craving, because it always begins where it ought to end.

4. But that other man, upright and pure, who has left the senate and the bar and all affairs of state, that he may retire to nobler affairs, cherishes those who have made it possible for him to do this in security; he is the only person who returns spontaneous thanks to them, the only person who owes them a great debt without their knowledge. Just as a man honours and reveres his teachers, by whose aid he has found release from his early wanderings, so the sage honours these men, also, under whose guardianship he can put his good theories into practice. **5.** But you answer: "Other men too are protected by a king's personal power." Perfectly true. But just as, out of a number of persons who have profited by the same stretch of calm weather, a man deems that his debt to Neptune is greater if his cargo during that voyage has been more extensive and valuable, and just as the vow is paid with more of a will by the merchant than by the passenger, and just as, from among the merchants themselves, heartier thanks are uttered by the dealer in spices, purple fabrics, and objects worth their weight in gold, than by him who has gathered cheap merchandise that will be nothing but ballast for his ship; similarly, the benefits of this peace, which extends to all, are more deeply appreciated by those who make good use of it.

6. For there are many of our toga-clad citizens to whom peace brings more trouble than war. Or do those, think you, owe as much as we do for the peace they enjoy, who spend it in drunkenness, or in lust, or in other vices which it were worth even a war to interrupt? No, not unless you think that the wise man is so unfair as to believe that as an individual he owes nothing in return for the advantages which he enjoys with all the rest. I owe a great debt to the sun and to the moon; and yet they do not rise for me alone. I am personally beholden to the seasons and to the god who controls them, although in no respect have they been apportioned for my benefit. **7.** The foolish greed of mortals makes a distinction between possession and ownership, and believes that it has ownership in nothing in which the general public has a share. But our philosopher considers nothing more truly his own than that which he shares in partnership with all mankind. For these things would not be common property, as indeed they are, unless every individual had his quota; even a joint interest based upon the slightest share makes one a partner. **8.** Again, the great and true goods are not divided in such a manner that each has but a slight interest; they belong in their entirety to each individual. At a distribution of grain men receive only the amount that has been promised to each person; the banquet and the meat-dole, or all else that a man can carry away with him, are divided into parts. These goods, however, are indivisible, – I mean peace and liberty, – and they belong in their entirety to all men just as much as they belong to each individual.

9. Therefore the philosopher thinks of the person who makes it possible for him to use and enjoy these things, of the person who exempts him when the state's dire need summons to arms, to sentry duty, to the defence of the walls, and to the manifold exactions of war; and he gives thanks to the helmsman of his state. This is what philosophy teaches most of all, – honourably to avow the debt of benefits received, and honourably to pay them; sometimes, however, the acknowledgment itself constitutes payment. **10.** Our philosopher will therefore acknowledge that he owes a large debt to the ruler who makes it possible, by his management and foresight, for him to enjoy rich leisure, control of his own time, and a tranquillity uninterrupted by public employments.

> Shepherd! a god this leisure gave to me,
> For he shall be my god eternally.

11. And if even such leisure as that of our poet owes a great debt to its author, though its greatest boon is this:

> As thou canst see,
> He let me turn my cattle out to feed,
> And play what fancy pleased on rustic reed;

how highly are we to value this leisure of the philosopher, which is spent among the gods, and makes us gods? **12.** Yes, this is what I mean, Lucilius; and I invite you to heaven by a short cut.

Sextius used to say that Jupiter had no more power than the good man. Of course, Jupiter has more gifts which he can offer to mankind; but when you are choosing between two good men, the richer is not necessarily the better, any more than, in the case of two pilots of equal skill in managing the tiller, you would call him the better whose ship is larger and more imposing. **13.** In what respect is Jupiter superior to our good man? His goodness lasts longer; but the wise man does not set a lower value upon himself, just because his virtues are limited by a briefer span. Or take two wise men; he who has died at a greater age is not happier than he whose virtue has been limited to fewer years: similarly, a god has no advantage over a wise man in point of happiness, even though he has such an advantage in point of years. That virtue is not greater which lasts longer. **14.** Jupiter possesses all things, but he has surely given over the possession of them to others; the only use of them which belongs to him is this: he is the cause of their use to all men. The wise man surveys and scorns all the possessions of others as calmly as does Jupiter, and regards himself with the greater esteem because, while Jupiter cannot make use of them, he, the wise man, does not wish to do so. **15.** Let us therefore believe Sextius when he shows us the path of perfect beauty, and cries: "This is 'the way to the stars' ; this is the way, by observing thrift, self-restraint, and courage!"

The gods are not disdainful or envious; they open the door to you; they lend a hand as you climb. **16.** Do you marvel that man goes to the gods? God comes to men; nay, he comes nearer, – he comes into men. No mind that has not God, is good. Divine seeds are scattered throughout our mortal bodies; if a good husbandman receives them, they spring up in the likeness of their source and of a parity with those from which they came. If, however, the husbandman be bad, like a barren or marshy soil, he kills the seeds, and causes tares to grow up instead of wheat. Farewell.

LXXIV. ON VIRTUE AS A REFUGE FROM WORLDLY DISTRACTIONS

1. Your letter has given me pleasure, and has roused me from sluggishness. It has also prompted my memory, which has been for some time slack and nerveless.

You are right, of course, my dear Lucilius, in deeming the chief means of attaining the happy life to consist in the belief that the only good lies in that which is honourable. For anyone who deems other things to be good, puts himself in the power of Fortune, and goes under the control of another; but he who has in every case defined the good by the honourable, is happy with an inward happiness.

2. One man is saddened when his children die; another is anxious when they become ill; a third is embittered when they do something disgraceful, or suffer a taint in their reputation. One man, you will observe, is tortured by passion for his neighbour's wife, another by passion for his own. You will find men who are completely upset by failure to win an election, and others who are actually plagued by the offices which they have won. **3.** But the largest throng of unhappy men among the host of mortals are those whom the expectation of death, which threatens them on every hand, drives to despair. For there is no quarter from which death may not approach. Hence, like soldiers scouting in the enemy's country, they must look about in all directions, and turn their heads at every sound; unless the breast be rid of this fear, one lives with a palpitating heart. **4.** You will readily recall those who have been driven into exile and dispossessed of their property. You will also recall (and this is the most serious kind of destitution) those who are poor in the midst of their riches. You will recall men who have suffered shipwreck, or those whose sufferings resemble shipwreck; for they were untroubled and at ease, when the anger or perhaps the envy of the populace, – a missile most deadly to those in high places, – dismantled them like a storm which is wont to rise when one is most confident of continued calm, or like a sudden stroke of lightning which even causes the region round about it to tremble. For just as anyone who stands near the bolt is stunned and resembles one who is struck so in these sudden and violent mishaps, although but one person is overwhelmed by the disaster, the rest are overwhelmed by fear, and the possibility that they may suffer makes them as downcast as the actual sufferer.

5. Every man is troubled in spirit by evils that come suddenly upon his neighbour. Like birds, who cower even at the whirr of an empty sling, we are distracted by mere sounds as well as by blows. No man therefore can be happy if he yields himself up to such foolish fancies. For nothing brings happiness unless it also brings calm; it is a bad sort of existence that is spent in apprehension. **6.** Whoever has largely surrendered himself to the power of Fortune has made for himself a huge web of disquietude, from which he cannot get free; if one would win a way to safety, there is but one road, – to despise externals and to be contented with that which is honourable. For those who regard anything as better than virtue, or believe that there is any good except virtue, are spreading their arms to gather in that which Fortune tosses abroad, and are anxiously awaiting her favours. **7.** Picture now to yourself that Fortune is holding a festival, and is showering down honours, riches, and influence upon this mob of mortals; some of these gifts have already been torn to pieces in the hands of those who try to snatch them, others have been divided up by treacherous partnerships, and still others have been seized to the great detriment of those into whose possession they have come. Certain of these favours have fallen to men while they were absent-minded; others have been lost to their seekers because they were snatching too eagerly for them, and, just because they are greedily seized upon, have been knocked from their hands. There is not a man among them all, however, – even he who has been lucky in the booty which has fallen to him, – whose joy in his spoil has lasted until the morrow.

The most sensible man, therefore, as soon as he sees the dole being brought in, runs from the theatre; for he knows that one pays a high price for small favours. No one will grapple with him on the way out, or strike him as he departs; the quarrelling takes place where the prizes are. **8.** Similarly with the gifts which Fortune tosses down to us; wretches that we are, we become excited, we are torn asunder, we wish that we had many hands, we look back now in this direction and now in that. All too slowly, as it seems, are the gifts thrown in our direction; they merely excite our cravings, since they can reach but few and are awaited by all. **9.** We are keen to intercept them as they fall down. We rejoice if we have laid hold of anything; and some have been mocked by the idle hope of laying hold; we have either paid a high price for worthless plunder with some disadvantage to ourselves, or else have been defrauded and are left in the lurch. Let us therefore withdraw from a game like this, and give way to the greedy rabble; let them gaze after such "goods," which hang suspended above them, and be themselves still more in suspense.

10. Whoever makes up his mind to be happy should conclude that the good consists only in that which is honourable. For if he regards anything else as good, he is, in the first place, passing an unfavourable judgment upon Providence because of the fact that upright men often suffer misfortunes, and that the time which is allotted to us is but short and scanty, if you compare it with the eternity which is allotted to the universe.

11. It is a result of complaints like these that we are unappreciative in our comments upon the gifts of heaven; we complain because they are not always granted to us, because they are few and unsure and fleeting. Hence we have not the will either to live or to die; we are possessed by hatred of life, by fear of death. Our plans are all at sea, and no amount of prosperity can satisfy us. And the reason for all this is that we have not yet attained to that good which is immeasurable and unsurpassable, in which all wishing on our part must cease, because there is no place beyond the highest. **12.** Do you ask why virtue needs nothing? Because it is pleased with what it has, and does not lust after that which it has not. Whatever is enough is abundant in the eyes of virtue.

Dissent from this judgment, and duty and loyalty will not abide. For one who desires to exhibit these two qualities must endure much that the world calls evil; we must sacrifice many things to which we are addicted, thinking them to be goods. **13.** Gone is courage, which should be continually testing itself; gone is greatness of soul, which cannot stand out clearly unless it has learned to scorn as trivial everything that the crowd covets as supremely important; and gone is kindness and the repaying of kindness, if we fear toil, if we have acknowledged anything to be more precious than loyalty, if our eyes are fixed upon anything except the best.

14. But to pass these questions by: either these so-called goods are not goods, or else man is more fortunate than God, because God has no enjoyment of the things which are given to us. For lust pertains not to God, nor do elegant banquets, nor wealth, nor any of the things that allure mankind and lead him on through the influence of degrading pleasure. Therefore, it is, either not incredible that there are goods which God does not possess, or else the very fact that God does not possess them is in itself a proof that these things are not goods. **15.** Besides, many things which are wont to be regarded as goods are granted to animals in fuller measure than to men. Animals eat their food with better appetite, are not in the same degree weakened by sexual indulgence, and have a greater and more uniform constancy in their strength. Consequently, they are much more fortunate than man. For there is no wickedness, no injury to themselves, in their way of living. They enjoy their pleasures and they take them more often and more easily, without any of the fear that results from shame or regret.

16. This being so, you should consider whether one has a right to call anything good in which God is outdone by man. Let us limit the Supreme Good to the soul; it loses its meaning if it is taken from the best part of us and applied to the worst, that is, if it is transferred to the senses; for the senses are more active in dumb beasts. The sum total of our happiness must not be placed in the flesh; the true goods are those which reason bestows, substantial and eternal; they cannot fall away, neither can they grow less or be diminished. **17.** Other things are goods according to opinion, and though they are called by the same name as the true goods, the essence of goodness is not in them. Let us therefore call them "advantages," and, to use our technical term, "preferred" things. Let us, however, recognize that they are our chattels, not parts of ourselves; and let us have them in our possession, but take heed to remember that they are outside ourselves. Even though they are in our possession, they are to be reckoned as things subordinate and poor, the possession of which gives no man a right to plume himself. For what is more foolish than being self-complacent about something which one has not accomplished by one's own efforts? **18.** Let everything of this nature be added to us, and not stick fast to us, so that, if it is withdrawn, it may come away without tearing off any part of us. Let us use these things, but not boast of them, and let us use them sparingly, as if they were given for safe-keeping and will be withdrawn. Anyone who does not employ reason in his possession of them never keeps them long; for prosperity of itself, if uncontrolled by reason, overwhelms itself. If anyone has put his trust in goods that are most fleeting, he is soon bereft of them, and, to avoid being bereft, he suffers distress. Few men have been permitted to lay aside prosperity gently. The rest all fall, together with the things amid which they have come into eminence, and they are weighted down by the very things which had before exalted them. **19.** For this reason foresight must be brought into play, to insist upon a limit or upon frugality in the use of these things, since license overthrows and destroys its own abundance. That which has no limit has never endured, unless reason, which sets limits, has held it in check. The fate of many cities will prove the truth of this; their sway has ceased at the very prime because they were given to luxury, and excess has ruined all that had been won by virtue. We should fortify ourselves against such calamities. But no wall can be erected against Fortune which she cannot take by storm; let us strengthen our inner defences. If the inner part be safe, man can be attacked, but never captured.

Do you wish to know what this weapon of defence is? **20.** It is the ability to refrain from chafing over whatever happens to one, of knowing that the very agencies which seem to bring harm are working for the preservation of the world, and are a part of the scheme for bringing to fulfilment the order of the universe and its functions. Let man be pleased with whatever has pleased God; let him marvel at himself and his own resources for this very reason, that he cannot be overcome, that he has the very powers of evil subject to his control, and that he brings into subjection chance and pain and wrong by means of that strongest of powers – reason. **21.** Love reason! The love of reason will arm you against the greatest hardships. Wild beasts dash against the hunter's spear through love of their young, and it is their wildness and their unpremeditated onrush that keep them from being tamed; often a desire for glory has stirred the mind of youth to despise both sword and stake; the mere vision and semblance of virtue impel certain men to a self-imposed death. In proportion as reason is stouter and steadier than ally of these emotions, so much the more forcefully will she make her way through the midst of utter terrors and dangers.

22. Men say to us: "You are mistaken if you maintain that nothing is a good except that which is honourable; a defence like this will not make you safe from Fortune and free from her assaults. For you maintain that dutiful children, and a well-governed country, and good parents, are to be reckoned as goods; but you cannot see these dear objects in danger and be yourself at ease. Your calm will be disturbed by a siege conducted against your country, by the death of your children, or by the enslaving of your parents." **23.** I will first state what we Stoics usually reply to these objectors, and then will add what additional answer should, in my opinion, be given.

The situation is entirely different in the case of goods whose loss entails some hardship substituted in their place; for example, when good health is impaired there is a change to ill-health; when the eye is put out, we are visited with blindness; we not only lose our speed when our leg-muscles are cut, but infirmity takes the place of speed. But no such danger is involved in the case of the goods to which we referred a moment ago. And why if I have lost a good friend, I have no false friend whom I must endure in his place; nor if I have buried a dutiful son, must I face in exchange unfilial conduct. **24.** In the second place, this does not mean to me the taking-off of a friend or of a child; it is the mere taking-off of their bodies. But a good can be lost in only one way, by changing into what is bad; and this is impossible according to the law of nature, because every virtue, and every work of virtue, abides uncorrupted. Again, even if friends have perished, or children of approved goodness who fulfil their father's prayers for them, there is something that can fill their place. Do you ask what this is? It is that which had made them good in the first place, namely, virtue. **25.** Virtue suffers no space in us to be unoccupied; it takes possession of the whole soul and removes all sense of loss. It alone is sufficient; for the strength and beginnings of all goods exist in virtue herself. What does it matter if running water is cut off and flows away, as long as the fountain from which it has flowed is unharmed? You will not maintain that a man's life is more just if his children are unharmed than if they have passed away, nor yet better appointed, nor more intelligent, nor more honourable; therefore, no better, either. The addition of friends does not make one wiser, nor does their taking away make one more foolish; therefore, not happier or more wretched, either. As long is your virtue is unharmed, you will not feel the loss of anything that has been withdrawn from you. **26.** You may say, "Come now; is not a man happier when girt about with a large company of friends and children?" Why should this be so? For the Supreme Good is neither impaired nor increased thereby; it abides within its own limits, no matter how Fortune has conducted herself. Whether a long old age falls to one's lot, or whether the end comes on this side of old age – the measure of the Supreme Good is unvaried, in spite of the difference in years.

27. Whether you draw a larger or a smaller circle, its size affects its area, not its shape. One circle may remain as it is for a long time while you may contract the other forthwith, or even merge it completely with the sand in which it was drawn; yet each circle has had the same shape. That which is straight is not judged by its size, or by its number, or by its duration; it can no more be made longer than it can be made shorter. Scale down the honourable life as much as you like from the full hundred years, and reduce it to a single day; it is equally honourable. **28.** Sometimes virtue is widespread, governing kingdoms, cities, and provinces, creating laws, developing friendships, and regulating the duties that hold good between relatives and children; at other times it is limited by the narrow bounds of poverty, exile, or bereavement. But it is no smaller when it is reduced from prouder heights to a private station, from a royal palace to a humble dwelling, or when from a general and broad jurisdiction it is gathered into the narrow limits of a private house or a tiny corner. **29.** Virtue is just as great, even when it has retreated within itself and is shut in on all sides. For its spirit is no less great and upright, its sagacity no less complete, its justice no less inflexible. It is, therefore, equally happy. For happiness has its abode in one place only, namely, in the mind itself, and is noble, steadfast, and calm; and this state cannot be attained without a knowledge of things divine and human.

30. The other answer, which I promised to make to your objection, follows from this reasoning. The wise man is not distressed by the loss of children or of friends. For he endures their death in the same spirit in which he awaits his own. And he fears the one as little as he grieves for the other. For the underlying principle of virtue is conformity; all the works of virtue are in harmony and agreement with virtue itself. But this harmony is lost if the soul, which ought to be uplifted, is cast down by grief or a sense of loss. It is ever a dishonour for a man to be troubled and fretted, to be numbed when there is any call for activity. For that which is honourable is free from care and untrammelled, is unafraid, and stands girt for action. **31.** "What," you ask, "will the wise man experience no emotion like disturbance of spirit? Will not his features change colour, his countenance be agitated, and his limbs grow cold? And there are other things which we do, not under the influence of the will, but unconsciously and as the result of a sort of natural impulse." I admit that this is true; but the sage will retain the firm belief that none of these things is evil, or important enough to make a healthy mind break down. **32.** Whatever shall remain to be done virtue can do with courage and readiness. For anyone would admit that it is a mark of folly to do in a slothful and rebellious spirit whatever one has to do, or to direct the body in one direction and the mind in another, and thus to be torn between utterly conflicting emotions. For folly is despised precisely because of the things for which she vaunts and admires herself, and she does not do gladly even those things in which she prides herself. But if folly fears some evil, she is burdened by it in the very moment of awaiting it, just as if it had actually come, – already suffering in apprehension whatever she fears she may suffer. **33.** Just as in the body symptoms of latent ill-health precede the disease – there is, for example, a certain weak sluggishness, a lassitude which is not the result of any work, a trembling, and a shivering that pervades the limbs, – so the feeble spirit is shaken by its ills a long time before it is overcome by them. It anticipates them, and totters before its time.

But what is greater madness than to be tortured by the future and not to save your strength for the actual suffering, but to invite and bring on wretchedness? If you cannot be rid of it, you ought at least to postpone it. **34.** Will you not understand that no man should be tormented by the future? The man who has been told that he will have to endure torture fifty years from now is not disturbed thereby, unless he has leaped over the intervening years, and has projected himself into the trouble that is destined to arrive a generation later. In the same way, souls that enjoy being sick and that seize upon excuses for sorrow are saddened by events long past and effaced from the records. Past and future are both absent; we feel neither of them. But there can be no pain except as the result of what you feel. Farewell.

LXXV. ON THE DISEASES OF THE SOUL

1. You have been complaining that my letters to you are rather carelessly written. Now who talks carefully unless he also desires to talk affectedly? I prefer that my letters should be just what my conversation would be if you and I were sitting in one another's company or taking walks together, spontaneous and easy; for my letters have nothing strained or artificial about them. **2.** If it were possible, I should prefer to show, rather than speak, my feelings. Even if I were arguing a point, I should not stamp my foot, or toss my arms about, or raise my voice; but I should leave that sort of thing to the orator, and should be content to have conveyed my feelings to you without having either embellished them or lowered their dignity. **3.** I should like to convince you entirely of this one fact, – that I feel whatever I say, that I not only feel it, but am wedded to it. It is one sort of kiss which a man gives his mistress and another which he gives his children; yet in the father's embrace also, holy and restrained as it is, plenty of affection is disclosed.

I prefer, however, that our conversation on matters so important should not be meagre and dry; for even philosophy does not renounce the company of cleverness. One should not, however, bestow very much attention upon mere words. **4.** Let this be the kernel of my idea: let us say what we feel, and feel what we say; let speech harmonize with life. That man has fulfilled his promise who is the same person both when you see him and when you hear him. **5.** We shall not fail to see what sort of man he is and how large a man he is, if only he is one and the same. Our words should aim not to please, but to help. If, however, you can attain eloquence without painstaking, and if you either are naturally gifted or can gain eloquence at slight cost, make the most of it and apply it to the noblest uses. But let it be of such a kind that it displays facts rather than itself. It and the other arts are wholly concerned with cleverness; but our business here is the soul.

6. A sick man does not call in a physician who is eloquent; but if it so happens that the physician who can cure him likewise discourses elegantly about the treatment which is to be followed, the patient will take it in good part. For all that, he will not find any reason to congratulate himself on having discovered a physician who is eloquent. For the case is no different from that of a skilled pilot who is also handsome. **7.** Why do you tickle my ears? Why do you entertain me? There is other business at hand; I am to be cauterized, operated upon, or put on a diet. That is why you were summoned to treat me!

You are required to cure a disease that is chronic and serious, – one which affects the general weal. You have as serious a business on hand as a physician has during a plague. Are you concerned about words? Rejoice this instant if you can cope with *things*. When shall you learn all that there is to learn? When shall you so plant in your mind that which you have learned, that it cannot escape? When shall you put it all into practice? For it is not sufficient merely to commit these things to memory, like other matters; they must be practically tested. He is not happy who only knows them, but he who does them. **8.** You reply: "What? Are there no degrees of happiness below your 'happy' man? Is there a sheer descent immediately below wisdom?" I think not. For though he who makes progress is still numbered with the fools, yet he is separated from them by a long interval. Among the very persons who are making progress there are also great spaces intervening. They fall into three classes, as certain philosophers believe. **9.** First come those who have not yet attained wisdom but have already gained a place near by. Yet even that which is not far away is still outside. These, if you ask me, are men who have already laid aside all passions and vices, who have learned what things are to be embraced; but their assurance is not yet tested. They have not yet put their good into practice, yet from now on they cannot slip back into the faults which they have escaped. They have already arrived at a point from which there is no slipping back, but they are not yet aware of the fact; as I remember writing in another letter, "They are ignorant of their knowledge." It has now been vouchsafed to them to enjoy their good, but not yet to be sure of it. **10.** Some define this class, of which I have been speaking, – a class of men who are making progress, – as having escaped the diseases of the mind, but not yet the passions, and as still standing upon slippery ground; because no one is beyond the dangers of evil except him who has cleared himself of it wholly. But no one has so cleared himself except the man who has adopted wisdom in its stead.

11. I have often before explained the difference between the diseases of the mind and its passions. And I shall remind you once more: the diseases are hardened and chronic vices, such as greed and ambition; they have enfolded the mind in too close a grip, and have begun to be permanent evils thereof. To give a brief definition: by "disease" we mean a persistent perversion of the judgment, so that things which are mildly desirable are thought to be highly desirable. Or, if you prefer, we may define it thus: to be too zealous in striving for things which are only mildly desirable or not desirable at all, or to value highly things which ought to be valued but slightly or valued not at all. **12.** "Passions" are objectionable impulses of the spirit, sudden and vehement; they have come so often, and so little attention has been paid to them, that they have caused a state of disease; just as a catarrh, when there has been but a single attack and the catarrh has not yet become habitual, produces a cough, but causes consumption when it has become regular and chronic. Therefore we may say that those who have made most progress are beyond the reach of the "diseases"; but they still feel the "passions" even when very near perfection.

13. The second class is composed of those who have laid aside both the greatest ills of the mind and its passions, but yet are not in assured possession of immunity. For they can still slip back into their former state. **14.** The third class are beyond the reach of many of the vices and particularly of the great vices, but not beyond the reach of all. They have escaped avarice, for example, but still feel anger; they no longer are troubled by lust, but are still troubled by ambition; they no longer have desire, but they still have fear. And just because they fear, although they are strong enough to withstand certain things, there are certain things to which they yield; they scorn death, but are in terror of pain.

15. Let us reflect a moment on this topic. It will be well with us if we are admitted to this class. The second stage is gained by great good fortune with regard to our natural gifts and by great and unceasing application to study. But not even the third type is to be despised. Think of the host of evils which you see about you; behold how there is no crime that is not exemplified, how far wickedness advances every day, and how prevalent are sins in home and commonwealth. You will see, therefore, that we are making a considerable gain, if we are not numbered among the basest.

16. "But as for me," you say, "I hope that it is in me to rise to a higher rank than that!" I should pray, rather than promise, that we may attain this; we have been forestalled. We hasten towards virtue while hampered by vices. I am ashamed to say it; but we worship that which is honourable only in so far as we have time to spare. But what a rich reward awaits us if only we break off the affairs which forestall us and the evils that cling to us with utter tenacity! **17.** Then neither desire nor fear shall rout us. Undisturbed by fears, unspoiled by pleasures, we shall be afraid neither of death nor of the gods; we shall know that death is no evil and that the gods are not powers of evil. That which harms has no greater power than that which receives harm, and things which are utterly good have no power at all to harm. **18.** There await us, if ever we escape from these low dregs to that sublime and lofty height, peace of mind and, when all error has been driven out, perfect liberty. You ask what this freedom is? It means not fearing either men or gods; it means not craving wickedness or excess; it means possessing supreme power over oneself And it is a priceless good to be master of oneself. Farewell.

LXXVI. ON LEARNING WISDOM IN OLD AGE

1. You have been threatening me with your enmity, if I do not keep you informed about all my daily actions. But see, now, upon what frank terms you and I live: for I shall confide even the following fact to your ears. I have been hearing the lectures of a philosopher; four days have already passed since I have been attending his school and listening to the harangue, which begins at two o'clock. "A fine time of life for that!" you say. Yes, fine indeed! Now what is more foolish than refusing to learn, simply because one has not been learning for a long time? **2.** "What do you mean? Must I follow the fashion set by the fops and youngsters?" But I am pretty well off if this is the only thing that discredits my declining years. Men of all ages are admitted to this class-room. You retort: "Do we grow old merely in order to tag after the youngsters?" But if I, an old man, go to the theatre, and am carried to the races, and allow no duel in the arena to be fought to a finish without my presence, shall I blush to attend a philosopher's lecture?

3. You should keep learning as long as you are ignorant, – even to the end of your life, if there is anything in the proverb. And the proverb suits the present case as well as any: "As long as you live, keep learning how to live." For all that, there is also something which I can teach in that school. You ask, do you, what I can teach? That even an old man should keep learning. **4.** But I am ashamed of mankind, as often as I enter the lecture-hall. On my way to the house of Metronax I am compelled to go, as you know, right past the Neapolitan Theatre. The building is jammed; men are deciding, with tremendous zeal, who is entitled to be called a good flute-player; even the Greek piper and the herald draw their crowds. But in the other place, where the question discussed is: "What is a good man?" and the lesson which we learn is "How to be a good man," very few are in attendance, and the majority think that even these few are engaged in no good business; they have the name of being empty-headed idler. I hope I may be blessed with that kind of mockery; for one should listen in an unruffled spirit to the railings of the ignorant; when one is marching toward the goal of honour, one should scorn scorn itself.

5. Proceed, then, Lucilius, and hasten, lest you yourself be compelled to learn in your old age, as is the case with me. Nay, you must hasten all the more, because for a long time you have not approached the subject, which is one that you can scarcely learn thoroughly when you are old. "How much progress shall I make?" you ask. Just as much as you try to make. **6.** Why do you wait? Wisdom comes haphazard to no man. Money will come of its own accord; titles will be given to you; influence and authority will perhaps be thrust upon you; but virtue will not fall upon you by chance. Either is knowledge thereof to be won by light effort or small toil; but toiling is worth while when one is about to win all goods at a single stroke. **7.** For there is but a single good, – namely, that which is honourable; in all those other things of which the general opinion approves, you will find no truth or certainty. Why it is, however, that there is but one good, namely, that which is honourable, I shall now tell you, inasmuch as you judge that in my earlier letter I did not carry the discussion far enough, and think that this theory was commended to you rather than proved. I shall also compress the remarks of other authors into narrow compass.

8. Everything is estimated by the standard of its own good. The vine is valued for its productiveness and the flavour of its wine, the stag for his speed. We ask, with regard to beasts of burden, how sturdy of back they are; for their only use is to bear burdens. If a dog is to find the trail of a wild beast, keenness of scent is of first importance; if to catch his quarry, swiftness of foot; if to attack and harry it, courage. In each thing that quality should be best for which the thing is brought into being and by which it is judged. **9.** And what quality is best in man? It is reason; by virtue of reason he surpasses the animals, and is surpassed only by the gods. Perfect reason is therefore the good peculiar to man; all other qualities he shares in some degree with animals and plants. Man is strong; so is the lion. Man is comely; so is the peacock. Man is swift; so is the horse. I do not say that man is surpassed in all these qualities. I am not seeking to find that which is greatest in him, but that which is peculiarly his own. Man has body; so also have trees. Man has the power to act and to move at will; so have beasts and worms. Man has a voice; but how much louder is the voice of the dog, how much shriller that of the eagle, how much deeper that of the bull, how much sweeter and more melodious that of the nightingale! **10.** What then is peculiar to man? Reason. When this is right and has reached perfection, man's felicity is complete. Hence, if everything is praiseworthy and has arrived at the end intended by its nature, when it has brought its peculiar good to perfection, and if man's peculiar good is reason; then, if a man has brought his reason to perfection, he is praiseworthy and has readied the end suited to his nature. This perfect reason is called virtue, and is likewise that which is honourable.

11. Hence that in man is alone a good which alone belongs to man. For we are not now seeking to discover what is a good, but what good is man's. And if there is no other attribute which belongs peculiarly to man except reason, then reason will be his one peculiar good, but a good that is worth all the rest put together. If any man is bad, he will, I suppose, be regarded with disapproval; if good, I suppose he will be regarded with approval. Therefore, that attribute of man whereby he is approved or disapproved is his chief and only good. **12.** You do not doubt whether this is a good; you merely doubt whether it is the sole good. If a man possess all other things, such as health, riches, pedigree, a crowded reception-hall, but is confessedly bad, you will disapprove of him. Likewise, if a man possess none of the things which I have mentioned, and lacks money, or an escort of clients, or rank and a line of grandfathers and great-grandfathers, but is confessedly good, you will approve of him. Hence, this is man's one peculiar good, and the possessor of it is to be praised even if he lacks other things; but he who does not possess it, though he possess everything else in abundance is condemned and rejected. **13.** The same thing holds good regarding men as regarding things. A ship is said to be good not when it is decorated with costly colours, nor when its prow is covered with silver or gold or its figure-head embossed in ivory, nor when it is laden with the imperial revenues or with the wealth of kings, but when it is steady and staunch and taut, with seams that keep out the water, stout enough to endure the buffeting of the waves' obedient to its helm, swift and caring naught for the winds. **14.** You will speak of a sword as good, not when its sword-belt is of gold, or its scabbard studded with gems, but when its edge is fine for cutting and its point will pierce any armour. Take the carpenter's rule: we do not ask how beautiful it is, but how straight it is. Each thing is praised in regard to that attribute which is taken as its standard, in regard to that which is its peculiar quality.

15. Therefore in the case of man also, it is not pertinent to the question to know how many acres he ploughs, how much money he has out at interest, how many callers attend his receptions, how costly is the couch on which he lies, how transparent are the cups from which he drinks, but how good he is. He is good, however, if his reason is well-ordered and right and adapted to that which his nature has willed. **16.** It is this that is called virtue; this is what we mean by "honourable"; it is man's unique good. For since reason alone brings man to perfection, reason alone, when perfected, makes man happy. This, moreover, is man's only good, the only means by which he is made happy. We do indeed say that those things also are goods which are furthered and brought together by virtue, – that is, all the works of virtue; but virtue itself is for this reason the only good, because there is no good without virtue. **17.** If every good is in the soul, then whatever strengthens, uplifts, and enlarges the soul, is a good; virtue, however, does make the soul stronger, loftier, and larger. For all other things, which arouse our desires, depress the soul and weaken it, and when we think that they are uplifting the soul, they are merely puffing it up and cheating it with much emptiness. Therefore, that alone is good which will make the soul better.

18. All the actions of life, taken as a whole, are controlled by the consideration of what is honourable or base; it is with reference to these two things that our reason is governed in doing or not doing a particular thing. I shall explain what I mean: A good man will do what he thinks it will be honourable for him to do, even if it involves toil; he will do it even if it involves harm to him; he will do it even if it involves peril; again, he will not do that which will be base, even if it brings him money, or pleasure, or power. Nothing will deter him from that which is honourable, and nothing will tempt him into baseness. **19.** Therefore, if he is determined invariably to follow that which is honourable, invariably to avoid baseness, and in every act of his life to have regard for these two things, deeming nothing else good except that which is honourable, and nothing else bad except that which is base; if virtue alone is unperverted in him and by itself keeps its even course, then virtue is that man's only good, and nothing can thenceforth happen to it which may make it anything else than good. It has escaped all risk of change; folly may creep upwards towards wisdom, but wisdom never slips back into folly.

20. You may perhaps remember my saying that the things which have been generally desired and feared have been trampled down by many a man in moments of sudden passion. There have been found men who would place their hands in the flames, men whose smiles could not be stopped by the torturer, men who would shed not a tear at the funeral of their children, men who would meet death unflinchingly. It is love, for example, anger, lust, which have challenged dangers. If a momentary stubbornness can accomplish all this when roused by some goad that pricks the spirit, how much more can be accomplished by virtue, which does not act impulsively or suddenly, but uniformly and with a strength that is lasting! **21.** It follows that the things which are often scorned by the men who are moved with a sudden passion, and are always scorned by the wise, are neither goods nor evils. Virtue itself is therefore the only good; she marches proudly between the two extremes of fortune, with great scorn for both.

22. If, however, you accept the view that there is anything good besides that which is honourable, all the virtues will suffer. For it will never be possible for any virtue to be won and held, if there is anything outside itself which virtue must take into consideration. If there is any such thing, then it is at variance with reason, from which the virtues spring, and with truth also, which cannot exist without reason. Any opinion, however, which is at variance with truth, is wrong. **23.** A good man, you will admit, must have the highest sense of duty toward the gods. Hence he will endure with an unruffled spirit whatever happens to him; for he will know that it has happened as a result of the divine law, by which the whole creation moves. This being so, there will be for him one good, and only one, namely, that which is honourable; for one of its dictates is that we shall obey the gods and not blaze forth in anger at sudden misfortunes or deplore our lot, but rather patiently accept fate and obey its commands. **24.** If anything except the honourable is good, we shall be hounded by greed for life, and by greed for the things which provide life with its furnishings, – an intolerable state, subject to no limits, unstable. The only good, therefore, is that which is honourable, that which is subject to bounds.

25. I have declared that man's life would be more blest than that of the gods, if those things which the gods do not enjoy are goods, – such as money and offices of dignity. There is this further consideration: if only it is true that our souls, when released from the body, still abide, a happier condition is in store for them than is theirs while they dwell in the body. And yet, if those things are goods which we make use of for our bodies' sake, our souls will be worse off when set free; and that is contrary to our belief, to say that the soul is happier when it is cabined and confined than when it is free and has betaken itself to the universe. 26. I also said that if those things which dumb animals possess equally with man are goods, then dumb animals also will lead a happy life; which is of course impossible. One must endure all things in defence of that which is honourable; but this would not be necessary if there existed any other good besides that which is honourable.

Although this question was discussed by me pretty extensively in a previous letter, I have discussed it summarily and briefly run through the argument. 27. But an opinion of this kind will never seem true to you unless you exalt your mind and ask yourself whether, at the call of duty, you would be willing to die for your country, and buy the safety of all your fellow-citizens at the price of your own; whether you would offer your neck not only with patience, but also with gladness. If you would do this, there is no other good in your eyes. For you are giving up everything in order to acquire this good. Consider how great is the power of that which is honourable: you will die for your country, even at a moment's notice, when you know that you ought to do so. 28. Sometimes, as a result of noble conduct, one wins great joy even in a very short and fleeting space of time; and though none of the fruits of a deed that has been done will accrue to the doer after he is dead and removed from the sphere of human affairs, yet the mere contemplation of a deed that is to be done is a delight, and the brave and upright man, picturing to himself the guerdons of his death, – guerdons such as the freedom of his country and the deliverance of all those for whom he is paying out his life, – partakes of the greatest pleasure and enjoys the fruit of his own peril. 29. But that man also who is deprived of this joy, the joy which is afforded by the contemplation of some last noble effort, will leap to his death without a moment's hesitation, content to act rightly and dutifully. Moreover, you may confront him with many discouragements; you may say: "Your deed will speedily be forgotten," or "Your fellow-citizens will offer you scant thanks." He will answer: "All these matters lie outside my task. My thoughts are on the deed itself. I know that this is honourable. Therefore, whithersoever I am led and summoned by honour, I will go."

30. This, therefore, is the only good, and not only is every soul that has reached perfection aware of it, but also every soul that is by nature noble and of right instincts; all other goods are trivial and mutable. For this reason we are harassed if we possess them. Even though, by the kindness of Fortune, they have been heaped together, they weigh heavily upon their owners, always pressing them down and sometimes crushing them. 31. None of those whom you behold clad in purple is happy, any more than one of these actors upon whom the play bestows a sceptre and a cloak while on the stage; they strut their hour before a crowded house, with

swelling port and buskined foot; but when once they make their exit the foot-gear is removed and they return to their proper stature. None of those who have been raised to a loftier height by riches and honours is really great. Why then does he seem great to you? It is because you are measuring the pedestal along with the man. A dwarf is not tall, though he stand upon a mountain-top; a colossal statue will still be tall, though you place it in a well. 32. This is the error under which we labour; this is the reason why we are imposed upon: we value no man at what he is, but add to the man himself the trappings in which he is clothed. But when you wish to inquire into a man's true worth, and to know what manner of man he is, look at him when he is naked; make him lay aside his inherited estate, his titles, and the other deceptions of fortune; let him even strip off his body. Consider his soul, its quality and its stature, and thus learn whether its greatness is borrowed, or its own.

33. If a man can behold with unflinching eyes the flash of a sword, if he knows that it makes no difference to him whether his soul takes flight through his mouth or through a wound in his throat, you may call him happy; you may also call him happy if, when he is threatened with bodily torture, whether it be the result of accident or of the might of the stronger, he can without concern hear talk of chains, or of exile, or of all the idle fears that stir men's minds, and can say:

> "O maiden, no new sudden form of toil
> Springs up before my eyes; within my soul
> I have forestalled and surveyed everything.

To-day it is you who threaten me with these terrors; but I have always threatened myself with them, and have prepared myself as a man to meet man's destiny." 34. If an evil has been pondered beforehand, the blow is gentle when it comes. To the fool, however, and to him who trusts in fortune, each event as it arrives "comes in a new and sudden form," and a large part of evil, to the inexperienced, consists in its novelty. This is proved by the fact that men endure with greater courage, when they have once become accustomed to them, the things which they had at first regarded as hardships. 35. Hence, the wise man accustoms himself to coming trouble, lightening by long reflection the evils which others lighten by long endurance. We sometimes hear the inexperienced say: "I knew that this was in store for me." But the wise man knows that all things are in store for him. Whatever happens, he says: "I knew it." Farewell.

LXXVII. ON TAKING ONE'S OWN LIFE

1. Suddenly there came into our view to-day the "Alexandrian" ships, – I mean those which are usually sent ahead to announce the coming of the fleet; they are called "mail-boats." The Campanians are glad to see them; all the rabble of Puteoli stand on the docks, and can recognize the "Alexandrian" boats, no matter how great the

crowd of vessels, by the very trim of their sails. For they alone may keep spread their topsails, which all ships use when out at sea, **2.** because nothing sends a ship along so well as its upper canvas; that is where most of the speed is obtained. So when the breeze has stiffened and becomes stronger than is comfortable, they set their yards lower; for the wind has less force near the surface of the water. Accordingly, when they have made Capreae and the headland whence

> Tall Pallas watches on the stormy peak,

all other vessels are bidden to be content with the mainsail, and the topsail stands out conspicuously on the "Alexandrian" mail-boats.

3. While everybody was bustling about and hurrying to the water-front, I felt great pleasure in my laziness, because, although I was soon to receive letters from my friends, I was in no hurry to know how my affairs were progressing abroad, or what news the letters were bringing; for some time now I have had no losses, nor gains either. Even if I were not an old man, I could not have helped feeling pleasure at this; but as it is, my pleasure was far greater. For, however small my possessions might be, I should still have left over more travelling-money than journey to travel, especially since this journey upon which we have set out is one which need not be followed to the end. **4.** An expedition will be incomplete if one stops half-way, or anywhere on this side of one's destination; but life is not incomplete if it is honourable. At whatever point you leave off living, provided you leave off nobly, your life is a whole. Often, however, one must leave off bravely, and our reasons therefore need not be momentous; for neither are the reasons momentous which hold us here.

5. Tullius Marcellinus, a man whom you knew very well, who in youth was a quiet soul and became old prematurely, fell ill of a disease which was by no means hopeless; but it was protracted and troublesome, and it demanded much attention; hence he began to think about dying. He called many of his friends together. Each one of them gave Marcellinus advice, – the timid friend urging him to do what he had made up his mind to do; the flattering and wheedling friend giving counsel which he supposed would be more pleasing to Marcellinus when he came to think the matter over; **6.** but our Stoic friend, a rare man, and, to praise him in language which he deserves, a man of courage and vigour admonished him best of all, as it seems to me. For he began as follows: "Do not torment yourself, my dear Marcellinus, as if the question which you are weighing were a matter of importance. It is not an important matter to live; all your slaves live, and so do all animals; but it is important to die honourably, sensibly, bravely. Reflect how long you have been doing the same thing: food, sleep, lust, – this is one's daily round. The desire to die may be felt, not only by the sensible man or the brave or unhappy man, but even by the man who is merely surfeited."

7. Marcellinus did not need someone to urge him, but rather someone to help him; his slaves refused to do his bidding. The Stoic therefore removed their fears, showing them that there was no risk involved for the household except when it was uncertain whether the master's death was self-sought or not; besides, it was as bad a practice to kill one's master as it was to prevent him forcibly from killing himself. **8.** Then he suggested to Marcellinus himself that it would be a kindly act to distribute gifts to those who had attended him throughout his whole life, when that life was finished, just as, when a banquet is finished, the remaining portion is divided among the attendants who stand about the table. Marcellinus was of a compliant and generous disposition, even when it was a question of his own property; so he distributed little sums among his sorrowing slaves, and comforted them besides. **9.** No need had he of sword or of bloodshed; for three days he fasted and had a tent put up in his very bedroom. Then a tub was brought in; he lay in it for a long time, and, as the hot water was continually poured over him, he gradually passed away, not without a feeling of pleasure, as he himself remarked, – such a feeling as a slow dissolution is wont to give. Those of us who have ever fainted know from experience what this feeling is.

10. This little anecdote into which I have digressed will not be displeasing to you. For you will see that your friend departed neither with difficulty nor with suffering. Though he committed suicide, yet he withdrew most gently, gliding out of life. The anecdote may also be of some use; for often a crisis demands just such examples. There are times when we ought to die and are unwilling; sometimes we die and are unwilling. **11.** No one is so ignorant as not to know that we must at some time die; nevertheless, when one draws near death, one turns to flight, trembles, and laments. Would you not think him an utter fool who wept because he was not alive a thousand years ago? And is he not just as much of a fool who weeps because he will not be alive a thousand years from now? It is all the same; you will not be, and you were not. Neither of these periods of time belongs to you. **12.** You have been cast upon this point of time; if you would make it longer, how much longer shall you make it? Why weep? Why pray? You are taking pains to no purpose.

> Give over thinking that your prayers can bend
> Divine decrees from their predestined end.

These decrees are unalterable and fixed; they are governed by a mighty and everlasting compulsion. Your goal will be the goal of all things. What is there strange in this to you? You were born to be subject to this law; this fate befell your father, your mother, your ancestors, all who came before you; and it will befall all who shall come after you. A sequence which cannot be broken or altered by any power binds all things together and draws all things in its course. **13.** Think of the multitudes of men doomed to death who will come after you, of the multitudes who will go with you! You would die more bravely, I suppose, in the company of many thousands; and yet there are many thousands, both of men and of animals, who at this very moment, while you are irresolute about death, are breathing their last, in their several ways. But you, – did you believe that you would not some day reach the goal towards which you have always been travelling? No journey but has its end.

14. You think, I suppose, that it is now in order for me to cite some examples of great men. No, I shall cite rather the case of a boy. The story of the Spartan lad has been preserved: taken captive while still a stripling, he kept crying in his Doric dialect, "I will not be a slave!" and he made good his word; for the very first time he was ordered to perform a menial and degrading service, – and the command was to fetch a chamber-pot, – he dashed out his brains against the wall. **15.** So near at hand is freedom, and is anyone still a slave? Would you not rather have your own son die thus than reach old age by weakly yielding? Why therefore are you distressed, when even a boy can die so bravely? Suppose that you refuse to follow him; you will be led. Take into your own control that which is now under the control of another. Will you not borrow that boy's courage, and say: "I am no slave!"? Unhappy fellow, you are a slave to men, you are a slave to your business, you are a slave to life. For life, if courage to die be lacking, is slavery.

16. Have you anything worth waiting for? Your very pleasures, which cause you to tarry and hold you back, have already been exhausted by you. None of them is a novelty to you, and there is none that has not already become hateful because you are cloyed with it. You know the taste of wine and cordials. It makes no difference whether a hundred or a thousand measures pass through your bladder; you are nothing but a wine-strainer. You are a connoisseur in the flavour of the oyster and of the mullet; your luxury has not left you anything untasted for the years that are to come; and yet these are the things from which you are torn away unwillingly. **17.** What else is there which you would regret to have taken from you? Friends? But who can be a friend to you? Country? What? Do you think enough of your country to be late to dinner? The light of the sun? You would extinguish it, if you could; for what have you ever done that was fit to be seen in the light? Confess the truth; it is not because you long for the senate chamber or the forum, or even for the world of nature, that you would fain put off dying; it is because you are loth to leave the fish-market, though you have exhausted its stores.

18. You are afraid of death; but how can you scorn it in the midst of a mushroom supper? You wish to live; well, do you know how to live? You are afraid to die. But come now: is this life of yours anything but death? Gaius Caesar was passing along the Via Latina, when a man stepped out from the ranks of the prisoners, his grey beard hanging down even to his breast, and begged to be put to death. "What!" said Caesar, "are you alive now?" That is the answer which should be given to men to whom death would come as a relief. "You are afraid to die; what! are you alive now?" **19.** "But," says one, "I wish to live, for I am engaged in many honourable pursuits. I am loth to leave life's duties, which I am fulfilling with loyalty and zeal." Surely you are aware that dying is also one of life's duties? You are deserting no duty; for there is no definite number established which you are bound to complete. **20.** There is no life that is not short. Compared with the world of nature, even Nestor's life was a short one, or Sattia's, the woman who bade carve on her tombstone that she had lived ninety and nine years. Some persons, you see, boast of their long lives; but who could have endured the old lady if she had had the luck to complete her hundredth year? It is with life as it is with a play, – it matters not how long the action is spun out, but how good the acting is. It makes no difference at what point you stop. Stop whenever you choose; only see to it that the closing period is well turned. Farewell.

LXXVIII. ON THE HEALING POWER OF THE MIND

1. That you are frequently troubled by the snuffling of catarrh and by short attacks of fever which follow after long and chronic catarrhal seizures, I am sorry to hear; particularly because I have experienced this sort of illness myself, and scorned it in its early stages. For when I was still young, I could put up with hardships and show a bold front to illness. But I finally succumbed, and arrived at such a state that I could do nothing but snuffle, reduced as I was to the extremity of thinness. **2.** I often entertained the impulse of ending my life then and there; but the thought of my kind old father kept me back. For I reflected, not how bravely I had the power to die, but how little power he had to bear bravely the loss of me. And so I commanded myself to live. For sometimes it is an act of bravery even to live.

3. Now I shall tell you what consoled me during those days, stating at the outset that these very aids to my peace of mind were as efficacious as medicine. Honourable consolation results in a cure; and whatever has uplifted the soul helps the body also. My studies were my salvation. I place it to the credit of philosophy that I recovered and regained my strength. I owe my life to philosophy, and that is the least of my obligations! **4.** My friends, too, helped me greatly toward good health; I used to be comforted by their cheering words, by the hours they spent at my bedside, and by their conversation. Nothing, my excellent Lucilius, refreshes and aids a sick man so much as the affection of his friends; nothing so steals away the expectation and the fear of death. In fact, I could not believe that, if they survived me, I should be dying at all. Yes, I repeat, it seemed to me that I should continue to live, not with them, but through them. I imagined myself not to be yielding up my soul, but to be making it over to them.

All these things gave me the inclination to succour myself and to endure any torture; besides, it is a most miserable state to have lost one's zest for dying, and to have no zest in living. **5.** These, then, are the remedies to which you should have recourse. The physician will prescribe your walks and your exercise; he will warn you not to become addicted to idleness, as is the tendency of the inactive invalid; he will order you to read in a louder voice and to exercise your lungs the passages and cavity of which are affected; or to sail and shake up your bowels by a little mild motion; he will recommend the proper food, and the suitable time for aiding your strength with wine or refraining from it in order to keep your cough from being irritated and hacking. But as for me, my counsel to you is this, – and it is a cure, not merely of this disease of yours, but of your whole life, – "Despise death." There is no sorrow in the world, when we have escaped from the fear of death. **6.** There are these three serious elements in every disease: fear of death, bodily pain, and interruption of pleasures. Concerning death enough has been said, and I shall add only a word: this fear is not a fear of disease, but a fear of nature. Disease has often postponed death, and a vision of dying has been many a man's salvation. You will die, not because you are ill, but because you are alive; even when you have been cured, the same end awaits you; when you have recovered, it will be not death, but ill-health, that you have escaped.

7. Let us now return to the consideration of the characteristic disadvantage of disease: it is accompanied by great suffering. The suffering, however, is rendered endurable by interruptions; for the strain of extreme pain must come to an end. No man can suffer both severely and for a long time; Nature, who loves us most tenderly, has so constituted us as to make pain either endurable or short. 8. The severest pains have their seat in the most slender parts of our body; nerves, joints, and any other of the narrow passages, hurt most cruelly when they have developed trouble within their contracted spaces. But these parts soon become numb, and by reason of the pain itself lose the sensation of pain, whether because the life-force, when checked in its natural course and changed for the worse, loses the peculiar power through which it thrives and through which it warns us, or because the diseased humours of the body, when they cease to have a place into which they may flow, are thrown back upon themselves, and deprive of sensation the parts where they have caused congestion. 9. So gout, both in the feet and in the hands, and all pain in the vertebrae and in the nerves, have their intervals of rest at the times when they have dulled the parts which they before had tortured; the first twinges, in all such cases, are what cause the distress, and their onset is checked by lapse of time, so that there is an end of pain when numbness has set in. Pain in the teeth, eyes, and ears is most acute for the very reason that it begins among the narrow spaces of the body, – no less acute, indeed, than in the head itself. But if it is more violent than usual, it turns to delirium and stupor. 10. This is, accordingly, a consolation for excessive pain, – that you cannot help ceasing to feel it if you feel it to excess. The reason, however, why the inexperienced are impatient when their bodies suffer is, that they have not accustomed themselves to be contented in spirit. They have been closely associated with the body. Therefore a high-minded and sensible man divorces soul from body, and dwells much with the better or divine part, and only as far as he must with this complaining and frail portion.

11. "But it is a hardship," men say, "to do without our customary pleasures, – to fast, to feel thirst and hunger." These are indeed serious when one first abstains from them. Later the desire dies down, because the appetites themselves which lead to desire are wearied and forsake us; then the stomach becomes petulant, then the food which we craved before becomes hateful. Our very wants die away. But there is no bitterness in doing without that which you have ceased to desire. 12. Moreover, every pain sometimes stops, or at any rate slackens; moreover, one may take precautions against its return, and, when it threatens, may check it by means of remedies. Every

variety of pain has its premonitory symptoms; this is true, at any rate, of pain that is habitual and recurrent. One can endure the suffering which disease entails, if one has come to regard its results with scorn. **13.** But do not of your own accord make your troubles heavier to bear and burden yourself with complaining. Pain is slight if opinion has added nothing to it; but if, on the other hand, you begin to encourage yourself and say, "It is nothing, – a trifling matter at most; keep a stout heart and it will soon cease"; then in thinking it slight, you will make it slight. Everything depends on opinion; ambition, luxury, greed, hark back to opinion. It is according to opinion that we suffer. **14.** A man is as wretched as he has convinced himself that he is. I hold that we should do away with complaint about past sufferings and with all language like this: "None has ever been worse off than I. What sufferings, what evils have I endured! No one has thought that I shall recover. How often have my family bewailed me, and the physicians given me over! Men who are placed on the rack are not torn asunder with such agony!" However, even if all this is true, it is over and gone. What benefit is there in reviewing past sufferings, and in being unhappy, just because once you were unhappy? Besides, every one adds much to his own ills, and tells lies to himself. And that which was bitter to bear is pleasant to have borne; it is natural to rejoice at the ending of one's ills.

Two elements must therefore be rooted out once for all, – the fear of future suffering, and the recollection of past suffering; since the latter no longer concerns me, and the former concerns me not yet. **15.** But when set in the very midst of troubles one should say:

> Perchance some day the memory of this sorrow
> Will even bring delight.

Let such a man fight against them with all his might: if he once gives way, he will be vanquished; but if he strives against his sufferings, he will conquer. As it is, however, what most men do is to drag down upon their own heads a falling ruin which they ought to try to support. If you begin to withdraw your support from that which thrusts toward you and totters and is ready to plunge, it will follow you and lean more heavily upon you; but if you hold your ground and make up your mind to push against it, it will be forced back. **16.** What blows do athletes receive on their faces and all over their bodies! Nevertheless, through their desire for fame they endure every torture, and they undergo these things not only because they are fighting but in order to be able to fight. Their very training means torture. So let us also win the way to victory in all our struggles, – for the reward is not a garland or a palm or a trumpeter who calls for silence at the proclamation of our names, but rather virtue, steadfastness of soul, and a peace that is won for all time, if fortune has once been utterly vanquished in any combat. You say, "I feel severe pain." **17.** What then; are you relieved from feeling it, if you endure it like a woman? Just as an enemy is more dangerous to a retreating army, so every trouble that fortune brings attacks us all the harder if we yield and turn our backs. "But the trouble is serious." What? Is it for this purpose that we are strong, – that we may have light burdens to bear? Would you have your illness long-drawn-out, or would you have it quick and short? If it is long, it means a respite, allows you a period for resting yourself, bestows upon you the boon of time in plenty; as it arises, so it must also subside. A short and rapid illness will do one of two things: it will quench or be quenched. And what difference does it make whether it is not or I am not? In either case there is an end of pain.

18. This, too, will help – to turn the mind aside to thoughts of other things and thus to depart from pain. Call to mind what honourable or brave deeds you have done; consider the good side of your own life. Run over in your memory those things which you have particularly admired. Then think of all the brave men who have conquered pain: of him who continued to read his book as he allowed the cutting out of varicose veins; of him who did not cease to smile, though that very smile so enraged his torturers that they tried upon him every instrument of their cruelty. If pain can be conquered by a smile, will it not be conquered by reason? 19. You may tell me now of whatever you like – of colds, bad coughing-spells that bring up parts of our entrails, fever that parches our very vitals, thirst, limbs so twisted that the joints protrude in different directions; yet worse than these are the stake, the rack, the red-hot plates, the instrument that reopens wounds while the wounds themselves are still swollen and that drives their imprint still deeper. Nevertheless there have been men who have not uttered a moan amid these tortures. "More yet!" says the torturer; but the victim has not begged for release. "More yet!" he says again; but no answer has come. "More yet!" the victim has smiled, and heartily, too. Can you not bring yourself, after an example like this, to make a mock at pain?

20. "But," you object, "my illness does not allow me to be doing anything; it has withdrawn me from all my duties." It is your body that is hampered by ill-health, and not your soul as well. It is for this reason that it clogs the feet of the runner and will hinder the handiwork of the cobbler or the artisan; but if your soul be habitually in practice, you will plead and teach, listen and learn, investigate and meditate. What more is necessary? Do you think that you are doing nothing if you possess self-control in your illness? You will be showing that a disease can be overcome, or at any rate endured. 21. There is, I assure you, a place for virtue even upon a bed of sickness. It is not only the sword and the battle-line that prove the soul alert and unconquered by fear; a man can display bravery even when wrapped in his bed-clothes. You have something to do: wrestle bravely with disease. If it shall compel you to nothing, beguile you to nothing, it is a notable example that you display. O what ample matter were there for renown, if we could have spectators of our sickness! Be your own spectator; seek your own applause.

22. Again, there are two kinds of pleasures. Disease checks the pleasures of the body, but does not do away with them. Nay, if the truth is to be considered, it serves to excite them; for the thirstier a man is, the more he enjoys a drink; the

hungrier he is, the more pleasure he takes in food. Whatever falls to one's lot after a period of abstinence is welcomed with greater zest. The other kind, however, the pleasures of the mind, which are higher and less uncertain, no physician can refuse to the sick man. Whoever seeks these and knows well what they are, scorns all the blandishments of the senses. **23.** Men say, "Poor sick fellow!" But why? Is it because he does not mix snow with his wine, or because he does not revive the chill of his drink – mixed as it is in a good-sized bowl – by chipping ice into it? Or because he does not have Lucrine oysters opened fresh at his table? Or because there is no din of cooks about his dining-hall, as they bring in their very cooking apparatus along with their viands? For luxury has already devised this fashion – of having the kitchen accompany the dinner, so that the food may not grow luke-warm, or fail to be hot enough for a palate which has already become hardened. **24.** "Poor sick fellow!" – he will eat as much as he can digest. There will be no boar lying before his eyes, banished from the table as if it were a common meat; and on his sideboard there will be heaped together no breast-meat of birds, because it sickens him to see birds served whole. But what evil has been done to you? You will dine like a sick man, nay, sometimes like a sound man.

25. All these things, however, can be easily endured – gruel, warm water, and anything else that seems insupportable to a fastidious man, to one who is wallowing in luxury, sick in soul rather than in body – if only we cease to shudder at death. And we shall cease, if once we have gained a knowledge of the limits of good and evil; then, and then only, life will not weary us, neither will death make us afraid. **26.** For surfeit of self can never seize upon a life that surveys all the things which are manifold, great, divine; only idle leisure is wont to make men hate their lives. To one who roams through the universe, the truth can never pall; it will be the untruths that will cloy. **27.** And, on the other hand, if death comes near with its summons, even though it be untimely in its arrival, though it cut one off in one's prime, a man has had a taste of all that the longest life can give. Such a man has in great measure come to understand the universe. He knows that honourable things do not depend on time for their growth; but any life must seem short to those who measure its length by pleasures which are empty and for that reason unbounded.

28. Refresh yourself with such thoughts as these, and meanwhile reserve some hours for our letters. There will come a time when we shall be united again and brought together; however short this time may be, we shall make it long by knowing how to employ it. For, as Posidonius says: "A single day among the learned lasts longer than the longest life of the ignorant." **29.** Meanwhile, hold fast to this thought, and grip it close: yield not to adversity; trust not to prosperity; keep before your eyes the full scope of Fortune's power, as if she would surely do whatever is in her power to do. That which has been long expected comes more gently. Farewell.

LXXIX. ON THE REWARDS OF SCIENTIFIC DISCOVERY

1. I have been awaiting a letter from you, that you might inform me what new matter was revealed to you during your trip round Sicily, and especially that you might give me further information regarding Charybdis itself. I know very well that Scylla is a rock – and indeed a rock not dreaded by mariners; but with regard to Charybdis I should like to have a full description, in order to see whether it agrees with the accounts in mythology; and, if you have by chance investigated it (for it is indeed worthy of your investigation), please enlighten me concerning the following: Is it lashed into a whirlpool by a wind from only one direction, or do all storms alike serve to disturb its depths? Is it true that objects snatched downwards by the whirlpool in that strait are carried for many miles under water, and then come to the surface on the beach near Tauromenium? **2.** If you will write me a full account of these matters, I shall then have the boldness to ask you to perform another task, – also to climb Aetna at my special request. Certain naturalists have inferred that the mountain is wasting away and gradually settling, because sailors used to be able to see it from a greater distance. The reason for this may be, not that the height of the mountain is decreasing, but because the flames have become dim and the eruptions less strong and less copious, and because for the same reason the smoke also is less active by day. However, either of these two things is possible to believe: that on the one hand the mountain is growing smaller because it is consumed from day to day, and that, on the other hand, it remains the same in size because the mountain is not devouring itself, but instead of this the matter which seethes forth collects in some subterranean valley and is fed by other material, finding in the mountain itself not the food which it requires, but simply a passage-way out. **3.** There is a well-known place in Lycia – called by the inhabitants "Hephaestion" – where the ground is full of holes in many places and is surrounded by a harmless fire, which does no injury to the plants that grow there. Hence the place is fertile and luxuriant with growth, because the flames do not scorch but merely shine with a force that is mild and feeble.

4. But let us postpone this discussion, and look into the matter when you have given me a description just how far distant the snow lies from the crater, – I mean the snow which does not melt even in summer, so safe is it from the adjacent fire. But there is no ground for your charging this work to my account; for you were about to gratify your own craze for fine writing, without a commission from anyone at all. **5.** Nay, what am I to offer you *not* merely to describe Aetna in your poem, and *not* to touch lightly upon a topic which is a matter of ritual for all poets? Ovid could not be prevented from using this theme simply because Vergil had already fully covered it; nor could either of these writers frighten off Cornelius Severus. Besides, the topic has served them all with happy results, and those who have gone before seem to me not to have forestalled all what could be said, but merely to have opened the way.

6. It makes a great deal of difference whether you approach a subject that has been exhausted, or one where the ground has merely been broken; in the latter case, the topic grows day by day, and what is already discovered does not hinder new discoveries. Besides, he who writes last has the best of the bargain; he finds already at hand words which, when marshalled in a different way, show a new face. And he is not pilfering them, as if they belonged to someone else, when he uses them, for they are common property. **7.** Now if Aetna does not make your mouth water, I am mistaken in you. You have for some time been desirous of writing something in the grand style and on the level of the older school. For your modesty does not allow you to set your hopes any higher; this quality of yours is so pronounced that, it sees to me, you are likely to curb the force of your natural ability, if there should be any danger of outdoing others; so greatly do you reverence the old masters. **8.** Wisdom has this advantage, among others, – that no man can be outdone by another, except during the climb. But when you have arrived at the top, it is a draw; there is no room for further ascent, the game is over. Can the sun add to his size? Can the moon advance beyond her usual fullness? The seas do not increase in bulk. The universe keeps the same character, the same limits. **9.** Things which have reached their full stature cannot grow higher. Men who have attained wisdom will therefore be equal and on the same footing. Each of them will possess his own peculiar gifts – one will be more affable, another more facile, another more ready of speech, a fourth more eloquent; but as regards the quality under discussion, – the element that produces happiness, – it is equal in them all. **10.** I do not know whether this Aetna of yours can collapse and fall in ruins, whether this lofty summit, visible for many miles over the deep sea, is wasted by the incessant power of the flames; but I do know that virtue will not be brought down to a lower plane either by flames or by ruins. Hers is the only greatness that knows no lowering; there can be for her no further rising or sinking. Her stature, like that of the stars in the heavens, is fixed. Let us therefore strive to raise ourselves to this altitude.

11. Already much of the task is accomplished; nay, rather, if I can bring myself to confess the truth, not much. For goodness does not mean merely being better than the lowest. Who that could catch but a mere glimpse of the daylight would boast his powers of vision? One who sees the sun shining through a mist may be contented meanwhile that he has escaped darkness, but he does not yet enjoy the blessing of light. **12.** Our souls will not have reason to rejoice in their lot until, freed from this darkness in which they grope, they have not merely glimpsed the brightness with feeble vision, but have absorbed the full light of day and have been restored to their place in the sky, – until, indeed, they have regained the place which they held at the allotment of their birth. The soul is summoned upward by its very origin. And it will reach that goal even before it is released from its prison below, as soon as it has cast off sin and, in purity and lightness, has leaped up into celestial realms of thought.

13. I am glad, beloved Lucilius, that we are occupied with this ideal, that we pursue it with all our might, even though few know it, or none. Fame is the shadow of virtue; it will attend virtue even against her will. But, as the shadow sometimes precedes and sometimes follows or even lags behind, so fame sometimes goes before us and shows herself in plain sight, and sometimes is in the rear, and is all the greater in proportion as she is late in coming, when once envy has beaten a retreat. **14.** How long did men believe Democritus to be mad! Glory barely came to Socrates. And how long did our state remain in ignorance of Cato! They rejected him, and did not know his worth until they had lost him. If Rutilius had not resigned himself to wrong, his innocence and virtue would have escaped notice; the hour of his suffering was the hour of his triumph. Did he not give thanks for his lot, and welcome his exile with open arms? I have mentioned thus far those to whom Fortune has brought renown at the very moment of persecution; but how many there are whose progress toward virtue has come to light only after their death! And how many have been ruined, not rescued, by their reputation? **15.** There is Epicurus, for example; mark how greatly he is admired, not only by the more cultured, but also by this ignorant rabble. This man, however, was unknown to Athens itself, near which he had hidden himself away. And so, when he had already survived by many years his friend Metrodorus, he added in a letter these last words, proclaiming with thankful appreciation the friendship that had existed between them: "So greatly blest were Metrodorus and I that it has been no harm to us to be unknown, and almost unheard of, in this well-known land of Greece." **16.** Is it not true, therefore, that men did not discover him until after he had ceased to be? Has not his renown shone forth, for all that? Metrodorus also admits this fact in one of his letters: that Epicurus and he were not well known to the public; but he declares that after the lifetime of Epicurus and himself any man who might wish to follow in their footsteps would win great and ready-made renown.

17. Virtue is never lost to view; and yet to have been lost to view is no loss. There will come a day which will reveal her, though hidden away or suppressed by the spite of her contemporaries. That man is born merely for a few, who thinks only of the people of his own generation. Many thousands of years and many thousands of peoples will come after you; it is to these that you should have regard. Malice may have imposed silence upon the mouths of all who were alive in your day; but there will come men who will judge you without prejudice and without favour. If there is any reward that virtue receives at the hands of fame, not even this can pass away. We ourselves, indeed, shall not be affected by the talk of posterity; nevertheless, posterity will cherish and celebrate us even though we are not conscious thereof. **18.** Virtue has never failed to reward a man, both during his life and after his death, provided he has followed her loyally, provided he has not decked himself out or painted himself up, but has been always the same, whether he appeared before men's eyes after being announced, or suddenly and without preparation. Pretence accomplishes nothing. Few are deceived by a mask that is easily drawn over the face. Truth is the same in every part. Things which deceive us have no real substance. Lies are thin stuff; they are transparent, if you examine them with care. Farewell.

LXXX. ON WORLDLY DECEPTIONS

1. To-day I have some free time, thanks not so much to myself as to the games, which have attracted all the bores to the boxing-match. No one will interrupt me or disturb the train of my thoughts, which go ahead more boldly as the result of my very confidence. My door has not been continually creaking on its hinges nor will my curtain be pulled aside; my thoughts may march safely on, – and that is all the more necessary for one who goes independently and follows out his own path. Do I then follow no predecessors? Yes, but I allow myself to discover something new, to alter, to reject. I am not a slave to them, although I give them my approval.

2. And yet that was a very bold word which I spoke when I assured myself that I should have some quiet, and some uninterrupted retirement. For lo, a great cheer comes from the stadium, and while it does not drive me distracted, yet it shifts my thought to a contrast suggested by this very noise. How many men, I say to myself, train their bodies, and how few train their minds! What crowds flock to the games, spurious as they are and arranged merely for pastime, – and what a solitude reigns where the good arts are taught! How feather-brained are the athletes whose muscles and shoulders we admire! **3.** The question which I ponder most of all is this; if the body can be trained to such a degree of endurance that it will stand the blows and kicks of several opponents at once and to such a degree that a man can last out the day and resist the scorching sun in the midst of the burning dust, drenched all the while with his own blood, – if this can be done, how much more easily might the mind be toughened so that it could receive the blows of Fortune and not be conquered, so that it might struggle to its feet again after it has been laid low, after it has been trampled under foot?

For although the body needs many things in order to be strong, yet the mind grows from within, giving to itself nourishment and exercise. Yonder athletes must have copious food, copious drink, copious quantities of oil, and long training besides; but you can acquire virtue without equipment and without expense. All that goes to make you a good man lies within yourself. **4.** And what do you need in order to become good? To wish it. But what better thing could you wish for than to break away from this slavery, a slavery that oppresses us all, a slavery which even chattels of the lowest estate, born amid such degradation, strive in every possible way to strip off? In exchange for freedom they pay out the savings which they have scraped together by cheating their own bellies; shall *you* not be eager to attain liberty at any price, seeing that you claim it as your birthright? **5.** Why cast glances toward your strong-box? Liberty cannot be bought. It is therefore useless to enter in your ledger the item of "Freedom," for freedom is possessed neither by those who have bought it, nor by those who have sold it. You must give this good to yourself, and seek it from yourself.

First of all, free yourself from the fear of death, for death puts the yoke about our necks; then free yourself from the fear of poverty. **6.** If you would know how little evil there is in poverty, compare the faces of the poor with those of the rich; the poor man smiles more often and more genuinely; his troubles do not go deep down; even if any anxiety comes upon him, it passes like a fitful cloud. But the merriment of those whom men call happy is feigned, while their sadness is heavy and festering, and all the heavier because they may not meanwhile display their grief, but must act the part of happiness in the midst of sorrows that eat out their very hearts. **7.** I often feel called upon to use the following illustration, and it seems to me that none expresses more effectively this drama of human life, wherein we are assigned the parts which we are to play so badly. Yonder is the man who stalks upon the stage with swelling port and head thrown back, and says:

> Lo, I am he whom Argos hails as lord,
> Whom Pelops left the heir of lands that spread
> From Hellespont and from th' Ionian sea
> E'en to the Isthmian straits.

And who is this fellow? He is but a slave; his wage is five measures of grain and five denarii. **8.** Yon other who, proud and wayward and puffed up by confidence in his power, declaims:

> Peace, Menelaus, or this hand shall slay thee!

receives a daily pittance and sleeps on rags. You may speak in the same way about all these dandies whom you see riding in litters above the heads of men and above the crowd; in every case their happiness is put on like the actor's mask. Tear it off, and you will scorn them.

9. When you buy a horse, you order its blanket to be removed; you pull off the garments from slaves that are advertised for sale, so that no bodily flaws may escape your notice; if you judge a man, do you judge him when he is wrapped in a disguise? Slave dealers hide under some sort of finery any defect which may give offence, and for that reason the very trappings arouse the suspicion of the buyer. If you catch sight of a leg or an arm that is bound up in cloths, you demand that it be stripped and that the body itself be revealed to you. **10.** Do you see yonder Scythian or Sarmatian king, his head adorned with the badge of his office? If you wish to see what he amounts to, and to know his full worth, take off his diadem; much evil lurks beneath it. But why do I speak of others? If you wish to set a value on yourself, put away your money, your estates, your honours, and look into your own soul. At present, you are taking the word of others for what you are. Farewell.

LXXXI. ON BENEFITS

1. You complain that you have met with an ungrateful person. If this is your first experience of that sort, you should offer thanks either to your good luck or to your caution. In this case, however, caution can effect nothing but to make you ungenerous. For if you wish to avoid such a danger, you will not confer benefits; and so, that benefits may not be lost with another man, they will be lost to yourself.

It is better, however, to get no return than to confer no benefits. Even after a poor crop one should sow again; for often losses due to continued barrenness of an unproductive soil have been made good by one year's fertility. **2.** In order to discover one grateful person, it is worth while to make trial of many ungrateful ones. No man has so unerring a hand when he confers benefits that he is not frequently deceived; it is well for the traveller to wander, that he may again cleave to the path. After a shipwreck, sailors try the sea again. The banker is not frightened away from the forum by the swindler. If one were compelled to drop everything that caused trouble, life would soon grow dull amid sluggish idleness; but in your case this very condition may prompt you to become more charitable. For when the outcome of any undertaking is unsure, you must try again and again, in order to succeed ultimately. **3.** I have, however, discussed the matter with sufficient fullness in the volumes which I have written, entitled "On Benefits."

What I think should rather be investigated is this, – a question which I feel has not been made sufficiently clear: "Whether he who has helped us has squared the account and has freed us from our debt, if he has done us harm later." You may add this question also, if you like: "when the harm done later has been more than the help rendered previously." **4.** If you are seeking for the formal and just decision of a strict judge, you will find that he checks off one act by the other, and declares: "Though the injuries outweigh the benefits, yet we should credit to the benefits anything that stands over even after the injury." The harm done was indeed greater, but the helpful act was done first. Hence the time also should be taken into account. **5.** Other cases are so clear that I need not remind you that you should also look into such points as: How gladly was the help offered, and how reluctantly was the harm done, – since benefits, as well as injuries, depend on the spirit. "I did not wish to confer the benefit; but I was won over by my respect for the man, or by the importunity of his request, or by hope." **6.** Our feeling about every obligation depends in each case upon the spirit in which the benefit is conferred; we weigh not the bulk of the gift, but the quality of the good-will which prompted it. So now let us do away with guess-work; the former deed was a benefit, and the latter, which transcended the earlier benefit, is an injury. The good man so arranges the two sides of his ledger that he voluntarily cheats himself by adding to the benefit and subtracting from the injury.

The more indulgent magistrate, however (and I should rather be such a one), will order us to forget the injury and remember the accommodation. **7.** "But surely," you say, "it is the part of justice to render to each that which is his due, – thanks in return for a benefit, and retribution, or at any rate ill-will, in return for an injury!" This, I say, will be true when it is one man who has inflicted the injury, and a different man who has conferred the benefit; for if it is the same man, the force of the injury is nullified by the benefit conferred. Indeed, a man who ought to be pardoned, even though there were no good deeds credited to him in the past, should receive something more than mere leniency if he commits a wrong when he has a benefit to his credit. **8.** I do not set an equal value on benefits and injuries. I reckon a benefit at a higher rate than an injury. Not all grateful persons know what it involves to be in debt for a benefit; even a thoughtless, crude fellow, one of the common herd, may know, especially soon after he has received the gift; but he does not know how deeply he stands in debt therefor. Only the wise man knows exactly what value should be put upon everything; for the fool whom I just mentioned, no matter how good his intentions may be, either pays less than he owes, or pays it at the wrong time or the wrong place. That for which he should make return he wastes and loses. **9.** There is a marvellously accurate phraseology applied to certain subjects, a long-established terminology which indicates certain acts by means of symbols that are most efficient and that serve to outline men's duties. We are, as you know, wont to speak thus: "A. has made a return for the favour bestowed by B." Making a return means handing over of your own accord that which you owe. We do not say, "He has paid back the favour"; for "pay back" is used of a man upon whom a demand for payment is made, of those who pay against their will. Of those who pay under any circumstances whatsoever, and of those who pay through a third party. We do not say, "He has 'restored' the benefit," or 'settled' it; we have never been satisfied with a word which applies properly to a debt of money. **10.** Making a return means offering something to him from whom you have received something. The phrase implies a voluntary return; he who has made such a return has served the writ upon himself.

The wise man will inquire in his own mind into all the circumstances: how much he has received, from whom, when, where, how. And so we declare that none but the wise man knows how to make return for a favour; moreover, none but the wise man knows how to confer a benefit, – that man, I mean, who enjoys the giving more than the recipient enjoys the receiving. **11.** Now some person will reckon this remark as one of the generally surprising statements such as we Stoics are wont to make and such as the Greeks call "paradoxes," and will say: "Do you maintain, then, that only the wise man knows how to return a favour? Do you maintain that no one else knows how to make restoration to a creditor for a debt? Or, on buying a commodity, to pay full value to the seller?" In order not to bring any odium upon myself, let me tell you that Epicurus says the same thing. At any rate, Metrodorus remarks that only the wise man knows how to return a favour. **12.** Again, the objector mentioned above wonders at our saying: "The wise man alone knows how to love, the wise man alone is a real friend." And yet it is a part of love and of friendship to return favours; nay, further, it is an ordinary act, and happens more frequently than real friendship. Again, this same objector wonders at our saying, "There is no loyalty except in the wise man," just as if he himself does not say the same thing! Or do you think that there is any loyalty in him who does not know how to return a favour? **13.** These men, accordingly, should cease to discredit us, just as if we were uttering an impossible boast; they should understand that the essence of honour resides in the wise man, while among the crowd we find only the ghost and the semblance of honour. None but the wise man knows how to return a favour. Even a fool can return it in proportion to his knowledge and his power; his fault would be a lack of knowledge rather than a lack of will or desire. To will does not come by teaching.

14. The wise man will compare all things with one another; for the very same object becomes greater or smaller, according to the time, the place, and the cause. Often the riches that are spent in profusion upon a palace cannot accomplish as much as a thousand *denarii* given at the right time. Now it makes a great deal of difference whether you give outright, or come to a man's assistance, whether your generosity saves him, or sets him up in life. Often the gift is small, but the consequences great. And what a distinction do you imagine there is between taking something which one lacks, – something which was offered, – and receiving a benefit in order to confer one in return?

15. But we should not slip back into the subject which we have already sufficiently investigated. In this balancing of benefits and injuries, the good man will, to be sure, judge with the highest degree of fairness, but he will incline towards the side of the benefit; he will turn more readily in this direction. **16.** Moreover, in affairs of this kind the person concerned is wont to count for a great deal. Men say: "You conferred a benefit upon me in that matter of the slave, but you did me an injury in the case of my father" or, "You saved my son, but robbed me of a father." Similarly, he will follow up all other matters in which comparisons can be made, and if the difference be very slight, he will pretend not to notice it. Even though the difference be great, yet if the concession can be made without impairment of duty and loyalty, our good man will overlook that is, provided the injury exclusively affects the good man himself. **17.** To sum up, the matter stands thus: the good man will be easy-going in striking a balance; he will allow too much to be set against his credit. He will be unwilling to pay a benefit by balancing the injury against it. The side towards which he will lean, the tendency which he will exhibit, is the desire to be under obligations for the favour, and the desire to make return therefor. For anyone who receives a benefit more gladly than he repays it is mistaken. By as much as he who pays is more light-hearted than he who borrows, by so much ought he to be more joyful who unburdens himself of the greatest debt – a benefit received – than he who incurs the greatest obligations. **18.** For ungrateful men make mistakes in this respect also: they have to pay their creditors both capital and interest, but they think that benefits are currency which they can use without interest. So the debts grow through postponement, and the later the action is postponed the more remains to be paid. A man is an ingrate if he repays a favour without interest. Therefore, interest also should be allowed for, when you compare your receipts and your expenses. **19.** We should try by all means to be as grateful as possible.

For gratitude is a good thing for ourselves, in a sense in which justice, that is commonly supposed to concern other persons, is not; gratitude returns in large measure unto itself. There is not a man who, when he has benefited his neighbour, has not benefited himself, – I do not mean for the reason that he whom you have aided will desire to aid you, or that he whom you have defended will desire to protect you, or that an example of good conduct returns in a circle to benefit the doer, just as examples of bad conduct recoil upon their authors, and as men find no pity if they suffer wrongs which they themselves have demonstrated the possibility of committing; but that the reward for all the virtues lies in the virtues themselves. For they are not practised with a view to recompense; the wages of a good deed is to have done it. **20.** I am grateful, not in order that my neighbour, provoked by the earlier act of kindness, may be more ready to benefit me, but simply in order that I may perform a most pleasant and beautiful act; I feel grateful, not because it profits me, but because it pleases me. And, to prove the truth of this to you, I declare that even if I may not be grateful without seeming ungrateful, even if I am able to retain a benefit only by an act which resembles an injury; even so, I shall strive in the utmost calmness of spirit toward the purpose which honour demands, in the very midst of disgrace. No one, I think, rates virtue higher or is more consecrated to virtue than he who has lost his reputation for being a good man in order to keep from losing the approval of his conscience. **21.** Thus, as I have said, your being grateful is more conducive to your own good than to your neighbour's good. For while your neighbour has had a common, everyday experience, – namely, receiving back the gift which he had bestowed, – you have had a great experience which is the outcome of an utterly happy condition of soul, – to have felt gratitude. For if wickedness makes men unhappy and virtue makes men blest, and if it is a virtue to be grateful, then the return which you have made is only the customary thing, but the thing to which you have attained is priceless, – the consciousness of gratitude, which comes only to the soul that is divine and blessed. The opposite feeling to this, however, is immediately attended by the greatest unhappiness; no man, if he be ungrateful, will be unhappy in the future. I allow him no day of grace; he is unhappy forthwith.

22. Let us therefore avoid being ungrateful, not for the sake of others but for our own sakes. When we do wrong, only the least and lightest portion of it flows back upon our neighbour; the worst and, if I may use the term, the densest portion of it stays at home and troubles the owner. My master Attalus used to say: "Evil herself drinks the largest portion of her own poison." The poison which serpents carry for the destruction of others, and secrete without harm to themselves, is not like this poison; for this sort is ruinous to the possessor. **23.** The ungrateful man tortures and torments himself; he hates the gifts which he has accepted, because he must make a return for them, and he tries to belittle their value, but he really enlarges and exaggerates the injuries which he has received. And what is more wretched than a man who forgets his benefits and clings to his injuries?

Wisdom, on the other hand, lends grace to every benefit, and of her own free will commends it to her own favour, and delights her soul by continued recollection thereof. **24.** Evil men have but one pleasure in benefits, and a very short-lived pleasure at that; it lasts only while they are receiving them. But the wise man derives therefrom an abiding and eternal joy. For he takes delight not so much in receiving the gift as in having received it; and this joy never perishes; it abides with him always. He despises the wrongs done him; he forgets them, not accidentally, but voluntarily. **25.** He does not put a wrong construction upon everything, or seek for someone whom he may hold responsible for each happening; he rather ascribes even the sins of men to chance. He will not misinterpret a word or a look; he makes light of all mishaps by interpreting them in a generous way. He does not remember an injury rather than a service. As far as possible, he lets his memory rest upon the earlier and the better deed, never changing his attitude towards those who have deserved well of him, except in climes where the bad deeds far outdistance the good, and the space between them is obvious even to one who closes his eyes to it; even then only to this extent, that he strives, after receiving the preponderant injury, to resume the attitude which he held before he received the benefit. For when the injury merely equals the benefit, a certain amount of kindly feeling is left over. **26.** Just as a defendant is acquitted when the votes are equal, and just as the spirit of kindliness always tries to bend every doubtful case toward the better interpretation, so the mind of the wise man, when another's merits merely equal his bad deeds, will, to be sure, cease to feel an obligation, but does not cease to desire to feel it, and acts precisely like the man who pays his debts even after they have been legally cancelled.

27. But no man can be grateful unless he has learned to scorn the things which drive the common herd to distraction; if you wish to make return for a favour, you must be willing to go into exile, – or to pour forth your blood, or to undergo poverty, or – and this will frequently happen, – even to let your very innocence be stained and exposed to shameful slanders. It is no slight price that a man must pay for being grateful. **28.** We hold nothing dearer than a benefit, so long as we are seeking one; we hold nothing cheaper after we have received it. Do you ask what it is that makes us forget benefits received? It is our extreme greed for receiving others. We consider not what we have obtained, but what we are to seek. We are deflected from the right course by riches, titles, power, and everything which is valuable in our opinion but worthless when rated at its real value. **29.** We do not know how to weigh matters; we should take counsel regarding them, not with their reputation but with their nature; those things possess no grandeur wherewith to enthral our minds, except the fact that we have become accustomed to marvel at them. For they are not praised because they ought to be desired, but they are desired because they have been praised; and when the error of individuals has once created error on the part of the public, then the public error goes on creating error on the part of individuals.

30. But just as we take on faith such estimates of values, so let us take on the faith of the people this truth that nothing is more honourable than a grateful heart. This phrase will be echoed by all cities, and by all races, even those from savage countries. Upon this point – good and bad will agree. **31.** Some praise pleasure, some prefer toil; some say that pain is the greatest of evils, some say it is no evil at all; some will include riches in the Supreme Good, others will say that their discovery meant harm to the human race, and that none is richer than he to whom Fortune has found nothing to give. Amid all this diversity of opinion all men will yet with one voice, as the saying is, vote "aye" to the proposition that thanks should be returned to those who have deserved well of us. On this question the common herd, rebellious as they are, will all agree, but at present we keep paying back injuries instead of benefits, and the primary reason why a man is ungrateful is that he has found it impossible to be grateful enough. **32.** Our madness has gone to such lengths that it is a very dangerous thing to confer great benefits upon a person; for just because he thinks it shameful not to repay, so he would have none left alive whom he should repay. "Keep for yourself what you have received; I do not ask it back – I do not demand it. Let it be safe to have conferred a favour." There is no worse hatred than that which springs from shame at the desecration of a benefit. Farewell.

LXXXII. ON THE NATURAL FEAR OF DEATH

1. I have already ceased to be anxious about you. "Whom then of the gods," you ask, "have you found as your voucher?" A god, let me tell you, who deceives no one, – a soul in love with that which is upright and good. The better part of yourself is on safe ground. Fortune can inflict injury upon you; what is more pertinent is that I have no fears lest you do injury to yourself. Proceed as you have begun, and settle yourself in this way of living, not luxuriously, but calmly. **2.** I prefer to be in trouble rather than in luxury; and you had better interpret the term "in trouble" as popular usage is wont to interpret it: living a "hard," "rough," "toilsome" life. We are wont to hear the lives of certain men praised as follows, when they are objects of unpopularity: "So-and-So lives luxuriously"; but by this they mean: "He is softened by luxury." For the soul is made womanish by degrees, and is weakened until it matches the ease and laziness in which it lies. Lo, is it not better for one who is really a man even to become hardened? Next, these same dandies fear that which they have made their own lives resemble. Much difference is there between lying idle and lying buried! **3.** "But," you say, "is it not better even to lie idle than to whirl round in these eddies of business distraction?" Both extremes are to be deprecated – both tension and sluggishness. I hold that he who lies on a perfumed couch is no less dead than he who is dragged along by the executioner's hook.

Leisure without study is death; it is a tomb for the living man. **4.** What then is the advantage of retirement? As if the real causes of our anxieties did not follow us across the seas! What hiding-place is there, where the fear of death does not enter?

What peaceful haunts are there, so fortified and so far withdrawn that pain does not fill them with fear? Wherever you hide yourself, human ills will make an uproar all around. There are many external things which compass us about, to deceive us or to weigh upon us; there are many things within which, even amid solitude, fret and ferment.

5. Therefore, gird yourself about with philosophy, an impregnable wall. Though it be assaulted by many engines, Fortune can find no passage into it. The soul stands on unassailable ground, if it has abandoned external things; it is independent in its own fortress; and every weapon that is hurled falls short of the mark. Fortune has not the long reach with which we credit her; she can seize none except him that clings to her. **6.** Let us then recoil from her as far as we are able. This will be possible for us only through knowledge of self and of the world of Nature. The soul should know whither it is going and whence it came, what is good for it and what is evil, what it seeks and what it avoids, and what is that Reason which distinguishes between the desirable and the undesirable, and thereby tames the madness of our desires and calms the violence of our fears.

7. Some men flatter themselves that they have checked these evils by themselves even without the aid of philosophy; but when some accident catches them off their guard, a tardy confession of error is wrung from them. Their boastful words perish from their lips when the torturer commands them to stretch forth their hands, and when death draws nearer! You might say to such a man: "It was easy for you to challenge evils that were not near-by; but here comes pain, which you declared you could endure; here comes death, against which you uttered many a courageous boast! The whip cracks, the sword flashes:

> Ah now, Aeneas, thou must needs be stout
> And strong of heart!"

8. This strength of heart, however, will come from constant study, provided that you practise, not with the tongue but with the soul, and provided that you prepare yourself to meet death. To enable yourself to meet death, you may expect no encouragement or cheer from those who try to make you believe, by means of their hair-splitting logic, that death is no evil. For I take pleasure, excellent Lucilius, in poking fun at the absurdities of the Greeks, of which, to my continual surprise, I have not yet succeeded in ridding myself. **9.** Our master Zeno uses a syllogism like this: "No evil is glorious; but death is glorious; therefore death is no evil." A cure, Zeno! I have been freed from fear; henceforth I shall not hesitate to bare my neck on the scaffold. Will you not utter sterner words instead of rousing a dying man to laughter? Indeed, Lucilius, I could not easily tell you whether he who thought that he was quenching the fear of death by setting up this syllogism was the more foolish, or he who attempted to refute it, just as if it had anything to do with the matter! **10.** For the refuter himself proposed a counter-syllogism, based upon the proposition that we regard death as "indifferent," – one of the things which the Greeks call ἀδιάφορα.

"Nothing," he says, "that is indifferent can be glorious; death is glorious; therefore death is not indifferent." You comprehend the tricky fallacy which is contained in this syllogism. – mere death is, in fact, not glorious; but a brave death is glorious. And when you say, "Nothing that is indifferent is glorious," I grant you this much, and declare that nothing is glorious except as it deals with indifferent things. I classify as "indifferent," – that is, neither good nor evil – sickness, pain, poverty, exile, death. **11.** None of these things is intrinsically glorious; but nothing can be glorious apart from them. For it is not poverty that we praise, it is the man whom poverty cannot humble or bend. Nor is it exile that we praise, it is the man who withdraws into exile in the spirit in which he would have sent another into exile. It is not pain that we praise, it is the man whom pain has not coerced. One praises not death, but the man whose soul death takes away before it can confound it. **12.** All these things are in themselves neither honourable nor glorious; but any one of them that virtue has visited and touched is made honourable and glorious by virtue; they merely lie in between, and the decisive question is only whether wickedness or virtue has laid hold upon them. For instance, the death which in Cato's case is glorious, is in the case of Brutus forthwith base and disgraceful. For this Brutus, condemned to death, was trying to obtain postponement; he withdrew a moment in order to ease himself; when summoned to die and ordered to bare his throat, he exclaimed: "I will bare my throat, if only I may live!" What madness it is to run away, when it is impossible to turn back! "I will bare my throat, if only I may live!" He came very near saying also: "even under Antony!" This fellow deserved indeed to be consigned to *life*!

13. But, as I was going on to remark, you see that death in itself is neither an evil nor a good; Cato experienced death most honourably, Brutus most basely. Everything, if you add virtue, assumes a glory which it did not possess before. We speak of a sunny room, even though the same room is pitch-dark at night. **14.** It is the day which fills it with light, and the night which steals the light away; thus it is with the things which we call indifferent and "middle," like riches, strength, beauty, titles, kingship, and their opposites, – death, exile, ill-health, pain, and all such evils, the fear of which upsets us to a greater or less extent; it is the wickedness or the virtue that bestows the name of good or evil. An object is not by its own essence either hot or cold; it is heated when thrown into a furnace, and chilled when dropped into water. Death is honourable when related to that which is honourable; by this I mean virtue and a soul that despises the worst hardships.

15. Furthermore, there are vast distinctions among these qualities which we call "middle." For example, death is not so indifferent as the question whether your hair should be worn evenly or unevenly. Death belongs among those things which are not indeed evils, but still have in them a semblance of evil; for there are implanted in us love of self, a desire for existence and self-preservation, and also an abhorrence of dissolution, because death seems to rob us of many goods and to withdraw us from the abundance to which we have become accustomed. And there is another element which estranges us from death, we are already familiar with the present, but are ignorant of the future into which we shall transfer ourselves, and we shrink from the unknown. Moreover, it is natural to fear the world of shades, whither death is supposed to lead. **16.** Therefore, although death is something indifferent, it is nevertheless not a thing which we can easily ignore. The soul must be hardened by long practice, so that it may learn to endure the sight and the approach of death.

Death ought to be despised more than it is wont to be despised. For we believe too many of the stories about death. Many thinkers have striven hard to increase its ill repute; they have portrayed the prison in the world below and the land overwhelmed by everlasting night, where

> Within his blood-stained cave Hell's warder huge
> Doth sprawl his ugly length on half-crunched bones,
> And terrifies the disembodied ghosts
> With never-ceasing bark.

Even if you can win your point and prove that these are mere stories and that nothing is left for the dead to fear, another fear steals upon you. For the fear of going to the underworld is equalled by the fear of going nowhere.

17. In the face of these notions, which long-standing opinion has dinned in our ears, how can brave endurance of death be anything else than glorious, and fit to rank among the greatest accomplishments of the human mind? For the mind will never rise to virtue if it believes that death is an evil; but it will so rise if it holds that death is a matter of indifference. It is not in the order of nature that a man shall proceed with a great heart to a destiny which he believes to be evil; he will go sluggishly and with reluctance. But nothing glorious can result from unwillingness and cowardice; virtue does nothing under compulsion. **18.** Besides, no deed that a man does is honourable unless he has devoted himself thereto and attended to it with all his heart, rebelling against it with no portion of his being. When, however, a man goes to face an evil, either through fear of worse evils or in the hope of goods whose attainment is of sufficient moment to him that he can swallow the one evil which he must endure, – in that case the judgment of the agent is drawn in two directions. On the one side is the motive which bids him carry out his purpose; on the other, the motive which restrains him and makes him flee from something which has aroused his apprehension or leads to danger. Hence he is torn in different directions; and if this happens, the glory of his act is gone. For virtue accomplishes its plans only when the spirit is in harmony with itself. There is no element of fear in any of its actions.

> Yield not to evils, but, still braver, go
> Where'er thy fortune shall allow.

19. You cannot "still braver go," if you are persuaded that those things are the real evils. Root out this idea from your soul; otherwise your apprehensions will remain undecided and will thus check the impulse to action. You will be pushed into that towards which you ought to advance like a soldier.

Those of our school, it is true, would have men think that Zeno's syllogism is correct, but that the second I mentioned, which is set up against his, is deceptive and wrong. But I for my part decline to reduce such questions to a matter of dialectical rules or to the subtleties of an utterly worn-out system. Away, I say, with all that sort of thing, which makes a man feel, when a question is propounded to him, that he is hemmed in, and forces him to admit a premiss, and then makes him say one thing in his answer when his real opinion is another. When truth is at stake, we must act more frankly; and when fear is to be combated, we must act more bravely. 20. Such questions, which the dialecticians involve in subtleties, I prefer to solve and weigh rationally, with the purpose of winning conviction and not of forcing the judgment.

When a general is about to lead into action an army prepared to meet death for their wives and children, how will he exhort them to battle? I remind you of the Fabii, who took upon a single clan a war which concerned the whole state. I point out to you the Lacedaemonians in position at the very pass of Thermopylae! They have no hope of victory, no hope of returning. The place where they stand is to be their tomb. 21. In what language do you encourage them to bar the way with their bodies and take upon themselves the ruin of their whole tribe, and to retreat from life rather than from their post? Shall you say: "That which is evil is not glorious; but death is glorious; therefore death is not an evil"? What a powerful discourse! After such words, who would hesitate to throw himself upon the serried spears of the foemen, and die in his tracks? But take Leonidas: how bravely did he address his men! He said: "Fellow-soldiers, let us to our breakfast, knowing that we shall sup in Hades!" The food of these men did not grow lumpy in their mouths, or stick in their throats, or slip from their fingers; eagerly did they accept the invitation to breakfast, and to supper also! 22. Think, too, of the famous Roman general; his soldiers had been dispatched to seize a position, and when they were about to make their way through a huge army of the enemy, he addressed them with the words: "You must go now, fellow-soldiers, to yonder place, whence there is no 'must' about your returning!"

You see, then, how straightforward and peremptory virtue is; but what man on earth can your deceptive logic make more courageous or more upright? Rather does it break the spirit, which should never be less straitened or forced to deal with petty and thorny problems than when some great work is being planned. 23. It is not the Three Hundred, – it is all mankind that should be relieved of the fear of death. But how can you prove to all those men that death is no evil? How can you overcome the notions of all our past life, – notions with which we are tinged from our very infancy? What succour can you discover for man's helplessness? What can you say that will make men rush, burning with zeal, into the midst of danger? By what persuasive speech can you turn aside this universal feeling of fear, by what strength of wit can you turn aside the conviction of the human race which steadfastly opposes you? Do you propose to construct catchwords for me, or to string together petty syllogisms? It takes great weapons to strike down great monsters. 24. You recall the fierce serpent in Africa, more frightful to the Roman legions than the war itself, and assailed in vain by arrows and slings; it could not be wounded even by "Pythius," since its huge size, and the toughness which matched its bulk, made spears, or any weapon hurled by the hand of man, glance off. It was finally destroyed by rocks equal in size to millstones. Are you, then, hurling petty weapons like yours even against death? Can you stop a lion's charge by an awl? Your arguments are indeed sharp; but there is nothing sharper than a stalk of grain. And certain arguments are rendered useless and unavailing by their very subtlety. Farewell.

LXXXIII. ON DRUNKENNESS

1. You bid me give you an account of each separate day, and of the whole day too; so you must have a good opinion of me if you think that in these days of mine there is nothing to hide. At any rate, it is thus that we should live, – as if we lived in plain sight of all men; and it is thus that we should think, – as if there were someone who could look into our inmost souls; and there is one who can so look. For what avails it that something is hidden from man? Nothing is shut off from the sight of God. He is witness of our souls, and he comes into the very midst of our thoughts – comes into them, I say, as one who may at any time depart. **2.** I shall therefore do as you bid, and shall gladly inform you by letter what I am doing, and in what sequence. I shall keep watching myself continually, and – a most useful habit – shall review each day. For this is what makes us wicked: that no one of us looks back over his own life. Our thoughts are devoted only to what we are about to do. And yet our plans for the future always depend on the past.

3. To-day has been unbroken; no one has filched the slightest part of it from me. The whole time has been divided between rest and reading. A brief space has been given over to bodily exercise, and on this ground I can thank old age – my exercise costs very little effort; as soon as I stir, I am tired. And weariness is the aim and end of exercise, no matter how strong one is. **4.** Do you ask who are my pacemakers? One is enough for me, – the slave Pharius, a pleasant fellow, as you know; but I shall exchange him for another. At my time of life I need one who is of still more tender years. Pharius, at any rate, says that he and I are at the same period of life; for we are both losing our teeth. Yet even now I can scarcely follow his pace as he runs, and within a very short time I shall not be able to follow him at all; so you see what profit we get from daily exercise. Very soon does a wide interval open between two persons who travel different ways. My slave is climbing up at the very moment when I am coming down, and you surely know how much quicker the latter is. Nay, I was wrong; for now my life is not coming down; it is falling outright. **5.** Do you ask, for all that, how our race resulted to-day? We raced to a tie, – something which rarely happens in a running contest. After tiring myself out in this way (for I cannot call it exercise), I took a cold bath; this, at my house, means just short of hot. I, the former cold-water enthusiast, who used to celebrate the new year by taking a plunge into the canal, who, just as naturally as I would set out to do some reading or writing, or to compose a speech, used to inaugurate the first of the year with a plunge into the Virgo aqueduct, have changed my allegiance, first to the Tiber, and then to my favourite tank, which is warmed only by the sun, at times when I am most robust and when there is not a flaw in my bodily processes. I have very little energy left for bathing. **6.** After the bath, some stale bread and breakfast without a table; no need to wash the hands after such a meal. Then comes a very short nap. You know my habit; I avail myself of a scanty bit of sleep, – unharnessing, as it were. For I am satisfied if I can just stop staying awake. Sometimes I know that I have slept; at other times, I have a mere suspicion.

7. Lo, now the din of the Races sounds about me! My ears are smitten with sudden and general cheering. But this does not upset my thoughts or even break their continuity. I can endure an uproar with complete resignation. The medley of voices blended in one note sounds to me like the dashing of waves, or like the wind that lashes the tree-tops, or like any other sound which conveys no meaning.

8. What is it, then, you ask, to which I have been giving my attention? I will tell you, a thought sticks in my mind, left over from yesterday, – namely, what men of the greatest sagacity have meant when they have offered the most trifling and intricate proofs for problems of the greatest importance, – proofs which may be true, but none the less resemble fallacies. **9.** Zeno, that greatest of men, the revered founder of our brave and holy school of philosophy, wishes to discourage us from drunkenness. Listen, then, to his arguments proving that the good man will not get drunk: "No one entrusts a secret to a drunken man; but one will entrust a secret to a good man; therefore, the good man will not get drunk." Mark how ridiculous Zeno is made when we set up a similar syllogism in contrast with his. There are many, but one will be enough: "No one entrusts a secret to a man when he is asleep; but one entrusts a secret to a good man; therefore, the good man does not go to sleep." **10.** Posidonius pleads the cause of our master Zeno in the only possible way; but it cannot, I hold, be pleaded even in this way. For Posidonius maintains that the word "drunken" is used in two ways, – in the one case of a man who is loaded with wine and has no control over himself; in the other, of a man who is accustomed to get drunk, and is a slave to the habit. Zeno, he says, meant the latter, – the man who is accustomed to get drunk, not the man who is drunk; and no one would entrust to this person any secret, for it might be blabbed out when the man was in his cups. **11.** This is a fallacy. For the first syllogism refers to him who is actually drunk and not to him who is about to get drunk. You will surely admit that there is a great difference between a man who is drunk and a drunkard. He who is actually drunk may be in this state for the first time and may not have the habit, while the drunkard is often free from drunkenness. I therefore interpret the word in its usual meaning, especially since the syllogism is set up by a man who makes a business of the careful use of words, and who weighs his language. Moreover, if this is what Zeno meant, and what he wished it to mean to us, he was trying to avail himself of an equivocal word in order to work in a fallacy; and no man ought to do this when truth is the object of inquiry.

12. But let us admit, indeed, that he meant what Posidonius says; even so, the conclusion is false, that secrets are not entrusted to an habitual drunkard. Think how many soldiers who are not always sober have been entrusted by a general or a captain or a centurion with messages which might not be divulged! With regard to the notorious plot to murder Gaius Caesar, – I mean the Caesar who conquered Pompey and got control of the state, – Tillius Cimber was trusted with it no less than Gaius Cassius. Now Cassius throughout his life drank water; while Tillius Cimber was a sot as well as a brawler. Cimber himself alluded to this fact, saying: "*I carry a master? I cannot carry my liquor!*" **13.** So let each one call to mind those who, to his knowledge, can be ill trusted with wine, but well trusted with the spoken word; and yet one case occurs to my mind, which I shall relate, lest it fall into oblivion. For life should be provided with conspicuous illustrations. Let us not always be harking back to the dim past.

14. Lucius Piso, the director of Public Safety at Rome, was drunk from the very time of his appointment. He used to spend the greater part of the night at banquets, and would sleep until noon. That was the way he spent his morning hours. Nevertheless, he applied himself most diligently to his official duties, which included the guardianship of the city. Even the sainted Augustus trusted him with secret orders when he placed him in command of Thrace. Piso conquered that country. Tiberius, too, trusted him when he took his holiday in Campania, leaving behind him in the city many a critical matter that aroused both suspicion and hatred. **15.** I fancy that it was because Piso's drunkenness turned out well for the Emperor that he appointed to the office of city prefect Cossus, a man of authority and balance, but so soaked and steeped in drink that once, at a meeting of the Senate, whither he had come after banqueting, he was overcome by a slumber from which he could not be roused, and had to be carried home. It was to this man that Tiberius sent many orders, written in his own hand, – orders which he believed he ought not to trust even to the officials of his household. Cossus never let a single secret slip out, whether personal or public.

16. So let us abolish all such harangues as this: "No man in the bonds of drunkenness has power over his soul. As the very vats are burst by new wine, and as the dregs at the bottom are raised to the surface by the strength of the fermentation; so, when the wine effervesces, whatever lies hidden below is brought up and made visible. As a man overcome by liquor cannot keep down his food when he has over-indulged in wine, so he cannot keep back a secret either. He pours forth impartially both his own secrets and those of other persons." **17.** This, of course, is what commonly happens, but so does this, – that we take counsel on serious subjects with those whom we know to be in the habit of drinking freely. Therefore this proposition, which is laid down in the guise of a defence of Zeno's syllogism, is false, – that secrets are not entrusted to the habitual drunkard.

How much better it is to arraign drunkenness frankly and to expose its vices! For even the middling good man avoids them, not to mention the perfect sage, who is satisfied with slaking his thirst; the sage, even if now and then he is led on by good cheer which, for a friend's sake, is carried somewhat too far, yet always stops short of drunkenness. **18.** We shall investigate later the question whether the mind of the sage is upset by too much wine and commits follies like those of the toper; but meanwhile, if you wish to prove that a good man ought not to get drunk, why work it out by logic? Show how base it is to pour down more liquor than one can carry, and not to know the capacity of one's own stomach; show how often the drunkard does things which make him blush when he is sober; state that drunkenness is nothing but a condition of insanity purposely assumed. Prolong the drunkard's condition to several days; will you have any doubt about his madness? Even as it is, the madness is no less; it merely lasts a shorter time. **19.** Think of Alexander of Macedon, who stabbed Clitus, his dearest and most loyal friend, at a banquet; after Alexander understood what he had done, he wished to die, and assuredly he ought to have died.

Drunkenness kindles and discloses every kind of vice, and removes the sense of shame that veils our evil undertakings. For more men abstain from forbidden actions because they are ashamed of sinning than because their inclinations are good. **20.** When the strength of wine has become too great and has gained control over the mind, every lurking evil comes forth from its hiding-place. Drunkenness does not create vice, it merely brings it into view; at such times the lustful man does not wait even for the privacy of a bedroom, but without postponement gives free play to the demands of his passions; at such times the unchaste man proclaims and publishes his malady; at such times your cross-grained fellow does not restrain his tongue or his hand. The haughty man increases his arrogance, the ruthless man his cruelty, the slanderer his spitefulness. Every vice is given free play and comes to the front. **21.** Besides, we forget who we are, we utter words that are halting and poorly enunciated, the glance is unsteady, the step falters, the head is dizzy, the very ceiling moves about as if a cyclone were whirling the whole house, and the stomach suffers torture when the wine generates gas and causes our very bowels to swell. However, at the time, these troubles can be endured, so long as the man retains his natural strength; but what can he do when sleep impairs his powers, and when that which was drunkenness becomes indigestion?

22. Think of the calamities caused by drunkenness in a nation! This evil has betrayed to their enemies the most spirited and warlike races; this evil has made breaches in walls defended by the stubborn warfare of many years; this evil has forced under alien sway peoples who were utterly unyielding and defiant of the yoke; this evil has conquered by the wine-cup those who in the field were invincible. **23.** Alexander, whom I have just mentioned, passed through his many marches, his many battles, his many winter campaigns (through which he worked his way by overcoming disadvantages of time or place), the many rivers which flowed from unknown sources, and the many seas, all in safety; it was intemperance in drinking that laid him low, and the famous death-dealing bowl of Hercules.

24. What glory is there in carrying much liquor? When you have won the prize, and the other banqueters, sprawling asleep or vomiting, have declined your challenge to still other toasts; when you are the last survivor of the revels; when you have vanquished every one by your magnificent show of prowess and there is no man who has proved himself of so great capacity as you, you are vanquished by the cask. **25.** Mark Antony was a great man, a man of distinguished ability; but what ruined him and drove him into foreign habits and un-Roman vices, if it was not drunkenness and – no less potent than wine – love of Cleopatra? This it was that made him an enemy of the state; this it was that rendered him no match for his enemies; this it was that made him cruel, when as he sat at table the heads of the leaders of the state were brought in; when amid the most elaborate feasts and royal luxury he would identify the faces and hands of men whom he had proscribed; when, though heavy with wine, he yet thirsted for blood. It was intolerable that he was getting drunk while he did such things; how much more intolerable that he did these things while actually drunk! **26.** Cruelty usually follows wine-bibbing; for a man's soundness of mind is corrupted and made savage. Just as a lingering illness makes men querulous and irritable and drives them wild at the least crossing of their desires, so continued bouts of drunkenness bestialize the soul. For when people are often beside themselves, the habit of madness lasts on, and the vices which liquor generated retain their power even when the liquor is gone.

27. Therefore you should state why the wise man ought not to get drunk. Explain by facts, and not by mere words, the hideousness of the thing, and its haunting evils. Do that which is easiest of all – namely, demonstrate that what men call pleasures are punishments as soon as they have exceeded due bounds. For if you try to prove that the wise man can souse himself with much wine and yet keep his course straight, even though he be in his cups, you may go on to infer by syllogisms that he will not die if he swallows poison, that he will not sleep if he takes a sleeping-potion, that he will not vomit and reject the matter which clogs his stomach when you give him hellebore. But, when a man's feet totter and his tongue is unsteady, what reason have you for believing that he is half sober and half drunk? Farewell.

LXXXIV. ON GATHERING IDEAS

1. The journeys to which you refer – journeys that shake the laziness out of my system – I hold to be profitable both for my health and for my studies. You see why they benefit my health: since my passion for literature makes me lazy and careless about my body, I can take exercise by deputy; as for my studies, I shall show you why my journeys help them, for I have not stopped my reading in the slightest degree. And reading, I hold, is indispensable – primarily, to keep me from being satisfied with myself alone, and besides, after I have learned what others have found out by their studies, to enable me to pass judgment on their discoveries and reflect upon discoveries that remain to be made. Reading nourishes the mind and refreshes it when it is wearied with study; nevertheless, this refreshment is not obtained without study. **2.** We ought not to confine ourselves either to writing or to reading; the one, continuous writing, will cast a gloom over our strength, and exhaust it; the other will make our strength flabby and watery. It is better to have recourse to them alternately, and to blend one with the other, so that the fruits of one's reading may be reduced to concrete form by the pen.

3. We should follow, men say, the example of the bees, who flit about and cull the flowers that are suitable for producing honey, and then arrange and assort in their cells all that they have brought in; these bees, as our Vergil says,

> pack close the flowing honey,
> And swell their cells with nectar sweet.

4. It is not certain whether the juice which they obtain from the flowers forms at once into honey, or whether they change that which they have gathered into this delicious object by blending something therewith and by a certain property of their breath. For some authorities believe that bees do not possess the art of making honey, but only of gathering it; and they say that in India honey has been found on the leaves of certain reeds, produced by a dew peculiar to that climate, or by the juice of the reed itself, which has an unusual sweetness, and richness. And in our own grasses too, they say, the same quality exists, although less clear and less evident; and a creature born to fulfil such a function could hunt it out and collect it. Certain others maintain that the materials which the bees have culled from the most delicate of blooming and flowering plants is transformed into this peculiar substance by a process of preserving and careful storing away, aided by what might be called fermentation, – whereby separate elements are united into one substance.

5. But I must not be led astray into another subject than that which we are discussing. We also, I say, ought to copy these bees, and sift whatever we have gathered from a varied course of reading, for such things are better preserved if they are kept separate; then, by applying the supervising care with which our nature has endowed us, – in other words, our natural gifts, – we should so blend those several flavours into one delicious compound that, even though it betrays its origin, yet it nevertheless is clearly a different thing from that whence it came. This is what we see nature doing in our own bodies without any labour on our part; **6.** the food we have eaten, as long as it retains its original quality and floats, in our stomachs as an undiluted mass, is a burden; but it passes into tissue and blood only when it has been changed from its original form. So it is with the food which nourishes our higher nature, – we should see to it that whatever we have absorbed should not be allowed to remain unchanged, or it will be no part of us. **7.** We must digest it; otherwise it will merely enter the memory and not the reasoning power. Let us loyally welcome such foods and make them our own, so that something that is one may be formed out of many elements, just as one number is formed of several elements whenever, by our reckoning, lesser sums, each different from the others, are brought together. This is what our mind should do: it should hide away all the materials by which it has been aided, and bring to light only what it has made of them. **8.** Even if there shall appear in you a likeness to him who, by reason of your admiration, has left a deep impress upon you, I would have you resemble him as a child resembles his father, and not as a picture resembles its original; for a picture is a lifeless thing.

"What," you say, "will it not be seen whose style you are imitating, whose method of reasoning, whose pungent sayings?" I think that sometimes it is impossible for it to be seen who is being imitated, if the copy is a true one; for a true copy stamps its own form upon all the features which it has drawn from what we may call the original, in such a way that they are combined into a unity. **9.** Do you not see how many voices there are in a chorus? Yet out of the many only one voice results. In that chorus one voice takes the tenor another the bass, another the baritone. There are women, too, as well as men, and the flute is mingled with them. In that chorus the voices of the individual singers are hidden; what we hear is the voices of all together. **10.** To be sure, I am referring to the chorus which the old-time philosophers knew; in our present-day exhibitions we have a larger number of singers than there used to be spectators in the theatres of old. All the aisles are filled with rows of singers; brass instruments surround the auditorium; the stage resounds with flutes and instruments of every description; and yet from the discordant sounds a harmony is produced.

I would have my mind of such a quality as this; it should be equipped with many arts, many precepts, and patterns of conduct taken from many epochs of history; but all should blend harmoniously into one. **11.** "How," you ask, "can this be accomplished?" By constant effort, and by doing nothing without the approval of reason. And if you are willing to hear her voice, she will say to you: "Abandon those pursuits which heretofore have caused you to run hither and thither. Abandon riches, which are either a danger or a burden to the possessor. Abandon the pleasures of the body and of the mind; they only soften and weaken you. Abandon your quest for office; it is a swollen, idle, and empty thing, a thing that has no goal, as anxious to see no one outstrip it as to see no one at its heels. It is afflicted with envy, and in truth with a twofold envy; and you see how wretched a man's plight is if he who is the object of envy feels envy also."

12. Do you behold yonder homes of the great, yonder thresholds uproarious with the brawling of those who would pay their respects? They have many an insult for you as you enter the door, and still more after you have entered. Pass by the steps that mount to rich men's houses, and the porches rendered hazardous by the huge throng; for there you will be standing, not merely on the edge of a precipice but also on slippery ground. Instead of this, direct your course hither to wisdom, and seek her ways, which are ways of surpassing peace and plenty. **13.** Whatever seems conspicuous in the affairs of men – however petty it may really be and prominent only by contrast with the lowest objects – is nevertheless approached by a difficult and toilsome pathway. It is a rough road that leads to the heights of greatness; but if you desire to scale this peak, which lies far above the range of Fortune, you will indeed look down from above upon all that men regard as most lofty, but none the less you can proceed to the top over level ground. Farewell.

LXXXV. ON SOME VAIN SYLLOGISMS

1. I had been inclined to spare you, and had omitted any knotty problems that still remained undiscussed; I was satisfied to give you a sort of taste of the views held by the men of our school, who desire to prove that virtue is of itself sufficiently capable of rounding out the happy life. But now you bid me include the entire bulk either of our own syllogisms or of those which have been devised by other schools for the purpose of belittling us. If I shall be willing to do this, the result will be a book, instead of a letter. And I declare again and again that I take no pleasure in such proofs. I am ashamed to enter the arena and undertake battle on behalf of gods and men armed only with an awl.

2. "He that possesses prudence is also self-restrained; he that possesses self-restraint is also unwavering; he that is unwavering is unperturbed; he that is unperturbed is free from sadness; he that is free from sadness is happy. Therefore, the prudent man is happy, and prudence is sufficient to constitute the happy life."

3. Certain of the Peripatetics reply to this syllogism by interpreting "unperturbed," "unwavering," and "free from sadness" in such a way as to make "unperturbed" mean one who is rarely perturbed and only to a moderate degree, and not one who is never perturbed. Likewise, they say that a person is called "free from sadness" who is not subject to sadness, one who falls into this objectionable state not often nor in too great a degree. It is not, they say, the way of human nature that a man's spirit should be exempt from sadness, or that the wise man is not overcome by grief but is merely touched by it, and other arguments of this sort, all in accordance with the teachings of their school. **4.** They do not abolish the passions in this way; they only moderate them. But how petty is the superiority which we attribute to the wise man, if he is merely braver than the most craven, happier than the most dejected, more self-controlled than the most unbridled, and greater than the lowliest! Would Ladas boast his swiftness in running by comparing himself with the halt and the weak?

> For she could skim the topmost blades of corn
> And touch them not, nor bruise the tender ears;
> Or travel over seas, well-poised above
> The swollen floods, nor dip her flying feet
> In ocean's waters.

This is speed estimated by its own standard, not the kind which wins praise by comparison with that which is slowest. Would you call a man well who has a light case of fever? No, for good health does not mean moderate illness. 5. They say, "The wise man is called unperturbed in the sense in which pomegranates are called mellow – not that there is no hardness at all in their seeds, but that the hardness is less than it was before." That view is wrong; for I am not referring to the gradual weeding out of evils in a good man, but to the complete absence of evils; there should be in him no evils at all, not even any small ones. For if there are any, they will grow, and as they grow will hamper him. Just as a large and complete cataract wholly blinds the eyes, so a medium-sized cataract dulls their vision.

6. If by your definition the wise man has any passions whatever, his reason will be no match for them and will be carried swiftly along, as it were, on a rushing stream, – particularly if you assign to him, not one passion with which he must wrestle, but all the passions. And a throng of such, even though they be moderate, can affect him more than the violence of one powerful passion. 7. He has a craving for money, although in a moderate degree. He has ambition, but it is not yet fully aroused. He has a hot temper, but it can be appeased. He has inconstancy, but not the kind that is very capricious or easily set in motion. He has lust, but not the violent kind. We could deal better with a person who possessed one full-fledged vice, than with one who possessed all the vices, but none of them in extreme form. 8. Again, it makes no difference how great the passion is; no matter what its size may be, it knows no obedience, and does not welcome advice. Just as no animal, whether wild or tamed and gentle, obeys reason, since nature made it deaf to advice; so the passions do not follow or listen, however slight they are. Tigers and lions never put off their wildness; they sometimes moderate it, and then, when you are least prepared, their softened fierceness is roused to madness. Vices are never genuinely tamed. 9. Again, if reason prevails, the passions will not even get a start; but if they get under way against the will of reason, they will maintain themselves against the will of reason. For it is easier to stop them in the beginning than to control them when they gather force. This half-way ground is accordingly misleading and useless; it is to be regarded just as the declaration that we ought to be "moderately" insane, or "moderately" ill. 10. Virtue alone possesses moderation; the evils that afflict the mind do not admit of moderation. You can more easily remove than control them. Can one doubt that the vices of the human mind, when they have become chronic and callous ("diseases" we call them), are beyond control, as, for example, greed, cruelty, and wantonness? Therefore the passions also are beyond control; for it is from the passions that we pass over to the vices. 11. Again, if you grant any privileges to sadness, fear, desire, and all the other wrong impulses, they will cease to lie within our jurisdiction. And why? Simply because the means of arousing them lie outside our own power. They will accordingly increase in proportion as the causes by which they are stirred up are greater or less. Fear will grow to greater proportions, if that which causes the terror is seen to be of greater magnitude or in closer proximity; and desire will grow keener in proportion as the hope of a greater gain has summoned it to action. 12. If the existence of the passions is not in our own control, neither is the extent of

their power; for if you once permit them to get a start, they will increase along with their causes, and they will be of whatever extent they shall grow to be. Moreover, no matter how small these vices are, they grow greater. That which is harmful never keeps within bounds. No matter how trifling diseases are at the beginning, they creep on apace; and sometimes the slightest augmentation of disease lays low the enfeebled body!

13. But what folly it is, when the beginnings of certain things are situated outside our control, to believe that their endings are within our control! How have I the power to bring something to a close, when I have not had the power to check it at the beginning? For it is easier to keep a thing out than to keep it under after you have let it in. **14.** Some men have made a distinction as follows, saying: "If a man has self-control and wisdom, he is indeed at peace as regards the attitude and habit of his mind, but not as regards the outcome. For, as far as his habit of mind is concerned, he is not perturbed, or saddened, or afraid; but there are many extraneous causes which strike him and bring perturbation upon him." **15.** What they mean to say is this: "So-and-so is indeed not a man of an angry disposition, but still he sometimes gives way to anger," and "He is not, indeed, inclined to fear, but still he sometimes experiences fear"; in other words, he is free from the fault, but is not free from the passion of fear. If, however, fear is once given an entrance, it will by frequent use pass over into a vice; and anger, once admitted into the mind, will alter the earlier habit of a mind that was formerly free from anger. **16.** Besides, if the wise man, instead of despising all causes that come from without, ever fears anything, when the time arrives for him to go bravely to meet the spear, or the flames, on behalf of his country, his laws, and his liberty, he will go forth reluctantly and with flagging spirit. Such inconsistency of mind, however, does not suit the character of a wise man.

17. Then, again, we should see to it that two principles which ought to be tested separately should not be confused. For the conclusion is reached independently that that alone is good which is honourable, and again independently the conclusion that virtue is sufficient for the happy life. If that alone is good which is honourable, everyone agrees that virtue is sufficient for the purpose of living happily; but, on the contrary, if virtue alone makes men happy, it will not be conceded that that alone is good which is honourable. **18.** Xenocrates and Speusippus hold that a man can become happy even by virtue alone, not, however, that that which is honourable is the only good. Epicurus also decides that one who possesses virtue is happy, but that virtue of itself is not sufficient for the happy life, because the pleasure that results from virtue, and not virtue itself, makes one happy. This is a futile distinction. For the same philosopher declares that virtue never exists without pleasure; and therefore, if virtue is always connected with pleasure and always inseparable therefrom, virtue is of itself sufficient. For virtue keeps pleasure in its company, and does not exist without it, even when alone. **19.** But it is absurd to say that a man will be happy by virtue alone, and yet not absolutely happy. I cannot discover how that may be, since the happy life contains in itself a good that is perfect and cannot be excelled, If a man has this good, life is completely happy.

Now if the life of the gods contains nothing greater or better, and the happy life is divine, then there is no further height to which a man can be raised. **20.** Also, if the happy life is in want of nothing, then every happy life is perfect; it is happy and at the same time most happy. Have you any doubt that the happy life is the Supreme Good? Accordingly, if it possesses the Supreme Good, it is supremely happy. Just as the Supreme Good does not admit of increase (for what will be superior to that which is supreme?), exactly so the happy life cannot be increased either; for it is not without the Supreme Good. If then you bring in one man who is "happier" than another, you will also bring in one who is "much happier"; you will then be making countless distinctions in the Supreme Good; although I understand the Supreme Good to be that good which admits of no degree above itself. **21.** If one person is less happy than another, it follows that he eagerly desires the life of that other and happier man in preference to his own. But the happy man prefers no other man's life to his own. Either of these two things is incredible: that there should be anything left for a happy man to wish for in preference to what is, or that he should not prefer the thing which is better than what he already has. For certainly, the more prudent he is, the more he will strive after the best, and he will desire to attain it by every possible means. But how can one be happy who is still able, or rather who is still bound, to crave something else? **22.** I will tell you what is the source of this error: men do not understand that the happy life is a unit; for it is its essence, and not its extent, that establishes such a life on the noblest Plane. Hence there is complete equality between the life that is long and the life that is short, between that which is spread out and that which is confined, between that whose influence is felt in many places and in many directions, and that which is restricted to one interest. Those who reckon life by number, or by measure, or by parts, rob it of its distinctive quality. Now, in the happy life, what is the distinctive quality? It is its fulness. **23.** Satiety, I think, is the limit to our eating or drinking. A eats more and B eats less; what difference does it make? Each is now sated. Or A drinks more and B drinks less; what difference does it make? Each is no longer thirsty, Again, A lives for many years and B for fewer; no matter, if only A's many years have brought as much happiness as B's few years. He whom you maintain to be "less happy" is not happy; the word admits of no diminution.

24. "He who is brave is fearless; he who is fearless is free from sadness; he who is free from sadness is happy." It is our own school which has framed this syllogism; they attempt to refute it by this answer, namely, that we Stoics are assuming as admitted a premiss which is false and distinctly controverted, – that the brave man is fearless. "What!" they say, "will the brave man have no fear of evils that threaten him? That would be the condition of a madman, a lunatic, rather than of a brave man. The brave man will, it is true, feel fear in only a very slight degree; but he is not absolutely free from fear." **25.** Now those who assert this are doubling back to their old argument, in that they regard vices of less degree as equivalent to virtues. For indeed the man who does feel fear, though he feels it rather seldom and to a slight degree, is not free from wickedness, but is merely troubled by it in a milder form. "Not so," is the reply, "for I hold that a man is mad if he does not fear evils which hang over his head." What you say is perfectly true, if the things which threaten are really evils; but if he knows that they are not evils and believes that the only evil is baseness, he will be bound to face dangers without anxiety and to despise things which other men cannot help fearing. Or, if it is the characteristic of a fool and a madman not to fear evils, then the wiser a man is the more he will fear such things! **26.** "It is the doctrine of you Stoics, then," they reply, "that a brave man will expose himself to dangers." By no means; he will merely not fear them, though he will avoid them. It is proper for him to be careful, but not to be fearful. "What then? Is he not to fear death, imprisonment, burning, and all the other missiles of Fortune?" Not at all; for he knows that they are not evils, but only seem to be. He reckons all these things as the bugbears of man's existence. **27.** Paint him a picture of slavery, lashes, chains, want, mutilation by disease or by torture, – or anything else you may care to mention; he will count all such things as terrors caused by the derangement of the mind. These things are only to be feared by those who are fearful. Or do you regard as an evil that to which some day we may be compelled to resort of our own free will?

28. What then, you ask, is an evil? It is the yielding to those things which are called evils; it is the surrendering of one's liberty into their control, when really we ought to suffer all things in order to preserve this liberty. Liberty is lost unless we despise those things which put the yoke upon our necks. If men knew what bravery was, they would have no doubts as to what a brave man's conduct should be. For bravery is not thoughtless rashness, or love of danger, or the courting of fear-inspiring objects; it is the knowledge which enables us to distinguish between that which is evil and that which is not. Bravery takes the greatest care of itself, and likewise endures with the greatest patience all things which have a false appearance of being evil. **29.** "What then?" is the query; "if the sword is brandished over your brave man's neck, if he is pierced in this place and in that continually, if he sees his entrails in his lap, if he is tortured again after being kept waiting in order that he may thus feel the torture more keenly, and if the blood flows afresh out of bowels where it has but lately ceased to flow, has he no fear? Shall you say that he has felt no pain either?" Yes, he has felt pain; for no human virtue can rid itself of feelings. But he has no fear; unconquered he looks down from a lofty height upon his sufferings. Do you ask me what spirit animates him in these circumstances? It is the spirit of one who is comforting a sick friend.

30. "That which is evil does harm; that which does harm makes a man worse. But pain and poverty do not make a man worse; therefore they are not evils." "Your proposition," says the objector, "is wrong; for what harms one does not necessarily make one worse. The storm and the squall work harm to the pilot, but they do not make a worse pilot of him for all that." **31.** Certain of the Stoic school reply to this argument as follows: "The pilot becomes a worse pilot because of storms or squalls, inasmuch as he cannot carry out his purpose and hold to his course; as far as his art is concerned, he becomes no worse a pilot, but in his work he does become worse." To this the Peripatetics retort: "Therefore, poverty will make even the wise man worse, and so will pain, and so will anything else of that sort. For although those things will not rob him of his virtue, yet they will hinder the work of virtue." **32.** This would be a correct statement, were it not for the fact that the pilot and the wise man are two different kinds of person. The wise man's purpose in conducting his life is not to accomplish at all hazards what he tries, but to do all things rightly; the pilot's purpose, however, is to bring his ship into port at all hazards. The arts are handmaids; they must accomplish what they promise to do. But wisdom is mistress and ruler. The arts render a slave's service to life; wisdom issues the commands.

33. For myself, I maintain that a different answer should be given: that the pilot's art is never made worse by the storm, nor the application of his art either. The pilot has promised you, not a prosperous voyage, but a serviceable performance of his task – that is, an expert knowledge of steering a ship. And the more he is hampered by the stress of fortune, so much the more does his knowledge become apparent. He who has been able to say, "Neptune, you shall never sink this ship except on an even keel," has fulfilled the requirements of his art; the storm does not interfere with the pilot's work, but only with his success. **34.** "What then," you say, "is not a pilot harmed by any circumstance which does not permit him to make port, frustrates all his efforts, and either carries him out to sea, or holds the ship in irons, or strips her masts?" No, it does not harm him as a pilot, but only as a voyager; otherwise, he is no pilot. It is indeed so far from hindering the pilot's art that it even exhibits the art; for anyone, in the words of the proverb, is a pilot on a calm sea. These mishaps obstruct the voyage but not the steersman *qua* steersman. **35.** A pilot has a double rôle: one he shares with all his fellow-passengers, for he also is a passenger; the other is peculiar to him, for he is the pilot. The storm harms him as a passenger, but not as a pilot. **36.** Again, the pilot's art is another's good – it concerns his passengers just as a physician's art concerns his patients. But the wise man's good is a common good – it belongs both to those in whose company he lives, and to himself also. Hence our pilot may perhaps be harmed, since his services, which have been promised to others, are hindered by the storm; **37.** but the wise man is not harmed by poverty, or by pain, or by any other of life's storms. For all his functions are not checked, but only those which pertain to others; he himself is always in action, and is greatest in performance at the very time when fortune has blocked his way. For then he is actually engaged in the business of wisdom; and this wisdom I have declared already to be, both the good of others, and also his own. **38.** Besides, he is not prevented from helping others, even at the time when constraining circumstances press him down. Because of his poverty he is prevented from showing how the State should be handled; but he teaches, none the less, how poverty should be handled. His work goes on throughout his whole life.

Thus no fortune, no external circumstance, can shut off the wise man from action. For the very thing which engages his attention prevents him from attending to other things. He is ready for either outcome: if it brings goods, he controls them; if evils, he conquers them. **39.** So thoroughly, I mean, has he schooled himself that he makes manifest his virtue in prosperity as well as in adversity, and keeps his eyes on virtue itself, not on the objects with which virtue deals. Hence neither poverty, nor pain, nor anything else that deflects the inexperienced and drives them headlong, restrains him from his course. **40.** Do you suppose that he is weighed down by evils? He makes use of them. It was not of ivory only that Phidias knew how to make statues; he also made statues of bronze. If you had given him marble, or a still meaner material, he would have made of it the best statue that the material would permit. So the wise man will develop virtue, if he may, in the midst of wealth, or, if not, in poverty; if possible, in his own country – if not, in exile; if possible, as a commander – if not, as a common soldier; if possible, in sound health – if not, enfeebled. Whatever fortune he finds, he will accomplish therefrom something noteworthy.

41. Animal-tamers are unerring; they take the most savage animals, which may well terrify those who encounter them, and subdue them to the will of man; not content with having driven out their ferocity, they even tame them so that they dwell in the same abode. The trainer puts his hand into the lion's mouth; the tiger is kissed by his keeper. The tiny Aethiopian orders the elephant to sink down on its knees, or to walk the rope. Similarly, the wise man is a skilled hand at taming evils. Pain, want, disgrace, imprisonment, exile, – these are universally to be feared; but when they encounter the wise man, they are tamed. Farewell.

LXXXVI. ON SCIPIO'S VILLA

1. I am resting at the country-house which once belonged to Scipio Africanus himself; and I write to you after doing reverence to his spirit and to an altar which I am inclined to think is the tomb of that great warrior. That his soul has indeed returned to the skies, whence it came, I am convinced, not because he commanded mighty armies – for Cambyses also had mighty armies, and Cambyses was a madman who made successful use of his madness – but because he showed moderation and a sense of duty to a marvellous extent. I regard this trait in him as more admirable after his withdrawal from his native land than while he was defending her; for there was the alternative: Scipio should remain in Rome, or Rome should remain free. **2.** "It is my wish," said he, "not to infringe in the least upon our laws, or upon our customs; let all Roman citizens have equal rights. O my country, make the most of the good that I have done, but without me. I have been the cause of your freedom, and I shall also be its proof; I go into exile, if it is true that I have grown beyond what is to your advantage!"

3. What can I do but admire this magnanimity, which led him to withdraw into voluntary exile and to relieve the state of its burden? Matters had gone so far that either liberty must work harm to Scipio, or Scipio to liberty. Either of these things was wrong in the sight of heaven. So he gave way to the laws and withdrew to Liternum, thinking to make the state a debtor for his own exile no less than for the exile of Hannibal.

4. I have inspected the house, which is constructed of hewn stone; the wall which encloses a forest; the towers also, buttressed out on both sides for the purpose of defending the house; the well, concealed among buildings and shrubbery, large enough to keep a whole army supplied; and the small bath, buried in darkness according to the old style, for our ancestors did not think that one could have a hot bath except in darkness. It was therefore a great pleasure to me to contrast Scipio's ways with our own. **5.** Think, in this tiny recess the "terror of Carthage," to whom Rome should offer thanks because she was not captured more than once, used to bathe a body wearied with work in the fields! For he was accustomed to keep himself busy and to cultivate the soil with his own hands, as the good old Romans were wont to do. Beneath this dingy roof he stood; and this floor, mean as it is, bore his weight.

6. But who in these days could bear to bathe in such a fashion? We think ourselves poor and mean if our walls are not resplendent with large and costly mirrors; if our marbles from Alexandria are not set off by mosaics of Numidian stone, if their borders are not faced over on all sides with difficult patterns, arranged in many colours like paintings; if our vaulted ceilings are not buried in glass; if our swimming-pools are not lined with Thasian marble, once a rare and wonderful sight in any temple pools into which we let down our bodies after they have been drained weak by abundant perspiration; and finally, if the water has not poured from silver spigots. **7.** I have so far been speaking of the ordinary bathing-establishments; what shall I say when I come to those of the freedmen? What a vast number of statues, of columns that support nothing, but are built for decoration, merely in order to spend money! And what masses of water that fall crashing from level to level! We have become so luxurious that we will have nothing but precious stones to walk upon.

8. In this bath of Scipio's there are tiny chinks – you cannot call them windows – cut out of the stone wall in such a way as to admit light without weakening the fortifications; nowadays, however, people regard baths as fit only for moths if they have not been so arranged that they receive the sun all day long through the widest of windows, if men cannot bathe and get a coat of tan at the same time, and if they cannot look out from their bath-tubs over stretches of land and sea. So it goes; the establishments which had drawn crowds and had won admiration when they were first opened are avoided and put back in the category of venerable antiques as soon as luxury has worked out some new device, to her own ultimate undoing. **9.** In the early days, however, there were few baths, and they were not fitted out with any display. For why should men elaborately fit out that which, costs a penny only, and was invented for use, not merely for delight? The bathers of those day did not have water poured over them, nor did it always run fresh as if from a hot spring; and they did not believe that it mattered at all how perfectly pure was the water into which they were to leave their dirt. 10. Ye gods, what a pleasure it is to enter that dark bath, covered with a common sort of roof, knowing that therein your hero Cato, as aedile, or Fabius Maximus, or one of the Cornelia, has warmed the water with his own hands! For this also used to be the duty of the noblest aediles – to enter these places to which the populace resorted, and to demand that they be cleaned and warmed to a heat required by considerations of use and health, not the heat that men have recently made fashionable, as great as a conflagration – so much so, indeed, that a slave condemned for some criminal offence now ought to be *bathed* alive! It seems to me that nowadays there is no difference between "the bath is on fire," and "the bath is warm."

11. How some persons nowadays condemn Scipio as a boor because he did not let daylight into his perspiring-room through wide windows, or because he did not roast in the strong sunlight and dawdle about until he could stew in the hot water! "Poor fool," they say, "he did not know how to live! He did not bathe in filtered water; it was often turbid, and after heavy rains almost muddy!" But it did not matter much to Scipio if he had to bathe in that way; he went there to wash off sweat, not ointment. 12. And how do you suppose certain persons will answer me? They will say: "I don't envy Scipio; that was truly an exile's life – to put up with baths like those!" Friend, if you were wiser, you would know that Scipio did not bathe every day. It is stated by those who have reported to us the old-time ways of Rome that the Romans washed only their arms and legs daily – because those were the members which gathered dirt in their daily toil – and bathed all over only once a week. Here someone will retort: "Yes; pretty dirty fellows they evidently were! How they must have smelled!" But they smelled of the camp, the farm, and heroism. Now that spick-and-span bathing establishments have been devised, men are really fouler than of yore. 13. What says Horatius Flaccus, when he wishes to describe a scoundrel, one who is notorious for his extreme luxury? He says. "Buccillus smells of perfume." Show me a Buccillus in these days; his smell would be the veritable goat-smell – he would take the place of the Gargonius with whom Horace in the same passage contrasted him. It is nowadays not enough to use ointment, unless you put on a fresh coat two or three times a day, to keep it from evaporating on the body. But why should a man boast of this perfume as if it were his own?

14. If what I am saying shall seem to you too pessimistic, charge it up against Scipio's country-house, where I have learned a lesson from Aegialus, a most careful householder and now the owner of this estate; he taught me that a tree can be transplanted, no matter how far gone in years. We old men must learn this precept; for there is none of us who is not planting an olive-yard for his successor. I have seen them bearing fruit in due season after three or four years of unproductiveness. 15. And you too shall be shaded by the tree which

> Is slow to grow, but bringeth shade to cheer
> Your grandsons in the far-off years,

as our poet Vergil says. Vergil sought, however, not what was nearest to the truth, but what was most appropriate, and aimed, not to teach the farmer, but to please the reader. **16.** For example, omitting all other errors of his, I will quote the passage in which it was incumbent upon me to-day to detect a fault:

> In spring sow beans then, too, O clover plant,
> Thou'rt welcomed by the crumbling furrows; and
> The millet calls for yearly care.

You may judge by the following incident whether those plants should be set out at the same time, or whether both should be sowed in the spring. It is June at the present writing, and we are well on towards July; and I have seen on this very day farmers harvesting beans and sowing millet.

17. But to return to our olive-yard again. I saw it planted in two ways. If the trees were large, Aegialus took their trunks and cut off the branches to the length of one foot each; he then transplanted along with the ball, after cutting off the roots, leaving only the thick part from which the roots hang. He smeared this with manure, and inserted it in the hole, not only heaping up the earth about it, but stamping and pressing it down. **18.** There is nothing, he says, more effective than this packing process; in other words, it keeps out the cold and the wind. Besides, the trunk is not shaken so much, and for this reason the packing makes it possible for the young roots to come out and get a hold in the soil. These are of necessity still soft; they have but a slight hold, and a very little shaking uproots them. This ball, moreover, Aegialus lops clean before he covers it up. For he maintains that new roots spring from all the parts which have been shorn. Moreover, the trunk itself should not stand more than three or four feet out of the ground. For there will thus be at once a thick growth from the bottom, nor will there be a large stump, all dry and withered, as is the case with old olive-yards. **19.** The second way of setting them out was the following: he set out in similar fashion branches that were strong and of soft bark, as those of young saplings are wont to be. These grow a little more slowly, but, since they spring from what is practically a cutting, there is no roughness or ugliness in them.

20. This too I have seen recently – an aged vine transplanted from its own plantation. In this case, the fibres also should be gathered together, if possible, and then you should cover up the vine-stem more generously, so that roots may spring up even from the stock. I have seen such plantings made not only in February, but at the very end of March; the plants take hold of and embrace alien elms. **21.** But all trees, he declares, which are, so to speak, "thick-stemmed," should be assisted with tank-water; if we have this help, we are our own rain-makers.

I do not intend to tell you any more of these precepts, lest, as Aegialus did with me, I may be training you up to be my competitor. Farewell.

LXXXVII. SOME ARGUMENTS IN FAVOUR OF THE SIMPLE LIFE

1. "I was shipwrecked before I got aboard." I shall not add how that happened, lest you may reckon this also as another of the Stoic paradoxes; and yet I shall, whenever you are willing to listen, nay, even though you be unwilling, prove to you that these words are by no means untrue, nor so surprising as one at first sight would think. Meantime, the journey showed me this: how much we possess that is superfluous; and how easily we can make up our minds to do away with things whose loss, whenever it is necessary to part with them, we do not feel.

2. My friend Maximus and I have been spending a most happy period of two days, taking with us very few slaves – one carriage-load – and no paraphernalia except what we wore on our persons. The mattress lies on the ground, and I upon the mattress. There are two rugs – one to spread beneath us and one to cover us. **3.** Nothing could have been subtracted from our luncheon; it took not more than an hour to prepare, and we were nowhere without dried figs, never without writing tablets. If I have bread, I use figs as a relish; if not, I regard figs as a substitute for bread. Hence they bring me a New Year feast every day, and I make the New Year happy and prosperous by good thoughts and greatness of soul; for the soul is never greater than when it has laid aside all extraneous things, and has secured peace for itself by fearing nothing, and riches by craving no riches. **4.** The vehicle in which I have taken my seat is a farmer's cart. Only by walking do the mules show that they are alive. The driver is barefoot, and not because it is summer either. I can scarcely force myself to wish that others shall think this cart mine. My false embarrassment about the truth still holds out, you see; and whenever we meet a more sumptuous party I blush in spite of myself – proof that this conduct which I approve and applaud has not yet gained a firm and steadfast dwelling-place within me. He who blushes at riding in a rattle-trap will boast when he rides in style.

5. So my progress is still insufficient. I have not yet the courage openly to acknowledge my thriftiness. Even yet I am bothered by what other travellers think of me. But instead of this, I should really have uttered an opinion counter to that in which mankind believe, saying, "You are mad, you are misled, your admiration devotes itself to superfluous things! You estimate no man at his real worth. When property is concerned, you reckon up in this way with most scrupulous calculation those to whom you shall lend either money or benefits; for by now you enter benefits also as payments in your ledger. **6.** You say. 'His estates are wide, but his debts are large.' 'He has a fine house, but he has built it on borrowed capital.' 'No man will display a more brilliant retinue on short notice, but he cannot meet his debts.' 'If he pays off his creditors, he will have nothing left.'" So you will feel bound to do in all other cases as well, – to find out by elimination the amount of every man's actual possessions.

7. I suppose you call a man rich just because his gold plate goes with him even on his travels, because he farms land in all the provinces, because he unrolls a large account-book, because he owns estates near the city so great that men would grudge his holding them in the waste lands of Apulia. But after you have mentioned all these facts, he is poor. And why? He is in debt. "To what extent?" you ask. For all that he has. Or perchance you think it matters whether one has borrowed from another man or from Fortune. **8.** What good is there in mules caparisoned in uniform livery? Or in decorated chariots and

> Steeds decked with purple and with tapestry,
> With golden harness hanging from their necks,
> Champing their yellow bits, all clothed in gold?

Neither master nor mule is improved by such trappings.

9. Marcus Cato the Censor, whose existence helped the state as much as did Scipio's, – for while Scipio fought against our enemies, Cato fought against our bad morals, – used to ride a donkey, and a donkey, at that, which carried saddle-bags containing the master's necessaries. O how I should love to see him meet today on the road one of our coxcombs, with his outriders and Numidians, and a great cloud of dust before him! Your dandy would no doubt seem refined and well-attended in comparison with Marcus Cato, – your dandy, who, in the midst of all his luxurious paraphernalia, is chiefly concerned whether to turn his hand to the sword or to the hunting-knife. **10.** O what a glory to the times in which he lived, for a general who had celebrated a triumph, a censor, and what is most noteworthy of all, a Cato, to be content with a single nag, and with less than a whole nag at that! For part of the animal was pre-empted by the baggage that hung down on either flank. Would you not therefore prefer Cato's steed, that single steed, saddle-worn by Cato himself, to the coxcomb's whole retinue of plump ponies, Spanish cobs, and trotters? **11.** I see that there will be no end in dealing with such a theme unless I make an end myself. So I shall now become silent, at least with reference to superfluous things like these; doubtless the man who first called them "hindrances" had a prophetic inkling that they would be the very sort of thing they now are. At present I should like to deliver to you the syllogisms, as yet very few, belonging to our school and bearing upon the question of virtue, which, in our opinion, is sufficient for the happy life.

12. "That which is good makes men good. For example, that which is good in the art of music makes the musician. But chance events do not make a good man; therefore, chance events are not goods." The Peripatetics reply to this by saying that the premiss is false; that men do not in every case become good by means of that which is good; that in music there is something good, like a flute, a harp, or an organ suited to accompany singing; but that none of these instruments makes the musician. **13.** We shall then reply: "You do not understand in what sense we have used the phrase 'that which is good in music.' For we do not mean that which equips the musician, but that which makes the musician; you, however, are referring to the instruments of the art, and not to the art itself. If, however, anything in the art of music is good, that will in every case make the musician." **14.** And I should like to put this idea still more clearly. We define the good in the art of music in two ways: first, that by which the performance of the musician is assisted, and second, that by which his art is assisted. Now the musical instruments have to do with his performance, – such as flutes and organs and harps; but they do not have to do with the musician's art itself. For he is an artist even without them; he may perhaps be lacking in the ability to practise his art. But the good in man is not in the same way twofold; for the good of man and the good of life are the same.

15. "That which can fall to the lot of any man, no matter how base or despised he may be, is not a good. But wealth falls to the lot of the pander and the trainer of gladiators; therefore wealth is not a good." "Another wrong premiss," they say, "for we notice that goods fall to the lot of the very lowest sort of men, not only in the scholar's art, but also in the art of healing or in the art of navigating." **16.** These arts, however, make no profession of greatness of soul; they do not rise to any heights nor do they frown upon what fortune may bring. It is virtue that uplifts man and places him superior to what mortals hold dear; virtue neither craves overmuch nor fears to excess that which is called good or that which is called bad. Chelidon, one of Cleopatra's eunuchs, possessed great wealth; and recently Natalis – a man whose tongue was as shameless as it was dirty, a man whose mouth used to perform the vilest offices – was the heir of many, and also made many his heirs. What then? Was it his money that made him unclean, or did he himself besmirch his money? Money tumbles into the hands of certain men as a shilling tumbles down a sewer. **17.** Virtue stands above all such things. It is appraised in coin of its own minting; and it deems none of these random windfalls to be good. But medicine and navigation do not forbid themselves and their followers to marvel at such things. One who is not a good man can nevertheless be a physician, or a pilot or a scholar, – yes just as well as he can be a cook! He to whose lot it falls to possess something which is not of a random sort, cannot be called a random sort of man: a person is of the same sort as that which he possesses. **18.** A strong-box is worth just what it holds; or rather, it is a mere accessory of that which it holds. Who ever sets any price upon a full purse except the price established by the count of the money deposited therein? This also applies to the owners of great estates: they are only accessories and incidentals to their possessions.

Why, then, is the wise man great? Because he has a great soul. Accordingly, it is true that that which falls to the lot even of the most despicable person is not a good. **19.** Thus, I should never regard inactivity as a good; for even the tree-frog and the flea possess this quality. Nor should I regard rest and freedom from trouble as a good; for what is more at leisure than a worm? Do you ask what it is that produces the wise man? That which produces a god. You must grant that the wise man has in an element of godliness, heavenliness, grandeur. The good does not come to every one, nor does it allow any random person to possess it. **20.** Behold:

> What fruits each country bears, or will not bear;
> Here corn, and there the vine, grow richlier.
> And elsewhere still the tender tree and grass
> Unbidden clothe themselves in green. Seest thou
> How Tmolus ships its saffron perfumes forth,
> And ivory comes from Ind; soft Sheba sends
> Its incense, and the unclad Chalybes
> Their iron.

21. These products are apportioned to separate countries in order that human beings may be constrained to traffic among themselves, each seeking something from his neighbour in his turn. So the Supreme Good has also its own abode. It does not grow where ivory grows, or iron. Do you ask where the Supreme Good dwells? In the soul. And unless the soul be pure and holy, there is no room in it for God.

22. "Good does not result from evil. But riches result from greed; therefore, riches are not a good." "It is not true," they say, "that good does not result from evil. For money comes from sacrilege and theft. Accordingly, although sacrilege and theft are evil, yet they are evil only because they work more evil than good. For they bring gain; but the gain is accompanied by fear, anxiety, and torture of mind and body." **23.** Whoever says this must perforce admit that sacrilege, though it be an evil because it works much evil, is yet partly good because it accomplishes a certain amount of good. What can be more monstrous than this? We have, to be sure, actually convinced the world that sacrilege, theft, and adultery are to be regarded as among the goods. How many men there are who do not blush at theft, how many who boast of having committed adultery! For petty sacrilege is punished, but sacrilege on a grand scale is honoured by a triumphal procession. **24.** Besides, sacrilege, if it is wholly good in some respect, will also be honourable and will be called right conduct; for it is conduct which concerns ourselves. But no human being, on serious consideration, admits this idea.

Therefore, goods cannot spring from evil. For if, as you object, sacrilege is an evil for the single reason that it brings on much evil, if you but absolve sacrilege of its punishment and pledge it immunity, sacrilege will be wholly good. And yet the worst punishment for crime lies in the crime itself. **25.** You are mistaken, I maintain, if you propose to reserve your punishments for the hangman or the prison; the crime is punished immediately after it is committed; nay, rather, at the moment when it is committed. Hence, good does not spring from evil, any more than figs grow from olive-trees. Things which grow correspond to their seed; and goods cannot depart from their class. As that which is honourable does not grow from that which is base, so neither does good grow from evil. For the honourable and the good are identical.

26. Certain of our school oppose this statement as follows: "Let us suppose that money taken from any source whatsoever is a good; even though it is taken by an act of sacrilege, the money does not on that account derive its origin from sacrilege.

You may get my meaning through the following illustration: In the same jar there is a piece of gold and there is a serpent. If you take the gold from the jar, it is not just because the serpent is there too, I say, that the jar yields me the gold – because it contains the serpent as well, – but it yields the gold in spite of containing the serpent also. Similarly, gain results from sacrilege, not just because sacrilege is a base and accursed act, but because it contains gain also. As the serpent in the jar is an evil, and not the gold which lies there, beside the serpent; so in an act of sacrilege it is the crime, not the profit, that is evil." **27.** But I differ from these men; for the conditions in each case are not at all the same. In the one instance I can take the gold without the serpent, in the other I cannot make the profit without committing the sacrilege. The gain in the latter case does not lie side by side with the crime; it is blended with the crime.

28. "That which, while we are desiring to attain it, involves us in many evils, is not a good. But while we are desiring to attain riches, we become involved in many evils; therefore, riches are not a good." "Your first premiss," they say, "contains two meanings; one is: we become involved in many evils while we are desiring to attain riches. But we also become involved in many evils while we are desiring to attain virtue. One man, while travelling in order to prosecute his studies, suffers shipwreck, and another is taken captive. **29.** The second meaning is as follows: that through which we become involved in evils is not a good. And it will not logically follow from our proposition that we become involved in evils through riches or through pleasure; otherwise, if it is through riches that we become involved in many evils, riches are not only not a good, but they are positively an evil. You, however, maintain merely that they are not a good. Moreover," the objector says, "you grant that riches are of some use. You reckon them among the advantages; and yet on this basis they cannot even be an advantage, for it is through the pursuit of riches that we suffer much disadvantage." **30.** Certain men answer this objection as follows: "You are mistaken if you ascribe disadvantages to riches. Riches injure no one; it is a man's own folly, or his neighbour's wickedness, that harms him in each case, just as a sword by itself does not slay; it is merely the weapon used by the slayer. Riches themselves do not harm you, just because it is on account of riches that you suffer harm."

31. I think that the reasoning of Posidonius is better: he holds that riches are a cause of evil, not because, of themselves, they do any evil, but because they goad men on so that they are ready to do evil. For the efficient cause, which necessarily produces harm at once, is one thing, and the antecedent cause is another. It is this antecedent cause which inheres in riches; they puff up the spirit and beget pride, they bring on unpopularity and unsettle the mind to such an extent that the mere reputation of having wealth, though it is bound to harm us, nevertheless affords delight. **32.** All goods, however, ought properly to be free from blame; they are pure, they do not corrupt the spirit, and they do not tempt us. They do, indeed, uplift and broaden the spirit, but without puffing it up. Those things which are goods produce confidence, but riches produce shamelessness. The things which are goods give us greatness of soul, but riches give us arrogance. And arrogance is nothing else than a false show of greatness.

33. "According to that argument," the objector says, "riches are not only not a good, but are a positive evil." Now they would be an evil if they did harm of themselves, and if, as I remarked, it were the efficient cause which inheres in them; in fact, however, it is the antecedent cause which inheres in riches, and indeed it is that cause which, so far from merely arousing the spirit, actually drags it along by force. Yes, riches shower upon us a semblance of the good, which is like the reality and wins credence in the eyes of many men. 34. The antecedent cause inheres in virtue also; it is this which brings on envy – for many men become unpopular because of their wisdom, and many men because of their justice. But this cause, though it inheres in virtue, is not the result of virtue itself, nor is it a mere semblance of the reality; nay, on the contrary, far more like the reality is that vision which is flashed by virtue upon the spirits of men, summoning them to love it and marvel thereat.

35. Posidonius thinks that the syllogism should be framed as follows: "Things which bestow upon the soul no greatness or confidence or freedom from care are not goods. But riches and health and similar conditions do none of these things; therefore, riches and health are not goods." This syllogism he then goes on to extend still farther in the following way: "Things which bestow upon the soul no greatness or confidence or freedom from care, but on the other hand create in it arrogance, vanity, and insolence, are evils. But things which are the gift of Fortune drive us into these evil ways. Therefore these things are not goods." 36. "But," says the objector, "by such reasoning, things which are the gift of Fortune will not even be advantages." No, advantages and goods stand each in a different situation. An advantage is that which contains more of usefulness than of annoyance. But a good ought to be unmixed and with no element in it of harmfulness. A thing is not good if it contains more benefit than injury, but only if it contains nothing but benefit. 37. Besides, advantages may be predicated of animals, of men who are less than perfect, and of fools. Hence the advantageous may have an element of disadvantage mingled with it, but the word "advantageous" is used of the compound because it is judged by its predominant element. The good, however, can be predicated of the wise man alone; it is bound to be without alloy,

38. Be of good cheer; there is only one knot left for you to untangle, though it is a knot for a Hercules: "Good does not result from evil. But riches result from numerous cases of poverty; therefore, riches are not a good." This syllogism is not recognized by our school, but the Peripatetics both concoct it and give its solution. Posidonius, however, remarks that this fallacy, which has been bandied about among all the schools of dialectic, is refuted by Antipater as follows: 39. "The word 'poverty' is used to denote, not the possession of something, but the non-possession or, as the ancients have put it, deprivation, (for the Greeks use the phrase 'by deprivation,' meaning

'negatively'). 'Poverty' states, not what a man has, but what he has not. Consequently there can be no fullness resulting from a multitude of voids; many positive things, and not many deficiencies, make up riches. You have," says he, "a wrong notion of the meaning of what poverty is. For poverty does not mean the possession of little, but the non-possession of much; it is used, therefore, not of what a man has, but of what he lacks." **40.** I could express my meaning more easily if there were a Latin word which could translate the Greek word which means "not-possessing." Antipater assigns this quality to poverty, but for my part I cannot see what else poverty is than the possession of little. If ever we have plenty of leisure, we shall investigate the question: what is the essence of riches, and what the essence of poverty; but when the time comes, we shall also consider whether it is not better to try to mitigate poverty, and to relieve wealth of its arrogance, than to quibble about the words as if the question of the things were already decided.

41. Let us suppose that we have been summoned to an assembly; an act dealing with the abolition of riches has been brought before the meeting. Shall we be supporting it, or opposing it, if we use these syllogisms? Will these syllogisms help us to bring it about that the Roman people shall demand poverty and praise it – poverty, the foundation and cause of their empire, – and, on the other hand, shall shrink in fear from their present wealth, reflecting that they have found it among the victims of their conquests, that wealth is the source from which office-seeking and bribery and disorder have burst into a city once characterized by the utmost scrupulousness and sobriety, and that because of wealth an exhibition all too lavish is made of the spoils of conquered nations; reflecting, finally, that whatever one people has snatched away from all the rest may still more easily be snatched by all away from one? Nay, it were better to support this law by our conduct and to subdue our desires by direct assault rather than to circumvent them by logic. If we can, let us speak more boldly; if not, let us speak more frankly.

LXXXVIII. ON LIBERAL AND VOCATIONAL STUDIES

1. You have been wishing to know my views with regard to liberal studies. My answer is this: I respect no study, and deem no study good, which results in money-making. Such studies are profit-bringing occupations, useful only in so far as they give the mind a preparation and do not engage it permanently. One should linger upon them only so long as the mind can occupy itself with nothing greater; they are our apprenticeship, not our real work. **2.** Hence you see why "liberal studies" are so called; it is because they are studies worthy of a free-born gentleman. But there is only one really liberal study, – that which gives a man his liberty. It is the study of wisdom, and that is lofty, brave, and great-souled. All other studies are puny and puerile. You surely do not believe that there is good in any of the subjects whose teachers are, as you see, men of the most ignoble and base stamp? We ought not to be learning such things; we should have done with learning them.

Certain persons have made up their minds that the point at issue with regard to the liberal studies is whether they make men good; but they do not even profess or aim at a knowledge of this particular subject. **3.** The scholar busies himself with investigations into language, and if it be his desire to go farther afield, he works on history, or, if he would extend his range to the farthest limits, on poetry. But which of these paves the way to virtue? Pronouncing syllables, investigating words, memorizing plays, or making rules for the scansion of poetry, what is there in all this that rids one of fear, roots out desire, or bridles the passions? **4.** The question is: do such men teach virtue, or not? If they do not teach it, then neither do they transmit it. If they do teach it, they are philosophers. Would you like to know how it happens that they have not taken the chair for the purpose of teaching virtue? See how unlike their subjects are; and yet their subjects would resemble each other if they taught the same thing.

5. It may be, perhaps, that they make you believe that Homer was a philosopher, although they disprove this by the very arguments through which they seek to prove it. For sometimes they make of him a Stoic, who approves nothing but virtue, avoids pleasures, and refuses to relinquish honour even at the price of immortality; sometimes they make him an Epicurean, praising the condition of a state in repose, which passes its days in feasting and song; sometimes a Peripatetic, classifying goodness in three ways; sometimes an Academic, holding that all things are uncertain. It is clear, however, that no one of these doctrines is to be fathered upon Homer, just because they are all there; for they are irreconcilable with one another. We may admit to these men, indeed, that Homer was a philosopher; yet surely he became a wise man before he had any knowledge of poetry. So let us learn the particular things that made Homer wise.

6. It is no more to the point, of course, for me to investigate whether Homer or Hesiod was the older poet, than to know why Hecuba, although younger than Helen, showed her years so lamentably. What, in your opinion, I say, would be the point in trying to determine the respective ages of Achilles and Patroclus? **7.** Do you raise the question, "Through what regions did Ulysses stray?" instead of trying to prevent ourselves from going astray at all times? We have no leisure to hear lectures on the question whether he was sea-tost between Italy and Sicily, or outside our known world (indeed, so long a wandering could not possibly have taken place within its narrow bounds); we ourselves encounter storms of the spirit, which toss us daily, and our depravity drives us into all the ills which troubled Ulysses. For us there is never lacking the beauty to tempt our eyes, or the enemy to assail us; on this side are savage monsters that delight in human blood, on that side the treacherous allurements of the ear, and yonder is shipwreck and all the varied category of misfortunes. Show me rather, by the example of Ulysses, how I am to love my country, my wife, my father, and how, even after suffering shipwreck, I am to sail toward these ends, honourable as they are. **8.** Why try to discover whether Penelope was a pattern of purity, or whether she had the laugh on her contemporaries? Or whether she suspected that the man in her presence was Ulysses, before she knew it was he? Teach me rather what purity is, and how great a good we have in it, and whether it is situated in the body or in the soul.

9. Now I will transfer my attention to the musician. You, sir, are teaching me how the treble and the bass are in accord with one another, and how, though the strings produce different notes, the result is a harmony; rather bring my soul into harmony with itself, and let not my purposes be out of tune. You are showing me what the doleful keys are; show me rather how, in the midst of adversity, I may keep from uttering a doleful note. **10.** The mathematician teaches me how to lay out the dimensions of my estates; but I should rather be taught how to lay out what is enough for a man to own. He teaches me to count, and adapts my fingers to avarice; but I should prefer him to teach me that there is no point in such calculations, and that one is none the happier for tiring out the book-keepers with his possessions – or rather, how useless property is to any man who would find it the greatest misfortune if he should be required to reckon out, by his own wits, the amount of his holdings. **11.** What good is there for me in knowing how to parcel out a piece of land, if I know not how to share it with my brother? What good is there in working out to a nicety the dimensions of an acre, and in detecting the error if a piece has so much as escaped my measuring-rod, if I am embittered when an ill-tempered neighbour merely scrapes off a bit of my land? The mathematician teaches me how I may lose none of my boundaries; I, however, seek to learn how to lose them all with a light heart. **12.** "But," comes the reply, "I am being driven from the farm which my father and grandfather owned!" Well? Who owned the land before your grandfather? Can you explain what people (I will not say what person) held it originally? You did not enter upon it as a master, but merely as a tenant. And whose tenant are you? If your claim is successful, you are tenant of the heir. The lawyers say that public property cannot be acquired privately by possession; what you hold and call your own is public property – indeed, it belongs to mankind at large. **13.** O what marvellous skill! You know how to measure the circle; you find the square of any shape which is set before you; you compute the distances between the stars; there is nothing which does not come within the scope of your calculations. But if you are a real master of your profession, measure me the mind of man! Tell me how great it is, or how puny! You know what a straight line is; but how does it benefit you if you do not know what is straight in this life of ours?

14. I come next to the person who boasts his knowledge of the heavenly bodies, who knows

> Whither the chilling star of Saturn hides,
> And through what orbit Mercury doth stray.

Of what benefit will it be to know this? That I shall be disturbed because Saturn and Mars are in opposition, or when Mercury sets at eventide in plain view of Saturn, rather than learn that those stars, wherever they are, are propitious, and that they are not subject to change? **15.** They are driven along by an unending round of destiny, on a course from which they cannot swerve. They return at stated seasons; they either set in motion, or mark the intervals of the whole world's work. But if they are responsible for whatever happens, how will it help you to know the secrets of the immutable? Or if they merely give indications, what good is there in foreseeing what you cannot escape? Whether you know these things or not, they will take place.

> **16.** Behold the fleeting sun,
> The stars that follow in his train, and thou
> Shalt never find the morrow play thee false,
> Or be misled by nights without a cloud.

It has, however, been sufficiently and fully ordained that I shall be safe from anything that may mislead me. **17.** "What," you say, "does the 'morrow never play me false'? Whatever happens without my knowledge plays me false." I, for my part, do not know what is to be, but I do know what may come to be. I shall have no misgivings in this matter; I await the future in its entirety; and if there is any abatement in its severity, I make the most of it. If the morrow treats me kindly, it is a sort of deception; but it does not deceive me even at that. For just as I know that all things can happen, so I know, too, that they will not happen in every case. I am ready for favourable events in every case, but I am prepared for evil.

18. In this discussion you must bear with me if I do not follow the regular course. For I do not consent to admit painting into the list of liberal arts, any more than sculpture, marble-working, and other helps toward luxury. I also debar from the liberal studies wrestling and all knowledge that is compounded of oil and mud; otherwise, I should be compelled to admit perfumers also, and cooks, and all others who lend their wits to the service of our pleasures. **19.** For what "liberal" element is there in these ravenous takers of emetics, whose bodies are fed to fatness while their minds are thin and dull? Or do we really believe that the training which they give is "liberal" for the young men of Rome, who used to be taught by our ancestors to stand straight and hurl a spear, to wield a pike, to guide a horse, and to handle weapons? Our ancestors used to teach their children nothing that could be learned while lying down. But neither the new system nor the old teaches or nourishes virtue. For what good does it do us to guide a horse and control his speed with the curb, and then find that our own passions, utterly uncurbed, bolt with us? Or to beat many opponents in wrestling or boxing, and then to find that we ourselves are beaten by anger?

20. "What then," you say, "do the liberal studies contribute nothing to our welfare?" Very much in other respects, but nothing at all as regards virtue. For even these arts of which I have spoken, though admittedly of a low grade – depending as they do upon handiwork – contribute greatly toward the equipment of life, but nevertheless have nothing to do with virtue. And if you inquire, "Why, then, do we educate our children in the liberal studies?" it is not because they can bestow virtue, but because they prepare the soul for the reception of virtue. Just as that "primary course," as the ancients called it, in grammar, which gave boys their elementary training, does not teach them the liberal arts, but prepares the ground for their early acquisition of these arts, so the liberal arts do not conduct the soul all the way to virtue, but merely set it going in that direction.

21. Posidonius divides the arts into four classes: first we have those which are common and low, then those which serve for amusement, then those which refer to the education of boys, and, finally, the liberal arts. The common sort belong to workmen and are mere hand-work; they are concerned with equipping life; there is in them no pretence to beauty or honour. **22.** The arts of amusement are those which aim to please the eye and the ear. To this class you may assign the stage-machinists, who invent scaffolding that goes aloft of its own accord, or floors that rise silently into the air, and many other surprising devices, as when objects that fit together then fall apart, or objects which are separate then join together automatically, or objects which stand erect then gradually collapse. The eye of the inexperienced is struck with amazement by these things; for such persons marvel at everything that takes place without warning, because they do not know the causes. **23.** The arts which belong to the education of boys, and are somewhat similar to the liberal arts, are those which the Greeks call the "cycle of studies," but which we Romans call the "liberal." However, those alone are really liberal – or rather, to give them a truer name, "free" – whose concern is virtue.

24. "But," one will say, "just as there is a part of philosophy which has to do with nature, and a part which has to do with ethics, and a part which has to do with reasoning, so this group of liberal arts also claims for itself a place in philosophy. When one approaches questions that deal with nature, a decision is reached by means of a word from the mathematician. Therefore mathematics is a department of that branch which it aids." **25.** But many things aid us and yet are not parts of ourselves. Nay, if they were, they would not aid us. Food is an aid to the body, but is not a part of it. We get some help from the service which mathematics renders; and mathematics is as indispensable to philosophy as the carpenter is to the mathematician. But carpentering is not a part of mathematics, nor is mathematics a part of philosophy. **26.** Moreover, each has its own limits; for the wise man investigates and learns the causes of natural phenomena, while the mathematician follows up and computes their numbers and their measurements. The wise man knows the laws by which the heavenly bodies persist, what powers belong to them, and what attributes; the astronomer merely notes their comings and goings, the rules which govern their settings and their risings, and the occasional periods during which they seem to stand still, although as a matter of fact no heavenly body can stand still. **27.** The wise man will know what causes the reflection in a mirror; but, the mathematician can merely tell you how far the body should be from the reflection, and what shape of mirror will produce a given reflection. The philosopher will demonstrate that the sun is a large body, while the astronomer will compute just how large, progressing in knowledge by his method of trial and experiment; but in order to progress, he must summon to his aid certain principles. No art, however, is sufficient unto itself, if the foundation upon which it rests depends upon mere favour. **28.** Now philosophy asks no favours from any other source; it builds everything on its own soil; but the science of numbers is, so to speak, a structure built on another man's land – it builds on everything on alien soil; It accepts first principles, and by their favour arrives at further conclusions. If it could march unassisted to the truth, if it were able to understand the nature of the universe, I should say that it would offer much assistance to our minds; for the mind grows by contact with things heavenly and draws into itself something from on high. There is but one thing that brings the soul to perfection – the unalterable knowledge of good and evil. But there is no other art which investigates good and evil.

I should like to pass in review the several virtues. **29.** Bravery is a scorner of things which inspire fear; it looks down upon, challenges, and crushes the powers of terror and all that would drive our freedom under the yoke. But do "liberal studies" strengthen this virtue? Loyalty is the holiest good in the human heart; it is forced into betrayal by no constraint, and it is bribed by no rewards. Loyalty cries: "Burn me, slay me, kill me! I shall not betray my trust; and the more urgently torture shall seek to find my secret, the deeper in my heart will I bury it!" Can the "liberal arts" produce such a spirit within us? Temperance controls our desires; some it hates and routs, others it regulates and restores to a healthy measure, nor does it ever approach our desires for their own sake. Temperance knows that the best measure of the appetites is not what you want to take, but what you ought to take. **30.** Kindliness forbids you to be over-bearing towards your associates, and it forbids you to be grasping. In words and in deeds and in feelings it shows itself gentle and courteous to all men. It counts no evil as another's solely. And the reason why it loves its own good is chiefly because it will some day be the good of another. Do "liberal studies" teach a man such character as this? No; no more than they teach simplicity, moderation and self-restraint, thrift and economy, and that kindliness which spares a neighbour's life as if it were one's own and knows that it is not for man to make wasteful use of his fellow-man.

31. "But," one says, "since you declare that virtue cannot be attained without the 'liberal studies,' how is it that you deny that they offer any assistance to virtue?" Because you cannot attain virtue without food, either; and yet food has nothing to do with virtue. Wood does not offer assistance to a ship, although a ship cannot be built except of wood. There is no reason, I say, why you should think that anything is made by the assistance of that without which it cannot be made. **32.** We might even make the statement that it is possible to attain wisdom without the "liberal studies"; for although virtue is a thing that must be learned, yet it is not learned by means of these studies.

What reason have I, however, for supposing that one who is ignorant of letters will never be a wise man, since wisdom is not to be found in letters? Wisdom communicates facts and not words; and it may be true that the memory is more to be depended upon when it has no support outside itself. **33.** Wisdom is a large and spacious thing. It needs plenty of free room. One must learn about things divine and human, the past and the future, the ephemeral and the eternal; and one must learn about Time. See how many questions arise concerning time alone: in the first place, whether it is anything in and by itself; in the second place, whether anything exists prior to time and without time; and again, did time begin along with the universe, or, because there was something even before the universe began, did time also exist then? **34.** There are countless questions concerning the soul alone: whence it comes, what is its nature, when it begins to exist, and how long it exists; whether it passes from one place to another and changes its habitation, being transferred successively from one animal shape to another, or whether it is a slave but once, roaming the universe after it is set free; whether it is corporeal or not; what will become of it when it ceases to use us as its medium; how it will employ its freedom when it has escaped from this present prison; whether it will forget all its past, and at that moment begin to know itself when, released from the body, it has withdrawn to the skies.

35. Thus, whatever phase of things human and divine you have apprehended, you will be wearied by the vast number of things to be answered and things to be learned. And in order that these manifold and mighty subjects may have free entertainment in your soul, you must remove therefrom all superfluous things. Virtue will not surrender herself to these narrow bounds of ours; a great subject needs wide space in which to move. Let all other things be driven out, and let the breast be emptied to receive virtue.

36. "But it is a pleasure to be acquainted with many arts." Therefore let us keep only as much of them as is essential. Do you regard that man as blameworthy who puts superfluous things on the same footing with useful things, and in his house makes a lavish display of costly objects, but do not deem him blameworthy who has allowed himself to become engrossed with the useless furniture of learning? This desire to know more than is sufficient is a sort of intemperance. **37.** Why? Because this unseemly pursuit of the liberal arts makes men troublesome, wordy, tactless, self-satisfied bores, who fail to learn the essentials just because they have learned the non-essentials. Didymus the scholar wrote four thousand books. I should feel pity for him if he had only read the same number of superfluous volumes. In these books he investigates Homer's birthplace, who was really the mother of Aeneas, whether Anacreon was more of a rake or more of a drunkard, whether Sappho was a bad lot, and other problems the answers to which, if found, were forthwith to be forgotten. Come now, do not tell me that life is long! **38.** Nay, when you come to consider our own countrymen also, I can show you many works which ought to be cut down with the axe.

It is at the cost of a vast outlay of time and of vast discomfort to the ears of others that we win such praise as this: "What a learned man you are!" Let us be content with this recommendation, less citified though it be: "What a good man you are!" **39.** Do I mean this? Well, would you have me unroll the annals of the world's history and try to find out who first wrote poetry? Or, in the absence of written records, shall I make an estimate of the number of years which lie between Orpheus and Homer? Or shall I make a study of the absurd writings of Aristarchus, wherein he branded the text of other men's verses, and wear my life away upon syllables? Shall I then wallow in the geometrician's dust? Have I so far forgotten that useful saw "Save your time"? Must I know these things? And what may I choose not to know?

40. Apion, the scholar, who drew crowds to his lectures all over Greece in the days of Gaius Caesar and was acclaimed a Homerid by every state, used to maintain that Homer, when he had finished his two poems, the *Iliad* and the *Odyssey*, added a preliminary poem to his work, wherein he embraced the whole Trojan war. The argument which Apion adduced to prove this statement was that Homer had purposely inserted in the opening line two letters which contained a key to the number of his books. **41.** A man who wishes to know many things must know such things as these, and must take no thought of all the time which one loses by ill-health, public duties, private duties, daily duties, and sleep. Apply the measure to the years of your life; they have no room for all these things.

42. I have been speaking so far of liberal studies; but think how much superfluous and unpractical matter the philosophers contain! Of their own accord they also have descended to establishing nice divisions of syllables, to determining the true meaning of conjunctions and prepositions; they have been envious of the scholars, envious of the mathematicians. They have taken over into their own art all the superfluities of these other arts; the result is that they know more about careful speaking than about careful living. **43.** Let me tell you what evils are due to over-nice exactness, and what an enemy it is of truth! Protagoras declares that one can take either side on any question and debate it with equal success – even on this very question, whether every subject can be debated from either point of view. Nausiphanes holds that in things which seem to exist, there is no difference between existence and non-existence. **44.** Parmenides maintains that nothing exists of all this which seems to exist, except the universe alone. Zeno of Elea removed all the difficulties by removing one; for he declares that nothing exists. The Pyrrhonean, Megarian, Eretrian, and Academic schools are all engaged in practically the same task; they have introduced a new knowledge, non-knowledge. **45.** You may sweep all these theories in with the superfluous troops of "liberal" studies; the one class of men give me a knowledge that will be of no use to me, the other class do away with any hope of attaining knowledge. It is better, of course, to know useless things than to know nothing. One set of philosophers offers no light by which I may direct my gaze toward the truth; the other digs out my very eyes and leaves me blind. If I cleave to Protagoras, there is nothing in the scheme of nature that is not doubtful; if I hold with Nausiphanes, I am sure only of this – that everything is unsure; if with Parmenides, there is nothing except the One; if with Zeno, there is not even the One.

46. What are we, then? What becomes of all these things that surround us, support us, sustain us? The whole universe is then a vain or deceptive shadow. I cannot readily say whether I am more vexed at those who would have it that we know nothing, or with those who would not leave us even this privilege. Farewell.

LXXXIX. ON THE PARTS OF PHILOSOPHY

1. It is a useful fact that you wish to know, one which is essential to him who hastens after wisdom – namely, the parts of philosophy and the division of its huge bulk into separate members. For by studying the parts we can be brought more easily to understand the whole. I only wish that philosophy might come before our eyes in all her unity, just as the whole expanse of the firmament is spread out for us to gaze upon! It would be a sight closely resembling that of the firmament. For then surely philosophy would ravish all mortals with love for her; we should abandon all those things which, in our ignorance of what is great, we believe to be great. Inasmuch, however, as this cannot fall to our lot, we must view philosophy just as men gaze upon the secrets of the firmament.

2. The wise man's mind, to be sure, embraces the whole framework of philosophy, surveying it with no less rapid glance than our mortal eyes survey the heavens; we, however, who must break through the gloom, we whose vision fails even for that which is near at hand, can be shown with greater ease each separate object even though we cannot yet comprehend the universe. I shall therefore comply with your demand, and shall divide philosophy into parts, but not into scraps. For it is useful that philosophy should be divided, but not chopped into bits. Just as it is hard to take in what is indefinitely large, so it is hard to take in what is indefinitely small. **3.** The people are divided into tribes, the army into centuries. Whatever has grown to greater size is more easily identified if it is broken up into parts; but the parts, as I have remarked, must not be countless in number and diminutive in size. For over-analysis is faulty in precisely the same way as no analysis at all; whatever you cut so fine that it becomes dust is as good as blended into a mass again.

4. In the first place, therefore, if you approve, I shall draw the distinction between wisdom and philosophy. Wisdom is the perfect good of the human mind; philosophy is the love of wisdom, and the endeavour to attain it. The latter strives toward the goal which the former has already reached. And it is clear why philosophy was so called. For it acknowledges by its very name the object of its love. **5.** Certain persons have defined wisdom as the knowledge of things divine and things human. Still others say: "Wisdom is knowing things divine and things human, and their causes also." This added phrase seems to me to be superfluous, since the causes of things divine and things human are a part of the divine system. Philosophy also has been defined in various ways; some have called it "the study of virtue," others have referred to it as "a study of the way to amend the mind," and some have named it "the search for right reason." **6.** One thing is practically settled, that there is some difference between philosophy and wisdom. Nor indeed is it possible that that which is sought and that which seeks are identical. As there is a great difference between avarice and wealth, the one being the subject of the craving and the other its object, so between philosophy and wisdom. For the one is a result and a reward of the other. Philosophy does the going, and wisdom is the goal. **7.** Wisdom is that which the Greeks call σοφία. The Romans also were wont to use this word in the sense in which they now use "philosophy" also. This will be proved to your satisfaction by our old national plays, as well as by the epitaph that is carved on the tomb of Dossennus:

Pause, stranger, and read the wisdom of Dossennus.

8. Certain of our school, however, although philosophy meant to them "the study of virtue," and though virtue was the object sought and philosophy the seeker, have maintained nevertheless that the two cannot be sundered. For philosophy cannot exist without virtue, nor virtue without philosophy. Philosophy is the study of virtue, by means, however, of virtue itself; but neither can virtue exist without the study of itself, nor can the study of virtue exist without virtue itself. For it is not like trying to hit a target at long range, where the shooter and the object to be shot at are in different places. Nor, as roads which lead into a city, are the approaches to virtue situated outside virtue herself; the path by which one reaches virtue leads by way of virtue herself; philosophy and virtue cling closely together.

9. The greatest authors, and the greatest number of authors, have maintained that there are three divisions of philosophy – moral, natural, and rational. The first keeps the soul in order; the second investigates the universe; the third works out the essential meanings of words, their combinations, and the proofs which keep falsehood from creeping in and displacing truth. But there have also been those who divided philosophy on the one hand into fewer divisions, on the other hand into more. **10.** Certain of the Peripatetic school have added a fourth division, "civil philosophy," because it calls for a special sphere of activity and is interested in a different subject matter. Some have added a department for which they use the Greek term "economics," the science of managing one's own household. Still others have made a distinct heading for the various kinds of life. There is no one of these subdivisions, however, which will not be found under the branch called "moral" philosophy.

11. The Epicureans held that philosophy was twofold, natural and moral; they did away with the rational branch. Then, when they were compelled by the facts themselves to distinguish between equivocal ideas and to expose fallacies that lay hidden under the cloak of truth they themselves also introduced a heading to which they give the name "forensic and regulative," which is merely "rational" under another name, although they hold that this section is accessory to the department of "natural" philosophy. **12.** The Cyrenaic school abolished the natural as well as the rational department, and were content with the moral side alone; and yet these philosophers also include under another title that which they have rejected. For they divide moral philosophy into five parts: (1) What to avoid and what to seek, (2) The Passions, (3) Actions, (4) Causes, (5) Proofs. Now the causes of things really belong to the "natural" division, the proofs to the "rational." **13.** Aristo of Chios remarked that the natural and the rational were not only superfluous, but were also contradictory. He even limited the "moral," which was all that was left to him; for he abolished that heading which embraced advice, maintaining that it was the business of the pedagogue, and not of the philosopher – as if the wise man were anything else than the pedagogue of the human race!

14. Since, therefore, philosophy is threefold, let us first begin to set in order the moral side. It has been agreed that this should be divided into three parts. First, we have the speculative part, which assigns to each thing its particular function and weighs the worth of each; it is highest in point of utility. For what is so indispensable as giving to everything its proper value? The second has to do with impulse, the third with actions. For the first duty is to determine severally what things are worth; the second, to conceive with regard to them a regulated and ordered impulse; the third, to make your impulse and your actions harmonize, so that under all these conditions you may be consistent with yourself. **15.** If any of the three be defective, there is confusion in the rest also. For what benefit is there in having all things appraised, each in its proper relations, if you go to excess in your impulses? What benefit is there in having checked your impulses and in having your desires in your own control, if when you come to action you are unaware of the proper times and seasons, and if you do not know when, where, and how each action should be carried out? It is one thing to understand the merits and the values of facts, another thing to know the precise moment for action, and still another to curb impulses and to proceed, instead of rushing, toward what is to be done. Hence life is in harmony with itself only when action has not deserted impulse, and when impulse toward an object arises in each case from the worth of the object, being languid or more eager as the case may be, according as the objects which arouse it are worth seeking.

16. The natural side of philosophy is twofold: bodily and non-bodily. Each is divided into its own grades of importance, so to speak. The topic concerning bodies deals, first, with these two grades: the creative and the created; and the created things are the elements. Now this very topic of the elements, as some writers hold, is integral; as others hold, it is divided into matter, the cause which moves all things, and the elements. **17.** It remains for me to divide rational philosophy into its parts. Now all speech is either continuous, or split up between questioner and answerer. It has been agreed upon that the former should be called rhetoric, and the latter dialectic. Rhetoric deals with words, and meanings, and arrangement. Dialectic is divided into two parts: words and their meanings, that is, into things which are said, and the words in which they are said. Then comes a subdivision of each – and it is of vast extent. Therefore I shall stop at this point, and

> But treat the climax of the story;

for if I should take a fancy to give the subdivisions, my letter would become a debater's handbook! **18.** I am not trying to discourage you, excellent Lucilius, from reading on this subject, provided only that you promptly relate to conduct all that you have read.

It is your conduct that you must hold in check; you must rouse what is languid in you, bind fast what has become relaxed, conquer what is obstinate, persecute your appetites, and the appetites of mankind, as much as you can; and to those who say: "How long will this unending talk go on?" answer with the words: **19.** "I ought to be asking you 'How long will these unending sins of yours go on?'" Do you really desire my remedies to stop before your vices? But I shall speak of my remedies all the more, and just because you offer objections I shall keep on talking. Medicine begins to do good at the time when a touch makes the diseased body tingle with pain. I shall utter words that will help men even against their will. At times you should allow words other than compliments to reach your ears, and because as individuals you are unwilling to hear the truth, hear it collectively. **20.** How far will you extend the boundaries of your estates? An estate which held a nation is too narrow for a single lord. How far will you push forward your ploughed fields – you who are not content to confine the measure of your farms even within the amplitude of provinces? You have noble rivers flowing down through your private grounds; you have mighty streams – boundaries of mighty nations – under your dominion from source to outlet. This also is too little for you unless you also surround whole seas with your estates, unless your steward holds sway on the other side of the Adriatic, the Ionian, and the Aegean seas, unless the islands, homes of famous chieftains, are reckoned by you as the most paltry of possessions! Spread them as widely as you will, if only you may have as a "farm" what was once called a kingdom; make whatever you can your own, provided only that it is more than your neighbour's!

21. And now for a word with you, whose luxury spreads itself out as widely as the greed of those to whom I have just referred. To you I say: "Will this custom continue until there is no lake over which the pinnacles of your country-houses do not tower? Until there is no river whose banks are not bordered by your lordly structures? Wherever hot waters shall gush forth in rills, there you will be causing new resorts of luxury to rise. Wherever the shore shall bend into a bay, there will you straightway be laying foundations, and, not content with any land that has not been made by art, you will bring the sea within your boundaries. On every side let your house-tops flash in the sun, now set on mountain peaks where they command an extensive outlook over sea and land, now lifted from the plain to the height of mountains; build your manifold structures, your huge piles, – you are nevertheless but individuals, and puny ones at that! What profit to you are your many bed-chambers? You sleep in one. No place is yours where you yourselves are not." **22.** "Next I pass to you, you whose bottomless and insatiable maw explores on the one hand the seas, on the other the earth, with enormous toil hunting down your prey, now with hook, now with snare, now with nets of various kinds; no animal has peace except when you are cloyed with it. And how slight a portion of those banquets of yours, prepared for you by so many hands, do you taste with your pleasure-jaded palate! How slight a portion of all that game, whose taking was fraught with danger, does the master's sick and squeamish stomach relish? How slight a portion of all those shell-fish, imported from so far, slips down that insatiable gullet? Poor wretches, do you not know that your appetites are bigger than your bellies?"

23. Talk in this way to other men, – provided that while you talk you also listen; write in this way, – provided that while you write you read, remembering that everything you hear or read, is to be applied to conduct, and to the alleviation of passion's fury. Study, not in order to add anything to your knowledge, but to make your knowledge better. Farewell.

XC. ON THE PART PLAYED BY PHILOSOPHY IN THE PROGRESS OF MAN

1. Who can doubt, my dear Lucilius, that life is the gift of the immortal gods, but that living well is the gift of philosophy? Hence the idea that our debt to philosophy is greater than our debt to the gods, in proportion as a good life is more of a benefit than mere life, would be regarded as correct, were not philosophy itself a boon which the gods have bestowed upon us. They have given the knowledge thereof to none, but the faculty of acquiring it they have given to all. **2.** For if they had made philosophy also a general good, and if we were gifted with understanding at our birth, wisdom would have lost her best attribute – that she is not one of the gifts of fortune. For as it is, the precious and noble characteristic of wisdom is that she does not advance to meet us, that each man is indebted to himself for her, and that we do not seek her at the hands of others.

What would there be in philosophy worthy of your respect, if she were a thing that came by bounty? **3.** Her sole function is to discover the truth about things divine and things human. From her side religion never departs, nor duty, nor justice, nor any of the whole company of virtues which cling together in close-united fellowship. Philosophy has taught us to worship that which is divine, to love that which is human; she has told us that with the gods lies dominion, and among men, fellowship. This fellowship remained unspoiled for a long time, until avarice tore the community asunder and became the cause of poverty, even in the case of those whom she herself had most enriched. For men cease to possess all things the moment they desire all things for their own.

4. But the first men and those who sprang from them, still unspoiled, followed nature, having one man as both their leader and their law, entrusting themselves to the control of one better than themselves. For nature has the habit of subjecting the weaker to the stronger. Even among the dumb animals those which are either biggest or fiercest hold sway. It is no weakling bull that leads the herd; it is one that has beaten the other males by his might and his muscle. In the case of elephants, the tallest goes first; among men, the best is regarded as the highest. That is why it was to the mind that a ruler was assigned; and for that reason the greatest happiness rested with those peoples among whom a man could not be the more powerful unless he were the better. For that man can safely accomplish what he will who thinks he can do nothing except what he ought to do.

5. Accordingly, in that age which is maintained to be the golden age, Posidonius holds that the government was under the jurisdiction of the wise. They kept their hands under control, and protected the weaker from the stronger. They gave advice, both to do and not to do; they showed what was useful and what was useless. Their forethought provided that their subjects should lack nothing; their bravery warded off dangers; their kindness enriched and adorned their subjects. For them ruling was a service, not an exercise of royalty. No ruler tried his power against those to whom he owed the beginnings of his power; and no one had the inclination, or the excuse, to do wrong, since the ruler ruled well and the subject obeyed well, and the king could utter no greater threat against disobedient subjects than that they should depart from the kingdom.

6. But when once vice stole in and kingdoms were transformed into tyrannies, a need arose for laws and these very laws were in turn framed by the wise. Solon, who established Athens upon a firm basis by just laws, was one of the seven men renowned for their wisdom. Had Lycurgus lived in the same period, an eighth would have been added to that hallowed number seven. The laws of Zaleucus and Charondas are praised; it was not in the forum or in the offices of skilled counsellors, but in the silent and holy retreat of Pythagoras, that these two men learned the principles of justice which they were to establish in Sicily (which at that time was prosperous) and throughout Grecian Italy.

7. Up to this point I agree with Posidonius; but that philosophy discovered the arts of which life makes use in its daily round I refuse to admit. Nor will I ascribe to it an artisan's glory. Posidonius says: "When men were scattered over the earth, protected by eaves or by the dug-out shelter of a cliff or by the trunk of a hollow tree, it was philosophy that taught them to build houses." But I, for my part, do not hold that philosophy devised these shrewdly-contrived dwellings of ours which rise story upon story, where city crowds against city, any more than that she invented the fish-preserves, which are enclosed for the purpose of saving men's gluttony from having to run the risk of storms, and in order that, no matter how wildly the sea is raging, luxury may have its safe harbours in which to fatten fancy breeds of fish. **8.** What! Was it philosophy that taught the use of keys and bolts? Nay, what was that except giving a hint to avarice? Was it philosophy that erected all these towering tenements, so dangerous to the persons who dwell in them? Was it not enough for man to provide himself a roof of any chance covering, and to contrive for himself some natural retreat without the help of art and without trouble? Believe me, that was a happy age, before the days of architects, before the days of builders! **9.** All this sort of thing was born when luxury was being born, – this matter of cutting timbers square and cleaving a beam with unerring hand as the saw made its way over the marked-out line.

> The primal man with wedges split his wood.

For they were not preparing a roof for a future banquet-hall; for no such use did they carry the pine trees or the firs along the trembling streets with a long row of drays – merely to fasten thereon panelled ceilings heavy with gold. **10.** Forked poles erected at either end propped up their houses. With close-packed branches and with leaves heaped up and laid sloping they contrived a drainage for even the heaviest rains. Beneath such dwellings, they lived, but they lived in peace. A thatched roof once covered free men; under marble and gold dwells slavery.

11. On another point also I differ from Posidonius, when he holds that mechanical tools were the invention of wise men. For on that basis one might maintain that those were wise who taught the arts

> Of setting traps for game, and liming twigs
> For birds, and girdling mighty woods with dogs.

It was man's ingenuity, not his wisdom, that discovered all these devices. **12.** And I also differ from him when he says that wise men discovered our mines of iron and copper, "when the earth, scorched by forest fires, melted the veins of ore which lay near the surface and caused the metal to gush forth." Nay, the sort of men who discover such things are the sort of men who are busied with them. **13.** Nor do I consider this question so subtle as Posidonius thinks, namely, whether the hammer or the tongs came first into use. They were both invented by some man whose mind was nimble and keen, but not great or exalted; and the same holds true of any other discovery which can only be made by means of a bent body and of a mind whose gaze is upon the ground.

The wise man was easy-going in his way of living. And why not? Even in our own times he would prefer to be as little cumbered as possible. **14.** How, I ask, can you consistently admire both Diogenes and Daedalus? Which of these two seems to you a wise man – the one who devised the saw, or the one who, on seeing a boy drink water from the hollow of his hand, forthwith took his cup from his wallet and broke it, upbraiding himself with these words: "Fool that I am, to have been carrying superfluous baggage all this time!" and then curled himself up in his tub and lay down to sleep? **15.** In these our own times, which man, pray, do you deem the wiser – the one who invents a process for spraying saffron perfumes to a tremendous height from hidden pipes, who fills or empties canals by a sudden rush of waters, who so cleverly constructs a dining-room with a ceiling of movable panels that it presents one pattern after another, the roof changing as often as the courses, – or the one who proves to others, as well as to himself, that nature has laid upon us no stern and difficult law when she tells us that we can live without the marble-cutter and the engineer, that we can clothe ourselves without traffic in silk fabrics, that we can have everything that is indispensable to our use, provided only that we are content with what the earth has placed on its surface? If mankind were willing to listen to this sage, they would know that the cook is as superfluous to them as the soldier. **16.** Those were wise men, or at any rate like the wise, who found the care of the body a problem easy to solve. The things that are indispensable require no elaborate pains for their acquisition; it is only the luxuries that call for labour. Follow nature, and you will need no skilled craftsmen.

Nature did not wish us to be harassed. For whatever she forced upon us, she equipped us. "But cold cannot be endured by the naked body." What then? Are there not the skins of wild beasts and other animals, which can protect us well enough, and more than enough, from the cold? Do not many tribes cover their bodies with the bark of trees? Are not the feathers of birds sewn together to serve for clothing? Even at the present day does not a large portion of the Scythian tribe garb itself in the skins of foxes and mice, soft to the touch and impervious to the winds? **17.** "For all that, men must have some thicker protection than the skin, in order to keep off the heat of the sun in summer." What then? Has not antiquity produced many retreats which, hollowed out either by the damage wrought by time or by any other occurrence you will, have opened into caverns? What then? Did not the very first-comers take twigs and weave them by hand into wicker mats, smear them with common mud, and then with stubble and other wild grasses construct a roof, and thus pass their winters secure, the rains carried off by means of the sloping gables? What then? Do not the peoples on the edge of the Syrtes dwell in dug-out houses and indeed all the tribes who, because of the too fierce blaze of the sun, possess no protection sufficient to keep off the heat except the parched soil itself?

18. Nature was not so hostile to man that, when she gave all the other animals an easy rôle in life, she made it impossible for him alone to live without all these artifices. None of these was imposed upon us by her; none of them had to be painfully sought out that our lives might be prolonged. All things were ready for us at our birth; it is we that have made everything difficult for ourselves, through our disdain for what is easy. Houses, shelter, creature comforts, food, and all that has now become the source of vast trouble, were ready at hand, free to all, and obtainable for trifling pains. For the limit everywhere corresponded to the need; it is we that have made all those things valuable, we that have made them admired, we that have caused them to be sought for by extensive and manifold devices. **19.** Nature suffices for what she demands. Luxury has turned her back upon nature; each day she expands herself, in all the ages she has been gathering strength, and by her wit promoting the vices. At first, luxury began to lust for what nature regarded as superfluous, then for that which was contrary to nature; and finally she made the soul a bondsman to the body, and bade it be an utter slave to the body's lusts. All these crafts by which the city is patrolled – or shall I say kept in uproar – are but engaged in the body's business; time was when all things were offered to the body as to a slave, but now they are made ready for it as for a master. Accordingly, hence have come the workshops of the weavers and the carpenters; hence the savoury smells of the professional cooks; hence the wantonness of those who teach wanton postures, and wanton and affected singing. For that moderation which nature prescribes, which limits our desires by resources restricted to our needs, has abandoned the field; it has now come to this – that to want only what is enough is a sign both of boorishness and of utter destitution.

20. It is hard to believe, my dear Lucilius, how easily the charm of eloquence wins even great men away from the truth. Take, for example, Posidonius – who, in my estimation, is of the number of those who have contributed most to philosophy – when he wishes to describe the art of weaving. He tells how, first, some threads are twisted and some drawn out from the soft, loose mass of wool; next, how the upright warp keeps the threads stretched by means of hanging weights; then, how the inserted thread of the woof, which softens the hard texture of the web which holds it fast on either side, is forced by the batten to make a compact union with the warp. He maintains that even the weaver's art was discovered by wise men, forgetting that the more complicated art which he describes was invented in later days – the art wherein

> The web is bound to frame; asunder now
> The reed doth part the warp. Between the threads
> Is shot the woof by pointed shuttles borne;
> The broad comb's well-notched teeth then drive it home.

Suppose he had had the opportunity of seeing the weaving of our own day, which produces the clothing that will conceal nothing, the clothing which affords – I will not say no protection to the body, but none even to modesty!

21. Posidonius then passes on to the farmer. With no less eloquence he describes the ground which is broken up and crossed again by the plough, so that the earth, thus loosened, may allow freer play to the roots; then the seed is sown, and the weeds plucked out by hand, lest any chance growth or wild plant spring up and spoil the crop. This trade also, he declares, is the creation of the wise, – just as if cultivators of the soil were not even at the present day discovering countless new methods of increasing the soil's fertility! **22.** Furthermore, not confining his attention to these arts, he even degrades the wise man by sending him to the mill. For he tells us how the sage, by imitating the processes of nature, began to make bread. "The grain," he says, "once taken into the mouth, is crushed by the flinty teeth, which meet in hostile encounter, and whatever grain slips out the tongue turns back to the selfsame teeth. Then it is blended into a mass, that it may the more easily pass down the slippery throat. When this has readied the stomach, it is digested by the stomach's equable heat; then, and not till then, it is assimilated with the body. **23.** Following this pattern," he goes on, "someone placed two rough stones, the one above the other, in imitation of the teeth, one set of which is stationary and awaits the motion of the other set. Then by the rubbing of the one stone against the other, the grain is crushed and brought back again and again, until by frequent rubbing it is reduced to powder. Then this man sprinkled the meal with water, and by continued manipulation subdued the mass and moulded the loaf. This loaf was, at first, baked by hot ashes or by an earthen vessel glowing hot; later on ovens were gradually discovered and the other devices whose heat will render obedience to the sage's will." Posidonius came very near declaring that even the cobbler's trade was the discovery of the wise man.

24. Reason did indeed devise all these things, but it was not right reason. It was man, but not the wise man, that discovered them; just as they invented ships, in which we cross rivers and seas – ships fitted with sails for the purpose of catching the force of the winds, ships with rudders added at the stern in order to turn the vessel's course in one direction or another. The model followed was the fish, which steers itself by its tail, and by its slightest motion on this side or on that bends its swift course. 25. "But," says Posidonius, "the wise man did indeed discover all these things; they were, however, too petty for him to deal with himself and so he entrusted them to his meaner assistants." Not so; these early inventions were thought out by no other class of men than those who have them in charge to-day. We know that certain devices have come to light only within our own memory – such as the use of windows which admit the clear light through transparent tiles, and such as the vaulted baths, with pipes let into their walls for the purpose of diffusing the heat which maintains an even temperature in their lowest as well as in their highest spaces. Why need I mention the marble with which our temples and our private houses are resplendent? Or the rounded and polished masses of stone by means of which we erect colonnades and buildings roomy enough for nations? Or our signs for whole words, which enable us to take down a speech, however rapidly uttered, matching speed of tongue by speed of hand? All this sort of thing has been devised by the lowest grade of slaves. 26. Wisdom's seat is higher; she trains not the hands, but is mistress of our minds.

Would you know what wisdom has brought forth to light, what she has accomplished? It is not the graceful poses of the body, or the varied notes produced by horn and flute, whereby the breath is received and, as it passes out or through, is transformed into voice. It is not wisdom that contrives arms, or walls, or instruments useful in war; nay, her voice is for peace, and she summons all mankind to concord. 27. It is not she, I maintain, who is the artisan of our indispensable implements of daily use. Why do you assign to her such petty things? You see in her the skilled artisan of life. The other arts, it is true, wisdom has under her control; for he whom life serves is also served by the things which equip life. But wisdom's course is toward the state of happiness; thither she guides us, thither she opens the way for us. 28. She shows us what things are evil and what things are seemingly evil; she strips our minds of vain illusion. She bestows upon us a greatness which is substantial, but she represses the greatness which is inflated, and showy but filled with emptiness; and she does not permit us to be ignorant of the difference between what is great and what is but swollen; nay, she delivers to us the knowledge of the whole of nature and of her own nature. She discloses to us what the gods are and of what sort they are; what are the nether gods, the household deities, and the protecting spirits; what are the souls which have been endowed with lasting life and have been admitted to the second class of divinities, where is their abode and what their activities, powers, and will.

Such are wisdom's rites of initiation, by means of which is unlocked, not a village shrine, but the vast temple of all the gods – the universe itself, whose true apparitions and true aspects she offers to the gaze of our minds. For the vision of our eyes is too dull for sights so great. **29.** Then she goes back to the beginnings of things, to the eternal Reason which was imparted to the whole, and to the force which inheres in all the seeds of things, giving them the power to fashion each thing according to its kind. Then wisdom begins to inquire about the soul, whence it comes, where it dwells, how long it abides, into how many divisions it falls. Finally, she has turned her attention from the corporeal to the incorporeal, and has closely examined truth and the marks whereby truth is known, inquiring next how that which is equivocal can be distinguished from the truth, whether in life or in language; for in both are elements of the false mingled with the true.

30. It is my opinion that the wise man has not withdrawn himself, as Posidonius thinks, from those arts which we were discussing, but that he never took them up at all. For he would have judged that nothing was worth discovering that he would not afterwards judge to be worth using always. He would not take up things which would have to be laid aside.

31. "But Anacharsis," says Posidonius, "invented the potter's wheel, whose whirling gives shape to vessels." Then because the potter's wheel is mentioned in Homer, people prefer to believe that Homer's verses are false rather than the story of Posidonius! But I maintain that Anacharsis was not the creator of this wheel; and even if he was, although he was a wise man when he invented it, yet he did not invent it *qua* "wise man" – just as there are a great many things which wise men do as men, not as wise men. Suppose, for example, that a wise man is exceedingly fleet of foot; he will outstrip all the runners in the race by virtue of being fleet, not by virtue of his wisdom. I should like to show Posidonius some glass-blower who by his breath moulds the glass into manifold shapes which could scarcely be fashioned by the most skilful hand. Nay, these discoveries have been made since we men have ceased to discover wisdom.

32. But Posidonius again remarks. "Democritus is said to have discovered the arch, whose effect was that the curving line of stones, which gradually lean toward each other, is bound together by the keystone." I am inclined to pronounce this statement false. For there must have been, before Democritus, bridges and gateways in which the curvature did not begin until about the top. **33.** It seems to have quite slipped your memory that this same Democritus discovered how ivory could be softened, how, by boiling, a pebble could be transformed into an emerald, – the same process used even to-day for colouring stones which are found to be amenable to this treatment! It may have been a wise man who discovered all such things, but he did not discover them by virtue of being a wise man; for he does many things which we see done just as well, or even more skilfully and dexterously, by men who are utterly lacking in sagacity.

34. Do you ask what, then, the wise man has found out and what he has brought to light? First of all there is truth, and nature; and nature he has not followed as the other animals do, with eyes too dull to perceive the divine in it. In the second place, there is the law of life, and life he has made to conform to universal principles; and he has taught us, not merely to know the gods, but to follow them, and to welcome the gifts of chance precisely as if they were divine commands. He has forbidden us to give heed to false opinions, and has weighed the value of each thing by a true standard of appraisement. He has condemned those pleasures with which remorse is intermingled, and has praised those goods which will always satisfy; and he has published the truth abroad that he is most happy who has no need of happiness, and that he is most powerful who has power over himself.

35. I am not speaking of that philosophy which has placed the citizen outside his country and the gods outside the universe, and which has bestowed virtue upon pleasure, but rather of that philosophy which counts nothing good except what is honourable, – one which cannot be cajoled by the gifts either of man or fortune, one whose value is that it cannot be bought for any value. That this philosophy existed in such a rude age, when the arts and crafts were still unknown and when useful things could only be learned by use, – this I refuse to believe.

36. Next there came the fortune-favoured period when the bounties of nature lay open to all, for men's indiscriminate use, before avarice and luxury had broken the bonds which held mortals together, and they, abandoning their communal existence, had separated and turned to plunder. The men of the second age were not wise men, even though they did what wise men should do. **37.** Indeed, there is no other condition of the human race that anyone would regard more highly; and if God should commission a man to fashion earthly creatures and to bestow institutions upon peoples, this man would approve of no other system than that which obtained among the men of that age, when

> No ploughman tilled the soil, nor was it right
> To portion off or bound one's property.
> Men shared their gains, and earth more freely gave
> Her riches to her sons who sought them not.

38. What race of men was ever more blest than that race? They enjoyed all nature in partnership. Nature sufficed for them, now the guardian, as before she was the parent, of all; and this her gift consisted of the assured possession by each man of the common resources. Why should I not even call that race the richest among mortals, since you could not find a poor person among them?

But avarice broke in upon a condition so happily ordained, and, by its eagerness to lay something away and to turn it to its own private use, made all things the property of others, and reduced itself from boundless wealth to straitened need. It was avarice that introduced poverty and, by craving much, lost all. **39.** And so, although she now tries to make good her loss, although she adds one estate to another, evicting a neighbour either by buying him out or by wronging him, although she extends her country-seats to the size of provinces and defines ownership as meaning extensive travel through one's own property, – in spite of all these efforts of hers no enlargement of our boundaries will bring us back to the condition from which we have departed.

When there is no more that we can do, we shall possess much; but we once possessed the whole world! **40.** The very soil was more productive when untilled, and yielded more than enough for peoples who refrained from despoiling one another. Whatever gift nature had produced, men found as much pleasure in revealing it to another as in having discovered it. It was possible for no man either to surpass another or to fall short of him; what there was, was divided among unquarrelling friends. Not yet had the stronger begun to lay hands upon the weaker; not yet had the miser, by hiding away what lay before him, begun to shut off his neighbour from even the necessities of life; each cared as much for his neighbour as for himself. **41.** Armour lay unused, and the hand, unstained by human blood, had turned all its hatred against wild beasts. The men of that day, who had found in some dense grove protection against the sun, and security against the severity of winter or of rain in their mean hiding-places, spent their lives under the branches of the trees and passed tranquil nights without a sigh. Care vexes us in our purple, and routs us from our beds with the sharpest of goads; but how soft was the sleep the hard earth bestowed upon the men of that day! **42.** No fretted and panelled ceilings hung over them, but as they lay beneath the open sky the stars glided quietly above them, and the firmament, night's noble pageant, marched swiftly by, conducting its mighty task in silence. For them by day, as well as by night, the visions of this most glorious abode were free and open. It was their joy to watch the constellations as they sank from mid-heaven and others, again, as they rose from their hidden abodes. **43.** What else but joy could it be to wander among the marvels which dotted the heavens far and wide? But you of the present day shudder at every sound your houses make, and as you sit among your frescoes the slightest creak makes you shrink in terror. *They* had no houses as big as cities. The air, the breezes blowing free through the open spaces, the flitting shade of crag or tree, springs crystal-clear and streams not spoiled by man's work, whether by water-pipe or by any confinement of the channel, but running at will, and meadows beautiful without the use of art, – amid such scenes were their rude homes, adorned with rustic hand. Such a dwelling was in accordance with nature; therein it was a joy to live, fearing neither the dwelling itself nor for its safety. In these days, however, our houses constitute a large portion of our dread.

44. But no matter how excellent and guileless was the life of the men of that age, they were not wise men; for that title is reserved for the highest achievement. Still, I would not deny that they were men of lofty spirit and – I may use the phrase – fresh from the gods. For there is no doubt that the world produced a better progeny before it was yet worn out. However, not all were endowed with mental faculties of highest perfection, though in all cases their native powers were more sturdy than ours and more fitted for toil. For nature does not bestow virtue; it is an art to become good. **45.** They, at least, searched not in the lowest dregs of the earth for gold, nor yet for silver or transparent stones; and they still were merciful even to the dumb animals – so far removed was that epoch from the custom of slaying man by man, not in anger or through fear, but just to make a show! They had as yet no embroidered garments nor did they weave cloth of gold; gold was not yet even mined.

46. What, then, is the conclusion of the matter? It was by reason of their ignorance of things that the men of those days were innocent; and it makes a great deal of difference whether one wills not to sin or has not the knowledge to sin. Justice was unknown to them, unknown prudence, unknown also self-control and bravery; but their rude life possessed certain qualities akin to all these virtues. Virtue is not vouchsafed to a soul unless that soul has been trained and taught, and by unremitting practice brought to perfection. For the attainment of this boon, but not in the possession of it, were we born; and even in the best of men, before you refine them by instruction, there is but the stuff of virtue, not virtue itself. Farewell.

XCI. ON THE LESSON TO BE DRAWN FROM THE BURNING OF LYONS

1. Our friend Liberalis is now downcast; for he has just heard of the fire which has wiped out the colony of Lyons. Such a calamity might upset anyone at all, not to speak of a man who dearly loves his country. But this incident has served to make him inquire about the strength of his own character, which he has trained, I suppose, just to meet situations that he thought might cause him fear. I do not wonder, however, that he was free from apprehension touching an evil so unexpected and practically unheard of as this, since it is without precedent. For fire has damaged many a city, but has annihilated none. Even when fire has been hurled against the walls by the hand of a foe, the flame dies out in many places, and although continually renewed, rarely devours so wholly as to leave nothing for the sword. Even an earthquake has scarcely ever been so violent and destructive as to overthrow whole cities. Finally, no conflagration has ever before blazed forth so savagely in any town that nothing was left for a second. **2.** So many beautiful buildings, any single one of which would make a single town famous, were wrecked in one night. In time of such deep peace an event has taken place worse than men can possibly fear even in time of war. Who can believe it? When weapons are everywhere at rest and when peace prevails throughout the world, Lyons, the pride of Gaul, is missing!

Fortune has usually allowed all men, when she has assailed them collectively, to have a foreboding of that which they were destined to suffer. Every great creation has had granted to it a period of reprieve before its fall; but in this case, only a single night elapsed between the city at its greatest and the city non-existent. In short, it takes me longer to tell you it has perished than it took for the city to perish.

3. All this has affected our friend Liberalis, bending his will, which is usually so steadfast and erect in the face of his own trials. And not without reason has he been shaken; for it is the unexpected that puts the heaviest load upon us. Strangeness adds to the weight of calamities, and every mortal feels the greater pain as a result of that which also brings surprise.

4. Therefore, nothing ought to be unexpected by us. Our minds should be sent forward in advance to meet all problems, and we should consider, not what is wont to happen, but what can happen. For what is there in existence that Fortune, when she has so willed, does not drag down from the very height of its prosperity? And what is there that she does not the more violently assail the more brilliantly it shines? What is laborious or difficult for her? **5.** She does not always attack in one way or even with her full strength; at one time she summons our own hands against us; at another time, content with her own powers, she makes use of no agent in devising perils for us. No time is exempt; in the midst of our very pleasures there spring up causes of suffering. War arises in the midst of peace, and that which we depended upon for protection is transformed into a cause of fear; friend becomes enemy, ally becomes foeman, The summer calm is stirred into sudden storms, wilder than the storms of winter. With no foe in sight we are victims of such fates as foes inflict, and if other causes of disaster fail, excessive good fortune finds them for itself. The most temperate are assailed by illness, the strongest by wasting disease, the most innocent by chastisement, the most secluded by the noisy mob.

Chance chooses some new weapon by which to bring her strength to bear against us, thinking we have forgotten her. **6.** Whatever structure has been reared by a long sequence of years, at the cost of great toil and through the great kindness of the gods, is scattered and dispersed by a single day. Nay, he who has said "a day" has granted too long a postponement to swift-coming misfortune; an hour, an instant of time, suffices for the overthrow of empires! It would be some consolation for the feebleness of our selves and our works, if all things should perish as slowly as they come into being; but as it is, increases are of sluggish growth, but the way to ruin is rapid. **7.** Nothing, whether public or private, is stable; the destinies of men, no less than those of cities, are in a whirl. Amid the greatest calm terror arises, and though no external agencies stir up commotion, yet evils burst forth from sources whence they were least expected. Thrones which have stood the shock of civil and foreign wars crash to the ground though no one sets them tottering. How few the states which have carried their good fortune through to the end!

We should therefore reflect upon all contingencies, and should fortify our minds against the evils which may possibly come. **8.** Exile, the torture of disease, wars, shipwreck, – we must think on these. Chance may tear you from your country or your country from you, or may banish you to the desert; this very place, where throngs are stifling, may become a desert. Let us place before our eyes in its entirety the nature of man's lot, and if we would not be overwhelmed, or even dazed, by those unwonted evils, as if they were novel, let us summon to our minds beforehand, not as great an evil as oftentimes happens, but the very greatest evil that possibly can happen. We must reflect upon fortune fully and completely.

9. How often have cities in Asia, how often in Achaia, been laid low by a single shock of earthquake! How many towns in Syria, how many in Macedonia, have been swallowed up! How often has this kind of devastation laid Cyprus in ruins! How often has Paphos collapsed! Not infrequently are tidings brought to us of the utter destruction of entire cities; yet how small a part of the world are we, to whom such tidings often come!

Let us rise, therefore, to confront the operations of Fortune, and whatever happens, let us have the assurance that it is not so great as rumour advertises it to be. **10.** A rich city has been laid in ashes, the jewel of the provinces, counted as one of them and yet not included with them; rich though it was, nevertheless it was set upon a single hill, and that not very large in extent. But of all those cities, of whose magnificence and grandeur you hear today, the very traces will be blotted out by time. Do you not see how, in Achaia, the foundations of the most famous cities have already crumbled to nothing, so that no trace is left to show that they ever even existed? **11.** Not only does that which has been made with hands totter to the ground, not only is that which has been set in place by man's art and man's efforts overthrown by the passing days; nay, the peaks of mountains dissolve, whole tracts have settled, and places which once stood far from the sight of the sea are now covered by the waves. The mighty power of fires has eaten away the hills through whose sides they used to glow, and has levelled to the ground peaks which were once most lofty – the sailor's solace and his beacon. The works of nature herself are harassed; hence we ought to bear with untroubled minds the destruction of cities. **12.** They stand but to fall! This doom awaits them, one and all; it may be that some internal force, and blasts of violence which are tremendous because their way is blocked, will throw off the weight which holds then down; or that a whirlpool of raging currents, mightier because they are hidden in the bosom of the earth, will break through that which resists its power; or that the vehemence of flames will burst asunder the framework of the earth's crust; or that time, from which nothing is safe, will reduce them little by little; or that a pestilential climate will drive their inhabitants away and the mould will corrode their deserted walls. It would be tedious to recount all the ways by which fate may come; but this one thing I know: all the works of mortal man have been doomed to mortality, and in the midst of things which have been destined to die, we live!

13. Hence it is thoughts like these, and of this kind, which I am offering as consolation to our friend Liberalis, who burns with a love for his country that is beyond belief. Perhaps its destruction has been brought about only that it may be raised up again to a better destiny. Oftentimes a reverse has but made room for more prosperous fortune. Many structures have fallen only to rise to a greater height. Timagenes, who had a grudge against Rome and her prosperity, used to say that the only reason he was grieved when conflagrations occurred in Rome was his knowledge that better buildings would arise than those which had gone down in the flames. 14. And probably in this city of Lyons, too, all its citizens will earnestly strive that everything shall be rebuilt better in size and security than what they have lost. May it be built to endure and, under happier auspices, for a longer existence! This is indeed but the hundredth year since this colony was founded – not the limit even of a man's lifetime. Led forth by Plancus, the natural advantages of its site have caused it to wax strong and reach the numbers which it contains to-day; and yet how many calamities of the greatest severity has it endured within the space of an old man's life!

15. Therefore let the mind be disciplined to understand and to endure its own lot, and let it have the knowledge that there is nothing which fortune does not dare – that she has the same jurisdiction over empires as over emperors, the same power over cities as over the citizens who dwell therein. We must not cry out at any of these calamities. Into such a world have we entered, and under such laws do we live. If you like it, obey; if not, depart whithersoever you wish. Cry out in anger if any unfair measures are taken with reference to you individually; but if this inevitable law is binding upon the highest and the lowest alike, be reconciled to fate, by which all things are dissolved. 16. You should not estimate our worth by our funeral mounds or by these monuments of unequal size which line the road; their ashes level all men! We are unequal at birth, but are equal in death. What I say about cities I say also about their inhabitants. Ardea was captured as well as Rome. The great founder of human law has not made distinctions between us on the basis of high lineage or of illustrious names, except while we live. When, however, we come to the end which awaits mortals, he says: "Depart, ambition! To all creatures that burden the earth let one and the same law apply!" For enduring all things, we are equal; no one is more frail than another, no one more certain of his own life on the morrow.

17. Alexander, king of Macedon, began to study geometry; unhappy man, because he would thereby learn how puny was that earth of which he had seized but a fraction! Unhappy man, I repeat, because he was bound to understand that he was bearing a false title. For who can be "great" in that which is puny? The lessons which were being taught him were intricate and could be learned only by assiduous application; they were not the kind to be comprehended by a madman, who let his thoughts range beyond the ocean. "Teach me something easy!" he cries; but his teacher answers: "These things are the same for all, as hard for one as for another."
18. Imagine that nature is saying to us: "Those things of which you complain are the same for all. I cannot give anything easier to any man, but whoever wishes will make things easier for himself." In what way? By equanimity. You must suffer pain, and thirst, and hunger, and old age too, if a longer stay among men shall be granted you; you must be sick, and you must suffer loss and death. 19. Nevertheless, you should

not believe those whose noisy clamour surrounds you; none of these things is an evil, none is beyond your power to bear, or is burdensome. It is only by common opinion that there is anything formidable in them. Your fearing death is therefore like your fear of gossip. But what is more foolish than a man afraid of words? Our friend Demetrius is wont to put it cleverly when he says: "For me the talk of ignorant men is like the rumblings which issue from the belly. For," he adds, "what difference does it make to me whether such rumblings come from above or from below?" **20.** What madness it is to be afraid of disrepute in the judgment of the disreputable! Just as you have had no cause for shrinking in terror from the talk of men, so you have no cause now to shrink from these things, which you would never fear had not their talk forced fear upon you. Does it do any harm to a good man to be besmirched by unjust gossip? **21.** Then let not this sort of thing damage death, either, in our estimation; death also is in bad odour. But no one of those who malign death has made trial of it.

Meanwhile it is foolhardy to condemn that of which you are ignorant. This one thing, however, you do know – that death is helpful to many, that it sets many free from tortures, want, ailments, sufferings, and weariness. We are in the power of nothing when once we have death in our own power! Farewell.

XCII. ON THE HAPPY LIFE

1. You and I will agree, I think, that outward things are sought for the satisfaction of the body, that the body is cherished out of regard for the soul, and that in the soul there are certain parts which minister to us, enabling us to move and to sustain life, bestowed upon us just for the sake of the primary part of us. In this primary part there is something irrational, and something rational. The former obeys the latter, while the latter is the only thing that is not referred back to another, but rather refers all things to itself. For the divine reason also is set in supreme command over all things, and is itself subject to none; and even this reason which we possess is the same, because it is derived from the divine reason. **2.** Now if we are agreed on this point, it is natural that we shall be agreed on the following also – namely, that the happy life depends upon this and this alone: our attainment of perfect reason. For it is naught but this that keeps the soul from being bowed down, that stands its ground against Fortune; whatever the condition of their affairs may be, it keeps men untroubled. And that alone is a good which is never subject to impairment. That man, I declare, is happy whom nothing makes less strong than he is; he keeps to the heights, leaning upon none but himself; for one who sustains himself by any prop may fall. If the case is otherwise, then things which do not pertain to us will begin to have great influence over us. But who desires Fortune to have the upper hand, or what sensible man prides himself upon that which is not his own?

3. What is the happy life? It is peace of mind, and lasting tranquillity. This will be yours if you possess greatness of soul; it will be yours if you possess the steadfastness that resolutely clings to a good judgment just reached. How does a man reach this condition? By gaining a complete view of truth, by maintaining, in all that he does, order, measure, fitness, and a will that is inoffensive and kindly, that is intent upon reason and never departs therefrom, that commands at the same time love and admiration. In short, to give you the principle in brief compass, the wise man's soul ought to be such as would be proper for a god. **4.** What more can one desire who possesses all honourable things? For if dishonourable things can contribute to the best estate, then there will be the possibility of a happy life under conditions which do not include an honourable life. And what is more base or foolish than to connect the good of a rational soul with things irrational? **5.** Yet there are certain philosophers who hold that the Supreme Good admits of increase because it is hardly complete when the gifts of fortune are adverse. Even Antipater, one of the great leaders of this school, admits that he ascribes some influence to externals, though only a very slight influence. You see, however, what absurdity lies in not being content with the daylight unless it is increased by a tiny fire. What importance can a spark have in the midst of this clear sunlight? **6.** If you are not contented with only that which is honourable, it must follow that you desire in addition either the kind of quiet which the Greeks call "undisturbedness," or else pleasure. But the former may be attained in any case. For the mind is free from disturbance when it is fully free to contemplate the universe, and nothing distracts it from the contemplation of nature. The second, pleasure, is simply the good of cattle. We are but adding the irrational to the rational, the dishonourable to the honourable. A pleasant physical sensation affects this life of ours; **7.** why, therefore, do you hesitate to say that all is well with a man just because all is well with his appetite? And do you rate, I will not say among heroes, but among men, the person whose Supreme Good is a matter of flavours and colours and sounds? Nay, let him withdraw from the ranks of this, the noblest class of living beings, second only to the gods; let him herd with the dumb brutes – an animal whose delight is in fodder!

8. The irrational part of the soul is twofold: the one part is spirited, ambitious, uncontrolled; its seat is in the passions; the other is lowly, sluggish, and devoted to pleasure. Philosophers have neglected the former, which, though unbridled, is yet better, and is certainly more courageous and more worthy of a man, and have regarded the latter, which is nerveless and ignoble, as indispensable to the happy life. **9.** They have ordered reason to serve this latter; they have made the Supreme Good of the noblest living being an abject and mean affair, and a monstrous hybrid, too, composed of various members which harmonize but ill. For as our Vergil, describing Scylla, says

> Above, a human face and maiden's breast,
> A beauteous breast, – below, a monster huge
> Of bulk and shapeless, with a dolphin's tail
> Joined to a wolf-like belly.

And yet to this Scylla are tacked on the forms of wild animals, dreadful and swift; but from what monstrous shapes have these wiseacres compounded wisdom! **10.** Man's primary art is virtue itself; there is joined to this the useless and fleeting flesh, fitted only for the reception of food, as Posidonius remarks. This divine virtue ends in foulness, and to the higher parts, which are worshipful and heavenly, there is fastened a sluggish and flabby animal. As for the second desideratum, – quiet, – although it would indeed not of itself be of any benefit to the soul, yet it would relieve the soul of hindrances; pleasure, on the contrary, actually destroys the soul and softens all its vigour. What elements so inharmonious as these can be found united? To that which is most vigorous is joined that which is most sluggish, to that which is austere that which is far from serious, to that which is most holy that which is unrestrained even to the point of impurity. **11.** "What, then," comes the retort, "if good health, rest, and freedom from pain are not likely to hinder virtue, shall you not seek all these?" Of course I shall seek them, but not because they are goods, – I shall seek them because they are according to nature and because they will be acquired through the exercise of good judgment on my part. What, then, will be good in them? This alone, – that it is a good thing to choose them. For when I don suitable attire, or walk as I should, or dine as I ought to dine, it is not my dinner, or my walk, or my dress that are goods, but the deliberate choice which I show in regard to them, as I observe, in each thing I do, a mean that conforms with reason. **12.** Let me also add that the choice of neat clothing is a fitting object of a man's efforts; for man is by nature a neat and well-groomed animal. Hence the choice of neat attire, and not neat attire in itself, is a good; since the good is not in the thing selected, but in the quality of the selection. Our actions are honourable, but not the actual things which we do. **13.** And you may assume that what I have said about dress applies also to the body. For nature has surrounded our soul with the body as with a sort of garment; the body is its cloak. But who has ever reckoned the value of clothes by the wardrobe which contained them? The scabbard does not make the sword good or bad. Therefore, with regard to the body I shall return the same answer to you, – that, if I have the choice, I shall choose health and strength, but that the good involved will be my judgment regarding these things, and not the things themselves.

14. Another retort is: "Granted that the wise man is happy; nevertheless, he does not attain the Supreme Good which we have defined, unless the means also which nature provides for its attainment are at his call. So, while one who possesses virtue cannot be unhappy, yet one cannot be perfectly happy if one lacks such natural gifts as health, or soundness of limb." **15.** But in saying this, you grant the alternative which seems the more difficult to believe, – that the man who is in the midst of unremitting and extreme pain is not wretched, nay, is even happy; and you deny that which is much less serious, – that he is completely happy. And yet, if virtue can keep a man from being wretched, it will be an easier task for it to render him completely happy. For the difference between happiness and complete happiness is less than that between wretchedness and happiness. Can it be possible that a thing which is so powerful as to snatch a man from disaster, and place him among the happy, cannot also accomplish what remains, and render him supremely happy? Does its strength fail at the very top of the climb? **16.** There are in life things which are advantageous and disadvantageous, – both beyond our control. If a good man, in spite of being weighed down by all kinds of disadvantages, is not wretched, how is he not supremely happy, no matter if he does lack certain advantages? For as he is not weighted down to wretchedness by his burden of disadvantages, so he is not withdrawn from supreme happiness through lack of any advantages; nay, he is just as supremely happy without the advantages as he is free from wretchedness though under the load of his disadvantages. Otherwise, if his good can be impaired, it can be snatched from him altogether.

17. A short space above, I remarked that a tiny fire does not add to the sun's light. For by reason of the sun's brightness any light that shines apart from the sunlight is blotted out. "But," one may say, "there are certain objects that stand in the way even of the sunlight." The sun, however, is unimpaired even in the midst of obstacles, and, though an object may intervene and cut off our view thereof, the sun sticks to his work and goes on his course. Whenever he shines forth from amid the clouds, he is no smaller, nor less punctual either, than when he is free from clouds; since it makes a great deal of difference whether there is merely something in the way of his light or something which interferes with his shining. **18.** Similarly, obstacles take nothing away from virtue; it is no smaller, but merely shines with less brilliancy. In our eyes, it may perhaps be less visible and less luminous than before; but as regards itself it is the same and, like the sun when he is eclipsed, is still, though in secret, putting forth its strength. Disasters, therefore, and losses, and wrongs, have only the same power over virtue that a cloud has over the sun.

19. We meet with one person who maintains that a wise man who has met with bodily misfortune is neither wretched nor happy. But he also is in error, for he is putting the results of chance upon a parity with the virtues, and is attributing only the same influence to things that are honourable as to things that are devoid of honour. But what is more detestable and more unworthy than to put contemptible things in the same class with things worthy of reverence! For reverence is due to justice, duty, loyalty, bravery, and prudence; on the contrary, those attributes are worthless with which the most worthless men are often blessed in fuller measure, – such as a sturdy leg, strong shoulders, good teeth, and healthy and solid muscles. **20.** Again, if the wise man whose body is a trial to him shall be regarded as neither wretched nor happy, but shall be left in a sort of half-way position, his life also will be neither desirable nor undesirable. But what is so foolish as to say that the wise man's life is not desirable? And what is so far beyond the bounds of credence as the opinion that any life is neither desirable nor undesirable? Again, if bodily ills do not make a man wretched, they consequently allow him to be happy. For things which have no power to change his condition for the worse, have not the power, either, to disturb that condition when it is at its best.

21. "But," someone will say, "we know what is cold and what is hot; a lukewarm temperature lies between. Similarly, A is happy, and B is wretched, and C is neither happy nor wretched." I wish to examine this figure, which is brought into play against us. If I add to your lukewarm water a larger quantity of cold water, the result will be cold water. But if I pour in a larger quantity of hot water, the water will finally become hot. In the case, however, of your man who is neither wretched nor happy, no matter how much I add to his troubles, he will not be unhappy, according to your argument; hence your figure offers no analogy. **22.** Again, suppose that I set before you a man who is neither miserable nor happy. I add blindness to his misfortunes; he is not rendered unhappy. I cripple him; he is not rendered unhappy. I add afflictions which are unceasing and severe; he is not rendered unhappy. Therefore, one whose life is not changed to misery by all these ills is not dragged by them, either, from his life of happiness. **23.** Then if, as you say, the wise man cannot fall from happiness to wretchedness, he cannot fall into non-happiness. For how, if one has begun to slip, can one stop at any particular place? That which prevents him from rolling to the bottom, keeps him at the summit. Why, you urge, may not a happy life possibly be destroyed? It cannot even be disjointed; and for that reason virtue is itself of itself sufficient for the happy life.

24. "But," it is said, "is not the wise man happier if he has lived longer and has been distracted by no pain, than one who has always been compelled to grapple with evil fortune?" Answer me now, – is he any better or more honourable? If he is not, then he is not happier either. In order to live more happily, he must live more rightly; if he cannot do that, then he cannot live more happily either. Virtue cannot be strained tighter, and therefore neither can the happy life, which depends on virtue. For virtue is so great a good that it is not affected by such insignificant assaults upon it as shortness of life, pain, and the various bodily vexations. For pleasure does not deserve that. virtue should even glance at it. **25.** Now what is the chief thing in virtue? It is the quality of not needing a single day beyond the present, and of not reckoning up the days that are ours; in the slightest possible moment of time virtue completes an eternity of good. These goods seem to us incredible and transcending man's nature; for we measure its grandeur by the standard of our own weakness, and we call our vices by the name of virtue. Furthermore, does it not seem just as incredible that any man in the midst of extreme suffering should say, "I am happy"? And yet this utterance was heard in the very factory of pleasure, when Epicurus said: "To-day and one other day have been the happiest of all!" although in the one case he was tortured by strangury, and in the other by the incurable pain of an ulcerated stomach. **26.** Why, then, should those goods which virtue bestows be incredible in the sight of us, who cultivate virtue, when they are found even in those who acknowledge pleasure as their mistress? These also, ignoble and base-minded as they are, declare that even in the midst of excessive pain and misfortune the wise man will be neither wretched nor happy. And yet this also is incredible, – nay, still more incredible, than the other case. For I do not understand how, if virtue falls from her heights, she can help being hurled all the way to the bottom. She either must preserve one in happiness, or, if driven from this position, she will not prevent us from becoming unhappy. If virtue only stands her ground, she cannot be driven from the field; she must either conquer or be conquered.

27. But some say: "Only to the immortal gods is given virtue and the happy life; we can attain but the shadow, as it were, and semblance of such goods as theirs. We approach them, but we never reach them." Reason, however, is a common attribute of both gods and men; in the gods it is already perfected, in us it is capable of being perfected. **28.** But it is our vices that bring us to despair; for the second class of rational being, man, is of an inferior order, – a guardian, as it were, who is too unstable to hold fast to what is best, his judgment still wavering and uncertain. He may require the faculties of sight and hearing, good health, a bodily exterior that is not loathsome, and, besides, greater length of days conjoined with an unimpaired constitution. **29.** Though by means of reason he can lead a life which will not bring regrets, yet there resides in this imperfect creature, man, a certain power that makes for badness, because he possesses a mind which is easily moved to perversity. Suppose, however, the badness which is in full view, and has previously been stirred to activity, to be removed; the man is still not a good man, but he is being moulded to goodness. One, however, in whom there is lacking any quality that makes for goodness, is bad.

30. But

> He in whose body virtue dwells, and spirit
> E'er present

is equal to the gods; mindful of his origin, he strives to return thither. No man does wrong in attempting to regain the heights from which he once came down. And why should you not believe that something of divinity exists in one who is a part of God? All this universe which encompasses us is one, and it is God; we are associates of God; we are his members. Our soul has capabilities, and is carried thither, if vices do not hold it down. Just as it is the nature of our bodies to stand erect and look upward to the sky, so the soul, which may reach out as far as it will, was framed by nature to this end, that it should desire equality with the gods. And if it makes use of its powers and stretches upward into its proper region it is by no alien path that it struggles toward the heights. **31.** It would be a great task to journey heavenwards; the soul but returns thither. When once it has found the road, it boldly marches on, scornful of all things. It casts, no backward glance at wealth; gold and silver – things which are fully worthy of the gloom in which they once lay – it values not by the sheen which smites the eyes of the ignorant, but by the mire of ancient days, whence our greed first detached and dug them out.

The soul, I affirm, knows that riches are stored elsewhere than in men's heaped-up treasure-houses; that it is the soul, and not the strong-box, which should be filled. **32.** It is the soul that men may set in dominion over all things, and may install as owner of the universe, so that it may limit its riches only by the boundaries of

East and West, and, like the gods, may possess all things; and that it may, with its own vast resources, look down from on high upon the wealthy, no one of whom rejoices as much in his own wealth as he resents the wealth of another. **33.** When the soul has transported itself to this lofty height, it regards the body also, since it is a burden which must be borne, not as a thing to love, but as a thing to oversee; nor is it subservient to that over which it is set in mastery. For no man is free who is a slave to his body. Indeed, omitting all the other masters which are brought into being by excessive care for the body, the sway which the body itself exercises is captious and fastidious. **34.** Forth from this body the soul issues, now with unruffled spirit, now with exultation, and, when once it has gone forth, asks not what shall be the end of the deserted day. No; just as we do not take thought for the clippings of the hair and the beard, even so that divine soul, when it is about to issue forth from the mortal man, regards the destination of its earthly vessel – whether it be consumed by fire, or shut in by a stone, or buried in the earth, or torn by wild beasts – as being of no more concern to itself than is the afterbirth to a child just born. And whether this body shall be cast out and plucked to pieces by birds, or devoured when

> thrown to the sea-dogs as prey,

how does that concern him who is nothing? **35.** Nay even when it is among the living, the soul fears nothing that may happen to the body after death; for though such things may have been threats, they were not enough to terrify the soul previous to the moment of death. It says; "I am not frightened by the executioner's hook, nor by the revolting mutilation of the corpse which is exposed to the scorn of those who would witness the spectacle. I ask no man to perform the last rites for me; I entrust my remains to none. Nature has made provision that none shall go unburied. Time will lay away one whom cruelty has cast forth." Those were eloquent words which Maecenas uttered:

> I want no tomb; for Nature doth provide
> For outcast bodies burial.

You would imagine that this was the saying of a man of strict principles. He was indeed a man of noble and robust native gifts, but in prosperity he impaired these gifts by laxness. Farewell.

XCIII. ON THE QUALITY, AS CONTRASTED WITH THE LENGTH, OF LIFE

1. While reading the letter in which you were lamenting the death of the philosopher Metronax as if he might have, and indeed ought to have, lived longer, I missed the spirit of fairness which abounds in all your discussions concerning men and things, but is lacking when you approach one single subject, – as is indeed the case with us all. In other words, I have noticed many who deal fairly with their fellow-men, but none who deals fairly with the gods. We rail every day at Fate, saying "Why has A. been carried off in the very middle of his career? Why is not B. carried off instead? Why should he prolong his old age, which is a burden to himself as well as to others?"

2. But tell me, pray, do you consider it fairer that you should obey Nature, or that Nature should obey you? And what difference does it make how soon you depart from a place which you must depart from sooner or later? We should strive, not to live long, but to live rightly; for to achieve long life you have need of Fate only, but for right living you need the soul. A life is really long if it is a full life; but fullness is not attained until the soul has rendered to itself its proper Good, that is, until it has assumed control over itself. **3.** What benefit does this older man derive from the eighty years he has spent in idleness? A person like him has not lived; he has merely tarried awhile in life. Nor has he died late in life; he has simply been a long time dying. He has lived eighty years, has he? That depends upon the date from which you reckon his death! Your other friend, however, departed in the bloom of his manhood. **4.** But he had fulfilled all the duties of a good citizen, a good friend, a good son; in no respect had he fallen short. His age may have been incomplete, but his life was complete. The other man has lived eighty years, has he? Nay, he has existed eighty years, unless perchance you mean by "he has lived" what we mean when we say that a tree "lives."

Pray, let us see to it, my dear Lucilius, that our lives, like jewels of great price, be noteworthy not because of their width but because of their weight. Let us measure them by their performance, not by their duration. Would you know wherein lies the difference between this hardy man who, despising Fortune, has served through every campaign of life and has attained to life's Supreme Good, and that other person over whose head many years have passed? The former exists even after his death; the latter has died even before he was dead.

5. We should therefore praise, and number in the company of the blest, that man who has invested well the portion of time, however little, that has been allotted to him; for such a one has seen the true light. He has not been one of the common herd. He has not only lived, but flourished. Sometimes he enjoyed fair skies; sometimes, as often happens, it was only through the clouds that there flashed to him the radiance of the mighty star. Why do you ask: "How long did he live?" He still lives! At one bound he has passed over into posterity and has consigned himself to the guardianship of memory.

6. And yet I would not on that account decline for myself a few additional years; although, if my life's space be shortened, I shall not say that I have lacked aught that is essential to a happy life. For I have not planned to live up to the very last day that my greedy hopes had promised me; nay, I have looked upon every day as if it were my last. Why ask the date of my birth, or whether I am still enrolled on the register of the younger men? What I have is my own. **7.** Just as one of small stature can be a perfect man, so a life of small compass can be a perfect life. Age ranks among the external things. How long I am to exist is not mine to decide, but how long I shall go on existing in my present way is in my own control. This is the only thing you have the right to require of me, – that I shall cease to measure out an inglorious age as it were in darkness, and devote myself to living instead of being carried along past life.

8. And what, you ask, is the fullest span of life? It is living until you possess wisdom. He who has attained wisdom has reached, not the furthermost, but the most important, goal. Such a one may indeed exult boldly and give thanks to the gods – aye, and to himself also – and he may count himself Nature's creditor for having lived. He will indeed have the right to do so, for he has paid her back a better life than he has received. He has set up the pattern of a good man, showing the quality and the greatness of a good man. Had another year been added, it would merely have been like the past.

9. And yet how long are we to keep living? We have had the joy of learning the truth about the universe. We know from what beginnings Nature arises; how she orders the course of the heavens; by what successive changes she summons back the year; how she has brought to an end all things that ever have been, and has established herself as the only end of her own being. We know that the stars move by their own motion, and that nothing except the earth stands still, while all the other bodies run on with uninterrupted swiftness. We know how the moon outstrips the sun; why it is that the slower leaves the swifter behind; in what manner she receives her light, or loses it again; what brings on the night, and what brings back the day. To that place you must go where you are to have a closer view of all these things. 10. "And yet," says the wise man, "I do not depart more valiantly because of this hope – because I judge the path lies clear before me to my own gods. I have indeed earned admission to their presence, and in fact have already been in their company; I have sent my soul to them as they had previously sent theirs to me. But suppose that I am utterly annihilated, and that after death nothing mortal remains; I have no less courage, even if, when I depart, my course leads – nowhere."

"But," you say, "he has not lived as many years as he might have lived." 11. There are books which contain very few lines, admirable and useful in spite of their size; and there are also the *Annals of Tanusius* – you know how bulky the book is, and what men say of it. This is the case with the long life of certain persons, – a state which resembles the *Annals of Tanusius*! 12. Do you regard as more fortunate the fighter who is slain on the last day of the games than one who goes to his death in the middle of the festivities? Do you believe that anyone is so foolishly covetous of life that he would rather have his throat cut in the dressing-room than in the amphitheatre? It is by no longer an interval than this that we precede one another. Death visits each and all; the slayer soon follows the slain. It is an insignificant trifle, after all, that people discuss with so much concern. And anyhow, what does it matter for how long a time you avoid that which you cannot escape? Farewell.

XCIV. ON THE VALUE OF ADVICE

1. That department of philosophy which supplies precepts appropriate to the individual case, instead of framing them for mankind at large – which, for instance, advises how a husband should conduct himself towards his wife, or how a father should bring up his children, or how a master should rule his slaves – this department of philosophy, I say, is accepted by some as the only significant part, while the other departments are rejected on the ground that they stray beyond the sphere of practical needs – as if any man could give advice concerning a portion of life without having first gained a knowledge of the sum of life as a whole!

2. But Aristo the Stoic, on the contrary, believes the above-mentioned department to be of slight import – he holds that it does not sink into the mind, having in it nothing but old wives' precepts, and that the greatest benefit is derived from the actual dogmas of philosophy and from the definition of the Supreme Good. When a man has gained a complete understanding of this definition and has thoroughly learned it, he can frame for himself a precept directing what is to be done in a given case. 3. Just as the student of javelin-throwing keeps aiming at a fixed target and thus trains the hand to give direction to the missile, and when, by instruction and practice, he has gained the desired ability he can then employ it against any target he wishes (having learned to strike not any random object, but precisely the object at which he has aimed), – he who has equipped himself for the whole of life does not need to be advised concerning each separate item, because he is now trained to meet his problem as a whole; for he knows not merely how he should live with his wife or his son, but how he should live aright. In this knowledge there is also included the proper way of living with wife and children.

4. Cleanthes holds that this department of wisdom is indeed useful, but that it is a feeble thing unless it is derived from general principles – that is, unless it is based upon a knowledge of the actual dogmas of philosophy and its main headings. This subject is therefore twofold, leading to two separate lines of inquiry: first, Is it useful or useless? and, and second, can it of itself produce a good man? – in other words, Is it superfluous, or does it render all other departments superfluous?

5. Those who urge the view that this department is superfluous argue as follows: "If an object that is held in front of the eyes interferes with the vision, it must be removed. For just as long as it is in the way, it is a waste of time to offer such precepts as these: 'Walk thus and so; extend your hand in that direction.' Similarly, when something blinds a man's soul and hinders it from seeing a line of duty clearly, there is no use in advising him: 'Live thus and so with your father, thus and so with your wife.' For precepts will be of no avail while the mind is clouded with error; only when the cloud is dispersed will it be clear what one's duty is in each case. Otherwise, you will merely be showing the sick man what he ought to do if he were well, instead of making him well. 6. Suppose you are trying to reveal to the poor man the art of 'acting rich'; how can the thing be accomplished as long as his poverty is unaltered?

You are trying to make clear to a starveling in what manner he is to act the part of one with a well-filled stomach; the first requisite, however, is to relieve him of the hunger that grips his vitals.

"The same thing, I assure you, holds good of all faults; the faults themselves must be removed, and precepts should not be given which cannot possibly be carried out while the faults remain. Unless you drive out the false opinions under which we suffer, the miser will never receive instruction as to the proper use of his money, nor the coward regarding the way to scorn danger. **7.** You must make the miser know that money is neither a good nor an evil; show him men of wealth who are miserable to the last degree. You must make the coward know that the things which generally frighten us out of our wits are less to be feared than rumour advertises them to be, whether the object of fear be suffering or death; that when death comes – fixed by law for us all to suffer – it is often a great solace to reflect that it can never come again; that in the midst of suffering resoluteness of soul will be as good as a cure, for the soul renders lighter any burden that it endures with stubborn defiance. Remember that pain has this most excellent quality: if prolonged it cannot be severe, and if severe it cannot be prolonged; and that we should bravely accept whatever commands the inevitable laws of the universe lay upon us.

8. "When by means of such doctrines you have brought the erring man to a sense of his own condition, when he has learned that the happy life is not that which conforms to pleasure, but that which conforms to Nature, when he has fallen deeply in love with virtue as man's sole good and has avoided baseness as man's sole evil, and when he knows that all other things – riches, office, health, strength, dominion – fall in between and are not to be reckoned either among goods or among evils, then he will not need a monitor for every separate action, to say to him: 'Walk thus and so, eat thus and so. This is the conduct proper for a man and that for a woman; this for a married man and that for a bachelor.' **9.** Indeed, the persons who take the greatest pains to proffer such advice are themselves unable to put it into practice. It is thus that the pedagogue advises the boy, and the grandmother her grandson; it is the hottest-tempered schoolmaster who contends that one should never lose one's temper. Go into an elementary school, and you will learn that just such pronouncements, emanating from high-browed philosophers, are to be found in the lesson-book for boys!

10. "Shall you then offer precepts that are clear, or precepts that are doubtful? Those which are clear need no counsellor, and doubtful precepts gain no credence; so the giving of precepts is superfluous. Indeed you should study the problem in this way: if you are counselling someone on a matter which is of doubtful clearness and doubtful meaning, you must supplement your precepts by proofs; and if you must resort to proofs, your means of proof are more effective and more satisfactory in themselves. **11.** 'It is thus that you must treat your friend, thus your fellow citizen, thus your associate.' And why? 'Because it is just.' Yet I can find all that material included under the head of Justice. I find there that fair play is desirable in itself, that we are not forced into it by fear nor hired to that end for pay, and that no man is just who is attracted by anything in this virtue other than the virtue itself. After convincing myself of this view and thoroughly absorbing it, what good can I obtain from such precepts, which only teach one who is already trained? To one who knows, it is superfluous to give precepts; to one who does not know, it is insufficient. For he must be told, not only what he is being instructed to do, but also why. **12.** I repeat, are such precepts useful to him who has correct ideas about good and evil, or to one who has them not? The latter will receive no benefit from you; for some idea that clashes with your counsel has already monopolized his attention. He who has made a careful decision as to what should be sought and what should be avoided knows what he ought to do, without a single word from you. Therefore, that whole department of philosophy may be abolished.

13. "There are two reasons why we go astray: either there is in the soul an evil quality which has been brought about by wrong opinions, or, even if not possessed by false ideas, the soul is prone to falsehood and rapidly corrupted by some outward appearance which attracts it in the wrong direction. For this reason it is our duty either to treat carefully the diseased mind and free it from faults, or to take possession of the mind when it is still unoccupied and yet inclined to what is evil. Both these results can be attained by the main doctrines of philosophy; therefore the giving of such precepts is of no use. **14.** Besides, if we give forth precepts to each individual, the task is stupendous. For one class of advice should be given to the financier, another to the farmer, another to the business man, another to one who cultivates the good graces of royalty, another to him who will seek the friendship of his equals, another to him who will court those of lower rank. **15.** In the case of marriage, you will advise one person how he should conduct himself with a wife who before her marriage was a maiden, and another how he should behave with a woman who had previously been wedded to another; how the husband of a rich woman should act, or another man with a dowerless spouse. Or do you not think that there is some difference between a barren woman and one who bears children, between one advanced in years and a mere girl, between a mother and a step-mother? We cannot include all the types, and yet each type requires separate treatment; but the laws of philosophy are concise and are binding in all cases. **16.** Moreover, the precepts of wisdom should be definite and certain: when things cannot be defined, they are outside the sphere of wisdom; for wisdom knows the proper limits of things.

"We should therefore do away with this department of precepts, because it cannot afford to all what it promises only to a few; wisdom, however, embraces all. **17.** Between the insanity of people in general and the insanity which is subject to medical treatment there is no difference, except that the latter is suffering from disease and the former from false opinions. In the one case, the symptoms of madness may be traced to ill-health; the other is the ill-health of the mind. If one should offer precepts to a madman – how he ought to speak, how he ought to walk, how he ought to conduct himself in public and private, he would be more of a lunatic than the person whom he was advising. What is really necessary is to treat the black bile and remove the essential cause of the madness. And this is what should also be done in the other case – that of the mind diseased. The madness itself must be shaken off; otherwise, your words of advice will vanish into thin air."

18. This is what Aristo says; and I shall answer his arguments one by one. First, in opposition to what he says about one's obligation to remove that which blocks the eye and hinders the vision. I admit that such a person does not need precepts in order to see, but that he needs treatment for the curing of his eyesight and the getting rid of the hindrance that handicaps him. For it is Nature that gives us our eyesight; and he who removes obstacles restores to Nature her proper function. But Nature does not teach us our duty in every case. 19. Again, if a man's cataract is cured, he cannot, immediately after his recovery, give back their eyesight to other men also; but when we are freed from evil we can free others also. There is no need of encouragement, or even of counsel, for the eye to be able to distinguish different colours; black and white can be differentiated without prompting from another. The mind, on the other hand, needs many precepts in order to see what it should do in life; although in eye-treatment also the physician not only accomplishes the cure, but gives advice into the bargain. 20. He says: "There is no reason why you should at once expose your weak vision to a dangerous glare; begin with darkness, and then go into half-lights, and finally be more bold, accustoming yourself gradually to the bright light of day. There is no reason why you should study immediately after eating; there is no reason why you should impose hard tasks upon your eyes when they are swollen and inflamed; avoid winds and strong blasts of cold air that blow into your face," – and other suggestions of the same sort, which are just as valuable as drugs themselves. The physician's art supplements remedies by advice.

21. "But," comes the reply, "error is the source of sin; precepts do not remove error, nor do they rout our false opinions on the subject of Good and Evil." I admit that precepts alone are not effective in overthrowing the mind's mistaken beliefs; but they do not on that account fail to be of service when they accompany other measures also. In the first place, they refresh the memory; in the second place, when sorted into their proper classes, the matters which showed themselves in a jumbled mass when considered as a whole, can be considered in this with greater care. According to our opponents theory, you might even say that consolation, and exhortation were superfluous. Yet they are not superfluous; neither, therefore, is counsel.

22. "But it is folly," they retort, "to prescribe what a sick man ought to do, just as if he were well, when you should really restore his health; for without health precepts are not worth a jot." But have not sick men and sound men something in common, concerning which they need continual advice? For example, not to grasp greedily after food, and to avoid getting over-tired. Poor and rich have certain precepts which fit them both. 23. "Cure their greed, then," people say, "and you will

not need to lecture either the poor or the rich, provided that in the case of each of them the craving has subsided." But is it not one thing to be free from lust for money, and another thing to know how to use this money? Misers do not know the proper limits in money matters, but even those who are not misers fail to comprehend its use. Then comes the reply: "Do away with error, and your precepts become unnecessary." That is wrong; for suppose that avarice is slackened, that luxury is confined, that rashness is reined in, and that laziness is pricked by the spur; even after vices are removed, we must continue to learn what we ought to do, and how we ought to do it.

24. "Nothing," it is said, "will be accomplished by applying advice to the more serious faults." No; and not even medicine can master incurable diseases; it is nevertheless used in some cases as a remedy, in others as a relief. Not even the power of universal philosophy, though it summon all its strength for the purpose, will remove from the soul what is now a stubborn and chronic disease. But Wisdom, merely because she cannot cure everything, is not incapable of making cures. **25.** People say: "What good does it do to point out the obvious?" A great deal of good; for we sometimes know facts without paying attention to them. Advice is not teaching; it merely engages the attention and rouses us, and concentrates the memory, and keeps it from losing grip. We miss much that is set before our very eyes. Advice is, in fact, a sort of exhortation. The mind often tries not to notice even that which lies before our eyes; we must therefore force upon it the knowledge of things that are perfectly well known. One might repeat here the saying of Calvus about Vatinius: "You all know that bribery has been going on, and everyone knows that you know it." **26.** You know that friendship should be scrupulously honoured, and yet you do not hold it in honour. You know that a man does wrong in requiring chastity of his wife while he himself is intriguing with the wives of other men; you know that, as your wife should have no dealings with a lover, neither should you yourself with a mistress; and yet you do not act accordingly. Hence, you must be continually brought to remember these facts; for they should not be in storage, but ready for use. And whatever is wholesome should be often discussed and often brought before the mind, so that it may be not only familiar to us, but also ready to hand. And remember, too, that in this way what is clear often becomes clearer.

27. "But if," comes the answer, "your precepts are not obvious, you will be bound to add proofs; hence the proofs, and not the precepts, will be helpful." But cannot the influence of the monitor avail even without proofs? It is like the opinions of a legal expert, which hold good even though the reasons for them are not delivered. Moreover, the precepts which are given are of great weight in themselves, whether they be woven into the fabric of song, or condensed into prose proverbs, like the famous *Wisdom of Cato* "Buy not what you need, but what you must have. That which you do not need, is dear even at a farthing." Or those oracular or oracular-like replies, such as **28.** "Be thrifty with time!" "Know thyself!" Shall you need to be told the meaning when someone repeats to you lines like these:

Forgetting trouble is the way to cure it.

Fortune favours the brave, but the coward is foiled by his faint heart.

Such maxims need no special pleader; they go straight to our emotions, and help us simply because Nature is exercising her proper function. **29.** The soul carries within itself the seed of everything that is honourable, and this seed is stirred to growth by advice, as a spark that is fanned by a gentle breeze develops its natural fire. Virtue is aroused by a touch, a shock. Moreover, there are certain things which, though in the mind, yet are not ready to hand but begin to function easily as soon as they are put into words. Certain things lie scattered about in various places, and it is impossible for the unpractised mind to arrange them in order. Therefore, we should bring them into unity, and join them, so that they may be more powerful and more of an uplift to the soul. **30.** Or, if precepts do not avail at all, then every method of instruction should be abolished, and we should be content with Nature alone.

Those who maintain this view do not understand that one man is lively and alert of wit, another sluggish and dull, while certainly some men have more intelligence than others. The strength of the wit is nourished and kept growing by precepts; it adds new points of view to those which are inborn and corrects depraved ideas. **31.** "But suppose," people retort, "that a man is not the possessor of sound dogmas, how can advice help him when he is chained down by vicious dogmas?" In this, assuredly, that he is freed there-from; for his natural disposition has not been crushed, but over-shadowed and kept down. Even so it goes on endeavouring to rise again, struggling against the influences that make for evil; but when it wins support and receives the aid of precepts, it grows stronger, provided only that the chronic trouble has not corrupted or annihilated the natural man. For in such a case, not even the training that comes from philosophy, striving with all its might, will make restoration. What difference, indeed, – is there between the dogmas of philosophy and precepts, unless it be this – that the former are general and the latter special? Both deal with advice – the one through the universal, the other through the particular.

32. Some say: "If one is familiar with upright and honourable dogmas, it will be superfluous to advise him." By no means; for this person has indeed learned to do things which he ought to do; but he does not see with sufficient clearness what these things are. For we are hindered from accomplishing praiseworthy deeds not only by our emotions, but also by want of practice in discovering the demands of a particular situation. Our minds are often under good control, and yet at the same time are inactive and untrained in finding the path of duty, – and advice makes this clear. **33.** Again, it is written: "Cast out all false opinions concerning Good and Evil, but replace them with true opinions; then advice will have no function to perform." Order in the soul can doubtless be established in this way; but these are not the only ways. For although we may infer by proofs just what Good and

Evil are, nevertheless precepts have their proper rôle. Prudence and justice consist of certain duties; and duties are set in order by precepts. 34. Moreover, judgment as to Good and Evil is itself strengthened by following up our duties, and precepts conduct us to this end. For both are in accord with each other; nor can precepts take the lead unless the duties follow. They observe their natural order; hence precepts clearly come first.

35. "Precepts," it is said "are numberless." Wrong again! For they are not numberless so far as concerns important and essential things. Of course there are slight distinctions, due to the time, or the place, or the person; but even in these cases, precepts are given which have a general application. 36. "No one, however," it is said, "cures madness by precepts, and therefore not wickedness either." There is a distinction; for if you rid a man of insanity, he becomes sane again, but if we have removed false opinions, insight into practical conduct does not at once follow. Even though it follows, counsel will none the less confirm one's right opinion concerning Good and Evil. And it is also wrong to believe that precepts are of no use to madmen. For though, by themselves, they are of no avail, yet they are a help towards the cure. Both scolding and chastening rein in a lunatic. Note that I here refer to lunatics whose wits are disturbed but not hopelessly gone.

37. "Still," it is objected, "laws do not always make us do what we ought to do; and what else are laws than precepts mingled with threats?" Now first of all, the laws do not persuade just because they threaten; precepts, however, instead of coercing, correct men by pleading. Again, laws frighten one out of communicating crime, while precepts urge a man on to his duty. Besides, the laws also are of assistance towards good conduct, at any rate if they instruct as well as command. 38. On this point I disagree with Posidonius, who says: "I do not think that Plato's *Laws* should have the preambles added to them. For a law should be brief, in order that the uninitiated may grasp it all the more easily. It should be a voice, as it were, sent down from heaven; it should command, not discuss. Nothing seems to me more dull or more foolish than a law with a preamble. Warn me, tell me what you wish me to do; I am not learning but obeying." But laws framed in this way are helpful; hence you will notice that a state with defective laws will have defective morals. 39. "But," it is said, "they are not of avail in every case." Well neither is philosophy; and yet philosophy is not on that account ineffectual and useless in the training of the soul. Furthermore, is not philosophy the Law of Life? Grant, if we will, that the laws do not avail; it does not necessarily follow that advice also should not avail. On this ground, you ought to say that consolation does not avail, and warning, and exhortation, and scolding, and praising; since they are all varieties of advice. It is by such methods that we arrive at a perfect condition of mind. 40. Nothing is more successful in bringing honourable influences to bear upon the mind, or in straightening out the wavering spirit that is prone to evil, than association with good men. For the frequent seeing, the frequent hearing of them little by little sinks into the heart and acquires the force of precepts.

We are indeed uplifted merely by meeting wise men; and one can be helped by a great man even when he is silent. **41.** I could not easily tell you how it helps us, though I am certain of the fact that I have received help in that way. Phaedo says: "Certain tiny animals do not leave any pain when they sting us; so subtle is their power, so deceptive for purposes of harm. The bite is disclosed by a swelling, and even in the swelling there is no visible wound." That will also be your experience when dealing with wise men, you will not discover how or when the benefit comes to you, but you will discover that you have received it. **42.** "What is the point of this remark?" you ask. It is, that good precepts, often welcomed within you, will benefit you just as much as good examples. Pythagoras declares that our souls experience a change when we enter a temple and behold the images of the gods face to face, and await the utterances of an oracle. **43.** Moreover, who can deny that even the most inexperienced are effectively struck by the force of certain precepts? For example, by such brief but weighty saws as: "Nothing in excess," "The greedy mind is satisfied by no gains," "You must expect to be treated by others as you yourself have treated them." We receive a sort if shock when we hear such sayings; no one ever thinks of doubting them or of asking "Why?" So strongly, indeed, does mere truth, unaccompanied by reason, attract us. **44.** If reverence reins in the soul and checks vice, why cannot counsel do the same? Also, if rebuke gives one a sense of shame, why has not counsel the same power, even though it does use bare precepts? The counsel which assists suggestion by reason – which adds the motive for doing a given thing and the reward which awaits one who carries out and obeys such precepts is – more effective and settles deeper into the heart. If commands are helpful, so is advice. But one is helped by commands; therefore one is helped also by advice.

45. Virtue is divided into two parts – into contemplation of truth, and conduct. Training teaches contemplation, and admonition teaches conduct. And right conduct both practises and reveals virtue. But if, when a man is about to act, he is helped by advice, he is also helped by admonition. Therefore, if right conduct is necessary to virtue, and if, moreover, admonition makes clear right conduct, then admonition also is an indispensable thing. **46.** There are two strong supports to the soul – trust in the truth and confidence; both are the result of admonition. For men believe it, and when belief is established, the soul receives great inspiration and is filled with confidence. Therefore, admonition is not superfluous.

Marcus Agrippa, a great-souled man, the only person among those whom the civil wars raised to fame and power whose prosperity helped the state, used to say that he was greatly indebted to the proverb "Harmony makes small things grow; lack of harmony makes great things decay." **47.** He held that he himself became the best of brothers and the best of friends by virtue of this saying. And if proverbs of such a kind, when welcomed intimately into the soul, can mould this very soul, why cannot the department of philosophy which consists of such proverbs possess equal influence? Virtue depends partly upon training and partly upon practice; you must learn first, and then strengthen your learning by action. If this be true, not only do the doctrines of wisdom help us but the precepts also, which check and banish our emotions by a sort of official decree.

48. It is said: "Philosophy is divided into knowledge and state of mind. For one who has learned and understood what he should do and avoid, is not a wise man until his mind is metamorphosed into the shape of that which he has learned. This third department – that of precept – is compounded from both the others, from dogmas of philosophy and state of mind. Hence it is superfluous as far as the perfecting of virtue is concerned; the other two parts are enough for the purpose." **49.** On that basis, therefore, even consolation would be superfluous, since this also is a combination of the other two, as likewise are exhortation, persuasion, and even proof itself. For proof also originates from a well-ordered and firm mental attitude. But, although these things result from a sound state of mind, yet the sound state of mind also results from them; it is both creative of them and resultant from them. **50.** Furthermore, that which you mention is the mark of an already perfect man, of one who has attained the height of human happiness. But the approach to these qualities is slow, and in the meantime in practical matters, the path should be pointed out for the benefit of one who is still short of perfection, but is making progress. Wisdom by her own agency may perhaps show herself this path without the help of admonition; for she has brought the soul to a stage where it can be impelled only in the right direction. Weaker characters, however, need someone to precede them, to say: "Avoid this," or "Do that." **51.** Moreover, if one awaits the time when one can know of oneself what the best line of action is, one will sometimes go astray and by going astray will be hindered from arriving at the point where it is possible to be content with oneself. The soul should accordingly be guided at the very moment when it is becoming able to guide itself. Boys study according to direction. Their fingers are held and guided by others so that they may follow the outlines of the letters; next, they are ordered to imitate a copy and base thereon a style of penmanship. Similarly, the mind is helped if it is taught according to direction. **52.** Such facts as these prove that this department of philosophy is not superfluous.

The question next arises whether this part alone is sufficient to make men wise. The problem shall be treated at the proper time; but at present, omitting all arguments, is it not clear that we need someone whom we may call upon as our preceptor in opposition to the precepts of men in general? **53.** There is no word which reaches our ears without doing us harm; we are injured both by good wishes and by curses. The angry prayers of our enemies instil false fears in us; and the affection of our friends spoils us through their kindly wishes. For this affection sets us a-groping after goods that are far away, unsure, and wavering, when we really might open the store of happiness at home. **54.** We are not allowed, I maintain, to travel a straight road. Our parents and our slaves draw us into wrong. Nobody confines his mistakes to himself; people sprinkle folly among their neighbours, and receive it from them in turn. For this reason, in an individual, you find the vices of nations, because the nation has given them to the individual. Each man, in corrupting others, corrupts himself; he imbibes, and then imparts, badness the result is a vast mass of wickedness, because the worst in every separate person is concentrated in one mass.

55. We should, therefore, have a guardian, as it were, to pluck us continually by the ear and dispel rumours and protest against popular enthusiasms. For you are mistaken if you suppose that our faults are inborn in us; they have come from without, have been heaped upon us. Hence, by receiving frequent admonitions, we can reject the opinions which din about our ears. **56.** Nature does not ally us with any vice; she produced us in health and freedom. She put before our eyes no object which might stir in us the itch of greed. She placed gold and silver beneath our feet, and bade those feet stamp down and crush everything that causes us to be stamped down and crushed. Nature elevated our gaze towards the sky and willed that we should look upward to behold her glorious and wonderful works. She gave us the rising and the setting sun, the whirling course of the on-rushing world which discloses the things of earth by day and the heavenly bodies by night, the movements of the stars, which are slow if you compare them with the universe, but most rapid if you reflect on the size of the orbits which they describe with unslackened speed; she showed us the successive eclipses of sun and moon, and other phenomena, wonderful because they occur regularly or because, through sudden causes they help into view – such as nightly trails of fire, or flashes in the open heavens unaccompanied by stroke or sound of thunder, or columns and beams and the various phenomena of flames. **57.** She ordained that all these bodies should proceed above our heads; but gold and silver, with the iron which, because of the gold and silver, never brings peace, she has hidden away, as if they were dangerous things to trust to our keeping. It is we ourselves that have dragged them into the light of day to the end that we might fight over them; it is we ourselves who, tearing away the superincumbent earth, have dug out the causes and tools of our own destruction; it is we ourselves who have attributed our own misdeeds to Fortune, and do not blush to regard as the loftiest objects those which once lay in the depths of earth. **58.** Do you wish to know how false is the gleam that has deceived your eyes? There is really nothing fouler or more involved in darkness than these things of earth, sunk and covered for so long a time in the mud where they belong. Of course they are foul; they have been hauled out through a long and murky mine-shaft. There is nothing uglier than these metals during the process of refinement and separation from the ore. Furthermore, watch the very workmen who must handle and sift the barren grade of dirt, the sort which comes from the bottom; see how soot-besmeared they are! **59.** And yet the stuff they handle soils the soul more than the body, and there is more foulness in the owner than in the workman.

It is therefore indispensable that we be admonished, that we have some advocate with upright mind, and, amid all the uproar and jangle of falsehood, hear one voice only. But what voice shall this be? Surely a voice which, amid all the tumult of self-seeking, shall whisper wholesome words into the deafened ear, saying: **60.** "You need not be envious of those whom the people call great and fortunate; applause need not disturb your composed attitude and your sanity of mind; you need not become disgusted with your calm spirit because you see a great man, clothed in purple, protected by the well-known symbols of authority; you need not judge the magistrate for whom the road is cleared to be any happier than yourself, whom his officer pushes from the road. If you would wield a command that is profitable to yourself, and injurious to nobody, clear your own faults out of the way. **61.** There are many who set fire to cities, who storm garrisons that have remained impregnable for generations and safe for numerous ages, who raise mounds as high as the walls they are besieging, who with battering-rams and engines shatter towers that have been reared to a wondrous height. There are many who can send their columns ahead and press destructively upon the rear of the foe, who can reach the Great Sea dripping with the blood of nations; but even these men, before they could conquer their foe, were conquered by their own greed. No one withstood their attack; but they themselves could not withstand desire for power and the impulse to cruelty; at the time when they seemed to be hounding others, they were themselves being hounded. **62.** Alexander was hounded into misfortune and dispatched to unknown countries by a mad desire to lay waste other men's territory. Do you believe that the man was in his senses who could begin by devastating Greece, the land where he received his education? One who snatched away the dearest guerdon of each nation, bidding Spartans be slaves, and Athenians hold their tongues? Not content with the ruin of all the states which Philip had either conquered or bribed into bondage, he overthrew various commonwealths in various places and carried his weapons all over the world; his cruelty was tired, but it never ceased – like a wild beast that tears to pieces more than its hunger demands. **63.** Already he has joined many kingdoms into one kingdom; already Greeks and Persians fear the same lord; already nations Darius had left free submit to the yoke: yet he passes beyond the Ocean and the Sun, deeming it shame that he should shift his course of victory from the paths which Hercules and Bacchus had trod; he threatens violence to Nature herself. He does not wish to go; but he cannot stay; he is like a weight that falls headlong, its course ending only when it lies motionless.

64. It was not virtue or reason which persuaded Gnaeus Pompeius to take part in foreign and civil warfare; it was his mad craving for unreal glory. Now he attacked Spain and the faction of Sertorius; now he fared forth to enchain the pirates and subdue the seas. These were merely excuses and pretexts for extending his power. **65.** What drew him into Africa, into the North, against Mithridates, into Armenia and all the corners of Asia? Assuredly it was his boundless desire to grow bigger; for only in his own eyes was he not great enough. And what impelled Gaius Caesar to the combined ruin of himself and of the state? Renown, self-seeking, and the setting no limit to pre-eminence over all other men. He could not allow a single person to outrank him, although the state allowed two men to stand at its head. **66.** Do you think that Gaius Marius, who was once consul (he received this office on one occasion, and stole it on all the others) courted all his perils by the inspiration of virtue when he was slaughtering the Teutons and the Cimbri, and pursuing Jugurtha through the wilds of Africa? Marius commanded armies, ambition Marius.

67. When such men as these were disturbing the world, they were themselves disturbed – like cyclones that whirl together what they have seized, but which are first whirled themselves and can for this reason rush on with all the greater force, having no control over themselves; hence, after causing such destruction to others, they feel in their own body the ruinous force which has enabled them to cause havoc to many. You need never believe that a man can become happy through the unhappiness of another. 68. We must unravel all such cases as are forced before our eyes and crammed into our ears; we must clear out our hearts, for they are full of evil talk. Virtue must be conducted into the place these have seized, – a kind of virtue which may root out falsehood and doctrines which contravene the truth, or may sunder us from the throng, in which we put too great trust, and may restore us to the possession of sound opinions. For this is wisdom – a return to Nature and a restoration to the condition from which man's errors have driven us. 69. It is a great part of health to have forsaken the counsellors of madness and to have fled far from a companionship that is mutually baneful.

That you may know the truth of my remark, see how different is each individual's life before the public from that of his inner self. A quiet life does not of itself give lessons in upright conduct; the countryside does not of itself teach plain living; no, but when witnesses and onlookers are removed, faults which ripen in publicity and display sink into the background. 70. Who puts on the purple robe for the sake of flaunting it in no man's eyes? Who uses gold plate when he dines alone? Who, as he flings himself down beneath the shadow of some rustic tree, displays in solitude the splendour of his luxury? No one makes himself elegant only for his own beholding, or even for the admiration of a few friends or relatives. Rather does he spread out his well-appointed vices in proportion to the size of the admiring crowd. 71. It is so: claqueurs and witnesses are irritants of all our mad foibles. You can make us cease to crave, if you only make us cease to display. Ambition, luxury, and waywardness need a stage to act upon; you will cure all those ills if you seek retirement.

72. Therefore, if our dwelling is situated amid the din of a city, there should be an adviser standing near us. When men praise great incomes, he should praise the person who can be rich with a slender estate and measures his wealth by the use he makes of it. In the face of those who glorify influence and power, he should of his own volition recommend a leisure devoted to study, and a soul which has left the external and found itself. 73. He should point out persons, happy in the popular estimation, who totter on their envied heights of power, who are dismayed and hold a far different opinion of themselves from what others hold of them. That which others think elevated, is to them a sheer precipice. Hence they are frightened and in a flutter whenever they look down the abrupt steep of their greatness. For they reflect that there are various

ways of falling and that the topmost point is the most slippery. **74.** Then they fear that for which they strove, and the good fortune which made them weighty in the eyes of others weighs more heavily upon themselves. Then they praise easy leisure and independence; they hate the glamour and try to escape while their fortunes are still unimpaired. Then at last you may see them studying philosophy amid their fear, and hunting sound advice when their fortunes go awry. For these two things are, as it were, at opposite poles – good fortune and good sense; that is why we are wiser when in the midst of adversity. It is prosperity that takes away righteousness. Farewell.

XCV. ON THE USEFULNESS OF BASIC PRINCIPLES

1. You keep asking me to explain without postponement a topic which I once remarked should be put off until the proper time, and to inform you by letter whether this department of philosophy which the Greeks call *paraenetic*, and we Romans call the "preceptorial," is enough to give us perfect wisdom. Now I know that you will take it in good part if I refuse to do so. But I accept your request all the more willingly, and refuse to let the common saying lose its point:

> Don't ask for what you'll wish you hadn't got.

2. For sometimes we seek with effort that which we should decline if offered voluntarily. Call that fickleness or call it pettishness, – we must punish the habit by ready compliance. There are many things that we would have men think that we wish, but that we really do not wish. A lecturer sometimes brings upon the platform a huge work of research, written in the tiniest hand and very closely folded; after reading off a large portion, he says: "I shall stop, if you wish;" and a shout arises: "Read on, read on!" from the lips of those who are anxious for the speaker to hold his peace then and there. We often want one thing and pray for another, not telling the truth even to the gods, while the gods either do not hearken, or else take pity on us. **3.** But I shall without pity avenge myself and shall load a huge letter upon your shoulders; for your part, if you read it with reluctance, you may say: "I brought this burden upon myself," and may class yourself among those men whose too ambitious wives drive them frantic, or those whom riches harass, earned by extreme sweat of the brow, or those who are tortured with the titles which they have sought by every sort of device and toil, and all others who are responsible for their own misfortunes.

4. But I must stop this preamble and approach the problem under consideration. Men say: "The happy life consists in upright conduct; precepts guide one to upright conduct; therefore precepts are sufficient for attaining the happy life." But they do not always guide us to upright conduct; this occurs only when the will is receptive; and sometimes they are applied in vain, when wrong opinions obsess the soul. **5.** Furthermore, a man may act rightly without knowing that he is acting rightly. For nobody, except he be trained from the start and equipped with complete reason, can develop to perfect proportions, understanding when he should do certain things, and to what extent, and in whose company, and how, and why. Without such training a man cannot strive with all his heart after that which is honourable, or even with steadiness or gladness, but will ever be looking back and wavering.

6. It is also said: "If honourable conduct results from precepts, then precepts are amply sufficient for the happy life; but the first of these statements is true; therefore the second is true also." We shall reply to these words that honourable conduct is, to be sure, brought about by precepts, but not by precepts alone. **7.** "Then," comes the reply, "if the other arts are content with precepts, wisdom will also be content therewith; for wisdom itself is an art of living. And yet the pilot is made by precepts which tell him thus and so to turn the tiller, set his sails, make use of a fair wind, tack, make the best of shifting and variable breezes – all in the proper manner. Other craftsmen also are drilled by precepts; hence precepts will be able to accomplish the same result in the case of our craftsman in the art of living." **8.** Now all these arts are concerned with the tools of life, but not with life as a whole. Hence there is much to clog these arts from without and to complicate them – such as hope, greed, fear. But that art which professes to teach the art of life cannot be forbidden by any circumstance from exercising its functions; for it shakes off complications and pierces through obstacles. Would you like to know how unlike its status is to the other arts? In the case of the latter, it is more pardonable to err voluntarily rather than by accident; but in the case of wisdom the worst fault is to commit sin wilfully. **9.** I mean something like this: A scholar will blush for shame, not if he makes a grammatical blunder intentionally, but if he makes it unintentionally; if a physician does not recognize that his patient is failing, he is a much poorer practitioner than if he recognizes the fact and conceals his knowledge. But in this art of living a voluntary mistake is the more shameful.

Furthermore, many arts, aye and the most liberal of them all, have their special doctrine, and not mere precepts of advice – the medical profession, for example. There are the different schools of Hippocrates, of Asclepiades, of Themison. **10.** And besides, no art that concerns itself with theories can exist without its own doctrines; the Greeks call them *dogmas*, while we Romans may use the term "doctrines," or "tenets," or "adopted principles," – such as you will find in geometry or astronomy. But philosophy is both theoretic and practical; it contemplates and at the same time acts. You are indeed mistaken if you think that philosophy offers you nothing but worldly assistance; her aspirations are loftier than that. She cries: "I investigate the whole universe, nor am I content, keeping myself within a mortal dwelling, to give you favourable or unfavourable advice. Great matters invite and such as are set far above you. In the words of Lucretius:

> **11.** To thee shall I reveal the ways of heaven
> And the gods, spreading before thine eyes
> The atoms, – whence all things are brought to birth,
> Increased, and fostered by creative power,
> And eke their end when Nature casts them off.

Philosophy, therefore, being theoretic, must have her doctrines. **12.** And why? Because no man can duly perform right actions except one who has been entrusted with reason, which will enable him, in all cases, to fulfil all the categories of duty. These categories he cannot observe unless he receives precepts for every occasion, and not for the present alone. Precepts by themselves are weak and, so to speak, rootless if they be assigned to the parts and not to the whole. It is the doctrines which will strengthen and support us in peace and calm, which will include simultaneously the whole of life and the universe in its completeness. There is the same difference between philosophical doctrines and precepts as there is between elements and members; the latter depend upon the former, while the former are the source both of the latter and of all things.

13. People say: "The old-style wisdom advised only what one should do and avoid; and yet the men of former days were better men by far. When savants have appeared, sages have become rare. For that frank, simple virtue has changed into hidden and crafty knowledge; we are taught how to debate, not how to live." **14.** Of course, as you say, the old-fashioned wisdom, especially in its beginnings, was crude; but so were the other arts, in which dexterity developed with progress. Nor indeed in those days was there yet any need for carefully-planned cures. Wickedness had not yet reached such a high point, or scattered itself so broadcast. Plain vices could be treated by plain cures; now, however, we need defences erected with all the greater care, because of the stronger powers by which we are attacked. **15.** Medicine once consisted of the knowledge of a few simples, to stop the flow of blood, or to heal wounds; then by degrees it reached its present stage of complicated variety. No wonder that in early days medicine had less to do! Men's bodies were still sound and strong; their food was light and not spoiled by art and luxury, whereas when they began to seek dishes not for the sake of removing, but of rousing, the appetite, and devised countless sauces to whet their gluttony, – then what before was nourishment to a hungry man became a burden to the full stomach. **16.** Thence come paleness, and a trembling of wine-sodden muscles, and a repulsive thinness, due rather to indigestion than to hunger. Thence weak tottering steps, and a reeling gait just like that of drunkenness. Thence dropsy, spreading under the entire skin, and the belly growing to a paunch through an ill habit of taking more than it can hold. Thence yellow jaundice, discoloured countenances, and bodies that rot inwardly, and fingers that grow knotty when the joints stiffen, and muscles that are numbed and without power of feeling, and palpitation of the heart with its ceaseless pounding. **17.** Why need I mention dizziness? Or speak of pain in the eye and in the ear, itching and aching in the fevered brain, and internal ulcers throughout the digestive system? Besides these, there are countless kinds of fever, some acute in their malignity, others creeping upon us with subtle damage, and still others which approach us with chills and severe ague. **18.** Why should I mention the other innumerable diseases, the tortures that result from high living?

Men used to be free from such ills, because they had not yet slackened their strength by indulgence, because they had control over themselves, and supplied their own needs. They toughened their bodies by work and real toil, tiring themselves out by running or hunting or tilling the earth. They were refreshed by food in which only a hungry man could take pleasure. Hence, there was no need for all our mighty medical paraphernalia, for so many instruments and pill-boxes. For plain reasons they enjoyed plain health; it took elaborate courses to produce elaborate diseases. **19.** Mark the number of things – all to pass down a single throat – that luxury mixes together, after ravaging land and sea. So many different dishes must surely disagree; they are bolted with difficulty and are digested with difficulty, each jostling against the other. And no wonder, that diseases which result from ill-assorted food are variable and manifold; there must be an overflow when so many unnatural combinations are jumbled together. Hence there are as many ways of being ill as there are of living. **20.** The illustrious founder of the guild and profession of medicine remarked that women never lost their hair or suffered from pain in the feet; and yet nowadays they run short of hair and are afflicted with gout. This does not mean that woman's physique has changed, but that it has been conquered; in rivalling male indulgences they have also rivalled the ills to which men are heirs. **21.** They keep just as late hours, and drink just as much liquor; they challenge men in wrestling and carousing; they are no less given to vomiting from distended stomachs and to thus discharging all their wine again; nor are they behind the men in gnawing ice, as a relief to their fevered digestions. And they even match the men in their passions, although they were created to feel love passively (may the gods and goddesses confound them!). They devise the most impossible varieties of unchastity, and in the company of men they play the part of men. What wonder, then, that we can trip up the statement of the greatest and most skilled physician, when so many women are gouty and bald! Because of their vices, women have ceased to deserve the privileges of their sex; they have put off their womanly nature and are therefore condemned to suffer the diseases of men.

22. Physicians of old time knew nothing about prescribing frequent nourishment and propping the feeble pulse with wine; they did not understand the practice of blood-letting and of easing chronic complaints with sweat-baths; they did not understand how, by bandaging ankles and arms, to recall to the outward parts the hidden strength which had taken refuge in the centre. They were not compelled to seek many varieties of relief, because the varieties of suffering were very few in number. **23.** Nowadays, however, to what a stage have the evils of ill-health advanced! This is the interest which we pay on pleasures which we have coveted beyond what is reasonable and right. You need not wonder that diseases are beyond counting: count the cooks! All intellectual interests are in abeyance; those who follow culture lecture to empty rooms, in out-of-the-way places. The halls of the professor and the philosopher are deserted; but what a crowd there is in the cafés! How many young fellows besiege the kitchens of their gluttonous friends! **24.** I shall not mention the troops of luckless boys who must put up with other shameful treatment after the banquet is over. I shall not mention the troops of catamites, rated according to nation and colour, who must all have the same smooth skin, and the same amount of youthful down on their cheeks, and the same way of dressing their hair, so that no boy with straight locks may get among the curly-heads. Nor shall I mention the medley of bakers, and the numbers of waiters who at a given signal scurry to carry in the courses. Ye gods! How many men are kept busy to humour a single belly! **25.** What? Do you imagine that those mushrooms, the epicure's poison, work no evil results in secret, even though they have had no immediate effect? What? Do you suppose that your summer snow does not harden the tissue of the liver? What? Do you suppose that those oysters, a sluggish food fattened on slime, do not weigh one down with mud-begotten heaviness? What? Do you not think that the so-called "Sauce from the Provinces," the costly extract of poisonous fish, burns up the stomach with its salted putrefaction? What? Do you judge that the corrupted dishes which a man swallows almost burning from the kitchen fire, are quenched in the digestive system without doing harm? How repulsive, then, and how unhealthy are their belchings, and how disgusted men are with themselves when they breathe forth the fumes of yesterday's debauch! You may be sure that their food is not being digested, but is rotting.

26. I remember once hearing gossip about a notorious dish into which everything over which epicures love to dally had been heaped together by a cookshop that was fast rushing into bankruptcy; there were two kinds of mussels, and oysters trimmed round at the line where they are edible, set off at intervals by sea-urchins; the whole was flanked by mullets cut up and served without the bones. **27.** In these days we are ashamed of separate foods; people mix many flavours into one. The dinner table does work which the stomach ought to do. I look forward next to food being served masticated! And how little we are from it already when we pick out shells and bones and the cook performs the office of the teeth!

They say: "It is too much trouble to take our luxuries one by one; let us have everything served at the same time and blended into the same flavour. Why should I help myself to a single dish? Let us have many coming to the table at once; the dainties of various courses should be combined and confounded. **28.** Those who used to declare that this was done for display and notoriety should understand that it is not done for show, but that it is an oblation to our sense of duty! Let us have at one time, drenched in the same sauce, the dishes that are usually served separately. Let there be no difference: let oysters, sea-urchins, shell-fish, and mullets be mixed together and cooked in the same dish." No vomited food could be jumbled up more helter-skelter. **29.** And as the food itself is complicated, so the resulting diseases are complex, unaccountable, manifold, variegated; medicine has begun to campaign against them in many ways and by many rules of treatment.

Now I declare to you that the same statement applies to philosophy. It was once more simple because men's sins were on a smaller scale, and could be cured with but slight trouble; in the face, however, of all this moral topsy-turvy men must leave no remedy untried. And would that this pest might so at last be overcome!

30. We are mad, not only individually, but nationally. We check manslaughter and isolated murders; but what of war and the much-vaunted crime of slaughtering whole peoples? There are no limits to our greed, none to our cruelty. And as long as such crimes are committed by stealth and by individuals, they are less harmful and less portentous; but cruelties are practised in accordance with acts of senate and popular assembly, and the public is bidden to do that which is forbidden to the individual. 31. Deeds that would be punished by loss of life when committed in secret, are praised by us because uniformed generals have carried them out. Man, naturally the gentlest class of being, is not ashamed to revel in the blood of others, to wage war, and to entrust the waging of war to his sons, when even dumb beasts and wild beasts keep the peace with one another. 32. Against this overmastering and widespread madness philosophy has become a matter of greater effort, and has taken on strength in proportion to the strength which is gained by the opposition forces.

It used to be easy to scold men who were slaves to drink and who sought out more luxurious food; it did not require a mighty effort to bring the spirit back to the simplicity from which it had departed only slightly. But now

33. One needs the rapid hand, the master-craft.

Men seek pleasure from every source. No vice remains within its limits; luxury is precipitated into greed. We are overwhelmed with forgetfulness of that which is honourable. Nothing that has an attractive value, is base. Man, an object of reverence in the eyes of man, is now slaughtered for jest and sport; and those whom it used to be unholy to train for the purpose of inflicting and enduring wounds, are thrust forth exposed and defenceless; and it is a satisfying spectacle to see a man made a corpse.

34. Amid this upset condition of morals, something stronger than usual is needed, – something which will shake off these chronic ills; in order to root out a deep-seated belief in wrong ideas, conduct must be regulated by doctrines. It is only when we add precepts, consolation, and encouragement to these, that they can prevail; by themselves they are ineffective. 35. If we would hold men firmly bound and tear them away from the ills which clutch them fast, they must learn what is evil and what is good. They must know that everything except virtue changes its name and becomes now good and now bad. Just as the soldier's primary bond of union is his oath of allegiance and his love for the flag, and a horror of desertion, and just as, after this stage, other duties can easily be demanded of him, and trusts given to him when once the oath has been administered; so it is with those whom you would bring to the happy life: the first foundations must be laid, and virtue worked into these men. Let them be held by a sort of superstitious worship of virtue; let them love her; let them desire to live with her, and refuse to live without her.

36. "But what, then," people say, "have not certain persons won their way to excellence without complicated training? Have they not made great progress by

obeying bare precepts alone?" Very true; but their temperaments were propitious, and they snatched salvation as it were by the way. For just as the immortal gods did not learn virtue having been born with virtue complete, and containing in their nature the essence of goodness – even so certain men are fitted with unusual qualities and reach without a long apprenticeship that which is ordinarily a matter of teaching, welcoming honourable things as soon as they hear them. Hence come the choice minds which seize quickly upon virtue, or else produce it from within themselves. But your dull, sluggish fellow, who is hampered by his evil habits, must have this soul-rust incessantly rubbed off. **37.** Now, as the former sort, who are inclined towards the good, can be raised to the heights more quickly: so the weaker spirits will be assisted and freed from their evil opinions if we entrust to them the accepted principles of philosophy; and you may understand how essential these principles are in the following way. Certain things sink into us, rendering us sluggish in some ways, and hasty in others. These two qualities, the one of recklessness and the other of sloth, cannot be respectively checked or roused unless we remove their causes, which are mistaken admiration and mistaken fear. As long as we are obsessed by such feelings, you may say to us: "You owe this duty to your father, this to your children, this to your friends, this to your guests"; but greed will always hold us back, no matter how we try. A man may know that he should fight for his country, but fear will dissuade him. A man may know that he should sweat forth his last drop of energy on behalf of his friends, but luxury will forbid. A man may know that keeping a mistress is the worst kind of insult to his wife, but lust will drive him in the opposite direction. **38.** It will therefore be of no avail to give precepts unless you first remove the conditions that are likely to stand in the way of precepts; it will do no more good than to place weapons by your side and bring yourself near the foe without having your hands free to use those weapons. The soul, in order to deal with the precepts which we offer, must first be set free. **39.** Suppose that a man is acting as he should; he cannot keep it up continuously or consistently, since he will not know the reason for so acting. Some of his conduct will result rightly because of luck or practice; but there will be in his hand no rule by which he may regulate his acts, and which he may trust to tell him whether that which he has done is right. One who is good through mere chance will not give promise of retaining such a character for ever. **40.** Furthermore, precepts will perhaps help you to do what should be done; but they will not help you to do it in the proper way; and if they do not help you to this end, they do not conduct you to virtue. I grant you that, if warned, a man will do what he should; but that is not enough, since the credit lies, not in the actual deed, but in the way it is done. **41.** What is more shameful than a costly meal which eats away the income even of a knight? Or what so worthy of the censor's condemnation as to be always indulging oneself and one's "inner man," if I may speak as the gluttons do? And yet often has an inaugural dinner cost the most careful man a cool million! The very sum that is called disgraceful if spent on the appetite, is beyond reproach if spent for official purposes! For it is not luxury but an expenditure sanctioned by custom.

42. A mullet of monstrous size was presented to the Emperor Tiberius. They say it weighed four and one half pounds (and why should I not tickle the palates of certain epicures by mentioning its weight?). Tiberius ordered it to be sent to the fish-market and put up for sale, remarking: "I shall be taken entirely by surprise, my friends, if either Apicius or P. Octavius does not buy that mullet." The guess came true beyond his expectation: the two men bid, and Octavius won, thereby acquiring a great reputation among his intimates because he had bought for five thousand sesterces a fish which the Emperor had sold, and which even Apicius did not succeed in buying. To pay such a price was disgraceful for Octavius, but not for the individual who purchased the fish in order to present it to Tiberius, – though I should be inclined to blame the latter as well; but at any rate he admired a gift of which he thought Caesar worthy.

When people sit by the bedsides of their sick friends, we honour their motives. 43. But when people do this for the purpose of attaining a legacy, they are like vultures waiting for carrion. The same act may be either shameful or honourable: the purpose and the manner make all the difference. Now each of our acts will be honourable if we declare allegiance to honour and judge honour and its results to be the only good that can fall to man's lot; for other things are only temporarily good. 44. I think, then, that there should be deeply implanted a firm belief which will apply to life as a whole: this is what I call a "doctrine." And as this belief is, so will be our acts and our thoughts. As our acts and our thoughts are, so will our lives be. It is not enough, when a man is arranging his existence as a whole, to give him advice about details. 45. Marcus Brutus, in the book which he has entitled *Concerning Duty*, gives many precepts to parents, children, and brothers; but no one will do his duty as he ought, unless he has some principle to which he may refer his conduct. We must set before our eyes the goal of the Supreme Good, towards which we may strive, and to which all our acts and words may have reference – just as sailors must guide their course according to a certain star. 46. Life without ideals is erratic: as soon as an ideal is to be set up, doctrines begin to be necessary. I am sure you will admit that there is nothing more shameful than uncertain and wavering conduct, than the habit of timorous retreat. This will be our experience in all cases unless we remove that which checks the spirit and clogs it, and keeps it from making an attempt and trying with all its might.

47. Precepts are commonly given as to how the gods should be worshipped. But let us forbid lamps to be lighted on the Sabbath, since the gods do not need light, neither do men take pleasure in soot. Let us forbid men to offer morning salutation and to throng the doors of temples; mortal ambitions are attracted by such ceremonies, but God is worshipped by those who truly know Him. Let us forbid bringing towels and flesh-scrapers to Jupiter, and proffering mirrors to Juno; for God seeks no servants. Of course not; he himself does service to mankind, everywhere and to all he is at hand to help. 48. Although a man hear what limit he should observe in sacrifice, and how far he should recoil from burdensome

superstitions, he will never make sufficient progress until he has conceived a right idea of God, – regarding Him as one who possesses all things, and allots all things, and bestows them without price. **49.** And what reason have the Gods for doing deeds of kindness? It is their nature. One who thinks that they are unwilling to do harm, is wrong; they cannot do harm. They cannot receive or inflict injury; for doing harm is in the same category as suffering harm. The universal nature, all-glorious and all-beautiful, has rendered incapable of inflicting ill those whom it has removed from the danger of ill.

50. The first way to worship the gods is to believe in the gods; the next to acknowledge their majesty, to acknowledge their goodness without which there is no majesty. Also, to know that they are supreme commanders in the universe, controlling all things by their power and acting as guardians of the human race, even though they are sometimes unmindful of the individual. They neither give nor have evil but they do chasten and restrain certain persons and impose penalties, and sometimes punish by bestowing that which seems good outwardly. Would you win over the gods? Then be a good man. Whoever imitates them, is worshipping them sufficiently. **51.** Then comes the second problem, – how to deal with men. What is our purpose? What precepts do we offer? Should we bid them refrain from bloodshed? What a little thing it is not to harm one whom you ought to help! It is indeed worthy of great praise, when man treats man with kindness! Shall we advise stretching forth the hand to the shipwrecked sailor, or pointing out the way to the wanderer, or sharing a crust with the starving? Yes, if I can only tell you first everything which ought to be afforded or withheld; meantime, I can lay down for mankind a rule, in short compass, for our duties in human relationships: **52.** all that you behold, that which comprises both god and man, is one – we are the parts of one great body. Nature produced us related to one another, since she created us from the same source and to the same end. She engendered in us mutual affection, and made us prone to friendships. She established fairness and justice; according to her ruling, it is more wretched to commit than to suffer injury. Through her orders, let our hands be ready for all that needs to be helped. **53.** Let this verse be in your heart and on your lips:

> I am a man; and nothing in man's lot
> Do I deem foreign to me.

Let us possess things in common; for birth is ours in common. Our relations with one another are like a stone arch, which would collapse if the stones did not mutually support each other, and which is upheld in this very way.

54. Next, after considering gods and men, let us see how we should make use of things. It is useless for us to have mouthed out precepts, unless we begin by reflecting what opinion we ought to hold concerning everything – concerning poverty, riches, renown, disgrace, citizenship, exile. Let us banish rumour and set a value upon each thing, asking what it is and not what it is called.

55. Now let us turn to a consideration of the virtues. Some persons will advise us to rate prudence very high, to cherish bravery, and to cleave more closely, if possible, to justice than to all other qualities. But this will do us no good if we do not know what virtue is, whether it is simple or compound, whether it is one or more than one, whether its parts are separate or interwoven with one another; whether he who has one virtue possesses the other virtues also; and just what are the distinctions between them. 56. The carpenter does not need to inquire about his art in the light of its origin or of its function, any more than a pantomime need inquire about the art of dancing; if these arts understand themselves, nothing is lacking, for they do not refer to life as a whole. But virtue means the knowledge of other things besides herself: if we would learn virtue we must learn all about virtue. 57. Conduct will not be right unless the will to act is right; for this is the source of conduct. Nor, again, can the will be right without a right attitude of mind; for this is the source of the will. Furthermore, such an attitude of mind will not be found even in the best of men unless he has learned the laws of life as a whole and has worked out a proper judgment about everything, and unless he has reduced facts to a standard of truth. Peace of mind is enjoyed only by those who have attained a fixed and unchanging standard of judgment; the rest of mankind continually ebb and flow in their decisions, floating in a condition where they alternately reject things and seek them. 58. And what is the reason for this tossing to and fro? It is because nothing is clear to them, because they make use of a most unsure criterion – rumour. If you would always desire the same things, you must desire the truth. But one cannot attain the truth without doctrines; for doctrines embrace the whole of life. Things good and evil, honourable and disgraceful, just and unjust, dutiful and undutiful, the virtues and their practice, the possession of comforts, worth and respect, health, strength, beauty, keenness of the senses – all these qualities call for one who is able to appraise them. One should be allowed to know at what value every object is to be rated on the list; 59. for sometimes you are deceived and believe that certain things are worth more than their real value; in fact, so badly are you deceived that you will find you should value at a mere pennyworth those things which we men regard as worth most of all – for example, riches, influence, and power.

You will never understand this unless you have investigated the actual standard by which such conditions are relatively rated. As leaves cannot flourish by their own efforts, but need a branch to which they may cling and from which they may draw sap, so your precepts, when taken alone, wither away; they must be grafted upon a school of philosophy. 60. Moreover, those who do away with doctrines do not understand that these doctrines are proved by the very arguments through which they seem to disprove them. For what are these men saying? They are saying that precepts are sufficient to develop life, and that the doctrines of wisdom (in other words, dogmas) are superfluous. And yet this very utterance of theirs is a doctrine just as if I should now remark that one must dispense with precepts on the ground that they are superfluous, that one must make use of doctrines, and that our studies should be directed solely towards this end; thus, by my very statement that precepts should not be taken seriously, I should be uttering a precept. **61.** There are certain matters in philosophy which need admonition; there are others which need proof, and a great deal of proof, too, because they are complicated and can scarcely be made clear with the greatest care and the greatest dialectic skill. If proofs are necessary, so are doctrines; for doctrines deduce the truth by reasoning. Some matters are clear, and others are vague: those which the senses and the memory can embrace are clear; those which are outside their scope are vague.

But reason is not satisfied by obvious facts; its higher and nobler function is to deal with hidden things. Hidden things need proof; proof cannot come without doctrines; therefore, doctrines are necessary. **62.** That which leads to a general agreement, and likewise to a perfect one, is an assured belief in certain facts; but if, lacking this assurance, all things are adrift in our minds, then doctrines are indispensable; for they give to our minds the means of unswerving decision. **63.** Furthermore, when we advise a man to regard his friends as highly as himself, to reflect that an enemy may become a friend, to stimulate love in the friend, and to check hatred in the enemy, we add: "This is just and honourable." Now the just and honourable element in our doctrines is embraced by reason; hence reason is necessary; for without it the doctrines cannot exist, either. **64.** But let us unite the two. For indeed branches are useless without their roots, and the roots themselves are strengthened by the growths which they have produced. Everyone can understand how useful the hands are; they obviously help us. But the heart, the source of the hands growth and power and motion, is hidden. And I can say the same thing about precepts: they are manifest, while the doctrines of wisdom are concealed. And as only the initiated know the more hallowed portion of the rites, so in philosophy the hidden truths are revealed only to those who are members and have been admitted to the sacred rites. But precepts and other such matters are familiar even to the uninitiated.

65. Posidonius holds that not only precept-giving (there is nothing to prevent my using this word), but even persuasion, consolation, and encouragement, are necessary. To these he adds the *investigation of causes* (but I fail to see why I should not dare to call it *aetiology*, since the scholars who mount guard over the Latin language thus use the term as having the right to do so). He remarks that it will also be useful to illustrate each particular virtue; this science Posidonius calls *ethology*, while others call it *characterization*. It gives the signs and marks which belong to each virtue and vice, so that by them distinction may be drawn between like things. **66.** Its function is the same as that of precept. For he who utters precepts says: "If you would have self-control, act thus and so!" He who illustrates, says "The man who acts thus and so, and refrains from certain other things, possesses self-control." If you ask what the difference here is, I say that the one gives the precepts of virtue, the other its embodiment. These illustrations, or, to use a commercial term, these *samples*, have, I confess, a certain utility; just put them up for exhibition well recommended, and you will find men to copy them. **67.** Would you, for instance, deem it a useful thing to have evidence given you by which you may recognize a thoroughbred horse, and not be cheated in your purchase or waste your time over a low-bred animal? But how much more useful it is to know the marks of a surpassingly fine soul – marks which one may appropriate from another for oneself!

> **68.** Straightway the foal of the high-bred drove, nursed up in the pastures,
> Marches with spirited step, and treads with a delicate motion;
> First on the dangerous pathway and into the threatening river,
> Trusting himself to the unknown bridge, without fear at its creakings,
> Neck thrown high in the air, and clear-cut head, and a belly
> Spare, back rounded, and breast abounding in courage and muscle.
> He, when the clashing of weapons is heard to resound in the distance,
> Leaps from his place, and pricks up his ears, and all in a tremble
> Pours forth the pent-up fire that lay close-shut in his nostrils.

69. Vergil's description, though referring to something else, might perfectly well be the portrayal of a brave man; at any rate, I myself should select no other simile for a hero. If I had to describe Cato, who was unterrified amid the din of civil war, who was first to attack the armies that were already making for the Alps, who plunged face-forward into the civil conflict, this is exactly the sort of expression and attitude which I should give him. **70.** Surely none could "march with more spirited step" than one who rose against Caesar and Pompey at the same time and, when some were supporting Caesar's party and others that of Pompey, issued a challenge to both leaders, thus showing that the republic also had some backers. For it is not enough to say of Cato "without fear at its creakings." Of course he is not afraid! He does not quail before real and imminent noises; in the face of ten legions, Gallic auxiliaries, and a motley host of citizens and foreigners, he utters words fraught with freedom, encouraging the Republic not to fail in the struggle for freedom, but to try all hazards; he declares that it is more honourable to fall into servitude than to fall in line with it. **71.** What force and energy are his! What confidence he displays amid the general panic! He knows that he is the only one whose standing is not in question, and that men do not ask whether Cato is free, but whether he is still *among* the free. Hence his contempt for danger and the sword. What a pleasure it is to say, in admiration of the unflinching steadiness of a hero who did not totter when the whole state was in ruins:

> A breast abounding in courage and muscle!

72. It will be helpful not only to state what is the usual quality of good men, and to outline their figures and features, but also to relate and set forth what men there have been of this kind. We might picture that last and bravest wound of Cato's, through which Freedom breathed her last; or the wise Laelius and his harmonious life with his friend Scipio; or the noble deeds of the Elder Cato at home and abroad; or the wooden couches of Tubero, spread at a public feast, goatskins instead of tapestry, and vessels of earthenware set out for the banquet before the very shrine of Jupiter! What else was this except consecrating poverty on the Capitol? Though I know no other deed of his for which to rank him with the Catos, is this one not enough? It was a censorship, not a banquet. **73.** How lamentably do those who covet glory fail to understand what glory is, or in what way it should be sought! On that day the Roman populace viewed the furniture of many men; it marvelled only at that of one! The gold and silver of all the others has been broken up and melted down times without number; but Tubero's earthenware will endure throughout eternity. Farewell.

XCVI. ON FACING HARDSHIPS

1. Spite of all do you still chafe and complain, not understanding that, in all the evils to which you refer, there is really only one – the fact that you *do* chafe and complain? If you ask me, I think that for a *man* there is no misery unless there be something in the universe which he thinks miserable. I shall not endure myself on that day when I find anything unendurable.

I am ill; but that is a part of my lot. My slaves have fallen sick, my income has gone off, my house is rickety, I have been assailed by losses, accidents, toil, and fear; this is a common thing. Nay, that was an understatement; it was an inevitable thing. **2.** Such affairs come by order, and not by accident. If you will believe me, it is my inmost emotions that I am just now disclosing to you: when everything seems to go hard and uphill, I have trained myself not merely to obey God, but to agree with His decisions. I follow Him because my soul wills it, and not because I must. Nothing will ever happen to me that I shall receive with ill humour or with a wry face. I shall pay up all my taxes willingly. Now all the things which cause us to groan or recoil, are part of the tax of life – things, my dear Lucilius, which you should never hope and never seek to escape.

3. It was disease of the bladder that made you apprehensive; downcast letters came from you; you were continually getting worse; I will touch the truth more closely, and say that you feared for your life. But come, did you not know, when you prayed for long life, that this was what you were praying for? A long life includes all these troubles, just as a long journey includes dust and mud and rain. **4.** "But," you cry, "I wished to live, and at the same time to be immune from all ills." Such a womanish cry does no credit to a man. Consider in what attitude you shall receive this prayer of mine (I offer it not only in a good, but in a noble spirit): "May gods and goddesses alike forbid that Fortune keep you in luxury!" **5.** Ask yourself voluntarily which you would choose if some god gave you the choice – a life in a café or life in a camp.

And yet life, Lucilius, is really a battle. For this reason those who are tossed about at sea, who proceed uphill and downhill over toilsome crags and heights, who go on campaigns that bring the greatest danger, are heroes and front-rank fighters;

but persons who live in rotten luxury and ease while others toil, are mere turtle-doves safe only because men despise them. Farewell.

XCVII. ON THE DEGENERACY OF THE AGE

1. You are mistaken, my dear Lucilius, if you think that luxury, neglect of good manners, and other vices of which each man accuses the age in which he lives, are especially characteristic of our own epoch; no, they are the vices of mankind and not of the times. No era in history has ever been free from blame. Moreover, if you once begin to take account of the irregularities belonging to any particular era, you will find – to man's shame be it spoken – that sin never stalked abroad more openly than in Cato's very presence. **2.** Would anyone believe that money changed hands in the trial when Clodius was defendant on the charge of secret adultery with Caesar's wife, when he violated the ritual of that sacrifice which is said to be offered on behalf of the people when all males are so rigorously removed outside the precinct, that even pictures of all male creatures are covered up? And yet, money was given to the jury, and, baser even than such a bargain, sexual crimes were demanded of married women and noble youths as a sort of additional contribution. **3.** The charge involved less sin than the acquittal; for the defendant on a charge of adultery parcelled out the adulteries, and was not sure of his own safety until he had made the jury criminals like himself. All this was done at the trial in which Cato gave evidence, although that was his sole part therein.

I shall quote Cicero's actual words, because the facts are so bad as to pass belief: **4.** "He made assignations, promises, pleas, and gifts. And more than this (merciful Heavens, what an abandoned state of affairs!) upon several of the jury, to round out their reward, he even bestowed the enjoyment of certain women and meetings with noble youths." **5.** It is superfluous to be shocked at the bribe; the additions to the bribe were worse. "Will you have the wife of that prig, A.? Very good. Or of B., the millionaire? I will guarantee that you shall lie with her. If you fail to commit adultery, condemn Clodius. That beauty whom you desire shall visit you. I assure you a night in that woman's company without delay; my promise shall be carried out faithfully within the legal time of postponement." It means more to parcel out such crimes than to commit them; it means blackmailing dignified matrons. **6.** These jurymen in the Clodius trial had asked the Senate for a guard – a favour which would have been necessary only for a jury about to convict the accused; and their request had been granted. Hence the witty remark of Catulus after the defendant had been acquitted: "Why did you ask us for the guard? Were you afraid of having your money stolen from you?" And yet, amid jests like these he got off unpunished who before the trial was an adulterer, during the trial a pander, and who escaped conviction more vilely than he deserved it.

7. Do you believe that anything could be more disgraceful than such moral standards – when lust could not keep its hands either from religious worship or from the courts of law, when, in the very inquiry which was held in special session by order of the Senate, more crime was committed than investigated? The question at issue was whether one could be safe after committing adultery; it was shown that one could not be safe without committing adultery! **8.** All this bargaining took place in the presence of Pompey and Caesar, of Cicero and Cato, – yes, that very Cato whose presence, it is said, caused the people to refrain from demanding the usual quips and cranks of naked actresses at the Floralia, – if you can believe that men were stricter in their conduct at a festival than in a court-room! Such things will be done in the future, as they have been done in the past; and the licentiousness of cities will sometimes abate through discipline and fear, never of itself.

9. Therefore, you need not believe that it is we who have yielded most to lust and least to law. For young men of to-day live far more simple lives than those of an epoch when a defendant would plead not guilty to an adultery charge before his judges, and his judges admit it before the defendant, when debauchery was practised to secure a verdict, and when Clodius, befriended by the very vices of which he was guilty, played the procurer during the actual hearing of the case. Could one believe this? He to whom one adultery brought condemnation was acquitted because of many. **10.** All ages will produce men like Clodius, but not all ages men like Cato. We degenerate easily, because we lack neither guides nor associates in our wickedness, and the wickedness goes on of itself, even without guides or associates. The road to vice is not only downhill, but steep; and many men are rendered incorrigible by the fact that, while in all other crafts errors bring shame to good craftsmen and cause vexation to those who go astray, the errors of life are a positive source of pleasure. **11.** The pilot is not glad when his ship is thrown on her beam-ends; the physician is not glad when he buries his patient; the orator is not glad when the defendant loses a case through the fault of his advocate; but on the other hand every man enjoys his own crimes. A. delights in an intrigue – for it was the very difficulty which attracted him thereto. B. delights in forgery and theft, and is only displeased with his sin when his sin has failed to hit the mark. And all this is the result of perverted habits.

12. Conversely, however, in order that you may know that there is an idea of good conduct present subconsciously in souls which have been led even into the most depraved ways, and that men are not ignorant of what evil is but indifferent – I say that all men hide their sins, and, even though the issue be successful, enjoy the results while concealing the sins themselves. A good conscience, however, wishes to come forth and be seen of men; wickedness fears the very shadows. **13.** Hence I hold Epicurus's saying to be most apt: "That the guilty may haply remain hidden is possible, that he should be sure of remaining hidden is not possible," or, if you think that the meaning can be made more clear in this way: "The reason that it is no advantage to wrong-doers to remain hidden is that even though they have the good fortune they have not the assurance of remaining so." This is what I mean: crimes can be well guarded; free from anxiety they cannot be.

14. This view, I maintain, is not at variance with the principles of our school, if it be so explained. And why? Because the first and worst penalty of sin is to have committed sin; and crime, though Fortune deck it out with her favours, though she protect and take it in her charge, can never go unpunished; since the punishment of crime lies in the crime itself. But none the less do these second penalties press close upon the heels of the first – constant fear, constant terror, and distrust in one's own security.

Why, then, should I set wickedness free from such a punishment? Why should I not always leave it trembling in the balance? **15.** Let us disagree with Epicurus on the one point, when he declares that there is no natural justice, and that crime should be avoided because one cannot escape the fear which results therefrom; let us agree with him on the other – that bad deeds are lashed by the whip of conscience, and that conscience is tortured to the greatest degree because unending anxiety drives and whips it on, and it cannot rely upon the guarantors of its own peace of mind. For this, Epicurus, is the very proof that we are by nature reluctant to commit crime, because even in circumstances of safety there is no one who does not feel fear. **16.** Good luck frees many men from punishment, but no man from fear. And why should this be if it were not that we have engrained in us a loathing for that which Nature has condemned? Hence even men who hide their sins can never count upon remaining hidden; for their conscience convicts them and reveals them to themselves. But it is the property of guilt to be in fear. It had gone ill with us, owing to the many crimes which escape the vengeance of the law and the prescribed punishments, were it not that those grievous offences against nature must pay the penalty in ready money, and that in place of suffering the punishment comes fear. Farewell.

XCVIII. ON THE FICKLENESS OF FORTUNE

1. You need never believe that anyone who depends upon happiness is happy! It is a fragile support – this delight in adventitious things; the joy which entered from without will some day depart. But that joy which springs wholly from oneself is leal and sound; it increases and attends us to the last; while all other things which provoke the admiration of the crowd are but temporary Goods. You may reply: "What do you mean? Cannot such things serve both for utility and for delight?" Of course. But only if they depend on us, and not we on them. **2.** All things that Fortune looks upon become productive and pleasant, only if he who possesses them is in possession also of himself, and is not in the power of that which belongs to him. For men make a mistake, my dear Lucilius, if they hold that anything good, or evil either, is bestowed upon us by Fortune; it is simply the raw material of Goods and Ills that she gives to us – the sources of things which, in our keeping, will develop into good or ill. For the soul is more powerful than any sort of Fortune; by its own agency it guides its affairs in either direction, and of its own power it can produce a happy life, or a wretched one.

3. A bad man makes everything bad – even things which had come with the appearance of what is best; but the upright and honest man corrects the wrongs of Fortune, and softens hardship and bitterness because he knows how to endure them; he likewise accepts prosperity with appreciation and moderation, and stands up against trouble with steadiness and courage. Though a man be prudent, though he conduct all his interests with well-balanced judgment, though he attempt nothing beyond his strength, he will not attain the Good which is unalloyed and beyond the reach of threats, unless he is sure in dealing with that which is unsure. **4.** For whether you prefer to observe other men (and it is easier to make up one's mind when judging the affairs of others), or whether you observe yourself, with all prejudice laid aside, you will perceive and acknowledge that there is no utility in all these desirable and beloved things, unless you equip yourself in opposition to the fickleness of chance and its consequences, and unless you repeat to yourself often and uncomplainingly, at every mishap, the words: "Heaven decreed it otherwise!" **5.** Nay rather, to adopt a phrase which is braver and nearer the truth – one on which you may more safely prop your spirit – say to yourself, whenever things turn out contrary to your expectation: "Heaven decreed *better!*"

If you are thus poised, nothing will affect you and a man will be thus poised if he reflects on the possible ups and downs in human affairs before he feels their force, and if he comes to regard children, or wife, or property, with the idea that he will not necessarily possess them always and that he will not be any more wretched just because he ceases to possess them. **6.** It is tragic for the soul to be apprehensive of the future and wretched in anticipation of wretchedness, consumed with an anxious desire that the objects which give pleasure may remain in its possession to the very end. For such a soul will never be at rest; in waiting for the future it will lose the present blessings which it might enjoy. And there is no difference between grief for something lost and the fear of losing it.

7. But I do not for this reason advise you to be indifferent. Rather do you turn aside from you whatever may cause fear. Be sure to foresee whatever can be foreseen by planning. Observe and avoid, long before it happens, anything that is likely to do you harm. To effect this your best assistance will be a spirit of confidence and a mind strongly resolved to endure all things. He who can bear Fortune, can also beware of Fortune. At any rate, there is no dashing of billows when the sea is calm. And there is nothing more wretched or foolish than premature fear. What madness it is to anticipate one's troubles! **8.** In fine, to express my thoughts in brief compass and portray to you those busybodies and self-tormentors – they are as uncontrolled in the midst of their troubles as they are before them. He suffers more than is necessary, who suffers before it is necessary; such men do not weigh the amount of their suffering, by reason of the same failing which prevents them from being ready for it; and with the same lack of restraint they fondly imagine that their luck will last for ever, and fondly imagine that their gains are bound to increase as well as merely continue. They forget this spring-board on which mortal things are tossed, and they guarantee for themselves exclusively a steady continuance of the gifts of chance.

9. For this very reason I regard as excellent the saying of Metrodorus, in a letter of consolation to his sister on the loss of her son, a lad of great promise: "All the Good of mortals is mortal." He is referring to those Goods towards which men rush in shoals. For the real Good does not perish; it is certain and lasting and it consists of wisdom and virtue; it is the only immortal thing that falls to mortal lot. **10.** But men are so wayward, and so forgetful of their goal and of the point toward which every day jostles them, that they are surprised at losing anything, although some day they are bound to lose everything. Anything of which you are entitled the owner is in your possession but is not your own; for there is no strength in that which is weak, nor anything lasting and invincible in that which is frail. We must lose our lives as surely as we lose our property, and this, if we understand the truth, is itself a consolation. Lose it with equanimity; for you must lose your life also.

11. What resource do we find, then, in the face of these losses? Simply this – to keep in memory the things we have lost, and not to suffer the enjoyment which we have derived from them to pass away along with them. To have may be taken from us, to have had, never. A man is thankless in the highest degree if, after losing something, he feels no obligation for having received it. Chance robs us of the thing, but leaves us its use and its enjoyment – and we have lost this if we are so unfair as to regret. **12.** Just say to yourself: "Of all these experiences that seem so frightful, none is insuperable. Separate trials have been overcome by many: fire by Mucius, crucifixion by Regulus, poison by Socrates, exile by Rutilius, and a sword-inflicted death by Cato; therefore, let us also overcome something." **13.** Again, those objects which attract the crowd under the appearance of beauty and happiness, have been scorned by many men and on many occasions. Fabricius when he was general refused riches, and when he was censor branded them with disapproval. Tubero deemed poverty worthy both of himself and of the deity on the Capitol when, by the use of earthenware dishes at a public festival, he showed that man should be satisfied with that which the gods could still use. The elder Sextius rejected the honours of office; he was born with an obligation to take part in public affairs, and yet would not accept the broad stripe even when the deified Julius offered it to him. For he understood that what can be given can also be taken away.

Let us also, therefore, carry out some courageous act of our own accord; let us be included among the ideal types of history. **14.** Why have we been slack? Why do we lose heart? That which could be done, can be done, if only we purify our souls and follow Nature; for when one strays away from Nature one is compelled to crave, and fear, and be a slave to the things of chance. We may return to the true path; we may be restored to our proper state; let us therefore be so, in order that we may be able to endure pain, in whatever form it attacks our bodies, and say to Fortune: "You have to deal with a man; seek someone whom you can conquer!"

had to endeavour rather to rejoice because you had possessed him than to mourn because you had lost him.

4. "But many men fail to count up how manifold their gains have been, how great their rejoicings. Grief like yours has this among other evils: it is not only useless, but thankless. Has it then all been for nothing that you have had such a friend? During so many years, amid such close associations, after such intimate communion of personal interests, has nothing been accomplished? Do you bury friendship along with a friend? And why lament having lost him, if it be of no avail to have possessed him? Believe me, a great part of those we have loved, though chance has removed their persons, still abides with us. The past is ours, and there is nothing more secure for us than that which has been. **5.** We are ungrateful for past gains, because we hope for the future, as if the future – if so be that any future is ours – will not be quickly blended with the past. People set a narrow limit to their enjoyments if they take pleasure only in the present; both the future and the past serve for our delight – the one with anticipation, and the other with memories but the one is contingent and may not come to pass, while the other must have been.

"What madness it is, therefore, to lose our grip on that which is the surest thing of all? Let us rest content with the pleasures we have quaffed in past days, if only, while we quaffed them, the soul was not pierced like a sieve, only to lose again whatever it had received. **6.** There are countless cases of men who have without tears buried sons in the prime of manhood – men who have returned from the funeral pyre to the Senate chamber, or to any other official duties, and have straightway busied themselves with something else. And rightly; for in the first place it is idle to grieve if you get no help from grief. In the second place, it is unfair to complain about what has happened to one man but is in store for all. Again, it is foolish to lament one's loss, when there is such a slight interval between the lost and the loser. Hence we should be more resigned in spirit, because we follow closely those whom we have lost.

7. "Note the rapidity of Time – that swiftest of things; consider the shortness of the course along which we hasten at top speed; mark this throng of humanity all straining toward the same point with briefest intervals between them – even when they seem longest; he whom you count as passed away has simply posted on ahead. And what is more irrational than to bewail your predecessor, when you yourself must travel on the same journey? **8.** Does a man bewail an event which he knew would take place? Or, if he did not think of death as man's lot, he has but cheated himself. Does a man bewail an event which he has been admitting to be unavoidable? Whoever complains about the death of anyone, is complaining that he was a man. Everyone is bound by the same terms: he who is privileged to be born, is destined to die. **9.** Periods of time separate us, but death levels us. The period which lies between our first day and our last is shifting and uncertain: if you reckon it by its troubles, it is long even to a lad, if by its speed, it is scanty even to a greybeard. Everything is slippery, treacherous, and more shifting than any weather. All things are tossed about and shift into their opposites at the bidding of Fortune; amid such a turmoil of mortal affairs nothing but death is surely in store for anyone. And yet all men complain about the one thing wherein none of them is deceived. **10.** 'But he died in boyhood.' I am not yet prepared to say that he who quickly comes to the end of his life has the better of the bargain; let us turn to consider the case of him who has grown to old age. How very little is he superior to the child! Place before your mind's eye the vast spread of time's abyss, and consider the universe; and then contrast our so-called human life with infinity: you will then see how scant is that for which we pray, and which we seek to lengthen. **11.** How much of this time is taken up with weeping, how much with worry! How much with prayers for death before death arrives, how much with our health, how much with our fears! How much is occupied by our years of inexperience or of useless endeavour! And half of all this time is wasted in sleeping. Add, besides, our toils, our griefs, our dangers – and you will comprehend that even in the longest life real living is the least portion thereof. **12.** Nevertheless, who will make such an admission as: 'A man is not better off who is allowed to return home quickly, whose journey is accomplished before he is wearied out'? Life is neither a Good nor an Evil; it is simply the place where good and evil exist. Hence this little boy has lost nothing except a hazard where loss was more assured than gain. He might have turned out temperate and prudent; he might, with your fostering care, have been moulded to a better standard; but (and this fear is more reasonable) he might have become just like the many. **13.** Note the youths of the noblest lineage whose extravagance has flung them into the arena; note those men who cater to the passions of themselves and others in mutual lust, whose days never pass without drunkenness or some signal act of shame; it will thus be clear to you that there was more to fear than to hope for.

"For this reason you ought not to invite excuses for grief or aggravate slight burdens by getting indignant. **14.** I am not exhorting you to make an effort and rise to great heights; for my opinion of you is not so low as to make me think that it is necessary for you to summon every bit of your virtue to face this trouble. Yours is not pain; it is a mere sting – and it is you yourself who are turning it into pain.

"Of a surety philosophy has done you much service if you can bear courageously the loss of a boy who was as yet better known to his nurse than to his father! **15.** And what, then? Now, at this time, am I advising you to be hard-hearted, desiring you to keep your countenance unmoved at the very funeral ceremony, and not allowing your soul even to feel the pinch of pain? By no means. That would mean lack of feeling rather than virtue – to behold the burial ceremonies of those near and dear to you with the same expression as you beheld their living forms, and to show no emotion over the first bereavement in your family. But suppose that I forbade you to show emotion; there are certain feelings which claim their own rights. Tears fall, no matter how we try to check them, and by being shed they ease the soul. **16.** What, then, shall we do? Let us allow them to fall, but let us not command them do so; let us according as emotion floods our eyes, but not as as mere imitation shall demand. Let us, indeed, add nothing to natural grief, nor augment it by following the example of others. The display of grief makes more demands than grief itself: how few men are sad in their own company! They lament the louder for being heard; persons who are reserved and silent when alone are stirred to new paroxysms of tears when they behold others near them! At such times they lay violent hands upon their own persons, – though they might have done this more easily if no one were present to check them; at such times they pray for death; at such times they toss themselves from their couches. But their grief slackens with the departure of onlookers. **17.** In this matter, as in others also, we are obsessed by this fault – conforming to the pattern of the many, and regarding convention rather than duty. We abandon nature and surrender to the mob – who are never good advisers in anything, and in this respect as in all others are most inconsistent. People see a man who bears his grief bravely: they call him undutiful and savage-hearted; they see a man who collapses and clings to his dead: they call him womanish and weak. **18.** Everything, therefore, should be referred to reason. But nothing is more foolish than to court a reputation for sadness and to sanction tears; for I hold that with a wise man some tears fall by consent, others by their own force.

"I shall explain the difference as follows: When the first news of some bitter loss has shocked us, when we embrace the form that will soon pass from our arms to the funeral flames – then tears are wrung from us by the necessity of Nature, and the life-force, smitten by the stroke of grief, shakes both the whole body, and the eyes also, from which it presses out and causes to flow the moisture that lies within. **19.** Tears like these fall by a forcing-out process, against our will; but different are the tears which we allow to escape when we muse in memory upon those whom we have lost. And there is in them a certain sweet sadness when we remember the sound of a pleasant voice, a genial conversation, and the busy duties of yore; at such a time the eyes are loosened, as it were, with joy. This sort of weeping we indulge; the former sort overcomes us.

20. "There is, then, no reason why, just because a group of persons is standing in your presence or sitting at your side, you should either check or pour forth your tears; whether restrained or outpoured, they are never so disgraceful as when feigned. Let them flow naturally. But it is possible for tears to flow from the eyes of those who are quiet and at peace. They often flow without impairing the influence of the wise man – with such restraint that they show no want either of feeling or of self-respect. **21.** We may, I assure you, obey Nature and yet maintain our dignity. I have seen men worthy of reverence, during the burial of those near and dear, with countenances upon which love was written clear even after the whole apparatus of mourning was removed, and who showed no other conduct than that which was allowed to genuine emotion. There is a comeliness even in grief. This should be cultivated by the wise man; even in tears, just as in other matters also, there is a certain sufficiency; it is with the unwise that sorrows, like joys, gush over.

22. "Accept in an unruffled spirit that which is inevitable. What can happen that is beyond belief? Or what that is new? How many men at this very moment are making arrangements for funerals! How many are purchasing grave-clothes! How many are mourning, when you yourself have finished mourning! As often as you reflect that your boy has ceased to be, reflect also upon man, who has no sure promise of anything, whom Fortune does not inevitably escort to the confines of old age, but lets him go at whatever point she sees fit. 23. You may, however, speak often concerning the departed, and cherish his memory to the extent of your power. This memory will return to you all the more often if you welcome its coming without bitterness; for no man enjoys converse with one who is sorrowful, much less with sorrow itself. And whatever words, whatever jests of his, no matter how much of a child he was, may have given you pleasure to hear – these I would have you recall again and again; assure yourself confidently that he might have fulfilled the hopes which you, his father, had entertained. 24. Indeed, to forget the beloved dead, to bury their memory along with their bodies, to bewail them bounteously and afterwards think of them but scantily – this is the mark of a soul below that of man. For that is the way in which birds and beasts love their young; their affection is quickly roused and almost reaches madness, but it cools away entirely when its object dies. This quality does not befit a man of sense; he should continue to remember, but should cease to mourn. 25. And in no wise do I approve of the remark of Metrodorus – that there is a certain pleasure akin to sadness, and that one should give chase thereto at such times as these. I am quoting the actual words of Metrodorus 26. I have no doubt what your feelings will be in these matters; for what is baser than to 'chase after' pleasure in the very midst of mourning – nay rather by means of mourning – and even amid one's tears to hunt out that which will give pleasure? These are the men who accuse us of too great strictness, slandering our precepts because of supposed harshness – because (say they) we declare that grief should either not be given place in the soul at all, or else should be driven out forthwith. But which is the more incredible or inhuman – to feel no grief at the loss of one's friend, or to go a-hawking after pleasure in the midst of grief? 27. That which we Stoics advise, is honourable; when emotion has prompted a moderate flow of tears, and has, so to speak, ceased to effervesce, the soul should not be surrendered to grief. But what do you mean, Metrodorus, by saying that with our very grief there should be a blending of pleasure? That is the sweetmeat method of pacifying children; that is the way we still the cries of infants, by pouring milk down their throats!

"Even at the moment when your son's body is on the pyre, or your friend breathing his last, will you not suffer your pleasure to cease, rather than tickle your very grief with pleasure? Which is the more honourable – to remove grief from your soul, or to admit pleasure even into the company of grief? Did I say 'admit'? Nay, I mean 'chase after,' and from the hands, too, of grief itself. 28. Metrodorus says: 'There is a certain pleasure which is related to sadness.' We Stoics may say that, but you may not. The only Good which you recognize, is pleasure, and the only Evil, pain; and what relationship can there be between a Good and an Evil? But suppose that such a relationship does exist; now, of all times, is it to be rooted out? Shall we examine grief also, and see with what elements of delight and pleasure it is surrounded? **29.** Certain remedies, which are beneficial for some parts of the body, cannot be applied to other parts because these are, in a way, revolting and unfit; and that which in certain cases would work to a good purpose without any loss to one's self-respect, may become unseemly because of the situation of the wound. Are you not, similarly, ashamed to cure sorrow by pleasure? No, this sore spot must be treated in a more drastic way. This is what you should preferably advise: that no sensation of evil can reach one who is dead; for if it can reach him, he is not dead. **30.** And I say that nothing can hurt him who is as naught; for if a man can be hurt, he is alive. Do you think him to be badly off because he is no more, or because he still exists as somebody? And yet no torment can come to him from the fact that he is no more – for what feeling can belong to one who does not exist? – nor from the fact that he exists; for he has escaped the greatest disadvantage that death has in it – namely, non-existence.

31. "Let us say this also to him who mourns and misses the untimely dead: that all of us, whether young or old, live, in comparison with eternity, on the same level as regards our shortness of life. For out of all time there comes to us less than what any one could call least, since 'least' is at any rate some part; but this life of ours is next to nothing, and yet (fools that we are!), we marshal it in broad array!

32. "These words I have written to you, not with the idea that you should expect a cure from me at such a late date – for it is clear to me that you have told yourself everything that you will read in my letter – but with the idea that I should rebuke you even for the slight delay during which you lapsed from your true self, and should encourage you for the future, to rouse your spirit against Fortune and to be on the watch for all her missiles, not as if they might possibly come, but as if they were bound to come." Farewell.

C. ON THE WRITINGS OF FABIANUS

1. You write me that you have read with the greatest eagerness the work by Fabianus Papirius entitled *The Duties of a Citizen*, and that it did not come up to your expectations; then, forgetting that you are dealing with a philosopher, you proceed to criticize his style.

Suppose, now, that your statement is true – that he pours forth rather than places his words; let me, however, tell you at the start that this trait of which you speak has a peculiar charm, and that it is a grace appropriate to a smoothly-gliding style. For, I maintain, it matters a great deal whether it tumbles forth, or flows along. Moreover, there is a deal of deference in this regard also – as I shall make clear to you: **2.** Fabianus seems to me to have not so much an "efflux" as a "flow" of words:

so copious is it, without confusion, and yet not without speed. This is indeed what his style declares and announces – that he has not spent a long time in working his matter over and twisting it into shape. But even supposing the facts are as you would have them; the man was building up character rather than words, and was writing those words for the mind rather than for the ear. **3.** Besides, had he been speaking them in his own person, you would not have had time to consider the details – the whole work would have so swept you along. For as a rule that which pleases by its swiftness is of less value when taken in hand for reading.

Nevertheless, this very quality, too, of attracting at first sight is a great advantage, no matter whether careful investigation may discover something to criticize. **4.** If you ask me, I should say that he who has forced approval is greater than he who has earned it; and yet I know that the latter is safer, I know that he can give more confident guarantees for the future. A meticulous manner of writing does not suit the philosopher; if he is timid as to words, when will he ever be brave and steadfast, when will he ever really show his worth? **5.** Fabianus's style was not careless, it was assured. That is why you will find nothing shoddy in his work: his words are well chosen and yet not hunted for; they are not unnaturally inserted and inverted, according to the present-day fashion; but they possess distinction, even though they are taken from ordinary speech. There you have honourable and splendid ideas, not fettered into aphorisms, but spoken with greater freedom. We shall of course notice passages that are not sufficiently pruned, not constructed with sufficient care, and lacking the polish which is in vogue nowadays; but after regarding the whole, you will see that there are no futile subtleties of argument. **6.** There may, doubtless, be no variety of marbles, no water-supply which flows from one apartment to another, no "pauper-rooms," or any other device that luxury adds when ill content with simple charms; but, in the vulgar phrase, it is "a good house to live in."

Furthermore, opinions vary with regard to the style. Some wish it to be polished down from all roughness; and some take so great a pleasure in the abrupt manner that they would intentionally break up any passage which may by chance spread itself out more smoothly, scattering the closing words in such a way that the sentences may result unexpectedly. **7.** Read Cicero: his style has unity; it moves with a modulated pace, and is gentle without being degenerate. The style of Asinius Pollio, on the other hand, is "bumpy," jerky, leaving off when you least expect it. And finally, Cicero always stops gradually; while Pollio breaks off, except in the very few cases where he cleaves to a definite rhythm and a single pattern.

8. In addition to this, you say that everything in Fabianus seems to you commonplace and lacking in elevation; but I myself hold that he is free from such a fault. For that style of his is not commonplace, but simply calm and adjusted to his peaceful and well-ordered mind – not on a low level but on an even plane. There is lacking the verve and spur of the orator (for which you are looking), and a sudden shock of epigrams. But look, please, at the whole work, how well-ordered it is: there is a distinction in it. His style does not possess, but will suggest, dignity.

9. Mention someone whom you may rank ahead of Fabianus. Cicero, let us say, whose books on philosophy are almost as numerous as those of Fabianus. I will concede this point; but it is no slight thing to be less than the greatest. Or Asinius Pollio, let us say. I will yield again, and content myself by replying: "It is a distinction to be third in so great a field." You may also include Livy; for Livy wrote both dialogues (which should be ranked as history no less than as philosophy), and works which professedly deal with philosophy. I shall yield in the case of Livy also. But consider how many writers Fabianus outranks, if he is surpassed by three only – and those three the greatest masters of eloquence!

10. But, it may be said, he does not offer everything: though his style is elevated, it is not strong; though it flows forth copiously, it lacks force and sweep; it is not translucent, but it is lucid. "One would fail," you urge, "to find therein any rugged denunciation of vice, any courageous words in the face of danger, any proud defiance of Fortune, any scornful threats against self-seeking. I wish to see luxury rebuked, lust condemned, waywardness crushed out. Let him show us the keenness of oratory, the loftiness of tragedy, the subtlety of comedy." You wish him to rely on that pettiest of things, phraseology; but he has sworn allegiance to the greatness of his subject and draws eloquence after him as a sort of shadow, but not of set purpose.

11. Our author will doubtless not investigate every detail, nor subject it to analysis, nor inspect and emphasize each separate word. This I admit. Many phrases will fall short, or will fail to strike home, and at times the style will slip along indolently; but there will be plenty of light throughout the work; there will be long stretches which will not weary the reader. And, finally, he will offer this quality of making it clear to you that he meant what he wrote. You will understand that his aim was to have you know what pleased him, rather than that he should please you. All his work makes for progress and for sanity, without any search for applause.

12. I do not doubt that his writings are of the kind I have described, although I am harking back to him rather than retaining a sure memory of him, and although the general tone of his writings remains in my mind, not from a careful and recent perusal, but in outline, as is natural after an acquaintance of long ago. But certainly, whenever I heard him lecture, such did his work seem to me – not solid but full, the kind which would inspire young men of promise and rouse their ambition to become like him, without making them hopeless of surpassing him; and this method of encouragement seems to me the most helpful of all. For it is disheartening to inspire in a man the desire, and to take away from him the hope, of emulation. At any rate, his language was fluent, and though one might not approve every detail, the general effect was noble. Farewell.

CI. ON THE FUTILITY OF PLANNING AHEAD

1. Every day and every hour reveal to us what a nothing we are, and remind us with some fresh evidence that we have forgotten our weakness; then, as we plan for eternity, they compel us to look over our shoulders at Death.

Do you ask me what this preamble means? It refers to Cornelius Senecio, a distinguished and capable Roman knight, whom you knew: from humble beginnings he had advanced himself to fortune, and the rest of the path already lay downhill before him. For it is easier to grow in dignity than to make a start; 2. and money is very slow to come where there is poverty; until it can creep out of that, it goes halting. Senecio was already bordering upon wealth, helped in that direction by two very powerful assets – knowing how to make money and how to keep it also; either one of these gifts might have made him a rich man. 3. Here was a person who lived most simply, careful of health and wealth alike. He had, as usual, called upon me early in the morning, and had then spent the whole day, even up to nightfall, at the bedside of a friend who was seriously and hopelessly ill. After a comfortable dinner, he was suddenly seized with an acute attack of quinsy, and, with the breath clogged tightly in his swollen throat, barely lived until daybreak. So within a very few hours after the time when he had been performing all the duties of a sound and healthy man, he passed away. 4. He who was venturing investments by land and sea, who had also entered public life and left no type of business untried, during the very realization of financial success and during the very onrush of the money that flowed into his coffers, was snatched from the world!

Graft now thy pears, Meliboeus, and set out thy vines in their order!

But how foolish it is to set out one's life, when one is not even owner of the morrow! O what madness it is to plot out far-reaching hopes! To say: "I will buy and build, loan and call in money, win titles of honour, and then, old and full of years, I will surrender myself to a life of ease." 5. Believe me when I say that everything is doubtful, even for those who are prosperous. No one has any right to draw for himself upon the future. The very thing that we grasp slips through our hands, and chance cuts into the actual hour which we are crowding so full. Time does indeed roll along by fixed law, but as in darkness; and what is it to me whether Nature's course is sure, when my own is unsure?

6. We plan distant voyages and long-postponed home-comings after roaming over foreign shores, we plan for military service and the slow rewards of hard campaigns, we canvass for governorships and the promotions of one office after another – and all the while death stands at our side; but since we never think of it except as it affects our neighbour, instances of mortality press upon us day by day, to remain in our minds only as long as they stir our wonder.

7. Yet what is more foolish than to wonder that something which may happen every day has happened on any one day? There is indeed a limit fixed for us, just

where the remorseless law of Fate has fixed it; but none of us knows how near he is to this limit. Therefore, let us so order our minds as if we had come to the very end. Let us postpone nothing. Let us balance life's account every day. **8.** The greatest flaw in life is that it is always imperfect, and that a certain part of it is postponed. One who daily puts the finishing touches to his life is never in want of time. And yet, from this want arise fear and a craving for the future which eats away the mind. There is nothing more wretched than worry over the outcome of future events; as to the amount or the nature of that which remains, our troubled minds are set aflutter with unaccountable fear.

9. How, then, shall we avoid this vacillation? In one way only, – if there be no reaching forward in our life, if it is withdrawn into itself. For he only is anxious about the future, to whom the present is unprofitable. But when I have paid my soul its due, when a soundly-balanced mind knows that a day differs not a whit from eternity – whatever days or problems the future may bring – then the soul looks forth from lofty heights and laughs heartily to itself when it thinks upon the ceaseless succession of the ages. For what disturbance can result from the changes and the instability of Chance, if you are sure in the face of that which is unsure?

10. Therefore, my dear Lucilius, begin at once to live, and count each separate day as a separate life. He who has thus prepared himself, he whose daily life has been a rounded whole, is easy in his mind; but those who live for hope alone find that the immediate future always slips from their grasp and that greed steals along in its place, and the fear of death, a curse which lays a curse upon everything else. Thence came that most debased of prayers, in which Maecenas does not refuse to suffer weakness, deformity, and as a climax the pain of crucifixion provided only that he may prolong the breath of life amid these sufferings:

> **11.** Fashion me with a palsied hand,
> Weak of foot, and a cripple;
> Build upon me a crook-backed hump;
> Shake my teeth till they rattle;
> All is well, if my life remains.
> Save, oh, save it, I pray you,
> Though I sit on the piercing cross!

12. There he is, praying for that which, if it had befallen him, would be the most pitiable thing in the world! And seeking a postponement of suffering, as if he were asking for life! I should deem him most despicable had he wished to live up to the very time of crucifixion: "Nay," he cries, "you may weaken my body if you will only leave the breath of life in my battered and ineffective carcass! Maim me if you will, but allow me, misshapen and deformed as I may be, just a little more time in the world! You may nail me up and set my seat upon the piercing cross!" Is it worth while to weigh down upon one's own wound, and hang impaled upon a gibbet, that one may but postpone something which is the balm of troubles, the end of punishment? Is it worth all this to possess the breath of life only to give it up? **13.** What would you ask for Maecenas but the indulgence of Heaven? What does he mean by such womanish and indecent verse? What does he mean by making terms with panic fear? What does he mean by begging so vilely for life? He cannot ever have heard Vergil read the words:

Tell me, is Death so wretched as that?

He asks for the climax of suffering, and – what is still harder to bear – prolongation and extension of suffering; and what does he gain thereby? Merely the boon of a longer existence. But what sort of life is a lingering death? **14.** Can anyone be found who would prefer wasting away in pain, dying limb by limb, or letting out his life drop by drop, rather than expiring once for all? Can any man be found willing to be fastened to the accursed tree, long sickly, already deformed, swelling with ugly tumours on chest and shoulders, and draw the breath of life amid long-drawn-out agony? I think he would have many excuses for dying even before mounting the cross!

Deny, now, if you can, that Nature is very generous in making death inevitable. **15.** Many men have been prepared to enter upon still more shameful bargains: to betray friends in order to live longer themselves, or voluntarily to debase their children and so enjoy the light of day which is witness of all their sins. We must get rid of this craving for life, and learn that it makes no difference when your suffering comes, because at some time you are bound to suffer. The point is, not how long you live, but how nobly you live. And often this living nobly means that you cannot live long. Farewell.

CII. ON THE INTIMATIONS OF OUR IMMORTALITY

1. Just as a man is annoying when he rouses a dreamer of pleasant dreams (for he is spoiling a pleasure which may be unreal but nevertheless has the appearance of reality), even so your letter has done me an injury. For it brought me back abruptly, absorbed as I was in agreeable meditation and ready to proceed still further if it had been permitted me. **2.** I was taking pleasure in investigating the immortality of souls, nay, in believing that doctrine. For I was lending a ready ear to the opinions of the great authors, who not only approve but promise this most pleasing condition. I was giving myself over to such a noble hope; for I was already weary of myself, beginning already to despise the fragments of my shattered existence, and feeling that I was destined to pass over into that infinity of time and the heritage of eternity, when I was suddenly awakened by the receipt of your letter, and lost my lovely dream. But, if I can once dispose of you, I shall reseek and rescue it.

3. There was a remark, at the beginning of your letter, that I had not explained the whole problem wherein I was endeavouring to prove one of the beliefs of our school, that the renown which falls to one's lot after death is a good; for I had not solved the problem with which we are usually confronted: "No good can consist of

15. By these words, and words of a like kind, the malignity of the ulcer is quieted down; and I hope indeed that it can be reduced, and either cured or brought to a stop, and grow old along with the patient himself. I am, however, comfortable in my mind regarding him; what we are now discussing is our own loss – the taking-off of a most excellent old man. For he himself has lived a full life, and anything additional may be craved by him, not for his own sake, but for the sake of those who need his services. **16.** In continuing to live, he deals generously. Some other person might have put an end to these sufferings; but our friend considers it no less base to flee from death than to flee towards death. "But," comes the answer, "if circumstances warrant, shall he not take his departure?" Of course, if he can no longer be of service to anyone, if all his business will be to deal with pain. **17.** This, my dear Lucilius, is what we mean by studying philosophy while applying it, by practising it on truth – note what courage a prudent man possesses against death, or against pain, when the one approaches and the other weighs heavily. What ought to be done must be learned from one who does it. **18.** Up to now we have dealt with arguments – whether any man can resist pain, or whether the approach of death can cast down even great souls. Why discuss it further? Here is an immediate fact for us to tackle – death does not make our friend braver to face pain, nor pain to face death. Rather does he trust himself in the face of both; he does not suffer with resignation because he hopes for death, nor does he die gladly because he is tired of suffering. Pain he endures, death he awaits. Farewell.

XCIX. ON CONSOLATION TO THE BEREAVED

1. I enclose a copy of the letter which I wrote to Marullus at the time when he had lost his little son and was reported to be rather womanish in his grief – a letter in which I have not observed the usual form of condolence: for I did not believe that he should be handled gently, since in my opinion he deserved criticism rather than consolation. When a man is stricken and is finding it most difficult to endure a grievous wound, one must humour him for a while; let him satisfy his grief or at any rate work off the first shock; **2.** but those who have assumed an indulgence in grief should be rebuked forthwith, and should learn that there are certain follies even in tears.

"Is it solace that you look for? Let me give you a scolding instead! You are like a woman in the way you take your son's death; what would you do if you had lost an intimate friend? A son, a little child of unknown promise, is dead; a fragment of time has been lost. **3.** We hunt out excuses for grief; we would even utter unfair complaints about Fortune, as if Fortune would never give us just reason for complaining! But I had really thought that you possessed spirit enough to deal with concrete troubles, to say nothing of the shadowy troubles over which men make moan through force of habit. Had you lost a friend (which is the greatest blow of all), you would have things that are distinct and separate; yet renown consists of such things." **4.** What you are asking about, my dear Lucilius, belongs to another topic of the same subject, and that is why I had postponed the arguments, not only on this one topic, but on other topics which also covered the same ground. For, as you know, certain logical questions are mingled with ethical ones. Accordingly, I handled the essential part of my subject which has to do with conduct – as to whether it is foolish and useless to be concerned with what lies beyond our last day, or whether our goods die with us and there is nothing left of him who is no more, or whether any profit can be attained or attempted beforehand out of that which, when it comes, we shall not be capable of feeling.

5. All these things have a view to conduct, and therefore they have been inserted under the proper topic. But the remarks of dialecticians in opposition to this idea had to be sifted out, and were accordingly laid aside. Now that you demand an answer to them all, I shall examine all their statements, and then refute them singly. **6.** Unless, however, I make a preliminary remark, it will be impossible to understand my rebuttals. And what is that preliminary remark? Simply this: there are certain continuous bodies, such as a man; there are certain composite bodies, – as ships, houses, and everything which is the result of joining separate parts into one sum total: there are certain others made up of things that are distinct, each member remaining separate – like an army, a populace, or a senate. For the persons who go to make up such bodies are united by virtue of law or function; but by their nature they are distinct and individual. Well, what further prefatory remarks do I still wish to make? **7.** Simply this: we believe that nothing is a good, if it be composed of things that are distinct. For a single good should be checked and controlled by a single soul; and the essential quality of each single good should be single. This can be proved of itself whenever you desire; in the meanwhile, however, it had to be laid aside, because our own weapons are being hurled at us.

8. Opponents speak thus: "You say, do you, that no good can be made up of things that are distinct? Yet this renown, of which you speak, is simply the favourable opinion of good men. For just as reputation does not consist of one person's remarks, and as ill repute does not consist of one person's disapproval, so renown does not mean that we have merely pleased one good person. In order to constitute renown, the agreement of many distinguished and praiseworthy men is necessary. But this results from the decision of a number – in other words, of persons who are distinct. Therefore, it is not a good. **9.** You say, again, that renown is the praise rendered to a good man by good men. Praise means speech: now speech is utterance with a particular meaning; and utterance, even from the lips of good men, is not a good in itself. For any act of a good man is not necessarily a good; he shouts his applause and hisses his disapproval, but one does not call the shouting or the hissing good – although his entire conduct may be admired and praised – any more than one would applaud a sneeze or a cough. Therefore, renown is not a good. **10.** Finally, tell us whether the good belongs to him who praises, or to him who is praised: if you say that the good belongs to him who is praised, you are on as foolish a quest as if you were to maintain that my neighbour's good health is my own. But to praise worthy men is an honourable action; thus the good is exclusively that of the man who does the praising, of the man who performs the action, and not of us, who are being praised. And yet this was the question under discussion."

11. I shall now answer the separate objections hurriedly. The first question still is, whether any good can consist of things that are distinct – and there are votes cast on both sides. Again, does renown need many votes? Renown can be satisfied with the decision of one good man: it is one good man who decides that we are good. **12.** Then the retort is: "What! Would you define reputation as the esteem of one individual, and ill-repute as the rancorous chatter of one man? Glory, too, we take to be more widespread, for it demands the agreement of many men." But the position of the "many" is different from that of "the one." And why? Because, if the good man thinks well of me, it practically amounts to my being thought well of by all good men; for they will all think the same, if they know me. Their judgment is alike and identical; the effect of truth on it is equal. They cannot disagree, which means that they would all hold the same view, being unable to hold different views. **13.** "One man's opinion," you say, "is not enough to create glory or reputation." In the former case, one judgment is a universal judgment, because all, if they were asked, would hold one opinion; in the other case, however, men of dissimilar character give divergent judgments. You will find perplexing emotions – everything doubtful, inconstant, untrustworthy. And can you suppose that all men are able to hold one opinion? Even an individual does not hold to a single opinion. With the good man it is truth that causes belief, and truth has but one function and one likeness; while among the second class of which I spoke, the ideas with which they agree are unsound. Moreover, those who are false are never steadfast: they are irregular and discordant. **14.** "But praise," says the objector, "is nothing but an utterance, and an utterance is not a good." When they say that renown is praise bestowed on the good by the good, what they refer to is not an utterance but a judgment. For a good man may remain silent; but if he decides that a certain person is worthy, of praise, that person is the object of praise. **15.** Besides, praise is one thing, and the giving of praise another; the latter demands utterance also. Hence no one speaks of "a funeral praise," but says "praise-giving" – for its function depends upon speech. And when we say that a man is worthy of praise, we assure human kindness to him, not in words, but in judgment. So the good opinion, even of one who in silence feels inward approval of a good man, is praise.

16. Again, as I have said, praise is a matter of the mind rather than of the speech; for speech brings out the praise that the mind has conceived, and publishes it forth to the attention of the many. To judge a man worthy of praise, is to praise him. And when our tragic poet sings to us that it is wonderful "to be praised by a well-praised hero," he means, "by one who is worthy of praise." Again, when an equally venerable bard says: "Praise nurtureth the arts," he does not mean the giving of praise, for that spoils the arts. Nothing has corrupted oratory and all other studies that depend on hearing so much as popular approval. **17.** Reputation necessarily demands words, but renown can be content with men's judgments, and suffice without the spoken word. It is satisfied not only amid silent approval, but even in the face of open protest. There is, in my opinion, this difference between renown and glory – the latter depends upon the judgments of the many; but renown on the judgments of good men. **18.** The retort comes: "But whose good is this renown, this praise rendered to a good man by good men? Is it of the one praised, or of the one who praises?" Of both, I say. It is my own good, in that I am praised, because I am naturally born to love all men, and I rejoice in having done good deeds and congratulate myself on having found men who express their ideas of my virtues with gratitude; that they are grateful, is a good to the many, but it is a good to me also. For my spirit is so ordered that I can regard the good of other men as my own – in any case those of whose good I am myself the cause. **19.** This good is also the good of those who render the praise, for it is applied by means of virtue; and every act of virtue is a good. My friends could not have found this blessing if I had not been a man of the right stamp. It is therefore a good belonging to both sides – this being praised when one deserves it – just as truly as a good decision is the good of him who makes the decision and also of him in whose favour the decision was given. Do you doubt that justice is a blessing to its possessor, as well as to the man to whom the just due was paid? To praise the deserving is justice; therefore, the good belongs to both sides.

20. This will be a sufficient answer to such dealers in subtleties. But it should not be our purpose to discuss things cleverly and to drag Philosophy down from her majesty to such petty quibbles. How much better it is to follow the open and direct road, rather than to map out for yourself a circuitous route which you must retrace with infinite trouble! For such argumentation is nothing else than the sport of men who are skilfully juggling with each other. **21.** Tell me rather how closely in accord with nature it is to let one's mind reach out into the boundless universe! The human soul is a great and noble thing; it permits of no limits except those which can be shared even by the gods. First of all, it does not consent to a lowly birthplace, like Ephesus or Alexandria, or any land that is even more thickly populated than these, and more richly spread with dwellings. The soul's homeland is the whole space that encircles the, height and breadth of the firmament, the whole rounded dome within which lie land and sea, within which the upper air that sunders the human from the divine also unites them, and where all the sentinel stars are taking their turn on duty. **22.** Again, the soul will not put up with a narrow span of existence. "All the years," says the soul, "are mine; no epoch is closed to great minds; all Time is open for the progress of thought. When the day comes to separate the heavenly from its earthly blend, I shall leave the body here where I found it, and shall of my own volition betake myself to the gods. I am not apart from them now, but am merely detained in a heavy and earthly prison." **23.** These delays of mortal existence are a prelude to the longer and better life. As the mother's womb holds us for ten months, making us ready, not for the womb itself, but for the existence into which we seem to be sent forth when at last we are fitted to draw breath and live in the open; just so, throughout the years extending between infancy and old age, we are making ourselves ready for another birth. A different beginning, a different condition, await us. **24.** We cannot yet, except at rare intervals, endure the light of heaven; therefore, look forward without fearing to that appointed hour, – the last hour of the body but not of the soul. Survey everything that lies about you, as if it were luggage in a guest-chamber: you must travel on. Nature strips you as bare at your departure as at your entrance. **25.** You may take away no more than you brought in; what is more, you must throw away the major portion of that which you brought with you into life: you will be stripped of the very skin which covers you – that which has been your last protection; you will be stripped of the flesh, and lose the blood which is suffuses and circulated through your body; you will be stripped of bones and sinews, the framework of these transitory and feeble parts.

26. That day, which you fear as being the end of all things, is the birthday of your eternity. Lay aside your burden – why delay? – just as if you had not previously left the body which was your hiding-place! You cling to your burden, you struggle; at your birth also great effort was necessary on your mother's part to set you free. You weep and wail; and yet this very weeping happens at birth also; but then it was to be excused – for you came into the world wholly ignorant and inexperienced. When you left the warm and cherishing protection of your mother's womb, a freer air breathed into your face; then you winced at the touch of a rough hand, and you looked in amaze at unfamiliar objects, still delicate and ignorant of all things.

27. But now it is no new thing for you to be sundered from that of which you have previously been a part; let go your already useless limbs with resignation and dispense with that body in which you have dwelt for so long. It will be torn asunder, buried out of sight, and wasted away. Why be downcast? This is what ordinarily happens: when we are born, the afterbirth always perishes. Why love such a thing as if it were your own possession? It was merely your covering. The day will come which will tear you forth and lead you away from the company of the foul and noisome womb. **28.** Withdraw from it now too as much as you can, and withdraw from pleasure, except such as may be bound up with essential and important things; estrange yourself from it even now, and ponder on something nobler and loftier. Some day the secrets of nature shall be disclosed to you, the haze will be shaken from your eyes, and the bright light will stream in upon you from all sides.

Picture to yourself how great is the glow when all the stars mingle their fires; no shadows will disturb the clear sky. The whole expanse of heaven will shine evenly; for day and night are interchanged only in the lowest atmosphere. Then you will say that you have lived in darkness, after you have seen, in your perfect state, the perfect light – that light which now you behold darkly with vision that is cramped to the last degree. And yet, far off as it is, you already look upon it in wonder; what do you think the heavenly light will be when you have seen it in its proper sphere?

29. Such thoughts permit nothing mean to settle in the soul, nothing low, nothing cruel. They maintain that the gods are witnesses of everything. They order us to meet the gods' approval, to prepare ourselves to join them at some future time, and to plan for immortality. He that has grasped this idea shrinks from no attacking army, is not terrified by the trumpet-blast, and is intimidated by no threats. **30.** How should it not be that a man feels no fear, if he looks forward to death? He also who believes that the soul abides only as long as it is fettered in the body, scatters it abroad forthwith when dissolved, so that it may be useful even after death. For though he is taken from men's sight, still

> Often our thoughts run back to the hero, and often the glory
> Won by his race recurs to the mind.

Consider how much we are helped by good example; you will thus understand that the presence of a noble man is of no less service than his memory. Farewell.

CIII. ON THE DANGERS OF ASSOCIATION WITH OUR FELLOW-MEN

1. Why are you looking about for troubles which may perhaps come your way, but which may indeed not come your way at all? I mean fires, falling buildings, and other accidents of the sort that are mere events rather than plots against us. Rather beware and shun those troubles which dog our steps and reach out their hands against us. Accidents, though they may be serious, are few – such as being shipwrecked or thrown from one's carriage; but it is from his fellow-man that a man's everyday danger comes. Equip yourself against that; watch that with an attentive eye. There is no evil more frequent, no evil more persistent, no evil more insinuating. **2.** Even the storm, before it gathers, gives a warning; houses crack before they crash; and smoke is the forerunner of fire. But damage from man is instantaneous, and the nearer it comes the more carefully it is concealed.

You are wrong to trust the countenances of those you meet. They have the aspect of men, but the souls of brutes; the difference is that only beasts damage you at the first encounter; those whom they have passed by they do not pursue. For nothing ever goads them to do harm except when need compels them: it is hunger or fear that forces them into a fight. But man delights to ruin man.

3. You must, however, reflect thus what danger you run at the hand of man, in order that you may deduce what is the duty of man. Try, in your dealings with others, to harm not, in order that you be not harmed. You should rejoice with all in their joys and sympathize with them in their troubles, remembering what you should offer and what you should withhold. **4.** And what may you attain by living such a life? Not necessarily freedom from harm at their hands, but at least freedom from deceit. In so far, however, as you are able, take refuge with philosophy: she will cherish you in her bosom, and in her sanctuary you shall be safe, or, at any rate, safer than before. People collide only when they are travelling the same path. **5.** But this very philosophy must never be vaunted by you; for philosophy when employed with insolence and arrogance has been perilous to many. Let her strip off your faults, rather than assist you to decry the faults of others. Let her not hold aloof from the customs of mankind, nor make it her business to condemn whatever she herself does not do. A man may be wise without parade and without arousing enmity. Farewell.

CIV. ON CARE OF HEALTH AND PEACE OF MIND

1. I have run off to my villa at Nomentum, for what purpose, do you suppose? To escape the city? No; to shake off a fever which was surely working its way into my system. It had already got a grip upon me. My physician kept insisting that when the circulation was upset and irregular, disturbing the natural poise, the disease was under way. I therefore ordered my carriage to be made ready at once, and insisted on departing in spite of my wife Paulina's efforts to stop me; for I remembered master Gallio's words, when he began to develop a fever in Achaia and took ship at once, insisting that the disease was not of the body but of the place. **2.** That is what I remarked to my dear Paulina, who always urges me to take care of my health. I know that her very life-breath comes and goes with my own, and I am beginning, in my solicitude for her, to be solicitous for myself. And although old age has made me braver to bear many things, I am gradually losing this boon that old age bestows. For it comes into my mind that in this old man there is a youth also, and youth needs tenderness. Therefore, since I cannot prevail upon her to love me any more heroically, she prevails upon me to cherish myself more carefully. **3.** For one must indulge genuine emotions; sometimes, even in spite of weighty reasons, the breath of life must be called back and kept at our very lips even at the price of great suffering, for the sake of those whom we hold dear; because the good man should not live as long as it pleases him, but as long as he ought. He who does not value his wife, or his friend, highly enough to linger longer in life – he who obstinately persists in dying is a voluptuary.

The soul should also enforce this command upon itself whenever the needs of one's relatives require; it should pause and humour those near and dear, not only when it desires, but even when it has begun, to die. **4.** It gives proof of a great heart to return to life for the sake of others; and noble men have often done this. But this procedure also, I believe, indicates the highest type of kindness: that although the greatest advantage of old age is the opportunity to be more negligent regarding self-preservation and to use life more adventurously, one should watch over one's old age with still greater care if one knows that such action is pleasing, useful, or desirable in the eyes of a person whom one holds dear. **5.** This is also a source of no mean joy and profit; for what is sweeter than to be so valued by one's wife that one becomes more valuable to oneself for this reason? Hence my dear Paulina is able to make me responsible, not only for her fears, but also for my own.

6. So you are curious to know the outcome of this prescription of travel? As soon as I escaped from the oppressive atmosphere of the city, and from that awful odour of reeking kitchens which, when in use, pour forth a ruinous mess of steam and soot, I perceived at once that my health was mending. And how much stronger do you think I felt when I reached my vineyards! Being, so to speak, let out to pasture, I regularly walked into my meals! So I am my old self again, feeling now no wavering languor in my system, and no sluggishness in my brain. I am beginning to work with all my energy.

7. But the mere place avails little for this purpose, unless the mind is fully master of itself, and can, at its pleasure, find seclusion even in the midst of business; the man, however, who is always selecting resorts and hunting for leisure, will find something to distract his mind in every place. Socrates is reported to have replied, when a certain person complained of having received no benefit from his travels: "It serves you right! You travelled in your own company!" **8.** O what a blessing it would be for some men to wander away from themselves! As it is, they cause themselves vexation, worry, demoralization, and fear! What profit is there in crossing the sea and in going from one city to another? If you would escape your troubles, you need not another place but another personality. Perhaps you have reached Athens, or perhaps Rhodes; choose any state you fancy, how does it matter what its character may be? You will be bringing to it your own.

9. Suppose that you hold wealth to be a good: poverty will then distress you, and, – which is most pitiable, – it will be an imaginary poverty. For you may be rich, and nevertheless, because your neighbour is richer, you suppose yourself to be poor exactly by the same amount in which you fall short of your neighbour. You may deem official position a good; you will be vexed at another's appointment or re-appointment to the consulship; you will be jealous whenever you see a name several times in the state records. Your ambition will be so frenzied that you will regard yourself last in the race if there is anyone in front of you. **10.** Or you may rate death as the worst of evils, although there is really no evil therein except that which precedes death's coming – fear. You will be frightened out of your wits, not only by real, but by fancied dangers, and will be tossed for ever on the sea of illusion. What benefit will it be to

> Have threaded all the towns of Argolis,
> A fugitive through midmost press of foes?

For peace itself will furnish further apprehension. Even in the midst of safety you will have no confidence if your mind has once been given a shock; once it has acquired the habit of blind panic, it is incapable of providing even for its own safety. For it does not avoid danger, but runs away. Yet we are more exposed to danger when we turn our backs.

11. You may judge it the most grievous of ills to lose any of those you love; while all the same this would be no less foolish than weeping because the trees which charm your eye and adorn your home lose their foliage. Regard everything that pleases you as if it were a flourishing plant; make the most of it while it is in leaf, for different plants at different seasons must fall and die. But just as the loss of leaves is a light thing, because they are born afresh, so it is with the loss of those whom you love and regard as the delight of your life; for they can be replaced even though they cannot be born afresh. 12. "New friends, however, will not be the same." No, nor will you yourself remain the same; you change with every day and every hour. But in other men you more readily see what time plunders; in your own case the change is hidden, because it will not take place visibly. Others are snatched from sight; we ourselves are being stealthily filched away from ourselves. You will not think about any of these problems, nor will you apply remedies to these wounds. You will of your own volition be sowing a crop of trouble by alternate hoping and despairing. If you are wise, mingle these two elements: do not hope without despair, or despair without hope.

13. What benefit has travel of itself ever been able to give anyone? No restraint upon pleasure, no bridling of desire, no checking of bad temper, no crushing of the wild assaults of passion, no opportunity to rid the soul of evil. Travelling cannot give us judgment, or shake off our errors; it merely holds our attention for a moment by a certain novelty, as children pause to wonder at something unfamiliar. 14. Besides, it irritates us, through the wavering of a mind which is suffering from an acute attack of sickness; the very motion makes it more fitful and nervous. Hence the spots we had sought most eagerly we quit still more eagerly, like birds that flit and are off as soon as they have alighted. 15. What travel will give is familiarity with other nations: it will reveal to you mountains of strange shape, or unfamiliar tracts of plain, or valleys that are watered by everflowing springs, or the characteristics of some river that comes to our attention. We observe how the Nile rises and swells in summer, or how the Tigris disappears, runs underground through hidden spaces, and then appears with unabated sweep; or how the Maeander, that oft-rehearsed theme and plaything of the poets, turns in frequent bendings, and often in winding comes close to its own channel before resuming its course. But this sort of information will not make better or sounder men of us.

16. We ought rather to spend our time in study, and to cultivate those who are masters of wisdom, learning something which has been investigated, but not settled; by this means the mind can be relieved of a most wretched serfdom, and won over to freedom. Indeed, as long as you are ignorant of what you should avoid or seek, or of what is necessary or superfluous, or of what is right or wrong, you will not be travelling, but merely wandering. 17. There will be no benefit to you in this hurrying to and fro; for you are travelling with your emotions and are followed by your afflictions. Would that they were indeed following you! In that case, they would be farther away; as it is, you are carrying and not leading them. Hence they

press about you on all sides, continually chafing and annoying you. It is medicine, not scenery, for which the sick man must go a-searching. **18.** Suppose that someone has broken a leg or dislocated a joint: he does not take carriage or ship for other regions, but he calls in the physician to set the fractured limb, or to move it back to its proper place in the socket. What then? When the spirit is broken or wrenched in so many places, do you think that change of place can heal it? The complaint is too deep-seated to be cured by a journey. **19.** Travel does not make a physician or an orator; no art is acquired by merely living in a certain place.

Where lies the truth, then? Can wisdom, the greatest of all the arts, be picked up on a journey? I assure you, travel as far as you like, you can never establish yourself beyond the reach of desire, beyond the reach of bad temper, or beyond the reach of fear; had it been so, the human race would long ago have banded together and made a pilgrimage to the spot. Such ills, as long as you carry with you their causes, will load you down and worry you to skin and bone in your wanderings over land and sea. **20.** Do you wonder that it is of no use to run away from them? That from which you are running, is within you. Accordingly, reform your own self, get the burden off your own shoulders, and keep within safe limits the cravings which ought to be removed. Wipe out from your soul all trace of sin. If you would enjoy your travels, make healthy the companion of your travels. As long as this companion is avaricious and mean, greed will stick to you; and while you consort with an overbearing man, your puffed-up ways will also stick close. Live with a hangman, and you will never be rid of your cruelty. If an adulterer be your club-mate, he will kindle the baser passions. **21.** If you would be stripped of your faults leave far behind you the patterns of the faults. The miser, the swindler, the bully, the cheat, who will do you much harm merely by being near you, are within you.

Change therefore to better associations: live with the Catos, with Laelius, with Tubero. Or, if you enjoy living with Greeks also, spend your time with Socrates and with Zeno: the former will show you how to die if it be necessary; the latter how to die before it is necessary. **22.** Live with Chrysippus, with Posidonius: they will make you acquainted with things earthly and things heavenly; they will bid you work hard over something more than neat turns of language and phrases mouthed forth for the entertainment of listeners; they will bid you be stout of heart and rise superior to threats. The only harbour safe from the seething storms of this life is scorn of the future, a firm stand, a readiness to receive Fortune's missiles full in the breast, neither skulking nor turning the back. **23.** Nature has brought us forth brave of spirit, and, as she has implanted in certain animals a spirit of ferocity, in others craft, in others terror, so she has gifted us with an aspiring and lofty spirit, which prompts us to seek a life of the greatest honour, and not of the greatest security, that most resembles the soul of the universe, which it follows and imitates as far as our mortal steps permit. This spirit thrusts itself forward, confident of commendation and esteem. **24.** It is superior to all, monarch of all it surveys; hence it should be subservient to nothing, finding no task too heavy, and nothing strong enough to weigh down the shoulders of a man.

> Shapes dread to look upon, of toil or death

are not in the least dreadful, if one is able to look upon them with unflinching gaze, and is able to pierce the shadows. Many a sight that is held a terror in the night-time, is turned to ridicule by day. "Shapes dread to look upon, of toil or death": our Vergil has excellently said that these shapes are dread, not in reality, but only "to look upon" – in other words, they seem terrible, but are not. **25.** And in these visions what is there, I say, as fear-inspiring as rumour has proclaimed? Why, pray, my dear Lucilius, should a man fear toil, or a mortal death? Countless cases occur to my mind of men who think that what they themselves are unable to do is impossible, who maintain that we utter words which are too big for man's nature to carry out. **26.** But how much more highly do I think of these men! They can do these things, but decline to do them. To whom that ever tried have these tasks proved false? To what man did they not seem easier in the doing? Our lack of confidence is not the result of difficulty. The difficulty comes from our lack of confidence.

27. If, however, you desire a pattern, take Socrates, a long-suffering old man, who was sea-tossed amid every hardship and yet was unconquered both by poverty (which his troubles at home made more burdensome) and by toil, including the drudgery of military service. He was much tried at home, whether we think of his wife, a woman of rough manners and shrewish tongue, or of the children whose intractability showed them to be more like their mother than their father. And if you consider the facts, he lived either in time of war, or under tyrants, or under a democracy, which is more cruel than wars and tyrants. **28.** The war lasted for twenty-seven years; then the state became the victim of the Thirty Tyrants, of whom many were his personal enemies. At the last came that climax of condemnation under the gravest of charges: they accused him of disturbing the state religion and corrupting the youth, for they declared that he had influenced the youth to defy the gods, to defy the council, and to defy the state in general. Next came the prison, and the cup of poison. But all these measures changed the soul of Socrates so little that they did not even change his features. What wonderful and rare distinction! He maintained this attitude up to the very end, and no man ever saw Socrates too much elated or too much depressed. Amid all the disturbance of Fortune, he was undisturbed.

29. Do you desire another case? Take that of the younger Marcus Cato, with whom Fortune dealt in a more hostile and more persistent fashion. But he withstood her, on all occasions, and in his last moments, at the point of death, showed that a brave man can live in spite of Fortune, can die in spite of her. His whole life was passed either in civil warfare, or under a political regime which was soon to breed civil war. And you may say that he, just as much as Socrates, declared allegiance to liberty in the midst of slavery – unless perchance you think that Pompey, Caesar, and Crassus were the allies of liberty! **30.** No one ever saw Cato change, no matter how often the state changed: he kept himself the same in all circumstances – in the praetorship, in defeat, under accusation, in his province, on the platform, in the army, in death. Furthermore, when the republic was in a crisis of terror, when Caesar was on one side with ten embattled legions at his call, aided by so many foreign nations. and when Pompey was on the other, satisfied to stand alone against all comers, and when the citizens were leaning towards either Caesar or Pompey, Cato alone established a definite party for the Republic. **31.** If you would obtain a mental picture of that period, you may imagine on one side the people and the whole proletariat eager for revolution – on the other the senators and knights, the chosen and honoured men of the commonwealth; and there were left between them but these two – the Republic and Cato.

I tell you, you will marvel when you see

> Atreus' son, and Priam, and Achilles, wroth at both.

Like Achilles, he scorns and disarms each faction. **32.** And this is the vote which he casts concerning them both: "If Caesar wins, I slay myself; if Pompey, I go into exile." What was there for a man to fear who, whether in defeat or in victory, had assigned to himself a doom which might have been assigned to him by his enemies in their utmost rage? So he died by his own decision.

33. You see that man can endure toil: Cato, on foot, led an army through African deserts. You see that thirst can be endured: he marched over sun-baked hills, dragging the remains of a beaten army and with no train of supplies, undergoing lack of water and wearing a heavy suit of armour; always the last to drink of the few springs which they chanced to find. You see that honour, and dishonour too, can be despised: for they report that on the very day when Cato was defeated at the elections, he played a game of ball. You see also that man can be free from fear of those above him in rank: for Cato attacked Caesar and Pompey simultaneously, at a time when none dared fall foul of the one without endeavouring to oblige the other. You see that death can be scorned as well as exile: Cato inflicted exile upon himself and finally death, and war all the while.

34. And so, if only we are willing to withdraw our necks from the yoke, we can keep as stout a heart against such terrors as these. But first and foremost, we must reject pleasures; they render us weak and womanish; they make great demands upon us, and, moreover, cause us to make great demands upon Fortune. Second, we must spurn wealth: wealth is the diploma of slavery. Abandon gold and silver, and whatever else is a burden upon our richly-furnished homes; liberty cannot be gained for nothing. If you set a high value on liberty, you must set a low value on everything else. Farewell.

CV. ON FACING THE WORLD WITH CONFIDENCE

1. I shall now tell you certain things to which you should pay attention in order to live more safely. Do you however, – such is my judgment, – hearken to my precepts just as if I were counselling you to keep safe your health in your country-place at Ardea.

Reflect on the things which goad man into destroying man: you will find that they are hope, envy, hatred, fear, and contempt. **2.** Now, of all these, contempt is the least harmful, so much so that many have skulked behind it as a sort of cure. When a man despises you, he works you injury, to be sure, but he passes on; and no one persistently or of set purpose does hurt to a person whom he despises. Even in battle, prostrate soldiers are neglected: men fight with those who stand their ground. **3.** And you can avoid the envious hopes of the wicked so long as you have nothing which can stir the evil desires of others, and so long as you possess nothing remarkable. For people crave even little things, if these catch the attention or are of rare occurrence.

You will escape envy if you do not force yourself upon the public view, if you do not boast your possessions, if you understand how to enjoy things privately. Hatred comes either from running foul of others: and this can be avoided by never provoking anyone; or else it is uncalled for: and common-sense will keep you safe from it. Yet it has been dangerous to many; some people have been hated without having had an enemy. **4.** As to not being feared, a moderate fortune and an easy disposition will guarantee you that; men should know that you are the sort of person who can be offended without danger; and your reconciliation should be easy and sure. Moreover, it is as troublesome to be feared at home as abroad; it is as bad to be feared by a slave as by a gentleman. For every one has strength enough to do you some harm. Besides, he who is feared, fears also; no one has been able to arouse terror and live in peace of mind.

5. Contempt remains to be discussed. He who has made this quality an adjunct of his own personality, who is despised because he wishes to be despised and not because he *must* be despised, has the measure of contempt under his control. Any inconveniences in this respect can be dispelled by honourable occupations and by friendships with men who have influence with an influential person; with these men it will profit you to engage but not to entangle yourself, lest the cure may cost you more than the risk. **6.** Nothing, however, will help you so much as keeping still – talking very little with others, and as much as may be with yourself. For there is a sort of charm about conversation, something very subtle and coaxing, which, like intoxication or love, draws secrets from us. No man will keep to himself what he hears. No one will tell another only as much as he has heard. And he who tells tales will tell names, too. Everyone has someone to whom he entrusts exactly what has been entrusted to him. Though he checks his own garrulity, and is content with one hearer, he will bring about him a nation, if that which was a secret shortly before becomes common talk.

7. The most important contribution to peace of mind is never to do wrong. Those who lack self-control lead disturbed and tumultuous lives; their crimes are balanced by their fears, and they are never at ease. For they tremble after the deed, and they are embarrassed; their consciences do not allow them to busy themselves with other matters, and continually compel them to give an answer. Whoever expects punishment, receives it, but whoever deserves it, expects it. **8.** Where there is an evil conscience something may bring safety, but nothing can bring ease; for a man imagines that, even if he is not under arrest, he may soon be arrested. His sleep is troubled; when he speaks of another man's crime, he reflects upon his own, which seems to him not sufficiently blotted out, not sufficiently hidden from view. A wrongdoer sometimes has the luck to escape notice but never the assurance thereof. Farewell.

CVI. ON THE CORPOREALITY OF VIRTUE

1. My tardiness in answering your letter was not due to press of business. Do not listen to that sort of excuse; I am at liberty, and so is anyone else who wishes to be at liberty. No man is at the mercy of affairs. He gets entangled in them of his own accord, and then flatters himself that being busy is a proof of happiness. Very well; you no doubt want to know why I did not answer the letter sooner? The matter about which you consulted me was being gathered into the fabric of my volume. **2.** For you know that I am planning to cover the whole of moral philosophy and to settle all the problems which concern it. Therefore I hesitated whether to make you wait until the proper time came for this subject, or to pronounce judgment out of the logical order; but it seemed more kindly not to keep waiting one who comes from such a distance. **3.** So I propose both to pick this out of the proper sequence of correlated matter, and also to send you, without waiting to be asked, whatever has to do with questions of the same sort.

Do you ask what these are? Questions regarding which knowledge pleases rather than profits; for instance, your question whether the good is corporeal. **4.** Now the good is active: for it is beneficial; and what is active is corporeal. The good stimulates the mind and, in a way, moulds and embraces that which is essential to the body. The goods of the body are bodily; so therefore must be the goods of the soul. For the soul, too, is corporeal. **5.** Ergo, man's good must be corporeal, since man himself is corporeal. I am sadly astray if the elements which support man and preserve or restore his health, are not bodily; therefore, his good is a body. You will have no doubt, I am sure, that emotions are bodily things (if I may be allowed to wedge in another subject not under immediate discussion), like wrath, love, sternness; unless you doubt whether they change our features, knot our foreheads, relax the countenance, spread blushes, or drive away the blood? What, then? Do you think that such evident marks of the body are stamped upon us by anything else than body? **6.** And if emotions are corporeal, so are the diseases of the spirit

– such as greed, cruelty, and all the faults which harden in our souls, to such an extent that they get into an incurable state. Therefore evil is also, and all its branches – spite, hatred, pride; **7.** and so also are goods, first because they are opposite poles of the bad, and second because they will manifest to you the same symptoms. Do you not see how a spirit of bravery makes the eye flash? How prudence tends toward concentration? How reverence produces moderation and tranquillity? How joy produces calm? How sternness begets stiffness? How gentleness produces relaxation? These qualities are therefore bodily; for they change the tones and the shapes of substances, exercising their own power in their own kingdoms.

Now all the virtues which I have mentioned are goods, and so are their results. **8.** Have you any doubt that whatever can touch is corporeal?

> Nothing but body can touch or be touched,

as Lucretius says. Moreover, such changes as I have mentioned could not affect the body without touching it. Therefore, they are bodily. **9.** Furthermore, any object that has power to move, force, restrain, or control, is corporeal. Come now! Does not fear hold us back? Does not boldness drive us ahead? Bravery spur us on, and give us momentum? Restraint rein us in and call us back? Joy raise our spirits? Sadness cast us down? **10.** In short, any act on our part is performed at the bidding of wickedness or virtue. Only a body can control or forcefully affect another body. The good of the body is corporeal; a man's good is related to his bodily good; therefore, it is bodily.

11. Now that I have humoured your wishes, I shall anticipate your remark, when you say: "What a game of pawns!" We dull our fine edge by such superfluous pursuits; these things make men clever, but not good. **12.** Wisdom is a plainer thing than that; nay, it is clearly better to use literature for the improvement of the mind, instead of wasting philosophy itself as we waste other efforts on superfluous things. Just as we suffer from excess in all things, so we suffer from excess in literature; thus we learn our lessons, not for life, but for the lecture-room. Farewell.

CVII. ON OBEDIENCE TO THE UNIVERSAL WILL

1. Where is that common-sense of yours? Where that deftness in examining things? That greatness of soul? Have you come to be tormented by a trifle? Your slaves regarded your absorption in business as an opportunity for them to run away. Well, if your friends deceived you (for by all means let them have the name which we mistakenly bestowed upon them, and so call them, that they may incur more shame by not being such friends) – if your friends, I repeat, deceived you, all your affairs would lack something; as it is, you merely lack men who damaged your own endeavours and considered you burdensome to your neighbours. **2.** None of these things is unusual or unexpected. It is as nonsensical to be put out by such events as to complain of being spattered in the street or at getting befouled in the mud.

The programme of life is the same as that of a bathing establishment, a crowd, or a journey: sometimes things will be thrown at you, and sometimes they will strike you by accident. Life is not a dainty business. You have started on a long journey; you are bound to slip, collide, fall, become weary, and cry out: "O for Death!" – or in other words, tell lies. At one stage you will leave a comrade behind you, at another you will bury someone, at another you will be apprehensive. It is amid stumblings of this sort that you must travel out this rugged journey.

3. Does one wish to die? Let the mind be prepared to meet everything; let it know that it has reached the heights round which the thunder plays. Let it know that it has arrived where –

> Grief and avenging Care have set their couch,
> And pallid sickness dwells, and drear Old Age.

With such messmates must you spend your days. Avoid them you cannot, but despise them you can. And you will despise them, if you often take thought and anticipate the future. 4. Everyone approaches courageously a danger which he has prepared himself to meet long before, and withstands even hardships if he has previously practised how to meet them. But, contrariwise, the unprepared are panic-stricken even at the most trifling things. We must see to it that nothing shall come upon us unforeseen. And since things are all the more serious when they are unfamiliar, continual reflection will give you the power, no matter what the evil may be, not to play the unschooled boy.

5. "My slaves have run away from me!" Yes, other men have been robbed, blackmailed, slain, betrayed, stamped under foot, attacked by poison or by slander; no matter what trouble you mention, it has happened to many. Again, there are manifold kinds of missiles which are hurled at us. Some are planted in us, some are being brandished and at this very moment are on the way, some which were destined for other men graze us instead. 6. We should not manifest surprise at any sort of condition into which we are born, and which should be lamented by no one, simply because it is equally ordained for all. Yes, I say, equally ordained; for a man might have experienced even that which he has escaped. And an equal law consists, not of that which all have experienced, but of that which is laid down for all. Be sure to prescribe for your mind this sense of equity; we should pay without complaint the tax of our mortality.

7. Winter brings on cold weather; and we must shiver. Summer returns, with its heat; and we must sweat. Unseasonable weather upsets the health; and we must fall ill. In certain places we may meet with wild beasts, or with men who are more destructive than any beasts. Floods, or fires, will cause us loss. And we cannot change this order of things; but what we can do is to acquire stout hearts, worthy of good men, thereby courageously enduring chance and placing ourselves in harmony with Nature. 8. And Nature moderates this world-kingdom which you see, by her changing seasons: clear weather follows cloudy; after a calm, comes the storm; the

winds blow by turns; day succeeds night; some of the heavenly bodies rise, and some set. Eternity consists of opposites.

9. It is to this law that our souls must adjust themselves, this they should follow, this they should obey. Whatever happens, assume that it was bound to happen, and do not be willing to rail at Nature. That which you cannot reform, it is best to endure, and to attend uncomplainingly upon the God under whose guidance everything progresses; for it is a bad soldier who grumbles when following his commander. **10.** For this reason we should welcome our orders with energy and vigour, nor should we cease to follow the natural course of this most beautiful universe, into which all our future sufferings are woven.

Let us address Jupiter, the pilot of this world-mass, as did our great Cleanthes in those most eloquent lines – lines which I shall allow myself to render in Latin, after the example of the eloquent Cicero. If you like them, make the most of them; if they displease you, you will understand that I have simply been following the practise of Cicero:

> **11.** Lead me, O Master of the lofty heavens,
> My Father, whithersoever thou shalt wish.
> I shall not falter, but obey with speed.
> And though I would not, I shall go, and suffer,
> In sin and sorrow what I might have done
> In noble virtue. Aye, the willing soul
> Fate leads, but the unwilling drags along.

12. Let us live thus, and speak thus; let Fate find us ready and alert. Here is your great soul – the man who has given himself over to Fate; on the other hand, that man is a weakling and a degenerate who struggles and maligns the order of the universe and would rather reform the gods than reform himself. Farewell.

CVIII. ON THE APPROACHES TO PHILOSOPHY

1. The topic about which you ask me is one of those where our only concern with knowledge is to have the knowledge. Nevertheless, because it does so far concern us, you are in a hurry; you are not willing to wait for the books which I am at this moment arranging for you, and which embrace the whole department of moral philosophy. I shall send you the books at once; but I shall, before doing that, write and tell you how this eagerness to learn, with which I see you are aflame, should be regulated, so that it may not get in its own way. **2.** Things are not to be gathered at random; nor should they be greedily attacked in the mass; one will arrive at a knowledge of the whole by studying the parts. The burden should be suited to your strength, nor should you tackle more than you can adequately handle. Absorb not all that you wish, but all that you can hold. Only be of a sound mind, and then you will be able to hold all that you wish. For the more the mind receives, the more does it expand.

3. This was the advice, I remember, which Attalus gave me in the days when I practically laid siege to his class-room, the first to arrive and the last to leave. Even as he paced up and down, I would challenge him to various discussions; for he not only kept himself accessible to his pupils, but met them half-way. His words were: "The same purpose should possess both master and scholar – an ambition in the one case to promote, and in the other to progress." **4.** He who studies with a philosopher should take away with him some one good thing every day: he should daily return home a sounder man, or in the way to become sounder. And he will thus return; for it is one of the functions of philosophy to help not only those who study her, but those also who associate with her. He that walks in the sun, though he walk not for that purpose, must needs become sunburned. He who frequents the perfumer's shop and lingers even for a short time, will carry with him the scent of the place. And he who follows a philosopher is bound to derive some benefit therefrom, which will help him even though he be remiss. Mark what I say: "remiss," not "recalcitrant."

5. "What then?" you say, "do we not know certain men who have sat for many years at the feet of a philosopher and yet have not acquired the slightest tinge of wisdom?" Of course I know such men. There are indeed persevering gentlemen who stick at it; I do not call them pupils of the wise, but merely "squatters." **6.** Certain of them come to hear and not to learn, just as we are attracted to the theatre to satisfy the pleasures of the ear, whether by a speech, or by a song, or by a play. This class, as you will see, constitutes a large part of the listeners, who regard the philosopher's lecture-room merely as a sort of lounging-place for their leisure. They do not set about to lay aside any faults there, or to receive a rule of life, by which they may test their characters; they merely wish to enjoy to the full the delights of the ear. And yet some arrive even with notebooks, not to take down the matter, but only the words, that they may presently repeat them to others with as little profit to these as they themselves received when they heard them. **7.** A certain number are stirred by high-sounding phrases, and adapt themselves to the emotions of the speaker with lively change of face and mind – just like the emasculated Phrygian priests who are wont to be roused by the sound of the flute and go mad to order. But the true hearer is ravished and stirred by the beauty of the subject matter, not by the jingle of empty words. When a bold word has been uttered in defiance of death, or a saucy fling in defiance of Fortune, we take delight in acting straightway upon that which we have heard. Men are impressed by such words, and become what they are bidden to be, should but the impression abide in the mind, and should the populace, who discourage honourable things, not immediately lie in wait to rob them of this noble impulse; only a few can carry home the mental attitude with which they were inspired. **8.** It is easy to rouse a listener so that he will crave righteousness; for Nature has laid the foundations and planted the seeds of virtue in us all. And we are all born to these general privileges; hence, when the stimulus is added, the good spirit is stirred as if it were freed from bonds. Have you not noticed how the theatre re-echoes whenever any words are spoken whose truth we appreciate generally and confirm unanimously.

> **9.** The poor lack much; the greedy man lacks all.
> A greedy man does good to none; he does
> Most evil to himself.

At such verses as these, your meanest miser claps applause and rejoices to hear his own sins reviled. How much more do you think this holds true, when such things are uttered by a philosopher, when he introduces verses among his wholesome precepts, that he may thus make those verses sink more effectively into the mind of the neophyte! **10.** Cleanthes used to say: "As our breath produces a louder sound when it passes through the long and narrow opening of the trumpet and escapes by a hole which widens at the end, even so the fettering rules of poetry clarify our meaning." The very same words are more carelessly received and make less impression upon us, when they are spoken in prose; but when metre is added and when regular prosody has compressed a noble idea, then the selfsame thought comes, as it were, hurtling with a fuller fling. **11.** We talk much about despising money, and we give advice on this subject in the lengthiest of speeches, that mankind may believe true riches to exist in the mind and not in one's bank account, and that the man who adapts himself to his slender means and makes himself wealthy on a little sum, is the truly rich man; but our minds are struck more effectively when a verse like this is repeated:

> He needs but little who desires but little.

or,

> He hath his wish, whose wish includeth naught
> Save that which is enough.

12. When we hear such words as these, we are led towards a confession of the truth.

Even men in whose opinion nothing is enough, wonder and applaud when they hear such words, and swear eternal hatred against money. When you see them thus disposed, strike home, keep at them, and charge them with this duty, dropping all double meanings, syllogisms, hair-splitting, and the other side-shows of ineffective smartness. Preach against greed, preach against high living; and when you notice that you have made progress and impressed the minds of your hearers, lay on still harder. You cannot imagine how much progress can be brought about by an address of that nature, when you are bent on curing your hearers and are absolutely devoted to their best interests. For when the mind is young, it may most easily be won over to desire what is honourable and upright; truth, if she can obtain a suitable pleader, will lay strong hands upon those who can still be taught, those who have been but superficially spoiled.

13. At any rate, when I used to hear Attalus denouncing sin, error, and the evils of life, I often felt sorry for mankind and regarded Attalus as a noble and majestic being – above our mortal heights. He called himself a king, but I thought him more than a king, because he was entitled to pass judgment on kings. **14.** And in truth, when he began to uphold poverty, and to show what a useless and dangerous burden was everything that passed the measure of our need, I often desired to leave his lecture-room a poor man. Whenever he castigated our pleasure-seeking lives, and extolled personal purity, moderation in diet, and a mind free from unnecessary, not to speak of unlawful, pleasures, the desire came upon me to limit my food and drink. **15.** And that is why some of these habits have stayed with me, Lucilius. For I had planned my whole life with great resolves. And later, when I returned to the duties of a citizen, I did indeed keep a few of these good resolutions. That is why I have forsaken oysters and mushrooms for ever: since they are not really food, but are relishes to bully the sated stomach into further eating, as is the fancy of gourmands and those who stuff themselves beyond their powers of digestion: down with it quickly, and up with it quickly! **16.** That is why I have also throughout my life avoided perfumes; because the best scent for the person is no scent at all. That is why my stomach is unacquainted with wine. That is why throughout my life I have shunned the bath, and have believed that to emaciate the body and sweat it into thinness is at once unprofitable and effeminate. Other resolutions have been broken, but after all in such a way that, in cases where I ceased to practice abstinence, I have observed a limit which is indeed next door to abstinence; perhaps it is even a little more difficult, because it is easier for the will to cut off certain things utterly than to use them with restraint.

17. Inasmuch as I have begun to explain to you how much greater was my impulse to approach philosophy in my youth than to continue it in my old age, I shall not be ashamed to tell you what ardent zeal Pythagoras inspired in me. Sotion used to tell me why Pythagoras abstained from animal food, and why, in later times, Sextius did also. In each case, the reason was different, but it was in each case a noble reason. **18.** Sextius believed that man had enough sustenance without resorting to blood, and that a habit of cruelty is formed whenever butchery is practised for pleasure. Moreover, he thought we should curtail the sources of our luxury; he argued that a varied diet was contrary to the laws of health, and was unsuited to our constitutions. **19.** Pythagoras, on the other hand, held that all beings were interrelated, and that there was a system of exchange between souls which transmigrated from one bodily shape into another. If one may believe him, no soul perishes or ceases from its functions at all, except for a tiny interval – when it is being poured from one body into another. We may question at what time and after what seasons of change the soul returns to man, when it has wandered through many a dwelling-place; but meantime, he made men fearful of guilt and parricide, since they might be, without knowing it, attacking the soul of a parent and injuring it with knife or with teeth – if, as is possible, the related spirit be dwelling temporarily in this bit of flesh! **20.** When Sotion had set forth this doctrine, supplementing it with his own proofs, he would say: "You do not believe that souls are assigned, first to one body and then to another, and that our so-called death is merely a change of abode? You do not believe that in cattle, or in wild beasts, or in creatures of the deep, the soul of him who was once a man may linger? You do not believe that nothing on this earth is annihilated, but only changes its haunts? And that animals also have cycles of progress and, so to speak, an orbit for their souls, no less than the heavenly bodies, which revolve in fixed circuits? Great men have put faith in this idea; **21.** therefore, while holding to your own view, keep the whole question in abeyance in your mind. If the theory is true, it is a mark of purity to refrain from eating flesh; if it be false, it is economy. And what harm does it do to you to give such credence? I am merely depriving you of food which sustains lions and vultures."

22. I was imbued with this teaching, and began to abstain from animal food; at the end of a year the habit was as pleasant as it was easy. I was beginning to feel that my mind was more active; though I would not to-day positively state whether it really was or not. Do you ask how I came to abandon the practice? It was this way: The days of my youth coincided with the early part of the reign of Tiberius Caesar. Some foreign rites were at that time being inaugurated, and abstinence from certain kinds of animal food was set down as a proof of interest in the strange cult. So at the request of my father, who did not fear prosecution, but who detested philosophy, I returned to my previous habits; and it was no very hard matter to induce me to dine more comfortably.

23. Attalus used to recommend a pillow which did not give in to the body; and now, old as I am, I use one so hard that it leaves no trace after pressure. I have mentioned all this in order to show you how zealous neophytes are with regard to their first impulses towards the highest ideals, provided that some one does his part in exhorting them and in kindling their ardour. There are indeed mistakes made, through the fault of our advisers, who teach us how to debate and not how to live; there are also mistakes made by the pupils, who come to their teachers to develop, not their souls, but their wits. Thus the study of wisdom has become the study of words.

24. Now it makes a great deal of difference what you have in mind when you approach a given subject. If a man is to be a scholar, and is examining the works of Vergil, he does not interpret the noble passage

> Time flies away, and cannot be restored

in the following sense: "We must wake up; unless we hasten, we shall be left behind. Time rolls swiftly ahead, and rolls us with it. We are hurried along ignorant of our destiny; we arrange all our plans for the future, and on the edge of a precipice are at our ease." Instead of this, he brings to our attention how often Vergil, in speaking of the rapidity of time, uses the word "flies" (*fugit*).

> The choicest days of hapless human life
> Fly first; disease and bitter eld succeed,
> And toil, till harsh death rudely snatches all.

25. He who considers these lines in the spirit of a philosopher comments on the words in their proper sense: "Vergil never says, 'Time goes,' but 'Time flies,' because the latter is the quickest kind of movement, and in every case our best days are the first to be snatched away; why, then, do we hesitate to bestir ourselves so that we may be able to keep pace with this swiftest of all swift things?" The good flies past and the bad takes its place. **26.** Just as the purest wine flows from the top of the jar and the thickest dregs settle at the bottom; so in our human life, that which is best comes first. Shall we allow other men to quaff the best, and keep the dregs for ourselves? Let this phrase cleave to your soul; you should be satisfied thereby as if it were uttered by an oracle:

> Each choicest day of hapless human life
> Flies first.

27. Why "choicest day?" Because what's to come is unsure. Why "choicest day"? Because in our youth we are able to learn; we can bend to nobler purposes minds that are ready and still pliable; because this is the time for work, the time for keeping our minds busied in study and in exercising our bodies with useful effort; for that which remains is more sluggish and lacking in spirit – nearer the end.

Let us therefore strive with all courage, omitting attractions by the way; let us struggle with a single purpose, lest, when we are left behind, we comprehend too late the speed of quick-flying time, whose course we cannot stay. Let every day, as soon as it comes, be welcome as being the choicest, and let it be made our own possession. **28.** We must catch that which flees. Now he who scans with a scholar's eye the lines I have just quoted, does not reflect that our first days are the best because disease is approaching and old age weighs upon us and hangs over our heads while we are still thinking about our youth. He thinks rather of Vergil's usual collocation of *disease and eld*; and indeed rightly. For old age is a disease which we cannot cure. **29.** "Besides," he says to himself, "think of the epithet that accompanies *eld*; Vergil calls it *bitter*," –

> Disease and bitter eld succeed.

And elsewhere Vergil says:

> There dwelleth pale disease and bitter eld.

There is no reason why you should marvel that each man can collect from the same source suitable matter for his own studies; for in the same meadow the cow grazes, the dog hunts the hare, and the stork the lizard. **30.** When Cicero's book *On the State* is opened by a philologist, a scholar, or a follower of philosophy, each man pursues his investigation in his own way. The philosopher wonders that so much could have been said therein against justice. The philologist takes up the same book and comments on the text as follows: There were two Roman kings – one without a father and one without a mother. For we cannot settle who was

Servius's mother, and Ancus, the grandson of Numa, has no father on record. **31.** The philologist also notes that the officer whom we call dictator, and about whom we read in our histories under that title, was named in old times the *magister populi*; such is the name existing to-day in the augural records, proved by the fact that he whom the dictator chose as second in command was called *magister equitum*. He will remark, too, that Romulus met his end during an eclipse; that there was an appeal to the people even from the kings (this is so stated in the pontiffs' register and is the opinion of others, including Fenestella). **32.** When the scholar unrolls this same volume, he puts down in his notebook the forms of words, noting that *reapse*, equivalent to *re ipsa*, is used by Cicero, and *sepse* just as frequently, which means *se ipse*. Then he turns his attention to changes in current usage. Cicero, for example, says: "Inasmuch as we are summoned back from the very calx by his interruption." Now the line in the circus which we call the *creta* was called the calx by men of old time. **33.** Again, he puts together some verses by Ennius, especially those which referred to Africanus:

> A man to whom nor friend nor foe could give
> Due meed for all his efforts and his deed.

From this passage the scholar declares that he infers the word *opem* to have meant formerly not merely *assistance*, but *efforts*. For Ennius must mean that neither friend nor foe could pay Scipio a reward worthy of his efforts. **34.** Next, he congratulates himself on finding the source of Vergil's words:

> Over whose head the mighty gate of Heaven
> Thunders,

remarking that Ennius stole the idea from Homer, and Vergil from Ennius. For there is a couplet by Ennius, preserved in this same book of Cicero's, *On the State*:

> If it be right for a mortal to scale the regions of Heaven,
> Then the huge gate of the sky opens in glory to *me*.

35. But that I, too, while engaged upon another task, may not slip into the department of the philologist or the scholar, my advice is this – that all study of philosophy and all reading should be applied to the idea of living the happy life, that we should not hunt out archaic or far-fetched words and eccentric metaphors and figures of speech, but that we should seek precepts which will help us, utterances of courage and spirit which may at once be turned into facts. We should so learn them that words may become deeds. **36.** And I hold that no man has treated mankind worse than he who has studied philosophy as if it were some marketable trade, who lives in a different manner from that which he advises. For those who are liable to every fault which they castigate advertise themselves as patterns of useless training. **37.** A teacher like that can help me no more than a sea-sick pilot can be efficient in a storm. He must hold the tiller when the waves are tossing him; he must wrestle, as it were, with the sea; he must furl his sails when the storm rages; what good is a frightened and vomiting steersman to *me*? And how much greater, think you, is the storm of life than that which tosses any ship! One must steer, not talk.

All the words that these men utter and juggle before a listening crowd, belong to others. 38. They have been spoken by Plato, spoken by Zeno, spoken by Chrysippus or by Posidonius, and by a whole host of Stoics as numerous as excellent. I shall show you how men can prove their words to be their own: it is by doing what they have been talking about. Since therefore I have given you the message I wished to pass on to you, I shall now satisfy your craving and shall reserve for a new letter a complete answer to your summons; so that you may not approach in a condition of weariness a subject which is thorny and which should be followed with an attentive and painstaking ear. Farewell.

CIX. ON THE FELLOWSHIP OF WISE MEN

1. You expressed a wish to know whether a wise man can help a wise man. For we say that the wise man is completely endowed with every good, and has attained perfection; accordingly, the question arises how it is possible for anyone to help a person who possesses the Supreme Good.

Good men are mutually helpful; for each gives practice to the other's virtues and thus maintains wisdom at its proper level. Each needs someone with whom he may make comparisons and investigations. **2.** Skilled wrestlers are kept up to the mark by practice; a musician is stirred to action by one of equal proficiency. The wise man also needs to have his virtues kept in action; and as he prompts himself to do things, so is he prompted by another wise man. **3.** How can a wise man help another wise man? He can quicken his impulses, and point out to him opportunities for honourable action. Besides, he can develop some of his own ideas; he can impart what he has discovered. For even in the case of the wise man something will always remain to discover, something towards which his mind may make new ventures.

4. Evil men harm evil men; each debases the other by rousing his wrath, by approving his churlishness, and praising his pleasures; bad men are at their worst stage when their faults are most thoroughly intermingled, and their wickedness has been, so to speak, pooled in partnership. Conversely, therefore, a good man will help another good man. "How?" you ask. **5.** Because he will bring joy to the other, he will strengthen his faith, and from the contemplation of their mutual tranquillity the delight of both will be increased. Moreover they will communicate to each other a knowledge of certain facts; for the wise man is not all-knowing. And even if he were all-knowing, someone might be able to devise and point out short cuts, by which the whole matter is more readily disseminated. **6.** The wise will help the wise, not, mark you, because of his own strength merely, but because of the strength of the man whom he assists. The latter, it is true, can by himself develop his own parts; nevertheless, even one who is running well is helped by one who cheers him on.

"But the wise man does not really help the wise; he helps himself. Let me tell you this: strip the one of his special powers, and the other will accomplish nothing." **7.** You might as well, on that basis, say that sweetness is not in the honey: for it is the person himself who is to eat it, that is so equipped, as to tongue and palate, for tasting this kind of food that the special flavour appeals to him, and anything else displeases. For there are certain men so affected by disease that they regard honey as bitter. Both men should be in good health, that the one may be helpful and the other a proper subject for help. **8.** Again they say: "When the highest degree of heat has been attained, it is superfluous to apply more heat; and when the Supreme Good has been attained, it is superfluous to have a helper. Does a completely stocked farmer ask for further supplies from his neighbours? Does a soldier who is sufficiently armed for going well-equipped into action need any more weapons? Very well, neither does the wise man; for he is sufficiently equipped and sufficiently armed for life." **9.** My answer to this is, that when one is heated to the highest degree, one must have continued heat to maintain the highest temperature. And if it be objected that heat is self-maintaining, I say that there are great distinctions among the things that you are comparing; for heat is a single thing, but helpfulness is of many kinds. Again, heat is not helped by the addition of further heat, in order to be hot; but the wise man cannot maintain his mental standard without intercourse with friends of his own kind – with whom he may share his goodness. **10.** Moreover, there is a sort of mutual friendship among all the virtues. Thus, he who loves the virtues of certain among his peers, and in turn exhibits his own to be loved, is helpful. Like things give pleasure, especially when they are honourable and when men know that there is mutual approval. **11.** And besides, none but a wise man can prompt another wise man's soul in an intelligent way, just as man can be prompted in a rational way by man only. As, therefore, reason is necessary for the prompting of reason, so, in order to prompt perfect reason, there is need of perfect reason.

12. Some say that we are helped even by those who bestow on us the so-called "indifferent" benefits, such as money, influence, security, and all the other valued or essential aids to living. If we argue in this way, the veriest fool will be said to help a wise man. Helping, however, really means prompting the soul in accordance with Nature, both by the prompter's excellence and by the excellence of him who is thus prompted. And this cannot take place without advantage to the helper also. For in training the excellence of another, a man must necessarily train his own. **13.** But, to omit from discussion supreme goods or the things which produce them, wise men can none the less be mutually helpful. For the mere discovery of a sage by a sage is in itself a desirable event; since everything good is naturally dear to the good man, and for this reason one feels congenial with a good man as one feels congenial with oneself.

14. It is necessary for me to pass from this topic to another, in order to prove my point. For the question is asked, whether the wise man will weigh his opinions, or whether he will apply to others for advice. Now he is compelled to do this when he approaches state and home duties – everything, so to speak, that is mortal. He needs outside advice on such matters, as does the physician, the pilot, the attorney, or the pleader of cases. Hence, the wise will sometimes help the wise; for they will persuade each other. But in these matters of great import also, – aye, of divine import, as I have termed them, – the wise man can also be useful by discussing honourable things in common, and by contributing his thoughts and ideas. **15.** Moreover, it is in accordance with Nature to show affection for our friends, and to rejoice in their advancement as if it were absolutely our own. For if we have not done this, even virtue, which grows strong only through exercising our perceptions, will not abide with us. Now virtue advises us to arrange the present well, to take thought regarding the future, to deliberate and apply our minds; and one who takes a friend into council with him, can more easily apply his mind and think out his problem.

Therefore he will seek either the perfect wise man or one who has progressed to a point bordering on perfection. The perfect wise man, moreover, will help us if he aids our counsels with ordinary good sense. **16.** They say that men see farther in the affairs of others than in their own. A defect of character causes this in those who are blinded by self-love, and whose fear in the hour of peril takes away their clear view of that which is useful; it is when a man is more at ease and freed from fear that he will begin to be wise. Nevertheless, there are certain matters where even wise men see the facts more clearly in the case of others than in their own. Moreover, the wise man will, in company with his fellow sage, confirm the truth of that most sweet and honourable proverb – "always desiring and always refusing the same things": it will be a noble result when they draw the load "with equal yoke."

17. I have thus answered your demand, although it came under the head of subjects which I include in my volumes *On Moral Philosophy*. Reflect, as I am often wont to tell you, that there is nothing in such topics for us except mental gymnastics. For I return again and again to the thought: "What good does this do me? Make me more brave now, more just, more restrained! I have not yet the opportunity to make use of my training; for I still need the physician. **18.** Why do you ask of me a useless knowledge? You have promised great things; test me, watch me! You assured me that I should be unterrified though swords were flashing round me, though the point of the blade were grazing my throat; you assured me that I should be at ease though fires were blazing round me, or though a sudden whirlwind should snatch up my ship and carry it over all the sea. Now make good for me such a course of treatment that I may despise pleasure and glory. Thereafter you shall teach me to work out complicated problems, to settle doubtful points, to see through that which is not clear; teach me now what it is necessary for me to know!" Farewell.

CX. ON TRUE AND FALSE RICHES

1. From my villa at Nomentum I send you greeting and bid you keep a sound spirit within you – in other words, gain the blessing of all the gods, for he is assured of their grace and favour who has become a blessing to himself. Lay aside for the present the belief of certain persons – that a god is assigned to each one of us as a sort of attendant – not a god of regular rank, but one of a lower grade – one of those whom Ovid calls "plebeian gods." Yet, while laying aside this belief, I would have you remember that our ancestors, who followed such a creed, have become Stoics; for they have assigned a Genius or a Juno to every individual. **2.** Later on we shall investigate whether the gods have enough time on their hands to care for the concerns of private individuals; in the meantime, you must know that whether we are allotted to special guardians, or whether we are neglected and consigned to Fortune, you can curse a man with no heavier curse than to pray that he may be at enmity with himself.

There is no reason, however, why you should ask the gods to be hostile to anyone whom you regard as deserving of punishment; they *are* hostile to such a person, I maintain, even though he seems to be advanced by their favour. **3.** Apply careful investigation, considering how our affairs actually stand, and not what men say of them; you will then understand that evils are more likely to help us than to harm us. For how often has so-called affliction been the source and the beginning of happiness! How often have privileges which we welcomed with deep thanksgiving built steps for themselves to the top of a precipice, still uplifting men who were already distinguished – just as if they had previously stood in a position whence they could fall in safety! **4.** But this very fall has in it nothing evil, if you consider the end, after which nature lays no man lower. The universal limit is near; yes, there is near us the point where the prosperous man is upset, and the point where the unfortunate is set free. It is we ourselves that extend both these limits, lengthening them by our hopes and by our fears.

If, however, you are wise, measure all things according to the state of man; restrict at the same time both your joys and your fears. Moreover, it is worth while not to rejoice at anything for long, so that you may not fear anything for long. **5.** But why do I confine the scope of this evil? There is no reason why you should suppose that anything is to be feared. All these things which stir us and keep us a-flutter, are empty things. None of us has sifted out the truth; we have passed fear on to one another; none has dared to approach the object which caused his dread, and to understand the nature of his fear – aye, the good behind it. That is why falsehood and vanity still gain credit – because they are not refuted. **6.** Let us account it worth while to look closely at the matter; then it will be clear how fleeting, how unsure, and how harmless are the things which we fear. The disturbance in our spirits is similar to that which Lucretius detected:

> Like boys who cower frightened in the dark,
> So grown-ups in the light of day feel fear.

What, then? Are we not more foolish than any child, we who "in the light of day feel fear"? **7.** But you were wrong, Lucretius; we are not afraid in the daylight; we have turned everything into a state of darkness. We see neither what injures nor what profits us; all our lives through we blunder along, neither stopping nor treading more carefully on this account. But you see what madness it is to rush ahead in the dark. Indeed, we are bent on getting ourselves called back from a greater distance; and though we do not know our goal, yet we hasten with wild speed in the direction whither we are straining.

8. The light, however, may begin to shine, provided we are willing. But such a result can come about only in one way – if we acquire by knowledge this familiarity with things divine and human, if we not only flood ourselves but steep ourselves therein, if a man reviews the same principles even though he understands them and applies them again and again to himself, if he has investigated what is good, what is evil, and what has falsely been so entitled; and, finally, if he has investigated honour and baseness, and Providence. **9.** The range of the human intelligence is not confined within these limits; it may also explore outside the universe – its destination and its source, and the ruin towards which all nature hastens so rapidly. We have withdrawn the soul from this divine contemplation and dragged it into mean and lowly tasks, so that it might be a slave to greed, so that it might forsake the universe and its confines, and, under the command of masters who try all possible schemes, pry beneath the earth and seek what evil it can dig up therefrom – discontented with that which was freely offered to it.

10. Now God, who is the Father of us all, has placed ready to our hands those things which he intended for our own good; he did not wait for any search on our part, and he gave them to us voluntarily. But that which would be injurious, he buried deep in the earth. We can complain of nothing but ourselves; for we have brought to light the materials for our destruction, against the will of Nature, who hid them from us. We have bound over our souls to pleasure, whose service is the source of all evil; we have surrendered ourselves to self-seeking and reputation, and to other aims which are equally idle and useless.

11. What, then, do I now encourage you to do? Nothing new – we are not trying to find cures for new evils – but this first of all: namely, to see clearly for yourself what is necessary and what is superfluous. What is necessary will meet you everywhere; what is superfluous has always to be hunted-out – and with great endeavour. **12.** But there is no reason why you should flatter yourself over-much if you despise gilded couches and jewelled furniture. For what virtue lies in despising useless things? The time to admire your own conduct is when you have come to despise the necessities. You are doing no great thing if you can live without royal pomp, if you feel no craving for boars which weigh a thousand pounds, or for flamingo tongues, or for the other absurdities of a luxury that already wearies of game cooked whole, and chooses different bits from separate animals; I shall admire you only when you have learned to scorn even the common sort of bread, when you have made yourself believe that grass grows for the needs of men as well as of cattle, when you have found out that food from the treetop can fill the belly – into which we cram things of value as if it could keep what it has received. We should satisfy our stomachs without being over-nice. How does it matter what the stomach receives, since it must lose whatever it has received? **13.** You enjoy the carefully arranged dainties which are caught on land and sea; some are more pleasing if they are brought fresh to the table, others, if after long feeding and forced fattening they almost melt and can hardly retain their own grease. You like the subtly devised flavour of these dishes. But I assure you that such carefully chosen and variously seasoned dishes, once they have entered the belly, will be overtaken alike by one and the same corruption. Would you despise the pleasures of eating? Then consider its result! **14.** I remember some words of Attalus, which elicited general applause:

"Riches long deceived me. I used to be dazed when I caught some gleam of them here and there. I used to think that their hidden influence matched their visible show. But once, at a certain elaborate entertainment, I saw embossed work in silver and gold equalling the wealth of a whole city, and colours and tapestry devised to match objects which surpassed the value of gold or of silver – brought not only from beyond our own borders, but from beyond the borders of our enemies; on one side were slave-boys notable for their training and beauty, on the other were throngs of slave-women, and all the other resources that a prosperous and mighty empire could offer after reviewing its possessions. **15.** What else is this, I said to myself, than a stirring-up of man's cravings, which are in themselves provocative of lust? What is the meaning of all this display of money? Did we gather merely to learn what greed was? For my own part I left the place with less craving than I had when I entered. I came to despise riches, not because of their uselessness, but because of their pettiness. **16.** Have you noticed how, inside a few hours, that programme, however slow-moving and carefully arranged, was over and done? Has a business filled up this whole life of ours, which could not fill up a whole day?

"I had another thought also: the riches seemed to me to be as useless to the possessors as they were to the onlookers. **17.** Accordingly, I say to myself, whenever a show of that sort dazzles my eyes, whenever I see a splendid palace with a well-groomed corps of attendants and beautiful bearers carrying a litter: Why wonder? Why gape in astonishment? It is all show; such things are displayed, not possessed; while they please they pass away. **18.** Turn thyself rather to the true riches. Learn to be content with little, and cry out with courage and with greatness of soul: 'We have water, we have porridge; let us compete in happiness with Jupiter himself.' And why not, I pray thee, make this challenge even without porridge and water? For it is base to make the happy life depend upon silver and gold, and just as base to make it depend upon water and porridge. 'But,' some will say, 'what could I do without such things?' **19.** Do you ask what is the cure for want? It is to make hunger satisfy hunger; for, all else being equal, what difference is there in the smallness or the largeness of the things that force you to be a slave? What matter how little it is that Fortune can refuse to you? **20.** Your very porridge and water can fall under another's jurisdiction; and besides, freedom comes, not to him over whom Fortune has slight power, but to him over whom she has no power at all. This is what I mean: you must crave nothing, if you would vie with Jupiter; for Jupiter craves nothing."

This is what Attalus told us. If you are willing to think often of these things, you will strive not to seem happy, but to be happy, and, in addition, to seem happy to yourself rather than to others. Farewell.

CXI. ON THE VANITY OF MENTAL GYMNASTICS

1. You have asked me to give you a Latin word for the Greek *sophismata*. Many have tried to define the term, but no name has stuck. This is natural, inasmuch as the thing itself has not been admitted to general use by us; the name, too, has met with opposition. But the word which Cicero used seems to me most suitable: he calls them *cavillationes*. **2.** If a man has surrendered himself to them, he weaves many a tricky subtlety, but makes no progress toward real living; he does not thereby become braver, or more restrained, or loftier of spirit.

He, however, who has practised philosophy to effect his own cure, becomes high-souled, full of confidence, invincible, and greater as you draw near him. **3.** This phenomenon is seen in the case of high mountains, which appear less lofty when beheld from afar, but which prove clearly how high the peaks are when you come near them; such, my dear Lucilius, is our true philosopher, true by his acts and not by his tricks. He stands in a high place, worthy of admiration, lofty, and really great. He does not stretch himself or walk on tiptoe like those who seek to improve their height by deceit, wishing to seem taller than they really are; he is content with his own greatness. **4.** And why should he not be content with having grown to such a height that Fortune cannot reach her hands to it? He is therefore above earthly things, equal to himself under all conditions, – whether the current of life runs free, or whether he is tossed and travels on troubled and desperate seas; but this steadfastness cannot be gained through such hair-splittings as I have just mentioned. The mind plays with them, but profits not a whit; the mind in such cases is simply dragging philosophy down from her heights to the level ground.

5. I would not forbid you to practise such exercises occasionally; but let it be at a time when you wish to do nothing. The worst feature, however, that these indulgences present is that they acquire a sort of self-made charm, occupying and holding the soul by a show of subtlety; although such weighty matters claim our attention, and a whole life seems scarcely sufficient to learn the single principle of despising life. "What? Did you not mean 'control' instead of 'despise'"? No; "controlling" is the second task; for no one has controlled his life aright unless he has first learned to despise it. Farewell.

CXII. ON REFORMING HARDENED SINNERS

1. I am indeed anxious that your friend be moulded and trained, according to your desire. But he has been taken in a very hardened state, or rather (and this is a more difficult problem), in a very soft state, broken down by bad and inveterate habits.

I should like to give you an illustration from my own handicraft. **2.** It is not every vine that admits the grafting process; if it be old and decayed, or if it be weak and slender, the vine either will not receive the cutting, or will not nourish it and make it a part of itself, nor will it accommodate itself to the qualities and nature of the grafted part. Hence we usually cut off the vine above ground, so that if we do not get results at first, we may try a second venture, and on a second trial graft it below the ground.

3. Now this person, concerning whom you have sent me your message in writing, has no strength; for he has pampered his vices. He has at one and the same time become flabby and hardened. He cannot receive reason, nor can he nourish it. "But," you say, "he desires reason of his own free will." Don't believe him. Of course I do not mean that he is lying to you; for he really thinks that he desires it. Luxury has merely upset his stomach; he will soon become reconciled to it again. **4.** "But he says that he is put out with his former way of living." Very likely. Who is not? Men love and hate their vices at the same time. It will be the proper season to pass judgment on him when he has given us a guarantee that he really hates luxury; as it is now, luxury and he are merely not on speaking terms. Farewell.

CXIII. ON THE VITALITY OF THE SOUL AND ITS ATTRIBUTES

1. You wish me to write to you my opinion concerning this question, which has been mooted by our school – whether justice, courage, foresight, and the other virtues, are living things. By such niceties as this, my beloved Lucilius, we have made people think that we sharpen our wits on useless objects, and waste our leisure time in discussions that will be unprofitable. I shall, however, do as you ask, and shall set forth the subject as viewed by our school. For myself, I confess to another belief: I hold that there are certain things which befit a wearer of white shoes and a Greek mantle. But what the beliefs are that have stirred the ancients, or those which the ancients have stirred up for discussion, I shall explain to you.

2. The soul, men are agreed, is a living thing, because of itself it can make us living things, and because "living things" have derived their name therefrom. But virtue is nothing else than a soul in a certain condition; therefore it is a living thing. Again, virtue is active, and no action can take place without impulse. And if a thing has impulse, it must be a living thing; for none except a living thing possesses impulse. **3.** A reply to this is: "If virtue is a living thing, then virtue itself possesses virtue." Of course it possesses its own self! Just as the wise man does everything by reason of virtue, so virtue accomplishes everything by reason of itself. "In that case," say they, "all the arts also are living things, and all our thoughts and all that the mind comprehends. It therefore follows that many thousands of living things dwell in man's tiny heart, and that each individual among us consists of, or at least contains, many living beings."

Are you gravelled for an answer to this remark? Each of these will be a living thing; but they will not be many separate living things. And why? I shall explain, if you will apply your subtlety and your concentration to my words. **4.** Each living thing must have a separate substance; but since all the things mentioned above have a single soul, consequently they can be separate living things but without plurality. I myself am a living thing, and a man; but you cannot say that there are two of me for that reason. And why? Because, if that were so, they would have to be two separate existences. This is what I mean: one would have to be sundered from the other so as to produce two. But whenever you have that which is manifold in one whole, it falls into the category of a single nature, and is therefore single.

5. My soul is a living thing, and so am I; but we are not two separate persons. And why? Because the soul is part of myself. It will only be reckoned as a definite thing in itself when it shall exist by itself. But as long as it shall be part of another, it cannot be regarded as different. And why? I will tell you: it is because that which is different, must be personal and peculiar to itself, a whole, and complete within itself. **6.** I myself have gone on record as being of a different opinion; for if one adopts this belief, not only the virtues will be living things, but so will their contrary vices, and the emotions, like wrath, fear, grief, and suspicion. Nay, the argument will carry us still further – all opinions and all thoughts will be living things. This is by no means admissible; since anything that man does is not necessarily the man himself. **7.** "What is Justice?" people say. Justice is a soul that maintains itself in a certain attitude. "Then if the soul is a living being, so is Justice." By no means. For Justice is really a state, a kind of power, of the soul; and this same soul is transformed into various likenesses and does not become a different kind of living thing as often as it acts differently. Nor is the result of soul-action a living thing. **8.** If Justice, Bravery, and the other virtues have actual life, do they cease to be living things and then begin life over again, or are they *always* living things?

But the virtues cannot cease to be. Therefore, there are many, nay countless, living things, sojourning in this one soul. **9.** "No," is the answer, "not many, because they are all attached to the one, being parts and members of a single whole." We are then portraying for ourselves an image of the soul like that of a many-headed hydra – each separate head fighting and destroying independently. And yet there is no separate living thing to each head; it is the head of a living thing, and the hydra itself is one single living thing. No one ever believed that the Chimaera contained a living lion or a living serpent; these were merely parts of the whole Chimaera; and parts are not living things. **10.** Then how can you infer that Justice is a living thing? "Justice," people reply, "is active and helpful; that which acts and is helpful, possesses impulse; and that which possesses impulse is a living thing."

True, if the impulse is its own; (but in the case of justice it is not its own;) the impulse comes from the soul. **11.** Every living thing exists as it began, until death; a man, until he dies, is a man, a horse is a horse, a dog a dog. They cannot change into anything else. Now let us grant that Justice – which is defined as "a soul in a certain attitude," is a living thing. Let us suppose this to be so. Then Bravery also is alive, being "a soul in a certain attitude." But which soul? That which was but now defined as Justice? The soul is kept within the first-named being, and cannot cross over into another; it must last out its existence in the medium where it had its origin. **12.** Besides, there cannot be one soul to two living things, much less to many living things. And if Justice, Bravery, Restraint, and all the other virtues, are living things, how will they have one soul? They must possess separate souls, or else they are not living things. **13.** Several living things cannot have one body; this is admitted by our very opponents. Now what is the "body" of justice? "The soul," they admit. And of bravery? "The soul also." And yet there cannot be one body of two living things. **14.** "The same soul, however," they answer, "assumes the guise of Justice, or Bravery, or Restraint." This would be possible if Bravery were absent when Justice was present, and if Restraint were absent when Bravery was present; as the case stands now, all the virtues exist at the same time. Hence, how can the separate virtues be living things, if you grant that there is one single soul, which cannot create more than one single living thing?

15. Again, no living thing is part of another living thing. But Justice is a part of the soul; therefore Justice is not a living thing. It looks as if I were wasting time over something that is an acknowledged fact; for one ought to decry such a topic rather than debate it. And no two living things are equal. Consider the bodies of all beings: every one has its particular colour, shape, and size. **16.** And among the other reasons for marvelling at the genius of the Divine Creator is, I believe, this, – that amid all this abundance there is no repetition; even seemingly similar things are, on comparison, unlike. God has created all the great number of leaves that we behold: each, however, is stamped with its special pattern. All the many animals: none resembles another in size – always some difference! The Creator has set himself the task of making unlike and unequal things that are different; but all the virtues, as your argument states, are equal. Therefore, they are not living things.

17. Every living thing acts of itself; but virtue does nothing of itself; it must act in conjunction with man. All living things either are gifted with reason, like men and gods, or else are irrational, like beasts and cattle. Virtues, in any case, are rational; and yet they are neither men nor gods; therefore they are not living things. **18.** Every living thing possessed of reason is inactive if it is not first stirred by some external impression; then the impulse comes, and finally assent confirms the impulse. Now what *assent* is, I shall explain. Suppose that I ought to take a walk: I *do* walk, but only after uttering the command to myself and approving this opinion of mine. Or suppose that I ought to seat myself; I *do* seat myself, but only after the same process. This assent is not a part of virtue. **19.** For let us suppose that it is Prudence; how will Prudence assent to the opinion: "I must take a walk"? Nature does not allow this. For Prudence looks after the interests of its possessor, and not of its own self. Prudence cannot walk or be seated. Accordingly, it does not possess the power of assent, and it is not a living thing possessed of reason. But if virtue is a living thing, it is rational. But it is not rational; therefore it is not a living thing. **20.** If virtue is a living thing, and virtue is a Good – is not, then, every Good a living thing? It is. Our school professes it.

Now to save a father's life is a Good; it is also a Good to pronounce one's opinion judiciously in the senate, and it is a Good to hand down just opinions; therefore the act of saving a father's life is a living thing, also the act of pronouncing judicious opinions. We have carried this absurd argument so far that you cannot keep from laughing outright: wise silence is a Good, and so is a frugal dinner; therefore silence and dining are living things. **21.** Indeed I shall never cease to tickle my mind and to make sport for myself by means of this nice nonsense. Justice and Bravery, if they are living things, are certainly of the earth. Now every earthly living thing gets cold or hungry or thirsty; therefore, Justice goes a-cold, Bravery is hungry, and Kindness craves a drink!

22. And what next? Should I not ask our honourable opponents what shape these living beings have? Is it that of man, or horse, or wild beast? If they are given a round shape, like that of a god, I shall ask whether greed and luxury and madness are equally round. For these, too, are "living things." If I find that they give a rounded shape to these also, I shall go so far as to ask whether a modest gait is a living thing; they must admit it, according to their argument, and proceed to say that a gait is a living thing, and a rounded living thing, at that!

23. Now do not imagine that I am the first one of our school who does not speak from rules but has his own opinion: Cleanthes and his pupil Chrysippus could not agree in defining the act of walking. Cleanthes held that it was spirit transmitted to the feet from the primal essence, while Chrysippus maintained that it was the primal essence in itself. Why, then, following the example of Chrysippus himself, should not every man claim his own freedom, and laugh down all these "living things," so numerous that the universe itself cannot contain them? **24.** One might say: "The virtues are not many living things, and yet they are living things. For just as an individual may be both poet and orator in one, even so these virtues are living things, but they are not many. The soul is the same; it can be at the same time just and prudent and brave, maintaining itself in a certain attitude towards each virtue." **25.** The dispute is settled, and we are therefore agreed. For I shall admit, meanwhile, that the soul is a living thing with the proviso that later on I may cast my final vote; but I deny that the acts of the soul are living beings. Otherwise, all words and all verses would be alive; for if prudent speech is a Good, and every Good a living thing, then speech is a living thing. A prudent line of poetry is a Good; everything alive is a Good; therefore, the line of poetry is a living thing. And so "Arms and the man I sing," is a living thing; but they cannot call it rounded, because it has six feet! **26.** "This whole proposition," you say, "which we are at this moment discussing, is a puzzling fabric." I split with laughter whenever I reflect that solecisms and barbarisms and syllogisms are living things, and, like an artist, I give to each a fitting likeness. Is this what we discuss with contracted brow and wrinkled forehead? I cannot say now, after Caelius, "What melancholy trifling!" It is more than this; it is absurd. Why do we not rather discuss something which is useful and wholesome to ourselves, seeking how we may attain the virtues, and finding the path which will take us in that direction?

27. Teach me, not whether Bravery be a living thing, but prove that no living thing is happy without bravery, that is, unless it has grown strong to oppose hazards and has overcome all the strokes of chance by rehearsing and anticipating their attack. And what is Bravery? It is the impregnable fortress for our mortal weakness; when a man has surrounded himself therewith, he can hold out free from anxiety during life's siege; for he is using his own strength and his own weapons. **28.** At this point I would quote you a saying of our philosopher Posidonius: "There are never any occasions when you need think yourself safe because you wield the weapons of Fortune; fight with your own! Fortune does not furnish arms against herself; hence men equipped against their foes are unarmed against Fortune herself."

29. Alexander, to be sure, harried and put to flight the Persians, the Hyrcanians, the Indians, and all the other races that the Orient spreads even to the Ocean; but he himself, as he slew one friend or lost another, would lie in the darkness lamenting sometimes his crime, and sometimes his loss; he, the conqueror of so many kings and nations, was laid low by anger and grief! For he had made it his aim to win control over everything except his emotions. **30.** Oh with what great mistakes are men obsessed, who desire to push their limits of empire beyond the seas, who judge themselves most prosperous when they occupy many provinces with their soldiery and join new territory to the old! Little do they know of that kingdom which is on an equality with the heavens in greatness! **31.** Self-Command is the greatest command of all. Let her teach me what a hallowed thing is the Justice which ever regards another's good and seeks nothing for itself except its own employment. It should have nothing to do with ambition and reputation; it should satisfy itself.

Let each man convince himself of this before all else – "I must be just without reward." And that is not enough; let him convince himself also of this: "May I take pleasure in devoting myself of my own free will to uphold this noblest of virtues." Let all his thoughts be turned as far as possible from personal interests. You need not look about for the reward of a just deed; a just deed in itself offers a still greater return. **32.** Fasten deep in your mind that which I remarked a short space above: that it makes no difference how many persons are acquainted with your uprightness. Those who wish their virtue to be advertised are not striving for virtue but for renown. Are you not willing to be just without being renowned? Nay, indeed you must often be just and be at the same time disgraced. And then, if you are wise, let ill repute, well won, be a delight. Farewell.

CXIV. ON STYLE AS A MIRROR OF CHARACTER

1. You have been asking me why, during certain periods, a degenerate style of speech comes to the fore, and how it is that men's wits have gone downhill into certain vices – in such a way that exposition at one time has taken on a kind of puffed-up strength, and at another has become mincing and modulated like the music of a concert piece. You wonder why sometimes bold ideas – bolder than one could believe – have been held in favour, and why at other times one meets with phrases that are disconnected and full of innuendo, into which one must read more meaning than was intended to meet the ear. Or why there have been epochs which maintained the right to a shameless use of metaphor. For answer, here is a phrase which you are wont to notice in the popular speech – one which the Greeks have made into a proverb: "Man's speech is just like his life." **2.** Exactly as each individual man's actions seem to speak, so people's style of speaking often reproduces the general character of the time, if the morale of the public has relaxed and has given itself over to effeminacy. Wantonness in speech is proof of public luxury, if it is popular and fashionable, and not confined to one or two individual instances. **3.** A man's ability cannot possibly be of one sort and his soul of another. If his soul be wholesome, well-ordered, serious, and restrained, his ability also is sound and sober. Conversely, when the one degenerates, the other is also contaminated. Do you not see that if a man's soul has become sluggish, his limbs drag and his feet move indolently? If it is womanish, that one can detect the effeminacy by his very gait? That a keen and confident soul quickens the step? That madness in the soul, or anger (which resembles madness), hastens our bodily movements from walking to rushing?

And how much more do you think that this affects one's ability, which is entirely interwoven with the soul, – being moulded thereby, obeying its commands, and deriving therefrom its laws! **4.** How Maecenas lived is too well-known for present comment. We know how he walked, how effeminate he was, and how he desired to display himself; also, how unwilling he was that his vices should escape notice. What, then? Does not the looseness of his speech match his ungirt attire? Are his habits, his attendants, his house, his wife, any less clearly marked than his words? He would have been a man of great powers, had he set himself to his task by a straight path, had he not shrunk from making himself understood, had he not been so loose in his style of speech also. You will therefore see that his eloquence was that of an intoxicated man – twisting, turning, unlimited in its slackness.

5. What is more unbecoming than the words: "A stream and a bank covered with long-tressed woods"? And see how "men plough the channel with boats and, turning up the shallows, leave gardens behind them." Or, "He curls his lady-locks, and bills and coos, and starts a-sighing, like a forest lord who offers prayers with down-bent neck." Or, "An unregenerate crew, they search out people at feasts, and assail households with the wine-cup, and, by hope, exact death." Or, "A Genius could hardly bear witness to his own festival"; or "threads of tiny tapers and crackling meal"; "mothers or wives clothing the hearth."

6. Can you not at once imagine, on reading through these words, that this was the man who always paraded through the city with a flowing tunic? For even if he was discharging the absent emperor's duties, he was always in undress when they asked him for the countersign. Or that this was the man who, as judge on the bench, or as an orator, or at any public function, appeared with his cloak wrapped about his head, leaving only the ears exposed, like the millionaire's runaway slaves in the farce? Or that this was the man who, at the very time when the state was embroiled in civil strife, when the city was in difficulties and under martial law, was attended in public by two eunuchs – both of them more men than himself? Or that this was the man who had but one wife, and yet was married countless times? **7.** These words of his, put together so faultily, thrown off so carelessly, and arranged in such marked contrast to the usual practice, declare that the character of their writer was equally unusual, unsound, and eccentric. To be sure, we bestow upon him the highest praise for his humanity; he was sparing with the sword and refrained from bloodshed; and he made a show of his power only in the course of his loose living; but he spoiled, by such preposterous finickiness of style, this genuine praise, which was his due. **8.** For it is evident that he was not really gentle, but effeminate, as is proved by his misleading word-order, his inverted expressions, and the surprising thoughts which frequently contain something great, but in finding expression have become nerveless. One would say that his head was turned by too great success.

This fault is due sometimes to the man, and sometimes to his epoch. **9.** When prosperity has spread luxury far and wide, men begin by paying closer attention to their personal appearance. Then they go crazy over furniture. Next, they devote attention to their houses – how to take up more space with them, as if they were country-houses, how to make the walls glitter with marble that has been imported over seas, how to adorn a roof with gold, so that it may match the brightness of the inlaid floors. After that, they transfer their exquisite taste to the dinner-table, attempting to court approval by novelty and by departures from the customary order of dishes, so that the courses which we are accustomed to serve at the end of the meal may be served first, and so that the departing guests may partake of the kind of food which in former days was set before them on their arrival.

10. When the mind has acquired the habit of scorning the usual things of life, and regarding as mean that which was once customary, it begins to hunt for novelties in speech also; now it summons and displays obsolete and old-fashioned words; now it coins even unknown words or misshapes them; and now a bold and frequent metaphorical usage is made a special feature of style, according to the fashion which has just become prevalent. **11.** Some cut the thoughts short, hoping to make a good impression by leaving the meaning in doubt and causing the hearer to suspect his own lack of wit. Some dwell upon them and lengthen them out. Others, too, approach just short of a fault – for a man must really do this if he hopes to attain an imposing effect – but actually love the fault for its own sake. In short, whenever you notice that a degenerate style pleases the critics, you may be sure that character also has deviated from the right standard.

Just as luxurious banquets and elaborate dress are indications of disease in the state, similarly a lax style, if it be popular, shows that the mind (which is the source of the word) has lost its balance. Indeed you ought not to wonder that corrupt speech is welcomed not merely by the more squalid mob but also by our more cultured throng; for it is only in their dress and not in their judgments that they differ. **12.** You may rather wonder that not only the effects of vices, but even vices themselves, meet with approval. For it has ever been thus: no man's ability has ever been approved without something being pardoned. Show me any man, however famous; I can tell you what it was that his age forgave in him, and what it was that his age purposely overlooked. I can show you many men whose vices have caused them no harm, and not a few who have been even helped by these vices. Yes, I will show you persons of the highest reputation, set up as models for our admiration; and yet if you seek to correct their errors, you destroy them; for vices are so intertwined with virtues that they drag the virtues along with them. **13.** Moreover, style has no fixed laws; it is changed by the usage of the people, never the same for any length of time. Many orators hark back to earlier epochs for their vocabulary, speaking in the language of the Twelve Tables. Gracchus, Crassus, and Curio, in their eyes, are too refined and too modern; so back to Appius and Coruncanius! Conversely, certain men, in their endeavour to maintain nothing but well-worn and common usages, fall into a humdrum style. **14.** These two classes, each in its own way, are degenerate; and it is no less degenerate to use no words except those which are conspicuous, high-sounding, and poetical, avoiding what is familiar and in ordinary usage. One is, I believe, as faulty as the other: the one class are unreasonably elaborate, the other are unreasonably negligent; the former depilate the leg, the latter not even the armpit.

15. Let us now turn to the arrangement of words. In this department, what countless varieties of fault I can show you! Some are all for abruptness and unevenness of style, purposely disarranging anything which seems to have a smooth flow of language. They would have jolts in all their transitions; they regard as strong and manly whatever makes an uneven impression on the ear. With some others it is not so much an "arrangement" of words as it is a setting to music; so wheedling and soft is their gliding style. **16.** And what shall I say of that arrangement in which words are put off and, after being long waited for, just manage to come in at the end of a period? Or again of that softly-concluding style, Cicero-fashion, with a gradual and gently poised descent always the same and always with the customary arrangement of the rhythm! Nor is the fault only in the style of the sentences, if they are either petty and childish, or debasing, with more daring than modesty should allow, or if they are flowery and cloying, or if they end in emptiness, accomplishing mere sound and nothing more.

17. Some individual makes these vices fashionable – some person who controls the eloquence of the day; the rest follow his lead and communicate the habit to each other. Thus when Sallust was in his glory, phrases were lopped off, words came to a close unexpectedly, and obscure conciseness was equivalent to elegance. L. Arruntius, a man of rare simplicity, author of a historical work on the Punic War, was a member and a strong supporter of the Sallust school. There is a phrase in Sallust: *exercitum argento fecit*, meaning thereby that he *recruited* an army by means of money. Arruntius began to like this idea; he therefore inserted the verb *facio* all through his book. Hence, in one passage, *fugam nostris fecere*; in another, *Hiero, rex Syracusanorum, bellum fecit*; and in another, *quae audita Panhormitanos dedere Romanis fecere*. **18.** I merely desired to give you a taste; his whole book is interwoven with such stuff as this. What Sallust reserved for occasional use, Arruntius makes into a frequent and almost continual habit – and there was a reason: for Sallust used the words as they occurred to his mind, while the other writer went afield in search of them. So you see the results of copying another man's vices. **19.** Again, Sallust said: *aquis hiemantibus*. Arruntius, in his first book on the Punic War, uses the words: *repente hiemavit tempestas*. And elsewhere, wishing to describe an exceptionally cold year, he says: *totus hiemavit annus*. And in another passage: *inde sexaginta onerarias leves praeter militem et necessarios nautarum hiemante aquilone misit*; and he continues to bolster many passages with this metaphor. In a certain place, Sallust gives the words: *inter arma civilia aequi bonique famas petit*; and Arruntius cannot restrain himself from mentioning at once, in the first book, that there were extensive "reminders" concerning Regulus.

20. These and similar faults, which imitation stamps upon one's style, are not necessarily indications of loose standards or of debased mind; for they are bound to be personal and peculiar to the writer, enabling one to judge thereby of a particular author's temperament; just as an angry man will talk in an angry way, an excitable man in a flurried way, and an effeminate man in a style that is soft and unresisting. **21.** You note this tendency in those who pluck out, or thin out, their beards, or who closely shear and shave the upper lip while preserving the rest of the hair and allowing it to grow, or in those who wear cloaks of outlandish colours, who wear transparent togas, and who never deign to do anything which will escape general notice; they endeavour to excite and attract men's attention, and they put up even with censure, provided that they can advertise themselves. That is the style of Maecenas and all the others who stray from the path, not by hazard, but consciously and voluntarily. **22.** This is the result of great evil in the soul. As in the case of drink, the tongue does not trip until the mind is overcome beneath its load and gives way or betrays itself; so that intoxication of style – for what else than this can I call it? – never gives trouble to anyone unless the soul begins to totter. Therefore, I say, take care of the soul; for from the soul issue our thoughts, from the soul our words, from the soul our dispositions, our expressions, and our very gait. When the soul is sound and strong, the style too is vigorous, energetic, manly; but if the soul lose its balance, down comes all the rest in ruins.

> **23.** If but the king be safe, your swarm will live
> Harmonious; if he die, the bees revolt.

The soul is our king. If it be safe, the other functions remain on duty and serve with obedience; but the slightest lack of equilibrium in the soul causes them to waver along with it. And when the soul has yielded to pleasure, its functions and actions grow weak, and any undertaking comes from a nerveless and unsteady source. **24.** To persist in my use of this simile – our soul is at one time a king, at another a tyrant. The king, in that he respects things honourable, watches over the welfare of the body which is entrusted to his charge, and gives that body no base, no ignoble commands. But an uncontrolled, passionate, and effeminate soul changes kingship into that most dread and detestable quality – tyranny; then it becomes a prey to the uncontrolled emotions, which dog its steps, elated at first, to be sure, like a populace idly sated with a largess which will ultimately be its undoing, and spoiling what it cannot consume. **25.** But when the disease has gradually eaten away the strength, and luxurious habits have penetrated the marrow and the sinews, such a soul exults at the sight of limbs which, through its overindulgence, it has made useless; instead of its own pleasures, it views those of others; it becomes the go-between and witness of the passions which, as the result of self-gratification, it can no longer feel. Abundance of delights is not so pleasing a thing to that soul as it is bitter, because it cannot send all the dainties of yore down through the over-worked throat and stomach, because it can no longer whirl in the maze of eunuchs and mistresses, and it is melancholy because a great part of its happiness is shut off, through the limitations of the body.

26. Now is it not madness, Lucilius, for none of us to reflect that he is mortal? Or frail? Or again that he is but one individual? Look at our kitchens, and the cooks, who bustle about over so many fires; is it, think you, for a single belly that all this bustle and preparation of food takes place? Look at the old brands of wine and storehouses filled with the vintages of many ages; is it, think you, a single belly that is to receive the stored wine, sealed with the names of so many consuls, and gathered from so many vineyards? Look, and mark in how many regions men plough the earth, and how many thousands of farmers are tilling and digging; is it, think you, for a single belly that crops are planted in Sicily and Africa? **27.** We should be sensible, and our wants more reasonable, if each of us were to take stock of himself, and to measure his bodily needs also, and understand how little he can consume, and for how short a time! But nothing will give you so much help toward moderation as the frequent thought that life is short and uncertain here below; whatever you are doing, have regard to death. Farewell.

CXV. ON THE SUPERFICIAL BLESSINGS

1. I wish, my dear Lucilius, that you would not be too particular with regard to words and their arrangement; I have greater matters than these to commend to your care. You should seek what to write, rather than how to write it – and even that not for the purpose of writing but of feeling it, that you may thus make what you have felt more your own and, as it were, set a seal on it. **2.** Whenever you notice a style that is too careful and too polished, you may be sure that the mind also is no less absorbed in petty things. The really great man speaks informally and easily; whatever he says, he speaks with assurance rather than with pains.

You are familiar with the young dandies, natty as to their beards and locks, fresh from the bandbox; you can never expect from them any strength or any soundness. Style is the garb of thought: if it be trimmed, or dyed, or treated, it shows that there are defects and a certain amount of flaws in the mind. Elaborate elegance is not a manly garb. **3.** If we had the privilege of looking into a good man's soul, oh what a fair, holy, magnificent, gracious, and shining face should we behold – radiant on the one side with justice and temperance, on another with bravery and wisdom! And, besides these, thriftiness, moderation, endurance, refinement, affability, and – though hard to believe – love of one's fellow-men, that Good which is so rare in man, all these would be shedding their own glory over that soul. There, too, forethought combined with elegance and, resulting from these, a most excellent greatness of soul (the noblest of all these virtues) – indeed what charm, O ye heavens, what authority and dignity would they contribute! What a wonderful combination of sweetness and power! No one could call such a face lovable without also calling it worshipful. **4.** If one might behold such a face, more exalted and more radiant than the mortal eye is wont to behold, would not one pause as if struck dumb by a visitation from above, and utter a silent prayer, saying: "May it be lawful to have looked upon it!"? And then, led on by the encouraging kindliness of his expression, should we not bow down and worship? Should we not, after much contemplation of a far superior countenance, surpassing those which we are wont to look upon, mild-eyed and yet flashing with life-giving fire – should we not then, I say, in reverence and awe, give utterance to those famous lines of our poet Vergil:

> **5.** O maiden, words are weak! Thy face is more
> Than mortal, and thy voice rings sweeter far
> Than mortal man's; . . . .
> Blest be thou; and, whoe'er thou art, relieve
> Our heavy burdens.

And such a vision will indeed be a present help and relief to us, if we are willing to worship it. But this worship does not consist in slaughtering fattened bulls, or in hanging up offerings of gold or silver, or in pouring coins into a temple treasury; rather does it consist in a will that is reverent and upright.

6. There is none of us, I declare to you, who would not burn with love for this vision of virtue, if only he had the privilege of beholding it; for now there are many things that cut off our vision, piercing it with too strong a light, or clogging it with too much darkness. If, however, as certain drugs are wont to be used for sharpening and clearing the eyesight, we are likewise willing to free our mind's eye from hindrances, we shall then be able to perceive virtue, though it be buried in the body – even though poverty stand in the way, and even though lowliness and disgrace block the path. We shall then, I say, behold that true beauty, no matter if it be smothered by unloveliness. **7.** Conversely, we shall get a view of evil and the deadening influences of a sorrow-laden soul – in spite of the hindrance that results from the widespread gleam of riches that flash round about, and in spite of the false light – of official position on the one side or great power on the other – which beats pitilessly upon the beholder.

8. Then it will be in our power to understand how contemptible are the things we admire – like children who regard every toy as a thing of value, who cherish necklaces bought at the price of a mere penny as more dear than their parents or than their brothers. And what, then, as Aristo says, is the difference between ourselves and these children, except that we elders go crazy over paintings and sculpture, and that our folly costs us dearer? Children are pleased by the smooth and variegated pebbles which they pick up on the beach, while we take delight in tall columns of veined marble brought either from Egyptian sands or from African deserts to hold up a colonnade or a dining-hall large enough to contain a city crowd; **9.** we admire walls veneered with a thin layer of marble, although we know the while what defects the marble conceals. We cheat our own eyesight, and when we have overlaid our ceilings with gold, what else is it but a lie in which we take such delight? For we know that beneath all this gilding there lurks some ugly wood.

Nor is such superficial decoration spread merely over walls and ceilings; nay, all the famous men whom you see strutting about with head in air, have nothing but a gold-leaf prosperity. Look beneath, and you will know how much evil lies under that thin coating of titles. **10.** Note that very commodity which holds the attention of so many magistrates and so many judges, and which creates both magistrates and judges – that money, I say, which ever since it began to be regarded with respect, has caused the ruin of the true honour of things; we become alternately merchants and merchandise, and we ask, not what a thing truly is, but what it costs; we fulfil duties if it pays, or neglect them if it pays, and we follow an honourable course as long as it encourages our expectations, ready to veer across to the opposite course if crooked conduct shall promise more. **11.** Our parents have instilled into us a respect for gold and silver; in our early years the craving has been implanted, settling deep within us and growing with our growth. Then too the whole nation, though at odds on every other subject, agrees upon this; this is what they regard, this is what they ask for their children, this is what they dedicate to the gods when they wish to show their gratitude – as if it were the greatest of all man's possessions! And finally, public opinion has come to such a pass that poverty is a hissing and a reproach, despised by the rich and loathed by the poor.

12. Verses of poets also are added to the account – verses which lend fuel to our passions, verses in which wealth is praised as if it were the only credit and glory of mortal man. People seem to think that the immortal gods cannot give any better gift than wealth – or even possess anything better:

> 13. The Sun-god's palace, set with pillars tall,
> And flashing bright with gold.

Or they describe the chariot of the Sun:

> Gold was the axle, golden eke the pole,
> And gold the tires that bound the circling wheels,
> And silver all the spokes within the wheels.

And finally, when they would praise an epoch as the best, they call it the "Golden Age." 14. Even among the Greek tragic poets there are some who regard pelf as better than purity, soundness, or good report:

> Call me a scoundrel, only call me rich!

> All ask how great my riches are, but none
> Whether my soul is good.

> None asks the means or source of your estate,
> But merely how it totals.

> All men are worth as much as what they own.

> What is most shameful for us to possess?
> Nothing!

> If riches bless me, I should love to live;
> Yet I would rather die, if poor.

> A man dies nobly in pursuit of wealth.

> Money, that blessing to the race of man,
> Cannot be matched by mother's love, or lisp
> Of children, or the honour due one's sire.

> And if the sweetness of the lover's glance
> Be half so charming, Love will rightly stir
> The hearts of gods and men to adoration.

15. When these last-quoted lines were spoken at a performance of one of the tragedies of Euripides, the whole audience rose with one accord to hiss the actor and the play off the stage. But Euripides jumped to his feet, claimed a hearing, and asked them to wait for the conclusion and see the destiny that was in store for this man

who gaped after gold. Bellerophon, in that particular drama, was to pay the penalty which is exacted of all men in the drama of life. **16.** For one must pay the penalty for all greedy acts; although the greed is enough of a penalty in itself. What tears and toil does money wring from us! Greed is wretched in that which it craves and wretched in that which it wins! Think besides of the daily worry which afflicts every possessor in proportion to the measure of his gain! The possession of riches means even greater agony of spirit than the acquisition of riches. And how we sorrow over our losses – losses which fall heavily upon us, and yet seem still more heavy! And finally, though Fortune may leave our property intact, whatever we cannot gain in addition, is sheer loss!

17. "But," you will say to me, "people call yonder man happy and rich; they pray that some day they may equal him in possessions." Very true. What, then? Do you think that there is any more pitiable lot in life than to possess misery and hatred also? Would that those who are bound to crave wealth could compare notes with the rich man! Would that those who are bound to seek political office could confer with ambitious men who have reached the most sought-after honours! They would then surely alter their prayers, seeing that these grandees are always gaping after new gain, condemning what is already behind them. For there is no one in the world who is contented with his prosperity, even if it comes to him on the run. Men complain about their plans and the outcome of their plans; they always prefer what they have failed to win.

18. So philosophy can settle this problem for you, and afford you, to my mind, the greatest boon that exists – absence of regret for your own conduct. This is a sure happiness; no storm can ruffle it; but you cannot be steered safely through by any subtly woven words, or any gently flowing language. Let words proceed as they please, provided only your soul keeps its own sure order, provided your soul is great and holds unruffled to its ideals, pleased with itself on account of the very things which displease others, a soul that makes life the test of its progress, and believes that its knowledge is in exact proportion to its freedom from desire and its freedom from fear. Farewell.

CXVI. ON SELF-CONTROL

1. The question has often been raised whether it is better to have moderate emotions, or none at all. Philosophers of our school reject the emotions; the Peripatetics keep them in check. I, however, do not understand how any half-way disease can be either wholesome or helpful. Do not fear; I am not robbing you of any privileges which you are unwilling to lose! I shall be kindly and indulgent towards the objects for which you strive – those which you hold to be necessary to our existence, or useful, or pleasant; I shall simply strip away the vice. For after I have issued my prohibitions against the desires, I shall still allow you to wish that you may do the same things fearlessly and with greater accuracy of judgment, and to feel even the pleasures more than before; and how can these pleasures help coming more readily to your call, if you are their lord rather than their slave!

2. "But," you object, "it is natural for me to suffer when I am bereaved of a friend; grant some privileges to tears which have the right to flow! It is also natural to be affected by men's opinions and to be cast down when they are unfavourable; so why should you not allow me such an honourable aversion to bad opinion?"

There is no vice which lacks some plea; there is no vice that at the start is not modest and easily entreated; but afterwards the trouble spreads more widely. If you allow it to begin, you cannot make sure of its ceasing. **3.** Every emotion at the start is weak. Afterwards, it rouses itself and gains strength by progress; it is more easy to forestall it than to forgo it. Who does not admit that all the emotions flow as it were from a certain natural source? We are endowed by Nature with an interest in our own well-being; but this very interest, when overindulged, becomes a vice. Nature has intermingled pleasure with necessary things – not in order that we should seek pleasure, but in order that the addition of pleasure may make the indispensable means of existence attractive to our eyes. Should it claim rights of its own, it is luxury.

Let us therefore resist these faults when they are demanding entrance, because, as I have said, it is easier to deny them admittance than to make them depart. **4.** And if you cry: "One should be allowed a certain amount of grieving, and a certain amount of fear." I reply that the "certain amount" can be too long-drawn-out, and that it will refuse to stop short when you so desire. The wise man can safely control himself without becoming over-anxious; he can halt his tears and his pleasures at will; but in our case, because it is not easy to retrace our steps, it is best not to push ahead at all. **5.** I think that Panaetius gave a very neat answer to a certain youth who asked him whether the wise man should become a lover: "As to the wise man, we shall see later; but you and I, who are as yet far removed from wisdom, should not trust ourselves to fall into a state that is disordered, uncontrolled, enslaved to another, contemptible to itself. If our love be not spurned, we are excited by its kindness; if it be scorned, we are kindled by our pride. An easily won love hurts us as much as one which is difficult to win; we are captured by that which is compliant, and we struggle with that which is hard. Therefore, knowing our weakness, let us remain quiet. Let us not expose this unstable spirit to the temptations of drink, or beauty, or flattery, or anything that coaxes and allures."

6. Now that which Panaetius replied to the question about love may be applied, I believe, to all the emotions. In so far as we are able, let us step back from slippery places; even on dry ground it is hard enough to take a sturdy stand. **7.** At this point, I know, you will confront me with that common complaint against the Stoics: "Your promises are too great, and your counsels too hard. We are mere manikins, unable to deny ourselves everything. We shall sorrow, but not to any great extent; we shall feel desires, but in moderation; we shall give way to anger, but we shall be appeased." **8.** And do you know why we have not the power to attain this Stoic ideal? It is because we refuse to believe in our power. Nay, of a surety, there is something else which plays a part: it is because we are in love with our vices; we uphold them and prefer to make excuses for them rather than shake them off. We mortals have been endowed with sufficient strength by nature, if only we use this strength, if only we concentrate our powers and rouse them all to help us or at least not to hinder us. The reason is unwillingness, the excuse, inability. Farewell.

CXVII. ON REAL ETHICS AS SUPERIOR TO SYLLOGISTIC SUBTLETIES

1. You will be fabricating much trouble for me, and you will be unconsciously embroiling me in a great discussion, and in considerable bother, if you put such petty questions as these; for in settling them I cannot disagree with my fellow-Stoics without impairing my standing among them, nor can I subscribe to such ideas without impairing my conscience. Your query is, whether the Stoic belief is true: that wisdom is a Good, but that *being wise* is not a Good. I shall first set forth the Stoic view, and then I shall be bold enough to deliver my own opinion.

2. We of the Stoic school believe that the Good is corporeal, because the Good is active, and whatever is active is corporeal. That which is good, is helpful. But, in order to be helpful, it must be active; so, if it is active, it is corporeal. They (the Stoics) declare that wisdom is a Good; it therefore follows that one must also call wisdom corporeal. **3.** But they do not think that *being wise* can be rated on the same basis. For it is incorporeal and accessory to something else, in other words, wisdom; hence it is in no respect active or helpful.

"What, then?" is the reply; "Why do we not say that *being wise* is a Good?" We do say so; but only by referring it to that on which it depends – in other words, wisdom itself. **4.** Let me tell you what answers other philosophers make to these objectors, before I myself begin to form my own creed and to take my place entirely on another side. "Judged in that light," they say, "not even *living happily* is a Good. Willy nilly, such persons ought to reply that the happy life is a Good, but that *living happily* is not a Good." **5.** And this objection is also raised against our school: "You wish to be wise. Therefore, *being wise* is a thing to be desired. And if it be a thing to be desired it is a Good." So our philosophers are forced to twist their words and insert another syllable into the word "desired," – a syllable which our language does not normally allow to be inserted. But, with your permission, I shall add it. "That which is good," they say, "is a thing to be desired; the *desirable* thing is that which falls to our lot after we have attained the Good. For the desirable is not sought as a Good; it is an accessory to the Good after the Good has been attained."

6. I myself do not hold the same view, and I judge that our philosophers have come down to this argument because they are already bound by the first link in the chain and for that reason may not alter their definition. People are wont to concede much to the things which all men take for granted; in our eyes the fact that all men agree upon something is a proof of its truth. For instance, we infer that the gods exist, for this reason, among others – that there is implanted in everyone an idea concerning deity, and there is no people so far beyond the reach of laws and customs that it does not believe at least in gods of some sort. And when we discuss the immortality of the soul, we are influenced in no small degree by the general opinion of mankind, who either fear or worship the spirits of the lower world. I make the most of this general belief: you can find no one who does not hold that wisdom is a Good, and being wise also. 7. I shall not appeal to the populace, like a conquered gladiator; let us come to close quarters, using our own weapons.

When something affects a given object, is it outside the object which it affects, or is it inside the object it affects? If it is inside the object it affects, it is as corporeal as the object which it affects. For nothing can affect another object without touching it, and that which touches is corporeal. If it is outside, it withdraws after having affected the object. And withdrawal means motion. And that which possesses motion, is corporeal. 8. You expect me, I suppose, to deny that "race" differs from "running," that "heat" differs from "being hot," that "light" differs from "giving light." I grant that these pairs vary, but hold that they are not in separate classes. If good health is an indifferent quality, then so is *being in good health*; if beauty is an indifferent quality, then so is *being beautiful*. If justice is a Good, then so is *being just*. And if baseness is an evil, then it is an evil to be base – just as much as, if sore eyes are an evil, the state of having sore eyes is also an evil. Neither quality, you may be sure, can exist without the other. He who is wise is a man of wisdom; he who is a man of wisdom is wise. So true it is that we cannot doubt the quality of the one to equal the quality of the other, that they are both regarded by certain persons as one and the same.

9. Here is a question, however, which I should be glad to put: granted that all things are either good or bad or indifferent – in what class does *being wise* belong? People deny that it is a Good; and, as obviously is not an evil, it must consequently be one of the "media." But we mean by the "medium," or the "indifferent" quality that which can fall to the lot of the bad no less than to the good – such things as money, beauty, or high social position. But the quality of *being wise* can fall to the lot of the good man alone; therefore *being wise* is not an indifferent quality. Nor is it an evil, either; because it cannot fall to the lot of the bad man; therefore, it is a Good. That which the good man alone can possess, is a Good; now *being wise* is the possession of the good man only; therefore it is a Good. **10.** The objector replies: "It is only an accessory of wisdom." Very well, then, I say, this quality which you call *being wise* – does it actively produce wisdom, or is it a passive concomitant of wisdom? It is corporeal in either case. For that which is acted upon and that which acts, are alike corporeal; and, if corporeal, each is a Good. The only quality which could prevent it from being a Good, would be incorporeality.

11. The Peripatetics believe that there is no distinction between *wisdom* and *being wise*, since either of these implies the other also. Now do you suppose that any man can *be wise* except one who possesses wisdom? Or that anyone who *is wise* does not possess wisdom? 12. The old masters of dialectic, however, distinguish between these two conceptions; and from them the classification has come right down to the Stoics. What sort of a classification this is, I shall explain: A field is one thing, and the possession of the field another thing; of course, because "possessing the field" refers to the possessor rather than to the field itself. Similarly, wisdom is one thing and *being wise* another. You will grant, I suppose, that these two are separate ideas – the possessed and the possessor: wisdom being that which one possesses, and he who *is wise* its possessor. Now wisdom is Mind perfected and developed to the highest and best degree. For it is the art of life. And what is *being wise*? I cannot call it "Mind Perfected," but rather that which falls to the lot of him who possesses a "mind perfected"; thus a good mind is one thing, and the so-called possession of a good mind another.

13. "There are," it is said, "certain natural classes of bodies; we say: 'This is a man,' 'this is a horse.' Then there attend on the bodily natures certain movements of the mind which declare something about the body. And these have a certain essential quality which is sundered from body; for example: 'I see Cato walking.' The senses indicate this, and the mind believes it. What I see, is *body*, and upon this I concentrate my eyes and my mind. Again, I say: 'Cato walks.' What I say," they continue, "is not body; it is a certain declarative fact concerning body – called variously an 'utterance,' a 'declaration,' a 'statement.' Thus, when we say 'wisdom,' we mean something *pertaining* to body; when we say '*he is wise*,' we are speaking *concerning* body. And it makes considerable difference whether you mention the person directly, or speak concerning the person."

14. Supposing for the present that these are two separate conceptions (for I am not yet prepared to give my own opinion); what prevents the existence of still a third – which is none the less a Good? I remarked a little while ago that a "field" was one thing, and the "possession of a field" another; of course, for possessor and possessed are of different natures; the latter is the land, and the former is the man who owns the land. But with regard to the point now under discussion, both are of the same nature – the possessor of wisdom, and wisdom itself. 15. Besides, in the one case that which is possessed is one thing, and he who possesses it is another; but in this case the possessed and the possessor come under the same category. The field is owned by virtue of law, wisdom by virtue of nature. The field can change hands and go into the ownership of another; but wisdom never departs from its owner. Accordingly, there is no reason why you should try to compare things that are so unlike one another. I had started to say that these can be two separate conceptions, and yet that both can be Goods – for instance, wisdom and the wise man being two separate things and yet granted by you to be equally good. And just as there is no objection to regarding both wisdom and the possessor of wisdom as Goods, so there is no objection to regarding as a good both wisdom and the possession of wisdom, – in other words, *being wise*. 16.

For I only wish to be a wise man in order to *be wise*. And what then? Is not that thing a Good without the possession of which a certain other thing cannot be a Good? You surely admit that wisdom, if given without the right to be used, is not to be welcomed! And wherein consists the use of wisdom? In *being wise*; that is its most valuable attribute; if you withdraw this, wisdom becomes superfluous. If processes of torture are evil, then being tortured is an evil – with this reservation, indeed, that if you take away the consequences, the former are not evil. Wisdom is a condition of "mind perfected," and *being wise* is the employment of this "mind perfected." How can the employment of that thing not be a Good, which without employment is not a Good? **17.** If I ask you whether wisdom is to be desired, you admit that it is. If I ask you whether the employment of wisdom is to be desired, you also admit the fact; for you say that you will not receive wisdom if you are not allowed to employ it. Now that which is to be desired is a Good. *Being wise* is the employment of wisdom, just as it is of eloquence to make a speech, or of the eyes to see things. Therefore, *being wise* is the employment of wisdom, and the employment of wisdom is to be desired. Therefore *being wise* is a thing to be desired; and if it is a thing to be desired, it is a Good.

18. Lo, these many years I have been condemning myself for imitating these men at the very time when I am arraigning them, and of wasting words on a subject that is perfectly clear. For who can doubt that, if heat is an evil, it is also an evil to be hot? Or that, if cold is an evil, it is an evil to be cold? Or that, if life is a Good, so is *being alive*? All such matters are on the outskirts of wisdom, not in wisdom itself. But our abiding-place should be in wisdom itself. **19.** Even though one takes a fancy to roam, wisdom has large and spacious retreats: we may investigate the nature of the gods, the fuel which feeds the constellations, or all the varied courses of the stars; we may speculate whether our affairs move in harmony with those of the stars, whether the impulse to motion comes from thence into the minds and bodies of all, and whether even these events which we call fortuitous are fettered by strict laws and nothing in this universe is unforeseen or unregulated in its revolutions. Such topics have nowadays been withdrawn from instruction in morals, but they uplift the mind and raise it to the dimensions of the subject which it discusses; the matters, however, of which I was speaking a while ago, wear away and wear down the mind, not (as you and yours maintain) whetting, but weakening it. **20.** And I ask you, are we to fritter away that necessary study which we owe to greater and better themes, in discussing a matter which may perhaps be wrong and is certainly of no avail? How will it profit me to know whether wisdom is one thing, and *being wise* another? How will it profit me to know that the one is, and the other is not, a Good? Suppose I take a chance, and gamble on this prayer: "Wisdom for you, and *being wise* for me!" We shall come out even.

21. Try rather to show me the way by which I may attain those ends. Tell me what to avoid, what to seek, by what studies to strengthen my tottering mind, how I may rebuff the waves that strike me abeam and drive me from my course, by what means I may be able to cope with all my evils, and by what means I can be rid of the calamities that have plunged in upon me and those into which I myself have plunged. Teach me how to bear the burden of sorrow without a groan on my part, and how to bear prosperity without making others groan; also, how to avoid waiting for the ultimate and inevitable end, and to beat a retreat of my own free will, when it seems proper to me to do so. 22. I think nothing is baser than to pray for death. For if you wish to live, why do you pray for death? And if you do not wish to live, why do you ask the gods for that which they gave you at birth? For even as, against your will, it has been settled that you must die some day, so the time when you shall wish to die is in your own hands. The one fact is to you a necessity, the other a privilege.

23. I read lately a most disgraceful doctrine, uttered (more shame to him!) by a learned gentleman: "So may I die as soon as possible!" Fool, thou art praying for something that is already thine own! "So may I die as soon as possible!" Perhaps thou didst grow old while uttering these very words! At any rate, what is there to hinder? No one detains thee; escape by whatsoever way thou wilt! Select any portion of Nature, and bid it provide thee with a means of departure! These, namely, are the elements, by which the world's work is carried on – water, earth, air. All these are no more the causes of life than they are the ways of death. **24.** "So may I die as soon as possible!" And what is thy wish with regard to this "as soon as possible"? What day dost thou set for the event? It may be sooner than thy prayer requests. Words like this come from a weak mind, from one that courts pity by such cursing; he who prays for death does not wish to die. Ask the gods for life and health; if thou art resolved to die, death's reward is to have done with prayers.

25. It is with such problems as these, my dear Lucilius, that we should deal, by such problems that we should mould our minds. This is wisdom, this is what *being wise* means – not to bandy empty subtleties in idle and petty discussions. Fortune has set before you so many problems – which you have not yet solved – and are you still splitting hairs? How foolish it is to practise strokes after you have heard the signal for the fight! Away with all these dummy-weapons; you need armour for a fight to the finish. Tell me by what means sadness and fear may be kept from disturbing my soul, by what means I may shift off this burden of hidden cravings. Do something! **26.** "Wisdom is a Good, but *being wise* is not a Good;" such talk results for us in the judgment that we are not wise, and in making a laughing-stock of this whole field of study – on the ground that it wastes its effort on useless things. Suppose you knew that this question was also debated: whether future wisdom is a Good? For, I beseech you, how could one doubt whether barns do not feel the weight of the harvest that is to come, and that boyhood does not have premonitions of approaching young manhood by any brawn and power? The sick person, in the intervening period, is not helped by the health that is to come, any more than a runner or a wrestler is refreshed by the period of repose that will follow many months later. **27.** Who does not know that what is yet to be is not a Good, for the very reason that it is yet to be? For that which is good is necessarily helpful. And unless things are in the present, they cannot be helpful; and if a thing is not helpful, it is not a Good; if helpful, it is already. I shall be a wise man some day; and this Good will be mine when I shall be a wise man, but in the meantime it is non-existent. A thing must exist first, then may be of a certain kind. **28.** How, I ask you, can that which is still nothing be already a Good? And in what better way do you wish it to be proved to you that a certain thing is not, than to say: "It is yet to be"? For it is clear that something which is on the way has not yet arrived. "Spring will follow": I know that winter is here now. "Summer will follow:" I know that it is not summer. The best proof to my mind that a thing is not yet present is that it is yet to be. **29.** I hope some day to be wise, but meanwhile I am not wise. For if I possessed that Good, I should now be free from this Evil. Some day I shall be wise; from this very fact you may understand that I am not yet wise. I cannot at the same time live in that state of Good and in this state of Evil; the two ideas do not harmonize, nor do Evil and Good exist together in the same person.

30. Let us rush past all this clever nonsense, and hurry on to that which will bring us real assistance. No man who is anxiously running after a midwife for his daughter in her birth-pangs will stop to read the praetor's edict or the order of events at the games. No one who is speeding to save his burning house will scan a checker-board to speculate how the imprisoned piece can be freed. **31.** But good heavens! – In your case all sorts of news are announced on all sides – your house afire, your children in danger, your country in a state of siege, your property plundered. Add to this shipwreck, earthquakes, and all other objects of dread; harassed amid these troubles, are you taking time for matters which serve merely for mental entertainment? Do you ask what difference there is between wisdom and *being wise*? Do you tie and untie knots while such a ruin is hanging over your head? **32.** Nature has not given us such a generous and free-handed space of time that we can have the leisure to waste any of it. Mark also how much is lost even when men are very careful: people are robbed of one thing by ill-health and of another thing by illness in the family; at one time private, at another public, business absorbs the attention; and all the while sleep shares our lives with us.

Out of this time, so short and swift, that carries us away in its flight, of what avail is it to spend the greater part on useless things? **33.** Besides, our minds are accustomed to entertain rather than to cure themselves, to make an aesthetic pleasure out of philosophy, when philosophy should really be a remedy. What the distinction is between wisdom and *being wise* I do not know; but I do know that it makes no difference to me whether I know such matters or am ignorant of them. Tell me: when I have found out the difference between wisdom and *being wise*, shall I be wise?

Why then do you occupy me with the words rather than with the works of wisdom? Make me braver, make me calmer, make me the equal of Fortune, make me her superior. And I can be her superior, if I apply to this end everything that I learn. Farewell.

CXVIII. ON THE VANITY OF PLACE-SEEKING

1. You have been demanding more frequent letters from me. But if we compare the accounts, you will not be on the credit side. We had indeed made the agreement that your part came first, that you should write the first letters, and that I should answer. However, I shall not be disagreeable; I know that it is safe to trust you, so I shall pay in advance, and yet not do as the eloquent Cicero bids Atticus do: "Even if you have nothing to say, write whatever enters your head." **2.** For there will always be something for me to write about, even omitting all the kinds of news with which Cicero fills his correspondence: what candidate is in difficulties, who is striving on borrowed resources and who on his own; who is a candidate for the consulship relying on Caesar, or on Pompey, or on his own strong-box; what a merciless usurer is Caecilius, out of whom his friends cannot screw a penny for less than one per cent each month.

But it is preferable to deal with one's own ills, rather than with another's – to sift oneself and see for how many vain things one is a candidate, and cast a vote for none of them. **3.** This, my dear Lucilius, is a noble thing, this brings peace and freedom – to canvass for nothing, and to pass by all the elections of Fortune. How can you call it enjoyable, when the tribes are called together and the candidates are making offerings in their favourite temples – some of them promising money gifts and others doing business by means of an agent, or wearing down their hands with the kisses of those to whom they will refuse the least finger-touch after being elected – when all are excitedly awaiting the announcement of the herald, do you call it enjoyable, I say, to stand idle and look on at this Vanity Fair without either buying or selling? **4.** How much greater joy does one feel who looks without concern, not merely upon the election of a praetor or of a consul, but upon that great struggle in which some are seeking yearly honours, and others permanent power, and others the triumph and the prosperous outcome of war, and others riches, or marriage and offspring, or the welfare of themselves and their relatives! What a great-souled action it is to be the only person who is canvassing for nothing, offering prayers to no man, and saying: "Fortune, I have nothing to do with you. I am not at your service. I know that men like Cato are spurned by you, and men like Vatinius made by you. I ask no favours." This is the way to reduce Fortune to the ranks.

5. These, then, are the things about which we may write in turn, and this is the ever fresh material which we may dig out as we scan the restless multitudes of men, who, in order to attain something ruinous, struggle on through evil to evil, and seek that which they must presently shun or even find surfeiting. **6.** For who was ever satisfied, after attainment, with that which loomed up large as he prayed for it? Happiness is not, as men think, a greedy thing; it is a lowly thing; for that reason it never gluts a man's desire. You deem lofty the objects you seek, because you are on a low level and hence far away from them; but they are mean in the sight of him who has reached them. And I am very much mistaken if he does not desire to climb still higher; that which you regard as the top is merely a rung on the ladder. **7.** Now all men suffer from ignorance of the truth; deceived by common report, they make for these ends as if they were good, and then, after having won their wish, and suffered much, they find them evil, or empty, or less important than they had expected. Most men admire that which deceives them at a distance, and by the crowd good things are supposed to be big things.

8. Now, lest this happen also in our own case, let us ask what is the Good. It has been explained in various ways; different men have described it in different ways. Some define it in this way. "That which attracts and calls the spirit to itself is a Good." But the objection at once comes up – what if it does attract, but straight to ruin? You know how seductive many evils are. That which is true differs from that which looks like the truth; hence the Good is connected with the true, for it is not good unless it is also true. But that which attracts and allures, is only *like* the truth; it steals your attention, demands your interest, and draws you to itself. **9.** Therefore, some have given this definition: "That is good which inspires desire for itself, or rouses towards itself the impulse of a struggling soul." There is the same objection to this idea; for many things rouse the soul's impulses, and yet the search for them is harmful to the seeker. The following definition is better: "That is good which rouses the soul's impulse towards itself in accordance with nature, and is worth seeking only when it begins to be thoroughly worth seeking." It is by this time an honourable thing; for that is a thing completely worth seeking.

10. The present topic suggests that I state the difference between the Good and the honourable. Now they have a certain quality which blends with both and is inseparable from either: nothing can be good unless it contains an element of the honourable, and the honourable is necessarily good. What, then, is the difference between these two qualities? The honourable is the perfect Good, and the happy life is fulfilled thereby; through its influence other things also are rendered good. **11.** I mean something like this: there are certain things which are neither good nor bad – as military or diplomatic service, or the pronouncing of legal decisions. When such pursuits have been honourably conducted, they begin to be good, and they change over from the "indifferent" class into the Good. The Good results from partnership with the honourable, but the honourable is good in itself. The Good springs from the honourable, but the latter from itself. What is good might have been bad; what is honourable could never have been anything but good.

12. Some have defined as follows: "That is good which is according to nature." Now attend to my own statement: that which is good is according to nature, but that which is according to nature does not also become immediately good; for many things harmonize with nature, but are so petty that it is not suitable to call them good. For they are unimportant and deserve to be despised. But there is no such thing as a very small and despicable good, for, as long as it is scanty, it is not good, and when it begins to be good, it ceases to be scanty. How, then, can the Good be recognized? Only if it is completely according to nature.

13. People say: "You admit that that which is good is according to nature; for this is its peculiar quality. You admit, too, that there are other things according to nature, which, however, are not good. How then can the former be good, and the latter not? How can there be an alteration in the peculiar quality of a thing, when each has, in common with the other, the special attribute of being in accord with nature?" **14.** Surely because of its magnitude. It is no new idea that certain objects change as they grow. A person, once a child, becomes a youth; his peculiar quality is transformed; for the child could not reason, but the youth possesses reason. Certain things not only grow in size as they develop, but grow into something else. **15.** Some reply: "But that which becomes greater does not necessarily become different. It matters not at all whether you pour wine into a flask or into a vat; the wine keeps its peculiar quality in both vessels. Small and large quantities of honey are not distinct in taste." But these are different cases which you mention; for wine and honey have a uniform quality; no matter how much the quantity is enlarged, the quality is the same. **16.** For some things endure according to their kind and their peculiar qualities, even when they are enlarged.

There are others, however, which, after many increments, are altered by the last addition; there is stamped upon them a new character, different from that of yore. One stone makes an archway – the stone which wedges the leaning sides and holds the arch together by its position in the middle. And why does the last addition, although very slight, make a great deal of difference? Because it does not increase; it fills up. **17.** Some things, through development, put off their former shape and are altered into a new figure. When the mind has for a long time developed some idea, and in the attempt to grasp its magnitude has become weary, that thing begins to be called "infinite." And then this has become something far different from what it was when it seemed great but finite. In the same way we have thought of something as difficult to divide; at the very end, as the task grows more and more hard, the thing is found to be "indivisible." Similarly, from that which could scarcely or with difficulty be moved we have advanced on and on – until we reach the "immovable." By the same reasoning a certain thing was according to nature; its greatness has altered it into some other peculiar quality and has rendered it a Good. Farewell.

CXIX. ON NATURE AS OUR BEST PROVIDER

1. Whenever I have made a discovery, I do not wait for you to cry "Shares!" I say it to myself in your behalf. If you wish to know what it is that I have found, open your pocket; it is clear profit. What I shall teach you is the ability to become rich as speedily as possible. How keen you are to hear the news! And rightly; I shall lead you by a short cut to the greatest riches. It will be necessary, however, for you to find a loan; in order to be able to do business, you must contract a debt, although I do not wish you to arrange the loan through a middle-man, nor do I wish the brokers to be discussing your rating. **2.** I shall furnish you with a ready creditor, Cato's famous one, who says: "Borrow from yourself!" No matter how small it is, it will be enough if we can only make up the deficit from our own resources. For, my dear Lucilius, it does not matter whether you crave nothing, or whether you possess something. The important principle in either case is the same – freedom from worry.

But I do not counsel you to deny anything to nature – for nature is insistent and cannot be overcome; she demands her due – but you should know that anything in excess of nature's wants is a mere "extra" and is not necessary. **3.** If I am hungry, I must eat. Nature does not care whether the bread is the coarse kind or the finest wheat; she does not desire the stomach to be entertained, but to be filled. And if I am thirsty, Nature does not care whether I drink water from the nearest reservoir, or whether I freeze it artificially by sinking it in large quantities of snow. Nature orders only that the thirst be quenched; and it does not matter whether it be a golden, or crystal, or murrine goblet, or a cup from Tibur, or the hollow hand. **4.** Look to the end, in all matters, and then you will cast away superfluous things. Hunger calls me; let me stretch forth my hand to that which is nearest; my very hunger has made attractive in my eyes whatever I can grasp. A starving man despises nothing.

5. Do you ask, then, what it is that has pleased me? It is this noble saying which I have discovered: "The wise man is the keenest seeker for the riches of nature." "What", you ask, "will you present me with an empty plate? What do you mean? I had already arranged my coffers; I was already looking about to see some stretch of water on which I might embark for purposes of trade, some state revenues that I might handle, and some merchandise that I might acquire. That is deceit – showing me poverty after promising me riches." But, friend, do you regard a man as poor to whom nothing is wanting? "It is, however," you reply, "thanks to himself and his endurance, and not thanks to his fortune." Do you, then, hold that such a man is not rich, just because his wealth can never fail? **6.** Would you rather have much, or enough? He who has much desires more – a proof that he has not yet acquired enough; but he who has enough has attained that which never fell to the rich man's lot – a stopping-point. Do you think that this condition to which I refer is not riches, just because no man has ever been proscribed as a result of possessing them? Or because sons and wives have never thrust poison down one's throat for that reason? Or because in war-time these riches are unmolested? Or because they bring leisure in time of peace? Or because it is not dangerous to possess them, or troublesome to invest them?

7. "But one possesses too little, if one is merely free from cold and hunger and thirst." Jupiter himself however, is no better off. Enough is never too little, and not-enough is never too much. Alexander was poor even after his conquest of Darius and the Indies. Am I wrong? He seeks something which he can really make his own, exploring unknown seas, sending new fleets over the Ocean, and, so to speak, breaking down the very bars of the universe. But that which is enough for nature, is not enough for man. **8.** There have been found persons who crave something more after obtaining everything; so blind are their wits and so readily does each man forget his start after he has got under way. He who was but lately the disputed lord of an unknown corner of the world, is dejected when, after reaching the limits of the globe, he must march back through a world which he has made his own. **9.** Money never made a man rich; on the contrary, it always smites men with a greater craving for itself. Do you ask the reason for this? He who possesses more begins to be able to possess still more.

To sum up, you may hale forth for our inspection any of the millionaires whose names are told off when one speaks of Crassus and Licinus. Let him bring along his rating and his present property and his future expectations, and let him add them all together: such a man, according to my belief, is poor; according to yours, he may be poor some day. **10.** He, however, who has arranged his affairs according to nature's demands, is free from the fear, as well as from the sensation, of poverty. And in order that you may know how hard it is to narrow one's interests down to the limits of nature – even this very person of whom we speak, and whom you call poor, possesses something actually superfluous. **11.** Wealth, however, blinds and attracts the mob, when they see a large bulk of ready money brought out of a man's house, or even his walls crusted with abundance of gold, or a retinue that is chosen for beauty of physique, or for attractiveness of attire. The prosperity of all these men looks to public opinion; but the ideal man, whom we have snatched from the control of the people and of Fortune, is happy inwardly. **12.** For as far as those persons are concerned, in whose minds bustling poverty has wrongly stolen the title of riches – these individuals have riches just as we say that we "have a fever," when really the fever has *us*. Conversely, we are accustomed to say: "A fever grips him." And in the same way we should say: "Riches grip him." There is therefore no advice – and of such advice no one can have too much – which I would rather give you than this: that you should measure all things by the demands of Nature; for these demands can be satisfied either without cost or else very cheaply. Only, do not mix any vices with these demands. **13.** Why need you ask how your food should be served, on what sort of table, with what sort of silver, with what well-matched and smooth-faced young servants? Nature demands nothing except mere food.

> Dost seek, when thirst inflames thy throat, a cup of gold?
> Dost scorn all else but peacock's flesh or turbot
> When the hunger comes upon thee?

14. Hunger is not ambitious; it is quite satisfied to come to an end; nor does it care very much what food brings it to an end. Those things are but the instruments of a luxury which is not "happiness"; a luxury which seeks how it may prolong hunger even after repletion, how to stuff the stomach, not to fill it, and how to rouse a thirst that has been satisfied with the first drink. Horace's words are therefore most excellent when he says that it makes no difference to one's thirst in what costly goblet, or with what elaborate state, the water is served. For if you believe it to be of importance how curly-haired your slave is, or how transparent is the cup which he offers you, you are not thirsty.

15. Among other things, Nature has bestowed upon us this special boon: she relieves sheer necessity of squeamishness. The superfluous things admit of choice; we say: "That is not suitable "; "this is not well recommended"; "that hurts my eyesight." The Builder of the universe, who laid down for us the laws of life, provided that we should exist in well-being, but not in luxury. Everything conducive to our well-being is prepared and ready to our hands; but what luxury requires can never be got together except with wretchedness and anxiety.

16. Let us therefore use this boon of Nature by reckoning it among the things of high importance; let us reflect that Nature's best title to our gratitude is that whatever we want because of sheer necessity we accept without squeamishness. Farewell.

CXX. MORE ABOUT VIRTUE

1. Your letter roamed, over several little problems, but finally dwelt upon this alone, asking for explanation: "How do we acquire a knowledge of that which is good and that which is honourable?" In the opinion of other schools, these two qualities are distinct; among our followers, however, they are merely divided. **2.** This is what I mean: Some believe the Good to be that which is useful; they accordingly bestow this title upon riches, horses, wine, and shoes; so cheaply do they view the Good, and to such base uses do they let it descend. They regard as honourable that which agrees with the principle of right conduct – such as taking dutiful care of an old father, relieving a friend's poverty, showing bravery on a campaign, and uttering prudent and well-balanced opinions. **3.** We, however, do make the Good and the honourable two things, but we make them out of one: only the honourable can be good; also, the honourable is necessarily good. I hold it superfluous to add the distinction between these two qualities, inasmuch as I have mentioned it so many times. But I shall say this one thing – that we regard nothing as good which can be put to wrong use by any person. And you see for yourself to what wrong uses many men put their riches, their high position, or their physical powers.

To return to the matter on which you desire information: "How we first acquire the knowledge of that which is good and that which is honourable." **4.** Nature could not teach us this directly; she has given us the seeds of knowledge, but not knowledge itself. Some say that we merely happened upon this knowledge; but it is unbelievable that a vision of virtue could have presented itself to anyone by mere chance. We believe that it is inference due to observation, a comparison of events that have occurred frequently; our school of philosophy hold that the honourable and the good have been comprehended by analogy. Since the word "analogy" has been admitted to citizen rank by Latin scholars, I do not think that it ought to be condemned, but I do think it should be brought into the citizenship which it can justly claim. I shall, therefore, make use of the word, not merely as admitted, but as established.

Now what this "analogy" is, I shall explain. **5.** We understood what bodily health was: and from this basis we deduced the existence of a certain mental health also. We knew, too, bodily strength, and from this basis we inferred the existence of mental sturdiness. Kindly deeds, humane deeds, brave deeds, had at times amazed us; so we began to admire them as if they were perfect. Underneath, however, there were many faults, hidden by the appearance and the brilliancy of certain conspicuous acts; to these we shut our eyes. Nature bids us amplify praiseworthy things – everyone exalts renown beyond the truth. And thus from such deeds we deduced the conception of some great good. **6.** Fabricius rejected King Pyrrhus's gold, deeming it greater than a king's crown to be able to scorn a king's money. Fabricius also, when the royal physician promised to give his master poison, warned Pyrrhus to beware of a plot. The selfsame man had the resolution to refuse either to be won over by gold or to win by poison. So we admired the hero, who could not be moved by the promises of the king or against the king, who held fast to a noble ideal, and who – is anything more difficult? – was in war sinless; for he believed that wrongs could be committed even against an enemy, and in that extreme poverty which he had made his glory, shrank from receiving riches as he shrank from using poison. "Live," he cried, "O Pyrrhus, thanks to me, and rejoice, instead of grieving as you have done till now, that Fabricius cannot be bribed!"

7. Horatius Cocles blocked the narrow bridge alone, and ordered his retreat to be cut off, that the enemy's path might be destroyed; then he long withstood his assailants until the crash of the beams, as they collapsed with a huge fall, rang in his ears. When he looked back and saw that his country, through his own danger, was free from danger, "Whoever," he cried, "wishes to pursue me this way, let him come!" He plunged headlong, taking as great care to come out arm'd from the midst of the dashing river-channel as he did to come out unhurt; he returned, preserving the glory of his conquering weapons, as safely as if he had come back over the bridge.

8. These deeds and others of the same sort have revealed to us a picture of virtue. I will add something which may perhaps astonish you: evil things have sometimes offered the appearance of what is honourable, and that which is best has been manifested through, its opposite. For there are, as you know, vices which are next-door to virtues; and even that which is lost and debased can resemble that which is upright. So the spendthrift falsely imitates the liberal man – although it matters a great deal whether a man knows how to give, or does not know how to save, his money. I assure you, my dear Lucilius, there are many who do not give, but simply throw away and I do not call a man liberal who is out of temper with his money. Carelessness looks like ease, and rashness like bravery. **9.** This resemblance has forced us to watch carefully and to distinguish between things which are by outward appearance closely connected, but which actually are very much at odds with one another; and in watching those who have become distinguished as a result of some noble effort, we have been forced to observe what persons have done some deed with noble spirit and lofty impulse, but have done it only once. We have marked one man who is brave in war and cowardly in civil affairs, enduring poverty courageously and disgrace shamefacedly; we have praised the deed but we have despised the man. **10.** Again, we have marked another man who is kind to his friends and restrained towards his enemies, who carries on his political and his personal business with scrupulous devotion, not lacking in long-suffering where there is anything that must be endured, and not lacking in prudence when action is to be taken. We have marked him giving with lavish hand when it was his duty to make a payment, and, when he had to toil, striving resolutely and lightening his bodily weariness by his resolution. Besides, he has always been the same, consistent in all his actions, not only sound in his judgment but trained by habit to such an extent that he not only can act rightly, but cannot help acting rightly. We have formed the conception that in such a man perfect virtue exists.

11. We have separated this perfect virtue into its several parts. The desires had to be reined in, fear to be suppressed, proper actions to be arranged, debts to be paid; we therefore included self-restraint, bravery, prudence, and justice – assigning to each quality its special function. How then have we formed the conception of virtue? Virtue has been manifested to us by this man's order, propriety, steadfastness, absolute harmony of action, and a greatness of soul that rises superior to everything. Thence has been derived our conception of the happy life, which flows along with steady course, completely under its own control. **12.** How then did we discover this fact? I will tell you: that perfect man, who has attained virtue, never cursed his luck, and never received the results of chance with dejection; he believed that he was citizen and soldier of the universe, accepting his tasks as if they were his orders. Whatever happened, he did not spurn it, as if it were evil and borne in upon him by hazard; he accepted it as if it were assigned to be his duty. "Whatever this may be," he says, "it is my lot; it is rough and it is hard, but I must work diligently at the task."

13. Necessarily, therefore, the man has shown himself great who has never grieved in evil days and never bewailed his destiny; he has given a clear conception of himself to many men; he has shone forth like a light in the darkness and has turned towards himself the thoughts of all men, because he was gentle and calm and equally compliant with the orders of man and of God. **14.** He possessed perfection of soul, developed to its highest capabilities, inferior only to the mind of God – from whom a part flows down even into this heart of a mortal. But this heart is never more divine than when it reflects upon its mortality, and understands that man was born for the purpose of fulfilling his life, and that the body is not a permanent dwelling, but a sort of inn (with a brief sojourn at that) which is to be left behind when one perceives that one is a burden to the host. **15.** The greatest proof, as I maintain, my dear Lucilius, that the soul proceeds from loftier heights, is if it judges its present situation lowly and narrow, and is not afraid to depart. For he who remembers whence he has come knows whither he is to depart. Do we not see how many discomforts drive us wild, and how ill-assorted is our fellowship with the flesh? **16.** We complain at one time of our headaches, at another of our bad digestions, at another of our hearts and our throats. Sometimes the nerves trouble us, sometimes the feet; now it is diarrhoea, and again it is catarrh; we are at one time full-blooded, at another anaemic; now this thing troubles us, now that, and bids us move away: it is just what happens to those who dwell in the house of another.

17. But we, to whom such corruptible bodies have been allotted, nevertheless set eternity before our eyes, and in our hopes grasp at the utmost space of time to which the life of man can be extended, satisfied with no income and with no influence. What can be more shameless or foolish than this? Nothing is enough for us, though we must die some day, or rather, are already dying; for we stand daily nearer the brink, and every hour of time thrusts us on towards the precipice over which we must fall. **18.** See how blind our minds are! What I speak of as in the future is happening at this minute, and a large portion of it has already happened; for it consists of our past lives. But we are mistaken in fearing the last day, seeing that each day, as it passes, counts just as much to the credit of death. The failing step does not produce, it merely announces, weariness. The last hour reaches, but every hour approaches, death. Death wears us away, but does not whirl us away.

For this reason the noble soul, knowing its better nature, while taking care to conduct itself honourably and seriously at the post of duty where it is placed, counts none of these extraneous objects as its own, but uses them as if they were a loan, like a foreign visitor hastening on his way. **19.** When we see a person of such steadfastness, how can we help being conscious of the image of a nature so unusual? Particularly if, as I remarked, it was shown to be true greatness by its consistency. It is indeed consistency that abides; false things do not last. Some men are like Vatinius or like Cato by turns; at times they do not think even Curius stern enough, or Fabricius poor enough, or Tubero sufficiently frugal and contented with simple things; while at other times they vie with Licinus in wealth, with Apicius in banqueting, or with Maecenas in daintiness. **20.** The greatest proof of an evil mind is unsteadiness, and continued wavering between pretence of virtue and love of vice.

> He'd have sometimes two hundred slaves at hand
>
> And sometimes ten. He'd speak of kings and grand
> Moguls and naught but greatness. Then he'd say:
>
> "Give me a three-legged table and a tray
> Of good clean salt, and just a coarse-wove gown
> To keep the cold out." If you paid him down
> (So sparing and content!) a million cool,
> In five short days he'd be a penceless fool.

21. The men I speak of are of this stamp; they are like the man whom Horatius Flaccus describes – a man never the same, never even like himself; to such an extent does he wander off into opposites. Did I say many are so? It is the case with almost all. Everyone changes his plans and prayers day by day. Now he would have a wife, and now a mistress; now he would be king, and again he strives to conduct himself so that no slave is more cringing; now he puffs himself up until he becomes unpopular; again, he shrinks and contracts into greater humility than those who are really unassuming; at one time he scatters money, at another he steals it. **22.** That is how a foolish mind is most clearly demonstrated: it shows first in this shape and then in that, and is never like itself – which is, in my opinion, the most shameful of qualities. Believe me, it is a great rôle – to play the rôle of one man. But nobody can be one person except the wise man; the rest of us often shift our masks. At times you will think us thrifty and serious, at other times wasteful and idle. We continually change our characters and play a part contrary to that which we have discarded. You should therefore force yourself to maintain to the very end of life's drama the character which you assumed at the beginning. See to it that men be able to praise you; if not, let them at least identify you. Indeed, with regard to the man whom you saw but yesterday, the question may properly be asked: "Who is he?" So great a change has there been! Farewell.

CXXI. ON INSTINCT IN ANIMALS

1. You will bring suit against me, I feel sure, when I set forth for you to-day's little problem, with which we have already fumbled long enough. You will cry out again: "What has this to do with character?" Cry out if you like, but let me first of all match you with other opponents, against whom you may bring suit – such as Posidonius and Archidemus; these men will stand trial. I shall then go on to say that whatever deals with character does not necessarily produce good character. **2.** Man needs one thing for his food, another for his exercise, another for his clothing, another for his instruction, and another for his pleasure. Everything, however, has reference to man's needs, although everything does not make him better. Character is affected by different things in different ways: some things serve to correct and regulate character, and others investigate its nature and origin. **3.** And when I seek the reason why Nature brought forth man, and why she set him above other animals, do you suppose that I have left character-study in the rear? No; that is wrong. For how are you to know what character is desirable, unless you have discovered what is best suited to man? Or unless you have studied his nature? You can find out what you should do and what you should avoid, only when you have learned what you owe to your own nature.

4. "I desire," you say, "to learn how I may crave less, and fear less. Rid me of my unreasoning beliefs. Prove to me that so-called felicity is fickle and empty, and that the word easily admits of a syllable's increase." I shall fulfil your want, encouraging your virtues and lashing your vices. People may decide that I am too zealous and reckless in this particular; but I shall never cease to hound wickedness, to check the most unbridled emotions, to soften the force of pleasures which will result in pain, and to cry down men's prayers. Of course I shall do this; for it is the greatest evils that we have prayed for, and from that which has made us give thanks comes all that demands consolation.

5. Meanwhile, allow me to discuss thoroughly some points which may seem now to be rather remote from the present inquiry. We were once debating whether all animals had any feelings about their "constitution." That this is the case is proved particularly by their making motions of such fitness and nimbleness that they seem to be trained for the purpose. Every being is clever in its own line. The skilled workman handles his tools with an ease born of experience; the pilot knows how to steer his ship skilfully; the artist can quickly lay on the colours which he has prepared in great variety for the purpose of rendering the likeness, and passes with ready eye and hand from palette to canvas. In the same way an animal is agile in all that pertains to the use of its body. 6. We are apt to wonder at skilled dancers because their gestures are perfectly adapted to the meaning of the piece and its accompanying emotions, and their movements match the speed of the dialogue. But that which art gives to the craftsman, is given to the animal by nature. No animal handles its limbs with difficulty, no animal is at a loss how to use its body. This function they exercise immediately at birth. They come into the world with this knowledge; they are born full-trained.

7. But people reply: "The reason why animals are so dexterous in the use of their limbs is that if they move them unnaturally, they will feel pain. They are *compelled* to do thus, according to your school, and it is fear rather than will-power which moves them in the right direction." This idea is wrong. Bodies driven by a compelling force move slowly; but those which move of their own accord possess alertness. The proof that it is not fear of pain which prompts them thus, is, that even when pain checks them they struggle to carry out their natural motions. 8. Thus the child who is trying to stand and is becoming used to carry his own weight, on beginning to test his strength, falls and rises again and again with tears until through painful effort he has trained himself to the demands of nature. And certain animals with hard shells, when turned on their backs, twist and grope with their feet and make motions sideways until they are restored to their proper position. The tortoise on his back feels no suffering; but he is restless because he misses his natural condition, and does not cease to shake himself about until he stands once more upon his feet.

9. So all these animals have a consciousness of their physical constitution, and for that reason can manage their limbs as readily as they do; nor have we any better proof that they come into being equipped with this knowledge than the fact that no animal is unskilled in the use of its body. 10. But some object as follows: "According to your account, one's constitution consists of a ruling power in the soul which has a certain relation towards the body. But how can a child comprehend

this intricate and subtle principle, which I can scarcely explain even to you? All living creatures should be born logicians, so as to understand a definition which is obscure to the majority of Roman citizens!" **11.** Your objection would be true if I spoke of living creatures as understanding "a definition of constitution," and not "their actual constitution." Nature is easier to understand than to explain; hence, the child of whom we were speaking does not understand what "constitution" is, but understands *its own* constitution. He does not know what "a living creature" is, but he feels that he is an animal. **12.** Moreover, that very constitution of his own he only understands confusedly, cursorily, and darkly. We also know that we possess souls, but we do not know the essence, the place, the quality, or the source, of the soul. Such as is the consciousness of our souls which we possess, ignorant as we are of their nature and position, even so all animals possess a consciousness of their own constitutions. For they must necessarily feel this, because it is the same agency by which they feel other things also; they must necessarily have a feeling of the principle which they obey and by which they are controlled. **13.** Every one of us understands that there is something which stirs his impulses, but he does not know what it is. He knows that he has a sense of striving, although he does not know what it is or its source. Thus even children and animals have a consciousness of their primary element, but it is not very clearly outlined or portrayed.

14. "You maintain, do you," says the objector, "that every living thing is at the start adapted to its constitution, but that man's constitution is a reasoning one, and hence man is adapted to himself not merely as a living, but as a reasoning, being? For man is dear to himself in respect of that wherein he is a man. How, then, can a child, being not yet gifted with reason, adapt himself to a reasoning constitution?" **15.** But each age has its own constitution, different in the case of the child, the boy, and the old man; they are all adapted to the constitution wherein they find themselves. The child is toothless, and he is fitted to this condition. Then his teeth grow, and he is fitted to that condition also. Vegetation also, which will develop into grain and fruits, has a special constitution when young and scarcely peeping over the tops of the furrows, another when it is strengthened and stands upon a stalk which is soft but strong enough to bear its weight, and still another when the colour changes to yellow, prophesies threshing-time, and hardens in the ear – no matter what may be the constitution into which the plant comes, it keeps it, and conforms thereto. **16.** The periods of infancy, boyhood, youth, and old age, are different; but I, who have been infant, boy, and youth, am still the same. Thus, although each has at different times a different constitution, the adaptation of each to its constitution is the same. For nature does not consign boyhood or youth, or old age, to me; it consigns me to them. Therefore, the child is adapted to that constitution which is his at the present moment of childhood, not to that which will be his in youth. For even if there is in store for him any higher phase into which he must be changed, the state in which he is born is also according to nature. **17.** First of all, the living being is adapted to itself, for there must be a pattern to which all other things may be referred. I seek pleasure;

for whom? For myself. I am therefore looking out for myself. I shrink from pain; on behalf of whom? Myself. Therefore, I am looking out for myself. Since I gauge all my actions with reference to my own welfare, I am looking out for myself before all else. This quality exists in all living beings – not engrafted but inborn.

18. Nature brings up her own offspring and does not cast them away; and because the most assured security is that which is nearest, every man has been entrusted to his own self. Therefore, as I have remarked in the course of my previous correspondence, even young animals, on issuing from the mother's womb or from the egg, know at once of their own accord what is harmful for them, and avoid death-dealing things. They even shrink when they notice the shadow of birds of prey which flit overhead.

No animal, when it enters upon life, is free from the fear of death. **19.** People may ask: "How can an animal at birth have an understanding of things wholesome or destructive?" The first question, however, is *whether* it can have such understanding, and not *how* it can understand. And it is clear that they have such understanding from the fact that, even if you add understanding, they will act no more adequately than they did in the first place. Why should the hen show no fear of the peacock or the goose, and yet run from the hawk, which is a so much smaller animal not even familiar to the hen? Why should young chickens fear a cat and not a dog.? These fowls clearly have a presentiment of harm – one not based on actual experiments; for they avoid a thing before they can possibly have experience of it. **20.** Furthermore, in order that you may not suppose this to be the result of chance, they do not shrink from certain other things which you would expect them to fear, nor do they ever forget vigilance and care in this regard; they all possess equally the faculty of avoiding what is destructive. Besides, their fear does not grow as their lives lengthen.

Hence indeed it is evident that these animals have not reached such a condition through experience; it is because of an inborn desire for self-preservation. The teachings of experience are slow and irregular; but whatever Nature communicates belongs equally to everyone, and comes immediately. **21.** If, however, you require an explanation, shall I tell you how it is that every living thing tries to understand that which is harmful? It feels that it is constructed of flesh; and so it perceives to what an extent flesh may be cut or burned or crushed, and what animals are equipped with the power of doing this damage; it is of animals of this sort that it derives an unfavourable and hostile idea. These tendencies are closely connected; for each animal at the same time consults its own safety, seeking that which helps it, and shrinks from that which will harm it. Impulses towards useful objects, and revulsion from the opposite, are according to nature; without any reflection to prompt the idea, and without any advice, whatever Nature has prescribed, is done.

22. Do you not see how skillful bees are in building their cells? How completely harmonious in sharing and enduring toil? Do you not see how the spider weaves a web so subtle that man's hand cannot imitate it; and what a task it is to arrange the threads, some directed straight towards the centre, for the sake of making the web solid, and others running in circles and lessening in thickness – for the purpose of tangling and catching in a sort of net the smaller insects for whose ruin the spider spreads the web? **23.** This art is born, not taught; and for this reason no animal is more skilled than any other. You will notice that all spider-webs are equally fine, and that the openings in all honeycomb cells are identical in shape. Whatever art communicates is uncertain and uneven; but Nature's assignments are always uniform. Nature has communicated nothing except the duty of taking care of themselves and the skill to do so; that is why living and learning begin at the same time. **24.** No wonder that living things are born with a gift whose absence would make birth useless. This is the first equipment that Nature granted them for the maintenance of their existence – the quality of adaptability and self-love. They could not survive except by desiring to do so. Nor would this desire alone have made them prosper, but without it nothing could have prospered. In no animal can you observe any low esteem, or even any carelessness, of self. Dumb beasts, sluggish in other respects, are clever at living. So you will see that creatures which are useless to others are alert for their own preservation. Farewell.

CXXII. ON DARKNESS AS A VEIL FOR WICKEDNESS

1. The day has already begun to lessen. It has shrunk considerably, but yet will still allow a goodly space of time if one rises, so to speak, with the day itself. We are more industrious, and we are better men if we anticipate the day and welcome the dawn; but we are base churls if we lie dozing when the sun is high in the heavens, or if we wake up only when noon arrives; and even then to many it seems not yet dawn. **2.** Some have reversed the functions of light and darkness; they open eyes sodden with yesterday's debauch only at the approach of night. It is just like the condition of those peoples whom, according to Vergil, Nature has hidden away and placed in an abode directly opposite to our own:

> When in our face the Dawn with panting steeds
> Breathes down, for them the ruddy evening kindles
> Her late-lit fires.

It is not the country of these men, so much as it is their life, that is "directly opposite" to our own. **3.** There may be Antipodes dwelling in this same city of ours who, in Cato's words, "have never seen the sun rise or set." Do you think that these men know how to live, if they do not know when to live? Do these men fear death, if they have buried themselves alive? They are as weird as the birds of night. Although they pass their hours of darkness amid wine and perfumes, although they spend the whole extent of their unnatural waking hours in eating dinners – and those too cooked separately to make up many courses – they are not really banqueting; they are conducting their own funeral services. And the dead at least have their banquets by daylight.

But indeed to one who is active no day is long. So let us lengthen our lives; for the duty and the proof of life consist in action. Cut short the night: use some of it for the day's business. **4.** Birds that are being prepared for the banquet, that they may be easily fattened through lack of exercise, are kept in darkness; and similarly, if men vegetate without physical activity, their idle bodies are overwhelmed with flesh, and in their self-satisfied retirement the fat of indolence grows upon them. Moreover, the bodies of those who have sworn allegiance to the hours of darkness have a loathsome appearance. Their complexions are more alarming than those of anaemic invalids; they are lackadaisical and flabby with dropsy; though still alive, they are already carrion. But this, to my thinking, would be among the least of their evils. How much more darkness there is in their souls! Such a man is internally dazed; his vision is darkened; he envies the blind. And what man ever had eyes for the purpose of seeing in the dark?

5. You ask me how this depravity comes upon the soul – this habit of reversing the daylight and giving over one's whole existence to the night? All vices rebel against Nature; they all abandon the appointed order. It is the motto of luxury to enjoy what is unusual, and not only to depart from that which is right, but to leave it as far behind as possible, and finally even take a stand in opposition thereto. **6.** Do you not believe that men live contrary to Nature who drink fasting, who take wine into empty veins, and pass to their food in a state of intoxication? And yet this is one of youth's popular vices – to perfect their strength in order to drink on the very threshold of the bath, amid the unclad bathers; nay even to soak in wine and then immediately to rub off the sweat which they have promoted by many a hot glass of liquor! To them, a glass after lunch or one after dinner is *bourgeois*; it is what the country squires do, who are not connoisseurs in pleasure. This unmixed wine delights them just because there is no food to float in it, because it readily makes its way into their muscles; this boozing pleases them just because the stomach is empty.

7. Do you not believe that men live contrary to Nature who exchange the fashion of their attire with women? Do not men live contrary to Nature who endeavour to look fresh and boyish at an age unsuitable for such an attempt? What could be more cruel or more wretched? Cannot time and man's estate ever carry such a person beyond an artificial boyhood? **8.** Do not men live contrary to Nature who crave roses in winter, or seek to raise a spring flower like the lily by means of hot-water heaters and artificial changes of temperature? Do not men live contrary to Nature who grow fruit-trees on the top of a wall? Or raise waving forests upon the roofs and battlements of their houses – the roots starting at a point to which it would be outlandish for the tree-tops to reach? Do not men live contrary to Nature who lay the foundations of bathrooms in the sea and do not imagine that they can enjoy their swim unless the heated pool is lashed as with the waves of a storm?

9. When men have begun to desire all things in opposition to the ways of Nature, they end by entirely abandoning the ways of Nature. They cry: "It is daytime – let us go to sleep! It is the time when men rest: now for exercise, now for our drive, now for our lunch! Lo, the dawn approaches: it is dinner-time! We should not do as mankind do. It is low and mean to live in the usual and conventional way. Let us abandon the ordinary sort of day. Let us have a morning that is a special feature of ours, peculiar to ourselves!" **10.** Such men are, in my opinion, as good as dead. Are they not all but present at a funeral – and before their time too – when they live amid torches and tapers? I remember that this sort of life was very fashionable at one time: among such men as Acilius Buta, a person of praetorian rank, who ran through a tremendous estate and on confessing his bankruptcy to Tiberius, received the answer: "You have waked up too late!" **11.** Julius Montanus was once reading a poem aloud he was a middling good poet, noted for his friendship with Tiberius, as well as his fall from favour. He always used to fill his poems with a generous sprinkling of sunrises and sunsets. Hence, when a certain person was complaining that Montanus had read all day long, and declared that no man should attend any of his readings, Natta Pinarius remarked: "I couldn't make a fairer bargain than this: I am ready to listen to him from sunrise to sunset!" **12.** Montanus was reading, and had reached the words:

> 'Gins the bright morning to spread forth his flames clear-burning; the red dawn
> Scatters its light; and the sad-eyed swallow returns to her nestlings,
> Bringing the chatterers' food, and with sweet bill sharing and serving.

Then Varus, a Roman knight, the hanger-on of Marcus Vinicius, and a sponger at elegant dinners which he earned by his degenerate wit, shouted: "Bed-time for Buta!" **13.** And later, when Montanus declaimed

> Lo, now the shepherds have folded their flocks, and the slow-moving darkness
> 'Gins to spread silence o'er lands that are drowsily lulled into slumber,

this same Varus remarked: "What? Night already? I'll go and pay my morning call on Buta!" You see, nothing was more notorious than Buta's upside-down manner of life. But this life, as I said, was fashionable at one time. **14.** And the reason why some men live thus is not because they think that night in itself offers any greater attractions, but because that which is normal gives them no particular pleasure; light being a bitter enemy of the evil conscience, and, when one craves or scorns all things in proportion as they have cost one much or little, illumination for which one does not pay is an object of contempt. Moreover, the luxurious person wishes to be an object of gossip his whole life; if people are silent about him, he thinks that he is wasting his time. Hence he is uncomfortable whenever any of his actions escape notoriety.

Many men eat up their property, and many men keep mistresses. If you would win a reputation among such persons, you must make your programme not only one of luxury but one of notoriety; for in such a busy community wickedness does not discover the ordinary sort of scandal. **15.** I heard Pedo Albinovanus, that most attractive story-teller, speaking of his residence above the town-house of Sextus

Papinius. Papinius belonged to the tribe of those who shun the light. "About nine o'clock at night I hear the sound of whips. I ask what is going on, and they tell me that Papinius is going over his accounts. About twelve there is a strenuous shouting; I ask what the matter is, and they say he is exercising his voice. About two A.M. I ask the significance of the sound of wheels; they tell me that he is off for a drive. **16.** And at dawn there is a tremendous flurry-calling of slaves and butlers, and pandemonium among the cooks. I ask the meaning of this also, and they tell me that he has called for his cordial and his appetizer, after leaving the bath. His dinner," said Pedo, "never went beyond the day, for he lived very sparingly; he was lavish with nothing but the night. Accordingly, if you believe those who call him tight-fisted and mean, you will call him also a 'slave of the lamp.'"

17. You should not be surprised at finding so many special manifestations of the vices; for vices vary, and there are countless phases of them, nor can all their various kinds be classified. The method of maintaining righteousness is simple; the method of maintaining wickedness is complicated, and has infinite opportunity to swerve. And the same holds true of character; if you follow nature, character is easy to manage, free, and with very slight shades of difference; but the sort of person I have mentioned possesses badly warped character, out of harmony with all things, including himself. **18.** The chief cause, however, of this disease seems to me to be a squeamish revolt from the normal existence. Just as such persons mark themselves off from others in their dress, or in the elaborate arrangement of their dinners, or in the elegance of their carriages; even so they desire to make themselves peculiar by their way of dividing up the hours of their day. They are unwilling to be wicked in the conventional way, because notoriety is the reward of their sort of wickedness. Notoriety is what all such men seek – men who are, so to speak, *living backwards*.

19. For this reason, Lucilius, let us keep to the way which Nature has mapped out for us, and let us not swerve therefrom. If we follow Nature, all is easy and unobstructed; but if we combat Nature, our life differs not a whit from that of men who row against the current. Farewell.

CXXIII. ON THE CONFLICT BETWEEN PLEASURE AND VIRTUE

1. Wearied with the discomfort rather than with the length of my journey, I have reached my Alban villa late at night, and I find nothing in readiness except myself. So I am getting rid of fatigue at my writing-table: I derive some good from this tardiness on the part of my cook and my baker. For I am communing with myself on this very topic – that nothing is heavy if one accepts it with a light heart, and that nothing need provoke one's anger if one does not add to one's pile of troubles by getting angry. **2.** My baker is out of bread; but the overseer, or the house-steward, or one of my tenants can supply me therewith. "Bad bread!" you say. But just wait for it; it will become good. Hunger will make even such bread delicate and of the finest flavour. For that reason I must not eat until hunger bids me; so I shall wait and shall not eat until I can either get good bread or else cease to be squeamish about it. **3.** It is necessary that one grow accustomed to slender fare: because there are many problems of time and place which will cross the path even of the rich man and one equipped for pleasure, and bring him up with a round turn. To have whatsoever he wishes is in no man's power; it is in his power not to wish for what he has not, but cheerfully to employ what comes to him. A great step towards independence is a good-humoured stomach, one that is willing to endure rough treatment.

4. You cannot imagine how much pleasure I derive from the fact that my weariness is becoming reconciled to itself; I am asking for no slaves to rub me down, no bath, and no other restorative except time. For that which toil has accumulated, rest can lighten. This repast, whatever it may be, will give me more pleasure than an inaugural banquet. **5.** For I have made trial of my spirit on a sudden – a simpler and a truer test. Indeed, when a man has made preparations and given himself a formal summons to be patient, it is not equally clear just how much real strength of mind he possesses; the surest proofs are those which one exhibits off-hand, viewing one's own troubles not only fairly but calmly, not flying into fits of temper or wordy wranglings, supplying one's own needs by not craving something which was really due, and reflecting that our habits may be unsatisfied, but never our own real selves. **6.** How many things are superfluous we fail to realize until they begin to be wanting; we merely used them not because we needed them but because we had them. And how much do we acquire simply because our neighbours have acquired such things, or because most men possess them! Many of our troubles may be explained from the fact that we live according to a pattern, and, instead of arranging our lives according to reason, are led astray by convention.

There are things which, if done by the few, we should refuse to imitate; yet when the majority have begun to do them, we follow along – just as if anything were more honourable because it is more frequent! Furthermore, wrong views, when they have become prevalent, reach, in our eyes, the standard of righteousness. **7.** Everyone now travels with Numidian outriders preceding him, with a troop of slave-runners to clear the way; we deem it disgraceful to have no attendants who will elbow crowds from the road, or will prove, by a great cloud of dust, that a high dignitary is approaching! Everyone now possesses mules that are laden with crystal and myrrhine cups carved by skilled artists of great renown; it is disgraceful for all your baggage to be made up of that which can be rattled along without danger. Everyone has pages who ride along with ointment-covered faces so that the heat or the cold will not harm their tender complexions; it is disgraceful that none of your attendant slave-boys should show a healthy cheek, not covered with cosmetics.

8. You should avoid conversation with all such persons: they are the sort that communicate and engraft their bad habits from one to another. We used to think that the very worst variety of these men were those who vaunted their words; but there are certain men who vaunt their wickedness. Their talk is very harmful; for even though it is not at once convincing, yet they leave the seeds of trouble in the soul, and the evil which is sure to spring into new strength follows us about even when we have parted from them. **9.** Just as those who have attended a concert carry about in their heads the melodies and the charm of the songs they have heard – a proceeding which interferes with their thinking and does not allow them to concentrate upon serious subjects, – even so the speech of flatterers and enthusiasts over that which is depraved sticks in our minds long after we have heard them talk. It is not easy to rid the memory of a catching tune; it stays with us, lasts on, and comes back from time to time. Accordingly, you should close your ears against evil talk, and right at the outset, too; for when such talk has gained an entrance and the words are admitted and are in our minds, they become more shameless. **10.** And then we begin to speak as follows: "Virtue, Philosophy, Justice – this is a jargon of empty words. The only way to be happy is to do yourself well. To eat, drink, and spend your money is the only real life, the only way to remind yourself that you are mortal. Our days flow on, and life – which we cannot restore – hastens away from us. Why hesitate to come to our senses? This life of ours will not always admit pleasures; meantime, while it can do so, while it clamours for them, what profit lies in imposing thereupon frugality? Therefore get ahead of death, and let anything that death will filch from you be squandered now upon yourself. You have no mistress, no favourite slave to make your mistress envious; you are sober when you make your daily appearance in public; you dine as if you had to show your account-book to 'Papa'; but *that* is not living, it is merely going shares in someone else's existence. **11.** And what madness it is to be looking out for the interests of your heir, and to deny yourself everything, with the result that you turn friends into enemies by the vast amount of the fortune you intend to leave! For the more the heir is to get from you, the more he will rejoice in your taking-off! All those sour fellows who criticize other men's lives in a spirit of priggishness and are real enemies to their own lives, playing schoolmaster to the world – you should not consider them as worth a farthing, nor should you hesitate to prefer good living to a good reputation."

12. These are voices which you ought to shun just as Ulysses did; he would not sail past them until he was lashed to the mast. They are no less potent; they lure men from country, parents, friends, and virtuous ways; and by a hope that, if not base, is ill-starred, they wreck them upon a life of baseness. How much better to follow a straight course and attain a goal where the words "pleasant" and "honourable" have the same meaning! **13.** This end will be possible for us if we understand that there are two classes of objects which either attract us or repel us. We are attracted by such things as riches, pleasures, beauty, ambition, and other such coaxing and pleasing objects; we are repelled by toil, death, pain, disgrace, or lives of greater frugality. We ought therefore to train ourselves so that we may avoid a fear of the one or a desire for the other. Let us fight in the opposite fashion: let us retreat from the objects that allure, and rouse ourselves to meet the objects that attack.

14. Do you not see how different is the method of descending a mountain from that employed in climbing upwards? Men coming down a slope bend backwards; men ascending a steep place lean forward. For, my dear Lucilius, to allow yourself to put your body's weight ahead when coming down, or, when climbing up, to throw it backward is to comply with vice. The pleasures take one down hill but one must work upwards toward that which is rough and hard to climb; in the one case let us throw our bodies forward, in the others let us put the check-rein on them.

15. Do you believe me to be stating now that only those men bring ruin to our ears, who praise pleasure, who inspire us with fear of pain – that element which is in itself provocative of fear? I believe that we are also in injured by those who masquerade under the disguise of the Stoic school and at the same time urge us on into vice. They boast that only the wise man and the learned is a lover. "He alone has wisdom in this art; the wise man too is best skilled in drinking and feasting. Our study ought to be this alone: up to what age the bloom of love can endure!"

16. All this may be regarded as a concession to the ways of Greece; we ourselves should preferably turn our attention to words like these: "No man is good by chance. Virtue is something which must be learned. Pleasure is low, petty, to be deemed worthless, shared even by dumb animals – the tiniest and meanest of whom fly towards pleasure. Glory is an empty and fleeting thing, lighter than air. Poverty is an evil to no man unless he kick against the goads. Death is not an evil; why need you ask? Death alone is the equal privilege of mankind. Superstition is the misguided idea of a lunatic; it fears those whom it ought to love; it is an outrage upon those whom it worships. For what difference is there between denying the gods and dishonouring them?"

17. You should learn such principles as these, nay rather you should learn them by heart; philosophy ought not to try to explain away vice. For a sick man, when his physician bids him live recklessly, is doomed beyond recall. Farewell.

CXXIV. ON THE TRUE GOOD AS ATTAINED BY REASON

1. Full many an ancient precept could I give,
Didst thou not shrink, and feel it shame to learn
Such lowly duties.

But you do not shrink, nor are you deterred by any subtleties of study. For your cultivated mind is not wont to investigate such important subjects in a free-and-easy manner. I approve your method in that you make everything count towards a certain degree of progress, and in that you are disgruntled only when nothing can be accomplished by the greatest degree of subtlety. And I shall take pains to show that this is the case now also. Our question is, whether the Good is grasped by the senses or by the understanding; and the corollary thereto is that it does not exist in dumb animals or little children.

2. Those who rate pleasure as the supreme ideal hold that the Good is a matter of the senses; but we Stoics maintain that it is a matter of the understanding, and we assign it to the mind. If the senses were to pass judgment on what is good, we should never reject any pleasure; for there is no pleasure that does not attract, no pleasure that does not please. Conversely, we should undergo no pain voluntarily; for there is no pain that does not clash with the senses. **3.** Besides, those who are too fond of pleasure and those who fear pain to the greatest degree would in that case not deserve reproof. But we condemn men who are slaves to their appetites and their lusts, and we scorn men who, through fear of pain, will dare no manly deed. But what wrong could such men be committing if they looked merely to the senses as arbiters of good and evil? For it is to the senses that you and yours have entrusted the test of things to be sought and things to be avoided!

4. Reason, however, is surely the governing element in such a matter as this; as reason has made the decision concerning the happy life, and concerning virtue and honour also, so she has made the decision with regard to good and evil. For with them the vilest part is allowed to give sentence about the better, so that the senses – dense as they are, and dull, and even more sluggish in man than in the other animals, – pass judgment on the Good. **5.** Just suppose that one should desire to distinguish tiny objects by the touch rather than by the eyesight! There is no special faculty more subtle and acute than the eye, that would enable us to distinguish between good and evil. You see, therefore, in what ignorance of truth a man spends his days and how abjectly he has overthrown lofty and divine ideals, if he thinks that the sense of touch can pass judgment upon the nature of the Supreme Good and the Supreme Evil! **6.** He says: "Just as every science and every art should possess an element that is palpable and capable of being grasped by the senses (their source of origin and growth), even so the happy life derives its foundation and its beginnings from things that are palpable, and from that which falls within the scope of the senses. Surely you admit that the happy life takes its beginnings from things palpable to the senses." **7.** But we define as "happy" those things that are in accord with Nature. And that which is in accord with Nature is obvious and can be seen at once – just as easily as that which is complete. That which is according to Nature, that which is given us as a gift immediately at our birth, is, I maintain, not a Good, but the beginning of a Good. You, however, assign the Supreme Good, pleasure, to mere babies, so that the child at its birth begins at the point whither the perfected man arrives. You are placing the tree-top where the root ought to be. **8.** If anyone should say that the child, hidden in its mother's womb, of unknown sex too, delicate, unformed, and shapeless – if one should say that this child is already in a state of goodness, he would clearly seem to be astray in his ideas. And yet how little difference is there between one who has just lately received the gift of life, and one who is still a hidden burden in the bowels of the mother! They are equally developed, as far as their understanding of good or evil is concerned; and a child is as yet no more capable of comprehending the Good than is a tree or any dumb beast.

But why is the Good non-existent in a tree or in a dumb beast? Because there is no reason there, either. For the same cause, then, the Good is non-existent in a child, for the child also has no reason; the child will reach the Good only when he reaches reason. **9.** There are animals without reason, there are animals not yet endowed with reason, and there are animals who possess reason, but only incompletely; in none of these does the Good exist, for it is reason that brings the Good in its company. What, then, is the distinction between the classes which I have mentioned? In that which does not possess reason, the Good will never exist. In that which is not yet endowed with reason, the Good cannot be existent at the time. And in that which possesses reason but only incompletely, the Good is capable of existing, but does not yet exist. **10.** This is what I mean, Lucilius: the Good cannot be discovered in any random person, or at any random age; and it is as far removed from infancy as last is from first, or as that which is complete from that which has just sprung into being. Therefore, it cannot exist in the delicate body, when the little frame has only just begun to knit together. Of course not – no more than in the seed. **11.** Granting the truth of this, we understand that there is a certain kind of Good of a tree or in a plant; but this is not true of its first growth, when the plant has just begun to spring forth out of the ground. There is a certain Good of wheat: it is not yet existent, however, in the swelling stalk, nor when the soft ear is pushing itself out of the husk, but only when summer days and its appointed maturity have ripened the wheat. Just as Nature in general does not produce her Good until she is brought to perfection, even so man's Good does not exist in man until both reason and man are perfected. **12.** And what is this Good? I shall tell you: it is a free mind, an upright mind, subjecting other things to itself and itself to nothing. So far is infancy from admitting this Good that boyhood has no hope of it, and even young manhood cherishes the hope without justification; even our old age is very fortunate if it has reached this Good after long and concentrated study. If this, then, is the Good, the good is a matter of the understanding.

13. "But," comes the retort, "you admitted that there is a certain Good of trees and of grass; then surely there can be a certain Good of a child also." But the true Good is not found in trees or in dumb animals the Good which exists in them is called good only by courtesy. "Then what is it?" you say. Simply that which is in accord with the nature of each. The real Good cannot find a place in dumb animals – not by any means; its nature is more blest and is of a higher class. And where there is no place for reason, the Good does not exist. **14.** There are four natures which we should mention here: of the tree, animal, man, and God. The last two, having reasoning power, are of the same nature, distinct only by virtue of the immortality of the one and the mortality of the other. Of one of these, then – to wit God – it is Nature that perfects the Good; of the other – to wit man – pains and study do so. All other things are perfect only in their particular nature, and not truly perfect, since they lack reason.

Indeed, to sum up, that alone is perfect which is perfect according to nature as a whole, and nature as a whole is possessed of reason. Other things can be perfect according to their kind. **15.** That which cannot contain the happy life cannot contain that which produces the happy life; and the happy life is produced by Goods alone. In dumb animals there is not a trace of the happy life, nor of the means whereby the happy life is produced; in dumb animals the Good does not exist. **16.** The dumb animal comprehends the present world about him through his senses alone. He remembers the past only by meeting with something which reminds his senses; a horse, for example, remembers the right road only when he is placed at the starting-point. In his stall, however, he has no memory of the road, no matter how often he may have stepped along it. The third state – the future – does not come within the ken of dumb beasts.

17. How, then, can we regard as perfect the nature of those who have no experience of time in its perfection? For time is three-fold, – past, present, and future. Animals perceive only the time which is of greatest moment to them within the limits of their coming and going – the present. Rarely do they recollect the past – and that only when they are confronted with present reminders. **18.** Therefore the Good of a perfect nature cannot exist in an imperfect nature; for if the latter sort of nature should possess the Good, so also would mere vegetation. I do not indeed deny that dumb animals have strong and swift impulses toward actions which seem according to nature, but such impulses are confused and disordered. The Good however, is never confused or disordered.

19. "What!" you say, "do dumb animals move in disturbed and ill-ordered fashion?" I should say that they moved in disturbed and ill-ordered fashion, if their nature admitted of order; as it is, they move in accordance with their nature. For that is said to be "disturbed" which can also at some other time be "not disturbed"; so, too, that is said to be in a state of trouble which can be in a state of peace. No man is vicious except one who has the capacity of virtue; in the case of dumb animals their motion is such as results from their nature. **20.** But, not to weary you, a certain sort of good will be found in a dumb animal, and a certain sort of virtue, and a certain sort of perfection – but neither the Good, nor virtue, nor perfection in the absolute sense. For this is the privilege of reasoning beings alone, who are permitted to know the cause, the degree, and the means. Therefore, good can exist only in that which possesses reason.

21. Do you ask now whither our argument is tending, and of what benefit it will be to your mind? I will tell you: it exercises and sharpens the mind, and ensures, by occupying it honourably, that it will accomplish some sort of good. And even that is beneficial which holds men back when they are hurrying into wickedness. However, I will say this also: I can be of no greater benefit to you than by revealing the Good that is rightly yours, by taking you out of the class of dumb animals, and by placing you on a level with God. **22.** Why, pray, do you foster and practise your bodily strength? Nature has granted strength in greater degree to cattle and wild beasts. Why cultivate your beauty? After all your efforts, dumb animals surpass you in comeliness. Why dress your hair with such unending attention? Though you let it down in Parthian fashion, or tie it up in the German style, or, as the Scythians do, let it flow wild – yet you will see a mane of greater thickness tossing upon any horse you choose, and a mane of greater beauty bristling upon the neck of any lion. And even after training yourself for speed, you will be no match for the hare. **23.** Are you not willing to abandon all these details – wherein you must acknowledge defeat, striving as you are for something that is not your own and come back to the Good that is really yours?

And what is this Good? It is a clear and flawless mind, which rivals that of God, raised far above mortal concerns, and counting nothing of its own to be outside itself. You are a reasoning animal. What Good, then, lies within you? Perfect reason. Are you willing to develop this to its farthest limits – to its greatest degree of increase? **24.** Only consider yourself happy when all your joys are born of reason, and when – having marked all the objects which men clutch at, or pray for, or watch over – you find nothing which you will desire; mind, I do not say *prefer*. Here is a short rule by which to measure yourself, and by the test of which you may feel that you have reached perfection: "You will come to your own when you shall understand that those whom the world calls fortunate are really the most unfortunate of all." Farewell.

ON BENEFITS

BOOK 1

1

Among the numerous faults of those who pass their lives recklessly and without due reflection, my good friend Liberalis, I should say that there is hardly anyone so hurtful to society as this, that we neither know how to bestow or how to receive a benefit. It follows from this that benefits are badly invested, and become bad debts: in these cases it is too late to complain of their not being returned, for they were thrown away when we bestowed them. Nor need we wonder that while the greatest vices are common, none is more common than ingratitude: for this I see is brought about by various causes. The first of these is, that we do not choose worthy persons upon whom to bestow our bounty, but although when we are about to lend money we first make a careful enquiry into the means and habits of life of our debtor, and avoid sowing seed in a worn-out or unfruitful soil, yet without any discrimination we scatter our benefits at random rather than bestow them. It is hard to say whether it is more dishonourable for the receiver to disown a benefit, or for the giver to demand a return of it: for a benefit is a loan, the repayment of which depends merely upon the good feeling of the debtor. To misuse a benefit like a spendthrift is most shameful, because we do not need our wealth but only our intention to set us free from the obligation of it; for a benefit is repaid by being acknowledged. Yet while they are to blame who do not even show so much gratitude as to acknowledge their debt, we ourselves are to blame no less. We find many men ungrateful, yet we make more men so, because at one time we harshly and reproachfully demand some return for our bounty, at another we are fickle and regret what we have given, at another we are peevish and apt to find fault with trifles. By acting thus we destroy all sense of gratitude, not only after we have given anything, but while we are in the act of giving it. Who has ever thought it enough to be asked for anything in an offhand manner, or to be asked only once? Who, when he suspected that he was going to be asked for anything, has not frowned, turned away his face, pretended to be busy, or purposely talked without ceasing, in order not to give his suitor a chance of preferring his request, and avoided by various tricks having to help his friend in his pressing need? and when driven into a corner, has not either put the matter off, that is, given a cowardly refusal, or promised his help ungraciously, with a wry face, and with unkind words, of which he seemed to grudge the utterance. Yet no one is glad to owe what he has not so much received from his benefactor, as wrung out of him. Who can be grateful for what has been disdainfully flung to him, or angrily cast at him, or been given him out of weariness, to avoid further trouble? No one need expect any return from those whom he has tired out with delays, or sickened with expectation. A benefit is received in the same temper in which it is given, and ought not, therefore, to be given carelessly, for a man thanks himself for that which he receives without the knowledge of the giver. Neither ought we to give after long delay, because in all good offices the will of the giver counts for much, and he who gives tardily must long have been unwilling to give at all. Nor, assuredly, ought we to give in offensive manner, because human nature is so constituted that insults sink deeper than kindnesses; the remembrance of the latter soon passes away, while that of the former is treasured in the memory; so what can a man expect who insults while he obliges? All the gratitude which he deserves is to be forgiven for helping us. On the other hand, the number of the ungrateful ought not to deter us from earning men's gratitude; for, in the first place, their number is increased by our own acts. Secondly, the sacrilege and indifference to religion of some men does not prevent even the immortal gods from continuing to shower their benefits upon us: for they act according to their divine nature and help all alike, among them even those who so ill appreciate their bounty. Let us take them for our guides as far as the weakness of our mortal nature permits; let us bestow benefits, not put them out at interest. The man who while he gives thinks of what he will get in return, deserves to be deceived. But what if the benefit turns out ill? Why, our wives and our children often disappoint our hopes, yet we marry—and bring up children, and are so obstinate in the face of experience that we fight after we have been beaten, and put to sea after we have been shipwrecked. How much more constancy ought we to show in bestowing benefits! If a man does not bestow benefits because he has not received any, he must have bestowed them in order to receive them in return, and he justifies ingratitude, whose disgrace lies in not returning benefits when able to do so. How many are there who are unworthy of the light of day? and nevertheless the sun rises. How many complain because they have been born? yet Nature is ever renewing our race, and even suffers men to live who wish that they had never lived. It is the property of a great and good mind to covet, not the fruit of good deeds, but good deeds themselves, and to seek for a good man even after having met with bad men. If there were no rogues, what glory would there be in doing good to many? As it is, virtue consists in bestowing benefits for which we are not certain of meeting with any return, but whose fruit is at once enjoyed by noble minds. So little influence ought this to have in restraining us from doing good actions, that even though I were denied the hope of meeting with a grateful man, yet the fear of not having my benefits returned would not prevent my bestowing them, because he who does not give, forestalls the vice of him who is ungrateful. I will explain what I mean. He who does not repay a benefit, sins more, but he who does not bestow one, sins earlier.

"If thou at random dost thy bounties waste,
Much must be lost, for one that's rightly placed."

2

In the former verse you may blame two things, for one should not cast them at random, and it is not right to waste anything, much less benefits; for unless they be given with judgement, they cease to be benefits, and, may be called by any other name you please. The meaning of the latter verse is admirable, that one benefit rightly bestowed makes amends for the loss of many that have been lost. See, I pray you, whether it be not truer and more worthy of the glory of the giver, that we should encourage him to give, even though none of his gifts should be worthily placed. "Much must be lost." Nothing is lost because he who loses had counted the cost before. The bookkeeping of benefits is simple: it is all expenditure; if anyone returns it, that is clear gain; if he does not return it, it is not lost, I gave it for the sake of giving. No one writes down his gifts in a ledger, or like a grasping creditor demands repayment to the day and hour. A good man never thinks of such matters, unless reminded of them by someone returning his gifts; otherwise they become like debts owing to him. It is a base usury to regard a benefit as an investment. Whatever may have been the result of your former benefits, persevere in bestowing others upon other men; they will be all the better placed in the hands of the ungrateful, whom shame, or a favourable opportunity, or imitation of others may some day cause to be grateful. Do not grow weary, perform your duty, and act as becomes a good man. Help one man with money, another with credit, another with your favour; this man with good advice, that one with sound maxims. Even wild beasts feel kindness, nor is there any animal so savage that good treatment will not tame it and win love from it. The mouths of lions are handled by their keepers with impunity; to obtain their food fierce elephants become as docile as slaves: so that constant unceasing kindness wins the hearts even of creatures who, by their nature, cannot comprehend or weigh the value of a benefit. Is a man ungrateful for one benefit? perhaps he will not be so after receiving a second. Has he forgotten two kindnesses? perhaps by a third he may be brought to remember the former ones also.

3

He who is quick to believe that he has thrown away his benefits, does really throw them away; but he who presses on and adds new benefits to his former ones, forces out gratitude even from a hard and forgetful breast. In the face of many kindnesses, your friend will not dare to raise his eyes; let him see you whithersoever he turns himself to escape from his remembrance of you; encircle him with your benefits. As for the power and property of these, I will explain it to you if first you will allow me to glance at a matter which does not belong to our subject, as to why the Graces are three in number, why they are sisters, why hand in hand, and why they are smiling and young, with a loose and transparent dress. Some writers think that there is one who bestows a benefit, one who receives it, and a third who returns it; others say that they represent the three sorts of benefactors, those who bestow, those who repay, and those who both receive and repay them. But take whichever you please to be true; what will this knowledge profit us? What is the meaning of this dance of sisters in a circle, hand in hand? It means that the course of a benefit is from hand to hand, back to the giver; that the beauty of the whole chain is lost if a single link fails, and that it is fairest when it proceeds in unbroken regular order. In the dance there is one esteemed beyond the others, who represents the givers of benefits. Their faces are cheerful, as those of men who give or receive benefits are wont to be. They are young, because the memory of benefits ought not to grow old. They are virgins, because benefits are pure and untainted, and held holy by all; in benefits there should be no strict or binding conditions, therefore the Graces wear loose flowing tunics, which are transparent, because benefits love to be seen. People who are not under the influence of Greek literature may say that all this is a matter of course; but there can be no one who would think that the names which Hesiod has given them bear upon our subject. He named the eldest Aglaia, the middle one Euphrosyne, the third Thalia. Everyone, according to his own ideas, twists the meaning of these names, trying to reconcile them with some system, though Hesiod merely gave his maidens their names from his own fancy. So Homer altered the name of one of them, naming her Pasithea, and betrothed her to a husband, in order that you may know that they are not vestal virgins.[1]

I could find another poet in whose writings they are girded, and wear thick or embroidered Phrygian robes. Mercury stands with them for the same reason, not because argument or eloquence commends benefits, but because the painter chose to do so. Also Chrysippus, that man of piercing intellect who saw to the very bottom of truth, who speaks only to the point, and makes use of no more words than are necessary to express his meaning, fills his whole treatise with these puerilities,

---

[1] I.e. not vowed to chastity.

insomuch that he says but very little about the duties of giving, receiving, and returning a benefit, and has not so much inserted fables among these subjects, as he has inserted these subjects among a mass of fables. For, not to mention what Hecaton borrows from him, Chrysippus tells us that the three Graces are the daughters of Jupiter and Eurynome, that they are younger than the Hours, and rather more beautiful, and that on that account they are assigned as companions to Venus. He also thinks that the name of their mother bears upon the subject, and that she is named Eurynome because to distribute benefits requires a wide inheritance; as if the mother usually received her name after her daughters, or as if the names given by poets were true. In truth, just as with a nomenclator, audacity supplies the place of memory, and he invents a name for everyone whose name he cannot recollect, so the poets think that it is of no importance to speak the truth, but are either forced by the exigencies of metre, or attracted by sweetness of sound, into calling everyone by whatever name runs neatly into verse. Nor do they suffer for it if they introduce another name into the list, for the next poet makes them bear what name he pleases. That you may know that this is so, for instance Thalia, our present subject of discourse, is one of the Graces in Hesiod's poems, while in those of Homer she is one of the Muses.

4

But lest I should do the very thing which I am blaming, I will pass over all these matters, which are so far from the subject that they are not even connected with it. Only do you protect me, if anyone attacks me for putting down Chrysippus, who, by Hercules, was a great man, but yet a Greek, whose intellect, too sharply pointed, is often bent and turned back upon itself; even when it seems to be in earnest it only pricks, but does not pierce. Here, however, what occasion is there for subtlety? We are to speak of benefits, and to define a matter which is the chief bond of human society; we are to lay down a rule of life, such that neither careless openhandedness may commend itself to us under the guise of goodness of heart, and yet that our circumspection, while it moderates, may not quench our generosity, a quality in which we ought neither to exceed nor to fall short. Men must be taught to be willing to give, willing to receive, willing to return; and to place before themselves the high aim, not merely of equalling, but even of surpassing those to whom they are indebted, both in good offices and in good feeling; because the man whose duty it is to repay, can never do so unless he outdoes his benefactor;[2] the one class must be taught to look for no return, the other to feel deeper gratitude. In this noblest of contests to outdo benefits by benefits, Chrysippus encourages us by bidding us beware lest, as the Graces are the daughters of Jupiter, to act ungratefully may not

---

[2] That is, he never comes up to his benefactor unless he leaves him behind: he can only make a dead heat of it by getting a start.

be a sin against them, and may not wrong those beauteous maidens. Do thou teach me how I may bestow more good things, and be more grateful to those who have earned my gratitude, and how the minds of both parties may vie with one another, the giver in forgetting, the receiver in remembering his debt. As for those other follies, let them be left to the poets, whose purpose is merely to charm the ear and to weave a pleasing story; but let those who wish to purify men's minds, to retain honour in their dealings, and to imprint on their minds gratitude for kindnesses, let them speak in sober earnest and act with all their strength; unless you imagine, perchance, that by such flippant and mythical talk, and such old wives' reasoning, it is possible for us to prevent that most ruinous consummation, the repudiation of benefits.

5

However, while I pass over what is futile and irrelevant I must point out that the first thing which we have to learn is, what we owe in return for a benefit received. One man says that he owes the money which he has received, another that he owes a consulship, a priesthood, a province, and so on. These, however, are but the outward signs of kindnesses, not the kindnesses themselves. A benefit is not to be felt and handled, it is a thing which exists only in the mind. There is a great difference between the subject matter of a benefit, and the benefit itself. Wherefore neither gold, nor silver, nor any of those things which are most highly esteemed, are benefits, but the benefit lies in the goodwill of him who gives them. The ignorant take notice only of that which comes before their eyes, and which can be owned and passed from hand to hand, while they disregard that which gives these things their value. The things which we hold in our hands, which we see with our eyes, and which our avarice hugs, are transitory, they may be taken from us by ill luck or by violence; but a kindness lasts even after the loss of that by means of which it was bestowed; for it is a good deed, which no violence can undo. For instance, suppose that I ransomed a friend from pirates, but another pirate has caught him and thrown him into prison. The pirate has not robbed him of my benefit, but has only robbed him of the enjoyment of it. Or suppose that I have saved a man's children from a shipwreck or a fire, and that afterwards disease or accident has carried them off; even when they are no more, the kindness which was done by means of them remains. All those things, therefore, which improperly assume the name of benefits, are means by which kindly feeling manifests itself. In other cases also, we find a distinction between the visible symbol and the matter itself, as when a general bestows collars of gold, or civic or mural crowns upon anyone. What value has the crown in itself? or the purple-bordered robe? or the fasces? or the judgment-seat and car of triumph? None of these things is in itself an honour, but is an emblem of honour. In like manner, that which is seen is not a benefit—it is but the trace and mark of a benefit.

6

What, then, is a benefit? It is the art of doing a kindness which both bestows pleasure and gains it by bestowing it, and which does its office by natural and spontaneous impulse. It is not, therefore, the thing which is done or given, but the spirit in which it is done or given, that must be considered, because a benefit exists, not in that which is done or given, but in the mind of the doer or giver. How great the distinction between them is, you may perceive from this, that while a benefit is necessarily good, yet that which is done or given is neither good nor bad. The spirit in which they are given can exalt small things, can glorify mean ones, and can discredit great and precious ones; the objects themselves which are sought after have a neutral nature, neither good nor bad; all depends upon the direction given them by the guiding spirit from which things receive their shape. That which is paid or handed over is not the benefit itself, just as the honour which we pay to the gods lies not in the victims themselves, although they be fat and glittering with gold,[3] but in the pure and holy feelings of the worshippers.

Thus good men are religious, though their offering be meal and their vessels of earthenware; whilst bad men will not escape from their impiety, though they pour the blood of many victims upon the altars.

7

If benefits consisted of things, and not of the wish to benefit, then the more things we received the greater the benefit would be. But this is not true, for sometimes we feel more gratitude to one who gives us trifles nobly, who, like Virgil's poor old soldier, "holds himself as rich as kings," if he has given us ever so little with a good will a man who forgets his own need when he sees mine, who has not only a wish but a longing to help, who thinks that he receives a benefit when he bestows one, who gives as though he would receive no return, receives a repayment as though he had originally given nothing, and who watches for and seizes an opportunity of being useful. On the other hand, as I said before, those gifts which are hardly wrung from the giver, or which drop unheeded from his hands, claim no gratitude from us, however great they may appear and may be. We prize much more what comes from a willing hand, than what comes from a full one. This man has given me but little, yet more he could not afford, while what that one has given is much indeed, but he hesitated, he put it off, he grumbled when he gave it, he gave it haughtily, or he proclaimed it aloud, and did it to please others, not to please the person to whom he gave it; he offered it to his own pride, not to me.

---

[3] Alluding to the practice of gilding the horns of the victims.

8

As the pupils of Socrates, each in proportion to his means, gave him large presents, Aeschines, a poor pupil, said, "I can find nothing to give you which is worthy of you; I feel my poverty in this respect alone. Therefore I present you with the only thing I possess, myself. I pray that you may take this my present, such as it is, in good part, and may remember that the others, although they gave you much, yet left for themselves more than they gave." Socrates answered, "Surely you have bestowed a great present upon me, unless perchance you set a small value upon yourself. I will accordingly take pains to restore you to yourself a better man than when I received you." By this present Aeschines outdid Alcibiades, whose mind was as great as his wealth, and all the splendour of the most wealthy youths of Athens.

9

You see how the mind even in the straitest circumstances finds the means of generosity. Aeschines seems to me to have said, "Fortune, it is in vain that you have made me poor; in spite of this I will find a worthy present for this man. Since I can give him nothing of yours, I will give him something of my own." Nor need you suppose that he held himself cheap; he made himself his own price. By a stroke of genius this youth discovered a means of presenting Socrates to himself. We must not consider how great presents are, but in what spirit they are given.

A rich man is well spoken of if he is clever enough to render himself easy of access to men of immoderate ambition, and although he intends to do nothing to help them, yet encourages their unconscionable hopes; but he is thought the worse of if he be sharp of tongue, sour in appearance, and displays his wealth in an invidious fashion. For men respect and yet loathe a fortunate man, and hate him for doing what, if they had the chance, they would do themselves.

Men nowadays no longer secretly, but openly outrage the wives of others, and allow to others access to their own wives. A match is thought countrified, uncivilized, in bad style, and to be protested against by all matrons, if the husband should forbid his wife to appear in public in a litter, and to be carried about exposed to the gaze of all observers. If a man has not made himself notorious by a liaison with some mistress, if he does not pay an annuity to someone else's wife, married women speak of him as a poor-spirited creature, a man given to low vice, a lover of servant girls. Soon adultery becomes the most respectable form of marriage, and widowhood and celibacy are commonly practised. No one takes a wife unless he takes her away from someone else. Now men vie with one another in wasting what they have stolen, and in collecting together what they have wasted with the keenest avarice; they become utterly reckless, scorn poverty in others, fear personal injury more than anything else, break the peace by their riots, and by violence and terror domineer over those who are weaker than themselves. No wonder that they plunder provinces and offer the seat of judgment for sale, knocking it down after an auction to the highest bidder, since it is the law of nations that you may sell what you have bought.

10

However, my enthusiasm has carried me further than I intended, the subject being an inviting one. Let me, then, end by pointing out that the disgrace of these crimes does not belong especially to our own time. Our ancestors before us have lamented, and our children after us will lament, as we do, the ruin of morality, the prevalence of vice, and the gradual deterioration of mankind; yet these things are really stationary, only moved slightly to and fro like the waves which at one time a rising tide washes further over the land, and at another an ebbing one restrains within a lower water mark. At one time the chief vice will be adultery, and licentiousness will exceed all bounds; at another time a rage for feasting will be in vogue, and men will waste their inheritance in the most shameful of all ways, by the kitchen; at another, excessive care for the body, and a devotion to personal beauty which implies ugliness of mind; at another time, injudiciously granted liberty will show itself in wanton recklessness and defiance of authority; sometimes there will be a reign of cruelty both in public and private, and the madness of the civil wars will come upon us, which destroy all that is holy and inviolable. Sometimes even drunkenness will be held in honour, and it will be a virtue to swallow most wine. Vices do not lie in wait for us in one place alone, but hover around us in changeful forms, sometimes even at variance one with another, so that in turn they win and lose the field; yet we shall always be obliged to pronounce the same verdict upon ourselves, that we are and always were evil, and, I unwillingly add, that we always shall be. There always will be homicides, tyrants, thieves, adulterers, ravishers, sacrilegious, traitors: worse than all these is the ungrateful man, except we consider that all these crimes flow from ingratitude, without which hardly any great wickedness has ever grown to full stature. Be sure that you guard against this as the greatest of crimes in yourself, but pardon it as the least of crimes in another. For all the injury which you suffer is this: you have lost the subject-matter of a benefit, not the benefit itself, for you possess unimpaired the best part of it, in that you have given it. Though we ought to be careful to bestow our benefits by preference upon those who are likely to show us gratitude for them, yet we must sometimes do what we have little hope will turn out well, and bestow benefits upon those who we not only think will prove ungrateful, but who we know have been so. For instance, if I should be able to save a man's children from a great danger with no risk to myself, I should not hesitate to do so. If a man be worthy I would defend him even with my blood, and would share his perils; if he be unworthy, and yet by merely crying for help I can rescue him from robbers, I would without reluctance raise the shout which would save a fellow-creature.

11

The next point to be defined is, what kind of benefits are to be given, and in what manner. First let us give what is necessary, next what is useful, and then what is pleasant, provided that they be lasting. We must begin with what is necessary, for those things which support life affect the mind very differently from those which adorn and improve it. A man may be nice, and hard to please, in things which he can easily do without, of which he can say, "Take them back; I do not want them, I am satisfied with what I have." Sometimes we wish not only to return what we have received, but even to throw it away. Of necessary things, the first class consists of things without which we cannot live; the second, of things without which we ought not to live; and the third, of things without which we should not care to live. The first class are, to be saved from the hands of the enemy, from the anger of tyrants, from proscription, and the various other perils which beset human life. By averting any one of these, we shall earn gratitude proportionate to the greatness of the danger, for when men think of the greatness of the misery from which they have been saved, the terror which they have gone through enhances the value of our services. Yet we ought not to delay rescuing anyone longer than we are obliged, solely in order to make his fears add weight to our services. Next come those things without which we can indeed live, but in such a manner that it would be better to die, such as liberty, chastity, or a good conscience. After these are what we have come to hold dear by connection and relationship and long use and custom, such as our wives and children, our household gods, and so on, to which the mind so firmly attaches itself that separation from them seems worse than death.

After these come useful things, which form a very wide and varied class; in which will be money, not in excess, but enough for living in a moderate style; public office, and, for the ambitious, due advancement to higher posts; for nothing can be more useful to a man than to be placed in a position in which he can benefit himself. All benefits beyond these are superfluous, and are likely to spoil those who receive them. In giving these we must be careful to make them acceptable by giving them at the appropriate time, or by giving things which are not common, but such as few people possess, or at any rate few possess in our times; or again, by giving things in such a manner, that though not naturally valuable, they become so by the time and place at which they are given. We must reflect what present will produce the most pleasure, what will most frequently come under the notice of the possessor of it, so that whenever he is with it he may be with us also; and in all cases we must be careful not to send useless presents, such as hunting weapons to a woman or old man, or books to a rustic, or nets to catch wild animals to a quiet literary man. On the other hand, we ought to be careful, while we wish to send what will please, that we do not send what will insultingly remind our friends of their failings, as, for example, if we send wine to a hard drinker or drugs to an invalid, for a present which contains an allusion to the shortcomings of the receiver, becomes an outrage.

12

If we have a free choice as to what to give, we should above all choose lasting presents, in order that our gift may endure as long as possible; for few are so grateful as to think of what they have received, even when they do not see it. Even the ungrateful remember us by our gifts, when they are always in their sight and do not allow themselves to be forgotten, but constantly obtrude and stamp upon the mind the memory of the giver. As we never ought to remind men of what we have given them, we ought all the more to choose presents that will be permanent; for the things themselves will prevent the remembrance of the giver from fading away. I would more willingly give a present of plate than of coined money, and would more willingly give statues than clothes or other things which are soon worn out. Few remain grateful after the present is gone: many more remember their presents only while they make use of them. If possible, I should like my present not to be consumed; let it remain in existence, let it stick to my friend and share his life. No one is so foolish as to need to be told not to send gladiators or wild beasts to one who has just given a public show, or not to send summer clothing in winter time, or winter clothing in summer. Common sense must guide our benefits; we must consider the time and the place, and the character of the receiver, which are the weights in the scale, which cause our gifts to be well or ill received. How far more acceptable a present is, if we give a man what he has not, than if we give him what he has plenty of! if we give him what he has long been searching for in vain, rather than what he sees everywhere! Let us make presents of things which are rare and scarce rather than costly, things which even a rich man will be glad of, just as common fruits, such as we tire of after a few days, please us if they have ripened before the usual season. People will also esteem things which no one else has given to them, or which we have given to no one else.

13

When the conquest of the East had flattered Alexander of Macedon into believing himself to be more than man, the people of Corinth sent an embassy to congratulate him, and presented him with the franchise of their city. When Alexander smiled at this form of courtesy, one of the ambassadors said, "We have never enrolled any stranger among our citizens except Hercules and yourself." Alexander willingly accepted the proffered honour, invited the ambassadors to his table, and showed them other courtesies. He did not think of who offered the citizenship, but to whom they had granted it; and being altogether the slave of glory, though he knew neither its true nature or its limits, had followed in the footsteps of Hercules and Bacchus, and had not even stayed his march where they ceased; so that he glanced aside from the givers of this honour to him with whom he shared it, and fancied that the heaven to which his vanity aspired was indeed opening before him when he was made equal to Hercules. In what indeed did that frantic youth, whose only merit was his lucky audacity, resemble Hercules? Hercules conquered nothing for himself; he travelled throughout the world, not coveting for himself but liberating the countries which he conquered, an enemy to bad men, a defender of the good, a peacemaker both by sea and land; whereas the other was from his boyhood a brigand and desolator of nations, a pest to his friends and enemies alike, whose greatest joy was to be the terror of all mankind, forgetting that men fear not only the fiercest but also the most cowardly animals, because of their evil and venomous nature.

14

Let us now return to our subject. He who bestows a benefit without discrimination, gives what pleases no one; no one considers himself to be under any obligation to the landlord of a tavern, or to be the guest of anyone with whom he dines in such company as to be able to say, "What civility has he shown to me? no more than he has shown to that man, whom he scarcely knows, or to that other, who is both his personal enemy and a man of infamous character. Do you suppose that he wished to do me any honour? not so, he merely wished to indulge his own vice of profusion." If you wish men to be grateful for anything, give it but seldom; no one can bear to receive what you give to all the world. Yet let no one gather from this that I wish to impose any bonds upon generosity; let her go to what lengths she will, so that she go a steady course, not at random. It is possible to bestow gifts in such a manner that each of those who receive them, although he shares them with many others, may yet feel himself to be distinguished from the common herd. Let each man have some peculiarity about his gift which may make him consider himself more highly favoured than the rest. He may say, "I received the same present that he did, but I never asked for it." "I received the same present, but mine was given me after a few days, whereas he had earned it by long service." "Others have the same present, but it was not given to them with the same courtesy and gracious words with which it was given to me." "That man got it because he asked for it; I did not ask." "That man received it as well as I, but then he could easily return it; one has great expectations from a rich man, old and childless, as he is; whereas in giving the same present to me he really gave more, because he gave it without the hope of receiving any return for it." Just as a courtesan divides her favours among many men, so that no one of her friends is without some proof of her affection, so let him who wishes his benefits to be prized consider how he may at the same time gratify many men, and nevertheless give each one of them some especial mark of favour to distinguish him from the rest.

15

I am no advocate of slackness in giving benefits: the more and the greater they are, the more praise they will bring to the giver. Yet let them be given with discretion; for what is given carelessly and recklessly can please no one. Whoever, therefore, supposes that in giving this advice I wish to restrict benevolence and to confine it to narrower limits, entirely mistakes the object of my warning. What virtue do we admire more than benevolence? Which do we encourage more? Who ought to applaud it more than we Stoics, who preach the brotherhood of the human race? What then is it? Since no impulse of the human mind can be approved of, even though it springs from a right feeling, unless it be made into a virtue by discretion, I forbid generosity to degenerate into extravagance. It is, indeed, pleasant to receive a benefit with open arms, when reason bestows it upon the worthy, not when it is flung hither or thither thoughtlessly and at random; this alone we care to display and claim as our own. Can you call anything a benefit, if you feel ashamed to mention the person who gave it you? How far more grateful is a benefit, how far more deeply does it impress itself upon the mind, never to be forgotten, when we rejoice to think not so much of what it is, as from whom we have received it! Crispus Passienus was wont to say that some men's advice was to be preferred to their presents, some men's presents to their advice; and he added as an example, "I would rather have received advice from Augustus than a present; I would rather receive a present from Claudius than advice." I, however, think that one ought not to wish for a benefit from any man whose judgement is worthless. What then? Ought we not to receive what Claudius gives? We ought; but we ought to regard it as obtained from fortune, which may at any moment turn against us. Why do we separate this which naturally is connected? That is not a benefit, to which the best part of a benefit, that it be bestowed with judgment, is wanting: a really great sum of money, if it be given neither with discernment nor with good will, is no more a benefit than if it remained hoarded. There are, however, many things which we ought not to reject, yet for which we cannot feel indebted.

BOOK 2

1

Let us consider, most excellent Liberalis, what still remains of the earlier part of the subject; in what way a benefit should be bestowed. I think that I can point out the shortest way to this; let us give in the way in which we ourselves should like to receive. Above all we should give willingly, quickly, and without any hesitation; a benefit commands no gratitude if it has hung for a long time in the hands of the giver, if he seems unwilling to part with it, and gives it as though he were being robbed of it. Even though some delay should intervene, let us by all means in our power strive not to seem to have been in two minds about giving it at all. To hesitate is the next thing to refusing to give, and destroys all claim to gratitude. For just as the sweetest part of a benefit is the kindly feeling of the giver, it follows that one who has by his very delay proved that he gives unwillingly, must be regarded not as having given anything, but as having been unable to keep it from an importunate suitor. Indeed, many men are made generous by want of firmness. The most acceptable benefits are those which are waiting for us to take them, which are easy to be received, and offer themselves to us, so that the only delay is caused by the modesty of the receiver. The best thing of all is to anticipate a person's wishes; the next, to follow them; the former is the better course, to be beforehand with our friends by giving them what they want before they ask us for it, for the value of a gift is much enhanced by sparing an honest man the misery of asking for it with confusion and blushes. He who gets what he asked for does not get it for nothing, for indeed, as our austere ancestors thought, nothing is so dear as that which is bought by prayers. Men would be much more modest in their petitions to heaven, if these had to be made publicly; so that even when addressing the gods, before whom we can with all honour bend our knees, we prefer to pray silently and within ourselves.

2

It is unpleasant, burdensome, and covers one with shame to have to say, "Give me." You should spare your friends, and those whom you wish to make your friends, from having to do this; however quick he may be, a man gives too late who gives what he has been asked for. We ought, therefore, to divine every man's wishes, and when we have discovered them, to set him free from the hard necessity of asking; you may be sure that a benefit which comes unasked will be delightful and will not be forgotten. If we do not succeed in anticipating our friends, let us at any rate cut them short when they ask us for anything, so that we may appear to be reminded of what we meant to do, rather than to have been asked to do it. Let us assent at once, and by our promptness make it appear that we meant to do so even before we were solicited. As in dealing with sick persons much depends upon when food is given, and plain water given at the right moment sometimes acts as a remedy, so a benefit, however slight and commonplace it may be, if it be promptly given without losing a moment of time, gains enormously in importance, and wins our gratitude more than a far more valuable present given after long waiting and deliberation. One who gives so readily must needs give with good will; he therefore gives cheerfully and shows his disposition in his countenance.

3

Many who bestow immense benefits spoil them by their silence or slowness of speech, which gives them an air of moroseness, as they say "yes" with a face which seems to say "no." How much better is it to join kind words to kind actions, and to enhance the value of our gifts by a civil and gracious commendation of them! To cure your friend of being slow to ask a favour of you, you may join to your gift the familiar rebuke, "I am angry with you for not having long ago let me know what you wanted, for having asked for it so formally, or for having made interest with a third party." "I congratulate myself that you have been pleased to make trial of me; hereafter, if you want anything, ask for it as your right; however, for this time I pardon your want of manners." By so doing you will cause him to value your friendship more highly than that, whatever it may have been, which he came to ask of you. The goodness and kindness of a benefactor never appears so great as when on leaving him one says, "I have today gained much; I am more pleased at finding him so kind than if I had obtained many times more of this, of which I was speaking, by some other means; I never can make any adequate return to this man for his goodness."

4

Many, however, there are who, by harsh words and contemptuous manner, make their very kindnesses odious, for by speaking and acting disdainfully they make us sorry that they have granted our requests. Various delays also take place after we have obtained a promise; and nothing is more heartbreaking than to be forced to beg for the very thing which you already have been promised. Benefits ought to be bestowed at once, but from some persons it is easier to obtain the promise of them than to get them. One man has to be asked to remind our benefactor of his purpose; another, to bring it into effect; and thus a single present is worn away in passing through many hands, until hardly any gratitude is left for the original promiser, since whoever we are forced to solicit after the giving of the promise receives some of the gratitude which we owe to the giver. Take care, therefore, if you wish your gifts to be esteemed, that they reach those to whom they are promised entire, and, as the saying is, without any deduction. Let no one intercept them or delay them; for no one can take any share of the gratitude due for your gifts without robbing you of it.

5

Nothing is more bitter than long uncertainty; some can bear to have their hopes extinguished better than to have them deferred. Yet many men are led by an unworthy vanity into this fault of putting off the accomplishment of their promises, merely in order to swell the crowd of their suitors, like the ministers of royalty, who delight in prolonging the display of their own arrogance, hardly thinking themselves possessed of power unless they let each man see for a long time how powerful they are. They do nothing promptly, or at one sitting; they are indeed swift to do mischief, but slow to do good. Be sure that the comic poet speaks the most absolute truth in the verses:—

> "Know you not this? If you your gifts delay,
> You take thereby my gratitude away."

And the following lines, the expression of virtuous pain—a high-spirited man's misery—

> "What thou doest, do quickly;"

and:—

> "Nothing in the world
> Is worth this trouble; I had rather you
> Refused it to me now."

When the mind begins through weariness to hate the promised benefit, or while it is wavering in expectation of it, how can it feel grateful for it? As the most refined cruelty is that which prolongs the torture, while to kill the victim at once is a kind of mercy, since the extremity of torture brings its own end with it—the interval is the worst part of the execution—so the shorter time a benefit hangs in the balance, the more grateful it is to the receiver. It is possible to look forward with anxious disquietude even to good things, and, seeing that most benefits consist in a release from some form of misery, a man destroys the value of the benefit which he confers, if he has the power to relieve us, and yet allows us to suffer or to lack pleasure longer than we need. Kindness is always eager to do good, and one who acts by love naturally acts at once; he who does us good, but does it tardily and with long delays, does not do so from the heart. Thus he loses two most important things: time, and the proof of his good will to us; for a lingering consent is but a form of denial.

6

The manner in which things are said or done, my Liberalis, forms a very important part of every transaction. We gain much by quickness, and lose much by slowness. Just as in darts, the strength of the iron head remains the same, but there is an immeasureable difference between the blow of one hurled with the full swing of the arm and one which merely drops from the hand, and the same sword either grazes or pierces according as the blow is delivered; so, in like manner, that which is given is the same, but the manner in which it is given makes the difference. How sweet, how precious is a gift, when he who gives does not permit himself to be thanked, and when while he gives he forgets that he has given! To reproach a man at the very moment that you are doing him a service is sheer madness; it is to mix insult with your favours. We ought not to make our benefits burdensome, or to add any bitterness to them. Even if there be some subject upon which you wish to warn your friend, choose some other time for doing so.

7

Fabius Verrucosus used to compare a benefit bestowed by a harsh man in an offensive manner to a gritty loaf of bread, which a hungry man is obliged to receive, but which is painful to eat. When Marius Nepos of the praetorian guard asked Tiberius Caesar for help to pay his debts, Tiberius asked him for a list of his creditors; this is calling a meeting of creditors, not paying debts. When the list was made out, Tiberius wrote to Nepos telling him that he had ordered the money to be paid, and adding some offensive reproaches. The result of this was that Nepos owed no debts, yet received no kindness; Tiberius, indeed, relieved him from his creditors, but laid him under no obligation. Tiberius, however, had some design in doing so; I imagine he did not wish more of his friends to come to him with the same request. His mode of proceeding was, perhaps, successful in restraining men's extravagant desires by shame, but he who wishes to confer benefits must follow quite a different path. In all ways you should make your benefit as acceptable as possible by presenting it in the most attractive form; but the method of Tiberius is not to confer benefits, but to reproach.

8

Moreover, if incidentally I should say what I think of this part of the subject, I do not consider that it is becoming even to an emperor to give merely in order to cover a man with shame. "And yet," we are told, "Tiberius did not even by this means attain his object; for after this a good many persons were found to make the same request. He ordered all of them to explain the reasons of their indebtedness before the senate, and when they did so, granted them certain definite sums of money." This is not an act of generosity, but a reprimand. You may call it a subsidy, or an imperial contribution; it is not a benefit, for the receiver cannot think of it without shame. I was summoned before a judge, and had to be tried at bar before I obtained what I asked for.

9

Accordingly, all writers on ethical philosophy tell us that some benefits ought to be given in secret, others in public. Those things which it is glorious to receive, such as military decorations or public offices, and whatever else gains in value the more widely it is known, should be conferred in public; on the other hand, when they do not promote a man or add to his social standing, but help him when in weakness, in want, or in disgrace, they should be given silently, and so as to be known only to those who profit by them.

10

Sometimes even the person who is assisted must be deceived, in order that he may receive our bounty without knowing the source from whence it flows. It is said that Arcesilaus had a friend who was poor, but concealed his poverty; who was ill, yet tried to hide his disorder, and who had not money for the necessary expenses of existence. Without his knowledge, Arcesilaus placed a bag of money under his pillow, in order that this victim of false shame might rather seem to find what he wanted than to receive. "What," say you, "ought he not to know from whom he received it?" Yes; let him not know it at first, if it be essential to your kindness that he should not; afterwards I will do so much for him, and give him so much that he will perceive who was the giver of the former benefit; or, better still, let him not know that he has received anything, provided I know that I have given it. "This," you say, "is to get too little return for one's goodness." True, if it be an investment of which you are thinking; but if a gift, it should be given in the way which will be of most service to the receiver. You should be satisfied with the approval of your own conscience; if not, you do not really delight in doing good, but in being seen to do good. "For all that," say you, "I wish him to know it." Is it a debtor that you seek for? "For all that, I wish him to know it." What! though it be more useful, more creditable, more pleasant for him not to know his benefactor, will you not consent to stand aside? "I wish him to know." So, then, you would not save a man's life in the dark? I do not deny that, whenever the matter admits of it, one ought to take into consideration the pleasure which we receive from the joy of the receiver of our kindness; but if he ought to have help and is ashamed to receive it—if what we bestow upon him pains him unless it be concealed—I forbear to make my benefits public. Why should I not refrain from hinting at my having given him anything, when the first and most essential rule is, never to reproach a man with what you have done for him, and not even to remind him of it. The rule for the giver and receiver of a benefit is, that the one should straightaway forget that he has given, the other should never forget that he has received it.

11

A constant reference to one's own services wounds our friend's feelings. Like the man who was saved from the proscription under the triumvirate by one of Caesar's friends, and afterwards found it impossible to endure his preserver's arrogance, they wish to cry, "Give me back to Caesar." How long will you go on saying, "I saved you, I snatched you from the jaws of death?" This is indeed life, if I remember it by my own will, but death if I remember it at yours; I owe you nothing, if you saved me merely in order to have someone to point at. How long do you mean to lead me about? how long do you mean to forbid me to forget my adventure? If I had been a defeated enemy, I should have been led in triumph but once. We ought not to speak of the benefits which we have conferred; to remind men of them is to ask them to return them. We should not obtrude them, or recall the memory of them; you should only remind a man of what you have given him by giving him something else. We ought not even to tell others of our good deeds. He who confers a benefit should be silent, it should be told by the receiver; for otherwise you may receive the retort which was made to one who was everywhere boasting of the benefit which he had conferred: "You will not deny," said his victim, "that you have received a return for it?" "When?" asked he. "Often," said the other, "and in many places, that is, wherever and whenever you have told the story." What need is there for you to speak, and to take the place which belongs to another? There is a man who can tell the story in a way much more to your credit, and thus you will gain glory for not telling it yourself. You would think me ungrateful if, through your own silence, no one is to know of your benefit. So far from doing this, even if anyone tells the story in our presence, we ought to make answer, "He does indeed deserve much more than this, and I am aware that I have not hitherto done any great things for him, although I wish to do so." This should not be said jokingly, nor yet with that air by which some persons repel those whom they especially wish to attract. In addition to this, we ought to act with the greatest politeness towards such persons. If the farmer ceases his labours after he has put in the seed, he will lose what he has sown; it is only by great pains that seeds are brought to yield a crop; no plant will bear fruit unless it be tended with equal care from first to last, and the same rule is true of benefits. Can any benefits be greater than those which children receive from their parents? Yet these benefits are useless if they be deserted while young, if the pious care of the parents does not for a long time watch over the gift which they have bestowed. So it is with other benefits; unless you help them, you will lose them; to give is not enough, you must foster what you have given. If you wish those whom you lay under an obligation to be grateful to you, you must not merely confer benefits upon them, but you must also love them. Above all, as I said before, spare their ears; you will weary them if you remind them of your goodness, if you reproach them with it you will make them hate you. Pride ought above all things to be avoided when you confer a benefit. What need have you for disdainful airs, or swelling phrases? the act itself will exalt you. Let us shun vain boasting: let us be silent, and let our deeds speak for us. A benefit conferred with haughtiness not only wins no gratitude, but causes dislike.

12

Gaius Caesar granted Pompeius Pennus his life, that is, if not to take away life be to grant it; then, when Pompeius was set free and returning thanks to him, he stretched out his left foot to be kissed. Those who excuse this action, and say that it was not done through arrogance, say that he wished to show him a gilded, nay a golden slipper studded with pearls. "Well," say they, "what disgrace can there be in a man of consular rank kissing gold and pearls, and what part of Caesar's whole body was it less pollution to kiss?" So, then, that man, the object of whose life was to change a free state into a Persian despotism, was not satisfied when a senator, an aged man, a man who had filled the highest offices in the State, prostrated himself before him in the presence of all the nobles, just as the vanquished prostrate themselves before their conqueror! He discovered a place below his knees down to which he might thrust liberty. What is this but trampling upon the commonwealth, and that, too, with the left foot, though you may say that this point does not signify? It was not a sufficiently foul and frantic outrage for the emperor to sit at the trial of a consular for his life wearing slippers, he must needs push his shoes into a senator's face.

13

O pride, the silliest fault of great good fortune! how pleasant it is to take nothing from thee! how dost thou turn all benefits into outrages! how dost thou delight in all excess! how ill all things become thee! The higher thou risest the lower thou art, and provest that the good things by which thou art so puffed up profit thee not; thou spoilest all that thou givest. It is worth while to inquire why it is that pride thus swaggers and changes the form and appearance of her countenance, so that she prefers a mask to her own face. It is pleasant to receive gifts when they are conferred in a kindly and gentle manner, when a superior in giving them does not exalt himself over me, but shows as much good feeling as possible, placing himself on a level with me, giving without parade, and choosing a time when I am glad of his help, rather than waiting till I am in the bitterest need. The only way by which you can prevail upon proud men not to spoil their gifts by their arrogance is by proving to them that benefits do not appear greater because they are bestowed with great pomp and circumstance; that no one will think them greater men for so doing, and that excessive pride is a mere delusion which leads men to hate even what they ought to love.

14

There are some things which injure those who receive them, things which it is not a benefit to give but to withhold; we should therefore consider the usefulness of our gift rather than the wish of the petitioner to receive it; for we often long for hurtful things, and are unable to discern how ruinous they are, because our judgment is biased by our feelings; when, however, the longing is past, when that frenzied impulse which masters our good sense has passed away, we abhor those who have given us hurtful gifts. As we refuse cold water to the sick, or swords to the grief-stricken or remorseful, and take from the insane whatever they might in their delirium use to their own destruction, so must we persist in refusing to give anything whatever that is hurtful, although our friends earnestly and humbly, nay, sometimes even most piteously beg for it. We ought to look at the end of our benefits as well as the beginning, and not merely to give what men are glad to receive, but what they will hereafter be glad to have received. There are many who say, "I know that this will do him no good, but what am I to do? he begs for it, I cannot withstand his entreaties. Let him see to it; he will blame himself, not me." Not so: you he will blame, and deservedly; when he comes to his right mind, when the frenzy which now excites him has left him, how can he help hating the man who has assisted him to harm and to endanger himself? It is a cruel kindness to allow oneself to be won over into granting that which injures those who beg for it. Just as it is the noblest of acts to save men from harm against their will, so it is but hatred, under the mask of civility, to grant what is harmful to those who ask for it. Let us confer benefits of such a kind, that the more they are made use of the better they please, and which never can turn into injuries. I never will give money to a man if I know that he will pay it to an adulteress, nor will I be found in connection with any wicked act or plan; if possible, I will restrain men from crime; if not, at least I will never assist them in it. Whether my friend be driven into doing wrong by anger, or seduced from the path of safety by the heat of ambition, he shall never gain the means of doing mischief except from himself, nor will I enable him one day to say, "He ruined me out of love for me." Our friends often give us what our enemies wish us to receive; we are driven by the unseasonable fondness of the former into the ruin which the latter hope will befall us. Yet, often as it is the case, what can be more shameful than that there should be no difference between a benefit and hatred?

15

Let us never bestow gifts which may recoil upon us to our shame. As the sum total of friendship consists in making our friends equal to ourselves, we ought to consider the interests of both parties; I must give to him that wants, yet so that I do not want myself; I must help him who is perishing, yet so that I do not perish myself, unless by so doing I can save a great man or a great cause. I must give no benefit which it would disgrace me to ask for. I ought not to make a small benefit appear a great one, nor allow great benefits to be regarded as small; for although it destroys all feeling of gratitude to treat what you give like a creditor, yet you do not reproach a man, but merely set off your gift to the best advantage by letting him know what it is worth. Every man must consider what his resources and powers are, so that we may not give either more or less than we are able. We must also consider the character and position of the person to whom we give, for some men are too great to give small gifts, while others are too small to receive great ones. Compare, therefore, the character both of the giver and the receiver, and weigh that which you give between the two, taking care that what is given be neither too burdensome nor too trivial for the one to give, nor yet such as the receiver will either treat with disdain as too small, or think too great for him to deal with.

16

Alexander, who was of unsound mind, and always full of magnificent ideas, presented somebody with a city. When the man to whom he gave it had reflected upon the scope of his own powers, he wished to avoid the jealousy which so great a present would excite, saying that the gift did not suit a man of his position. "I do not ask," replied Alexander, "what is becoming for you to receive, but what is becoming for me to give." This seems a spirited and kingly speech, yet really it is a most foolish one. Nothing is by itself a becoming gift for anyone: all depends upon who gives it, to whom he gives it, when, for what reason, where, and so forth, without which details it is impossible to argue about it. Inflated creature! if it did not become him to receive this gift, it could not become thee to give it. There should be a proportion between men's characters and the offices which they fill; and as virtue in all cases should be our measure, he who gives too much acts as wrongly as he who gives too little. Even granting that fortune has raised you so high, that, where other men give cups, you give cities (which it would show a greater mind in you not to take than to take and squander), still there must be some of your friends who are not strong enough to put a city in their pockets.

17

A certain cynic asked Antigonus for a talent. Antigonus answered that this was too much for a cynic to ask for. After this rebuff he asked for a penny. Antigonus answered that this was too little for a king to give. "This kind of hair splitting" (you say) "is contemptible: he found the means of giving neither. In the matter of the penny he thought of the king, in that of the talent he thought of the cynic, whereas with respect to the cynic it would have been right to receive the penny, with respect to the king it would have been right to give the talent. Though there may be things which are too great for a cynic to receive, yet nothing is so small, that it does not become a gracious king to bestow it." If you ask me, I applaud Antigonus; for it is not to be endured that a man who despises money should ask for it. Your cynic has publicly proclaimed his hatred of money, and assumed the character of one who despises it: let him act up to his professions. It is most inconsistent for him to earn money by glorifying his poverty. I wish to use Chrysippus's simile of the game of ball, in which the ball must certainly fall by the fault either of the thrower or of the catcher; it only holds its course when it passes between the hands of two persons who each throw it and catch it suitably. It is necessary, however, for a good player to send the ball in one way to a comrade at a long distance, and in another to one at a short distance. So it is with a benefit: unless it be suitable both for the giver and the receiver, it will neither leave the one nor reach the other as it ought. If we have to do with a practised and skilled player, we shall throw the ball more recklessly, for however it may come, that quick and agile hand will send it back again; if we are playing with an unskilled novice, we shall not throw it so hard, but far more gently, guiding it straight into his very hands, and we shall run to meet it when it returns to us. This is just what we ought to do in conferring benefits; let us teach some men how to do so, and be satisfied if they attempt it, if they have the courage and the will to do so. For the most part, however, we make men ungrateful, and encourage them to be so, as if our benefits were only great when we cannot receive any gratitude for them; just as some spiteful ballplayers purposely put out their companion, of course to the ruin of the game, which cannot be carried on without entire agreement. Many men are of so depraved a nature that they had rather lose the presents which they make than be thought to have received a return for them, because they are proud, and like to lay people under obligations: yet how much better and more kindly would it be if they tried to enable the others also to perform their parts, if they encouraged them in returning gratitude, put the best construction upon all their acts, received one who wished to thank them just as cordially as if he came to repay what he had received, and easily lent themselves to the belief that those whom they have laid under an obligation wish to repay it. We blame usurers equally when they press harshly for payment, and when they delay and make difficulties about taking back the money which they have lent; in the same way, it is just as right that a benefit should be returned, as it is wrong to ask anyone to return it. The best man is he who gives readily, never asks for any return, and is delighted when the return is made, because, having really and truly forgotten what he gave, he receives it as though it were a present.

18

Some men not only give, but even receive benefit haughtily, a mistake into which we ought not to fall: for now let us cross over to the other side of the subject, and consider how men should behave when they receive benefits. Every function which is performed by two persons makes equal demands upon both: after you have considered what a father ought to be, you will perceive that there remains an equal task, that of considering what a son ought to be: a husband has certain duties, but those of a wife are no less important. Each of these give and take equally, and each require a similar rule of life, which, as Hecaton observes, is hard to follow: indeed, it is difficult for us to attain to virtue, or even to anything that comes near virtue: for we ought not only to act virtuously but to do so upon principle. We ought to follow this guide throughout our lives, and to do everything great and small according to its dictates: according as virtue prompts us we ought both to give and to receive. Now she will declare at the outset that we ought not to receive benefits from every man. "From whom, then, ought we to receive them?" To answer you briefly, I should say, from those to whom we have given them. Let us consider whether we ought not to be even more careful in choosing to whom we should owe than to whom we should give. For even supposing that no unpleasantness should result (and very much always does), still it is a great misery to be indebted to a man to whom you do not wish to be under an obligation; whereas it is most delightful to receive a benefit from one whom you can love even after he has wronged you, and when the pleasure which you feel in his friendship is justified by the grounds on which it is based. Nothing is more wretched for a modest and honourable man than to feel it to be his duty to love one whom it does not please him to love. I must constantly remind you that I do not speak of wise men, who take pleasure in everything that is their duty, who have their feelings under command, and are able to lay down whatever law they please to themselves and keep it, but that I speak of imperfect beings struggling to follow the right path, who often have trouble in bending their passions to their will. I must therefore choose the man from whom I will accept a benefit; indeed, I ought to be more careful in the choice of my creditor for a benefit than for money; for I have only to pay the latter as much as I received of him, and when I have paid it I am free from all obligation; but to the other I must both repay more, and even when I have repaid his kindness we remain connected, for when I have paid my debt I ought again to renew it, while our friendship endures unbroken. Thus, as I ought not to make an unworthy man my friend, so I ought not to admit an unworthy man into that most holy bond of gratitude for benefits, from which friendship arises. You reply, "I cannot always say 'No': sometimes I must receive a benefit even against my will. Suppose I were given something by a cruel and easily offended tyrant, who would take it as an affront if his bounty were slighted? am I not to accept it? Suppose it were offered by a pirate, or a brigand, or a king of the temper of a pirate or brigand. What ought I to do? Such a man is not a worthy object for me to owe a benefit to." When I say that you ought to choose, I except *vis major* and fear, which destroy all power of choice. If you are free, if it lies with you to decide whether you will or not, then you will turn over in your own mind whether you will take a gift from a man or not; but if your position makes it impossible for you to choose, then be assured that you do not receive a gift, you merely obey orders. No one incurs any obligation by receiving what it was not in his power to refuse; if you want to know whether I wish to take it, arrange matters so that I have the power of saying "No." "Yet suppose he gave you your life." It does not matter what the gift was, unless it be given and received with good will: you are not my preserver because you have saved my life. Poison sometimes acts as a medicine, yet it is not on that account regarded as wholesome. Some things benefit us but put us under no obligation: for instance a man who intended to kill a tyrant, cut with his sword a tumour from which he suffered: yet the tyrant did not show him gratitude because by wounding him he had healed a disease which surgeons had feared to meddle with.

19

You see that the actual thing itself is not of much importance, because it is not regarded as a benefit at all, if you do good when you intended to do evil; in such a case the benefit is done by chance, the man did harm. I have seen a lion in the amphitheatre, who recognized one of the men who fought with wild beasts, who once had been his keeper, and protected him against the attacks of the other animals. Are we, then, to say that this assistance of the brute was a benefit? By no means, because it did not intend to do it, and did not do it with kindly intentions. You may class the lion and your tyrant together: each of them saved a man's life, yet neither conferred a benefit. Because it is not a benefit to be forced to receive one, neither is it a benefit to be under an obligation to a man to whom we do not wish to be indebted. You must first give me personal freedom of decision, and then your benefit.

20

The question has been raised, whether Marcus Brutus ought to have received his life from the hands of Julius Caesar, who, he had decided, ought to be put to death.

As to the grounds upon which he put him to death, I shall discuss them elsewhere; for to my mind, though he was in other respects a great man, in this he seems to have been entirely wrong, and not to have followed the maxims of the Stoic philosophy. He must either have feared the name of "King," although a state thrives best under a good king, or he must have hoped that liberty could exist in a state where some had so much to gain by reigning, and others had so much to gain by becoming slaves. Or, again, he must have supposed that it would be possible to restore the ancient constitution after all the ancient manners had been lost, and that citizens could continue to possess equal rights, or laws remain inviolate, in a state in which he had seen so many thousands of men fighting to decide, not whether they should be slaves or free, but which master they should serve. How forgetful he seems to have been, both of human nature and of the history of his own country, in supposing that when one despot was destroyed another of the same temper would not take his place, though, after so many kings had perished by lightning and the sword, a Tarquin was found to reign! Yet Brutus did right in receiving his life from Caesar, though he was not bound thereby to regard Caesar as his father, since it was by a wrong that Caesar had come to be in a position to bestow this benefit. A man does not save your life who does not kill you; nor does he confer a benefit, but merely gives you your discharge.[4]

21

It seems to offer more opportunity for debate to consider what a captive ought to do, if a man of abominable vices offers him the price of his ransom? Shall I permit myself to be saved by a wretch? When safe, what recompense can I make to him? Am I to live with an infamous person? Yet, am I not to live with my preserver? I will tell you my opinion. I would accept money, even from such a person, if it were to save my life; yet I would only accept it as a loan, not as a benefit. I would repay him the money, and if I were ever able to preserve him from danger I would do so. As for friendship, which can only exist between equals, I would not condescend to be such a man's friend; nor would I regard him as my preserver, but merely as a moneylender, to whom I am only bound to repay what I borrowed from him.

A man may be a worthy person for me to receive a benefit from, but it will hurt him to give it. For this reason I will not receive it, because he is ready to help me to his own prejudice, or even danger. Suppose that he is willing to plead for me in court, but by so doing will make the king his enemy. I should be his enemy, if, when he is willing to risk himself for me, if I were not to risk myself without him, which moreover is easier for me to do.

As an instance of this, Hecaton calls the case of Arcesilaus silly, and not to the purpose. Arcesilaus, he says, refused to receive a large sum of money which was offered to him by a son, lest the son should offend his penurious father. What did he do deserving of praise, in not receiving stolen goods, in choosing not to receive

---

[4] The "discharge" alluded to is that which was granted to the beaten one of a pair of gladiators, when their duel was not to the death.

them, instead of returning them? What proof of self-restraint is there in refusing to receive another man's property? If you want an instance of magnanimity, take the case of Julius Graecinus, whom Caius Caesar put to death merely on the ground that he was a better man than it suited a tyrant for anyone to be. This man, when he was receiving subscriptions from many of his friends to cover his expenses in exhibiting public games, would not receive a large sum which was sent him by Fabius Persicus; and when he was blamed for rejecting it by those who think more of what is given than of who gives it, he answered, "Am I to accept a present from a man when I would not accept his offer to drink a glass of wine with him?"

A consular named Rebilius, a man of equally bad character, sent a yet larger sum to Graecinus, and pressed him to receive it. "I must beg," answered he, "that you will excuse me. I did not take money from Persicus either." Ought we to call this receiving presents, or rather taking one's pick of the senate?

22

When we have decided to accept, let us accept with cheerfulness, showing pleasure, and letting the giver see it, so that he may at once receive some return for his goodness: for as it is a good reason for rejoicing to see our friend happy, it is a better one to have made him so. Let us, therefore, show how acceptable a gift is by loudly expressing our gratitude for it; and let us do so, not only in the hearing of the giver, but everywhere. He who receives a benefit with gratitude, repays the first instalment of it.

23

There are some, who only like to receive benefits privately: they dislike having any witnesses and confidants. Such men, we may believe, have no good intentions. As a giver is justified in dwelling upon those qualities of his gift which will please the receiver, so a man, when he receives, should do so publicly; you should not take from a man what you are ashamed to owe him. Some return thanks to one stealthily, in a corner, in a whisper. This is not modesty, but a kind of denying of the debt: it is the part of an ungrateful man not to express his gratitude before witnesses. Some object to any accounts being kept between them and their benefactors, and wish no brokers to be employed or witnesses to be called, but merely to give their own signature to a receipt. Those men do the like, who take care to let as few persons as possible know of the benefits which they have received. They fear to receive them in public, in order that their success may be attributed rather to their own talents than to the help of others: they are very seldom to be found in attendance upon those to whom they owe their lives and their fortunes, and thus, while avoiding the imputation of servility, they incur that of ingratitude.

24

Some men speak in the most offensive terms of those to whom they owe most. There are men whom it is safer to affront than to serve, for their dislike leads them to assume the airs of persons who are not indebted to us: although nothing more is expected of them than that they should remember what they owe us, refreshing their memory from time to time, because no one can be grateful who forgets a kindness, and he who remembers it, by so doing proves his gratitude. We ought neither to receive benefits with a fastidious air, nor yet with a slavish humility: for if a man does not care for a benefit when it is freshly bestowed—a time at which all presents please us most—what will he do when its first charms have gone off? Others receive with an air of disdain, as much as to say. "I do not want it; but as you wish it so very much, I will allow you to give it to me." Others take benefits languidly, and leave the giver in doubt as to whether they know that they have received them; others barely open their lips in thanks, and would be less offensive if they said nothing. One ought to proportion one's thanks to the importance of the benefit received, and to use the phrases, "You have laid more of us than you think under an obligation," for everyone likes to find his good actions extend further than he expected. "You do not know what it is that you have done for me; but you ought to know how much more important it is than you imagine." It is in itself an expression of gratitude to speak of oneself as overwhelmed by kindness; or "I shall never be able to thank you sufficiently; but, at any rate, I will never cease to express everywhere my inability to thank you."

25

By nothing did Furnius gain greater credit with Augustus, and make it easy for him to obtain anything else for which he might ask, than by merely saying, when at his request Augustus pardoned his father for having taken Antonius's side, "One wrong alone I have received at your hands, Caesar; you have forced me to live and to die owing you a greater debt of gratitude than I can ever repay." What can prove gratitude so well as that a man should never be satisfied, should never even entertain the hope of making any adequate return for what he has received? By these and similar expressions we must try not to conceal our gratitude, but to display it as clearly as possible. No words need be used; if we only feel as we ought, our thankfulness will be shown in our countenances. He who intends to be grateful, let him think how he shall repay a kindness while he is receiving it. Chrysippus says that such a man must watch for his opportunity, and spring forward whenever it offers, like one who has been entered for a race, and who stands at the starting-point waiting for the barriers to be thrown open; and even then he must use great exertions and great swiftness to catch the other, who has a start of him.

26

We must now consider what is the main cause of ingratitude. It is caused by excessive self-esteem, by that fault innate in all mortals, of taking a partial view of ourselves and our own acts, by greed, or by jealousy.

Let us begin with the first of these. Everyone is prejudiced in his own favour, from which it follows that he believes himself to have earned all that he receives, regards it as payment for his services, and does not think that he has been appraised at a valuation sufficiently near his own. "He has given me this," says he, "but how late, after how much toil? how much more might I have earned if I had attached myself to So and so, or to So and so? I did not expect this; I have been treated like one of the herd; did he really think that I only deserved so little? why, it would have been less insulting to have passed me over altogether."

27

The augur Cnaeus Lentulus, who, before his freedmen reduced him to poverty, was one of the richest of men, who saw himself in possession of a fortune of four hundred millions—I say advisedly, "saw," for he never did more than see it—was as barren and contemptible in intellect as he was in spirit. Though very avaricious, yet he was so poor a speaker that he found it easier to give men coins than words. This man, who owed all his prosperity to the late Emperor Augustus, to whom he had brought only poverty, encumbered with a noble name, when he had risen to be the chief man in Rome, both in wealth and influence, used sometimes to complain that Augustus had interrupted his legal studies, observing that he had not received anything like what he had lost by giving up the study of eloquence. Yet the truth was that Augustus, besides loading him with other gifts, had set him free from the necessity of making himself ridiculous by labouring at a profession in which he never could succeed.

Greed does not permit anyone to be grateful; for what is given is never equal to its base desires, and the more we receive the more we covet, for avarice is much more eager when it has to deal with great accumulations of wealth, just as the power of a flame is enormously greater in proportion to the size of the conflagration from which it springs. Ambition in like manner suffers no man to rest satisfied with that measure of public honours, to gain which was once the limit of his wildest hope; no one is thankful for becoming tribune, but grumbles at not being at once promoted to the post of praetor; nor is he grateful for this if the consulship does not follow; and even this does not satisfy him if he be consul but once. His greed ever stretches itself out further, and he does not understand the greatness of his success because he always looks forward to the point at which he aims, and never back towards that from which he started.

28

A more violent and distressing vice than any of these is jealousy which disturbs us by suggesting comparisons. "He gave me this, but he gave more to that man, and he gave it to him before me;" after which he sympathises with no one, but pushes his own claims to the prejudice of everyone else. How much more straightforward and modest is it to make the most of what we have received, knowing that no man is valued so highly by anyone else as by his own self! "I ought to have received more, but it was not easy for him to give more; he was obliged to distribute his liberality among many persons. This is only the beginning; let me be contented, and by my gratitude encourage him to show me more favour; he has not done as much as he ought, but he will do so the more frequently; he certainly preferred that man to me, but he has preferred me before many others; that man is not my equal either in virtue or in services, but he has some charm of his own: by complaining I shall not make myself deserve to receive more, but shall become unworthy of what I have received. More has been given to those most villainous men than has been given to me; well, what is that to the purpose? how seldom does Fortune show judgment in her choice? We complain every day of the success of bad men; very often the hail passes over the estates of the greatest villains and strikes down the crops of the best of men; every man has to take his chance, in friendship as well as in everything else." There is no benefit so great that spitefulness can pick no holes in it, none so paltry that it cannot be made more of by friendly interpretation. We shall never want a subject for complaint if we look at benefits on their wrong side.

29

See how unjustly the gifts of heaven are valued even by some who profess themselves philosophers, who complain that we are not as big as elephants, as swift as stags, as light as birds, as strong as bulls; that the skins of seals are stronger, of hinds prettier, of bears thicker, of beavers softer than ours; that dogs excel us in delicacy of scent, eagles in keenness of sight, crows in length of days, and many beasts in ease of swimming. And although nature itself does not allow some qualities, as for example strength and swiftness, to be combined in the same person, yet they call it a monstrous thing that men are not compounded of different and inconsistent good qualities, and call the gods neglectful of us because we have not been given health which even our vices cannot destroy, or knowledge of the future. They scarcely refrain from rising to such a pitch of impudence as to hate nature because we are below the gods, and not on an equality with them. How much better is it to turn to the contemplation of so many great blessings, and to be thankful that the gods have been pleased to give us a place second only to themselves in this most beautiful abode, and that they have appointed us to be the lords of the Earth! Can anyone compare us with the animals over whom we rule? Nothing has been denied us except what could not have been granted. In like manner, thou that takest an unfair view of the lot of mankind, think what blessings our Father has bestowed upon us, how far more powerful animals than ourselves we have broken to harness, how we catch those which are far swifter, how nothing that has life is placed beyond the reach of our weapons! We have received so many excellencies, so many crafts, above all our mind, which can pierce at once whatever it is directed against, which is swifter than the stars in their courses, for it arrives before them at the place which they will reach after many ages; and besides this, so many fruits of the earth, so much treasure, such masses of various things piled one upon another. You may go through the whole order of nature, and since you find no entire creature which you would prefer to be, you may choose from each, the special qualities which you would like to be given to yourself; then, if you rightly appreciate the partiality of nature for you, you cannot but confess yourself to be her spoiled child. So it is; the immortal gods have unto this day always held us most dear, and have bestowed upon us the greatest possible honour, a place nearest to themselves. We have indeed received great things, yet not too great.

30

I have thought it necessary, my friend Liberalis, to state these facts, both because when speaking of small benefits one ought to make some mention of the greatest, and because also this shameless and hateful vice (of ingratitude), starting with these, transfers itself from them to all the rest. If a man scorn these, the greatest of all benefits, to whom will he feel gratitude, what gift will he regard as valuable or deserving to be returned: to whom will he be grateful for his safety or his life, if he denies that he has received from the gods that existence which he begs from them daily? He, therefore, who teaches men to be grateful, pleads the cause not only of men, but even of the gods, for though they, being placed above all desires, cannot be in want of anything, yet we can nevertheless offer them our gratitude.

No one is justified in seeking an excuse for ingratitude in his own weakness or poverty, or in saying, "What am I to do, and how? When can I repay my debt to my superiors the lords of heaven and earth?" Avaricious as you are, it is easy for you to give them thanks, without expense; lazy though you be, you can do it without labour. At the same instant at which you received your debt towards them, if you wish to repay it, you have done as much as anyone can do, for he returns a benefit who receives it with good will.

31

This paradox of the Stoic philosophy, that he returns a benefit who receives it with good will, is, in my opinion, either far from admirable, or else it is incredible. For if we look at everything merely from the point of view of our intentions, every man has done as much as he chose to do; and since filial piety, good faith, justice, and in short every virtue is complete within itself, a man may be grateful in intention even though he may not be able to lift a hand to prove his gratitude. Whenever a man obtains what he aimed at, he receives the fruit of his labour. When a man bestows a benefit, at what does he aim? clearly to be of service and afford pleasure to him upon whom he bestows it. If he does what he wishes, if his purpose reaches me and fills us each with joy, he has gained his object. He does not wish anything to be given to him in return, or else it becomes an exchange of commodities, not a bestowal of benefits. A man steers well who reaches the port for which he started: a dart hurled by a steady hand performs its duty if it hits the mark; one who bestows a benefit wishes it to be received with gratitude; he gets what he wanted if it be well received. "But," you say, "he hoped for some profit also." Then it was not a benefit, the property of which is to think nothing of any repayment. I receive what was given me in the same spirit in which it was given: then I have repaid it. If this be not true, then this best of deeds has this worst of conditions attached to it, that it depends entirely upon fortune whether I am grateful or not, for if my fortune is adverse I can make no repayment. The intention is enough. "What then? am I not to do whatever I may be able to repay it, and ought I not ever to be on the watch for an opportunity of filling the bosom[5] of him from whom I have received any kindness? True; but a benefit is in an evil plight if we cannot be grateful for it even when we are empty-handed.

32

"A man," it is argued, "who has received a benefit, however gratefully he may have received it, has not yet accomplished all his duty, for there remains the part of repayment; just as in playing at ball it is something to catch the ball cleverly and carefully, but a man is not called a good player unless he can handily and quickly send back the ball which he has caught." This analogy is imperfect; and why? Because to do this creditably depends upon the movement and activity of the body, and not upon the mind: and an act of which we judge entirely by the eye, ought to be all clearly displayed. But if a man caught the ball as he ought to do, I should not call him a bad player for not returning it, if his delay in returning it was not caused by his own fault. "Yet," say you, "although the player is not wanting in skill, because he did one part of his duty, and was able to do the other part, yet in such a case the game is imperfect, for its perfection lies in sending the ball backwards and forwards." I am unwilling to expose this fallacy further; let us think that it is the game, not the player that is imperfect: so likewise in the subject which we are discussing, the thing which is given lacks something, because another equal thing ought to be returned for it,

---

[5] *Sinus*, the fold of the toga over the breast, used as a pocket by the Romans. The great French actor Talma, when dressed for the first time in correct classical costume, indignantly asked where he was to put his snuffbox.

but the mind of the giver lacks nothing, because it has found another mind equal to itself, and as far as intentions go, has effected what it wished.

33

A man bestows a benefit upon me: I receive it just as he wished it to be received: then he gets at once what he wanted, and the only thing which he wanted, and therefore I have proved myself grateful. After this it remains for me to enjoy my own resources, with the addition of an advantage conferred upon me by one whom I have obliged; this advantage is not the remainder of an imperfect service, but an addition to a perfected service.[6] For example, Phidias makes a statue. Now the product of an art is one thing, and that of a trade is another. It is the business of the art to make the thing which he wished to make, and that of the trade to make it with a profit. Phidias has completed his work, even though he does not sell it. The product, therefore, of his work is threefold: there is the consciousness of having made it, which he receives when his work is completed; there is the fame which he receives; and thirdly, the advantage which he obtains by it, in influence, or by selling it, or otherwise. In like manner the first fruit of a benefit is the consciousness of it, which we feel when we have bestowed it upon the person whom we chose; secondly and thirdly there is the credit which we gain by doing so, and there are those things which we may receive in exchange for it. So when a benefit has been graciously received, the giver has already received gratitude, but has not yet received recompense for it: that which we owe in return is therefore something apart from the benefit itself, for we have paid for the benefit itself when we accept it in a grateful spirit.

34

"What," say you, "can a man repay a benefit, though he does nothing?" He has taken the first step, he has offered you a good thing with good feeling, and, which is the characteristic of friendship, has placed you both on the same footing. In the next place, a benefit is not repaid in the same manner as a loan: you have no reason for expecting me to offer you any payment; the account between us depends upon the feelings alone. What I say will not appear difficult, although it may not at first accord with your ideas, if you will do me the favour to remember that there are more things than there are words to express them. There is an enormous mass of things without names, which we do not speak of under distinctive names of their own, but by the names of other things transferred to them. We speak of our own foot, of the foot of a couch, of a sail, or of a poem; we apply the word "dog" to a hound, a fish, and a star. Because we have not enough words to assign a separate name to each thing, we

---

[6] Nothing is wanted to make a benefit, conferred from good motives, perfect: if it is returned, the gratitude is to be counted as net profit.

borrow a name whenever we want one. Bravery is the virtue which rightly despises danger, or the science of repelling, sustaining, or inviting dangers: yet we call a brave man a gladiator, and we use the same word for a good-for-nothing slave, who is led by rashness to defy death. Economy is the science of avoiding unnecessary expenditure, or the art of using one's income with moderation: yet we call a man of mean and narrow mind, most economical, although there is an immeasurable distance between moderation and meanness. These things are naturally distinct, yet the poverty of our language compels us to call both these men economical, just as he who views slight accidents with rational contempt, and he who without reason runs into danger are alike called brave. Thus a benefit is both a beneficent action, and also is that which is bestowed by that action, such as money, a house, an office in the State: there is but one name for them both, though their force and power are widely different.

35

Wherefore, give me your attention, and you will soon perceive that I say nothing to which you can object. That benefit which consists of the action is repaid when we receive it graciously; that other, which consists of something material, we have not then repaid, but we hope to do so. The debt of goodwill has been discharged by a return of goodwill; the material debt demands a material return. Thus, although we may declare that he who has received a benefit with goodwill has returned the favour, yet we counsel him to return to the giver something of the same kind as that which he has received. Some part of what we have said departs from the conventional line of thought, and then rejoins it by another path. We declare that a wise man cannot receive an injury; yet, if a man hits him with his fist, that man will be found guilty of doing him an injury. We declare that a fool can possess nothing; yet if a man stole anything from a fool, we should find that man guilty of theft. We declare that all men are mad, yet we do not dose all men with hellebore; but we put into the hands of these very persons, whom we call madmen, both the right of voting and of pronouncing judgment. Similarly, we say that a man who has received a benefit with goodwill has returned the favour, yet we leave him in debt nevertheless—bound to repay it even though he has repaid it. This is not to disown benefits, but is an encouragement to us neither to fear to receive benefits, nor to faint under the too great burden of them. "Good things have been given to me; I have been preserved from starving; I have been saved from the misery of abject poverty; my life, and what is dearer than life, my liberty, has been preserved. How shall I be able to repay these favours? When will the day come upon which I can prove my gratitude to him?" When a man speaks thus, the day has already come. Receive a benefit, embrace it, rejoice, not that you have received it, but that you have to owe it and return it; then you will never be in peril of the great sin of being rendered ungrateful by mischance. I will not enumerate any difficulties to you, lest you should despair, and faint at the prospect of a long and laborious servitude. I do not refer you to the future; do it with what means you have at hand. You never will be grateful unless you are so straightaway. What, then, will you do? You need not take up arms, yet perhaps you may have to do so; you need not cross the seas, yet it may be that you will pay your debt, even when the wind threatens to blow a gale. Do you wish to return the benefit? Then receive it graciously; you have then returned the favour—not, indeed, so that you can think yourself to have repaid it, but so that you can owe it with a quieter conscience.

BOOK 3

1

Not to return gratitude for benefits, my Æbutius Liberalis, is both base in itself, and is thought base by all men; wherefore even ungrateful men complain of ingratitude, and yet what all condemn is at the same time rooted in all; and so far do men sometimes run into the other extreme that some of them become our bitterest enemies, not merely after receiving benefits from us, but because they have received them. I cannot deny that some do this out of sheer badness of nature; but more do so because lapse of time destroys their remembrance, for time gradually effaces what they felt vividly at the moment. I remember having had an argument with you about this class of persons, whom you wished to call forgetful rather than ungrateful, as if that which caused a man to be ungrateful was any excuse for his being so, or as if the fact of this happening to a man prevented his being ungrateful, when we know that it only happens to ungrateful men. There are many classes of the ungrateful, as there are of thieves or of homicides, who all have the same fault, though there is a great variety in its various forms. The man is ungrateful who denies that he has received a benefit; who pretends that he has not received it; who does not return it. The most ungrateful man of all is he who forgets it. The others, though they do not repay it, yet feel their debt, and possess some traces of worth, though obstructed by their bad conscience. They may by some means and at some time be brought to show their gratitude, if, for instance, they be pricked by shame, if they conceive some noble ambition such as occasionally rises even in the breasts of the wicked, if some easy opportunity of doing so offers; but the man from whom all recollection of the benefit has passed away can never become grateful. Which of the two do you call the worse—he who is ungrateful for kindness, or he who does not even remember it? The eyes which fear to look at the light are diseased, but those which cannot see it are blind. It is filial impiety not to love one's parents, but not to recognise them is madness.

2

Who is so ungrateful as he who has so completely laid aside and cast away that which ought to be in the forefront of his mind and ever before him, that he knows it not? It is clear that if forgetfulness of a benefit steals over a man, he cannot have often thought about repaying it.

In short, repayment requires gratitude, time, opportunity, and the help of fortune; whereas, he who remembers a benefit is grateful for it, and that too without expenditure. Since gratitude demands neither labour, wealth, nor good fortune, he who fails to render it has no excuse behind which to shelter himself; for he who places a benefit so far away that it is out of his sight, never could have meant to be grateful for it. Just as those tools which are kept in use, and are daily touched by the hand, are never in danger of growing rusty, while those which are not brought before our eyes, and lie as if superfluous, not being required for common use, collect dirt by the mere lapse of time, so likewise that which our thoughts frequently turn over and renew never passes from our memory, which only loses those things to which it seldom directs its eyes.

3

Besides this, there are other causes which at times erase the greatest services from our minds. The first and most powerful of these is that, being always intent upon new objects of desire, we think, not of what we have, but of what we are striving to obtain. Those whose mind is fixed entirely upon what they hope to gain, regard with contempt all that is their own already. It follows that since men's eagerness for something new makes them undervalue whatever they have received, they do not esteem those from whom they have received it. As long as we are satisfied with the position we have gained, we love our benefactor, we look up to him, and declare that we owe our position entirely to him; then we begin to entertain other aspirations, and hurry forward to attain them after the manner of human beings, who when they have gained much always covet more; straightaway all that we used to regard as benefits slip from our memory, and we no longer consider the advantages which we enjoy over others, but only the insolent prosperity of those who have outstripped us. Now no one can at the same time be both jealous and grateful, because those who are jealous are querulous and sad, while the grateful are joyous. In the next place, since none of us think of any time but the present, and but few turn back their thoughts to the past, it results that we forget our teachers, and all the benefits which we have obtained from them, because we have altogether left our childhood behind us: thus, all that was done for us in our youth perishes unremembered, because our youth itself is never reviewed. What has been is regarded by everyone, not only as past, but as gone; and for the same reason, our memory is weak for what is about to happen in the future.

4

Here I must do Epicurus the justice to say that he constantly complains of our ingratitude for past benefits, because we cannot bring back again, or count among our present pleasures, those good things which we have received long ago, although no pleasures can be more undeniable than those which cannot be taken from us. Present good is not yet altogether complete, some mischance may interrupt it; the future is in suspense, and uncertain; but what is past is laid up in safety. How can any man feel gratitude for benefits, if he skips through his whole life entirely engrossed with the present and the future? It is remembrance that makes men grateful; and the more men hope, the less they remember.

5

In the same way, my Liberalis, as some things remain in our memory as soon as they are learned, while to know others it is not enough to have learned them, for our knowledge slips away from us unless it be kept up—I allude to geometry and astronomy, and such other sciences as are hard to remember because of their intricacy—so the greatness of some benefits prevents their being forgotten, while others, individually less, though many more in number, and bestowed at different times, pass from our minds, because, as I have stated above, we do not constantly think about them, and do not willingly recognize how much we owe to each of our benefactors. Listen to the words of those who ask for favours. There is not one of them who does not declare that his remembrance will be eternal, who does not vow himself your devoted servant and slave, or find, if he can, some even greater expression of humility with which to pledge himself. After a brief space of time these same men avoid their former expressions, thinking them abject, and scarcely befitting freeborn men; afterwards they arrive at the same point to which, as I suppose, the worst and most ungrateful of men come—that is, they forget. So little does forgetfulness excuse ingratitude, that even the remembrance of a benefit may leave us ungrateful.

6

The question has been raised, whether this most odious vice ought to go unpunished; and whether the law commonly made use of in the schools, by which we can proceed against a man for ingratitude, ought to be adopted by the State also, since all men agree that it is just. "Why not?" you may say, "seeing that even cities cast in each other's teeth the services which they have performed to one another, and demand from the children some return for benefits conferred upon their fathers?" On the other hand, our ancestors, who were most admirable men, made demands upon their enemies alone, and both gave and lost their benefits with magnanimity. With the exception of Macedonia, no nation has ever established an action at law for ingratitude. And this is a strong argument against its being established, because all agree in blaming crime; and homicide, poisoning, parricide, and sacrilege are visited with different penalties in different countries, but everywhere with some penalty; whereas this most common vice is nowhere punished, though it is everywhere blamed. We do not acquit it; but as it would be most difficult to reckon accurately the penalty for so varying a matter, we condemn it only to be hated, and place it upon the list of those crimes which we refer for judgment to the gods.

7

Many arguments occur to me which prove that this vice ought not to come under the action of the law. First of all, the best part of a benefit is lost if the benefit can be sued for at law, as in the case of a loan, or of letting and hiring. Indeed, the finest part of a benefit is that we have given it without considering whether we shall lose it or not, that we have left all this to the free choice of him who receives it: if I call him before a judge, it begins to be not a benefit, but a loan. Next, though it is a most honourable thing to show gratitude, it ceases to be honourable if it be forced, for in that case no one will praise a grateful man any more than he praises him who restores the money which was deposited in his keeping, or who pays what he borrowed without the intervention of a judge. We should therefore spoil the two finest things in human life—a grateful man and a beneficent man; for what is there admirable in one who does not give but merely lends a benefit, or in one who repays it, not because he wishes, but because he is forced to do so? There is no credit in being grateful, unless it is safe to be ungrateful. Besides this, all the courts would hardly be enough for the action of this one law. Who would not plead under it? Who would not be pleaded against? for everyone exalts his own merits, everyone magnifies even the smallest matters which he has bestowed upon another. Besides this, those things which form the subject of a judicial inquiry can be distinctly defined, and cannot afford unlimited licence to the judge; wherefore a good cause is in a better position if it be tried before a judge than before an arbitrator, because the words of the law tie down a judge and define certain limits beyond which he may not pass, whereas the conscience of an arbitrator is free and not fettered by any rules, so that he can either give or take away, and can arrange his decision, not according to the precepts of law and justice, but just as his own kindly feeling or compassion may prompt him. An action for ingratitude would not bind a judge, but would place him in the position of an autocrat. It cannot be known what or how great a benefit is; all that would be really important would be, how indulgently the judge might interpret it. No law defines an ungrateful person, often, indeed, one who repays what he has received is ungrateful, and one who has not returned it is grateful. Even an unpractised judge can give his vote upon some matters; for instance, when the thing to be determined is whether something has or has not been done, when a dispute is terminated by the parties giving written bonds, or when the casting up of accounts decides between the disputants. When, however, motives have to be guessed at, when matters upon which wisdom alone can decide, are brought into court, they cannot be tried by a judge taken at random from the list of "select judges,"[7] whom property and the inheritance of an equestrian fortune[8] has placed upon the roll.

8

Ingratitude, therefore, is not only matter unfit to be brought into court, but no judge could be found fit to try it; and this you will not be surprised at, if you examine the difficulties of anyone who should attempt to prosecute a man upon such a charge. One man may have given a large sum of money, but he is rich and would not feel it; another may have given it at the cost of his entire inheritance. The sum given is the same in each case, but the benefit conferred is not the same. Add another instance: suppose that to redeem a debtor from slavery one man paid money from his own private means, while another man paid the same sum, but had to borrow it or beg for it, and allow himself to be laid under a great obligation to someone; would you rank the man who so easily bestowed his benefit on an equality with him who was obliged to receive a benefit himself before he could bestow it? Some benefits are great, not because of their amount, but because of the time at which they are bestowed; it is a benefit to give an estate whose fertility can bring down the price of corn, and it is a benefit to give a loaf of bread in time of famine; it is a benefit to give provinces through which flow vast navigable rivers, and it is a benefit, when men are parched with thirst, and can scarcely draw breath through their dry throats, to show them a spring of water. Who will compare these cases with one another, or weigh one against the other? It is hard to give a decision when it is not the thing given, but its meaning, which has to be considered; though what is given is the same, yet if it be given under different circumstances it has a different value. A man may have bestowed a benefit upon me, but unwillingly; he may have complained of having given it; he may have looked at me with greater haughtiness than he was wont to do; he may have been so slow in giving it, that he would have done me a greater service if he had promptly refused it. How could a judge estimate the value of these things, when words, hesitation, or looks can destroy all their claim to gratitude?

9

What, again, could he do, seeing that some things are called benefits because they are unduly coveted, whilst others are not benefits at all, according to this common

---

[7] See Smith's *Dictionary of Antiquities*, s.v.
[8] 400,000 sesterces.

valuation, yet are of even greater value, though not so showy? You call it a benefit to cause a man to be adopted as a member of a powerful city, to get him enrolled among the knights, or to defend one who is being tried for his life: what do you say of him who gives useful advice? of him who holds you back when you would rush into crime? of him who strikes the sword from the hands of the suicide? of him who by his power of consolation brings back to the duties of life one who was plunged in grief, and eager to follow those whom he had lost? of him who sits at the bedside of the sick man, and who, when health and recovery depend upon seizing the right moment, administers food in due season, stimulates the failing veins with wine, or calls in the physician to the dying man? Who can estimate the value of such services as these? who can bid us weigh dissimilar benefits one with another? "I gave you a house," says one. Yes, but I forewarned you that your own house would come down upon your head. "I gave you an estate," says he. True, but I gave a plank to you when shipwrecked. "I fought for you and received wounds for you," says another. But I saved your life by keeping silence. Since a benefit is both given and returned differently by different people, it is hard to make them balance.

10

Besides this, no day is appointed for repayment of a benefit, as there is for borrowed money; consequently he who has not yet repaid a benefit may do so hereafter: for tell me, pray, within what time a man is to be declared ungrateful? The greatest benefits cannot be proved by evidence; they often lurk in the silent consciousness of two men only; are we to introduce the rule of not bestowing benefits without witnesses? Next, what punishment are we to appoint for the ungrateful? is there to be one only for all, though the benefits which they have received are different? or should the punishment be varying, greater or less according to the benefit which each has received? Are our valuations to be restricted to pecuniary fines? what are we to do, seeing that in some cases the benefit conferred is life, and things dearer than life? What punishment is to be assigned to ingratitude for these? One less than the benefit? That would be unjust. One equal to it; death? What could be more inhuman than to cause benefits to result in cruelty?

11

It may be argued, "Parents have certain privileges: these are regarded as exempt from the action of ordinary rules, and so also ought to be the case with other beneficent persons." Nay; mankind has assigned a peculiar sanctity to the position of parents, because it was advantageous that children should be reared, and people had to be tempted into undergoing the toil of doing so, because the issue of their experiment was doubtful. One cannot say to them, as one does to others who bestow benefits, "Choose the man to whom you give: you must only blame yourself if you are deceived; help the deserving." In rearing children nothing depends upon the judgment of those who rear them; it is a matter of hope: in order, therefore, that people may be more willing to embark upon this lottery, it was right that they should be given a certain authority; and since it is useful for youth to be governed, we have placed their parents in the position of domestic magistrates, under whose guardianship their lives may be ruled. Moreover, the position of parents differs from that of other benefactors, for their having given formerly to their children does not stand in the way of their giving now and hereafter; and also, there is no fear of their falsely asserting that they have given: with others one has to inquire not only whether they have received, but whether they have given; but the good deeds of parents are placed beyond doubt. In the next place, one benefit bestowed by parents is the same for all, and might be counted once for all; while the others which they bestow are of various kinds, unlike one to another, differing from one another by the widest possible intervals; they can therefore come under no regular rule, since it would be more just to leave them all unrewarded than to give the same reward to all.

12

Some benefits cost much to the givers, some are of much value to the receivers but cost the givers nothing. Some are bestowed upon friends, others on strangers: now although that which is given be the same, yet it becomes more when it is given to one with whom you are beginning to be acquainted through the benefits which you have previously conferred upon him. One man may give us help, another distinctions, a third consolation. You may find one who thinks nothing pleasanter or more important than to have someone to save him from distress; you may again find one who would rather be helped to great place than to security; while some consider themselves more indebted to those who save their lives than to those who save their honour. Each of these services will be held more or less important, according as the disposition of our judge inclines to one or the other of them. Besides this, I choose my creditors for myself, whereas I often receive benefits from those from whom I would not, and sometimes I am laid under an obligation without my knowledge. What will you do in such a case? When a man has received a benefit unknown to himself, and which, had he known of it, he would have refused to receive, will you call him ungrateful if he does not repay it, however he may have received it? Suppose that someone has bestowed a benefit upon me, and that the same man has afterwards done me some wrong; am I to be bound by his one bounty to endure with patience any wrong that he may do me, or will it be the same as if I had repaid it, because he himself has by the subsequent wrong cancelled his own benefit? How, in that case, would you decide which was the greater; the present which the man has received, or the injury which has been done him? Time would fail me if I attempted to discuss all the difficulties which would arise.

13

It may be argued that "we render men less willing to confer benefits by not supporting the claim of those which have been bestowed to meet with gratitude, and by not punishing those who repudiate them." But you would find, on the other hand, that men would be far less willing to receive benefits, if by so doing they were likely to incur the danger of having to plead their cause in court, and having more difficulty in proving their integrity. This legislation would also render us less willing to give: for no one is willing to give to those who are unwilling to receive, but one who is urged to acts of kindness by his own good nature and by the beauty of charity, will give all the more freely to those who need make no return unless they choose. It impairs the credit of doing a service, if in doing it we are carefully protected from loss.

14

"Benefits, then, will be fewer, but more genuine: well, what harm is there in restricting people from giving recklessly?" Even those who would have no legislation upon the subject follow this rule, that we ought to be somewhat careful in giving, and in choosing those upon whom we bestow favours. Reflect over and over again to whom you are giving: you will have no remedy at law, no means of enforcing repayment. You are mistaken if you suppose that the judge will assist you: no law will make full restitution to you, you must look only to the honour of the receiver. Thus only can benefits retain their influence, and thus only are they admirable: you dishonour them if you make them the grounds of litigation. "Pay what you owe" is a most just proverb; and one which carries with it the sanction of all nations; but in dealing with benefits it is most shameful. "Pay!" How is a man to pay who owes his life, his position, his safety, or his reason to another? None of the greatest benefits can be repaid. "Yet," it is said, "you ought to give in return for them something of equal value." This is just what I have been saying, that the grandeur of the act is ruined if we make our benefits commercial transactions. We ought not to encourage ourselves in avarice, in discontent, or in quarrels; the human mind is prone enough to these by nature. As far as we are able, let us check it, and cut off the opportunities for which it seeks.

15

Would that we could indeed persuade men to receive back money which they have lent from those debtors only who are willing to pay! would that no agreement ever bound the buyer to the seller, and that their interests were not protected by sealed covenants and agreements, but rather by honour and a sense of justice! However, men prefer what is needful to what is truly best, and choose rather to force their creditors to keep faith with them than to trust that they will do so. Witnesses are called on both sides; the one, by calling in brokers, makes several names appear in his accounts as his debtors instead of one; the other is not content with the legal forms of question and answer unless he holds the other party by the hand. What a shameful admission of the dishonesty and wickedness of mankind! men trust more to our signet-rings than to our intentions. For what are these respectable men summoned? for what do they impress their seals? it is in order that the borrower may not deny that he has received what he has received. You regard these men, I suppose, as above bribes, as maintainers of the truth: well, these very men will not be entrusted with money except on the same terms. Would it not, then, be more honourable to be deceived by some than to suspect all men of dishonesty? To fill up the measure of avarice one thing only is lacking, that we should bestow no benefit without a surety. To help, to be of service, is the part of a generous and noble mind; he who gives acts like a god, he who demands repayment acts like a moneylender. Why then, by trying to protect the rights of the former class, should we reduce them to the level of the basest of mankind?

16

"More men," our opponent argues, "will be ungrateful, if no legal remedy exists against ingratitude." Nay, fewer, because then benefits will be bestowed with more discrimination. In the next place, it is not advisable that it should be publicly known how many ungrateful men there are: for the number of sinners will do away with the disgrace of the sin, and a reproach which applies to all men will cease to be dishonourable. Is any woman ashamed of being divorced, now that some noble ladies reckon the years of their lives, not by the number of the consuls, but by that of their husbands, now that they leave their homes in order to marry others, and marry only in order to be divorced? Divorce was only dreaded as long as it was unusual; now that no gazette appears without it, women learn to do what they hear so much about. Can anyone feel ashamed of adultery, now that things have come to such a pass that no woman keeps a husband at all unless it be to pique her lover? Chastity merely implies ugliness. Where will you find any woman so abject, so repulsive, as to be satisfied with a single pair of lovers, without having a different one for each hour of the day; nor is the day long enough for all of them, unless she has taken her airing in the grounds of one, and passes the night with another. A woman is frumpish and old-fashioned if she does not know that "adultery with one paramour is nicknamed marriage." Just as all shame at these vices has disappeared since the vice itself became so widely spread, so if you made the ungrateful begin to count their own numbers, you would both make them more numerous, and enable them to be ungrateful with greater impunity.

17

"What then? shall the ungrateful man go unpunished?" What then, I answer, shall we punish the undutiful, the malicious, the avaricious, the headstrong, and the cruel? Do you imagine that those things which are loathed are not punished, or do you suppose that any punishment is greater than the hate of all men? It is a punishment not to dare receive a benefit from anyone, not to dare to bestow one, to be, or to fancy that you are a mark for all men's eyes, and to lose all appreciation of so excellent and pleasant a matter. Do you call a man unhappy who has lost his sight, or whose hearing has been impaired by disease, and do you not call him wretched who has lost the power of feeling benefits? He fears the gods, the witnesses of all ingratitude; he is tortured by the thought of the benefit which he has misapplied, and, in fine, he is sufficiently punished by this great penalty, that, as I said before, he cannot enjoy the fruits of this most delightful act. On the other hand, he who takes pleasure in receiving a benefit, enjoys an unvarying and continuous happiness, which he derives from consideration, not of the thing given, but of the intention of the giver. A benefit gives perpetual joy to a grateful man, but pleases an ungrateful one only for a moment. Can the lives of such men be compared, seeing that the one is sad and gloomy—as it is natural that a denier of his debts and a defrauder should be, a man who does not give his parents, his nurses, or his teachers the honour which is their due—while the other is joyous, cheerful, on the watch for an opportunity of proving his gratitude, and gaining much pleasure from this frame of mind itself? Such a man has no wish to become bankrupt, but only to make the fullest and most copious return for benefits, and that not only to parents and friends, but also to more humble persons; for even if he receives a benefit from his own slave, he does not consider from whom he receives it, but what he receives.

18

It has, however, been doubted by Hecaton and some other writers, whether a slave can bestow a benefit upon his master. Some distinguish between benefits, duties, and services, calling those things benefits which are bestowed by a stranger—that is, by one who could discontinue them without blame—while duties are performed by our children, our wives, and those whom relationship prompts and orders to afford us help; and, thirdly, services are performed by slaves, whose position is such that nothing which they do for their master can give them any claim upon him. ...

Besides this, he who affirms that a slave does not sometimes confer a benefit upon his master is ignorant of the rights of man; for the question is, not what the station in life of the giver may be, but what his intentions are. The path of virtue is closed to no one, it lies open to all; it admits and invites all, whether they be freeborn men, slaves or freedmen, kings or exiles; it requires no qualifications of family or of property, it is satisfied with a mere man. What, indeed, should we have to trust to for defence against sudden misfortunes, what could a noble mind promise to itself to keep unshaken, if virtue could be lost together with prosperity? If a slave cannot confer a benefit upon his master, then no subject can confer a benefit upon his king, and no soldier upon his general; for so long as the man is subject to supreme authority, the form of authority can make no difference. If main force, or the fear of death and torture, can prevent a slave from gaining any title to his master's gratitude, they will also prevent the subjects of a king, or the soldiers of a general from doing so, for the same things may happen to either of these classes of men, though under different names.

Yet men do bestow benefits upon their kings and their generals; therefore slaves can bestow benefits upon their masters. A slave can be just, brave, magnanimous; he can therefore bestow a benefit, for this is also the part of a virtuous man. So true is it that slaves can bestow benefits upon their masters, that the masters have often owed their lives to them.

19

There is no doubt that a slave can bestow a benefit upon anyone; why, then, not upon his master? "Because," it is argued, "he cannot become his master's creditor if he gives him money. If this be not so, he daily lays his master under an obligation to him; he attends him when on a journey, he nurses him when sick, he works most laboriously at the cultivation of his estate; yet all these, which would be called benefits if done for us by anyone else, are merely called service when done by a slave. A benefit is that which someone bestows who has the option of withholding it: now a slave has no power to refuse, so that he does not afford us his help, but obeys our orders, and cannot boast of having done what he could not leave undone." Even under these conditions I shall win the day, and will place a slave in such positions, that for many purposes he will be free; in the meanwhile, tell me, if I give you an instance of a slave fighting for his master's safety without regard to himself, pierced through with wounds, yet spending the last drops of his blood, and gaining time for his master to escape by the sacrifice of his life, will you say that this man did not bestow a benefit upon his master because he was a slave? If I give an instance of one who could not be bribed to betray his master's secrets by any of the offers of a tyrant, who was not terrified by any threats, nor overpowered by any tortures, but who, as far as he was able, placed his questioners upon a wrong scent, and, paid for his loyalty with his life; will you say that this man did not confer a benefit upon his master because he was a slave? Consider, rather, whether an example of virtue in a slave be not all the greater because it is rarer than in free men, and whether it be not all the more gratifying that, although to be commanded is odious, and all submission to authority is irksome, yet in some particular cases love for a master has been more powerful than men's general dislike to servitude. A benefit does not, therefore, cease to be a benefit because it is bestowed by a slave, but is all the greater on that account, because not even slavery could restrain him from bestowing it.

20

It is a mistake to imagine that slavery pervades a man's whole being; the better part of him is exempt from it: the body indeed is subjected and in the power of a master, but the mind is independent, and indeed is so free and wild, that it cannot be restrained even by this prison of the body, wherein it is confined, from following its own impulses, dealing with gigantic designs, and soaring into the infinite, accompanied by all the host of heaven. It is, therefore, only the body which misfortune hands over to a master, and which he buys and sells; this inward part cannot be transferred as a chattel. Whatever comes from this, is free; indeed, we are not allowed to order all things to be done, nor are slaves compelled to obey us in all things; they will not carry out treasonable orders, or lend their hands to an act of crime.

21

There are some things which the law neither enjoins nor forbids; it is in these that a slave finds the means of bestowing benefits. As long as we only receive what is generally demanded from a slave, that is mere service; when more is given than a slave need afford us, it is a benefit; as soon as what he does begins to partake of the affection of a friend, it can no longer be called service. There are certain things with which a master is bound to provide his slave, such as food and clothing; no one calls this a benefit; but supposing that he indulges his slave, educates him above his station, teaches him arts which freeborn men learn, that is a benefit. The converse is true in the case of the slave; anything which goes beyond the rules of a slave's duty, which is done of his own free will, and not in obedience to orders, is a benefit, provided it be of sufficient importance to be called by such a name if bestowed by any other person.

22

It has pleased Chrysippus to define a slave as "a hireling for life." Just as a hireling bestows a benefit when he does more than he engaged himself to do, so when a slave's love for his master raises him above his condition and urges him to do something noble—something which would be a credit even to men more fortunate by birth—he surpasses the hopes of his master, and is a benefit found in the house. Do you think it is just that we should be angry with our slaves when they do less than their duty, and that we should not be grateful to them when they do more? Do you wish to know when their service is not a benefit? When the question can be asked, "What if he had refused to do it?" When he does that which he might have refused to do, we must praise his good will. Benefits and wrongs are opposites; a slave can bestow a benefit upon his master, if he can receive a wrong from his master. Now an official has been appointed to hear complaints of the wrongs done by masters to their slaves, whose duty it is to restrain cruelty and lust, or avarice in providing them with the necessaries of life. What follows, then? Is it the master who receives a benefit from his slave? nay, rather, it is one man who receives it from another. Lastly, he did all that lay in his power; he bestowed a benefit upon his master; it lies in your power to receive or not to receive it from a slave. Yet who is so exalted, that fortune may not make him need the aid even of the lowliest?

23

I shall now quote a number of instances of benefits, not all alike, some even contradictory. Some slaves have given their master life, some death; have saved him when perishing, or, as if that were not enough, have saved him by their own death; others have helped their master to die, some have saved his life by stratagem. Claudius Quadrigarius tells us in the eighteenth book of his *Annals*, that when Grumentum was being besieged, and had been reduced to the greatest straits, two slaves deserted to the enemy, and did valuable service. Afterwards, when the city was taken, and the victors were rushing wildly in every direction, they ran before everyone else along the streets, which they well knew, to the house in which they had been slaves, and drove their mistress before them; when they were asked who she might be, they answered that she was their mistress, and a most cruel one, and that they were leading her away for punishment. They led her outside the walls, and concealed her with the greatest care until the fighting was over; then, as the soldiery, satisfied with the sack of the city, quickly resumed the manners of Romans, they also returned to their own countrymen, and themselves restored their mistress to them. She manumitted each of them on the spot, and was not ashamed to receive her life from men over whom she had held the power of life and death. She might, indeed, especially congratulate herself upon this; for had she been saved otherwise, she would merely have received a common and hackneyed piece of kindness, whereas, by being saved as she was, she became a glorious legend, and an example to two cities. In the confusion of the captured city, when everyone was thinking only of his own safety, all deserted her except these deserters; but they, that they might prove what had been their intentions in effecting that desertion, deserted again from the victors to the captive, wearing the masks of unnatural murderers.

They thought—and this was the greatest part of the service which they rendered—they were content to seem to have murdered their mistress, if thereby their mistress might be saved from murder. Believe me, it is the mark of no slavish soul to purchase a noble deed by the semblance of crime.

When Vettius, the praetor of the Marsi, was being led into the presence of the Roman general, his slave snatched a sword from the soldier who was dragging him along, and first slew his master. Then he said, "It is now time for me to look to myself; I have already set my master free," and with these words transfixed himself with one blow. Can you tell me of anyone who saved his master more gloriously?

24

When Caesar was besieging Corfinium, Domitius, who was shut up in the city, ordered a slave of his own, who was also a physician, to give him poison. Observing the man's hesitation, he said, "Why do you delay, as though the whole business was in your power? I ask for death with arms in my hands." Then the slave assented, and gave him a harmless drug to drink. When Domitius fell asleep after drinking this, the slave went to his son, and said, "Give orders for my being kept in custody until you learn from the result whether I have given your father poison or no." Domitius lived, and Caesar saved his life; but his slave had saved it before.

25

During the civil war, a slave hid his master, who had been proscribed, put on his rings and clothes, met the soldiers who were searching for him, and, after declaring that he would not stoop to entreat them not to carry out their orders, offered his neck to their swords. What a noble spirit it shows in a slave to have been willing to die for his master, at a time when few were faithful enough to wish their master to live! to be found kind when the State was cruel, faithful when it was treacherous! to be eager for the reward of fidelity, though it was death, at a time when such rich rewards were offered for treachery!

26

I will not pass over the instances which our own age affords. In the reign of Tiberius Caesar, there was a common and almost universal frenzy for informing, which was more ruinous to the citizens of Rome than the whole civil war; the talk of drunkards, the frankness of jesters, was alike reported to the government; nothing was safe; every opportunity of ferocious punishment was seized, and men no longer waited to hear the fate of accused persons, since it was always the same. One Paulus, of the Praetorian guard, was at an entertainment, wearing a portrait of Tiberius Caesar engraved in relief upon a gem. It would be absurd for me to beat about the bush for some delicate way of explaining that he took up a chamberpot, an action which was at once noticed by Maro, one of the most notorious informers of that time, and the slave of the man who was about to fall into the trap, who drew the ring from the finger of his drunken master. When Maro called the guests to witness that Paulus had dishonoured the portrait of the emperor, and was already drawing up an act of accusation, the slave showed the ring upon his own finger. Such a man no more deserves to be called a slave, than Maro deserved to be called a guest.

27

In the reign of Augustus men's own words were not yet able to ruin them, yet they sometimes brought them into trouble. A senator named Rufus, while at dinner, expressed a hope that Caesar would not return safe from a journey for which he was preparing, and added that all bulls and calves wished the same thing. Some of those present carefully noted these words. At daybreak, the slave who had stood at his feet during the dinner, told him what he had said in his cups, and urged him to be the first to go to Caesar, and denounce himself. Rufus followed this advice, met Caesar as he was going down to the forum, and, swearing that he was out of his mind the day before, prayed that what he had said might fall upon his own head and that of his children; he then begged Caesar pardon him, and to take him back into favour. When Caesar said that he would do so, he added, "No one will believe that you have taken me back into favour unless you make me a present of something;" and he asked for and obtained a sum of money so large, that it would have been a gift not to be slighted even if bestowed by an unoffended prince. Caesar added: "In future I will take care never to quarrel with you, for my own sake." Caesar acted honourably in pardoning him, and in being liberal as well as forgiving; no one can hear this anecdote without praising Caesar, but he must praise the slave first. You need not wait for me to tell you that the slave who did his master this service was set free; yet his master did not do this for nothing, for Caesar had already paid him the price of the slave's liberty.

28

After so many instances, can we doubt that a master may sometimes receive a benefit from a slave? Why need the person of the giver detract from the thing which he gives? why should not the gift add rather to the glory of the giver? All men descend from the same original stock; no one is better born than another, except in so far as his disposition is nobler and better suited for the performance of good actions. Those who display portraits of their ancestors in their halls, and set up in the entrance to their houses the pedigree of their family drawn out at length, with many complicated collateral branches, are they not notorious rather than noble? The universe is the one parent of all, whether they trace their descent from this primary source through a glorious or a mean line of ancestors. Be not deceived when men who are reckoning up their genealogy, wherever an illustrious name is wanting, foist in that of a god in its place. You need despise no one, even though he bears a commonplace name, and owes little to fortune. Whether your immediate ancestors were freedmen, or slaves, or foreigners, pluck up your spirits boldly, and leap over any intervening disgraces of your pedigree; at its source, a noble origin awaits you. Why should our pride inflate us to such a degree that we think it beneath us to receive benefits from slaves, and think only of their position, forgetting their good deeds? You, the slave of lust, of gluttony, of a harlot, nay, who are owned as a joint chattel by harlots, can you call anyone else a slave? Call a man a slave? why, I pray you, whither are you being hurried by those bearers who carry your litter? whither are these men with their smart military-looking cloaks carrying you? is it not to the door of some doorkeeper, or to the gardens of someone who has not even a subordinate office? and then you, who regard the salute of another man's slave as a benefit, declare that you cannot receive a benefit from your own slave. What inconsistency is this? At the same time you despise and fawn upon slaves, you are haughty and violent at home, while out of doors you are meek, and as much despised as you despise your slaves; for none abase themselves lower than those who unconscionably give themselves airs, nor are any more prepared to trample upon others than those who have learned how to offer insults by having endured them.

29

I felt it my duty to say this, in order to crush the arrogance of men who are themselves at the mercy of fortune, and to claim the right of bestowing a benefit for slaves, in order that I may claim it also for sons. The question arises, whether children can ever bestow upon their parents greater benefits than those which they have received from them.

It is granted that many sons become greater and more powerful than their parents, and also that they are better men. If this be true, they may give better gifts to their fathers than they have received from them, seeing that their fortune and their good nature are alike greater than that of their father. "Whatever a father receives from his son," our opponent will urge, "must in any case be less than what the son received from him, because the son owes to his father the very power of giving. Therefore the father can never be surpassed in the bestowal of benefits, because the benefit which surpasses his own is really his." I answer, that some things derive their first origin from others, yet are greater than those others; and a thing may be greater than that from which it took its rise, although without that thing to start from it never could have grown so great. All things greatly outgrow their beginnings. Seeds are the causes of all things, and yet are the smallest part of the things which they produce. Look at the Rhine, or the Euphrates, or any other famous rivers; how small they are, if you only view them at the place from whence they take their rise? they gain all that makes them terrible and renowned as they flow along. Look at the trees which are tallest if you consider their height, and the broadest if you look at their thickness and the spread of their branches; compared with all this, how small a part of them is contained in the slender fibres of the root? Yet take away their roots, and no more groves will arise, nor great mountains be clothed with trees. Temples and cities are supported by their foundations; yet what is built as the foundation of the entire building lies out of sight. So it is in other matters; the subsequent greatness of a thing ever eclipses its origin. I could never have obtained anything without having previously received the boon of existence from my parents; yet it does not follow from this that whatever I obtain is less than that without which I could not obtain it. If my nurse had not fed me when I was a child, I should not have been able to conduct any of those enterprises which I now carry on, both with my head and with my hand, nor should I ever have obtained the fame which is due to my labours both in peace and war; would you on that account argue that the services of a nurse were more valuable than the most important undertakings? Yet is not the nurse as important as the father, since without the benefits which I have received from each of them alike, I should have been alike unable to effect anything? If I owe all that I now can do to my original beginning, I cannot regard my father or my grandfather as being this original beginning; there always will be a spring further back, from which the spring next below is derived. Yet no one will argue that I owe more to unknown and forgotten ancestors than to my father; though really I do owe them more, if I owe it to my ancestors that my father begat me.

30

"Whatever I have bestowed upon my father," says my opponent, "however great it may be, yet is less valuable than what my father has bestowed upon me, because if he had not begotten me, it never could have existed at all." By this mode of reasoning, if a man has healed my father when ill, and at the point of death, I shall not be able to bestow anything upon him equivalent to what I have received from him; for had my father not been healed, he could not have begotten me. Yet think whether it be not nearer the truth to regard all that I can do, and all that I have done, as mine, due to my own powers and my own will? Consider what the fact of my birth is in itself; you will see that it is a small matter, the outcome of which is dubious, and that it may lead equally to good or to evil; no doubt it is the first step to everything, but because it is the first, it is not on that account more important than all the others. Suppose that I have saved my father's life, raised him to the highest honours, and made him the chief man in his city, that I have not merely made him illustrious by my own deeds, but have furnished him himself with an opportunity of performing great exploits, which is at once important, easy, and safe, as well as glorious; that I have loaded him with appointments, wealth, and all that attracts men's minds; still, even when I surpass all others, I am inferior to him. Now if you say, "You owe to your father the power of doing all this," I shall answer, "Quite true, if to do all this it is only necessary to be born; but if life is merely an unimportant factor in the art of living well, and if you have bestowed upon me only that which I have in common with wild beasts and the smallest, and some of the foulest of creatures, do not claim for yourself what did not come into being in consequence of the benefits which you bestowed, even though it could not have come into being without them."

31

Suppose, father, that I have saved your life, in return for the life which I received from you: in this case also I have outdone your benefit, because I have given life to one who understands what I have done, and because I understood what I was doing, since I gave you your life not for the sake of, or by the means of my own pleasure; for just as it is less terrible to die before one has time to fear death, so it is a much greater boon to preserve one's life than to receive it. I have given life to one who will at once enjoy it, you gave it to one who knew not if he should ever live; I have given life to one who was in fear of death, your gift of life merely enables me to die; I have given you a life complete, perfect; you begat me without intelligence, a burden upon others. Do you wish to know how far from a benefit it was to give life under such conditions? You should have exposed me as a child, for you did me a wrong in begetting me. What do I gather from this? That the cohabitation of a father and mother is the very least of benefits to their child, unless in addition this beginning of kindnesses be followed up by others, and confirmed by other services. It is not a good thing to live, but to live well. "But," say you, "I do live well." True, but I might have lived ill; so that your part in me is merely this, that I live. If you claim merit to yourself for giving me mere life, bare and helpless, and boast of it as a great boon, reflect that this you claim merit for giving me is a boon which I possess in common with flies and worms. In the next place, if I say no more than that I have applied myself to honourable pursuits, and have guided the course of my life along the path of rectitude, then you have received more from your benefit than you gave; for you gave me to myself ignorant and unlearned, and I have returned to you a son such as you would wish to have begotten.

32

My father supported me. If I repay this kindness, I give him more than I received, because he has the pleasure, not only of being supported, but of being supported by a son, and receives more delight from my filial devotion than from the food itself, whereas the food which he used to give me merely affected my body. What? if any man rises so high as to become famous among nations for his eloquence, his justice, or his military skill, if much of the splendour of his renown is shed upon his father also, and by its clear light dispels the obscurity of his birth, does not such a man confer an inestimable benefit upon his parents? Would anyone have heard of Aristo and Gryllus except through Xenophon and Plato, their sons? Socrates keeps alive the memory of Sophroniscus. It would take long to recount the other men whose names survive for no other reason than that the admirable qualities of their sons have handed them down to posterity. Did the father of Marcus Agrippa, of whom nothing was known, even after Agrippa became famous, confer the greater benefit upon his son, or was that greater which Agrippa conferred upon his father when he gained the glory, unique in the annals of war, of a naval crown, and when he raised so many vast buildings in Rome, which not only surpassed all former grandeur, but have been surpassed by none since? Did Octavius confer a greater benefit upon his son, or the Emperor Augustus upon his father, obscured as he was by the intervention of an adoptive father? What joy would he have experienced, if, after the putting down of the civil war, he had seen his son ruling the State in peace and security? He would not have recognized the good which he had himself bestowed, and would hardly have believed, when he looked back upon himself, that so great a man could have been born in his house. Why should I go on to speak of others who would now be forgotten, if the glory of their sons had not raised them from obscurity, and kept them in the light until this day? In the next place, as we are not considering what son may have given back to his father greater benefits than he received from him, but whether a son can give back greater benefits, even if the examples which I have quoted are not sufficient, and such benefits do not outweigh the benefits bestowed by the parents, if no age has produced an actual example, still it is not in the nature of things impossible. Though no solitary act can outweigh the deserts of a parent, yet many such acts combined by one son may do so.

33

Scipio, while under seventeen years of age, rode among the enemy in battle, and saved his father's life. Was it not enough, that in order to reach his father he despised so many dangers when they were pressing hardest upon the greatest generals, that he, a novice in his first battle, made his way through so many obstacles, over the bodies of so many veteran soldiers, and showed strength and courage beyond his years? Add to this, that he also defended his father in court, and saved him from a plot of his powerful enemies, that he heaped upon him a second and a third consulship and other posts which were coveted even by consulars, that when his father was poor he bestowed upon him the plunder which he took by military licence, and that he made him rich with the spoils of the enemy, which is the greatest honour of a soldier. If even this did not repay his debt, add to it that he caused him to be constantly employed in the government of provinces and in special commands, add, that after he had destroyed the greatest cities, and became without a rival either in the east or in the west, the acknowledged protector and second founder of the Roman Empire, he bestowed upon one who was already of noble birth the higher title of "the father of Scipio;" can we doubt that the commonplace benefit of his birth was outdone by his exemplary conduct, and by the valour which was at once the glory and the protection of his country? Next, if this be not enough, suppose that a son were to rescue his father from the torture, or to undergo it in his stead. You can suppose the benefits returned by the son as great as you please, whereas the gift he received from his father was of one sort only, was easily performed, and was a pleasure to the giver; that he must necessarily have given the same thing to many others, even to some to whom he knows not that he has given it, that he had a partner in doing so, and that he had in view the law, patriotism, the rewards bestowed upon fathers of families by the State, the maintenance of his house and family: everything rather than him to whom he was giving life. What? supposing that anyone were to learn philosophy and teach it to his father, could it be any longer disputed that the son had given him something greater than he had received from him, having returned to his father a happy life, whereas he had received from him merely life?

34

"But," says our opponent, "whatever you do, whatever you are able to give to your father, is part of his benefit bestowed upon you." So it is the benefit of my teacher that I have become proficient in liberal studies; yet we pass on from those who taught them to us, at any rate from those who taught us the alphabet; and although no one can learn anything without them, yet it does not follow that whatsoever success one subsequently obtains, one is still inferior to those teachers. There is a great difference between the beginning of a thing and its final development; the beginning is not equal to the thing at its greatest, merely upon the ground that, without the beginning, it could never have become so great.

35

It is now time for me to bring forth something, so to speak, from my own mint. So long as there is something better than the benefit which a man bestows, he may be outdone. A father gives life to his son; there is something better than life; therefore a father may be outdone, because there is something better than the benefit which he has bestowed. Still further, he who has given anyone his life, if he be more than once saved from peril of death by him, has received a greater benefit than he bestowed. Now, a father has given life to his son: if, therefore, he be more than once saved from peril by his son, he can receive a greater benefit than he gave. A benefit becomes greater to the receiver in proportion to his need of it. Now he who is alive needs life more than he who has not been born, seeing that such a one can have no need at all; consequently a father, if his life is saved by his son, receives a greater benefit than his son received from him by being born. It is said, "The benefits conferred by fathers cannot be outdone by those returned by their sons." Why? "Because the son received life from his father, and had he not received it, he could not have returned any benefits at all." A father has this in common with all those who have given any men their lives; it is impossible that these men could repay the debt if they had not received their life. Then I suppose one cannot overpay one's debt to a physician, for a physician gives life as well as a father; or to a sailor who has saved us when shipwrecked? Yet the benefits bestowed by these and by all the others who give us life in whatever fashion, can be outdone: consequently those of our fathers can be outdone. If anyone bestows upon me a benefit which requires the help of benefits from many other persons, whereas I give him what requires no one to help it out, I have given more than I have received; now a father gave to his son a life which, without many accessories to preserve it, would perish; whereas a son, if he gives life to his father, gives him a life which requires no assistance to make it lasting; therefore the father who receives life from his son, receives a greater benefit than he himself bestowed upon his son.

36

These considerations do not destroy the respect due to parents, or make their children behave worse to them, nay, better; for virtue is naturally ambitious, and wishes to outstrip those who are before it. Filial piety will be all the more eager, if, in returning a father's benefits, it can hope to outdo them; nor will this be against the will or the pleasure of the father, since in many contests it is to our advantage to be outdone. How does this contest become so desirable? How comes it to be such happiness to parents that they should confess themselves outdone by the benefits bestowed by their children? Unless we decide the matter thus, we give children an excuse, and make them less eager to repay their debt, whereas we ought to spur them on, saying, "Noble youths, give your attention to this! You are invited to contend in an honourable strife between parents and children, as to which party has received more than it has given. Your fathers have not necessarily won the day because they are first in the field: only take courage, as befits you, and do not give up the contest; you will conquer if you wish to do so. In this honourable warfare you will have no lack of leaders who will encourage you to perform deeds like their own, and bid you follow in their footsteps upon a path by which victory has often before now been won over parents.

37

Æneas conquered his father in well doing, for he himself had been but a light and a safe burden for him when he was a child, yet he bore his father, when heavy with age, through the midst of the enemy's lines and the crash of the city which was falling around him, albeit the devout old man, who bore the sacred images and the household gods in his hands, pressed him with more than his own weight; nevertheless (what cannot filial piety accomplish!) Æneas bore him safe through the blazing city, and placed him in safety, to be worshipped as one of the founders of the Roman Empire. Those Sicilian youths outdid their parents whom they bore away safe, when Aetna, roused to unusual fury, poured fire over cities and fields throughout a great part of the island. It is believed that the fires parted, and that the flames retired on either side, so as to leave a passage for these youths to pass through, who certainly deserved to perform their daring task in safety. Antigonus outdid his father when, after having conquered the enemy in a great battle, he transferred the fruits of it to him, and handed over to him the empire of Cyprus. This is true kingship, to choose not to be a king when you might. Manlius conquered his father, imperious[9] though he was, when, in spite of his having previously been banished for a time by his father on account of his dullness and stupidity as a boy, he came to an interview which he had demanded with the tribune of the people, who had filed an action against his father. The tribune had granted him the interview, hoping that he would betray his hated father, and believed that he had earned the gratitude of the youth, having, amongst other matters, reproached old Manlius with sending him into exile, treating it as a very serious accusation; but the youth, having caught him alone, drew a sword which he had hidden in his robe, and said, "Unless you swear to give up your suit against my father, I will run you through with this sword. It is in your power to decide how my father shall be freed from his prosecutor." The tribune swore, and kept his oath; he related the reason of his abandonment of his action to an assembly at the Rostra. No other man was ever permitted to put down a tribune with impunity.

38

There are instances without number of men who have saved their parents from danger, have raised them from the lowest to the highest station, and, taking them from the nameless mass of the lower classes, have given them a name glorious throughout all ages. By no force of words, by no power of genius, can one rightly express how desirable, how admirable, how never to be erased from human memory it is to be able to say, "I obeyed my parents, I gave way to them, I was submissive to their authority whether it was just, or unjust and harsh; the only point in which I resisted them was, not to be conquered by them in benefits." Continue this struggle, I beg of you, and even though weary, yet re-form your ranks. Happy are they who conquer, happy are they who are conquered. What can be more glorious than the youth who can say to himself—it would not be right to say it to another—"I have conquered my father with benefits"? What is more fortunate than that old man who declares everywhere to everyone that he has been conquered in benefits by his son? What, again, is more blissful than to be overcome in such a contest?

---

[9] There is an allusion to the surname of both the father and the son, "Imperiosus," given them on account of their severity.

BOOK 4

1

Of all the matters which we have discussed, Aebutius Liberalis, there is none more essential, or which, as Sallust says, ought to be stated with more care than that which is now before us: whether the bestowal of benefits and the return of gratitude for them are desirable objects in themselves. Some men are found who act honourably from commercial motives, and who do not care for unrewarded virtue, though it can confer no glory if it brings any profit. What can be more base than for a man to consider what it costs him to be a good man, when virtue neither allures by gain nor deters by loss, and is so far from bribing anyone with hopes and promises, that on the other hand she bids them spend money upon herself, and often consists in voluntary gifts? We must go to her, trampling what is merely useful under our feet: whithersoever she may call us or send us we must go, without any regard for our private fortunes, sometimes without sparing even our own blood, nor must we ever refuse to obey any of her commands. "What shall I gain," says my opponent, "if I do this bravely and gratefully?" You will gain the doing of it—the deed itself is your gain. Nothing beyond this is promised. If any advantage chances to accrue to you, count it as something extra. The reward of honourable dealings lies in themselves. If honour is to be sought after for itself, since a benefit is honourable, it follows that because both of these are of the same nature, their conditions must also be the same. Now it has frequently and satisfactorily been proved, that honour ought to be sought after for itself alone.

2

In this part of the subject we oppose the Epicureans, an effeminate and dreamy sect who philosophize in their own paradise, amongst whom virtue is the handmaid of pleasures, obeys them, is subject to them, and regards them as superior to itself. You say, "there is no pleasure without virtue." But wherefore is it superior to virtue? Do you imagine that the matter in dispute between them is merely one of precedence? Nay, it is virtue itself and its powers which are in question. It cannot be virtue if it can follow; the place of virtue is first, she ought to lead, to command, to stand in the highest rank; you bid her look for a cue to follow. "What," asks our opponent, "does that matter to you? I also declare that happiness is impossible without virtue. Without virtue I disapprove of and condemn the very pleasures which I pursue, and to which I have surrendered myself. The only matter in dispute is this, whether virtue be the cause of the highest good, or whether it be itself the highest good." Do you suppose, though this be the only point in question, that it is a mere matter of precedence? It is a confusion and obvious blindness to prefer the last to the first. I am not angry at virtue being placed below pleasure, but at her being mixed up at all with pleasure, which she despises, whose enemy she is, and from which she separates herself as far as possible, being more at home with labour and sorrow, which are manly troubles, than with your womanish good things.

3

It was necessary to insert this argument, my Liberalis, because it is the part of virtue to bestow those benefits which we are now discussing, and it is most disgraceful to bestow benefits for any other purpose than that they should be free gifts. If we give with the hope of receiving a return, we should give to the richest men, not to the most deserving: whereas we prefer a virtuous poor man to an unmannerly rich one. That is not a benefit, which takes into consideration the fortune of the receiver. Moreover, if our only motive for benefiting others was our own advantage, those who could most easily distribute benefits, such as rich and powerful men, or kings, and persons who do not stand in need of the help of others, ought never to do so at all; the gods would not bestow upon us the countless blessings which they pour upon us unceasingly by night and by day, for their own nature suffices them in all respects, and renders them complete, safe, and beyond the reach of harm; they will, therefore, never bestow a benefit upon anyone, if self and self interest be the only cause for the bestowal of benefits. To take thought, not where your benefit will be best bestowed, but where it may be most profitably placed at interest, from whence you will most easily get it back, is not bestowal of benefits, but usury. Now the gods have nothing to do with usury; it follows, therefore, that they cannot be liberal; for if the only reason for giving is the advantage of the giver, since God cannot hope to receive any advantages from us, there is no cause why God should give anything.

4

I know what answer may be made to this. "True; therefore God does not bestow benefits, but, free from care and unmindful of us, He turns away from our world and either does something else, or else does nothing, which Epicurus thought the greatest possible happiness, and He is not affected either by benefits or by injuries." The man who says this cannot surely hear the voices of worshippers, and of those who all around him are raising their hands to heaven and praying for the success both of their private affairs and those of the State; which certainly would not be the case, all men would not agree in this madness of appealing to deaf and helpless gods, unless we knew that their benefits are sometimes bestowed upon us unasked, sometimes in answer to our prayers, and that they give us both great and seasonable gifts, which shield us from the most terrible dangers. Who is there so poor, so uncared for, born to sorrow by so unkind a fate, as never to have felt the vast generosity of the Gods? Look even at those who complain and are discontented with their lot; you will find that they are not altogether without a share in the bounty of heaven, that there is no one upon whom something has not been shed from that most gracious fount. Is the gift which is bestowed upon all alike, at their birth, not enough? However unequally the blessings of after life may be dealt out to us, did nature give us too little when she gave us herself?

5

It is said, "God does not bestow benefits." Whence, then, comes all that you possess, that you give or refuse to give, that you hoard or steal? whence come these innumerable delights of our eyes, our ears, and our minds? whence the plenty which provides us even with luxury—for it is not our bare necessities alone against which provision is made; we are loved so much as actually to be pampered—whence so many trees bearing various fruits, so many wholesome herbs, so many different sorts of food distributed throughout the year, so that even the slothful may find sustenance in the chance produce of the earth? Then, too, whence come the living creatures of all kinds, some inhabiting the dry land, others the waters, others alighting from the sky, that every part of nature may pay us some tribute; the rivers which encircle our meadows with most beauteous bends, the others which afford a passage to merchant fleets as they flow on, wide and navigable, some of which in summer time are subject to extraordinary overflowings in order that lands lying parched under a glowing sun may suddenly be watered by the rush of a midsummer torrent?

What of the fountains of medicinal waters? What of the bursting forth of warm waters upon the seashore itself? Shall I

> "Tell of the seas round Italy that flow,
> Which laves her shore above, and which below;
> Or of her lakes, unrivalled Larius, thee,
> Or thee, Benacus, roaring like a sea?"

6

If anyone gave you a few acres, you would say that you had received a benefit; can you deny that the boundless extent of the Earth is a benefit? If anyone gave you money, and filled your chest, since you think that so important, you would call that a benefit. God has buried countless mines in the earth, has poured out from the earth countless rivers, rolling sands of gold; He has concealed in every place huge masses of silver, copper and iron, and has bestowed upon you the means of discovering them, placing upon the surface of the Earth signs of the treasures hidden below; and yet do you say that you have received no benefit? If a house were given you, bright with marble, its roof beautifully painted with colours and gilding, you would call it no small benefit. God has built for you a huge mansion that fears no fire or ruin, in which you see no flimsy veneers, thinner than the very saw with which they are cut, but vast blocks of most precious stone, all composed of those various and different substances whose paltriest fragments you admire so much; he has built a roof which glitters in one fashion by day, and in another by night; and yet do you say that you have received no benefit? When you so greatly prize what you possess, do you act the part of an ungrateful man, and think that there is no one to whom you are indebted for them? Whence comes the breath which you draw? the light by which you arrange and perform all the actions of your life? the blood by whose circulation your vital warmth is maintained? those meats which excite your palate by their delicate flavour after your hunger is appeased? those provocatives which rouse you when wearied with pleasure? that repose in which you are rotting and mouldering? Will you not, if you are grateful, say—

> " 'Tis to a god that this repose I owe,
> For him I worship, as a god below.
> Oft on his altar shall my firstlings bleed,
> See, by his bounty here with rustic reed
> I play the airs I love the livelong day,
> The while my oxen round about me stray."

The true God is he who has placed, not a few oxen, but all the herds on their pastures throughout the world; who furnishes food to the flocks wherever they wander; who has ordained the alternation of summer and winter pasturage, and has taught us not merely to play upon a reed, and to reduce to some order a rustic and artless song, but who has invented so many arts and varieties of voice, so many notes to make music, some with our own breath, some with instruments. You cannot call our inventions our own any more than you call our growth our own, or the various bodily functions which correspond to each stage of our lives; at one time comes the loss of childhood's teeth, at another, when our age is advancing and growing into robuster manhood, puberty and the last wisdom-tooth marks the end of our youth.

We have implanted in us the seeds of all ages, of all arts, and God our master brings forth our intellects from obscurity.

7

"Nature," says my opponent, "gives me all this." Do you not perceive when you say this that you merely speak of God under another name? for what is nature but God and divine reason, which pervades the universe and all its parts? You may address the author of our world by as many different titles as you please; you may rightly call him Jupiter, Best and Greatest, and the Thunderer, or the Stayer, so called, not because, as the historians tell us, he stayed the flight of the Roman army in answer to the prayer of Romulus, but because all things continue in their stay through his goodness. If you were to call this same personage Fate, you would not lie; for since fate is nothing more than a connected chain of causes, he is the first cause of all upon which all the rest depend. You will also be right in applying to him any names that you please which express supernatural strength and power: he may have as many titles as he has attributes.

8

Our school regards him as Father Liber, and Hercules, and Mercurius: he is Father Liber because he is the parent of all, who first discovered the power of seed, and our being led by pleasure to plant it; he is Hercules, because his might is unconquered, and when it is wearied after completing its labours, will retire into fire; he is Mercurius, because in him is reasoning, and numbers, and system, and knowledge. Whither-soever you turn yourself you will see him meeting you: nothing is void of him, he himself fills his own work. Therefore, most ungrateful of mortals, it is in vain that you declare yourself indebted, not to God, but to nature, because there can be no God without nature, nor any nature without God; they are both the same thing, differing only in their functions. If you were to say that you owe to Annaeus or to Lucius what you received from Seneca, you would not change your creditor, but only his name, because he remains the same man whether you use his first, second, or third name. So whether you speak of nature, fate, or fortune, these are all names of the same God, using his power in different ways. So likewise justice, honesty, discretion, courage, frugality, are all the good qualities of one and the same mind; if you are pleased with any one of these, you are pleased with that mind.

9

However, not to drift aside into a distinct controversy, God bestows upon us very many and very great benefits without hope of receiving any return; since he does not require any offering from us, and we are not capable of bestowing anything upon him: wherefore, a benefit is desirable in itself. In it the advantage of the receiver is all that is taken into consideration: we study this without regarding our own interests. "Yet," argues our opponent, "you say that we ought to choose with care the persons upon whom we bestow benefits, because neither do husbandmen sow seed in the sand: now if this be true, we follow our own interest in bestowing benefits, just as much as in ploughing and sowing: for sowing is not desirable in itself. Besides this you inquire where and how you ought to bestow a benefit, which would not need to be done if the bestowal of a benefit was desirable in itself: because in whatever place and whatever manner it might be bestowed, it still would be a benefit." We seek to do honourable acts, solely because they are honourable; yet even though we need think of nothing else, we consider to whom we shall do them, and when, and how; for in these points the act has its being. In like manner, when I choose upon whom I shall bestow a benefit, and when I aim at making it a benefit; because if it were bestowed upon a base person, it could neither be a benefit nor an honourable action.

10

To restore what has been entrusted to one is desirable in itself; yet I shall not always restore it, nor shall I do so in any place or at any time you please. Sometimes it makes no difference whether I deny that I have received it, or return it openly. I shall consider the interests of the person to whom I am to return it, and shall deny that I have received a deposit, which would injure him if returned. I shall act in the same manner in bestowing a benefit: I shall consider when to give it, to whom, in what manner, and on what grounds. Nothing ought to be done without a reason: a benefit is not truly so, if it be bestowed without a reason, since reason accompanies all honorable action. How often do we hear men reproaching themselves for some thoughtless gift, and saying, "I had rather have thrown it away than have given it to him!" What is thoughtlessly given away is lost in the most discreditable manner, and it is much worse to have bestowed a benefit badly than to have received no return for it; that we receive no return is the fault of another; that we did not choose upon whom we should bestow it, is our own. In choosing a fit person, I shall not, as you expect, pay the least attention to whether I am likely to get any return from him, for I choose one who will be grateful, not one who will return my goodness, and it often happens that the man who makes no return is grateful, while he who returns a benefit is ungrateful for it. I value men by their hearts alone, and, therefore, I shall pass over a rich man if he be unworthy, and give to a good man though he be poor; for he will be grateful however destitute he may be, since whatever he may lose, his heart will still be left him.

11

I do not fish for gain, for pleasure, or for credit, by bestowing benefits: satisfied in doing so with pleasing one man alone, I shall give in order to do my duty. Duty, however, leaves one some choice; do you ask me, how I am to choose? I shall choose an honest, plain, man, with a good memory, and grateful for kindness; one who keeps his hands off other men's goods, yet does not greedily hold to his own, and who is kind to others; when I have chosen such a man, I shall have acted to my mind, although Fortune may have bestowed upon him no means of returning my kindness. If my own advantage and mean calculation made me liberal, if I did no one any service except in order that he might in turn do a service to me, I should never bestow a benefit upon one who was setting out for distant and foreign countries, never to return; I should not bestow a benefit upon one who was so ill as to be past hope of recovery, nor should I do so when I myself was failing, because I should not live long enough to receive any return. Yet, that you may know that to do good is desirable in itself, we afford help to strangers who put into our harbour only to leave it straightaway; we give a ship and fit it out for a shipwrecked stranger to sail back in to his own country. He leaves us hardly knowing who it was who saved him, and, as he will never return to our presence, he hands over his debt of gratitude to the gods, and beseeches them to fulfil it for him: in the meanwhile we rejoice in the barren knowledge that we have done a good action. What? when we stand upon the extreme verge of life, and make our wills, do we not assign to others benefits from which we ourselves shall receive no advantage? How much time we waste, how long we consider in secret how much property we are to leave, and to whom! What then? does it make any difference to us to whom we leave our property, seeing that we cannot expect any return from anyone? Yet we never give anything with more care, we never take such pains in deciding upon our verdict, as when, without any views of personal advantage, we think only of what is honourable, for we are bad judges of our duty as long as our view of it is distorted by hope and fear, and that most indolent of vices, pleasure: but when death has shut off all these, and brought us as incorrupt judges to pronounce sentence, we seek for the most worthy men to leave our property to, and we never take more scrupulous care than in deciding what is to be done with what does not concern us. Yet, by Hercules, then there steals over us a great satisfaction as we think, "I shall make this man richer, and by bestowing wealth upon that man I shall add lustre to his high position." Indeed, if we never give without expecting some return, we must all die without making our wills.

12

It may be said, "You define a benefit as a loan which cannot be repaid: now a loan is not a desirable thing in itself." When we speak of a loan, we make use of a figure, or comparison, just as we speak of law as; the standard of right and wrong, although a standard is not a thing to be desired for its own sake. I have adopted this phrase in order to illustrate my subject: when I speak of a loan, I must be understood to mean something resembling a loan. Do you wish to know how it differs from one? I add the words "which cannot be repaid," whereas every loan both can and ought to be repaid. It is so far from being right to bestow a benefit for one's own advantage, that often, as I have explained, it is one's duty to bestow it when it involves one's own loss and risk: for instance, if I assist a man when beset by robbers, so that he gets away from them safely, or help some victim of power, and bring upon myself the party spite of a body of influential men, very probably incurring myself the same disgrace from which I saved him, although I might have taken the other side, and looked on with safety at struggles with which I have nothing to do: if I were to give bail for one who has been condemned, and when my friend's goods were advertised for sale I were to give a bond to the effect that I would make restitution to the creditors, if, in order to save a proscribed person I myself run the risk of being proscribed. No one, when about to buy a villa at Tusculum or Tibur, for a summer retreat, because of the health of the locality, considers how many years' purchase he gives for it; this must be looked to by the man who makes a profit by it. The same is true with benefits; when you ask what return I get for them, I answer, the consciousness of a good action. "What return does one get for benefits?" Pray tell me what return one gets for righteousness, innocence, magnanimity, chastity, temperance? If you wish for anything beyond these virtues, you do not wish for the virtues themselves. For what does the order of the universe bring round the seasons? for what does the sun make the day now longer and now shorter? all these things are benefits, for they take place for our good. As it is the duty of the universe to maintain the round of the seasons, as it is the duty of the sun to vary the points of his rising and setting, and to do all these things by which we profit, without any reward, so is it the duty of man, amongst other things, to bestow benefits. Wherefore then does he give? He gives for fear that he should not give, lest he might lose an opportunity of doing a good action.

13

You Epicureans take pleasure in making a study of dull torpidity, in seeking for a repose which differs little from sound sleep, in lurking beneath the thickest shade, in amusing with the feeblest possible trains of thought that sluggish condition of your languid minds which you term tranquil contemplation, and in stuffing with food and drink, in the recesses of your gardens, your bodies which are pallid with want of exercise; we Stoics, on the other hand, take pleasure in bestowing benefits, even though they cost us labour, provided that they lighten the labours of others; though they lead us into danger, provided that they save others, though they straiten our means, if they alleviate the poverty and distresses of others. What difference does it make to me whether I receive benefits or not? even if I receive them, it is still my duty to bestow them. A benefit has in view the advantage of him upon whom we bestow it, not our own; otherwise we merely bestow it upon ourselves. Many things, therefore, which are of the greatest possible use to others lose all claim to gratitude by being paid for. Merchants are of use to cities, physicians to invalids, dealers to slaves; yet all these have no claim to the gratitude of those whom they benefit, because they seek their own advantage through that of others. That which is bestowed with a view to profit is not a benefit. "I will give this in order that I may get a return for it" is the language of a broker.

14

I should not call a woman modest, if she rebuffed her lover in order to increase his passion, or because she feared the law or her husband; as Ovid says:

> "She that denies, because she does not dare
> To yield, in spirit grants her lover's prayer."

Indeed, the woman who owes her chastity, not to her own virtue, but to fear, may rightly be classed as a sinner. In the same manner, he who merely gave in order that he might receive, cannot be said to have given. Pray, do we bestow benefits upon animals when we feed them for our use or for our table? do we bestow benefits upon trees when we tend them that they may not suffer from drought or from hardness of ground? No one is moved by righteousness and goodness of heart to cultivate an estate, or to do any act in which the reward is something apart from the act itself; but he is moved to bestow benefits, not by low and grasping motives, but by a kind and generous mind, which even after it has given is willing to give again, to renew its former bounties by fresh ones, which thinks only of how much good it can do the man to whom it gives; whereas to do anyone a service because it is our interest to do so is a mean action, which deserves no praise, no credit. What grandeur is there in loving oneself, sparing oneself, gaining profit for oneself? The true love of giving calls us away from all this, forcibly leads us to put up with loss, and foregoes its own interest, deriving its greatest pleasure from the mere act of doing good.

15

Can we doubt that the converse of a benefit is an injury? As the infliction of injuries is a thing to be avoided, so is the bestowal of benefits to be desired for its own sake. In the former, the disgrace of crime outweighs all the advantages which incite us to commit it; while we are urged to the latter course by the appearance of honour, in itself a powerful incentive to action, which attends it.

I should not lie if I were to affirm that everyone takes pleasure in the benefits which he has bestowed, that everyone loves best to see the man whom he has most largely benefited. Who does not think that to have bestowed one benefit is a reason for bestowing a second? and would this be so, if the act of giving did not itself give us pleasure? How often you may hear a man say, "I cannot bear to desert one whose life I have preserved, whom I have saved from danger. True, he asks me to plead his cause against men of great influence. I do not wish to do so, yet what am I to do? I have already helped him once, nay twice." Do you not perceive how very powerful this instinct must be, if it leads us to bestow benefits first because it is right to do so, and afterwards because we have already bestowed somewhat? Though at the outset a man may have had no claim upon us, we yet continue to give to him because we have already given to him. So untrue is it that we are urged to bestow benefits by our own interest, that even when our benefits prove failures we continue to nurse them and encourage them out of sheer love of benefiting, which has a natural weakness even for what has been ill-bestowed, like that which we feel for our vicious children.

16

These same adversaries of ours admit that they are grateful, yet not because it is honourable, but because it is profitable to be so. This can be proved to be untrue all the more easily, because it can be established by the same arguments by which we have established that to bestow a benefit is desirable for its own sake. All our arguments start from this settled point, that honour is pursued for no reason except because it is honour. Now, who will venture to raise the question whether it be honourable to be grateful? who does not loathe the ungrateful man, useless as he is even to himself? How do you feel when anyone is spoken of as being ungrateful for great benefits conferred upon him by a friend? Is it as though he had done something base, or had merely neglected to do something useful and likely to be profitable to himself? I imagine that you think him a bad man, and one who deserves punishment, not one who needs a guardian; and this would not be the case, unless gratitude were desirable in itself and honourable. Other qualities, it may be, manifest their importance less clearly, and require an explanation to prove whether they be honourable or no; this is openly proved to be so in the sight of all, and is too beautiful for anything to obscure or dim its glory. What is more praiseworthy, upon what are all men more universally agreed, than to return gratitude for good offices?

17

Pray tell me, what is it that urges us to do so? Is it profit? Why, unless a man despises profit, he is not grateful. Is it ambition? why, what is there to boast of in having paid what you owe? Is it fear? The ungrateful man feels none, for against this one crime we have provided no law, as though nature had taken sufficient precautions against it. Just as there is no law which bids parents love and indulge their children, seeing that it is superfluous to force us into the path which we naturally take, just as no one needs to be urged to love himself, since self-love begins to act upon him as soon as he is born, so there is no law bidding us to seek that which is honourable in itself; for such things please us by their very nature, and so attractive is virtue that the disposition even of bad men leads them to approve of good rather than of evil. Who is there who does not wish to appear beneficent, who does not even when steeped in crime and wrongdoing strive after the appearance of goodness, does not put some show of justice upon even his most intemperate acts, and endeavour to seem to have conferred a benefit even upon those whom he has injured? Consequently, men allow themselves to be thanked by those whom they have ruined, and pretend to be good and generous, because they cannot prove themselves so; and this they never would do were it not that a love of honour for its own sake forces them to seek a reputation quite at variance with their real character, and to conceal their baseness, a quality whose fruits we covet, though we regard it itself with dislike and shame. No one has ever so far rebelled against the laws of nature and put off human feeling as to act basely for mere amusement. Ask any of those who live by robbery whether he would not rather obtain what he steals and plunders by honest means; the man whose trade is highway robbery and the murder of travellers would rather find his booty than take it by force; you will find no one who would not prefer to enjoy the fruits of wickedness without acting wickedly. Nature bestows upon us all this immense advantage, that the light of virtue shines into the minds of all alike; even those who do not follow her, behold her.

18

A proof that gratitude is desirable for itself lies in the fact that ingratitude is to be avoided for itself, because no vice more powerfully rends asunder and destroys the union of the human race. To what do we trust for safety, if not in mutual good offices one to another? It is by the interchange of benefits alone that we gain some measure of protection for our lives, and of safety against sudden disasters. Taken singly, what should we be? a prey and quarry for wild beasts, a luscious and easy banquet; for while all other animals have sufficient strength to protect themselves, and those which are born to a wandering solitary life are armed, man is covered by a soft skin, has no powerful teeth or claws with which to terrify other creatures, but weak and naked by himself is made strong by union.

God has bestowed upon him two gifts, reason and union, which raise him from weakness to the highest power; and so he, who if taken alone would be inferior to every other creature, possesses supreme dominion. Union has given him sovereignty over all animals; union has enabled a being born upon the Earth to assume power over a foreign element, and bids him be lord of the sea also; it is union which has checked the inroads of disease, provided supports for our old age, and given us relief from pain; it is union which makes us strong, and to which we look for protection against the caprices of fortune. Take away union, and you will rend asunder the association by which the human race preserves its existence; yet you will take it away if you succeed in proving that ingratitude is not to be avoided for itself, but because something is to be feared for it; for how many are there who can with safety be ungrateful? In fine, I call every man ungrateful who is merely made grateful by fear.

19

No sane man fears the gods; for it is madness to fear what is beneficial, and no man loves those whom he fears. You, Epicurus, ended by making God unarmed; you stripped him of all weapons, of all power, and, lest anyone should fear him, you banished him out of the world. There is no reason why you should fear this being, cut off as he is, and separated from the sight and touch of mortals by a vast and impassable wall; he has no power either of rewarding or of injuring us; he dwells alone halfway between our heaven and that of another world, without the society either of animals, of men, or of matter, avoiding the crash of worlds as they fall in ruins above and around him, but neither hearing our prayers nor interested in us. Yet you wish to seem to worship this being just as a father, with a mind, I suppose, full of gratitude; or, if you do not wish to seem grateful, why should you worship him, since you have received no benefit from him, but have been put together entirely at random and by chance by those atoms and mites of yours? "I worship him," you answer, "because of his glorious majesty and his unique nature." Granting that you do this, you clearly do it without the attraction of any reward, or any hope; there is therefore something which is desirable for itself, whose own worth attracts you, that is, honour. Now what is more honourable than gratitude? the means of practising this virtue are as extensive as life itself.

20

"Yet," argues he, "there is also a certain amount of profit inherent in this virtue." In what virtue is there not? But that which we speak of as desirable for itself is such, that although it may possess some attendant advantages, yet it would be desirable even if stripped of all these. It is profitable to be grateful; yet I will be grateful even though it harm me. What is the aim of the grateful man? is it that his gratitude may win for him more friends and more benefits? What then? If a man is likely to meet with affronts by showing his gratitude, if he knows that far from gaining anything by it, he must lose much even of what he has already acquired, will he not cheerfully act to his own disadvantage? That man is ungrateful who, in returning a kindness, looks forward to a second gift—who hopes while he repays. I call him ungrateful who sits at the bedside of a sick man because he is about to make a will, when he is at leisure to think of inheritances and legacies. Though he may do everything which a good and dutiful friend ought to do, yet, if any hope of gain be floating in his mind, he is a mere legacy-hunter, and is angling for an inheritance. Like the birds which feed upon carcases, which come close to animals weakened by disease, and watch till they fall, so these men are attracted by death and hover around a corpse.

21

A grateful mind is attracted only by a sense of the beauty of its purpose. Do you wish to know this to be so, and that it is not bribed by ideas of profit? There are two classes of grateful men: a man is called grateful who has made some return for what he received; this man may very possibly display himself in this character, he has something to boast of, to refer to. We also call a man grateful who receives a benefit with goodwill, and owes it to his benefactor with goodwill; yet this man's gratitude lies concealed within his own mind. What profit can accrue to him from this latent feeling? yet this man, even though he is not able to do anything more than this, is grateful; he loves his benefactor, he feels his debt to him, he longs to repay his kindness; whatever else you may find wanting, there is nothing wanting in the man. He is like a workman who has not the tools necessary for the practice of his craft, or like a trained singer whose voice cannot be heard through the noise of those who interrupt him. I wish to repay a kindness: after this there still remains something for me to do, not in order that I may become grateful, but that I may discharge my debt; for, in many cases, he who returns a kindness is ungrateful for it, and he who does not return it is grateful. Like all other virtues, the whole value of gratitude lies in the spirit in which it is done; so, if this man's purpose be loyal, any shortcomings on his part are due not to himself, but to fortune. A man who is silent may, nevertheless, be eloquent; his hands may be folded or even bound, and he may yet be strong; just as a pilot is a pilot even when upon dry land, because his knowledge is complete, and there is nothing wanting to it, though there may be obstacles which prevent his making use of it. In the same way, a man is grateful who only wishes to be so, and who has no one but himself who can bear witness to his frame of mind. I will go even further than this: a man sometimes is grateful when he appears to be ungrateful, when ill-judging report has declared him to be so. Such a man can look to nothing but his own conscience, which can please him even when overwhelmed by calumny, which contradicts the mob and common rumour, relies only upon itself, and though it beholds a vast crowd of the other way of thinking opposed to it, does not count heads, but wins by its own vote alone. Should it see its own good faith meet with the punishment due to treachery, it will not descend from its pedestal, and will remain superior to its punishment. "I have," it says, "what I wished, what I strove for. I do not regret it, nor shall I do so; nor shall Fortune, however unjust she may be, ever hear me say, 'What did I want? What now is the use of having meant well?' " A good conscience is of value on the rack, or in the fire; though fire be applied to each of our limbs, gradually encircle our living bodies, and burst our heart, yet if our heart be filled with a good conscience, it will rejoice in the fire which will make its good faith shine before the world.

22

Now let that question also which has been already stated be again brought forward; Why is it that we should wish to be grateful when we are dying, that we should carefully weigh the various services rendered us by different individuals, and carefully review our whole life, that we may not seem to have forgotten any kindness? Nothing then remains for us to hope for; yet when on the very threshold, we wish to depart from human life as full of gratitude as possible. There is in truth an immense reward for this thing merely in doing it, and what is honourable has great power to attract men's minds, which are overwhelmed by its beauty and carried off their balance, enchanted by its brilliancy and splendour. "Yet," argues our adversary, "from it many advantages take their rise, and good men obtain a safer life and love, and the good opinion of the better class, while their days are spent in greater security when accompanied by innocence and gratitude."

Indeed, nature would have been most unjust had she rendered this great blessing miserable, uncertain, and fruitless. But consider this point, whether you would make your way to that virtue, to which it is generally safe and easy to attain, even though the path lay over rocks and precipices, and were beset with fierce beasts and venomous serpents. A virtue is none the less to be desired for its own sake, because it has some adventitious profit connected with it: indeed, in most cases the noblest virtues are accompanied by many extraneous advantages, but it is the virtues that lead the way, and these merely follow in their train.

23

Can we doubt that the climate of this abode of the human race is regulated by the motion of the sun and moon in their orbits? that our bodies are sustained, the hard earth loosened, excessive moisture reduced, and the surly bonds of winter broken by the heat of the one, and that crops are brought to ripeness by the effectual all-pervading warmth of the other? that the fertility of the human race corresponds to the courses of the moon? that the sun by its revolution marks out the year, and that the moon, moving in a smaller orbit, marks out the months? Yet, setting aside all this, would not the sun be a sight worthy to be contemplated and worshipped, if he did no more than rise and set? would not the moon be worth looking at, even if it passed uselessly through the heavens? Whose attention is not arrested by the universe itself, when by night it pours forth its fires and glitters with innumerable stars? Who, while he admires them, thinks of their being of use to him? Look at that great company gliding over our heads, how they conceal their swift motion under the semblance of a fixed and immovable work. How much takes place in that night which you make use of merely to mark and count your days! What a mass of events is being prepared in that silence! What a chain of destiny their unerring path is forming! Those which you imagine to be merely strewn about for ornament are really one and all at work. Nor is there any ground for your belief that only seven stars revolve, and that the rest remain still: we understand the orbits of a few, but countless divinities, further removed from our sight, come and go; while the greater part of those whom our sight reaches move in a mysterious manner and by an unknown path.

24

What then? would you not be captivated by the sight of such a stupendous work, even though it did not cover you, protect you, cherish you, bring you into existence and penetrate you with its spirit? Though these heavenly bodies are of the very first importance to us, and are, indeed, essential to our life, yet we can think of nothing but their glorious majesty, and similarly all virtue, especially that of gratitude, though it confers great advantages upon us, does not wish to be loved for that reason; it has something more in it than this, and he who merely reckons it among useful things does not perfectly comprehend it. A man, you say, is grateful because it is to his advantage to be so. If this be the case, then his advantage will be the measure of his gratitude. Virtue will not admit a covetous lover; men must approach her with open purse. The ungrateful man thinks, "I did wish to be grateful, but I fear the expense and danger and insults to which I should expose myself: I will rather consult my own interest." Men cannot be rendered grateful and ungrateful by the same line of reasoning: their actions are as distinct as their purposes. The one is ungrateful, although it is wrong, because it is his interest; the other is grateful, although it is not his interest, because it is right.

25

It is our aim to live in harmony with the scheme of the universe, and to follow the example of the gods. Yet in all their acts the gods have no object in view other than the act itself, unless you suppose that they obtain a reward for their work in the smoke of burnt sacrifices and the scent of incense. See what great things they do every day, how much they divide amongst us, with how great crops they fill the earth, how they move the seas with convenient winds to carry us to all shores, how by the fall of sudden showers they soften the ground, renew the dried-up springs of fountains, and call them into new life by unseen supplies of water. All this they do without reward, without any advantage accruing to themselves. Let our line of conduct, if it would not depart from its model, preserve this direction, and let us not act honourably because we are hired to do so. We ought to feel ashamed that any benefit should have a price: we pay nothing for the gods.

26

"If," our adversary may say, "you wish to imitate the gods, then bestow benefits upon the ungrateful as well as the grateful; for the sun rises upon the wicked as well as the good, the seas are open even to pirates." By this question he really asks whether a good man would bestow a benefit upon an ungrateful person, knowing him to be ungrateful. Allow me here to introduce a short explanation, that we may not be taken in by a deceitful question. Understand that according to the system of the Stoics there are two classes of ungrateful persons. One man is ungrateful because he is a fool; a fool is a bad man; a man who is bad possesses every vice: therefore he is ungrateful. In the same way we speak of all bad men as dissolute, avaricious, luxurious, and spiteful, not because each man has all these vices in any great or remarkable degree, but because he might have them; they are in him, even though they be not seen. The second form of ungrateful person is he who is commonly meant by the term, one who is inclined by nature to this vice. In the case of him who has the vice of ingratitude just as he has every other, a wise man will bestow a benefit, because if he sets aside all such men there will be no one left for him to bestow it on. As for the ungrateful man who habitually misapplies benefits and acts so by choice, he will no more bestow a benefit upon him than he would lend money to a spendthrift, or place a deposit in the hands of one who had already often refused to many persons to give up the property with which they had entrusted him.

27

We call some men timid because they are fools: in this they are like the bad men who are steeped in all vices without distinction. Strictly speaking, we call those persons timid who are alarmed even at unmeaning noises. A fool possesses all vices, but he is not equally inclined by nature to all; one is prone to avarice, another to luxury, and another to insolence. Those persons, therefore, are mistaken, who ask the Stoics, "What do you say, then? is Achilles timid? Aristides, who received a name for justice, is he unjust? Fabius, who 'by delays retrieved the day,' is he rash? Does Decius fear death? Is Mucius a traitor? Camillus a betrayer?" We do not mean that all vices are inherent in all men in the same way in which some especial ones are noticeable in certain men, but we declare that the bad man and the fool possess all vices; we do not even acquit them of fear when they are rash, or of avarice when they are extravagant. Just as a man has all his senses, yet all men have not on that account as keen a sight as Lynceus, so a man that is a fool has not all vices in so active and vigorous a form as some persons have some of them, yet he has them all. All vices exist in all of them, yet all are not prominent in each individual. One man is naturally prone to avarice, another is the slave of wine, a third of lust; or, if not yet enslaved by these passions, he is so fashioned by nature that this is the direction in which his character would probably lead him. Therefore, to return to my original proposition, every bad man is ungrateful, because he has the seeds of every villainy in him; but he alone is rightly so called who is naturally inclined to this vice. Upon such a person as this, therefore, I shall not bestow a benefit. One who betrothed his daughter to an ill-tempered man from whom many women had sought a divorce, would be held to have neglected her interests; a man would be thought a bad father if he entrusted the care of his patrimony to one who had lost his own family estate, and it would be the act of a madman to make a will naming as the guardian of one's son a man who had already defrauded other wards. So will that man be said to bestow benefits as badly as possible, who chooses ungrateful persons, in whose hands they will perish.

28

"The gods," it may be said, "bestow much, even upon the ungrateful." But what they bestow they had prepared for the good, and the bad have their share as well, because they cannot be separated. It is better to benefit the bad as well, for the sake of benefiting the good, than to stint the good for fear of benefiting the bad. Therefore the gods have created all that you speak of, the day, the sun, the alternations of winter and summer, the transitions through spring and autumn from one extreme to the other, showers, drinking fountains, and regularly blowing winds for the use of all alike; they could not except individuals from the enjoyment of them. A king bestows honours upon those who deserve them, but he gives largesse to the undeserving as well. The thief, the bearer of false witness, and the adulterer, alike receive the public grant of corn, and all are placed on the register without any examination as to character; good and bad men share alike in all the other privileges which a man receives, because he is a citizen, not because he is a good man. God likewise has bestowed certain gifts upon the entire human race, from which no one is shut out. Indeed, it could not be arranged that the wind which was fair for good men should be foul for bad ones, while it is for the good of all men that the seas should be open for traffic and the kingdom of mankind be enlarged; nor could any law be appointed for the showers, so that they should not fall upon the fields of wicked and evil men. Some things are given to all alike: cities are founded for good and bad men alike; works of genius reach, by publication, even unworthy men; medicine points out the means of health even to the wicked; no one has checked the making up of wholesome remedies for fear that the undeserving should be healed. You must seek for examination and preference of individuals in such things as are bestowed separately upon those who are thought to deserve them; not in these, which admit the mob to share them without distinction. There is a great difference between not shutting a man out and choosing him. Even a thief receives justice; even murderers enjoy the blessings of peace; even those who have plundered others can recover their own property; assassins and private bravoes are defended against the common enemy by the city wall; the laws protect even those who have sinned most deeply against them. There are some things which no man could obtain unless they were given to all; you need not, therefore, cavil about those matters in which all mankind is invited to share. As for things which men receive or not at my discretion, I shall not bestow them upon one whom I know to be ungrateful.

29

"Shall we, then," argues he, "not give our advice to an ungrateful man when he is at a loss, or refuse him a drink of water when he is thirsty, or not show him the path when he has lost his way? or would you do him these services and yet not give him anything?" Here I will draw a distinction, or at any rate endeavour to do so. A benefit is a useful service, yet all useful service is not a benefit; for some are so trifling as not to claim the title of benefits. To produce a benefit two conditions must concur. First, the importance of the thing given; for some things fall short of the dignity of a benefit. Who ever called a hunch of bread a benefit, or a farthing dole tossed to a beggar, or the means of lighting a fire? yet sometimes these are of more value than the most costly benefits; still their cheapness detracts from their value even when, by the exigency of time, they are rendered essential. The next condition, which is the most important of all, must necessarily be present, namely, that I should confer the benefit for the sake of him whom I wish to receive it, that I should judge him worthy of it, bestow it of my own free will, and receive pleasure from my own gift, none of which conditions are present in the cases of which we have just now spoken; for we do not bestow such things as those upon these who are worthy of them, but we give them carelessly, as trifles, and do not give them so much to a man as to humanity.

30

I shall not deny that sometimes I would give even to the unworthy, out of respect for others; as, for instance, in competition for public offices, some of the basest of men are preferred on account of their noble birth, to industrious men of no family, and that for good reasons; for the memory of great virtues is sacred, and more men will take pleasure in being good, if the respect felt for good men does not cease with their lives. What made Cicero's son a consul, except his father? What lately brought Cinna[10] out of the camp of the enemy and raised him to the consulate? What made Sextus Pompeius and the other Pompeii consuls, unless it was the greatness of one man, who once was raised so high that, by his very fall, he sufficiently exalted all his relatives. What lately made Fabius Persicus a member of more than one college of priests, though even profligates avoided his kiss? Was it not Verrucosus, and Allobrogicus, and the three hundred who to serve their

---

[10] See "On Clemency," Book I, Chapter IX

country blocked the invader's path with the force of a single family? It is our duty to respect the virtuous, not only when present with us, but also when removed from our sight: as they have made it their study not to bestow their benefits upon one age alone, but to leave them existing after they themselves have passed away, so let us not confine our gratitude to a single age. If a man has begotten great men, he deserves to receive benefits, whatever he himself may be: he has given us worthy men. If a man descends from glorious ancestors, whatever he himself may be, let him find refuge under the shadow of his ancestry. As mean places are lighted up by the rays of the sun, so let the degenerate shine in the light of their forefathers.

31

In this place, my Liberalis, I wish to speak in defence of the gods. We sometimes say, "What could Providence mean by placing an Arrhidaeus upon the throne?" Do you suppose that the crown was given to Arrhidaeus? nay, it was given to his father and his brother. Why did Heaven bestow the empire of the world upon Caius Caesar, the most bloodthirsty of mankind, who was wont to order blood to be shed in his presence as freely as if he wished to drink of it? Why do you suppose that it was given to him? It was given to his father, Germanicus, to his grandfather, his great grandfather, and to others before them, no less illustrious men, though they lived as private citizens on a footing of equality with others. Why, when you yourself were making Mamercus Scaurus consul, were you ignorant of his vices? did he himself conceal them? did he wish to appear decent?

Did you admit a man who was so openly filthy to the fasces and the tribunal? Yes, it was because you were thinking of the great old Scaurus, the chief of the Senate, and were unwilling that his descendant should be despised.

32

It is probable that the gods act in the same manner, that they show greater indulgence to some for the sake of their parents and their ancestry, and to others for the sake of their children and grandchildren, and a long line of descendants beyond them; for they know the whole course of their works, and have constant access to the knowledge of all that shall hereafter pass through their hands. These things come upon us from the unknown future, and the gods have foreseen and are familiar with the events by which we are startled. "Let these men," says Providence, "be kings, because their ancestors were good kings, because they regarded righteousness and temperance as the highest rule of life, because they did not devote the State to themselves, but devoted themselves to the State. Let these others reign, because some one of their ancestors before them was a good man, who bore a soul superior to fortune, who preferred to be conquered rather than to conquer in civil strife, because it was more to the advantage of the State.[11] It was not possible to make a sufficient return to him for this during so long a time; let this other, therefore, out of regard for him, be chief of the people, not because he knows how, or is capable, but because the other has earned it for him. This man is misshapen, loathsome to look upon, and will disgrace the insignia of his office. Men will presently blame me, calling me blind and reckless, not knowing upon whom I am conferring what ought to be given to the greatest and noblest of men; but I know that, in giving this dignity to one man, I am paying an old debt to another. How should the men of today know that ancient hero, who so resolutely avoided the glory which pressed upon him, who went into danger with the same look which other men wear when they have escaped from danger, who never regarded his own interest as apart from that of the commonwealth?" "Where," you ask, "or who is he? whence does he come?" "You know him not; it lies with me to balance the debit and credit account in such cases as these; I know how much I owe to each man; I repay some after a long interval, others beforehand, according as my opportunities and the exigencies of my social system permit." I shall, therefore, sometimes bestow somewhat upon an ungrateful man, though not for his own sake.

33

"What," argues he, "if you do not know whether your man be ungrateful or grateful—will you wait until you know, or will you not lose the opportunity of bestowing a benefit? To wait is a long business—for, as Plato says, it is hard to form an opinion about the human mind—not to wait, is rash." To this objector we shall answer, that we never should wait for absolute knowledge of the whole case, since the discovery of truth is an arduous task, but should proceed in the direction in which truth appeared to direct us. All our actions proceed in this direction: it is thus that we sow seed, that we sail upon the sea, that we serve in the army, marry, and bring up children. The result of all these actions is uncertain, so we take that course from which we believe that good results may be hoped for. Who can guarantee a harvest to the sower, a harbour to the sailor, victory to the soldier, a modest wife to the husband, dutiful children to the father? We proceed in the way in which reason, not absolute truth, directs us. Wait, do nothing that will not turn out well, form no opinion until you have searched but the truth, and your life will pass in absolute inaction. Since it is only the appearance of truth, not truth itself, which leads me hither or thither, I shall confer benefits upon the man who apparently will be grateful.

---

[11] Gertz, "Stud. Crit.," p. 159, note.

34

"Many circumstances," argues he, "may arise which may enable a bad man to steal into the place of a good one, or may cause a good man to be disliked as though he were a bad one; for appearances, to which we trust, are deceptive." Who denies it? Yet I can find nothing else by which to guide my opinion. I must follow these tracks in my search after truth, for I have none more trustworthy than these; I will take pains to weigh the value of these with all possible care, and will not hastily give my assent to them. For instance, in a battle, it may happen that my hand may be deceived by some mistake into turning my weapon against my comrade, and sparing my enemy as though he were on my side; but this will not often take place, and will not take place through any fault of mine, for my object is to strike the enemy, and defend my countryman. If I know a man to be ungrateful, I shall not bestow a benefit upon him. But the man has passed himself off as a good man by some trick, and has imposed upon me. Well, this is not at all the fault of the giver, who gave under the impression that his friend was grateful. "Suppose," asks he, "that you were to promise to bestow a benefit, and afterwards were to learn that your man was ungrateful, would you bestow it or not? If you do, you do wrong knowingly, for you give to one to whom you ought not; if you refuse, you do wrong likewise, for you do not give to him to whom you promised to give. This case upsets your consistency, and that proud assurance of yours that the wise man never regrets his actions, or amends what he has done, or alters his plans." The wise man never changes his plans while the conditions under which he formed them remain the same; therefore, he never feels regret, because at the time nothing better than what he did could have been done, nor could any better decision have been arrived at than that which was made; yet he begins everything with the saving clause, "If nothing shall occur to the contrary." This is the reason why we say that all goes well with him, and that nothing happens contrary to his expectation, because he bears in mind the possibility of something happening to prevent the realization of his projects. It is an imprudent confidence to trust that fortune will be on our side. The wise man considers both sides: he knows how great is the power of errors, how uncertain human affairs are, how many obstacles there are to the success of plans. Without committing himself, he awaits the doubtful and capricious issue of events, and weighs certainty of purpose against uncertainty of result. Here also, however, he is protected by that saving clause, without which he decides upon nothing, and begins nothing.

35

When I promise to bestow a benefit, I promise it, unless something occurs which makes it my duty not to do so. What if, for example, my country orders me to give to her what I had promised to my friend? or if a law be passed forbidding anyone to do what I had promised to do for him? Suppose that I have promised you my daughter in marriage, that then you turn out to be a foreigner, and that I have no right of intermarriage with foreigners; in this case, the law, by which I am forbidden to fulfil my promise, forms my defence. I shall be treacherous, and hear myself blamed for inconsistency, only if I do not fulfil my promise when all conditions remain the same as when I made it; otherwise, any change makes me free to reconsider the entire case, and absolves me from my promise. I may have promised to plead a cause; afterwards it appears that this cause is designed to form a precedent for an attack upon my father. I may have promised to leave my country, and travel abroad; then news comes that the road is beset with robbers. I was going to an appointment at some particular place; but my son's illness, or my wife's confinement, prevented me. All conditions must be the same as they were when I made the promise, if you mean to hold me bound in honour to fulfil it. Now what greater change can take place than that I should discover you to be a bad and ungrateful man? I shall refuse to an unworthy man that which I had intended to give him supposing him to be worthy, and I shall also have reason to be angry with him for the trick which he has put upon me.

36

I shall nevertheless look into the matter, and consider what the value of the thing promised may be. If it be trifling, I shall give it, not because you are worthy of it, but because I promised it, and I shall not give it as a present, but merely in order to make good my words and give myself a twitch of the ear. I will punish my own rashness in promising by the loss of what I gave. "See how grieved you are; mind you take more care what you say in future." As the saying is, I will take tongue money from you. If the matter be important, I will not, as Maecenas said, let ten million sesterces reproach me. I will weigh the two sides of the question one against the other: there is something in abiding by what you have promised; on the other hand, there is a great deal in not bestowing a benefit upon one who is unworthy of it. Now, how great is this benefit? If it is a trifling one, let us wink and let it pass; but if it will cause me much loss or much shame to give it, I had rather excuse myself once for refusing it than have to do so ever after for giving it. The whole point, I repeat, depends upon how much the thing given is worth: let the terms of my promise be appraised. Not only shall I refuse to give what I may have promised rashly, but I shall also demand back again what I may have wrongly bestowed: a man must be mad who keeps a promise made under a mistake.

37

Philip, king of the Macedonians, had a hardy soldier whose services he had found useful in many campaigns. From time to time he made this man presents of part of the plunder as the reward of his valour, and used to excite his greedy spirit by his frequent gifts. This man was cast by shipwreck upon the estate of a certain Macedonian, who as soon as he heard the news hastened to him, restored his breath, removed him to his own farmhouse, gave up his own bed to him, nursed him out of his weakened and half-dead condition, took care of him at his own expense for thirty days, restored him to health and gave him a sum of money for his journey, as the man kept constantly saying, "If only I can see my chief, I will repay your kindness." He told Philip of his shipwreck, said nothing about the help which he had received, and at once demanded that a certain man's estate should be given to him. The man was a friend of his: it was that very man by whom he had been rescued and restored to health. Sometimes, especially in time of war, kings bestow many gifts with their eyes shut. One just man cannot deal with such a mass of armed selfishness. It is not possible for anyone to be at the same time a good man and a good general. How are so many thousands of insatiable men to be satiated? What would they have, if every man had his own? Thus Philip reasoned with himself while he ordered the man to be put in possession of the property which he asked for. However, the other, when driven out of his estate, did not, like a peasant, endure his wrongs in silence, thankful that he himself was not given away also, but sent a sharp and outspoken letter to Philip, who, on reading it, was so much enraged that he straightaway ordered Pausanias to restore the property to its former owner, and to brand that wickedest of soldiers, that most ungrateful of guests, that greediest of shipwrecked men, with letters bearing witness to his ingratitude. He, indeed, deserved to have the letters not merely branded but carved in his flesh, for having reduced his host to the condition in which he himself had been when he lay naked and shipwrecked upon the beach; still, let us see within what limits one ought to keep in punishing him. Of course what he had so villainously seized ought to be taken from him. But who would be affected by the spectacle of his punishment? The crime which he had committed would prevent his being pitied even by any humane person.

38

Will Philip then give you a thing because he has promised to give it, even though he ought not to do so, even though he will commit a wrong by doing so, nay, a crime, even though by this one act he will make it impossible for shipwrecked men to reach the shore? There is no inconsistency in giving up an intention which we have discovered to be wrong and have condemned as wrong; we ought candidly to admit, "I thought that it was something different; I have been deceived." It is mere pride and folly to persist, "what I once have said, be it what it may, shall remain unaltered and settled." There is no disgrace in altering one's plans according to circumstances. Now, if Philip had left this man in possession of that seashore which he obtained by his shipwreck, would he not have practically pronounced sentence of banishment against all unfortunates for the future? "Rather," says Philip, "do thou carry upon thy forehead of brass those letters, that they may be impressed upon the eyes of all throughout my kingdom. Go, let men see how sacred a thing is the table of hospitality; show them your face, that upon it they may read the decree which prevents its being a capital crime to give refuge to the unfortunate under one's roof. The order will be more certainly respected by this means than if I had inscribed it upon tablets of brass."

39

"Why then," argues our adversary, "did your Stoic philosopher Zeno, when he had promised a loan of five hundred denarii to some person, whom he afterwards discovered to be of doubtful character, persist in lending it, because of his promise, though his friends dissuaded him from doing so?" In the first place a loan is on a different footing to a benefit. Even when we have lent money to an undesirable person we can recall it; I can demand payment upon a certain day, and if he becomes bankrupt, I can obtain my share of his property; but a benefit is lost utterly and instantly. Besides, the one is the act of a bad man, the other that of a bad father of a family. In the next place, if the sum had been a larger one, not even Zeno would have persisted in lending it. It was five hundred denarii; the sort of sum of which one says, "May he spend it in sickness," and it was worth paying so much to avoid breaking his promise. I shall go out to supper, even though the weather be cold, because I have promised to go; but I shall not if snow be falling. I shall leave my bed to go to a betrothal feast, although I may be suffering from indigestion; but I shall not do so if I am feverish. I will become bail for you, because I promised; but not if you wish me to become bail in some transaction of uncertain issue, if you expose me to forfeiting my money to the State. There runs through all these cases, I argue, an implied exception; if I am able, provided it is right for me to do so, if these things be so and so. Make the position the same when you ask me to fulfil my promise, as it was when I gave it, and it will be mere fickleness to disappoint you; but if something new has taken place in the meanwhile, why should you wonder at my intentions being changed when the conditions under which I gave the promise are changed? Put everything back as it was, and I shall be the same as I was. We enter into recognizances to appear, yet if we fail to do so an action will not in all cases lie against us, for we are excused for making default if forced to do so by a power which we cannot resist.

40

You may take the same answer to the question as to whether we ought in all cases to show gratitude for kindness, and whether a benefit ought in all cases to be repaid. It is my duty to show a grateful mind, but in some cases my own poverty, in others the prosperity of the friend to whom I owe some return, will not permit me to give it. What, for instance, am I, a poor man, to give to a king or a rich man in return for his kindness, especially as some men regard it as a wrong to have their benefits repaid, and are wont to pile one benefit upon another? In dealing with such persons, what more can I do than wish to repay them? Yet I ought not to refuse to receive a new benefit, because I have not repaid the former one. I shall take it as freely as it is given, and will offer myself to my friend as a wide field for the exercise of his good nature: he who is unwilling to receive new benefits must be dissatisfied with what he has already received. Do you say, "I shall not be able to return them?" What is that to the purpose? I am willing enough to do so if opportunity or means were given me. He gave it to me, of course, having both opportunity and means: is he a good man or a bad one? if he is a good man, I have a good case against him, and I will not plead if he be a bad one. Neither do I think it right to insist on making repayment, even though it be against the will of those whom we repay, and to press it upon them however reluctant they may be; it is not repayment to force an unwilling man to resume what you were once willing to take. Some people, if any trifling present be sent to them, afterwards send back something else for no particular reason, and then declare that they are under no obligation; to send something back at once, and balance one present by another, is the next thing to refusing to receive it. On some occasions I shall not return a benefit, even though I be able to do so. When? When by so doing I shall myself lose more than he will gain, or if he would not notice any advantage to himself in receiving that which it would be a great loss to me to return. The man who is always eager to repay under all circumstances, has not the feeling of a grateful man, but of a debtor; and, to put it shortly, he who is too eager to repay, is unwilling to be in his friend's debt; he who is unwilling, and yet is in his friend's debt, is ungrateful.

BOOK 5

1

In the preceding books I seem to have accomplished the object which I proposed to myself, since in them I have discussed how a benefit ought to be bestowed, and how it ought to be received. These are the limits of this action; when I dwell upon it further I am not obeying the orders, but the caprices of my subject which ought to be followed whither it leads, not whither it allures us to wander; for now and then something will arise, which, although it is all but unconnected with the subject, instead of being a necessary part of it, still thrills the mind with a certain charm. However, since you wish it to be so, let us go on, after having completed our discussion of the heads of the subject itself, to investigate those matters which, if you wish for truth, I must call adjacent to it, not actually connected with it; to examine which carefully is not one worth one's while, and yet is not labour in vain. No praise, however, which I can give to benefits does justice to you, Aebutius Liberalis, a man of excellent disposition and naturally inclined to bestow them. Never have I seen anyone esteem even the most trifling services more kindly; indeed, your good-nature goes so far as to regard whatever benefit is bestowed upon anyone as bestowed upon yourself; you are prepared to pay even what is owed by the ungrateful, that no one may regret having bestowed benefits. You yourself are so far from any boastfulness, you are so eager at once to free those whom you serve from any feeling of obligation to you, that you like, when giving anything to anyone, to seem not so much to be giving a present as returning one; and therefore what you give in this manner will all the more fully he repaid to you: for, as a rule, benefits come to one who does not demand repayment of them; and just as glory follows those who avoid it, so men receive a more plentiful harvest in return for benefits bestowed upon those who had it in their power to be ungrateful. With you there is no reason why those who have received benefits from you should not ask for fresh ones; nor would you refuse to bestow others, to overlook and conceal what you have given, and to add to it more and greater gifts, since it is the aim of all the best men and the noblest dispositions to bear with an ungrateful man until you make him grateful. Be not deceived in pursuing this plan; vice, if you do not too soon begin to hate it, will yield to virtue.

2

Thus it is that you are especially pleased with what you think the grandly-sounding phrase, "It is disgraceful to be worsted in a contest of benefits." Whether this be true or not deserves to be investigated, and it means something quite different from what you imagine; for it is never disgraceful to be worsted in any honourable contest, provided that you do not throw down your arms, and that even when conquered you wish to conquer. All men do not strive for a good object with the same strength, resources, and good fortune, upon which depend at all events the issues of the most admirable projects, though we ought to praise the will itself which makes an effort in the right direction. Even though another passes it by with swifter pace, yet the palm of victory does not, as in publicly-exhibited races, declare which is the better man; though even in the games chance frequently brings an inferior man to the front. As far as loyalty of feeling goes, which each man wishes to be possessed in the fullest measure on his own side, if one of the two be the more powerful, if he have at his disposal all the resources which he wishes to use, and be favoured by fortune in his most ambitious efforts, while the other, although equally willing, can only return less than he receives, or perhaps can make no return at all, but still wishes to do so and is entirely devoted to this object; then the latter is no more conquered than he who dies in arms, whom the enemy found it easier to slay than to turn back. To be conquered, which you consider disgraceful, cannot happen to a good man; for he will never surrender, never give up the contest, to the last day of his life he will stand prepared and in that posture he will die, testifying that though he has received much, yet that he had the will to repay as much as he had received.

3

The Lacedaemonians forbid their young men to contend in the pancratium, or with the *caestus*, in which games the defeated party has to acknowledge himself beaten. The winner of a race is he who first reaches the goal; he outstrips the others in swiftness, but not in courage. The wrestler who has been thrown three times loses the palm of victory, but does not yield it up. Since the Lacedaemonians thought it of great importance that their countrymen should be invincible, they kept them away from those contests in which victory is assigned, not by the judge, or by the issue of the contest itself, but by the voice of the vanquished begging the victor to spare him as he falls. This attribute of never being conquered, which they so jealously guard among their citizens, can be attained by all men through virtue and goodwill, because even when all else is vanquished, the mind remains unconquered. For this cause no one speaks of the three hundred Fabii as conquered, but slaughtered. Regulus was taken captive by the Carthaginians, not conquered; and so were all other men who have not yielded in spirit when overwhelmed by the strength and weight of angry Fortune.

So is it with benefits. A man may have received more than he gave, more valuable ones, more frequently bestowed; yet is he not vanquished. It may be that, if you compare the benefits with one another, those which he has received will outweigh those which he has bestowed; but if you compare the giver and the receiver, whose intentions also ought to be considered apart, neither will prove the victor. It often happens that even when one combatant is pierced with many wounds, while the other is only slightly injured, yet they are said to have fought a drawn battle, although the former may appear to be the worse man.

4

No one, therefore, can be conquered in a contest of benefits, if he knows how to owe a debt, if he wishes to make a return for what he has received, and raises himself to the same level with his friend in spirit, though he cannot do so in material gifts. As long as he remains in this temper of mind, as long as he has the wish to declare by proofs that he has a grateful mind, what difference does it make upon which side we can count the greater number of presents? You are able to give much; I can do nothing but receive. Fortune abides with you, goodwill alone with me; yet I am as much on an equality with you as naked or lightly armed men are with a large body armed to the teeth. No one, therefore, is worsted by benefits, because each man's gratitude is to be measured by his will. If it be disgraceful to be worsted in a contest of benefits, you ought not to receive a benefit from very powerful men whose kindness you cannot return, I mean such as princes and kings, whom fortune has placed in such a station that they can give away much, and can only receive very little and quite inadequate returns for what they give. I have spoken of kings and princes, who alone can cause works to be accomplished, and whose superlative power depends upon the obedience and services of inferiors; but some there are, free from all earthly lusts, who are scarcely affected by any human objects of desire, upon whom Fortune herself could bestow nothing. I must be worsted in a contest of benefits with Socrates, or with Diogenes, who walked naked through the treasures of Macedonia, treading the king's wealth under his feet. In good sooth, he must then rightly have seemed, both to himself and to all others whose eyes were keen enough to perceive the real truth, to be superior even to him at whose feet all the world lay. He was far more powerful, far richer even than Alexander, who then possessed everything; for there was more that Diogenes could refuse to receive than that Alexander was able to give.

5

It is not disgraceful to be worsted by these men, for I am not the less brave because you pit me against an invulnerable enemy, nor does fire not burn because you throw into it something over which flames have no power, nor does iron lose its power of cutting, though you may wish to cut up a stone which is hard, impervious to blows, and of such a nature that hard tools are blunted upon it. I give you the same answer about gratitude. A man is not disgracefully worsted in a contest of benefits if he lays himself under an obligation to such persons as these, whose enormous wealth or admirable virtue shut out all possibility of their benefits being returned. As a rule we are worsted by our parents; for while we have them with us, we regard them as severe, and do not understand what they do for us. When our age begins to bring us a little sense, and we gradually perceive that they deserve our love for those very things which used to prevent our loving them, their advice, their punishments, and the careful watch which they used to keep over our youthful recklessness, they are taken from us. Few live to reap any real fruit from children; most men feel their sons only as a burden. Yet there is no disgrace in being worsted by one's parent in bestowing benefits; how should there be, seeing that there is no disgrace in being worsted by anyone. We are equal to some men, and yet not equal; equal in intention, which is all that they care for, which is all that we promise to be, but unequal in fortune. And if fortune prevents anyone from repaying a kindness, he need not, therefore, blush, as though he were vanquished; there is no disgrace in failing to reach your object, provided you attempt to reach it. It often is necessary, that before making any return for the benefits which we have received, we should ask for new ones; yet, if so, we shall not refrain from asking for them, nor shall we do so as though disgraced by so doing, because, even if we do not repay the debt, we shall owe it; because, even if something from without befalls us to prevent our repaying it, it will not be our fault if we are not grateful. We can neither be conquered in intention, nor can we be disgraced by yielding to what is beyond our strength to contend with.

6

Alexander, the king of the Macedonians, used to boast that he had never been worsted by anybody in a contest of benefits. If so, it was no reason why, in the fullness of his pride, he should despise the Macedonians, Greeks, Carians, Persians, and other tribes of whom his army was composed, nor need he imagine that it was this that gave him an empire reaching from a corner of Thrace to the shore of the unknown sea. Socrates could make the same boast, and so could Diogenes, by whom Alexander was certainly surpassed; for was he not surpassed on the day when, swelling as he was beyond the limits of merely human pride, he beheld one to whom he could give nothing, from whom he could take nothing? King Archelaus invited Socrates to come to him. Socrates is reported to have answered that he should be sorry to go to one who would bestow benefits upon him, since he should not be able to make him an adequate return for them. In the first place, Socrates was at liberty not to receive them; next, Socrates himself would have been the first to bestow a benefit, for he would have come when invited, and would have given to

Archelaus that for which Archelaus could have made no return to Socrates. Even if Archelaus were to give Socrates gold and silver, if he learned in return for them to despise gold and silver, would not Socrates be able to repay Archelaus? Could Socrates receive from him as much value as he gave, in displaying to him a man skilled in the knowledge of life and of death, comprehending the true purpose of each? Suppose that he had found this king, as it were, groping his way in the clear sunlight, and had taught him the secrets of nature, of which he was so ignorant, that when there was an eclipse of the sun, he shut up his palace, and shaved his son's head,[12] which men are wont to do in times of mourning and distress. What a benefit it would have been if he had dragged the terror-stricken king out of his hiding-place, and bidden him be of good cheer, saying, "This is not a disappearance of the sun, but a conjunction of two heavenly bodies; for the moon, which proceeds along a lower path, has placed her disk beneath the sun, and hidden it by the interposition of her own mass. Sometimes she only hides a small portion of the sun's disk, because she only grazes it in passing; sometimes she hides more, by placing more of herself before it; and sometimes she shuts it out from our sight altogether, if she passes in an exactly even course between the sun and the Earth. Soon, however, their own swift motion will draw these two bodies apart; soon the Earth will receive back again the light of day. And this system will continue throughout centuries, having certain days, known beforehand, upon which the sun cannot display all rays, because of the intervention of the moon. Wait only for a short time; he will soon emerge, he will soon leave that seeming cloud, and freely shed abroad his light without any hindrances." Could Socrates not have made an adequate return to Archelaus, if he had taught him to reign? as though Socrates would not benefit him sufficiently, merely by enabling him to bestow a benefit upon Socrates. Why, then, did Socrates say this? Being a joker and a speaker in parables—a man who turned all, especially the great, into ridicule—he preferred giving him a satirical refusal, rather than an obstinate or haughty one, and therefore said that he did not wish to receive benefits from one to whom he could not return as much as he received. He feared, perhaps, that he might be forced to receive something which he did not wish, he feared that it might be something unfit for Socrates to receive. Someone may say, "He ought to have said that he did not wish to go." But by so doing he would have excited against himself the anger of an arrogant king, who wished everything connected with himself to be highly valued. It makes no difference to a king whether you be unwilling to give anything to him or to accept anything from him; he is equally incensed at either rebuff, and to be treated with disdain is more bitter to a proud spirit than not to be feared. Do you wish to know what Socrates really meant? He, whose freedom of speech could not be borne even by a free state, was not willing of his own choice to become a slave.

---

[12] Gertz very reasonably conjectures that he shaved his own head which reading would require a very trifling alteration of the text.

7

I think that we have sufficiently discussed this part of the subject, whether it be disgraceful to be worsted in a contest of benefits. Whoever asks this question must know that men are not wont to bestow benefits upon themselves, for evidently it could not be disgraceful to be worsted by oneself. Yet some of the Stoics debate this question, whether anyone can confer a benefit upon himself, and whether one ought to return one's own kindness to oneself. This discussion has been raised in consequence of our habit of saying, "I am thankful to myself," "I can complain of no one but myself," "I am angry with myself," "I will punish myself," "I hate myself," and many other phrases of the same sort, in which one speaks of oneself as one would of some other person. "If," they argue, "I can injure myself, why should I not be able also to bestow a benefit upon myself? Besides this, why are those things not called benefits when I bestow them upon myself which would be called benefits if I bestowed them upon another? If to receive a certain thing from another would lay me under an obligation to him, how is it that if I give it to myself, I do not contract an obligation to myself? why should I be ungrateful to my own self, which is no less disgraceful than it is to be mean to oneself, or hard and cruel to oneself, or neglectful of oneself? The procurer is equally odious whether he prostitutes others or himself. We blame a flatterer, and one who imitates another man's mode of speech, or is prepared to give praise whether it be deserved or not; we ought equally to blame one who humours himself and looks up to himself, and so to speak is his own flatterer. Vices are not only hateful when outwardly practised, but also when they are repressed within the mind. Whom would you admire more than he who governs himself and has himself under command? It is easier to rule savage nations, impatient of foreign control, than to restrain one's own mind and keep it under one's own control. Plato, it is argued, was grateful to Socrates for having been taught by him; why should not Socrates be grateful to himself for having taught himself? Marcus Cato said, "Borrow from yourself whatever you lack;" why, then, if I can lend myself anything, should I be unable to give myself anything? The instances in which usage divides us into two persons are innumerable; we are wont to say, "Let me converse with myself," and, "I will give myself a twitch of the ear;"[13] and if it be true that one can do so, then a man ought to be grateful to himself, just as he is angry with himself; as he blames himself, so he ought to praise himself; since he can impoverish himself, he can also enrich himself. Injuries and benefits are the converse of one another: if we say of a man, "he has done himself an injury," we can also say, "he has bestowed upon himself a benefit?"

---

[13] See Book IV, Chapter XXXVI.

8

It is natural that a man should first incur an obligation, and then that he should return gratitude for it; a debtor cannot exist without a creditor, any more than a husband without a wife, or a son without a father; someone must give in order that someone may receive. Just as no one carries himself, although he moves his body and transports it from place to place; as no one, though he may have made a speech in his own defence, is said to have stood by himself, or erects a statue to himself as his own patron; as no sick man, when by his own care he has regained his health, asks himself for a fee; so in no transaction, even when a man does what is useful to himself, need he return thanks to himself, because there is no one to whom he can return them. Though I grant that a man can bestow a benefit upon himself, yet at the same time that he gives it, he also receives it; though I grant that a man may receive a benefit from himself, yet he receives it at the same time that he gives it. The exchange takes place within doors, as they say, and the transfer is made at once, as though the debt were a fictitious one; for he who gives is not a different person to he who receives, but one and the same. The word "to owe" has no meaning except as between two persons; how then can it apply to one man who incurs an obligation, and by the same act frees himself from it? In a disk or a ball there is no top or bottom, no beginning or end, because the relation of the parts is changed when it moves, what was behind coming before, and what went down on one side coming up on the other, so that all the parts, in whatever direction they may move, come back to the same position. Imagine that the same thing takes place in a man; into however many pieces you may divide him, he remains one. If he strikes himself, he has no one to call to account for the insult; if he binds himself and locks himself up, he cannot demand damages; if he bestows a benefit upon himself, he straightaway returns it to the giver. It is said that there is no waste in nature, because everything which is taken from nature returns to her again, and nothing can perish, because it cannot fall out of nature, but goes round again to the point from whence it started. You ask, "What connection has this illustration with the subject?" I will tell you. Imagine yourself to be ungrateful; the benefit bestowed upon you is not lost, he who gave it has it; suppose that you are unwilling to receive it, it still belongs to you before it is returned. You cannot lose anything, because what you take away from yourself, you nevertheless gain yourself. The matter revolves in a circle within yourself; by receiving you give, by giving you receive.

9

"It is our duty," argues our adversary, "to bestow benefits upon ourselves; therefore we ought also to be grateful to ourselves." The original axiom, upon which the inference depends, is untrue, for no one bestows benefits upon himself, but obeys the dictates of his nature, which disposes him to affection for himself, and which makes him take the greatest pains to avoid hurtful things, and to follow after those things which are profitable to him. Consequently, the man who gives to himself is not generous, nor is he who pardons himself forgiving, nor is he who is touched by his own misfortunes tenderhearted; it is natural to do those things to oneself which when done to others become generosity, clemency, and tenderness of heart. A benefit is a voluntary act, but to do good to oneself is an instinctive one. The more benefits a man bestows, the more beneficent he is, yet who ever was praised for having been of service to himself? or for having rescued himself from brigands? No one bestows a benefit upon himself any more than he bestows hospitality upon himself; no one gives himself anything, any more than he lends himself anything. If each man bestows benefits upon himself, is always bestowing them, and bestows them without any cessation, then it is impossible for him to make any calculation of the number of his benefits; when then can he show his gratitude, seeing that by the very act of doing so he would bestow a benefit? for what distinction can you draw between giving himself a benefit or receiving a benefit for himself, when the whole transaction takes place in the mind of the same man? Suppose that I have freed myself from danger, then I have bestowed a benefit upon myself; suppose I free myself a second time, by so doing do I bestow or repay a benefit? In the next place, even if I grant the primary axiom, that we can bestow benefits upon ourselves, I do not admit that which follows; for even if we can do so, we ought not to do so. Wherefore? Because we receive a return for them at once. It is right for me to receive a benefit, then to lie under an obligation, then to repay it; now here there is no time for remaining under an obligation, because we receive the return without any delay. No one really gives except to another, no one owes except to another, no one repays except to another. An act which always requires two persons cannot take place within the mind of one.

10

A benefit means the affording of something useful, and the word "affording" implies other persons. Would not a man be thought mad if he said that he had sold something to himself, because selling means alienation, and the transferring of a thing and of one's rights in that thing to another person? Yet giving, like selling anything, consists in making it pass away from you, handing over what you yourself once owned into the keeping of someone else.

If this be so, no one ever gave himself a benefit, because no one gives to himself; if not, two opposites coalesce, so that it becomes the same thing to give and to receive. Yet there is a great difference between giving and receiving; how should there not be, seeing that these words are the converse of one another? Still, if anyone can give himself a benefit, there can be no difference between giving and receiving. I said a little before that some words apply only to other persons, and are so constituted that their whole meaning lies apart from ourselves; for instance, I am a brother, but a brother of some other man, for no one is his own brother; I am an equal, but equal to somebody else, for who is equal to himself? A thing which is compared to another thing is unintelligible without that other thing; a thing which is joined to something else does not exist apart from it; so that which is given does not exist without the other person, nor can a benefit have any existence without another person. This is clear from the very phrase which describes it, "to do good," yet no one does good to himself, any more than he favours himself or is on his own side. I might enlarge further upon this subject and give many examples. Why should benefits not be included among those acts which require two persons to perform them? Many honourable, most admirable and highly virtuous acts cannot take place without a second person. Fidelity is praised and held to be one of the chief blessings known among men, yet was anyone ever on that account said to have kept faith with himself?

11

I come now to the last part of this subject. The man who returns a kindness ought to expend something, just as he who repays expends money; but the man who returns a kindness to himself expends nothing, just as he who receives a benefit from himself gains nothing. A benefit and gratitude for it must pass to and fro between two persons; their interchange cannot take place within one man. He who returns a kindness does good in his turn to him from whom he has received something; but the man who returns his own kindness, to whom does he do good? To himself? Is there anyone who does not regard the returning of a kindness, and the bestowal of a benefit, as distinct acts? "He who returns a kindness to himself does good to himself." Was any man ever unwilling to do this, even though he were ungrateful? nay, who ever was ungrateful from any other motive than this? "If," it is argued, "we are right in thanking ourselves, we ought to return our own kindness;" yet we say, "I am thankful to myself for having refused to marry that woman," or "for having refused to join a partnership with that man." When we speak thus, we are really praising ourselves, and make use of the language of those who return thanks to approve our own acts. A benefit is something which, when given, may or may not be returned. Now, he who gives a benefit to himself must needs receive what he gives; therefore, this is not a benefit. A benefit is received at one time, and is returned at another; (but when a man bestows a benefit upon himself, he both receives it and returns it at the same time). In a benefit, too, what we commend and admire is, that a man has for the time being forgotten his own interests, in order that he may do good to another; that he has deprived himself of something, in order to bestow it upon another. Now, he who bestows a benefit upon himself does not do this. The bestowal of a benefit is an act of companionship—it wins some man's friendship, and lays some man under an obligation; but to bestow it upon oneself is no act of companionship—it wins no man's friendship, lays no man under an obligation, raises no man's hopes, or leads him to say, "This man must be courted; he bestowed a benefit upon that person, perhaps he will bestow one upon me also." A benefit is a thing which one gives not for one's own sake, but for the sake of him to whom it is given; but he who bestows a benefit upon himself, does so for his own sake; therefore, it is not a benefit.

12

Now I seem to you not to have made good what I said at the beginning of this book. You say that I am far from doing what is worth anyone's while; nay, that in real fact I have thrown away all my trouble. Wait, and soon you will be able to say this more truly, for I shall lead you into covert lurking-places, from which when you have escaped, you will have gained nothing except that you will have freed yourself from difficulties with which you need never have hampered yourself. What is the use of laboriously untying knots which you yourself have tied, in order that you might untie them? Yet, just as some knots are tied in fun and for amusement, so that a tyro may find difficulty in untying them, which knots he who tied them can loose without any trouble, because he knows the joinings and the difficulties of them, and these nevertheless afford us some pleasure, because they test the sharpness of our wits, and engross our attention; so also these questions, which seem subtle and tricky, prevent our intellects becoming careless and lazy, for they ought at one time to have a field given them to level, in order that they may wander about it, and at another to have some dark and rough passage thrown in their way for them to creep through, and make their way with caution. It is said by our opponent that no one is ungrateful; and this is supported by the following arguments: "A benefit is that which does good; but, as you Stoics say, no one can do good to a bad man; therefore, a bad man does not receive a benefit. (If he does not receive it, he need not return it; therefore, no bad man is ungrateful.) Furthermore, a benefit is an honourable and commendable thing. No honourable or commendable thing can find any place with a bad man; therefore, neither can a benefit. If he cannot receive one, he need not repay one; therefore, he does not become ungrateful. Moreover, as you say, a good man does everything rightly; if he does everything rightly, he cannot be ungrateful. A good man returns a benefit, a bad man does not receive one. If this be so, no man, good or bad, can be ungrateful. Therefore, there is no such thing in nature as an ungrateful man: the word is meaningless." We Stoics have only one kind of good, that which is honourable. This cannot come to a bad man, for he would cease to be bad if virtue entered into him; but as long as he is bad, no one can bestow a benefit upon him, because good and bad are contraries, and cannot exist together. Therefore, no one can do good to such a man, because whatever he receives is corrupted by his vicious way of using it. Just as the stomach, when disordered by disease and secreting bile, changes all the food which it receives, and turns every kind of sustenance into a source of pain, so whatever you entrust to an ill-regulated mind becomes to it a burden, an annoyance, and a source of misery. Thus the most prosperous and the richest men have the most trouble; and the more property they have to perplex them, the less likely they are to find out what they really are. Nothing, therefore, can reach bad men which would do them good; nay, nothing which would not do them harm. They change whatever falls to their lot into their own evil nature; and things which elsewhere would, if given to better men, be both beautiful and profitable, are ruinous to them. They cannot, therefore, bestow benefits, because no one can give what he does not possess, and, therefore, they lack the pleasure of doing good to others.

13

But, though this be so, yet even a bad man can receive some things which resemble benefits, and he will be ungrateful if he does not return them. There are good things belonging to the mind, to the body, and to fortune. A fool or a bad man is debarred from the first—those, that is, of the mind; but he is admitted to a share in the two latter, and, if he does not return them, he is ungrateful. Nor does this follow from our (Stoic) system alone the Peripatetics, also, who widely extend the boundaries of human happiness, declare that trifling benefits reach bad men, and that he who does not return them is ungrateful. We therefore do not agree that things which do not tend to improve the mind should be called benefits, yet do not deny that these things are convenient and desirable. Such things as these a bad man may bestow upon a good man, or may receive from him—such, for example, as money, clothes, public office, or life; and, if he makes no return for these, he will come under the denomination of ungrateful. "But how can you call a man ungrateful for not returning that which you say is not a benefit?" Some things, on account of their similarity, are included under the same designation, although they do not really deserve it. Thus we speak of a silver or golden box;[14] thus we call a man illiterate, although he may not be utterly ignorant, but only not acquainted with the higher branches of literature; thus, seeing a badly-dressed ragged man we say that we have seen a naked man. These things of which we spoke are not benefits, but they possess the appearance of benefits. "Then, just as they are quasi-benefits, so your man is quasi-ungrateful, not really ungrateful." This is untrue, because both he who gives and he who receives them speaks of them as benefits; so he who fails to return the semblance of a real benefit is as much an ungrateful man as he who mixes a sleeping draught, believing it to be poison, is a poisoner.

---

[14] "The original word is *pyx*, which means a box made of boxwood."

14

Cleanthes speaks more impetuously than this. "Granted," says he, "that what he received was not a benefit, yet he is ungrateful, because he would not have returned a benefit if he had received one." So he who carries deadly weapons and has intentions of robbing and murdering, is a brigand even before he has dipped his hands in blood; his wickedness consists and is shown in action, but does not begin thereby. Men are punished for sacrilege, although no one's hands can reach to the gods. "How," asks our opponent, "can anyone be ungrateful to a bad man, since a bad man cannot bestow a benefit?" In the same way, I answer, because that which he received was not a benefit, but was called one; if anyone receives from a bad man any of those things which are valued by the ignorant, and of which bad men often possess great store, it becomes his duty to make a return in the same kind, and to give back as though they were truly good those things which he received as though they were truly good. A man is said to be in debt, whether he owes gold pieces or leather marked with a state stamp, such as the Lacedaemonians used, which passes for coined money. Pay your debts in that kind in which you incurred them. You have nothing to do with the definition of benefits, or with the question whether so great and noble a name ought to be degraded by applying it to such vulgar and mean matters as these, nor do we seek for truth that we may use it to the disadvantage of others; do you adjust your minds to the semblance of truth, and while you are learning what is really honourable, respect everything to which the name of honour is applied.

15

"In the same way," argues our adversary, "that your school proves that no one is ungrateful, you afterwards prove that all men are ungrateful. For, as you say, all fools are bad men; he who has one vice has all vices; all men are both fools and bad men; therefore all men are ungrateful." Well, what then? Are they not? Is not this the universal reproach of the human race? is there not a general complaint that benefits are thrown away, and that there are very few men who do not requite their benefactors with the basest ingratitude? Nor need you suppose that what we say is merely the grumbling of men who think every act wicked and depraved which falls short of an ideal standard of righteousness. Listen! I know not who it is who speaks, yet the voice with which he condemns mankind proceeds not from the schools of philosophers, but from the midst of the crowd:

> "Host is not safe from guest;
> Father-in-law from son; but seldom love
> Exists 'twixt brothers; wives long to destroy
> Their husbands; husbands long to slay their wives."

This goes even further: according to this, crimes take the place of benefits, and men do not shrink from shedding the blood of those for whom they ought to shed their own; we requite benefits by steel and poison. We call laying violent hands upon our own country, and putting down its resistance by the fasces of its own lictors, gaining power and great place; every man thinks himself to be in a mean and degraded position if he has not raised himself above the constitution; the armies which are received from the State are turned against her, and a general now says to his men, "Fight against your wives, fight against your children, march in arms against your altars, your hearths and homes!" Yes,[15] you, who even when about to triumph ought not to enter the city at the command of the senate, and who have often, when bringing home a victorious army, been given an audience outside the walls, you now, after slaughtering your countrymen, stained with the blood of your kindred, march into the city with standards erect. "Let liberty," say you, "be silent amidst the ensigns of war, and now that wars are driven far away and no ground for terror remains, let that people which conquered and civilized all nations be beleaguered within its own walls, and shudder at the sight of its own eagles."

16

Coriolanus was ungrateful, and became dutiful late, and after repenting of his crime; he did indeed lay down his arms, but only in the midst of his unnatural warfare. Catilina was ungrateful; he was not satisfied with taking his country captive without overturning it, without despatching the hosts of the Allobroges against it, without bringing an enemy from beyond the Alps to glut his old inborn hatred, and to offer Roman generals as sacrifices which had been long owing to the tombs of the Gaulish dead. Caius Marius was ungrateful, when, after being raised from the ranks to the consulship, he felt that he would not have wreaked his vengeance upon fortune, and would sink to his original obscurity, unless he slaughtered Romans as freely as he had slaughtered the Cimbri, and not merely gave the signal, but was himself the signal for civil disasters and butcheries. Lucius Sulla was ungrateful, for he saved his country by using remedies worse than the perils with which it was threatened, when he marched through human blood all the way from the citadel of Praeneste to the Colline Gate, fought more battles and caused more slaughter afterwards within the city, and most cruelly after the victory was won, most wickedly after quarter had been promised them, drove two legions into a corner and put them to the sword, and, great gods! invented a proscription by which he who slew a Roman citizen received indemnity, a sum of money, everything but a civic crown! Cnaeus Pompeius was ungrateful, for the return which he made to his country for three consulships, three triumphs, and the innumerable public offices into most of which

---

[15] I believe, in spite of Gertz, that this is part of the speech of the Roman general, and that the conjecture of Muretus, "without the command of the senate," gives better sense.

he thrust himself when under age, was to lead others also to lay hands upon her under the pretext of thus rendering his own power less odious; as though what no one ought to do became right if more than one person did it. Whilst he was coveting extraordinary commands, arranging the provinces so as to have his own choice of them, and dividing the whole State with a third person,[16] in such a manner as to leave two-thirds of it in the possession of his own family,[17] he reduced the Roman people to such a condition that they could only save themselves by submitting to slavery. The foe and conqueror[18] of Pompeius was himself ungrateful; he brought war from Gaul and Germany to Rome, and he, the friend of the populace, the champion of the commons, pitched his camp in the Circus Flaminus, nearer to the city than Porsena's camp had been. He did, indeed, use the cruel privileges of victory with moderation; as was said at the time, he protected his countrymen, and put to death no man who was not in arms. Yet what credit is there in this? Others used their arms more cruelly, but flung them away when glutted with blood, while he, though he soon sheathed the sword, never laid it aside. Antonius was ungrateful to his dictator, who he declared was rightly slain, and whose murderers he allowed to depart to their commands in the provinces; as for his country, after it had been torn to pieces by so many proscriptions, invasions, and civil wars, he intended to subject it to kings, not even of Roman birth, and to force that very state to pay tribute to eunuchs,[19] which had itself restored sovereign rights, autonomy, and immunities, to the Achaeans, the Rhodians, and the people of many other famous cities.

17

The day would not be long enough for me to enumerate those who have pushed their ingratitude so far as to ruin their native land. It would be as vast a task to mention how often the State has been ungrateful to its best and most devoted lovers, although it has done no less wrong than it has suffered. It sent Camillus and Scipio into exile; even after the death of Catiline it exiled Cicero, destroyed his house, plundered his property, and did everything which Catiline would have done if victorious; Rutilius found his virtue rewarded with a hiding-place in Asia; to Cato the Roman people refused the praetorship, and persisted in refusing the consulship. We are ungrateful in public matters; and if every man asks himself, you will find that there is no one who has not some private ingratitude to complain of. Yet it is impossible that all men should complain, unless all were deserving of complaint, therefore all men are

---

[16] Crassus.

[17] Pompey was married to Caesar's daughter. Cf. Virgil, *Æneid*, VI, 831, sq., and Lucan's beautiful verses, *Pharsalia*, I, 114.

[18] Seneca is careful to avoid the mention of Caesar's name, which might have given offence to the emperors under whom he lived, who used the name as a title.

[19] The allusion is to Antonius's connection with Cleopatra. Cf. Virgil, *Æneid*, VIII, 688.

ungrateful. Are they ungrateful alone? nay, they are also all covetous, all spiteful, and all cowardly, especially those who appear daring; and, besides this, all men fawn upon the great, and all are impious. Yet you need not be angry with them; pardon them, for they are all mad. I do not wish to recall you to what is not proved, or to say, "See how ungrateful is youth! what young man, even if of innocent life, does not long for his father's death? even if moderate in his desires, does not look forward to it? even if dutiful, does not think about it? How few there are who fear the death even of the best of wives, who do not even calculate the probabilities of it. Pray, what litigant, after having been successfully defended, retains any remembrance of so great a benefit for more than a few days?" All agree that no one dies without complaining. Who on his last day dares to say,

"I've lived, I've done the task which Fortune set me."

Who does not leave the world with reluctance, and with lamentations? Yet it is the part of an ungrateful man not to be satisfied with the past. Your days will always be few if you count them. Reflect that length of time is not the greatest of blessings; make the best of your time, however short it may be; even if the day of your death be postponed, your happiness will not be increased, for life is merely made longer, not pleasanter, by delay. How much better is it to be thankful for the pleasures which one has received, not to reckon up the years of others, but to set a high value upon one's own, and score them to one's credit, saying, "God thought me worthy of this; I am satisfied with it; he might have given me more, but this, too, is a benefit." Let us be grateful towards both gods and men, grateful to those who have given us anything, and grateful even to those who have given anything to our relatives.

18

"You render me liable to an infinite debt of gratitude," says our opponent, "when you say 'even to those who have given anything to our relations,' so fix some limit. He who bestows a benefit upon the son, according to you, bestows it likewise upon the father: this is the first question I wish to raise. In the next place I should like to have a clear definition of whether a benefit, if it be bestowed upon your friend's father as well as upon himself, is bestowed also upon his brother? or upon his uncle? or his grandfather? or his wife and his father-in-law? tell me where I am to stop, how far I am to follow out the pedigree of the family?"

Seneca: If I cultivate your land, I bestow a benefit upon you; if I extinguish your house when burning, or prop it so as to save it from falling, I shall bestow a benefit upon you; if I heal your slave, I shall charge it to you; if I save your son's life, will you not thereby receive a benefit from me?

19

The Adversary: Your instances are not to the purpose, for he who cultivates my land, does not benefit the land, but me; he who props my house so that it does not fall, does this service to me, for the house itself is without feeling, and as it has none, it is I who am indebted to him; and he who cultivates my land does so because he wishes to oblige me, not to oblige the land. I should say the same of a slave; he is a chattel owned by me; he is saved for my advantage, therefore I am indebted for him. My son is himself capable of receiving a benefit; so it is he who receives it; I am gratified at a benefit which comes so near to myself, but am not laid under any obligation.

Seneca: Still I should like you, who say that you are under no obligation, to answer me this. The good health, the happiness, and the inheritance of a son are connected with his father; his father will be more happy if he keeps his son safe, and more unhappy if he loses him. What follows, then? when a man is made happier by me and is freed from the greatest danger of unhappiness, does he not receive a benefit?

The Adversary: No, because there are some things which are bestowed upon others, and yet flow from them so as to reach ourselves; yet we must ask the person upon whom it was bestowed for repayment; as for example, money must be sought from the man to whom it was lent, although it may, by some means, have come into my hands. There is no benefit whose advantages do not extend to the receiver's nearest friends, and sometimes even to those less intimately connected with him; yet we do not enquire whither the benefit has proceeded from him to whom it was first given, but where it was first placed. You must demand repayment from the defendant himself personally.

Seneca: Well, but I pray you, do you not say, "you have preserved my son for me; had he perished, I could not have survived him?" Do you not owe a benefit for the life of one whose safety you value above your own? Moreover, should I save your son's life, you would fall down before my knees, and would pay vows to heaven as though you yourself had been saved; you would say, "It makes no difference whether you have saved mine or me; you have saved us both, yet me more than him." Why do you say this, if you do not receive a benefit?

The Adversary: Because, if my son were to contract a loan, I should pay his creditor, yet I should not, therefore, be indebted to him; or if my son were taken in adultery, I should blush, yet I should not, therefore, be an adulterer. I say that I am under an obligation to you for saving my son, not because I really am, but because I am willing to constitute myself your debtor of my own free will. On the other hand I have derived from his safety the greatest possible pleasure and advantage, and I have escaped that most dreadful blow, the loss of my child. True, but we are not now discussing whether you have done me any good or not, but whether you have bestowed a benefit upon me; for animals, stones, and herbs can do one good, but do not bestow benefits, which can only be given by one who wishes well to the receiver.

Now you do not wish well to the father, but only to the son; and sometimes you do not even know the father. So when you have said, "Have I not bestowed a benefit upon the father by saving the son?" you ought to meet this with, "Have I, then, bestowed a benefit upon a father whom I do not know, whom I never thought of?" And what will you say when, as is sometimes the case, you hate the father, and yet save his son? Can you be thought to have bestowed a benefit upon one whom you hated most bitterly while you were bestowing it?

However, if I were to lay aside the bickering of dialogue, and answer you as a lawyer, I should say that you ought to consider the intention of the giver, you must regard his benefit as bestowed upon the person upon whom he meant to bestow it. If he did it in honour of the father, then the father received the benefit; if he thought only of the son, then the father is not laid under any obligation: by the benefit which was conferred upon the son, even though the father derives pleasure from it. Should he, however, have an opportunity, he will himself wish to give you something, yet not as though he were forced to repay a debt, but rather as if he had grounds for beginning an exchange of favours. No return for a benefit ought to be demanded from the father of the receiver; if he does you any kindness in return for it, he should be regarded as a righteous man, but not as a grateful one. For there is no end to it; if I bestow a benefit on the receiver's father, do I likewise bestow it upon his mother, his grandfather, his maternal uncle, his children, relations, friends, slaves, and country? Where, then, does a benefit begin to stop? for there follows it this endless chain of people, to whom it is hard to assign bounds, because they join it by degrees, and are always creeping on towards it.

20

A common question is, "Two brothers are at variance. If I save the life of one, do I confer a benefit upon the other, who will be sorry that his hated brother did not perish?" There can be no doubt that it is a benefit to do good to a man, even against that man's will, just as he, who against his own will does a man good, does not bestow a benefit upon him. "Do you," asks our adversary, "call that by which he is displeased and hurt a benefit?" Yes; many benefits have a harsh and forbidding appearance, such as cutting or burning to cure disease, or confining with chains. We must not consider whether a man is grieved at receiving a benefit, but whether he ought to rejoice: a coin is not bad because it is refused by a savage who is unacquainted with its proper stamp. A man receives a benefit even though he hates what is done, provided that it does him good, and that the giver bestowed it in order to do him good. It makes no difference if he receives a good thing in a bad spirit. Consider the converse of this. Suppose that a man hates his brother, though it is to his advantage to have a brother, and I kill this brother, this is not a benefit, though he may say that it is, and be glad of it. Our most artful enemies are those whom we thank for the wrongs which they do us.

"I understand; a thing which does good is a benefit, a thing which does harm is not a benefit. Now I will suggest to you an act which neither does good nor harm, and yet is a benefit. Suppose that I find the corpse of someone's father in a wilderness, and bury it, then I certainly have done him no good, for what difference could it make to him in what manner his body decayed? Nor have I done any good to his son, for what advantage does he gain by my act?" I will tell you what he gains. He has by my means performed a solemn and necessary rite; I have performed a service for his father which he would have wished, nay, which it would have been his duty to have performed himself. Yet this act is not a benefit, if I merely yielded to those feelings of pity and kindliness which would make me bury any corpse whatever, but only if I recognized this body, and buried it, with the thought in my mind that I was doing this service to the son; but, by merely throwing earth over a dead stranger, I lay no one under an obligation for an act performed on general principles of humanity.

It may be asked, "Why are you so careful in inquiring upon whom you bestow benefits, as though some day you meant to demand repayment of them? Some say that repayment should never be demanded; and they give the following reasons. An unworthy man will not repay the benefit which he has received, even if it be demanded of him, while a worthy man will do so of his own accord. Consequently, if you have bestowed it upon a good man, wait; do not outrage him by asking him for it, as though of his own accord he never would repay it. If you have bestowed it upon a bad man, suffer for it, but do not spoil your benefit by turning it into a loan. Moreover the law, by not authorizing you, forbids you, by implication, to demand the repayment of a benefit." All this is nonsense. As long as I am in no pressing need, as long as I am not forced by poverty, I will lose my benefits rather than ask for repayment; but if the lives of my children were at stake, if my wife were in danger, if my regard for the welfare of my country and for my own liberty were to force me to adopt a course which I disliked, I should overcome my delicacy, and openly declare that I had done all that I could to avoid the necessity of receiving help from an ungrateful man; the necessity of obtaining repayment of one's benefit will in the end overcome one's delicacy about asking for it. In the next place, when I bestow a benefit upon a good man, I do so with the intention of never demanding repayment, except in case of absolute necessity.

21

"But," argues he, "by not authorizing you, the law forbids you to exact repayment." There are many things which are not enforced by any law or process, but which the conventions of society, which are stronger than any law, compel us to observe. There is no law forbidding us to divulge our friend's secrets; there is no law which bids us keep faith even with an enemy; pray what law is there which binds us to stand by what we have promised? There is none. Nevertheless I should remonstrate with one who did not keep a secret, and I should be indignant with one who pledged his word and broke it. "But," he argues, "you are turning a benefit into a loan." By no means, for I do not insist upon repayment, but only demand it; nay, I do not even demand it, but remind my friend of it. Even the direst need will not bring me to apply for help to one with whom I should have to undergo a long struggle.

If there be anyone so ungrateful that it is not sufficient to remind him of his debt, I should pass him over, and think that he did not deserve to be made grateful by force. A moneylender does not demand repayment from his debtors if he knows they have become bankrupt, and, to their shame, have nothing but shame left to lose; and I, like him, should pass over those who are openly and obstinately ungrateful, and would demand repayment only from those who were likely to give it me, not from those from whom I should have to extort it by force.

22

There are many who cannot deny that they have received a benefit, yet cannot return it—men who are not good enough to be termed grateful, nor yet bad enough to be termed ungrateful; but who are dull and sluggish, backward debtors, though not defaulters. Such men as these I should not ask for repayment, but forcibly remind them of it, and, from a state of indifference, bring them back to their duty. They would at once reply, "Forgive me; I did not know, by Hercules, that you missed this, or I would have offered it of my own accord, I beg that you will not think me ungrateful; I remember your goodness to me." Why need I hesitate to make such men as these better to themselves and to me? I would prevent anyone from doing wrong, if I were able; much more would I prevent a friend, both lest he should do wrong, and lest he should do wrong to me in particular. I bestow a second benefit upon him by not permitting him to be ungrateful; and I should not reproach him harshly with what I had done for him, but should speak as gently as I could. In order to afford him an opportunity of returning my kindness, I should refresh his remembrance of it, and ask for a benefit; he would understand that I was asking for repayment. Sometimes I would make use of somewhat severe language, if I had any hope that by it he might be amended; though I would not irritate a hopelessly ungrateful man, for fear that I might turn him into an enemy. If we spare the ungrateful even the affront of reminding them of their conduct, we shall render them more backward in returning benefits; and although some might be cured of their evil ways, and be made into good men, if their consciences were stung by remorse, yet we shall allow them to perish for want of a word of warning, with which a father sometimes corrects his son, a wife brings back to herself an erring husband, or a man stimulates the wavering fidelity of his friend.

23

To awaken some men, it is only necessary to stir them, not to strike them; in like manner, with some men, the feeling of honour about returning a benefit is not extinct, but slumbering. Let us rouse it. "Do not," they will say, "make the kindness you have done me into a wrong: for it is a wrong, if you do not demand some return from me, and so make me ungrateful. What if I do not know what sort of repayment you wish for? if I am so occupied by business, and my attention is so much diverted to other subjects that I have not been able to watch for an opportunity of serving you? Point out to me what I can do for you, what you wish me to do. Why do you despair, before making a trial of me? Why are you in such haste to lose both your benefit and your friend? How can you tell whether I do not wish, or whether I do not know how to repay you: whether it be in intention or in opportunity that I am wanting? Make a trial of me." I would therefore remind him of what I had done, without bitterness, not in public, or in a reproachful manner, but so that he may think that he himself has remembered it rather than that it has been recalled to him.

24

One of Julius Caesar's veterans was once pleading before him against his neighbours, and the cause was going against him. "Do you remember, general," said he, "that in Spain you dislocated your ankle near the river Sucro?"[20] When Caesar said that he remembered it, he continued, "Do you remember that when, during the excessive heat, you wished to rest under a tree which afforded very little shade, as the ground in which that solitary tree grew was rough and rocky, one of your comrades spread his cloak under you?"

Caesar answered, "Of course, I remember; indeed, I was perishing with thirst; and since I was unable to walk to the nearest spring, I would have crawled thither on my hands and knees, had not my comrade, a brave and active man, brought me water in his helmet."

"Could you, then, my general, recognize that man or that helmet?"

Caesar replied that he could not remember the helmet, but that he could remember the man well; and he added, I fancy in anger at being led away to this old story in the midst of a judicial enquiry, "At any rate, you are not he."

"I do not blame you, Caesar," answered the man, "for not recognizing me; for when this took place, I was unwounded; but afterwards, at the battle of Munda, my eye was struck out, and the bones of my skull crushed. Nor would you recognize that helmet if you saw it, for it was split by a Spanish sword." Caesar would not permit this man to be troubled with lawsuits, and presented his old soldier with the fields through which a village right of way had given rise to the dispute.

---

[20] Xucar.

25

In this case, what ought he to have done? Because his commander's memory was confused by a multitude of incidents, and because his position as the leader of vast armies did not permit him to notice individual soldiers, ought the man not to have asked for a return for the benefit which he had conferred? To act as he did is not so much to ask for a return as to take it when it lies in a convenient position ready for us, although we have to stretch out our hands in order to receive it. I shall therefore ask for the return of a benefit, whenever I am either reduced to great straits, or where by doing so I shall act to the advantage of him from whom I ask it. Tiberius Caesar, when someone addressed him with the words, "Do you remember … ?" answered, before the man could mention any further proofs of former acquaintance, "I do not remember what I was." Why should it not be forbidden to demand of this man repayment of former favours? He had a motive for forgetting them: he denied all knowledge of his friends and comrades, and wished men only to see, to think, and to speak of him as emperor. He regarded his old friend as an impertinent meddler.

We ought to be even more careful to choose a favorable opportunity when we ask for a benefit to be repaid to us than when we ask for one to be bestowed upon us. We must be temperate in our language, so that the grateful may not take offence, or the ungrateful pretend to do so. If we lived among wise men, it would be our duty to wait in silence until our benefits were returned. Yet even to wise men it would be better to give some hint of what our position required. We ask for help even from the gods themselves, from whose knowledge nothing is hid, although our prayers cannot alter their intentions towards us, but can only recall them to their minds. Homer's priest,[21] I say, recounts even to the gods his duteous conduct and his pious care of their altars. The second best form of virtue is to be willing and able to take advice.[22] A horse who is docile and prompt to obey can be guided hither and thither by the slightest movement of the reins. Very few men are led by their own reason: those who come next to the best are those who return to the right path in consequence of advice; and these we must not deprive of their guide. When our eyes are covered they still possess sight; but it is the light of day which, when admitted to them, summons them to perform their duty: tools lie idle, unless the workman uses them to take part in his work. Similarly men's minds contain a good feeling, which, however, lies torpid, either through luxury and disuse, or through ignorance of its duties. This we ought to render useful, and not to get into a passion with it, and leave it in its wrong doing, but bear with it patiently, just as schoolmasters bear patiently with the blunders of forgetful scholars; for as by the prompting of a word or two their memory is often recalled to the text of the speech which they have to repeat, so men's goodwill can be brought to return kindness by reminding them of it.

---

[21] *The Iliad*, I, 39 sqq.
[22] Hesiod, *Opera et Dies*, 291.

BOOK 6

1

There are some things, my most excellent Liberalis, which lie completely outside of our actual life, and which we only inquire into in order to exercise our intellects, while others both give us pleasure while we are discovering them, and are of use when discovered. I will place all these in your hands; you, at your own discretion, may order them either to be investigated thoroughly, or to be reserved, and be used as agreeable interludes. Something will be gained even by those which you dismiss at once, for it is advantageous even to know what subjects are not worth learning. I shall be guided, therefore, by your face: according to its expression, I shall deal with some questions at greater length, and drive others out of court, and put an end to them at once.

2

It is a question whether a benefit can be taken away from one by force. Some say that it cannot, because it is not a thing, but an act. A gift is not the same as the act of giving, any more than a sailor is the same as the act of sailing. A sick man and a disease are not the same thing, although no one can be ill without disease; and, similarly, a benefit itself is one thing, and what any of us receive through a benefit is another. The benefit itself is incorporeal, and never becomes invalid; but its subject-matter changes owners, and passes from hand to hand. So, when you take away from anyone what you have given him, you take away the subject-matter only of the benefit, not the benefit itself. Nature herself cannot recall what she has given. She may cease to bestow benefits, but cannot take them away: a man who dies, yet has lived; a man who becomes blind, nevertheless has seen. She can cut off her blessings from us in the future, but she cannot prevent our having enjoyed them in the past. We are frequently not able to enjoy a benefit for long, but the benefit is not thereby destroyed. Let Nature struggle as hard as she please, she cannot give herself retrospective action. A man may lose his house, his money, his property—everything to which the name of benefit can be given—yet the benefit itself will remain firm and unmoved; no power can prevent his benefactor's having bestowed them, or his having received them.

3

I think that a fine passage in Rabirius's poem, where M. Antonius, seeing his fortune deserting him, nothing left him except the privilege of dying, and even that only on condition that he used it promptly, exclaims,

"What I have given, that I now possess!"

How much he might have possessed, had he chosen! These are riches to be depended upon, which through all the turmoil of human life will remain steadfast; and the greater they are, the less envy they will attract. Why are you sparing of your property, as though it were your own? You are but the manager of it. All those treasures, which make you swell with pride, and soar above mere mortals, till you forget the weakness of your nature; all that which you lock up in iron-grated treasuries, and guard in arms, which you win from other men with their lives, and defend at the risk of your own; for which you launch fleets to dye the sea with blood, and shake the walls of cities, not knowing what arrows fortune may be preparing for you behind your back; to gain which you have so often violated all the ties of relationship, of friendship, and of colleagueship, till the whole world lies crushed between the two combatants: all these are not yours; they are a kind of deposit, which is on the point of passing into other hands: your enemies, or your heirs, who are little better, will seize upon them. "How," do you ask, "can you make them your own?" "By giving them away." Do, then, what is best for your own interests, and gain a sure enjoyment of them, which cannot be taken from you, making them at once more certainly yours, and more honorable to you. That which you esteem so highly, that by which you think that you are made rich and powerful, owns but the shabby title of "house," "slave," or "money;" but when you have given it away, it becomes a benefit.

4

"You admit," says our adversary, "that we sometimes are under no obligation to him from whom we have received a benefit. In that case it has been taken by force." Nay, there are many things which would cause us to cease to feel gratitude for a benefit, not because the benefit has been taken from me, but because it has been spoiled. Suppose that a man has defended me in a lawsuit, but has forcibly outraged my wife; he has not taken away the benefit which he conferred upon me, but by balancing it with an equivalent wrong, he has set me free from my debt; indeed, if he has injured me more than he had previously benefited me, he not only puts an end to my gratitude, but makes me free to revenge myself upon him, and to complain of him, when the wrong outweighs the benefit; in such a case the benefit is not taken away, but is overcome. Why, are not some fathers so cruel and so wicked that it is right and proper for their sons to turn away from them, and disown them? Yet, pray, have they taken away the life which they gave? No, but their unnatural conduct in later years has destroyed all the gratitude which was due to them for their original benefit. In these cases it is not a benefit itself, but the gratitude owing for a benefit which is taken away, and the result is, not that one does not possess the benefit, but that one is not laid under any obligation by it. It is as though a man were to lend me money, and then burn my house down; the advantage of the loan is balanced by the damage which he has caused: I do not repay him, and yet I am not in his debt. In like manner anyone who may have acted kindly and generously to me, and who afterwards has shown himself haughty, insulting, and cruel, places me in just the same position as though I never had received anything from him: he has murdered his own benefits. Though the lease may remain in force, still a man does not continue to be a tenant if his landlord tramples down his crops, or cuts down his orchard; their contract is at an end, not because the landlord has received the rent which was agreed upon, but because he has made it impossible that he should receive it. So, too, a creditor often has to pay money to his debtor, should he have taken more property from him in other transactions than he claims as having lent him. The judge does not sit merely to decide between debtor and creditor, when he says, "You did lend the man money; but then, what followed? You have driven away his cattle, you have murdered his slave, you have in your possession plate which you have not paid for. After valuing what each has received, I order you, who came to this court as a creditor, to leave it as a debtor." In like manner a balance is struck between benefits and injuries. In many cases, I repeat, a benefit is not taken away from him who receives it, and yet it lays him under no obligation, if the giver has repented of giving it, called himself unhappy because he gave it, sighed or made a wry face while he gave it; if he thought that he was throwing it away rather than giving it, if he gave it to please himself, or to please anyone except me, the receiver; if he persistently makes himself offensive by boasting of what he has done, if he brags of his gift everywhere, and makes it a misery to me, then indeed the benefit remains in my hands, but I owe him nothing for it, just as sums of money to which a creditor has no legal right are owed to him, but cannot be claimed by him.

5

Though you have bestowed a benefit upon me, yet you have since done me a wrong; the benefit demanded gratitude, the wrong required vengeance: the result is that I do not owe you gratitude, nor do you owe me compensation—each is cancelled by the other. When we say, "I returned him his benefit," we do not mean that we restored to him the very thing which we had received, but something else in its place. To return is to give back one thing instead of another, because, of course, in all repayment it is not the thing itself, but its equivalent which is returned. We are said to have returned money even though we count out gold pieces instead of silver ones, or even if no money passes between us, but the transaction be effected verbally by the assignment of a debt.

I think I see you say, "You are wasting your time; of what use is it to me to know whether what I do not owe to another still remains in my hands or not? These are like the ingenious subtleties of the lawyers, who declare that one cannot acquire an inheritance by prescription, but can only acquire those things of which the inheritance consists, as though there were any difference between the heritage and the things of which it consists. Rather decide this point for me, which may be of use. If the same man confers a benefit upon me, and afterwards does me a wrong, is it my duty to return the benefit to him, and nevertheless to avenge myself upon him, having, as it were, two distinct accounts open with him, or to mix them both together, and do nothing, leaving the benefit to be wiped out by the injury, the injury by the benefit? I see that the former course is adopted by the law of the land; you know best what the law may be among you Stoic philosophers in such a case. I suppose that you keep the action which I bring against another distinct from that which he brings against me, and the two processes are not merged into one? For instance, if a man entrusts me with money, and afterwards robs me, I shall bring an action against him for theft, and he will bring one against me for unlawfully detaining his property?"

6

The cases which you have mentioned, my Liberalis, come under well-established laws, which it is necessary for us to follow. One law cannot be merged in another: each one proceeds its own way. There is a particular action which deals with deposits just as there is one which deals with theft. A benefit is subject to no law; it depends upon my own arbitration. I am at liberty to contrast the amount of good or harm which anyone may have done me, and then to decide which of us is indebted to the other. In legal processes we ourselves have no power, we must go whither they lead us; in the case of a benefit the supreme power is mine, I pronounce sentence. Consequently I do not separate or distinguish between benefits and wrongs, but send them before the same judge. Unless I did so, you would bid me love and hate, give thanks and make complaints at the same time, which human nature does not admit of. I would rather compare the benefit and the injury with one another, and see whether there were any balance in my favour. If anybody puts lines of other writing upon my manuscript he conceals, though he does not take away, the letters which were there before, and in like manner a wrong coming after a benefit does not allow it to be seen.

7

Your face, by which I have agreed to be guided, now becomes wrinkled with frowns, as though I were straying too widely from the subject. You seem to say to me:

"Why steer to seaward? Hither bend thy course,
Hug close the shore …"

I do hug it as close as possible. So now, if you think that we have dwelt sufficiently upon this point, let us proceed to the consideration of the next—that is, whether we are at all indebted to anyone who does us good without wishing to do so. I might have expressed this more clearly, if it were not right that the question should be somewhat obscurely stated, in order that by the distinction immediately following it may be shown that we mean to investigate the case both of him who does us good against his will, and that of him who does us good without knowing it. That a man who does us good by acting under compulsion does not thereby lay us under any obligation, is so clear, that no words are needed to prove it. Both this question, and any other of the like character which may be raised, can easily be settled if in each case we bear in mind that, for anything to be a benefit, it must reach us in the first place through some thought, and secondly through the thought of a friend and well-wisher. Therefore we do not feel any gratitude towards rivers, albeit they may bear large ships, afford an ample and unvarying stream for the conveyance of merchandise, or flow beauteously and full of fish through fertile fields. No one conceives himself to be indebted for a benefit to the Nile, any more than he would owe it a grudge if its waters flooded his fields to excess, and retired more slowly than usual; the wind does not bestow benefits, gentle and favorable though it may be, nor does wholesome and useful food; for he who would bestow a benefit upon me, must not only do me good, but must wish to do so. No obligation can therefore be incurred towards dumb animals; yet how many men have been saved from peril by the swiftness of a horse!—nor yet towards trees—yet how many sufferers from summer heat have been sheltered by the thick foliage of a tree! What difference can it make, whether I have profited by the act of one who did not know that he was doing me good, or one who could not know it, when in each case the will to do me good was wanting? You might as well bid me be grateful to a ship, a carriage, or a lance for saving me from danger, as bid me be grateful to a man who may have done me good by chance, but with no more intention of doing me good than those things could have.

8

Some men may receive benefits without knowing it, but no man can bestow them without knowing it. Many sick persons have been cured by chance circumstances, which do not therefore become specific remedies; as, for instance, one man was restored to health by falling into a river during very cold weather, as another was set free from a quartan fever by means of a flogging, because the sudden terror turned his attention into a new channel, so that the dangerous hours passed unnoticed. Yet none of these are remedies, even though they may have been successful; and in like manner some men do us good, though they are unwilling—indeed, because they are unwilling to do so—yet we need not feel grateful to them as though we had received a benefit from them, because fortune has changed the evil which they intended into good. Do you suppose that I am indebted to a man who strikes my enemy with a blow which he aimed at me, who would have injured me had he not missed his mark? It often happens that by openly perjuring himself a man makes even trustworthy witnesses disbelieved, and renders his intended victim an object of compassion, as though he were being ruined by a conspiracy. Some have been saved by the very power which was exerted to crush them, and judges who would have condemned a man by law, have refused to condemn him by favour. Yet they did not confer a benefit upon the accused, although they rendered him a service, because we must consider at what the dart was aimed, not what it hits, and a benefit is distinguished from an injury not by its result, but by the spirit in which it was meant. By contradicting himself, by irritating the judge by his arrogance, or by rashly allowing his whole case to depend upon the testimony of one witness, my opponent may have saved my cause. I do not consider whether his mistakes benefited me or not, for he wished me ill.

9

In order that I may be grateful, I must wish to do what my benefactor must have wished in order that he might bestow a benefit. Can anything be more unjust than to bear a grudge against a person who may have trodden upon one's foot in a crowd, or splashed one, or pushed one the way which one did not wish to go? Yet it was by his act that we were injured, and we only refrain from complaining of him, because he did not know what he was doing. The same reason makes it possible for men to do us good without conferring benefits upon us, or to harm us without doing us wrong, because it is intention which distinguishes our friends from our enemies. How many have been saved from service in the army by sickness! Some men have been saved from sharing the fall of their house, by being brought up upon their recognizances to a court of law by their enemies; some have been saved by shipwreck from falling into the hands of pirates; yet we do not feel grateful to such things, because chance has no feeling of the service it renders, nor are we grateful to our enemy, though his lawsuit, while it harassed and detained us, still saved our lives. Nothing can be a benefit which does not proceed from good will, and which is not meant as such by the giver. If anyone does me a service, without knowing it, I am under no obligation to him; should he do so, meaning to injure me, I shall imitate his conduct.

10

Let us turn our attention to the first of these. Can you desire me to do anything to express my gratitude to a man who did nothing in order to confer a benefit upon me? Passing on to the next, do you wish me to show my gratitude to such a man, and of my own will to return to him what I received from him against his will? What am I to say of the third, he who, meaning to do an injury, blunders into bestowing a benefit? That you should have wished to confer a benefit upon me is not sufficient to render me grateful; but that you should have wished not to do so is enough to set me free from any obligation to you. A mere wish does not constitute a benefit; and just as the best and heartiest wish is not a benefit when fortune prevents its being carried into effect, neither is what fortune bestows upon us a benefit, unless good wishes preceded it. In order to lay me under an obligation, you must not merely do me a service, but you must do so intentionally.

11

Cleanthes makes use of the following example:—"I sent," says he, "two slaves to look for Plato and bring him to me from the Academy. One of them searched through the whole of the colonnade, and every other place in which he thought that he was likely to be found, and returned home alike weary and unsuccessful; the other sat down among the audience of a mountebank close by, and, while amusing himself in the society of other slaves like a careless vagabond as he was, found Plato, without seeking for him, as he happened to pass that way. We ought," says he, "to praise that slave who, as far as lay in his power, did what he was ordered, and we ought to punish the other whose laziness turned out so fortunate." It is goodwill alone which does one real service; let us then consider under what conditions it lays us under obligations. It is not enough to wish a man well, without doing him good; nor is it enough to do him good without wishing him well. Suppose that someone wished to give me a present, but did not give it; I have his good will, but I do not have his benefit, which consists of subject matter and goodwill together. I owe nothing to one who wished to lend me money but did not do so, and in like manner I shall be the friend of one who wished but was not able to bestow a benefit upon me, but I shall not be under any obligation to him. I also shall wish to bestow something upon him, even as he did upon me; but if fortune be more favorable to me than to him, and I succeed in bestowing something upon him, my doing so will be a benefit bestowed upon him, not a repayment out of gratitude for what he did for me. It will become his duty to be grateful to me; I shall have begun the interchange of benefits; the series must be counted from my act.

12

I already understand what you wish to ask; there is no need for you to say anything, your countenance speaks for you. "If anyone does us good for his own sake, are we," you ask, "under an obligation to him? I often hear you complain that there are some things which men make use of themselves, but which they put down to the account of others." I will tell you, my Liberalis; but first let me distinguish between the two parts of your question, and separate what is fair from what is unfair. It makes a great difference whether anyone bestows a benefit upon us for his own sake, or whether he does so partly for his own sake and partly for ours. He who looks only to his own interests, and who does us good because he cannot otherwise make a profit for himself, seems to me to be like the farmer who provides winter and summer fodder for his flocks, or like the man who feeds up the captives whom he has bought in order that they may fetch a better price in the slave market, or who crams and currycombs fat oxen for sale; or like the keeper of a school of arms, who takes great pains in exercising and equipping his gladiators. As Cleanthes says, there is a great difference between benefits and trade.

13

On the other hand, I am not so unjust as to feel no gratitude to a man, because, while helping me, he helped himself also; for I do not insist upon his consulting my interests to the exclusion of his own—nay, I should prefer that the benefit which I receive may be of even greater advantage to the giver, provided that he thought of us both when giving it, and meant to divide it between me and himself. Even should he possess the larger portion of it, still, if he admits me to a share, if he meant it for both of us, I am not only unjust but ungrateful, if I do not rejoice in what has benefited me benefiting him also. It is the essence of spitefulness to say that nothing can be a benefit which does not cause some inconvenience to the giver.

As for him who bestows a benefit for his own sake, I should say to him, "You have made use of me, and how can you say that you have bestowed a benefit upon me, rather than I upon you?" "Suppose," answers he, "that I cannot obtain a public office except by ransoming ten citizens out of a great number of captives, will you owe me nothing for setting you free from slavery and bondage? Yet I shall do so for my own sake." To this I should answer, "You do this partly for my sake, partly for your own. It is for your own sake that you ransom captives, but it is for my sake that you ransom me; for to serve your purpose it would be enough for you to ransom anyone. I am therefore your debtor, not for ransoming me but for choosing me, since you might have attained the same result by ransoming someone else instead of me. You divide the advantages of the act between yourself and me, and you confer upon me a benefit by which both of us profit. What you do entirely for my sake is, that you choose me in preference to others. If therefore you were to be made praetor for ransoming ten captives, and there were only ten of us captives, none of us would be under any obligation to you, because there is nothing for which you can ask any one of us to give you credit apart from your own advantage. I do not regard a benefit jealously and wish it to be given to myself alone, but I wish to have a share in it."

14

"Well, then," says he, "suppose that I were to order all your names to be put into a ballot-box, and that your name was drawn among those who were to be ransomed, would you owe me nothing?" Yes, I should owe you something, but very little: how little, I will explain to you. By so doing you do something for my sake, in that you grant me the chance of being ransomed; I owe to fortune that my name was drawn, all I owe to you is that my name could be drawn. You have given me the means of obtaining your benefit. For the greater part of that benefit I am indebted to fortune; that I could be so indebted, I owe to you.

I shall take no notice whatever of those whose benefits are bestowed in a mercenary spirit, who do not consider to whom, but upon what terms they give, whose benefits are entirely selfish. Suppose that someone sells me corn; I cannot live unless I buy it; yet I do not owe my life to him because I have bought it. I do not consider how essential it was to me, and that I could not live without it; but how little thanks are due for it, since I could not have had it without paying for it, and since the merchant who imported it did not consider how much good he would do me, but how much he would gain for himself, I owe nothing for what I have bought and paid for.

15

"According to this reasoning," says my opponent, "you would say that you owe nothing to a physician beyond his paltry fee, nor to your teacher, because you have paid him some money; yet these persons are all held very dear, and are very much respected." In answer to this I should urge that some things are of greater value than the price which we pay for them. You buy of a physician life and good health, the value of which cannot be estimated in money; from a teacher of the liberal sciences you buy the education of a gentleman and mental culture; therefore you pay these persons the price, not of what they give us, but of their trouble in giving it; you pay them for devoting their attention to us, for disregarding their own affairs to attend to us: they receive the price, not of their services, but of the expenditure of their time. Yet this may be more truly stated in another way, which I will at once lay before you, having first pointed out how the above may be confuted. Our adversary would say, "If some things are of greater value than the price which we pay for them, then, though you may have bought them, you still owe me something more for them." I answer, in the first place, what does their real value matter, since the buyer and seller have settled the price between them? Next, I did not buy it at its own price, but at yours. "It is," you say, "worth more than its sale price." True, but it cannot be sold for more. The price of everything varies according to circumstances; after you have well praised your wares, they are worth only the highest price at which you can sell them; a man who buys things cheap is not on that account under any obligation to the seller. In the next place, even if they are worth more, there is no generosity in your letting them go for less, since the price is settled by custom and the rate of the market, not by the uses and powers of the merchandise. What would you state to be the proper payment of a man who crosses the seas, holding a true course through the midst of the waves after the land has sunk out of sight, who foresees coming storms, and suddenly, when no one expects danger, orders sails to be furled, yards to be lowered, and the crew to stand at their posts ready to meet the fury of the unexpected gale? and yet the price of such great skill is fully paid for by the passage money. At what sum can you estimate the value of a lodging in a wilderness, of a shelter in the rain, of a bath or fire in cold weather? Yet I know on what terms I shall be supplied with these when I enter an inn. How much the man does for us who props our house when it is about to fall, and who, with a skill beyond belief, suspends in the air a block of building which has begun to crack at the foundation; yet we can contract for underpinning at a fixed and cheap rate. The city wall keeps us safe from our enemies, and from sudden inroads of brigands; yet it is well known how much a day a smith would earn for erecting towers and scaffoldings[23] to provide for the public safety.

16

I might go on forever collecting instances to prove that valuable things are sold at a low price. What then? why is it that I owe something extra both to my physician and to my teacher, and that I do not acquit myself of all obligation to them by paying them their fee? It is because they pass from physicians and teachers into friends, and lay us under obligations, not by the skill which they sell to us, but by kindly and familiar good will. If my physician does no more than feel my pulse and class me among those whom he sees in his daily rounds, pointing out what I ought to do or to avoid without any personal interest, then I owe him no more than his fee, because he views me with the eye not of a friend, but of a commander.[24] Neither have I any reason for loving my teacher, if he has regarded me merely as one of the mass of his scholars, and has not thought me worthy of taking especial pains with by myself, if he has never fixed his attention upon me, and if when he discharged his knowledge

---

[23] See Viollet-le-Duc's *Dictionnaire d'Architecture*, articles "Architecture Militaire" and "Hourds," for the probable meaning of *propugnacula*.

[24] I read *"Non tamquam amicus videt sed tamquam imperator."*

on the public, I might be said rather to have picked it up than to have learnt it from him. What then is our reason for owing them much? It is, not that what they have sold us is worth more than we paid for it, but that they have given something to us personally. Suppose that my physician has spent more consideration upon my case than was professionally necessary; that it was for me, not for his own credit, that he feared: that he was not satisfied with pointing out remedies, but himself applied them, that he sat by my bedside among my anxious friends, and came to see me at the crises of my disorder; that no service was too troublesome or too disgusting for him to perform; that he did not hear my groans unmoved; that among the numbers who called for him I was his favourite case; and that he gave the others only so much time as his care of my health permitted him: I should feel obliged to such a man not as to a physician, but as to a friend. Suppose again that my teacher endured labour and weariness in instructing me; that he taught me something more than is taught by all masters alike; that he roused my better feelings by his encouragement, and that at one time he would raise my spirits by praise, and at another warn me to shake off slothfulness: that he laid his hand, as it were, upon my latent and torpid powers of intellect and drew them out into the light of day; that he did not stingily dole out to me what he knew, in order that he might be wanted for a longer time, but was eager, if possible, to pour all his learning into me; then I am ungrateful, if I do not love him as much as I love my nearest relatives and my dearest friends.

17

We give something additional even to those who teach the meanest trades, if their efforts appear to be extraordinary; we bestow a gratuity upon pilots, upon workmen who deal with the commonest materials and hire themselves out by the day. In the noblest arts, however, those which either preserve or beautify our lives, a man would be ungrateful who thinks he owes the artist no more than he bargained for. Besides this, the teaching of such learning as we have spoken of blends mind with mind; now when this takes place, both in the case of the physician and of the teacher the price of his work is paid, but that of his mind remains owing.

18

Plato once crossed a river, and as the ferryman did not ask him for anything, he supposed that he had let him pass free out of respect, and said that the ferryman had laid Plato under an obligation. Shortly afterwards, seeing the ferryman take one person after another across the river with the same pains, and without charging anything, Plato declared that the ferryman had not laid him under an obligation. If you wish me to be grateful for what you give, you must not merely give it to me, but show that you mean it specially for me; you cannot make any claim upon one for having given him what you fling away broadcast among the crowd. What then?

shall I owe you nothing for it? Nothing, as an individual; I will pay, when the rest of mankind do, what I owe no more than they.

19

"Do you say," inquires my opponent, "that he who carries me gratis in a boat across the river Po, does not bestow any benefit upon me?" I do. He does me some good, but he does not bestow a benefit upon me; for he does it for his own sake, or at any rate not for mine; in short, he himself does not imagine that he is bestowing a benefit upon me, but does it for the credit of the State, or of the neighbourhood, or of himself, and expects some return for doing so, different from what he would receive from individual passengers. "Well," asks my opponent, "if the emperor were to grant the franchise to all the Gauls, or exemption from taxes to all the Spaniards, would each individual of them owe him nothing on that account?" Of course he would: but he would be indebted to him, not as having personally received a benefit intended for himself alone, but as a partaker in one conferred upon his nation. He would argue, "The emperor had no thought of me at the time when he benefited us all; he did not care to give me the franchise separately, he did not fix his attention upon me; why then should I be grateful to one who did not have me in his mind when he was thinking of doing what he did? In answer to this, I say that when he thought of doing good to all the Gauls, he thought of doing good to me also, for I was a Gaul, and he included me under my national, if not under my personal appellation. In like manner, I should feel grateful to him, not as for a personal, but for a general benefit; being only one of the people, I should regard the debt of gratitude as incurred, not by myself, but by my country, and should not pay it myself, but only contribute my share towards doing so. I do not call a man my creditor because he has lent money to my country, nor should I include that money in a schedule of my debts were I either a candidate for a public office, or a defendant in the courts; yet I would pay my share towards extinguishing such a debt. Similarly, I deny that I am laid under an obligation by a gift bestowed upon my entire nation, because although the giver gave it to me, yet he did not do so for my sake, but gave it without knowing whether he was giving it to me or not: nevertheless I should feel that I owed something for the gift, because it did reach me, though not directly. To lay me under an obligation, a thing must be done for my sake alone.

20

"According to this," argues our opponent, "you are under no obligation to the sun or the moon; for they do not move for your sake alone." No, but since they move with the object of preserving the balance of the universe, they move for my sake also, seeing that I am a fraction of the universe. Besides, our position and theirs is not the same, for he who does me good in order that he may by my means do good to himself, does not bestow a benefit upon me, because he merely makes use of me as an instrument for his own advantage; whereas the sun and the moon, even if they do us good for their own sakes, still cannot do good to us in order that by our means they may do good to themselves, for what is there which we can bestow upon them?

21

"I should be sure," replies he, "that the sun and the moon wished to do us good, if they were able to refuse to do so; but they cannot help moving as they do. In short, let them stop and discontinue their work."

See now, in how many ways this argument may be refuted. One who cannot refuse to do a thing may nevertheless wish to do it; indeed there is no greater proof of a fixed desire to do anything, than not to be able to alter one's determination. A good man cannot leave undone what he does: for unless he does it he will not be a good man. Is a good man, then, not able to bestow a benefit, because he does what he ought to do, and is not able not to do what he ought to do? Besides this, it makes a great difference whether you say, "He is not able not to do this, because he is forced to do it," or "He is not able to wish not to do it;" for, if he could not help doing it, then I am not indebted for it to him, but to the person who forced him to do it; if he could not help wishing for it because he had nothing better to wish for, then it is he who forces himself to do it, and in this case the debt which as acting under compulsion he could not claim, is due to him as compelling himself.

"Let the sun and moon cease to wish to benefit us," says our adversary. I answer, "Remember what has been said. Who can be so crazy as to refuse the name of free-will to that which has no danger of ceasing to act, and of adopting the opposite course, since, on the contrary, he whose will is fixed forever, must be thought to wish more earnestly than anyone else. Surely if he, who may at any moment change his mind, can be said to wish, we must not deny the existence of will in a being whose nature does not admit of change of mind.

22

"Well," says he, "let them stop, if it be possible." What you say is this:—"Let all those heavenly bodies, placed as they are at vast distances from each other, and arranged to preserve the balance of the universe, leave their appointed posts: let sudden confusion arise, so that constellations may collide with constellations, that the established harmony of all things may be destroyed and the works of God be shaken into ruin; let the whole frame of the rapidly moving heavenly bodies abandon in mid career those movements which we were assured would endure for ages, and let those which now by their regular advance and retreat keep the world at a moderate temperature, be instantly consumed by fire, so that instead of the infinite variety of the seasons all may be reduced to one uniform condition; let fire rage everywhere, followed by dull night, and let the bottomless abyss swallow up all the gods." Is it worth while to destroy all this merely in order to refute you? Even though you do not wish it, they do you good, and they wheel in their courses for your sake, though their motion may be due to some earlier and more important cause.

23

Besides this, the gods act under no external constraint, but their own will is a law to them for all time. They have established an order which is not to be changed, and consequently it is impossible that they should appear to be likely to do anything against their will, since they wish to continue doing whatever they cannot cease from doing, and they never regret their original decision. No doubt it is impossible for them to stop short, or to desert to the other side, but it is so for no other reason than that their own force holds them to their purpose. It is from no weakness that they persevere; no, they have no mind to leave the best course, and by this it is fated that they should proceed. When, at the time of the original creation, they arranged the entire universe, they paid attention to us as well as to the rest, and took thought about the human race; and for this reason we cannot suppose that it is merely for their own pleasure that they move in their orbits and display their work, since we also are a part of that work. We are, therefore, under an obligation to the sun and moon and the rest of the heavenly host, because, although they may rise in order to bestow more important benefits than those which we receive from them, yet they do bestow these upon us as they pass on their way to greater things. Besides this, they assist us of set purpose, and, therefore, lay us under an obligation, because we do not in their case stumble by chance upon a benefit bestowed by one who knew not what he was doing, but they knew that we should receive from them the advantages which we do; so that, though they may have some higher aim, though the result of their movements may be something of greater importance than the preservation of the human race, yet from the beginning thought has been directed to our comforts, and the scheme of the world has been arranged in a fashion which proves that our interests were neither their least nor last concern. It is our duty to show filial love for our parents, although many of them had no thought of children when they married. Not so with the gods: they cannot but have known what they were doing when they furnished mankind with food and comforts. Those for whose advantage so much was created, could not have been created without design. Nature conceived the idea of us before she formed us, and, indeed, we are no such trifling piece of work as could have fallen from her hands unheeded. See how great privileges she has bestowed upon us, how far beyond the human race the empire of mankind extends; consider how widely she allows us to roam, not having restricted us to the land alone, but permitted us to traverse every part of herself; consider, too, the audacity of our intellect, the only one which knows of the gods or seeks for them, and how we can raise our mind high above the Earth, and commune with those divine influences: you will perceive that man is not a hurriedly put together, or an unstudied piece of work. Among her noblest products nature has none of which she can boast more than man, and assuredly no other which can comprehend her boast. What madness is this, to call the gods in question for their bounty? If a man declares that he has received nothing when he is receiving all the while, and from those who will always be giving without ever receiving anything in return, how will he be grateful to those whose kindness cannot be returned without expense? and how great a mistake is it not to be thankful to a giver, because he is good even to him who disowns him, or to use the fact of his bounty being poured upon us in an uninterrupted stream, as an argument to prove that he cannot help bestowing it. Suppose that such men as these say, "I do not want it," "Let him keep it to himself," "Who asks him for it?" and so forth, with all the other speeches of insolent minds: still, he whose bounty reaches you, although you say that it does not, lays you under an obligation nevertheless; indeed, perhaps the greatest part of the benefit which he bestows is that he is ready to give even when you are complaining against him.

24

Do you not see how parents force children during their infancy to undergo what is useful for their health? Though the children cry and struggle, they swathe them and bind their limbs straight lest premature liberty should make them grow crooked, afterwards instill into them a liberal education, threatening those who are unwilling to learn, and finally, if spirited young men do not conduct themselves frugally, modestly, and respectably, they compel them to do so. Force and harsh measures are used even to youths who have grown up and are their own masters, if they, either from fear or from insolence, refuse to take what is good for them. Thus the greatest benefits that we receive, we receive either without knowing it, or against our will, from our parents.

25

Those persons who are ungrateful and repudiate benefits, not because they do not wish to receive them, but in order that they may not be laid under an obligation for them, are like those who fall into the opposite extreme, and are over grateful, who pray that some trouble or misfortune may befall their benefactors to give them an opportunity of proving how gratefully they remember the benefit which they have received. It is a question whether they are right, and show a truly dutiful feeling; their state of mind is morbid, like that of frantic lovers who long for their mistress to be exiled, that they may accompany her when she leaves her country forsaken by all her friends, or that she may be poor in order that she may the more need what they give her, or who long that she may be ill in order that they may sit by her bedside, and who, in short, out of sheer love form the same wishes as her enemies would wish for her. Thus the results of hatred and of frantic love are very nearly the same; and these lovers are very like those who hope that their friends may meet with difficulties which they may remove, and who thus do a wrong that they may bestow a benefit, whereas it would have been much better for them to do nothing, than by a crime to gain an opportunity of doing good service. What should we say of a pilot who prayed to the gods for dreadful storms and tempests, in order that danger might make his skill more highly esteemed? what of a general who should pray that a vast number of the enemy surround his camp, fill the ditches by a sudden charge, tear down the rampart round his panic-stricken army, and plant its hostile standards at the very gates, in order that he might gain more glory by restoring his broken ranks and shattered fortunes? All such men confer their benefits upon us by odious means, for they beg the gods to harm those whom they mean to help, and wish them to be struck down before they raise them up; it is a cruel feeling, brought about by a distorted sense of gratitude, to wish evil to befall one whom one is bound in honour to succour.

26

"My wish," argues our opponent, "does him no harm, because when I wish for the danger I wish for the rescue at the same time." What you mean by this is not that you do no wrong, but that you do less than if you wished that the danger might befall him, without wishing for the rescue. It is wicked to throw a man into the water in order that you may pull him out, to throw him down that you may raise him up, or to shut him up that you may release him. You do not bestow a benefit upon a man by ceasing to wrong him, nor can it ever be a piece of good service to anyone to remove from him a burden which you yourself imposed on him. True, you may cure the hurt which you inflict, but I had rather that you did not hurt me at all. You may gain my gratitude by curing me because I am wounded, but not by wounding me in order that you may cure me: no man likes scars except as compared with wounds, which he is glad to see thus healed, though he had rather not have received them. It would be cruel to wish such things to befall one from whom you had never received a kindness; how much more cruel is it to wish that they may befall one in whose debt you are.

27

"I pray," replies he, "at the same time, that I may be able to help him." In the first place, if I stop you short in the middle of your prayer, it shows at once that you are ungrateful: I have not yet heard what you wish to do for him; I have heard what you wish him to suffer. You pray that anxiety and fear and even worse evil than this may come upon him. You desire that he may need aid: this is to his disadvantage; you desire that he may need your aid: this is to your advantage. You do not wish to help him, but to be set free from your obligation to him: for when you are eager to repay your debt in such a way as this, you merely wish to be set free from the debt, not to repay it. So the only part of your wish that could be thought honourable proves to be the base and ungrateful feeling of unwillingness to lie under an obligation: for what you wish for is, not that you may have an opportunity of repaying his kindness, but that he may be forced to beg you to do him a kindness. You make yourself the superior, and you wickedly degrade beneath your feet the man who has done you good service. How much better would it be to remain in his debt in an honourable and friendly manner, than to seek to discharge the debt by these evil means! You would be less to blame if you denied that you had received it, for your benefactor would then lose nothing more than what he gave you, whereas now you wish him to be rendered inferior to you, and brought by the loss of his property and social position into a condition below his own benefits. Do you think yourself grateful? Just utter your wishes in the hearing of him to whom you wish to do good. Do you call that a prayer for his welfare, which can be divided between his friend and his enemy, which, if the last part were omitted, you would not doubt was pronounced, by one who opposed and hated him? Enemies in war have sometimes wished to capture certain towns in order to spare them, or to conquer certain persons in order to pardon, them, yet these were the wishes of enemies, and what was the kindest part of them began by cruelty. Finally, what sort of prayers do you think those can be which he, on whose behalf they are made, hopes more earnestly than anyone else may not be granted? In hoping that the gods may injure a man, and that you may help him, you deal most dishonourably with him, and you do not treat the gods themselves fairly, for you give them the odious part to play, and reserve the generous one for yourself: the gods must do him wrong in order that you may do him a service. If you were to suborn an informer to accuse a man, and afterwards withdrew him, if you engaged a man in a lawsuit and afterwards gave it up, no one would hesitate to call you a villain: what difference does it make, whether you attempt to do this by chicanery or by prayer, unless it be that by prayer you raise up more powerful enemies to him than by the other means? You cannot say, "Why, what harm do I do him?" your prayer is either futile or harmful, indeed it is harmful even though nothing comes of it. You do your friend wrong by wishing him harm: you must thank the gods that you do him no harm. The fact of your wishing it is enough: we ought to be just as angry with you as if you had effected it.

28

"If," argues our adversary, "my prayers had any efficacy, they would also have been efficacious to save him from danger." In the first place, I reply, the danger into which you wish me to fall is certain, the help which I should receive is uncertain. Or call them both certain; it is that which injures me that comes first. Besides, *you* understand the terms of your wish; *I* shall be tossed by the storm without being sure that I have a haven of rest at hand.

Think what torture it must have been to me, even if I receive your help, to have stood in need of it: if I escape safely, to have trembled for myself; if I be acquitted, to have had to plead my cause. To escape from fear, however great it may be, can never be so pleasant as to live in sound unassailable safety. Pray that you may return my kindnesses when I need their return, but do not pray that I may need them. You would have done what you prayed for, had it been in your power.

29

How far more honourable would a prayer of this sort be: "I pray that he may remain in such a position as that he may always bestow benefits and never need them: may he be attended by the means of giving and helping, of which he makes such a bountiful use; may he never want benefits to bestow, or be sorry for any which he has bestowed; may his nature, fitted as it is for acts of pity, goodness, and clemency, be stimulated and brought out by numbers of grateful persons, whom I trust he will find without needing to make trial of their gratitude; may he refuse to be reconciled to no one, and may no one require to be reconciled to him: may fortune so uniformly continue to favour him that no one may be able to return his kindness in any way except by feeling grateful to him."

How far more proper are such prayers as these, which do not put you off to some distant opportunity, but express your gratitude at once? What is there to prevent your returning your benefactor's kindness, even while he is in prosperity? How many ways are there by which we can repay what we owe even to the affluent—for instance, by honest advice, by constant intercourse, by courteous conversation, pleasing him without flattering him, by listening attentively to any subject which he may wish to discuss, by keeping safe any secret that he may impart to us, and by social intercourse. There is no one so highly placed by fortune as not to want a friend all the more because he wants nothing.

30

The other is a melancholy opportunity, and one which we ought always to pray may be kept far from us: must the gods be angry with a man in order that you may prove your gratitude to him? Do you not perceive that you are doing wrong, from the very fact that those to whom you are ungrateful fare better? Call up before your mind dungeons, chains, wretchedness, slavery, war, poverty: these are the opportunities for which you pray; if anyone has any dealings with you, it is by means of these that you square your account. Why not rather wish that he to whom you owe most may be powerful and happy? for, as I have just said, what is there to prevent your returning the kindness even of those who enjoy the greatest prosperity? to do which, ample and various opportunities will present themselves to you. What! do you not know that a debt can be paid even to a rich man? Nor will I trouble you with many instances of what you may do. Though a man's riches and prosperity may prevent your making him any other repayment, I will show you what the highest in the land stand in need of, what is wanting to those who possess everything. They want a man to speak the truth, to save them from the organized mass of falsehood by which they are beset, which so bewilders them with lies that the habit of hearing only what is pleasant instead of what is true, prevents their knowing what truth really is. Do you not see how such persons are driven to ruin by the want of candour among their friends, whose loyalty has degenerated into slavish obsequiousness? No one, when giving them his advice, tells them what he really thinks, but each vies with the other in flattery; and while the man's friends make it their only object to see who can most pleasantly deceive him, he himself is ignorant of his real powers, and, believing himself to be as great a man as he is told that he is, plunges the State in useless wars, which bring disasters upon it, breaks off a useful and necessary peace, and, through a passion of anger which no one checks, spills the blood of numbers of people, and at last sheds his own. Such persons assert what has never been investigated as certain facts, consider that to modify their opinion is as dishonourable as to be conquered, believe that institutions which are just flickering out of existence will last forever, and, thus overturn great States, to the destruction of themselves and all who are connected with them. Living as they do in a fool's paradise, resplendent with unreal and short-lived advantages, they forget that, as soon as they put it out of their power to hear the truth, there is no limit to the misfortunes which they may expect.

31

When Xerxes declared war against Greece, all his courtiers encouraged his boastful temper, which forgot how unsubstantial his grounds for confidence were. One declared that the Greeks would not endure to hear the news of the declaration of war, and would take to flight at the first rumour of his approach; another, that with such a vast army Greece could not only be conquered, but utterly overwhelmed, and that it was rather to be feared that they would find the Greek cities empty and abandoned, and that the panic flight of the enemy would leave them only vast deserts, where no use could be made of their enormous forces. Another told him that the world was hardly large enough to contain him, that the seas were too narrow for his fleets, the camps would not take in his armies, the plains were not wide enough to deploy his cavalry in, and that the sky itself was scarcely large enough to enable all his troops to hurl their darts at once. While much boasting of this sort was going on around him, raising his already overweening self-confidence to a frantic pitch, Demaratus, the Lacedaemonian, alone told him that the disorganized and unwieldy multitude in which he trusted, was in itself a danger to its chief, because it possessed only weight without strength; for an army which is too large cannot be governed, and one which cannot be governed, cannot long exist. "The Lacedaemonians," said he, "will meet you upon the first mountain in Greece, and will give you a taste of their quality. All these thousands of nations of yours will be held in check by three hundred men: they will stand firm at their posts, they will defend the passes entrusted to them with their weapons, and block them up with their bodies: all Asia will not force them to give way; few as they are, they will stop all this terrible invasion, attempted though it be by nearly the whole human race. Though the laws of nature may give way to you, and enable you to pass from Europe to Asia, yet you will stop short in a bypath; consider what your losses will be afterwards, when you have reckoned up the price which you have to pay for the pass of Thermopylae; when you learn that your march can be stayed, you will discover that you may be put to flight. The Greeks will yield up many parts of their country to you, as if they were swept out of them by the first terrible rush of a mountain torrent; afterwards they will rise against you from all quarters and will crush you by means of your own strength. What people say, that your warlike preparations are too great to be contained in the countries which you intend to attack, is quite true; but this is to our disadvantage. Greece will conquer you for this very reason, that she cannot contain you; you cannot make use of the whole of your force. Besides this, you will not be able to do what is essential to victory—that is, to meet the manoeuvres of the enemy at once, to support your own men if they give way, or to confirm and strengthen them when their ranks are wavering; long before you know it, you will be defeated. Moreover, you should not think that because your army is so large that its own chief does not know its numbers, it is therefore irresistible; there is nothing so great that it cannot perish; nay, without any other cause, its own excessive size may prove its ruin." What Demaratus predicted came to pass. He whose power gods and men obeyed, and who swept away all that opposed him, was bidden to halt by three hundred men, and the Persians, defeated in every part of Greece, learned how great a difference there is between a mob and an army. Thus it came to pass that Xerxes, who suffered more from the shame of his failure than from the losses which he sustained, thanked Demaratus for having been the only man who told him the truth, and permitted him to ask what boon he pleased. He asked to be allowed to drive a chariot into Sardis, the largest city in Asia, wearing a tiara erect upon his head, a privilege which was enjoyed by kings alone. He deserved his reward before he asked for it, but how wretched must the nation have been, in which there was no one who would speak the truth to the king except one man who did not speak it to himself.

32

The late Emperor Augustus banished his daughter, whose conduct went beyond the shame of ordinary immodesty, and made public the scandals of the imperial house.

Led away by his passion, he divulged all these crimes which, as emperor, he ought to have kept secret with as much care as he punished them, because the shame of some deeds asperses even him who avenges them. Afterwards, when by lapse of time shame took the place of anger in his mind, he lamented that he had not kept silence about matters which he had not learned until it was disgraceful to speak of them, and often used to exclaim, "None of these things would have happened to me, if either Agrippa or Maecenas had lived!" So hard was it for the master of so many thousands of men to repair the loss of two. When his legions were slaughtered, new ones were at once enrolled; when his fleet was wrecked, within a few days another was afloat; when the public buildings were consumed by fire, finer ones arose in their stead; but the places of Agrippa and Maecenas remained unfilled throughout his life. What am I to imagine? that there were not any men like these, who could take their place, or that it was the fault of Augustus himself, who preferred mourning for them to seeking for their likes? We have no reason for supposing that it was the habit of Agrippa or Maecenas to speak the truth to him; indeed, if they had lived they would have been as great dissemblers as the rest. It is one of the habits of kings to insult their present servants by praising those whom they have lost, and to attribute the virtue of truthful speaking to those from whom there is no further risk of hearing it.

33

However, to return to my subject, you see how easy it is to return the kindness of the prosperous, and even of those who occupy the highest places of all mankind. Tell them not what they wish to hear, but what they will wish that they always had heard; though their ears be stopped by flatteries, yet sometimes truth may penetrate them; give them useful advice. Do you ask what service you can render to a prosperous man? Teach him not to rely upon his prosperity, and to understand that it ought to be supported by the hands of many trusty friends. Will you not have done much for him, if you take away his foolish belief that his influence will endure forever, and teach him that what we gain by chance passes away soon, and at a quicker rate than it came; that we cannot fall by the same stages by which we rose to the height of good fortune, but that frequently between it and ruin there is but one step? You do not know how great is the value of friendship, if you do not understand how much you give to him to whom you give a friend, a commodity which is scarce not only in men's houses, but in whole centuries, and which is nowhere scarcer than in the places where it is thought to be most plentiful. Pray, do you suppose that those books of names, which your nomenclator[25] can hardly carry or remember, are those of friends? It is not your friends who crowd to knock at your door, and who are admitted to your greater or lesser levees.

---

[25] The "nomenclator" was a slave who attended his master in canvassing and on similar occasions, for the purpose of telling him the names of whom he met in the street.

34

To divide one's friends into classes is an old trick of kings and their imitators; it shows great arrogance to think that to touch or to pass one's threshold can be a valuable privilege, or to grant as an honour that you should sit nearer one's front door than others, or enter house before them, although within the house there are many more doors, which shut out even those who have been admitted so far. With us Gaius Gracchus, and shortly after him Livius Drusus, were the first to keep themselves apart from the mass of their adherents, and to admit some to their privacy, some to their more select, and others to their general receptions. These men consequently had friends of the first and second rank, and so on, but in none had they true friends. Can you apply the name of friend to one who is admitted in his regular order to pay his respects to you? or can you expect perfect loyalty from one who is forced to slip into your presence through a grudgingly-opened door? How can a man arrive at using bold freedom of speech with you, if he is only allowed in his proper turn to make use of the common phrase, "Hail to you," which is used by perfect strangers? Whenever you go to any of these great men, whose levees interest the whole city, though you find all the streets beset with throngs of people, and the passersby hardly able to make their way through the crowd, you may be sure that you have come to a place where there are many men, but no friends of their patron. We must not seek our friends in our entrance hall, but in our own breast; it is there that he ought to be received, there retained, and hoarded up in our minds. Teach this, and you will have repaid your debt of gratitude.

35

If you are useful to your friend only when he is in distress, and are superfluous when all goes well with him, you form a mean estimate of your own value. As you can bear yourself wisely both in doubtful, in prosperous, and in adverse circumstances, by showing prudence in doubtful cases, courage in misfortune, and self-restraint in good fortune, so in all circumstances you can make yourself useful to your friend. Do not desert him in adversity, but do not wish that it may befall him: the various incidents of human life will afford you many opportunities of proving your loyalty to him without wishing him evil. He who prays that another may become rich, in order that he may share his riches, really has a view to his own advantage, although his prayers are ostensibly offered in behalf of his friend; and similarly he who wishes that his friend may get into some trouble from which his own friendly assistance may extricate him—a most ungrateful wish—prefers himself to his friend, and thinks it worthwhile that his friend should be unhappy, in order that he may prove his gratitude. This very wish makes him ungrateful, for he wishes to rid himself of his gratitude as though it were a heavy burden. In returning a kindness it makes a great difference whether you are eager to bestow a benefit, or merely to free yourself from a debt. He who wishes to return a benefit will study his friend's interests, and will hope that a suitable occasion will arise; he who only wishes to free himself from an obligation will be eager to do so by any means whatever, which shows very bad feeling. "Do you say," we may be asked, "that eagerness to repay kindness belongs to a morbid feeling of gratitude?" I cannot explain my meaning more clearly than by repeating what I have already said. You do not want to repay, but to escape from the benefit which you have received. You seem to say, "When shall I get free from this obligation? I must strive by any means in my power to extinguish my debt to him." You would be thought to be far from grateful, if you wished to pay a debt to him with his own money; yet this wish of yours is even more unjust; for you invoke curses upon him, and call down terrible imprecations upon the head of one who ought to be held sacred by you. No one, I suppose, would have any doubt of your wickedness if you were openly to pray that he might suffer poverty, captivity, hunger, or fear; yet what is the difference between openly praying for some of these things, and silently wishing for them? for you do wish for some of these. Go, and enjoy your belief that this is gratitude, to do what not even an ungrateful man would do, supposing he confined himself to repudiating the benefit, and did not go so far as to hate his benefactor.

36

Who would call Aeneas pious, if he wished that his native city might be captured, in order that he might save his father from captivity? Who would point to the Sicilian youths as good examples for his children, if they had prayed that Aetna might flame with unusual heat and pour forth a vast mass of fire in order to afford them an opportunity of displaying their filial affection by rescuing their parents from the midst of the conflagration? Rome owes Scipio nothing if he kept the Punic War alive in order that he might have the glory of finishing it; she owes nothing to the Decii if they prayed for public disasters, to give themselves an opportunity of displaying their brave self-devotion. It is the greatest scandal for a physician to make work for himself; and many who have aggravated the diseases of their patients that they may have the greater credit for curing them, have either failed to cure them at all or have done so at the cost of the most terrible suffering to their victims.

37

It is said (at any rate Hecaton tells us) that when Callistratus with many others was driven into exile by his factious and licentiously free country, someone prayed that such trouble might befall the Athenians that they would be forced to recall the exiles, on hearing which, he prayed that God might forbid his return upon such terms. When someone tried to console our own countryman, Rutilius, for his exile, pointing out that civil war was at hand, and that all exiles would soon be restored to

Rome, he answered with even greater spirit, "What harm have I done you, that you should wish that I may return to my country more unhappily than I quit it? My wish is, that my country should blush at my being banished, rather than that she should mourn at my having returned." An exile, of which everyone is more ashamed than the sufferer, is not exile at all. These two persons, who did not wish to be restored to their homes at the cost of a public disaster, but preferred that two should suffer unjustly than that all should suffer alike, are thought to have acted like good citizens; and in like manner it does not accord with the character of a grateful man, to wish that his benefactor may fall into troubles which he may dispel; because, even though he may mean well to him, yet he wishes him evil. To put out a fire which you yourself have lighted, will not even gain acquittal for you, let alone credit.

38

In some states an evil wish was regarded as a crime. It is certain that at Athens Demades obtained a verdict against one who sold furniture for funerals, by proving that he had prayed for great gains, which he could not obtain without the death of many persons. Yet it is a stock question whether he was rightly found guilty. Perhaps he prayed, not that he might sell his wares to many persons, but that he might sell them dear, or that he might procure what he was going to sell, cheaply. Since his business consisted of buying and selling, why should you consider his prayer to apply to one branch of it only, although he made profit from both? Besides this, you might find everyone of his trade guilty, for they all wish, that is, secretly pray, as he did. You might, moreover, find a great part of the human race guilty, for who is there who does not profit by his neighbour's wants? A soldier, if he wishes for glory, must wish for war; the farmer profits by corn being dear; a large number of litigants raises the price of forensic eloquence; physicians make money by a sickly season; dealers in luxuries are made rich by the effeminacy of youth; suppose that no storms and no conflagrations injured our dwellings, the builder's trade would be at a standstill. The prayer of one man was detected, but it was just like the prayers of all other men. Do you imagine that Arruntius and Haterius, and all other professional legacy-hunters do not put up the same prayers as undertakers and gravediggers? though the latter know not whose death it is that they wish for, while the former wish for the death of their dearest friends, from whom, on account of their intimacy, they have most hopes of inheriting a fortune. No one's life does the undertaker any harm, whereas these men starve if their friends are long about dying; they do not, therefore, merely wish for their deaths in order that they may receive what they have earned by a disgraceful servitude, but in order that they may be set free from a heavy tax. There can, therefore, be no doubt that such persons repeat with even greater earnestness the prayer for which the undertaker was condemned, for whoever is likely to profit such men by dying, does them an injury by living. Yet the wishes of all these are alike well known and unpunished. Lastly, let every man examine his own self, let him look into the secret thoughts of his heart and consider what it is that he silently hopes for; how many of his prayers he would blush to acknowledge, even to himself; how few there are which we could repeat in the presence of witnesses!

39

Yet we must not condemn everything which we find worthy of blame, as, for instance, this wish about our friends which we have been discussing, arises from a misdirected feeling of affection, and falls into the very error which it strives to avoid, for the man is ungrateful at the very time when he hurries to prove his gratitude. He prays aloud, "May he fall into my power, may he need my influence, may not be able to be safe and respectable without my aid, may he be so unfortunate that whatever return I make to him may be regarded as a benefit." To the gods alone he adds, "May domestic treasons encompass him, which can be quelled by me alone; may some powerful and virulent enemy, some excited and armed mob, assail him; may he be set upon by a creditor or an informer."

40

See, how just you are; you would never have wished any of these misfortunes to befall him, if he had not bestowed a benefit upon you. Not to speak of the graver guilt which you incur by returning evil for good, you distinctly do wrong in not waiting for the fitting time for each action, for it is as wrong to anticipate this as it is not to take it when it comes. A benefit ought not always to be accepted, and ought not in all cases to be returned. If you were to return it to me against my will, you would be ungrateful, how much more ungrateful are you, if you force me to wish for it? Wait patiently; why are you unwilling to let my bounty abide with you? Why do you chafe at being laid under an obligation? why, as though you were dealing with a harsh usurer, are you in such a hurry to sign and seal an equivalent bond? Why do you wish me to get into trouble? Why do you call upon the gods to ruin me? If this is your way of returning a kindness, what would you do if you were exacting repayment of a debt?

41

Above all, therefore, my Liberalis, let us learn to live calmly under an obligation to others, and watch for opportunities of repaying our debt without manufacturing them. Let us remember that this anxiety to seize the first opportunity of setting ourselves free shows ingratitude; for no one repays with good will that which he is unwilling to owe, and his eagerness to get it out of his hands shows that he regards it as a burden rather than as a favour. How much better and more righteous is it to bear in mind what we owe to our friends, and to offer repayment, not to obtrude it, nor to think ourselves too much indebted; because a benefit is a common bond which connects two persons. Say "I do not delay to repay your kindness to me; I hope that you will accept my gratitude cheerfully. If irresistible fate hangs over either of us, and destiny rules either that you must receive your benefit back again, or that I must receive a second benefit, why then, of us two, let him give that was wont to give. I am ready to receive it.

" 'Tis not the part of Turnus to delay."

That is the spirit which I shall show whenever the time comes; in the meanwhile the gods shall be my witnesses.

42

I have noted in you, my Liberalis, and as it were touched with my hand a feeling of fussy anxiety not to be behindhand in doing what is your duty. This anxiety is not suitable to a grateful mind, which, on the contrary, produces the utmost confidence in oneself, and which drives away all trouble by the consciousness of real affection towards one's benefactor. To say "Take back what you gave me," is no less a reproach than to say "You are in my debt." Let this be the first privilege of a benefit, that he who bestowed it may choose the time when he will have it returned. "But I fear that men may speak ill of me." You do wrong if you are grateful only for the sake of your reputation, and not to satisfy your conscience. You have in this matter two judges, your benefactor, whom you ought not, and yourself, whom you cannot deceive. "But," say you, "if no occasion of repayment offers, am I always to remain in his debt?" Yes; but you should do so openly, and willingly, and should view with great pleasure what he has entrusted to you. If you are vexed at not having yet returned a benefit, you must be sorry that you ever received it; but if he deserved that you should receive a benefit from him, why should he not deserve that you should long remain in his debt?

43

Those persons are much mistaken who regard it as a proof of a great mind to make offers to give, and to fill many men's pockets and houses with their presents, for sometimes these are due not to a great mind, but to a great fortune; they do not know how far more great and more difficult it sometimes is to receive than to lavish gifts. I must disparage neither act; it is as proper to a noble heart to owe as to receive, for both are of equal value when done virtuously; indeed, to owe is the more difficult, because it requires more pains to keep a thing safe than to give it away. We ought not therefore to be in a hurry to repay, nor need we seek to do so out of due season, for to hasten to make repayment at the wrong time is as bad as to be slow to do so at the right time. My benefactor has entrusted his bounty to me: I ought not to have any fears either on his behalf or on my own. He has a sufficient security; he cannot lose it except he loses me—nay, not even if he loses me. I have returned thanks to him for it—that is, I have requited him. He who thinks too much about repaying a benefit must suppose that his friend thinks too much about receiving repayment. Make no difficulty about either course. If he wishes to receive his benefit back again, let us return it cheerfully; if he prefers to leave it in our hands, why should we dig up his treasure? why should we decline to be its guardians? he deserves to be allowed to do whichever he pleases. As for fame and reputation, let us regard them as matters which ought to accompany, but which ought not to direct our actions.

BOOK 7

1

Be of good cheer, my Liberalis:

> "Our port is close, and I will not delay,
> Nor by digressions wander from the way."

This book collects together all that has been omitted, and in it, having exhausted my subject, I shall consider not what I am to say, but what there is which I have not yet said. If there be anything superfluous in it, I pray you take it in good part, since it is for you that it is superfluous. Had I wished to set off my work to the best advantage, I ought to have added to it by degrees, and to have kept for the last that part which would be eagerly perused even by a sated reader. However, instead of this, I have collected together all that was essential in the beginning; I am now collecting together whatever then escaped me; nor, by Hercules, if you ask me, do I think that, after the rules which govern our conduct have been stated, it is very much to the purpose to discuss the other questions which have been raised more for the exercise of our intellects than for the health of our minds. The cynic Demetrius, who in my opinion was a great man even if compared with the greatest philosophers, had an admirable saying about this, that one gained more by having a few wise precepts ready and in common use than by learning many without having them at hand. "The best wrestler," he would say, "is not he who has learned thoroughly all the tricks and twists of the art, which are seldom met with in actual wrestling, but he who has well and carefully trained himself in one or two of them, and watches keenly for an opportunity of practising them. It does not matter how many of them he knows, if he knows enough to give him the victory; and so in this subject of ours there are many points of interest, but few of importance. You need not know what is the system of the ocean tides, why each seventh year leaves its mark upon the human body, why the more distant parts of a long portico do not keep their true proportion, but seem to approach one another until at last the spaces between the columns disappear, how it can be that twins are conceived separately, though they are born together, whether both result from one, or each from a separate act, why those whose birth was the same should have such different fates in life, and dwell at the greatest possible distance from one another, although they were born touching one another; it will not do you much harm to pass over matters which we are not permitted to know, and which we should not profit by knowing. Truths so obscure may be neglected with impunity.[26] Nor can we complain that nature deals hardly with us, for there is nothing which is hard to discover except those things by which we gain nothing beyond the credit of having discovered them; whatever things tend to make us better or happier are either obvious or easily discovered. Your mind can rise superior to the accidents of life, if it can raise itself above fears and not greedily covet boundless wealth, but has learned to seek for riches within itself; if it has cast out the fear of men and gods, and has learned that it has not much to fear from man, and nothing to fear from God; if by scorning all those things which make life miserable while they adorn it, the mind can soar to such a height as to see clearly that death cannot be the beginning of any trouble, though it is the end of many; if it can dedicate itself to righteousness and think any path easy which leads to it; if, being a gregarious creature, and born for the common good, it regards the world as the universal home, if it keeps its conscience clear towards God and lives always as though in public, fearing itself more than other men, then it avoids all storms, it stands on firm ground in fair daylight, and has brought to perfection its knowledge of all that is useful and essential. All that remains serves merely to amuse our leisure; yet, when once anchored in safety, the mind may consider these matters also, though it can derive no strength, but only culture from their discussion."

2

The above are the rules which my friend Demetrius bids him who would make progress in philosophy to clutch with both hands, never to let go, but to cling to them, and make them a part of himself, and by daily meditation upon them to bring himself into such a state of mind, that these wholesome maxims occur to him of their own accord, that wherever he may be, they may straightaway be ready for use when required, and that the criterion of right and wrong may present itself to him without delay. Let him know that nothing is evil except what is base, and nothing good except what is honourable: let him guide his life by this rule: let him both act and expect others to act in accordance with this law, and let him regard those whose minds are steeped in indolence, and who are given up to lust and gluttony, as the most pitiable of mankind, no matter how splendid their fortunes may be. Let him say to himself, "Pleasure is uncertain, short, apt to pall upon us, and the more eagerly we indulge in it, the sooner we bring on a reaction of feeling against it; we must necessarily afterwards blush for it, or be sorry for it, there is nothing grand about it, nothing worthy of man's nature, little lower as it is than that of the

---

[26] The old saying, "Truth lurks deep in a well (or abyss)."

gods; pleasure is a low act, brought about by the agency of our inferior and baser members, and shameful in its result. True pleasure, worthy of a human being and of a man, is, not to stuff or swell his body with food and drink, nor to excite lusts which are least hurtful when they are most quiet, but to be free from all forms of mental disturbance, both those which arise from men's ambitious struggles with one another, and those which come from on high and are more difficult to deal with, which flow from our taking the traditional view of the gods, and estimating them by the analogy of our own vices." This equable, secure, uncloying pleasure is enjoyed by the man now described; a man skilled, so to say, in the laws of gods and men alike. Such a man enjoys the present without anxiety for the future: for he who depends upon what is uncertain can rely confidently upon nothing. Thus he is free from all those great troubles which unhinge the mind, he neither hopes for, nor covets anything, and engages in no uncertain adventures, being satisfied with what he has. Do not suppose that he is satisfied with a little; for everything is his, and that not in the sense in which all was Alexander's, who, though he reached the shore of the Red Sea, yet wanted more territory than that through which he had come. He did not even own those countries which he held or had conquered, while Onesicritus, whom he had sent on before him to discover new countries, was wandering about the ocean and engaging in war in unknown seas. Is it clear that he who pushed his armies beyond the bounds of the universe, who with reckless greed dashed headlong into a boundless and unexplored sea, must in reality have been full of wants? It matters not how many kingdoms he may have seized or given away, or how great a part of the world may pay him tribute; such a man must be in need of as much as he desires.

3

This was not the vice of Alexander alone, who followed with a fortunate audacity in the footsteps of Bacchus and Hercules, but it is common to all those whose covetousness is whetted rather than appeased by good fortune. Look at Cyrus and Cambyses and all the royal house of Persia: can you find one among them who thought his empire large enough, or was not at the last gasp still aspiring after further conquests? We need not wonder at this, for whatever is obtained by covetousness is simply swallowed up and lost, nor does it matter how much is poured into its insatiable maw. Only the wise man possesses everything without having to struggle to retain it; he alone does not need to send ambassadors across the seas, measure out camps upon hostile shores, place garrisons in commanding forts, or manoeuvre legions and squadrons of cavalry. Like the immortal gods, who govern their realm without recourse to arms, and from their serene and lofty heights protect their own, so the wise man fulfils his duties, however far-reaching they may be, without disorder, and looks down upon the whole human race, because he himself is the greatest and most powerful member thereof. You may laugh at him, but if you in your mind survey the east and the west, reaching even to the regions separated from us by vast wildernesses, if you think of all the creatures of the Earth, all the riches which the bounty of nature lavishes, it shows a great spirit to be able to say, as though you were a god, "All these are mine." Thus it is that he covets nothing, for there is nothing which is not contained in everything, and everything is his.

4

"This," say you, "is the very thing that I wanted! I have caught you! I shall be glad to see how you will extricate yourself from the toils into which you have fallen of your own accord. Tell me, if the wise man possesses everything, how can one give anything to a wise man? for even what you give him is his already. It is impossible, therefore, to bestow a benefit upon a wise man, if whatever is given him comes from his own store; yet you Stoics declare that it is possible to give to a wise man. I make the same inquiry about friends as well: for you say that friends own everything in common, and if so, no one can give anything to his friend, for he gives what his friend owned already in common with himself."

There is nothing to prevent a thing belonging to a wise man, and yet being the property of its legal owner. According to law everything in a state belongs to the king, yet all that property over which the king has rights of possession is parcelled out among individual owners, and each separate thing belongs to somebody: and so one can give the king a house, a slave, or a sum of money without being said to give him what was his already; for the king has rights over all these things, while each citizen has the ownership of them. We speak of the country of the Athenians, or of the Campanians, though the inhabitants divide them amongst themselves into separate estates; the whole region belongs to one state or another, but each part of it belongs to its own individual proprietor; so that we are able to give our lands to the State, although they are reckoned as belonging to the State, because we and the State own them in different ways. Can there be any doubt that all the private savings of a slave belong to his master as well as he himself? yet he makes his master presents. The slave does not therefore possess nothing, because if his master chose he might possess nothing; nor does what he gives of his own free will cease to be a present, because it might have been wrung from him against his will. As for how we are to prove that the wise man possesses all things, we shall see afterwards; for the present we are both agreed to regard this as true; we must gather together something to answer the question before us, which is, how any means remain of acting generously towards one who already possesses all things? All things that a son has belong to his father, yet who does not know that in spite of this a son can make presents to his father? All things belong to the gods; yet we make presents and bestow alms even upon the gods. What I have is not necessarily not mine because it belongs to you; for the same thing may belong both to me and to you.

"He to whom courtesans belong," argues our adversary, "must be a procurer: now courtesans are included in all things, therefore courtesans belong to the wise man. But he to whom courtesans belong is a procurer; therefore the wise man is a procurer." Yes! by the same reasoning, our opponents would forbid him to buy anything, arguing, "No man buys his own property. Now all things are the property of the wise man; therefore the wise man buys nothing." By the same reasoning they object to his borrowing, because no one pays interest for the use of his own money. They raise endless quibbles, although they perfectly well understand what we say.

5

For, when I say that the wise man possesses everything, I mean that he does so without thereby impairing each man's individual rights in his own property, in the same way as in a country ruled by a good king, everything belongs to the king, by the right of his authority, and to the people by their several rights of ownership. This I shall prove in its proper place; in the mean time it is a sufficient answer to the question to declare that I am able to give to the wise man that which is in one way mine, and in another way his. Nor is it strange that I should be able to give anything to one who possesses everything. Suppose I have hired a house from you: some part of that house is mine, some is yours; the house itself is yours, the use of your house belongs to me. Crops may ripen upon your land, but you cannot touch them against the will of your tenant; and if corn be dear, or at famine price, you will

"In vain another's mighty store behold,"

grown upon your land, lying upon your land, and to be deposited in your own barns. Though you be the landlord, you must not enter my hired house, nor may you take away your own slave from me if I have contracted for his services; nay, if I hire a carriage from you, I bestow a benefit by allowing you to take your seat in it, although it is your own. You see, therefore, that it is possible for a man to receive a present by accepting what is his own.

6

In all the cases which I have mentioned, each party is the owner of the same thing. How is this? It is because the one owns the thing, the other owns the use of the thing. We speak of the books of Cicero. Dorus, the bookseller, calls these same books his own; the one claims them because he wrote them, the other because he bought them; so that they may quite correctly be spoken of as belonging to either of the two, for they do belong to each, though in a different manner. Thus Titus Livius may receive as a present, or may buy his own books from Dorus. Although the wise man possesses everything, yet I can give him what I individually possess; for though, king-like, he in his mind possesses everything, yet the ownership of all things is divided among various individuals, so that he can both receive a present and owe one; can buy, or hire things. Everything belongs to Caesar; yet he has no private property beyond his own privy purse; as Emperor all things are his, but nothing is his own except what he inherits. It is possible, without treason, to discuss what is and what is not his; for even what the court may decide not to be his, from another point of view is his. In the same way the wise man in his mind possesses everything, in actual right and ownership he possesses only his own property.

7

Bion is able to prove by argument at one time that everyone is sacrilegious, at another that no one is. When he is in a mood for casting all men down the Tarpeian rock, he says, "Whosoever touches that which belongs to the gods, and consumes it or converts it to his own uses, is sacrilegious; but all things belong to the gods, so that whatever thing anyone touches belongs to them to whom all belongs; whoever, therefore, touches anything is sacrilegious." Again, when he bids men break open temples and pillage the Capitol without fear of the wrath of heaven, he declares that no one can be sacrilegious; because, whatever a man takes away, he takes from one place which belongs to the gods into another place which belongs to the gods. The answer to this is that all places do indeed belong to the gods, but all are not consecrated to them, and that sacrilege can only be done in places solemnly dedicated to heaven. Thus, also, the whole world is a temple of the immortal gods, and, indeed, the only one worthy of their greatness and splendour, and yet there is a distinction between things sacred and profane; all things which it is lawful to do under the sky and the stars are not lawful to do within consecrated walls. The sacrilegious man cannot do God any harm, for He is placed beyond his reach by His divine nature; yet he is punished because he seems to have done Him harm: his punishment is demanded by our feeling on the matter, and even by his own. In the same way, therefore, as he who carries off any sacred things is regarded as sacrilegious, although that which he stole is nevertheless within the limits of the world, so it is possible to steal from a wise man: for in that case it will be some, not of that universe which he possesses, but some of those things of which he is the acknowledged owner, and which are severally his own property, which will be stolen from him. The former of these possessions he will recognize as his own, the latter he will be unwilling, even if he be able to possess; he will say, as that Roman commander said, when, to reward his courage and good service to the State, he was assigned as much land as he could inclose in one day's ploughing. "You do not," said he, "want a citizen who wants more than is enough for one citizen." Do you not think that it required a much greater man to refuse this reward than to earn it? for many have taken away the landmarks of other men's property, but no one sets up limits to his own.

8

When, then, we consider that the mind of the truly wise man has power over all things and pervades all things, we cannot help declaring that everything is his, although, in the estimation of our common law, it may chance that he may be rated as possessing no property whatever. It makes a great difference whether we estimate what he owns by the greatness of his mind, or by the public register. He would pray to be delivered from that possession of everything of which you speak. I will not remind you of Socrates, Chrysippus, Zeno, and other great men, all the greater, however, because envy prevents no one from praising the ancients. But a short time ago I mentioned Demetrius, who seems to have been placed by nature in our times that he might prove that we could neither corrupt him nor be corrected by him; a man of consummate wisdom, though he himself disclaimed it, constant to the principles which he professed, of an eloquence worthy to deal with the mightiest subjects, scorning mere prettinesses and verbal niceties, but expressing with infinite spirit, the ideas which inspired it. I doubt not that he was endowed by divine providence with so pure a life and such power of speech in order that our age might neither be without a model nor a reproach. Had some god wished to give all our wealth to Demetrius on the fixed condition that he should not be permitted to give it away, I am sure that he would have refused to accept it, and would have said,

9

"I do not intend to fasten upon my back a burden like this, of which I never can rid myself, nor do I, nimble and lightly equipped as I am, mean to hinder my progress by plunging into the deep morass of business transactions. Why do you offer to me what is the bane of all nations? I would not accept it even if I meant to give it away, for I see many things which it would not become me to give. I should like to place before my eyes the things which fascinate both kings and peoples, I wish to behold the price of your blood and your lives. First bring before me the trophies of Luxury, exhibiting them as you please, either in succession, or, which is better, in one mass. I see the shell of the tortoise, a foul and slothful brute, bought for immense sums and ornamented with the most elaborate care, the contrast of colours which is admired in it being obtained by the use of dyes resembling the natural tints. I see tables and pieces of wood valued at the price of a senator's estate, which are all the more precious, the more knots the tree has been twisted into by disease. I see crystal vessels, whose price is enhanced by their fragility, for among the ignorant the risk of losing things increases their value instead of lowering it, as it ought. I see murrhine cups, for luxury would be too cheap if men did not drink to one another out of hollow gems the wine to be afterwards thrown up again. I see more than one large pearl placed in each ear; for now our ears are trained to carry burdens, pearls are hung from them in pairs, and each pair has other single ones fastened above it. This womanish folly is not exaggerated enough for the men of our time, unless they hang two or three estates upon each ear. I see ladies' silk dresses, if those deserve to be called dresses which can neither cover their body or their shame; when wearing which, they can scarcely with a good conscience, swear that they are not naked. These are imported at a vast expense from nations unknown even to trade, in order that our matrons may show as much of their persons in public as they do to their lovers in private."

10

"What are you doing, Avarice? see how many things there are whose price exceeds that of your beloved gold: all those which I have mentioned are more highly esteemed and valued. I now wish to review your wealth, those plates of gold and silver which dazzle our covetousness. By Hercules, the very Earth, while she brings forth upon the surface everything that is of use to us, has buried these, sunk them deep, and rests upon them with her whole weight, regarding them as pernicious substances, and likely to prove the ruin of mankind if brought into the light of day. I see that iron is brought out of the same dark pits as gold and silver, in order that we may lack neither the means nor the reward of murder. Thus far we have dealt with actual substances; but some forms of wealth deceive our eyes and minds alike. I see there letters of credit, promissory notes, and bonds, empty phantoms of property, ghosts of sick Avarice, with which she deceives our minds, which delight in unreal fancies; for what are these things, and what are interest, and account books, and usury, except the names of unnatural developments of human covetousness? I might complain of nature for not having hidden gold and silver deeper, for not having laid over it a weight too heavy to be removed: but what are your documents, your sale of time, your bloodsucking twelve percent interest? these are evils which we owe to our own will, which flow merely from our perverted habit, having nothing about them which can be seen or handled, mere dreams of empty avarice. Wretched is he who can take pleasure in the size of the audit book of his estate, in great tracts of land cultivated by slaves in chains, in huge flocks and herds which require provinces and kingdoms for their pasture ground, in a household of servants, more in number than some of the most warlike nations, or in a private house whose extent surpasses that of a large city! After he has carefully reviewed all his wealth, in what it is invested, and on what it is spent, and has rendered himself proud by the thoughts of it, let him compare what he has with what he wants: he becomes a poor man at once. Let me go: restore me to those riches of mine. I know the kingdom of wisdom, which is great and stable: I possess everything, and in such a manner that it belongs to all men nevertheless."

11

When, therefore, Gaius Caesar offered him two hundred thousand sesterces, he laughingly refused it, thinking it unworthy of himself to boast of having refused so small a sum. Ye gods and goddesses, what a mean mind must the emperor have had, if he hoped either to honour or to corrupt him. I must here repeat a proof of his magnanimity. I have heard that when he was expressing his wonder at the folly of Gaius at supposing that he could be influenced by such a bribe, he said, "If he meant to tempt me, he ought to have tried to do so by offering his entire kingdom."

12

It is possible, then, to give something to the wise man, although all things belong to the wise man. Similarly, though we declare that friends have all things in common, it is nevertheless possible to give something to a friend: for I have not everything in common with a friend in the same manner as with a partner, where one part belongs to him, and another to me, but rather as a father and a mother possess their children in common when they have two, not each parent possessing one child, but each possessing both. First of all I will prove that any chance would-be partner of mine has nothing in common with me: and why? Because this community of goods can only exist between wise men, who are alone capable of friendship: other men can neither be friends nor partners one to another. In the next place, things may be owned in common in various ways. The knights' seats in the theatre belong to all the Roman knights; yet of these the seat which I occupy becomes my own, and if I yield it up to anyone, although I only yield him a thing which we own in common, still I appear to have given him something. Some things belong to certain persons under particular conditions. I have a place among the knights, not to sell, or to let, or to dwell in, but simply to see the spectacle from, wherefore I do not tell an untruth when I say that I have a place among the knights' seats. Yet if, when I come into the theatre, the knights' seats are full, I both have a seat there by right, because I have the privilege of sitting there, and I have not a seat there, because my seat is occupied by those who share my right to those places. Suppose that the same thing takes place between friends; whatever our friend possesses, is common to us, but is the property of him who owns it; I cannot make use of it against his will. "You are laughing at me," say you; "if what belongs to my friend is mine, I am able to sell it." You are not able; for you are not able to sell your place among the knights' seats, and yet they are in common between you and the other knights. Consequently, the fact that you cannot sell a thing, or consume it, or exchange it for the better or the worse does not prove that it is not yours; for that which is yours under certain conditions is yours nevertheless.

13

I have received, but certainly not less. Not to detain you longer than is necessary, a benefit can be no more than a benefit; but the means employed to convey benefits may be both greater and more numerous. I mean those things by which kindness expresses and gives vent to itself, like lovers, whose many kisses and close embraces do not increase their love but give it play.

14

The next question which arises has been thoroughly threshed out in the former books, so here it shall only be touched on shortly; for the arguments which have been used for other cases can be transferred to it.

The question is, whether one who has done everything in his power to return a benefit, has returned it. "You may know," says our adversary, "that he has not returned it, because he did everything in his power to return it; it is evident, therefore, that he did not do that which he did not have an opportunity of doing. A man who searches everywhere for his creditor without finding him does not thereby pay him what he owes." Some are in such a position that it is their duty to effect something material; in the case of others to have done all in their power to effect it is as good as effecting it. If a physician has done all in his power to heal his patient he has performed his duty; an advocate who employs his whole powers of eloquence on his client's behalf, performs his duty even though his client be convicted; the generalship even of a beaten commander is praised if he has prudently, laboriously, and courageously exercised his functions. Your friend has done all in his power to return your kindness, but your good fortune stood in his way; no adversity befell you in which he could prove the truth of his friendship; he could not give you money when you were rich, or nurse you when you were in health, or help you when you were succeeding; yet he repaid your kindness, even though you did not receive a benefit from him. Moreover, this man, being always eager, and on the watch for an opportunity of doing this, as he has expended much anxiety and much trouble upon it, has really done more than he who quickly had an opportunity of repaying your kindness. The case of a debtor is not the same, for it is not enough for him to have tried to find the money unless he pays it; in his case a harsh creditor stands over him who will not let a single day pass without charging him interest; in yours there is a most kind friend, who seeing you busy, troubled, and anxious would say.

" 'Dismiss this trouble from thy breast;'

leave off disturbing yourself; I have received from you all that I wish; you wrong me, if you suppose that I want anything further; you have fully repaid me in intention."

"Tell me," says our adversary, "if he had repaid the benefit you would say that he had returned your kindness: is, then, he who repays it in the same position as he who does not repay it?"

On the other hand, consider this: if he had forgotten the benefit which he had received, if he had not even attempted to be grateful, you would say that he had not returned the kindness; but this man has laboured day and night to the neglect of all his other duties in his devoted care to let no opportunity of proving his gratitude escape him; is then he who took no pains to return a kindness to be classed with this man who never ceased to take pains? you are unjust, if you require a material payment from me when you see that I am not wanting in intention.

15

In short, suppose that when you are taken captive, I have borrowed money, made over my property as security to my creditor, that I have sailed in a stormy winter season along coasts swarming with pirates, that I have braved all the perils which necessarily attend a voyage even on a peaceful sea, that I have wandered through all wildernesses seeking for those men whom all others flee from, and that when I have at length reached the pirates, someone else has already ransomed you: will you say that I have not returned your kindness? Even if during this voyage I have lost by shipwreck the money that I had raised to save you, even if I myself have fallen into the prison from which I sought to release you, will you say that I have not returned your kindness? No, by Hercules! the Athenians call Harmodius and Aristogiton tyrannicides; the hand of Mucius which he left on the enemy's altar was equivalent to the death of Porsena, and valour struggling against fortune is always illustrious, even if it falls short of accomplishing its design. He who watches each opportunity as it passes, and tries to avail himself of one after another, does more to show his gratitude than he whom the first opportunity enabled to be grateful without any trouble whatever. "But," says our adversary, "he gave you two things, material help and kindly feeling; you, therefore, owe him two." You might justly say this to one who returns your kindly feeling without troubling himself further; this man is really in your debt; but you cannot say so of one who wishes to repay you, who struggles and leaves no stone unturned to do so; for, as far as in him lies, he repays you in both kinds; in the next place, counting is not always a true test, sometimes one thing is equivalent to two; consequently so intense and ardent a wish to repay takes the place of a material repayment. Indeed, if a feeling of gratitude has no value in repaying a kindness without giving something material, then no one can be grateful to the gods, whom we can repay by gratitude alone. "We cannot," says our adversary, "give the gods anything else." Well, but if I am not able to give this man, whose kindness I am bound to return, anything beside my gratitude, why should that which is all that I can bestow on a god be insufficient to prove my gratitude towards a man?

16

If, however, you ask me what I really think, and wish me to give a definite answer, I should say that the one party ought to consider his benefit to have been returned, while the other ought to feel that he has not returned it; the one should release his friend from the debt, the other should hold himself bound to pay it; the one should say, "I have received;" the other should answer, "I owe." In our whole investigation, we ought to look entirely to the public good; we ought to prevent the ungrateful having any excuses in which they can take refuge, and under cover of which they can disown their debts. "I have done all in my power," say you. Well, keep on doing so still. Do you suppose that our ancestors were so foolish, as not to understand that it is most unjust that the man who has wasted the money which he received from his creditor on debauchery, or gambling, should be classed with one who has lost his own property as well as that of others in a fire, by robbery, or some sadder mischance? They would take no excuse, that men might understand that they were always bound to keep their word; it was thought better that even a good excuse should not be accepted from a few persons, than that all men should be led to try to make excuses. You say that you have done all in your power to repay your debt; this ought to be enough for your friend, but not enough for you. He to whom you owe a kindness, is unworthy of gratitude if he lets all your anxious care and trouble to repay it go for nothing; and so, too, if your friend takes your good will as a repayment, you are ungrateful if you are not all the more eager to feel the obligation of the debt which he has forgiven you. Do not snap up his receipt, or call witnesses to prove it; rather seek opportunities for repaying not less than before; repay the one man because he asks for repayment, the other because he forgives you your debt; the one because he is good, the other because he is bad. You, need not, therefore, think that you have anything to do with the question whether a man be bound to repay the benefit which he has received from a wise man, if that man has ceased to be wise and has turned into a bad man. You would return a deposit which you had received from a wise man; you would return a loan even to a bad man; what grounds have you for not returning a benefit also? Because he has changed, ought he to change you? What? if you had received anything from a man when healthy, would you not return it to him when he was sick, though we always are more bound to treat our friends with more kindness when they are ailing? So, too, this man is sick in his mind; we ought to help him, and bear with him; folly is a disease of the mind.

17

I think here we ought to make a distinction, in order to render this point more intelligible. Benefits are of two kinds: one, the perfect and true benefit, which can only be bestowed by one wise man upon another; the other, the common vulgar form which ignorant men like ourselves interchange. With regard to the latter, there is no doubt that it is my duty to repay it whether my friend turns out to be a murderer, a thief, or an adulterer. Crimes have laws to punish them; criminals are better reformed by judges than by ingratitude; a man ought not to make you bad by being so himself. I will fling a benefit back to a bad man, I will return it to a good man; I do so to the latter, because I owe it to him; to the former, that I may not be in his debt.

18

With regard to the other class of benefit, the question arises whether if I was not able to take it without being a wise man, I am able to return it, except to a wise man. For suppose I do return it to him, he cannot receive it, he is not any longer able to receive such a thing, he has lost the knowledge of how to use it. You would not bid me throw back[27] a ball to a man who has lost his hand; it is folly to give anyone what he cannot receive. If I am to begin to reply to the last argument, I say that I should not give him what he is unable to take; but I would return it, even though he is not able to receive it. I cannot lay him under an obligation unless he takes my bounty; but by returning it I can free myself from my obligations to him. You say, "he will not be able to use it." Let him see to that; the fault will lie with him, not with me.

19

"To return a thing," says our adversary, "is to hand it over to one who can receive it. Why, if you owed some wine to any man, and he bade you pour it into a net or a sieve, would you say that you had returned it? or would you be willing to return it in such a way that in the act of returning it was lost between you?" To return is to give that which you owe back to its owner when he wishes for it. It is not my duty to perform more than this; that he should possess what he has received from me is a matter for further consideration; I do not owe him the safekeeping of his property, but the honourable payment of my debt, and it is much better that he should not have it, than that I should not return it to him. I would repay my creditor, even though he would at once take what I paid him to the market; even if he deputed an adulteress to receive the money from me, I would pay it to her; even if he were to pour the coins which he receives into a loose fold of his cloak, I would pay it. It is my business to return it to him, not to keep it and save it for him after I have returned it; I am bound to take care of his bounty when I have received it, but not when I have returned it to him. While it remains with me, it must be kept safe; but when he asks for it again I must give it to him, even though it slips out of his hands as he takes it. I will repay a good man when it is convenient; I will repay a bad man when he asks me to do so.

---

[27] I.e. in the game of ball.

"You cannot," argues our adversary, "return him a benefit of the same kind as that which you received; for you received it from a wise man, and you are returning it to a fool." Do I not return to him such a benefit, as he is now able to receive? It is not my fault if I return it to him worse than I received it, the fault lies with him, and so, unless he regains his former wisdom, I shall return it in such a form as he in his fallen condition is able to receive. "But what," asks he, "if he become not only bad, but savage and ferocious, like Apollodorus or Phalaris, would you return even to such a man as this a benefit which you had received from him?" I answer, Nature does not admit of so great a change in a wise man. Men do not change from the best to the worst; even in becoming bad, he would necessarily retain some traces of goodness; virtue is never so utterly quenched as not to imprint on the mind marks which no degradation can efface. If wild animals bred in captivity escape into the woods, they still retain something of their original tameness, and are as remote from the gentlest in the one extreme as they are in the other from those which have always been wild, and have never endured to be touched by man's hand. No one who has ever applied himself to philosophy ever becomes completely wicked; his mind becomes so deeply coloured with it, that its tints can never be entirely spoiled and blackened. In the next place, I ask whether this man of yours be ferocious merely in intent, or whether he breaks out into actual outrages upon mankind? You have instanced the tyrants Apollodorus and Phalaris; if the bad man restrains their evil likeness within himself, why should I not return his benefit to him, in order to set myself free from any further dealings with him? If, however, he not only delights in human blood, but feeds upon it; if he exercises his insatiable cruelty in the torture of persons of all ages, and his fury is not prompted by anger, but by a sort of delight in cruelty, if he cuts the throats of children before the eyes of their parents; if, not satisfied with merely killing his victims, he tortures them, and not only burns but actually roasts them; if his castle is always wet with freshly shed blood; then it is not enough not to return his benefits. All connection between me and such a man has been broken off by his destruction of the bonds of human society. If he had bestowed something upon me, but were to invade my native country, he would have lost all claim to my gratitude, and it would be counted a crime to make him any return; if he does not attack my country, but is the scourge of his own; if he has nothing to do with my nation, but torments and cuts to pieces his own, then in the same manner such depravity, though it does not render him my personal enemy, yet renders him hateful to me, and the duty which I owe to the human race is anterior to and more important than that which I owe to him as an individual.

20

However, although this be so, and although I am freed from all obligation towards him, from the moment when, by outraging all laws, he rendered it impossible for any man to do him a wrong, nevertheless, I think I ought to make the following distinction in dealing with him. If my repayment of his benefit will neither increase nor maintain his powers of doing mischief to mankind, and is of such a character that I can return it to him without disadvantage to the public, I would return it: for instance, I would save the life of his infant child; for what harm can this benefit do to any of those who suffer from his cruelty? But I would not furnish him with money to pay his bodyguard. If he wishes for marbles, or fine clothes, the trappings of his luxury will harm no one; but with soldiers and arms I would not furnish him. If he demands, as a great boon, actors and courtesans and such things as will soften his savage nature, I would willingly bestow them upon him. I would not furnish him with triremes and brass-beaked ships of war, but I would send him fast sailing and luxuriously-fitted vessels, and all the toys of kings who take their pleasure on the sea. If his health was altogether despaired of, I would by the same act bestow a benefit on all men and return one to him; seeing that for such characters death is the only remedy, and that he who never will return to himself, had best leave himself. However, such wickedness as this is uncommon, and is always regarded as a portent, as when the earth opens, or when fires break forth from caves under the sea; so let us leave it, and speak of those vices which we can hate without shuddering at them. As for the ordinary bad man, whom I can find in the marketplace of any town, who is feared only by individuals, I would return to him a benefit which I had received from him. It is not right that I should profit by his wickedness; let me return what is not mine to its owner. Whether he be good or bad makes no difference; but I would consider the matter most carefully, if I were not returning but bestowing it.

21

This point requires to be illustrated by a story. A certain Pythagoraean bought a fine pair of shoes from a shoemaker; and as they were an expensive piece of work, he did not pay ready money for them. Some time afterwards he came to the shop to pay for them, and after he had long been knocking at the closed door, someone said to him, "Why do you waste your time? The shoemaker whom you seek has been carried out of his house and buried; this is a grief to us who lose our friends forever, but by no means so to you, who know that he will be born again," jeering at the Pythagoraean. Upon this our philosopher not unwillingly carried his three or four denarii home again, shaking them every now and then; afterwards, blaming himself for the pleasure which he had secretly felt at not paying his debt, and perceiving that he enjoyed having made this trifling gain, he returned to the shop, and saying, "the man lives for you, pay him what you owe," he passed four denarii into the shop through the crack of the closed door, and let them fall inside, punishing himself for his unconscionable greediness that he might not form the habit of appropriating that which is not his own.

22

If you owe anything, seek for someone to whom you may repay it, and if no one demands it, dun your own self; whether the man be good or bad is no concern of yours; repay him, and then blame him. You have forgotten how your several duties are divided: it is right for him to forget it, but we have bidden you bear it in mind. When, however, we say that he who bestows a benefit ought to forget it, it is a mistake to suppose that we rob him of all recollection of the business, though it is most creditable to him; some of our precepts are stated over strictly in order to reduce them to their true proportions. When we say that he ought not to remember it, we mean he ought not to speak publicly, or boast of it offensively. There are some, who, when they have bestowed a benefit, tell it in all societies, talk of it when sober, cannot be silent about it when drunk, force it upon strangers, and communicate it to friends; it is to quell this excessive and reproachful consciousness that we bid him who gave it forget it, and by commanding him to do this, which is more than he is able, encourage him to keep silence.

23

When you distrust those whom you order to do anything, you ought to command them to do more than enough in order that they may do what is enough. The purpose of all exaggeration is to arrive at the truth by falsehood. Consequently, he who spoke of horses as being:

"Whiter than snows and swifter than the winds,"

said what could not possibly be in order that they might be thought to be as much so as possible. And he who said:

"More firm than crags, more headlong than the stream,"

did not suppose that he should make anyone believe that a man could ever be as firm as a crag. Exaggeration never hopes all its daring flights to be believed, but affirms what is incredible, that thereby it may convey what is credible. When we say, "let the man who has bestowed a benefit, forget it," what we mean is, "let him be as though he had forgotten it; let not his remembrance of it appear or be seen." When we say that repayment of a benefit ought not to be demanded, we do not utterly forbid its being demanded; for repayment must often be extorted from bad men, and even good men require to be reminded of it. Am I not to point out a means of repayment to one who does not perceive it? Am I not to explain my wants to one does not know them? Why should he (if a bad man) have the excuse, or (if a good man) have the sorrow of not knowing them? Men ought sometimes to be reminded of their debts, though with modesty, not in the tone of one demanding a legal right.

24

Socrates once said in the hearing of his friends: "I would have bought a cloak, if I had had the money for it." He asked no one for money, but he reminded them all to give it. There was a rivalry between them, as to who should give it; and how should there not be? Was it not a small thing which Socrates received? Yes, but it was a great thing to be the man from whom Socrates received it. Could he blame them more gently? "I would," said he, "have bought a cloak if I had had the money for it." After this, however eager anyone was to give, he gave too late; for he had already been wanting in his duty to Socrates. Because some men harshly demand repayment of debts, we forbid it, not in order that it may never be done, but that it may be done sparingly.

25

Aristippus once, when enjoying a perfume, said: "Bad luck to those effeminate persons who have brought so nice a thing into disrepute." We also may say, "Bad luck to those base extortioners who pester us for a fourfold return of their benefits, and have brought into disrepute so nice a thing as reminding our friends of their duty." I shall nevertheless make use of this right of friendship, and I shall demand the return of a benefit from any man from whom I would not have scrupled to ask for one, such a man as would regard the power of returning a benefit as equivalent to receiving a second one. Never, not even when complaining of him, would I say,

> "A wretch forlorn upon the shore he lay,
> His ship, his comrades, all were swept away;
> Fool that I was, I pitied his despair,
> And even gave him of my realm a share."

This is not to remind, but to reproach; this is to make one's benefits odious to enable him, or even to make him wish to be ungrateful. It is enough, and more than enough, to remind him of it gently and familiarly:

> "If aught of mine hath e'er deserved thy thanks."

To this his answer would be, "Of course you have deserved my thanks; you took me up, 'a wretch forlorn upon the shore.'"

26

"But," says our adversary, "suppose that we gain nothing by this; suppose that he pretends that he has forgotten it, what ought I to do?" You now ask a very necessary question, and one which fitly concludes this branch of the subject, how, namely, one ought to bear with the ungrateful. I answer, calmly, gently, magnanimously. Never let anyone's discourtesy, forgetfulness, or ingratitude, enrage you so much that you do not feel any pleasure at having bestowed a benefit upon him; never let your wrongs drive you into saying, "I wish I had not done it." You ought to take pleasure even in the ill-success of your benefit; he will always be sorry for it, even though you are not even now sorry for it. You ought not to be indignant, as if something strange had happened; you ought rather to be surprised if it had not happened. Some are prevented by difficulties, some by expense, and some by danger from returning your bounty; some are hindered by a false shame, because by returning it, they would confess that they had received it; with others ignorance of their duty, indolence, or excess of business, stands in the way. Reflect upon the insatiability of men's desires. You need not be surprised if no one repays you in a world in which no one ever gains enough. What man is there of so firm and trustworthy a mind that you can safely invest your benefits in him? One man is crazed with lust, another is the slave of his belly, another gives his whole soul to gain, caring nothing for the means by which he amasses it; some men's minds are disturbed by envy, some blinded by ambition till they are ready to fling themselves on the sword's point. In addition to this, one must reckon sluggishness of mind and old age; and also the opposites of these, restlessness and disturbance of mind, also excessive self-esteem and pride in the very things for which a man ought to be despised. I need not mention obstinate persistence in wrongdoing, or frivolity which cannot remain constant to one point; besides all this, there is headlong rashness, there is timidity which never gives us trustworthy counsel, and the numberless errors with which we struggle, the rashness of the most cowardly, the quarrels of our best friends, and that most common evil of trusting in what is most uncertain, and of undervaluing, when we have obtained it, that which we once never hoped to possess. Amidst all these restless passions, how can you hope to find a thing so full of rest as good faith?

27

If a true picture of our life were to rise before your mental vision, you would, I think, behold a scene like that of a town just taken by storm, where decency and righteousness were no longer regarded, and no advice is heard but that of force, as if universal confusion were the word of command. Neither fire nor sword are spared; crime is unpunished by the laws; even religion, which saves the lives of suppliants in the very midst of armed enemies, does not check those who are rushing to secure plunder. Some men rob private houses, some public buildings; all places, sacred or profane, are alike stripped; some burst their way in, others climb over; some open a wider path for themselves by overthrowing the walls that keep them out, and make their way to their booty over ruins; some ravage without murdering, others brandish spoils dripping with their owner's blood; everyone carries off his neighbours' goods. In this greedy struggle of the human race surely you forget the common lot of all mankind, if you seek among these robbers for one who will return what he has got.

If you are indignant at men being ungrateful, you ought also to be indignant at their being luxurious, avaricious and lustful; you might as well be indignant with sick men for being ugly, or with old men for being pale. It is, indeed, a serious vice, it is not to be borne, and sets men at variance with one another; nay, it rends and destroys that union by which alone our human weakness can be supported; yet it is so absolutely universal, that even those who complain of it most are not themselves free from it.

28

Consider within yourself, whether you have always shown gratitude to those to whom you owe it, whether no one's kindness has ever been wasted upon you, whether you constantly bear in mind all the benefits which you have received. You will find that those which you received as a boy were forgotten before you became a man; that those bestowed upon you as a young man slipped from your memory when you became an old one. Some we have lost, some we have thrown away, some have by degrees passed out of our sight, to some we have wilfully shut our eyes. If I am to make excuses for your weakness, I must say in the first place that human memory is a frail vessel, and is not large enough to contain the mass of things placed in it; the more it receives, the more it must necessarily lose; the oldest things in it give way to the newest. Thus it comes to pass that your nurse has hardly any influence with you, because the lapse of time has set the kindness which you received from her at so great a distance; thus it is that you no longer look upon your teacher with respect; and that now when you are busy about your candidature for the consulate or the priesthood, you forget those who supported you in your election to the quaestorship. If you carefully examine yourself, perhaps you will find the vice of which you complain in your own bosom; you are wrong in being angry with a universal failing, and foolish also, for it is your own as well; you must pardon others, that you may yourself be acquitted. You will make your friend a better man by bearing with him, you will in all cases make him a worse one by reproaching him. You can have no reason for rendering him shameless; let him preserve any remnants of modesty which he may have. Too loud reproaches have often dispelled a modesty which might have borne good fruit. No man fears to be that which all men see that he is; when his fault is made public, he loses his sense of shame.

29

You say, "I have lost the benefit which I bestowed." Yet do we say that we have lost what we consecrate to heaven, and a benefit well bestowed, even though we get an ill return for it, is to be reckoned among things consecrated. Our friend is not such a man as we hoped he was; still, let us, unlike him, remain the same as we were. The loss did not take place when he proved himself so; his ingratitude cannot be made public without reflecting some shame upon us, since to complain of the loss of a benefit is a sign that it was not well bestowed. As far as we are able we ought to plead with ourselves on his behalf: "Perhaps he was not able to return it, perhaps he did not know of it, perhaps he will still do so." A wise and forbearing creditor prevents the loss of some debts by encouraging his debtor and giving him time. We ought to do the same, we ought to deal tenderly with a weakly sense of honour.

30

"I have lost," say you, "the benefit which I bestowed." You are a fool, and do not understand when your loss took place; you have indeed lost it, but you did so when you gave it, the fact has only now come to light. Even in the case of those benefits which appear to be lost, gentleness will do much good; the wounds of the mind ought to be handled as tenderly as those of the body. The string, which might be disentangled by patience, is often broken by a rough pull. What is the use of abuse, or of complaints? why do you overwhelm him with reproaches? why do you set him free from his obligation? even if he be ungrateful he owes you nothing after this. What sense is there in exasperating a man on whom you have conferred great favours, so as out of a doubtful friend to make a certain enemy, and one, too, who will seek to support his own cause by defaming you, or to make men say, "I do not know what the reason is that he cannot endure a man to whom he owes so much; there must be something in the background?" Any man can asperse, even if he does not permanently stain the reputation of his betters by complaining of them; nor will anyone be satisfied with imputing small crimes to them, when it is only by the enormity of his falsehood that he can hope to be believed.

31

What a much better way is that by which the semblance of friendship, and, indeed, if the other regains to his right mind, friendship itself is preserved! Bad men are overcome by unwearying goodness, nor does anyone receive kindness in so harsh and hostile a spirit as not to love good men even while he does them wrong, when they lay him under the additional obligation of requiring no return for their kindness. Reflect, then, upon this: you say, "My kindness has met with no return, what am I to do? I ought to imitate the gods, those noblest disposers of all events, who begin to bestow their benefits on those who know them not, and persist in bestowing them on those who are ungrateful for them. Some reproach them with neglect of us, some with injustice towards us; others place them outside of their own world, in sloth and indifference, without light, and without any functions; others declare that the sun itself, to whom we owe the division of our times of labour and of rest, by whose means we are saved from being plunged in the darkness of eternal night; who, by his circuit, orders the seasons of the year, gives strength to our bodies, brings forth our crops and ripens our fruits, is merely a mass of stone, or a fortuitous collection of fiery particles, or anything rather than a god. Yet, nevertheless, like the kindest of parents, who only smile at the spiteful words of their children, the gods do not cease to heap benefits upon those who doubt from what source their benefits are derived, but continue impartially distributing their bounty among all the peoples and nations of the Earth. Possessing only the power of doing good, they moisten the land with seasonable showers, they put the seas in movement by the winds, they mark time by the course of the constellations, they temper the extremes of heat and cold, of summer and winter, by breathing a milder air upon us; and they graciously and serenely bear with the faults of our erring spirits. Let us follow their example; let us give, even if much be given to no purpose, let us, in spite of this, give to others; nay, even to those upon whom our bounty has been wasted. No one is prevented by the fall of a house from building another; when one home has been destroyed by fire, we lay the foundations of another before the site has had time to cool; we rebuild ruined cities more than once upon the same spots, so untiring are our hopes of success. Men would undertake no works either on land or sea if they were not willing to try again what they have failed in once.

32

Suppose a man is ungrateful: he does not injure me, but himself; I had the enjoyment of my benefit when I bestowed it upon him. Because he is ungrateful, I shall not be slower to give but more careful; what I have lost with him, I shall receive back from others. But I will bestow a second benefit upon this man himself, and will overcome him even as a good husbandman overcomes the sterility of the soil by care and culture; if I do not do so my benefit is lost to me, and he is lost to mankind. It is no proof of a great mind to give and to throw away one's bounty; the true test of a great mind is to throw away one's bounty and still to give."

ON ANGER

BOOK 1

1

You have demanded of me, Novatus, that I should write how anger may be soothed, and it appears to me that you are right in feeling especial fear of this passion, which is above all others hideous and wild: for the others have some alloy of peace and quiet, but this consists wholly in action and the impulse of grief, raging with an utterly inhuman lust for arms, blood and tortures, careless of itself provided it hurts another, rushing upon the very point of the sword, and greedy for revenge even when it drags the avenger to ruin with itself. Some of the wisest of men have in consequence of this called anger a short madness: for it is equally devoid of self control, regardless of decorum, forgetful of kinship, obstinately engrossed in whatever it begins to do, deaf to reason and advice, excited by trifling causes, awkward at perceiving what is true and just, and very like a falling rock which breaks itself to pieces upon the very thing which it crushes. That you may know that they whom anger possesses are not sane, look at their appearance; for as there are distinct symptoms which mark madmen, such as a bold and menacing air, a gloomy brow, a stern face, a hurried walk, restless hands, changed colour, quick and strongly-drawn breathing; the signs of angry men, too, are the same: their eyes blaze and sparkle, their whole face is a deep red with the blood which boils up from the bottom of their heart, their lips quiver, their teeth are set, their hair bristles and stands on end, their breath is laboured and hissing, their joints crack as they twist them about, they groan, bellow, and burst into scarcely intelligible talk, they often clap their hands together and stamp on the ground with their feet, and their whole body is highly-strung and plays those tricks which mark a distraught mind, so as to furnish an ugly and shocking picture of self-perversion and excitement. You cannot tell whether this vice is more execrable or more disgusting. Other vices can be concealed and cherished in secret; anger shows itself openly and appears in the countenance, and the greater it is, the more plainly it boils forth. Do you not see how in all animals certain signs appear before they proceed to mischief, and how their entire bodies put off their usual quiet appearance and stir up their ferocity? Boars foam at the mouth and sharpen their teeth by rubbing them against trees, bulls toss their horns in the air and scatter the sand with blows of their feet, lions growl, the necks of enraged snakes swell, mad dogs have a sullen look—there is no animal so hateful and venomous by nature that it does not, when seized by anger, show additional fierceness. I know well that the other passions can hardly be concealed, and that lust, fear, and boldness give signs of their presence and may be discovered beforehand, for there is no one of the stronger passions that does not affect the countenance: what then is the difference between them and anger? Why, that the other passions are visible, but that this is conspicuous.

2

Next, if you choose to view its results and the mischief that it does, no plague has cost the human race more dear: you will see slaughterings and poisonings, accusations and counter-accusations, sacking of cities, ruin of whole peoples, the persons of princes sold into slavery by auction, torches applied to roofs, and fires not merely confined within city-walls but making whole tracts of country glow with hostile flame. See the foundations of the most celebrated cities hardly now to be discerned; they were ruined by anger. See deserts extending for many miles without an inhabitant: they have been desolated by anger. See all the chiefs whom tradition mentions as instances of ill fate; anger stabbed one of them in his bed, struck down another, though he was protected by the sacred rights of hospitality, tore another to pieces in the very home of the laws and in sight of the crowded forum, bade one shed his own blood by the parricide hand of his son, another to have his royal throat cut by the hand of a slave, another to stretch out his limbs on the cross: and hitherto I am speaking merely of individual cases. What, if you were to pass from the consideration of those single men against whom anger has broken out to view whole assemblies cut down by the sword, the people butchered by the soldiery let loose upon it, and whole nations condemned to death in one common ruin[28] as though by men who either freed themselves from our charge or despised

---

[28] Here a leaf or more has been lost, including the fragment cited in Lactantius, *De Ira Dei*, 17: "*Ira est cupiditas,*" etc. The entire passage is:—"But the Stoics did not perceive that there is a difference between right and wrong; that there is just and unjust anger: and as they could find no remedy for it, they wished to extirpate it. The Peripatetics, on the other hand, declared that it ought not to be destroyed, but restrained. These I have sufficiently answered in the sixth book of my *Institutiones*. It is clear that the philosophers did not comprehend the reason of anger, from the definitions of it which Seneca has enumerated in the books 'On Anger' which

our authority? Why, wherefore is the people angry with gladiators, and so unjust as to think itself wronged if they do not die cheerfully? It thinks itself scorned, and by looks, gestures, and excitement turns itself from a mere spectator into an adversary. Everything of this sort is not anger, but the semblance of anger, like that of boys who want to beat the ground when they have fallen upon it, and who often do not even know why they are angry, but are merely angry without any reason or having received any injury, yet not without some semblance of injury received, or without some wish to exact a penalty for it. Thus they are deceived by the likeness of blows, and are appeased by the pretended tears of those who deprecate their wrath, and thus an unreal grief is healed by an unreal revenge.

3

"We often are angry," says our adversary, "not with men who have hurt us, but with men who are going to hurt us: so you may be sure that anger is not born of injury." It is true that we are angry with those who are going to hurt us, but they do already hurt us in intention, and one who is going to do an injury is already doing it. "The weakest of men," argues he, "are often angry with the most powerful: so you may be sure that anger is not a desire to punish their antagonist—for men do not desire to punish him when they cannot hope to do so." In the first place, I spoke of a desire to inflict punishment, not a power to do so: now men desire even what they cannot obtain. In the next place, no one is so low in station as not to be able to hope to inflict punishment even upon the greatest of men: we all are powerful for mischief. Aristotle's definition differs little from mine: for he declares anger to be a desire to repay suffering. It would be a long task to examine the differences between his definition and mine: it may be urged against both of them that wild beasts become angry without being excited by injury, and without any idea of punishing others or requiting them with pain: for, even though they do these things, these are not what they aim at doing. We must admit, however, that neither wild beasts nor any other creature except man is subject to anger: for, whilst anger is the foe of reason, it nevertheless does not arise in any place where reason cannot dwell. Wild beasts have impulses, fury, cruelty, combativeness: they have not anger any more than they have luxury: yet they indulge in some pleasures with less self-control than human beings. Do not believe the poet who says:

"The boar his wrath forgets, the stag forgets the hounds,
The bear forgets how 'midst the herd he leaped with frantic bounds."[29]

---

he has written. 'Anger,' he says, 'is the desire of avenging an injury.' Others, as Posidonius says, call it 'a desire to punish one by whom you think that you have been unjustly injured.' Some have defined it thus: 'Anger is an impulse of the mind to injure him who either has injured you or has sought to injure you.' Aristotle's definition differs but little from our own. He says, 'that anger is a desire to repay suffering,' " etc.

[29] Ovid, *Metamorphoses*, VII, 545–6.

When he speaks of beasts being angry he means that they are excited, roused up: for indeed they know no more how to be angry than they know how to pardon. Dumb creatures have not human feelings, but have certain impulses which resemble them: for if it were not so, if they could feel love and hate, they would likewise be capable of friendship and enmity, of disagreement and agreement. Some traces of these qualities exist even in them, though properly all of them, whether good or bad, belong to the human breast alone. To no creature besides man has been given wisdom, foresight, industry, and reflection. To animals not only human virtues but even human vices are forbidden: their whole constitution, mental and bodily, is unlike that of human beings: in them the royal[30] and leading principle is drawn from another source, as, for instance, they possess a voice, yet not a clear one, but indistinct and incapable of forming words: a tongue, but one which is fettered and not sufficiently nimble for complex movements: so, too, they possess intellect, the greatest attribute of all, but in a rough and inexact condition. It is, consequently, able to grasp those visions and semblances which rouse it to action, but only in a cloudy and indistinct fashion. It follows from this that their impulses and outbreaks are violent, and that they do not feel fear, anxieties, grief, or anger, but some semblances of these feelings: wherefore they quickly drop them and adopt the converse of them: they graze after showing the most vehement rage and terror, and after frantic bellowing and plunging they straightaway sink into quiet sleep.

4

What anger is has been sufficiently explained. The difference between it and irascibility is evident: it is the same as that between a drunken man and a drunkard; between a frightened man and a coward. It is possible for an angry man not to be irascible; an irascible man may sometimes not be angry. I shall omit the other varieties of anger, which the Greeks distinguish by various names, because we have no distinctive words for them in our language, although we call men bitter and harsh, and also peevish, frantic, clamorous, surly and fierce: all of which are different forms of irascibility. Among these you may class sulkiness, a refined form of irascibility; for there are some sorts of anger which go no further than noise, while some are as lasting as they are common: some are fierce in deed, but inclined to be sparing of words: some expend themselves in bitter words and curses: some do not go beyond complaining and turning one's back: some are great, deep-seated, and brood within a man: there are a thousand other forms of a multiform evil.

5

We have now finished our enquiry as to what anger is, whether it exists in any other creature besides man, what the difference is between it and irascibility, and how

---

[30] τό ἡγεμονικόν of the Stoics.

many forms it possesses. Let us now enquire whether anger be in accordance with nature, and whether it be useful and worth entertaining in some measure.

Whether it be according to nature will become evident if we consider man's nature, than which what is more gentle while it is in its proper condition? Yet what is more cruel than anger? What is more affectionate to others than man? Yet what is more savage against them than anger? Mankind is born for mutual assistance, anger for mutual ruin: the former loves society, the latter estrangement. The one loves to do good, the other to do harm; the one to help even strangers, the other to attack even its dearest friends. The one is ready even to sacrifice itself for the good of others, the other to plunge into peril provided it drags others with it. Who, then, can be more ignorant of nature than he who classes this cruel and hurtful vice as belonging to her best and most polished work? Anger, as we have said, is eager to punish; and that such a desire should exist in man's peaceful breast is least of all according to his nature; for human life is founded on benefits and harmony and is bound together into an alliance for the common help of all, not by terror, but by love towards one another.

6

"What, then? Is not correction sometimes necessary?" Of course it is; but with discretion, not with anger; for it does not injure, but heals under the guise of injury. We char crooked spearshafts to straighten them, and force them by driving in wedges, not in order to break them, but to take the bends out of them; and, in like manner, by applying pain to the body or mind we correct dispositions which have been rendered crooked by vice. So the physician at first, when dealing with slight disorders, tries not to make much change in his patient's daily habits, to regulate his food, drink, and exercise, and to improve his health merely by altering the order in which he takes them. The next step is to see whether an alteration in their amount will be of service. If neither alteration of the order or of the amount is of use, he cuts off some and reduces others. If even this does not answer, he forbids food, and disburdens the body by fasting. If milder remedies have proved useless he opens a vein; if the extremities are injuring the body and infecting it with disease he lays his hands upon the limbs; yet none of his treatment is considered harsh if its result is to give health. Similarly, it is the duty of the chief administrator of the laws, or the ruler of a state, to correct ill-disposed men, as long as he is able, with words, and even with gentle ones, that he may persuade them to do what they ought, inspire them with a love of honour and justice, and cause them to hate vice and set store upon virtue. He must then pass on to severer language, still confining himself to advising and reprimanding; last of all he must betake himself to punishments, yet still making them slight and temporary. He ought to assign extreme punishments only to extreme crimes, that no one may die unless it be even to the criminal's own advantage that he should die. He will differ from the physician in one point alone; for whereas physicians render it easy to die for those to whom they cannot grant the boon of life, he will drive the condemned out of life with ignominy and disgrace, not because he takes pleasure in any man's being punished, for the wise man is far from such inhuman ferocity, but that they may be a warning to all men, and that, since they would not be useful when alive, the State may at any rate profit by their death. Man's nature is not, therefore, desirous of inflicting punishment; neither, therefore, is anger in accordance with man's nature, because that is desirous of inflicting punishment. I will also adduce Plato's argument—for what harm is there in using other men's arguments, so far as they are on our side? "A good man," says he, "does not do any hurt: it is only punishment which hurts. Punishment, therefore, does not accord with a good man: wherefore anger does not do so either, because punishment and anger accord one with another. If a good man takes no pleasure in punishment, he will also take no pleasure in that state of mind to which punishment gives pleasure: consequently anger is not natural to man."

7

May it not be that, although anger be not natural, it may be right to adopt it, because it often proves useful? It rouses the spirit and excites it; and courage does nothing grand in war without it, unless its flame be supplied from this source; this is the goad which stirs up bold men and sends them to encounter perils. Some therefore consider it to be best to control anger, not to banish it utterly, but to cut off its extravagances, and force it to keep within useful bounds, so as to retain that part of it without which action will become languid and all strength and activity of mind will die away.

In the first place, it is easier to banish dangerous passions than to rule them; it is easier not to admit them than to keep them in order when admitted; for when they have established themselves in possession of the mind they are more powerful than the lawful ruler, and will in no wise permit themselves to be weakened or abridged. In the next place, Reason herself, who holds the reins, is only strong while she remains apart from the passions; if she mixes and befouls herself with them she becomes no longer able to restrain those whom she might once have cleared out of her path; for the mind, when once excited and shaken up, goes whither the passions drive it. There are certain things whose beginnings lie in our own power, but which, when developed, drag us along by their own force and leave us no retreat. Those who have flung themselves over a precipice have no control over their movements, nor can they stop or slacken their pace when once started, for their own headlong and irremediable rashness has left no room for either reflection or remorse, and they cannot help going to lengths which they might have avoided. So, also, the mind, when it has abandoned itself to anger, love, or any other passion, is unable to check itself: its own weight and the downward tendency of vices must needs carry the man off and hurl him into the lowest depth.

8

The best plan is to reject straightaway the first incentives to anger, to resist its very beginnings, and to take care not to be betrayed into it: for if once it begins to carry us away, it is hard to get back again into a healthy condition, because reason goes for nothing when once passion has been admitted to the mind, and has by our own free will been given a certain authority, it will for the future do as much as it chooses, not only as much as you will allow it. The enemy, I repeat, must be met and driven back at the outermost frontier-line: for when he has once entered the city and passed its gates, he will not allow his prisoners to set bounds to his victory. The mind does not stand apart and view its passions from without, so as not to permit them to advance further than they ought, but it is itself changed into a passion, and is therefore unable to check what once was useful and wholesome strength, now that it has become degenerate and misapplied: for passion and reason, as I said before, have not distinct and separate provinces, but consist of the changes of the mind itself for better or for worse. How then can reason recover itself when it is conquered and held down by vices, when it has given way to anger? or how can it extricate itself from a confused mixture, the greater part of which consists of the lower qualities? "But," argues our adversary, "some men when in anger control themselves." Do they so far control themselves that they do nothing which anger dictates, or somewhat? If they do nothing thereof, it becomes evident that anger is not essential to the conduct of affairs, although your sect advocated it as possessing greater strength than reason. Finally, I ask, is anger stronger or weaker than reason? If stronger, how can reason impose any check upon it, since it is only the less powerful that obey: if weaker, then reason is competent to effect its ends without anger, and does not need the help of a less powerful quality. "But some angry men remain consistent and control themselves." When do they do so? It is when their anger is disappearing and leaving them of its own accord, not when it was red-hot, for then it was more powerful than they. "What then? do not men, even in the height of their anger, sometimes let their enemies go whole and unhurt, and refrain from injuring them?" They do: but when do they do so? It is when one passion overpowers another, and either fear or greed gets the upper hand for a while. On such occasions, it is not thanks to reason that anger is stilled, but owing to an untrustworthy and fleeting truce between the passions.

9

In the next place, anger has nothing useful in itself, and does not rouse up the mind to warlike deeds: for a virtue, being self-sufficient, never needs the assistance of a vice: whenever it needs an impetuous effort, it does not become angry, but rises to the occasion, and excites or soothes itself as far as it deems requisite, just as the machines which hurl darts may be twisted to a greater or lesser degree of tension at the manager's pleasure. "Anger," says Aristotle, "is necessary, nor can any fight be won without it, unless it fills the mind, and kindles up the spirit. It must, however, be made use of, not as a general, but as a soldier." Now this is untrue; for if it listens to reason and follows whither reason leads, it is no longer anger, whose characteristic is obstinacy: if, again, it is disobedient and will not be quiet when ordered, but is carried away by its own willful and headstrong spirit, it is then as useless an aid to the mind as a soldier who disregards the sounding of the retreat would be to a general. If, therefore, anger allows limits to be imposed upon it, it must be called by some other name, and ceases to be anger, which I understand to be unbridled and unmanageable: and if it does not allow limits to be imposed upon it, it is harmful and not to be counted among aids: wherefore either anger is not anger, or it is useless: for if any man demands the infliction of punishment, not because he is eager for the punishment itself, but because it is right to inflict it, he ought not to be counted as an angry man: that will be the useful soldier, who knows how to obey orders: the passions cannot obey any more than they can command.

10

For this cause reason will never call to its aid blind and fierce impulses, over whom she herself possesses no authority, and which she never can restrain save by setting against them similar and equally powerful passions, as for example, fear against anger, anger against sloth, greed against timidity. May virtue never come to such a pass, that reason should fly for aid to vices! The mind can find no safe repose there, it must needs be shaken and tempest-tossed if it be safe only because of its own defects, if it cannot be brave without anger, diligent without greed, quiet without fear: such is the despotism under which a man must live if he becomes the slave of a passion. Are you not ashamed to put virtues under the patronage of vices? Then, too, reason ceases to have any power if she can do nothing without passion, and begins to be equal and like unto passion; for what difference is there between them if passion without reason be as rash as reason without passion is helpless? They are both on the same level, if one cannot exist without the other. Yet who could endure that passion should be made equal to reason? "Then," says our adversary, "passion is useful, provided it be moderate." Nay, only if it be useful by nature: but if it be disobedient to authority and reason, all that we gain by its moderation is that the less there is of it, the less harm it does: wherefore a moderate passion is nothing but a moderate evil.

11

"But," argues he, "against our enemies anger is necessary." In no case is it less necessary; since our attacks ought not to be disorderly, but regulated and under control. What, indeed, is it except anger, so ruinous to itself, that overthrows barbarians, who have so much more bodily strength than we, and are so much better able to endure fatigue? Gladiators, too, protect themselves by skill, but expose themselves to wounds when they are angry. Moreover, of what use is anger, when the same end can be arrived at by reason? Do you suppose that a hunter is angry with the beasts he kills? Yet he meets them when they attack him, and follows them when they flee from him, all of which is managed by reason without anger. When so many thousands of Cimbri and Teutones poured over the Alps, what was it that caused them to perish so completely, that no messenger, only common rumour, carried the news of that great defeat to their homes, except that with them anger stood in the place of courage? and anger, although sometimes it overthrows and breaks to pieces whatever it meets, yet is more often its own destruction. Who can be braver than the Germans? who charge more boldly? who have more love of arms, among which they are born and bred, for which alone they care, to the neglect of everything else? Who can be more hardened to undergo every hardship, since a large part of them have no store of clothing for the body, no shelter from the continual rigour of the climate: yet Spaniards and Gauls, and even the unwarlike races of Asia and Syria cut them down before the main legion comes within sight, nothing but their own irascibility exposing them to death. Give but intelligence to those minds, and discipline to those bodies of theirs, which now are ignorant of vicious refinements, luxury, and wealth—to say nothing more, we should certainly be obliged to go back to the ancient Roman habits of life. By what did Fabius restore the shattered forces of the State, except by knowing how to delay and spin out time, which angry men know not how to do? The empire, which then was at its last gasp, would have perished if Fabius had been as daring as anger urged him to be: but he took thought about the condition of affairs, and after counting his force, no part of which could be lost without everything being lost with it, he laid aside thoughts of grief and revenge, turning his sole attention to what was profitable and to making the most of his opportunities, and conquered his anger before he conquered Hannibal. What did Scipio do? Did he not leave behind Hannibal and the Carthaginian army, and all with whom he had a right to be angry, and carry over the war into Africa with such deliberation that he made his enemies think him luxurious and lazy? What did the second Scipio do? Did he not remain a long, long time before Numantia, and bear with calmness the reproach to himself and to his country that Numantia took longer to conquer than Carthage? By blockading and investing his enemies, he brought them to such straits that they perished by their own swords. Anger, therefore, is not useful even in wars or battles: for it is prone to rashness, and while trying to bring others into danger, does not guard itself against danger. The most trustworthy virtue is that which long and carefully considers itself, controls itself, and slowly and deliberately brings itself to the front.

12

"What, then," asks our adversary, "is a good man not to be angry if he sees his father murdered or his mother outraged?" No, he will not be angry, but will avenge them, or protect them. Why do you fear that filial piety will not prove a sufficient spur to him even without anger? You may as well say—"What then? When a good man sees his father or his son being cut down, I suppose he will not weep or faint," as we see women do whenever any trifling rumour of danger reaches them. The good man will do his duty without disturbance or fear, and he will perform the duty of a good man, so as to do nothing unworthy of a man. My father will be murdered: then I will defend him: he has been slain, then I will avenge him, not because I am grieved, but because it is my duty. "Good men are made angry by injuries done to their friends." When you say this, Theophrastus, you seek to throw discredit upon more manly maxims; you leave the judge and appeal to the mob: because everyone is angry when such things befall his own friends, you suppose that men will decide that it is their duty to do what they do: for as a rule every man considers a passion which he recognises to be a righteous one. But he does the same thing if the hot water is not ready for his drink, if a glass be broken, or his shoe splashed with mud. It is not filial piety, but weakness of mind that produces this anger, as children weep when they lose their parents, just as they do when they lose their toys. To feel anger on behalf of one's friends does not show a loving, but a weak mind: it is admirable and worthy conduct to stand forth as the defender of one's parents, children, friends, and countrymen, at the call of duty itself, acting of one's own free will, forming a deliberate judgment, and looking forward to the future, not in an impulsive, frenzied fashion. No passion is more eager for revenge than anger, and for that very reason it is unapt to obtain it: being over hasty and frantic, like almost all desires, it hinders itself in the attainment of its own object, and therefore has never been useful either in peace or war: for it makes peace like war, and when in arms forgets that Mars belongs to neither side, and falls into the power of the enemy, because it is not in its own. In the next place, vices ought not to be received into common use because on some occasions they have effected somewhat: for so also fevers are good for certain kinds of ill-health, but nevertheless it is better to be altogether free from them: it is a hateful mode of cure to owe one's health to disease. Similarly, although anger, like poison, or falling headlong, or being shipwrecked, may have unexpectedly done good, yet it ought not on that account to be classed as wholesome, for poisons have often proved good for the health.

13

Moreover, qualities which we ought to possess become better and more desirable the more extensive they are: if justice is a good thing, no one will say that it would be better if any part were subtracted from it; if bravery is a good thing, no one would wish it to be in any way curtailed: consequently the greater anger is, the better it is, for whoever objected to a good thing being increased? But it is not expedient that anger should be increased: therefore it is not expedient that it should exist at all, for that which grows bad by increase cannot be a good thing. "Anger is useful," says our adversary, "because it makes men more ready to fight." According to that mode of reasoning, then, drunkenness also is a good thing, for it makes men insolent and daring, and many use their weapons better when the worse for liquor: nay, according to that reasoning, also, you may call frenzy and madness essential to strength, because madness often makes men stronger. Why, does not fear often by the rule of contraries make men bolder, and does not the terror of death rouse up even arrant cowards to join battle? Yet anger, drunkenness, fear, and the like, are base and temporary incitements to action, and can furnish no arms to virtue, which has no need of vices, although they may at times be of some little assistance to sluggish and cowardly minds. No man becomes braver through anger, except one who without anger would not have been brave at all: anger does not therefore come to assist courage, but to take its place. What are we to say to the argument that, if anger were a good thing it would attach itself to all the best men? Yet the most irascible of creatures are infants, old men, and sick people. Every weakling is naturally prone to complaint.

14

It is impossible, says Theophrastus, for a good man not to be angry with bad men. By this reasoning, the better a man is, the more irascible he will be: yet will he not rather be more tranquil, more free from passions, and hating no one: indeed, what reason has he for hating sinners, since it is error that leads them into such crimes? now it does not become a sensible man to hate the erring, since if so he will hate himself: let him think how many things he does contrary to good morals, how much of what he has done stands in need of pardon, and he will soon become angry with himself also, for no righteous judge pronounces a different judgment in his own case and in that of others. No one, I affirm, will be found who can acquit himself. Everyone when he calls himself innocent looks rather to external witnesses than to his own conscience. How much more philanthropic it is to deal with the erring in a gentle and fatherly spirit, and to call them into the right course instead of hunting them down? When a man is wandering about our fields because he has lost his way, it is better to place him on the right path than to drive him away.

15

The sinner ought, therefore, to be corrected both by warning and by force, both by gentle and harsh means, and may be made a better man both towards himself and others by chastisement, but not by anger: for who is angry with the patient whose wounds he is tending? "But they cannot be corrected, and there is nothing in them that is gentle or that admits of good hope." Then let them be removed from mortal society, if they are likely to deprave everyone with whom they come in contact, and let them cease to be bad men in the only way in which they can: yet let this be done without hatred: for what reason have I for hating the man to whom I am doing the greatest good, since I am rescuing him from himself? Does a man hate his own limbs when he cuts them off? That is not an act of anger, but a lamentable method of healing. We knock mad dogs on the head, we slaughter fierce and savage bulls, and we doom scabby sheep to the knife, lest they should infect our flocks: we destroy monstrous births, and we also drown our children if they are born weakly or unnaturally formed; to separate what is useless from what is sound is an act, not of anger, but of reason. Nothing becomes one who inflicts punishment less than anger, because the punishment has all the more power to work reformation if the sentence be pronounced with deliberate judgment. This is why Socrates said to the slave, "I would strike you, were I not angry." He put off the correction of the slave to a calmer season; at the moment, he corrected himself. Who can boast that he has his passions under control, when Socrates did not dare to trust himself to his anger?

16

We do not, therefore, need an angry chastiser to punish the erring and wicked: for since anger is a crime of the mind, it is not right that sins should be punished by sin. "What! am I not to be angry with a robber, or a poisoner?" No: for I am not angry with myself when I bleed myself. I apply all kinds of punishment as remedies. You are as yet only in the first stage of error, and do not go wrong seriously, although you do so often: then I will try to amend you by a reprimand given first in private and then in public.[31] You, again, have gone too far to be restored to virtue by words alone; you must be kept in order by disgrace. For the next, some stronger measure is required, something that he can feel must be branded upon him; you, sir, shall be sent into exile and to a desert place. The next man's thorough villainy needs harsher remedies: chains and public imprisonment must be applied to him. You, lastly, have an incurably vicious mind, and add crime to crime: you have come to such a pass, that you are not influenced by the arguments which are never wanting to recommend evil, but sin itself is to you a sufficient reason for sinning: you have so steeped your whole heart in wickedness, that wickedness cannot be taken from you

---

[31] The gospel rule, Matt, xviii, 15.

without bringing your heart with it. Wretched man! you have long sought to die; we will do you good service, we will take away that madness from which you suffer, and to you who have so long lived a misery to yourself and to others, we will give the only good thing which remains, that is, death. Why should I be angry with a man just when I am doing him good: sometimes the truest form of compassion is to put a man to death. If I were a skilled and learned physician, and were to enter a hospital, or a rich[32] man's house, I should not have prescribed the same treatment for all the patients who were suffering from various diseases. I see different kinds of vice in the vast number of different minds, and am called in to heal the whole body of citizens: let us seek for the remedies proper for each disease. This man may be cured by his own sense of honour, that one by travel, that one by pain, that one by want, that one by the sword. If, therefore, it becomes my duty as a magistrate to put on black[33] robes, and summon an assembly by the sound of a trumpet,[34] I shall walk to the seat

---

[32] *Divitis* (where there might be an army of slaves).

[33] "Lorsque le Preteur devoit prononcer la sentence d'un coupable, il se depouilloit de la robe pretexte, et se revètoit alors d'une simple tunique, ou d'une autre robe, presque usee, et d'un blanc sale (sordida) ou d'un gris très foncé tirant sur le noir (toga pulla), telle qu'en portoient à Rome le peuple et les pauvres (pullaque paupertas). Dans les jours solemnelles et marqués par un deuil public, les Senateurs quittoient le laticlave, et les Magistrats la pretexte. La pourpre, la hache, les faisceaux, aucun de ces signes extérieurs de leur dignité ne les distinguoient alors des autres citoyens: sine insignibus Magistratus. Mais ce n'étoit pas seulement pendant le temps ou la ville était plongée dans le deuil et dans l'affliction, que les magistrats s'habilloient comme le peuple (sordidam vestem induebant); ils en usoient de même lorsqu'ils devoient condamner à mort un citoyen. C'est dans ces tristes circonstances qu'ils quittoient la prétexte et prenoient la robe de deuil: perversam vestem. (No doubt "inside out."—J. E. B. M.)

"On pourrait supposer avec assez de vraisemblance que par cette expression, Séneque a voulu faire allusion à ce changement ... Peut-être les Magistrats qui devoient juger à mort un citoyen, portoient ils aussi leur robe renversée, ou la jettoient ils de travers ou confusément sur leurs épaules, pour mieux peindre par ce desordre le trouble de leur esprit. Si cette conjecture est vraie, comme je serais assez porté à croire, l'expression perversa vestis, dont Séneque s'est servi ici, indiqueroit plus d'un simple changement d'habit," etc. (La Grange's translation of Seneca, edited by J. A. Naigeon. Paris, 1778.)

[34] "Ceci fait allusion à une coutume que Caius Gracchus prétend avoir été pratiquée de tout tems à Rome. 'Lorsqu'un citoyen,' dit il, 'avoit un procès criminel qui alloit à la mort, s'il refusoit d'obéir aux sommations qui lui étoient faites; le jour qu'on devoit le juger, en envoyoit des le matin à la porte de sa maison un Officier l'appeller au son de la trompette, et jamais avant que cette cérémonie eût été observée, les Juges ne donneroient leur voix contre lui: tant ces hommes sages,' ajoute ce hardi Tribun, 'avoient de retenue et de precaution dans leurs jugements, quand il s'agissoit de la vie d'un citoyen.'"

"C'étoit de même au son de la trompette que l'on convoquoit le peuple, lorsqu'on devoit faire mourir un citoyen, afin qu'il fût témoin de ce triste spectacle, et que la supplice du coupable pût lui servir d'exemple. Tacite dit qu'un Astrologue, nommé P. Marcius, fût exécuté, selon l'ancien usage, hors de la porte Esquiline, en presence du peuple Romain que les Consuls firent convoquer au son de la trompette. (Tacitus, Annals, II, 32.) L. Grom.

of judgment not in a rage or in a hostile spirit, but with the countenance of a judge; I shall pronounce the formal sentence in a grave and gentle rather than a furious voice, and shall bid them proceed sternly, yet not angrily. Even when I command a criminal to be beheaded, when I sew a parricide up in a sack, when I send a man to be punished by military law, when I fling a traitor or public enemy down the Tarpeian Rock, I shall be free from anger, and shall look and feel just as though I were crushing snakes and other venomous creatures. "Anger is necessary to enable us to punish." What? Do you think that the law is angry with men whom it does not know, whom it has never seen, who it hopes will never exist? We ought, therefore, to adopt the law's frame of mind, which does not become angry, but merely defines offences: for, if it is right for a good man to be angry at wicked crimes, it will also be right for him to be moved with envy at the prosperity of wicked men: what, indeed, is more scandalous than that in some cases the very men, for whose deserts no fortune could be found bad enough, should flourish and actually be the spoiled children of success? Yet he will see their affluence without envy, just as he sees their crimes without anger: a good judge condemns wrongful acts, but does not hate them. "What then? when the wise man is dealing with something of this kind, will his mind not be affected by it and become excited beyond its usual wont?" I admit that it will: he will experience a slight and trifling emotion; for, as Zeno says, "Even in the mind of the wise man, a scar remains after the wound is quite healed." He will, therefore, feel certain hints and semblances of passions; but he will be free from the passions themselves.

17

Aristotle says that "certain passions, if one makes a proper use of them, act as arms": which would be true if, like weapons of war, they could be taken up or laid aside at the pleasure of their wielder. These arms, which Aristotle assigns to virtue, fight of their own accord, do not wait to be seized by the hand, and possess a man instead of being possessed by him. We have no need of external weapons, nature has equipped us sufficiently by giving us reason. She has bestowed this weapon upon us, which is strong, imperishable, and obedient to our will, not uncertain or capable of being turned against its master. Reason suffices by itself not merely to take thought for the future, but to manage our affairs:[35] what, then, can be more foolish than for reason to beg anger for protection, that is, for what is certain to beg of what is uncertain? what is trustworthy of what is faithless? what is whole of what is sick? What, indeed? since reason is far more powerful by itself even in performing those operations in which the help of anger seems especially needful: for when reason has decided that a particular thing should be done, she perseveres in doing it; not being able to find anything better than herself to exchange with. She, therefore, abides by her

---

[35] I.e., not only for counsel, but for action.

purpose when it has once been formed; whereas anger is often overcome by pity: for it possesses no firm strength, but merely swells like an empty bladder, and makes a violent beginning, just like the winds which rise from the earth and are caused by rivers and marshes, which blow furiously without any continuance: anger begins with a mighty rush, and then falls away, becoming fatigued too soon: that which but lately thought of nothing but cruelty and novel forms of torture, is become quite softened and gentle when the time comes for punishment to be inflicted. Passion soon cools, whereas reason is always consistent: yet even in cases where anger has continued to burn, it often happens that although there may be many who deserve to die, yet after the death of two or three it ceases to slay. Its first onset is fierce, just as the teeth of snakes when first roused from their lair are venomous, but become harmless after repeated bites have exhausted their poison. Consequently those who are equally guilty are not equally punished, and often he who has done less is punished more, because he fell in the way of anger when it was fresher. It is altogether irregular; at one time it runs into undue excess, at another it falls short of its duty: for it indulges its own feelings and gives sentence according to its caprices, will not listen to evidence, allows the defence no opportunity of being heard, clings to what it has wrongly assumed, and will not suffer its opinion to be wrested from it, even when it is a mistaken one.

18

Reason gives each side time to plead; moreover, she herself demands adjournment, that she may have sufficient scope for the discovery of the truth; whereas anger is in a hurry: reason wishes to give a just decision; anger wishes its decision to be thought just: reason looks no further than the matter in hand; anger is excited by empty matters hovering on the outskirts of the case: it is irritated by anything approaching to a confident demeanour, a loud voice, an unrestrained speech, dainty apparel, high-flown pleading, or popularity with the public. It often condemns a man because it dislikes his patron; it loves and maintains error even when truth is staring it in the face. It hates to be proved wrong, and thinks it more honourable to persevere in a mistaken line of conduct than to retract it. I remember Gnaeus Piso, a man who was free from many vices, yet of a perverse disposition, and one who mistook harshness for consistency. In his anger he ordered a soldier to be led off to execution because he had returned from furlough without his comrade, as though he must have murdered him if he could not show him. When the man asked for time for search, he would not grant it: the condemned man was brought outside the rampart, and was just offering his neck to the axe, when suddenly there appeared his comrade who was thought to be slain. Hereupon the centurion in charge of the execution bade the guardsman sheathe his sword, and led the condemned man back to Piso, to restore to him the innocence which Fortune had restored to the soldier. They were led into his presence by their fellow soldiers amid the great joy of the whole camp, embracing one another and accompanied by a vast crowd. Piso mounted the tribunal in a fury and ordered them both to be executed, both him who had not murdered and him who had not been slain. What could be more unworthy than this? Because one was proved to be innocent, two perished. Piso even added a third: for he actually ordered the centurion, who had brought back the condemned man, to be put to death. Three men were set up to die in the same place because one was innocent. O, how clever is anger at inventing reasons for its frenzy! "You," it says, "I order to be executed, because you have been condemned to death: you, because you have been the cause of your comrade's condemnation, and you, because when ordered to put him to death you disobeyed your general." He discovered the means of charging them with three crimes, because he could find no crime in them.

19

Irascibility, I say, has this fault—it is loath to be ruled: it is angry with the truth itself, if it comes to light against its will: it assails those whom it has marked for its victims with shouting and riotous noise and gesticulation of the entire body, together with reproaches and curses. Not thus does reason act: but if it must be so, she silently and quietly wipes out whole households, destroys entire families of the enemies of the State, together with their wives and children, throws down their very dwellings, levels them with the ground, and roots out the names of those who are the foes of liberty. This she does without grinding her teeth or shaking her head, or doing anything unbecoming to a judge, whose countenance ought to be especially calm and composed at the time when he is pronouncing an important sentence. "What need is there," asks Hieronymus, "for you to bite your own lips when you want to strike someone?" What would he have said, had he seen a proconsul leap down from the tribunal, snatch the fasces from the lictor, and tear his own clothes because those of others were not torn as fast as he wished. Why need you upset the table, throw down the drinking cups, knock yourself against the columns, tear your hair, smite your thigh and your breast? How vehement do you suppose anger to be, if it thus turns back upon itself, because it cannot find vent on another as fast as it wishes? Such men, therefore, are held back by the bystanders and are begged to become reconciled with themselves. But he who while free from anger assigns to each man the penalty which he deserves, does none of these things. He often lets a man go after detecting his crime, if his penitence for what he has done gives good hope for the future, if he perceives that the man's wickedness is not deeply rooted in his mind, but is only, as the saying is, skindeep. He will grant impunity in cases where it will hurt neither the receiver nor the giver. In some cases he will punish great crimes more leniently than lesser ones, if the former were the result of momentary impulse, not of cruelty, while the latter were instinct with secret, underhand, long-practised craftiness. The same fault, committed by two separate men, will not be visited by him with the same penalty, if the one was guilty of it through carelessness, the other with a premeditated intention of doing mischief. In all dealing with crime he will remember that the one form of punishment is meant to make bad men better, and the other to put them out of the way. In either case he will look to the future, not to the past: for, as Plato says, "no wise man punishes anyone because he has sinned, but that he may sin no more: for what is past cannot be recalled, but what is to come may be checked." Those, too, whom he wishes to make examples of the ill success of wickedness, he executes publicly, not merely in order that they themselves may die, but that by dying they may deter others from doing likewise. You see how free from any mental disturbance a man ought to be who has to weigh and consider all this, when he deals with a matter which ought to be handled with the utmost care, I mean, the power of life and death. The sword of justice is ill-placed in the hands of an angry man.

20

Neither ought it to be believed that anger contributes anything to magnanimity: what it gives is not magnanimity but vain glory. The increase which disease produces in bodies swollen with morbid humours is not healthy growth, but bloated corpulence. All those whose madness raises them above human considerations, believe themselves to be inspired with high and sublime ideas; but there is no solid ground beneath, and what is built without foundation is liable to collapse in ruin. Anger has no ground to stand upon, and does not rise from a firm and enduring foundation, but is a windy, empty quality, as far removed from true magnanimity as foolhardiness from courage, boastfulness from confidence, gloom from austerity, cruelty from strictness. There is, I say, a great difference between a lofty and a proud mind: anger brings about nothing grand or beautiful. On the other hand, to be constantly irritated seems to me to be the part of a languid and unhappy mind, conscious of its own feebleness, like folk with diseased bodies covered with sores, who cry out at the lightest touch. Anger, therefore, is a vice which for the most part affects women and children. "Yet it affects men also." Because many men, too, have womanish or childish intellects. "But what are we to say? do not some words fall from angry men which appear to flow from a great mind?" Yes, to those who know not what true greatness is: as, for example, that foul and hateful saying, "Let them hate me, provided they fear me," which you may be sure was written in Sulla's time. I know not which was the worse of the two things he wished for, that he might be hated or that he might be feared. It occurs to his mind that someday people will curse him, plot against him, crush him: what prayer does he add to this? May all the gods curse him—for discovering a cure for hate so worthy of it. "Let them hate." How? "Provided they obey me?" No! "Provided they approve of me?" No! How then? "Provided they fear me!" I would not even be loved upon such terms. Do you imagine that this was a very spirited saying? You are wrong: this is not greatness, but monstrosity. You should not believe the words of angry men, whose speech is very loud and menacing, while their mind within them is as timid as possible: nor need you suppose that the most eloquent of men, Titus Livius, was right in describing somebody as being "of a great rather than a good disposition." The things cannot be separated: he must either be good or else he cannot be great, because I take greatness of mind to mean that it is unshaken, sound throughout, firm and uniform to its very foundation; such as cannot exist in evil dispositions. Such dispositions may be terrible, frantic, and destructive, but cannot possess greatness; because greatness rests upon goodness, and owes its strength to it. "Yet by speech, action, and all outward show they will make one think them great." True, they will say something which you may think shows a great spirit, like Gaius Caesar, who when angry with heaven because it interfered with his ballet-dancers, whom he imitated more carefully than he attended to them when they acted, and because it frightened his revels by its thunders, surely ill-directed,[36] challenged Jove to fight, and that to the death, shouting the Homeric verse:—

"Carry me off, or I will carry thee!"

How great was his madness! He must have believed either that he could not be hurt even by Jupiter himself, or that he could hurt even Jupiter itself. I imagine that this saying of his had no small weight in nerving the minds of the conspirators for their task: for it seemed to be the height of endurance to bear one who could not bear Jupiter.

21

There is therefore nothing great or noble in anger, even when it seems to be powerful and to contemn both gods and men alike. Anyone who thinks that anger produces greatness of mind, would think that luxury produces it: such a man wishes to rest on ivory, to be clothed with purple, and roofed with gold; to remove lands, embank seas, hasten the course of rivers, suspend woods in the air. He would think that avarice shows greatness of mind: for the avaricious man broods over heaps of gold and silver, treats whole provinces as merely fields on his estate, and has larger tracts of country under the charge of single bailiffs than those which consuls once drew lots to administer. He would think that lust shows greatness of mind: for the lustful man swims across straits, castrates troops of boys, and puts himself within reach of the swords of injured husbands with complete scorn of death. Ambition, too, he would think shows greatness of mind: for the ambitious man is not content with office once a year, but, if possible, would fill the calendar of dignities with his name alone, and cover the whole world with his titles. It matters nothing to what heights or lengths these passions may proceed: they are narrow, pitiable, grovelling. Virtue alone is lofty and sublime, nor is anything great which is not at the same time tranquil.

---

[36] *Prorsus parum certis.* (I.e., the thunderbolts missed their aim in not striking him dead.)

BOOK 2

1

My first book, Novatus, had a more abundant subject: for carriages roll easily down hill:[37] now we must proceed to drier matters. The question before us is whether anger arises from deliberate choice or from impulse, that is, whether it acts of its own accord or like the greater part of those passions which spring up within us without our knowledge. It is necessary for our debate to stoop to the consideration of these matters, in order that it may afterwards be able to rise to loftier themes; for likewise in our bodies the parts which are first set in order are the bones, sinews, and joints, which are by no means fair to see, albeit they are the foundation of our frame and essential to its life: next to them come the parts of which all beauty of face and appearance consists; and after these, colour, which above all else charms the eye, is applied last of all, when the rest of the body is complete. There is no doubt that anger is roused by the appearance of an injury being done: but the question before us is, whether anger straightaway follows the appearance, and springs up without assistance from the mind, or whether it is roused with the sympathy of the mind. Our (the Stoics') opinion is, that anger can venture upon nothing by itself, without the approval of mind: for to conceive the idea of a wrong having been done, to long to avenge it, and to join the two propositions, that we ought not to have been injured and that it is our duty to avenge our injuries, cannot belong to a mere impulse which is excited without our consent. That impulse is a simple act; this is a complex one, and composed of several parts. The man understands something to have happened: he becomes indignant thereat: he condemns the deed; and he avenges it. All these things cannot be done without his mind agreeing to those matters which touched him.

2

Whither, say you, does this inquiry tend? That we may know what anger is: for if it springs up against our will, it never will yield to reason: because all the motions which take place without our volition are beyond our control and unavoidable, such

---

[37] "*Vehiculorum ridicule* Koch," says Gertz, justly, "*viliorum* makes excellent sense."—J. E. B. M.

as shivering when cold water is poured over us, or shrinking when we are touched in certain places. Men's hair rises up at bad news, their faces blush at indecent words, and they are seized with dizziness when looking down a precipice; and as it is not in our power to prevent any of these things, no reasoning can prevent their taking place. But anger can be put to flight by wise maxims; for it is a voluntary defect of the mind, and not one of those things which are evolved by the conditions of human life, and which, therefore, may happen even to the wisest of us. Among these and in the first place must be ranked that thrill of the mind which seizes us at the thought of wrongdoing. We feel this even when witnessing the mimic scenes of the stage, or when reading about things that happened long ago. We often feel angry with Clodius for banishing Cicero, and with Antonius for murdering him. Who is not indignant with the wars of Marius, the proscriptions of Sulla? who is not enraged against Theodotus and Achillas and the boy king who dared to commit a more than boyish crime?[38] Sometimes songs excite us, and quickened rhythm and the martial noise of trumpets; so, too, shocking pictures and the dreadful sight of tortures, however well deserved, affect our minds. Hence it is that we smile when others are smiling, that a crowd of mourners makes us sad, and that we take a glowing interest in another's battles; all of which feelings are not anger, any more than that which clouds our brow at the sight of a stage shipwreck is sadness, or what we feel, when we read how Hannibal after Cannae beset the walls of Rome, can be called fear. All these are emotions of minds which are loath to be moved, and are not passions, but rudiments which may grow into passions. So, too, a soldier starts at the sound of a trumpet, although he may be dressed as a civilian and in the midst of a profound peace, and camp horses prick up their ears at the clash of arms. It is said that Alexander, when Xenophantus was singing, laid his hand upon his weapons.

3

None of these things which casually influence the mind deserve to be called passions: the mind, if I may so express it, rather suffers passions to act upon itself than forms them. A passion, therefore, consists not in being affected by the sights which are presented to us, but in giving way to our feelings and following up these chance promptings: for whoever imagines that paleness, bursting into tears, lustful feelings, deep sighs, sudden flashes of the eyes, and so forth, are signs of passion and betray the state of the mind, is mistaken, and does not understand that these are merely impulses of the body. Consequently, the bravest of men often turns pale while he is putting on his armour; when the signal for battle is given, the knees of the boldest soldier shake for a moment; the heart even of a great general leaps into his mouth just before the lines clash together, and the hands and feet even of the

---

[38] The murder of Pompeius, bc 48. Achillas and Theodotus acted under the nominal orders of Ptolemy XII, Cleopatra's brother, then about seventeen years of age.

most eloquent orator grow stiff and cold while he is preparing to begin his speech. Anger must not merely move, but break out of bounds, being an impulse: now, no impulse can take place without the consent of the mind: for it cannot be that we should deal with revenge and punishment without the mind being cognisant of them. A man may think himself injured, may wish to avenge his wrongs, and then may be persuaded by some reason or other to give up his intention and calm down: I do not call that anger, it is an emotion of the mind which is under the control of reason. Anger is that which goes beyond reason and carries her away with it: wherefore the first confusion of a man's mind when struck by what seems an injury is no more anger than the apparent injury itself: it is the subsequent mad rush, which not only receives the impression of the apparent injury, but acts upon it as true, that is anger, being an exciting of the mind to revenge, which proceeds from choice and deliberate resolve. There never has been any doubt that fear produces flight, and anger a rush forward; consider, therefore, whether you suppose that anything can be either sought or avoided without the participation of the mind.

4

Furthermore, that you may know in what manner passions begin and swell and gain spirit, learn that the first emotion is involuntary, and is, as it were, a preparation for a passion, and a threatening of one. The next is combined with a wish, though not an obstinate one, as, for example, "It is my duty to avenge myself, because I have been injured," or "It is right that this man should be punished, because he has committed a crime." The third emotion is already beyond our control, because it overrides reason, and wishes to avenge itself, not if it be its duty, but whether or no. We are not able by means of reason to escape from that first impression on the mind, any more than we can escape from those things which we have mentioned as occurring to the body: we cannot prevent other people's yawns temping us to yawn:[39] we cannot help winking when fingers are suddenly darted at our eyes. Reason is unable to overcome these habits, which perhaps might be weakened by practice and constant watchfulness: they differ from an emotion which is brought into existence and brought to an end by a deliberate mental act.

5

We must also enquire whether those whose cruelty knows no bounds, and who delight in shedding human blood, are angry when they kill people from whom they have received no injury, and who they themselves do not think have done them any injury; such as were Apollodorus or Phalaris. This is not anger, it is ferocity:

---

[39] "On Clemency," Book II, 6, 4, I emended many years ago ἑνὸς χανότος με ΤΕΣΧΗΚεν into ἑ. χ., με ΤΑΚΕΧΗΝεν ὕτερος: "when one has yawned, the other yawns."—J. E. B. M

for it does not do hurt because it has received injury: but is even willing to receive injury, provided it may do hurt. It does not long to inflict stripes and mangle bodies to avenge its wrongs, but for its own pleasure. What then are we to say? This evil takes its rise from anger; for anger, after it has by long use and indulgence made a man forget mercy, and driven all feelings of human fellowship from his mind, passes finally into cruelty. Such men therefore laugh, rejoice, enjoy themselves greatly, and are as unlike as possible in countenance to angry men, since cruelty is their relaxation. It is said that when Hannibal saw a trench full of human blood, he exclaimed, "O, what a beauteous sight!" How much more beautiful would he have thought it, if it had filled a river or a lake? Why should we wonder that you should be charmed with this sight above all others, you who were born in bloodshed and brought up amid slaughter from a child? Fortune will follow you and favour your cruelty for twenty years, and will display to you everywhere the sight that you love. You will behold it both at Trasumene and at Cannae, and lastly at your own city of Carthage. Volesus, who not long ago, under the Emperor Augustus, was proconsul of Asia Minor, after he had one day beheaded three hundred persons, strutted out among the corpses with a haughty air, as though he had performed some grand and notable exploit, and exclaimed in Greek, "What a kingly action!" What would this man have done, had he been really a king? This was not anger, but a greater and an incurable disease.

6

"Virtue," argues our adversary, "ought to be angry with what is base, just as she approves of what is honourable." What should we think if he said that virtue ought to be both mean and great; yet this is what he means, when he wants her to be raised and lowered, because joy at a good action is grand and glorious, while anger at another's sin is base and befits a narrow mind: and virtue will never be guilty of imitating vice while she is repressing it; she considers anger to deserve punishment for itself, since it often is even more criminal than the faults with which it is angry. To rejoice and be glad is the proper and natural function of virtue: it is as much beneath her dignity to be angry, as to mourn: now, sorrow is the companion of anger, and all anger ends in sorrow, either from remorse or from failure. Secondly, if it be the part of the wise man to be angry with sins, he will be more angry the greater they are, and will often be angry: from which it follows that the wise man will not only be angry but irascible. Yet if we do not believe that great and frequent anger can find any place in the wise man's mind, why should we not set him altogether free from this passion? for there can be no limit, if he ought to be angry in proportion to what every man does: because he will either be unjust if he is equally angry at unequal crimes, or he will be the most irascible of men, if he blazes into wrath as often as crimes deserve his anger.

7

What, too, can be more unworthy of the wise man, than that his passions should depend upon the wickedness of others? If so, the great Socrates will no longer be able to return home with the same expression of countenance with which he set out. Moreover, if it be the duty of the wise man to be angry at base deeds, and to be excited and saddened at crimes, then is there nothing more unhappy than the wise man, for all his life will be spent in anger and grief. What moment will there be at which he will not see something deserving of blame? whenever he leaves his house, he will be obliged to walk among men who are criminals, misers, spendthrifts, profligates, and who are happy in being so: he can turn his eyes in no direction without their finding something to shock them. He will faint, if he demands anger from himself as often as reason calls for it. All these thousands who are hurrying to the law courts at break of day, how base are their causes, and how much baser their advocates? One impugns his father's will, when he would have done better to deserve it; another appears as the accuser of his mother; a third comes to inform against a man for committing the very crime of which he himself is yet more notoriously guilty. The judge, too, is chosen to condemn men for doing what he himself has done, and the audience takes the wrong side, led astray by the fine voice of the pleader.

8

Why need I dwell upon individual cases? Be assured, when you see the forum crowded with a multitude, the Saepta[40] swarming with people, or the great Circus, in which the greater part of the people find room to show themselves at once, that among them there are as many vices as there are men. Among those whom you see in the garb of peace there is no peace: for a small profit any one of them will attempt the ruin of another: no one can gain anything save by another's loss. They hate the fortunate and despise the unfortunate: they grudgingly endure the great, and oppress the small: they are fired by diverse lusts: they would wreck everything for the sake of a little pleasure or plunder: they live as though they were in a school of gladiators, fighting with the same people with whom they live: it is like a society of wild beasts, save that beasts are tame with one another, and refrain from biting their own species, whereas men tear one another, and gorge themselves upon one another. They differ from dumb animals in this alone, that the latter are tame with those who feed them, whereas the rage of the former preys on those very persons by whom they were brought up.

---

[40] The voting-place in the Campus Martius.

9

The wise man will never cease to be angry, if he once begins, so full is every place of vices and crimes. More evil is done than can be healed by punishment: men seem engaged in a vast race of wickedness. Every day there is greater eagerness to sin, less modesty. Throwing aside all reverence for what is better and more just, lust rushes whithersoever it thinks fit, and crimes are no longer committed by stealth, they take place before our eyes, and wickedness has become so general and gained such a footing in everyone's breast that innocence is no longer rare, but no longer exists. Do men break the law singly, or a few at a time? Nay, they rise in all quarters at once, as though obeying some universal signal, to wipe out the boundaries of right and wrong.

> "Host is not safe from guest,
> Father-in-law from son; but seldom love
> Exists 'twixt brothers; wives long to destroy
> Their husbands, husbands long to slay their wives,
> Stepmothers deadly aconite prepare
> And child-heirs wonder when their sires will die."

And how small a part of men's crimes are these! The poet[41] has not described one people divided into two hostile camps, parents and children enrolled on opposite sides, Rome set on fire by the hand of a Roman, troops of fierce horsemen scouring the country to track out the hiding-places of the proscribed, wells defiled with poison, plagues created by human hands, trenches dug by children round their beleaguered parents, crowded prisons, conflagrations that consume whole cities, gloomy tyrannies, secret plots to establish despotisms and ruin peoples, and men glorying in those deeds which, as long as it was possible to repress them, were counted as crimes—I mean rape, debauchery, and lust ... Add to these, public acts of national bad faith, broken treaties, everything that cannot defend itself carried off as plunder by the stronger, knaveries, thefts, frauds, and disownings of debt such as three of our present law-courts would not suffice to deal with. If you want the wise man to be as angry as the atrocity of men's crimes requires, he must not merely be angry, but must go mad with rage.

10

You will rather think that we should not be angry with people's faults; for what shall we say of one who is angry with those who stumble in the dark, or with deaf people who cannot hear his orders, or with children, because they forget their

---

[41] Ovid, *Metamorphoses*, I, 144, sqq. The same lines are quoted in the essay *On Benefits*, Book V, Chapter 15.

duty and interest themselves in the games and silly jokes of their companions? What shall we say if you choose to be angry with weaklings for being sick, for growing old, or becoming fatigued? Among the other misfortunes of humanity is this, that men's intellects are confused, and they not only cannot help going wrong, but love to go wrong. To avoid being angry with individuals, you must pardon the whole mass, you must grant forgiveness to the entire human race. If you are angry with young and old men because they do wrong, you will be angry with infants also, for they soon will do wrong. Does anyone become angry with children, who are too young to comprehend distinctions? Yet, to be a human being is a greater and a better excuse than to be a child. Thus are we born, as creatures liable to as many disorders of the mind as of the body; not dull and slow-witted, but making a bad use of our keenness of wit, and leading one another into vice by our example. He who follows others who have started before him on the wrong road is surely excusable for having wandered on the highway.[42] A general's severity may be shown in the case of individual deserters; but where a whole army deserts, it must needs be pardoned. What is it that puts a stop to the wise man's anger? It is the number of sinners. He perceives how unjust and how dangerous it is to be angry with vices which all men share. Heraclitus, whenever he came out of doors and beheld around him such a number of men who were living wretchedly, nay, rather perishing wretchedly, used to weep: he pitied all those who met him joyous and happy. He was of a gentle but too weak disposition: and he himself was one of those for whom he ought to have wept. Democritus, on the other hand, is said never to have appeared in public without laughing; so little did men's serious occupations appear serious to him. What room is there for anger? Everything ought either to move us to tears or to laughter. The wise man will not be angry with sinners. Why not? Because he knows that no one is born wise, but becomes so: he knows that very few wise men are produced in any age, because he thoroughly understands the circumstances of human life. Now, no sane man is angry with nature: for what should we say if a man chose to be surprised that fruit did not hang on the thickets of a forest, or to wonder at bushes and thorns not being covered with some useful berry? No one is angry when nature excuses a defect. The wise man, therefore, being tranquil, and dealing candidly with mistakes, not an enemy to but an improver of sinners, will go abroad every day in the following frame of mind:—"Many men will meet me who are drunkards, lustful, ungrateful, greedy, and excited by the frenzy of ambition." He will view all these as benignly as a physician does his patients. When a man's ship leaks freely through its opened seams, does he become angry with the sailors or the ship itself? No; instead of that, he tries to remedy it: he shuts out some water, bales out some other, closes all the holes that he can see, and by ceaseless labour counteracts those which are out of sight and which let water into the hold; nor does he relax his efforts because

---

[42] I.e., he can plead that he kept the beaten track.

as much water as he pumps out runs in again. We need a long-breathed struggle against permanent and prolific evils; not, indeed, to quell them, but merely to prevent their overpowering us.

11

"Anger," says our opponent, "is useful, because it avoids contempt, and because it frightens bad men." Now, in the first place, if anger is strong in proportion to its threats, it is hateful for the same reason that it is terrible: and it is more dangerous to be hated than to be despised. If, again, it is without strength, it is much more exposed to contempt, and cannot avoid ridicule: for what is more flat than anger when it breaks out into meaningless ravings? Moreover, because some things are somewhat terrible, they are not on that account desirable: nor does wisdom wish it to be said of the wise man, as it is of a wild beast, that the fear which he inspires is as a weapon to him. Why, do we not fear fever, gout, consuming ulcers? and is there, for that reason, any good in them? nay; on the other hand, they are all despised and thought to be foul and base, and are for this very reason feared. So, too, anger is in itself hideous and by no means to be feared; yet it is feared by many, just as a hideous mask is feared by children. How can we answer the fact that terror always works back to him who inspired it, and that no one is feared who is himself at peace? At this point it is well that you should remember that verse of Laberius, which, when pronounced in the theatre during the height of the civil war, caught the fancy of the whole people as though it expressed the national feeling:—

"He must fear many, whom so many fear."

Thus has nature ordained, that whatever becomes great by causing fear to others is not free from fear itself. How disturbed lions are at the faintest noises! How excited those fiercest of beasts become at strange shadows, voices, or smells! Whatever is a terror to others, fears for itself. There can be no reason, therefore, for any wise man to wish to be feared, and no one need think that anger is anything great because it strikes terror, since even the most despicable things are feared, as, for example, noxious vermin whose bite is venomous: and since a string set with feathers stops the largest herds of wild beasts and guides them into traps, it is no wonder that from its effect it should be named a "Scarer."[43] Foolish creatures are frightened by foolish things: the movement of chariots and the sight of their wheels turning round drives lions back into their cage: elephants are frightened at the cries of pigs: and so also we fear anger just as children fear the dark, or wild beasts fear red feathers: it has in itself nothing solid or valiant, but it affects feeble minds.

---

[43] "On Clemency," Book I, 12, 5.

12

"Wickedness," says our adversary, "must be removed from the system of nature, if you wish to remove anger: neither of which things can be done." In the first place, it is possible for a man not to be cold, although according to the system of nature it may be wintertime, nor yet to suffer from heat, although it be summer according to the almanac. He may be protected against the inclement time of the year by dwelling in a favoured spot, or he may have so trained his body to endurance that it feels neither heat nor cold. Next, reverse this saying:—You must remove anger from your mind before you can take virtue into the same, because vices and virtues cannot combine, and none can at the same time be both an angry man and a good man, any more than he can be both sick and well. "It is not possible," says he, "to remove anger altogether from the mind, nor does human nature admit of it." Yet there is nothing so hard and difficult that the mind of man cannot overcome it, and with which unremitting study will not render him familiar, nor are there any passions so fierce and independent that they cannot be tamed by discipline. The mind can carry out whatever orders it gives itself: some have succeeded in never smiling: some have forbidden themselves wine, sexual intercourse, or even drink of all kinds. Some, who are satisfied with short hours of rest, have learned to watch for long periods without weariness. Men have learned to run upon the thinnest ropes even when slanting, to carry huge burdens, scarcely within the compass of human strength, or to dive to enormous depths and suffer themselves to remain under the sea without any chance of drawing breath. There are a thousand other instances in which application has conquered all obstacles, and proved that nothing which the mind has set itself to endure is difficult. The men whom I have just mentioned gain either no reward or one that is unworthy of their unwearied application; for what great thing does a man gain by applying his intellect to walking upon a tight rope? or to placing great burdens upon his shoulders? or to keeping sleep from his eyes? or to reaching the bottom of the sea? and yet their patient labour brings all these things to pass for a trifling reward. Shall not we then call in the aid of patience, we whom such a prize awaits, the unbroken calm of a happy life? How great a blessing is it to escape from anger, that chief of all evils, and therewith from frenzy, ferocity, cruelty, and madness, its attendants?

13

There is no reason why we should seek to defend such a passion as this or excuse its excesses by declaring it to be either useful or unavoidable. What vice, indeed, is without its defenders? yet this is no reason why you should declare anger to be ineradicable. The evils from which we suffer are curable, and since we were born with a natural bias towards good, nature herself will help us if we try to amend our lives. Nor is the path to virtue steep and rough, as some think it to be: it may be reached on level ground. This is no untrue tale which I come to tell you: the road to happiness is easy; do you only enter upon it with good luck and the good help of the gods themselves. It is much harder to do what you are doing. What is more restful than a mind at peace, and what more toilsome than anger? What is more at leisure than clemency, what fuller of business than cruelty? Modesty keeps holiday while vice is overwhelmed with work. In fine, the culture of any of the virtues is easy, while vices require a great expense. Anger ought to be removed from our minds: even those who say that it ought to be kept low admit this to some extent: let it be got rid of altogether; there is nothing to be gained by it. Without it we can more easily and more justly put an end to crime, punish bad men, and amend their lives. The wise man will do his duty in all things without the help of any evil passion, and will use no auxiliaries which require watching narrowly lest they get beyond his control.

14

Anger, then, must never become a habit with us, but we may sometimes affect to be angry when we wish to rouse up the dull minds of those whom we address, just as we rouse up horses who are slow at starting with goads and firebrands. We must sometimes apply fear to persons upon whom reason makes no impression: yet to be angry is of no more use than to grieve or to be afraid. "What? do not circumstances arise which provoke us to anger?" Yes: but at those times above all others we ought to choke down our wrath. Nor is it difficult to conquer our spirit, seeing that athletes, who devote their whole attention to the basest parts of themselves, nevertheless are able to endure blows and pain, in order to exhaust the strength of the striker, and do not strike when anger bids them, but when opportunity invites them. It is said that Pyrrhus, the most celebrated trainer for gymnastic contests, used habitually to impress upon his pupils not to lose their tempers: for anger spoils their science, and thinks only how it can hurt: so that often reason counsels patience while anger counsels revenge, and we, who might have survived our first misfortunes, are exposed to worse ones. Some have been driven into exile by their impatience of a single contemptuous word, have been plunged into the deepest miseries because they would not endure the most trifling wrong in silence, and have brought upon themselves the yoke of slavery because they were too proud to give up the least part of their entire liberty.

15

"That you may be sure," says our opponent, "that anger has in it something noble, pray look at the free nations, such as the Germans and Scythians, who are especially prone to anger." The reason of this is that stout and daring intellects are liable to anger before they are tamed by discipline; for some passions engraft themselves upon the better class of dispositions only, just as good land, even when waste, grows strong brushwood, and the trees are tall which stand upon a fertile soil. In like manner, dispositions which are naturally bold produce irritability, and, being hot and fiery, have no mean or trivial qualities, but their energy is misdirected, as happens with all those who without training come to the front by their natural advantages alone, whose minds, unless they be brought under control, degenerate from a courageous temper into habits of rashness and reckless daring. "What? are not milder spirits linked with gentler vices, such as tenderness of heart, love, and bashfulness?" Yes, and therefore I can often point out to you a good disposition by its own faults: yet their being the proofs of a superior nature does not prevent their being vices. Moreover, all those nations which are free because they are wild, like lions or wolves, cannot command any more than they can obey: for the strength of their intellect is not civilized, but fierce and unmanageable: now, no one is able to rule unless he is also able to be ruled. Consequently, the empire of the world has almost always remained in the hands of those nations who enjoy a milder climate. Those who dwell near the frozen north have uncivilized temper

"Just on the model of their native skies,"

as the poet has it.

16

Those animals, urges our opponent, are held to be the most generous who have large capacity for anger. He is mistaken when he holds up creatures who act from impulse instead of reason as patterns for men to follow, because in man reason takes the place of impulse. Yet even with animals, all do not alike profit by the same thing. Anger is of use to lions, timidity to stags, boldness to hawks, flight to doves. What if I declare that it is not even true that the best animals are the most prone to anger? I may suppose that wild beasts, who gain their food by rapine, are better the angrier they are; but I should praise oxen and horses who obey the rein for their patience. What reason, however, have you for referring mankind to such wretched models, when you have the universe and God, whom he alone of animals imitates because he alone comprehends Him? "The most irritable men," says he, "are thought to be the most straightforward of all." Yes, because they are compared with swindlers and sharpers, and appear to be simple because they are outspoken. I should not call such men simple, but heedless. We give this title of "simple" to all fools, gluttons, spendthrifts, and men whose vices lie on the surface.

17

"An orator," says our opponent, "sometimes speaks better when he is angry." Not so, but when he pretends to be angry: for so also actors bring down the house by their playing, not when they are really angry, but when they act the angry man well: and in like manner, in addressing a jury or a popular assembly, or in any other position in which the minds of others have to be influenced at our pleasure, we must ourselves pretend to feel anger, fear, or pity before we can make others feel them, and often the pretence of passion will do what the passion itself could not have done. "The mind which does not feel anger," says he, "is feeble." True, if it has nothing stronger than anger to support it. A man ought to be neither robber nor victim, neither tenderhearted nor cruel. The former belongs to an over-weak mind, the latter to an over-hard one. Let the wise man be moderate, and when things have to be done somewhat briskly, let him call force, not anger, to his aid.

18

Now that we have discussed the questions propounded concerning anger, let us pass on to the consideration of its remedies. These, I imagine, are twofold: the one class preventing our becoming angry, the other preventing our doing wrong when we are angry. As with the body we adopt a certain regimen to keep ourselves in health, and use different rules to bring back health when lost, so likewise we must repel anger in one fashion and quench it in another. That we may avoid it, certain general rules of conduct which apply to all men's lives must be impressed upon us. We may divide these into such as are of use during the education of the young and in afterlife. Education ought to be carried on with the greatest and most salutary assiduity: for it is easy to mould minds while they are still tender, but it is difficult to uproot vices which have grown up with ourselves.

19

A hot mind is naturally the most prone to anger: for as there are four elements,[44] consisting of fire, air, earth, and water, so there are powers corresponding and equivalent to each of these, namely, hot, cold, dry, and moist. Now the mixture of the elements is the cause of the diversities of lands and of animals, of bodies and of character, and our dispositions incline to one or the other of these according as the strength of each element prevails in us. Hence it is that we call some regions wet or dry, warm or cold. The same distinctions apply likewise to animals and mankind; it makes a great difference how much moisture or heat a man contains; his character will partake of whichever element has the largest share in him. A warm temper of mind will make men prone to anger; for fire is full of movement and vigour; a mixture of coldness makes men cowards, for cold is sluggish and contracted.

---

[44] Compare Shakespeare, *Julius Caesar*, Act V, Scene 5:—

"His life was gentle, and the elementsSo mixed in him, that nature might stand upAnd say to all the world, *this was a man!*"

See Mr. Aldis Wright's note upon the passage.

Because of this, some of our Stoics think that anger is excited in our breasts by the boiling of the blood round the heart: indeed, that place is assigned to anger for no other reason than because the breast is the warmest part of the whole body. Those who have more moisture in them become angry by slow degrees, because they have no heat ready at hand, but it has to be obtained by movement; wherefore the anger of women and children is sharp rather than strong, and arises on lighter provocation. At dry times of life anger is violent and powerful, yet without increase, and adding little to itself, because as heat dies away cold takes its place. Old men are testy and full of complaints, as also are sick people and convalescents, and all whose store of heat has been consumed by weariness or loss of blood. Those who are wasted by thirst or hunger are in the same condition, as also are those whose frame is naturally bloodless and faints from want of generous diet. Wine kindles anger, because it increases heat; according to each man's disposition, some fly into a passion when they are heavily drunk, some when they are slightly drunk: nor is there any other reason than this why yellow-haired, ruddy-complexioned people should be excessively passionate, seeing that they are naturally of the colour which others put on during anger; for their blood is hot and easily set in motion.

20

But just as nature makes some men prone to anger, so there are many other causes which have the same power as nature. Some are brought into this condition by disease or bodily injury, others by hard work, long watching, nights of anxiety, ardent longings, and love: and everything else which is hurtful to the body or the spirit inclines the distempered mind to find fault. All these, however, are but the beginning and causes of anger. Habit of mind has very great power, and, if it be harsh, increases the disorder. As for nature, it is difficult to alter it, nor may we change the mixture of the elements which was formed once for all at our birth: yet knowledge will be so far of service, that we should keep wine out of the reach of hot-tempered men, which Plato thinks ought also to be forbidden to boys, so that fire be not made fiercer. Neither should such men be overfed: for if so, their bodies will swell, and their minds will swell with them. Such men ought to take exercise, stopping short, however, of fatigue, in order that their natural heat may be abated, but not exhausted, and their excess of fiery spirit may be worked off. Games also will be useful: for moderate pleasure relieves the mind and brings it to a proper balance. With those temperaments which incline to moisture, or dryness and stiffness, there is no danger of anger, but there is fear of greater vices, such as cowardice, moroseness, despair, and suspiciousness: such dispositions therefore ought to be softened, comforted, and restored to cheerfulness: and since we must make use of different remedies for anger and for sullenness, and these two vices require not only unlike, but absolutely opposite modes of treatment, let us always attack that one of them which is gaining the mastery.

21

It is, I assure you, of the greatest service to boys that they should be soundly brought up, yet to regulate their education is difficult, because it is our duty to be careful neither to cherish a habit of anger in them, nor to blunt the edge of their spirit. This needs careful watching, for both qualities, both those which are to be encouraged, and those which are to be checked, are fed by the same things; and even a careful watcher may be deceived by their likeness. A boy's spirit is increased by freedom and depressed by slavery: it rises when praised, and is led to conceive great expectations of itself: yet this same treatment produces arrogance and quickness of temper: we must therefore guide him between these two extremes, using the curb at one time and the spur at another. He must undergo no servile or degrading treatment; he never must beg abjectly for anything, nor must he gain anything by begging; let him rather receive it for his own sake, for his past good behaviour, or for his promises of future good conduct. In contests with his comrades we ought not to allow him to become sulky or fly into a passion: let us see that he be on friendly terms with those whom he contends with, so that in the struggle itself he may learn to wish not to hurt his antagonist but to conquer him: whenever he has gained the day or done something praiseworthy, we should allow him to enjoy his victory, but not to rush into transports of delight: for joy leads to exultation, and exultation leads to swaggering and excessive self-esteem. We ought to allow him some relaxation, yet not yield him up to laziness and sloth, and we ought to keep him far beyond the reach of luxury, for nothing makes children more prone to anger than a soft and fond bringing-up, so that the more only children are indulged, and the more liberty is given to orphans, the more they are corrupted. He to whom nothing is ever denied, will not be able to endure a rebuff, whose anxious mother always wipes away his tears, whose *paedagogus*[45] is made to pay for his shortcomings. Do you not observe how a man's anger becomes more violent as he rises in station? This shows itself especially in those who are rich and noble, or in great place, when the favouring gale has roused all the most empty and trivial passions of their minds. Prosperity fosters anger, when a man's proud ears are surrounded by a mob of flatterers, saying, "That man answers you! you do not act according to your dignity, you lower yourself." And so forth, with all the language which can hardly be resisted even by healthy and originally well-principled minds. Flattery, then, must be kept well out of the way of children. Let a child hear the truth, and sometimes fear it: let him always reverence it. Let him rise in the presence of his elders. Let him obtain nothing by flying into a passion: let him be given when he is quiet what was refused him when he cried for it: let him behold, but not make use of his father's wealth: let him be reproved for what he does wrong. It will be advantageous to furnish boys with even-tempered teachers

---

[45] *Paedagogus* was a slave who accompanied a boy to school, etc., to keep him out of mischief; he did not teach him anything.

and *paedagogi*: what is soft and unformed clings to what is near, and takes its shape: the habits of young men reproduce those of their nurses and *paedagogi*. Once, a boy who was brought up in Plato's house went home to his parents, and, on seeing his father shouting with passion, said, "I never saw anyone at Plato's house act like that." I doubt not that he learned to imitate his father sooner than he learned to imitate Plato. Above all, let his food be scanty, his dress not costly, and of the same fashion as that of his comrades: if you begin by putting him on a level with many others, he will not be angry when someone is compared with him.

22

These precepts, however, apply to our children: in ourselves the accident of birth and our education no longer admits of either mistakes or advice; we must deal with what follows. Now we ought to fight against the first causes of evil: the cause of anger is the belief that we are injured; this belief, therefore, should not be lightly entertained. We ought not to fly into a rage even when the injury appears to be open and distinct: for some false things bear the semblance of truth. We should always allow some time to elapse, for time discloses the truth. Let not our ears be easily lent to calumnious talk: let us know and be on our guard against this fault of human nature, that we are willing to believe what we are unwilling to listen to, and that we become angry before we have formed our opinion. What shall I say? we are influenced not merely by calumnies but by suspicions, and at the very look and smile of others we may fly into a rage with innocent persons because we put the worst construction upon it. We ought, therefore, to plead the cause of the absent against ourselves, and to keep our anger in abeyance: for a punishment which has been postponed may yet be inflicted, but when once inflicted cannot be recalled.

23

Everyone knows the story of the tyrannicide who, being caught before he had accomplished his task, and being tortured by Hippias to make him betray his accomplices, named the friends of the tyrant who stood around, and everyone to whom he knew the tyrant's safety was especially dear. As the tyrant ordered each man to be slain as he was named, at last the man, being asked if anyone else remained, said, "You remain alone, for I have left no one else alive to whom you are dear." Anger had made the tyrant lend his assistance to the tyrant-slayer, and cut down his guards with his own sword. How far more spirited was Alexander, who after reading his mother's letter warning him to beware of poison from his physician, Philip, nevertheless drank undismayed the medicine which Philip gave him! He felt more confidence in his friend: he deserved that his friend should be innocent, and deserved that his conduct should make him innocent. I praise Alexander's doing this all the more because he was above all men prone to anger; but the rarer moderation is among kings, the more it deserves to be praised. The great Gaius Caesar, who proved such a merciful conqueror in the civil war, did the same thing; he burned a packet of letters addressed to Gnaeus Pompeius by persons who had been thought to be either neutrals or on the other side. Though he was never violent in his anger, yet he preferred to put it out of his power to be angry: he thought that the kindest way to pardon each of them was not to know what his offence had been.

24

Readiness to believe what we hear causes very great mischief; we ought often not even to listen, because in some cases it is better to be deceived than to suspect deceit. We ought to free our minds of suspicion and mistrust, those most untrustworthy causes of anger. "This man's greeting was far from civil; that one would not receive my kiss; one cut short a story I had begun to tell; another did not ask me to dinner; another seemed to view me with aversion." Suspicion will never lack grounds: what we want is straightforwardness, and a kindly interpretation of things. Let us believe nothing unless it forces itself upon our sight and is unmistakable, and let us reprove ourselves for being too ready to believe, as often as our suspicions prove to be groundless: for this discipline will render us habitually slow to believe what we hear.

25

Another consequence of this will be, that we shall not be exasperated by the slightest and most contemptible trifles. It is mere madness to be put out of temper because a slave is not quick, because the water we are going to drink is lukewarm or because our couch is disarranged or our table carelessly laid. A man must be in a miserably bad state of health if he shrinks from a gentle breath of wind; his eyes must be diseased if they are distressed by the sight of white clothing; he must be broken down with debauchery if he feels pain at seeing another man work. It is said that there was one Mindyrides, a citizen of Sybaris, who one day seeing a man digging and vigorously brandishing a mattock, complained that the sight made him weary, and forbade the man to work where he could see him. The same man complained that he had suffered from the rose-leaves upon which he lay being folded double. When pleasures have corrupted both the body and the mind, nothing seems endurable, not indeed because it is hard, but because he who has to bear it is soft: for why should we be driven to frenzy by anyone's coughing and sneezing, or by a fly not being driven away with sufficient care, or by a dog's hanging about us, or a key dropping from a careless servant's hand? Will one whose ears are agonised by the noise of a bench being dragged along the floor be able to endure with unruffled mind the rude language of party strife, and the abuse which speakers in the forum or the senate house heap upon their opponents? Will he who is angry with his slave for icing his drink badly, be able to endure hunger, or the thirst of a long march in summer? Nothing, therefore, nourishes anger more than excessive and dissatisfied luxury: the mind ought to be hardened by rough treatment, so as not to feel any blow that is not severe.

26

We are angry, either with those who can, or with those who cannot do us an injury. To the latter class belong some inanimate things, such as a book, which we often throw away when it is written in letters too small for us to read, or tear up when it is full of mistakes, or clothes which we destroy because we do not like them. How foolish to be angry with such things as these, which neither deserve nor feel our anger! "But of course it is their makers who really affront us." I answer that, in the first place, we often become angry before making this distinction clear in our minds, and secondly, perhaps even the makers might put forward some reasonable excuses: one of them, it may be, could not make them any better than he did, and it is not through any disrespect to you that he was unskilled in his trade: another may have done his work so without any intention of insulting you: and, finally, what can be more crazy than to discharge upon things the ill-feeling which one has accumulated against persons? Yet as it is the act of a madman to be angry with inanimate objects, so also is it to be angry with dumb animals, which can do us no wrong because they are not able to form a purpose; and we cannot call anything a wrong unless it be done intentionally. They are, therefore, able to hurt us, just as a sword or a stone may do so, but they are not able to do us a wrong. Yet some men think themselves insulted when the same horses which are docile with one rider are restive with another, as though it were through their deliberate choice, and not through habit and cleverness of handling that some horses are more easily managed by some men than by others. And as it is foolish to be angry with them, so it is to be angry with children, and with men who have little more sense than children: for all these sins, before a just judge, ignorance would be as effective an excuse as innocence.

27

There are some things which are unable to hurt us, and whose power is exclusively beneficial and salutary, as, for example, the immortal gods, who neither wish nor are able to do harm: for their temperament is naturally gentle and tranquil, and no more likely to wrong others than to wrong themselves. Foolish people who know not the truth hold them answerable for storms at sea, excessive rain, and long winters, whereas all the while these phenomena by which we suffer or profit take place without any reference whatever to us: it is not for our sake that the universe causes summer and winter to succeed one another; these have a law of their own, according to which their divine functions are performed. We think too much of ourselves, when we imagine that we are worthy to have such prodigious revolutions effected for our sake: so, then, none of these things take place in order to do us an injury, nay, on the contrary, they all tend to our benefit. I have said that there are some things which cannot hurt us, and some which would not. To the latter class belong good men in authority, good parents, teachers, and judges, whose punishments ought to be submitted to by us in the same spirit in which we undergo the surgeon's knife, abstinence from food, and suchlike things which hurt us for our benefit. Suppose that we are being punished; let us think not only of what we suffer, but of what we have done: let us sit in judgement on our past life. Provided we are willing to tell ourselves the truth, we shall certainly decide that our crimes deserve a harder measure than they have received.

28

If we desire to be impartial judges of all that takes place, we must first convince ourselves of this, that no one of us is faultless: for it is from this that most of our indignation proceeds. "I have not sinned, I have done no wrong." Say, rather, you do not admit that you have done any wrong. We are infuriated at being reproved, either by reprimand or actual chastisement, although we are sinning at that very time, by adding insolence and obstinacy to our wrongdoings. Who is there that can declare himself to have broken no laws? Even if there be such a man, what a stinted innocence it is, merely to be innocent by the letter of the law. How much further do the rules of duty extend than those of the law! how many things which are not to be found in the statute book, are demanded by filial feeling, kindness, generosity, equity, and honour? Yet we are not able to warrant ourselves even to come under that first narrowest definition of innocence: we have done what was wrong, thought what was wrong, wished for what was wrong, and encouraged what was wrong: in some cases we have only remained innocent because we did not succeed. When we think of this, let us deal more justly with sinners, and believe that those who scold us are right: in any case let us not be angry with ourselves (for with whom shall we not be angry, if we are angry even with our own selves?), and least of all with the gods: for whatever we suffer befalls us not by any ordinance of theirs but of the common law of all flesh. "But diseases and pains attack us." Well, people who live in a crazy dwelling must have some way of escape from it. Someone will be said to have spoken ill of you: think whether you did not first speak ill of him: think of how many persons you have yourself spoken ill. Let us not, I say, suppose that others are doing us a wrong, but are repaying one which we have done them, that some are acting with good intentions, some under compulsion, some in ignorance, and let us believe that even he who does so intentionally and knowingly did not wrong us merely for the sake of wronging us, but was led into doing so by the attraction of saying something witty, or did whatever he did, not out of any spite against us, but because he himself could not succeed unless he pushed us back. We are often offended by flattery even while it is being lavished upon us: yet whoever recalls to his mind how often he himself has been the victim of undeserved suspicion, how often fortune has given his true service an appearance of wrongdoing, how many persons he has begun by hating and ended by loving, will be able to keep himself from becoming angry straightaway, especially if he silently says to himself when each offence is committed: "I have done this very thing myself." Where, however, will you find so impartial a judge? The same man who lusts after everyone's wife, and thinks that a woman's belonging to someone else is a sufficient reason for adoring her, will not allow anyone else to look at his own wife. No man expects such exact fidelity as a traitor: the perjurer himself takes vengeance of him who breaks his word: the pettifogging lawyer is most indignant at an action being brought against him: the man who is reckless of his own chastity cannot endure any attempt upon that of his slaves. We have other men's vices before our eyes, and our own behind our backs: hence it is that a father, who is worse than his son, blames the latter for giving extravagant feasts,[46] and disapproves of the least sign of luxury in another, although he was wont to set no bounds to it in his own case; hence it is that despots are angry with homicides, and thefts are punished by those who despoil temples. A great part of mankind is not angry with sins, but with sinners. Regard to our own selves[47] will make us more moderate, if we inquire of ourselves:—have we ever committed any crime of this sort? have we ever fallen into this kind of error? is it for our interest that we should condemn this conduct?

29

The greatest remedy for anger is delay: beg anger to grant you this at the first, not in order that it may pardon the offence, but that it may form a right judgment about it:—if it delays, it will come to an end. Do not attempt to quell it all at once, for its first impulses are fierce; by plucking away its parts we shall remove the whole. We are made angry by some things which we learn at secondhand, and by some which we ourselves hear or see. Now, we ought to be slow to believe what is told us. Many tell lies in order to deceive us, and many because they are themselves deceived. Some seek to win our favour by false accusations, and invent wrongs in order that they may appear angry at our having suffered them. One man lies out of spite, that he may set trusting friends at variance; some because they are suspicious,[48] and wish to see sport, and watch from a safe distance those whom they have set by the ears. If you were about to give sentence in court about ever so small a sum of money, you would take nothing as proved without a witness, and a witness would count for nothing except on his oath. You would allow both sides to be heard: you would allow them time: you would not despatch the matter at one sitting, because the

---

[46] *Tempestiva*, beginning before the usual hour.
[47] Fear of self-condemnation.
[48] Lipsius conjectures *supprocax*, mischievous.

oftener it is handled the more distinctly the truth appears. And do you condemn your friend offhand? Are you angry with him before you hear his story, before you have cross-examined him, before he can know either who is his accuser or with what he is charged. Why then, just now, in the case which you just tried, did you hear what was said on both sides? This very man who has informed against your friend, will say no more if he be obliged to prove what he says. "You need not," says he, "bring me forward as a witness; if I am brought forward I shall deny what I have said; unless you excuse me from appearing I shall never tell you anything." At the same time he spurs you on and withdraws himself from the strife and battle. The man who will tell you nothing save in secret hardly tells you anything at all. What can be more unjust than to believe in secret, and to be angry openly?

30

Some offences we ourselves witness: in these cases let us examine the disposition and purpose of the offender. Perhaps he is a child; let us pardon his youth, he knows not whether he is doing wrong: or he is a father; he has either rendered such great services, as to have won the right even to wrong us—or perhaps this very act which offends us is his chief merit: or a woman; well, she made a mistake. The man did it because he was ordered to do it. Who but an unjust person can be angry with what is done under compulsion? You had hurt him: well, there is no wrong in suffering the pain which you have been the first to inflict. Suppose that your opponent is a judge; then you ought to take his opinion rather than your own: or that he is a king; then, if he punishes the guilty, yield to him because he is just, and if he punishes the innocent, yield to him because he is powerful. Suppose that it is a dumb animal or as stupid as a dumb animal: then, if you are angry with it, you will make yourself like it. Suppose that it is a disease or a misfortune; it will take less effect upon you if you bear it quietly: or that it is a god; then you waste your time by being angry with him as much as if you prayed him to be angry with someone else. Is it a good man who has wronged you? do not believe it: is it a bad one? do not be surprised at this; he will pay to someone else the penalty which he owes to you—indeed, by his sin he has already punished himself.

31

There are, as I have stated, two cases which produce anger: first, when we appear to have received an injury, about which enough has been said, and, secondly, when we appear to have been treated unjustly: this must now be discussed. Men think some things unjust because they ought not to suffer them, and some because they did not expect to suffer them: we think what is unexpected is beneath our deserts. Consequently, we are especially excited at what befalls us contrary to our hope and expectation: and this is why we are irritated at the smallest trifles in our own domestic affairs, and why we call our friends' carelessness deliberate injury. How is it, then, asks our opponent, that we are angered by the injuries inflicted by our enemies? It is because we did not expect those particular injuries, or, at any rate, not on so extensive a scale. This is caused by our excessive self-love: we think that we ought to remain uninjured even by our enemies: every man bears within his breast the mind of a despot, and is willing to commit excesses, but unwilling to submit to them. Thus it is either ignorance or arrogance that makes us angry: ignorance of common facts; for what is there to wonder at in bad men committing evil deeds? what novelty is there in your enemy hurting you, your friend quarrelling with you, your son going wrong, or your servant doing amiss? Fabius was wont to say that the most shameful excuse a general could make was "I did not think." I think it the most shameful excuse that a man can make. Think of everything, expect everything: even with men of good character something queer will crop up: human nature produces minds that are treacherous, ungrateful, greedy, and impious: when you are considering what any man's morals may be, think what those of mankind are. When you are especially enjoying yourself, be especially on your guard: when everything seems to you to be peaceful, be sure that mischief is not absent, but only asleep. Always believe that something will occur to offend you. A pilot never spreads all his canvas abroad so confidently as not to keep his tackle for shortening sail ready for use. Think, above all, how base and hateful is the power of doing mischief, and how unnatural in man, by whose kindness even fierce animals are rendered tame. See how bulls yield their necks to the yoke, how elephants[49] allow boys and women to dance on their backs unhurt, how snakes glide harmlessly over our bosoms and among our drinking-cups, how within their dens bears and lions submit to be handled with complacent mouths, and wild beasts fawn upon their master: let us blush to have exchanged habits with wild beasts. It is a crime to injure one's country: so it is, therefore, to injure any of our countrymen, for he is a part of our country; if the whole be sacred, the parts must be sacred too. Therefore it is also a crime to injure any man: for he is your fellow-citizen in a larger state. What, if the hands were to wish to hurt the feet? or the eyes to hurt the hands? As all the limbs act in unison, because it is the interest of the whole body to keep each one of them safe, so men should spare one another, because they are born for society. The bond of society, however, cannot exist unless it guards and loves all its members. We should not even destroy vipers and water-snakes and other creatures whose teeth and claws are dangerous, if we were able to tame them as we do other animals, or to prevent their being a peril to us: neither ought we, therefore, to hurt a man because he has done wrong, but lest he should do wrong, and our punishment should always look to the future, and never to the past, because it is inflicted in a spirit of precaution, not of anger: for if everyone who has a crooked and vicious disposition were to be punished, no one would escape punishment.

---

[49] I have adopted the transposition of Haase and Koch.

32

"But anger possesses a certain pleasure of its own, and it is sweet to pay back the pain you have suffered." Not at all; it is not honourable to requite injuries by injuries, in the same way as it is to repay benefits by benefits. In the latter case it is a shame to be conquered; in the former it is a shame to conquer. Revenge and retaliation are words which men use and even think to be righteous, yet they do not greatly differ from wrongdoing, except in the order in which they are done: he who renders pain for pain has more excuse for his sin; that is all. Someone who did not know Marcus Cato struck him in the public bath in his ignorance, for who would knowingly have done him an injury? Afterwards when he was apologizing, Cato replied, "I do not remember being struck." He thought it better to ignore the insult than to revenge it. You ask, "Did no harm befall that man for his insolence?" No, but rather much good; he made the acquaintance of Cato. It is the part of a great mind to despise wrongs done to it; the most contemptuous form of revenge is not to deem one's adversary worth taking vengeance upon. Many have taken small injuries much more seriously to heart than they need, by revenging them: that man is great and noble who like a large wild animal hears unmoved the tiny curs that bark at him.

33

"We are treated," says our opponent, "with more respect if we revenge our injuries." If we make use of revenge merely as a remedy, let us use it without anger, and not regard revenge as pleasant, but as useful: yet often it is better to pretend not to have received an injury than to avenge it. The wrongs of the powerful must not only be borne, but borne with a cheerful countenance: they will repeat the wrong if they think they have inflicted it. This is the worst trait of minds rendered arrogant by prosperity, they hate those whom they have injured. Everyone knows the saying of the old courtier, who, when someone asked him how he had achieved the rare distinction of living at court till he reached old age, replied, "By receiving wrongs and returning thanks for them." It is often so far from expedient to avenge our wrongs, that it will not do even to admit them. Gaius Caesar, offended at the smart clothes and well-dressed hair of the son of Pastor, a distinguished Roman knight, sent him to prison. When the father begged that his son might suffer no harm, Gaius, as if reminded by this to put him to death, ordered him to be executed, yet, in order to mitigate his brutality to the father, invited him that very day to dinner. Pastor came with a countenance which betrayed no ill will. Caesar pledged him in a glass of wine, and set a man to watch him. The wretched creature went through his part, feeling as though he were drinking his son's blood: the emperor sent him some perfume and a garland, and gave orders to watch whether he used them: he did so. On the very day on which he had buried, nay, on which he had not even buried his son, he sat down as one of a hundred guests, and, old and gouty as he was, drank to an extent which would have been hardly decent on a child's birthday; he shed no tear the while; he did not permit his grief to betray itself by the slightest sign; he dined just as though his entreaties had gained his son's life. You ask me why he did so? he had another son. What did Priam do in the *Iliad*? Did he not conceal his wrath and embrace the knees of Achilles? did he not raise to his lips that death-dealing hand, stained with the blood of his son, and sup with his slayer? True! but there were no perfumes and garlands, and his fierce enemy encouraged him with many soothing words to eat, not to drain huge goblets with a guard standing over him to see that he did it. Had he only feared for himself, the father would have treated the tyrant with scorn: but love for his son quenched his anger: he deserved the emperor's permission to leave the banquet and gather up the bones of his son: but, meanwhile, that kindly and polite youth the emperor would not even permit him to do this, but tormented the old man with frequent invitations to drink, advising him thereby to lighten his sorrows. He, on the other hand, appeared to be in good spirits, and to have forgotten what had been done that day: he would have lost his second son had he proved an unacceptable guest to the murderer of his eldest.

34

We must, therefore, refrain from anger, whether he who provokes us be on a level with ourselves, or above us, or below us. A contest with one's equal is of uncertain issue, with one's superior is folly, and with one's inferior is contemptible. It is the part of a mean and wretched man to turn and bite one's biter: even mice and ants show their teeth if you put your hand to them, and all feeble creatures think that they are hurt if they are touched. It will make us milder tempered to call to mind any services which he with whom we are angry may have done us, and to let his deserts balance his offence. Let us also reflect, how much credit the tale of our forgiveness will confer upon us, how many men may be made into valuable friends by forgiveness. One of the lessons which Sulla's cruelty teaches us is not to be angry with the children of our enemies, whether they be public or private; for he drove the sons of the proscribed into exile. Nothing is more unjust than that anyone should inherit the quarrels of his father. Whenever we are loath to pardon anyone, let us think whether it would be to our advantage that all men should be inexorable. He who refuses to pardon, how often has he begged it for himself? how often has he grovelled at the feet of those whom he spurns from his own? How can we gain more glory than by turning anger into friendship? what more faithful allies has the Roman people than those who have been its most unyielding enemies? where would the empire be today, had not a wise foresight united the conquered and the conquerors? If anyone is angry with you, meet his anger by returning benefits for it: a quarrel which is only taken up on one side falls to the ground: it takes two men to fight. But[50] suppose that there is an angry struggle on both sides, even then, he is the better man who first gives way; the winner is the real loser. He struck you; well then, do you fall back: if you strike him in turn you will give him both an opportunity and an excuse for striking you again: you will not be able to withdraw yourself from the struggle when you please.

35

Does anyone wish to strike his enemy so hard, as to leave his own hand in the wound, and not to be able to recover his balance after the blow? yet such a weapon is anger: it is scarcely possible to draw it back. We are careful to choose for ourselves light weapons, handy and manageable swords: shall we not avoid these clumsy, unwieldy,[51] and never-to-be-recalled impulses of the mind? The only swiftness of which men approve is that which, when bidden, checks itself and proceeds no further, and which can be guided, and reduced from a run to a walk: we know that the sinews are diseased when they move against our will. A man must be either aged or weakly who runs when he wants to walk: let us think that those are the most powerful and the soundest operations of our minds, which act under our own control, not at their own caprice. Nothing, however, will be of so much service as to consider, first, the hideousness, and, secondly, the danger of anger. No passion bears a more troubled aspect: it befouls the fairest face, makes fierce the expression which before was peaceful. From the angry "all grace has fled;" though their clothing may be fashionable, they will trail it on the ground and take no heed of their appearance; though their hair be smoothed down in a comely manner by nature or art, yet it will bristle up in sympathy with their mind. The veins become swollen, the breast will be shaken by quick breathing, the man's neck will be swelled as he roars forth his frantic talk: then, too, his limbs will tremble, his hands will be restless, his whole body will sway hither and thither. What, think you, must be the state of his mind within him, when its appearance without is so shocking? how far more dreadful a countenance he bears within his own breast, how far keener pride, how much more violent rage, which will burst him unless it finds some vent? Let us paint anger looking like those who are dripping with the blood of foemen or savage beasts, or those who are just about to slaughter them—like those monsters of the nether world fabled by the poet to be girt with serpents and breathing flame, when they sally forth from hell, most frightful to behold, in order that they may kindle wars, stir up strife between nations, and overthrow peace; let us paint her eyes glowing with fire, her voice hissing, roaring, grating, and making worse sounds if worse there be, while she brandishes weapons in both hands, for she cares not to protect herself, gloomy, stained with blood, covered

---

[50] I adopt Vahlen's reading. See his Preface, p. viii, ed. Jenae, 1879.
[51] I read *onerosos* with Vahlen. See his Preface, p. viii, ed. Jenae, 1879.

with scars and livid with her own blows, reeling like a maniac, wrapped in a thick cloud, dashing hither and thither, spreading desolation and panic, loathed by everyone and by herself above all, willing, if otherwise she cannot hurt her foe, to overthrow alike earth, sea, and heaven, harmful and hateful at the same time. Or, if we are to see her, let her be such as our poets have described her—"There with her bloodstained scourge Bellona fights, And Discord in her riven robe delights,"[52] or, if possible, let some even more dreadful aspect be invented for this dreadful passion.

36

Some angry people, as Sextius remarks, have been benefited by looking at the glass: they have been struck by so great an alteration in their own appearance: they have been, as it were, brought into their own presence and have not recognized themselves: yet how small a part of the real hideousness of anger did that reflected image in the mirror reproduce? Could the mind be displayed or made to appear through any substance, we should be confounded when we beheld how black and stained, how agitated, distorted, and swollen it looked: even at present it is very ugly when seen through all the screens of blood, bones, and so forth: what would it be, were it displayed uncovered? You say, that you do not believe that anyone was ever scared out of anger by a mirror: and why not? because when he came to the mirror to change his mind, he had changed it already: to angry men no face looks fairer than one that is fierce and savage and such as they wish to look like. We ought rather to consider, how many men anger itself has injured. Some in their excessive heat have burst their veins; some by straining their voices beyond their strength have vomited blood, or have injured their sight by too violently injecting humours into their eyes, and have fallen sick when the fit passed off. No way leads more swiftly to madness: many have, consequently, remained always in the frenzy of anger, and, having once lost their reason, have never recovered it. Ajax was driven mad by anger, and driven to suicide by madness. Men, frantic with rage, call upon heaven to slay their children, to reduce themselves to poverty, and to ruin their houses, and yet declare that they are not either angry or insane. Enemies to their best friends, dangerous to their nearest and dearest, regardless of the laws save where they injure, swayed by the smallest trifles, unwilling to lend their ears to the advice or the services of their friends, they do everything by main force, and are ready either to fight with their swords or to throw themselves upon them, for the greatest of all evils, and one which surpasses all vices, has gained possession of them. Other passions gain a footing in the mind by slow degrees: anger's conquest is sudden and complete, and, moreover, it makes all other passions subservient to itself. It conquers the warmest love: men have thrust

---

[52] The lines are from Virgil, *Æneid*, VIII, 702, but are inaccurately quoted.

swords through the bodies of those whom they loved, and have slain those in whose arms they have lain. Avarice, that sternest and most rigid of passions, is trampled underfoot by anger, which forces it to squander its carefully collected wealth and set fire to its house and all its property in one heap. Why, has not even the ambitious man been known to fling away the most highly valued ensigns of rank, and to refuse high office when it was offered to him? There is no passion over which anger does not bear absolute rule.

BOOK 3

1

We will now, my Novatus, attempt to do that which you so especially long to do, that is, to drive out anger from our minds, or at all events to curb it and restrain its impulses. This may sometimes be done openly and without concealment, when we are only suffering from a slight attack of this mischief, and at other times it must be done secretly, when our anger is excessively hot, and when every obstacle thrown in its way increases it and makes it blaze higher. It is important to know how great and how fresh its strength may be, and whether it can be driven forcibly back and suppressed, or whether we must give way to it until its first storm blow over, lest it sweep away with it our remedies themselves. We must deal with each case according to each man's character: some yield to entreaties, others are rendered arrogant and masterful by submission: we may frighten some men out of their anger, while some may be turned from their purpose by reproaches, some by acknowledging oneself to be in the wrong, some by shame, and some by delay, a tardy remedy for a hasty disorder; which we ought only to use when all others have failed: for other passions admit of having their case put off, and may be healed at a later time; but the eager and self-destructive violence of anger does not grow up by slow degrees, but reaches its full height as soon as it begins. Nor does it, like other vices, merely disturb men's minds, but it takes them away, and torments them till they are incapable of restraining themselves and eager for the common ruin of all men, nor does it rage merely against its object, but against every obstacle which it encounters on its way. The other vices move our minds; anger hurls them headlong. If we are not able to withstand our passions, yet at any rate our passions ought to stand firm: but anger grows more and more powerful, like lightning flashes or hurricanes, or any other things which cannot stop themselves because they do not proceed along, but fall from above. Other vices affect our judgment, anger affects our sanity: others come in mild attacks and grow unnoticed, but men's minds plunge abruptly into anger. There is no passion that is more frantic, more destructive to its own self; it is arrogant if successful, and frantic if it fails. Even when defeated it does not grow weary, but if chance places its foe beyond its reach, it turns its teeth against itself. Its intensity is in no way regulated by its origin: for it rises to the greatest heights from the most trivial beginnings.

2

It passes over no time of life; no race of men is exempt from it: some nations have been saved from the knowledge of luxury by the blessing of poverty; some through their active and wandering habits have escaped from sloth; those whose manners are unpolished and whose life is rustic know not chicanery and fraud and all the evils to which the courts of law give birth: but there is no race which is not excited by anger, which is equally powerful with Greeks and barbarians, and is just as ruinous among law-abiding folk as among those whose only law is that of the stronger. Finally, the other passions seize upon individuals anger is the only one which sometimes possesses a whole state. No entire people ever fell madly in love with a woman, nor did any nation ever set its affections altogether upon gain and profit. Ambition attacks single individuals; ungovernable rage is the only passion that affects nations. People often fly into a passion by troops; men and women, old men and boys, princes and populace all act alike, and the whole multitude, after being excited by a very few words, outdoes even its exciter: men betake themselves straightaway to fire and sword, and proclaim a war against their neighbours or wage one against their countrymen. Whole houses are burned with the entire families which they contain, and he who but lately was honoured for his popular eloquence now finds that his speech moves people to rage. Legions aim their darts at their commander; the whole populace quarrels with the nobles; the senate, without waiting for troops to be levied or appointing a general, hastily chooses leaders, for its anger chases wellborn men through the houses of Rome, and puts them to death with its own hand. Ambassadors are outraged, the law of nations violated, and an unnatural madness seizes the State. Without allowing time for the general excitement to subside, fleets are straightaway launched and laden with a hastily enrolled soldiery. Without organization, without taking any auspices, the populace rushes into the field guided only by its own anger, snatches up whatever comes first to hand by way of arms, and then atones by a great defeat for the reckless audacity of its anger. This is usually the fate of savage nations when they plunge into war: as soon as their easily excited minds are roused by the appearance of wrong having been done them, they straightaway hasten forth, and, guided only by their wounded feelings, fall like an avalanche upon our legions, without either discipline, fear, or precaution, and willfully seeking for danger. They delight in being struck, in pressing forward to meet the blow, writhing their bodies along the weapon, and perishing by a wound which they themselves make.

3

"No doubt," you say, "anger is very powerful and ruinous: point out, therefore, how it may be cured." Yet, as I stated in my former books, Aristotle stands forth in defence of anger, and forbids it to be uprooted, saying that it is the spur of virtue, and that when it is taken away, our minds become weaponless, and slow to attempt great exploits. It is therefore essential to prove its unseemliness and ferocity, and to place distinctly before our eyes how monstrous a thing it is that one man should rage against another, with what frantic violence he rushes to destroy alike himself and his foe, and overthrows those very things whose fall he himself must share. What, then? can anyone call this man sane, who, as though caught up by a hurricane, does not go but is driven, and is the slave of a senseless disorder? He does not commit to another the duty of revenging him, but himself exacts it, raging alike in thought and deed, butchering those who are dearest to him, and for whose loss he himself will ere long weep. Will anyone give this passion as an assistant and companion to virtue, although it disturbs calm reason, without which virtue can do nothing? The strength which a sick man owes to a paroxysm of disease is neither lasting nor wholesome, and is strong only to its own destruction. You need not, therefore, imagine that I am wasting time over a useless task in defaming anger, as though men had not made up their minds about it, when there is someone, and he, too, an illustrious philosopher, who assigns it services to perform, and speaks of it as useful and supplying energy for battles, for the management of business, and indeed for everything which requires to be conducted with spirit. Lest it should delude anyone into thinking that on certain occasions and in certain positions it may be useful, we must show its unbridled and frenzied madness, we must restore to it its attributes, the rack, the cord, the dungeon, and the cross, the fires lighted round men's buried bodies, the hook[53] that drags both living men and corpses, the different kinds of fetters, and of punishments, the mutilations of limbs, the branding of the forehead, the dens of savage beasts. Anger should be represented as standing among these her instruments, growling in an ominous and terrible fashion, herself more shocking than any of the means by which she gives vent to her fury.

4

There may be some doubt about the others, but at any rate no passion has a worse look. We have described the angry man's appearance in our former books, how sharp and keen he looks, at one time pale as his blood is driven inwards and backwards, at

---

[53] The hook alluded to was fastened to the neck of condemned criminals, and by it they were dragged to the Tiber. Also the bodies of dead gladiators were thus dragged out of the arena. The hook by which the dead bull is drawn away at a modern Spanish bullfight is probably a survival of this custom.

another with all the heat and fire of his body directed to his face, making it reddish-coloured as if stained with blood, his eyes now restless and starting out of his head, now set motionless in one fixed gaze. Add to this his teeth, which gnash against one another, as though he wished to eat somebody, with exactly the sound of a wild boar sharpening his tusks: add also the cracking of his joints, the involuntary wringing of his hands, the frequent slaps he deals himself on the chest, his hurried breathing and deep-drawn sighs, his reeling body, his abrupt broken speech, and his trembling lips, which sometimes he draws tight as he hisses some curse through them. By Hercules, no wild beast, neither when tortured by hunger, or with a weapon struck through its vitals, not even when it gathers its last breath to bite its slayer, looks so shocking as a man raging with anger. Listen, if you have leisure, to his words and threats: how dreadful is the language of his agonized mind! Would not every man wish to lay aside anger when he sees that it begins by injuring himself? When men employ anger as the most powerful of agents, consider it to be a proof of power, and reckon a speedy revenge among the greatest blessings of great prosperity, would you not wish me to warn them that he who is the slave of his own anger is not powerful, nor even free? Would you not wish me to warn all the more industrious and circumspect of men, that while other evil passions assail the base, anger gradually obtains dominion over the minds even of learned and in other respects sensible men? So true is that, that some declare anger to be a proof of straightforwardness, and it is commonly believed that the best-natured people are prone to it.

5

You ask me, whither does all this tend? To prove, I answer, that no one should imagine himself to be safe from anger, seeing that it rouses up even those who are naturally gentle and quiet to commit savage and violent acts. As strength of body and assiduous care of the health avail nothing against a pestilence, which attacks the strong and weak alike, so also steady and good-humoured people are just as liable to attacks of anger as those of unsettled character, and in the case of the former it is both more to be ashamed of and more to be feared, because it makes a greater alteration in their habits. Now as the first thing is not to be angry, the second to lay aside our anger, and the third to be able to heal the anger of others as well as our own, I will set forth first how we may avoid falling into anger; next, how we may set ourselves free from it, and, lastly, how we may restrain an angry man, appease his wrath, and bring him back to his right mind.

We shall succeed in avoiding anger, if from time to time we lay before our minds all the vices connected with anger, and estimate it at its real value: it must be prosecuted before us and convicted: its evils must be thoroughly investigated and exposed. That we may see what it is, let it be compared with the worst vices. Avarice scrapes together and amasses riches for some better man to use: anger spends money;

few can indulge in it for nothing. How many slaves an angry master drives to run away or to commit suicide! how much more he loses by his anger than the value of what he originally became angry about! Anger brings grief to a father, divorce to a husband, hatred to a magistrate, failure to a candidate for office. It is worse than luxury, because luxury enjoys its own pleasure, while anger enjoys another's pain. It is worse than either spitefulness or envy; for they wish that someone may become unhappy, while anger wishes to make him so: they are pleased when evil befalls one by accident, but anger cannot wait upon fortune; it desires to injure its victim personally, and is not satisfied merely with his being injured. Nothing is more dangerous than jealousy: it is produced by anger. Nothing is more ruinous than war: it is the outcome of powerful men's anger; and even the anger of humble private persons, though without arms or armies, is nevertheless war. Moreover, even if we pass over its immediate consequences, such as heavy losses, treacherous plots, and the constant anxiety produced by strife, anger pays a penalty at the same moment that it exacts one: it forswears human feelings. The latter urge us to love, anger urges us to hatred: the latter bid us do men good, anger bids us do them harm. Add to this that, although its rage arises from an excessive self-respect and appears to show high spirit, it really is contemptible and mean: for a man must be inferior to one by whom he thinks himself despised, whereas the truly great mind, which takes a true estimate of its own value, does not revenge an insult because it does not feel it. As weapons rebound from a hard surface, and solid substances hurt those who strike them, so also no insult can make a really great mind sensible of its presence, being weaker than that against which it is aimed. How far more glorious is it to throw back all wrongs and insults from oneself, like one wearing armour of proof against all weapons, for revenge is an admission that we have been hurt. That cannot be a great mind which is disturbed by injury. He who has hurt you must be either stronger or weaker than yourself. If he be weaker, spare him: if he be stronger, spare yourself.

6

There is no greater proof of magnanimity than that nothing which befalls you should be able to move you to anger. The higher region of the universe, being more excellently ordered and near to the stars, is never gathered into clouds, driven about by storms, or whirled round by cyclones: it is free from all disturbance: the lightnings flash in the region below it. In like manner a lofty mind, always placid and dwelling in a serene atmosphere, restraining within itself all the impulses from which anger springs, is modest, commands respect, and remains calm and collected: none of which qualities will you find in an angry man: for who, when under the influence of grief and rage, does not first get rid of bashfulness? who, when excited and confused and about to attack someone, does not fling away any habits of shamefacedness he may have possessed? what angry man attends to the number or routine of his duties? who uses moderate language? Who keeps any part of his body quiet? who can guide himself when in full career? We shall find much profit in that sound maxim of Democritus which defines peace of mind to consist in not labouring much, or too much for our strength, either in public or private matters. A man's day, if he is engaged in many various occupations, never passes so happily that no man or no thing should give rise to some offence which makes the mind ripe for anger. Just as when one hurries through the crowded parts of the city one cannot help jostling many people, and one cannot help slipping at one place, being hindered at another, and splashed at another, so when one's life is spent in disconnected pursuits and wanderings, one must meet with many troubles and many accusations. One man deceives our hopes, another delays their fulfillment, another destroys them: our projects do not proceed according to our intention. No one is so favoured by Fortune as to find her always on his side if he tempts her often: and from this it follows that he who sees several enterprises turn out contrary to his wishes becomes dissatisfied with both men and things, and on the slightest provocation flies into a rage with people, with undertakings, with places, with fortune, or with himself. In order, therefore, that the mind may be at peace, it ought not to be hurried hither and thither, nor, as I said before, wearied by labour at great matters, or matters whose attainment is beyond its strength. It is easy to fit one's shoulder to a light burden, and to shift it from one side to the other without dropping it: but we have difficulty in bearing the burdens which others' hands lay upon us, and when overweighted by them we fling them off upon our neighbours. Even when we do stand upright under our load, we nevertheless reel beneath a weight which is beyond our strength.

7

Be assured that the same rule applies both to public and private life: simple and manageable undertakings proceed according to the pleasure of the person in charge of them, but enormous ones, beyond his capacity to manage, are not easily undertaken. When he has got them to administer, they hinder him, and press hard upon him, and just as he thinks that success is within his grasp, they collapse, and carry him with them: thus it comes about that a man's wishes are often disappointed if he does not apply himself to easy tasks, yet wishes that the tasks which he undertakes may be easy. Whenever you would attempt anything, first form an estimate both of your own powers, of the extent of the matter which you are undertaking, and of the means by which you are to accomplish it: for if you have to abandon your work when it is half done, the disappointment will sour your temper. In such cases, it makes a difference whether one is of an ardent or of a cold and unenterprising temperament: for failure will rouse a generous spirit to anger, and will move a sluggish and dull one to sorrow. Let our undertakings, therefore, be neither petty nor yet presumptuous and reckless: let our hopes not range far from home: let us attempt nothing which if we succeed will make us astonished at our success.

8

Since we know not how to endure an injury, let us take care not to receive one: we should live with the quietest and easiest-tempered persons, not with anxious or with sullen ones: for our own habits are copied from those with whom we associate, and just as some bodily diseases are communicated by touch, so also the mind transfers its vices to its neighbours. A drunkard leads even those who reproach him to grow fond of wine: profligate society will, if permitted, impair the morals even of robust-minded men: avarice infects those nearest it with its poison. Virtues do the same thing in the opposite direction, and improve all those with whom they are brought in contact: it is as good for one of unsettled principles to associate with better men than himself as for an invalid to live in a warm country with a healthy climate. You will understand how much may be effected this way, if you observe how even wild beasts grow tame by dwelling among us, and how no animal, however ferocious, continues to be wild, if it has long been accustomed to human companionship: all its savageness becomes softened, and amid peaceful scenes is gradually forgotten. We must add to this, that the man who lives with quiet people is not only improved by their example, but also by the fact that he finds no reason for anger and does not practise his vice: it will, therefore, be his duty to avoid all those who he knows will excite his anger. You ask, who these are: many will bring about the same thing by various means; a proud man will offend you by his disdain, a talkative man by his abuse, an impudent man by his insults, a spiteful man by his malice, a quarrelsome man by his wrangling, a braggart and liar by his vain-gloriousness: you will not endure to be feared by a suspicious man, conquered by an obstinate one, or scorned by an ultra-refined one: Choose straightforward, good-natured, steady people, who will not provoke your wrath, and will bear with it. Those whose dispositions are yielding, polite and suave, will be of even greater service, provided they do not flatter, for excessive obsequiousness irritates bad-tempered men. One of my own friends was a good man indeed, but too prone to anger, and it was as dangerous to flatter him as to curse him. Caelius the orator, it is well known, was the worst-tempered man possible. It is said that once he was dining in his own chamber with an especially long-suffering client, but had great difficulty when thrown thus into a man's society to avoid quarrelling with him. The other thought it best to agree to whatever he said, and to play second fiddle, but Caelius could not bear his obsequious agreement, and exclaimed, "Do contradict me in something, that there may be two of us!" Yet even he, who was angry at not being angry, soon recovered his temper, because he had no one to fight with. If, then, we are conscious of an irascible disposition, let us especially choose for our friends those who will look and speak as we do: they will pamper us and lead us into a bad habit of listening to nothing that does not please us, but it will be good to give our anger respite and repose. Even those who are naturally crabbed and wild will yield to caresses: no creature continues either angry or frightened if you pat him. Whenever a controversy seems likely to be longer or more keenly disputed than usual, let us check its first beginnings, before it gathers strength. A dispute nourishes itself as it proceeds, and takes hold of those who plunge too deeply into it: it is easier to stand aloof than to extricate oneself from a struggle.

9

Irascible men ought not to meddle with the more serious class of occupations, or, at any rate, ought to stop short of weariness in the pursuit of them; their mind ought not to be engaged upon hard subjects, but handed over to pleasing arts: let it be softened by reading poetry, and interested by legendary history: let it be treated with luxury and refinement. Pythagoras used to calm his troubled spirit by playing upon the lyre: and who does not know that trumpets and clarions are irritants, just as some airs are lullabies and soothe the mind? Green is good for wearied eyes, and some colours are grateful to weak sight, while the brightness of others is painful to it. In the same way cheerful pursuits soothe unhealthy minds. We must avoid law courts, pleadings, verdicts, and everything else that aggravates our fault, and we ought no less to avoid bodily weariness; for it exhausts all that is quiet and gentle in us, and rouses bitterness. For this reason those who cannot trust their digestion, when they are about to transact business of importance always allay their bile with food, for it is peculiarly irritated by fatigue, either because it draws the vital heat into the middle of the body, and injures the blood and stops its circulation by the clogging of the veins, or else because the worn-out and weakened body reacts upon the mind: this is certainly the reason why those who are broken by ill health or age are more irascible than other men. Hunger also and thirst should be avoided for the same reason; they exasperate and irritate men's minds: it is an old saying that "a weary man is quarrelsome": and so also is a hungry or a thirsty man, or one who is suffering from any cause whatever: for just as sores pain one at the slightest touch, and afterwards even at the fear of being touched, so an unsound mind takes offence at the slightest things, so that even a greeting, a letter, a speech, or a question, provokes some men to anger.

10

That which is diseased can never bear to be handled without complaining: it is best, therefore, to apply remedies to oneself as soon as we feel that anything is wrong, to allow oneself as little licence as possible in speech, and to restrain one's impetuosity: now it is easy to detect the first growth of our passions: the symptoms precede the disorder. Just as the signs of storms and rain come before the storms themselves, so there are certain forerunners of anger, love, and all the storms which torment our minds. Those who suffer from epilepsy know that the fit is coming on if their extremities become cold, their sight fails, their sinews tremble, their memory deserts them, and their head swims: they accordingly check the growing disorder by applying the usual remedies: they try to prevent the loss of their senses by smelling or tasting some drug; they battle against cold and stiffness of limbs by hot fomentations; or, if all remedies fail, they retire apart, and faint where no one sees them fall. It is useful for a man to understand his disease, and to break its strength before it becomes developed. Let us see what it is that especially irritates us. Some men take offence at insulting words, others at deeds: one wishes his pedigree, another his person, to be treated with respect. This man wishes to be considered especially fashionable, that man to be thought especially learned: one cannot bear pride, another cannot bear obstinacy. One thinks it beneath him to be angry with his slaves, another is cruel at home, but gentle abroad. One imagines that he is proposed for office because he is unpopular, another thinks himself insulted because he is not proposed. People do not all take offence in the same way; you ought then to know what your own weak point is, that you may guard it with especial care.

11

It is better not to see or to hear everything: many causes of offence may pass by us, most of which are disregarded by the man who ignores them. Would you not be irascible? then be not inquisitive. He who seeks to know what is said about him, who digs up spiteful tales even if they were told in secret, is himself the destroyer of his own peace of mind. Some stories may be so construed as to appear to be insults: wherefore it is best to put some aside, to laugh at others, and to pardon others. There are many ways in which anger may be checked; most things may be turned into jest. It is said that Socrates when he was given a box on the ear, merely said that it was a pity a man could not tell when he ought to wear his helmet out walking. It does not so much matter how an injury is done, as how it is borne; and I do not see how moderation can be hard to practise, when I know that even despots, though success and impunity combine to swell their pride, have sometimes restrained their natural ferocity. At any rate, tradition informs us that once, when a guest in his cups bitterly reproached Pisistratus, the despot of Athens, for his cruelty, many of those present offered to lay hands on the traitor, and one said one thing and one another to kindle his wrath, he bore it coolly, and replied to those who were egging him on, that he was no more angry with the man than he should be with one who ran against him blindfold.

12

A large part of mankind manufacture their own grievances either by entertaining unfounded suspicions or by exaggerating trifles. Anger often comes to us, but we often go to it. It ought never to be sent for: even when it falls in our way it ought to be flung aside. No one says to himself, "I myself have done or might have done this very thing which I am angry with another for doing." No one considers the intention of the doer, but merely the thing done: yet we ought to think about him, and whether he did it intentionally or accidentally, under compulsion or under a mistake, whether he did it out of hatred for us, or to gain something for himself, whether he did it to please himself or to serve a friend. In some cases the age, in others the worldly fortunes of the culprit may render it humane or advantageous to bear with him and put up with what he has done. Let us put ourselves in the place of him with whom we are angry: at present an overweening conceit of our own importance makes us prone to anger, and we are quite willing to do to others what we cannot endure should be done to ourselves. No one will postpone his anger: yet delay is the best remedy for it, because it allows its first glow to subside, and gives time for the cloud which darkens the mind either to disperse or at any rate to become less dense. Of these wrongs which drive you frantic, some will grow lighter after an interval, not of a day, but even of an hour: some will vanish altogether. Even if you gain nothing by your adjournment, still what you do after it will appear to be the result of mature deliberation, not of anger. If you want to find out the truth about anything, commit the task to time: nothing can be accurately discerned at a time of disturbance. Plato, when angry with his slave, could not prevail upon himself to wait, but straightaway ordered him to take off his shirt and present his shoulders to the blows which he meant to give him with his own hand: then, when he perceived that he was angry, he stopped the hand which he had raised in the air, and stood like one in act to strike. Being asked by a friend who happened to come in, what he was doing, he answered: "I am making an angry man expiate his crime." He retained the posture of one about to give way to passion, as if struck with astonishment at its being so degrading to a philosopher, forgetting the slave, because he had found another still more deserving of punishment. He therefore denied himself the exercise of authority over his own household, and once, being rather angry at some fault, said, "Speusippus, will you please to correct that slave with stripes; for I am in a rage." He would not strike him, for the very reason for which another man would have struck him. "I am in a rage," said he; "I should beat him more than I ought: I should take more pleasure than I ought in doing so: let not that slave fall into the power of one who is not in his own power." Can anyone wish to grant the power of revenge to an angry man, when Plato himself gave up his own right to exercise it? While you are angry, you ought not to be allowed to do anything. "Why?" do you ask? Because when you are angry there is nothing that you do not wish to be allowed to do.

13

Fight hard with yourself, and if you cannot conquer anger, do not let it conquer you: you have begun to get the better of it if it does not show itself, if it is not given vent. Let us conceal its symptoms, and as far as possible keep it secret and hidden. It will give us great trouble to do this, for it is eager to burst forth, to kindle our eyes and to transform our face; but if we allow it to show itself in our outward appearance, it is our master. Let it rather be locked in the innermost recesses of our breast, and be borne by us, not bear us: nay, let us replace all its symptoms by their opposites; let us make our countenance more composed than usual, our voice milder, our step slower. Our inward thoughts gradually become influenced by our outward demeanour. With Socrates it was a sign of anger when he lowered his voice, and became sparing of speech; it was evident at such times that he was exercising restraint over himself. His friends, consequently, used to detect him acting thus, and convict him of being angry; nor was he displeased at being charged with concealment of anger; indeed, how could he help being glad that many men should perceive his anger, yet that none should feel it? they would however, have felt it had not he granted to his friends the same right of criticizing his own conduct which he himself assumed over theirs. How much more needful is it for us to do this? let us beg all our best friends to give us their opinion with the greatest freedom at the very time when we can bear it least, and never to be compliant with us when we are angry. While we are in our right senses, while we are under our own control, let us call for help against so powerful an evil, and one which we regard with such unjust favour. Those who cannot carry their wine discreetly, and fear to be betrayed into some rash and insolent act, give their slaves orders to take them away from the banquet when they are drunk; those who know by experience how unreasonable they are when sick give orders that no one is to obey them when they are in ill health. It is best to prepare obstacles beforehand for vices which are known, and above all things so to tranquilize our mind that it may bear the most sudden and violent shocks either without feeling anger, or, if anger be provoked by the extent of some unexpected wrong, that it may bury it deep, and not betray its wound. That it is possible to do this will be seen, if I quote a few of an abundance of examples, from which we may learn both how much evil there is in anger, when it exercises entire dominion over men in supreme power, and how completely it can control itself when overawed by fear.

14

King Cambyses[54] was excessively addicted to wine. Præxaspes was the only one of his closest friends who advised him to drink more sparingly, pointing out how shameful a thing drunkenness was in a king, upon whom all eyes and ears were fixed. Cambyses answered, "That you may know that I never lose command of myself, I will presently prove to you that both my eyes and my hands are fit for service after I have been drinking." Hereupon he drank more freely than usual, using larger cups, and when heavy and besotted with wine ordered his reprover's son to go beyond the threshold and stand there with his left hand raised above

---

[54] Heroditus, iii, 34, 35.

his head; then he bent his bow and pierced the youth's heart, at which he had said that he aimed. He then had his breast cut open, showed the arrow sticking exactly into the heart, and, looking at the boy's father, asked whether his hand was not steady enough. He replied that Apollo himself could not have taken better aim. God confound such a man, a slave in mind, if not in station! He actually praised an act which he ought not to have endured to witness. He thought that the breast of his son being torn asunder, and his heart quivering with its wound, gave him an opportunity of making a complimentary speech. He ought to have raised a dispute with him about his success, and have called for another shot, that the king might be pleased to prove upon the person of the father that his hand was even steadier than when he shot the son. What a savage king! what a worthy mark for all his follower's arrows! Yet though we curse him for making his banquet end in cruelty and death, still it was worse to praise that arrow-shot than to shoot it. We shall see hereafter how a father ought to bear himself when standing over the corpse of his son, whose murder he had both caused and witnessed: the matter which we are now discussing, has been proved, I mean, that anger can be suppressed. He did not curse the king, he did not so much as let fall a single inauspicious word, though he felt his own heart as deeply wounded as that of his son. He may be said to have done well in choking down his words; for though he might have spoken as an angry man, yet he could not have expressed what he felt as a father. He may, I repeat, be thought to have behaved with greater wisdom on that occasion than when he tried to regulate the drink of one who was better employed in drinking wine than in drinking blood, and who granted men peace while his hands were busy with the wine cup. He, therefore, added one more to the number of those who have shown to their bitter cost how little kings care for their friends' good advice.

15

I have no doubt that Harpagus must have given some such advice to the king of the Persians and of himself, in anger at which the king placed Harpagus's own children before him on the dinner-table for him to eat, and asked him from time to time, whether he liked the seasoning. Then, when he saw that he was satiated with his own misery, he ordered their heads to be brought to him, and asked him how he liked his entertainment. The wretched man did not lose his readiness of speech; his face did not change. "Every kind of dinner," said he, "is pleasant at the king's table." What did he gain by this obsequiousness? He avoided being invited a second time to dinner, to eat what was left of them. I do not forbid a father to blame the act of his king, or to seek for some revenge worthy of so bloodthirsty a monster, but in the meanwhile I gather from the tale this fact, that even the anger which arises from unheard of outrages can be concealed, and forced into using language which is the very reverse of its meaning. This way of curbing anger is necessary, at least for those who have chosen this sort of life and who are admitted to dine at a king's table; this is how they must eat and drink, this is how they must answer, and how they must laugh at their own deaths. Whether life is worth having at such a price, we shall see hereafter; that is another question. Let us not console so sorry a crew, or encourage them to submit to the orders of their butchers; let us point out that however slavish a man's condition may be, there is always a path to liberty open to him, unless his mind be diseased. It is a man's own fault if he suffers, when by putting an end to himself he can put an end to his misery. To him whose king aimed arrows at the breasts of his friends, and to him whose master gorged fathers with the hearts of their children, I would say "Madman, why do you groan? for what are you waiting? for some enemy to avenge you by the destruction of your entire nation, or for some powerful king to arrive from a distant land? Wherever you turn your eyes you may see an end to your woes. Do you see that precipice? Down that lies the road to liberty; do you see that sea? that river? that well? Liberty sits at the bottom of them. Do you see that tree? stunted, blighted, dried up though it be, yet liberty hangs from its branches. Do you see your own throat, your own neck, your own heart? they are so many ways of escape from slavery. Are these modes which I point out too laborious, and needing much strength and courage? do you ask what path leads to liberty? I answer, any vein[55] in your body."

16

As long, however, as we find nothing in our life so unbearable as to drive us to suicide, let us, in whatever position we may be, set anger far from us: it is destructive to those who are its slaves. All its rage turns to its own misery, and authority becomes all the more irksome the more obstinately it is resisted. It is like a wild animal whose struggles only pull the noose by which it is caught tighter; or like birds who, while flurriedly trying to shake themselves free, smear birdlime onto all their feathers. No yoke is so grievous as not to hurt him who struggles against it more than him who yields to it: the only way to alleviate great evils is to endure them and to submit to do what they compel. This control of our passions, and especially of this mad and unbridled passion of anger, is useful to subjects, but still more useful to kings. All is lost when a man's position enables him to carry out whatever anger prompts him to do; nor can power long endure if it be exercised to the injury of many, for it becomes endangered as soon as common fear draws together those who bewail themselves separately. Many kings, therefore, have fallen victims, some to single individuals, others to entire peoples, who have been forced by general indignation to make one man the minister of their wrath. Yet many kings have indulged their anger as though it were a privilege of royalty,

---

[55] Seneca's own death, by opening his veins, gives a melancholy interest to this passage.

like Darius, who, after the dethronement of the Magian, was the first ruler of the Persians and of the greater part of the East: for when he declared war[56] against the Scythians who bordered on the empire of the East, Oeobazus, an aged noble, begged that one of his three sons might be left at home to comfort his father, and that the king might be satisfied with the services of two of them. Darius promised him more than he asked for, saying that he would allow all three to remain at home, and flung their dead bodies before their father's eyes. He would have been harsh, had he taken them all to the war with him. How much more good-natured was Xerxes,[57] who, when Pythias, the father of five sons, begged for one to be excused from service, permitted him to choose which he wished for. He then tore the son whom the father had chosen into two halves, placed one on each side of the road, and, as it were, purified his army by means of this propitiatory victim. He therefore had the end which he deserved, being defeated, and his army scattered far and wide in utter rout, while he in the midst of it walked among the corpses of his soldiers, seeing on all sides the signs of his own overthrow.

17

So ferocious in their anger were those kings who had no learning, no tincture of polite literature: now I will show you King Alexander (the Great), fresh from the lap of Aristotle, who with his own hand while at table stabbed Clitus, his dearest friend, who had been brought up with him, because he did not flatter him enough, and was too slow in transforming himself from a free man and a Macedonian into a Persian slave. Indeed he shut up Lysimachus,[58] who was no less his friend than Clitus, in a cage with a lion; yet did this make Lysimachus, who escaped by some happy chance from the lion's teeth, any gentler when he became a king? Why, he mutilated his own friend, Telesphorus the Rhodian, cutting off his nose and ears, and kept him for a long while in a den, like some new and strange animal, after the hideousness of his hacked and disfigured face had made him no longer appear to be human, assisted by starvation and the squalid filth of a body left to wallow in its own dung! Besides this, his hands and knees, which the narrowness of his abode forced him to use instead of his feet, became hard and callous, while his sides were covered with sores by rubbing against the walls, so that his appearance was no less shocking than frightful, and his punishment turned him into so monstrous a creature that he was not even pitied. Yet, however unlike a man he was who suffered this, even more unlike was he who inflicted it.

---

[56] Heroditus, iv, 84.
[57] Heroditus, vii, 38, 39.
[58] Plutarch, *Life of Demetrius*, 27.

18

Would to heaven that such savagery had contented itself with foreign examples, and that barbarity in anger and punishment had not been imported with other outlandish vices into our Roman manners! Marcus Marius, to whom the people erected a statue in every street, to whom they made offerings of incense and wine, had, by the command of Lucius Sulla, his legs broken, his eyes pulled out, his hands cut off, and his whole body gradually torn to pieces limb by limb, as if Sulla killed him as many times as he wounded him. Who was it who carried out Sulla's orders? who but Catiline, already practising his hands in every sort of wickedness? He tore him to pieces before the tomb of Quintus Catulus, an unwelcome burden to the ashes of that gentlest of men, above which one who was no doubt a criminal, yet nevertheless the idol of the people, and who was not undeserving of love, although men loved him beyond all reason, was forced to shed his blood drop by drop. Though Marius deserved such tortures, yet it was worthy of Sulla to order them, and of Catiline to execute them; but it was unworthy of the State to be stabbed by the swords of her enemy and her avenger alike. Why do I pry into ancient history? quite lately Gaius Caesar flogged and tortured Sextus Papinius, whose father was a consular, Betilienas Bassus, his own quaestor, and several others, both senators and knights, on the same day, not to carry out any judicial inquiry, but merely to amuse himself. Indeed, so impatient was he of any delay in receiving the pleasure which his monstrous cruelty never delayed in asking, that when walking with some ladies and senators in his mother's gardens, along the walk between the colonnade and the river, he struck off some of their heads by lamplight. What did he fear? what public or private danger could one night threaten him with? how very small a favour it would have been to wait until morning, and not to kill the Roman people's senators in his slippers?

19

It is to the purpose that we should know how haughtily his cruelty was exercised, although someone might suppose that we are wandering from the subject and embarking on a digression; but this digression is itself connected with unusual outbursts of anger. He beat senators with rods; he did it so often that he made men able to say, "It is the custom." He tortured them with all the most dismal engines in the world, with the cord, the boots, the rack, the fire, and the sight of his own face. Even to this we may answer, "To tear three senators to pieces with stripes and fire like criminal slaves was no such great crime for one who had thoughts of butchering the entire Senate, who was wont to wish that the Roman people had but one neck, that he might concentrate into one day and one blow all the wickedness which he divided among so many places and times. Was there ever anything so unheard-of as an execution in the nighttime? Highway robbery seeks for the shelter of darkness, but the more public an execution is, the more power it has as an example and lesson. Here I shall be met by: "This, which you are so surprised at, was the daily habit of that monster; this was what he lived for, watched for, sat up at night for." Certainly one could find no one else who would have ordered all those whom he condemned to death to have their mouths closed by a sponge being fastened in them, that they might not have the power even of uttering a sound. What dying man was ever forbidden to groan? He feared that the last agony might find too free a voice, that he might hear what would displease him. He knew, moreover, that there were countless crimes, with which none but a dying man would dare to reproach him. When sponges were not forthcoming, he ordered the wretched men's clothes to be torn up, and the rags stuffed into their mouths. What savagery was this? Let a man draw his last breath: give room for his soul to escape through: let it not be forced to leave the body through a wound. It becomes tedious to add to this that in the same night he sent centurions to the houses of the executed men and made an end of their fathers also, that is to say, being a compassionate-minded man, he set them free from sorrow: for it is not my intention to describe the ferocity of Gaius, but the ferocity of anger, which does not merely vent its rage upon individuals, but rends in pieces whole nations, and even lashes cities, rivers, and things which have no sense of pain.

20

Thus, the king of the Persians cut off the noses of a whole nation in Syria, wherefore the place is called Rhinocolura. Do you think that he was merciful, because he did not cut their heads off altogether? no, he was delighted at having invented a new kind of punishment. Something of the same kind would have befallen the Æthiopians,[59] who on account of their prodigiously long lives are called Macrobiotae; for, because they did not receive slavery with hands uplifted to heaven in thankfulness, and sent an embassy which used independent, or what kings call insulting language, Cambyses became wild with rage, and, without any store of provisions, or any knowledge of the roads, started with all his fighting men through an arid and trackless waste, where during the first day's march the necessaries of life failed, and the country itself furnished nothing, being barren and uncultivated, and untrodden by the foot of man. At first the tenderest parts of leaves and shoots of trees relieved their hunger, then hides softened by fire, and anything else that their extremity drove them to use as food. When as they proceeded neither roots nor herbs were to be found in the sand, and they found a wilderness destitute even of animal life, they chose each tenth man by lot and made of him a meal which was more cruel than hunger. Rage still drove the king madly forwards, until after he had lost one part of his army and eaten another he began to fear that he also might be called upon to draw the lot for

---

[59] Heroditus, iii, 17, sqq.

his life; then at last he gave the order for retreat. Yet all the while his well-bred hawks were not sacrificed, and the means of feasting were carried for him on camels, while his soldiers were drawing lots for who should miserably perish, and who should yet more miserably live.

21

This man was angry with an unknown and inoffensive nation, which nevertheless was able to feel his wrath; but Cyrus[60] was angry with a river. When hurrying to besiege Babylon, since in making war it is above all things important to seize one's opportunity, he tried to ford the widespread river Gyndes, which it is hardly safe to attempt even when the river has been dried up by the summer heat and is at its lowest. Here one of the white horses which drew the royal chariot was washed away, and his loss moved the king to such violent rage, that he swore to reduce the river which had carried off his royal retinue to so low an ebb that even women should walk across it and trample upon it. He thereupon devoted all the resources of his army to this object, and remained working until by cutting one hundred and eighty channels across the bed of the river he divided it into three hundred and sixty brooks, and left the bed dry, the waters flowing through other channels. Thus he lost time, which is very important in great operations, and lost, also, the soldiers' courage, which was broken by useless labour, and the opportunity of falling upon his enemy unprepared, while he was waging against the river the war which he had declared against his foes. This frenzy, for what else can you call it, has befallen Romans also, for G. Caesar destroyed a most beautiful villa at Herculaneum because his mother was once imprisoned in it, and has thus made the place notorious by its misfortune; for while it stood, we used to sail past it without noticing it, but now people inquire why it is in ruins.

22

These should be regarded as examples to be avoided, and what I am about to relate, on the contrary, to be followed, being examples of gentle and lenient conduct in men who both had reasons for anger and power to avenge themselves. What could have been easier than for Antigonus to order those two common soldiers to be executed who leaned against their king's tent while doing what all men especially love to do, and run the greatest danger by doing, I mean while they spoke evil of their king. Antigonus heard all they said, as was likely, since there was only a piece of cloth between the speakers and the listener, who gently raised it, and said, "Go a little further off, for fear the king should hear you." He also on one night, hearing some of his soldiers invoking everything that was evil upon their king for having

---

[60] Heroditus, i, 189, 190.

brought them along that road and into that impassable mud, went to those who were in the greatest difficulties, and having extricated them without their knowing who was their helper, said, "Now curse Antigonus, by whose fault you have fallen into this trouble, but bless the man who has brought you out of this slough." This same Antigonus bore the abuse of his enemies as good-naturedly as that of his countrymen; thus when he was besieging some Greeks in a little fort, and they, despising their enemy through their confidence in the strength of their position, cut many jokes upon the ugliness of Antigonus, at one time mocking him for his shortness of stature, at another for his broken nose, he answered, "I rejoice, and expect some good fortune because I have a Silenus in my camp." After he had conquered these witty folk by hunger, his treatment of them was to form regiments of those who were fit for service, and sell the rest by public auction; nor would he, said he, have done this had it not been better that men who had such evil tongues should be under the control of a master.

23

This man's grandson[61] was Alexander, who used to hurl his lance at his guests, who, of the two friends which I have mentioned above, exposed one to the rage of a wild beast, and the other to his own; yet of these two men, he who was exposed to the lion survived. He did not derive this vice from his grandfather, nor even from his father; for it was an especial virtue of Philip's to endure insults patiently, and was a great safeguard of his kingdom. Demochares, who was surnamed Parrhesiastes on account of his unbridled and impudent tongue, came on an embassy to him with other ambassadors from Athens. After graciously listening to what they had to say, Philip said to them, "Tell me, what can I do that will please the Athenians?" Demochares took him up, and answered, "Hang yourself." All the bystanders expressed their indignation at so brutal an answer, but Philip bade them be silent, and let this Thersites depart safe and sound. "But do you," said he, "you other ambassadors, tell the Athenians that those who say such things are much more arrogant than those who hear them without revenging themselves." The late Emperor Augustus also did and said many memorable things, which prove that he was not under the dominion of anger. Timagenes, the historical writer, made some remarks upon him, his wife, and his whole family: nor did his jests fall to the ground, for nothing spreads more widely or is more in people's mouths than reckless wit. Caesar often warned him to be less audacious in his talk, and as he continued to offend, forbade him his house. Timagenes after this passed the later years of his life as the guest of Asinius Pollio, and was the favourite of the whole city: the closing of Caesar's door did not close any other door against him. He read aloud the history which he wrote after this, but burned the books which contained

---

[61] A mistake: Antigonus (Monophthalmus) was one of Alexander's generals.

the doings of Augustus Caesar. He was at enmity with Caesar, but yet no one feared to be his friend, no one shrank from him as though he were blasted by lightning: although he fell from so high a place, yet someone was found to catch him in his lap. Caesar, I say, bore this with patience, and was not even irritated by the historian's having laid violent hands upon his own glories and acts: he never complained of the man who afforded his enemy shelter, but merely said to Asinius Pollio, "You are keeping a wild beast:" then, when the other would have excused his conduct, he stopped him, and said "Enjoy, my Pollio, enjoy his friendship." When Pollio said, "If you order me, Caesar, I will straightaway forbid him my house," he answered, "Do you think that I am likely to do this, after having made you friends again?" for formerly Pollio had been angry with Timagenes, and ceased to be angry with him for no other reason than that Caesar began to be so.

24

Let everyone, then, say to himself, whenever he is provoked, "Am I more powerful than Philip? yet he allowed a man to curse him with impunity. Have I more authority in my own house than the Emperor Augustus possessed throughout the world? yet he was satisfied with leaving the society of his maligner. Why should I make my slave atone by stripes and manacles for having answered me too loudly or having put on a stubborn look, or muttered something which I did not catch? Who am I, that it should be a crime to shock my ears? Many men have forgiven their enemies: shall I not forgive men for being lazy, careless, and gossipping?" We ought to plead age as an excuse for children, sex for women, freedom for a stranger, familiarity for a houseservant. Is this his first offence? think how long he has been acceptable. Has he often done wrong, and in many other cases? then let us continue to bear what we have borne so long. Is he a friend? then he did not intend to do it. Is he an enemy? then in doing it he did his duty. If he be a sensible man, let us believe his excuses; if a fool, let us grant him pardon; whatever he may be, let us say to ourselves on his behalf, that even the wisest of men are often in fault, that no one is so alert that his carefulness never betrays itself, that no one is of so ripe a judgment that his serious mind cannot be goaded by circumstances into some hotheaded action, that, in fine, no one, however much he may fear to give offence, can help doing so even while he tries to avoid it.

25

As it is a consolation to a humble man in trouble that the greatest are subject to reverses of fortune, and a man weeps more calmly over his dead son in the corner of his hovel if he sees a piteous[62] funeral proceed out of the palace as well; so one bears injury or insult more calmly if one remembers that no power is so great as to be above the reach

---

[62] *Acerbum* = ἄωρον; the funeral of one who has been cut off in the flower of this youth.

of harm. Indeed, if even the wisest do wrong, who cannot plead a good excuse for his faults? Let us look back upon our own youth, and think how often we then were too slothful in our duty, too impudent in our speech, too intemperate in our cups. Is anyone angry? then let us give him enough time to reflect upon what he has done, and he will correct his own self. But suppose he ought to pay the penalty of his deeds: well, that is no reason why we should act as he does. It cannot be doubted that he who regards his tormentor with contempt raises himself above the common herd and looks down upon them from a loftier position: it is the property of true magnanimity not to feel the blows which it may receive. So does a huge wild beast turn slowly and gaze at yelping curs: so does the wave dash in vain against a great cliff. The man who is not angry remains unshaken by injury: he who is angry has been moved by it. He, however, whom I have described as being placed too high for any mischief to reach him, holds as it were the highest good in his arms: he can reply, not only to any man, but to Fortune herself: "Do what you will, you are too feeble to disturb my serenity: this is forbidden by reason, to whom I have entrusted the guidance of my life: to become angry would do me more harm than your violence can do me. 'More harm?' say you. Yes, certainly: I know how much injury you have done me, but I cannot tell to what excesses anger might not carry me."

26

You say, "I cannot endure it: injuries are hard to bear." You lie; for how can anyone not be able to bear injury, if he can bear to be angry? Besides, what you intend to do is to endure both injury and anger. Why do you bear with the delirium of a sick man, or the ravings of a madman, or the impudent blows of a child? Because, of course, they evidently do not know what they are doing: a man be not responsible for his actions, what does it matter by what malady he became so: the plea of ignorance holds equally good in every case. "What then?" say you, "shall he not be punished?" He will be, even supposing that you do not wish it: for the greatest punishment for having done harm is the sense of having done it, and no one is more severely punished than he who is given over to the punishment of remorse. In the next place, we ought to consider the whole state of mankind, in order to pass a just judgment on all the occurrences of life: for it is unjust to blame individuals for a vice which is common to all. The colour of an Æthiop is not remarkable amongst his own people, nor is any man in Germany ashamed of red hair rolled into a knot.

You cannot call anything peculiar or disgraceful in a particular man if it is the general characteristic of his nation. Now, the cases which I have quoted are defended only by the usage of one out-of-the-way quarter of the world: see now, how far more deserving of pardon those crimes are which are spread abroad among all mankind. We all are hasty and careless, we all are untrustworthy, dissatisfied, and ambitious: nay, why do I try to hide our common wickedness by a too partial description? we all are bad. Every one of us therefore will find in his own breast the vice which he blames in another. Why do you remark how pale this man, or how lean that man is? there is a general pestilence. Let us therefore be more gentle one to another: we are bad men, living among bad men: there is only one thing which can afford us peace, and that is to agree to forgive one another. "This man has already injured me," say you, "and I have not yet injured him." No, but you have probably injured someone else, and you will injure him some day. Do not form your judgment by one hour, or one day: consider the whole tendency of your mind: even though you have done no evil, yet you are capable of doing it.

27

How far better is it to heal an injury than to avenge it? Revenge takes up much time, and throws itself in the way of many injuries while it is smarting under one. We all retain our anger longer than we feel our hurt: how far better it were to take the opposite course and not meet one mischief by another. Would anyone think himself to be in his perfect mind if he were to return kicks to a mule or bites to a dog? "These creatures," you say, "know not that they are doing wrong." Then, in the first place, what an unjust judge you must be if a man has less chance of gaining your forgiveness than a beast! Secondly, if animals are protected from your anger by their want of reason, you ought to treat all foolish men in the like manner: for if a man has that mental darkness which excuses all the wrongdoings of dumb animals, what difference does it make if in other respects he be unlike a dumb animal? He has sinned. Well, is this the first time, or will this be the last time? Why, you should not believe him even if he said, "Never will I do so again." He will sin, and another will sin against him, and all his life he will wallow in wickedness. Savagery must be met by kindness: we ought to use, to a man in anger, the argument which is so effective with one in grief, that is, "Shall you leave off this at some time, or never? If you will do so at some time, how better is it that you should abandon anger than that anger should abandon you? Or, will this excitement never leave you? Do you see to what an unquiet life you condemn yourself? for what will be the life of one who is always swelling with rage?" Add to this, that after you have worked yourself up into a rage, and have from time to time renewed the causes of your excitement, yet your anger will depart from you of its own accord, and time will sap its strength: how much better then is it that it should be overcome by you than by itself?

28

If you are angry, you will quarrel first with this man, and then with that: first with slaves, then with freedmen: first with parents, then with children: first with acquaintances, then with strangers: for there are grounds for anger in every case, unless your mind steps in and intercedes with you: your frenzy will drag you from one place to another, and from thence to elsewhere, your madness will constantly meet with newly-occurring irritants, and will never depart from you. Tell me, miserable man, what time you will have for loving? O, what good time you are wasting on an evil thing! How much better it would be to win friends, and disarm enemies: to serve the State, or to busy oneself with one's private affairs, rather than to cast about for what harm you can do to somebody, what wound you can inflict either upon his social position, his fortune, or his person, although you cannot succeed in doing so without a struggle and risk to yourself, even if your antagonist be inferior to you. Even supposing that he were handed over to you in chains, and that you were at liberty to torture him as much as you please, yet even then excessive violence in striking a blow often causes us to dislocate a joint, or entangles a sinew in the teeth which it has broken. Anger makes many men cripples, or invalids, even when it meets with an unresisting victim: and besides this, no creature is so weak that it can be destroyed without any danger to its destroyer: sometimes grief, sometimes chance, puts the weakest on a level with the strongest. What shall we say of the fact that the greater part of the things which enrage us are insults, not injuries? It makes a great difference whether a man thwarts my wishes or merely fails to carry them out, whether he robs me or does not give me anything: yet we count it all the same whether a man takes anything from us or refuses to give anything to us, whether he extinguishes our hope or defers it, whether his object be to hinder us or to help himself, whether he acts out of love for someone or out of hatred for us. Some men are bound to oppose us not only on the ground of justice, but of honour: one is defending his father, another his brother, another his country, another his friend: yet we do not forgive men for doing what we should blame them for not doing; nay, though one can hardly believe it, we often think well of an act, and ill of the man who did it. But, by Hercules, a great and just man looks with respect at the bravest of his enemies, and the most obstinate defender of his freedom and his country, and wishes that he had such a man for his own countryman and soldier.

29

It is shameful to hate him whom you praise: but how much more shameful is it to hate a man for something for which he deserves to be pitied? If a prisoner of war, who has suddenly been reduced to the condition of a slave, still retains some remnants of liberty, and does not run nimbly to perform foul and toilsome tasks, if, having grown slothful by long rest, he cannot run fast enough to keep pace with his master's horse or carriage, if sleep overpowers him when weary with many days and nights of watching, if he refuses to undertake farm work, or does not do it heartily when brought away from the idleness of city service and put to hard labour, we ought to make a distinction between whether a man cannot or will not do it: we should pardon many slaves, if we began to judge them before we began to be angry with them: as it is, however, we obey our first impulse, and then, although we may prove to have been excited about mere trifles, yet we continue to be angry, lest we should seem to have begun to be angry without cause; and, most unjust of all, the injustice of our anger makes us persist in it all the more; for we nurse it and inflame it, as though to be violently angry proved our anger to be just.

30

How much better is it to observe how trifling, how inoffensive are the first beginnings of anger? You will see that men are subject to the same influences as dumb animals: we are put out by trumpery, futile matters. Bulls are excited by red colour, the asp raises its head at a shadow, bears or lions are irritated at the shaking of a rag, and all creatures who are naturally fierce and wild are alarmed at trifles. The same thing befalls men both of restless and of sluggish disposition; they are seized by suspicions, sometimes to such an extent that they call slight benefits injuries: and these form the most common and certainly the most bitter subject for anger: for we become angry with our dearest friends for having bestowed less upon us than we expected, and less than others have received from them: yet there is a remedy at hand for both these grievances. Has he favoured our rival more than ourselves? then let us enjoy what we have without making any comparisons. A man will never be well off to whom it is a torture to see anyone better off than himself. Have I less than I hoped for? well, perhaps I hoped for more than I ought. This it is against which we ought to be especially on our guard: from hence arises the most destructive anger, sparing nothing, not even the holiest. The Emperor Julius was not stabbed by so many enemies as by friends whose insatiable hopes he had not satisfied. He was willing enough to do so, for no one ever made a more generous use of victory, of whose fruits he kept nothing for himself save the power of distributing them; but how could he glut such unconscionable appetites, when each man coveted as much as any one man could possess? This was why he saw his fellow-soldiers standing round his chair with drawn swords, Tillius Cimber, though he had a short time before been the keenest defender of his party, and others who only became Pompeians after Pompeius was dead. This it is which has turned the arms of kings against them, and made their trustiest followers meditate the death of him for whom and before whom[63] they once would have been glad to die.

31

No man is satisfied with his own lot if he fixes his attention on that of another: and this leads to our being angry even with the gods, because somebody precedes us, though we forget of how many we take precedence, and that when a man envies few

---

[63] In point of time.

people, he must be followed in the background by a huge crowd of people who envy him. Yet so churlish is human nature, that, however much men may have received, they think themselves wronged if they are able to receive still more. "He gave me the praetorship. Yes, but I had hoped for the consulship. He bestowed the twelve axes upon me: true, but he did not make me a regular[64] consul. He allowed me to give my name to the year, but he did not help me to the priesthood. I have been elected a member of the college: but why only of one? He has bestowed upon me every honour that the State affords: yes, but he has added nothing to my private fortune. What he gave me he was obliged to give to somebody: he brought out nothing from his own pocket." Rather than speak thus, thank him for what you have received: wait for the rest, and be thankful that you are not yet too full to contain more: there is a pleasure in having something left to hope for. Are you preferred to everyone? then rejoice at holding the first place in the thoughts of your friend. Or are many others preferred before you? then think how many more are below you than there are above you. Do you ask, what is your greatest fault? It is, that you keep your accounts wrongly: you set a high value upon what you give, and a low one upon what you receive.

32

Let different qualities in different people keep us from quarrelling with them: let us fear to be angry with some, feel ashamed of being angry with others, and disdain to be angry with others. We do a fine thing, indeed, when we send a wretched slave to the workhouse! Why are we in such a hurry to flog him at once, to break his legs straightaway? we shall not lose our boasted power if we defer its exercise. Let us wait for the time when we ourselves can give orders: at present we speak under constraint from anger. When it has passed away we shall see what amount of damage has been done; for this is what we are especially liable to make mistakes about: we use the sword, and capital punishment, and we appoint chains, imprisonment, and starvation to punish a crime which deserves only flogging with a light scourge. "In what way," say you, "do you bid us look at those things by which we think ourselves injured, that we may see how paltry, pitiful, and childish they are?" Of all things I would charge you to take to yourself a magnanimous spirit, and behold how low and sordid all these matters are about which we squabble and run to and fro till we are out of breath; to anyone who entertains any lofty and magnificent ideas, they are not worthy of a thought.

---

[64] *Consul ordinarius*, a regular consul, one who administered in office from the first of January, in opposition to *consul suffectus*, one chosen in the course of the year in the place of one who had died. The *consul ordinarius* gave his name to the year.

33

The greatest hullabaloo is about money: this it is which wearies out the law-courts, sows strife between father and son, concocts poisons, and gives swords to murderers just as to soldiers: it is stained with our blood: on account of it husbands and wives wrangle all night long, crowds press round the bench of magistrates, kings rage and plunder, and overthrow communities which it has taken the labour of centuries to build, that they may seek for gold and silver in the ashes of their cities. Do you like to look at your moneybags lying in the corner? it is for these that men shout till their eyes start from their heads, that the law-courts ring with the din of trials, and that jurymen brought from great distances sit to decide which man's covetousness is the more equitable. What shall we say if it be not even for a bag of money, but for a handful of coppers or a shilling scored up by a slave that some old man, soon to die without an heir, bursts with rage? what if it be an invalid moneylender whose feet are distorted by the gout, and who can no longer use his hands to count with, who calls for his interest of one thousandth a month,[65] and by his sureties demands his pence even during the paroxysms of his disease? If you were to bring to me all the money from all our mines, which we are at this moment sinking, if you were to bring tonight all that is concealed in hoards, where avarice returns money to the earth from whence it came, and pity that it ever was dug out—all that mass I should not think worthy to cause a wrinkle on the brow of a good man. What ridicule those things deserve which bring tears into our eyes!

34

Come now, let us enumerate the other causes of anger: they are food, drink, and the showy apparatus connected with them, words, insults, disrespectful movements of the body, suspicions, obstinate cattle, lazy slaves, and spiteful construction put upon other men's words, so that even the gift of language to mankind becomes reckoned among the wrongs of nature. Believe me, the things which cause us such great heat are trifles, the sort of things that children fight and squabble over: there is nothing serious, nothing important in all that we do with such gloomy faces. It is, I repeat, the setting a great value on trifles that is the cause of your anger and madness. This man wanted to rob me of my inheritance, that one has brought a charge against me before persons[66] whom I had long courted with great expectations, that one has coveted my mistress. A wish for the same things, which ought to have been a bond of friendship, becomes a source of quarrels and hatred. A narrow path causes quarrels among those who pass up and down it; a wide and broadly spread road may be used by whole tribes without jostling. Those objects of desire of yours cause strife

---

[65] It seems inconceivable that so small an interest, 1⅕ percent per annum, can be meant.
[66] *Captatis*, Madvig. Adv., II, 394.

and disputes among those who covet the same things, because they are petty, and cannot be given to one man without being taken away from another.

35

You are indignant at being answered back by your slave, your freedman, your wife, or your client: and then you complain of the State having lost the freedom which you have destroyed in your own house: then again if he is silent when you question him, you call it sullen obstinacy. Let him both speak and be silent, and laugh too. "In the presence of his master?" you ask. Nay, say rather "in the presence of the housefather." Why do you shout? why do you storm? why do you in the middle of dinner call for a whip, because the slaves are talking, because a crowd as large as a public meeting is not as silent as the wilderness? You have ears, not merely that you may listen to musical sounds, softly and sweetly drawn out and harmonized: you ought to hear laughter and weeping, coaxing and quarrelling, joy and sorrow, the human voice and the roaring and barking of animals. Miserable one! why do you shudder at the noise of a slave, at the rattling of brass or the banging of a door? you cannot help hearing the thunder, however refined you may be. You may apply these remarks about your ears with equal truth to your eyes, which are just as dainty, if they have been badly schooled: they are shocked at stains and dirt, at silver plate which is not sufficiently bright, or at a pool whose water is not clear down to the bottom. Those same eyes which can only endure to see the most variegated marble, and that which has just been scoured bright, which will look at no table whose wood is not marked with a network of veining, and which at home are loath to tread upon anything that is not more precious than gold, will, when out of doors, gaze most calmly upon rough and miry paths, will see unmoved that the greater number of persons that meet them are shabbily dressed, and that the walls of the houses are rotten, full of cracks, and uneven. What, then, can be the reason that they are not distressed out of doors by sights which would shock them in their own home, unless it be that their temper is placid and long-suffering in one case, sulky and faultfinding in the other?

36

All our senses should be educated into strength: they are naturally able to endure much, provided that the spirit forbears to spoil them. The spirit ought to be brought up for examination daily. It was the custom of Sextius when the day was over, and he had betaken himself to rest, to inquire of his spirit: "What bad habit of yours have you cured today? what vice have you checked? in what respect are you better?" Anger will cease, and become more gentle, if it knows that every day it will have to appear before the judgment seat. What can be more admirable than this fashion of discussing the whole of the day's events? how sweet is the sleep which follows this self-examination? how calm, how sound, and careless is it when our spirit has either received praise or reprimand, and when our secret inquisitor and censor has made his report about our morals? I make use of this privilege, and daily plead my cause before myself: when the lamp is taken out of my sight, and my wife, who knows my habit, has ceased to talk, I pass the whole day in review before myself, and repeat all that I have said and done: I conceal nothing from myself, and omit nothing: for why should I be afraid of any of my shortcomings, when it is in my power to say, "I pardon you this time: see that you never do that anymore? In that dispute you spoke too contentiously: do not for the future argue with ignorant people: those who have never been taught are unwilling to learn. You reprimanded that man with more freedom than you ought, and consequently you have offended him instead of amending his ways: in dealing with other cases of the kind, you should look carefully, not only to the truth of what you say, but also whether the person to whom you speak can bear to be told the truth." A good man delights in receiving advice: all the worst men are the most impatient of guidance.

37

At the dinner-table some jokes and sayings intended to give you pain have been directed against you: avoid feasting with low people. Those who are not modest even when sober become much more recklessly impudent after drinking. You have seen your friend in a rage with the porter of some lawyer or rich man, because he has sent him back when about to enter, and you yourself on behalf of your friend have been in a rage with the meanest of slaves. Would you then be angry with a chained house-dog? Why, even he, after a long bout of barking, becomes gentle if you offer him food. So draw back and smile; for the moment your porter fancies himself to be somebody, because he guards a door which is beset by a crowd of litigants; for the moment he who sits within is prosperous and happy, and thinks that a street-door through which it is hard to gain entrance is the mark of a rich and powerful man; he knows not that the hardest door of all to open is that of the prison. Be prepared to submit to much. Is anyone surprised at being cold in winter? at being sick at sea? or at being jostled in the street? The mind is strong enough to bear those evils for which it is prepared. When you are not given a sufficiently distinguished place at table you have begun to be angry with your fellow-guests, with your host, and with him who is preferred above you. Idiot! What difference can it make what part of the couch you rest upon? Can a cushion give you honour or take it away? You have looked askance at somebody, because he has spoken slightingly of your talents; will you apply this rule to yourself? If so, Ennius, whose poetry you do not care for, would have hated you. Hortensius, if you had found fault with his speeches, would have quarreled with you, and Cicero, if you had laughed at his poetry, would have been your enemy. A candidate for office, will you resent men's votes?

38

Someone has offered you an insult? Not a greater one, probably, than was offered to the Stoic philosopher Diogenes, in whose face an insolent young man spat just when he was lecturing upon anger. He bore it mildly and wisely. "I am not angry," said he, "but I am not sure that I ought not to be angry." Yet how much better did our Cato behave? When he was pleading, one Lentulus, whom our fathers remember as a demagogue and passionate man, spat all the phlegm he could muster upon his forehead. Cato wiped his face, and said, "Lentulus, I shall declare to all the world that men are mistaken when they say that you are wanting in cheek."

39

We have now succeeded, my Novatus, in properly regulating our own minds: they either do not feel anger or are above it: let us next see how we may soothe the wrath of others, for we do not only wish to be whole, but to heal. You should not attempt to allay the first burst of anger by words: it is deaf and frantic: we must give it scope; our remedies will only be effective when it slackens. We do not meddle with men's eyes when they are swollen, because we should only irritate their hard stiffness by touching them, nor do we try to cure other diseases when at their height: the best treatment in the first stage of illness is rest. "Of how very little value," say you, "is your remedy, if it appeases anger which is subsiding of its own accord?" In the first place, I answer, it makes it end quicker: in the next, it prevents a relapse. It can render harmless even the violent impulse which it dares not soothe: it will put out of the way all weapons which might be used for revenge: it will pretend to be angry, in order that its advice may have more weight as coming from an assistant and comrade in grief. It will invent delays, and postpone immediate punishment while a greater one is being sought for: it will use every artifice to give the man a respite from his frenzy. If his anger be unusually strong, it will inspire him with some irresistible feeling of shame or of fear: if weak, it will make use of conversation on amusing or novel subjects, and by playing upon his curiosity lead him to forget his passion. We are told that a physician, who was forced to cure the king's daughter, and could not without using the knife, conveyed a lancet to her swollen breast concealed under the sponge with which he was fomenting it. The same girl, who would have shrunk from the remedy if he had applied it openly, bore the pain because she did not expect it. Some diseases can only be cured by deceit.

40

To one class of men you will say, "Beware, lest your anger give pleasure to your foes:" to the other, "Beware, lest your greatness of mind and the reputation it bears among most people for strength become impaired. I myself, by Hercules, am scandalized at your treatment and am grieved beyond measure, but we must wait for a proper opportunity. He shall pay for what he has done; be well assured of that: when you are able you shall return it to him with interest." To reprove a man when he is angry is to add to his anger by being angry oneself. You should approach him in different ways and in a compliant fashion, unless perchance you be so great a personage that you can quash his anger, as the Emperor Augustus did when he was dining with Vedius Pollio.[67] One of the slaves had broken a crystal goblet of his: Vedius ordered him to be led away to die, and that too in no common fashion: he ordered him to be thrown to feed the *muraenae*, some of which fish, of great size, he kept in a tank. Who would not think that he did this out of luxury? but it was out of cruelty. The boy slipped through the hands of those who tried to seize him, and flung himself at Caesar's feet in order to beg for nothing more than that he might die in some different way, and not be eaten. Caesar was shocked at this novel form of cruelty, and ordered him to be let go, and, in his place, all the crystal ware which he saw before him to be broken, and the tank to be filled up. This was the proper way for Caesar to reprove his friend: he made a good use of his power. What are you, that when at dinner you order men to be put to death, and mangled by an unheard-of form of torture? Are a man's bowels to be torn asunder because your cup is broken? You must think a great deal of yourself, if even when the emperor is present you order men to be executed.

41

If anyone's power is so great that he can treat anger with the tone of a superior let him crush it out of existence, but only if it be of the kind of which I have just spoken, fierce, inhuman, bloodthirsty, and incurable save by fear of something more powerful than itself … let us give the mind that peace which is given by constant meditation upon wholesome maxims, by good actions, and by a mind directed to the pursuit of honour alone. Let us set our own conscience fully at rest, but make no efforts to gain credit for ourselves: so long as we deserve well, let us be satisfied, even if we should be ill spoken of. "But the common herd admires spirited actions, and bold men are held in honour, while quiet ones are thought to be indolent." True, at first sight they may appear to be so: but as soon as the even tenor of their life proves that this quietude arises not from dullness but from peace of mind, then that same populace respects and reverences them. There is, then, nothing useful in that hideous and destructive passion of anger, but on the contrary, every kind of evil, fire and sword. Anger tramples self-restraint underfoot, steeps its hands in slaughter, scatters abroad the limbs of its children: it leaves no place unsoiled by crime, it has no thoughts of glory, no fears of disgrace, and when once anger has hardened into hatred, no amendment is possible.

---

[67] See "On Clemency," Book I, 18, 2.

42

Let us be free from this evil, let us clear our minds of it, and extirpate root and branch a passion which grows again wherever the smallest particle of it finds a resting-place. Let us not moderate anger, but get rid of it altogether: what can moderation have to do with an evil habit? We shall succeed in doing this, if only we exert ourselves. Nothing will be of greater service than to bear in mind that we are mortal: let each man say to himself and to his neighbour, "Why should we, as though we were born to live forever, waste our tiny span of life in declaring anger against anyone? why should days, which we might spend in honourable enjoyment, be misapplied in grieving and torturing others? Life is a matter which does not admit of waste, and we have no spare time to throw away. Why do we rush into the fray? why do we go out of our way to seek disputes? why do we, forgetful of the weakness of our nature, undertake mighty feuds, and, frail though we be, summon up all our strength to cut down other men? Ere long, fever or some other bodily ailment will make us unable to carry on this warfare of hatred which we so implacably wage: death will soon part the most vigorous pair of combatants. Why do we make disturbances and spend our lives in rioting? fate hangs over our heads, scores up to our account the days as they pass, and is ever drawing nearer and nearer. The time which you have marked for the death of another perhaps includes your own."

43

Instead of acting thus, why do you not rather draw together what there is of your short life, and keep it peaceful for others and for yourself? why do you not rather make yourself beloved by everyone while you live, and regretted by everyone when you die? Why do you wish to tame that man's pride, because he takes too lofty a tone with you? why do you try with all your might to crush that other who snaps and snarls at you, a low and contemptible wretch, but spiteful and offensive to his betters? Master, why are you angry with your slave? Slave, why are you angry with your master? Client, why are you angry with your patron? Patron, why are you angry with your client? Wait but a little while. See, here comes death, who will make you all equals. We often see at a morning performance in the arena a battle between a bull and a bear, fastened together, in which the victor, after he has torn the other to pieces, is himself slain. We do just the same thing: we worry someone who is connected with us, although the end of both victor and vanquished is at hand, and that soon. Let us rather pass the little remnant of our lives in peace and quiet: may no one loathe us when we lie dead. A quarrel is often brought to an end by a cry of "Fire!" in the neighbourhood, and the appearance of a wild beast parts the highwayman from the traveller: men have no leisure to battle with minor evils when menaced by some overpowering terror. What have we to do with fighting and ambuscades? do you want anything more than death to befall him with whom you are angry? well, even though you sit quiet, he will be sure to die. You waste your pains: you want to do what is certain to be done. You say, "I do not wish necessarily to kill him, but to punish him by exile, or public disgrace, or loss of property." I can more easily pardon one who wishes to give his enemy a wound than one who wishes to give him a blister: for the latter is not only bad, but petty-minded. Whether you are thinking of extreme or slighter punishments, how very short is the time during which either your victim is tortured or you enjoy an evil pleasure in another's pain? This breath that we hold so dear will soon leave us: in the meantime, while we draw it, while we live among human beings, let us practise humanity: let us not be a terror or a danger to anyone. Let us keep our tempers in spite of losses, wrongs, abuse or sarcasm, and let us endure with magnanimity our shortlived troubles: while we are considering what is due to ourselves, as the saying is, and worrying ourselves, death will be upon us.

ON THE SHORTNESS OF LIFE

1

The greater part of mankind, my Paulinus, complains of the unkindness of Nature, because we are born only for a short space of time, and that this allotted period of life runs away so swiftly, nay so hurriedly, that with but few exceptions men's life comes to an end just as they are preparing to enjoy it: nor is it only the common herd and the ignorant vulgar who mourn over this universal misfortune, as they consider it to be: this reflection has wrung complaints even from great men. Hence comes that well-known saying of physicians, that art is long but life is short: hence arose that quarrel, so unbefitting a sage, which Aristotle picked with Nature, because she had indulged animals with such length of days that some of them lived for ten or fifteen centuries, while man, although born for many and such great exploits, had the term of his existence cut so much shorter. We do not have a very short time assigned to us, but we lose a great deal of it: life is long enough to carry out the most important projects: we have an ample portion, if we do but arrange the whole of it aright: but when it all runs to waste through luxury and carelessness, when it is not devoted to any good purpose, then at the last we are forced to feel that it is all over, although we never noticed how it glided away. Thus it is: we do not receive a short life, but we make it a short one, and we are not poor in days, but wasteful of them. When great and kinglike riches fall into the hands of a bad master, they are dispersed straightaway, but even a moderate fortune, when bestowed upon a wise guardian, increases by use: and in like manner our life has great opportunities for one who knows how to dispose of it to the best advantage.

2

Why do we complain of Nature? she has dealt kindly with us. Life is long enough, if you know how to use it. One man is possessed by an avarice which nothing can satisfy, another by a laborious diligence in doing what is totally useless: another is sodden by wine: another is benumbed by sloth: one man is exhausted by an ambition which makes him court the good will of others:[68] another, through his eagerness as a merchant, is led to visit every land and every sea by the hope of gain: some are plagued by the love of soldiering, and are always either endangering other men's lives or in trembling for their own: some wear away their lives in that voluntary slavery, the unrequited service of great men: many are occupied either in laying claim to other men's fortune or in complaining of their own: a great number have no settled purpose, and are tossed from one new scheme to another by a rambling, inconsistent, dissatisfied, fickle habit of mind: some care for no object sufficiently to try to attain it, but lie lazily yawning until their fate comes upon them: so that I cannot doubt the truth of that verse which the greatest of poets has dressed in the guise of an oracular response—

"We live a small part only of our lives."

But all duration is time, not life: vices press upon us and surround us on every side, and do not permit us to regain our feet, or to raise our eyes and gaze upon truth, but when we are down keep us prostrate and chained to low desires. Men who are in this condition are never allowed to come to themselves: if ever by chance they obtain any rest, they roll to and fro like the deep sea, which heaves and tosses after a gale, and they never have any respite from their lusts. Do you suppose that I speak of those whose ills are notorious? Nay, look at those whose prosperity all men run to see: they are choked by their own good things. To how many men do riches prove a heavy burden? how many men's eloquence and continual desire to display their own cleverness has cost them their lives?[69] how many are sallow with constant sensual indulgence? how many have no freedom left them by the tribe of clients that surges around them? Look through all these, from the lowest to the highest:—this man calls his friends to support him, this one is present in court, this one is the defendant, this one pleads for him, this one is on the jury: but no one lays claim to his own self, everyone wastes his time over someone else. Investigate those men, whose names are in everyone's mouth: you will find that they bear just the same marks: A is devoted to B, and B to C: no one belongs to himself. Moreover some men are full of most irrational anger: they complain of the insolence of their chiefs, because they have not granted them an audience when they wished for it; as if a man had any right to complain of being so haughtily shut out by another, when he never has leisure to give his own conscience a hearing. This chief of yours, whoever he is, though he may look at you in an offensive manner, still will some day look at you, open his ears to your words, and give you a seat by his side: but you never design to look upon yourself, to listen to your own grievances. You ought not, then, to claim

---

[68] "*L'un se consume en projets d'ambition, dont le succès dépend du suffrage de l'autrui.*" —La Grange.

[69] "*Combien d'orateurs qui s'épuisent de sang et de forces pour faire montrer de leur génie!*" —La Grange.

these services from another, especially since while you yourself were doing so, you did not wish for an interview with another man, but were not able to obtain one with yourself.[70]

3

Were all the brightest intellects of all time to employ themselves on this one subject, they never could sufficiently express their wonder at this blindness of men's minds: men will not allow anyone to establish himself upon their estates, and upon the most trifling dispute about the measuring of boundaries, they betake themselves to stones and cudgels; yet they allow others to encroach upon their lives, nay, they themselves actually lead others in to take possession of them. You cannot find anyone who wants to distribute his money; yet among how many people does everyone distribute his life? men covetously guard their property from waste, but when it comes to waste of time, they are most prodigal of that of which it would become them to be sparing. Let us take one of the elders, and say to him, "We perceive that you have arrived at the extreme limits of human life: you are in your hundredth year, or even older. Come now, reckon up your whole life in black and white: tell us how much of your time has been spent upon your creditors, how much on your mistress, how much on your king, how much on your clients, how much in quarrelling with your wife, how much in keeping your slaves in order, how much in running up and down the city on business. Add to this the diseases which we bring upon us with our own hands, and the time which has laid idle without any use having been made of it; you will

---

[70] "*Pour vous, jamais vous ne daignâtes vous regarder seulement, ou vous entendre. Ne faites pas non plus valoir votre condescendance a écouter les autres. Lorsque vous vous y prétez, ce n'est pas que vous aimiez a vous communiquer aux autres; c'est que vous craignez de vous trouver avec vous-même.*"—La Grange.

"It is a folly therefore beyond Sence,
When great men will not give us Audience
To count them proud; how dare we call it pride
When we the same have to ourselves deny'd.
Yet they how great, how proud so e're, have bin
Sometimes so courteous as to call thee in,
And hear thee speak; but thou could'st nere afford
Thyself the leisure of a look or word.
Thou should'st not then herein another blame,
Because when thou thyself do'st do the same,
Thou would'st not be with others, but we see
Plainly thou can'st not with thine own self be."

L. Annaeus Seneca, the Philosopher, his book of the Shortness of Life, translated into an English poem. Imprinted at London, by William Goldbird, for the Author.

see that you have not lived as many years as you count. Look back in your memory and see how often you have been consistent in your projects, how many days passed as you intended them to do when you were at your own disposal, how often you did not change colour and your spirit did not quail, how much work you have done in so long a time, how many people have without your knowledge stolen parts of your life from you, how much you have lost, how large a part has been taken up by useless grief, foolish gladness, greedy desire, or polite conversation; how little of yourself is left to you: you will then perceive that you will die prematurely." What, then, is the reason of this? It is that people live as though they would live forever: you never remember your human frailty; you never notice how much of your time has already gone by: you spend it as though you had an abundant and overflowing store of it, though all the while that day which you devote to some man or to some thing is perhaps your last. You fear everything, like mortals as you are, and yet you desire everything as if you were immortals. You will hear many men say, "After my fiftieth year I will give myself up to leisure: my sixtieth shall be my last year of public office": and what guarantee have you that your life will last any longer? who will let all this go on just as you have arranged it? are you not ashamed to reserve only the leavings of your life for yourself, and appoint for the enjoyment of your own right mind only that time which you cannot devote to any business? How late it is to begin life just when we have to be leaving it! What a foolish forgetfulness of our mortality, to put off wholesome counsels until our fiftieth or sixtieth year, and to choose that our lives shall begin at a point which few of us ever reach.

4

You will find that the most powerful and highly-placed men let fall phrases in which they long for leisure, praise it, and prefer it to all the blessings which they enjoy. Sometimes they would fain descend from their lofty pedestal, if it could be safely done: for fortune collapses by its own weight, without any shock or interference from without. The late Emperor Augustus, upon whom the gods bestowed more blessings than on anyone else, never ceased to pray for rest and exemption from the troubles of empire: he used to enliven his labours with this sweet, though unreal consolation, that he would some day live for himself alone. In a letter which he addressed to the Senate, after promising that his rest shall not be devoid of dignity nor discreditable to his former glories, I find the following words:—"These things, however, it is more honourable to do than to promise: but my eagerness for that time, so earnestly longed for, has led me to derive a certain pleasure from speaking about it, though the reality is still far distant."[71] He thought leisure so important, that

---

[71] "*Dans une lettre qu'il envoya au Sénat apres avoir promis que son repos n'aura rièn indigne de la gloire de ses premières années, il ajoute: Mais l'execution y mettra un prix, que ne peuvent y mettre les promesses. J'obeis cependant à la vive passion que j'ai, de me voir a ce temps si*

though he could not actually enjoy it, yet he did so by anticipation and by thinking about it. He, who saw everything depending upon himself alone, who swayed the fortunes of men and of nations, thought that his happiest day would be that on which he laid aside his greatness. He knew by experience how much labour was involved in that glory that shone through all lands, and how much secret anxiety was concealed within it: he had been forced to assert his rights by war, first with his countrymen, next with his colleagues, and lastly with his own relations, and had shed blood both by sea and by land: after marching his troops under arms through Macedonia, Sicily, Egypt, Syria, Asia Minor, and almost all the countries of the world, when they were weary with slaughtering Romans he had directed them against a foreign foe. While he was pacifying the Alpine regions, and subduing the enemies whom he found in the midst of the Roman empire, while he was extending its boundaries beyond the Rhine, the Euphrates, and the Danube, at Rome itself the swords of Murena, Caepio, Lepidus, Egnatius, and others were being sharpened to slay him. Scarcely had he escaped from their plot, when his already failing age was terrified by his daughter and all the noble youths who were pledged to her cause by adultery with her by way of oath of fidelity. Then there was Paulus and Antonius's mistress, a second time to be feared by Rome: and when he had cut out these ulcers from his very limbs, others grew in their place: the empire, like a body overloaded with blood, was always breaking out somewhere. For this reason he longed for leisure: all his labours were based upon hopes and thoughts of leisure: this was the wish of him who could accomplish the wishes of all other men.

5

While tossed hither and thither by Catiline and Clodius, Pompeius and Crassus, by some open enemies and some doubtful friends, while he struggled with the struggling republic and kept it from going to ruin, when at last he was banished, being neither able to keep silence in prosperity nor to endure adversity with patience, how often must Marcus Cicero have cursed that consulship of his which he never ceased to praise, and which nevertheless deserved it? What piteous expressions he uses in a letter to Atticus when Pompeius the father had been defeated, and his son was recruiting his shattered forces in Spain? "Do you ask," writes he, "what I am doing here? I am living in my Tusculan villa almost as a prisoner." He adds

---

désiré; et puisque l'heureuse situation d'affaires m'en tient encore éloigné, j'ai voulu du moins me satisfaire en partie, par la douceur que je trouve à vous en parler."—La Grange.

"Such words I find. But these things rather ought
Be done, then said; yet so far hath the thought
Of that wish'd time prevail'd, that though the glad
Fruition of the thing be not yet had,
Yet I,"

more afterwards, wherein he laments his former life, complains of the present, and despairs of the future. Cicero called himself "half a prisoner," but, by Hercules, the wise man never would have come under so lowly a title: he never would be half a prisoner, but would always enjoy complete and entire liberty, being free, in his own power, and greater than all others: for what can be greater than the man who is greater than Fortune?

6

When Livius Drusus, a vigorous and energetic man, brought forward bills for new laws and radical measures of the Gracchus pattern, being the centre of a vast mob of all the peoples of Italy, and seeing no way to solve the question, since he was not allowed to deal with it as he wished, and yet was not free to throw it up after having once taken part in it, complained bitterly of his life, which had been one of unrest from the very cradle, and said, we are told, that "he was the only person who had never had any holidays even when he was a boy." Indeed, while he was still under age and wearing the *praetexta*, he had the courage to plead the cause of accused persons in court, and to make use of his influence so powerfully that it is well known that in some causes his exertions gained a verdict. Where would such precocious ambition stop? You may be sure that one who showed such boldness as a child would end by becoming a great pest both in public and in private life: it was too late for him to complain that he had had no holidays, when from his boyhood he had been a firebrand and a nuisance in the courts. It is a stock question whether he committed suicide: for he fell by a sudden wound in the groin, and some doubted whether his death was caused by his own hand, though none disputed its having happened most seasonably. It would be superfluous to mention more who, while others thought them the happiest of men, have themselves borne true witness to their own feelings, and have loathed all that they have done for all the years of their lives: yet by these complaints they have effected no alteration either in others or in themselves: for after these words have escaped them their feelings revert to their accustomed frame. By Hercules, that life of you great men, even though it should last for more than a thousand years, is still a very short one: those vices of yours would swallow up any extent of time: no wonder if this our ordinary span, which, though Nature hurries on, can be enlarged by common sense, soon slips away from you: for you do not lay hold of it or hold it back, and try to delay the swiftest of all things, but you let it pass as though it were a useless thing and you could supply its place.

7

Among these I reckon in the first place those who devote their time to nothing but drinking and debauchery: for no men are busied more shamefully: the others, although the glory which they pursue is but a counterfeit, still deserve some credit for their pursuit of it—though you may tell me of misers, of passionate men, of men who hate and who even wage war without a cause—yet all such men sin like men: but the sin of those who are given up to gluttony and lust is a disgraceful one. Examine all the hours of their lives: consider how much time they spend in calculation, how much in plotting, how much in fear, how much in giving and receiving flattery, how much in entering into recognizances for themselves or for others, how much in banquets, which indeed become a serious business, you will see that they are not allowed any breathing time either by their pleasures or their pains. Finally, all are agreed that nothing, neither eloquence nor literature, can be done properly by one who is occupied with something else; for nothing can take deep root in a mind which is directed to some other subject, and which rejects whatever you try to stuff into it. No man knows less about living than a business man: there is nothing about which it is more difficult to gain knowledge. Other arts have many folk everywhere who profess to teach them: some of them can be so thoroughly learned by mere boys, that they are able to teach them to others: but one's whole life must be spent in learning how to live, and, which may perhaps surprise you more, one's whole life must be spent in learning how to die. Many excellent men have freed themselves from all hindrances, have given up riches, business, and pleasure, and have made it their duty to the very end of their lives to learn how to live: and yet the larger portion of them leave this life confessing that they do not yet know how to live, and still less know how to live as wise men. Believe me, it requires a great man and one who is superior to human frailties not to allow any of his time to be filched from him: and therefore it follows that his life is a very long one, because he devotes every possible part of it to himself: no portion lies idle or uncultivated, or in another man's power; for he finds nothing worthy of being exchanged for his time, which he husbands most grudgingly. He, therefore, had time enough: whereas those who gave up a great part of their lives to the people of necessity had not enough. Yet you need not suppose that the latter were not sometimes conscious of their loss: indeed, you will hear most of those who are troubled with great prosperity every now and then cry out amid their hosts of clients, their pleadings in court, and their other honourable troubles, "I am not allowed to live my own life." Why is he not allowed? because all those who call upon you to defend them, take you away from yourself. How many of your days have been spent by that defendant? by that candidate for office? by that old woman who is weary with burying her heirs? by that man who pretends to be ill, in order to excite the greed of those who hope to inherit his property? by that powerful friend of yours, who uses you to swell his train, not to be his friend? Balance your account, and run over all the days of your life; you will see that only a very few days, and only those which were useless for any other purpose, have been left to you. He who has obtained the fasces[72] for which he longed, is eager to get rid of them, and is constantly saying, "When will this year be over?" Another

---

[72] The rods carried by the lictors as symbols of office. See Smith's *Dictionary of Antiquities*, s.v.

exhibits public games, and once would have given a great deal for the chance of doing so, but now "when," says he, "shall I escape from this?" Another is an advocate who is fought for in all the courts, and who draws immense audiences, who crowd all the forum to a far greater distance than they can hear him; "When," says he, "will vacation-time come?" Every man hurries through his life, and suffers from a yearning for the future, and a weariness of the present: but he who disposes of all his time for his own purposes, who arranges all his days as though he were arranging the plan of his life, neither wishes for nor fears the morrow: for what new pleasure can any hour now bestow upon him? he knows it all, and has indulged in it all even to satiety. Fortune may deal with the rest as she will, his life is already safe from her: such a man may gain something, but cannot lose anything: and, indeed, he can only gain anything in the same way as one who is already glutted and filled can get some extra food which he takes although he does not want it. You have no grounds, therefore, for supposing that anyone has lived long, because he has wrinkles or grey hairs: such a man has not lived long, but has only been long alive. Why! would you think that a man had voyaged much if a fierce gale had caught him as soon as he left his port, and he had been driven round and round the same place continually by a succession of winds blowing from opposite quarters? such a man has not travelled much, he has only been much tossed about.

8

I am filled with wonder when I see some men asking others for their time, and those who are asked for it most willing to give it: both parties consider the object for which the time is given, but neither of them thinks of the time itself, as though in asking for this one asked for nothing, and in giving it one gave nothing: we play with what is the most precious of all things: yet it escapes men's notice, because it is an incorporeal thing, and because it does not come before our eyes; and therefore it is held very cheap, nay, hardly any value whatever is put upon it. Men set the greatest store upon presents or pensions, and hire out their work, their services, or their care in order to gain them: no one values time: they give it much more freely, as though it cost nothing. Yet you will see these same people clasping the knees of their physician as suppliants when they are sick and in present peril of death, and if threatened with a capital charge willing to give all that they possess in order that they may live: so inconsistent are they. Indeed, if the number of every man's future years could be laid before him, as we can lay that of his past years, how anxious those who found that they had but few years remaining would be to make the most of them? Yet it is easy to arrange the distribution of a quantity, however small, if we know how much there is: what you ought to husband most carefully is that which may run short you know not when. Yet you have no reason to suppose that they do not know how dear a thing time is: they are wont to say to those whom they especially love that they are ready to give them a part of their own years. They do give them, and know not that they are giving them; but they give them in such a manner that they themselves lose them without the others gaining them. They do not, however, know whence they obtain their supply, and therefore they are able to endure the waste of what is not seen: yet no one will give you back your years, no one will restore them to you again: your life will run its course when once it has begun, and will neither begin again or efface what it has done. It will make no disturbance, it will give you no warning of how fast it flies: it will move silently on: it will not prolong itself at the command of a king, or at the wish of a nation: as it started on its first day, so it will run: it will never turn aside, never delay. What follows, then? Why! you are busy, but life is hurrying on: death will be here some time or other, and you must attend to him, whether you will or no.

9

Can anything be mentioned which is more insane than the ideas of leisure of those people who boast of their worldly wisdom? They live laboriously, in order that they may live better; they fit themselves out for life at the expense of life itself, and cast their thoughts a long way forwards: yet postponement is the greatest waste of life: it wrings day after day from us, and takes away the present by promising something hereafter: there is no such obstacle to true living as waiting, which loses today while it is depending on the morrow. You dispose of that which is in the hand of Fortune, and you let go that which is in your own. Whither are you looking, whither are you stretching forward? everything future is uncertain: live now straightaway. See how the greatest of bards cries to you and sings in wholesome verse as though inspired with celestial fire:—

> "The best of wretched mortals' days is that
> Which is the first to fly."

Why do you hesitate, says he, why do you stand back? unless you seize it it will have fled: and even if you do seize it, it will still fly. Our swiftness in making use of our time ought therefore to vie with the swiftness of time itself, and we ought to drink of it as we should of a fast-running torrent which will not be always running. The poet, too, admirably satirizes our boundless thoughts, when he says, not "the first age," but "the first day." Why are you careless and slow while time is flying so fast, and why do you spread out before yourself a vision of long months and years, as many as your greediness requires? he talks with you about one day, and that a fast-fleeting one. There can, then, be no doubt that the best days are those which fly first for wretched, that is, for busy mortals, whose minds are still in their childhood when old age comes upon them, and they reach it unprepared and without arms to combat it. They have never looked forward: they have all of a sudden stumbled upon old age: they never noticed that it was stealing upon them day by day. As conversation, or reading, or deep thought deceives travellers, and they find themselves at their journey's end before they knew that it was drawing near, so in this fast and never-ceasing journey of life, which we make at the same pace whether we are asleep or awake, busy people never notice that they are moving till they are at the end of it.

10

If I chose to divide this proposition into separate steps, supported by evidence, many things occur to me by which I could prove that the lives of busy men are the shortest of all. Fabianus, who was none of your lecture-room philosophers, but one of the true antique pattern, used to say, "We ought to fight against the passions by main force, not by skirmishing, and upset their line of battle by a home charge, not by inflicting trifling wounds: I do not approve of dallying with sophisms; they must be crushed, not merely scratched." Yet, in order that sinners may be confronted with their errors, they must be taught, and not merely mourned for. Life is divided into three parts: that which has been, that which is, and that which is to come: of these three stages, that which we are passing through is brief, that which we are about to pass is uncertain, and that which we have passed is certain: this it is over which Fortune has lost her rights, and which can fall into no other man's power: and this is what busy men lose: for they have no leisure to look back upon the past, and even if they had, they take no pleasure in remembering what they regret: they are, therefore, unwilling to turn their minds to the contemplation of ill-spent time, and they shrink from reviewing a course of action whose faults become glaringly apparent when handled a second time, although they were snatched at when we were under the spell of immediate gratification. No one, unless all his acts have been submitted to the infallible censorship of his own conscience, willingly turns his thoughts back upon the past. He who has ambitiously desired, haughtily scorned, passionately vanquished, treacherously deceived, greedily snatched, or prodigally wasted much, must needs fear his own memory; yet this is a holy and consecrated part of our time, beyond the reach of all human accidents, removed from the dominion of Fortune, and which cannot be disquieted by want, fear, or attacks of sickness: this can neither be troubled nor taken away from one: we possess it forever undisturbed. Our present consists only of single days, and those, too, taken one hour at a time: but all the days of past times appear before us when bidden, and allow themselves to be examined and lingered over, albeit busy men cannot find time for so doing. It is the privilege of a tranquil and peaceful mind to review all the parts of its life: but the minds of busy men are like animals under the yoke, and cannot bend aside or look back. Consequently, their life passes away into vacancy, and as you do no good however much you may pour into a vessel which cannot keep or hold what you put there, so also it matters not how much time you give men if it can find no place to settle in, but leaks away through the chinks and holes of their minds. Present time is very short, so much so that to some it seems to be no time at all; for it is always in motion, and runs swiftly away: it ceases to exist before it comes, and can no more brook delay than can the universe or the host of heaven, whose unresting movement never lets them pause on their way. Busy men, therefore, possess present time alone, that being so short that they cannot grasp it, and when they are occupied with many things they lose even this.

11

In a word, do you want to know for how short a time they live? see how they desire to live long: broken-down old men beg in their prayers for the addition of a few more years: they pretend to be younger than they are: they delude themselves with their own lies, and are as willing to cheat themselves as if they could cheat Fate at the same time: when at last some weakness reminds them that they are mortal, they die as it were in terror: they may rather be said to be dragged out of this life than to depart from it. They loudly exclaim that they have been fools and have not lived their lives, and declare that if they only survive this sickness they will spend the rest of their lives at leisure: at such times they reflect how uselessly they have laboured to provide themselves with what they have never enjoyed, and how all their toil has gone for nothing: but those whose life is spent without any engrossing business may well find it ample: no part of it is made over to others, or scattered here and there; no part is entrusted to fortune, is lost by neglect, is spent in ostentatious giving, or is useless: all of it is, so to speak, invested at good interest. A very small amount of it, therefore, is abundantly sufficient, and so, when his last day arrives, the wise man will not hang back, but will walk with a steady step to meet death.

12

Perhaps you will ask me whom I mean by "busy men"? you need not think that I allude only to those who are hunted out of the courts of justice with dogs at the close of the proceedings, those whom you see either honourably jostled by a crowd of their own clients or contemptuously hustled in visits of ceremony by strangers, who call them away from home to hang about their patron's doors, or who make use of the praetor's sales by auction to acquire infamous gains which some day will prove their own ruin. Some men's leisure is busy: in their country house or on their couch, in complete solitude, even though they have retired from all men's society, they still continue to worry themselves: we ought not to say that such men's life is one of leisure, but their very business is sloth. Would you call a man idle who expends anxious finicking care in the arrangement of his Corinthian bronzes, valuable only through the mania of a few connoisseurs? and who passes the greater part of his days among plates of rusty metal? who sits in the palaestra (shame, that our very vices should be foreign) watching boys wrestling? who distributes his gangs of fettered slaves into pairs according to their age and colour? who keeps athletes of the latest fashion? Why do you call those men idle, who pass many hours at the barber's while the growth of the past night is being plucked out by the roots, holding councils over each several hair, while the scattered locks are arranged in order and those which fall back are forced forward on to the forehead? How angry they become if the shaver is a little careless, as though he were shearing a *man*! what a white heat they work themselves into if some of their mane is cut away, if some part of it is ill-arranged, if all their ringlets do not lie in regular order! who of them would not rather that the state were overthrown than that his hair should be ruffled? who does not care more for the appearance of his head than for his health? who would not prefer ornament to honour? Do you call these men idle, who make a business of the comb and looking-glass? what of those who devote their lives to composing, hearing, and learning songs who twist their voices, intended by Nature to sound best and simplest when used straightforwardly, through all the turns of futile melodies; whose fingers are always beating time to some music on which they are inwardly meditating; who, when invited to serious and even sad business may be heard humming an air to themselves?—such people are not at leisure, but are busy about trifles. As for their banquets, by Hercules, I cannot reckon them among their unoccupied times when I see with what anxious care they set out their plate, how laboriously they arrange the girdles of their waiters' tunics, how breathlessly they watch to see how the cook dishes up the wild boar, with what speed, when the signal is given, the slave-boys run to perform their duties, how skilfully birds are carved into pieces of the right size, how painstakingly wretched youths wipe up the spittings of drunken men. By these means men seek credit for taste and grandeur, and their vices follow them so far into their privacy that they can neither eat nor drink without a view to effect. Nor should I count those men idle who have themselves carried hither and thither in sedans and litters, and who look forward to their regular hour for taking this exercise as though they were not allowed to omit it: men who are reminded by someone else when to bathe, when to swim, when to dine: they actually reach such a pitch of languid effeminacy as not to be able to find out for themselves whether they are hungry. I have heard one of these luxurious folk—if indeed, we ought to give the name of luxury to unlearning the life and habits of a man—when he was carried in men's arms out of the bath and placed in his chair, say inquiringly, "Am I seated?" Do you suppose that such a man as this, who did not know when he was seated, could know whether he was alive, whether he could see, whether he was at leisure? I can hardly say whether I pity him more if he really did not know or if he pretended not to know this. Such people do really become unconscious of much, but they behave as though they were unconscious of much more: they delight in some failings because they consider them to be proofs of happiness: it seems the part of an utterly low and contemptible man to know what he is doing. After this, do you suppose that playwrights draw largely upon their imaginations in their burlesques upon luxury: by Hercules, they omit more than they invent; in this age, inventive in this alone, such a number of incredible vices have been produced, that already you are able to reproach the playwrights with omitting to notice them. To think that there should be anyone who had so far lost his senses through luxury as to take someone else's opinion as to whether he was sitting or not? This man certainly is not at leisure: you must bestow a different title on him: he is sick, or rather dead: he only is at leisure who feels that he is at leisure: but this creature is only half alive, if he wants someone to tell him what position his body is in. How can such a man be able to dispose of any time?

13

It would take long to describe the various individuals who have wasted their lives over playing at draughts, playing at ball, or toasting their bodies in the sun: men are not at leisure if their pleasures partake of the character of business, for no one will doubt that those persons are laborious triflers who devote themselves to the study of futile literary questions, of whom there is already a great number in Rome also. It used to be a peculiarly Greek disease of the mind to investigate how many rowers Ulysses had, whether the *Iliad* or the *Odyssey* was written first, and furthermore, whether they were written by the same author, with other matters of the same stamp, which neither please your inner consciousness if you keep them to yourself, nor make you seem more learned, but only more troublesome, if you publish them abroad. See, already this vain longing to learn what is useless has taken hold of the Romans: the other day I heard somebody telling who was the first Roman general who did this or that: Duillius was the first who won a sea-fight, Curius Dentatus was the first who drove elephants in his triumph: moreover, these stories, though they add nothing to real glory, do nevertheless deal with the great deeds of our countrymen: such knowledge is not profitable, yet it claims our attention as a fascinating kind of folly. I will even pardon those who want to know who first persuaded the Romans to go on board ship. It was Claudius, who for this reason was surnamed Caudex, because any piece of carpentry formed of many planks was called *caudex* by the ancient Romans, for which reason public records are called *codices*, and by old custom the ships which ply on the Tiber with provisions are called *codicariae*. Let us also allow that it is to the point to tell how Valerius Corvinus was the first to conquer Messana, and first of the family of the Valerii transferred the name of the captured city to his own, and was called Messana, and how the people gradually corrupted the pronunciation and called him Messalla: or would you let anyone find interest in Lucius Sulla having been the first to let lions loose in the circus, they having been previously exhibited in chains, and hurlers of darts having been sent by King Bocchus to kill them? This may be permitted to their curiosity: but can it serve any useful purpose to know that Pompeius was the first to exhibit eighteen elephants in the circus, who were matched in a mimic battle with some convicts? The leading man in the State, and one who, according to tradition, was noted among the ancient leaders of the State for his transcendent goodness of heart, thought it a notable kind of show to kill men in a manner hitherto unheard of. Do they fight to the death? that is not cruel enough: are they torn to pieces? that is not cruel enough: let them be crushed flat by animals of enormous bulk. It would be much better that such a thing should be forgotten, for fear that hereafter some potentate might hear of it and envy its refined barbarity. O, how doth excessive prosperity blind our intellects! at the moment at which he was casting so many troops of wretches to be trampled on by outlandish beasts, when he was proclaiming war between such different creatures, when he was shedding so much blood before the eyes of the Roman people, whose blood he himself was soon to shed even more freely, he thought himself the master of the whole world; yet he afterwards, deceived by the treachery of the Alexandrians, had to offer himself to the dagger of the vilest of slaves, and then at last discovered what an empty boast was his surname of "The Great." But to return to the point from which I have digressed, I will prove that even on this very subject some people expend useless pains. The same author tells us that Metellus, when he triumphed after having conquered the Carthaginians in Sicily, was the only Roman who ever had a hundred and twenty captured elephants led before his car: and that Sulla was the last Roman who extended the *pomoerium*[73] which it was not the custom of the ancients to extend on account of the conquest of provincial, but only of Italian territory. Is it more useful to know this, than to know that the Mount Aventine, according to him, is outside of the *pomoerium*, for one of two reasons, either because it was thither that the plebeians seceded, or because when Remus took his auspices on that place the birds which he saw were not propitious: and other stories without number of the like sort, which are either actual falsehoods or much the same as falsehoods? for even if you allow that these authors speak in all good faith, if they pledge themselves for the truth of what they write, still, whose mistakes will be made fewer by such stories? whose passions will be restrained? whom will they make more brave, more just, or more gentlemanly? My friend Fabianus used to say that he was not sure that it was not better not to apply oneself to any studies at all than to become interested in these.

14

The only persons who are really at leisure are those who devote themselves to philosophy: and they alone really live: for they do not merely enjoy their own lifetime, but they annex every century to their own: all the years which have passed before them belong to them. Unless we are the most ungrateful creatures in the world, we shall regard these noblest of men, the founders of divine schools of thought, as having been born for us, and having prepared life for us: we are led by the labour of others to behold most beautiful things which have been brought out of darkness into light: we are not shut out from any period, we can make our way into every subject, and, if only we can summon up sufficient strength of mind to overstep the narrow

---

[73] See Smith's *Dictionary of Antiquities*.

limit of human weakness, we have a vast extent of time wherein to disport ourselves: we may argue with Socrates, doubt with Carneades, repose with Epicurus, overcome human nature with the Stoics, exceed it with the Cynics. Since Nature allows us to commune with every age, why do we not abstract ourselves from our own petty fleeting span of time, and give ourselves up with our whole mind to what is vast, what is eternal, what we share with better men than ourselves? Those who gad about in a round of calls, who worry themselves and others, after they have indulged their madness to the full, and crossed every patron's threshold daily, leaving no open door unentered, after they have hawked about their interested greetings in houses of the most various character—after all, how few people are they able to see out of so vast a city, divided among so many different ruling passions: how many will be moved by sloth, self-indulgence, or rudeness to deny them admittance: how many, after they have long plagued them, will run past them with feigned hurry? how many will avoid coming out through their entrance-hall with its crowds of clients, and will escape by some concealed backdoor? as though it were not ruder to deceive their visitor than to deny him admittance!—how many, half asleep and stupid with yesterday's debauch, can hardly be brought to return the greeting of the wretched man who has broken his own rest in order to wait on that of another, even after his name has been whispered to them for the thousandth time, save by a most offensive yawn of his half-opened lips. We may truly say that those men are pursuing the true path of duty, who wish every day to consort on the most familiar terms with Zeno, Pythagoras, Democritus, and the rest of those high priests of virtue, with Aristotle and with Theophrastus. None of these men will be "engaged," none of these will fail to send you away after visiting him in a happier frame of mind and on better terms with yourself, none of them will let you leave him empty-handed: yet their society may be enjoyed by all men, and by night as well as by day.

15

None of these men will force you to die, but all of them will teach you how to die: none of these will waste your time, but will add his own to it. The talk of these men is not dangerous, their friendship will not lead you to the scaffold, their society will not ruin you in expenses: you may take from them whatsoever you will; they will not prevent your taking the deepest draughts of their wisdom that you please. What blessedness, what a fair old age awaits the man who takes these for his patrons! he will have friends with whom he may discuss all matters, great and small, whose advice he may ask daily about himself, from whom he will hear truth without insult, praise without flattery, and according to whose likeness he may model his own character. We are wont to say that we are not able to choose who our parents should be, but that they were assigned to us by chance; yet we may be born just as we please: there are several families of the noblest intellects: choose which you would like to belong to: by your adoption you will not receive their name only, but also their property, which is not intended to be guarded in a mean and miserly spirit: the more persons you divide it among the larger it becomes. These will open to you the path which leads to eternity, and will raise you to a height from whence none shall cast you down. By this means alone can you prolong your mortal life, nay, even turn it into an immortal one. High office, monuments, all that ambition records in decrees or piles up in stone, soon passes away: lapse of time casts down and ruins everything; but those things on which Philosophy has set its seal are beyond the reach of injury: no age will discard them or lessen their force, each succeeding century will add somewhat to the respect in which they are held: for we look upon what is near us with jealous eyes, but we admire what is further off with less prejudice. The wise man's life, therefore, includes much: he is not hedged in by the same limits which confine others: he alone is exempt from the laws by which mankind is governed: all ages serve him like a god. If any time be past, he recalls it by his memory; if it be present, he uses it; if it be future, he anticipates it: his life is a long one because he concentrates all times into it.

16

Those men lead the shortest and unhappiest lives who forget the past, neglect the present, and dread the future: when they reach the end of it the poor wretches learn too late that they were busied all the while that they were doing nothing. You need not think, because sometimes they call for death, that their lives are long: their folly torments them with vague passions which lead them into the very things of which they are afraid: they often, therefore, wish for death because they live in fear. Neither is it, as you might think, a proof of the length of their lives that they often find the days long, that they often complain how slowly the hours pass until the appointed time arrives for dinner: for whenever they are left without their usual business, they fret helplessly in their idleness, and know not how to arrange or to spin it out. They betake themselves, therefore, to some business, and all the intervening time is irksome to them; they would wish, by Hercules, to skip over it, just as they wish to skip over the intervening days before a gladiatorial contest or some other time appointed for a public spectacle or private indulgence: all postponement of what they wish for is grievous to them. Yet the very time which they enjoy is brief and soon past, and is made much briefer by their own fault: for they run from one pleasure to another, and are not able to devote themselves consistently to one passion: their days are not long, but odious to them: on the other hand, how short they find the nights which they spend with courtesans or over wine? Hence arises that folly of the poets who encourage the errors of mankind by their myths, and declare that Jupiter to gratify his voluptuous desires doubled the length of the night. Is it not adding fuel to our vices to name the gods as their authors, and to offer our distempers free scope by giving them deity for an example? How can the nights for which men pay so dear fail to appear of the shortest? they lose the day in looking forward to the night, and lose the night through fear of the dawn.

17

Such men's very pleasures are restless and disturbed by various alarms, and at the most joyous moment of all there rises the anxious thought: "How long will this last?" This frame of mind has led kings to weep over their power, and they have not been so much delighted at the grandeur of their position, as they have been terrified by the end to which it must some day come. That most arrogant Persian king,[74] when his army stretched over vast plains and could not be counted but only measured, burst into tears at the thought that in less than a hundred years none of all those warriors would be alive: yet their death was brought upon them by the very man who wept over it, who was about to destroy some of them by sea, some on land, some in battle, and some in flight, and who would in a very short space of time put an end to those about whose hundredth year he showed such solicitude. Why need we wonder at their very joys being mixed with fear? they do not rest upon any solid grounds, but are disturbed by the same emptiness from which they spring. What must we suppose to be the misery of such times as even they acknowledge to be wretched, when even the joys by which they elevate themselves and raise themselves above their fellows are of a mixed character. All the greatest blessings are enjoyed with fear, and no thing is so untrustworthy as extreme prosperity: we require fresh strokes of good fortune to enable us to keep that which we are enjoying, and even those of our prayers which are answered require fresh prayers. Everything for which we are dependent on chance is uncertain: the higher it rises, the more opportunities it has of falling. Moreover, no one takes any pleasure in what is about to fall into ruin: very wretched, therefore, as well as very short must be the lives of those who work very hard to gain what they must work even harder to keep: they obtain what they wish with infinite labour, and they hold what they have obtained with fear and trembling. Meanwhile they take no account of time, of which they will never have a fresh and larger supply: they substitute new occupations for old ones, one hope leads to another, one ambition to another: they do not seek for an end to their wretchedness, but they change its subject. Do our own preferments trouble us? nay, those of other men occupy more of our time. Have we ceased from our labours in canvassing? then we begin others in voting. Have we got rid of the trouble of accusation? then we begin that of judging. Has a man ceased to be a judge? then he becomes an examiner. Has he grown old in the salaried management of other people's property? then he becomes occupied with his own. Marius is discharged from military service; he becomes consul many times: Quintius is eager to reach the end of his dictatorship; he will be called a second time from the plough: Scipio marched against the Carthaginians before he was of years sufficient for so great an undertaking; after he has conquered Hannibal, conquered Antiochus, been the glory of his own consulship and the surety for that of his brother, he might, had he wished it, have been set on the same pedestal with Jupiter; but civil factions will

---

[74] Xerxes.

vex the saviour of the State, and he who when a young man disdained to receive divine honours, will take pride as an old man in obstinately remaining in exile. We shall never lack causes of anxiety, either pleasurable or painful: our life will be pushed along from one business to another: leisure will always be wished for, and never enjoyed.

18

Wherefore, my dearest Paulinus, tear yourself away from the common herd, and since you have seen more rough weather than one would think from your age, betake yourself at length to a more peaceful haven: reflect what waves you have sailed through, what storms you have endured in private life, and brought upon yourself in public. Your courage has been sufficiently displayed by many toilsome and wearisome proofs; try how it will deal with leisure: the greater, certainly the better part of your life, has been given to your country; take now some part of your time for yourself as well. I do not urge you to practise a dull or lazy sloth, or to drown all your fiery spirit in the pleasures which are dear to the herd: that is not rest: you can find greater works than all those which you have hitherto so manfully carried out, upon which you may employ yourself in retirement and security. You manage the revenues of the entire world, as unselfishly as though they belonged to another, as laboriously as if they were your own, as scrupulously as though they belonged to the public: you win love in an office in which it is hard to avoid incurring hatred; yet, believe me, it is better to understand your own mind than to understand the corn-market. Take away that keen intellect of yours, so well capable of grappling with the greatest subjects, from a post which may be dignified, but which is hardly fitted to render life happy, and reflect that you did not study from childhood all the branches of a liberal education merely in order that many thousand tons of corn might safely be entrusted to your charge: you have given us promise of something greater and nobler than this. There will never be any want of strict economists or of laborious workers: slow-going beasts of burden are better suited for carrying loads than well-bred horses, whose generous swiftness no one would encumber with a heavy pack. Think, moreover, how full of risk is the great task which you have undertaken: you have to deal with the human stomach: a hungry people will not endure reason, will not be appeased by justice, and will not hearken to any prayers. Only just a few days ago, when G. Caesar perished, grieving for nothing so much (if those in the other world can feel grief) as that the Roman people did not die with him, there was said to be only enough corn for seven or eight days' consumption: while he was making bridges with ships[75] and playing with the resources of the empire, want of provisions,

---

[75] "Sénèque parle ici du pont que Caligula fit construire sur le golphe de Baies, l'an de Rome 791, 40 de J. C. ... Il rassembla et fit entrer dans la construction de son pont tous les vaisseaux qui se trouverent dans les ports d'Italie et des contrées voisines. Il n'excepta pas même ceux qui etoient destinés a y apporter des grains étrangers," etc.—La Grange.

the worst evil that can befall even a besieged city, was at hand: his imitation of a crazy outlandish and misproud king very nearly ended in ruin, famine, and the general revolution which follows famine. What must then have been the feelings of those who had the charge of supplying the city with corn, who were in danger of stoning, of fire and sword, of Gaius himself? With consummate art they concealed the vast internal evil by which the State was menaced, and were quite right in so doing; for some diseases must be cured without the patient's knowledge: many have died through discovering what was the matter with them.

19

Betake yourself to these quieter, safer, larger fields of action; do you think that there can be any comparison between seeing that corn is deposited in the public granary without being stolen by the fraud or spoilt by the carelessness of the importer, that it does not suffer from damp or overheating, and that it measures and weighs as much as it ought, and beginning the study of sacred and divine knowledge, which will teach you of what elements the gods are formed, what are their pleasures, their position, their form? to what changes your soul has to look forward? where Nature will place us when we are dismissed from our bodies? what that principle is which holds all the heaviest particles of our universe in the middle, suspends the lighter ones above, puts fire highest of all, and causes the stars to rise in their courses, with many other matters, full of marvels? Will you not[76] cease to grovel on Earth and turn your mind's eye on these themes? nay, while your blood still flows swiftly, before your knees grow feeble, you ought to take the better path. In this course of life there await you many good things, such as love and practice of the virtues, forgetfulness of passions, knowledge of how to live and die, deep repose. The position of all busy men is unhappy, but most unhappy of all is that of those who do not even labour at their own affairs, but have to regulate their rest by another man's sleep, their walk by another man's pace, and whose very love and hate, the freest things in the world, are at another's bidding. If such men wish to know how short their lives are, let them think how small a fraction of them is their own.

20

When, therefore, you see a man often wear the purple robes of office, and hear his name often repeated in the forum, do not envy him: he gains these things by losing so much of his life. Men throw away all their years in order to have one year named after them as consul: some lose their lives during the early part of the struggle, and never reach the height to which they aspired: some after having submitted to a thousand indignities in order to reach the crowning dignity, have the miserable reflection that

---

[76] For *vis tu* see Juvenal V, *vis tu consuetis*, etc. Mayor's note.

the only result of their labours will be the inscription on their tombstone. Some, while telling off extreme old age, like youth, for new aspirations, have found it fail from sheer weakness amid great and presumptuous enterprises. It is a shameful ending, when a man's breath deserts him in a court of justice, while, although well stricken in years, he is still striving to gain the sympathies of an ignorant audience for some obscure litigant: it is base to perish in the midst of one's business, wearied with living sooner than with working; shameful, too, to die in the act of receiving payments, amid the laughter of one's long-expectant heir. I cannot pass over an instance which occurs to me: Turannius was an old man of the most painstaking exactitude, who after entering upon his ninetieth year, when he had by Gr. Caesar's own act been relieved of his duties as collector of the revenue, ordered himself to be laid out on his bed and mourned for as though he were dead. The whole house mourned for the leisure of its old master, and did not lay aside its mourning until his work was restored to him. Can men find such pleasure in dying in harness? Yet many are of the same mind: they retain their wish for labour longer than their capacity for it, and fight against their bodily weakness; they think old age an evil for no other reason than because it lays them on the shelf. The law does not enroll a soldier after his fiftieth year, or require a senator's attendance after his sixtieth: but men have more difficulty in obtaining their own consent than that of the law to a life of leisure. Meanwhile, while they are plundering and being plundered, while one is disturbing another's repose, and all are being made wretched alike, life remains without profit, without pleasure, without any intellectual progress: no one keeps death well before his eyes, no one refrains from far-reaching hopes. Some even arrange things which lie beyond their own lives, such as huge sepulchral buildings, the dedication of public works, and exhibitions to be given at their funeral-pyre, and ostentatious processions: but, by Hercules, the funerals of such men ought to be conducted by the light of torches and wax tapers,[77] as though they had lived but a few days.

---

[77] As those of children were.

ON A HAPPY LIFE

1

All men, brother Gallio, wish to live happily, but are dull at perceiving exactly what it is that makes life happy: and so far is it from being easy to attain the happiness that the more eagerly a man struggles to reach it the further he departs from it, if he takes the wrong road; for, since this leads in the opposite direction, his very swiftness carries him all the further away. We must therefore first define clearly what it is at which we aim: next we must consider by what path we may most speedily reach it, for on our journey itself, provided it be made in the right direction, we shall learn how much progress we have made each day, and how much nearer we are to the goal towards which our natural desires urge us. But as long as we wander at random, not following any guide except the shouts and discordant clamours of those who invite us to proceed in different directions, our short life will be wasted in useless roamings, even if we labour both day and night to get a good understanding. Let us not therefore decide whither we must tend, and by what path, without the advice of some experienced person who has explored the region which we are about to enter, because this journey is not subject to the same conditions as others; for in them some distinctly understood track and inquiries made of the natives make it impossible for us to go wrong, but here the most beaten and frequented tracks are those which lead us most astray. Nothing, therefore, is more important than that we should not, like sheep, follow the flock that has gone before us, and thus proceed not whither we ought, but whither the rest are going. Now nothing gets us into greater troubles than our subservience to common rumour, and our habit of thinking that those things are best which are most generally received as such, of taking many counterfeits for truly good things, and of living not by reason but by imitation of others. This is the cause of those great heaps into which men rush till they are piled one upon another. In a great crush of people, when the crowd presses upon itself, no one can fall without drawing someone else down upon him, and those who go before cause the destruction of those who follow them. You may observe the same thing in human life: no one can merely go wrong by himself, but he must become both the cause and adviser of another's wrong doing. It is harmful to follow the march of those who go before us, and since everyone had rather believe another than form his own opinion, we never pass a deliberate judgment upon life, but some traditional error always entangles us and brings us to ruin, and we perish because we follow other men's examples: we should be cured of this if we were to disengage ourselves from the herd; but as it is, the mob is ready to fight against reason in defence of its own mistake. Consequently the same thing happens as at elections, where, when the fickle breeze of popular favour has veered round, those who have been chosen consuls and praetors are viewed with admiration by the very men who made them so. That we should all approve and disapprove of the same things is the end of every decision which is given according to the voice of the majority.

2

When we are considering a happy life, you cannot answer me as though after a division of the House, "This view has most supporters;" because for that very reason it is the worse of the two: matters do not stand so well with mankind that the majority should prefer the better course: the more people do a thing the worse it is likely to be. Let us therefore inquire, not what is most commonly done, but what is best for us to do, and what will establish us in the possession of undying happiness, not what is approved of by the vulgar, the worst possible exponents of truth. By "the vulgar" I mean both those who wear woollen cloaks and those who wear crowns;[78] for I do not regard the colour of the clothes with which they are covered: I do not trust my eyes to tell me what a man is: I have a better and more trustworthy light by which I can distinguish what is true from what is false: let the mind find out what is good for the mind. If a man ever allows his mind some breathing space and has leisure for communing with himself, what truths he will confess to himself, after having been put to the torture by his own self! He will say, "Whatever I have hitherto done I wish were undone: when I think over what I have said, I envy dumb people: whatever I have longed for seems to have been what my enemies would pray might befall me: good heaven, how far more endurable what I have feared seems to be than what I have lusted after. I have been at enmity with many men, and have changed my dislike of them into friendship, if friendship can exist between bad men: yet I have not yet become reconciled to myself. I have striven with all my strength to raise myself above the common herd, and to make myself remarkable for some talent: what have I effected save to make myself a mark for the arrows of my enemies, and show those who hate me where to wound me? Do you see those who praise your eloquence, who covet your wealth, who court your favour, or who vaunt your power? All these either are, or, which comes to the same thing, may be your enemies: the number of those who envy you is as great as that of those who

---

[78] Lipsius's conjecture, "those who are dressed in white as well as those who are dressed in coloured clothes," alluding to the white robes of candidates for office, seems reasonable.

admire you; why do I not rather seek for some good thing which I can use and feel, not one which I can show? these good things which men gaze at in wonder, which they crowd to see, which one points out to another with speechless admiration, are outwardly brilliant, but within are miseries to those who possess them."

3

Let us seek for some blessing, which does not merely look fine, but is sound and good throughout alike, and most beautiful in the parts which are least seen: let us unearth this. It is not far distant from us; it can be discovered: all that is necessary is to know whither to stretch out your hand: but, as it is, we behave as though we were in the dark, and reach out beyond what is nearest to us, striking as we do so against the very things that we want. However, that I may not draw you into digressions, I will pass over the opinions of other philosophers, because it would take a long time to state and confute them all: take ours. When, however, I say "ours," I do not bind myself to any one of the chiefs of the Stoic school, for I too have a right to form my own opinion. I shall, therefore, follow the authority of some of them, but shall ask some others to discriminate their meaning:[79] perhaps, when after having reported all their opinions, I am asked for my own, I shall impugn none of my predecessors' decisions, and shall say, "I will also add somewhat to them." Meanwhile I follow nature, which is a point upon which every one of the Stoic philosophers are agreed: true wisdom consists in not departing from nature and in moulding our conduct according to her laws and model. A happy life, therefore, is one which is in accordance with its own nature, and cannot be brought about unless in the first place the mind be sound and remain so without interruption, and next, be bold and vigorous, enduring all things with most admirable courage, suited to the times in which it lives, careful of the body and its appurtenances, yet not troublesomely careful. It must also set due value upon all the things which adorn our lives, without overestimating any one of them, and must be able to enjoy the bounty of Fortune without becoming her slave. You understand without my mentioning it that an unbroken calm and freedom ensue, when we have driven away all those things which either excite us or alarm us: for in the place of sensual pleasures and those slight perishable matters which are connected with the basest crimes, we thus gain an immense, unchangeable, equable joy, together with peace, calmness and greatness of mind, and kindliness: for all savageness is a sign of weakness.

---

[79] The Latin words are literally "to divide" their vote, that is, "to separate things of different kinds comprised in a single vote so that they might be voted for separately."—Andrews.
"Sénèque fait allusion ici à une coutume pratiquée dans les assemblés du Sénat; et il nous explique lui-même ailleurs d'un manière très claire: 'Si quelqu'un dans le Sénat,' dit il, 'ouvre un avis, dont une partie me convienne, je le somme de la détacher du reste, et j'y adhère.'"
Ep. 21—La Grange.

4

Our highest good may also be defined otherwise; that is to say, the same idea may be expressed in different language. Just as the same army may at one time be extended more widely, at another contracted into a smaller compass, and may either be curved towards the wings by a depression in the line of the centre, or drawn up in a straight line, while, in whatever figure it be arrayed, its strength and loyalty remain unchanged; so also our definition of the highest good may in some cases be expressed diffusely and at great length, while in others it is put into a short and concise form. Thus, it will come to the same thing, if I say, "The highest good is a mind which despises the accidents of fortune, and takes pleasure in virtue": or, "It is an unconquerable strength of mind, knowing the world well, gentle in its dealings, showing great courtesy and consideration for those with whom it is brought into contact." Or we may choose to define it by calling that man happy who knows good and bad only in the form of good or bad minds: who worships honour, and is satisfied with his own virtue, who is neither puffed up by good fortune nor cast down by evil fortune, who knows no other good than that which he is able to bestow upon himself, whose real pleasure lies in despising pleasures. If you choose to pursue this digression further, you can put this same idea into many other forms, without impairing or weakening its meaning: for what prevents our saying that a happy life consists in a mind which is free, upright, undaunted, and steadfast, beyond the influence of fear or desire, which thinks nothing good except honour, and nothing bad except shame, and regards everything else as a mass of mean details which can neither add anything to nor take anything away from the happiness of life, but which come and go without either increasing or diminishing the highest good? A man of these principles, whether he will or no, must be accompanied by a continual cheerfulness, a high happiness, which comes indeed from on high because he delights in what he has, and desires no greater pleasures than those which his home affords. Is he not right in allowing these to turn the scale against petty, ridiculous and shortlived movements of his wretched body? on the day on which he becomes proof against pleasure he also becomes proof against pain. See, on the other hand, how evil and guilty a slavery the man is forced to serve who is dominated in turn by pleasures and pains, those most untrustworthy and passionate of masters. We must, therefore, escape from them into freedom. This nothing will bestow upon us save contempt of fortune: but if we attain to this, then there will dawn upon us those invaluable blessings, the repose of a mind that is at rest in a safe haven, its lofty imaginings, its great and steady delight at casting out errors and learning to know the truth, its courtesy, and its cheerfulness, in all of which we shall take delight, not regarding them as good things, but as proceeding from the proper good of man.

5

Since I have begun to make my definitions without a too strict adherence to the letter, a man may be called "happy" who, thanks to reason, has ceased either to hope or to fear: but rocks also feel neither fear nor sadness, nor do cattle, yet no one would call those things happy which cannot comprehend what happiness is. With them you may class men whose dull nature and want of self-knowledge reduces them to the level of cattle, mere animals: there is no difference between the one and the other, because the latter have no reason, while the former have only a corrupted form of it, crooked and cunning to their own hurt. For no one can be styled happy who is beyond the influence of truth: and consequently a happy life is unchangeable, and is founded upon a true and trustworthy discernment; for the mind is uncontaminated and freed from all evils only when it is able to escape not merely from wounds but also from scratches, when it will always be able to maintain the position which it has taken up, and defend it even against the angry assaults of Fortune: for with regard to sensual pleasures, though they were to surround one on every side, and use every means of assault, trying to win over the mind by caresses and making trial of every conceivable stratagem to attract either our entire selves or our separate parts, yet what mortal that retains any traces of human origin would wish to be tickled day and night, and, neglecting his mind, to devote himself to bodily enjoyments?

6

"But," says our adversary, "the mind also will have pleasures of its own." Let it have them, then, and let it sit in judgment over luxury and pleasures; let it indulge itself to the full in all those matters which give sensual delights: then let it look back upon what it enjoyed before, and with all those faded sensualities fresh in its memory let it rejoice and look eagerly forward to those other pleasures which it experienced long ago, and intends to experience again, and while the body lies in helpless repletion in the present, let it send its thoughts onward towards the future, and take stock of its hopes: all this will make it appear, in my opinion, yet more wretched, because it is insanity to choose evil instead of good: now no insane person can be happy, and no one can be sane if he regards what is injurious as the highest good and strives to obtain it. The happy man, therefore, is he who can make a right judgment in all things: he is happy who in his present circumstances, whatever they may be, is satisfied and on friendly terms with the conditions of his life. That man is happy, whose reason recommends to him the whole posture of his affairs.

7

Even those very people who declare the highest good to be in the belly, see what a dishonourable position they have assigned to it: and therefore they say that pleasure cannot be parted from virtue, and that no one can either live honourably without living cheerfully, nor yet live cheerfully without living honourably. I do not see how these very different matters can have any connection with one another. What is there, I pray you, to prevent virtue existing apart from pleasure? of course the reason is that all good things derive their origin from virtue, and therefore even those things which you cherish and seek for come originally from its roots. Yet, if they were entirely inseparable, we should not see some things to be pleasant, but not honourable, and others most honourable indeed, but hard and only to be attained by suffering. Add to this, that pleasure visits the basest lives, but virtue cannot coexist with an evil life; yet some unhappy people are not without pleasure, nay, it is owing to pleasure itself that they are unhappy; and this could not take place if pleasure had any connection with virtue, whereas virtue is often without pleasure, and never stands in need of it. Why do you put together two things which are unlike and even incompatible one with another? virtue is a lofty quality, sublime, royal, unconquerable, untiring: pleasure is low, slavish, weakly, perishable; its haunts and homes are the brothel and the tavern. You will meet virtue in the temple, the marketplace, the senate house, manning the walls, covered with dust, sunburnt, horny-handed: you will find pleasure skulking out of sight, seeking for shady nooks at the public baths, hot chambers, and places which dread the visits of the aedile, soft, effeminate, reeking of wine and perfumes, pale or perhaps painted and made up with cosmetics. The highest good is immortal: it knows no ending, and does not admit of either satiety or regret: for a right-thinking mind never alters or becomes hateful to itself, nor do the best things ever undergo any change: but pleasure dies at the very moment when it charms us most: it has no great scope, and therefore it soon cloys and wearies us, and fades away as soon as its first impulse is over: indeed, we cannot depend upon anything whose nature is to change. Consequently it is not even possible that there should be any solid substance in that which comes and goes so swiftly, and which perishes by the very exercise of its own functions, for it arrives at a point at which it ceases to be, and even while it is beginning always keeps its end in view.

8

What answer are we to make to the reflection that pleasure belongs to good and bad men alike, and that bad men take as much delight in their shame as good men in noble things? This was why the ancients bade us lead the highest, not the most pleasant life, in order that pleasure might not be the guide but the companion of a right-thinking and honourable mind; for it is Nature whom we ought to make our guide: let our reason watch her, and be advised by her. To live happily, then, is the same thing as to live according to Nature: what this may be, I will explain. If we guard the endowments of the body and the advantages of nature with care and fearlessness, as things soon to depart and given to us only for a day; if we do not fall under their dominion, nor allow ourselves to become the slaves of what is no part of our own being; if we assign to all bodily pleasures and external delights the same position which is held by auxiliaries and light-armed troops in a camp; if we make them our servants, not our masters—then and then only are they of value to our minds. A man should be unbiased and not to be conquered by external things: he ought to admire himself alone, to feel confidence in his own spirit, and so to order his life as to be ready alike for good or for bad fortune. Let not his confidence be without knowledge, nor his knowledge without steadfastness: let him always abide by what he has once determined, and let there be no erasure in his doctrines. It will be understood, even though I append it not, that such a man will be tranquil and composed in his demeanour, high-minded and courteous in his actions. Let reason be encouraged by the senses to seek for the truth, and draw its first principles from thence: indeed it has no other base of operations or place from which to start in pursuit of truth: it must fall back upon itself. Even the all-embracing universe and God who is its guide extends himself forth into outward things, and yet altogether returns from all sides back to himself. Let our mind do the same thing: when, following its bodily senses it has by means of them sent itself forth into the things of the outward world, let it remain still their master and its own. By this means we shall obtain a strength and an ability which are united and allied together, and shall derive from it that reason which never halts between two opinions, nor is dull in forming its perceptions, beliefs, or convictions. Such a mind, when it has ranged itself in order, made its various parts agree together, and, if I may so express myself, harmonized them, has attained to the highest good: for it has nothing evil or hazardous remaining, nothing to shake it or make it stumble: it will do everything under the guidance of its own will, and nothing unexpected will befall it, but whatever may be done by it will turn out well, and that, too, readily and easily, without the doer having recourse to any underhand devices: for slow and hesitating action are the signs of discord and want of settled purpose. You may, then, boldly declare that the highest good is singleness of mind: for where agreement and unity are, there must the virtues be: it is the vices that are at war one with another.

9

"But," says our adversary, "you yourself only practise virtue because you hope to obtain some pleasure from it." In the first place, even though virtue may afford us pleasure, still we do not seek after her on that account: for she does not bestow this, but bestows this to boot, nor is this the end for which she labours, but her labour wins this also, although it be directed to another end. As in a tilled-field, when ploughed for corn, some flowers are found amongst it, and yet, though these posies may charm the eye, all this labour was not spent in order to produce them—the man who sowed the field had another object in view, he gained this over and above it—so pleasure is not the reward or the cause of virtue, but comes in addition to it; nor do we choose virtue because she gives us pleasure, but she gives us pleasure also if we choose her. The highest good lies in the act of choosing her, and in the attitude of the noblest minds, which when once it has fulfilled its function and established itself within its own limits has attained to the highest good, and needs nothing more: for there is nothing outside of the whole, any more than there is anything beyond the end. You are mistaken, therefore, when you ask me what it is on account of which I seek after virtue: for you are seeking for something above the highest. Do you ask what I seek from virtue? I answer, Herself: for she has nothing better; she is her own reward. Does this not appear great enough, when I tell you that the highest good is an unyielding strength of mind, wisdom, magnanimity, sound judgment, freedom, harmony, beauty? Do you still ask me for something greater, of which these may be regarded as the attributes? Why do you talk of pleasures to me? I am seeking to find what is good for man, not for his belly; why, cattle and whales have larger ones than he.

10

"You purposely misunderstand what I say," says he, "for I too say that no one can live pleasantly unless he lives honorably also, and this cannot be the case with dumb animals who measure the extent of their happiness by that of their food. I loudly and publicly proclaim that what I call a pleasant life cannot exist without the addition of virtue." Yet who does not know that the greatest fools drink the deepest of those pleasures of yours? or that vice is full of enjoyments, and that the mind itself suggests to itself many perverted, vicious forms of pleasure?—in the first place arrogance, excessive self-esteem, swaggering precedence over other men, a shortsighted, nay, a blind devotion to his own interests, dissolute luxury, excessive delight springing from the most trifling and childish causes, and also talkativeness, pride that takes a pleasure in insulting others, sloth, and the decay of a dull mind which goes to sleep over itself. All these are dissipated by virtue, which plucks a man by the ear, and measures the value of pleasures before she permits them to be used; nor does she set much store by those which she allows to pass current, for she merely allows their use, and her cheerfulness is not due to her use of them, but to her moderation in using them. "Yet when moderation lessens pleasure, it impairs the highest good." You devote yourself to pleasures, I check them; you indulge in pleasure, I use it; you think that it is the highest good, I do not even think it to be good: for the sake of pleasure I do nothing, you do everything.

11

When I say that I do nothing for the sake of pleasure, I allude to that wise man, whom alone you admit to be capable of pleasure: now I do not call a man wise who is overcome by anything, let alone by pleasure: yet, if engrossed by pleasure, how will he resist toil, danger, want, and all the ills which surround and threaten the life of man? How will he bear the sight of death or of pain? How will he endure the tumult of the world, and make head against so many most active foes, if he be conquered by so effeminate an antagonist? He will do whatever pleasure advises him: well, do you not see how many things it will advise him to do? "It will not," says our adversary, "be able to give him any bad advice, because it is combined with virtue?" Again, do you not see what a poor kind of highest good that must be which requires a guardian to ensure its being good at all? and how is virtue to rule pleasure if she follows it, seeing that to follow is the duty of a subordinate, to rule that of a commander? do you put that which commands in the background? According to your school, virtue has the dignified office of preliminary tester of pleasures. We shall, however, see whether virtue still remains virtue among those who treat her with such contempt, for if she leaves her proper station she can no longer keep her proper name: in the meanwhile, to keep to the point, I will show you many men beset by pleasures, men upon whom Fortune has showered all her gifts, whom you must needs admit to be bad men. Look at Nomentanus and Apicius, who digest all the good things, as they call them, of the sea and land, and review upon their tables the whole animal kingdom. Look at them as they lie on beds of roses gloating over their banquet, delighting their ears with music, their eyes with exhibitions, their palates with flavours: their whole bodies are titillated with soft and soothing applications, and lest even their nostrils should be idle, the very place in which they solemnized[80] the rites of luxury is scented with various perfumes. You will say that these men live in the midst of pleasures. Yet they are ill at ease, because they take pleasure in what is not good.

12

"They are ill at ease," replies he, "because many things arise which distract their thoughts, and their minds are disquieted by conflicting opinions." I admit that this is true: still these very men, foolish, inconsistent, and certain to feel remorse as they are, do nevertheless receive great pleasure, and we must allow that in so doing they are as far from feeling any trouble as they are from forming a right judgment, and that, as is the case with many people, they are possessed by a merry madness, and laugh while they rave. The pleasures of wise men, on the other hand, are mild, decorous, verging on dullness, kept under restraint and scarcely noticeable, and are neither invited to come nor received with honour when they come of their own accord, nor are they welcomed with any delight by those whom they visit, who mix them up with their lives and fill up empty spaces with them, like an amusing farce in

---

[80] *Parentatur* seems to mean where an offering is made to luxury—where they sacrifice to luxury. Perfumes were used at funerals. Lipsius suggests that these feasts were like funerals because the guests were carried away from them dead drunk.

the intervals of serious business. Let them no longer, then, join incongruous matters together, or connect pleasure with virtue, a mistake whereby they court the worst of men. The reckless profligate, always in liquor and belching out the fumes of wine, believes that he lives with virtue, because he knows that he lives with pleasure, for he hears it said that pleasure cannot exist apart from virtue; consequently he dubs his vices with the title of wisdom and parades all that he ought to conceal. So, men are not encouraged by Epicurus to run riot, but the vicious hide their excesses in the lap of philosophy, and flock to the schools in which they hear the praises of pleasure. They do not consider how sober and temperate—for so, by Hercules, I believe it to be—that "pleasure" of Epicurus is, but they rush at his mere name, seeking to obtain some protection and cloak for their vices. They lose, therefore, the one virtue which their evil life possessed, that of being ashamed of doing wrong: for they praise what they used to blush at, and boast of their vices. Thus modesty can never reassert itself, when shameful idleness is dignified with an honourable name. The reason why that praise which your school lavishes upon pleasure is so hurtful, is because the honourable part of its teaching passes unnoticed, but the degrading part is seen by all.

13

I myself believe, though my Stoic comrades would be unwilling to hear me say so, that the teaching of Epicurus was upright and holy, and even, if you examine it narrowly, stern: for this much talked of pleasure is reduced to a very narrow compass, and he bids pleasure submit to the same law which we bid virtue do—I mean, to obey nature. Luxury, however, is not satisfied with what is enough for nature. What is the consequence? Whoever thinks that happiness consists in lazy sloth, and alternations of gluttony and profligacy, requires a good patron for a bad action, and when he has become an Epicurean, having been led to do so by the attractive name of that school, he follows, not the pleasure which he there hears spoken of, but that which he brought thither with him, and, having learned to think that his vices coincide with the maxims of that philosophy, he indulges in them no longer timidly and in dark corners, but boldly in the face of day. I will not, therefore, like most of our school, say that the sect of Epicurus is the teacher of crime, but what I say is: it is ill spoken of, it has a bad reputation, and yet it does not deserve it. "Who can know this without having been admitted to its inner mysteries?" Its very outside gives opportunity for scandal, and encourages men's baser desires: it is like a brave man dressed in a woman's gown: your chastity is assured, your manhood is safe, your body is submitted to nothing disgraceful, but your hand holds a drum (like a priest of Cybele). Choose, then, some honourable superscription for your school, some writing which shall in itself arouse the mind: that which at present stands over your door has been invented by the vices. He who ranges himself on the side of virtue gives thereby a proof of a noble disposition: he who follows pleasure appears to be weakly, worn out, degrading his manhood, likely to fall into infamous vices unless someone discriminates his pleasures for him, so that he may know which remain within the bounds of natural desire, which are frantic and boundless, and become all the more insatiable the more they are satisfied. But come! let virtue lead the way: then every step will be safe. Too much pleasure is hurtful: but with virtue we need fear no excess of any kind, because moderation is contained in virtue herself. That which is injured by its own extent cannot be a good thing: besides, what better guide can there be than reason for beings endowed with a reasoning nature? so if this combination pleases you, if you are willing to proceed to a happy life thus accompanied, let virtue lead the way, let pleasure follow and hang about the body like a shadow: it is the part of a mind incapable of great things to hand over virtue, the highest of all qualities, as a handmaid to pleasure.

14

Let virtue lead the way and bear the standard: we shall have pleasure for all that, but we shall be her masters and controllers; she may win some concessions from us, but will not force us to do anything. On the contrary, those who have permitted pleasure to lead the van, have neither one nor the other: for they lose virtue altogether, and yet they do not possess pleasure, but are possessed by it, and are either tortured by its absence or choked by its excess, being wretched if deserted by it, and yet more wretched if overwhelmed by it, like those who are caught in the shoals of the Syrtes and at one time are left on dry ground and at another tossed on the flowing waves. This arises from an exaggerated want of self-control, and a hidden love of evil: for it is dangerous for one who seeks after evil instead of good to attain his object. As we hunt wild beasts with toil and peril, and even when they are caught find them an anxious possession, for they often tear their keepers to pieces, even so are great pleasures: they turn out to be great evils and take their owners prisoner. The more numerous and the greater they are, the more inferior and the slave of more masters does that man become whom the vulgar call a happy man. I may even press this analogy further: as the man who tracks wild animals to their lairs, and who sets great store on—

"Seeking with snares the wandering brutes to noose,"

and

"Making their hounds the spacious glade surround,"

that he may follow their tracks, neglects far more desirable things, and leaves many duties unfulfilled, so he who pursues pleasure postpones everything to it, disregards that first essential, liberty, and sacrifices it to his belly; nor does he buy pleasure for himself, but sells himself to pleasure.

15

"But what," asks our adversary, "is there to hinder virtue and pleasure being combined together, and a highest good being thus formed, so that honour and pleasure may be the same thing?" Because nothing except what is honourable can form a part of honour, and the highest good would lose its purity if it were to see within itself anything unlike its own better part. Even the joy which arises from virtue, although it be a good thing, yet is not a part of absolute good, any more than cheerfulness or peace of mind, which are indeed good things, but which merely follow the highest good, and do not contribute to its perfection, although they are generated by the noblest causes. Whoever on the other hand forms an alliance, and that, too, a one-sided one, between virtue and pleasure, clogs whatever strength the one may possess by the weakness of the other, and sends liberty under the yoke, for liberty can only remain unconquered as long as she knows nothing more valuable than herself: for he begins to need the help of Fortune, which is the most utter slavery: his life becomes anxious, full of suspicion, timorous, fearful of accidents, waiting in agony for critical moments of time. You do not afford virtue a solid immoveable base if you bid it stand on what is unsteady: and what can be so unsteady as dependence on mere chance, and the vicissitudes of the body and of those things which act on the body? How can such a man obey God and receive everything which comes to pass in a cheerful spirit, never complaining of fate, and putting a good construction upon everything that befalls him, if he be agitated by the petty pinpricks of pleasures and pains? A man cannot be a good protector of his country, a good avenger of her wrongs, or a good defender of his friends, if he be inclined to pleasures. Let the highest good, then, rise to that height from whence no force can dislodge it, whither neither pain can ascend, nor hope, nor fear, nor anything else that can impair the authority of the "highest good." Thither virtue alone can make her way: by her aid that hill must be climbed: she will bravely stand her ground and endure whatever may befall her not only resignedly, but even willingly: she will know that all hard times come in obedience to natural laws, and like a good soldier she will bear wounds, count scars, and when transfixed and dying will yet adore the general for whom she falls: she will bear in mind the old maxim, "Follow God." On the other hand, he who grumbles and complains and bemoans himself is nevertheless forcibly obliged to obey orders, and is dragged away, however much against his will, to carry them out: yet what madness is it to be dragged rather than to follow? as great, by Hercules, as it is folly and ignorance of one's true position to grieve because one has not got something or because something has caused us rough treatment, or to be surprised or indignant at those ills which befall good men as well as bad ones, I mean diseases, deaths, illnesses, and the other cross accidents of human life. Let us bear with magnanimity whatever the system of the universe makes it needful for us to bear: we are all bound by this oath: "To bear the ills of mortal life, and to submit with a good grace to what we cannot avoid." We have been born into a monarchy: our liberty is to obey God.

16

True happiness, therefore, consists in virtue: and what will this virtue bid you do? Not to think anything bad or good which is connected neither with virtue nor with wickedness: and in the next place, both to endure unmoved the assaults of evil, and, as far as is right, to form a god out of what is good. What reward does she promise you for this campaign? an enormous one, and one that raises you to the level of the gods: you shall be subject to no restraint and to no want; you shall be free, safe, unhurt; you shall fail in nothing that you attempt; you shall be debarred from nothing; everything shall turn out according to your wish; no misfortune shall befall you; nothing shall happen to you except what you expect and hope for. "What! does virtue alone suffice to make you happy?" why, of course, consummate and godlike virtue such as this not only suffices, but more than suffices: for when a man is placed beyond the reach of any desire, what can he possibly lack? if all that he needs is concentred in himself, how can he require anything from without? He, however, who is only on the road to virtue, although he may have made great progress along it, nevertheless needs some favour from Fortune while he is still struggling among mere human interests, while he is untying that knot, and all the bonds which bind him to mortality. What, then, is the difference between them? it is that some are tied more or less tightly by these bonds, and some have even tied themselves with them as well; whereas he who has made progress towards the upper regions and raised himself upwards drags a looser chain, and though not yet free, is yet as good as free.

17

If, therefore, any one of those dogs who yelp at philosophy were to say, as they are wont to do, "Why, then, do you talk so much more bravely than you live? why do you check your words in the presence of your superiors, and consider money to be a necessary implement: why are you disturbed when you sustain losses, and weep on hearing of the death of your wife or your friend? Why do you pay regard to common rumour, and feel annoyed by calumnious gossip? why is your estate more elaborately kept than its natural use requires? why do you not dine according to your own maxims? why is your furniture smarter than it need be? why do you drink wine that is older than yourself? why are your grounds laid out? Why do you plant trees which afford nothing except shade? why does your wife wear in her ears the price of a rich man's house? why are your children at school dressed in costly clothes? why is it a science to wait upon you at table? why is your silver plate not set down anyhow or at random, but skillfully disposed in regular order, with a superintendent to preside over the carving of the viands?" Add to this, if you like, the questions "Why do you own property beyond the seas? why do you own more than you know of? it is a shame to you not to know your slaves by sight: for you must be very neglectful of them if you only own a few, or very extravagant if you have too many for your memory to retain." I will add some reproaches afterwards, and will bring more accusations against myself than you think of: for the present I will make you the following answer. "I am not a wise man, and I will not be one in order to feed your spite: so do not require me to be on a level with the best of men, but merely to be better than the worst: I am satisfied, if every day I take away something from my vices and correct my faults. I have not arrived at perfect soundness of mind, indeed, I never shall arrive at it: I compound palliatives rather than remedies for my gout, and am satisfied if it comes at rarer interval—and does not shoot so painfully. Compared with your feet, which are lame, I am a racer." I make this speech, not on my own behalf, for I am steeped in vices of every kind, but on behalf of one who has made some progress in virtue.

18

"You talk one way," objects our adversary, "and live another." You most spiteful of creatures, you who always show the bitterest hatred to the best of men, this reproach was flung at Plato, at Epicurus, at Zeno: for all these declared how they ought to live, not how they did live. I speak of virtue, not of myself, and when I blame vices, I blame my own first of all: when I have the power, I shall live as I ought to do: spite, however deeply steeped in venom, shall not keep me back from what is best: that poison itself with which you bespatter others, with which you choke yourselves, shall not hinder me from continuing to praise that life which I do not, indeed, lead, but which I know I ought to lead, from loving virtue and from following after her, albeit a long way behind her and with halting gait. Am I to expect that evil speaking will respect anything, seeing that it respected neither Rutilius nor Cato? Will anyone care about being thought too rich by men for whom Diogenes the Cynic was not poor enough? That most energetic philosopher fought against all the desires of the body, and was poorer even than the other Cynics, in that besides having given up possessing anything he had also given up asking for anything: yet they reproached him for not being sufficiently in want: as though forsooth it were poverty, not virtue, of which he professed knowledge.

19

They say that Diodorus, the Epicurean philosopher, who within these last few days put an end to his life with his own hand, did not act according to the precepts of Epicurus, in cutting his throat: some choose to regard this act as the result of madness, others of recklessness; he, meanwhile, happy and filled with the consciousness of his own goodness, has borne testimony to himself by his manner of departing from life, has commended the repose of a life spent at anchor in a safe harbour, and has said what you do not like to hear, because you too ought to do it.

"I've lived, I've run the race which Fortune set me."

You argue about the life and death of another, and yelp at the name of men whom some peculiarly noble quality has rendered great, just as tiny curs do at the approach of strangers: for it is to your interest that no one should appear to be good, as if virtue in another were a reproach to all your crimes. You enviously compare the glories of others with your own dirty actions, and do not understand how greatly to your disadvantage it is to venture to do so: for if they who follow after virtue be greedy, lustful, and fond of power, what must you be, who hate the very name of virtue? You say that no one acts up to his professions, or lives according to the standard which he sets up in his discourses: what wonder, seeing that the words which they speak are brave, gigantic, and able to weather all the storms which wreck mankind, whereas they themselves are struggling to tear themselves away from crosses into which each one of you is driving his own nail. Yet men who are crucified hang from one single pole, but these who punish themselves are divided between as many crosses as they have lusts, but yet are given to evil speaking, and are so magnificent in their contempt of the vices of others that I should suppose that they had none of their own, were it not that some criminals when on the gibbet spit upon the spectators.

20

"Philosophers do not carry into effect all that they teach." No; but they effect much good by their teaching, by the noble thoughts which they conceive in their minds: would, indeed, that they could act up to their talk: what could be happier than they would be? but in the meanwhile you have no right to despise good sayings and hearts full of good thoughts. Men deserve praise for engaging in profitable studies, even though they stop short of producing any results. Why need we wonder if those who begin to climb a steep path do not succeed in ascending it very high? yet, if you be a man, look with respect on those who attempt great things, even though they fall. It is the act of a generous spirit to proportion its efforts not to its own strength but to that of human nature, to entertain lofty aims, and to conceive plans which are too vast to be carried into execution even by those who are endowed with gigantic intellects, who appoint for themselves the following rules: "I will look upon death or upon a comedy with the same expression of countenance: I will submit to labours, however great they may be, supporting the strength of my body by that of my mind: I will despise riches when I have them as much as when I have them not; if they be elsewhere I will not be more gloomy, if they sparkle around me I will not be more lively than I should otherwise be: whether Fortune comes or goes I will take no notice of her: I will view all lands as though they belong to me, and my own as though they belonged to all mankind: I will so live as to remember that I was born for others, and will thank Nature on this account: for in what fashion could she have done better for me? she has given me alone to all, and all to me alone. Whatever I may possess, I will neither hoard it greedily nor squander it recklessly. I will think that I have no possessions so real as those which I have given away to deserving people: I will not reckon benefits by their magnitude or number, or by anything except the value set upon them by the receiver: I never will consider a gift to be a large one if it be bestowed upon a worthy object. I will do nothing because of public opinion, but everything because of conscience: whenever I do anything alone by myself I will believe that the eyes of the Roman people are upon me while I do it. In eating and drinking my object shall be to quench the desires of Nature, not to fill and empty my belly. I will be agreeable with my friends, gentle and mild to my foes: I will grant pardon before I am asked for it, and will meet the wishes of honourable men half way: I will bear in mind that the world is my native city, that its governors are the gods, and that they stand above and around me, criticizing whatever I do or say. Whenever either Nature demands my breath again, or reason bids me dismiss it, I will quit this life, calling all to witness that I have loved a good conscience, and good pursuits; that no one's freedom, my own least of all, has been impaired through me." He who sets up these as the rules of his life will soar aloft and strive to make his way to the gods: of a truth, even though he fails, yet he

"Fails in a high emprise."[81]

But you, who hate both virtue and those who practise it, do nothing at which we need be surprised, for sickly lights cannot bear the sun, nocturnal creatures avoid the brightness of day, and at its first dawning become bewildered and all betake themselves to their dens together: creatures that fear the light hide themselves in crevices. So croak away, and exercise your miserable tongues in reproaching good men: open wide your jaws, bite hard: you will break many teeth before you make any impression.

21

"But how is it that this man studies philosophy and nevertheless lives the life of a rich man? Why does he say that wealth ought to be despised and yet possess it? that life should be despised, and yet live? that health should be despised, and yet guard it with the utmost care, and wish it to be as good as possible? Does he consider banishment to be an empty name, and say, 'What evil is there in changing one country for another?' and yet, if permitted, does he not grow old in his native land? does he declare that there is no difference between a longer and a shorter time, and yet, if he be not prevented, lengthen out his life and flourish in a green old age?" His answer is, that these things ought to be despised, not that he should not possess them, but that he should not possess them with fear and trembling: he does not drive them away from him, but when they leave him he follows after them unconcernedly. Where, indeed, can Fortune invest riches more securely than

---

[81] The quotation is from the epitaph on Phaeton. See Ovid, *Metamorphoses*, II, 327.

in a place from whence they can always be recovered without any squabble with their trustee? Marcus Cato, when he was praising Curius and Coruncanius and that century in which the possession of a few small silver coins were an offence which was punished by the Censor, himself owned four million sesterces; a less fortune, no doubt, than that of Crassus, but larger than of Cato the Censor. If the amounts be compared, he had outstripped his great-grandfather further than he himself was outdone by Crassus, and if still greater riches had fallen to his lot, he would not have spurned them: for the wise man does not think himself unworthy of any chance presents: he does not love riches, but he prefers to have them; he does not receive them into his spirit, but only into his house: nor does he cast away from him what he already possesses, but keeps them, and is willing that his virtue should receive a larger subject-matter for its exercise.

22

Who can doubt, however, that the wise man, if he is rich, has a wider field for the development of his powers than if he is poor, seeing that in the latter case the only virtue which he can display is that of neither being perverted nor crushed by his poverty, whereas if he has riches, he will have a wide field for the exhibition of temperance, generosity, laboriousness, methodical arrangement, and grandeur. The wise man will not despise himself, however short of stature he may be, but nevertheless he will wish to be tall: even though he be feeble and one-eyed he may be in good health, yet he would prefer to have bodily strength, and that too, while he knows all the while that he has something which is even more powerful: he will endure illness, and will hope for good health: for some things, though they may be trifles compared with the sum total, and though they may be taken away without destroying the chief good, yet add somewhat to that constant cheerfulness which arises from virtue. Riches encourage and brighten up such a man just as a sailor is delighted at a favourable wind that bears him on his way, or as people feel pleasure at a fine day or at a sunny spot in the cold weather. What wise man, I mean of our school, whose only good is virtue, can deny that even these matters which we call neither good nor bad have in themselves a certain value, and that some of them are preferable to others? to some of them we show a certain amount of respect, and to some a great deal. Do not, then, make any mistake: riches belong to the class of desirable things. "Why then," say you, "do you laugh at me, since you place them in the same position that I do?" Do you wish to know how different the position is in which we place them? If my riches leave me, they will carry away with them nothing except themselves: you will be bewildered and will seem to be left without yourself if they should pass away from you: with me riches occupy a certain place, but with you they occupy the highest place of all. In fine, my riches belong to me, you belong to your riches.

23

Cease, then, forbidding philosophers to possess money: no one has condemned wisdom to poverty. The philosopher may own ample wealth, but will not own wealth that which has been torn from another, or which is stained with another's blood: his must be obtained without wronging any man, and without its being won by base means; it must be alike honourably come by and honourably spent, and must be such as spite alone could shake its head at. Raise it to whatever figure you please, it will still be an honourable possession, if, while it includes much which every man would like to call his own, there be nothing which anyone can say is his own. Such a man will not forfeit his right to the favour of Fortune, and will neither boast of his inheritance nor blush for it if it was honourably acquired: yet he will have something to boast of, if he throw his house open, let all his countrymen come among his property, and say, "If anyone recognizes here anything belonging to him, let him take it." What a great man, how excellently rich will he be, if after this speech he possesses as much as he had before! I say, then, that if he can safely and confidently submit his accounts to the scrutiny of the people, and no one can find in them any item upon which he can lay hands, such a man may boldly and unconcealedly enjoy his riches. The wise man will not allow a single ill-won penny to cross his threshold: yet he will not refuse or close his door against great riches, if they are the gift of fortune and the product of virtue: what reason has he for grudging them good quarters: let them come and be his guests: he will neither brag of them nor hide them away: the one is the part of a silly, the other of a cowardly and paltry spirit, which, as it were, muffles up a good thing in its lap. Neither will he, as I said before, turn them out of his house: for what will he say? will he say, "You are useless," or, "I do not know how to use riches?" As he is capable of performing a journey upon his own feet, but yet would prefer to mount a carriage, just so he will be capable of being poor, yet will wish to be rich; he will own wealth, but will view it as an uncertain possession which will someday fly away from him. He will not allow it to be a burden either to himself or to anyone else: he will give it—why do you prick up your ears? why do you open your pockets?—he will give it either to good men or to those whom it may make into good men. He will give it after having taken the utmost pains to choose those who are fittest to receive it, as becomes one who bears in mind that he ought to give an account of what he spends as well as of what he receives. He will give for good and commendable reasons, for a gift ill bestowed counts as a shameful loss: he will have an easily opened pocket, but not one with a hole in it, so that much may be taken out of it, yet nothing may fall out of it.

24

He who believes giving to be an easy matter, is mistaken: it offers very great difficulties, if we bestow our bounty rationally, and do not scatter it impulsively and at random. I do this man a service, I requite a good turn done me by that one: I help this other, because I pity him: this man, again, I teach to be no fit object for poverty to hold down or degrade. I shall not give some men anything, although they are in want, because, even if I do give to them they will still be in want: I shall proffer my bounty to some, and shall forcibly thrust it upon others: I cannot be neglecting my own interests while I am doing this: at no time do I make more people in my debt than when I am giving things away. "What?" say you, "do you give that you may receive again?" At any rate I do not give that I may throw my bounty away: what I give should be so placed that although I cannot ask for its return, yet it may be given back to me. A benefit should be invested in the same manner as a treasure buried deep in the earth, which you would not dig up unless actually obliged. Why, what opportunities of conferring benefits the mere house of a rich man affords? for who considers generous behaviour due only to those who wear the toga? Nature bids me do good to mankind—what difference does it make whether they be slaves or freemen, freeborn or emancipated, whether their freedom be legally acquired or bestowed by arrangement among friends? Wherever there is a human being, there is an opportunity for a benefit: consequently, money may be distributed even within one's own threshold, and a field may be found there for the practice of freehandedness, which is not so called because it is our duty towards free men, but because it takes its rise in a freeborn mind. In the case of the wise man, this never falls upon base and unworthy recipients, and never becomes so exhausted as not, whenever it finds a worthy object, to flow as if its store was undiminished. You have, therefore, no grounds for misunderstanding the honourable, brave, and spirited language which you hear from those who are studying wisdom: and first of all observe this, that a student of wisdom is not the same thing as a man who has made himself perfect in wisdom. The former will say to you, "In my talk I express the most admirable sentiments, yet I am still weltering amid countless ills. You must not force me to act up to my rules: at the present time I am forming myself, moulding my character, and striving to rise myself to the height of a great example. If I should ever succeed in carrying out all that I have set myself to accomplish, you may then demand that my words and deeds should correspond." But he who has reached the summit of human perfection will deal otherwise with you, and will say, "In the first place, you have no business to allow yourself to sit in judgment upon your betters:" I have already obtained one proof of my righteousness in having become an object of dislike to bad men: however, to make you a rational answer, which I grudge to no man, listen to what I declare, and at what price I value all things. Riches, I say, are not a good thing; for if they were, they would make men good: now since that which is found even among bad men cannot be termed good, I do not allow them to be called so: nevertheless I admit that they are desirable and useful and contribute great comforts to our lives.

25

Learn, then, since we both agree that they are desirable, what my reason is amongst counting them among good things, and in what respects I should behave differently to you if I possessed them. Place me as master in the house of a very rich man: place me where gold and silver plate is used for the commonest purposes; I shall not think more of myself because of things which even though they are in my house are yet no part of me. Take me away to the wooden bridge[82] and put me down there among the beggars: I shall not despise myself because I am sitting among those who hold out their hands for alms: for what can the lack of a piece of bread matter to one who does not lack the power of dying? Well, then? I prefer the magnificent house to the beggar's bridge. Place me among magnificent furniture and all the appliances of luxury: I shall not think myself any happier because my cloak is soft, because my guests rest upon purple. Change the scene: I shall be no more miserable if my weary head rests upon a bundle of hay, if I lie upon a cushion from the circus, with all the stuffing on the point of coming out through its patches of threadbare cloth. Well, then? I prefer, as far as my feelings go, to show myself in public dressed in woollen and in robes of office, rather than with naked or half-covered shoulders: I should like every day's business to turn out just as I wish it to do, and new congratulations to be constantly following upon the former ones: yet I will not pride myself upon this: change all this good fortune for its opposite, let my spirit be distracted by losses, grief, various kinds of attacks: let no hour pass without some dispute: I shall not on this account, though beset by the greatest miseries, call myself the most miserable of beings, nor shall I curse any particular day, for I have taken care to have no unlucky days. What, then, is the upshot of all this? it is that I prefer to have to regulate joys than to stifle sorrows. The great Socrates would say the same thing to you. "Make me," he would say, "the conqueror of all nations: let the voluptuous car of Bacchus bear me in triumph to Thebes from the rising of the sun: let the kings of the Persians receive laws from me: yet I shall feel myself to be a man at the very moment when all around salute me as a God. Straightaway connect this lofty height with a headlong fall into misfortune: let me be placed upon a foreign chariot that I may grace the triumph of a proud and savage conqueror: I will follow another's car with no more humility than I showed when I stood in my own. What then? In spite of all this, I had rather be a conqueror than a captive. I despise the whole dominion of Fortune, but still, if I were given my choice, I would choose its better parts. I shall make whatever befalls me become a good thing, but I prefer that what befalls me should be comfortable and pleasant and unlikely to cause me annoyance: for you need not suppose that any virtue exists without labour, but some virtues need spurs, while others need the curb. As we have to check our body on a downward path, and to urge

---

[82] The "Pons Sublicius," or "pile bridge," was built over the Tiber by Ancus Martius, one of the early kings of Rome, and was always kept in repair out of a superstitious feeling.

it to climb a steep one; so also the path of some virtues leads downhill, that of others uphill. Can we doubt that patience, courage, constancy, and all the other virtues which have to meet strong opposition, and to trample fortune under their feet, are climbing, struggling, winning their way up a steep ascent? Why! is it not equally evident that generosity, moderation, and gentleness glide easily downhill? With the latter we must hold in our spirit, lest it run away with us: with the former we must urge and spur it on. We ought, therefore to apply these energetic, combative virtues to poverty, and to riches those other more thrifty ones which trip lightly along, and merely support their own weight. This being the distinction between them, I would rather have to deal with those which I could practise in comparative quiet, than those of which one can only make trial through blood and sweat. "Wherefore," says the sage, "I do not talk one way and live another: but you do not rightly understand what I say: the sound of my words alone reaches your ears, you do not try to find out their meaning."

26

"What difference, then, is there between me, who am a fool, and you, who are a wise man?" "All the difference in the world: for riches are slaves in the house of a wise man, but masters in that of a fool. You accustom yourself to them and cling to them as if somebody had promised that they should be yours forever, but a wise man never thinks so much about poverty as when he is surrounded by riches. No general ever trusts so implicitly in the maintenance of peace as not to make himself ready for a war, which, though it may not actually be waged, has nevertheless been declared; you are rendered overproud by a fine house, as though it could never be burned or fall down, and your heads are turned by riches as though they were beyond the reach of all dangers and were so great that Fortune has not sufficient strength to swallow them up. You sit idly playing with your wealth and do not foresee the perils in store for it, as savages generally do when besieged, for, not understanding the use of siege artillery, they look on idly at the labours of the besiegers and do not understand the object of the machines which they are putting together at a distance: and this is exactly what happens to you: you go to sleep over your property, and never reflect how many misfortunes loom menacingly around you on all sides, and soon will plunder you of costly spoils, but if one takes away riches from the wise man, one leaves him still in possession of all that is his: for he lives happy in the present, and without fear for the future. The great Socrates, or anyone else who had the same superiority to and power to withstand the things of this life, would say, 'I have no more fixed principle than that of not altering the course of my life to suit your prejudices: you may pour your accustomed talk upon me from all sides: I shall not think that you are abusing me, but that you are merely wailing like poor little babies.' " This is what the man will say who possesses wisdom, whose mind, being free from vices, bids him reproach others, not because he hates them, but in order to improve them: and to this he will add, "Your opinion of me affects me with pain, not for my own sake but for yours, because to hate perfection and to assail virtue is in itself a resignation of all hope of doing well. You do me no harm; neither do men harm the gods when they overthrow their altars: but it is clear that your intention is an evil one and that you will wish to do harm even where you are not able. I bear with your prating in the same spirit in which Jupiter, best and greatest, bears with the idle tales of the poets, one of whom represents him with wings, another with horns, another as an adulterer staying out all night, another is dealing harshly with the gods, another as unjust to men, another as the seducer of noble youths whom he carries off by force, and those, too, his own relatives, another as a parricide and the conqueror of another's kingdom, and that his father's. The only result of such tales is that men feel less shame at committing sin if they believe the gods to be guilty of such actions. But although this conduct of yours does not hurt me, yet, for your own sakes, I advise you, respect virtue: believe those who having long followed her cry aloud that what they follow is a thing of might, and daily appears mightier. Reverence her as you would the gods, and reverence her followers as you would the priests of the gods: and whenever any mention of sacred writings is made, *favete linguis*, favour us with silence: this word is not derived, as most people imagine, from *favour*, but commands silence, that divine service may be performed without being interrupted by any words of evil omen. It is much more necessary that you should be ordered to do this, in order that whenever utterance is made by that oracle, you may listen to it with attention and in silence. Whenever anyone beats a *sistrum*,[83] pretending to do so by divine command, any proficient in grazing his own skin covers his arms and shoulders with blood from light cuts, anyone crawls on his knees howling along the street, or any old man clad in linen comes forth in daylight with a lamp and laurel branch and cries out that one of the gods is angry, you crowd round him and listen to his words, and each increases the other's wonderment by declaring him to be divinely inspired.

27

Behold! from that prison of his, which by entering he cleansed from shame and rendered more honourable than any senate house, Socrates addresses you, saying: "What is this madness of yours? what is this disposition, at war alike with gods and men, which leads you to calumniate virtue and to outrage holiness with malicious accusations? Praise good men, if you are able: if not, pass them by in silence: if indeed you take pleasure in this offensive abusiveness, fall foul of one another: for when you rave against Heaven, I do not say that you commit sacrilege, but you waste your time. I once afforded Aristophanes with the subject of a jest: since then all the crew of comic poets have made me a mark for their envenomed wit: my virtue has

---

[83] A metallic rattle used by the Egyptians in celebrating the rites of Isis, etc.—Andrews.

been made to shine more brightly by the very blows which have been aimed at it, for it is to its advantage to be brought before the public and exposed to temptation, nor do any people understand its greatness more than those who by their assaults have made trial of its strength. The hardness of flint is known to none so well as to those who strike it. I offer myself to all attacks, like some lonely rock in a shallow sea, which the waves never cease to beat upon from whatever quarter they may come, but which they cannot thereby move from its place nor yet wear away, for however many years they may unceasingly dash against it. Bound upon me, rush upon me, I will overcome you by enduring your onset: whatever strikes against that which is firm and unconquerable merely injures itself by its own violence.

Wherefore, seek some soft and yielding object to pierce with your darts. But have you leisure to peer into other men's evil deeds and to sit in judgment upon anybody? to ask how it is that this philosopher has so roomy a house, or that one so good a dinner?

Do you look at other people's pimples while you yourselves are covered with countless ulcers? This is as though one who was eaten up by the mange were to point with scorn at the moles and warts on the bodies of the handsomest men. Reproach Plato with having sought for money, reproach Aristotle with having obtained it,

Democritus with having disregarded it, Epicurus with having spent it: cast Phaedrus and Alcibiades in my own teeth, you who reach the height of enjoyment whenever you get an opportunity of imitating our vices! Why do you not rather cast your eyes around yourselves at the ills which tear you to pieces on every side, some attacking you from without, some burning in your own bosoms? However little you know your own place, mankind has not yet come to such a pass that you can have leisure to wag your tongues to the reproach of your betters.

28

This you do not understand, and you bear a countenance which does not befit your condition, like many men who sit in the circus or the theatre without having learned that their home is already in mourning: but I, looking forward from a lofty standpoint, can see what storms are either threatening you, and will burst in torrents upon you somewhat later, or are close upon you and on the point of sweeping away all that you possess. Why, though you are hardly aware of it, is there not a whirling hurricane at this moment spinning round and confusing your minds, making them seek and avoid the very same things, now raising them aloft and now dashing them below?

ON LEISURE

1

... why do they with great unanimity recommend vices to us? even though we attempt nothing else that would do us good, yet retirement in itself will be beneficial to us: we shall be better men when taken singly—and if so, what an advantage it will be to retire into the society of the best of men, and to choose some example by which we may guide our lives! This cannot be done without leisure: with leisure we can carry out that which we have once for all decided to be best, when there is no one to interfere with us and with the help of the mob pervert our as yet feeble judgment: with leisure only can life, which we distract by aiming at the most incompatible objects, flow on in a single gentle stream. Indeed, the worst of our various ills is that we change our very vices, and so we have not even the advantage of dealing with a well-known form of evil: we take pleasure first in one and then in another, and are, besides, troubled by the fact that our opinions are not only wrong, but lightly formed; we toss as it were on waves, and clutch at one thing after another: we let go what we just now sought for, and strive to recover what we have let go. We oscillate between desire and remorse, for we depend entirely upon the opinions of others, and it is that which many people praise and seek after, not that which deserves to be praised and sought after, which we consider to be best. Nor do we take any heed of whether our road be good or bad in itself, but we value it by the number of footprints upon it, among which there are none of any who have returned. You will say to me, "Seneca, what are you doing? do you desert your party? I am sure that our Stoic philosophers say we must be in motion up to the very end of our life, we will never cease to labour for the general good, to help individual people, and when stricken in years to afford assistance even to our enemies. We are the sect that gives no discharge for any number of years' service, and in the words of the most eloquent of poets:—

'We wear the helmet when our locks are grey.'[84]

We are they who are so far from indulging in any leisure until we die, that if circumstances permit it, we do not allow ourselves to be at leisure even when we are dying. Why do you preach the maxims of Epicurus in the very headquarters of Zeno? nay, if you are ashamed of your party, why do you not go openly altogether over to the enemy rather than betray your own side?" I will answer this question straightaway: What more can you wish than that I should imitate my leaders? What then follows? I shall go whither they lead me, not whither they send me.

2

Now I will prove to you that I am not deserting the tenets of the Stoics: for they themselves have not deserted them: and yet I should be able to plead a very good excuse even if I did follow, not their precepts, but their examples. I shall divide what I am about to say into two parts: first, that a man may from the very beginning of his life give himself up entirely to the contemplation of truth; secondly, that a man when he has already completed his term of service, has the best of rights, that of his shattered health, to do this, and that he may then apply his mind to other studies after the manner of the Vestal virgins, who allot different duties to different years, first learn how to perform the sacred rites, and when they have learned them teach others.

3

I will show that this is approved of by the Stoics also, not that I have laid any commandment upon myself to do nothing contrary to the teaching of Zeno and Chrysippus, but because the matter itself allows me to follow the precepts of those men; for if one always follows the precepts of one man, one ceases to be a debater and becomes a partisan. Would that all things were already known, that truth were unveiled and recognized, and that none of our doctrines required modification! but as it is we have to seek for truth in the company of the very men who teach it. The two sects of Epicureans and Stoics differ widely in most respects, and on this point among the rest, nevertheless, each of them consigns us to leisure, although by a different road. Epicurus says, "The wise man will not take part in politics, except

---

[84] Virgil, *Æneid*, IX, 612. Compare Sir Walter Scott, *Lay of the Last Minstrel*, canto IV:—
"And still, in age, he spurned at rest,
And still his brows the helmet pressed,
Albeit the blanched looks below
Were white as Dinlay's spotless snow,"
etc.

upon some special occasion;" Zeno says, "The wise man will take part in politics, unless prevented by some special circumstance." The one makes it his aim in life to seek for leisure, the other seeks it only when he has reasons for so doing: but this word "reasons" has a wide signification. If the State is so rotten as to be past helping, if evil has entire dominion over it, the wise man will not labour in vain or waste his strength in unprofitable efforts. Should he be deficient in influence or bodily strength, if the State refuse to submit to his guidance, if his health stand in the way, then he will not attempt a journey for which he is unfit, just as he would not put to sea in a worn-out ship, or enlist in the army if he were an invalid. Consequently, one who has not yet suffered either in health or fortune has the right, before encountering any storms, to establish himself in safety, and thenceforth to devote himself to honourable industry and inviolate leisure, and the service of those virtues which can be practiced even by those who pass the quietest of lives. The duty of a man is to be useful to his fellow-men; if possible, to be useful to many of them; failing this, to be useful to a few; failing this, to be useful to his neighbours, and, failing them, to himself: for when he helps others, he advances the general interests of mankind. Just as he who makes himself a worse man does harm not only to himself but to all those to whom he might have done good if he had made himself a better one, so he who deserves well of himself does good to others by the very fact that he is preparing what will be of service to them.

4

Let us grasp the fact that there are two republics, one vast and truly "public," which contains alike gods and men, in which we do not take account of this or that nook of land, but make the boundaries of our state reach as far as the rays of the sun: and another to which we have been assigned by the accident of birth. This may be that of the Athenians or Carthaginians, or of any other city which does not belong to all men but to some especial ones. Some men serve both of these states, the greater and the lesser, at the same time; some serve only the lesser, some only the greater. We can serve the greater commonwealth even when we are at leisure; indeed I am not sure that we cannot serve it better when we are at leisure to inquire into what virtue is, and whether it be one or many: whether it be nature or art that makes men good: whether that which contains the earth and sea and all that in them is be one, or whether God has placed therein many bodies of the same species: whether that out of which all things are made be continuous and solid, or containing interstices and alternate empty and full spaces: whether God idly looks on at His handiwork, or directs its course: whether He is without and around the world, or whether He pervades its entire surface: whether the world be immortal, or doomed to decay and belonging to the class of things which are born only for a time? What service does he who meditates upon these questions render to God? He prevents these His great works having no one to witness them.

5

We have a habit of saying that the highest good is to live according to nature: now nature has produced us for both purposes, for contemplation and for action. Let us now prove what we said before: nay, who will not think this proved if he bethinks himself how great a passion he has for discovering the unknown? how vehemently his curiosity is roused by every kind of romantic tale. Some men make long voyages and undergo the toils of journeying to distant lands for no reward except that of discovering something hidden and remote. This is what draws people to public shows, and causes them to pry into everything that is closed, to puzzle out everything that is secret, to clear up points of antiquity, and to listen to tales of the customs of savage nations. Nature has bestowed upon us an inquiring disposition, and being well aware of her own skill and beauty, has produced us to be spectators of her vast works, because she would lose all the fruits of her labour if she were to exhibit such vast and noble works of such complex construction, so bright and beautiful in so many ways, to solitude alone. That you may be sure that she wishes to be gazed upon, not merely looked at, see what a place she has assigned to us: she has placed us in the middle of herself and given us a prospect all around. She has not only set man erect upon his feet, but also with a view to making it easy for him to watch the heavens, she has raised his head on high and connected it with a pliant neck, in order that he might follow the course of the stars from their rising to their setting, and move his face round with the whole heaven. Moreover, by carrying six constellations across the sky by day, and six by night, she displays every part of herself in such a manner that by what she brings before man's eyes she renders him eager to see the rest also. For we have not beheld all things, nor yet the true extent of them, but our eyesight does but open to itself the right path for research, and lay the foundation, from which our speculations may pass from what is obvious to what is less known, and find out something more ancient than the world itself, from whence those stars came forth: inquire what was the condition of the universe before each of its elements were separated from the general mass: on what principle its confused and blended parts were divided: who assigned their places to things, whether it was by their own nature that what was heavy sunk downwards, and what was light flew upwards, or whether besides the stress and weight of bodies some higher power gave laws to each of them: whether that greatest proof that the spirit of man is divine be true, the theory, namely, that some parts and as it were sparks of the stars have fallen down upon earth and stuck there in a foreign substance. Our thought bursts through the battlements of heaven, and is not satisfied with knowing only what is shown to us: "I investigate," it says, "that which lies without the world, whether it be a bottomless abyss, or whether it also is confined within boundaries of its own: what the appearance of the things outside may be, whether they be shapeless and vague, extending equally in every direction, or whether they also are arranged in a certain kind of order: whether they are connected with this world of ours, or are widely separated from it and welter about in empty space: whether they consist of distinct atoms, of which everything that is and that is to be, is made, or whether their substance is uninterrupted and all of it capable of change: whether the elements are naturally opposed to one another, or whether they are not at variance, but work towards the same end by different means." Since man was born for such speculations as these, consider how short a time he has been given for them, even supposing that he makes good his claims to the whole of it, allows no part of it to be wrested from him through good nature, or to slip away from him through carelessness; though he watches over all his hours with most miserly care, though he live to the extreme confines of human existence, and though misfortune take nothing away from what Nature bestowed upon him, even then man is too mortal for the comprehension of immortality. I live according to Nature, therefore, if I give myself entirely up to her, and if I admire and reverence her. Nature, however, intended me to do both, to practise both contemplation and action: and I do both, because even contemplation is not devoid of action.

6

"But," say you, "it makes a difference whether you adopt the contemplative life for the sake of your own pleasure, demanding nothing from it save unbroken contemplation without any result: for such a life is a sweet one and has attractions of its own." To this I answer you: It makes just as much difference in what spirit you lead the life of a public man, whether you are never at rest, and never set apart any time during which you may turn your eyes away from the things of Earth to those of Heaven. It is by no means desirable that one should merely strive to accumulate property without any love of virtue, or do nothing but hard work without any cultivation of the intellect, for these things ought to be combined and blended together; and, similarly, virtue placed in leisure without action is but an incomplete and feeble good thing, because she never displays what she has learned. Who can deny that she ought to test her progress in actual work, and not merely think what ought to be done, but also sometimes use her hands as well as her head, and bring her conceptions into actual being? But if the wise man be quite willing to act thus, if it be the things to be done, not the man to do them that are wanting, will you not then allow him to live to himself? What is the wise man's purpose in devoting himself to leisure? He knows that in leisure as well as in action he will accomplish something by which he will be of service to posterity. Our school at any rate declares that Zeno and Chrysippus have done greater things than they would have done had they been in command of armies, or filled high offices, or passed laws: which latter indeed they did pass, though not for one single state, but for the whole human race. How then can it be unbecoming to a good man to enjoy a leisure such as this, by whose means he gives laws to ages to come, and addresses himself not to a few persons but to all men of all nations, both now and hereafter? To sum up the matter, I ask you whether Cleanthes, Chrysippus, and Zeno lived in accordance with their doctrine? I am sure that you will answer that they lived in the manner in which they taught that men ought to live: yet no one of them governed a state. "They had not," you reply, "the amount of property or social position which as a rule enables people to take part in public affairs." Yet for all that they did not live an idle life: they found the means of making their retirement more useful to mankind than the perspirings and runnings to and fro of other men: wherefore these persons are thought to have done great things, in spite of their having done nothing of a public character.

7

Moreover, there are three kinds of life, and it is a stock question which of the three is the best: the first is devoted to pleasure, the second to contemplation, the third to action. First, let us lay aside all disputatiousness and bitterness of feeling, which, as we have stated, causes those whose paths in life are different to hate one another beyond all hope of reconciliation, and let us see whether all these three do not come to the same thing, although under different names: for neither he who decides for pleasure is without contemplation, nor is he who gives himself up to contemplation without pleasure: nor yet is he, whose life is devoted to action, without contemplation. "It makes," you say, "all the difference in the world, whether a thing is one's main object in life, or whether it be merely an appendage to some other object." I admit that the difference is considerable, nevertheless the one does not exist apart from the other: the one man cannot live in contemplation without action, nor can the other act without contemplation: and even the third, of whom we all agree in having a bad opinion, does not approve of passive pleasure, but of that which he establishes for himself by means of reason: even this pleasure-seeking sect itself, therefore, practises action also. Of course it does, since Epicurus himself says that at times he would abandon pleasure and actually seek for pain, if he became likely to be surfeited with pleasure, or if he thought that by enduring a slight pain he might avoid a greater one. With what purpose do I state this? To prove that all men are fond of contemplation. Some make it the object of their lives: to us it is an anchorage, but not a harbour.

8

Add to this that, according to the doctrine of Chrysippus, a man may live at leisure: I do not say that he ought to endure leisure, but that he ought to choose it. Our Stoics say that the wise man would not take part in the government of any state. What difference does it make by what path the wise man arrives at leisure, whether it be because the State is wanting to him, or he is wanting to the State? If the State is to be wanting to all wise men (and it always will be found wanting by refined thinkers), I ask you, to what state should the wise man betake himself; to that of the Athenians, in which Socrates is condemned to death, and from which Aristotle goes into exile lest he should be condemned to death? where virtues are borne down by jealousy? You will tell me that no wise man would join such a state. Shall then the wise man go to the commonwealth of the Carthaginians, where faction never ceases to rage, and liberty is the foe of all the best men, where justice and goodness are held of no account, where enemies are treated with inhuman cruelty and natives are treated like enemies: he will flee from this state also. If I were to discuss each one separately, I should not be able to find one which the wise man could endure, or which could endure the wise man. Now if such a state as we have dreamed of cannot be found on Earth, it follows that leisure is necessary for everyone, because the one thing which might be preferred to leisure is nowhere to be found. If anyone says that to sail is the best of things, and then says that we ought not to sail in a sea in which shipwrecks were common occurrences, and where sudden storms often arise which drive the pilot back from his course, I should imagine that this man, while speaking in praise of sailing, was really forbidding me to unmoor my ship.

ON PEACE OF MIND

1

(Serenus)

When I examine myself, Seneca, some vices appear on the surface, and so that I can lay my hands upon them, while others are less distinct and harder to reach, and some are not always present, but recur at intervals: and these I should call the most troublesome, being like a roving enemy that assails one when he sees his opportunity, and who will neither let one stand on one's guard as in war, nor yet take one's rest without fear as in peace. The position in which I find myself more especially (for why should I not tell you the truth as I would to a physician), is that of neither being thoroughly set free from the vices which I fear and hate, nor yet quite in bondage to them: my state of mind, though not the worst possible, is a particularly discontented and sulky one: I am neither ill nor well. It is of no use for you to tell me that all virtues are weakly at the outset, and that they acquire strength and solidity by time, for I am well aware that even those which do but help our outward show, such as grandeur, a reputation for eloquence, and everything that appeals to others, gain power by time. Both those which afford us real strength and those which do but trick us out in a more attractive form, require long years before they gradually are adapted to us by time. But I fear that custom, which confirms most things, implants this vice more and more deeply in me. Long acquaintance with both good and bad people leads one to esteem them all alike. What this state of weakness really is, when the mind halts between two opinions without any strong inclination towards either good or evil, I shall be better able to show you piecemeal than all at once. I will tell you what befalls me, you must find out the name of the disease. I have to confess the greatest possible love of thrift: I do not care for a bed with gorgeous hangings, nor for clothes brought out of a chest, or pressed under weights and made glossy by frequent manglings, but for common and cheap ones, that require no care either to keep them or to put them on. For food I do not want what needs whole troops of servants to prepare it and admire it, nor what is ordered many days before and served up by many hands, but something handy and easily come at, with nothing farfetched or costly about it, to be had in every part of the world, burdensome neither to one's fortune nor one's body, not likely to go out of the body by the same path by which it came in. I like[85] a rough and unpolished homebred servant, I like my servant born in my house: I like my country-bred father's heavy silver plate stamped with no maker's name: I do not want a table that is beauteous with dappled spots, or known to all the town by the number of fashionable people to whom it has successively belonged, but one which stands merely for use, and which causes no guest's eye to dwell upon it with pleasure or to kindle at it with envy. While I am well satisfied with this, I am reminded of the clothes of a certain schoolboy, dressed with no ordinary care and splendour, of slaves bedecked with gold and a whole regiment of glittering attendants. I think of houses too, where one treads on precious stones, and where valuables lie about in every corner, where the very roof is brilliantly painted, and a whole nation attends and accompanies an inheritance on the road to ruin. What shall I say of waters, transparent to the very bottom, which flow round the guests, and banquets worthy of the theatre in which they take place? Coming as I do from a long course of dull thrift, I find myself surrounded by the most brilliant luxury, which echoes around me on every side: my sight becomes a little dazzled by it: I can lift up my heart against it more easily than my eyes. When I return from seeing it I am a sadder, though not a worse man, I cannot walk amid my own paltry possessions with so lofty a step as before, and silently there steals over me a feeling of vexation, and a doubt whether that way of life may not be better than mine. None of these things alter my principles, yet all of them disturb me. At one time I would obey the maxims of our school and plunge into public life, I would obtain office and become consul, not because the purple robe and lictor's axes attract me, but in order that I may be able to be of use to my friends, my relatives, to all my countrymen, and indeed to all mankind. Ready and determined, I follow the advice of Zeno, Cleanthes, and Chrysippus, all of whom bid one take part in public affairs, though none of them ever did so himself: and then, as soon as something disturbs my mind, which is not used to receiving shocks, as soon as something occurs which is either disgraceful, such as often occurs in all men's lives, or which does not proceed quite easily, or when subjects of very little importance require me to devote a great deal of time to them, I go back to my life of leisure, and, just as even tired cattle go faster when they are going home, I wish to retire and pass my life within the walls of my house. "No one," I say, "that will give me no compensation worth such a loss shall ever rob me of a day. Let my mind be contained within itself and improve itself: let it take no part with other men's affairs, and do nothing which depends on the approval of others: let me enjoy a tranquility undisturbed by either public or private troubles." But whenever my spirit is roused by reading some brave words, or some noble example spurs me into action, I want to rush into the law courts, to place my voice at one man's disposal, my services at another's, and to try to help him even

---

[85] Cf. Juvenal II, 150.

though I may not succeed, or to quell the pride of some lawyer who is puffed up by ill-deserved success: but I think, by Hercules, that in philosophical speculation it is better to view things as they are, and to speak of them on their own account, and as for words, to trust to things for them, and to let one's speech, simply follow whither they lead. "Why do you want to construct a fabric that will endure for ages? Do you not wish to do this in order that posterity may talk of you: yet you were born to die, and a silent death is the least wretched. Write something therefore in a simple style, merely to pass the time, for your own use, and not for publication. Less labour is needed when one does not look beyond the present." Then again, when the mind is elevated by the greatness of its thoughts, it becomes ostentatious in its use of words, the loftier its aspirations, the more loftily it desires to express them, and its speech rises to the dignity of its subject. At such times I forget my mild and moderate determination and soar higher than is my wont, using a language that is not my own. Not to multiply examples, I am in all things attended by this weakness of a well-meaning mind, to whose level I fear that I shall be gradually brought down, or what is even more worrying, that I may always hang as though about to fall, and that there may be more the matter with me than I myself perceive: for we take a friendly view of our own private affairs, and partiality always obscures our judgment. I fancy that many men would have arrived at wisdom had they not believed themselves to have arrived there already, had they not purposely deceived themselves as to some parts of their character, and passed by others with their eyes shut: for you have no grounds for supposing that other people's flattery is more ruinous to us than our own. Who dares to tell himself the truth? Who is there, by however large a troop of caressing courtiers he may be surrounded, who in spite of them is not his own greatest flatterer? I beg you, therefore, if you have any remedy by which you could stop this vacillation of mine, to deem me worthy to owe my peace of mind to you. I am well aware that these oscillations of mind are not perilous and that they threaten me with no serious disorder: to express what I complain of by an exact simile, I am not suffering from a storm, but from seasickness. Take from me, then, this evil, whatever it may be, and help one who is in distress within sight of land.

2

(Seneca)

I have long been silently asking myself, my friend Serenus, to what I should liken such a condition of mind, and I find that nothing more closely resembles it than the conduct of those who, after having recovered from a long and serious illness, occasionally experience slight touches and twinges, and, although they have passed through the final stages of the disease, yet have suspicions that it has not left them, and though in perfect health yet hold out their pulse to be felt by the physician, and whenever they feel warm suspect that the fever is returning. Such men, Serenus, are not unhealthy, but they are not accustomed to being healthy; just as even a quiet sea or lake nevertheless displays a certain amount of ripple when its waters are subsiding after a storm. What you need, therefore, is, not any of those harsher remedies to which allusion has been made, not that you should in some cases check yourself, in others be angry with yourself, in others sternly reproach yourself, but that you should adopt that which comes last in the list, have confidence in yourself, and believe that you are proceeding on the right path, without being led aside by the numerous divergent tracks of wanderers which cross it in every direction, some of them circling about the right path itself. What you desire, to be undisturbed, is a great thing, nay, the greatest thing of all, and one which raises a man almost to the level of a god. The Greeks call this calm steadiness of mind *euthymia*, and Democritus's treatise upon it is excellently written: I call it peace of mind: for there is no necessity for translating so exactly as to copy the words of the Greek idiom: the essential point is to mark the matter under discussion by a name which ought to have the same meaning as its Greek name, though perhaps not the same form. What we are seeking, then, is how the mind may always pursue a steady, unruffled course, may be pleased with itself, and look with pleasure upon its surroundings, and experience no interruption of this joy, but abide in a peaceful condition without being ever either elated or depressed: this will be "peace of mind." Let us now consider in a general way how it may be attained: then you may apply as much as you choose of the universal remedy to your own case. Meanwhile we must drag to light the entire disease, and then each one will recognize his own part of it: at the same time you will understand how much less you suffer by your self-depreciation than those who are bound by some showy declaration which they have made, and are oppressed by some grand title of honour, so that shame rather than their own free will forces them to keep up the pretence. The same thing applies both to those who suffer from fickleness and continual changes of purpose, who always are fondest of what they have given up, and those who merely yawn and dawdle: add to these those who, like bad sleepers, turn from side to side, and settle themselves first in one manner and then in another, until at last they find rest through sheer weariness: in forming the habits of their lives they often end by adopting some to which they are not kept by any dislike of change, but in the practice of which old age, which is slow to alter, has caught them living: add also those who are by no means fickle, yet who must thank their dullness, not their consistency for being so, and who go on living not in the way they wish, but in the way they have begun to live. There are other special forms of this disease without number, but it has but one effect, that of making people dissatisfied with themselves. This arises from a distemperature of mind and from desires which one is afraid to express or unable to fulfill, when men either dare not attempt as much as they wish to do, or fail in their efforts and depend entirely upon hope: such people are always fickle and changeable, which is a necessary consequence of living in a state of suspense: they take any way to arrive at their ends, and teach and force themselves to use both dishonourable and difficult means to do so, so that when their toil has been in vain they are made wretched by the disgrace of failure, and do not regret having longed for what was wrong, but having longed for it in vain. They then begin to feel sorry for what they have done, and afraid to begin again, and their mind falls by degrees into a state of endless vacillation, because they can neither command nor obey their passions, of hesitation, because their life cannot properly develop itself, and of decay, as the mind becomes stupefied by disappointments. All these symptoms become aggravated when their dislike of a laborious misery has driven them to idleness and to secret studies, which are unendurable to a mind eager to take part in public affairs, desirous of action and naturally restless, because, of course, it finds too few resources within itself: when therefore it loses the amusement which business itself affords to busy men, it cannot endure home, loneliness, or the walls of a room, and regards itself with dislike when left to itself. Hence arises that weariness and dissatisfaction with oneself, that tossing to and fro of a mind which can nowhere find rest, that unhappy and unwilling endurance of enforced leisure. In all cases where one feels ashamed to confess the real cause of one's suffering, and where modesty leads one to drive one's sufferings inward, the desires pent up in a little space without any vent choke one another. Hence comes melancholy and drooping of spirit, and a thousand waverings of the unsteadfast mind, which is held in suspense by unfulfilled hopes, and saddened by disappointed ones: hence comes the state of mind of those who loathe their idleness, complain that they have nothing to do, and view the progress of others with the bitterest jealousy: for an unhappy sloth favours the growth of envy, and men who cannot succeed themselves wish everyone else to be ruined. This dislike of other men's progress and despair of one's own produces a mind angered against fortune, addicted to complaining of the age in which it lives to retiring into corners and brooding over its misery, until it becomes sick and weary of itself: for the human mind is naturally nimble and apt at movement: it delights in every opportunity of excitement and forgetfulness of itself, and the worse a man's disposition the more he delights in this, because he likes to wear himself out with busy action, just as some sores long for the hands that injure them and delight in being touched, and the foul itch enjoys anything that scratches it. Similarly I assure you that these minds over which desires have spread like evil ulcers, take pleasure in toils and troubles, for there are some things which please our body while at the same time they give it a certain amount of pain, such as turning oneself over and changing one's side before it is wearied, or cooling oneself in one position after another. It is like Homer's Achilles lying first upon its face, then upon its back, placing itself in various attitudes, and, as sick people are wont, enduring none of them for long, and using changes as though they were remedies. Hence men undertake aimless wanderings, travel along distant shores, and at one time at sea, at another by land, try to soothe that fickleness of disposition which always is dissatisfied with the present. "Now let us make for Campania: now I am sick of rich cultivation: let us see wild regions, let us thread the passes of Bruttii and Lucania: yet amid this wilderness one wants some thing of beauty to relieve our pampered eyes after so long dwelling on savage wastes: let us seek Tarentum with its famous harbour, its mild winter climate, and its district, rich enough to support even the great hordes of ancient times. Let us now return to town: our ears have too long missed its shouts and noise: it would be pleasant also to enjoy the sight of human bloodshed." Thus one journey succeeds another, and one sight is changed for another. As Lucretius says:—

"Thus every mortal from himself doth flee;"

but what does he gain by so doing if he does not escape from himself? he follows himself and weighs himself down by his own most burdensome companionship. We must understand, therefore, that what we suffer from is not the fault of the places but of ourselves: we are weak when there is anything to be endured, and cannot support either labour or pleasure, either one's own business or anyone else's for long. This has driven some men to death, because by frequently altering their purpose they were always brought back to the same point, and had left themselves no room for anything new. They had become sick of life and of the world itself, and as all indulgences palled upon them they began to ask themselves the question, "How long are we to go on doing the same thing?"

3

You ask me what I think we had better make use of to help us to support this ennui. "The best thing," as Athenodorus says, "is to occupy oneself with business, with the management of affairs of state and the duties of a citizen: for as some pass the day in exercising themselves in the sun and in taking care of their bodily health, and athletes find it most useful to spend the greater part of their time in feeding up the muscles and strength to whose cultivation they have devoted their lives; so too for you who are training your mind to take part in the struggles of political life, it is far more honourable to be thus at work than to be idle. He whose object is to be of service to his countrymen and to all mortals, exercises himself and does good at the same time when he is engrossed in business and is working to the best of his ability both in the interests of the public and of private men. But," continues he, "because innocence is hardly safe among such furious ambitions and so many men who turn one aside from the right path, and it is always sure to meet with more hindrance than help, we ought to withdraw ourselves from the forum and from public life, and a great mind even in a private station can find room wherein to expand freely. Confinement in dens restrains the springs of lions and wild creatures, but this does not apply to human beings, who often effect the most important works in retirement. Let a man, however, withdraw himself only in such a fashion that wherever he spends his leisure his wish may still be to benefit individual men and mankind alike, both with his intellect, his voice, and his advice. The man that does good service to the State is not only he who brings forward candidates for public office, defends accused persons, and gives his vote on questions of peace and war, but he who encourages young men in well-doing, who supplies the present dearth of good teachers by instilling into their minds the principles of virtue, who seizes and holds back those who are rushing wildly in pursuit of riches and luxury, and, if he does nothing else, at least checks their course—such a man does service to the public though in a private station. Which does the most good, he who decides between foreigners and citizens (as *praetor peregrinus*), or, as *praetor urbanus*, pronounces sentence to the suitors in his court at his assistant's dictation, or he who shows them what is meant by justice, filial feeling, endurance, courage, contempt of death and knowledge of the gods, and how much a man is helped by a good conscience? If then you transfer to philosophy the time which you take away from the public service, you will not be a deserter or have refused to perform your proper task. A soldier is not merely one who stands in the ranks and defends the right or the left wing of the army, but he also who guards the gates—a service which, though less dangerous, is no sinecure—who keeps watch, and takes charge of the arsenal: though all these are bloodless duties, yet they count as military service. As soon as you have devoted yourself to philosophy, you will have overcome all disgust at life: you will not wish for darkness because you are weary of the light, nor will you be a trouble to yourself and useless to others: you will acquire many friends, and all the best men will be attracted towards you: for virtue, in however obscure a position, cannot be hidden, but gives signs of its presence: anyone who is worthy will trace it out by its footsteps: but if we give up all society, turn our backs upon the whole human race, and live communing with ourselves alone, this solitude without any interesting occupation will lead to a want of something to do: we shall begin to build up and to pull down, to dam out the sea, to cause waters to flow through natural obstacles, and generally to make a bad disposal of the time which Nature has given us to spend: some of us use it grudgingly, others wastefully; some of us spend it so that we can show a profit and loss account, others so that they have no assets remaining: than which nothing can be more shameful. Often a man who is very old in years has nothing beyond his age by which he can prove that he has lived a long time."

4

To me, my dearest Serenus, Athenodorus seems to have yielded too completely to the times, to have fled too soon: I will not deny that sometimes one must retire, but one ought to retire slowly, at a foot's pace, without losing one's ensigns or one's honour as a soldier: those who make terms with arms in their hands are more respected by their enemies and more safe in their hands. This is what I think ought to be done by virtue and by one who practises virtue: if Fortune get the upper hand and deprive him of the power of action, let him not straightaway turn his back to the enemy, throw away his arms, and run away seeking for a hiding-place, as if there were any place whither Fortune could not pursue him, but let him be more sparing in his acceptance of public office, and after due deliberation discover some means by which he can be of use to the State. He is not able to serve in the army: then let him become a candidate for civic honours: must he live in a private station? then let him be an advocate: is he condemned to keep silence? then let him help his countrymen with silent counsel. Is it dangerous for him even to enter the forum? then let him prove himself a good comrade, a faithful friend, a sober guest in people's houses, at public shows, and at wine-parties. Suppose that he has lost the status of a citizen; then let him exercise that of a man: our reason for magnanimously refusing to confine ourselves within the walls of one city, for having gone forth to enjoy intercourse with all lands and for professing ourselves to be citizens of the world is that we may thus obtain a wider theatre on which to display our virtue. Is the bench of judges closed to you, are you forbidden to address the people from the hustings, or to be a candidate at elections? then turn your eyes away from Rome, and see what a wide extent of territory, what a number of nations present themselves before you. Thus, it is never possible for so many outlets to be closed against your ambition that more will not remain open to it: but see whether the whole prohibition does not arise from your own fault. You do not choose to direct the affairs of the State except as consul or prytanis[86] or meddix[87] or sufes:[88] what should we say if you refused to serve in the army save as general or military tribune? Even though others may form the first line, and your lot may have placed you among the veterans of the third, do your duty there with your voice, encouragement, example, and spirit: even though a man's hands be cut off, he may find means to help his side in a battle, if he stands his ground and cheers on his comrades. Do something of that sort yourself: if Fortune removes you from the front rank, stand your ground nevertheless and cheer on your comrades, and if somebody stops your mouth, stand nevertheless and help your side in silence. The services of a good citizen are never thrown away: he does good by being heard and seen, by his expression, his gestures, his silent determination, and his very walk. As some remedies benefit us by their smell as well as by their their taste and touch, so virtue even when concealed and at a distance sheds usefulness around. Whether she moves at her ease and enjoys her just rights, or can only appear abroad on sufferance and is forced to shorten sail to the tempest, whether it be unemployed, silent, and pent up in a narrow lodging, or openly displayed, in whatever guise she may appear, she always does good. What? do you think that the example of one who can rest nobly has no value? It is by far the best plan, therefore, to mingle leisure with business, whenever chance impediments or the state of public affairs forbid one's leading an active life: for one is never so cut off from all pursuits as to find no room left for honourable action.

---

[86] The chief magistrate of the Greeks.

[87] The chief magistrate of the Uscans.

[88] The chief magistrate of the Carthaginians.

5

Could you anywhere find a miserable city than that of Athens when it was being torn to pieces by the thirty tyrants? they slew thirteen hundred citizens, all the best men, and did not leave off because they had done so, but their cruelty became stimulated by exercise. In the city which possessed that most reverend tribunal, the Court of the Areopagus, which possessed a Senate, and a popular assembly which was like a Senate, there met daily a wretched crew of butchers, and the unhappy Senate House was crowded with tyrants. A state, in which there were so many tyrants that they would have been enough to form a bodyguard for one, might surely have rested from the struggle; it seemed impossible for men's minds even to conceive hopes of recovering their liberty, nor could they see any room for a remedy for such a mass of evil: for whence could the unhappy state obtain all the Harmodiuses it would need to slay so many tyrants? Yet Socrates was in the midst of the city, and consoled its mourning Fathers, encouraged those who despaired of the republic, by his reproaches brought rich men, who feared that their wealth would be their ruin, to a tardy repentance of their avarice, and moved about as a great example to those who wished to imitate him, because he walked a free man in the midst of thirty masters. However, Athens herself put him to death in prison, and Freedom herself could not endure the freedom of one who had treated a whole band of tyrants with scorn: you may know, therefore, that even in an oppressed state a wise man can find an opportunity for bringing himself to the front, and that in a prosperous and flourishing one wanton insolence, jealousy, and a thousand other cowardly vices bear sway. We ought therefore, to expand or contract ourselves according as the State presents itself to us, or as Fortune offers us opportunities: but in any case we ought to move and not to become frozen still by fear: nay, he is the best man who, though peril menaces him on every side and arms and chains beset his path, nevertheless neither impairs nor conceals his virtue: for to keep oneself safe does not mean to bury oneself. I think that Curius Dentatus spoke truly when he said that he would rather be dead than alive: the worst evil of all is to leave the ranks of the living before one dies; yet it is your duty, if you happen to live in an age when it is not easy to serve the State, to devote more time to leisure and to literature. Thus, just as though you were making a perilous voyage, you may from time to time put into harbour, and set yourself free from public business without waiting for it to do so.

6

We ought, however, first to examine our own selves, next the business which we propose to transact, next those for whose sake or in whose company we transact it.

It is above all things necessary to form a true estimate of oneself, because as a rule we think that we can do more than we are able: one man is led too far through confidence in his eloquence, another demands more from his estate than it can produce, another burdens a weakly body with some toilsome duty. Some men are too shamefaced for the conduct of public affairs, which require an unblushing front: some men's obstinate pride renders them unfit for courts: some cannot control their anger, and break into unguarded language on the slightest provocation: some cannot rein in their wit or resist making risky jokes: for all these men leisure is better than employment: a bold, haughty and impatient nature ought to avoid anything that may lead it to use a freedom of speech which will bring it to ruin. Next we must form an estimate of the matter which we mean to deal with, and compare our strength with the deed we are about to attempt: for the bearer ought always to be more powerful than his load: indeed, loads which are too heavy for their bearer must of necessity crush him: some affairs also are not so important in themselves as they are prolific and lead to much more business, which employments, as they involve us in new and various forms of work, ought to be refused. Neither should you engage in anything from which you are not free to retreat: apply yourself to something which you can finish, or at any rate can hope to finish: you had better not meddle with those operations which grow in importance, while they are being transacted, and which will not stop where you intended them to stop.

7

In all cases one should be careful in one's choice of men, and see whether they be worthy of our bestowing a part of our life upon them, or whether we shall waste our own time and theirs also: for some even consider us to be in their debt because of our services to them. Athenodorus said that "he would not so much as dine with a man who would not be grateful to him for doing so": meaning, I imagine, that much less would he go to dinner with those who recompense the services of their friends by their table, and regard courses of dishes as donatives, as if they overate themselves to do honour to others. Take away from these men their witnesses and spectators: they will take no pleasure in solitary gluttony. You must decide whether your disposition is better suited for vigorous action or for tranquil speculation and contemplation, and you must adopt whichever the bent of your genius inclines you for. Socrates laid hands upon Ephorus and led him away from the forum, thinking that he would be more usefully employed in compiling chronicles; for no good is done by forcing one's mind to engage in uncongenial work: it is vain to struggle against Nature. Yet nothing delights the mind so much as faithful and pleasant friendship: what a blessing it is when there is one whose breast is ready to receive all your secrets with safety, whose knowledge of your actions you fear less than your own conscience, whose conversation removes your anxieties, whose advice assists your plans, whose cheerfulness dispels your gloom, whose very sight delights you! We should choose for our friends men who are, as far as possible, free from strong desires: for vices are contagious, and pass from a man to his neighbour, and injure those who touch them. As, therefore, in times of pestilence we have to be careful not to sit near people who are infected and in whom the disease is raging, because by so doing, we shall run into danger and catch the plague from their very breath; so, too, in choosing our friends' dispositions, we must take care to select those who are as far as may be unspotted by the world; for the way to breed disease is to mix what is sound with what is rotten. Yet I do not advise you to follow after or draw to yourself no one except a wise man: for where will you find him whom for so many centuries we have sought in vain? in the place of the best possible man take him who is least bad. You would hardly find any time that would have enabled you to make a happier choice than if you could have sought for a good man from among the Platos and Xenophons and the rest of the produce of the brood of Socrates, or if you had been permitted to choose one from the age of Cato: an age which bore many men worthy to be born in Cato's time (just as it also bore many men worse than were ever known before, planners of the blackest crimes: for it needed both classes in order to make Cato understood: it wanted both good men, that he might win their approbation, and bad men, against whom he could prove his strength): but at the present day, when there is such a dearth of good men, you must be less squeamish in your choice. Above all, however, avoid dismal men who grumble at whatever happens, and find something to complain of in everything. Though he may continue loyal and friendly towards you, still one's peace of mind is destroyed by a comrade whose mind is soured and who meets every incident with a groan.

8

Let us now pass on to the consideration of property, that most fertile source of human sorrows: for if you compare all the other ills from which we suffer—deaths, sicknesses, fears, regrets, endurance of pains and labours–with those miseries which our money inflicts upon us, the latter will far outweigh all the others. Reflect, then, how much less a grief it is never to have had any money than to have lost it: we shall thus understand that the less poverty has to lose, the less torment it has with which to afflict us: for you are mistaken if you suppose that the rich bear their losses with greater spirit than the poor: a wound causes the same amount of pain to the greatest and the smallest body. It was a neat saying of Bion's, "that it hurts bald men as much as hairy men to have their hairs pulled out": you may be assured that the same thing is true of rich and poor people, that their suffering is equal: for their money clings to both classes, and cannot be torn away without their feeling it: yet it is more endurable, as I have said, and easier not to gain property than to lose it, and therefore you will find that those upon whom Fortune has never smiled are more cheerful than those whom she has deserted. Diogenes, a man of infinite spirit, perceived this, and made it impossible that anything should be taken from him. Call this security from loss poverty, want, necessity, or any contemptuous name you please: I shall consider such a man to be happy, unless you find me another who can lose nothing. If I am not mistaken, it is a royal attribute among so many misers, sharpers, and robbers, to be the one man who cannot be injured. If anyone doubts the happiness of Diogenes, he would doubt whether the position of the immortal gods was one of sufficient happiness, because they have no farms or gardens, no valuable estates let to strange tenants, and no large loans in the money market. Are you not ashamed of yourself, you who gaze upon riches with astonished admiration? Look upon the universe: you will see the gods quite bare of property, and possessing nothing though they give everything. Do you think that this man who has stripped himself of all fortuitous accessories is a pauper, or one like to the immortal gods? Do you call Demetrius, Pompeius's freedman, a happier man, he who was not ashamed to be richer than Pompeius, who was daily furnished with a list of the number of his slaves, as a general is with that of his army, though he had long deserved that all his riches should consist of a pair of underlings, and a roomier cell than the other slaves? But Diogenes's only slave ran away from him, and when he was pointed out to Diogenes, he did not think him worth fetching back. "It is a shame," he said, "that Manes should be able to live without Diogenes, and that Diogenes should not be able to live without Manes." He seems to me to have said, "Fortune, mind your own business: Diogenes has nothing left that belongs to you. Did my slave run away? nay, he went away from me as a free man." A household of slaves requires food and clothing: the bellies of so many hungry creatures have to be filled: we must buy raiment for them, we must watch their most thievish hands, and we must make use of the services of people who weep and execrate us. How far happier is he who is indebted to no man for anything except for what he can deprive himself of with the greatest ease! Since we, however, have not such strength of mind as this, we ought at any rate to diminish the extent of our property, in order to be less exposed to the assaults of fortune: those men whose bodies can be within the shelter of their armour, are more fitted for war than those whose huge size everywhere extends beyond it, and exposes them to wounds: the best amount of property to have is that which is enough to keep us from poverty, and which yet is not far removed from it.

9

We shall be pleased with this measure of wealth if we have previously taken pleasure in thrift, without which no riches are sufficient, and with which none are insufficient, especially as the remedy is always at hand, and poverty itself by calling in the aid of thrift can convert itself into riches. Let us accustom ourselves to set aside mere outward show, and to measure things by their uses, not by their ornamental trappings: let our hunger be tamed by food, our thirst quenched by drinking, our lust confined within needful bounds; let us learn to use our limbs, and to arrange our dress and way of life according to what was approved of by our ancestors, not in imitation of newfangled models: let us learn to increase our continence, to repress luxury, to set bounds to our pride, to assuage our anger, to look upon poverty without prejudice, to practise thrift, albeit many are ashamed to do so, to apply cheap remedies to the wants of nature, to keep all undisciplined hopes and aspirations as it were under lock and key, and to make it our business to get our riches from ourselves and not from Fortune. We never can so thoroughly defeat the vast diversity and malignity of misfortune with which we are threatened as not to feel the weight of many gusts if we offer a large spread of canvas to the wind: we must draw our affairs into a small compass, to make the darts of Fortune of no avail. For this reason, sometimes slight mishaps have turned into remedies, and more serious disorders have been healed by slighter ones. When the mind pays no attention to good advice, and cannot be brought to its senses by milder measures, why should we not think that its interests are being served by poverty, disgrace, or financial ruin being applied to it? one evil is balanced by another. Let us then teach ourselves to be able to dine without all Rome to look on, to be the slaves of fewer slaves, to get clothes which fulfill their original purpose, and to live in a smaller house. The inner curve is the one to take, not only in running races and in the contests of the circus, but also in the race of life; even literary pursuits, the most becoming thing for a gentleman to spend money upon, are only justifiable as long as they are kept within bounds. What is the use of possessing numberless books and libraries, whose titles their owner can hardly read through in a lifetime? A student is overwhelmed by such a mass, not instructed, and it is much better to devote yourself to a few writers than to skim through many. Forty thousand books were burned at Alexandria: some would have praised this library as a most noble memorial of royal wealth, like Titus Livius, who says that it was "a splendid result of the taste and attentive care of the kings."[89] It had nothing to do with taste or care, but was a piece of learned luxury, nay, not even learned, since they amassed it, not for the sake of learning, but to make a show, like many men who know less about letters than a slave is expected to know, and who uses his books not to help him in his studies but to ornament his dining-room. Let a man, then, obtain as many books as he wants, but none for show. "It is more respectable," say you, "to spend one's money on such books than on vases of Corinthian brass and paintings." Not so: everything that is carried to excess is wrong. What excuses can you find for a man who is eager to buy bookcases of ivory and citrus wood, to collect the works of unknown or discredited authors, and who sits yawning amid so many thousands of books, whose backs and titles please him more than any other part of them? Thus in the houses of the laziest of men you will see the works of all the orators and historians stacked upon bookshelves reaching right up to the ceiling. At the present day a library has become as necessary an appendage to a house as a hot and cold bath. I would excuse them straightaway if they really were carried away by

---

[89] "Livy himself styled the Alexandrian library *elegantiae regum curaeque egregium opus*: a liberal encomium, for which he is pertly criticised by the narrow stoicism of Seneca ('On Peace of Mind,' Chapter II), whose wisdom, on this occasion, deviates into nonsense."
—Gibbon, Decline and Fall, Chapter LI, note.

an excessive zeal for literature; but as it is, these costly works of sacred genius, with all the illustrations that adorn them, are merely bought for display and to serve as wall-furniture.

10

Suppose, however, that your life has become full of trouble, and that without knowing what you were doing you have fallen into some snare which either public or private fortune has set for you, and that you can neither untie it nor break it: then remember that fettered men suffer much at first from the burdens and clogs upon their legs: afterwards, when they have made up their minds not to fret themselves about them, but to endure them, necessity teaches them to bear them bravely, and habit to bear them easily. In every station of life you will find amusements, relaxations, and enjoyments; that is, provided you be willing to make light of evils rather than to hate them. Knowing to what sorrows we were born, there is nothing for which Nature more deserves our thanks than for having invented habit as an alleviation of misfortune, which soon accustoms us to the severest evils. No one could hold out against misfortune if it permanently exercised the same force as at its first onset. We are all chained to fortune: some men's chain is loose and made of gold, that of others is tight and of meaner metal: but what difference does this make? we are all included in the same captivity, and even those who have bound us are bound themselves, unless you think that a chain on the left side is lighter to bear: one man may be bound by public office, another by wealth: some have to bear the weight of illustrious, some of humble birth: some are subject to the commands of others, some only to their own: some are kept in one place by being banished thither, others by being elected to the priesthood. All life is slavery: let each man therefore reconcile himself to his lot, complain of it as little as possible, and lay hold of whatever good lies within his reach. No condition can be so wretched that an impartial mind can find no compensations in it. Small sites, if ingeniously divided, may be made use of for many different purposes, and arrangement will render ever so narrow a room habitable. Call good sense to your aid against difficulties: it is possible to soften what is harsh, to widen what is too narrow, and to make heavy burdens press less severely upon one who bears them skillfully. Moreover, we ought not to allow our desires to wander far afield, but we must make them confine themselves to our immediate neighbourhood, since they will not endure to be altogether locked up. We must leave alone things which either cannot come to pass or can only be effected with difficulty, and follow after such things as are near at hand and within reach of our hopes, always remembering that all things are equally unimportant, and that though they have a different outward appearance, they are all alike empty within. Neither let us envy those who are in high places: the heights which look lofty to us are steep and rugged. Again, those whom unkind fate has placed in critical situations will be safer if they show as little pride in their proud position as may be, and do all they are able to bring down their fortunes to the level of other men's. There are many who must needs cling to their high pinnacle of power, because they cannot descend from it save by falling headlong: yet they assure us that their greatest burden is being obliged to be burdensome to others, and that they are nailed to their lofty post rather than raised to it: let them then, by dispensing justice, clemency, and kindness with an open and liberal hand, provide themselves with assistance to break their fall, and looking forward to this maintain their position more hopefully. Yet nothing sets as free from these alternations of hope and fear so well as always fixing some limit to our successes, and not allowing fortune to choose when to stop our career, but to halt of our own accord long before we apparently need do so. By acting thus certain desires will rouse up our spirits, and yet being confined within bounds, will not lead us to embark on vast and vague enterprises.

11

These remarks of mine apply only to imperfect, commonplace, and unsound natures, not to the wise man, who needs not to walk with timid and cautious gait: for he has such confidence in himself that he does not hesitate to go directly in the teeth of Fortune, and never will give way to her. Nor indeed has he any reason for fearing her, for he counts not only chattels, property, and high office, but even his body, his eyes, his hands, and everything whose use makes life dearer to us, nay, even his very self, to be things whose possession is uncertain; he lives as though he had borrowed them, and is ready to return them cheerfully whenever they are claimed. Yet he does not hold himself cheap, because he knows that he is not his own, but performs all his duties as carefully and prudently as a pious and scrupulous man would take care of property left in his charge as trustee. When he is bidden to give them up, he will not complain of Fortune, but will say, "I thank you for what I have had possession of: I have managed your property so as largely to increase it, but since you order me, I give it back to you and return it willingly and thankfully. If you still wish me to own anything of yours, I will keep it for you: if you have other views, I restore into your hands and make restitution of all my wrought and coined silver, my house and my household. Should Nature recall what she previously entrusted us with, let us say to her also: 'Take back my spirit, which is better than when you gave it me: I do not shuffle or hang back. Of my own free will I am ready to return what you gave me before I could think: take me away.' " What hardship can there be in returning to the place from whence one came? a man cannot live well if he knows not how to die well. We must, therefore, take away from this commodity its original value, and count the breath of life as a cheap matter. "We dislike gladiators," says Cicero, "if they are eager to save their lives by any means whatever: but we look favourably upon them if they are openly reckless of them." You may be sure that the same thing occurs with us: we often die because we are afraid of death. Fortune, which regards our lives as a show in the arena for her own enjoyment, says, "Why should I spare you, base and cowardly creature that you are? you will be pierced and hacked with all the more wounds because you know not how to offer your throat to the knife: whereas you, who receive the stroke without drawing away your neck or putting up your hands to stop it, shall both live longer and die more quickly." He who fears death will never act as becomes a living man: but he who knows that this fate was laid upon him as soon as he was conceived will live according to it, and by this strength of mind will gain this further advantage, that nothing can befall him unexpectedly: for by looking forward to everything which can happen as though it would happen to him, he takes the sting out of all evils, which can make no difference to those who expect it and are prepared to meet it: evil only comes hard upon those who have lived without giving it a thought and whose attention has been exclusively directed to happiness. Disease, captivity, disaster, conflagration, are none of them unexpected: I always knew with what disorderly company Nature had associated me. The dead have often been wailed for in my neighbourhood: the torch and taper have often been borne past my door before the bier of one who has died before his time: the crash of falling buildings has often resounded by my side: night has snatched away many of those with whom I have become intimate in the forum, the Senate-house, and in society, and has sundered the hands which were joined in friendship: ought I to be surprised if the dangers which have always been circling around me at last assail me? How large a part of mankind never think of storms when about to set sail? I shall never be ashamed to quote a good saying because it comes from a bad author. Publilius, who was a more powerful writer than any of our other playwrights, whether comic or tragic, whenever he chose to rise above farcical absurdities and speeches addressed to the gallery, among many other verses too noble even for tragedy, let alone for comedy, has this one:—

"What one hath suffered may befall us all."

If a man takes this into his inmost heart and looks upon all the misfortunes of other men, of which there is always a great plenty, in this spirit, remembering that there is nothing to prevent their coming upon him also, he will arm himself against them long before they attack him. It is too late to school the mind to endurance of peril after peril has come. "I did not think this would happen," and "Would you ever have believed that this would have happened?" say you. But why should it not? Where are the riches after which want, hunger, and beggary do not follow? what office is there whose purple robe, augur's staff, and patrician reins have not as their accompaniment rags and banishment, the brand of infamy, a thousand disgraces, and utter reprobation? what kingdom is there for which ruin, trampling under foot, a tyrant and a butcher are not ready at hand? nor are these matters divided by long periods of time, but there is but the space of an hour between sitting on the throne ourselves and clasping the knees of someone else as suppliants. Know then that every station of life is transitory, and that what has ever happened to anybody may happen to you also. You are wealthy: are you wealthier than Pompeius?[90] Yet when Gaius,[91] his old relative and new host, opened Caesar's house to him in order that he might close his own, he lacked both bread and water: though he owned so many rivers which both rose and discharged themselves within his dominions, yet he had to beg for drops of water: he perished of hunger and thirst in the palace of his relative, while his heir was contracting for a public funeral for one who was in want of food. You have filled public offices: were they either as important, as unlooked for, or as all-embracing as those of Sejanus? Yet on the day on which the Senate disgraced him, the people tore him to pieces: the executioner[92] could find no part left large enough to drag to the Tiber, of one upon whom gods and men had showered all that could be given to man. You are a king: I will not bid you go to Croesus for an example, he who while yet alive saw his funeral pile both lighted and extinguished, being made to outlive not only his kingdom but even his own death, nor to Jugurtha, whom the people of Rome beheld as a captive within the year in which they had feared him. We have seen Ptolemaeus King of Africa, and Mithridates King of Armenia, under the charge of Gaius's[93] guards: the former was sent into exile, the latter chose it in order to make his exile more honourable. Among such continual topsy-turvy changes, unless you expect that whatever can happen will happen to you, you give adversity power against you, a power which can be destroyed by anyone who looks at it beforehand.

12

The next point to these will be to take care that we do not labour for what is vain, or labour in vain: that is to say, neither to desire what we are not able to obtain, nor yet, having obtained our desire too late, and after much toil to discover the folly of our wishes: in other words, that our labour may not be without result, and that the result may not be unworthy of our labour: for as a rule sadness arises from one of these two things, either from want of success or from being ashamed of having succeeded. We must limit the running to and fro which most men practise, rambling about houses, theatres, and marketplaces. They mind other men's business, and always seem as though they themselves had something to do. If you ask one of them as he comes out of his own door, "Whither are you going?" he will answer, "By Hercules, I do not know: but I shall see some people and do something." They wander purposelessly seeking for something to do, and do, not what they have made up their minds to do, but what has casually fallen in their way. They move uselessly and without any plan,

---

[90] Haase reads "Ptolemaeus."
[91] Caligula.
[92] It was the duty of the executioner to fasten a hook to the neck of condemned criminals, by which they were dragged to the Tiber.
[93] Caligula.

just like ants crawling over bushes, which creep up to the top and then down to the bottom again without gaining anything. Many men spend their lives in exactly the same fashion, which one may call a state of restless indolence. You would pity some of them when you see them running as if their house was on fire: they actually jostle all whom they meet, and hurry along themselves and others with them, though all the while they are going to salute someone who will not return their greeting, or to attend the funeral of someone whom they did not know: they are going to hear the verdict on one who often goes to law, or to see the wedding of one who often gets married: they will follow a man's litter, and in some places will even carry it: afterwards returning home weary with idleness, they swear that they themselves do not know why they went out, or where they have been, and on the following day they will wander through the same round again. Let all your work, therefore, have some purpose, and keep some object in view: these restless people are not made restless by labour, but are driven out of their minds by mistaken ideas: for even they do not put themselves in motion without any hope: they are excited by the outward appearance of something, and their crazy mind cannot see its futility. In the same way every one of those who walk out to swell the crowd in the streets, is led round the city by worthless and empty reasons; the dawn drives him forth, although he has nothing to do, and after he has pushed his way into many men's doors, and saluted their nomenclators one after the other, and been turned away from many others, he finds that the most difficult person of all to find at home is himself. From this evil habit comes that worst of all vices, talebearing and prying into public and private secrets, and the knowledge of many things which it is neither safe to tell nor safe to listen to.

13

It was, I imagine, following out this principle that Democritus taught that "he who would live at peace must not do much business either public or private," referring of course to unnecessary business: for if there be any necessity for it we ought to transact not only much but endless business, both public and private; in cases, however, where no solemn duty invites us to act, we had better keep ourselves quiet: for he who does many things often puts himself in Fortune's power, and it is safest not to tempt her often, but always to remember her existence, and never to promise oneself anything on her security. I will set sail unless anything happens to prevent me, I shall be praetor, if nothing hinders me, my financial operations will succeed, unless anything goes wrong with them. This is why we say that nothing befalls the wise man which he did not expect—we do not make him exempt from the chances of human life, but from its mistakes, nor does everything happen to him as he wished it would, but as he thought it would: now his first thought was that his purpose might meet with some resistance, and the pain of disappointed wishes must affect a man's mind less severely if he has not been at all events confident of success.

14

Moreover, we ought to cultivate an easy temper, and not become over fond of the lot which fate has assigned to us, but transfer ourselves to whatever other condition chance may lead us to, and fear no alteration, either in our purposes or our position in life, provided that we do not become subject to caprice, which of all vices is the most hostile to repose: for obstinacy, from which Fortune often wrings some concession, must needs be anxious and unhappy, but caprice, which can never restrain itself, must be more so. Both of these qualities, both that of altering nothing, and that of being dissatisfied with everything, are enemies to repose. The mind ought in all cases to be called away from the contemplation of external things to that of itself: let it confide in itself, rejoice in itself, admire its own works; avoid as far as may be those of others, and devote itself to itself; let it not feel losses, and put a good construction even upon misfortunes. Zeno, the chief of our school, when he heard the news of a shipwreck, in which all his property had been lost, remarked, "Fortune bids me follow philosophy in lighter marching order." A tyrant threatened Theodorus with death, and even with want of burial. "You are able to please yourself," he answered, "my half pint of blood is in your power: for, as for burial, what a fool you must be if you suppose that I care whether I rot above ground or under it." Julius Kanus, a man of peculiar greatness, whom even the fact of his having been born in this century does not prevent our admiring, had a long dispute with Gaius, and when as he was going away that Phalaris of a man said to him, "That you may not delude yourself with any foolish hopes, I have ordered you to be executed," he answered, "I thank you, most excellent prince." I am not sure what he meant: for many ways of explaining his conduct occur to me. Did he wish to be reproachful, and to show him how great his cruelty must be if death became a kindness? or did he upbraid him with his accustomed insanity? for even those whose children were put to death, and whose goods were confiscated, used to thank him: or was it that he willingly received death, regarding it as freedom? Whatever he meant, it was a magnanimous answer. Someone may say, "After this Gaius might have let him live." Kanus had no fear of this: the good faith with which Gaius carried out such orders as these was well known. Will you believe that he passed the ten intervening days before his execution without the slightest despondency? it is marvellous how that man spoke and acted, and how peaceful he was. He was playing at draughts when the centurion in charge of a number of those who were going to be executed bade him join them: on the summons he counted his men and said to his companion, "Mind you do not tell a lie after my death, and say that you won;" then, turning to the centurion, he said, "You will bear me witness that I am one man ahead of him." Do you think that Kanus played upon that draught-board? nay, he played with it. His friends were sad at being about to lose so great a man: "Why," asked he, "are you sorrowful? you are enquiring whether our souls are immortal, but I shall presently know." Nor did he up to the very end cease his search after truth, and raised arguments upon the subject of his own death. His own teacher of philosophy accompanied him, and they were not far from the hill on which the daily sacrifice to Caesar our god was offered, when he said, "What are you thinking of now, Kanus? or what are your ideas?" "I have decided," answered Kanus, "at that most swiftly-passing moment of all to watch whether the spirit will be conscious of the act of leaving the body." He promised, too, that if he made any discoveries, he would come round to his friends and tell them what the condition of the souls of the departed might be. Here was peace in the very midst of the storm: here was a soul worthy of eternal life, which used its own fate as a proof of truth, which when at the last step of life experimented upon his fleeting breath, and did not merely continue to learn until he died, but learned something even from death itself. No man has carried the life of a philosopher further. I will not hastily leave the subject of a great man, and one who deserves to be spoken of with respect: I will hand thee down to all posterity, thou most noble heart, chief among the many victims of Gaius.

15

Yet we gain nothing by getting rid of all personal causes of sadness, for sometimes we are possessed by hatred of the human race. When you reflect how rare simplicity is, how unknown innocence, how seldom faith is kept, unless it be to our advantage, when you remember such numbers of successful crimes, so many equally hateful losses and gains of lust, and ambition so impatient even of its own natural limits that it is willing to purchase distinction by baseness, the mind seems as it were cast into darkness, and shadows rise before it as though the virtues were all overthrown and we were no longer allowed to hope to possess them or benefited by their possession. We ought therefore to bring ourselves into such a state of mind that all the vices of the vulgar may not appear hateful to us, but merely ridiculous, and we should imitate Democritus rather than Heraclitus. The latter of these, whenever he appeared in public, used to weep, the former to laugh: the one thought all human doings to be follies, the other thought them to be miseries. We must take a higher view of all things, and bear with them more easily: it better becomes a man to scoff at life than to lament over it. Add to this that he who laughs at the human race deserves better of it than he who mourns for it, for the former leaves it some good hopes of improvement, while the latter stupidly weeps over what he has given up all hopes of mending. He who after surveying the universe cannot control his laughter shows, too, a greater mind than he who cannot restrain his tears, because his mind is only affected in the slightest possible degree, and he does not think that any part of all this apparatus is either important, or serious, or unhappy. As for the several causes which render us happy or sorrowful, let everyone describe them for himself, and learn the truth of Bion's saying, "That all the doings of men were very like what he began with, and that there is nothing in their lives which is more holy or decent than their conception." Yet it is better to accept public morals and human vices calmly without bursting into either laughter or tears; for to be hurt by the sufferings of others is to be forever miserable, while to enjoy the sufferings of others is an inhuman pleasure, just as it is a useless piece of humanity to weep and pull a long face because someone is burying his son. In one's own misfortunes, also, one ought so to conduct oneself as to bestow upon them just as much sorrow as reason, not as much as custom requires: for many shed tears in order to show them, and whenever no one is looking at them their eyes are dry, but they think it disgraceful not to weep when everyone does so. So deeply has this evil of being guided by the opinion of others taken root in us, that even grief, the simplest of all emotions, begins to be counterfeited.

16

There comes now a part of our subject which is wont with good cause to make one sad and anxious: I mean when good men come to bad ends; when Socrates is forced to die in prison, Rutilius to live in exile, Pompeius and Cicero to offer their necks to the swords of their own followers, when the great Cato, that living image of virtue, falls upon his sword and rips up both himself and the republic, one cannot help being grieved that Fortune should bestow her gifts so unjustly: what, too, can a good man hope to obtain when he sees the best of men meeting with the worst fates. Well, but see how each of them endured his fate, and if they endured it bravely, long in your heart for courage as great as theirs; if they died in a womanish and cowardly manner, nothing was lost: either they deserved that you should admire their courage, or else they did not deserve that you should wish to imitate their cowardice: for what can be more shameful than that the greatest men should die so bravely as to make people cowards. Let us praise one who deserves such constant praises, and say, "The braver you are the happier you are! You have escaped from all accidents, jealousies, diseases: you have escaped from prison: the gods have not thought you worthy of ill fortune, but have thought that fortune no longer deserved to have any power over you": but when anyone shrinks back in the hour of death and looks longingly at life, we must lay hands upon him. I will never weep for a man who dies cheerfully, nor for one who dies weeping: the former wipes away my tears, the latter by his tears makes himself unworthy that any should be shed for him. Shall I weep for Hercules because he was burned alive, or for Regulus because he was pierced by so many nails, or for Cato because he tore open his wounds a second time? All these men discovered how at the cost of a small portion of time they might obtain immortality, and by their deaths gained eternal life.

17

It also proves a fertile source of troubles if you take pains to conceal your feelings and never show yourself to anyone undisguised, but, as many men do, live an artificial life, in order to impose upon others: for the constant watching of himself becomes a torment to a man, and he dreads being caught doing something at variance with his usual habits, and, indeed, we never can be at our ease if we imagine that everyone who looks at us is weighing our real value: for many things occur which strip people of their disguise, however reluctantly they may part with it, and even if all this trouble about oneself is successful, still life is neither happy nor safe when one always has to wear a mask. But what pleasure there is in that honest straightforwardness which is its own ornament, and which conceals no part of its character? Yet even this life, which hides nothing from anyone runs some risk of being despised; for there are people who disdain whatever they come close to: but there is no danger of virtue's becoming contemptible when she is brought near our eyes, and it is better to be scorned for one's simplicity than to bear the burden of unceasing hypocrisy. Still, we must observe moderation in this matter, for there is a great difference between living simply and living slovenly. Moreover, we ought to retire a great deal into ourselves: for association with persons unlike ourselves upsets all that we had arranged, rouses the passions which were at rest, and rubs into a sore any weak or imperfectly healed place in our minds. Nevertheless we ought to mix up these two things, and to pass our lives alternately in solitude and among throngs of people; for the former will make us long for the society of mankind, the latter for that of ourselves, and the one will counteract the other: solitude will cure us when we are sick of crowds, and crowds will cure us when we are sick of solitude. Neither ought we always to keep the mind strained to the same pitch, but it ought sometimes to be relaxed by amusement. Socrates did not blush to play with little boys, Cato used to refresh his mind with wine after he had wearied it with application to affairs of state, and Scipio would move his triumphal and soldierly limbs to the sound of music, not with a feeble and halting gait, as is the fashion nowadays, when we sway in our very walk with more than womanly weakness, but dancing as men were wont in the days of old on sportive and festal occasions, with manly bounds, thinking it no harm to be seen so doing even by their enemies. Men's minds ought to have relaxation: they rise up better and more vigorous after rest. We must not force crops from rich fields, for an unbroken course of heavy crops will soon exhaust their fertility, and so also the liveliness of our minds will be detroyed by unceasing labour, but they will recover their strength after a short period of rest and relief: for continuous toil produces a sort of numbness and sluggishness. Men would not be so eager for this, if play and amusement did not possess natural attractions for them, although constant indulgence in them takes away all gravity and all strength from the mind: for sleep, also, is necessary for our refreshment, yet if you prolong it for days and nights together it will become death. There is a great difference between slackening your hold of a thing and letting it go. The founders of our laws appointed festivals, in order that men might be publicly encouraged to be cheerful, and they thought it necessary to vary our labours with amusements, and, as I said before, some great men have been wont to give themselves a certain number of holidays in every month, and some divided every day into playtime and work-time. Thus, I remember that great orator Asinius Pollio would not attend to any business after the tenth hour:

he would not even read letters after that time for fear some new trouble should arise, but in those two hours[94] used to get rid of the weariness which he had contracted during the whole day. Some rest in the middle of the day, and reserve some light occupation for the afternoon. Our ancestors, too, forbade any new motion to be made in the Senate after the tenth hour. Soldiers divide their watches, and those who have just returned from active service are allowed to sleep the whole night undisturbed. We must humour our minds and grant them rest from time to time, which acts upon them like food, and restores their strength. It does good also to take walks out of doors, that our spirits may be raised and refreshed by the open air and fresh breeze: sometimes we gain strength by driving in a carriage, by travel, by change of air, or by social meals and a more generous allowance of wine: at times we ought to drink even to intoxication, not so as to drown, but merely to dip ourselves in wine: for wine washes away troubles and dislodges them from the depths of the mind, and acts as a remedy to sorrow as it does to some diseases. The inventor of wine is called Liber, not from the licence which he gives to our tongues, but because he liberates the mind from the bondage of cares, and emancipates it, animates it, and renders it more daring in all that it attempts. Yet moderation is wholesome both in freedom and in wine. It is believed that Solon and Arcesilaus used to drink deep. Cato is reproached with drunkenness: but whoever casts this in his teeth will find it easier to turn his reproach into a commendation than to prove that Cato did anything wrong: however, we ought not to do it often, for fear the mind should contract evil habits, though it ought sometimes to be forced into frolic and frankness, and to cast off dull sobriety for a while. If we believe the Greek poet, "it is sometimes pleasant to be mad"; again, Plato always knocked in vain at the door of poetry when he was sober; or, if we trust Aristotle, no great genius has ever been without a touch of insanity. The mind cannot use lofty language, above that of the common herd, unless it be excited. When it has spurned aside the commonplace environments of custom, and rises sublime, instinct with sacred fire, then alone can it chant a song too grand for mortal lips: as long as it continues to dwell within itself it cannot rise to any pitch of splendour: it must break away from the beaten track, and lash itself to frenzy, till it gnaws the curb and rushes away bearing up its rider to heights whither it would fear to climb when alone.

I have now, my beloved Serenus, given you an account of what things can preserve peace of mind, what things can restore it to us, what can arrest the vices which secretly undermine it: yet be assured, that none of these is strong enough to enable us to retain so fleeting a blessing, unless we watch over our vacillating mind with intense and unremitting care.

---

[94] The Romans reckoned twelve hours from sunrise to sunset. These "two hours" were therefore the two last of the day.

ON PROVIDENCE

1

You have asked me, Lucilius, why, if the world be ruled by providence, so many evils befall good men? The answer to this would be more conveniently given in the course of this work, after we have proved that providence governs the universe, and that God is amongst us: but, since you wish me to deal with one point apart from the whole, and to answer one replication before the main action has been decided, I will do what is not difficult, and plead the cause of the gods. At the present time it is superfluous to point out that it is not without some guardian that so great a work maintains its position, that the assemblage and movements of the stars do not depend upon accidental impulses, or that objects whose motion is regulated by chance often fall into confusion and soon stumble, whereas this swift and safe movement goes on, governed by eternal law, bearing with it so many things both on sea and land, so many most brilliant lights shining in order in the skies; that this regularity does not belong to matter moving at random, and that particles brought together by chance could not arrange themselves with such art as to make the heaviest weight, that of the Earth, remain unmoved, and behold the flight of the heavens as they hasten round it, to make the seas pour into the valleys and so temper the climate of the land, without any sensible increase from the rivers which flow into them, or to cause huge growths to proceed from minute seeds. Even those phenomena which appear to be confused and irregular, I mean showers of rain and clouds, the rush of lightning from the heavens, fire that pours from the riven peaks of mountains, quakings of the trembling Earth, and everything else which is produced on Earth by the unquiet element in the universe, do not come to pass without reason, though they do so suddenly: but they also have their causes, as also have those things which excite our wonder by the strangeness of their position, such as warm springs amidst the waves of the sea, and new islands that spring up in the wide ocean. Moreover, anyone who has watched how the shore is laid bare by the retreat of the sea into itself, and how within a short time it is again covered, will believe that it is in obedience to some hidden law of change that the waves are at one time contracted and driven inwards, at another burst forth and regain their bed with a strong current, since all the while they wax in regular proportion, and come up at their appointed day and hour greater or less, according as the moon, at whose pleasure the ocean flows, draws them. Let these matters be set aside for discussion at their own proper season, but I, since you do not doubt the existence of providence but complain of it, will on that account more readily reconcile you to gods who are most excellent to excellent men: for indeed the nature of things does not ever permit good to be injured by good. Between good men and the gods there is a friendship which is brought about by virtue—friendship do I say? nay, rather relationship and likeness, since the good man differs from a god in time alone, being his pupil and rival and true offspring, whom his glorious parent trains more severely than other men, insisting sternly on virtuous conduct, just as strict fathers do. When therefore you see men who are good and acceptable to the gods toiling, sweating, painfully struggling upwards, while bad men run riot and are steeped in pleasures, reflect that modesty pleases us in our sons, and forwardness in our house-born slave-boys; that the former are held in check by a somewhat stern rule, whereas the boldness of the latter is encouraged. Be thou sure that God acts in like manner: He does not pet the good man: He tries him, hardens him, and fits him for Himself.

2

Why do many things turn out badly for good men? Why, no evil can befall a good man; contraries cannot combine. Just as so many rivers, so many showers of rain from the clouds, such a number of medicinal springs, do not alter the taste of the sea, indeed, do not so much as soften it, so the pressure of adversity does not affect the mind of a brave man; for the mind of a brave man maintains its balance and throws its own complexion over all that takes place, because it is more powerful than any external circumstances. I do not say that he does not feel them, but he conquers them, and on occasion calmly and tranquilly rises superior to their attacks, holding all misfortunes to be trials of his own firmness. Yet who is there who, provided he be a man and have honourable ambition, does not long for due employment, and is not eager to do his duty in spite of danger? Is there any hardworking man to whom idleness is not a punishment? We see athletes, who study only their bodily strength, engage in contests with the strongest of men, and insist that those who train them for the arena should put out their whole strength when practising with them: they endure blows and maltreatment, and, if they cannot find any single person who is their match, they engage with several at once: their strength and courage droop without an antagonist: they can only prove how great and how mighty it is by proving how much they can endure. You should know that good men ought to act in like manner, so as not to fear troubles and difficulties, nor to lament their hard fate, to take in good part whatever befalls them, and force it to become a blessing to them. It does not matter what you bear, but how you bear it. Do you not see how differently fathers and mothers indulge their children? How the former urge them to begin their tasks betimes, will not suffer them to be idle even on holidays, and exercise them till they perspire, and sometimes till they shed tears—while their mothers want to cuddle them in their laps, and keep them out of the sun, and never wish them to be vexed, or to cry, or to work. God bears a fatherly mind towards good men, and loves them in a manly spirit. "Let them," says He, "be exercised by labours, sufferings, and losses, that so they may gather true strength." Those who are surfeited with ease break down not only with labour, but with mere motion and by their own weight. Unbroken prosperity cannot bear a single blow; but he who has waged an unceasing strife with his misfortunes has gained a thicker skin by his sufferings, yields to no disaster, and even though he fall yet fights on his knee. Do you wonder that God, who so loves the good, who would have them attain the highest goodness and preeminence, should appoint Fortune to be their adversary? I should not be surprised if the gods sometimes experience a wish to behold great men struggling with some misfortune. We sometimes are delighted when a youth of steady courage receives on his spear the wild beast that attacks him; or when he meets the charge of a lion without flinching; and the more eminent the man is who acts thus,[95] the more attractive is the sight: yet these are not matters which can attract the attention of the gods, but are mere pastime and diversions of human frivolity. Behold a sight worthy to be viewed by a god interested in his own work, behold a pair[96] worthy of a god, a brave man matched with evil fortune, especially if he himself has given the challenge. I say, I do not know what nobler spectacle Jupiter could find on Earth, should he turn his eyes thither, than that of Cato, after his party had more than once been defeated, still standing upright amid the ruins of the commonwealth. Quoth he, "What though all be fallen into one man's power, though the land be guarded by his legions, the sea by his fleets, though Caesar's soldiers beset the city gate? Cato has a way out of it: with one hand he will open a wide path to freedom; his sword, which he has borne unstained by disgrace and innocent of crime even in a civil war, will still perform good and noble deeds; it will give to Cato that freedom which it could not give to his country. Begin, my soul, the work which thou so long hast contemplated, snatch thyself away from the world of man. Already Petreius and Juba have met and fallen, each slain by the other's hand—a brave and noble compact with fate, yet not one befitting my greatness: it is as disgraceful for Cato to beg his death of anyone as it would be for him to beg his life."

It is clear to me that the gods must have looked on with great joy, while that man, his own most ruthless avenger, took thought for the safety of others and arranged the escape of those who departed, while even on his last night he pursued his studies, while he drove the sword into his sacred breast, while he tore forth his vitals and laid his hand

---

[95] *Honestior* is opposed to the gladiator—the loftier the station of the combatant. The Gracchus of Juvenal, *Satires* II and VIII, illustrates the passage.

[96] *Par*, a technical term in the language of sport (worthy of such a spectator).

upon that most holy life which was unworthy to be defiled by steel. This, I am inclined to think, was the reason that his wound was not well-aimed and mortal: the gods were not satisfied with seeing Cato die once: his courage was kept in action and recalled to the stage, that it might display itself in a more difficult part: for it needs a greater mind to return a second time to death. How could they fail to view their pupil with interest when leaving his life by such a noble and memorable departure? Men are raised to the level of the gods by a death which is admired even by those who fear them.

3

However, as my argument proceeds, I shall prove that what appear to be evils are not so; for the present I say this, that what you call hard measure, misfortunes, and things against which we ought to pray, are really to the advantage, firstly, of those to whom they happen, and secondly, of all mankind, for whom the gods care more than for individuals; and next, that these evils befall them with their own good will, and that men deserve to endure misfortunes, if they are unwilling to receive them. To this I shall add, that misfortunes proceed thus by destiny, and that they befall good men by the same law which makes them good. After this, I shall prevail upon you never to pity any good man; for though he may be called unhappy, he cannot be so.

Of all these propositions that which I have stated first appears the most difficult to prove, I mean, that the things which we dread and shudder at are to the advantage of those to whom they happen. "Is it," say you, "to their advantage to be driven into exile, to be brought to want, to carry out to burial their children and wife, to be publicly disgraced, to lose their health?" Yes! if you are surprised at these being to any man's advantage, you will also be surprised at any man being benefited by the knife and cautery, or by hunger and thirst as well. Yet if you consider that some men, in order to be cured, have their bones scraped, and pieces of them extracted, that their veins are pulled out, and that some have limbs cut off, which could not remain in their place without ruin to the whole body, you will allow me to prove to you this also, that some misfortunes are for the good of those to whom they happen, just as much, by Hercules, as some things which are praised and sought after are harmful to those who enjoy them, like indigestions and drunkenness and other matters which kill us through pleasure. Among many grand sayings of our Demetrius is this, which I have but just heard, and which still rings and thrills in my ears: "No one," said he, "seems to me more unhappy than the man whom no misfortune has ever befallen." He never has had an opportunity of testing himself; though everything has happened to him according to his wish, nay, even before he has formed a wish, yet the gods have judged him unfavourably; he has never been deemed worthy to conquer ill fortune, which avoids the greatest cowards, as though it said, "Why should I take that man for my antagonist? He will straightaway lay down his arms: I shall not need all my strength against him: he will be put to flight by a mere menace: he dares not even face me; let me look around for some other with whom I may fight hand to hand: I blush to join battle with one who is prepared to be beaten." A gladiator deems it a disgrace to be matched with an inferior, and knows that to win without danger is to win without glory. Just so doth Fortune; she seeks out the bravest to match herself with, passes over some with disdain, and makes for the most unyielding and upright of men, to exert her strength against them. She tried Mucius by fire, Fabricius by poverty, Rutilius by exile, Regulus by torture, Socrates by poison, Cato by death: it is ill fortune alone that discovers these glorious examples. Was Mucius unhappy, because he grasped the enemy's fire with his right hand, and of his own accord paid the penalty of his mistake? because he overcame the King with his hand when it was burned, though he could not when it held a sword? Would he have been happier, if he had warmed his hand in his mistress's bosom; Was Fabricius unhappy, because when the State could spare him, he dug his own land? because he waged war against riches as keenly as against Pyrrhus? because he supped beside his hearth off the very roots and herbs which he himself, though an old man, and one who had enjoyed a triumph, had grubbed up while clearing his field of weeds? What then? would he have been happier if he had gorged himself with fishes from distant shores, and birds caught in foreign lands? if he had roused the torpor of his queasy stomach with shellfish from the upper and the lower sea? if he had piled a great heap of fruits round game of the first head, which many huntsmen had been killed in capturing? Was Rutilius unhappy, because those who condemned him will have to plead their cause for all ages? because he endured the loss of his country more composedly than that of his banishment? because he was the only man who refused anything to Sulla the dictator, and when recalled from exile all but went further away and banished himself still more. "Let those," said he, "whom thy fortunate reign catches at Rome, see to the forum drenched with blood,[97] and the heads of Senators above the Pool of Servilius—the place where the victims of Sulla's proscriptions were stripped—the bands of assassins roaming at large through the city, and many thousands of Roman citizens slaughtered in one place, after, nay, by means of a promise of quarter. Let those who are unable to go into exile behold these things." Well! is Lucius Sulla happy, because when he comes down into the forum room is made for him with sword-strokes, because he allows the heads of consulars to be shown to him, and counts out the price of blood through the quaestor and the state exchequer? And this, this was the man who passed the Lex Cornelia! Let us now come to Regulus: what injury did Fortune do him when she made him an example of good faith, an example of endurance? They pierce his skin with nails: wherever he leans his weary body, it rests on a wound; his eyes are fixed forever open; the greater his sufferings, the greater is his glory. Would you know how far he is from regretting that he valued his honour at such a price? Heal his wounds and send him again into the senate-house; he will give the same advice. So, then, you think Maecenas a happier man, who when troubled by love, and weeping at the daily repulses of his ill-natured

---

[97] *Vidirint*—Let them see to it: it is no matter of mine.

wife, sought for sleep by listening to distant strains of music? Though he drug himself with wine, divert himself with the sound of falling waters, and distract his troubled thoughts with a thousand pleasures, yet Maecenas will no more sleep on his down cushions than Regulus on the rack. Yet it consoles the latter that he suffers for the sake of honour, and he looks away from his torments to their cause: whilst the other, jaded with pleasures and sick with over-enjoyment, is more hurt by the cause of his sufferings than by the sufferings themselves. Vice has not so utterly taken possession of the human race that, if men were allowed to choose their destiny, there can be any doubt but that more would choose to be Reguluses than to be Maecenases: or if there were anyone who dared to say that he would prefer to be born Maecenas than Regulus, that man, whether he says so or not, would rather have been Terentia (than Cicero).

Do you consider Socrates to have been badly used, because he took that draught which the State assigned to him as though it were a charm to make him immortal, and argued about death until death itself? Was he ill treated, because his blood froze and the current of his veins gradually stopped as the chill of death crept over them? How much more is this man to be envied than he who is served on precious stones, whose drink a creature trained to every vice, a eunuch or much the same, cools with snow in a golden cup? Such men as these bring up again all that they drink, in misery and disgust at the taste of their own bile, while Socrates cheerfully and willingly drains his poison. As for Cato, enough has been said, and all men must agree that the highest happiness was reached by one who was chosen by Nature herself as worthy to contend with all her terrors: "The enmity," says she, "of the powerful is grievous, therefore let him be opposed at once by Pompeius, Caesar, and Crassus: it is grievous, when a candidate for public offices, to be defeated by one's inferiors; therefore let him be defeated by Vatinius: it is grievous to take part in civil wars, therefore let him fight in every part of the world for the good cause with equal obstinacy and ill-luck: it is grievous to lay hands upon oneself, therefore let him do so. What shall I gain by this? That all men may know that these things, which I have deemed Cato worthy to undergo, are not real evils."

4

"Prosperity comes to the mob, and to low-minded men as well as to great ones; but it is the privilege of great men alone to send under the yoke[98] the disasters and terrors of

---

[98] That is, to triumph over.

"Two spears were set upright ... and a third was fastened across them at the top; and through this gateway the vanquished army marched out, as a token that they had been conquered in war, and owed their lives to the enemy's mercy. It was no peculiar insult devised for this occasion, but a common usage, so far as appears, in similar cases; like the modern ceremony of piling arms when a garrison or army surrender themselves as prisoners of war."

—Arnold's *History of Rome*, Chapter XXXI.

mortal life: whereas to be always prosperous, and to pass through life without a twinge of mental distress, is to remain ignorant of one half of nature. You are a great man; but how am I to know it, if fortune gives you no opportunity of showing your virtue? You have entered the arena of the Olympic games, but no one else has done so: you have the crown, but not the victory: I do not congratulate you as I would a brave man, but as one who has obtained a consulship or praetorship. You have gained dignity. I may say the same of a good man, if troublesome circumstances have never given him a single opportunity of displaying the strength of his mind. I think you unhappy because you never have been unhappy: you have passed through your life without meeting an antagonist: no one will know your powers, not even you yourself." For a man cannot know himself without a trial; no one ever learnt what he could do without putting himself to the test; for which reason many have of their own free will exposed themselves to misfortunes which no longer came in their way, and have sought for an opportunity of making their virtue, which otherwise would have been lost in darkness, shine before the world. Great men, I say, often rejoice at crosses of fortune just as brave soldiers do at wars. I remember to have heard Triumphus, who was a gladiator[99] in the reign of Tiberius Caesar, complaining about the scarcity of prizes. "What a glorious time," said he, "is past." Valour is greedy of danger, and thinks only of whither it strives to go, not of what it will suffer, since even what it will suffer is part of its glory. Soldiers pride themselves on their wounds, they joyously display their blood flowing over their breastplate.[100] Though those who return unwounded from battle may have done as bravely, yet he who returns wounded is more admired. God, I say, favours those whom He wishes to enjoy the greatest honours, whenever He affords them the means of performing some exploit with spirit and courage, something which is not easily to be accomplished: you can judge of a pilot in a storm, of a soldier in a battle. How can I know with how great a spirit you could endure poverty, if you overflow with riches? How can I tell with how great firmness you could bear up against disgrace, dishonour, and public hatred, if you grow old to the sound of applause, if popular favour cannot be alienated from you, and seems to flow to you by the natural bent of men's minds? How can I know how calmly you would endure to be childless, if you see all your children around you? I have heard what you said when you were consoling others: then I should have seen whether you could have consoled yourself, whether you could have forbidden yourself to grieve. Do not, I beg you, dread those things which the immortal gods apply to our minds like spurs: misfortune is virtue's opportunity. Those men may justly be called unhappy who are stupified with excess of enjoyment, whom sluggish contentment keeps as it were becalmed in a quiet sea: whatever befalls them will come strange to them. Misfortunes press hardest on those who are unacquainted with them: the yoke feels heavy to the tender neck. The recruit turns pale at the thought of a wound: the veteran, who knows that he has often won the victory after losing

---

[99] He was a *mirmillo*, a kind of gladiator who was armed with a Gaulish helmet.
[100] *E lorica*.

blood, looks boldly at his own flowing gore. In like manner God hardens, reviews, and exercises those whom He tests and loves: those whom He seems to indulge and spare, He is keeping out of condition to meet their coming misfortunes: for you are mistaken if you suppose that anyone is exempt from misfortune: he who has long prospered will have his share some day; those who seem to have been spared them have only had them put off. Why does God afflict the best of men with ill-health, or sorrow, or other troubles? Because in the army the most hazardous services are assigned to the bravest soldiers: a general sends his choicest troops to attack the enemy in a midnight ambuscade, to reconnoitre his line of march, or to drive the hostile garrisons from their strong places. No one of these men says as he begins his march, "The general has dealt hardly with me," but "He has judged well of me." Let those who are bidden to suffer what makes the weak and cowardly weep, say likewise, "God has thought us worthy subjects on whom to try how much suffering human nature can endure." Avoid luxury, avoid effeminate enjoyment, by which men's minds are softened, and in which, unless something occurs to remind them of the common lot of humanity, they lie unconscious, as though plunged in continual drunkenness. He whom glazed windows have always guarded from the wind, whose feet are warmed by constantly renewed fomentations, whose dining-room is heated by hot air beneath the floor and spread through the walls, cannot meet the gentlest breeze without danger. While all excesses are hurtful, excess of comfort is the most hurtful of all; it affects the brain; it leads men's minds into vain imaginings; it spreads a thick cloud over the boundaries of truth and falsehood. Is it not better, with virtue by one's side, to endure continual misfortune, than to burst with an endless surfeit of good things? It is the overloaded stomach that is rent asunder: death treats starvation more gently. The gods deal with good men according to the same rule as schoolmasters with their pupils, who exact most labour from those of whom they have the surest hopes. Do you imagine that the Lacedaemonians, who test the mettle of their children by public flogging, do not love them? Their own fathers call upon them to endure the strokes of the rod bravely, and when they are torn and half dead, ask them to offer their wounded skin to receive fresh wounds. Why then should we wonder if God tries noble spirits severely? There can be no easy proof of virtue. Fortune lashes and mangles us: well, let us endure it: it is not cruelty, it is a struggle, in which the oftener we engage the braver we shall become. The strongest part of the body is that which is exercised by the most frequent use: we must entrust ourselves to Fortune to be hardened by her against herself: by degrees she will make us a match for herself. Familiarity with danger leads us to despise it. Thus the bodies of sailors are hardened by endurance of the sea, and the hands of farmers by work; the arms of soldiers are powerful to hurl darts, the legs of runners are active: that part of each man which he exercises is the strongest: so by endurance the mind becomes able to despise the power of misfortunes. You may see what endurance might effect in us if you observe what labour does among tribes that are naked and rendered stronger by want. Look at all the nations that dwell beyond the Roman Empire: I mean the Germans and all the nomad tribes that war against us along the Danube. They suffer from eternal winter, and a dismal climate, the barren soil grudges them sustenance, they keep off the rain with leaves or thatch, they bound across frozen marshes, and hunt wild beasts for food. Do you think them unhappy? There is no unhappiness in what use has made part of one's nature: by degrees men find pleasure in doing what they were first driven to do by necessity. They have no homes and no resting-places save those which weariness appoints them for the day; their food, though coarse, yet must be sought with their own hands; the harshness of the climate is terrible, and their bodies are unclothed. This, which you think a hardship, is the mode of life of all these races: how then can you wonder at good men being shaken, in order that they may be strengthened? No tree which the wind does not often blow against is firm and strong; for it is stiffened by the very act of being shaken, and plants its roots more securely: those which grow in a sheltered valley are brittle: and so it is to the advantage of good men, and causes them to be undismayed, that they should live much amidst alarms, and learn to bear with patience what is not evil save to him who endures it ill.

5

Add to this that it is to the advantage of everyone that the best men should, so to speak, be on active service and perform labours: God has the same purpose as the wise man, that is, to prove that the things which the herd covets and dreads are neither good nor bad in themselves. If, however, He only bestows them upon good men, it will be evident that they are good things, and bad, if He only inflicts them upon bad men. Blindness would be execrable if no one lost his eyes except those who deserve to have them pulled out; therefore let Appius and Metellus be doomed to darkness. Riches are not a good thing: therefore let Elius the pander possess them, that men who have consecrated money in the temple, may see the same in the brothel: for by no means can God discredit objects of desire so effectually as by bestowing them upon the worst of men, and removing them from the best. "But," you say, "it is unjust that a good man should be enfeebled, or transfixed, or chained, while bad men swagger at large with a whole skin." What! is it not unjust that brave men should bear arms, pass the night in camps, and stand on guard along the rampart with their wounds still bandaged, while within the city eunuchs and professional profligates live at their ease? what? is it not unjust that maidens of the highest birth should be roused at night to perform Divine service, while fallen women enjoy the soundest sleep? Labour calls for the best men: the senate often passes the whole day in debate, while at the same time every scoundrel either amuses his leisure in the Campus Martius, or lurks in a tavern, or passes his time in some pleasant society. The same thing happens in this great commonwealth (of the world): good men labour, spend and are spent, and that too of their own free will; they are not dragged along by Fortune, but follow her and take equal steps with her; if they knew how, they would outstrip her. I remember, also, to have heard this spirited saying of that stoutest-hearted of men, Demetrius. "Ye immortal Gods," said he, "the only complaint which I have to make of you is that you did not make your will known to me earlier; for then I would sooner have gone into that state of life to which I now have been called. Do you wish to take my children? it was for you that I brought them up. Do you wish to take some part of my body? take it: it is no great thing that I am offering you, I shall soon have done with the whole of it. Do you wish for my life? why should I hesitate to return to you what you gave me? whatever you ask you shall receive with my good will: nay, I would rather give it than be forced to hand it over to you: what need had you to take away what you did? you might have received it from me: yet even as it is you cannot take anything from me, because you cannot rob a man unless he resists."

I am constrained to nothing, I suffer nothing against my will, nor am I God's slave, but his willing follower, and so much the more because I know that everything is ordained and proceeds according to a law that endures forever. The fates guide us, and the length of every man's days is decided at the first hour of his birth: every cause depends upon some earlier cause: one long chain of destiny decides all things, public or private. Wherefore, everything must be patiently endured, because events do not fall in our way, as we imagine, but come by a regular law. It has long ago been settled at what you should rejoice and at what you should weep, and although the lives of individual men appear to differ from one another in a great variety of particulars, yet the sum total comes to one and the same thing: we soon perish, and the gifts which we receive soon perish. Why, then, should we be angry? why should we lament? we are prepared for our fate: let nature deal as she will with her own bodies; let us be cheerful whatever befalls, and stoutly reflect that it is not anything of our own that perishes. What is the duty of a good man? To submit himself to fate: it is a great consolation to be swept away together with the entire universe: whatever law is laid upon us that thus we must live and thus we must die, is laid upon the gods also: one unchangeable stream bears along men and gods alike: the creator and ruler of the universe himself, though he has given laws to the fates, yet is guided by them: he always obeys, he only once commanded. "But why was God so unjust in His distribution of fate, as to assign poverty, wounds, and untimely deaths to good men?" The workman cannot alter his materials: this is their nature. Some qualities cannot be separated from some others: they cling together; are indivisible. Dull minds, tending to sleep or to a waking state exactly like sleep, are composed of sluggish elements: it requires stronger stuff to form a man meriting careful description. His course will not be straightforward; he must go upwards and downwards, be tossed about, and guide his vessel through troubled waters: he must make his way in spite of fortune: he will meet with much that is hard which he must soften, much that is rough that he must make smooth. Fire tries gold, misfortune tries brave men. See how high virtue has to climb: you may be sure that it has no safe path to tread.

> "Steep is the path at first: the steeds, though strong,
> Fresh from their rest, can hardly crawl along;
> The middle part lies through the topmost sky,
> Whence oft, as I the earth and sea descry,
> I shudder, terrors through my bosom thrill.
> The ending of the path is sheer down hill,
> And needs the careful guidance of the rein,
> Forever when I sink beneath the main,
> Old Tethys trembles in her depths below
> Lest headlong down upon her I should go."[101]

When the spirited youth heard this, he said, "I have no fault to find with the road: I will mount it, it is worthwhile to go through these places, even though one fall." His father did not cease from trying to scare his brave spirit with terrors:—

> "Then, too, that thou may'st hold thy course aright,
> And neither turn aside to left nor right,
> Straight through the Bull's fell horns thy path must go,
> Through the fierce Lion, and the Archer's bow."

After this Phaethon says:—

> "Harness the chariot which you yield to me,

I am encouraged by these things with which you think to scare me: I long to stand where the Sun himself trembles to stand." It is the part of grovellers and cowards to follow the safe track; courage loves a lofty path.

6

"Yet, why does God permit evil to happen to good men?" He does not permit it: he takes away from them all evils, such as crimes and scandalous wickedness, daring thoughts, grasping schemes, blind lusts, and avarice coveting its neighbour's goods. He protects and saves them. Does anyone besides this demand that God should look after the baggage of good men also? Why, they themselves leave the care of this to God: they scorn external accessories. Democritus forswore riches, holding them to be a burden to a virtuous mind: what wonder then, if God permits that to happen to a good man, which a good man sometimes chooses should happen to himself? Good men, you say, lose their children: why should they not, since sometimes they even put them to death? They are banished: why should they not be, since sometimes they leave their country of their own free will, never to return? They are

---

[101] The lines occur in Ovid's *Metamorphoses*, II, 63. Phoebus is telling Phaethon how to drive the chariot of the Sun.

slain: why not, since sometimes they choose to lay violent hands on themselves? Why do they suffer certain miseries? it is that they may teach others how to do so. They are born as patterns. Conceive, therefore, that God says:—"You, who have chosen righteousness, what complaint can you make of me? I have encompassed other men with unreal good things, and have deceived their inane minds as it were by a long and misleading dream: I have bedecked them with gold, silver, and ivory, but within them there is no good thing. Those men whom you regard as fortunate, if you could see, not their outward show, but their hidden life, are really unhappy, mean, and base, ornamented on the outside like the walls of their houses: that good fortune of theirs is not sound and genuine: it is only a veneer, and that a thin one. As long, therefore, as they can stand upright and display themselves as they choose, they shine and impose upon one; when something occurs to shake and unmask them, we see how deep and real a rottenness was hidden by that factitious magnificence. To you I have given sure and lasting good things, which become greater and better the more one turns them over and views them on every side: I have granted to you to scorn danger, to disdain passion. You do not shine outwardly, all your good qualities are turned inwards; even so does the world neglect what lies without it, and rejoices in the contemplation of itself. I have placed every good thing within your own breasts: it is your good fortune not to need any good fortune. 'Yet many things befall you which are sad, dreadful, hard to be borne.' Well, as I have not been able to remove these from your path, I have given your minds strength to combat all: bear them bravely. In this you can surpass God himself; He is beyond suffering evil; you are above it. Despise poverty; no man lives as poor as he was born: despise pain; either it will cease or you will cease: despise death; it either ends you or takes you elsewhere: despise fortune; I have given her no weapon that can reach the mind. Above all, I have taken care that no one should hold you captive against your will: the way of escape lies open before you: if you do not choose to fight, you may fly. For this reason, of all those matters which I have deemed essential for you, I have made nothing easier for you than to die. I have set man's life as it were on a mountain side: it soon slips down.[102] Do but watch, and you will see how short

---

[102] Compare Walter Scott:

"All ... must have felt that but for the dictates of religion, or the natural recoil of the mind from the idea of dissolution, there have been times when they would have been willing to throw away life as a child does a broken toy. I am sure I know one who has often felt so. O God! what are we?—Lords of nature?—Why, a tile drops from a housetop, which an elephant would not feel more than a sheet of pasteboard, and there lies his lordship. Or something of inconceivably minute origin, the pressure of a bone, or the inflammation of a particle of the brain takes place, and the emblem of the Deity destroys himself or someone else. We hold our health and our reason on terms slighter than anyone would desire, were it in their choice, to hold an Irish cabin."

—Lockhart's *Life of Sir Walter Scott*, Volume VII, p. 11.

and how ready a path leads to freedom. I have not imposed such long delays upon those who quit the world as upon those who enter it: were it not so, fortune would hold a wide dominion over you, if a man died as slowly as he is born. Let all time, let every place teach you, how simple it is to renounce nature, and to fling back her gifts to her: before the altar itself and during the solemn rites of sacrifice, while life is being prayed for, learn how to die. Fat oxen fall dead with a tiny wound; a blow from a man's hand fells animals of great strength: the sutures of the neck are severed by a thin blade, and when the joint which connects the head and neck is cut, all that great mass falls. The breath of life is not deep seated, nor only to be let forth by steel—the vitals need not be searched throughout by plunging a sword among them to the hilt: death lies near the surface. I have not appointed any particular spot for these blows—the body may be pierced wherever you please. That very act which is called dying, by which the breath of life leaves the body, is too short for you to be able to estimate its quickness: whether a knot crushes the windpipe, or water stops your breathing: whether you fall headlong from a height and perish upon the hard ground below, or a mouthful of fire checks the drawing of your breath—whatever it is, it acts swiftly. Do you not blush to spend so long a time in dreading what takes so short a time to do?"

ON CLEMENCY

BOOK 1

1

I have determined to write a book upon clemency, Nero Caesar, in order that I may as it were serve as a mirror to you, and let you see yourself arriving at the greatest of all pleasures. For although the true enjoyment of good deeds consists in the performance of them, and virtues have no adequate reward beyond themselves, still it is worth your while to consider and investigate a good conscience from every point of view, and afterwards to cast your eyes upon this enormous mass of mankind—quarrelsome, factious, and passionate as they are; likely, if they could throw off the yoke of your government, to take pleasure alike in the ruin of themselves and of one another—and thus to commune with yourself:—"Have I of all mankind been chosen and thought fit to perform the office of a god upon Earth? I am the arbiter of life and death to mankind: it rests with me to decide what lot and position in life each man possesses: Fortune makes use of my mouth to announce what she bestows on each man: cities and nations are moved to joy by my words: no region anywhere can flourish without my favour and good will: all these thousands of swords now restrained by my authority, would be drawn at a sign from me: it rests with me to decide which tribes shall be utterly exterminated, which shall be moved into other lands, which shall receive and which shall be deprived of liberty, what kings shall be reduced to slavery and whose heads shall be crowned, what cities shall be destroyed and what new ones shall be founded. In this position of enormous power I am not tempted to punish men unjustly by anger, by youthful impulse, by the recklessness and insolence of men, which often overcomes the patience even of the best regulated minds, not even that terrible vanity, so common among great sovereigns, of displaying my power by inspiring terror. My sword is sheathed, nay, fixed in its sheath: I am sparing of the blood even of the lowest of my subjects: a man who has nothing else to recommend him, will nevertheless find favour in my eyes because he is a man. I keep harshness concealed, but I have clemency always at hand: I watch myself as carefully as though I had to give an account of my actions to those laws which I have brought out of darkness and neglect into the light of day. I have been moved to compassion by the youth of one culprit, and the age of another: I have spared one man because of his great place, another on account of his insignificance: when I could find no reason for showing mercy, I have had mercy upon myself. I am prepared this day, should the gods demand it, to render to them an account of the human race." You, Caesar, can boldly say that everything which has come into your charge has been kept safe, and that the State has neither openly nor secretly suffered any loss at your hands. You have coveted a glory which is most rare, and which has been obtained by no emperor before you, that of innocence. Your remarkable goodness is not thrown away, nor is it ungratefully or spitefully undervalued. Men feel gratitude towards you: no one person ever was so dear to another as you are to the people of Rome, whose great and enduring benefit you are. You have, however, taken upon yourself a mighty burden: no one any longer speaks of the good times of the late Emperor Augustus, or the first years of the reign of Tiberius, or proposes for your imitation any model outside yourself: yours is a pattern reign. This would have been difficult had your goodness of heart not been innate, but merely adopted for a time; for no one can wear a mask for long, and fictitious qualities soon give place to true ones. Those which are founded upon truth, and which, so to speak, grow out of a solid basis, only become greater and better as time goes on. The Roman people were in a state of great hazard as long as it was uncertain how your generous[103] disposition would turn out; now, however, the prayers of the community are sure of an answer, for there is no fear that you should suddenly forget your own character. Indeed, excess of happiness makes men greedy, and our desires are never so moderate as to be bounded by what they have obtained: great successes become the stepping-stones to greater ones, and those who have obtained more than they hoped, entertain even more extravagant hopes than before; yet by all your countrymen we hear it admitted that they are now happy, and moreover, that nothing can be added to the blessings that they enjoy, except that they should be eternal. Many circumstances force this admission from them, although it is the one which men are least willing to make: we enjoy a profound and prosperous peace, the power of the law has been openly asserted in the sight of all men, and raised beyond the reach of any violent interference: the form of our government is so happy, as to contain all the essentials of liberty except the power of destroying itself. It is nevertheless your clemency which is most especially admired by the high and low alike: every man enjoys or hopes to enjoy the other blessings of your rule according to the measure of his own personal good fortune, whereas from your clemency all hope alike: no one has so much confidence in his own innocence,

---

[103] *Nobilis.*

as not to feel glad that in your presence stands a clemency which is ready to make allowance for human errors.

2

I know, however, that there are some who imagine that clemency only saves the life of every villain, because clemency is useless except after conviction, and alone of all the virtues has no function among the innocent. But in the first place, although a physician is only useful to the sick, yet he is held in honour among the healthy also; and so clemency, though she be invoked by those who deserve punishment, is respected by innocent people as well. Next, she can exist also in the person of the innocent, because sometimes misfortune takes the place of crime; indeed, clemency not only succours the innocent, but often the virtuous, since in the course of time it happens that men are punished for actions which deserve praise. Besides this, there is a large part of mankind which might return to virtue if the hope of pardon were not denied them. Yet it is not right to pardon indiscriminately; for when no distinction is made between good and bad men, disorder follows, and all vices break forth; we must therefore take care to distinguish those characters which admit of reform from those which are hopelessly depraved. Neither ought we to show an indiscriminate and general, nor yet an exclusive clemency; for to pardon everyone is as great cruelty as to pardon none; we must take a middle course; but as it is difficult to find the true mean, let us be careful, if we depart from it, to do so upon the side of humanity.

3

But these matters will be treated of better in their own place. I will now divide this whole subject into three parts. The first will be of gentleness of temper:[104] the second will be that which explains the nature and disposition of clemency; for since there are certain vices which have the semblance of virtue, they cannot be separated unless you stamp upon them the marks which distinguish them from one another: in the third place we shall inquire how the mind may be led to practise this virtue, how it may strengthen it, and by habit make it its own.

That clemency, which is the most humane of virtues, is that which best befits a man, is necessarily an axiom, not only among our own sect, which regards man as a social animal, born for the good of the whole community, but even among those philosophers who give him up entirely to pleasure, and whose words and actions have no other aim than their own personal advantage. If man, as they argue, seeks for quiet and repose, what virtue is there which is more agreeable to his nature

---

[104] The text is corrupt. I have followed Gertz's conjectural emendation, *mansuefactionis*, but I believe that Lipsius is right in thinking that a great deal more than one word has been lost here.

than clemency, which loves peace and restrains him from violence? Now clemency becomes no one more than a king or a prince; for great power is glorious and admirable only when it is beneficent; since to be powerful only for mischief is the power of a pestilence. That man's greatness alone rests upon a secure foundation, whom all men know to be as much on their side as he is above them, of whose watchful care for the safety of each and all of them they receive daily proofs, at whose approach they do not fly in terror, as though some evil and dangerous animal had sprung out from its den, but flock to him as they would to the bright and health-giving sunshine. They are perfectly ready to fling themselves upon the swords of conspirators in his defence, to offer their bodies if his only path to safety must be formed of corpses: they protect his sleep by nightly watches, they surround him and defend him on every side, and expose themselves to the dangers which menace him. It is not without good reason that nations and cities thus agree in sacrificing their lives and property for the defence and the love of their king whenever their leader's safety demands it; men do not hold themselves cheap, nor are they insane when so many thousands are put to the sword for the sake of one man, and when by so many deaths they save the life of one man alone, who not unfrequently is old and feeble. Just as the entire body is commanded by the mind, and although the body be so much larger and more beautiful while the mind is impalpable and hidden, and we are not certain as to where it is concealed, yet the hands, feet, and eyes work for it, the skin protects it; at its bidding we either lie still or move restlessly about; when it gives the word, if it be an avaricious master, we scour the sea in search of gain, or if it be ambitious we straightaway place our right hand in the flames like Mucius, or leap into the pit like Curtius, so likewise this enormous multitude which surrounds one man is directed by his will, is guided by his intellect, and would break and hurl itself into ruin by its own strength, if it were not upheld by his wisdom.

4

Men therefore love their own safety, when they draw up vast legions in battle on behalf of one man, when they rush to the front, and expose their breasts to wounds, for fear that their leader's standards should be driven back. He is the bond which fastens the commonwealth together, he is the breath of life to all those thousands, who by themselves would become merely an encumbrance and a source of plunder if that directing mind were withdrawn:—

> Bees have but one mind, till their king doth die,
> But when he dies, disorderly they fly.

Such a misfortune will be the end of the peace of Rome, it will wreck the prosperity of this great people; the nation will be free from this danger as long as it knows how to endure the reins: should it ever break them, or refuse to have them replaced if they were to fall off by accident, then this mighty whole, this complex fabric of government will fly asunder into many fragments, and the last day of Rome's empire will be that upon which it forgets how to obey. For this reason we need not wonder that princes, kings, and all other protectors of a state, whatever their titles may be, should be loved beyond the circle of their immediate relatives; for since right-thinking men prefer the interests of the State to their own, it follows that he who bears the burden of state affairs must be dearer to them than their own friends. Indeed, the emperor long ago identified himself so thoroughly with the State, that neither of them could be separated without injury to both, because the one requires power, while the other requires a head.

5

My argument seems to have wandered somewhat far from the subject, but, by Hercules, it really is very much to the point. For if, as we may infer from what has been said, you are the soul of the State, and the State is your body, you will perceive, I imagine, how necessary clemency is; for when you appear to spare another, you are really sparing yourself. You ought therefore to spare even blameworthy citizens, just as you spare weakly limbs; and when bloodletting becomes necessary, you must hold your hand, lest you should cut deeper than you need. Clemency therefore, as I said before, naturally befits all mankind, but more especially rulers, because in their case there is more for it to save, and it is displayed upon a greater scale. Cruelty in a private man can do but very little harm; but the ferocity of princes is war. Although there is a harmony between all the virtues, and no one is better or more honourable than another, yet some virtues befit some persons better than others. Magnanimity befits all mortal men, even the humblest of all; for what can be greater or braver than to resist ill fortune? Yet this virtue of magnanimity occupies a wider room in prosperity, and shows to greater advantage on the judgment seat than on the floor of the court. On the other hand, clemency renders every house into which it is admitted happy and peaceful; but though it is more rare, it is on that account even more admirable in a palace. What can be more remarkable than that he whose anger might be indulged without fear of the consequences, whose decision, even though a harsh one, would be approved even by those who were to suffer by it, whom no one can interrupt, and of whom indeed, should he become violently enraged, no one would dare to beg for mercy, should apply a check to himself and use his power in a better and calmer spirit, reflecting: "Anyone may break the law to kill a man, no one but I can break it to save him"? A great position requires a great mind, for unless the mind raises itself to and even above the level of its station, it will degrade its station and draw it down to the earth; now it is the property of a great mind to be calm and tranquil and to look down upon outrages and insults with contempt. It is a womanish thing to rage with passion; it is the part of wild beasts, and that, too, not of the most noble ones, to bite and worry the fallen. Elephants and lions pass by those whom they have struck down; inveteracy is the quality of ignoble animals.

Fierce and implacable rage does not befit a king, because he does not preserve his superiority over the man to whose level he descends by indulging in rage; but if he grants their lives and honours to those who are in jeopardy and who deserve to lose them, he does what can only be done by an absolute ruler; for life may be torn away even from those who are above us in station, but can never be granted save to those who are below us. To save men's lives is the privilege of the loftiest station, which never deserves admiration so much as when it is able to act like the gods, by whose kindness good and bad men alike are brought into the world. Thus a prince, imitating the mind of a god, ought to look with pleasure on some of his countrymen because they are useful and good men, while he ought to allow others to remain to fill up the roll; he ought to be pleased with the existence of the former, and to endure that of the latter.

6

Look at this city of Rome, in which the widest streets become choked whenever anything stops the crowds which unceasingly pour through them like raging torrents, in which the people streaming to three theatres demand the roads at the same time, in which the produce of the entire world is consumed, and reflect what a desolate waste it would become if only those were left in it whom a strict judge would acquit. How few magistrates are there who ought not to be condemned by the very same laws which they administer? How few prosecutors are themselves faultless? I imagine, also, that few men are less willing to grant pardon, than those who have often had to beg it for themselves. We have all of us sinned, some more deeply than others, some of set purpose, some either by chance impulse or led away by the wickedness of others; some of us have not stood bravely enough by our good resolutions, and have lost our innocence, although unwillingly and after a struggle; nor have we only sinned, but to the very end of our lives we shall continue to sin. Even if there be anyone who has so thoroughly cleansed his mind that nothing can hereafter throw him into disorder or deceive him, yet even he has reached this state of innocence through sin.

7

Since I have made mention of the gods, I shall state the best model on which a prince may mould his life to be, that he deal with his countrymen as he would that the gods may deal with himself. Is it then desirable that the gods should show no mercy upon sins and mistakes, and that they should harshly pursue us to our ruin? In that case what king will be safe? Whose limbs will not be torn asunder and collected by the soothsayers? If, on the other hand, the gods are placable and kind, and do not at once avenge the crimes of the powerful with thunderbolts, is it not far more just that a man set in authority over other men should exercise his power in a spirit of clemency and should consider whether the condition of the world is more beauteous and pleasant to the eyes on a fine calm day, or when everything is shaken with frequent thunderclaps and when lightning flashes on all sides! Yet the appearance of a peaceful and constitutional reign is the same as that of the calm and brilliant sky. A cruel reign is disordered and hidden in darkness, and while all shake with terror at the sudden explosions, not even he who caused all this disturbance escapes unharmed. It is easier to find excuses for private men who obstinately claim their rights; possibly they may have been injured, and their rage may spring from their wrongs; besides this, they fear to be despised, and not to return the injuries which they have received looks like weakness rather than clemency; but one who can easily avenge himself, if he neglects to do so, is certain to gain praise for goodness of heart. Those who are born in a humble station may with greater freedom exercise violence, go to law, engage in quarrels, and indulge their angry passions; even blows count for little between two equals; but in the case of a king, even loud clamour and unmeasured talk are unbecoming.

8

You think it a serious matter to take away from kings the right of free speech which the humblest enjoy. "This," you say, "is to be a subject, not a king." What, do you not find that we have the command, you the subjection? Your position is quite different to that of those who lie hid in the crowd which they never leave, whose very virtues cannot be manifested without a long struggle, and whose vices are shrouded in obscurity; rumour catches up your acts and sayings, and therefore no persons ought to be more careful of their reputation than those who are certain to have a great one, whatsoever one they may have deserved. How many things there are that you may not do which, thanks to you, we may do! I am able to walk alone without fear in any part of Rome whatever, although no companion accompanies me, though there is no guard at my house no sword by my side. You must live armed in the peace which you maintain.[105] You cannot stray away from your position; it besets you, and follows you with mighty pomp wherever you go. This slavery of not being able to sink one's rank belongs to the highest position of all; yet it is a burden which you share with the gods. They too are held fast in heaven, and it is no more possible for them to come down than it is safe[106] for you; you are chained to your lofty pinnacle. Of our movements few persons are aware; we can go forth and return home and change our dress without its being publicly known; but you are no more able to hide yourself than the sun. A strong light is all around you, the eyes of all are turned towards it. Do you think you are leaving your house? nay, you are dawning upon the world. You cannot speak without all nations everywhere hearing your voice; you cannot be

---

[105] *Pace.*
[106] *Tutum.*

angry, without making everything tremble, because you can strike no one without shaking all around him. Just as thunderbolts when they fall endanger few men but terrify all, so the chastisement inflicted by great potentates terrify more widely than they injure, and that for good reasons; for in the case of one whose power is absolute, men do not think of what he has done, so much as of what he may do. Add to this that private men endure wrongs more tamely, because they have already endured others; the safety of kings on the other hand is more surely founded on kindness, because frequent punishment may crush the hatred of a few, but excites that of all. A king ought to wish to pardon while he has still grounds for being severe; if he acts otherwise, just as lopped trees sprout forth again with numberless boughs, and many kinds of crops are cut down in order that they may grow more thickly, so a cruel king increases the number of his enemies by destroying them; for the parents and children of those who are put to death, and their relatives and friends, step into the place of each victim.

9

I wish to prove the truth of this by an example drawn from your own family. The late Emperor Augustus was a mild prince, if in estimating his character one reckons from the era of his reign; yet he appealed to arms while the state was shared among the triumvirate. When he was just of your age, at the end of his twenty-second year, he had already hidden daggers under the clothes of his friends, he had already conspired to assassinate Marcus Antonius, the consul, he had already taken part in the proscription. But when he had passed his sixtieth[107] year, and was staying in Gaul, intelligence was brought to him that Lucius Cinna, a dull man, was plotting against him: the plot was betrayed by one of the conspirators, who told him where, when, and in what manner Cinna meant to attack him. Augustus

---

[107] Gertz reads *sexagesimum*, his sixtieth year, which he calls "the not very audacious conjecture of Wesseling," and adds that he does so because of the words at the beginning of Chapter XI and the authority of Dion Cassius. The ordinary reading is *quadragesimum*, "his fortieth year," and this is the date to which Cinna's conspiracy is referred to by Merivale, *History of the Romans under the Empire*, Volume IV, Chapter 37. "A plot," he says, "was formed for his destruction, at the head of which was Cornelius Cinna, described as a son of Faustus Sulla by a daughter of the Great Pompeius." The story of Cinna's conspiracy is told by Seneca, "On Clemency" Book I, 9, and Dion IV, 14, foll. They agree in the main fact; but Seneca is our authority for the details of the interview between Augustus and his enemy, while Dion has doubtless invented his long conversation between the emperor and Livia. Seneca, however, calls the conspirator Lucius, and places the event in the fortieth year of Augustus (auc 731), the scene in Gaul: Dion, on the other, gives the names of Gnaeus, and supposes the circumstances to have occurred twenty-six years later, and at Rome. It may be observed that a son of Faustus Sulla must have been at least fifty at this latter date, nor do we know why he should bear the name of Cinna, though an adoption is not impossible.

determined to consult his own safety against this man, and ordered a council of his own friends to be summoned. He passed a disturbed night, reflecting that he would be obliged to condemn to death a youth of noble birth, who was guilty of no crime save this one, and who was the grandson of Gnaeus Pompeius. He, who had sat at dinner and heard M. Antonius[108] read aloud his edict for the proscription, could not now bear to put one single man to death. With groans he kept at intervals making various inconsistent exclamations:—"What! shall I allow my assassin to walk about at his ease while I am racked by fears? Shall the man not be punished who has plotted not merely to slay but actually to sacrifice at the altar" (for the conspirators intended to attack him when he was sacrificing), "now when there is peace by land and sea, that life which so many civil wars have sought in vain, which has passed unharmed through so many battles of fleets and armies?"

Then, after an interval of silence, he would say to himself in a far louder, angrier tone than he had used to Cinna, "Why do you live, if it be to so many men's advantage that you should die? Is there no end to these executions? to this bloodshed? I am a figure set up for nobly-born youths to sharpen their swords on. Is life worth having, if so many must perish to prevent my losing it?" At last his wife Livia interrupted him, saying: "Will you take a woman's advice? Do as the physicians do, who, when the usual remedies fail, try their opposites. Hitherto you have gained nothing by harsh measures: Salvidienus has been followed by Lepidus, Lepidus by Muraena, Muraena by Caepio, and Caepio by Egnatius, not to mention others of whom one feels ashamed of their having dared to attempt so great a deed. Now try what effect clemency will have: pardon Lucius Cinna. He has been detected, he cannot now do you any harm, and he can do your reputation much good." Delighted at finding someone to support his own view of the case, he thanked his wife, straightaway ordered his friends, whose counsel he had asked for, to be told that he did not require their advice, and summoned Cinna alone. After ordering a second seat to be placed for Cinna, he sent everyone else out of the room, and said:—"The first request which I have to make of you is, that you will not interrupt me while I am speaking to you: that you will not cry out in the middle of my address to you: you shall be allowed time to speak freely in answer to me. Cinna, when I found you in the enemy's camp, you who had not become but were actually born my enemy, I saved your life, and restored to you the whole of your father's estate. You are now so prosperous and so rich, that many of the victorious party envy you, the vanquished one: when you were a candidate for the priesthood I passed over many others whose parents had served with me in the wars, and gave it to you: and now, after I have deserved so well of you, you have made up your mind to kill me." When at this word the man exclaimed that he was

---

[108] See Shakespeare's *Julius Caesar*, Act IV, Scene 1.

far from being so insane, Augustus replied, "You do not keep your promise, Cinna; it was agreed upon between us that you should not interrupt me. I repeat, you are preparing to kill me." He then proceeded to tell him of the place, the names of his accomplices, the day, the way in which they had arranged to do the deed, and which of them was to give the fatal stab. When he saw Cinna's eyes fixed upon the ground, and that he was silent, no longer because of the agreement, but from consciousness of his guilt, he said, "What is your intention in doing this? is it that you yourself may be emperor? The Roman people must indeed be in a bad way if nothing but my life prevents your ruling over them. You cannot even maintain the dignity of your own house: you have recently been defeated in a legal encounter by the superior influence of a freedman: and so you can find no easier task than to call your friends to rally round you against Ceesar. Come, now, if you think that I alone stand in the way of your ambition; will Paulus and Fabius Maximus, will the Cossi and the Servilii and all that band of nobles, whose names are no empty pretence, but whose ancestry really renders them illustrious—will they endure that you should rule over them?" Not to fill up the greater part of this book by repeating the whole of his speech—for he is known to have spoken for more than two hours, lengthening out this punishment, which was the only one which he intended to inflict—he said at last: "Cinna, I grant you your life for the second time: when I gave it you before you were an open enemy, you are now a secret plotter and parricide.[109] From this day forth let us be friends: let us try which of us is the more sincere, I in giving you your life, or you in owing your life to me." After this he of his own accord bestowed the consulship upon him, complaining of his not venturing to offer himself as a candidate for that office, and found him ever afterwards his most grateful and loyal adherent. Cinna made the emperor his sole heir, and no one ever again formed any plot against him.

10

Your great-great-grandfather spared the vanquished: for whom could he have ruled over, had he not spared them? He recruited Sallustins, the Cocceii, the Deillii, and the whole inner circle of his court from the camp of his opponents. Soon afterwards his clemency gave him a Domitius, a Messala, an Asinius, a Cicero, and all the flower of the State. For what a long time he waited for Lepidus to die: for years he allowed him to retain all the insignia of royalty, and did not allow the office of Pontifex Maximus to be conferred upon himself until after Lepidus's death; for he wished it to be called a honourable office rather than a spoil stripped from a vanquished foe. It was this clemency which made him end his days in safety and security: this it was which rendered him popular and beloved,

---

[109] An allusion to the title of "Father of his country," bestowed by the Senate upon Augustus. See Merivale, Chapter 33.

although he had laid his hands on the neck of the Romans when they were still unused to bearing the yoke: this gives him even at the present day a reputation such as hardly any prince has enjoyed during his own lifetime. "We believe him to be a god, and not merely because we are bidden to do so. We declare that Augustus was a good emperor, and that he was well worthy to bear his parent's name, for no other reason than because he did not even show cruelty in avenging personal insults, which most princes feel more keenly than actual injuries; because he smiled at scandalous jests against himself, because it was evident that he himself suffered when he punished others, because he was so far from putting to death even those whom he had convicted of intriguing with his daughter, that when they were banished he gave them passports to enable them to travel more safely. When you know that there will be many who will take your quarrel upon themselves, and will try to gain your favour by the murder of your enemies, you do indeed pardon them if you not only grant them their lives but ensure that they shall not lose them.

11

Such was Augustus when an old man, or when growing old: in his youth he was hasty and passionate, and did many things upon which he looked back with regret. No one will venture to compare the rule of the blessed Augustus to the mildness of your own, even if your youth be compared with his more than ripe old age: he was gentle and placable, but it was after he had dyed the sea at Actium with Roman blood; after he had wrecked both the enemy's fleet and his own at Sicily; after the holocaust of Perusia and the proscriptions. But I do not call it clemency to be wearied of cruelty; true clemency, Caesar, is that which you display, which has not begun from remorse at its past ferocity, on which there is no stain, which has never shed the blood of your countrymen: this, when combined with unlimited power, shows the truest self-control and all-embracing love of the human race as of oneself, not corrupted by any low desires, any extravagant ideas, or any of the bad examples of former emperors into trying, by actual experiment, how great a tyranny you would be allowed to exercise over his countrymen, but inclining rather to blunting your sword of empire. You, Caesar, have granted us the boon of keeping our state free from bloodshed, and that of which you boast, that you have not caused one single drop of blood to flow in any part of the world, is all the more magnanimous and marvellous because no one ever had the power of the sword placed in his hands at an earlier age. Clemency, then, makes princes safer as well as more respected, and is a glory to empires besides being their most trustworthy means of preservation. Why have legitimate sovereigns grown old on the throne, and bequeathed their power to their children and grandchildren, while the sway of despotic usurpers is both hateful and shortlived? What is the difference between the tyrant and the king—for their outward symbols of authority and their powers are the same—except it be that tyrants take delight in cruelty, whereas kings are only cruel for good reasons and because they cannot help it.[110]

12

"What, then," say you, "do not kings also put men to death?" They do, but only when that measure is recommended by the public advantage: tyrants enjoy cruelty. A tyrant differs from a king in deeds, not in title: for the elder Dionysius deserves to be preferred before many kings, and what can prevent our styling Lucius Sulla a tyrant, since he only left off slaying because he had no more enemies to slay? Although he laid down his dictatorship and resumed the garb of a private citizen, yet what tyrant ever drank human blood as greedily as he, who ordered seven thousand Roman citizens to be butchered, and who, on hearing the shrieks of so many thousands being put to the sword as he sat in the temple of Bellona, said to the terror-stricken Senate, "Let us attend to our business, Conscript Fathers; it is only a few disturbers of the public peace who are being put to death by my orders." In saying this he did not lie: they really seemed few to Sulla. But we shall speak of Sulla presently, when we consider how we ought to feel anger against our enemies, at any rate when our own countrymen, members of the same community as ourselves, have been torn away from it and assumed the name of enemies: in the meanwhile, as I was saying, clemency is what makes the great distinction between kings and tyrants. Though each of them may be equally fenced around by armed soldiers, nevertheless the one uses his troops to safeguard the peace of his kingdom, the other uses them to quell great hatred by great terror: and yet he does not look with any confidence upon those to whose hands he entrusts himself. He is driven in opposite directions by conflicting passions: for since he is hated because he is feared, he wishes to be feared because he is hated: and he acts up to the spirit of that odious verse, which has cast so many headlong from their thrones—

"Why, let them hate me, if they fear me too!"—

not knowing how frantic men become when their hatred becomes excessive: for a moderate amount of fear restrains men, but a constant and keen apprehension of the worst tortures rouses up even the most grovelling spirits to deeds of reckless courage, and causes them to hesitate at nothing. Just so a string stuck full of feathers[111] will prevent wild beasts escaping: but should a horseman begin to shoot at them from another quarter, they will attempt to escape over the very thing that scared them,

---

[110] This whole comparison, which reads so meaninglessly both in Latin and in English, is borrowed from the eternal declamations of Plutarch and the Greek philosophers about βασιλετς and τύραννοι. See Plutarch, *Lives of Philopoemen and Aratus*, Plato, *Gorgias* and *Politicus*; Arnold, *Appendix to Thucydides*, Volume I, and *Dictionary of Antiquities*, s.v.
[111] "On Anger," Book II, Chapter 2.

and will trample the cause of their alarm underfoot. No courage is so great as that which is born of utter desperation. In order to keep people down by terror, you must grant them a certain amount of security, and let them see that they have far more to hope for than to fear: for otherwise, if a man is in equal peril whether he sits still or takes action, he will feel actual pleasure in risking his life, and will fling it away as lightly as though it were not his own.

13

A calm and peaceful king trusts his guards, because he makes use of them to ensure the common safety of all his subjects, and his soldiers, who see that the security of the State depends upon their labours, cheerfully undergo the severest toil and glory in being the protectors of the father of their country: whereas your harsh and murderous tyrant must needs be disliked even by his own janissaries. No man can expect willing and loyal service from those whom he uses like the rack and the axe, as instruments of torture and death, to whom he casts men as he would cast them to wild beasts. No prisoner at the bar is so full of agony and anxiety as a tyrant; for while he dreads both gods and men because they have witnessed, and will avenge his crimes, he has at the same time so far committed himself to this course of action that he is not able to alter it. This is perhaps the very worst quality of cruelty: a man must go on exercising it, and it is impossible for him to retrace his steps and start in a better path; for crimes must be safeguarded by fresh crimes. Yet who can be more unhappy than he who is actually compelled to be a villain? How greatly he ought to be pitied: I mean, by himself, for it would be impious for others to pity a man who has made use of his power to murder and ravage, who has rendered himself mistrusted by everyone at home and abroad, who fears the very soldiers to whom he flees for safety, who dare not rely upon the loyalty of his friends or the affection of his children: who, whenever he considers what he has done, and what he is about to do, and calls to mind all the crimes and torturings with which his conscience is burdened, must often fear death, and yet must often wish for it, for he must be even more hateful to himself than he is to his subjects. On the other hand, he who takes an interest in the entire State, who watches over every department of it with more or less care, who attends to all the business of the State as well as if it were his own, who is naturally inclined to mild measures, and shows, even when it is to his advantage to punish, how unwilling he is to make use of harsh remedies; who has no angry or savage feelings, but wields his authority calmly and beneficially, being anxious that even his subordinate officers shall be popular with his countrymen, who thinks his happiness complete if he can make the nation share his prosperity, who is courteous in language, whose presence is easy of access, who looks obligingly upon his subjects, who is disposed to grant all their reasonable wishes, and does not treat their unreasonable wishes with harshness—such a prince is loved, protected, and worshipped by his whole empire. Men talk of such a one in private in the same words which they use in public: they are eager to bring up families under his reign, and they put an end to the childlessness which public misery had previously rendered general: everyone feels that he will indeed deserve that his children should be grateful to him for having brought them into so happy an age. Such a prince is rendered safe by his own beneficence; he has no need of guards, their arms serve him merely as decorations.

14

What, then, is his duty? It is that of good parents, who sometimes scold their children good naturedly, sometimes threaten them, and sometimes even flog them. No man in his senses disinherits his son for his first offence: he does not pass this extreme sentence upon him unless his patience has been worn out by many grievous wrongs, unless he fears that his son will do something worse than that which he punishes him for having done; before doing this he makes many attempts to lead his son's mind into the right way while it is still hesitating between good and evil and has only taken its first steps in depravity; it is only when its case is hopeless that he adopts this extreme measure. No one demands that people should be executed until after he has failed to reform them. This which is the duty of a parent, is also that of the prince whom with no unmeaning flattery we call "The Father of our Country." Other names are given as titles of honour: we have styled some men "The Great," "The Fortunate," or "The August" and have thus satisfied their passion for grandeur by bestowing upon them all the dignity that we could: but when we style a man "The Father of his Country" we give him to understand that we have entrusted him with a father's power over us, which is of the mildest character for a father takes thought for his children and subordinates his own interests to theirs. It is long before a father will cut off a member of his own body: even after he has cut it off he longs to replace it, and in cutting it off he laments and hesitates much and long: for he who condemns quickly is not far from being willing to condemn; and he who inflicts too great punishment comes very near to punishing unjustly.

15

Within my own recollection the people stabbed in the forum with their writing-styles a Roman knight named Tricho, because he had flogged his son to death: even the authority of Augustus Caesar could hardly save him from the angry clutches of both fathers and sons: but everyone admired Tarius, who, on discovering that his son meditated parricide, tried him, convicted him, and was then satisfied with punishing him by exile, and that, too, to that pleasant place of exile, Marseilles, where he made him the same yearly allowance which he had done while he was innocent: the result of this generosity was that even in a city where every villain finds someone to defend him, no one doubted that he was justly condemned, since even the father who was unable to hate him, nevertheless had condemned him. In this very same instance I will give you an example of a good prince, which you may compare with a good father. Tarius, when about to sit in judgement on his son, invited Augustus Caesar to assist in trying him: Augustus came into his private house, sat beside the father, took part in another man's family council, and did not say, "Nay, let him rather come to my house," because if he had done so, the trial would have been conducted by Caesar and not by the father. When the cause had been heard, after all that the young man pleaded in his own defence and all that was alleged against him had been thoroughly discussed, the emperor begged that each man would write his sentence (instead of pronouncing it aloud), in order that they might not all follow Caesar in giving sentence: then, before the tablets were opened, he declared that if Tarius, who was a rich man, made him his heir, he would not accept the bequest. One might say, "It showed a paltry mind in him to fear that people would think that he condemned the son in order to enable himself to inherit the estate." I am of a contrary opinion—any one of us ought to have sufficient trust in the consciousness of his own integrity to defend him against calumny, but princes must take great pains to avoid even the appearance of evil. He swore that he would not accept the property. On that day Tarius lost two heirs to his estate, but Caesar gained the liberty of forming an unbiased judgement: and when he had proved that his severity was disinterested, a point of which a prince should never lose sight, he gave sentence that the son should be banished to whatever place the father might choose. He did not sentence him to the sack and the snakes, or to prison, because he thought, not of who it was upon whom he was passing sentence, but of who it was with whom he was sitting in judgement: he said that a father ought to be satisfied with the mildest form of punishment for his stripling son, who had been seduced into a crime which he had attempted so fainteartedly as to be almost innocent of it, and that he ought to be removed from Rome and out of his father's sight.

16

How worthy was he to be invited by fathers to join their family councils: how worthy to be made co-heir with innocent children! This is the sort of clemency which befits a prince; wherever he goes, let him make everyone more charitable. In the king's sight, no one ought to be so despicable that he should not notice whether he lives or dies: be his character what it may, he is a part of the empire. Let us take examples for great kingdoms from smaller ones. There are many forms of royalty: a prince reigns over his subjects, a father over his children, a teacher over his scholars, a tribune or centurion over his soldiers. Would not he, who constantly punished his children by beating them for the most trifling faults, be thought the worst of fathers? Which is worthier to impart a liberal education: he who flays his scholars alive if their memory be weak, or if their eyes do not run quickly along the lines as they read, or he who prefers to improve and instruct them by kindly warnings and moral influence? If a tribune or a centurion is harsh, he will make men deserters, and one cannot blame them for desertion. It is never right to rule a human being more harshly and cruelly than we rule dumb animals; yet a skilled horse-breaker will not scare a horse by frequent blows, because he will become timid and vicious if you do not soothe him with pats and caresses. So also a huntsman, both when he is teaching puppies to follow the tracks of wild animals, and when he uses dogs already trained to drive them from their lairs and hunt them, does not often threaten to beat them, for, if he does, he will break their spirit, and make them stupid and currish with fear; though, on the other hand, he will not allow them to roam and range about unrestrained. The same is the case with those who drive the slower draught cattle, which, though brutal treatment and wretchedness is their lot from their birth, still, by excessive cruelty may be made to refuse to draw.

17

No creature is more self-willed, requires more careful management, or ought to be treated with greater indulgence than man. What, indeed, can be more foolish than that we should blush to show anger against dogs or beasts of burden, and yet wish one man to be most abominably ill-treated by another? We are not angry with diseases, but apply remedies to them: but this also is a disease of the mind, and requires soothing medicine and a physician who is anything but angry with his patient. It is the part of a bad physician to despair of effecting a cure: he, to whom the care of all men's well-being is entrusted, ought to act like a good physician, and not be in a hurry to give up hope or to declare that the symptoms are mortal: he should wrestle with vices, withstand them, reproach some with their distemper, and deceive others by a soothing mode of treatment, because he will cure his patient more quickly and more thoroughly if the medicines which he administers escape his notice: a prince should take care not only of the recovery of his people, but also that their scars should be honourable. Cruel punishments do a king no honour: for who doubts that he is able to inflict them? but, on the other hand, it does him great honour to restrain his powers, to save many from the wrath of others, and sacrifice no one to his own.

18

It is creditable to a man to keep within reasonable bounds in his treatment of his slaves. Even in the case of a human chattel one ought to consider, not how much one can torture him with impunity, but how far such treatment is permitted by natural goodness and justice, which prompts us to act kindly towards even prisoners of war and slaves bought for a price (how much more towards freeborn, respectable gentlemen?), and not to treat them with scornful brutality as human chattels, but as persons somewhat below ourselves in station, who have been placed under our protection rather than assigned to us as servants. Slaves are allowed to run and take sanctuary at the statue of a god, though the laws allows a slave to be ill-treated to any extent, there are nevertheless some things which the common laws of life forbid us to do to a human being. Who does not hate Vedius Pollio[112] more even than his own slaves did, because he used to fatten his lampreys with human blood, and ordered those who had offended him in any way to be cast into his fishpond, or rather snake-pond? That man deserved to die a thousand deaths, both for throwing his slaves to be devoured by the lampreys which he himself meant to eat, and for keeping lampreys that he might feed them in such a fashion. Cruel masters are pointed at with disgust in all parts of the city, and are hated and loathed; the wrongdoings of kings are enacted on a wider theatre: their shame and unpopularity endures for ages: yet how far better it would have been never to have been born than to be numbered among those who have been born to do their country harm!

19

Nothing can be imagined which is more becoming to a sovereign than clemency, by whatever title and right he may be set over his fellow citizens. The greater his power, the more beautiful and admirable he will confess his clemency to be: for there is no reason why power should do any harm, if only it be wielded in accordance with the laws of nature. Nature herself has conceived the idea of a king, as you may learn from various animals, and especially from bees, among whom the king's cell is the roomiest, and is placed in the most central and safest part of the hive; moreover, he does no work, but employs himself in keeping the others up to their work. If the king be lost, the entire swarm disperses: they never endure to have more than one king at a time, and find out which is the better by making them fight with one another: moreover the king is distinguished by his statelier appearance, being both larger and more brilliantly coloured than the other bees. The most remarkable distinction, however, is the following: bees are very fierce, and for their size are the most pugnacious of creatures, and leave their stings in the wounds which they make, but the king himself has no sting: nature does not wish him to be savage or to seek revenge at so dear a rate, and so has deprived him of his weapon and disarmed his rage. She has offered him as a pattern to great sovereigns, for she is wont to practice herself in small matters, and to scatter abroad tiny models of the hugest structures. We ought to be ashamed of not learning a lesson in behaviour from these small creatures, for a man, who has so much more power of doing harm than they, ought

---

[112] Vedius Pollio had a villa on the mountain now called Punta di Posilippo, which projects into the sea between Naples and Puteoli, which he left to Augustus, and which was afterwards possessed by the Emperor Trajan. He was a freedman by birth, and remarkable for nothing except his riches and his cruelty. Cf. Dion Cassius, LIV, 23; Pliny, *Naturalis Historia*, IX, 23; and Seneca, "On Anger," Book III, Chapter 40.

to show a correspondingly greater amount of self-control. Would that human beings were subject to the same law, and that their anger destroyed itself together with its instrument, so that they could only inflict a wound once, and would not make use of the strength of others to carry out their hatreds: for their fury would soon grow faint if it carried its own punishment with it, and could only give rein to its violence at the risk of death. Even as it is, however, no one can exercise it with safety, for he must needs feel as much fear as he hopes to cause, he must watch everyone's movements, and even when his enemies are not laying violent hands upon him he must bear in mind that they are plotting to do so, and he cannot have a single moment free from alarm. Would anyone endure to live such a life as this, when he might enjoy the privileges of his high station to the general joy of all men, without injuring anyone, and for that very reason have no one to fear? for it is a mistake to suppose that the king can be safe in a state where nothing is safe from the king: he can only purchase a life without anxiety for himself by guaranteeing the same for his subjects. He need not pile up lofty citadels, escarp steep hills, cut away the sides of mountains, and fence himself about with many lines of walls and towers: clemency will render a king safe even upon an open plain. The one fortification which cannot be stormed is the love of his countrymen. What can be more glorious than a life which everyone spontaneously and without official pressure hopes may last long? to excite men's fears, not their hopes, if one's health gives way a little? to know that no one holds anything so dear that he would not be glad to give it in exchange for the health of his sovereign? "O, may no evil befall him!" they would cry: "he must live for his own sake, not only for ours: his constant proofs of goodness have made him belong to the State instead of the State belonging to him." Who would dare to plot any danger to such a king? Who would not rather, if he could, keep misfortune far from one under whom justice, peace, decency, security and merit flourish, under whom the State grows rich with an abundance of all good things, and looks upon its ruler in the same spirit of adoration and respect with which we should look upon the immortal gods, if they allowed us to behold them as we behold him? Why! does not that man come very close to the gods who acts in a godlike manner, and who is beneficent, openhanded, and powerful for good? Your aim and your pride ought to lie in being thought the best, as well as the greatest of mankind.

20

A prince generally inflicts punishment for one of two reasons: he wishes either to assert his own rights or those of another. I will first discuss the case in which he is personally concerned, for it is more difficult for him to act with moderation when he acts under the impulse of actual pain than when he merely does so for the sake of the example. It is unnecessary in this place to remind him to be slow to believe what he hears, to ferret out the truth, to show favour to innocence, and to bear in mind that to prove it is as much the business of the judge as that of the prisoner;

for these considerations are connected with justice, not with clemency: what we are now encouraging him to do is not to lose control over his feelings when he receives an unmistakeable injury, and to forego punishing it if he possibly can do so with safety, if not, to moderate the severity of the punishment, and to show himself far more unwilling to forgive wrongs done to others than those done to himself: for, just as the truly generous man is not he who gives away what belongs to others, but he who deprives himself of what he gives to another, so also I should not call a prince clement who looked good naturedly upon a wrong done to someone else, but one who is unmoved even by the sting of a personal injury, who understands how magnanimous it is for one whose power is unlimited to allow himself to be wronged, and that there is no more noble spectacle than that of a sovereign who has received an injury without avenging it.

21

Vengeance effects two purposes: it either affords compensation to the person to whom the wrong was done, or it ensures him against molestation for the future. A prince is too rich to need compensation, and his power is too evident for him to require to gain a reputation for power by causing anyone to suffer. I mean, when he is attacked and injured by his inferiors, for if he sees those who once were his equals in a position of inferiority to himself he is sufficiently avenged. A king may be killed by a slave, or a serpent, or an arrow: but no one can be saved except by someone who is greater than him whom he saves. He, therefore, who has the power of giving and of taking away life ought to use such a great gift of heaven in a spirited manner. Above all, if he once obtains this power over those who he knows were once on a level with himself, he has completed his revenge, and done all that he need to towards the punishment of his adversary: for he who owes his life to another must have lost it, and he who has been cast down from on high and lies at his enemy's feet with his kingdom and his life depending upon the pleasure of another, adds to the glory of his preserver if he be allowed to live, and increases his reputation much more by remaining unhurt than if he were put out of the way. In the former case he remains as an everlasting testimony to the valour of his conqueror; whereas if led in the procession of a triumph he would have soon passed out of sight.[113] If, however, his kingdom also may be safely left in his hands and he himself replaced upon the throne from which he has fallen, such a measure confers an immense increase of luster on him who scorned to take anything from a conquered king beyond the glory of having conquered him. To do this is to triumph even over one's own victory, and to declare that one has found nothing among the vanquished which it was worth the victor's while to take. As for his countrymen, strangers, and persons of

---

[113] The conquered princes who were led through Rome in triumphs were as a rule put to death when the procession was over.

mean condition, he ought to treat them with all the less severity because it costs so much less to overcome them. Some you would be glad to spare, against some you would disdain to assert your rights, and would forbear to touch them as you would to touch little insects which defile your hands when you crush them: but in the case of men upon whom all eyes are fixed, whether they be spared or condemned, you should seize the opportunity of making your clemency widely known.

22

Let us now pass on to the consideration of wrongs done to others, in avenging which the law has aimed at three ends, which the prince will do well to aim at also: they are, either that it may correct him whom it punishes, or that his punishment may render other men better, or that, by bad men being put out of the way, the rest may live without fear. You will more easily correct the men themselves by a slight punishment, for he who has some part of his fortune remaining untouched will behave less recklessly; on the other hand, no one cares about respectability after he has lost it: it is a species of impunity to have nothing left for punishment to take away. It is conducive, however, to good morals in a state, that punishment should seldom be inflicted: for where there is a multitude of sinners men become familiar with sin, shame is less felt when shared with a number of fellow-criminals, and severe sentences, if frequently pronounced, lose the influence which constitutes their chief power as remedial measures. A good king establishes a good standard of morals for his kingdom and drives away vices if he is long-suffering with them, not that he should seem to encourage them, but to be very unwilling and to suffer much when he is forced to chastise them. Clemency in a sovereign even makes men ashamed to do wrong: for punishment seems far more grievous when inflicted by a merciful man.

23

Besides this, you will find that sins which are frequently punished are frequently committed. Your father sewed up more parricides in sacks during five years, than we hear of in all previous centuries. As long as the greatest of crimes remained without any special law, children were much more timid about committing it. Our wise ancestors, deeply skilled in human nature, preferred to pass over this as being a wickedness too great for belief, and beyond the audacity of the worst criminal, rather than teach men that it might be done by appointing a penalty for doing it: parricides, consequently, were unknown until a law was made against them, and the penalty showed them the way to the crime. Filial affection soon perished, for since that time we have seen more men punished by the sack than by the cross. Where men are seldom punished innocence becomes the rule, and is encouraged as a public benefit. If a state thinks itself innocent, it will be innocent: it will be all the more angry with those who corrupt the general simplicity of manners if it sees that they are few in number. Believe me, it is a dangerous thing to show a state how great a majority of bad men it contains.

24

A proposal was once made in the Senate to distinguish slaves from free men by their dress: it was then discovered how dangerous it would be for our slaves to be able to count our numbers. Be assured that the same thing would be the case if no one's offence is pardoned: it will quickly be discovered how far the number of bad men exceeds that of the good. Many executions are as disgraceful to a sovereign as many funerals are to a physician: one who governs less strictly is better obeyed. The human mind is naturally self-willed, kicks against the goad, and sets its face against authority; it will follow more readily than it can be led. As well-bred and high-spirited horses are best managed with a loose rein, so mercy gives men's minds a spontaneous bias towards innocence, and the public think that it is worth observing. Mercy, therefore, does more good than severity.

25

Cruelty is far from being a human vice, and is unworthy of man's gentle mind: it is mere bestial madness to take pleasure in blood and wounds, to cast off humanity and transform oneself into a wild beast of the forest. Pray, Alexander, what is the difference between your throwing Lysimachus into a lion's den and tearing his flesh with your own teeth? it is you that have the lion's maw, and the lion's fierceness. How pleased you would be if you had claws instead of nails, and jaws that were capable of devouring men! We do not expect of you that your hand, the sure murderer of your best friends, should restore health to anyone; or that your proud spirit, that inexhaustible source of evil to all nations, should be satisfied with anything short of blood and slaughter: we rather call it mercy that your friend should have a human being chosen to be his butcher. The reason why cruelty is the most hateful of all vices is that it goes first beyond the ordinary limits, and then beyond those of humanity; that it devises new kinds of punishments, calls ingenuity to aid it in inventing devices for varying and lengthening men's torture, and takes delight in their sufferings: this accursed disease of the mind reaches its highest pitch of madness when cruelty itself turns into pleasure, and the act of killing a man becomes enjoyment. Such a ruler is soon cast down from his throne; his life is attempted by poison one day and by the sword the next; he is exposed to as many dangers as there are men to whom he is dangerous, and he is sometimes destroyed by the plots of individuals, and at others by a general insurrection. Whole communities are not roused to action by unimportant outrages on private persons; but cruelty which takes a wider range, and from which no one is safe, becomes a mark for all men's weapons. Very small snakes escape our notice, and the whole country does not combine to destroy them; but when one of them exceeds the usual size and grows into a monster, when it poisons fountains with its spittle, scorches herbage with its breath, and spreads ruin wherever it crawls, we shoot at it with military engines. Trifling evils may cheat us and elude our observation, but we gird up our loins to attack great ones. One sick person does not so much as disquiet the house in which he lies; but when frequent deaths show that a plague is raging, there is a general outcry, men take to flight and shake their fists angrily at the very gods themselves. If a fire breaks out under one single roof, the family and the neighbours pour water upon it; but a wide conflagration which has consumed many houses must be smothered under the ruins of a whole quarter of a city.

26

The cruelty even of private men has sometimes been revenged by their slaves in spite of the certainty that they will be crucified: whole kingdoms and nations when oppressed by tyrants or threatened by them, have attempted their destruction. Sometimes their own guards have risen in revolt, and have used against their master all the deceit, disloyalty, and ferocity which they have learned from him. What, indeed, can he expect from those whom he has taught to be wicked? A bad man will not long be obedient, and will not do only as much evil as he is ordered. But even if the tyrant may be cruel with safety, how miserable his kingdom must be: it must look like a city taken by storm, like some frightful scene of general panic. Everywhere sorrow, anxiety, disorder; men dread even their own pleasures; they cannot even dine with one another in safety when they have to keep watch over their tongues even when in their cups, nor can they safely attend the public shows when informers are ready to find grounds for their impeachment in their behaviour there. Although the spectacles be provided at an enormous expense, with royal magnificence and with world-famous artists, yet who cares for amusement when he is in prison? Ye gods! what a miserable life it is to slaughter and to rage, to delight in the clanking of chains, and to cut off one's countrymen's heads, to cause blood to flow freely wherever one goes, to terrify people, and make them flee away out of one's sight! It is what would happen if bears or lions were our masters, if serpents and all the most venomous creatures were given power over us. Even these animals, devoid of reason as they are, and accused by us of cruel ferocity, spare their own kind, and wild beasts themselves respect their own likeness: but the fury of tyrants does not even stop short at their own relations, and they treat friends and strangers alike, only becoming more violent the more they indulge their passions. By insensible degrees he proceeds from the slaughter of individuals to the ruin of nations, and thinks it a sign of power to set roofs on fire and to plough up the sites of ancient cities: he considers it unworthy of an emperor to order only one or two people to be put to death, and thinks that his cruelty is unduly restrained if whole troops of wretches are not sent to execution together. True happiness, on the other hand, consists in saving many men's lives, in calling them back from the very gates of death, and in being so merciful as to deserve a civic crown.[114] No decoration is more worthy or more becoming to a prince's rank than that crown for saving the lives of fellow-citizens: not trophies torn from a vanquished enemy, not chariots wet with their savage owner's blood, not spoils captured in war. This power which saves men's lives by crowds and by nations, is godlike: the power of extensive and indiscriminate massacre is the power of downfall and conflagration.

---

[114] The "civic" crown of oak-leaves was bestowed on him who had saved the life of a fellow-citizen in war. It was bestowed upon Augustus, and after him upon the other emperors, as preservers of the State.

BOOK 2

1

I have been especially led to write about clemency, Nero Caesar, by a saying of yours, which I remember having heard with admiration and which I afterwards told to others: a noble saying, showing a great mind and great gentleness, which suddenly burst from you without premeditation, and was not meant to reach any ears but your own, and which displayed the conflict which was raging between your natural goodness and your imperial duties. Your prefect Burrus, an excellent man who was born to be the servant of such an emperor as you are, was about to order two brigands to be executed, and was pressing you to write their names and the grounds on which they were to be put to death: this had often been put off, and he was insisting that it should then be done. When he reluctantly produced the document and put it into your equally reluctant hands, you exclaimed: "Would that I had never learned my letters!" O what a speech, how worthy to be heard by all nations, both those who dwell within the Roman Empire, those who enjoy a debatable independence upon its borders, and those who either in will or in deed fight against it! It is a speech which ought to be spoken before a meeting of all mankind, whose words all kings and princes ought to swear to obey: a speech worthy of the days of human innocence, and worthy to bring back that golden age. Now in truth we ought all to agree to love righteousness and goodness; covetousness, which is the root of all evil, ought to be driven away, piety and virtue, good faith and modesty ought to resume their interrupted reign, and the vices which have so long and so shamefully ruled us ought at last to give way to an age of happiness and purity.

2

To a great extent, Caesar, we may hope and expect that this will come to pass. Let your own goodness of heart be gradually spread and diffused throughout the whole body of the empire, and all parts of it will mould themselves into your likeness. Good health proceeds from the head into all the members of the body: they are all either brisk and erect, or languid and drooping, according as their guiding spirit blooms or withers. Both Romans and allies will prove worthy of this goodness of yours, and good morals will return to all the world: your hands will everywhere find less to do. Allow me to dwell somewhat upon this saying of yours, not because it is a pleasant subject for your ears (indeed, this is not my way; I would rather offend by telling the truth than curry favour by flattery). What, then, is my reason? Besides wishing that you should be as familiar as possible with your own good deeds and good words, in order that what is now untutored impulse may grow into matured decision, I remember that many great but odious sayings have become part of human life and are familiar in men's mouths, such as that celebrated, "Let them hate me, provided that they fear me," which is like that Greek verse, "ἐμοῦ θανούτος γαῖα μιχθήτω πυρί," in which a man bids the Earth perish in flame after he is dead, and others of the like sort. I know not how it is, but certainly human ingenuity seems to have found it easier to find emphatic and ardent expression for monstrous and cynical sentiments: I have never hitherto heard any spirited saying from a good and gentle person. What, then, is the upshot of all this? It is that, albeit seldom and against your will, and after much hesitation, you sometimes nevertheless must write that which made you hate your letters, but that you ought to do so with great hesitation and after many postponements, even as you now do.

3

But lest the plausible word "mercy" should sometimes deceive us and lead us into the opposite extreme, let us consider what mercy is, what its qualities are, and within what limits it is confined. Mercy is "a restraining of the mind from vengeance when it is in its power to avenge itself," or it is "gentleness shown by a powerful man in fixing the punishment of a weaker one." It is safer to have more than one definition, since one may not include the whole subject, and may, so to speak, lose its cause: mercy, therefore, may likewise be termed a tendency towards mildness in inflicting punishment. It is possible to discover certain inconsistencies in the definition which comes nearer the truth than all the rest, which is to call mercy "self-restraint, which remits some part of a fine which it deserves to receive and which is due to it." To this it will be objected that no virtue ever gives any man less than his due. However, all men understand mercy to consist in coming short of the penalty which might with justice be inflicted.

4

The unlearned think that its opposite is strictness: but no virtue is the opposite of another virtue. What, then, is the opposite of mercy? Cruelty: which is nothing more than obstinacy in exacting punishments. "But," say you, "some men do not exact punishments, and nevertheless are cruel, such as those who kill the strangers whom they meet, not in order to rob them, but for killing's sake, and men who are not satisfied with killing, but kill with savage tortures, like the famous Busiris,[115] and Procrustes, and pirates who flog their captives and burn them alive." This appears to be cruelty: but as it is not the result of vengeance (for it has received no wrong), and is not excited by any offence (for no crime has preceded it), it does not come within our definition, which was limited to "extravagance in exacting the penalties of wrongdoing." We may say that this is not cruelty, but ferocity, which finds pleasure in savagery: or we may call it madness; for madness is of various kinds, and there is no truer madness than that which takes to slaughtering and mutilating human beings. I shall, therefore, call those persons cruel who have a reason for punishing but who punish without moderation, like Phalaris, who is not said to have tortured innocent men, but to have tortured criminals with inhuman and incredible barbarity. We may avoid hairsplitting by defining cruelty to be "a tendency of the mind towards harsh measures." Mercy repels cruelty and bids it be far from her: with strictness she is on terms of amity.

At this point it is useful to inquire into what pity is; for many praise it as a virtue, and say that a good man is full of pity. This also is a disease of the mind. Both of these stand close to mercy and to strictness, and both ought to be avoided, lest under the name of strictness we be led into cruelty, and under the name of mercy into pity. It is less dangerous to make the latter mistake, but both lead us equally far away from the truth.

5

Just as the gods are worshipped by religion, but are dishonoured by superstition, so all good men will show mercy and mildness, but will avoid pity, which is a vice incident to weak minds which cannot endure the sight of another's sufferings. It is, therefore, most commonly found in the worst people; there are old women and girls[116] who are affected by the tears of the greatest criminals, and who, if they could, would let them out of prison. Pity considers a man's misfortunes and does not consider to what they are due: mercy is combined with reason. I know that the doctrine of the Stoics is unpopular among the ignorant as being excessively severe and not at all likely to give kings and princes good advice; it is blamed because it declares that the wise man knows not how to feel pity or to grant pardon. These doctrines, if taken separately, are indeed odious, for they appear to give men no hope of repairing their mistakes but exact a penalty for every slip. If this were true, how can it be true wisdom to bid us put off human feeling, and to exclude

---

[115] A king of Egypt, who sacrificed strangers, and was himself slain by Hercules.

[116] "Three or four wenches where I stood, cried 'Alas, good soul!' and forgave him with all their hearts: but there's no heed to be taken of them; if Caesar had stabbed their mothers, they would have done no less."
—*Julius Caesar*, Act I, Scene 2.

us from mutual help, that surest haven of refuge against the attacks of Fortune? But no school of philosophy is more gentle and benignant, none is more full of love towards man or more anxious to promote the happiness of all, seeing that its maxims are, to be of service and assistance to others, and to consult the interests of each and all, not of itself alone. Pity is a disorder of the mind caused by the sight of other men's miseries, or it is a sadness caused by the evils with which it believes others to be undeservedly afflicted: but the wise man cannot be affected by any disorder: his mind is calm, and nothing can possibly happen to ruffle it. Moreover, nothing becomes a man more than magnanimity: but magnanimity cannot coexist with sorrow. Sorrow overwhelms men's minds, casts them down, contracts them: now this cannot happen to the wise man even in his greatest misfortunes, but he will beat back the rage of Fortune and triumph over it: he will always retain the same calm, undisturbed expression of countenance, which he never could do were he accessible to sorrow.

6

Add to this, that the wise man provides for the future and always has a distinct plan of action ready: yet nothing clear and true can flow from a disturbed source. Sorrow is awkward at reviewing the position of affairs, at devising useful expedients, avoiding dangerous courses, and weighing the merits of fair and just ones: therefore the wise man will not feel pity, because this cannot happen to a man unless his mind is disturbed. He will do willingly and high-mindedly all that those who feel pity are wont to do; he will dry the tears of others, but will not mingle his own with them; he will stretch out his hand to the shipwrecked mariner, will offer hospitality to the exile, and alms to the needy—not in the offensive way in which most of those who wish to be thought tenderhearted fling their bounty to those whom they assist and shrink from their touch, but as one man would give another something out of the common stock—he will restore children to their weeping mothers, will loose the chains of the captive, release the gladiator from his bondage, and even bury the carcass of the criminal, but he will perform all this with a calm mind and unaltered expression of countenance. Thus the wise man will not pity men, but will help them and be of service to them, seeing that he is born to be a help to all men and a public benefit, of which he will bestow a share upon everyone. He will even grant a proportional part of his bounty to those sufferers who deserve blame and correction; but he will much more willingly help those whose troubles and adversities are caused by misfortune. Whenever he is able he will interpose between Fortune and her victims: for what better employment can he find for his wealth or his strength than in setting up again what chance has overthrown? He will not show or feel any disgust at a man's having withered legs, or a flabby wrinkled skin, or supporting his aged body upon a staff; but he will do good to those who deserve it, and will, like a god, look benignantly upon all who are in trouble. Pity borders upon misery: it is partly composed of it and partly derived from it. You know that eyes must be weak, if they fill with rheum at the sight of another's blearedness, just as it is not real merriment but hysteria which makes people laugh because others laugh, and yawn whenever others open their jaws: pity is a defect in the mind of people who are extraordinarily affected by suffering, and he who requires a wise man to exhibit it is not far from requiring him to lament and groan when strangers are buried.

7

But why should he not pardon?[117] Let us decide by exact definition this other slippery matter, the true nature of pardon, and we shall then perceive that the wise man ought not to grant it. Pardon is the remitting of a deserved punishment. The reasons why the wise man ought not to grant this remission are given at length by those of whom this question is specially asked: I will briefly say, as though it were no concern of mine to decide this point, "A man grants pardon to one whom he ought to punish: now the wise man does nothing which he ought not to do, and omits to do nothing which he ought to do: he does not, therefore, remit any punishment which he ought to exact. But the wise man will bestow upon you in a more honourable way that which you wish to obtain by pardon, for he will make allowances for you, will consult your interests, and will correct your bad habits: he will act just as though he were pardoning you, but nevertheless he will not pardon you, because he who pardons admits that in so doing he has neglected a part of his duty. He will only punish some people by reprimanding them, and will inflict no further penalty if he considers that they are of an age which admits of reformation: some people who are undeniably implicated in an odious charge he will acquit, because they were deceived into committing, or were not sober when they committed the offence with which they are charged: he will let his enemies depart unharmed, sometimes even with words of commendation, if they have taken up arms to defend their honour, their covenants with others, their freedom, or on any other honourable ground. All these doings come under the head of mercy, not of pardon. Mercy is free to come to what decision it pleases: she gives her decision, not under any statute, but according to equity and goodness: she may acquit the defendant, or impose what damages she pleases. She does not do any of these things as though she were doing less than justice requires, but as though the justest possible course were that which she adopts. On the other hand, to pardon is not to punish a man whom you have decided ought to be punished; pardon is the remission of a punishment which ought to be inflicted. The first advantage which mercy has over it is that she does not tell those whom she lets off that they ought to have suffered: she is more complete, more honourable than pardon."

---

[117] See "On Clemency," Book II, Chapter 5.

In my opinion, this is a mere dispute about words, and we are agreed about the thing itself. The wise man will remit many penalties, and will save many who are wicked, but whose wickedness is not incurable. He will act like good husbandmen, who do not cultivate only straight and tall trees, but also apply props to straighten those which have been rendered crooked by various causes; they trim some, lest the luxuriance of their boughs should hinder their upward growth, they nurse those which have been weakened by being planted in an unsuitable position, and they give air to those which are overshadowed by the foliage of others. The wise man will see the several treatments suitable to several dispositions, and how what is crooked may be straightened. ...

TO MARCIA, ON CONSOLATION

1

Did I not know, Marcia, that you have as little of a woman's weakness of mind as of her other vices, and that your life was regarded as a pattern of antique virtue, I should not have dared to combat your grief, which is one that many men fondly nurse and embrace, nor should I have conceived the hope of persuading you to hold fortune blameless, having to plead for her at such an unfavorable time, before so partial a judge, and against such an odious charge. I derive confidence, however, from the proved strength of your mind, and your virtue, which has been proved by a severe test. All men know how well you behaved towards your father, whom you loved as dearly as your children in all respects, save that you did not wish him to survive you: indeed, for all that I know you may have wished that also: for great affection ventures to break some of the golden rules of life. You did all that lay in your power to avert the death of your father, Aulus Cremutius Cordus;[118] but when it became clear that, surrounded as he was by the myrmidons of Sejanus, there was no other way of escape from slavery, you did not indeed approve of his resolution, but gave up all attempts to oppose it; you shed tears openly, and choked down your sobs, yet did not screen them behind a smiling face; and you did all this in the present century, when not to be unnatural towards one's parents is considered the height of filial affection. When the changes of our times gave you an opportunity, you restored to the use of man that genius of your father for which he had suffered, and made him in real truth immortal by publishing as an eternal memorial of him those books which that bravest of men had written with his own blood. You have done a great service to Roman literature: a large part of Cordus's books had been burned; a great service to posterity, who will receive a true account of events, which cost its author so dear; and a great service to himself, whose memory flourishes and ever will flourish, as long as men set any value upon the facts of Roman history, as long as anyone lives who wishes to review the deeds of our fathers, to know what a true Roman was like—one who still remained unconquered when all other necks were broken in to receive the yoke of Sejanus, one who was free in every thought, feeling,

---

[118] See Merivale's *History of the Romans under the Empire*, Chapter XIV.

and act. By Hercules, the state would have sustained a great loss if you had not brought him forth from the oblivion to which his two splendid qualities, eloquence and independence, had consigned him: he is now read, is popular, is received into men's hands and bosoms, and fears no old age: but as for those who butchered him, before long men will cease to speak even of their crimes, the only things by which they are remembered. This greatness of mind in you has forbidden me to take into consideration your sex or your face, still clouded by the sorrow by which so many years ago it was suddenly overcast. See; I shall do nothing underhand, nor try to steal away your sorrows: I have reminded you of old hurts, and to prove that your present wound may be healed, I have shown you the scar of one which was equally severe. Let others use soft measures and caresses; I have determined to do battle with your grief, and I will dry those weary and exhausted eyes, which already, to tell you the truth, are weeping more from habit than from sorrow. I will effect this cure, if possible, with your goodwill: if you disapprove of my efforts, or dislike them, then you must continue to hug and fondle the grief which you have adopted as the survivor of your son. What, I pray you, is to be the end of it? All means have been tried in vain: the consolations of your friends, who are weary of offering them, and the influence of great men who are related to you: literature, a taste which your father enjoyed and which you have inherited from him, now finds your ears closed, and affords you but a futile consolation, which scarcely engages your thoughts for a moment. Even time itself, nature's greatest remedy, which quiets the most bitter grief, loses its power with you alone. Three years have already passed, and still your grief has lost none of its first poignancy, but renews and strengthens itself day by day, and has now dwelt so long with you that it has acquired a domicile in your mind, and actually thinks that it would be base to leave it. All vices sink into our whole being, if we do not crush them before they gain a footing; and in like manner these sad, pitiable, and discordant feelings end by feeding upon their own bitterness, until the unhappy mind takes a sort of morbid delight in grief. I should have liked, therefore, to have attempted to effect this cure in the earliest stages of the disorder, before its force was fully developed; it might have been checked by milder remedies, but now that it has been confirmed by time it cannot be beaten without a hard struggle. In like manner, wounds heal easily when the blood is fresh upon them: they can then be cleared out and brought to the surface, and admit of being probed by the finger: when disease has turned them into malignant ulcers, their cure is more difficult. I cannot now influence so strong a grief by polite and mild measures: it must be broken down by force.

2

I am aware that all who wish to give anyone advice begin with precepts, and end with examples: but it is sometimes useful to alter this fashion, for we must deal differently with different people. Some are guided by reason, others must be confronted with authority and the names of celebrated persons, whose brilliancy dazzles their mind and destroys their power of free judgment. I will place before your eyes two of the greatest examples belonging to your sex and your century: one, that of a woman who allowed herself to be entirely carried away by grief; the other, one who, though afflicted by a like misfortune, and an even greater loss, yet did not allow her sorrows to reign over her for a very long time, but quickly restored her mind to its accustomed frame. Octavia and Livia, the former Augustus's sister, the latter his wife, both lost their sons when they were young men, and when they were certain of succeeding to the throne. Octavia lost Marcellus, whom both his father-in-law and his uncle had begun to depend upon, and to place upon his shoulders the weight of the empire—a young man of keen intelligence and firm character, frugal and moderate in his desires to an extent which deserved especial admiration in one so young and so wealthy, strong to endure labour, averse to indulgence, and able to bear whatever burden his uncle might choose to lay, or I may say to pile upon his shoulders. Augustus had well chosen him as a foundation, for he would not have given way under any weight, however excessive. His mother never ceased to weep and sob during her whole life, never endured to listen to wholesome advice, never even allowed her thoughts to be diverted from her sorrow. She remained during her whole life just as she was during the funeral, with all the strength of her mind intently fixed upon one subject. I do not say that she lacked the courage to shake off her grief, but she refused to be comforted, thought that it would be a second bereavement to lose her tears, and would not have any portrait of her darling son, nor allow any allusion to be made to him. She hated all mothers, and raged against Livia with especial fury, because it seemed as though the brilliant prospect once in store for her own child was now transferred to Livia's son. Passing all her days in darkened rooms and alone, not conversing even with her brother, she refused to accept the poems which were composed in memory of Marcellus, and all the other honours paid him by literature, and closed her ears against all consolation. She lived buried and hidden from view, neglecting her accustomed duties, and actually angry with the excessive splendour of her brother's prosperity, in which she shared. Though surrounded by her children and grandchildren, she would not lay aside her mourning garb, though by retaining it she seemed to put a slight upon all her relations, in thinking herself bereaved in spite of their being alive.

3

Livia lost her son Drusus, who would have been a great emperor, and was already a great general: he had marched far into Germany, and had planted the Roman standards in places where the very existence of the Romans was hardly known. He died on the march, his very foes treating him with respect, observing a reciprocal truce, and not having the heart to wish for what would do them most service. In addition to his dying thus in his country's service, great sorrow for him was expressed by the citizens, the provinces, and the whole of Italy, through which his corpse was attended by the people of the free towns and colonies, who poured out to perform the last sad offices to him, till it reached Rome in a procession which resembled a triumph. His mother was not permitted to receive his last kiss and gather the last fond words from his dying lips: she followed the relics of her Drusus on their long journey, though every one of the funeral pyres with which all Italy was glowing seemed to renew her grief, as though she had lost him so many times. When, however, she at last laid him in the tomb, she left her sorrow there with him, and grieved no more than was becoming to a Caesar or due to a son. She did not cease to make frequent mention of the name of her Drusus, to set up his portrait in all places, both public and private, and to speak of him and listen while others spoke of him with the greatest pleasure: she lived with his memory; which none can embrace and consort with who has made it painful to himself.[119] Choose, therefore, which of these two examples you think the more commendable: if you prefer to follow the former, you will remove yourself from the number of the living; you will shun the sight both of other people's children and of your own, and even of him whose loss you deplore; you will be looked upon by mothers as an omen of evil; you will refuse to take part in honourable, permissible pleasures, thinking them unbecoming for one so afflicted; you will be loath to linger above ground, and will be especially angry with your age, because it will not straightaway bring your life abruptly to an end. I here put the best construction on what is really most contemptible and foreign to your character. I mean that you will show yourself unwilling to live, and unable to die. If, on the other hand, showing a milder and better regulated spirit, you try to follow the example of the latter most exalted lady, you will not be in misery, nor will you wear your life out with suffering. Plague on it! what madness this is, to punish oneself because one is unfortunate, and not to lessen, but to increase one's ills! You ought to display, in this matter also, that decent behaviour and modesty which has characterised all your life: for there is such a thing as self-restraint in grief also. You will show more respect for the youth himself, who well deserves that it should make you glad to speak and think of him, if you make him able to meet his mother with a cheerful countenance, even as he was wont to do when alive.

4

I will not invite you to practise the sterner kind of maxims, nor bid you bear the lot of humanity with more than human philosophy; neither will I attempt to dry a mother's eyes on the very day of her son's burial. I will appear with you before an arbitrator: the matter upon which we shall join issue is, whether grief ought to be deep or unceasing. I doubt not that you will prefer the example of Julia Augusta,

---

[119] If it is a pain to dwell upon the thought of lost friends, of course you do not continually refresh the memory of them by speaking of them.

who was your intimate friend: she invites you to follow her method: she, in her first paroxysm, when grief is especially keen and hard to bear, betook herself for consolation to Areus, her husband's teacher in philosophy, and declared that this did her much good; more good than the thought of the Roman people, whom she was unwilling to sadden by her mourning; more than Augustus, who, staggering under the loss of one of his two chief supporters, ought not to be yet more bowed down by the sorrow of his relatives; more even than her son Tiberius, whose affection during that untimely burial of one for whom whole nations wept made her feel that she had only lost one member of her family. This was, I imagine, his introduction to and grounding in philosophy of a woman peculiarly tenacious of her own opinion:—"Even to the present day, Julia, as far as I can tell—and I was your husband's constant companion, and knew not only what all men were allowed to know, but all the most secret thoughts of your hearts—you have been careful that no one should find anything to blame in your conduct; not only in matters of importance, but even in trifles you have taken pains to do nothing which you could wish common fame, that most frank judge of the acts of princes, to overlook. Nothing, I think, is more admirable than that those who are in high places should pardon many shortcomings in others, and have to ask it for none of their own. So also in this matter of mourning you ought to act up to your maxim of doing nothing which you could wish undone, or done otherwise.

5

"In the next place, I pray and beseech you not to be self-willed and beyond the management of your friends. You must be aware that none of them know how to behave, whether to mention Drusus in your presence or not, as they neither wish to wrong a noble youth by forgetting him nor to hurt you by speaking of him. When we leave you and assemble together by ourselves, we talk freely about his sayings and doings, treating them with the respect which they deserve: in your presence deep silence is observed about him, and thus you lose that greatest of pleasures, the hearing the praises of your son, which I doubt not you would be willing to hand down to all future ages, had you the means of so doing, even at the cost of your own life. Wherefore endure to listen to, nay, encourage conversation of which he is the subject, and let your ears be open to the name and memory of your son. You ought not to consider this painful, like those who in such a case think that part of their misfortune consists in listening to consolation.

As it is, you have altogether run into the other extreme, and, forgetting the better aspects of your lot, look only upon its worse side: you pay no attention to the pleasure you have had in your son's society and your joyful meetings with him, the sweet caresses of his babyhood, the progress of his education: you fix all your attention upon that last scene of all: and to this, as though it were not shocking enough, you add every horror you can. Do not, I implore you, take a perverse pride in appearing the most unhappy of women: and reflect also that there is no great credit in behaving bravely in times of prosperity, when life glides easily with a favouring current: neither does a calm sea and fair wind display the art of the pilot: some foul weather is wanted to prove his courage.

Like him, then, do not give way, but rather plant yourself firmly, and endure whatever burden may fall upon you from above; scared though you may have been at the first roar of the tempest. There is nothing that fastens such a reproach[120] on Fortune as resignation." After this he points out to her the son who is yet alive: he points out grandchildren from the lost one.

6

It is your trouble, Marcia, which has been dealt with here: it is beside your couch of mourning that Areus has been sitting: change the characters, and it is you whom he has been consoling. But, on the other hand, Marcia, suppose that you have sustained a greater loss than ever mother did before you: see, I am not soothing you or making light of your misfortune: if fate can be overcome by tears, let us bring tears to bear upon it: let every day be passed in mourning, every night be spent in sorrow instead of sleep: let your breast be torn by your own hands, your very face attacked by them, and every kind of cruelty be practised by your grief, if it will profit you. But if the dead cannot be brought back to life, however much we may beat our breasts, if destiny remains fixed and immoveable forever, not to be changed by any sorrow, however great, and death does not loose his hold of anything that he once has taken away, then let our futile grief be brought to an end. Let us, then, steer our own course, and no longer allow ourselves to be driven to leeward by the force of our misfortune. He is a sorry pilot who lets the waves wring his rudder from his grasp, who leaves the sails to fly loose, and abandons the ship to the storm: but he who boldly grasps the helm and clings to it until the sea closes over him, deserves praise even though he be shipwrecked.

7

"But," say you, "sorrow for the loss of one's own children is natural." Who denies it? provided it be reasonable? for we cannot help feeling a pang, and the stoutest-hearted of us are cast down not only at the death of those dearest to us, but even when they leave us on a journey. Nevertheless, the mourning which public opinion enjoins is more than nature insists upon. Observe how intense and yet how brief are the sorrows of dumb animals: we hear a cow lowing for one or two days, nor do

---

[120] See my note on *invidiam facere alicui* in Juvenal 15. —J. E. B. Mayor. *Dead Souls*. (Translator's note.)

mares pursue their wild and senseless gallops for longer: wild beasts after they have tracked their lost cubs throughout the forest, and often visited their plundered dens, quench their rage within a short space of time. Birds circle round their empty nests with loud and piteous cries, yet almost immediately resume their ordinary flight in silence; nor does any creature spend long periods in sorrowing for the loss of its offspring, except man, who encourages his own grief, the measure of which depends not upon his sufferings, but upon his will. You may know that to be utterly broken down by grief is not natural, by observing that the same bereavement inflicts a deeper wound upon women than upon men, upon savages than upon civilized and cultivated persons, upon the unlearned than upon the learned: yet those passions which derive their force from nature are equally powerful in all men: therefore it is clear that a passion of varying strength cannot be a natural one. Fire will burn all people equally, male and female, of every rank and every age: steel will exhibit its cutting power on all bodies alike: and why? Because these things derive their strength from nature, which makes no distinction of persons. Poverty, grief, and ambition,[121] are felt differently by different people, according as they are influenced by habit: a rooted prejudice about the terrors of these things, though they are not really to be feared, makes a man weak and unable to endure them.

8

Moreover, that which depends upon nature is not weakened by delay, but grief is gradually effaced by time. However obstinate it may be, though it be daily renewed and be exasperated by all attempts to soothe it, yet even this becomes weakened by time, which is the most efficient means of taming its fierceness. You, Marcia, have still a mighty sorrow abiding with you, nevertheless it already appears to have become blunted: it is obstinate and enduring, but not so acute as it was at first: and this also will be taken from you piecemeal by succeeding years. Whenever you are engaged in other pursuits your mind will be relieved from its burden: at present you keep watch over yourself to prevent this. Yet there is a great difference between allowing and forcing yourself to grieve. How much more in accordance with your cultivated taste it would be to put an end to your mourning instead of looking for the end to come, and not to wait for the day when your sorrow shall cease against your will: dismiss it of your own accord.

9

"Why then," you ask, "do we show such persistence in mourning for our friends, if it be not nature that bids us do so?" It is because we never expect that any evil will befall ourselves before it comes, we will not be taught by seeing the misfortunes of

---

[121] Koch declares that this cannot be the true reading, and suggests *deminutio*, "degradation."

others that they are the common inheritance of all men, but imagine that the path which we have begun to tread is free from them and less beset by dangers than that of other people. How many funerals pass our houses? yet we do not think of death. How many untimely deaths? we think only of our son's coming of age, of his service in the army, or of his succession to his father's estate. How many rich men suddenly sink into poverty before our very eyes, without its ever occurring to our minds that our own wealth is exposed to exactly the same risks? When, therefore, misfortune befalls us, we cannot help collapsing all the more completely, because we are struck as it were unawares: a blow which has long been foreseen falls much less heavily upon us. Do you wish to know how completely exposed you are to every stroke of fate, and that the same shafts which have transfixed others are whirling around yourself? Then imagine that you are mounting without sufficient armour to assault some city wall or some strong and lofty position manned by a great host, expect a wound, and suppose that all those stones, arrows, and darts which fill the upper air are aimed at your body: whenever anyone falls at your side or behind your back, exclaim, "Fortune, you will not outwit me, or catch me confident and heedless: I know what you are preparing to do: you have struck down another, but you aimed at me." Whoever looks upon his own affairs as though he were at the point of death? which of us ever dares to think about banishment, want, or mourning? who, if advised to meditate upon these subjects, would not reject the idea like an evil omen, and bid it depart from him and alight on the heads of his enemies, or even on that of his untimely adviser? "I never thought it would happen!" How can you think that anything will not happen, when you know that it may happen to many men, and has happened to many? That is a noble verse, and worthy of a nobler source than the stage:—

"What one hath suffered may befall us all."

That man has lost his children: you may lose yours. That man has been convicted: your innocence is in peril. We are deceived and weakened by this delusion, when we suffer what we never foresaw that we possibly could suffer: but by looking forward to the coming of our sorrows we take the sting out of them when they come.

10

My Marcia, all these adventitious circumstances which glitter around us, such as children, office in the State, wealth, large halls, vestibules crowded with clients seeking vainly for admittance, a noble name, a wellborn or beautiful wife, and every other thing which depends entirely upon uncertain and changeful fortune, are but furniture which is not our own, but entrusted to us on loan: none of these things are given to us outright: the stage of our lives is adorned with properties gathered from various sources, and soon to be returned to their several owners: some of them will be taken away on the first day, some on the second, and but few will remain till the end. We have, therefore, no grounds for regarding ourselves with complacency, as though the things which surround us were our own: they are only borrowed: we have the use and enjoyment of them for a time regulated by the lender, who controls his own gift: it is our duty always to be able to lay our hands upon what has been lent us with no fixed date for its return, and to restore it when called upon without a murmur: the most detestable kind of debtor is he who rails at his creditor. Hence all our relatives, both those who by the order of their birth we hope will outlive ourselves, and those who themselves most properly wish to die before us, ought to be loved by us as persons whom we cannot be sure of having with us forever, nor even for long. We ought frequently to remind ourselves that we must love the things of this life as we would what is shortly to leave us, or indeed in the very act of leaving us. Whatever gift Fortune bestows upon a man, let him think while he enjoys it, that it will prove as fickle as the goddess from whom it came. Snatch what pleasure you can from your children, allow your children in their turn to take pleasure in your society, and drain every pleasure to the dregs without any delay. We cannot reckon on tonight, nay, I have allowed too long a delay, we cannot reckon on this hour: we must make haste: the enemy presses on behind us: soon that society of yours will be broken up, that pleasant company will be taken by assault and dispersed. Pillage is the universal law: unhappy creatures, know you not that life is but a flight? If you grieve for the death of your son, the fault lies with the time when he was born, for at his birth he was told that death was his doom: it is the law under which he was born, the fate which has pursued him ever since he left his mother's womb. We have come under the dominion of Fortune, and a harsh and unconquerable dominion it is: at her caprice we must suffer all things whether we deserve them or not. She maltreats our bodies with anger, insult, and cruelty: some she burns, the fire being sometimes applied as a punishment and sometimes as a remedy: some she imprisons, allowing it to be done at one time by our enemies, at another by our countrymen: she tosses others naked on the changeful seas, and after their struggle with the waves will not even cast them out upon the sand or the shore, but will entomb them in the belly of some huge sea-monster: she wears away others to a skeleton by diverse kinds of disease, and keeps them long in suspense between life and death: she is as capricious in her rewards and punishments as a fickle, whimsical, and careless mistress is with those of her slaves.

11

Why need we weep over parts of our life? the whole of it calls for tears: new miseries assail us before we have freed ourselves from the old ones. You, therefore, who allow them to trouble you to an unreasonable extent ought especially to restrain yourselves, and to muster all the powers of the human breast to combat your fears and your pains. Moreover, what forgetfulness of your own position and that of mankind is this? You were born a mortal, and you have given birth to mortals: yourself a weak and fragile body, liable to all diseases, can you have hoped to produce anything strong and lasting from such unstable materials? Your son has died: in other words he has reached that goal towards which those whom you regard as more fortunate than your offspring are still hastening: this is the point towards which move at different rates all the crowds which are squabbling in the law courts, sitting in the theatres, praying in the temples. Those whom you love and those whom you despise will both be made equal in the same ashes. This is the meaning of that command, know thyself, which is written on the shrine of the Pythian oracle. What is man? a potter's vessel, to be broken by the slightest shake or toss: it requires no great storm to rend you asunder: you fall to pieces wherever you strike. What is man? a weakly and frail body, naked, without any natural protection, dependent on the help of others, exposed to all the scorn of Fortune; even when his muscles are well trained he is the prey and the food of the first wild beast he meets, formed of weak and unstable substances, fair in outward feature, but unable to endure cold, heat, or labour, and yet falling to ruin if kept in sloth and idleness, fearing his very victuals, for he is starved if he has them not, and bursts if he has too much. He cannot be kept safe without anxious care, his breath only stays in the body on sufferance, and has no real hold upon it; he starts at every sudden danger, every loud and unexpected noise that reaches his ears. Ever a cause of anxiety to ourselves, diseased and useless as we are, can we be surprised at the death of a creature which can be killed by a single hiccup? Is it a great undertaking to put an end to us? why, smells, tastes, fatigue and want of sleep, food and drink, and the very necessaries of life, are mortal. Whithersoever he moves he straightaway becomes conscious of his weakness, not being able to bear all climates, falling sick after drinking strange water, breathing an air to which he is not accustomed, or from other causes and reasons of the most trifling kind, frail, sickly, entering upon his life with weeping: yet nevertheless what a disturbance this despicable creature makes! what ideas it conceives, forgetting its lowly condition! It exercises its mind upon matters which are immortal and eternal, and arranges the affairs of its grandchildren and great-grandchildren, while death surprises it in the midst of its far-reaching schemes, and what we call old age is but the round of a very few years.

12

Supposing that your sorrow has any method at all, is it your own sufferings or those of him who is gone that it has in view? Why do you grieve over your lost son? is it because you have received no pleasure from him, or because you would have received more had he lived longer? If you answer that you have received no pleasure from him you make your loss more endurable: for men miss less when lost what has given them no enjoyment or gladness. If, again, you admit that you have received much pleasure, it is your duty not to complain of that part which you have lost, but to return thanks for that which you have enjoyed. His rearing alone ought to have brought you a sufficient return for your labours, for it can hardly be that those who take the greatest pains to rear puppies, birds, and suchlike paltry objects of amusement derive a certain pleasure from the sight and touch and fawning caresses of these dumb creatures, and yet that those who rear children should not find their reward in doing so. Thus, even though his industry may have gained nothing for you, his carefulness may have saved nothing for you, his foresight may have given you no advice, yet you found sufficient reward in having owned him and loved him. "But," say you, "it might have lasted longer." True, but you have been better dealt with than if you had never had a son, for, supposing you were given your choice, which is the better lot, to be happy for a short time or not at all? It is better to enjoy pleasures which soon leave us than to enjoy none at all. Which, again, would you choose? to have had one who was a disgrace to you, and who merely filled the position and owned the name of your son, or one of such noble character as your son's was? a youth who soon grew discreet and dutiful, soon became a husband and a father, soon became eager for public honours, and soon obtained the priesthood, winning his way to all these admirable things with equally admirable speed. It falls to scarcely anyone's lot to enjoy great prosperity, and also to enjoy it for a long time: only a dull kind of happiness can last for long and accompany us to the end of our lives. The immortal gods, who did not intend to give you a son for long, gave you one who was straightaway what another would have required long training to become. You cannot even say that you have been specially marked by the gods for misfortune because you have had no pleasure in your son. Look at any company of people, whether they be known to you or not: everywhere you will see some who have endured greater misfortunes than your own. Great generals and princes have undergone like bereavements: mythology tells us that the gods themselves are not exempt from them, its aim, I suppose, being to lighten our sorrow at death by the thought that even deities are subject to it. Look around, I repeat, at everyone: you cannot mention any house so miserable as not to find comfort in the fact of another being yet more miserable. I do not, by Hercules, think so ill of your principles as to suppose that you would bear your sorrow more lightly were I to show you an enormous company of mourners: that is a spiteful sort of consolation which we derive from the number of our fellow-sufferers: nevertheless I will quote some instances, not indeed in order to teach you that this often befalls men, for it is absurd to multiply examples of man's mortality, but to let you know that there have been many who have lightened their misfortunes by patient endurance of them. I will begin with the luckiest man of all. Lucius Sulla lost his son, yet this did not impair either the spitefulness or the brilliant valour which he displayed at the expense of his enemies and his countrymen alike, nor did it make him appear to have assumed his well-known title untruly that he did so after his son's death, fearing neither the hatred of men, by whose sufferings that excessive prosperity of his was purchased, nor the ill-will of the gods, to whom it was a reproach that Sulla should be so truly The Fortunate. What, however, Sulla's real character was may pass among questions still undecided: even his enemies will admit that he took up arms with honour, and laid them aside with honour: his example proves the point at issue, that an evil which befalls even the most prosperous cannot be one of the first magnitude.

13

That Greece cannot boast unduly of that father who, being in the act of offering sacrifice when he heard the news of his son's death, merely ordered the flute-player to be silent, and removed the garland from his head, but accomplished all the rest of the ceremony in due form, is due to a Roman, Pulvillus the high priest. When he was in the act of holding the doorpost[122] and dedicating the Capitol the news of his son's death was brought to him. He pretended not to hear it, and pronounced the form of words proper for the high priest on such an occasion, without his prayer being interrupted by a single groan, begging that Jupiter would show himself gracious, at the very instant that he heard his son's name mentioned as dead. Do you imagine that this man's mourning knew no end, if the first day and the first shock could not drive him, though a father, away from the public altar of the State, or cause him to mar the ceremony of dedication by words of ill omen? Worthy, indeed, of the most exalted priesthood was he who ceased not to revere the gods even when they were angry. Yet he, after he had gone home, filled his eyes with tears, said a few words of lamentation, and performed the rites with which it was then customary to honour the dead, resumed the expression of countenance which he had worn in the Capitol.

Paulus,[123] about the time of his magnificent triumph, in which he drove Perses in chains before his car, gave two of his sons to be adopted into other families, and buried those whom he had kept for himself. What, think you, must those whom he kept have been, when Scipio was one of those whom he gave away? It was not without emotion that the Roman people looked upon Paulus's empty chariot:[124] nevertheless he made a speech to them, and returned thanks to the gods for having granted his prayer: for he had prayed that, if any offering to Nemesis were due in consequence of the stupendous victory which he had won, it might be paid at his own expense rather than at that of his country. Do you see how magnanimously he bore his loss? he even congratulated himself on being left childless, though who had

---

[122] This seems to have been part of the ceremony of dedication. Pulvillus was dedicating the Temple of Jupiter in the Capitol. See Livy, II, 8; Cicero, *Pro Domo*, paragraph cxxi.

[123] Lucius Æmilius Paullus conquered Perses, the last King of Macedonia, bc 168.

[124] "For he had four sons, two, as has been already related, adopted into other families, Scipio and Fabius; and two others, who were still children, by his second wife, who lived in his own house. Of these, one died five days before Æmilius's triumph, at the age of fourteen, and the other, twelve years old, died three days after it: so that there was no Roman that did not grieve for him," etc.

—Plutarch, *Life of Æmilius*, Chapter XXXV

more to suffer by such a change? he lost at once his comforters and his helpers. Yet Perses did not have the pleasure of seeing Paulus look sorrowful.

14

Why should I lead you on through the endless series of great men and pick out the unhappy ones, as though it were not more difficult to find happy ones? For how few households have remained possessed of all their members until the end? what one is there that has not suffered some loss? Take any one year you please and name the consuls for it: if you like, that of[125] Lucius Bibulus and Gaius Caesar; you will see that, though these colleagues were each other's bitterest enemies, yet their fortunes agreed. Lucius Bibulus, a man more remarkable for goodness than for strength of character, had both his sons murdered at the same time, and even insulted by the Egyptian soldiery, so that the agent of his bereavement was as much a subject for tears as the bereavement itself. Nevertheless Bibulus, who during the whole of his year of office had remained hidden in his house, to cast reproach upon his colleague Caesar on the day following that upon which he heard of both his sons' deaths, came forth and went through the routine business of his magistracy. Who could devote less than one day to mourning for two sons? Thus soon did he end his mourning for his children, although he had mourned a whole year for his consulship. Gaius Caesar, after having traversed Britain, and not allowed even the ocean to set bounds to his successes, heard of the death of his daughter, which hurried on the crisis of affairs. Already Gnaeus Pompeius stood before his eyes, a man who would ill endure that anyone besides himself should become a great power in the State, and one who was likely to place a check upon his advancement, which he had regarded as onerous even when each gained by the other's rise: yet within three days' time he resumed his duties as general, and conquered his grief as quickly as he was wont to conquer everything else.

15

Why need I remind you of the deaths of the other Caesars, whom Fortune appears to me sometimes to have outraged in order that even by their deaths they might be useful to mankind, by proving that not even they, although they were styled "sons of gods," and "fathers of gods to come," could exercise the same power over their own fortunes which they did over those of others? The Emperor Augustus lost his children and his grandchildren, and after all the family of Caesar had perished was obliged to prop his empty house by adopting a son: yet he bore his losses as bravely as though he were already personally concerned in the honour of the gods, and as though it were especially to his interest that no one should complain of the injustice

---

[125] auc 695, bc 59.

of Heaven. Tiberius Caesar lost both the son whom he begot and the son whom he adopted, yet he himself pronounced a panegyric upon his son from the Rostra, and stood in full view of the corpse, which merely had a curtain on one side to prevent the eyes of the high priest resting upon the dead body, and did not change his countenance, though all the Romans wept: he gave Sejanus, who stood by his side, a proof of how patiently he could endure the loss of his relatives. See you not what numbers of most eminent men there have been, none of whom have been spared by this blight which prostrates us all: men, too, adorned with every grace of character, and every distinction that public or private life can confer. It appears as though this plague moved in a regular orbit, and spread ruin and desolation among us all without distinction of persons, all being alike its prey. Bid any number of individuals tell you the story of their lives: you will find that all have paid some penalty for being born.

16

I know what you will say: "You quote men as examples: you forget that it is a woman that you are trying to console." Yet who would say that nature has dealt grudgingly with the minds of women, and stunted their virtues? Believe me, they have the same intellectual power as men, and the same capacity for honourable and generous action. If trained to do so, they are just as able to endure sorrow or labour. Ye good gods, do I say this in that very city in which Lucretia and Brutus removed the yoke of kings from the necks of the Romans? We owe liberty to Brutus, but we owe Brutus to Lucretia—in which Cloelia, for the sublime courage with which she scorned both the enemy and the river, has been almost reckoned as a man. The statue of Cloelia, mounted on horseback, in that busiest of thoroughfares, the Sacred Way, continually reproaches the youth of the present day, who never mount anything but a cushioned seat in a carriage, with journeying in such a fashion through that very city in which we have enrolled even women among our knights. If you wish me to point out to you examples of women who have bravely endured the loss of their children, I shall not go far afield to search for them: in one family I can quote two Cornelias, one the daughter of Scipio, and the mother of the Gracchi, who made acknowledgment of the birth of her twelve children by burying them all: nor was it so hard to do this in the case of the others, whose birth and death were alike unknown to the public, but she beheld the murdered and unburied corpses of both Tiberius Gracchus and Gaius Gracchus, whom even those who will not call them good must admit were great men. Yet to those who tried to console her and called her unfortunate, she answered, "I shall never cease to call myself happy, because I am the mother of the Gracchi." Cornelia, the wife of Livius Drusus, lost by the hands of an unknown assassin a young son of great distinction, who was treading in the footsteps of the Gracchi, and was murdered in his own house just when he had so many bills half way through the process of becoming law: nevertheless she bore the untimely and unavenged death of her son with as lofty a spirit as he had shown in carrying his laws. Will you not, Marcia, forgive Fortune because she has not refrained from striking you with the darts with which she launched at the Scipios, and the mothers and daughters of the Scipios, and with which she has attacked the Caesars themselves? Life is full of misfortunes; our path is beset with them: no one can make a long peace, nay, scarcely an armistice with Fortune. You, Marcia, have borne four children: now they say that no dart which is hurled into a close column of soldiers can fail to hit one—ought you then to wonder at not having been able to lead along such a company without exciting the ill-will of Fortune, or suffering loss at her hands? "But," say you, "Fortune has treated me unfairly, for she not only has bereaved me of my son, but chose my best beloved to deprive me of." Yet you never can say that you have been wronged, if you divide the stakes equally with an antagonist who is stronger than yourself: Fortune has left you two daughters, and their children: she has not even taken away altogether him who you now mourn for, forgetful of his elder brother: you have two daughters by him, who if you support them ill will prove great burdens, but if well, great comforts to you. You ought to prevail upon yourself, when you see them, to let them remind you of your son, and not of your grief. When a husbandman's trees have either been torn up, roots and all, by the wind, or broken off short by the force of a hurricane, he takes care of what is left of their stock, straightaway plants seeds or cuttings in the place of those which he has lost, and in a moment—for time is as swift in repairing losses as in causing them—more nourishing trees are growing than were there before. Take, then, in the place of your Metilius these his two daughters, and by their twofold consolation lighten your single sorrow. True, human nature is so constituted as to love nothing so much as what it has lost, and our yearning after those who have been taken from us makes us judge unfairly of those who are left to us: nevertheless, if you choose to reckon up how merciful Fortune has been to you even in her anger, you will feel that you have more than enough to console you. Look at all your grandchildren, and your two daughters: and say also, Marcia:—"I should indeed be cast down, if everyone's fortune followed his deserts, and if no evil ever befell good men: but as it is I perceive that no distinction is made, and that the bad and the good are both harassed alike."

17

"Still, it is a sad thing to lose a young man whom you have brought up, just as he was becoming a defence and a pride both to his mother and to his country." No one denies that it is sad: but it is the common lot of mortals. You were born to lose others, to be lost, to hope, to fear, to destroy your own peace and that of others, to fear and yet to long for death, and, worst of all, never to know what your real position is. If you were about to journey to Syracuse, and someone were to say:— "Learn beforehand all the discomforts, and all the pleasures of your coming voyage, and then set sail. The sights which you will enjoy will be as follows: first, you will see the island itself, now separated from Italy by a narrow strait, but which, we know, once formed part of the mainland. The sea suddenly broke through, and

> 'Sever'd Sicilia from the western shore.'[126]

Next, as you will be able to sail close to Charybdis, of which the poets have sung, you will see that greediest of whirlpools, quite smooth if no south wind be blowing, but whenever there is a gale from that quarter, sucking down ships into a huge and deep abyss. You will see the fountain of Arethusa, so famed in song, with its waters bright and pellucid to the very bottom, and pouring forth an icy stream which it either finds on the spot or else plunges it under ground, conveys it thither as a separate river beneath so many seas, free from any mixture of less pure water, and there brings it again to the surface. You will see a harbour which is more sheltered than all the others in the world, whether they be natural or improved by human art for the protection of shipping; so safe, that even the most violent storms are powerless to disturb it. You will see the place where the power of Athens was broken, where that natural prison, hewn deep among precipices of rock, received so many thousands of captives: you will see the great city itself, occupying a wider site than many capitals, an extremely warm resort in winter, where not a single day passes without sunshine: but when you have observed all this, you must remember that the advantages of its winter climate are counterbalanced by a hot and pestilential summer: that here will be the tyrant Dionysius, the destroyer of freedom, of justice, and of law, who is greedy of power even after conversing with Plato, and of life even after he has been exiled; that he will burn some, flog others, and behead others for slight offences; that he will exercise his lust upon both sexes ... You have now heard all that can attract you thither, all that can deter you from going: now, then, either set sail or remain at home!" If, after this declaration, anybody were to say that he wished to go to Syracuse, he could blame no one but himself for what befell him there, because he would not stumble upon it unknowingly, but would have gone thither fully aware of what was before him. To everyone Nature says: "I do not deceive any person. If you choose to have children, they may be handsome, or they may be deformed; perhaps they will be born dumb. One of them may perhaps prove the saviour of his country, or perhaps its betrayer. You need not despair of their being raised to such honour that for their sake no one will dare to speak evil of you: yet remember that they may reach such a pitch of infamy as themselves to become curses to you. There is nothing to prevent their performing the last offices for you, and your panegyric being spoken by your children: but hold yourself prepared nevertheless to place a son as boy, man, or greybeard, upon the funeral pyre: for years have nothing to do with the matter, since every sort of funeral in which a parent buries his child must

---

[126] Virgil, *Æneid*, III, 418.

alike be untimely.[127] If you still choose to rear children, after I have explained these conditions to you, you render yourself incapable of blaming the gods, for they never guaranteed anything to you."

18

You may make this simile apply to your whole entrance into life. I have explained to you what attractions and what drawbacks there would be if you were thinking of going to Syracuse: now suppose that I were to come and give you advice when you were going to be born. "You are about," I should say, "to enter a city of which both gods and men are citizens, a city which contains the whole universe, which is bound by irrevocable and eternal laws, and wherein the heavenly bodies run their unwearied courses: you will see therein innumerable twinkling stars, and the sun, whose single light pervades every place, who by his daily course marks the times of day and night, and by his yearly course makes a more equal division between summer and winter. You will see his place taken by night by the moon, who borrows at her meetings with her brother a gentle and softer light, and who at one time is invisible, at another hangs full faced above the Earth, ever waxing and waning, each phase unlike the last. You will see five stars, moving in the opposite direction to the others, stemming the whirl of the skies towards the West: on the slightest motions of these depend the fortunes of nations, and according as the aspect of the planets is auspicious or malignant, the greatest empires rise and fall: you will see with wonder the gathering clouds, the falling showers, the zigzag lightning, the crashing together of the heavens. When, sated with the wonders above, you turn your eyes towards the Earth, they will be met by objects of a different yet equally admirable aspect: on one side a boundless expanse of open plains, on another the towering peaks of lofty and snow-clad mountains: the downward course of rivers, some streams running eastward, some westward from the same source: the woods which wave even on the mountain tops, the vast forests with all the creatures that dwell therein, and the confused harmony of the birds: the variously-placed cities, the nations which natural obstacles keep secluded from the world, some of whom withdraw themselves to lofty mountains, while others dwell in fear and trembling on the sloping banks of rivers: the crops which are assisted by cultivation, and the trees which bear fruit even without it: the rivers that flow gently through the meadows, the lovely bays and shores that curve inwards to form harbours: the countless islands scattered over the main, which break and spangle the seas. What of the brilliancy of stones and gems, the gold that rolls amid the sands of rushing streams, the heaven-born fires that burst forth from the midst of the earth and even from the midst of the sea; the ocean itself, that binds land to land, dividing the nations by its threefold indentations, and boiling up with mighty rage? Swimming upon its waves, making them disturbed and

---

[127] See Mayor's note on Juvenal I, and above, Chapter 16, §4.

swelling without wind, you will see animals exceeding the size of any that belong to the land, some clumsy and requiring others to guide their movements, some swift and moving faster than the utmost efforts of rowers, some of them that drink in the waters and blow them out again to the great perils of those who sail near them: you will see here ships seeking for unknown lands: you will see that man's audacity leaves nothing unattempted, and you will yourself be both a witness and a sharer in great attempts. You will both learn and teach the arts by which men's lives are supplied with necessaries, are adorned, and are ruled: but in this same place there will be a thousand pestilences fatal to both body and mind, there will be wars and highway robberies, poisonings and shipwrecks, extremes of climate and excesses of body, untimely griefs for our dearest ones, and death for ourselves, of which we cannot tell whether it will be easy or by torture at the hands of the executioner. Now consider and weigh carefully in your own mind which you would choose. If you wish to enjoy these blessings you must pass through these pains. Do you answer that you choose to live? "Of course." Nay, I thought you would not enter upon that of which the least diminution causes pain. Live, then, as has been agreed on. You say, "No one has asked my opinion." Our parents' opinion was taken about us, when, knowing what the conditions of life are, they brought us into it.

19

But, to come to topics of consolation, in the first place consider if you please to what our remedies must be applied, and next, in what way. It is regret for the absence of his loved one which causes a mourner to grieve: yet it is clear that this in itself is bearable enough; for we do not weep at their being absent or intending to be absent during their lifetime, although when they leave our sight we have no more pleasure in them. What tortures us, therefore, is an idea. Now every evil is just as great as we consider it to be: we have, therefore, the remedy in our own hands. Let us suppose that they are on a journey, and let us deceive ourselves: we have sent them away, or, rather, we have sent them on in advance to a place whither we shall soon follow them.[128] Besides this, mourners are wont to suffer from the thought, "I shall have no one to protect me, no one to avenge me when I am scorned." To use a very disreputable but very true mode of consolation, I may say that in our country the loss of children bestows more influence than it takes away, and loneliness, which used to bring the aged to ruin, now makes them so powerful that some old men have pretended to pick quarrels with their sons, have disowned their own children, and have made themselves childless by their own act. I know what you will say: "My own losses do not grieve me:" and indeed a man does not deserve to be consoled if he is sorry for his son's death as he would

---

[128] Lipsius points out that this idea is borrowed from the comic poet Antiphanes. See Meineke's *Comic Fragments*, p. 3.

be for that of a slave, who is capable of seeing anything in his son beyond his son's self. What then, Marcia, is it that grieves you? is it that your son has died, or that he did not live long? If it be his having died, then you ought always to have grieved, for you always knew that he would die. Reflect that the dead suffer no evils, that all those stories which make us dread the nether world are mere fables, that he who dies need fear no darkness, no prison, no blazing streams of fire, no river of Lethe, no judgment seat before which he must appear, and that Death is such utter freedom that he need fear no more despots. All that is a fantasy of the poets, who have terrified us without a cause. Death is a release from and an end of all pains: beyond it our sufferings cannot extend: it restores us to the peaceful rest in which we lay before we were born. If anyone pities the dead, he ought also to pity those who have not been born. Death is neither a good nor a bad thing, for that alone which is something can be a good or a bad thing: but that which is nothing, and reduces all things to nothing, does not hand us over to either fortune, because good and bad require some material to work upon. Fortune cannot take hold of that which Nature has let go, nor can a man be unhappy if he is nothing. Your son has passed beyond the border of the country where men are forced to labour; he has reached deep and everlasting peace. He feels no fear of want, no anxiety about his riches, no stings of lust that tears the heart in guise of pleasure: he knows no envy of another's prosperity, he is not crushed by the weight of his own; even his chaste ears are not wounded by any ribaldry: he is menaced by no disaster, either to his country or to himself. He does not hang, full of anxiety, upon the issue of events, to reap even greater uncertainty as his reward: he has at last taken up a position from which nothing can dislodge him, where nothing can make him afraid.

20

O how little do men understand their own misery, that they do not praise and look forward to death as the best discovery of Nature, whether because it hedges in happiness, or because it drives away misery: because it puts an end to the sated weariness of old age, cuts down youth in its bloom while still full of hope of better things, or calls home childhood before the harsher stages of life are reached: it is the end of all men, a relief to many, a desire to some, and it treats none so well as those to whom it comes before they call for it. Death frees the slave though his master wills it not, it lightens the captive's chains: it leads out of prison those whom headstrong power has forbidden to quit it: it points out to exiles, whose minds and eyes are ever turned towards their own country, that it makes no difference under what people's soil one lies. When Fortune has unjustly divided the common stock, and has given over one man to another, though they were born with equal rights, Death makes them all equal. After Death no one acts any more at another's bidding: in death no man suffers any more from the sense of his low position. It is open to all: it was what your father, Marcia, longed for: it is this, I say, that renders it no misery to be born, which enables me to face the threatenings of misfortune without quailing, and to keep my mind unharmed and able to command itself. I have a last appeal. I see before me crosses not all alike, but differently made by different peoples: some hang a man head downwards, some force a stick upwards through his groin, some stretch out his arms on a forked gibbet. I see cords, scourges, and instruments of torture for each limb and each joint: but I see Death also. There are bloodthirsty enemies, there are overbearing fellow-countrymen, but where they are there I see Death also. Slavery is not grievous if a man can gain his freedom by one step as soon as he becomes tired of thralldom. Life, it is thanks to Death that I hold thee so dear. Think how great a blessing is a timely death, how many have been injured by living longer than they ought. If sickness had carried off that glory and support of the empire Gnaeus Pompeius, at Naples, he would have died the undoubted head of the Roman people, but as it was, a short extension of time cast him down from his pinnacle of fame: he beheld his legions slaughtered before his eyes: and what a sad relic of that battle, in which the Senate formed the first line, was the survival of the general. He saw his Egyptian butcher, and offered his body, hallowed by so many victories, to a guardsman's sword, although even had he been unhurt, he would have regretted his safety: for what could have been more infamous than that a Pompeius should owe his life to the clemency of a king? If Marcus Cicero had fallen at the time when he avoided those daggers which Catiline aimed equally at him and at his country, he might have died as the saviour of the commonwealth which he had set free: if his death had even followed upon that of his daughter, he might have died happy. He would not then have seen swords drawn for the slaughter of Roman citizens, the goods of the murdered divided among the murderers, that men might pay from their own purse the price of their own blood, the public auction of the consul's spoil in the civil war, the public letting out of murder to be done, brigandage, war, pillage, hosts of Catilines. Would it not have been a good thing for Marcus Cato if the sea had swallowed him up when he was returning from Cyprus after sequestrating the king's hereditary possessions, even if that very money which he was bringing to pay the soldiers in the civil war had been lost with him? He certainly would have been able to boast that no one would dare to do wrong in the presence of Cato: as it was, the extension of his life for a very few more years forced one who was born for personal and political freedom to flee from Caesar and to become Pompeius's follower. Premature death therefore did him no evil: indeed, it put an end to the power of any evil to hurt him.

21

"Yet," say you, "he perished too soon and untimely." In the first place, suppose that he had lived to extreme old age: let him continue alive to the extreme limits of human existence: how much is it after all? Born for a very brief space of time, we regard this life as an inn which we are soon to quit that it may be made ready for the coming guest. Do I speak of our lives, which we know roll away incredibly fast? Reckon up the centuries of cities: you will find that even those which boast of their antiquity have not existed for long. All human works are brief and fleeting; they take up no part whatever of infinite time. Tried by the standard of the universe, we regard this Earth of ours, with all its cities, nations, rivers, and seaboard as a mere point: our life occupies less than a point when compared with all time, the measure of which exceeds that of the world, for indeed the world is contained many times in it. Of what importance, then, can it be to lengthen that which, however much you add to it, will never be much more than nothing? We can only make our lives long by one expedient, that is, by being satisfied with their length: you may tell me of long-lived men, whose length of days has been celebrated by tradition, you may assign a hundred and ten years apiece to them: yet when you allow your mind to conceive the idea of eternity, there will be no difference between the shortest and the longest life, if you compare the time during which anyone has been alive with that during which he has not been alive. In the next place, when he died his life was complete: he had lived as long as he needed to live: there was nothing left for him to accomplish. All men do not grow old at the same age, nor indeed do all animals: some are wearied out by life at fourteen years of age, and what is only the first stage of life with man is their extreme limit of longevity. To each man a varying length of days has been assigned: no one dies before his time, because he was not destined to live any longer than he did. Everyone's end is fixed, and will always remain where it has been placed: neither industry nor favour will move it on any further. Believe, then, that you lost him by advice: he took all that was his own,

"And reached the goal allotted to his life,"

so you need not burden yourself with the thought, "He might have lived longer." His life has not been cut short, nor does chance ever cut short our years: every man receives as much as was promised to him: the Fates go their own way, and neither add anything nor take away anything from what they have once promised. Prayers and endeavours are all in vain: each man will have as much life as his first day placed to his credit: from the time when he first saw the light he has entered on the path that leads to death, and is drawing nearer to his doom: those same years which were added to his youth were subtracted from his life. We all fall into this mistake of supposing that it is only old men, already in the decline of life, who are drawing near to death, whereas our first infancy, our youth, indeed every time of life leads thither. The Fates ply their own work: they take from us the consciousness of our death, and, the better to conceal its approaches, death lurks under the very names we give to life: infancy changes into boyhood, maturity swallows up the boy, old age the man: these stages themselves, if you reckon them properly, are so many losses.

22

Do you complain, Marcia, that your son did not live as long as he might have done? How do you know that it was to his advantage to live longer? whether his interest was not served by this death? Whom can you find at the present time whose fortunes are grounded on such sure foundations that they have nothing to fear in the future? All human affairs are evanescent and perishable, nor is any part of our life so frail and liable to accident as that which we especially enjoy. We ought, therefore, to pray for death when our fortune is at its best, because so great is the uncertainty and turmoil in which we live, that we can be sure of nothing but what is past. Think of your son's handsome person, which you had guarded in perfect purity among all the temptations of a voluptuous capital. Who could have undertaken to keep that clear of all diseases, so that it might preserve its beauty of form unimpaired even to old age? Think of the many taints of the mind: for fine dispositions do not always continue to their life's end to make good the promise of their youth, but have often broken down: either extravagance, all the more shameful for being indulged in late in life, takes possession of men and makes their well-begun lives end in disgrace, or they devote their entire thoughts to the eating-house and the belly, and they become interested in nothing save what they shall eat and what they shall drink. Add to this conflagrations, falling houses, shipwrecks, the agonizing operations of surgeons, who cut pieces of bone out of men's living bodies, plunge their whole hands into their entrails, and inflict more than one kind of pain to effect the cure of shameful diseases. After these comes exile; your son was not more innocent than Rutilius: imprisonment; he was not wiser than Socrates: the piercing of one's breast by a self-inflicted wound; he was not of holier life than Cato. When you look at these examples, you will perceive that nature deals very kindly with those whom she puts speedily in a place of safety because there awaited them the payment of some such price as this for their lives. Nothing is so deceptive, nothing is so treacherous as human life; by Hercules, were it not given to men before they could form an opinion, no one would take it. Not to be born, therefore, is the happiest lot of all, and the nearest thing to this, I imagine, is that we should soon finish our strife here and be restored again to our former rest. Recall to your mind that time, so painful to you, during which Sejanus handed over your father as a present to his client Satrius Secundus: he was angry with him about something or other which he had said with too great freedom, because he was not able to keep silence and see Sejanus climbing up to take his seat upon our necks, which would have been bad enough had he been placed there by his master. He was decreed the honour of a statue, to be set up in the theatre of Pompeius, which had been burned down and was being restored by Caesar. Cordus exclaimed that "Now the theatre was really destroyed." What then? should he not burst with spite at a Sejanus being set up over the ashes of Gnaeus Pompeius, at a faithless soldier being commemorated within the memorial of a consummate commander?

The inscription was put up:[129] and those keen-scented hounds whom Sejanus used to feed on human blood, to make them tame towards himself and fierce to all the world beside, began to bay around their victim and even to make premature snaps at him. What was he to do? If he chose to live, he must gain the consent of Sejanus; if to die, he must gain that of his daughter; and neither of them could have been persuaded to grant it: he therefore determined to deceive his daughter, and having taken a bath in order to weaken himself still further, he retired to his bedchamber on the pretence of taking a meal there. After dismissing his slaves he threw some of the food out of the window, that he might appear to have eaten it: then he took no supper, making the excuse that he had already had enough food in his chamber. This he continued to do on the second and the third day: the fourth betrayed his condition by his bodily weakness; so, embracing you, "My dearest daughter," said he, "from whom I have never throughout your whole life concealed aught but this, I have begun my journey towards death, and have already travelled halfway thither. You cannot and you ought not to call me back." So saying he ordered all light to be excluded from the room and shut himself up in the darkness. When his determination became known there was a general feeling of pleasure at the prey being snatched out of the jaws of those ravening wolves. His prosecutors, at the instance of Sejanus, went to the judgment-seat of the consuls, complained that Cordus was dying, and begged the consuls to interpose to prevent his doing what they themselves had driven him to do; so true was it that Cordus appeared to them to be escaping: an important matter was at stake, namely, whether the accused should lose the right to die. While this point was being debated, and the prosecutors were going to attend the court a second time, he had set himself free from them. Do you see, Marcia, how suddenly evil days come upon a man? and do you weep because one of your family could not avoid dying? one of your family was within a very little of not being allowed to die.

23

Besides the fact that everything that is future is uncertain, and the only certainty is that it is more likely to turn out ill than well, our spirits find the path to the Gods above easiest when it is soon allowed to leave the society of mankind, because it has then contracted fewest impurities to weigh it down: if set free before they become hardened worldlings, before earthly things have sunk too deep into them, they fly all the more lightly back to the place from whence they came, and all the more easily wash away the stains and defilements which they may have contracted. Great minds never love to linger long in the body: they are eager to burst its bonds and escape from it, they chafe at the narrowness of their prison, having been wont to wander

---

[129] This I believe to be the meaning of the text, but Koch reasonably conjectures that the true reading is *editur subscriptio*, "an indictment was made out against him." See *On Benefits*, Book III, Chapter 26.

through space, and from aloft in the upper air to look down with contempt upon human affairs. Hence it is that Plato declares that the wise man's mind is entirely given up to death, longs for it, contemplates it, and through his eagerness for it is always striving after things which lie beyond this life. Why, Marcia, when you saw him while yet young displaying the wisdom of age, with a mind that could rise superior to all sensual enjoyments, faultless and without a blemish, able to win riches without greediness, public office without ambition, pleasure without extravagance, did you suppose it would long be your lot to keep him safe by your side? Whatever has arrived at perfection, is ripe for dissolution. Consummate virtue flees away and betakes itself out of our sight, and those things which come to maturity in the first stage of their being do not wait for the last. The brighter a fire glows, the sooner it goes out: it lasts longer when it is made up with bad and slowly burning fuel, and shows a dull light through a cloud of smoke: its being poorly fed makes it linger all the longer. So also the more brilliant men's minds, the shorter lived they are: for when there is no room for further growth, the end is near.

Fabianus tells us, what our parents themselves have seen, that there was at Rome a boy of gigantic stature, exceeding that of a man: but he soon died, and every sensible person always said that he would soon die, for he could not live to reach the age which he had assumed before it was due. So it is: too complete maturity is a proof that destruction is near and the end approaches when growth is over.

24

Begin to reckon his age, not by years, but by virtues: he lived long enough. He was left as a ward in the care of guardians up to his fourteenth year, and never passed out of that of his mother: when he had a household of his own he was loath to leave yours, and continued to dwell under his mother's roof, though few sons can endure to live under their father's. Though a youth whose height, beauty, and vigour of body destined him for the army, yet he refused to serve, that he might not be separated from you. Consider, Marcia, how seldom mothers who live in separate houses see their children: consider how they lose and pass in anxiety all those years during which they have sons in the army, and you will see that this time, none of which you lost, was of considerable extent: he never went out of your sight: it was under your eyes that he applied himself to the cultivation of an admirable intellect and one which would have rivaled that of his grandfather, had it not been hindered by shyness, which has concealed many men's accomplishments: though a youth of unusual beauty, and living among such throngs of women who made it their business to seduce men, he gratified the wishes of none of them, and when the effrontery of some led them so far as actually to tempt him, he blushed as deeply at having found favour in their eyes as though he had been guilty. By this holiness of life he caused himself, while yet quite a boy, to be thought worthy of the priesthood, which no doubt he owed to his mother's influence; but even his mother's influence would have had no weight if the candidate for whom it was exerted had been unfit for the post. Dwell upon these virtues, and nurse your son as it were in your lap: now he is more at leisure to respond to your caresses, he has nothing to call him away from you, he will never be an anxiety or a sorrow to you. You have grieved at the only grief so good a son could cause you: all else is beyond the power of fortune to harm, and is full of pleasure, if only you know how to make use of your son, if you do but know what his most precious quality was. It is merely the outward semblance of your son that has perished, his likeness, and that not a very good one; he himself is immortal, and is now in a far better state, set free from the burden of all that was not his own, and left simply by himself: all this apparatus which you see about us of bones and sinews, this covering of skin, this face, these our servants the hands, and all the rest of our environment, are but chains and darkness to the soul: they overwhelm it, choke it, corrupt it, fill it with false ideas, and keep it at a distance from its own true sphere: it has to struggle continually against this burden of the flesh, lest it be dragged down and sunk by it. It ever strives to rise up again to the place from whence it was sent down on Earth: there eternal rest awaits it, there it will behold what is pure and clear, in place of what is foul and turbid.

25

You need not, therefore, hasten to the burial-place of your son: that which lies there is but the worst part of him and that which gave him most trouble, only bones and ashes, which are no more parts of him than clothes or other coverings of his body. He is complete, and without leaving any part of himself behind on Earth has taken wing and gone away altogether: he has tarried a brief space above us while his soul was being cleansed and purified from the vices and rust which all mortal lives must contract, and from thence he will rise to the high heavens and join the souls of the blessed: a saintly company will welcome him thither—Scipios and Catos; and among the rest of those who have held life cheap and set themselves free, thanks to death, albeit all there are alike akin, your father, Marcia, will embrace his grandson as he rejoices in the unwonted light, will teach him the motion of the stars which are so near to them, and introduce him with joy into all the secrets of nature, not by guesswork but by real knowledge. Even as a stranger is grateful to one who shows him the way about an unknown city, so is a searcher after the causes of what he sees in the heavens to one of his own family who can explain them to him. He will delight in gazing deep down upon the Earth, for it is a delight to look from aloft at what one has left below. Bear yourself, therefore, Marcia, as though you were placed before the eyes of your father and your son, yet not such as you knew them, but far loftier beings, placed in a higher sphere. Blush, then, to do any mean or common action, or to weep for those your relatives who have been changed for the better. Free to roam through the open, boundless realms of the ever-living universe, they are not hindered in their course by intervening seas, lofty mountains, impassable valleys, or the treacherous flats of the Syrtes: they find a level path everywhere, are swift and ready of motion, and are permeated in their turn by the stars and dwell together with them.

26

Imagine then, Marcia, that your father, whose influence over you was as great as yours over your son, no longer in that frame of mind in which he deplored the civil wars, or in which he forever proscribed those who would have proscribed him, but in a mood as much more joyful as his abode now is higher than of old, is saying, as he looks down from the height of heaven, "My daughter, why does this sorrow possess you for so long? why do you live in such ignorance of the truth, as to think that your son has been unfairly dealt with because he has returned to his ancestors in his prime, without decay of body or mind, leaving his family flourishing? Do you not know with what storms Fortune unsettles everything? how she proves kind and compliant to none save to those who have the fewest possible dealings with her? Need I remind you of kings who would have been the happiest of mortals had death sooner withdrawn them from the ruin which was approaching them? or of Roman generals, whose greatness, had but a few years been taken from their lives, would have wanted nothing to render it complete? or of men of the highest distinction and noblest birth who have calmly offered their necks to the stroke of a soldier's sword? Look at your father and your grandfather: the former fell into the hands of a foreign murderer: I allowed no man to take any liberties with me, and by abstinence from food showed that my spirit was as great as my writings had represented it. Why, then, should that member of our household who died most happily of all be mourned in it the longest? We have all assembled together, and, not being plunged in utter darkness, we see that with you on Earth there is nothing to be wished for, nothing grand or magnificent, but all is mean, sad, anxious, and hardly receives a fractional part of the clear light in which we dwell. I need not say that here are no frantic charges of rival armies, no fleets shattering one another, no parricides, actual or meditated, no courts where men babble over lawsuits for days together, here is nothing underhand, all hearts and minds are open and unveiled, our life is public and known to all, and that we command a view of all time and of things to come. I used to take pleasure in compiling the history of what took place in one century among a few people in the most out-of-the-way corner of the world: here I enjoy the spectacle of all the centuries, the whole chain of events from age to age as long as years have been. I may view kingdoms when they rise and when they fall, and behold the ruin of cities and the new channels made by the sea. If it will be any consolation to you in your bereavement to know that it is the common lot of all, be assured that nothing will continue to stand in the place in which it now stands, but that time will lay everything low and bear it away with itself: it will sport, not only with men—for how small a part are they of the dominion of Fortune?—but with districts, provinces, quarters of the world: it will efface entire mountains, and in other places will pile new rocks on high: it will dry up seas, change the course of rivers, destroy the intercourse of nation with nation, and break up the communion and fellowship of the human race: in other regions it will swallow up cities by opening vast chasms in the earth, will shake them with earthquakes, will breathe forth pestilence from the nether world, cover all habitable ground with inundations and destroy every creature in the flooded world, or burn up all mortals by a huge conflagration. When the time shall arrive for the world to be brought to an end, that it may begin its life anew, all the forces of nature will perish in conflict with one another, the stars will be dashed together, and all the lights which now gleam in regular order in various parts of the sky will then blaze in one fire with all their fuel burning at once. Then we also, the souls of the blest and the heirs of eternal life, whenever God thinks fit to reconstruct the universe, when all things are settling down again, we also, being a small accessory to the universal wreck,[130] shall be changed into our old elements. Happy is your son, Marcia, in that he already knows this."

---

[130] *Ruinae*; Koch's *urinae* is a misprint.

TO HELVIA, ON CONSOLATION

1

My best of mothers, I have often felt eager to console you, and have as often checked that impulse. Many things urged me to make the attempt: in the first place, I thought that if, though I might not be able to restrain your tears, yet that if I could even wipe them away, I should set myself free from all my own sorrows: then I was quite sure that I should rouse you from your grief with more authority if I had first shaken it off myself. I feared, too, lest fortune, though overcome by me, might nevertheless overcome someone of my family. Then I endeavoured to crawl and bind up your wounds in the best way I could, holding my hand over my own wound; but then again other considerations occurred to me which held me back: I knew that I must not oppose your grief during its first transports, lest my very attempts at consolation might irritate it, and add fuel to it: for in diseases, also, there is nothing more hurtful than medicine applied too soon. I waited, therefore, until it exhausted itself by its own violence, and being weakened by time, so that it was able to bear remedies, would allow itself to be handled and touched. Beside this, while turning over all the works which the greatest geniuses have composed, for the purpose of soothing and pacifying grief, I could not find any instance of one who had offered consolation to his relatives, while he himself was being sorrowed over by them. Thus, the subject being a new one, I hesitated and feared that instead of consoling, I might embitter your grief. Then here was the thought that a man who had only just raised his head after burying his child, and who wished to console his friends, would require to use new phrases not taken from our common everyday words of comfort: but every sorrow of more than usual magnitude must needs prevent one's choosing one's words, seeing that it often prevents one's using one's very voice. However this may be, I will make the attempt, not trusting in my own genius, but because my consolation will be most powerful since it is I who offer it. You never would deny me anything, and I hope, though all grief is obstinate, that you will surely not refuse me this request, that you will allow me to set bounds to your sorrow.

2

See how far I have presumed upon your indulgence: I have no doubts about my having more power over you than your grief, than which nothing has more power over the unhappy. In order, therefore, to avoid encountering it straightaway, I will at first take its part and offer it every encouragement: I will rip up and bring to light again wounds already scarred. Someone may say, "What sort of consolation is this, for a man to rake up buried evils, and to bring all its sorrows before a mind which scarcely can bear the sight of one?" but let him reflect that diseases which are so malignant that they do but gather strength from ordinary remedies, may often be cured by the opposite treatment: I will, therefore, display before your grief all its woes and miseries: this will be to effect a cure, not by soothing measures, but by cautery and the knife. What shall I gain by this? I shall make the mind that could overcome so many sorrows, ashamed to bewail one wound more in a body so full of scars. Let those whose feeble minds have been enervated by a long period of happiness, weep and lament for many days, and faint away on receiving the slightest blow: but those whose years have all been passed amid catastrophes should bear the severest losses with brave and unyielding patience. Continual misfortune has this one advantage, that it ends by rendering callous those whom it is always scourging. Ill fortune has given you no respite, and has not left even your birthday free from the bitterest grief: you lost your mother as soon as you were born, nay, while you were being born, and you came into life, as it were, an outcast: you grew up under a stepmother, whom you made into a mother by all the obedience and respect which even a real daughter could have bestowed upon her: and even a good stepmother costs everyone dear. You lost your most affectionate uncle, a brave and excellent man, just when you were awaiting his return: and, lest fortune should weaken its blows by dividing them, within a month you lost your beloved husband, by whom you had become the mother of three children. This sorrowful news was brought you while you were already in mourning, while all your children were absent, so that all your misfortunes seemed to have been purposely brought upon you at a time when your grief could nowhere find any repose. I pass over all the dangers and alarms which you have endured without any respite: it was but the other day that you received the bones of three of your grandchildren in the bosom from which you had sent them forth: less than twenty days after you had buried my child, who perished in your arms and amid your kisses, you heard that I had been exiled: you wanted only this drop in your cup, to have to weep for those who still lived.

3

The last wound is, I admit, the severest that you have ever yet sustained: it has not merely torn the skin, but has pierced you to the very heart: yet as recruits cry aloud when only slightly wounded, and shudder more at the hands of the surgeon than at the sword, while veterans even when transfixed allow their hurts to be dressed without a groan, and as patiently as if they were in someone else's body, so now you ought to offer yourself courageously to be healed. Lay aside lamentations and wailings, and all the usual noisy manifestations of female sorrow: you have gained nothing by so many misfortunes, if you have not learned how to suffer. Now, do I seem not to have spared you? nay, I have not passed over any of your sorrows, but have placed them all together in a mass before you.

4

I have done this by way of a heroic remedy: for I have determined to conquer this grief of yours, not merely to limit it; and I shall conquer it, I believe, if in the first place I can prove that I am not suffering enough to entitle me to be called unhappy, let alone to justify me in rendering my family unhappy: and, secondly, if I can deal with your case and prove that even your misfortune, which comes upon you entirely through me, is not a severe one. The point to which I shall first address myself is that of which your motherly love longs to hear, I mean, that I am not suffering: if I can, I will make it clear to you that the events by which you think that I am overwhelmed, are not unendurable: if you cannot believe this, I at any rate shall be all the more pleased with myself for being happy under circumstances which could make most men miserable. You need not believe what others say about me: that you may not be puzzled by any uncertainty as to what to think, I distinctly tell you that I am not miserable: I will add, for your greater comfort, that it is not possible for me to be made miserable.

5

We are born to a comfortable position enough, if we do not afterwards lose it: the aim of Nature has been to enable us to live well without needing a vast apparatus to enable us to do so: every man is able by himself to make himself happy. External circumstances have very little importance either for good or for evil: the wise man is neither elated by prosperity nor depressed by adversity; for he has always endeavoured to depend chiefly upon himself and to derive all his joys from himself. Do I, then, call myself a wise man? far from it: for were I able to profess myself wise, I should not only say that I was not unhappy, but should avow myself to be the most fortunate of men, and to be raised almost to the level of a god: as it is, I have applied myself to the society of wise men, which suffices to lighten all sorrows, and, not being as yet able to rely upon my own strength, I have betaken myself for refuge to the camp of others, of those, namely, who can easily defend both themselves and their friends. They have ordered me always to stand as it were on guard, and to mark the attacks and charges of Fortune long before she delivers them; she is only terrible to those whom she catches unawares; he who is always looking out for her assault, easily sustains it: for so also an invasion of the enemy overthrows those by whom it is unexpected, but those who have prepared themselves for the coming war before it broke out, stand in their ranks fully equipped and repel with ease the first, which is always the most furious onset. I never have trusted in Fortune, even when she seemed most peaceful. I have accepted all the gifts of wealth, high office, and influence, which she has so bountifully bestowed upon me, in such a manner that she can take them back again without disturbing me: I have kept a great distance between them and myself: and therefore she has taken them, not painfully torn them away from me. No man loses anything by the frowns of Fortune unless he has been deceived by her smiles: those who have enjoyed her bounty as though it were their own heritage forever, and who have chosen to take precedence of others because of it, lie in abject sorrow when her unreal and fleeting delights forsake their empty childish minds, that know nothing about solid pleasure: but he who has not been puffed up by success, does not collapse after failure: he possesses a mind of tried constancy, superior to the influences of either state; for even in the midst of prosperity he has experimented upon his powers of enduring adversity. Consequently I have always believed that there was no real good in any of those things which all men desire: I then found that they were empty, and merely painted over with artificial and deceitful dyes, without containing anything within which corresponds to their outside: I now find nothing so harsh and fearful as the common opinion of mankind threatened me with in this which is known as adversity: the word itself, owing to the prevalent belief and ideas current about it, strikes somewhat unpleasantly upon one's ears, and thrills the hearers as something dismal and accursed, for so hath the vulgar decreed that it should be: but a great many of the decrees of the vulgar are reversed by the wise.

6

Setting aside, then, the verdict of the majority, who are carried away by the first appearance of things and the usual opinion about them, let us consider what is meant by exile: clearly a changing from one place to another. That I may not seem to be narrowing its force, and taking away its worst parts, I must add, that this changing of place is accompanied by poverty, disgrace, and contempt. Against these I will combat later on: meanwhile I wish to consider what there is unpleasant in the mere act of changing one's place of abode. "It is unbearable," men say, "to lose one's native land." Look, I pray you, on these vast crowds, for whom all the countless roofs of Rome can scarcely find shelter: the greater part of those crowds have lost their native land: they have flocked hither from their country towns and colonies, and in fine from all parts of the world. Some have been brought by ambition, some by the exigencies of public office, some by being entrusted with embassies, some by luxury which seeks a convenient spot, rich in vices, for its exercise, some by their wish for a liberal education, others by a wish to see the public shows. Some have been led hither by friendship, some by industry, which finds here a wide field for the display of its powers. Some have brought their beauty for sale, some their eloquence: people of every kind assemble themselves together in Rome, which sets a high price both upon virtues and vices. Bid them all to be summoned to answer to their names, and ask each one from what home he has come: you will find that the greater part of them have left their own abodes, and journeyed to a city which, though great and beauteous beyond all others, is nevertheless not their own. Then leave this city, which may be said to be the common property of all men, and visit all other towns: there is not one of them which does not contain a large proportion of aliens. Pass away from those whose delightful situation and convenient position attracts many settlers: examine wildernesses and the most rugged islands, Sciathus and Seriphus, Gyarus and Corsica: you will find no place of exile where someone does not dwell for his own pleasure. What can be found barer or more precipitous on every side than this rock? what more barren in respect of food? what more uncouth in its inhabitants? more mountainous in its configuration? or more rigorous in its climate? yet even here there are more strangers than natives. So far, therefore, is the mere change of place from being irksome, that even this place has allured some away from their country. I find some writers who declare that mankind has a natural itch for change of abode and alteration of domicile: for the mind of man is wandering and unquiet; it never stands still, but spreads itself abroad and sends forth its thoughts into all regions, known or unknown; being nomadic, impatient of repose, and loving novelty beyond everything else. You need not be surprised at this, if you reflect upon its original source: it is not formed from the same elements as the heavy and earthly body, but from heavenly spirit: now heavenly things are by their nature always in motion, speeding along and flying with the greatest swiftness. Look at the luminaries which light the world: none of them stands still. The sun is perpetually in motion, and passes from one quarter to another, and although he revolves with the entire heaven, yet nevertheless he has a motion in the contrary direction to that of the universe itself, and passes through all the constellations without remaining in any: his wandering is incessant, and he never ceases to move from place to place. All things continually revolve and are forever changing; they pass from one position to another in accordance with natural and unalterable laws: after they have completed a certain circuit in a fixed space of time, they begin again the path which they had previously trodden. Be not surprised, then, if the human mind, which is formed from the same seeds as the heavenly bodies, delights in change and wandering, since the divine nature itself either takes pleasure in constant and exceeding swift motion or perhaps even preserves its existence thereby.

7

Come now, turn from divine to human affairs: you will see that whole tribes and nations have changed their abodes. What is the meaning of Greek cities in the midst of barbarous districts? or of the Macedonian language existing among the Indians and the Persians? Scythia and all that region which swarms with wild and uncivilized tribes boasts nevertheless Achaean cities along the shores of the Black Sea. Neither the rigours of eternal winter, nor the character of men as savage as their climate, has prevented people migrating thither. There is a mass of Athenians in Asia Minor. Miletus has sent out into various parts of the world citizens enough to populate seventy-five cities. That whole coast of Italy which is washed by the Lower Sea is a part of what once was "Greater Greece." Asia claims the Tuscans as her own: there are Tyrians living in Africa, Carthaginians in Spain; Greeks have pushed in among the Gauls, and Gauls among the Greeks. The Pyrenees have proved no barrier to the Germans: human caprice makes its way through pathless and unknown regions: men drag along with them their children, their wives, and their aged and worn-out parents. Some have been tossed hither and thither by long wanderings, until they have become too wearied to choose an abode, but have settled in whatever place was nearest to them: others have made themselves masters of foreign countries by force of arms: some nations while making for parts unknown have been swallowed up by the sea: some have established themselves in the place in which they were originally stranded by utter destitution. Nor have all men had the same reasons for leaving their country and for seeking for a new one: some have escaped from their cities when destroyed by hostile armies, and having lost their own lands have been thrust upon those of others: some have been cast out by domestic quarrels: some have been driven forth in consequence of an excess of population, in order to relieve the pressure at home: some have been forced to leave by pestilence, or frequent earthquakes, or some unbearable defects of a barren soil: some have been seduced by the fame of a fertile and overpraised clime. Different people have been led away from their homes by different causes; but in all cases it is clear that nothing remains in the same place in which it was born: the movement of the human race is perpetual: in this vast world some changes take place daily. The foundations of new cities are laid, new names of nations arise, while the former ones die out, or become absorbed by more powerful ones. And yet what else are all these general migrations but the banishments of whole peoples? Why should I lead you through all these details? what is the use of mentioning Antenor the founder of Padua, or Evander who established his kingdom of Arcadian settlers on the banks of the Tiber? or Diomedes and the other heroes, both victors and vanquished, whom the Trojan war scattered over lands which were not their own? It is a fact that the Roman Empire itself traces its origin back to an exile as its founder, who, fleeing from his country after its conquest, with what few relics he had saved from the wreck, had been brought to Italy by hard necessity and fear of his conqueror, which bade him seek distant lands. Since then, how many colonies has this people sent forth into every province? wherever the Roman conquers, there he dwells. These migrations always found people eager to take part in them, and veteran soldiers desert their native hearths and follow the flag of the colonists across the sea. The matter does not need illustrations by any more examples: yet I will add one more which I have before my eyes: this very island[131] has often changed its inhabitants. Not to mention more ancient events, which have become obscure from their antiquity, the Greeks who inhabit Marseilles at the present day, when they left Phocaea, first settled here, and it is doubtful what drove them hence, whether it was the rigour of the climate, the sight of the more powerful land of Italy, or the want of harbours on the coast: for the fact of their having placed themselves in the midst of what were then the most savage and uncouth tribes of Gaul proves that they were not driven hence by the ferocity of the natives. Subsequently the Ligurians came over into this same island, and also the Spaniards,[132] which is proved by the resemblance of their customs: for they wear the same head-coverings and the same sort of shoes as the Cantabrians, and some of their words are the same: for by association with Greeks and Ligurians they have entirely lost their native speech. Hither since then have been brought two Roman colonies, one by Marius, the other by Sulla: so often has the population of this barren and thorny rock been changed. In fine, you will scarcely find any land which is still in the hands of its original inhabitants: all peoples have become confused and intermingled: one has come after another: one has wished for what another scorned: some have been driven out of the land which they took from another. Thus fate has decreed that nothing should ever enjoy an uninterrupted course of good fortune.

8

Varro, that most learned of all the Romans, thought that for the mere change of place, apart from the other evils attendant on exile, we may find a sufficient remedy in the thought that wherever we go we always have the same Nature to deal with. Marcus Brutus thought that there was sufficient comfort in the thought that those who go into exile are permitted to carry their virtues thither with them. Though one might think that neither of these alone were able to console an exile, yet it must be confessed that when combined they have great power: for how very little it is that we lose! whithersoever we betake ourselves two most excellent things will accompany us, namely, a common Nature and our own especial virtue. Believe me, this is the work of whoever was the Creator of the universe, whether he be an all-powerful deity, an incorporeal mind which effects vast works, a divine spirit by which all things from the greatest to the smallest are equally pervaded, or fate and an unalterable connected sequence of events, this, I say, is its work, that nothing above the very lowest can ever fall into the power of another: all that is best for a man's enjoyment lies beyond human power, and can neither be bestowed or taken away: this world, the greatest and the most beautiful of Nature's productions, and its noblest part, a mind which can behold and admire it, are our own property, and will remain with us as long as we ourselves endure. Let us therefore briskly

---

[131] Corsica.

[132] Seneca himself was of Spanish extraction.

and cheerfully hasten with undaunted steps whithersoever circumstances call us: let us wander over whatever countries we please; no place of banishment can be found in the whole world in which man cannot find a home. I can raise my eyes from the earth to the sky in one place as well as in another; the heavenly bodies are everywhere equally near to mankind: accordingly, as long as my eyes are not deprived of that spectacle of which they never can have their fill, as long as I am allowed to gaze on the sun and moon, to dwell upon the other stars, to speculate upon their risings and settings, their periods, and the reasons why they move faster or slower, to see so many stars glittering throughout the night, some fixed, some not moving in a wide orbit but revolving in their own proper track, some suddenly diverging from it, some dazzling our eyes by a fiery blaze as though they were falling, or flying along drawing after them a long trail of brilliant light: while I am permitted to commune with these, and to hold intercourse, as far as a human being may, with all the company of heaven, while I can raise my spirit aloft to view its kindred sparks above, what does it matter upon what soil I tread?

9

"But this country does not produce beautiful or fruit-bearing trees; it is not watered by the courses of large or navigable rivers; it bears nothing which other nations would covet, since its produce barely suffices to support its inhabitants: no precious marbles are quarried here, no veins of gold and silver are dug out." What of that! It must be a narrow mind that takes pleasure in things of the Earth: it ought to be turned away from them to the contemplation of those which can be seen everywhere, which are equally brilliant everywhere: we ought to reflect, also, that these vulgar matters by a mistaken perversion of ideas prevent really good things reaching us: the further men stretch out their porticos, the higher they raise their towers, the more widely they extend their streets, the deeper they sink their retreats from the heats of summer, the more ponderous the roofs with which they cover their banqueting halls, the more there will be to obstruct their view of heaven. Fortune has cast you into a country in which there is no lodging more splendid than a cottage: you must indeed have a poor spirit, and one which seeks low sources of consolation, if you endure this bravely because you have seen the cottage of Romulus: say, rather, "Should that lowly barn be entered by the virtues, it will straightaway become more beautiful than any temple, because within it will be seen justice, self-restraint, prudence, love, a right division of all duties, a knowledge of all things on Earth and in heaven. No place can be narrow, if it contains such a company of the greatest virtues; no exile can be irksome in which one can be attended by these companions." Brutus, in the book which he wrote upon virtue, says that he saw Marcellus in exile at Mytilene, living as happily as it is permitted to man to live, and never keener in his pursuit of literature than at that time. He consequently adds the reflection: "I seemed rather to be going into exile myself when I had to return without him, than to be leaving him in exile." O how much more fortunate was Marcellus at that time, when Brutus praised him for his exile, than when Rome praised him for his consulship! what a man that must have been who made anyone think himself exiled because he was leaving him in exile! what a man that must have been who attracted the admiration of one whom even his friend Cato admired! Brutus goes on to say:—"Gaius Caesar sailed past Mytilene without landing, because he could not bear to see a fallen man." The Senate did indeed obtain his recall by public petition, being so anxious and sorrowful the while, that you would have thought that they all were of Brutus's mind that day, and were not pleading the cause of Marcellus, but their own, that they might not be sent into exile by being deprived of him: yet he gained far greater glory on the day when Brutus could not bear to leave him in exile, and Caesar could not bear to see him: for each of them bore witness to his worth: Brutus grieved, and Caesar blushed at going home without Marcellus. Can you doubt that so great a man as Marcellus frequently encouraged himself to endure his exile patiently in some such terms as these: "The loss of your country is no misery to you: you have so steeped yourself in philosophic lore, as to know that all the world is the wise man's country? What! was not this very man who banished you absent from his country for ten successive years? he was, no doubt, engaged in the extension of the empire, but for all that he was absent from his country. Now see how his presence is required in Africa, which threatens to rekindle the war, in Spain which is nursing up again the strength of the broken and shattered opposite faction, in treacherous Egypt, in fine, in all the parts of the world, for all are watching their opportunity to seize the empire at a disadvantage. Which will he go to meet first? which part of the universal conspiracy will he first oppose? His victory will drag him through every country in the world. Let nations look up to him and worship him: do thou live satisfied with the admiration of Brutus."

10

Marcellus, then, nobly endured his exile, and his change of place made no change in his mind, even though it was accompanied by poverty, in which every man who has not fallen into the madness of avarice and luxury, which upset all our ideas, sees no harm. Indeed, how very little is required to keep a man alive? and who, that has any virtue whatever, will find this fail him? As for myself, I do not feel that I have lost my wealth, but my occupation: the wants of the body are few: it wants protection from the cold, and the means of allaying hunger and thirst: all desires beyond these are vices, not necessities. There is no need for prying into all the depths of the sea, for loading one's stomach with heaps of slaughtered animals, or for tearing up shellfish[133] from the unknown shore of the furthest sea: may the gods and goddesses bring ruin upon those whose luxury transcends the bounds of an empire which

---

[133] Qu. oysters from Britain.

is already perilously wide. They want to have their ostentatious kitchens supplied with game from the other side of the Phasis, and though Rome has not yet obtained satisfaction from the Parthians, they are not ashamed to obtain birds from them: they bring together from all regions everything, known or unknown, to tempt their fastidious palate: food, which their stomach, worn out with delicacies, can scarcely retain, is brought from the most distant ocean: they vomit that they may eat, and eat that they may vomit, and do not even deign to digest the banquets which they ransack the globe to obtain. If a man despises these things, what harm can poverty do him? If he desires them, then poverty even does him good, for he is cured in spite of himself, and though he will not receive remedies even upon compulsion, yet while he is unable to fulfill his wishes he is as though he had them not. Gaius Caesar, whom in my opinion Nature produced in order to show what unlimited vice would be capable of when combined with unlimited power, dined one day at a cost of ten millions of sesterces: and though in this he had the assistance of the intelligence of all his subjects, yet he could hardly find how to make one dinner out of the tribute-money of three provinces. How unhappy are they whose appetite can only be aroused by costly food! and the costliness of food depends not upon its delightful flavour and sweetness of taste, but upon its rarity and the difficulty of procuring it: otherwise, if they chose to return to their sound senses, what need would they have of so many arts which minister to the stomach? of so great a commerce? of such ravaging of forests? of such ransacking of the depths of the sea? Food is to be found everywhere, and has been placed by Nature in every part of the world, but they pass it by as though they were blind, and wander through all countries, cross the seas, and excite at a great cost the hunger which they might allay at a small one. One would like to say: Why do you launch ships? why do you arm your hands for battle both with men and wild beasts? why do you run so riotously hither and thither? why do you amass fortune after fortune? Are you unwilling to remember how small our bodies are? is it not frenzy and the wildest insanity to wish for so much when you can contain so little? Though you may increase your income, and extend the boundaries of your property, yet you never can enlarge your own bodies: when your business transactions have turned out well, when you have made a successful campaign, when you have collected the food for which you have hunted through all lands, you will have no place in which to bestow all these superfluities. Why do you strive to obtain so much? Do you think that our ancestors, whose virtue supports our vices even to the present day, were unhappy, though they dressed their food with their own hands, though the earth was their bed, though their roofs did not yet glitter with gold, nor their temples with precious stones? and so they used then to swear with scrupulous honesty by earthenware gods; those who called these gods to witness would go back to the enemy for certain death rather than break their word.[134] Do you suppose that our dictator who granted an audience to the ambassadors of

---

[134] The allusion is evidently to Regulus.

the Samnites, while he roasted the commonest food before the fire himself with that very hand with which he had so often smitten the enemy, and with which he had placed his laurel wreath upon the lap of Capitolian Jove, enjoyed life less than the Apicius who lived in our own days, whose habits tainted the entire century, who set himself up as a professor of gastronomy in that very city from which philosophers once were banished as corrupters of youth? It is worthwhile to know his end. After he had spent a hundred millions of sesterces on his kitchen, and had wasted on each single banquet a sum equal to so many presents from the reigning emperors, and the vast revenue which he drew from the Capitol being overburdened with debt, he then for the first time was forced to examine his accounts: he calculated that he would have ten millions left of his fortune, and, as though he would live a life of mere starvation on ten millions, put an end to his life by poison. How great must the luxury of that man have been, to whom ten millions signified want? Can you think after this that the amount of money necessary to make a fortune depends upon its actual extent rather than on the mind of the owner? Here was a man who shuddered at the thought of a fortune of ten million sesterces, and escaped by poison from a prospect which other men pray for. Yet, for a mind so diseased, that last draught of his was the most wholesome: he was really eating and drinking poisons when he was not only enjoying, but boasting of his enormous banquets, when he was flaunting his vices, when he was causing his country to follow his example, when he was inviting youths to imitate him, albeit youth is quick to learn evil, without being provided with a model to copy. This is what befalls those who do not use their wealth according to reason, which has fixed limits, but according to vicious fashion, whose caprices are boundless and immeasurable. Nothing is sufficient for covetous desire, but Nature can be satisfied even with scant measure. The poverty of an exile, therefore, causes no inconvenience, for no place of exile is so barren as not to produce what is abundantly sufficient to support a man.

11

Next, need an exile regret his former dress and house? If he only wishes for these things because of their use to him, he will want neither roof nor garment, for it takes as little to cover the body as it does to feed it: Nature has annexed no difficult conditions to anything which man is obliged to do. If, however, he sighs for a purple robe steeped in floods of dye, interwoven with threads of gold and with many coloured artistic embroideries, then his poverty is his own fault, not that of fortune: even though you restored to him all that he has lost, you would do him no good; for he would have more unsatisfied ambitions, if restored, than he had unsatisfied wants when he was an exile. If he longs for furniture glittering with silver vases, plate which boasts the signature of antique artists, bronze which the mania of a small clique has rendered costly, slaves enough to crowd however large a house, purposely overfed horses, and precious stones of all countries: whatever collections he may make of these, he never will satisfy his insatiable appetite, any more than any amount of liquor will quench a thirst which arises not from the need of drink but from the burning heat within a man; for this is not thirst but disease. Nor does this take place only with regard to money and food, but every want which is caused by vice and not by necessity is of this nature: however much you supply it with you do not quench it but intensify it. He who restrains himself within the limits prescribed by nature, will not feel poverty; he who exceeds them will always be poor, however great his wealth may be. Even a place of exile suffices to provide one with necessaries; whole kingdoms do not suffice to provide one with superfluities. It is the mind which makes men rich: this it is that accompanies them into exile, and in the most savage wildernesses, after having found sufficient sustenance for the body, enjoys its own overflowing resources: the mind has no more connection with money than the immortal gods have with those things which are so highly valued by untutored intellects, sunk in the bondage of the flesh. Gems, gold, silver, and vast polished round tables are but earthly dross, which cannot be loved by a pure mind that is mindful of whence it came, is unblemished by sin, and which, when released from the body, will straightaway soar aloft to the highest heaven: meanwhile, as far as it is permitted by the hindrances of its mortal limbs and this heavy clog of the body by which it is surrounded, it examines divine things with swift and airy thought. From this it follows that no freeborn man, who is akin to the gods, and fit for any world and any age, can ever be in exile: for his thoughts are directed to all the heavens and to all times past and future: this trumpery body, the prison and fetter of the spirit, may be tossed to this place or to that; upon it tortures, robberies, and diseases may work their will: but the spirit itself is holy and eternal, and upon it no one can lay hands.

12

That you may not suppose that I merely use the maxims of the philosophers to disparage the evils of poverty, which no one finds terrible, unless he thinks it so; consider in the first place how many more poor people there are than rich, and yet you will not find that they are sadder or more anxious than the rich: nay, I am not sure that they are not happier, because they have fewer things to distract their minds. From these poor men, who often are not unhappy at their poverty, let us pass to the rich. How many occasions there are on which they are just like poor men! When they are on a journey their baggage is cut down, whenever they are obliged to travel fast their train of attendants is dismissed. When they are serving in the army, how small a part of their property can they have with them, since camp discipline forbids superfluities! Nor is it only temporary exigencies or desert places that put them on the same level as poor men: they have some days on which they become sick of their riches, dine reclining on the ground, put away all their gold and silver plate, and use earthenware. Madmen! they are always afraid of this for which they sometimes wish. O how dense a stupidity, how great an ignorance of the truth they show when they flee from this thing and yet amuse themselves by playing with it! Whenever I look back to the great examples of antiquity, I feel ashamed to seek consolation for my poverty, now that luxury has advanced so far in the present age, that the allowance of an exile is larger than the inheritance of the princes of old. It is well known that Homer had one slave, that Plato had three, and that Zeno, who first taught the stern and masculine doctrine of the Stoics, had none: yet could anyone say that they lived wretchedly without himself being thought a most pitiable wretch by all men? Menenius Agrippa, by whose mediation the patricians and plebeians were reconciled, was buried by public subscription. Attilius Regulus, while he was engaged in scattering the Carthaginians in Africa, wrote to the Senate that his hired servant had left him, and that consequently his farm was deserted: whereupon it was decreed that as long as Regulus was absent, it should be cultivated at the expense of the State. Was it not worth his while to have no slave, if thereby he obtained the Roman people for his farm-bailiff? Scipio's daughters received their dowries from the Treasury, because their father had left them none: by Hercules, it was right for the Roman people to pay tribute to Scipio for once, since he had exacted it forever from Carthage. O how happy were those girls' husbands, who had the Roman people for their father-in-law. Can you think that those whose daughters dance in the ballet, and marry with a settlement of a million sesterces, are happier than Scipio, whose children received their dowry of old-fashioned brass money from their guardian the Senate? Can anyone despise poverty, when she has such a noble descent to boast of? can an exile be angry at any privation, when Scipio could not afford a portion for his daughters, Regulus could not afford a hired labourer, Menenius could not afford a funeral? when all these men's wants were supplied in a manner which rendered them a source of additional honour? Poverty, when such men as these plead its cause, is not only harmless, but positively attractive.

13

To this one may answer: "Why do you thus ingeniously divide what can indeed be endured if taken singly, but which all together are overwhelming? Change of place can be borne if nothing more than one's place be changed: poverty can be borne if it be without disgrace, which is enough to cow our spirits by itself." If anyone were to endeavour to frighten me with the number of my misfortunes, I should answer him as follows: If you have enough strength to resist any one part of your ill fortune, you will have enough to resist it all. If virtue has once hardened your mind, it renders it impervious to blows from any quarter: if avarice, that greatest pest of the human race, has left it, you will not be troubled by ambition: if you regard the end of your days not as a punishment, but as an ordinance of nature, no fear of anything else will dare to enter the breast which has cast out the fear of death. If you consider sexual passion to have been bestowed on mankind not for the sake of pleasure, but for the continuance of the race, all other desires will pass harmlessly by one who is safe even from this secret plague, implanted in our very bosoms. Reason does not conquer vices one by one, but all together: if reason is defeated, it is utterly defeated once for all. Do you suppose that any wise man, who relies entirely upon himself, who has set himself free from the ideas of the common herd, can be wrought upon by disgrace? A disgraceful death is worse even than disgrace: yet Socrates bore the same expression of countenance with which he had rebuked thirty tyrants, when he entered the prison and thereby took away the infamous character of the place; for the place which contained Socrates could not be regarded as a prison. Was anyone ever so blind to the truth as to suppose that Marcus Cato was disgraced by his double defeat in his candidature for the praetorship and the consulship? that disgrace fell on the praetorship and consulship which Cato honoured by his candidature. No one is despised by others unless he be previously despised by himself: a grovelling and abject mind may fall an easy prey to such contempt: but he who stands up against the most cruel misfortunes, and overcomes those evils by which others would have been crushed—such a man, I say, turns his misfortunes into badges of honour, because we are so constituted as to admire nothing so much as a man who bears adversity bravely. At Athens, when Aristides was being led to execution, everyone who met him cast down his eyes and groaned, as though not merely a just man but justice herself was being put to death. Yet one man was found who spat in his face: he might have been disturbed at this, since he knew it could only be a foul-mouthed fellow that would have the heart to do so; he, however, wiped his face, and with a smile asked the magistrate who accompanied him to warn that man not to open his mouth so rudely again. To act thus was to treat contumely itself with contempt. I know that some say that there is nothing more terrible than disgrace, and that they would prefer death. To such men I answer that even exile is often accompanied by no disgrace whatever: if a great man falls, he remains a great man after his fall, you can no more suppose that he is disgraced than when people tread upon the walls of a ruined temple, which the pious treat with as much respect as when they were standing.

14

Since, then, my dearest mother, you have no reason for endless weeping on my account, it follows that your tears must flow on your own: there are two causes for this, either your having lost my protection, or your not being able to bear the mere fact of separation. The first of these I shall only touch upon lightly, for I know that your heart loves nothing belonging to your children except themselves. Let other mothers look to that, who make use of their sons' authority with a woman's passion, who are ambitious through their sons because they cannot bear office themselves, who spend their sons' inheritance, and yet are eager to inherit it, and who weary their sons by lending their eloquence to others: you have always rejoiced exceedingly in the successes of your sons, and have made no use of them whatever: you have always set bounds to our generosity, although you set none to your own: you, while a minor under the power of the head of the family, still used to make presents to your wealthy sons: you managed our inheritances with as much care as if you were working for your own, yet refrained from touching them as scrupulously as if they belonged to strangers: you have spared to use our influence, as though you enjoyed other means of your own, and you have taken no part in the public offices to which we have been elected beyond rejoicing in our success and paying our expenses: your indulgence has never been tainted by any thought of profit, and you cannot regret the loss of your son for a reason which never had any weight with you before his exile.

15

All my powers of consolation must be directed to the other point, the true source of your maternal grief. You say, "I am deprived of the embraces of my darling son, I cannot enjoy the pleasure of seeing him and of hearing him talk. Where is he at whose sight I used to smooth my troubled brow, in whose keeping I used to deposit all my cares? Where is his conversation, of which I never could have enough? his studies, in which I used to take part with more than a woman's eagerness, with more than a mother's familiarity? Where are our meetings? The boyish delight which he always showed at the sight of his mother?" To all this you add the actual places of our merrymakings and conversation, and, what must needs have more power to move you than anything else, the traces of our late social life, for fortune treated you with the additional cruelty of allowing you to depart on the very third day before my ruin, without a trace of anxiety, and not fearing anything of the kind. It was well that we had been separated by a vast distance: it was well that an absence of some years had prepared you to bear this blow: you came home, not to take any pleasure in your son, but to get rid of the habit of longing for him. Had you been absent long before, you would have borne it more bravely, as the very length of your absence would have moderated your longing to see me: had you never gone away, you would at any rate have gained one last advantage in seeing your son for two days longer: as it was, cruel Fate so arranged it that you were not present with me during my good fortune, and yet have not become accustomed to my absence. But the harder these things are to bear, the more virtue you must summon to your aid, and the more bravely you must struggle as it were with an enemy whom you know well, and whom you have already often conquered. This blood did not flow from a body previously unhurt: you have been struck through the scar of an old wound.

16

You have no grounds for excusing yourself on the ground of being a woman, who has a sort of right to weep without restraint, though not without limit. For this reason our ancestors allotted a space of ten months' mourning for women who had lost their husbands, thus settling the violence of a woman's grief by a public ordinance.

They did not forbid them to mourn, but they set limits to their grief: for while it is a foolish weakness to give way to endless grief when you lose one of those dearest to you, yet it shows an unnatural hardness of heart to express no grief at all: the best middle course between affection and hard common sense is both to feel regret and to restrain it. You need not look at certain women whose sorrow, when once begun, has been ended only by death: you know some who after the loss of their sons have never laid aside the garb of mourning: you are constitutionally stronger than these, and from you more is required. You cannot avail yourself of the excuse of being a woman, for you have no womanish vices. Unchastity, the greatest evil of the age, has never classed you with the majority of women; you have not been tempted either by gems or by pearls; riches have not allured you into thinking them the greatest blessing that man can own; respectably brought up as you were in an old-fashioned and strict household, you have never been led astray by that imitation of others which is so full of danger even to virtuous women. You have never been ashamed of your fruitfulness as though it were a reproach to your youth: you never concealed the signs of pregnancy as though it were an unbecoming burden, nor did you ever destroy your expected child within your womb after the fashion of many other women, whose attractions are to be found in their beauty alone. You never defiled your face with paints or cosmetics: you never liked clothes which showed the figure as plainly as though it were naked: your sole ornament has been a consummate loveliness which no time can impair, your greatest glory has been your modesty. You cannot, therefore, plead your womanhood as an excuse for your grief, because your virtues have raised you above it: you ought to be as superior to womanish tears as you are to womanish vices. Even women would not allow you to pine away after receiving this blow, but would bid you quickly and calmly go through the necessary amount of mourning, and then to arise and shake it off: I mean, if you are willing to take as your models those women whose eminent virtue has given them a place among even great men. Misfortune reduced the number of Cornelia's children from twelve to two: if you count the number of their deaths, Cornelia had lost ten: if you weigh them, she had lost the Gracchi: nevertheless, when her friends were weeping around her and using too bitter imprecations against her fate, she forbade them to blame fortune for having deprived[135] her of her sons the Gracchi. Such ought to have been the mother of him who, when speaking in the forum, said, "Would you speak evil of the mother who bore me?" The mother's speech seems to me to show a far greater spirit: the son set a high value on the birth of the Gracchi; the mother set an equal value on their deaths. Rutilia followed her son Cotta into exile, and was so passionately attached to him that she could bear exile better than absence from him; nor did she return home before her son did so: after he had been restored, and had

---

[135] I think Madvig's *ademisset* spoils the sense. *Dedisset* means: "when you bid me mourn the loss of the Gracchi you bid me blame fortune for having given me such sons." " 'Tis better to have loved and lost than to have never loved at all."—J. E. B. M.

been raised to honour in the republic, she bore his death as bravely as she had borne his exile. No one saw any traces of tears upon her cheeks after she had buried her son: she displayed her courage when he was banished, her wisdom when he died: she allowed no considerations either to interfere with her affection, or to force her to protract a useless and foolish mourning. These are the women with whom I wish you to be numbered: you have the best reasons for restraining and suppressing your sorrow as they did, because you have always imitated their lives.

17

I am aware that this is a matter which is not in our power, and that none of the passions, least of all that which arises from grief, are obedient to our wishes; indeed, it is overbearing and obstinate, and stubbornly rejects all remedies: we sometimes wish to crush it, and to swallow our emotion, but, nevertheless, tears flow over our carefully arranged and made-up countenance. Sometimes we occupy our minds with public spectacles and shows of gladiators; but during the very sights by which it is amused, the mind is wrung by slight touches of sorrow. It is better, therefore, to conquer it than to cheat it; for a grief which has been deceived and driven away either by pleasure or by business rises again, and its period of rest does but give it strength for a more terrible attack; but a grief which has been conquered by reason is appeased forever. I shall not, then, give you the advice which so many, I know, adopt, that you should distract your thoughts by a long journey, or amuse them by a beautiful one; that you should spend much of your time in the careful examination of accounts, and the management of your estate, and that you should keep constantly engaging in new enterprises: all these things avail but little, and do not cure, but merely obstruct our sorrow. I had rather it should be brought to an end than that it should be cheated: and, therefore, I would fain lead you to the study of philosophy, the true place of refuge for all those who are flying from the cruelty of Fortune: this will heal your wounds and take away all your sadness: to this you would now have to apply yourself, even though you had never done so before; but as far as my father's old-fashioned strictness permitted, you have gained a superficial, though not a thorough knowledge of all liberal studies. Would that my father, most excellent man that he was, had been less devoted to the customs of our ancestors, and had been willing to have you thoroughly instructed in the elements of philosophy, instead of receiving a mere smattering of it! I should not now need to be providing you with the means of struggling against Fortune, but you would offer them to me: but he did not allow you to pursue your studies far, because some women use literature to teach them luxury instead of wisdom. Still, thanks to your keen intellectual appetite, you learned more than one could have expected in the time: you laid the foundations of all good learning: now return to them: they will render you safe, they will console you, and charm you. If once they have thoroughly entered into your mind, grief, anxiety, the distress of vain suffering will never gain admittance thither: your breast will not be open to any of these; against all other vices it has long been closed. Philosophy is your most trustworthy guardian, and it alone can save you from the attacks of Fortune.

18

Since, however, you require something to lean upon until you can reach that haven of rest which philosophy offers to you, I wish in the meantime to point out to you the consolations which you have. Look at my two brothers—while they are safe, you have no grounds for complaint against Fortune; you can derive pleasure from the virtues of each of them, different as they are; the one has gained high office by attention to business, the other has philosophically despised it. Rejoice in the great place of one of your sons, in the peaceful retirement of the other, in the filial affection of both. I know my brothers' most secret motives: the one adorns his high office in order to confer lustre upon you, the other has withdrawn from the world into his life of quiet, and contemplation, that he may have full enjoyment of your society. Fortune has consulted both your safety and your pleasure in her disposal of your two sons: you may be protected by the authority of the one, and delighted by the literary leisure of the other. They will vie with one another in dutiful affection to you, and the loss of one son will be supplied by the love of two others. I can confidently promise that you will find nothing wanting in your sons except their number. Now, then, turn your eyes from them to your grandchildren; to Marcus, that most engaging child, whose sight no sorrow can withstand. No grief can be so great or so fresh in anyone's bosom as not to be charmed away by his presence. Where are the tears which his joyousness could not dry? whose heart is so nipped by sorrow that his animation would not cause it to dilate? who would not be rendered mirthful by his playfulness? who would not be attracted and made to forget his gloomy thoughts by that prattle to which no one can ever be weary of listening? I pray the gods that he may survive us: may all the cruelty of fate exhaust itself on me and go no further; may all the sorrow destined for my mother and my grandmother fall upon me; but let all the rest flourish as they do now: I shall make no complaints about my childlessness or my exile, if only my sacrifice may be received as a sufficient atonement, and my family suffer nothing more. Hold in your bosom Novatilla, who soon will present you with great-grandchildren, she whom I had so entirely adopted and made my own, that, now that she has lost me, she seems like an orphan, even though her father is alive. Love her for my sake as well as for her own: Fortune has lately deprived her of her mother: your affection will be able to prevent her really feeling the loss of the mother whom she mourns. Take this opportunity of forming and strengthening her principles; nothing sinks so deeply into the mind as the teaching which we receive in our earliest years; let her become accustomed to hearing your discourses; let her character be moulded according to your pleasure: she will gain much even if you give her nothing more than your example. This continually recurring duty will be a remedy in itself: for when your mind is full of maternal sorrow, nothing can distract it from its grief except either philosophic argument or honourable work. I should count your father among your greatest consolations, were he not absent: as it is, judge from your affection for me what his affection is for you, and then you will see how much more just it is that you should be preserved for him than that you should be sacrificed to me. Whenever your keenest paroxysms of grief assail you and bid you give way to them, think of your father. By giving him so many grandchildren and great-grandchildren you have made yourself no longer his only daughter; but you alone can crown his prosperous life by a happy end: as long as he is alive it is impiety for you to regret having been born.

19

I have hitherto said nothing of your chief source of consolation, your sister, that most faithful heart which shares all your sorrows as fully as your own, and who feels for all of us like a mother. With her you have mingled your tears, on her bosom you have tasted your first repose: she always feels for your troubles, and when I am in the case she does not grieve for you alone. It was in her arms that I was carried into Rome: by her affectionate and motherly nursing I regained my strength after a long period of sickness: she enlarged her influence to obtain the office of quaestor for me, and her fondness for me made her conquer a shyness which at other times made her shrink from speaking to, or loudly greeting her friends. Neither her retired mode of life, nor her country-bred modesty, at a time when so many women display such boldness of manner, her placidity, nor her habits of solitary seclusion prevented her from becoming actually ambitious on my account. Here, my dearest mother, is a source from which you may gain true consolation: join yourself, as far as you are able, to her, bind yourself to her by the closest embraces. Those who are in sorrow are wont to flee from those who are dearest to them, and to seek liberty for the indulgence of their grief: do you let her share your every thought: if you wish to nurse your grief, she will be your companion, if you wish to lay it aside she will bring it to an end. If, however, I rightly understand the wisdom of that most perfect woman, she will not suffer you to waste your life in unprofitable mourning, and will tell you what happened in her own instance, which I myself witnessed. During a sea-voyage she lost a beloved husband, my uncle, whom she married when a maiden; she endured at the same time grief for him and fear for herself, and at last, though shipwrecked, nevertheless rescued his body from the vanquished tempest. How many noble deeds are unknown to fame! If only she had had the simple-minded ancients to admire her virtues, how many brilliant intellects would have vied with one another in singing the praises of a wife who forgot the weakness of her sex, forgot the perils of the sea, which terrify even the boldest, exposed herself to death in order to lay him in the earth, and who was so eager to give him decent burial that she cared nothing about whether she shared it or no. All the poets have made the wife[136] famous who gave herself to death instead of her husband: my aunt did more when she

---

[136] Alcestis.

risked her life in order to give her husband a tomb: it shows greater love to endure the same peril for a less important end. After this, no one need wonder that for sixteen years, during which her husband governed the province of Egypt, she was never beheld in public, never admitted any of the natives to her house, never begged any favour of her husband, and never allowed anyone to beg one of her. Thus it came to pass that a gossiping province, ingenious in inventing scandal about its rulers, in which even the blameless often incurred disgrace, respected her as a singular example of uprightness,[137] never made free with her name—a remarkable piece of self-restraint among a people who will risk everything rather than forego a jest—and that at the present time it hopes for another governor's wife like her, although it has no reasonable expectation of ever seeing one. It would have been greatly to her credit if the province had approved her conduct for a space of sixteen years: it was much more creditable to her that it knew not of her existence. I do not remind you of this in order to celebrate her praises, for to take such scanty notice of them is to curtail them, but in order that you may understand the magnanimity of a woman who has not yielded either to ambition or to avarice, those twin attendants and scourges of authority, who, when her ship was disabled and her own death was impending, was not restrained by fear from keeping fast hold of her husband's dead body, and who sought not how to escape from the wreck, but how to carry him out of it with her. You must now show a virtue equal to hers, recall your mind from grief, and take care that no one may think that you are sorry that you have borne a son.

20

However, since it is necessary, whatever you do, that your thoughts should sometimes revert to me, and that I should now be present to your mind more often than your other children, not because they are less dear to you, but because it is natural to lay one's hands more often upon a place that pains one; learn how you are to think of me: I am as joyous and cheerful as in my best days: indeed these days are my best, because my mind is relieved from all pressure of business and is at leisure to attend to its own affairs, and at one time amuses itself with lighter studies, at another eagerly presses its inquiries into its own nature and that of the universe: first it considers the countries of the world and their position: then the character of the sea which flows between them, and the alternate ebbings and flowings of its tides; next it investigates all the terrors which hang between heaven and earth, the region which is torn asunder by thunderings, lightnings, gusts of wind, vapour, showers of snow and hail. Finally, having traversed every one of the realms below, it soars to the highest heaven, enjoys the noblest of all spectacles, that of things divine, and, remembering itself to be eternal, reviews all that has been and all that will be forever and ever.

---

[137] The context shows that *sanctitas* is opposed to "rapacity," "taking bribes," like the Celaeno of Juvenal viii. —J. E. B. M.

TO POLYBIUS, ON CONSOLATION

1

... compared with ours is firm and lasting; but if you transfer it to the domain of Nature, which destroys everything and calls everything back to the place from whence it came, it is transitory. What, indeed, have mortal hands made that is not mortal? The seven wonders of the world, and any even greater wonders which the ambition of later ages has constructed, will be seen some day leveled with the ground. So it is: nothing lasts forever, few things even last for long: all are susceptible of decay in one way or another. The ways in which things come to an end are manifold, but yet everything that has a beginning has an end also. Some threaten the world with death, and, though you may think the thought to be impious, this entire universe, containing gods and men and all their works will someday be swept away and plunged a second time into its original darkness and chaos. Weep, if you can, after this, over the loss of any individual life! Can we mourn the ashes of Carthage, Numantia, Corinth, or any city that has fallen from a high estate, when we know that the world must perish, albeit it has no place into which it can fall. Weep, if you can, because Fate has not spared you, she who someday will dare to work so great a wickedness! Who can be so haughtily and peevishly arrogant as to expect that this law of nature by which everything is brought to an end will be set aside in his own case, and that his own house will be exempted from the ruin which menaces the whole world itself? It is, therefore, a great consolation to reflect that what has happened to us has happened to everyone before us and will happen to everyone after us. In my opinion, Nature has made her cruellest acts affect all men alike, in order that the universality of their lot might console them for its hardship.

2

It will also be no small assistance to you to reflect that grief can do no good either to him whom you have lost or to yourself, and you would not wish to protract what is useless: for if we could gain anything by sorrow, I should not refuse to bestow upon your misfortunes whatever tears my own have left at my disposal: I would force some drops to flow from these eyes, exhausted as they are with weeping over my own domestic afflictions, were it likely to be of any service to you. Why do you hesitate? let us lament together, and I will even make this quarrel my own:—"Fortune, whom everyone thinks most unjust, you seemed hitherto to have restrained yourself from attacking one who by your favour had become the object of such universal respect that—rare distinction for anyone—his prosperity had excited no jealousy: but now, behold! you have dealt him the cruelest wound which, while Caesar lives, he could receive, and after reconnoitering him from all sides you have discovered that on this point alone he was exposed to your strokes. What else indeed could you have done to him? should you take away his wealth? he never was its slave: now he has even as far as possible put it away from him, and the chief thing that he has gained by his unrivalled facilities for amassing money has been to despise it. Should you take away his friends? you knew that he was of so loveable a disposition that he could easily gain others to replace those whom he might lose: for of all the powerful officers of the Imperial household he seems to me to be the only one whom all men wish to have for their friend without considering how advantageous his friendship would be. Should you take away his reputation? it is so firmly established, that even you could not shake it. Should you take away his health? you knew that his mind was so grounded on philosophical studies, in whose schools he was born as well as bred, that it would rise superior to any sufferings of the body. Should you take away his breath? how small an injury would that be to him? fame promised his genius one of the longest of lives: he himself has taken care that his better part should remain alive, and has guarded himself against death by the composition of his admirable works of eloquence: as long as literature shall be held in any honour, as long as the vigour of the Latin or the grace of the Greek language shall endure, he will flourish together with their greatest writers, with whose genius he has measured, or, if his modesty will not let me say this, has connected his own. This, then, was the only means you could devise of doing him a great injury. The better a man is, the more frequently he is wont to suffer from your indiscriminate rage, you who are to be feared even when you are bestowing benefits upon one. How little it would have cost you to avert this blow from one upon whom your favours seemed to be conferred according to some regular plan, and not to be flung at random in your wonted fashion!"

3

Let us add, if you please, to these grounds of complaint the disposition of the youth himself, cut off in the midst of its first growth. He was worthy to be your brother: you most certainly did not deserve to be given any pain through your brother, even though he had been unworthy. All men alike bear witness to his merits: he is regretted for your sake, and is praised for his own. He had no qualities which you would not be glad to recognize. You would indeed have been good to a worse brother, but to him your fraternal love was given all the more freely because in him it found so fitting a field for its exercise. No one ever was made to feel his influence by receiving wrongs at his hands, he never used the fact of your being his brother to threaten anyone: he had moulded his character after the pattern of your modesty, and reflected how great a glory and how great a burden you were to your family: the burden he was able to sustain; but, O pitiless Fate, always unjust to virtue—before your brother could taste the happiness of his position, he was called away. I am well aware that I express my feelings inadequately; for nothing is harder than to find words which adequately represent great grief: still, let us again lament for him, if it be of any use to do so:—"What did you mean, Fortune, by being so unjust and so savage? did you so soon repent you of your favour? What cruelty it was to fall upon brothers, to break up so loving a circle by so deadly an attack; why did you bring mourning into a house so plenteously stocked with admirable youths, in which no brother came short of the high standard of the rest, and without any cause pluck one of them away? So, then, scrupulous innocency of life, old-fashioned frugality, the power of amassing vast wealth wielded with the greatest self-denial, a true and imperishable love of literature, a mind free from the least spot of sin, all avail nothing: Polybius is in mourning, and, warned by the fate of one brother what he may have to dread for the rest, he fears for the very persons who soothe his grief. O shame! Polybius is in mourning, and mourns even though he still enjoys the favour of Caesar. No doubt, Fortune, what you aimed at in your impotent rage was to prove that no one could be protected from your attacks, not even by Caesar himself."

4

We might go on blaming fate much longer, but we cannot alter it: it stands harsh and inexorable: no one can move it by reproaches, by tears, or by justice. Fate never spares anyone, never makes allowances to anyone. Let us, then, refrain from unprofitable tears: for our grief will carry us away to join him sooner than it will bring him back to us: and if it tortures us without helping us, we ought to lay it aside as soon as possible, and restore the tone of our minds after their indulgence in that vain solace and the bitter luxury of woe: for unless reason puts an end to our tears, fortune will not do so. Look around, I pray you, upon all mortals: everywhere there is ample and constant reason for weeping: one man is driven to daily labour by toilsome poverty, another is tormented by never-resting ambition, another fears the very riches that he once wished for, and suffers from the granting of his own prayer: one man is made wretched by loneliness, another by labour, another by the crowds which always besiege his antechamber. This man mourns because he has children, that one because he has lost them. Tears will fail us sooner than causes for shedding them. Do you not see what sort of a life it must be that Nature has promised to us men when she makes us weep as soon as we are born? We begin life in this fashion, and all the chain of years that follow it is in harmony with it. Thus we pass our lives, and consequently we ought to be sparing in doing what we have to do so often, and when we look back upon the mass of sorrows that hangs over us, we ought, if not to end our tears, at any rate to reserve them. There is nothing that we ought to husband more carefully than this, which we are so often obliged to expend.

5

It will also be no small assistance to you to consider that there is no one to whom your grief is more offensive than he upon whom it is nominally bestowed: he either does not wish you to suffer or does not understand why you suffer. There is, therefore, no reason for a service which is useless if it is not felt by him who is the object of it, and which is displeasing to him if it is. I can boldly affirm that there is no one in the whole world who derives any pleasure from your tears. What then? do you suppose that your brother has a feeling against you which no one else has, that he wishes you to be injured by your self-torture, that he desires to separate you from the business of your life, that is, from philosophy and from Caesar? that is not likely: for he always gave way to you as a brother, respected you as a parent, courted you as a superior. He wishes to be fondly remembered by you, but not to be a source of agony to you. Why, then, should you insist upon pining away with a grief which, if the dead have any feelings, your brother wishes to bring to an end? If it were any other brother about whose affection there could be any question, I should put all this vaguely, and say, "If your brother wishes you to be tortured with endless mourning, he does not deserve such affection: if he does not wish it, dismiss the grief which affects you both: an unnatural brother ought not, a good brother would not wish to be so mourned for," but with one whose brotherly love has been so clearly proved, we may be quite sure that nothing could hurt him more than that you should be hurt by his loss, that it should agonize you, that your eyes, most undeserving as they are of such a fate, should be by the same cause continually filled and drained of never-ceasing tears.

Nothing however will restrain your loving nature from these useless tears so effectually as the reflection that you ought to show your brothers an example by bearing this outrage of fortune bravely. You ought to imitate great generals in times of disaster, when they are careful to affect a cheerful demeanour, and conceal misfortunes by a counterfeited joyousness, lest, if the soldiers saw their leader cast down, they should themselves become dispirited. This must now be done by you also. Put on a countenance that does not reflect your feelings, and if you possibly can, cast out completely all of your grief; if not, conceal it within you and hide it away so that it may not be seen, and take care that your brothers, who will think everything honourable that they see you doing, imitate you in this and take courage from the sight of your looks. It is your duty to be both their comfort and their consoler; but you will have no power to check their grief if you humour your own.

6

It may also keep you from excessive grief if you remind yourself that nothing which you do can be done in secret: all men agree in regarding you as an important personage, and you must keep up this character: you are encompassed by all that mass of offerers of consolation who all are peering into your mind to learn how much strength it has to resist grief, and whether you merely know how to avail yourself cunningly of prosperity, or whether you can also bear adversity with a manly spirit: the expression of your very eyes is watched. Those who are able to conceal their feelings may indulge them more freely; but you are not free to have any secrecy: your fortune has set you in so brilliant a position, that nothing which you do can be hid: all men will know how you have borne this wound of yours, whether you laid down your arms at the first shock or whether you stood your ground. Long ago the love of Caesar raised you, and your own literary pursuits brought you, to the highest rank in the State: nothing vulgar, nothing mean befits you: yet what can be meaner or more womanish than to make oneself a victim to grief? Although your sorrow is as great as that of your brothers, yet you may not indulge it as much as they: the ideas which the public have formed about your philosophic learning and your character make many things impossible for you. Men demand much, and expect much from you: you ought not to have drawn all eyes upon yourself, if you wished to be allowed to act as you pleased: as it is, you must make good that of which you have given promise. All those, who praise the works of your genius, who make copies of them, who need your genius if they do not need your fortune, are as guards set over your mind: you cannot, therefore, ever do anything unworthy of the character of a thorough philosopher and sage, without many men feeling sorry that they ever admired you. You may not weep beyond reason: nor is this the only thing that you may not do: you may not so much as remain asleep after daybreak, or retreat from the noisy troubles of public business to the peaceful repose of the country, or refresh yourself with a pleasure tour when wearied by constant attendance to the duties of your toilsome post, or amuse yourself with beholding various shows, or even arrange your day according to your own wish. Many things are forbidden to you which are permitted to the poorest beggars that lie about in holes and corners. A great fortune is a great slavery; you may not do anything according to your wish: you must give audiences to all those thousands of people, you must take charge of all those petitions: you must cheer yourself up, in order that all this mass of business which flows hither from every part of the world may be offered in due order for the consideration of our excellent emperor. I repeat, you yourself are forbidden to weep, that you may be able to listen to so many weeping petitioners: your own tears must be dried, in order that the tears of those who are in peril and who desire to obtain the gracious pardon of the kindest-hearted of Caesars may be dried.

7

These reflections will serve you as partial remedies for your grief, but if you wish to forget it altogether, remember Caesar: think with what loyalty, with what industry you are bound to requite the favours which he has shown you: you will then see that you can no more sink beneath your burden than could he of whom the myths tells us, he whose shoulders upheld the world. Even Caesar, who may do all things, may not do many things for this very reason: his watchfulness protects all men's sleep, his labour guarantees their leisure, his toil ensures their pleasures, his work preserves their holidays. On the day on which Caesar devoted his services to the universe, he lost them for himself, and like the planets which ever unrestingly pursue their course, he can never halt or attend to any affair of his own. After a certain fashion this prohibition is imposed upon you also; you may not consider your own interests, or devote yourself to your own studies: while Caesar owns the world, you cannot allow either joy or grief, or anything else to occupy any part of you: you owe your entire self to Caesar. Add to this that, since you have always declared that Caesar was dearer to you than your own life, you have no right to complain of misfortune as long as Caesar is alive: while he is safe all your friends are alive, you have lost nothing, your eyes ought not only to be dry, but glad. In him is your all, he stands in the place of all else to you: you are not grateful enough for your present happy state (which God forbid that one of your most wise and loyal disposition should be) if you permit yourself to weep at all while Caesar is safe.

8

I will now point out to you yet another remedy, of a more domestic, though not of a more efficacious character. Your sorrow is most to be feared when you have retired to your own home: for as long as your divinity is before your eyes, it can find no means of access to you, but Caesar will possess your entire being; when you have left his presence, grief, as though it then had an opportunity of attack, will lie in ambush for you in your loneliness, and creep by degrees over your mind as it rests from its labours. You ought not, therefore, to allow any moment to be unoccupied by literary pursuits: at such times let literature repay to you the debt which your long and faithful love has laid upon it, let it claim you for its high priest and worshipper: at such times let Homer[138] and Virgil be much in your company, those poets to whom the human race owes as much as everyone owes to you, and

---

[138] "The Latins had four versions of Homer (Fabric, tom. i l. ii ch. 3, p. 297), yet, in spite of the phraises of Seneca, 'Consolations' chapter 26 (viii), they appear to have been more successful in imitating than in translating the Greek poets."
—Gibbon's *Decline and Fall*, Chapter 41, ad initium, note.
Polybius had made a prose translation of Homer, and a prose paraphrase of Virgil.

they especially, because you have made them known to a wider circle than that for which they wrote. All time which you entrust to their keeping will be safe. At such times, as far as you are able, compile an account of your Caesar's acts, that they may be read by all future ages in a panegyric written by one of his own household: for he himself will afford you both the noblest subject and the noblest example for putting together and composing a history. I dare not go so far as to advise you to write in your usual elegant style a version of Æsop's fables, a work which no Roman intellect has hitherto attempted. It is hard, no doubt, for a mind which has received so rude a shock to betake itself so quickly to these livelier pursuits: but if it is able to pass from more serious studies to these lighter ones, you must regard it as a proof that it has recovered its strength, and is itself again. In the former case, although it may suffer and hang back, still it will be led on by the serious nature of the subject under consideration to take an interest in it: but, unless it has thoroughly recovered, it will not endure to treat of subjects which must be written of in a cheerful spirit. You ought, therefore, first to exercise your mind upon grave studies, and then to enliven it with gayer ones.

9

It will also be a great solace to you if you often ask yourself: "Am I grieving on my own account or on that of him who is gone? if on my own, I have no right to boast of my affectionate sensibility; grief is only excusable as long as it is honourable; but when it is only caused by personal interests, it no longer springs from tenderness: nothing can be less becoming to a good man than to make a calculation about his grief for his brother. If I grieve on his account, I must necessarily take one of the two following views: if the dead retain no feeling whatever, my brother has escaped from all the troubles of life, has been restored to the place which he occupied before his birth, and, being free from every kind of ill, can neither fear, nor desire, nor suffer: what madness then for me never to cease grieving for one who will never grieve again? If the dead have any feeling, then my brother is now like one who has been let out of a prison in which he has long been confined, who at last is free and his own master, and who enjoys himself, amuses himself with viewing the works of Nature, and looks down from above the Earth upon all human things, while he looks at things divine, whose meaning he has long sought in vain, from a much nearer standpoint. Why then am I wasting away with grief for one who is either in bliss or nonexistent? it would be envy to weep for one who is in bliss, it would be madness to weep for one who has no existence whatever." Are you affected by the thought that he appears to have been deprived of great blessings just at the moment when they came crowding upon him? after thinking how much he has lost, call to mind how much more he has ceased to fear: anger will never more wring his heart, disease will not crush him, suspicion will not disquiet him, the gnawing pain of envy which we feel at the successes of others will not attend him, terror will not make him wretched, the fickleness of Fortune who quickly transfers her favours from one man to another will not alarm him. If you reckon it up properly, he has been spared more than he has lost. He will not enjoy wealth, or your influence at Court, or his own: he will not receive benefits, and will not confer them: do you imagine him to be unhappy, because he has lost these things, or happy because he does not miss them? Believe me, he who does not need good fortune is happier than he on whom it attends: all those good things which charm us by the attractive but unreal pleasures which they afford, such as money, high office, influence, and many other things which dazzle the stupid greed of mankind, require hard labour to keep, are regarded by others with bitter jealousy, and are more of a menace than an advantage to those who are bedecked and encumbered by them. They are slippery and uncertain; one never can enjoy them in comfort; for, even setting aside anxiety about the future, the present management of great prosperity is an uneasy task. If we are to believe some profound seekers after truth, life is all torment: we are flung, as it were, into this deep and rough sea, whose tides ebb and flow, at one time raising us aloft by sudden accessions of fortune, at another bringing down low by still greater losses, and forever tossing us about, never letting us rest on firm ground. We roll and plunge upon the waves, and sometimes strike against one another, sometimes are shipwrecked, always are in terror. For those who sail upon this stormy sea, exposed as it is to every gale, there is no harbour save death. Do not, then, grudge your brother his rest: he has at last become free, safe, and immortal: he leaves surviving him Caesar and all his family, yourself, and his and your brothers. He left Fortune before she had ceased to regard him with favour, while she stood still by him, offering him gifts with a full hand. He now ranges free and joyous through the boundless heavens; he has left this poor and low-lying region, and has soared upwards to that place, whatever it may be, which receives in its happy bosom the souls which have been set free from the chains of matter: he now roams there at liberty, and enjoys with the keenest delight all the blessings of Nature. You are mistaken! your brother has not lost the light of day, but has obtained a more enduring light: whither he has gone, we all alike must go: why then do we weep for his fate? He has not left us, but has gone on before us. Believe me, there is great happiness in a happy death. We cannot be sure of anything even for one whole day: since the truth is so dark and hard to come at, who can tell whether death came to your brother out of malice or out of kindness?

10

One who is as just in all things as you are, must find comfort in the thought that no wrong has been done you by the loss of so noble a brother, but that you have received a benefit by having been permitted for so long a time to enjoy his affection. He who will not allow his benefactor to choose his own way of bestowing a gift upon him, is unjust: he who does not reckon what he receives as gain, and yet reckons what he gives back again as loss, is greedy: he who says that he has been wronged, because his pleasure has come to an end, is ungrateful: he who thinks that we gain nothing from good things beyond the present enjoyment of them, is a fool, because he finds no pleasure in past joys, and does not regard those which are gone as his most certain possessions, since he need not fear that they will come to an end. A man limits his pleasures too narrowly if he believes that he enjoys those things only which he touches and sees, if he counts the having enjoyed them for nothing: for all pleasure quickly leaves us, seeing that it flows away, flits across our lives, and is gone almost before it has come. We ought, therefore, to make our mind travel back over past time, to bring back whatever we once took pleasure in, and frequently to ruminate over it in our thoughts: the remembrance of pleasures is truer and more trustworthy than their reality. Regard it, then, among your greatest blessings that you have had an excellent brother: you need not think for how much longer you might have had him, but for how long you did have him. Nature gave him to you, as she gives others to other brothers, not as an absolute property, but as a loan: afterwards when she thought proper she took him back again, and followed her own rules of action, instead of waiting until you had indulged your love to satiety. If anyone were to be indignant at having to repay a loan of money, especially if he had been allowed to use it without having to pay any interest, would he not be thought an unreasonable man? Nature gave your brother his life, just as she gave you yours: exercising her lawful rights, she has chosen to ask one of you to repay her loan before the other: she cannot be blamed for this, for you knew the conditions on which you received it: you must blame the greedy hopes of mortal men's minds, which every now and then forget what Nature is, and never remember their own lot unless reminded of it. Rejoice, then, that you have had so good a brother, and be grateful for having had the use and enjoyment of him, though it was for a shorter time than you wished. Reflect that what you have had of him was most delightful, that your having lost him is an accident common to mankind. There is nothing more inconsistent than that a man should grieve that so good a brother was not long enough with him, and should not rejoice that he nevertheless has been with him.

11

"But," you say, "he was taken away unexpectedly." Every man is deceived by his own willingness to believe what he wishes, and he chooses to forget that those whom he loves are mortal: yet Nature gives us clear proofs that she will not suspend her laws in favour of anyone: the funeral processions of our friends and of strangers alike pass daily before our eyes, yet we take no notice of them, and when an event happens which our whole life warns us will someday happen, we call it sudden. This is not, therefore, the injustice of fate, but the perversity and insatiable universal greediness of the human mind, which is indignant at having to leave a place to which it was only admitted on sufferance. How far more righteous was he who, on hearing of the death of his son, made a speech worthy of a great man, saying: "When I begat him, I knew that he would die some day." Indeed, you need not be surprised at the son of such a man being able to die bravely. He did not receive the tidings of his son's death as news: for what is there new in a man's dying, when his whole life is merely a journey towards death? "When I begat him, I knew that he would die some day," said he: and then he added, what showed even more wisdom and courage, "It was for this that I brought him up." It is for this that we have all been brought up: everyone who is brought into life is intended to die. Let us enjoy what is given to us, and give it back when it is asked for: the Fates lay their hands on some men at some times, and on other men at other times, but they will never pass anyone by altogether. Our mind ought always to be on the alert, and while it ought never to fear what is certain to happen, it ought always to be ready for what may happen at any time. Why need I tell you of generals and the children of generals, of men ennobled by many consulships and triumphs, who have succumbed to pitiless fate? Whole kingdoms together with their kings, whole nations with all their component tribes, have all submitted to their doom. All men, nay, all things look forward to an end of their days: yet all do not come to the same end: one man loses his life in the midst of his career, another at the very beginning of it, another seems hardly able to free himself from it when worn out with extreme old age, and eager to be released: we are all going to the same place, but we all go thither at different times. I know not whether it is more foolish not to know the law of mortality, or more presumptuous to refuse to obey it. Come, take into your hands the poems of whichever you please of those two authors upon whom your genius has expended so much labour, whom you have so well paraphrased, that although the structure of the verse be removed, its charm nevertheless is preserved; for you have transferred them from one language to another so well as to effect the most difficult matter of all, that of making all the beauties of the original reappear in a foreign speech: among their works you will find no volume which will not offer you numberless instances of the vicissitudes of human life, of the uncertainty of events, and of tears shed for various reasons. Read with what fire you have thundered out their swelling phrases: you will feel ashamed of suddenly failing and falling short of the elevation of their magnificent language. Do not commit the fault of making everyone, who according to his ability admires your writings, ask how so frail a mind can have formed such stable and well-connected ideas.

12

Turn yourself away from these thoughts which torment you, and look rather at those numerous and powerful sources of consolation which you possess: look at your excellent brothers, look at your wife and your son. It is to guarantee the safety of all these that Fortune[139] has struck you in this this quarter: you have many left

---

[139] "Fortune hath parted stakes with thee, in taking away thy brother, and leaving thee all the rest in securtie and safetie." —Lodge.

in whom you can take comfort. Guard yourself from the shame of letting all men think that a single grief has more power with you than these many consolations. You see all of them cast down into the same despondency as yourself, and you know that they cannot help you, nay, that on the other hand they look to you to encourage them: wherefore, the less learning and the less intellect they possess, the more vigorously you ought to withstand the evil which has fallen upon you all. The very fact of one's grief being shared by many persons acts as a consolation, because if it be distributed among such a number the share of it which falls upon you must be small. I shall never cease to recall your thoughts to Caesar. While he governs the Earth, and shows how far better the empire may be maintained by kindnesses than by arms, while he presides over the affairs of mankind, there is no danger of your feeling that you have lost anything: in this fact alone you will find ample help and ample consolation; raise yourself up, and fix your eyes upon Caesar whenever tears rise to them; they will become dry on beholding that greatest and most brilliant light; his splendour will attract them and firmly attach them to himself, so that they are able to see nothing else. He whom you behold both by day and by night, from whom your mind never deviates to meaner matters, must occupy your thoughts and be your defence against Fortune; indeed, so kind and gracious as he is towards all his followers that he has already, I doubt not, laid many healing balms upon this wound of yours, and furnished you with many antidotes for your sorrow. Why, even had he done nothing of the kind, is not the mere sight and thought of Caesar in itself your greatest consolation? May the gods and goddesses long spare him to the Earth: may he rival the deeds of the Emperor Augustus, and surpass him in length of days! As long as he remains among mortals, may he never be reminded that any of his house are mortal: may he train up his son by long and faithful service to be the ruler of the Roman people, and see him share his father's power before he succeeds to it: may the day on which his kindred shall claim him for heaven be far distant, and may our grandchildren alone be alive to see it.

13

Fortune, refrain your hands from him, and show your power over him only in doing him good: allow him to heal the long sickness from which mankind has suffered; to replace and restore whatever has been shattered by the frenzy of our late sovereign: may this star, which has shed its rays upon a world overthrown and cast into darkness, ever shine brightly: may he give peace to Germany, open Britain to us, and lead through the city triumphs, both over the nations whom his fathers conquered, and over new ones. Of these his clemency, the first of his many virtues, gives me hopes of being a spectator: for he has not so utterly cast me down that he will never raise me up again; nay, he has not cast me down at all; rather he has supported me when I was struck by evil fortune and was tottering, and has gently used his godlike hand to break my headlong fall: he pleaded with the Senate on my behalf, and not only gave me my life but even begged it for me. He will see to my cause: let him judge my cause to be such as he would desire; let his justice pronounce it good or his clemency so regard it: his kindness to me will be equal in either case, whether he knows me to be innocent or chooses that I should be thought so. Meanwhile it is a great comfort to me for my own miseries to behold his pardons travelling throughout the world: even from the corner in which I am confined his mercy has unearthed and restored to light many exiles who had been buried and forgotten here for long years, and I have no fear that I alone shall be passed over by it. He best knows the time at which he ought to show favour to each man: I will use my utmost efforts to prevent his having to blush when he comes to me. O how blessed is your clemency, Caesar, which makes exiles live more peacefully during your reign than princes did in that of Gaius! We do not tremble or expect the fatal stroke every hour, nor are we terrified whenever a ship comes in sight: you have set bounds to the cruelty of Fortune towards us, and have given us present peace and hopes of a happier future. You may indeed be sure that those thunderbolts alone are just which are worshipped even by those who are struck by them.

14

Thus this prince, who is the universal consoler of all men, has, unless I am altogether mistaken, already revived your spirit and applied more powerful remedies to so severe a wound than I can: he has already strengthened you in every way: his singularly retentive memory has already furnished you with all the examples which will produce tranquility: his practised eloquence has already displayed before you all the precepts of sages. No one therefore could console you as well as he: when he speaks his words have greater weight, as though they were the utterances of an oracle: his divine authority will crush all the strength of your grief. Think, then, that he speaks to you as follows:—"Fortune has not chosen you as the only man in the world to receive so severe a blow: there is no house in all the Earth, and never has been one, that has not something to mourn for: I will pass over examples taken from the common herd, which, while they are of less importance, are also endless in number, and I will direct your attention to the Calendar and the State Chronicles. Do you see all these images which fill the hall of the Caesars? there is not one of these men who was not especially afflicted by domestic sorrows: no one of those men who shine there as the ornament of the ages was not either tortured by grief for some of his family or most bitterly mourned for by those whom he left behind. Why need I remind you of Scipio Africanus, who heard the news of his brother's death when he was himself in exile? he who saved his brother from prison could not save him from his fate. Yet all men saw how impatient Africanus's brotherly affection was even of equal law: on the same day on which Scipio Africanus rescued his brother from the hands of the apparitor, he, although not holding any office, protested against the action of the tribune of the people. He mourned for his brother as magnanimously as he had defended him. Why need I remind you of Scipio Æmilianus,[140] who almost at one and the same time beheld his father's triumph and the funeral of his two brothers? yet, although a stripling and hardly more than a boy, he bore the sudden bereavement which befell his family at the very time of Paulus's triumph with all the courage which beseemed one who was born that Rome might not be without a Scipio and that she might be without a Carthage.

15

Why should I speak of the intimacy of the two Luculli, which was broken only by their death? or of the Pompeii? whom the cruelty of Fortune did not even allow to perish by the same catastrophe; for Sextus Pompeius in the first place survived his sister,[141] by whose death the firmly knit bond of peace in the Roman empire was broken, and he also survived his noble brother, whom Fortune had raised so high in order that she might cast him down from as great a height as she had already cast down his father; yet after this great misfortune Sextus Pompeius was able not only to endure his grief but even to make war. Innumerable instances occur to me of brothers who were separated by death: indeed on the other hand we see very few pairs of brothers growing old together: however, I shall content myself with examples from my own family. No one can be so devoid of feeling or of reason as to complain of Fortune's having thrown him into mourning when he learns that she has coveted the tears of the Caesars themselves. The Emperor Augustus lost his darling sister Octavia, and though Nature destined him for heaven, yet she did not relax her laws to spare him from mourning while on Earth: nay, he suffered every kind of bereavement, losing his sister's son,[142] who was intended to be his heir. In fine, not to mention his sorrows in detail, he lost his son-in-law, his children, and his grandchildren, and, while he remained among men, no mortal was more often reminded that he was a man. Yet his mind, which was able to bear all things, bore all these heavy sorrows, and the blessed Augustus was the conqueror, not only of foreign nations, but also of his own sorrows. Gaius Caesar,[143] the grandson of the blessed Augustus, my maternal great uncle, in the first years of manhood, when Prince of the Roman Youth, as he was preparing for the Parthian war, lost his darling brother Lucius[144] who was also "Prince of the Roman Youth," and suffered more thereby in his mind than he did afterwards in his body, though he bore both afflictions with the greatest piety and fortitude. Tiberius Caesar, my paternal uncle,

---

[140] See *On Benefits*, Book V, Chapter 16.
[141] Scipio Africanus Minor, the son of Paulus Æmilius.
[142] Marcellus. See Virgil's well-known lines, *Æneid*, VI, 869, sqq., and "Consolatio ad Marciam," Chapter 2.
[143] G. Caesar, d. at Limyra, ad 4.
[144] Lucius Caesar, d. at Marseilles, ad 2.

lost his younger brother Drusus Germanicus,[145] my father, when he was opening out the innermost fastnesses of Germany, and bringing the fiercest tribes under the dominion of the Roman empire; he embraced him and received his last kiss, but he nevertheless restrained not only his own grief but that of others, and when the whole army, not merely sorrowful but heartbroken, claimed the corpse of their Drusus for themselves, he made them grieve only as it became Romans to grieve, and taught them that they must observe military discipline not only in fighting but also in mourning. He could not have checked the tears of others had he not first repressed his own.

16

"Marcus Antonius, my grandfather, who was second to none save his conqueror, received the news of his brother's execution at the very time when the State was at his disposal, and when, as a member of the triumvirate, he saw no one in the world superior to himself in power, nay, when, with the exception of his two colleagues, every man was subordinate to himself. O wanton Fortune, what sport you make for yourself out of human sorrows! At the very time when Marcus Antonius was enthroned with power of life and death over his countrymen, Marcus Antonius's brother was being led to his death: yet Antonius bore this cruel wound with the same greatness of mind with which he had endured all his other crosses; and he mourned for his brother by offering the blood of twenty legions to his manes. However, to pass by all other instances, not to speak of the other deaths which have occurred in my own house, Fortune has twice assailed me through the death of a brother; she has twice learned that she could wound me but could not overthrow me. I lost my brother Germanicus, whom I loved in a manner which anyone will understand if he thinks how affectionate brothers love one another; yet I so restrained my passion of grief as neither to leave undone anything which a good brother could be called upon to do, nor yet to do anything which a sovereign could be blamed for doing." Think, then, that our common parent quotes these instances to you, and that he points out to you how nothing is respected or held inviolable by Fortune, who actually dares to send out funeral processions from the very house in which she will have to look for gods: so let no one be surprised at her committing any act of cruelty or injustice; for how could she show any humanity or moderation in her dealings with private families, when her pitiless

---

[145] Drusus died by a fall from his horse, bc 9. "A monument was erected in his honour at Moguntiacum (Mayence), and games and military spectacles were exhibited there on the anniversary of his death. An altar had already been raised in his honour on the banks of the Lippe." Tacitus, *Annals*, II, 7. "The soldiers began now to regard themselves as a distinct people, with rites and heroes of their own. Augustus required them to surrender the body of their beloved chief as a matter of discipline." Merivale, Chapter 36.

fury has so often hung the very throne[146] itself with black? She will not change her habits even though reproached, not by my voice alone, but by that of the entire nation: she will hold on her course in spite of all prayers and complaints. Such has Fortune always been, and such she ever will be in connection with human affairs: she has never shrunk from attacking anything, and she will never let anything alone: she will rage everywhere terribly, as she has always been wont to do: she will dare to enter for evil purposes into those houses whose entrance lies through the temples of the gods, and will hang signs of mourning upon laurelled doorposts. However, if she has not yet determined to destroy the human race: if she still looks with favour upon the Roman nation, may our public and private prayers prevail upon her to regard as sacred from her violence this prince, whom all men think to be sacred, who has been granted them by heaven to give them rest after their misfortunes: let her learn clemency from him, and let the mildest of all sovereigns teach her mildness.

17

You ought, therefore, to fix your eyes upon all the persons whom I have just mentioned, who have either been deified or were nearly related to those who have been deified, and when Fortune lays her hands upon you to bear it calmly, seeing that she does not even respect those by whose names we swear. It is your duty to imitate their constancy in enduring and triumphing over suffering, as far as it is permitted to a mere man to follow in the footsteps of the immortals. Albeit in all other matters rank and birth make great distinctions between men, yet virtue is open to all; she despises no one provided he thinks himself worthy to possess her. Surely you cannot do better than follow the example of those who, though they might have been angry at not being exempt from this evil, nevertheless have decided to regard this, the only thing which brings them down to the level of other men, not as a wrong done to themselves, but as the law of our mortal nature, and to bear what befalls them without undue bitterness and wrath, and yet in no base or cowardly spirit: for it is not human not to feel our sorrows, while it is unmanly not to bear them. When I glance through the roll of all the Caesars whom fate has bereaved of sisters or brothers, I cannot pass over that one who is unworthy to figure on the list of Caesars, whom Nature produced to be the ruin and the shame of the human race, who utterly wrecked and destroyed the State which is now recovering under the gentle rule of the most benign of princes. On losing his sister Drusilla, Gaius Caesar, a man who could neither mourn nor rejoice as becomes a prince, shrank from seeing and speaking to his countrymen, was not present at his sister's funeral, did not pay her the conventional tribute of respect, but tried to forget the sorrows

---

[146] *Pulvinaria*. This word properly means "a couch made of cushions, and spread over with a splendid covering, for the gods or persons who received divine honours."

caused by this most distressing death by playing at dice in his Alban villa, and by sitting on the judgment-seat, and the like customary engagements. What a disgrace to the Empire! a Roman emperor solaced himself by gambling for his grief at the loss of his sister! This same Gaius, with frantic levity, at one time let his beard and hair grow long, at another wandered aimlessly along the coast of Italy and Sicily. He never clearly made up his mind whether he wished his sister to be mourned for or to be worshipped, and during all the time that he was raising temples and shrines[147] in her honour he punished those who did not manifest sufficient sorrow with the most cruel tortures:[148] for his mind was so ill-balanced, that he was as much cast down by adversity as he was unbecomingly elated and puffed up by success. Far be it from every Roman to follow such an example, either to divert his mind from his grief by unreasonable amusements, to stimulate it by unseemly squalor and neglect, or to be so inhuman as to console himself by taking pleasure in the sufferings of others.

18

You, however, need change none of your ordinary habits, since you have taught yourself to love those studies which, while they are preeminently fitted for perfecting our happiness, at the same time teach us how we may bear misfortune most lightly, and which are at the same time a man's greatest honour and greatest comfort. Now, therefore, immerse yourself even more deeply in your studies, now surround your mind with them like fortifications, so that grief may not find any place at which it can gain entrance. At the same time, prolong the remembrance of your brother by inserting some memoir of him among your other writings: for that is the only sort of monument that can be erected by man which no storm can injure, no time destroy. The others, which consist of piles of stone, masses of marble, or huge mounds of earth heaped on high, cannot preserve his memory for long, because they themselves perish; but the memorials which genius raises are everlasting. Lavish these upon your brother, embalm him in these: you will do better to immortalise him by an everlasting work of genius than to mourn over him with useless grief. As for Fortune herself, although I cannot just now plead her cause before you, because all that she has given us is now hateful to you, because she has taken something away from you, yet I will plead her cause as soon as time shall have rendered you a more impartial judge of her action: indeed she has bestowed much upon you to make amends for the injury which she has done you, and she will give more hereafter by

---

[147] *Pulvinaria.* This word properly means "a couch made of cushions, and spread over with a splendid covering, for the gods or persons who received divine honours."
[148] Merivale, following Suetonius and Dion Cassius, says: "He declared that if any man dared to mourn for his sister's death, he should be punished, for she had become a goddess: if anyone ventured to rejoice at her deification, he should be punished also, for she was dead." The passage in the text, he remarks, gives a less extravagant turn to the story.

way of atonement for it: and, after all, it was she herself who gave you this brother whom she has taken away. Forbear, then, to display your abilities against your own self, or to take part with your grief against yourself: your eloquence, can, no doubt, make trifles appear great, and, conversely, can disparage and depreciate great things until they seem the merest trifles; but let it reserve those powers and use them on some other subject, and at the present time devote its entire strength to the task of consoling you. Yet see whether even this task be not unnecessary. Nature demands from us a certain amount of grief, our imagination adds some more to it; but I will never forbid you to mourn at all. I know, indeed, that there are some men, whose wisdom is of a harsh rather than a brave character, who say that the wise man never would mourn. It seems to me that they never can have been in the position of mourners, for otherwise their misfortune would have shaken all their haughty philosophy out of them, and, however much against their will, would have forced them to confess their sorrow. Reason will have done enough if she does but cut off from our grief all that is superfluous and useless: as for her not allowing us to grieve at all, that we ought neither to expect nor to wish for. Let her rather restrain us within the bounds of a chastened grief, which partakes neither of indifference nor of madness, and let her keep our minds in that attitude which becomes affection without excitement: let your tears flow, but let them some day cease to flow: groan as deeply as you will, but let your groans cease some day: regulate your conduct so that both philosophers and brothers may approve of it. Make yourself feel pleasure in often thinking about your brother, talk constantly about him, and keep him ever present in your memory; which you cannot succeed in doing unless you make the remembrance of him pleasant rather than sad: for it is but natural that the mind should shrink from a subject which it cannot contemplate without sadness. Think of his retiring disposition, of his abilities for business, his diligence in carrying it out, his loyalty to his word. Tell other men of all his sayings and doings, and remind your own self of them: think how good he was and how great you hoped he might become: for what success is there which you might not safely have wagered that such a brother would win?

I have thrown together these reflections in the best way that I could, for my mind is dimmed and stupefied with the tedium of my long exile: if, therefore, you should find them unworthy of the consideration of a person of your intelligence, or unable to console you in your grief, remember how impossible it is for one who is full of his own sorrows to find time to minister to those of others, and how hard it is to express oneself in the Latin language, when all around one hears nothing but a rude foreign jargon, which even barbarians of the more civilised sort regard with disgust.

www.ingramcontent.com/pod-product-compliance
Lightning Source LLC
LaVergne TN
LVHW091610070526
838199LV00044B/744